2001

American Treaties
and Alliances

American Treaties
and Alliances

ALAN AXELROD

CQ PRESS

A Division of Congressional Quarterly Inc.
WASHINGTON, D.C.

CQ Press

A Division of Congressional Quarterly Inc.
1414 22nd Street, N.W.
Washington, D.C. 20037

(202) 822-1475; (800) 638-1710

www.cqpress.com

Produced by The Ian Samuel Group, Inc.

Printed in the United States of America

04 03 02 01 00   5 4 3 2 1

LIBRARY OF CONGRESS CATALOGING-IN-PUBLICATION DATA:

In process

ISBN: 1-56802-440-1

Cover illustrations:
BACKGROUND IMAGE: Treaty of Paris, 1783, detail of the signature page.
Source: National Archives and Records Administration. INSET IMAGE: British
prime minister Tony Blair (left) and U.S. president Bill Clinton shake hands
in front of NATO secretary general Javier Solana (right) at NATO's fiftieth
anniversary summit in April 1999. Also pictured are French president
Jacques Chirac (between Blair and Clinton) and Czech president Vaclav
Havel. *Source: Win McNamee, Reuters.*

CONTENTS

SECTION I: SETTLEMENT, UNION, EXPANSION, AND BOUNDARIES

1.1 General

1.2 Indian Treaties

SECTION II: WARS AND MILITARY ALLIANCES

2.1 French and Indian War

2.2 American Revolution

2.3 U.S.-Barbary States Wars, Quasi-War with France, and War of 1812

2.4 U.S.-Mexican War

2.5 Civil War

2.6 Spanish-American War

2.7 Boxer Rebellion

2.8 World War I

2.9 World War II

2.10 Cold War, Korea, and Vietnam

SECTION III: DIPLOMACY AND INTERNATIONAL ORGANIZATIONS

3.1 Arms Limitation

3.2 War Crimes and Rules of Warfare

3.3 Criminal Law, Civil Law, and Extradition

3.4 Cultural Property and Cultural Relations

3.5 Diplomatic Relations

3.6 International Dispute Resolution

3.7 Organization of American States and Other Pan-American Matters

3.8 Rights and Duties of States

3.9 Terrorism

3.10 UN Establishing Document

3.11 U.S. as Peacemaker

SECTION IV: TRADE, COMMERCE, AND TRANSPORTATION

4.1 Aviation and Space Exploration

4.2 Commerce, Trade, and Standardization Issues

4.3 Communication and Postal Agreements and Conventions

4.4 Copyrights, Patents, Industrial Property, and Intellectual Property

4.5 Customs, Transport, and Immigration Issues

4.6 Finance

4.7 Labor Matters

4.8 Navigation and Law of the Sea

SECTION V: HUMAN AND POLITICAL RIGHTS

5.1 General Assistance and Disaster Relief Cooperation

5.2 Health

5.3 Human Rights, Equality, Slavery, and Genocide Issues

5.4 Rights and Welfare of Children

5.5 Rights of Women

SECTION VI: SCIENCE AND ENVIRONMENT

6.1 Conservation and Environment

6.2 Meteorological, Scientific, and Technological Cooperation

How to Use This Book

We are accustomed to thinking of history in terms of people and events, but we actually come to know "history" through documents, and no historical documents are of greater moment than treaties, the instruments through which tribes, states, and nations have traditionally sought to define themselves and their relation to others. As important as treaties are, both to our current lives and to our understanding of history, few people other than professional diplomats and professional historians have much direct contact with these documents, which are typically encountered only at second or third hand through brief allusions and summaries in narrative histories or, perhaps, as nothing more than footnotes here or there. It is the purpose of this book to provide the general reader with ready, convenient, *first-hand* access to key American treaties, agreements, conventions, declarations, and acts, beginning with the *Mayflower* Compact of 1620 and continuing through some of the most recent multilateral treaties to which the United States is a signatory. Also included are certain notable documents important to the United States, but which it did not sign (such as the **Treaty of Versailles** of 1919 and the **Convention on the Prohibition of the Use, Stockpiling, Production and Transfer of Anti-Personnel Mines and on Their Destruction** of 1997).

The United States is party to thousands of treaties currently in force. Add to this the historical treaties, no longer in force, to which colonial America and the United States have been party, and the figure is much higher. This book presents 747 of the historical and current treaties of greatest significance to the United States, through history and at the present time.

The following criteria were used to determine which documents are of "greatest significance":

- Historical importance by consensus. The treaties and agreements associated with major wars, with the settlement of major boundary questions, with the enablement of national expansion (for example, treaties and conventions relating to the Louisiana Purchase), with major trading alliances, and with the foundation of major international organizations (such as the League of Nations and the United Nations) are all included.
- Basic documents. These include treaties of obvious historical importance, with an emphasis on documents of enduring and/or current effect.
- Representative documents. The collection in this volume

includes treaties, agreements, and conventions representative of a wide variety of circumstances, subjects, and cosignatories.

Most of the documents represented here have been or currently are treaties signed and ratified by the United States. (We discuss below the significance of signature, ratification, and accession.) However, also included are a number of documents to which the United States is not a signatory or, although a signatory, failed to ratify. Additionally, a few treaties (such as **Secret Treaty on the Retrocession of Louisiana** of 1800, between France and Spain) do not include the United States at all. In most of these cases, despite the non-participation of the United States, the document in question significantly or even profoundly affected this nation. In a few instances, the very fact that the United States did not participate is in itself of historic significance (as with the **Treaty of Versailles** and the **Convention on the Prohibition of the Use, Stockpiling, Production and Transfer of Anti-Personnel Mines and on Their Destruction**).

Section 3.11: U.S. as Peacemaker consists of yet another special category of treaty, those to which the United States is not a principal signatory, but nevertheless played a key intermediary role in the creation of (as it did, for example, in the 1905 **Treaty of Portsmouth [between Japan and Russia],** ending the Russo-Japanese War, and the 1978 **Camp David Accords [between Egypt and Israel]** or the 1979 **Egyptian-Israeli Peace Treaty**).

A quick glance at the table of contents reveals that this book is hardly limited to war-related treaties but also includes a great many political, diplomatic, and commercial treaties, as well as conventions and declarations relating to human rights, the environment, international law, and many other issues. It should also be noted that many of the documents included here are not even called *treaties*, but bear such designations as *convention, agreement, note, exchange of notes constituting an agreement,* and *declaration.* In a few cases, examples of domestic legislation and presidential proclamation have also been included. Regardless of designation, all of the documents included here convey the practical force of a treaty—that is, a formal agreement between two or more states or between a state and some other entity, such as an Indian tribe or an international organization.

Why, then, the differences among the designations of these documents?

There are no absolute rules governing the use of various terms to describe international agreements, and, in most cases, *treaty* is an adequate generic label to describe most of them; however, the following rules of thumb apply in distinguishing among the terms:

- *Treaty* is best applied to the most formal, solemn, and enduring of international agreements. In most countries, the chief executive or his or her designated representative officer or officers may negotiate and sign a treaty, but, before it can enter into force, a deliberative body (in the United States, the Senate) must ratify the document. In some countries (but not the United States), some treaties are ratified by popular vote, called a *plebiscite*.

- Whereas a treaty usually defines relations (or some aspect of relations) between states, a *convention* typically focuses less on relations than on a specific subject, issue, set of rules, or body of procedures—for example, a convention on the treatment of prisoners of war. Usually, but not always, acceptance of a convention requires signature as well as ratification.

- *Agreement* generally applies to accords made at a lower level than that of a treaty. Usually, an agreement addresses a very specific and temporary issue, such as (for example) an agreement to make a foreign-aid loan. As such, an agreement resembles a contract between states more than it does a treaty. Usually agreements require nothing beyond signature by duly authorized officials of the governments involved; ratification is usually not required. Many agreements take the form of a *note*, a *letter*, an *exchange of notes constituting an agreement*, or an *exchange of letters constituting an agreement*. An agreement is a solemn legal document, but it does not carry the full diplomatic force of a treaty.

- A *declaration* is a statement of the position of a government or several governments on a particular subject. Ratification is generally not required to put the declaration into force.

- A *communiqué* is a statement, typically made by two governments, on a particular subject. Generally, a communiqué has little, if any, legal force under international law.

- A *proclamation* is issued by the president of the United States concerning issues in which the president is constitutionally the competent authority. In American history, some proclamations have had a force at least analogous to that of a treaty, as in the proclamations relating to the end of the Civil War and to the granting of amnesty to the southern states.

- This volume includes a few legislative acts that, in the context of history, have had a force analogous to that of a treaty, as has, for example, the **Indian Removal Act of** 1830 (Section 1.2). Also included are a few *legislative acts* bearing directly on international agreements, such as the **Lend Lease Act** of 1941 (Section 2.9).

As mentioned earlier, most treaties require a two-step acceptance or approval process. The first step is *signature* by a competent national authority, which may be an ambassador or a designated negotiator, or may be the chief executive. The second step is *ratification*. In the United States, this requires a two-thirds majority vote by the Senate. Other forms of approval or acceptance are sometimes also possible:

- A state may sign and ratify some treaties *with reservation or reservations*, modifying or even exempting certain provisions.

- A state may sign and ratify some treaties *with declaration* or *declarations*. This may modify some portion of the treaty or may express regret that some provision has been included or excluded from the treaty.

- A state may *accept* or *accede to* a treaty. In this case, a state agrees to abide by the terms of a treaty without signing it. Accession to a treaty requires ratification. Acceptance and accession generally apply only to multilateral treaties, conventions, and other agreements.

Finally, many treaties and conventions include a *denunciation clause*, laying down the procedure by which a state may legally opt out of or abrogate the agreement. Usually, the only requirement for a legal denunciation is a stated period of advance notice of intent to denounce the treaty.

The treaties included in this book are grouped according to subjects or categories the author believes will be most immediately useful to general researchers, students, and other users of the volume. Within each category or subject section, the entries are arranged chronologically. Related entries are indicated by boldface cross-references within each entry. Most sections include both *bilateral agreements* (between two states or sovereign entities) as well as *multilateral agreements* (among three or more states or sovereign entities).

Treaty names often present difficulties because a given treaty may be known by more than one name (for example, the **Panama Canal Treaty** of 1977 is also often called the Torrijos-Carter Treaty) or may be better known by a "familiar" name than by its official name: *the Treaty to Settle and to Find the Boundaries between the Territories of the United States in the Possessions of Her Britannic Majesty in North America; for the Final Suppression of the African Slave Trade, and for the Giving Up of Criminals, Fugitive from Justice, in Certain Cases* is much better known as the **Webster-Ashburton Treaty.** In this book, entry headings always give the name by which the treaty is best known. If the treaty has an official title that differs from this familiar name, the full official title is given following the subhead **"Official title."** For treaties that have long or cumbersome official names, but no generally used familiar name, a more concisely descriptive title is generally substituted in the entry heading, and, again, the full official title follows the **"Official title"** subhead. In the instance of most bilateral treaty names, to increase clarity, the name of the cosignatory is parenthetically included—for example, **Treaty (with France) for the Cession of Louisiana.**

In addition to furnishing the treaty's familiar (or convenient) name and, where necessary, the official title, each entry also supplies the following information:

- Following the subhead **"Signed"** are the date and place of signature. In the case of multilateral treaties with many signatories signing on various dates, the date given is the date on which the treaty was opened for signature. (In a few special cases, **"Adopted"** or **"Drafted"** are used in place of **"Signed."**)
- Following the subhead **"Signatories"** are the signatory states and/or sovereign entities, listed in alphabetical order. Occasionally, reservations or other information regarding the status of signatures is noted. Note that many recent multilateral treaties included in this book remain open for signature. In all cases, the signatories listed are those as of December 1999.
- Following the subhead **"In force"** is the date on which the treaty entered into force. In the case of bilateral treaties, this is usually the date on which both parties ratified the treaty or the president of the United States proclaimed (officially announced) the Senate's ratification of the treaty. Sometimes the date of entry into force follows ratification by some period specified in the treaty itself. In the case of multilateral treaties, the date of entry into force is usually that on which a certain number of states have ratified the document. In some cases, however, the date of entry into force is explicitly specified by a provision of the treaty. In cases where the date on which a multilateral treaty *generally* entered into force differs from that on which the treaty entered into force *for the United States,* both dates are given. In cases where entry into force coincides with signature, the phrase "On signing" follows the subhead **"In force."** Finally, in the case of treaties

that had not entered into force as of December 1999, the phrase "Not yet in force" follows the subhead **"In force."**

- Following the subhead **"Overview"** is a brief statement of the main subject of the treaty.
- Following the subhead **"Discussion"** is a more or less extended consideration of the treaty and its significance. The length of the discussion depends on the importance and complexity of the document in question, but discussion typically includes historical background or context and a summary of the chief provisions of the treaty, the issues it addresses, any problems created by the treaty, and, where appropriate, the history of the treaty, including its current status. Where warranted, extended quotation from the treaty text is included following this subhead.
- Following the subhead **"References"** will be found books relevant to the treaty and/or to the historical and subject context of the treaty. (More general books on treaties are listed in **Appendix C: Bibliography.**)

Following the entries, in the back of the book, are three appendixes.

- **Appendix A: Depositories** lists the principal places researchers can find American treaty texts and information relating to the treaties.
- **Appendix B: Web Sources** lists sites on the World Wide Web that serve up significant offerings relating to treaties, including, in many cases, full treaty texts.
- **Appendix C: Bibliography** includes general works on treaties, which are not listed in the **References** section of the entries themselves.

In addition to historical events, subjects, personal names, and country names, the **Index** at the end of the book lists all of the treaties, using all of the names by which they are known.

Settlement, Union, Expansion, and Boundaries

SECTION 1.1

General

Overview of the Documents

The treaties and agreements in this section include some of the most basic documents in American history, in that they establish early government, define and describe boundaries, and formalize expansion.

The *Mayflower* Compact of 1620 is generally regarded as the first political "constitution" to be drawn up by Europeans on the North American continent, while **The Articles of Confederation of the United Colonies of New England** (1643) must be considered the first serious attempt to unite the disparate and disputatious English colonies, albeit for the limited purpose of common defense. Similarly limited was the abortive **Albany Plan of Union** (1754), a proposal for political unity among the English during the crisis of the French and Indian War.

Other key documents relating to the unification of the colonies include **Virginia's Cession of Western Lands** (1783) and **The Northwest Ordinance** (1787). By the **Cession,** Virginia renounced its claims to extensive tracts of western land (claims based on broad interpretation of original royal grants), which conflicted with the claims of other states and delayed ratification of the Articles of Confederation. The cession removed a stumbling block to ratification of the Articles. The **Northwest Ordinance,** the most important piece of United States legislation passed under the Articles of Confederation, is presented here as, in effect, a treaty between the government of the United States and the Northwest Territory, defining the relationship among the territory, the government, and the several states, while also laying down basic laws for the region.

Except for the two "contracts" between France and the United States (**Contract between the King [of France] and the Thirteen United States of North America** of 1782 and of 1783), which lay down the terms of two post-Revolutionary War loans to the United States, the remaining treaties and agreements in this section either define boundaries or accompany and enable expansion of the nation.

The **Proclamation of 1763,** promulgated by King George III of England, attempted to set a limit to the western settlement of the colonies, mainly in an effort to bring costly Indian warfare to an end. The proclamation was successful in relieving some of the pressures of encroachment that created conflict between frontier colonists and the Indians; however, the document also contributed to the growing disaffection of the frontier regions and their alienation from colonial government headquartered in the Tidewater as well as the royal government across the Atlantic. Thus this attempt to control and limit colonial expansion helped kindle the fires of revolution.

Jay's Treaty with Great Britain (1794) is a key post-Revolutionary document that guaranteed British evacuation of western outposts and, therefore, successfully asserted United States sovereignty over the Old Northwest. While the Jay treaty settled matters of sovereignty with the British (at least in principle and temporarily), the **Treaty of San Lorenzo (Pinckney's Treaty),** concluded a year later, fixed the southern boundary of the United States (the boundary with Spain's colonies) at 31°N latitude and established commercial arrangements with Spain favorable to the United States, including free navigation of the Mississippi River through Spanish territory.

A group of two treaties and three conventions bears indirectly and directly on the single greatest expansion of the United States, the acquisition of the Louisiana Territory from France. The **Secret Treaty on the Retrocession of Louisiana** (1800) did not directly involve the United States, but effected Spain's return of the territory to France, thereby making the sale possible. **Louisiana Purchase: First Convention, Louisiana Purchase: Second Convention,** and **Treaty (with France) for the Cession of Louisiana,** all of 1803, are the documents that formally concluded the sale and purchase of the territory.

Convention (with Britain Regarding Canada) Respecting Fisheries, Boundary, and the Restoration of Slaves (1818) was one of a series of treaties seeking to define the boundary between British Canada and the United States, and the **Adams-Oñis Treaty** (1819) further defined the border with Spain's possessions, confirming the Spanish cession of Florida to the United States and the Spanish renunciation of the Oregon country in exchange for U.S. recognition of Spanish sovereignty over Texas. Within a few years of these treaties, the United States would look beyond the continent, concluding the 1826 **Treaty between Hawaii and the United States,** which, by establishing amity and commerce with Hawaii (then called the Sandwich Islands), created a first American political foothold in the Pacific.

In 1821, the Mexican Revolution liberated Mexico from Spain, thereby rendering moot the provision of the Adams-Oñis Treaty recognizing Spanish sovereignty over Texas. Fifteen years later, Texas, in turn, won its independence from Mexico (**Treaty of Velasco,** 1836) and concluded a boundary treaty with the United States (**Texas-American Boundary Convention,** 1838), thereby securing the U.S. government's de facto recognition of its sovereignty. After much debate, controversy, and anxiety, generated both by fears of provoking war with Mexico and by admitting to the union a new slaveholding state, **The Treaty of Annexation (of Texas)** was concluded in 1844, paving the way to statehood for the young republic.

Two years earlier, in 1842, the **Webster-Ashburton Treaty** settled the thorny question of the northeastern boundary between the United States and Canada (while also providing for Anglo-American cooperation in the suppression of the slave trade). Two years after the Texas annexation, in 1846, the **Oregon Treaty** made diplomatically important, if not geopolitically definitive, strides toward resolving the disputed boundary between the United States and Canada in the Northwest. While these two treaties defined limits, the **Gadsden Treaty** (1853) and the **Alaska Purchase** (1867) added large territories to the nation. The Gadsden Treaty formalized the so-called Gadsden Purchase of some 29,670 square miles of northern Mexican territory, which now constitutes southern Arizona and southern New Mexico. By the Alaska Purchase, the United States acquired the vast territory of Alaska from the czar of Russia.

Between 1849 and 1898, a series of documents brought Hawaii into the American orbit and then into the American grasp (**Treaty between Hawaii and the United States,** 1849; **Treaty of Reciprocity between the United States of America and the Hawaiian Kingdom,** 1875; **Supplementary Convention to the Treaty of Reciprocity between the United States of America and the Hawaiian Kingdom,** 1884;, **Treaty of Annexation [of Hawaii],** 1897; and the **Newlands Resolution [Annexation of Hawaii],** 1898).

Some of the treaties in sections 2.4, 2.6, and 2.7 also deal with United States expansion and imperialism, but the major moves in this regard had all been made by the end of the nineteenth century. Nevertheless, border issues persisted well into the twentieth century. Two examples of twentieth-century border agreements, **Convention between the United States and Mexico: Equitable Distribution of the Waters of the Rio Grande** (1906) and **Treaty to Resolve Pending Boundary Differences and Maintain the Rio Grande and Colorado Rivers as the International Boundaries** (1970) are included in this section.

Mayflower Compact

SIGNED: November 11, 1620, Cape Cod, New England
IN FORCE: On signing
SIGNATORIES: Puritan "Separatists" (later popularly known as "Pilgrims") vs. the "Strangers" (non-Puritan settlers, with the Separatists, of the Plymouth colony); in all, 41 colonists signed the document
OVERVIEW: Drawn up as the *Mayflower* rode at anchor off the

New England coast, this document, a "plantation covenant," is often called the first American constitution. It was an agreement between two sets of differently motivated colonists to cooperate in forming a temporary government for the Plymouth colony.

DISCUSSION:
Beginning during the reign of Elizabeth I, some members of the Church of England objected to what they deemed compromises with Catholic practice. When James I ascended the throne in 1603, Puritan leaders called for reform, including the abolition of bishops. James refused, but Puritanism—as the reform movement was called—continued to gain a substantial following. The government, wedded to mainstream Anglicanism, reacted with repression and persecution of the Puritans, which prompted some to leave England for religiously tolerant Holland. Those who left were called Separatists. Facing economic hardship and distressed that their children were growing up Dutch rather than English, some of the Separatists voted to immigrate to America. On September 16, 1620, 102 persons (among them 37 Separatists) embarked on the *Mayflower,* bound for America. Although land was sighted on November 19, rough seas off Nantucket (apparently) forced the *Mayflower's* skipper, Captain Christopher Jones, to steer away from the intended landing place at the mouth of the Hudson River, to Cape Cod. This location was well beyond the jurisdiction of the Virginia Company (also called the London Company), from which the *Mayflower* party had obtained authorization to establish a colony.

Some historians believe that a Separatist bribe, not adverse winds, caused Captain Jones to alter course. These historians argue that the Separatists wished to make their group independent of external authority, so purposely put themselves beyond the reach of the Virginia Company. Whether or not this was the case, it is also true that the change in landing place created anxiety among at least some of the Separatists that the non-Separatist "Strangers" among them would exploit the fact that they had landed outside the authorized land grant as a motive to challenge Separatist authority in matters of governance. To allay these fears and to create an equitable relationship between the Separatist and Stranger groups, the Separatists drew up the *Mayflower* Compact, by which both groups agreed to create a "Civil Body Politic," a temporary government, and to abide by laws created for the good of the colony.

The original document has not come down to us, and it is known through a copy of it in an early Separatist account called *Mourt's Relation* (1622). It was also reproduced by William Bradford, in his narrative history, *Of Plymouth Plantation,* which was written in the seventeenth century, but not printed until 1856. The following is Bradford's version:

> In the name of God, Amen. We, whose names are underwritten, the loyal subjects of our dread sovereigne Lord, King James, by the grace

of God, of Great Britaine, France, and Ireland king, defender of the faith, etc., having undertaken, for the glory of God, and advancement of the Christian faith, and honour of our king and country, a voyage to plant the first colony in the Northerne parts of Virginia, doe, by these presents, solemnly and mutually in the presence of God, and one of another, covenant and combine ourselves together into a civill body politick, for our better ordering and preservation and furtherance of the ends aforesaid; and by virtue hereof to enacte, constitute, and frame such just and equall laws, ordinances, acts, constitutions, and offices, from time to time, as shall be thought most meete and convenient for the generall good of the Colonie unto which we promise all due submission and obedience. In witness whereof we have hereunder subscribed our names at Cap-Codd the 11, of November, in the year of the raigne of our sovereigne lord, King James, of England, France, and Ireland, the eighteenth, and of Scotland the fiftie-fourth. Anno. Dom. 1620.

REFERENCES:

Bradford, William, *Of Plymouth Plantation 1620-1647.* Edited by Samuel Eliot Morison. New York: Scribner's, 1963.

Donovan, Frank Robert. *The Mayflower Compact.* New York: Grosset and Dunlap, 1968.

Walsh, John E. *The Mayflower Compact, November 11, 1620: The First Democratic Document in America.* New York: Franklin Watts, 1971

The Articles of Confederation of the United Colonies of New England

SIGNED: May 19, 1643, at Boston

SIGNATORIES: "the Plantations under the Government of the Massachusetts, the Plantations under the Government of New Plymouth, the Plantations under the Government of Connecticut, and the Government of New Haven with the Plantations in Combination therewith"

IN FORCE: From September 7, 1643

OVERVIEW: After the **Mayflower Compact,** the first important document of colonial unity.

DISCUSSION:

The idea of colonial unity was slow in coming. By and large, the various English colonies, even those concentrated in the region known as New England, regarded themselves not only as separate, but as competitors for land and for trade with the mother country as well as with the Indians. It was nothing less than grim necessity that drove the colonies to draw up very limited articles of confederation, as the preamble to the 1643 document explains:

Whereas we all came into these parts of America with one and the same end and aim, namely, to advance the Kingdom of our Lord Jesus Christ and to enjoy the liberties of the Gospel in purity with peace; and whereas in our settling (by a wise providence of God) we are further dispersed upon the sea coasts and rivers than was at first intended, so that we can not according to our desire with convenience communicate in one government and jurisdiction; and whereas we live encompassed with people of several nations and strange languages which

hereafter may prove injurious to us or our posterity. And forasmuch as the natives have formerly committed sundry Insolence and outrages upon several Plantations of the English and have of late combined themselves against us: and seeing by reason of those sad distractions in England which they have heard of, and by which they know vie are hindered from that humble way of seeking advice, or reaping those comfortable fruits of protection, which at other times we might well expect. We therefore do conceive it our bounden duty, without delay to enter into a present Consocation amongst ourselves, for mutual help and strength in all our future concernments: That, as in nation and religion, so in other respects, we be and continue one according to the tenor and true meaning of the ensuing articles: Wherefore it is fully agreed and concluded by and between the parties or Jurisdictions above named, and they jointly and severally do by these presents agree and conclude that they all be and henceforth be called by the name of the United Colonies of New England.

The Indian "Insolence and outrages" to which the document refers includes primarily the conflict historians call the Pequot War (1636-1637), although violent conflict between colonists and Indians was frequent.

The principal text that follows the preamble is reproduced here:

2. The said United Colonies for themselves and their posterities do jointly and severally hereby enter into a firm and perpetual league of friendship and amity for offence and defence, mutual advice and succor upon all just occasions both for preserving and propagating the truth and liberties of the Gospel and for their own mutual safety and welfare.

3. It is further agreed that the Plantations which at present are or hereafter shall be settled within the limits of the Massachusetts shall be forever under the Massachusetts and shall have peculiar jurisdiction among themselves in all cases as an entire body, and that Plymouth, Connecticut, and New Haven shall each of them have like peculiar jurisdiction and government within their limits; and in reference to the Plantations which already are settled, or shall hereafter be erected, or shall settle within their limits respectively; provided no other Jurisdiction shall hereafter be taken in as a distinct head or member of this Confederation, nor shall any other Plantation or Jurisdiction in present being, and not already in combination or under the jurisdiction of any of these Confederates, be received by any of them; nor shall any two of the Confederates join in one Jurisdiction without consent of the rest, which consent to be interpreted as is expressed in the sixth article ensuing.

4. It is by these Confederates agreed that the charge of all just wars, whether offensive or defensive, upon what part or member of this Confederation soever they fall, shall both in men, provisions and all other disbursements be borne by all the parts of this Confederation in different proportions according to their different ability in manner following, namely, that the Commissioners for each Jurisdiction from time to time, as there shall be occasion, bring a true account and number of all their males in every Plantation, or any way belonging to or under their several Jurisdictions, of what quality or condition soever they be, from sixteen years old to threescore, being inhabitants there. And that according to the different numbers which from time to time shall be found in each Jurisdiction upon a true and just account, the service of men and all charges of the war be borne by the

poll: each Jurisdiction or Plantation being left to their own just course and custom of rating themselves and people according to their different estates with due respects to their qualities and exemptions amongst themselves though the Confederation take no notice of any such privilege: and that according to their different charge of each Jurisdiction and Plantation the whole advantage of the war (if it please God so to bless their endeavors) whether it be in lands, goods, or persons, shall be proportionately divided among the said Confederates.

5. It is further agreed, that if any of these Jurisdictions or any Plantation under or in combination with them, be invaded by any enemy whomsoever, upon notice and request of any three magistrates of that Jurisdiction so invaded, the rest of the Confederates without any further meeting or expostulation shall forthwith send aid to the Confederate in danger but in different proportions; namely, the Massachusetts an hundred men sufficiently armed and provided for such a service and journey, and each of the rest, forty-five so armed and provided, or any less number, if less be required according to this proportion. But if such Confederate in danger may be supplied by their next Confederates, not exceeding the number hereby agreed, they may crave help there, and seek no further for the present: the charge to be borne as in this article is expressed: and at the return to be victualled and supplied with powder and shot for their journey (if there be need) by that Jurisdiction which employed or sent for them; but none of the Jurisdictions to exceed these numbers until by a meeting of the Commissioners for this Confederation a greater aid appear necessary. And this proportion to continue till upon knowledge of greater numbers in each Jurisdiction which shall be brought to the next meeting, some other proportion be ordered. But in any such case of sending men for present aid, whether before or after such order or alteration, it is agreed that at the meeting of the Commissioners for this Confederation, the cause of such war or invasion be duly considered: and if it appear that the fault lay in the parties so invaded then that Jurisdiction or Plantation make just satisfaction, both to the invaders whom they have injured, and bear all the charges of the war themselves, without requiring any allowance from the rest of the Confederates towards the same. And further that if any Jurisdiction see any danger of invasion approaching, and there be time for a meeting, that in such a case three magistrates of the Jurisdiction may summon a meeting at such convenient place as themselves shall think meet, to consider and provide against the threatened danger; provided when they are met they may remove to what place they please; only whilst any of these four Confederates have but three magistrates in their Jurisdiction, their requests, or summons, from any two of them shall be accounted of equal force with the three mentioned in both the clauses of this article, till there be an increase of magistrates there.

6. It is also agreed, that for the managing and concluding of all Affairs and concerning the whole Confederation two Commissioners shall be chosen by and out of each of these four Jurisdictions: namely, two for the Massachusetts, two for Plymouth, two for Connecticut, and two for New Haven, being all in Church-fellowship with us, which shall bring full power from their several General Courts respectively to hear, examine, weigh, and determine all affairs of our war, or peace, leagues, aids, charges, and numbers of men for war, division of spoils and whatsoever is gotten by conquest, receiving of more Confederates for Plantations into combination with any of the Confederates, and all things of like nature, which are the proper concomitants or conse-

quents of such a Confederation for amity, offense, and defence: not intermeddling with the government of any of the Jurisdictions, which by the third article is preserved entirely to themselves. But if these eight Commissioners when they meet shall not all agree yet it [is] concluded that any six of the eight agreeing shall have power to settle and determine the business in question. But if six do not agree, that then such propositions with their reasons so far as they have been debated, be sent and referred to the four General Courts; namely, the Massachusetts, Plymouth, Connecticut, and New Haven; and if at all the said General Courts the business so referred be concluded, then to be prosecuted by the Confederates and all their members. It is further agreed that these eight Commissioners shall meet once every year besides extraordinary meetings (according to the fifth article) to consider, treat, and conclude of all affairs belonging to this Confederation, which meeting shall ever be the first Thursday in September. And that the next meeting after the date of these presents, which shall be accounted the second meeting, shall be at Boston in the Massachusetts, the third at Hartford, the fourth at New Haven, the fifth at Plymouth, the sixth and seventh at Boston; and then Hartford, New Haven, and Plymouth, and so n course successively, if in the meantime some middle place be not found out and agreed on, which may be commodious for all the Jurisdictions.

7. It is further agreed that at each meeting of these eight Commissioners, whether ordinary or extraordinary, they or six of them agreeing as before, may choose their President out of themselves whose office work shall be to take care and direct for order and a comely carrying on of all proceedings in the present meeting: but he shall be invested with no such power or respect, as by which he shall hinder the propounding or progress of any business, or any way cast the scales otherwise than in the precedent article is agreed.

8. It is also agreed that the Commissioners for this Confederation hereafter at their meetings, whether ordinary or extraordinary, as they may have commission or opportunity, do endeavor to frame and establish agreements and orders in general cases of a civil nature, wherein all the Plantations are interested, for preserving of peace among themselves, for preventing as much as may be all occasion of war or differences with others, as about the free and speedy passage of justice in every Jurisdiction, to all the Confederates equally as to their own, receiving those that remove from one Plantation to another without due certificate, how all the Jurisdictions may carry it towards the Indians, that they neither grow insolent nor be injured without due satisfaction, lest war break in upon the Confederates through such miscarriages. It is also agreed that if any servant run away from his master into any other of these confederated Jurisdictions, that in such case, upon the certificate of one magistrate in the Jurisdiction out of which the said servant fled, or upon other due proof; the said servant shall be delivered, either to his master, or any other that pursues and brings such certificate or proof. And that upon the escape of any prisoner whatsoever, or fugitive for any criminal cause, whether breaking prison, or getting from the officer, or otherwise escaping, upon the certificate of two magistrates of the Jurisdiction out of which the escape is made, that he was a prisoner, or such an offender at the time of the escape, the magistrates, or some of them of that Jurisdiction where for the present the said prisoner or fugitive abideth, shall forthwith grant such a warrant as the case will bear, for the apprehending of any such person, and the delivery of him into the hands of the officer or other person who pursues him. And if there be

help required, for the safe returning of any such offender, then it shall be granted to him that craves the same, he paying the charges thereof.

9. And for that the justest wars may be of dangerous consequence, especially to the smaller Plantations in these United Colonies, it is agreed that neither the Massachusetts, Plymouth, Connecticut, nor New Haven, nor any of the members of them, shall at any time hereafter begin, undertake, or engage themselves, or this Confederation, or any part thereof in any war whatsoever (sudden exigencies, with the necessary consequents thereof excepted), which are also to be moderated as much as the case will permit, without the consent and agreement of the forementioned eight Commissioners, or at least six of them, as in the sixth article is provided: and that no charge be required of any of the Confederates, in case of a defensive war, till the said Commissioners have met, and approved the justice of the war, and have agreed upon the sum of money to be levied, which sum is then to be paid by the several Confederates in proportion according to the fourth article

10. That in extraordinary occasions, when meetings are summoned by three magistrats of any Jurisdiction, or two as in the fifth article, ii) any of the Commissioners come not, due warning being given or sent, it is agreed that four of the Commissioners shall have power to direct a war which cannot be delayed, and to send for due proportions of men out of each Jurisdiction, as well as six might do if all met; but not less than six shall determine the justice of the war, or allow the demands or bills of charges, or cause any levies to be made for the same.

11. It is further agreed that if any of the Confederates shall hereafter break any of these present articles, or be any other ways injurious to any one of the other Jurisdictions; such breach of agreement or injury shall be duly considered and ordered by the Commissioners for the other Jurisdictions, that both peace and this present Confederation may be entirely preserved without violation.

12. Lastly, this perpetual Confederation, and the several articles and agreements thereof being read and seriously considered, both by the General Court for the Massachusetts, and by the Commissioners for Plymouth, Connecticut, and New Haven, were fully allowed and confirmed by three of the forenamed Confederates, namely, the Massachusetts, Connecticut, and New Haven; only the Commissioners for Plymouth having no commission to concludes desired respite until they might advise with their General Court; whereupon it was agreed and concluded by the said Court of the Massachusetts, and the Commissioners for the other two Confederates, that, if Plymouth consent, then the whole treaty as it stands in these present articles is, and shall continue, firm and stable without alteration: but if Plymouth come not in yet the other three Confederates do by these presents confirm the whole Confederation, and all the articles thereof; only in September next when the second meeting of the Commissioners is to be at Boston, new consideration may be taken of the sixth article, which concerns number of Commissioners for meeting and concluding the affairs of this Confederation to the satisfaction of the Court of the Massachusetts, and the Commissioners for the other two Confederates, but the rest to stand unquestioned.

REFERENCE:
Hubbard, William. *The History of the Indian Wars in New England.* 1677; reprint ed., New York: Kraus, 1969.

Albany Plan of Union

PROPOSED: By Benjamin Franklin at the Congress of Albany, 1754
SIGNATORIES: None
IN FORCE: Not enacted
OVERVIEW: The first substantive proposal and plan for a union of Britain's North American colonies.

DISCUSSION:
The Congress of Albany was convened in 1754 by the British Board of Trade in an effort to secure the loyalty of the Iroquois Confederacy, which was wavering between alliance with the French and the British at the opening of the French and Indian War. Benjamin Franklin, a delegate to the congress, formulated and proposed a plan for union, primarily with the purpose of promoting more effective military coordination and cooperation among the colonies, which were suffering greatly in the war. Although the plan came to nothing and was never submitted to the king or to Parliament, it is important for the scheme of government and representation it proposed:

- A general government of what was then eleven colonies, to be administered by a royally appointed president-general and a Grand Council, "to be chosen by the representatives of the people of the several Colonies met in their respective assemblies."
- Representation in the Grand Council was to be proportional to the population of each colony.
- " . . . assent of the President-General [was to be] requisite to all acts of the Grand Council . . ."
- The president-general was to make all Indian treaties, "with the advice of the Grand Council."
- The Grand Council was to make most laws locally and directly affecting the colonies (albeit with the assent of the president-general).
- Laws enacted by the Grand Council "shall not be repugnant, but, as near as may be, agreeable to the laws of England, and shall be transmitted to the King in Council for approbation . . ."

The Plan of Union was to be flexible and loose, with "the particular military as well as civil establishments in each Colony [to] remain in their present state, the general constitution notwithstanding . . ." In the event of emergency, "any Colony may defend itself, and lay accounts of expense thence arising before the President-General and Grand Council . . ."

REFERENCE:
Jennings, Francis. *Empire of Fortune: Crowns, Colonies, and Tribes in the Even Years War in America.* New York: W.W. Norton, 1988.

Proclamation of 1763

PROCLAIMED: October 7, 1763, at London
SIGNATORY: King George III of England
IN FORCE: Upon proclamation
OVERVIEW: In an effort to curb Indian hostility, the Proclamation of 1763 limited white colonial settlement to territory east of the Appalachian Mountains, thereby provoking the defiant ire of frontier settlers.

DISCUSSION:

During the French and Indian War (1754-63) British authorities concluded the Treaty of Easton (1758) with the Iroquois tribes and the Delawares, guaranteeing that white settlement would proceed no farther west than the Allegheny Mountains. Settlers violated this agreement almost immediately. Just as the French and Indian War ended, a violent spasm of Indian raids, known as Pontiac's Rebellion, convulsed the frontier. In an effort to bring peace to te colonies at last, the government of King George III proclaimed a new settlement boundary, this one through the Appalachian Mountains.

After making declarations relevant to the government of the colonies, the Proclamation of 1763 defines the limit of settlement:

And whereas it is just and reasonable and essential to our interest and the security of our colonies that the several nations or tribes of Indians with whom we are connected, and who live under our protection should not be molested or disturbed in the possession of such parts of our dominions and territories as, not having been ceded to or purchased by us, are reserved to them, or any of them, as their hunting grounds; we do therefore, with the advice of our Privy Council, declare it to be our royal will and pleasure that no governor or commander in chief, in any of our colonies of Quebec, East Florida, or West Florida, do presume, upon any pretense whatever, to grant warrants of survey or pass any patents for lands beyond the bounds of their respective governments, as described in their commissions; as also that no governor or commander in chief of our other colonies or plantations in America do presume for the present, and until our further pleasure be known, to grant warrants of survey or pass patents for any lands beyond the heads or sources of any of the rivers which fall into the Atlantic Ocean from the west or northwest; or upon any lands whatever which, not having been ceded to or purchased by us, as aforesaid, are reserved to the said Indians or any of them.

The "heads or sources" of the longest rivers from the west or northwest are at the eastern continental divide of Appalachians. The Proclamation continues:

And we do further strictly enjoin and require all persons whatever who have either willfully or inadvertently seated themselves upon any lands within the countries above described, or upon any other lands which, not having been ceded to or purchased by us, are still reserved to the said Indians as aforesaid, forthwith to remove themselves from such settlements. And whereas great frauds and abuses have been committed in the purchasing lands of the Indians, to the great prejudice of our interests and to the great dissatisfaction of the said Indians; in order, therefore, to prevent such irregularities for the future, and to the end that the Indians may be convinced of our justice and determined resolution to remove all reasonable cause of discontent, we do, with the advice of our Privy Council, strictly enjoin and require that no private person do presume to make any purchase from the said Indians of any lands reserved to the said Indians within those parts of our colonies where we have thought proper to allow settlement . . .

The so-called "Proclamation Line" did bring a brief period of peace with the Indians, but, like the earlier Easton boundary, was soon breached by settlers, who also demanded that the royal government protect them from Indian depredations. The government often declined to protect settlers who had defied the proclamation, and the result was growing resentment toward the "mother country," which contributed to the spirit of rebellion that ultimately resulted in the American Revolution.

REFERENCE:
The Annals of America, vol. 2 (Chicago: Encyclopaedia Britannica, Inc., 1976).

Contract between the King (of France) and the Thirteen United States of North America

SIGNED: July 16, 1782
SIGNATORIES: France vs. "the Thirteen United States of America"
In force: Within nine months from signing
OVERVIEW: An accounting of the sums loaned by France to the United States in prosecution of the American Revolution, together with a repayment agreement.

DISCUSSION:

Negotiated between Benjamin Franklin, for the United States, and Charles Gravier de Vergennes, for King Louis XVI, the contract stipulated the sums of money disbursed by France to the United States and specified "the periods at which the Congress of the United States have engaged to repay them to His Majesty's royal treasury." The additional object of the contract was "to state this matter in such a way as for the future to prevent all difficulties capable of interrupting the good harmony which His Majesty is resolved to maintain and preserve between him and the said United States."

REFERENCES:
Boatner, Mark M. *Encyclopedia of the American Revolution.* New York: D. McKay, 1966.
Commager, Henry Steele, and Morris, Richard B., eds. *The Spirit of 'Seventy-Six: The Story of the American Revolution as Told by Participants.* New York: Harper & Row, 1958.
Morris, Richard B. *The Forging of the Union, 1781-1789.* New York: Harper & Row, 1987.
Smith, Page. *A New Age Now Begins: A People's History of the American Revolution,* 2 vols. New York: Penguin, 1976.

Contract between the King (of France) and the Thirteen United States of North America

SIGNED: February 25, 1783

SIGNATORIES: France vs. "the Thirteen United States of North America"

IN FORCE: Within nine months from signing

OVERVIEW: The instrument by which France loaned to the United States 6 million livres after the Revolution, in addition to the sums loaned during the Revolution (see **Contract between the King [of France] and the Thirteen United States of North America** [1782]).

DISCUSSION:

"The reestablished peace between the belligerent powers, the advantages of a free commerce to all parts of the globe, and the independence of the thirteen United States of North America, acknowledged and founded on a solid and honorable basis, rendered it probable that the said States would be in a condition to provide hereafter for their necessities, by means of the resources within themselves, without being compelled to implore the continuation of the succors which the King has so liberally granted during the war; but the Minister Plenipotentiary of the said United States to His Majesty having represented to him the exhausted state to which they have been reduced by a long and disastrous war, His Majesty has condescended to take into consideration the request made by the aforesaid Minister in the name of the Congress of the said States for a new advance of money to answer numerous purposes of urgent and indispensable expenses in the course of the present year; His Majesty has, in consequence, determined, notwithstanding the no less pressing necessities of his own service, to grant to Congress a new pecuniary assistance, which he has fixed at the sum of six millions livres tournois ..."

The contract recapitulated the early agreement of 1782 and further specified a repayment schedule.

REFERENCES:
Boatner, Mark M. *Encyclopedia of the American Revolution.* New York: D. McKay, 1966.
Commager, Henry Steele, and Morris, Richard B., eds. *The Spirit of 'Seventy-Six: The Story of the American Revolution as Told by Participants.* New York: Harper & Row, 1958.
Morris, Richard B. *The Forging of the Union, 1781-1789.* New York: Harper & Row, 1987.
Smith, Page. *A New Age Now Begins: A People's History of the American Revolution,* 2 vols. New York: Penguin, 1976.

Virginia's Cession of Western Lands

SIGNED: December 20, 1783, at Williamsburg, Virginia

SIGNATORIES: General Assembly of Virginia vs. United States

IN FORCE: From signing

OVERVIEW: When Virginia's claims to extensive tracts of western land (based on broad interpretation of original royal grants) conflicted with the claims of other states and delayed ratification of the Articles of Confederation, Virginia ceded to the federal government its claims north of the Ohio River, thereby removing a roadblock to ratification.

DISCUSSION:

In addition to promoting ratification of the Articles of Confederation, Virginia's cession of its Ohio country claims was a profound acknowledgment of federal union because the cession was not made from one colony or state to another, but from a state to the nation. For this reason, Virginia's Cession is a key American agreement.

The document reads in part:

Be it enacted by the General Assembly that it shall and may be lawful for the delegates of this state to the Congress of the United States, or such of them as shall be assembled in Congress, and the said delegates, or such of them so assembled, are hereby fully authorized and empowered, for and on behalf of this state, by proper deeds or instrument in writing, under their hands and seals, to convey, transfer, assign, and make over unto the United States in Congress assembled, for the benefit of the said states, all right, title, and claim, as well of soil as jurisdiction, which this Commonwealth has to the territory or tract of country within the limits of the Virginia charter, situated, lying, and being to the northwest of the River Ohio, subject to the terms and conditions contained in the before-recited act of Congress of the 13th day of September last, that is to say:

Upon condition that the territory so ceded shall be laid out and formed into states, containing a suitable extent of territory, not less than 100 nor more than 150 miles square, or as near thereto as circumstances will admit; and that the states so formed shall be distinct republican states, and admitted members of the federal Union, have the same rights of sovereignty, freedom, and independence as the other states...

REFERENCES:
The Annals of America, vol. 2. Chicago: Encyclopaedia Britannica, 1976.
Jensen, Merrill. *The Articles of Confederation: An Interpretation of the Social-Constitutional History of the American Revolution, 1774-1781.* Madison: University of Wisconsin Press, 1970.

Northwest Ordinance

ENACTED: July 13, 1787

SIGNATORIES: Legislation of Congress under the Articles of Confederation

IN FORCE: From enactment

OVERVIEW: The Northwest Ordinance specified how territories were to become states and ensured that democratic government would prevail in the territories.

DISCUSSION:

Given the nature of the United States under the Articles of Confederation, a collection of states bound in amity and cooperation rather than mere political divisions subordinate to a central government, the Northwest Ordinance may be considered a treaty or covenant among separate states.

The ordinance specified the division of the "Old Northwest"—the vast region bounded by the Ohio and Mississippi rivers and by the Great Lakes—into three to five territories. Congress was empowered to appoint a governor, a secretary, and three judges to govern each of the territories. When the adult male population of a territory reached 5,000, elections would be held in the territory to form a territorial legislature and to send a nonvoting representative to Congress. When its adult male population reached 60,000, a territory could write a constitution and apply for statehood.

One of the causes of the American Revolution was Britain's refusal to make its American colonies full members of a national commonwealth. The Northwest Ordinance ensured that the frontier regions would never be mere colonies of the more established Tidewater region, but would become full partners in a common enterprise.

In addition to providing for the representation and statehood of territories, the Northwest Ordinance enumerated the democratic rights of the region's citizens, years in advance of the Constitution and its first ten amendments, the Bill of Rights:

> *Art. 2.* The inhabitants of the said territory shall always be entitled to the benefits of the writ of habeas corpus, and of the trial by jury; of a proportionate representation of the people in the legislature; and of judicial proceedings according to the course of the common law. All persons shall be bailable, unless for capital offenses, where the proof shall be evident or the presumption great. All fines shall be moderate; and no cruel or unusual punishments shall be inflicted. No man shall be deprived of his liberty or property, but by the judgment of his peers or the law of the land; and, should the public exigencies make it necessary, for the common preservation, to take any person's property, or to demand his particular services, full compensation shall be made for the same. And, in the just preservation of rights and property, it is understood and declared, that no law ought ever to be made, or have force in the said territory, that shall, in any manner whatever, interfere with or affect private contracts or engagements, *bona fide*, and without fraud, previously formed.

The final article of the document, Article 6, prohibited the extension of slavery into the territories—the first stand the federal government took against slavery. Nevertheless, any fugitive slave escaping into the territories was subject to recovery by "the person claiming his or her service."

REFERENCES:

Burnett, Edmund Cody. *The Continental Congress.* 1941; reprint ed., Westport, CT: Greenwood Press, 1975.

Farrand, Max, ed. *The Records of the Federal Convention of 1787.* New Haven, CT: Yale University Press, 1911, 1986. 4 vols.

Hutson, James, ed. *Supplement to Max Farrand's "The Records of the Federal Convention of 1787.* New Haven, CT: Yale University Press, 1987.

Jensen, Merrill. *The Articles of Confederation.* Madison, WI: University of Wisconsin Press, 1940, 1970.

____. *The New Nation: A History of the United States during the Confederation, 1781-1789.* 1950; Reprint ed., Boston, MA: Northeastern University Press, 1981.

Madison, James. *Notes of Debates in the Federal Convention of 1787.* Athens, OH: Ohio University Press, 1987.

Morris, Richard B. *The Forging of the Union, 1781-1789.* New York: Harper & Row, 1987.

Rossiter, Clinton L. *1787: The Grand Convention.* New York: W. W. Norton, 1987.

Jay's Treaty with Great Britain

SIGNED: November 19, 1794, at London

IN FORCE: October 28, 1795

SIGNATORIES: United States vs. Great Britain

OVERVIEW: By the **Treaty of Paris (1783)**, which ended the Revolution, Britain recognized the independence and sovereignty of the United States; however, friction between the two nations developed in large part because British interests continued to occupy outposts in the Old Northwest. Jay's Treaty resolved this matter, preserving U.S. sovereignty while averting renewed war.

DISCUSSION:

One condition of the Treaty of Paris was the British evacuation of outposts on the western frontier. Not only did the British government fail to enforce this provision, American settlers in the region believed that British interests were inducing the Indians to raid. Additionally, the boundaries between British North America and United States territory were also hotly disputed. For their part, the British also had grievances, chief among which was a claim that Americans were repudiating prerevolutionary debts owed British creditors and that the federal government had not compensated Loyalists for property confiscated during the Revolution. When Britain began routinely intercepting American merchant ships on the high seas and "impressing" certain American sailors deemed to be British subjects into service in the Royal Navy, the Anglo-American crisis reached a critical point.

John Jay, chief justice of the Supreme Court and George Washington's specially appointed minister in this matter, negotiated a "Treaty of Amity, Commerce, and Navigation," which not only averted war, but accomplished the following:

• It laid a firm foundation for Anglo-American trade.
• It secured the British evacuation of the frontier forts.
• It secured the limited right of American ships to trade in the British West Indies.

Although it achieved much, Jay's Treaty temporized on two other critical matters, referring the question of repaying prerevolutionary debts and the disputed boundaries to joint "commissioners to be appointed." The boundary would remain in dispute and would be the subject of additional negotiations and treaties well into the nineteenth century. Even more serious, however, was the treaty's failure to settle the following:

- Issues relating to British-allied Indians
- The compensation claims of Loyalists
- Impressment on the high seas

Unresolved, these issues would ultimately bring about the War of 1812.

Jay's Treaty was not well received by the public, who believed Jay had conceded too much to the British. But President Washington endorsed it, urging and obtaining Senate ratification, albeit with deletion of a provision that limited American trade in the West Indies.

REFERENCES:
The Annals of America, vol. 2. Chicago: Encyclopaedia Britannica, Inc., 1976.
Bemis, Samuel Flagg. *Jay's Treaty.* Westport, CT: Greenwood Publishing, 1975.

Treaty of San Lorenzo (Pinckney's Treaty)

OFFICIAL TITLE: Treaty of Friendship, Limits, and Navigation between Spain and the United States
SIGNED: October 27, 1795, at San Lorenzo el Real, Spain
Signatories: Spain vs. United States
In force: From August 2, 1796
OVERVIEW: The treaty fixed the southern boundary of the United States at 31°N latitude and established commercial arrangements with Spain favorable to the United States, including free navigation of the Mississippi River through Spanish territory.

DISCUSSION:
In addition to fixing the boundary between the Spanish colonies and the United States and securing free navigation of the Mississippi, the treaty granted Americans the right of tax-free deposit—temporary warehousing of goods—at New Orleans. Additionally, each side agreed to attempt to restrain Indians within its borders from attacks on the other. Important provisions related to maintaining freedom of the seas, including a pledge of either party to defend the vessels of the other.

In the United States, the treaty is named for Thomas Pinckney, the United States envoy to Spain.

REFERENCE:
Miller, Hunter, ed. *Treaties and other International Acts of the United States of America.* vol. 2. Washington: Government Printing Office, 1931.

Secret Treaty on the Retrocession of Louisiana

OFFICIAL TITLE: Preliminary and Secret Treaty between the French Republic and His Catholic Majesty the King of Spain, Concerning the Aggrandizement of His Royal Highness the Infant Duke of Parma in Italy and the Retrocession of Louisiana
SIGNED: October 1, 1800
SIGNATORIES: France vs. Spain
IN FORCE: March 21, 1801
OVERVIEW: The ambiguous and secret retrocession of the Louisiana Territory by Spain to France.

DISCUSSION:
Although the United States was not a party to this secret treaty, the document played a key role in the Louisiana Purchase. See the entry on the **Treaty [with France] for the Cession of Louisiana** for the background of the present treaty and the role it played in the purchase.

The basis of the retrocession was a secret exchange. Napoleon undertook to acquire, by conquest, Tuscany, which he would turn over to the infant Duke of Parma—in effect delivering it into the control of Spain—in exchange for the retrocession. Napoleon considered the retrocession a fait accompli, although he did not campaign to conquer Tuscany for the infant Duke of Parma. Spain continued to exercise control over the territory, as if the retrocession had not occurred, closing the Mississippi to American navigation in 1802. As explained in the entry on the **Treaty [with France] for the Cession of Louisiana**, this action prompted President Thomas Jefferson's bid either to stop the retrocession or to purchase New Orleans from France. By the time negotiations began, France was willing to sell all of the vast Louisiana Territory.

REFERENCES:
Houck, Louis. *The Boundaries of the Louisiana Purchase.* Reprint ed., North Stratford, NH: Ayer, 1971.
Palmer, Michael A. *Stoddert's War: Naval Operations During the Quasi-War with France,* 1798-1801. 1987; reprint ed., Annapolis, MD: United States Naval Institute, 1999.
Richard, Carl J. *The Louisiana Purchase.* Lafayette: University of Southwestern Louisiana, Center for Louisiana Studies, 1995.

Louisiana Purchase: First Convention

SIGNED: April 30, 1803, at Paris
SIGNATORIES: France vs. United States
IN FORCE: Six months from signing
OVERVIEW: One of two conventions specifying the terms of payment for the French cession of Louisiana to the United States. (See **Treaty [with France] for the Cession of Louisiana and Louisiana Purchase: Second Convention.**)

DISCUSSION:
The main text of the brief First Convention follows:

ARTICLE 1
The Government of the United States engages to pay to the French government in the manner Specified in the following article the sum

of Sixty millions of francs independent of the Sum which Shall be fixed by another Convention for the payment of the debts due by France to citizens of the United States.

ARTICLE 2

For the payment of the Sum of Sixty millions of francs mentioned in the preceding article the United States shall create a Stock of eleven millions, two hundred and fifty thousand Dollars bearing an interest of Six per cent per annum payable half yearly in London Amsterdam or Paris amounting by the half year to three hundred and thirty Seven thousand five hundred Dollars, according to the proportions which Shall be determined by the french Government to be paid at either place: The principal of the Said Stock to be reimbursed at the treasury of the United States in annual payments of not less than three millions of Dollars each; of which the first payment Shall commence fifteen years after the date of the exchange of ratifications: —this Stock Shall be transferred to the government of France or to Such person or persons as Shall be authorized to receive it in three months at most after the exchange of ratifications of this treaty and after Louisiana Shall be taken possession of in the name of the Government of the United States.

It is further agreed that if the french Government Should be desirous of disposing of the Said Stock to receive the capital in Europe at Shorter terms that its measures for that purpose Shall be taken So as to favour in the greatest degree possible the credit of the United States, and to raise to the highest price the Said Stock.

ARTICLE 3

It is agreed that the Dollar of the United States Specified in the present Convention shall be fixed at five francs 3333/100000 or five livres eight sous tournois.

REFERENCES:

Houck, Louis. *The Boundaries of the Louisiana Purchase*. Reprint ed., North Stratford, NH: Ayer, 1971.

Richard, Carl J. *The Louisiana Purchase*. Lafayette: University of Southwestern Louisiana, Center for Louisiana Studies, 1995.

Louisiana Purchase: Second Convention

SIGNED: April 30, 1803, at Paris
SIGNATORIES: France vs. United States
IN FORCE: Six months from signing
OVERVIEW: One of two conventions specifying the terms of payment for the French cession of Louisiana to the United States. (See **Treaty [with France] for the Cession of Louisiana** and **Louisiana Purchase: First Convention.**)

DISCUSSION:

In the Second Convention, as part of the purchase price paid for the Louisiana Territory, the United States agreed to assume certain debts owed by French citizens to citizens of the United States. The convention established a means of adjudicating claims and questions arising from these debts.

REFERENCES:

Houck, Louis. *The Boundaries of the Louisiana Purchase*. Reprint ed.,

North Stratford, NH: Ayer, 1971.

Richard, Carl J. *The Louisiana Purchase*. Lafayette: University of Southwestern Louisiana, Center for Louisiana Studies, 1995.

Treaty (with France) for the Cession of Louisiana

SIGNED: April 30, 1803, at Paris
SIGNATORIES: France vs. United States
IN FORCE: Six months from signing
OVERVIEW: The principal instrument by which France ceded to the United States the Louisiana Territory, encompassing the western half of the Mississippi River basin, some 828,000 square miles of land.

DISCUSSION:

As a result of its defeat in the French and Indian War (1754-1763), France ceded Louisiana west of the Mississippi River to Spain and in 1763 transferred almost all of its remaining North American territories to Great Britain. On October 1, 1800, Napoleon secretly negotiated the retrocession of Louisiana to France (**Secret Treaty on the Retrocession of Louisiana**), in force from March 21, 1801).

Americans saw the retrocession as a threat to the freedom of American settlers in the valleys of the Cumberland, Tennessee, and Ohio rivers to navigate the Mississippi. By the **Treaty of San Lorenzo (Pinckney's Treaty)** (1795), Spain had granted to the United States the right to ship goods on the Mississippi and to use New Orleans for temporary storage ("right of deposit"). Americans feared that the French might not honor this agreement. They soon found that they had even more to fear from Spain. The Spanish king had made a verbal agreement with Napoleon that France would never alienate the territory to a third power. Concerned that this would indeed now happen, Spain, in 1802, leaving the retrocession ambiguous, revoked the right of deposit it had guaranteed in 1795.

In response to this confusing and perilous situation, President Thomas Jefferson instructed Robert R. Livingston, U.S. minister to France, to discuss with Charles Maurice de Talleyrand, Napoleon's minister, the possibility of preventing the retrocession, if it had not already occurred, or of purchasing New Orleans, if that property had actually been transferred from Spain to France. With great diplomatic aplomb, Livingston let it be known that the United States might well seek an alliance with Great Britain. Fearing this, having suffered defeat in military campaigns in Santo Domingo, and seeing an opportunity to neutralize an impending British threat in America without military effort, Napoleon suddenly instructed Talleyrand to offer the United States not just New Orleans, but all of the Louisiana Territory.

At this point James Monroe arrived in Paris as Jefferson's minister plenipotentiary, and negotiations were swiftly carried to conclusion. The treaty was signed on May 2 but antedated to

April 30. The treaty specified the following:

- The Louisiana Territory, as France had received it from Spain, was sold to the United States.
- The United States agreed to pay $11,250,000 outright and to assume claims of its citizens against France in the amount of $3,750,000.
- The United States agreed to a schedule of interest payments incidental to the final settlement, which made the total selling price $27,267,622 (about 3 cents per acre).

The treaty presented several problems:

- The boundaries of the purchased territory were very vague. The treaty did not specify that West Florida was to be considered a part of Louisiana. Not did it delineate the southwest boundary of the purchase.

Boundaries would not be fixed until separate treaties were negotiated with Spain and Britain. (See **Adams-Oñis Treaty**, for the settlement with Spain, and the **Convention [with Britain Regarding Canada] Respecting Fisheries, Boundary, and the Restoration of Slaves**, for the settlement with Britain.) Of more immediate concern were questions about the constitutionality of the purchase. It was not clear whether the Constitution allowed such a purchase; nevertheless, the Senate approved the treaty by a vote of 24 to 7, and the United States was instantly doubled in the size of its territory, a course of western expansion was fixed, the nation made a giant stride toward occupation of the entire continent.

Two conventions, **Louisiana Purchase: First Convention** and **Louisiana Purchase: Second Convention**, accompanied the treaty, specifying details of payment.

REFERENCES:

Houck, Louis. *The Boundaries of the Louisiana Purchase.* Reprint ed., North Stratford, NH: Ayer, 1971.
Richard, Carl J. *The Louisiana Purchase.* Lafayette: University of Southwestern Louisiana, Center for Louisiana Studies, 1995.

Convention (with Britain Regarding Canada) Respecting Fisheries, Boundary, and the Restoration of Slaves

SIGNED: October 20, 1818, at London
SIGNATORIES: Great Britain vs. United States
In force: From January 30, 1819
Overview: A treaty addressing issues of fishing rights, boundary, and the restoration of slaves left unresolved by the Treaty of Ghent.

DISCUSSION:

The **Treaty of Ghent** (See Section 2.3), ending the War of 1812, failed fully to resolve American fishing rights off Newfoundland,

which were guaranteed by the **Treaty of Paris** (See Section 2.2) of 1783, ending the American Revolution. The **Treaty of Ghent** also did not adequately define the boundary between Canada and the United States, and it left ambiguous the issue of the restoration of slaves "who, at the date of the Exchange of the Ratifications of the [**Treaty of Ghent**] were in any Territory, Places, or Possessions whatsoever directed by the said Treaty to be restored to the United States."

The 1818 convention laid down the following:

- A definition of the extent of American fishing rights off the coast of Newfoundland
- A precise description of the boundary between Canada in the Northeast (which was finally and definitively defined by the **Webster-Ashburton Treaty**
- A temporary compromise on the disputed boundary between Canada and the United States in the Northwest: "It is agreed, that any Country that may be claimed by either Party on the North West Coast of America, Westward of the Stony Mountains, shall, together with it's Harbours, Bays, and Creeks, and the Navigation of all Rivers within the same, be free and open, for the term of ten Years from the date of the Signature of the present Convention, to the Vessels, Citizens, and Subjects of the Two Powers: it being well understood, that this Agreement is not to be construed to the Prejudice of any Claim, which either of the Two High Contracting Parties may have to any part of the said Country, nor shall it be taken to affect the Claims of any other Power or State to any part of the said Country; the only Object of The High Contracting Parties, in that respect, being to prevent disputes and differences amongst Themselves."
- An agreement to refer the issue of the restoration of slaves to "to some Friendly Sovereign or State to be named for that purpose; and The High Contracting Parties further engage to consider the decision of such Friendly Sovereign or State, to be final and conclusive on all the Matters referred."

REFERENCES:

Merk, Frederick. *The Oregon Question: Essays in Anglo-American Diplomacy and Politics.* Cambridge, MA: Harvard University Press, 1967.
Scott, Geraldine Tidd. *Ties of Common Blood: A History of Maine's Northeast Boundary Dispute with Great Britain, 1783-1842.* Bowie, MD: Heritage Books, 1992.
VanderZwaag, David L. *The Fish Feud: The U.S. and Canadian Boundary Dispute.* Lexington, MA: Lexington Books, 1983.

Adams-Oñis Treaty

OFFICIAL TITLE: Treaty of Amity, Settlement, and Limits Between the United States of America and His Catholic Majesty
SIGNED: February 22, 1819
SIGNATORIES: Spain vs. United States
IN FORCE: From February 22, 1821

OVERVIEW: The treaty confirmed the Spanish cession of Florida to the United States and the Spanish renunciation of the Oregon country in exchange for United States recognition of Spanish sovereignty over Texas.

DISCUSSION:

Also familiarly called the *Transcontinental Treaty* or *The Purchase of Florida*, the Adams-Oñis Treaty stands as the crowning triumph of John Quincy Adams's diplomacy as secretary of state under President James Monroe. By persuading Spain to cede all of its territory east of the Mississippi and renounce claims to Oregon, Adams succeeded in extending the territorial boundaries of the United States from Atlantic to Pacific. As a result of the treaty, the United States and Spain divided their North American claims along a line from the southeastern corner of what is now Louisiana, north and west to what is now Wyoming, and thence west along the latitude 42° N to the Pacific.

The treaty resolved the so-called "West Florida controversy," created by the Spanish cession of Louisiana to France (**Secret Treaty on the Retrocession of Louisiana, 1800**) and the Louisiana Purchase by the United States (**Treaty of Paris**, 1803). Spain held that its cession to France comprehended only the territory that was denominated Louisiana at the time of the cession; the United States held that the Louisiana Territory encompassed the territory ultimately defined by the Adams-Oñis Treaty.

REFERENCES:
Merk, Frederick. *The Oregon Question: Essays in Anglo-American Diplomacy and Politics.* Cambridge, MA: Harvard University Press, 1967.
Thorpe, Francis Newton, comp. and ed. *The Federal and State Constitutions, Colonial Charters, and other Organic Laws of the States, Territories, and Colonies Now or Heretofore Forming the United States of America.* Washington: Government Printing Office, 1909.

The Monroe Doctrine

PROCLAIMED: December 2, 1823, in the Message to Congress of President James Monroe
SIGNATORIES: Unilateral declaration
IN FORCE: From proclamation
OVERVIEW: In his December 2, 1823, Message to Congress, President James Monroe declared United States policy in opposition to interference in the affairs of the hemisphere by powers from outside of the hemisphere.

DISCUSSION:

The so-called Monroe Doctrine was never presented as a self-standing proclamation, but was part of the president's December 2, 1823 message to Congress:

> The American continents, by the free and independent condition which they have assumed and maintain, are henceforth not to be considered as subject for future colonization by any European power. ... We would not view any interposition for the purpose of oppressing [the nations of the Americas or] controlling in any other manner their destiny by any European power in any other light than as the manifestation of an unfriendly disposition toward the United States.

The message of the Monroe Doctrine, that the United States would respond to any unfriendly move against any American state as a move against itself, was reiterated by President James K. Polk on December 2, 1845 and, most forcefully, by Theodore Roosevelt in his "Corollary to the Monroe Doctrine" in May 1904:

> In the Western Hemisphere the adherence of the United States to the Monroe doctrine may force the United States, however, reluctantly, in flagrant cases of such wrongdoing or interference, to the exercise of an international police power.

The Monroe Doctrine and the Roosevelt Corollary form the foundation of United States policy with regard to the hemisphere (although, pursuant to President Franklin D. Roosevelt's "Good Neighbor Policy," the Roosevelt Corollary was officially renounced in the 1930s).

REFERENCES:
Ferrell, Robert H. *American Diplomacy: A History.* New York: W.W. Norton, 1959.
Perkins, Dexter. *The Monroe Doctrine, 1823-1826.* Reprint ed., Gloucester, MA: Peter Smith, 1965.
Wilbur, W. Allan. *The Monroe Doctrine.* Boston: Heath, 1965.

Treaty between Hawaii and the United States

SIGNED: December 23, 1826, at Oahu
SIGNATORIES: Hawaii (Sandwich Islands) vs. United States
IN FORCE: From signing
OVERVIEW: A brief treaty establishing amity and commerce between Hawaii (then called the Sandwich Islands) and the United States.

DISCUSSION:
The text of the brief treaty follows:

Art: 1st
The peace and friendship subsisting between the United States, and their Majesties, the Queen Regent, and Kauikeaouli, King of the Sandwich Islands, and their subjects and people, are hereby confirmed, and declared to be perpetual.

Art: 2nd
The ships and vessels of the United States (as well as their Consuls and all other citizens within the territorial jurisdiction of the Sandwich Islands, together with all their property), shall be inviolably protected against all Enemies of the United States in time of war.

Art: 3rd
The contracting parties being desirous to avail themselves of the bounties of Divine Providence, by promoting the commercial inter-

course and friendship subsisting between the respective Nations, for the better security of these desirable objects, Their Majesties bind themselves to receive into their Ports and Harbours all ships and vessels of the United States; and to protect, to the utmost of their capacity, all such ships and vessels, their cargoes officers and crews, so long as they shall behave themselves peacefully, and not infringe the established laws of the land, the citizens of the United States being permitted to trade freely with the people of the Sandwich Islands.

Art: 4th

Their Majesties do further agree to extend the fullest protection, within their control, to all ships and vessels of the United States which may be wrecked on their shores; and to render every assistance in their power to save the wreck and her apparel and cargo; and as a reward for the assistance and protection which the people of the Sandwich Islands shall afford to all such distressed vessels of the United States, they shall be entitled to a salvage, or a portion of the property so saved; but such salvage shall, in no case, exceed one third of the value saved; which valuation is to be fixed by a commission of disinterested persons who shall be chosen equally by the Parties.

Art: 5th

Citizens of the United States, whether resident or transient, engaged in commerce, or trading to the Sandwich Islands, shall be inviolably protected in their lawful pursuits; and shall be allowed to sue for, and recover by judgment, all claims against the subjects of His Majesty The King, according to strict principles of equity, and the acknowledged practice of civilized nations.

Art: 6th

Their Majesties do further agree and bind themselves to discountenance and use all practicable means to prevent desertion from all American ships which visit the Sandwich Islands; and to that end it shall be made the duty of all Governors, Magistrates, Chiefs of Districts, and all others in authority, to apprehend all deserters; and to deliver them over to the master of the vessel from which they have deserted; and for the apprehension of every such deserter, who shall be delivered over as aforesaid, the master, owner, or agent, shall pay to the person or persons apprehending such deserter, the sum of six Dollars, if taken on the side of the Island near which the vessel is anchored; but if taken on the opposite side of the Island, the sum shall be twelve Dollars; and if taken on any other Island, the reward shall be twenty four Dollars, and shall be a just charge against the wages of every such deserter.

Art: 7th

No tonnage dues or impost shall be exacted of any Citizen of the United States which is not paid by the Citizens or subjects of the nation most favored in commerce with the Sandwich Island; and the citizens of subjects of the Sandwich Islands shall be allowed to trade with the United States, and her territories, upon principles of equal advantage with the most favored nation.

REFERENCES:

Coffman, Tom. *Nation Within: The Story of America's Annexation of the Nation of Hawaii.* Kane'ohe, HA: Tom Coffman/EPI Center, 1998.

Osborne, Thomas J. *"Empire Can Wait": American Opposition to Hawaiian Annexation, 1893-1898.* Kent, OH: Kent State University Press, 1981.

Pratt, Julius William. *Expansionists of 1898: The Acquisition of Hawaii and the Spanish Islands.* 1936; reprint ed., New York: Peter Smith, 1951.

Russ, William Adam. *The Hawaiian Republic (1894-98) and its Struggle to Win Annexation.* Selinsgrove, PA: Susquehanna University Press, 1992.

Thurston, Lorrin Andrews. *A Hand-Book of the Annexation of Hawaii.* St. Joseph, MI: N. Pub., 1897.

Treaty of Velasco (Texas Independence)

SIGNED: May 14, 1836, at the Port of Velasco, Mexico
SIGNATORIES: Mexico vs. Republic of Texas
IN FORCE: From signing
OVERVIEW: The treaty ending the Texan War for Independence and acknowledging the independence of the Republic of Texas from Mexico.

DISCUSSION:

The Louisiana Purchase of 1803 had sparked interest in Texas among many Americans, but several private projects to colonize this Mexican state came to nothing until 1820, when a visionary entrepreneur named Moses Austin secured a grant from the Spanish government to establish a colony of Americans in Mexico. Austin fell ill and died in 1821, before he could begin the project of settlement. On his deathbed, he asked his son, Stephen F. Austin, to carry out his plans. In the meantime, Mexico had won independence form Spain in the revolution of 1821 and, under terms established by a special act of the new Mexican government in 1824 (as well as additional agreements negotiated in 1825, 1827, and 1828), Austin brought more than 1,200 American families to Texas. Colonization was so successful, that by 1836 the American population of Texas was 50,000, while that of the Mexicans was a mere 3,500.

By the 1830s, the American majority was chafing under Mexican rule—especially because Mexican laws forbade slavery—and violent conflicts between settlers and military garrisons became frequent. Austin struggled to negotiate peace with the tumultuous Mexican government, and even drew up a proposed constitution to make Texas a Mexican state. In 1833, however, when he traveled to Mexico City to present his proposal to Antonio López de Santa Anna, the country's new president, he was not only spurned, but arrested and imprisoned in Mexico City for two years. Released in 1835, Austin returned to Texas embittered and broken in health. He urged Texans to support a Mexican revolt against Santa Anna, and this, in turn, triggered the Texan War for Independence.

Santa Anna led troops into Texas during January 1836 and reached San Antonio in February. There, against the advice of independence leader Sam Houston (1793-1863), a force of 187 Texans under militia colonel William B. Travis, took a defensive stand behind the walls of a decayed Spanish mission formally called San Antonio de Valero, but nicknamed the Alamo because it was close to a grove of cottonwoods (called. in Spanish, alamos). The small Texas band, which included such renowned frontier figures as Jim Bowie and Davy Crockett, held off five thousand of Santa Anna's troops for ten days, hoping desperately that, somehow, the American nation would rally and rush to their aid. But the hope proved forlorn, and, on March 6, the Mexican troops breached the mission's wall and slaughtered everyone inside.

This Mexican "victory" produced the martyrdom that united Texans under the battle cry of "Remember the Alamo!" Sam Houston brilliantly led a ragtag army against Santa Anna at the Battle of San Jacinto on April 21, and resulting victory gave Texas its independence.

The following treaty formalized the terms by which the war was ended and independence acknowledged:

Article 1st

General Antonio Lopez de Santa Anna agrees that he will not take up arms, nor will he exercise his influence to cause them to be taken up against the people of Texas, during the present war of Independence.

Article 2nd

All hostilities between the mexican and texian troops will cease immediately both on land and water.

Article 3rd

The mexican troops will evacuate the Territory of Texas, passing to the other side of the Rio Grande del Norte.

Article 4th

The mexican Army in its retreat shall not take the property of any person without his consent and just indemnification, using only such articles as may be necessary for its subsistence, in cases when the owner may not be present, and remitting to the commander of the army of Texas or to the commissioner to be appointed for the adjustment of such matters, an account of the value of the property consumed—the place where taken, and the name of the owner, if it can be ascertained.

Article 5th

That all private property including cattle, horses, negro slaves or indentured persons of whatever denomination, that may have been captured by any portion of the mexican army or may have taken refuge in the said army since the commencement of the late invasion, shall be restored to the Commander of the Texian army, or to such other persons as may be appointed by the Government of Texas to receive them.

Article 6th

The troops of both armies will refrain from coming into contact with each other, and to this end the Commander of the army of Texas will be careful not to approach within a shorter distance of the mexican army than five leagues.

Article 7th

The mexican army shall not make any other delay on its march, than that which is necessary to take up their hospitals, baggage, and to cross the rivers—any delay not necessary to these purposes to be considered an infraction of this agreement.

Article 8th

By express to be immediately dispatched, this agreement shall be sent to General Filisola and to General T. J. Rusk, commander of the texian Army, in order that they may be apprised of its stipulations, and to this and they will exchange engagements to comply with the same.

Article 9th

That all texian prisoners now in possession of the mexican Army or its authorities be forthwith released and furnished with free passports to return to their homes, in consideration of which a corresponding number of Mexican prisoners, rank and file, now in possession of the Government of Texas shall be immediately released. The remainder of the mexican prisoners that continue in possession of the Government of Texas to be treated with due humanity—any extraordinary comforts that may be furnished them to be at the charge of the Government of Mexico.

Article 10th

General Antonio Lopez de Santa Anna will be sent to Veracruz as soon as it shall be deemed proper.

The contracting parties sign this Instrument for the above mentioned purposes, by duplicate, at the Port of Velasco this fourteenth day of May 1836.

REFERENCE:

Nofi, Albert A. *The Alamo and the Texas War of Independence.* Reprint ed., New York: Da Capo, 1994.

Texas-American Boundary Convention

SIGNED: April 25, 1838

SIGNATORIES: Republic of Texas vs. United States

IN FORCE: From October 13, 1838

OVERVIEW: A convention calling for a survey of the boundary between the United States and the newly independent Republic of Texas, constituting United States recognition of the republic.

DISCUSSION:

The **Adams-Oñis Treaty** of 1819 had established the boundary between the United States and Mexico, which included within Mexico the present state of Texas. Within months of ratification of the treaty Stephen F. Austin founded a colony of American settlers in this Mexican state, and within ten years, some 20,000 Americans lived there, far outnumbering the Mexican residents. In 1836, Texas won its independence from Mexico and established the Republic of Texas under the presidency of Sam Houston. Two years later, the United States officially recognized Texas independence by virtue of this boundary convention.

The convention alludes to a Treaty of Limits (January 12, 1828) between the United States and Mexico, which elaborated on the boundary definitions of the 1819 treaty. Inasmuch as Texas was a state of Mexico in 1828, the present convention assumes that the boundary definition of the 1828 treaty is binding on the Republic of Texas. "And whereas it is deemed proper and expedient, in order to prevent future disputes and collisions between the United States and Texas in regard to the boundary between the two countries as designated by the said treaty, . . . a portion of the same should be run and marked with out unnecessary delay." The rest of the convention lays down the procedure by which boundary commissioners will be appointed and do their work.

REFERENCES:
Fletcher & Boeselt. *The Republic of Texas Annexation and Statehood, 1845*. San Antonio, TX: Fletcher & Boeselt, 1992.
Garber, Paul N. *The Gadsden Treaty*. Philadelphia: Press of the University of Pennsylvania, 1923.
Smith, Justin Harvey. *The Annexation of Texas*. Corrected ed. New York: Barnes and Noble, 1941.
___. *The Policy of England and France in Reference to the Annexation of Texas*. New York: Baker and Taylor, 1911.
Treaties and Conventions between the United States of America and Other Powers Since July 4, 1776. Washington: Government Printing Office, 1871.
Tutorow, Norman E. *Texas Annexation and the Mexican War: A Political Study of the Old Northwest*. Palo Alto, CA: Chadwick House, 1978.

Webster-Ashburton Treaty

OFFICIAL TITLE: Treaty to Settle and to Find the Boundaries Between the Territories of United States in the Possessions of Her Britannica Majesty in North America; for the Final Suppression of the African Slave Trade, and for the Giving up of Criminals, Fugitive from Justice, in Certain Cases
SIGNED: August 9, 1842, at Washington
SIGNATORIES: Great Britain vs. United States
IN FORCE: From November 10, 1842
OVERVIEW: Established the northeastern boundary between the United States and Canada and provided for Anglo-American cooperation in the suppression of the slave trade.

DISCUSSION:
The treaty, negotiated by Daniel Webster, U.S. secretary of state under President John Tyler, and Alexander Baring, 1st Baron Ashburton, settled the thorny issue of the northeastern boundary between the United States and Canada, which had been left unsettled by the 1783 **Treaty of Paris** (See Section 2.2), which ended the American Revolution. The first two articles stipulated the boundary, and Article III specified that the St. John River, separating New Brunswick from Maine, would be free for purposes of navigation and trade by Canadians as well as Americans.

In addition to settling the boundary dispute, the treaty (Articles VIII and IX) included a program for Anglo-American cooperation in suppressing the slave trade. (Although slavery was practiced in the United States, the importation of slaves had been ended in 1808 by Article I, Section 9 of the Constitution.) Article X was an agreement for the extradition of fugitive felons.

REFERENCES:
Boundary, Slave Trade, and Extradition (Webster-Ashburton Treaty). Washington, D.C.: U.S. Government Printing Office, 1942.
Jones, Howard. *To the Webster-Ashburton Treaty: A Study in Anglo-American Relations, 1783-1843*. Chapel Hill: University of North Carolina Press, 1977.

The Treaty of Annexation (of Texas)

SIGNED: April 12, 1844
SIGNATORIES: Republic of Texas vs. United States
IN FORCE: The treaty failed of ratification by the Senate, June 8, 1844, and never came into force
OVERVIEW: Amid fears of adding another slave-holding state to the union and unwilling to provoke war with Mexico, the Senate failed to muster the two-thirds majority necessary for ratification of this treaty.

DISCUSSION:
The treaty begins: "The people of Texas having, at the time of adopting their constitution, expressed by an almost unanimous vote, their desire to be incorporated into the Union of the United States, and being still desirous of the same with equal unanimity, in order to provide more effectually for their security and prosperity; and the United States, actuated solely by the desire to add to their own security and prosperity, and to meet the wishes of the Government and people of Texas, have determined to accomplish, by treaty, objects so important to their mutual and permanent welfare . . ."

The language is significant: Annexation is portrayed as the product of the wishes of the people of the Republic of Texas and is animated, on the part of the United States, "solely by the desire" to accede to their wishes and to augment their "security and prosperity." The object of this language was to justify an action that would likely provoke war with Mexico, which would interpret the annexation of Texas as a violation of boundary agreements made in the **Adams-Oñis Treaty** (1819) and the Treaty of Limits (1828).

Yet provoking war with Mexico was actually the lesser of the two reasons that ultimately prevented Senate ratification of the Treaty of Annexation. It was understood that Texas, annexed as a territory, would immediately be eligible for admission as a state and that it would seek admission as a slave-holding state. In the tense decades leading up to the Civil War, maintaining the balance between slave-holding and free states was a matter of great difficulty and delicacy. Many Senators were unwilling to upset the delicate balance, and the treaty failed to receive the two-thirds majority vote necessary for ratification.

The rejection of the treaty proved a temporary setback only. Popular sentiment both in Texas and the United States pressed Congress to exercise its prerogative of annexing territory, without treaty, by a simple majority vote. Congress so voted on February 28, 1845, and the Congress of the Republic of Texas accepted annexation on June 23, 1845, after the United States pledged to protect Texas from Mexican invasion. The United States declared war on Mexico (May 9, 1846) after Mexican forces attacked United States troops sent to hold the Texas-Mexican boundary at the Rio Grande.

There were two important differences between the terms of annexation presented in the treaty and the terms the United States Congress ultimately presented to the Texas Congress:

- The treaty had called for the cession of Texas public lands to the United States; the congressional resolution allowed Texas to retain title to its public lands.
- The treaty called for the United States to "assume and agree to pay the public debts and liabilities of Texas, however created"; the congressional resolution called for Texas to retain responsibility for all debts it incurred as an independent republic.

Statehood rapidly followed annexation, Texas becoming the twenty-eighth state on December 29, 1845.

REFERENCES:

Fletcher & Boeselt. *The Republic of Texas Annexation and Statehood, 1845.* San Antonio, TX: Fletcher & Boeselt, 1992.

Garber, Paul N. *The Gadsden Treaty.* Philadelphia: Press of the University of Pennsylvania, 1923.

Smith, Justin Harvey. *The Annexation of Texas.* Corrected ed. New York: Barnes and Noble, 1941.

___. *The Policy of England and France in Reference to the Annexation of Texas.* New York: Baker and Taylor, 1911.

Treaties and Conventions between the United States of America and Other Powers Since July 4, 1776. Washington: Government Printing Office, 1871.

Tutorow, Norman E. *Texas Annexation and the Mexican War: A Political Study of the Old Northwest.* Palo Alto, CA: Chadwick House, 1978.

Oregon Treaty

OFFICIAL TITLE: Treaty with Great Britain, in Regard to Limits Westward of the Rocky Mountains
SIGNED: June 15, 1846, at Washington
SIGNATORIES: Great Britain vs. United States
IN FORCE: From July 17, 1846
OVERVIEW: The treaty attempted to resolve the disputed boundary between the United States and Canada in the Northwest.

DISCUSSION:

The treaty set the 49th parallel as the boundary between the Oregon Territory and Canada. The dispute over possession of the Pacific Northwest originally involved Spain, Russia, the United States, and Great Britain. Spain was the first to vacate its claims by the Nootka Sound Convention of 1790 with Britain and the **Adams-Oñis Treaty** of 1819 with the United States. By

the **Convention (with Britain Regarding Canada) Respecting Fisheries, Boundary, and the Restoration of Slaves** of 1818, Great Britain and the United States established a joint claim over the Oregon Country, which was later defined as lying below latitude 54° 40′ N, above latitude 42° N, and west of the Continental Divide. In the meantime, Russia abandoned its claim to the area (1824-1825).

In 1844, James K. Polk ran for president under the slogan "Fifty-four forty or fight," a platform that demanded United States possession of the Oregon Country up to 54° 44′. The Oregon Treaty was a compromise, which pushed the boundary down to 49° N and guaranteed British navigation rights on the Columbia River. The full text of the principal articles of the treaty follows:

ARTICLE I.

From the point on the forty-ninth parallel of north latitude, where the boundary laid down in existing treaties and conventions between the United States and Great Britain terminates, the line of boundary between the territories of the United States and those of her Britannic Majesty shall be continued westward along the said forty-ninth parallel of north latitude to the middle of the channel which separates the continent from Vancouver's Island, and thence southerly through the middle of the said channel, and of Fuca's Straits, to the Pacific Ocean: Provided, however, That the navigation of the whole of the said channel and straits, south of the forty-ninth parallel of north latitude, remain free and open to both parties.

ARTICLE II.

From the point at which the forty-ninth parallel of north latitude shall be found to intersect the great northern branch of the Columbia River, the navigation of the said branch shall be free and open to the Hudson's Bay Company, and to all British subjects trading with the same, to the point where the said branch meets the main stream of the Columbia, and thence down the said main stream to the ocean, with Fee access into and through the said river or rivers, it being understood that all the usual portages along the line thus described shall, in like manner, be free and open. In navigating the said river or rivers, British subjects, with their goods and produce, shall be treated on the same footing as citizens of the United States; it being, however, always understood that nothing in this article shall be construed as preventing, or intended to prevent, the government of the United States from making any regulations respecting the navigation of the said river or rivers not inconsistent with the present treaty.

ARTICLE III

In the future appropriation of the territory south of the forty-ninth parallel of north latitude, as provided in the first article of this treaty, the possessory rights of the Hudson's Bay Company, and of all British subjects who may be already in the occupation of land or other property lawfully acquired within the said territory, shall be respected.

ARTICLE IV.

The farms, lands, and other property of every description, belonging to the Puget's Sound Agricultural Company, on the north side of the Columbia River, shall be confirmed to the said company. In case, however, the situation of those farms and lands should be considered by the United States to be of public and political importance, and the

United States government should signify a desire to obtain possession of the whole, or of any part thereof, the property so required shall be transferred to the said government, at a proper valuation, to be agreed upon between the parties.

ARTICLE V.

The present treaty shall be ratified by the President of the United States, by and with the advice and consent of the Senate thereof, and by her Britannic Majesty; and the ratifications shall be exchanged at London, at the expiration of six months from the date hereof, or sooner, if possible.

It was not until the 1870s that the marine portion of the boundary south of Vancouver Island was definitively established.

REFERENCES:
Merk, Frederick. *The Oregon Question: Essays in Anglo-American Diplomacy and Politics.* Cambridge, MA: Harvard University Press, 1967.

Treaty between Hawaii and the United States

SIGNED: December 20, 1849, at Washington
SIGNATORIES: Hawaii (Sandwich Islands) vs. United States
IN FORCE: From signing
OVERVIEW: A treaty of amity and commerce that extends and further defines the commercial provisions of the **Treaty between Hawaii and the United States** of 1826 and adds a postal provision and an article regarding freedom of religion.

DISCUSSION:

This treaty reflected the desire of the United States to bring Hawaii more intimately within its circle of commercial interests and was a step closer to annexation, which would come in 1898.

In addition to general trade and commercial provisions, the treaty provided for "free access" to Hawaiian ports for "steam vessels of the United States . . . carrying . . . public mails across the Pacific Ocean" (Article VI), access of United States whaling ships to the ports of Hilo, Kealakekua, and Hanalei "for the purposes of refitment and refreshment, as well as to the ports of Honolulu and Lahaina" (Article VII).

Since the 1820s, Hawaii had drawn increasing numbers of American missionaries, who, by the 1840s, had become a strong cultural and political force on the islands. Article XI stipulated "that perfect and entire liberty of conscience shall be enjoyed by the citizens and subjects of both the contracting parties, in the countries of the one and the other, without their being liable to be disturbed or molested no account of their religious belief." As many Hawaiians resented the dilution of their native culture and religion, the article further stipulated that "nothing contained in this article shall be construed to interfere with the exclusive right of the Hawaiian government to regulate for itself the

schools which it may establish or support within its jurisdiction."

Article XV established a postal convention between Hawaii and the United States: "So soon as steam or other mail packets under the flag of either of the contracting parties shall have commenced running between their respective ports of entry, the contracting parties agree to receive at the post-offices of those ports all mailable matter, and to forward it as directed, the destination being to same regular post-office of either country, charging thereupon the regular postal rates an established by law in the territories of either party receiving said mailable matter, in addition to the original postage of the office whence the mail was sent. . . ."

REFERENCES:
Coffman, Tom. *Nation Within: The Story of America's Annexation of the Nation of Hawaii.* Kane'ohe, HA: Tom Coffman/EPI Center, 1998.
Osborne, Thomas J. *"Empire Can Wait": American Opposition to Hawaiian Annexation, 1893-1898.* Kent, OH: Kent State University Press, 1981.
Pratt, Julius William. *Expansionists of 1898: The Acquisition of Hawaii and the Spanish Islands.* 1936; reprint ed., New York: Peter Smith, 1951.
Russ, William Adam. *The Hawaiian Republic (1894-98) and its Struggle to Win Annexation.* Selinsgrove, PA: Susquehanna University Press, 1992.
Thurston, Lorrin Andrews. *A Hand-Book of the Annexation of Hawaii.* St. Joseph, MI: N. Pub., 1897.

Gadsden Treaty

SIGNED: December 30, 1853, at Mexico City (revised treaty ratified by the Senate April 25, 1854)
IN FORCE: From June 30, 1854
SIGNATORIES: United States vs. Mexico
OVERVIEW: The United States victory in the U.S.-Mexican War (1846-1848) resulted in the conquest of much of northern Mexico (See **Treaty of Guadalupe-Hidalgo**, 1848, in Section 2.4); James Gadsden, United States minister to Mexico, negotiated the purchase of an additional 29,670 square miles of northern Mexican territory, which is now southern Arizona and southern New Mexico. This treaty formalizes the "Gasden Purchase."

DISCUSSION:

Shortly after operation of the Baltimore and Ohio, the first steam railway in the United States, was inaugurated in 1827, American entrepreneurs and legislators began contemplating construction of a rail line that would span the continent.
During the late 1840s and early 1850s, Congress authorized a series of western expeditions to determine the most practical route for such a railroad.

In the charged climate of the decades preceding the Civil War, defining what was "practical" involved as many political as geographical and topographical considerations. Jefferson Davis, the Mississippian who would, after secession, become president of the Confederacy, had been appointed secretary of war by President Franklin Pierce in 1853. Secretary Davis pressed for selection of an extreme southerly route for the transcontinental railroad, which would be of great economic as well as military advantage to whatever region it passed through. When a survey made it clear that an extensive portion of Davis's proposed route ran through territory that had not been acquired from Mexico by the Treaty of Guadalupe Hidalgo ending the Mexican War (1846-1848), Secretary Davis prevailed on President Pierce to commission James Gadsden, U.S. minister (ambassador) to Mexico, to negotiate purchase of the additional required territory.

Gadsden opened negotiations with Mexican officials on May 19, 1853, with an offer of $15 million for nearly 30,000 square miles of territory in the Mesilla Valley, south of the Gila River. By the time the treaty was concluded, on December 30, 1853, Gadsden had driven a harder bargain, which reduced the total purchase price to $10 million, although a full $7 million was to be paid upfront, the remainder withheld until an extensive survey had been completed and approved.

The main purpose of the treaty was to formalize the Gasden Purchase, which also established the present Mexican-American boundary. The Gadsden Treaty also abrogated Article XI of the **Treaty of Guadalupe Hidalgo**, in which the United States had pledged to prevent Indians from leaving territory acquired by that treaty and settling (or raiding) in territory still held by Mexico. The abrogation of this article corrected what was now seen as a serious defect in the Guadalupe Hidalgo agreement. Practically speaking, the treaty condition was impossible to satisfy and certainly would have required huge expenditures of military resources. Secondarily, lawmakers objected to the forcible restraint of anyone from leaving the country. Not only was this morally repugnant, but, although Indians were not considered citizens of the United States, it raised serious constitutional issues.

REFERENCES:
Eisenhower, John D. *So Far From God*. New York: Random House, 1989.
Israel, Fred L. *Major Peace Treaties of Modern History, 1648-1967, vol. 2*. New York: Chelsea House and McGraw-Hill, 1967.

Alaska Purchase

OFFICIAL TITLE: Treaty concerning the Cession of the Russian Possessions in North America by his Majesty the Emperor of all the Russias to the United States of America
SIGNED: March 30, 1867
SIGNATORIES: Russia vs. United States
IN FORCE: From June 20, 1867
OVERVIEW: The treaty by which the United States purchased Alaska from Russia.

DISCUSSION:

The purchase of Alaska from Russia, negotiated by Secretary of State William H. Seward and derided by many Americans as "Seward's folly" (Alaska itself was referred to as "Seward's ice box"), would prove to be a political and economic triumph. Rich in mineral and other natural resources, Alaska passed from territorial to statehood status on January 3, 1959, becoming the forty-ninth state.

Purchased for $7,200,000 (Article VI), about two cents an acre, Alaska was a real estate bargain on a par with the Louisiana Purchase more than half a century earlier.

Article I stipulates the immediate cession of the territory, the extent and boundaries of which it defines. Article II lays down:

In the cession of territory and dominion made by the preceding article are included the right of property in all public lots and squares, vacant lands, and all public buildings, fortifications, barracks, and other edifices which are not private individual property. It is, however, understood and agreed, that the churches which have been built in the ceded territory by the Russian government, shall remain the property of such members of the Greek Oriental Church resident in the territory, as may choose to worship therein....

Article III deals with the people of Alaska:

The inhabitants of the ceded territory, according to their choice, reserving their natural allegiance, may return to Russia within three years; but if they should prefer to remain in the ceded territory, they, with the exception of uncivilized native tribes, shall be admitted to the enjoyment of all the rights, advantages, and immunities of citizens of the United States, and shall be maintained and protected in the free enjoyment of their liberty, property, and religion. The uncivilized tribes will be subject to such laws and regulations as the United States may, from time to time, adopt in regard to aboriginal tribes of that country.

REFERENCES:
Cohen, Daniel. *The Alaska Purchase*. Brookfield, CT: Millbrook Press, 1996.
Fermon, David. K. *The Alaska Purchase in American History*. Springfield, NJ: Enslow, 1999.
Jensen, Ronald J. *The Alaska Purchase and Russian-American Relations*. Seattle: University of Washington Press, 1975.

Treaty of Reciprocity between the United States of America and the Hawaiian Kingdom

SIGNED: May 31, 1875
SIGNATORIES: Hawaiian Kingdom vs. United States
IN FORCE: From signing
OVERVIEW: A convention of commercial reciprocity, whereby the signatories agreed to allow the duty-free importation of a wide variety of goods.

DISCUSSION:

Although reciprocal, the relief from import duties was of greater benefit to the United States than to Hawaii, allowing producers based in the United States to export freely to Hawaii and for United States-owned plantation producers in Hawaii to export freely to the mainland.

Hawaiian produce to be imported duty free into the United States included: "Arrow-root; Castor oil; Bananas; Nuts; Vegetables, dried and undried, preserved and unpreserved; Hides and skins, undressed; Rice; Pulu; Seeds; Plants, Shrubs, or Trees; Muscovado, brown, and all other unrefined Sugar, meaning hereby the grade of sugar heretofore commonly imported from the Hawaiian Islands, and now known in the markets of San Francisco and Portland as 'Sandwich Island sugar'; syrups of Sugar-cane, Melado, and Molasses; Tallow."

United States goods to be imported duty free into Hawaii included: "Agricultural Implements; Animals; Beef, Bacon, Pork, Ham, and all fresh, smoked, or preserved meats; Boots and Shoes; Grain, flour, meal, and Bran. Bread and Breadstuff, of all kinds; Bricks, Lime, and Cement; Butter, Cheese, Lard, Tallow; Bullion; Coal; Cordage, Naval Stores, including Tar, Pitch, Resin, Turpentine raw and rectified; Copper and Composition Sheeting; Nails and Bolts; Cotton and manufactures of cotton, bleached and unbleached, and whether or not colored, stained, painted, or printed; Eggs; Fish and Oysters, and all other creatures living in the water, and the produce thereof; Fruits, Nuts, and Vegetables, green, dried, or undried, preserved or unpreserved; Hardware; Hides, Furs, Skins and Pelts, dressed or undressed; Hoop iron and Rivets, Nails, Spikes and Bolts, Tacks, Brads, or Sprigs; Ice; Iron and Steel and manufactures thereof; Leather; Lumber and Timber of all kinds, round, hewed, sawed and unmanufactured, in hole or in part; Doors, Sashes, and Blinds; Machinery of all kinds, Engines and parts thereof; Oats and Hay; Paper, Stationary, and Books, and all manufactures of Paper or Paper and Wood; Petroleum and all oils for lubricating or illuminating purposes; Plants, Shrubs, Trees, and Seeds; Rice; Sugar, refined or unrefined; Salt; Soap; Shooks, Staves, and Headings; Wool and manufactures of wool, other than ready made clothing; Wagons and Carts for the purposes of agriculture or of dryage; Wood and manufacture of Wood, or of Wood and Metal, except furniture either upholstered or carved, and carriages; Textile manufactures made of a combination of wool, cotton, silk, or linen, or of any two or more of them other than when ready-made clothing; harness and all manufactures of leather; starch; and tobacco, whether in leaf or manufactured."

The term of the reciprocity treaty, set at seven years, was extended for seven more years by the **Supplementary Convention to the Treaty of Reciprocity Between the United States of America and the Hawaiian Kingdom** of 1884.

REFERENCES:
Coffman, Tom. *Nation Within: The Story of America's Annexation of the Nation of Hawaii.* Kane'ohe, HA: Tom Coffman/EPI Center, 1998.
Osborne, Thomas J. *"Empire Can Wait": American Opposition to Hawaiian Annexation, 1893-1898.* Kent, OH: Kent State University Press, 1981.
Pratt, Julius William. *Expansionists of 1898: The Acquisition of Hawaii and the Spanish Islands.* 1936; reprint ed., New York: Peter Smith, 1951.
Russ, William Adam. *The Hawaiian Republic (1894-98) and its Struggle to Win Annexation.* Selinsgrove, PA: Susquehanna University Press, 1992.
Thurston, Lorrin Andrews. *A Hand-Book of the Annexation of Hawaii.* St. Joseph, MI: N. Pub., 1897.

Supplementary Convention to the Treaty of Reciprocity between the United States of America and the Hawaiian Kingdom

SIGNED: December 6, 1884, at Washington
SIGNATORIES: Hawaiian Kingdom vs. United States
IN FORCE: From signing
OVERVIEW: A convention extending for seven years the **Treaty of Reciprocity Between the United States of America and the Hawaiian Kingdom** of 1875.

REFERENCES:
Coffman, Tom. *Nation Within: The Story of America's Annexation of the Nation of Hawaii.* Kane'ohe, HA: Tom Coffman/EPI Center, 1998.
Osborne, Thomas J. *"Empire Can Wait": American Opposition to Hawaiian Annexation, 1893-1898.* Kent, OH: Kent State University Press, 1981.
Pratt, Julius William. *Expansionists of 1898: The Acquisition of Hawaii and the Spanish Islands.* 1936; reprint ed., New York: Peter Smith, 1951.
Russ, William Adam. *The Hawaiian Republic (1894-98) and its Struggle to Win Annexation.* Selinsgrove, PA: Susquehanna University Press, 1992.
Thurston, Lorrin Andrews. *A Hand-Book of the Annexation of Hawaii.* St. Joseph, MI: N. Pub., 1897.

Treaty of Annexation (of Hawaii)

SIGNED: June 16, 1897, at Washington D. C.
SIGNATORIES: Hawaii vs. United States
IN FORCE: From July 7, 1898
OVERVIEW: The treaty by which Hawaii was ceded to and annexed to the United States.

DISCUSSION:

The rationale for the cession of Hawaii to the United States is given in the preamble to the treaty: "The Republic of Hawaii and the United States of America, in view of the natural dependence of the Hawaiian Islands upon the United States, of their geographical proximity thereto, of the preponderant share acquired by the United States and its citizens in the industries and trade of said Islands, and of the expressed desire of the government of the Republic of Hawaii that those Islands should be incorporated into the United States as an integral part thereof, and under its sovereignty, have determined to accomplish by treaty an object so important to their mutual and permanent welfare."

The major articles of the treaty follow:

ARTICLE I.

The Republic of Hawaii hereby cedes absolutely and without reserve to the United States of America all rights of sovereignty of whatsoever kind in and over the Hawaiian Islands and their dependencies: and it is agreed that all the territory of and appertaining to the Republic of Hawaii is hereby annexed to the United States of America under the name of the Territory of Hawaii.

ARTICLE II.

The Republic of Hawaii also cedes and hereby transfers to the United States the absolute fee and ownership of all public, government or crown lands, public buildings or edifices, ports, harbors, military equipment, and all other public property of every kind and description belonging to the government of the Hawaiian Islands, together with every right and appurtenance thereunto appertaining.

The existing laws of the United States relative to public lands shall not apply to such lands in the Hawaiian Islands: but the Congress of the United States shall enact special laws for their management and disposition. Provided: that all revenue from or proceeds of the same, except as regards such part thereof as may be used or occupied for the civil, military or naval purposes of the United States, or may be assigned for the use of the local government, shall be used solely for the benefit of the inhabitants of the Hawaiian islands for educational and other public purposes.

ARTICLE III.

Until Congress shall provide for the government of such Islands, all the civil, judicial and military powers exercised by the officers of the existing government in said Islands, shall be vested in such person or person, and shall be exercised in such manner as the President of the United States shall direct: and the President shall have power to remove said officers and fill the vacancies so occasioned.

The existing treaties of the Hawaiian Islands with foreign nations shall forthwith cease and terminate, being replaced by such treaties as may exist, or as may be hereafter concluded between the United States and such foreign nations. The municipal legislation of the Hawaiian Islands, not enacted for the fulfillment of the treaty so extinguished, and not inconsistent with this treaty, not contrary to the Constitution of the United States, nor to any existing treaty of the United States, shall remain in force until the Congress of the United States shall otherwise determine.

Until legislation shall be enacted extending the United States Customs laws and regulations to the Hawaiian Islands, the existing Customs relations of the Hawaiian islands with the United States and other countries shall remain unchanged.

ARTICLE IV.

The public debt of the Republic of Hawaii, lawfully existing at the date of the exchange of the ratification of this Treaty, including the amounts due to depositors in the Hawaiian Postal savings Bank, is hereby assumed by the Government of the United States: but the liability of the United States in this regard shall in no case exceed $4,000.000. So long, however, as the existing government and the present commercial relations of the Hawaiian Islands are continued, as herein before provided, said Government shall continue to pay the interest on said debt.

ARTICLE V.

There shall be no further immigration of Chinese into the Hawaiian Islands, except upon such conditions as are now or may hereafter be allowed by the laws of the United States, and no Chinese by reason of anything herein contained shall be allowed to enter the United States from the Hawaiian Islands.

ARTICLE VI.

The President shall appoint Commissioners, at least two of whom shall be residents of the Hawaiian Islands, who shall, as soon as reasonably practical recommend to Congress such legislation concerning the Territory of Hawaii as they shall deem necessary or proper.

ARTICLE VII.

This treaty shall be ratified by the President of the Republic of Hawaii, by and with the advice and consent of the Senate, in accordance with the Constitution of the said Republic, on the one part: and by the President of the United States, by and with the advice and consent of the Senate, on the other: and the ratifications hereof shall be exchanged at Washington as soon as possible.

The treaty was ratified by the Hawaiian Senate on September 9, 1897, and by the United States Congress on July 7, 1898 with the **Newlands Resolution (Annexation of Hawaii)**. Hawaii remained a territory of the United States until it was granted statehood in 1959.

REFERENCES:

Coffman, Tom. *Nation Within: The Story of America's Annexation of the Nation of Hawaii.* Kane'ohe, HA: Tom Coffman/EPI Center, 1998.

Osborne, Thomas J. *"Empire Can Wait": American Opposition to Hawaiian Annexation, 1893-1898.* Kent, OH: Kent State University Press, 1981.

Pratt, Julius William. *Expansionists of 1898: The Acquisition of Hawaii and the Spanish Islands.* 1936; reprint ed., New York: Peter Smith, 1951.

Russ, William Adam. *The Hawaiian Republic (1894-98) and its Struggle to Win Annexation.* Selinsgrove, PA: Susquehanna University Press, 1992.

Thurston, Lorrin Andrews. *A Hand-Book of the Annexation of Hawaii.* St. Joseph, MI: N. Pub., 1897.

Newlands Resolution (Annexation of Hawaii)

OFFICIAL TITLE: Newlands Resolution to Provide for Annexing the Hawaiian Islands to the United States.

SIGNED: July 7, 1898

SIGNATORIES: Resolution of Congress

IN FORCE: From signing

OVERVIEW: A resolution accepting, ratifying, and confirming the cession of the "Hawaiian Islands and their dependencies" and annexing them "as a part of the territory of the United States."

DISCUSSION:

With the approval of the **Treaty of Annexation (of Hawaii)** by the Hawaiian Senate, Hawaii was ceded to the United States as a territory. The resolution of annexation provided as follows:

The existing laws of the United States relative to public lands shall not apply to such lands in the Hawaiian Islands; but the Congress of the United States shall enact special laws for their management and disposition: *Provided,* That all revenue from or proceeds of the same, except as regards such part thereof as may be used or occupied for the civil, military, or naval purposes of the United States, or may be assigned for the use of the local government, shall be used solely for the benefit of the inhabitants of the Hawaiian Islands for educational and other public purposes.

Until Congress shall provide for the government of such islands all the civil, judicial, and military powers exercised by the officers of the existing government in said islands shall be vested in such person or persons and shall be exercised in such manner as the President of the United States shall direct; and the President shall have the power to remove said officers and fill the vacancies so occasioned.

With annexation, Hawaii's sovereignty, in both a national and international sense, was terminated:

The existing treaties of the Hawaiian Islands with foreign nations shall forthwith cease and determine, being replaced by such treaties as may exist, or as may be hereafter concluded, between the United States and such foreign nations. The municipal legislation of the Hawaiian Islands, not enacted for the fulfillment of the treaties so extinguished, and not inconsistent with this joint resolution nor contrary to the Constitution of the United States nor to any existing treaty of the United States, shall remain in force until the Congress of the United States shall otherwise determine.

Until legislation shall be enacted extending the United States customs laws and regulations to the Hawaiian Islands the existing customs relations of the Hawaiian Islands with the United States and other countries shall remain unchanged.

The United States agreed to assume "the public debt of the Republic of Hawaii, lawfully existing at the date of the passage of this joint resolution, including the amounts due to depositors in the Hawaiian Postal Savings Bank, is hereby assumed by the Government of the United States; but the liability of the United States in this regard shall in no case exceed four million dollars."

In 1882, Congress had passed the Chinese Exclusion Act, barring Chinese immigration into the United States for a period of ten years (the act was regularly renewed until 1920), and the Newlands Resolution reflected this legislation:

There shall be no further immigration of Chinese into the Hawaiian Islands, except upon such conditions as are now or may hereafter be allowed by the laws of the United States; no Chinese, by reason of anything herein contained, shall be allowed to enter the United States from the Hawaiian Islands.

The resolution concludes by providing for the presidential appointment of "five commissioners, at least two of whom shall be residents of the Hawaiian Islands, who shall, as soon as reasonably practicable, recommend to Congress such legislation concerning the Hawaiian Islands as they shall deem necessary or proper."

REFERENCES:

Coffman, Tom. *Nation Within: The Story of America's Annexation of the Nation of Hawaii.* Kane'ohe, HA: Tom Coffman/EPI Center, 1998.

Osborne, Thomas J. *"Empire Can Wait": American Opposition to Hawaiian Annexation, 1893-1898.* Kent, OH: Kent State University Press, 1981.

Pratt, Julius William. *Expansionists of 1898: The Acquisition of Hawaii and the Spanish Islands.* 1936; reprint ed., New York: Peter Smith, 1951.

Russ, William Adam. *The Hawaiian Republic (1894-98) and its Struggle to Win Annexation.* Selinsgrove, PA: Susquehanna University Press, 1992.

Thurston, Lorrin Andrews. *A Hand-Book of the Annexation of Hawaii.* St. Joseph, MI: N. Pub., 1897.

Convention between the United States and Mexico: Equitable Distribution of the Waters of the Rio Grande

SIGNED: May 21, 1906, at Washington

SIGNATORIES: Mexico vs. United States

IN FORCE: From January 16, 1907

OVERVIEW: "…a Convention…providing for the equitable distribution of the waters of the Rio Grande for irrigation purposes, and to remove all causes of controversy…in respect thereto."

DISCUSSION:

Distribution of water from the Rio Grande has often been a source of contention between the United States and Mexico. Article 1 of the treaty lays down the proposed remedy for the inequitable distribution: "After the completion of the proposed storage dam near Engle, New Mexico, and the distributing system auxiliary thereto, and as soon as water shall be available in said system for the purpose, the United States shall deliver to Mexico a total of 60,000 acre-feet of water annually, in the bed of the Rio Grande at the point where the head works of the Acequia Madre, known as the Old Mexican Canal, now exit above the city of Juarez, Mexico." The treaty also stipulated a monthly schedule, by volume, for delivery of the water.

REFERENCES:
Proceedings of the International (Water) Boundary Commission. Washington, D.C.: U.S. Government Printing Office, 1903.

Agreement (with Mexico) on the Utilization of Waters of the Colorado and Tijuana Rivers and of the Rio Grande

SIGNED: February 3, 1944, at Washington; protocol signed, November 14, 1944
SIGNATORIES: Mexico vs. United States
IN FORCE: From November 8, 1945
OVERVIEW: A treaty to "fix and delimit the rights of the two countries with respect to the waters of the Colorado and Tijuana Rivers, and of the Rio Grande (Rio Bravo) from Fort Quitman, Texas, United States of America, to the Gulf of Mexico, in order to obtain the most complete and satisfactory utilization thereof."

DISCUSSION:

Recognizing that the bed of the Rio Grande—and, consequently the border between the United States and Mexico—is subject to continual change, the treaty extends indefinitely the operation of the International Boundary Commission and further defines its mission, jurisdiction, and composition. Section II of the treaty specifies in detail the allocation of the waters of the Rio Grande between the two nations and further specifies how each nation would construct dams to accomplish the desired distribution. Section III lays down details of distribution (together with specifications for dam projects) of the waters of the Colorado River, and Section IV, the Tijuana River.

Similar in spirit to the **Convention Between the United States and Mexico: Equitable Distribution of the Waters of the Rio Grande** of 1906, the 1944 document is far more detailed and entails a program of extensive construction cooperation between the two signatories, whereas, in the 1906 document, the burden of creating the distribution rested solely with the United States.

See also **Treaty to Resolve Pending Boundary Differences and Maintain the Rio Grande and Colorado River as the International Boundary.**

REFERENCES:
Demarcation of the New International Boundary. Washington, D.C.: U.S. Government Printing Office, 1968.
Proceedings of the International (Water) Boundary Commission. Washington, D.C.: U.S. Government Printing Office, 1903.

Treaty to Resolve Pending Boundary Differences and Maintain the Rio Grande and Colorado River as the International Boundary

SIGNED: November 29, 1970, at Mexico City
SIGNATORIES: Mexico vs. United States
IN FORCE: From April 18, 1972
OVERVIEW: A treaty to resolve "pending boundary differences" resulting from changes in the beds of the Colorado River and the Rio Grande.

DISCUSSION:

The United States of America and the United Mexican States, Animated by a spirit of close friendship and mutual respect and desiring to:

Resolve all pending boundary differences between the two countries,

Restore to the Rio Grande its character of international boundary in the reaches where that character has been lost, and preserve for the Rio Grande and Colorado River the character of international boundaries ascribed to them by the boundary treaties in force,

Minimize changes in the channels of these rivers, and should these changes occur, attempt to resolve the problems arising therefrom promptly and equitably,

Resolve problems relating to sovereignty over existing or future islands in the Rio Grande,

And finally, considering that it is in the interest of both countries to delimit clearly their maritime boundaries in the Gulf of Mexico and in the Pacific Ocean,

Have resolved to conclude this Treaty concerning their fluvial and maritime boundaries . . .

The treaty precisely redefines the boundary between the United States and Mexico so that the Colorado River and the Rio Grande remain the true border. Such redefinition was made necessary by the continual shifting evolution of the beds of these rivers.

REFERENCES:
Demarcation of the New International Boundary. Washington, D.C.: U.S. Government Printing Office, 1968.
Proceedings of the International (Water) Boundary Commission. Washington, D.C.: U.S. Government Printing Office, 1903.

SECTION 1.2

Indian Treaties

Overview of the Indian Treaties

Columbus, as everyone knows, landed in the Bahamas on October 12, 1492. He set sail on a return voyage to Spain early the next year, leaving behind a small garrison. Shortly after Columbus's departure, the garrison attacked the local Indians, whom they mistakenly judged peaceful to the point of total passivity, and were in turn attacked and wiped out. Thus the first violent clash between whites and Indians occurred almost immediately after contact, and warfare between the two peoples would continue, endemically in North America, for the next four centuries, culminating in the so-called "Battle" of Wounded Knee, Dakota Territory, on December 29, 1890, and followed by the formal surrender of the Sioux nation at White Clay Creek on January 15, 1891.

If four hundred years of white-Indian contact in North America produced almost continual warfare, those years also yielded a torrent of treaties and agreements, of which a small fraction is represented here. The vast majority of treaties represent attempts to end either a particular war or a chronic, generalized state of violent hostility. Yet, of course, the continued warfare, in spite of the treaties, affirms a truth that surprises no one who has even a nodding acquaintance with American history: Treaties between whites and Indians were usually violated almost as soon as they were signed.

It is a simple matter to ascribe the violations to Euro-American avarice and perfidy. While the settlement of North America was, from the European perspective, a natural expansion of "empire" or "civilization," from the perspective of Native America, this same movement was neither more nor less than an invasion. And what can be expected from treaties struck with invaders?

Indeed, it *was* often the case that white governments, colonial or federal, entered into treaties with deliberate bad faith. More often, however, the treaty commissioners came to the peace table with at least reasonably good intentions, perhaps wishing to drive a hard bargain, and perhaps willing to use coercion and intimidation to extract Indian signatures, yet also fully confident that their own side would abide by the terms of the agreement they hammered out. Such confidence, more often than not, was without basis in fact. It was rare that colonial or federal authorities commanded the means to compel the compliance of the people they governed. Settlers in frontier regions, hungry for Indian lands but also vulnerable to Indian

attack, typically felt little allegiance to the eastern seats of colonial government, let alone to governments ensconced in Europe. Even in the nineteenth century, federal treaties often proved difficult or impossible to enforce, as states, territories, individual military commanders, militia forces, or bands of settlers might, at any time, take matters into their own hands and do as they pleased. During the era of what the United States Army called the "Indian Wars," roughly from the end of the Civil War in 1865 through the early 1880s, the federal military presence in the West was feeble. After rapidly demobilizing at the end of the Civil War, so that an army of over a million was instantly reduced to a mere 30,000, the size of the force was increased to a peak of 56,815 in 1867, but fully one-third of these troops were required to oversee Reconstruction in the South. Through the 1870s, cutbacks were severe. In 1874, a ceiling of 27,000 was placed on army strength, but effective strength (allowing for casualties and deserters) was closer to 19,000. These meager forces were apportioned into 430 companies to man some 200 posts, of which 100 were widely dispersed throughout the West. The result was that the army was rarely able to fight Indians with decisive effect, and it was also inadequate to enforce upon local white citizens and local white officials the conditions agreed to by treaty.

The inadequacy of the federal government to enforce treaty obligations was compounded by the official attitude toward the administration of Indian policy. Many Indian treaties required the signatory tribes to retire to prescribed reservations in exchange for a promise of government-funded building supplies, agricultural equipment, food, an annuity, and other essentials. However, throughout the nineteenth century and well into the twentieth, the system of reservations and Indian agencies was administered with scandalous inconsistency, inefficiency, heartlessness, and rampant corruption.

Nevertheless, problems with Indian treaties were not exclusively the fault of the Euro-American or government signatories. The nature of Indian tribal government also created difficult conditions for treaty making and the fulfilment of treaty terms. Tribal organization was characteristically loose and democratic to the point of anarchy. So-called chiefs were seldom sovereigns in the Euro-American sense, but were, instead, merely men who enjoyed authority and respect. From the tribe's perspective, the chief's decisions might carry little if any legal or political weight. A particular chief might assent to a treaty, but his action was not necessarily binding on anyone else in the tribe. Moreover, tribes were often severely splintered into "peace" factions and "war" factions, usually with the older men constituting the former, and the young warriors belonging to the latter. Often, government treaty commissioners either ignored such factionalism or tried to use the ambiguity of authority to their advantage. For example, **Treaty with the Chickasaw** (1830) is typical of several treaties concluded pursuant to the **Indian Removal Act** (1830). By this treaty, the Chickasaw "voluntarily" agreed to their "removal" from their eastern homelands to designated "Indian Territory" (a region encompassing present-day Oklahoma and parts of other states) in return for various considerations. The treaty, like many of the other removal treaties, was concluded exclusively with the tribal faction that favored peaceful removal. This notwithstanding, the government then deemed the treaty binding on all Chickasaws and used it, wherever necessary, as a legal basis for effecting the forcible removal of recalcitrant tribal members. In the case of the treaty concluded with the Cherokee (not represented in this collection), the tribe's so-called Treaty Party—Indian supporters of removal—were outnumbered seventeen to one by the "National Party," which opposed removal. The administration of President Andrew Jackson chose simply to ignore the majority, no matter how substantial.

Such instances of outright deception and willful misinterpretation were hardly rare in the creation of Indian treaties, but, more often, ambiguity was accidental. Nevertheless, these accidents created nothing but confusion and ill will. And even the treaty ceremonies themselves created ambiguities. Some signing ceremonies were relatively relaxed occasions, almost always solemnized by the presentation of gifts. Clearly, Indian chiefs often signed a treaty just to obtain the accompanying gifts, which were not the beads and trinkets of cliché and folklore but, more often, such sorely needed items as firearms, ammunition, food, and clothing. Other treaty signings were tense affairs presided over by whatever show of military might the government could muster. The message of these was clear enough: sign or die. Under such duress, Indians assented with little or no intention of abiding by the terms to which they agreed.

Treaties, like all aspects of Indian-white relations, were plagued by essential cultural differences, the most important of which centered on concepts of ownership and property. Most Indian cultures did not embrace concepts of private property and exclusive ownership. No one "owned" a particular parcel of land. A given tribe might claim the right to hunt, trap, farm, and otherwise dwell in a region and might defend that right by force of arms; however, most tribes were willing to make agreements allowing other tribes or individuals to hunt or trap on "their" land. Such agreements did not convey ownership of the land to the other party. How could they? For elements of the natural world—the air one breathed, the water one drank, the

earth one trod—could neither be bought nor sold. Nevertheless, treaties persistently ignored the profound cultural gulf dividing the Indian world view from that of the Euro-Americans.

The Taunton Agreement

SIGNED: April 10, 1671, at Taunton, Plymouth Colony (now in Massachusetts)
IN FORCE: From 1671 to 1675; abrogated by King Philip's War
SIGNATORIES: Plymouth Colony vs. the Wampanoag Indians of Massachusetts
OVERVIEW: This brief document—just over 200 words—is typical of the legal instruments by which European colonists in America sought to dominate their Native American neighbors, both to neutralize them as military threats and to exploit them as "clients" or even "subjects" in order to legitimate questionable claims to territory and sovereignty. The humiliating terms Plymouth Colony imposed on King Philip through the Taunton Agreement led directly to King Philip's War (1675-76), proportionate to population, the costliest war in American history.

DISCUSSION:

Massasoit, chief of the Wampanoags and longtime friend of the Plymouth colonists, died in 1661 at the age of eighty-one. His son Wamsutta, whom the English called Alexander, succeeded him and continued the tradition of friendship. However, under Wamsutta, the Wampanoags divided their loyalty between two English colonies, Rhode Island and Plymouth, which competed for the purchase of Indian lands and which both sought to establish a protectorate over the Wampanoags in order to put backbone into their weak and tenuous charters. Plymouth officials sought to intimidate Alexander by forcibly taking him to Duxbury to pressure him into selling land to Plymouth in preference to Rhode Island. During his captivity, Alexander fell ill and, though released, died on the journey home. Alexander's twenty-four-year-old brother, Metacom or Metacomet, whom the English called Philip, succeeded Wamsutta as chief and broadcast the opinion that the colonists had poisoned Alexander. From this point on, friction between Plymouth Colony and King Philip steadily increased. A skilled diplomat, forceful speaker, and charismatic leader, King Philip patiently forged alliances with neighboring tribes. Plymouth authorities, fearful of his activities and seeking to intimidate him as they had Alexander, summoned King Philip to Plymouth Town on August 6, 1664, to answer charges of plotting against the colony. He denied the accusations, but signed a document pledging to seek permission from the colony before selling any land.

Peaceful if uneasy relations prevailed between the Indians and the English until 1665, when a land dispute between colonists and the Narragansett Indians brought the region to the brink of war. Seizing a chance to exploit the rift between the English and a rival tribe, King Philip warned New York colonial authorities that the Narragansetts were plotting war against them. The Narragansett chief, Ninigret, responded by accusing Philip of hostile designs, and in 1667 Philip was again summoned to Plymouth. This time, he was defiant. "Your governor is but a subject," he declared, "I shal treat only with my brother, King Charles of England. When he comes, I am ready."

For four more years, the mutual animosity intensified. Early in 1671, Philip, outraged when a new Plymouth settlement, Swansea, encroached on his land, staged an armed display for the benefit of the town's citizens. On April 10, 1671, he was summoned to Taunton, to sign an agreement acknowledging and apologizing for such "plotting." The document, given below in its entirety, bound the Wampanoags to surrender their arms and compelled King Philip to In force: acknowledge submission to the British Crown and to Plymouth Colony.

Whereas my Father, my Brother, and my self, have formally submitted ourselves and our People unto the Kings Majesty of England, and to the Colony of New Plimouth, by solemn Covenant under our Hand; but I having of late through my Indiscretion, and the Naughtiness of my Heart, violated and broken this my Covenant with my Friends, by taking up Arms, with evil intent against them, and that groundlessly; I being now deeply sensible of my Unfaithfulness and Folly, so desire at this Time solemnly to renew my Covenant with my ancient Friends, my Fathers Friends above mentioned, and do desire that this may testifie to the World against me if ever I shall again fail in my Faithfulness towards them (that I have now, and at all Times found so kind to me) or any other of the English Colonies; and as a real Pledge of my true Intentions for the Future to be Faithful and Friendly, I do freely engage to resign up unto the Government of New Plimouth, all my English Arms, to be kept by them for their Security, so long as they shall see Reason. For true Performance of the Premises, I have hereunto set my Hand, together with the Rest of my Council.

After signing the document, Philip attempted to incite a dispute between Plymouth and Massachusetts by pointing out that his retroactive pledge to Plymouth undermined the validity of land titles Massachusetts had earlier secured from the Wampanoags. Canny though this strategy was, it backfired, serving to unite the two colonies against Philip. Toward the end of September the chief was once more haled into a Plymouth court, where he was tried for breaking the Taunton Agreement. Fined £100, he was now forbidden to wage war against other Indians without authority from the colonial government.

Philip, outraged and offended, bided his time, sealing an alliance against the English with the Nipmuck Indians as well as with his tribe's former rivals, the Narragansetts. Early in 1675, King Philip probably murdered John Sassamon, an Indian employed by the colonists to spy on him. Summoned to answer charges of murder, Philip made no secret of his contempt for his accusers, who were compelled at length to release him for lack of evidence. On June 11, 1675, shortly after his release, the Wampanoags armed near Swansea and Plymouth Town. Cattle

were killed and houses looted in the outlying settlements, from which colonists began to retreat. Although it would not be declared officially by the "United Colonies" (Massachusetts, Plymouth, Rhode Island, Connecticut, New Hampshire, and Maine) until September 9, 1675, King Philip's War had begun. Before it ended—with Philip's defeat and death on August 12, 1676—it would devastate half the towns of New England, virtually bankrupt the fledgling colonies, and kill one in sixteen men of military age, as well as many older men, women, and children. At least three thousand Indians perished in the war—mostly Wampanoags, Narragansetts, and Nipmucks—and many who did not die were deported to the West Indies as slaves. In proportion to population, King Philip's War must be counted as the costliest in American history.

REFERENCES:

Axelrod, Alan. *Chronicle of the Indian Wars: From Colonial Times to Wounded Knee.* New York: Prentice Hall Press, 1993.

Hubbard, William. *The History of the Indian Wars in New England from the First Settlement to the Termination of the War with King Philip, in 1677.* 1814; reprint ed., New York: Krauss, 1969.

King Philip's War Narratives (facsimiles of *The Present State of New-England, with Respect to the Indian War* [1675]; *A Continuation of the State of New-England, Being a Farther Account of the Indian War* [1676]; *A New and Further Narrative of the State of New-England, Being a Continued Account of the Bloody Indian War* [1676]; *A True Account of the Most Considerable Occurrences that Have Hapned in the Warre between the English and the Indians in New-England* [1676]; and *The War in New-England Visibly Ended* [1677]. Ann Arbor, Mich.: Readex Microprint, 1966.

Slotkin, Richard., and James K. Folsom, eds. *So Dreadfull a Judgement: Puritan Responses to King Philip's War, 1676-1677.* Middletown, Conn.: Wesleyan University Press, 1978.

Delaware Indian Treaty

SIGNED: September 17, 1778, Fort Pitt (present-day Pittsburgh, Pennsylvania)

IN FORCE: From 1778, but frequently violated

SIGNATORIES: United States vs. Delaware Indians

OVERVIEW: During the American Revolution, most combatant Indian tribes sided with the British. Among the most important of Britain's Indian allies were the Delawares. This treaty sought to end that alliance and establish one with the United States.

DISCUSSION:

During the American Revolution, most Indian tribes and groups sought to remain neutral, but of those who were combatants, the majority sided with the British against the Americans. Their reasoning was sound. As they saw it, a British victory would result in enforcement of the Proclamation of 1763, by which King George III barred white settlement west of the Appalachian Mountains. In contrast, an American victory would bring a western invasion of white settlers.

Most of the Delawares cooperated with the British in devastating attacks on the frontier regions of the Cherry Valley, the Mohawk Valley, and the Wyoming Valley of New York and Pennsylvania. These attacks were worst during 1778, and the Fort Pitt treaty sought an end to them as well as an alliance with the Delawares that would preempt their collaboration with the British.

The Delaware Indian Treaty provided for equitable adjudication of criminal cases involving whites and Indians, and sought to establish a sound and ongoing basis of trade. Article VI of the treaty pledged restraint in white settlement of Delaware lands.

Like many treaties between Indians and the United States, the Delaware Indian Treaty seems just, reasonable, and unambiguous. However, also like most such treaties, it would prove ineffective. If the colonial administration of King George III had been incapable of enforcing the 1763 Proclamation Line, how could the struggling and distracted revolutionary government of the United States expect to be effective in restraining expansion of settlement into Indian lands? For their part, many Delaware groups continued to fight alongside the British, treaty or no treaty, and many Delaware leaders had not signed the treaty. The most prominent of these, Joseph Brant (Thayendanegea), led highly effective raids against Patriot settlers in the Ohio Valley during 1781.

The Delaware Indian Treaty is an important early example of the failing that would plague perhaps the majority of treaties between the United States and Indians. Euro-American treaty negotiators wrongly assumed that tribes were analogous to sovereign states. In fact, tribal organization was typically far less formal, cultural rather than political, and loosely structured to a point that many Euro-Americans would deem anarchy. The so-called chiefs or sachems with whom Euro-American treaty commissioners negotiated were not sovereigns, rulers, or chief executives in the European or American sense. They led factions—rarely entire tribes—and, moreover, their leadership was based largely on consensus, not on any absolute decree, policy, law, or even tradition. Thus the word or signature of a chief might or might not be perceived as binding by any number of tribal members. For this reason, Indian treaties were frequently repudiated or simply ignored, as in the case of this 1778 document.

REFERENCES:

Axelrod, Alan, *Chronicle of the Indian Wars: From Colonial Times to Wounded Knee*. New York: Macmillan General Reference, 1993.

Israel, Fred L. *Major Peace Treaties of Modern History, 1648–1967*, vol. 1. New York: Chelsea House and McGraw-Hill, 1967.

Prucha, Francis Paul, ed. *Documents of United States Indian Policy*, 2d ed., expanded. Lincoln: University of Nebraska Press, 1990.

Treaty with the Six Nations (Treaty of Fort Stanwix)

SIGNED: October 22, 1784

SIGNATORIES: "United States, in Congress assembled" vs. "the Sachems and Warriors of the Six Nations" (the Iroquois Confederation, consisting of the Mohawk, Oneida, Onondaga, Cayuga, Seneca, and Tuscarora tribes)

IN FORCE: From signing

OVERVIEW: The treaty secured large cessions of territory from the Six Nations in return for peaceful occupation of certain lands and an unspecified present of "goods . . . for [the] use and comfort" of the Six Nations.

DISCUSSION:

The Iroquois Confederation, or Six Nations, was torn apart by the Revolution, with most tribal members siding with the British, but a significant minority allying themselves with the Americans. Having suffered severely in the war and in continued frontier violence following it, the Iroquois relinquished a large tract of territory in return for peace and aid in the form of goods. The treaty is very brief and may be reproduced in full:

The United States of America give peace to the Senecas, Mohawks, Onondagas and Cayugas, and receive them into their protection upon the following conditions:

ARTICLE I.

Six hostages shall be immediately delivered to the commissioners by the said nations, to remain in possession of the United States, till all the prisoners, white and black, which were taken by the said Senecas, Mohawks, Onondagas and Cayugas, or by any of them, in the late war, from among the people of the United States, shall be delivered up.

ARTICLE II.

The Oneida and Tuscarora nations shall be secured in the possession of the lands on which they are settled.

ARTICLE III.

A line shall be drawn, beginning at the mouth of a creek about four miles east of Niagara, called Oyonwayea, or Johnston's Landing-Place, upon the lake named by the Indians Oswego, and by us Ontario; from thence southerly in a direction always four miles east of the carrying-path, between Lake Erie and Ontario, to the mouth of Tehoseroron or Buffaloe Creek on Lake Erie; thence south to the north boundary of the state of Pennsylvania; thence west to the end of the said north boundary; thence south along the west boundary of the said state, to the river Ohio; the said line from the mouth of the Oyonwayea to the Ohio, shall be the western boundary of the lands of the Six Nations, so that the Six Nations shall and do yield to the United States, all claims to the country west of the said boundary, and then they shall be secured in the peaceful possession of the lands they inhabit east and north of the same, reserving only six miles square round the fort of Oswego, to the United States, for the support of the same.

ARTICLE IV.

The Commissioners of the United States, in consideration of the present circumstances of the Six Nations, and in execution of the humane and liberal views of the United States upon the signing of the above articles, will order goods to be delivered to the said Six Nations for their use and comfort.

REFERENCES:

Axelrod, Alan. *Chronicle of the Indian Wars: From Colonial Times to Wounded Knee.* New York: Macmillan General Reference, 1993.

Kappler, Charles J., comp. and ed., *Indian Affairs: Laws and Treaties,* vol. 2. Washington, D.C.: Government Printing Office, 1904.

Treaty of Fort McIntosh

SIGNED: January 21, 1785, at Fort McIntosh

SIGNATORIES: United States vs. sachems and warriors of the Wyandot, Delaware, Chippewa, and Ottawa nations

IN FORCE: From signing

OVERVIEW: A peace treaty following the Revolution, in which the Indians acknowledge the "protection" of the United States and agree to boundary lines.

DISCUSSION:

The treaty not only called for peace between these tribes of the Old Northwest and the United States, but established boundaries between Indian and white settlement and obtained the Indians' acknowledgment of the authority and protection of the United States. The treaty specified that the Indians were not to settle on lands belonging to the United States and that "any person not being an Indian" who attempts to settle on lands allotted to the Indians "shall forfeit the protection of the United States, and the Indians may punish him as they please."

Like most Indian-white treaties, the Treaty of Fort McIntosh proved unenforceable and had little positive effect. It was confirmed and augmented by the **Treaty of Fort Harmar**, which was more effective because it provided for payment to the Indians for land ceded to the United States.

REFERENCE:

Prucha, Francis Paul. *Documents of United States Indian Policy,* 2d ed., expanded. Lincoln: University of Nebraska Press, 1990.

Treaty with the Cherokee

SIGNED: November 28, 1785

SIGNATORIES: United States vs. "headmen and Warriors of all the Cherokees"

IN FORCE: From signing

OVERVIEW: A treaty concluding hostilities with the Cherokees at the end of the American Revolution and establishing territorial boundaries.

DISCUSSION:

Most Indian tribes that did not manage to remain neutral during the American Revolution sided with the British and Loyalists against the Patriot forces, largely in the belief that a British-Loyalist victory would pose less of a danger to their lands than a Patriot triumph would. The American victory over the British, which brought the Revolution to an end, left much Indian hostility unresolved. In the South, separate peace treaties were made with factions of the closely allied Creek and Cherokee tribes. The text of the first post-Revolutionary treaty with the Cherokees follows:

ARTICLE I.

The Head Men and Warriors of all the Cherokees shall restore all the prisoners, citizens of the United States, or subjects of their allies, to their entire liberty: They shall also restore all the Negroes, and all other property taken during the late war from the citizens, to such person, and at such time and place, as the Commissioners shall appoint.

ARTICLE II.

The Commissioners of the United States in Congress assembled, shall restore all the prisoners taken from the Indians, during the late war, to the Head-Men and Warriors of the Cherokees, as early as is practicable.

The United States treaty commissioners were particularly anxious to assert authority over the Cherokee, to have the Cherokee acknowledge that authority, and to have them renounce allegiance to any other sovereign:

ARTICLE III.

The said Indians for themselves and their respective tribes and towns do acknowledge all the Cherokees to be under the protection of the United States of America, and of no other sovereign whosoever.

A common theme of many United States-Indian treaties is the definition of territorial boundaries:

ARTICLE IV.

The boundary allotted to the Cherokees for their hunting grounds, between the said Indians and the citizens of the United States, within the limits of the United States of America, is, and shall be the following, viz. Beginning at the mouth of Duck river, on the Tennessee; thence running north-east to the ridge dividing the waters running into Cumberland from those running into the Tennessee; thence eastwardly along the said ridge to a north-east line to be run, which shall strike the river Cumberland forty miles above Nashville; thence along the said line to the river; thence up the said river to the ford where the Kentucky road crosses the river; thence to Campbell's line, near Cumberland gap; thence to the mouth of Claud's creek on Holstein; thence to the Chimney-top mountain; thence to Camp-creek, near the mouth of Big Limestone, on Nolichuckey; thence a southerly course six miles to a mountain; thence south to the North-Carolina line; thence to the South-Carolina Indian boundary, and along the same south-west over the top of the Oconee mountain till it shall strike Tugaloo river; thence a direct line to the top of the Currohee mountain; thence to the head of the south fork of Oconee river.

ARTICLE V.

If any citizen of the United States, or other person not being an Indian, shall attempt to settle on any of the lands westward or southward of the said boundary which are hereby allotted to the Indians for their hunting grounds, or having already settled and will not remove from the same within six months after the ratification of this treaty, such person shall forfeit the protection of the United States, and the Indians may punish him or not as they please: Provided nevertheless, That this article shall not extend to the people settled between the fork of French Broad and Holstein rivers, whose particular situation shall be transmitted to the United States in Congress assembled for their decision thereon, which the Indians agree to abide by.

Law enforcement and the administration of justice are also common themes:

ARTICLE VI.

If any Indian or Indians, or person residing among them, or who shall take refuge in their nation, shall commit a robbery, or murder, or other capital crime, on any citizen of the United States, or person under their protection, the nation, or the tribe to which such offender or offenders may belong, shall be bound to deliver him or them up to be punished Cording to the ordinances of the United States; provided, that the punishment shall not be greater than if the robbery or murder, or other capital crime had been committed by a citizen on a citizen.

ARTICLE VII.

If any citizen of the United States, or person under their protection, shall commit a robbery or murder, or other capital crime, on any Indian, such offender or offenders shall be punished in the same manner as if the murder or robbery, or other capital crime, had been committed on a citizen of the United States; and the punishment shall be in presence of some of the Cherokees, if any shall attend at the time and place, and that they may have an opportunity so to do, due notice of the time of such intended punishment shall be sent to some one of the tribes.

ARTICLE VIII.

It is understood that the punishment of the innocent under the idea of retaliation, is unjust, and shall not be practiced on either side, except where there is a manifest violation of this treaty; and then it shall be preceded first by a demand of justice, and if refused, then by a declaration of hostilities.

In Article IX, the federal government asserts the right to regulate trade with the Indians. In part, this was an attempt to control the Indians, but, equally important, it was a recognition that private individuals, local authorities, and state governments frequently coerced, cheated, and swindled the Indians, thereby creating the conditions in which violence and even warfare developed:

ARTICLE IX.

For the benefit and comfort of the Indians, and for the prevention of injuries or oppressions on the part of the citizens or Indians, the United States in Congress assembled shall have the sole and exclusive right of regulating the trade with the Indians, and managing all their affairs in such manner as they think proper.

ARTICLE X.

Until the pleasure of Congress be known, respecting the ninth article, all traders, citizens of the United States, shall have liberty to go to any of the tribes or towns of the Cherokees to trade with them, and they shall be protected in their persons and property, and kindly treated.

Article XI binds the Indians to "give notice to the citizens of the United States, of any designs which they may know or suspect to be formed in any neighboring tribe, or by any person whosoever, against the peace, trade or interest of the United States." And Article XII gives them "the right to send a deputy of their choice, whenever they think fit, to Congress."

By Article XIII, peace is sworn:

The hatchet shall be forever buried, and the peace given by the United States, and friendship re-established between the said states on the one part, and all the Cherokees on the other, shall be universal; and the contracting parties shall use their utmost endeavors to maintain the peace given as aforesaid, and friendship re-established.

In many places, trading relationships between non-Indians and Cherokees were profitable, and a high degree of social and cultural integration prevailed. However, hostilities were repeatedly renewed, especially in Georgia, where abuses of Cherokee rights, especially property rights, were sanctioned by and, in some cases, perpetrated by the state government.

REFERENCES:

Axelrod, Alan. *Chronicle of the Indian Wars: From Colonial Times to Wounded Knee*. New York: Macmillan General Reference, 1993.

Coupler, Charles J., ed. *Indian Treaties, 1778-1883*. New York: Interland, 1972.

Fairbanks, Charles H. *Chickasaw, Cherokee, Creek*. New York: Garland, 1974.

Prucha, Francis Paul, ed. *Documents of United States Indian Policy*, 2d ed. Lincoln: University of Nebraska Press, 1990.

Treaties between the United States of America and the Cherokee Nation, from 1785. Tahlequah, Cherokee Nation: National Printing Office, 1870.

Tyler, Lyman S. *A History of Indian Policy*. Washington, D.C.: U.S. Government Printing Office, 1973.

Treaty with the Choctaw

SIGNED: January 3, 1786, at Hopewell

SIGNATORIES: United States vs. "Commissioners Plenipotentiary of all the Choctaw Nation"

IN FORCE: From signing

OVERVIEW: A treaty restoring peace between the United States and the Choctaw following the American Revolution.

DISCUSSION:

The Choctaw were among those Indian tribes who sided with the British and the Loyalists during the American Revolution. The peace treaty concluded with them establishes boundaries of Choctaw lands and contains the Choctaws' acknowledgment of United States authority over them.

The administration of criminal justice is addressed in three straightforward articles:

ARTICLE V.

If any Indian or Indians, or persons, residing among them. or who shall take refuge in their nation, shall commit a robbery or murder or other capital crime on any citizen of the United States of America, or person under their protection, the tribe to which such offender may belong, or the nation, shall be bound to deliver him or them up to be punished according to the ordinances of the United States in Congress assembled: Provided, that the punishment shall not be greater than if the robbery or murder, or other capital crime, had been committed by a citizen on a citizen.

ARTICLE VI.

If any citizen of the United States of America, or person under their protection, shall commit a robbery or murder, or other capital crime, on any Indian, such offender or offenders shall be punished in the same manner as if the robbery or murder, or other capital crime, had been committed on a citizen of the United States of America; and the punishment shall be in presence of some of the Choctaws, if any will attend at the time and place; and that they may have an opportunity so to do, due notice, if practicable, of the time of such intended punishment, shall be sent to some one of the tribes.

ARTICLE VII.

It is understood that the punishment of the innocent, under the idea of retaliation, is unjust, and shall not be practiced on either side, except where there is a manifest violation of this treaty; and then it shall be preceded, first by a demand of justice, and if refused, then by a declaration of hostilities.

Article VIII gives Congress full authority in regulating trade with the Choctaw: "For the benefit and comfort of the Indians, and for the prevention of injuries or oppressions on the part of the citizens or Indians, the United States in Congress assembled, shall have the sole and exclusive right of regulating the trade with the Indians, and managing all their affairs in such manner as they think proper." And a general peace is established, in Article IX, by a phrase that was standard in early United States-Indian treaties: "The hatchet shall be forever buried."

REFERENCES:

Axelrod, Alan. *Chronicle of the Indian Wars: From Colonial Times to Wounded Knee.* New York: Macmillan General Reference, 1993.

Constitution, Treaties, and Laws of the Choctaw Nation. Sedalia, MO: Democrat Steam Print, 1887.

Coupler, Charles J., ed. *Indian Treaties, 1778-1883.* New York: Interland, 1972.

Fairbanks, Charles H. *Chickasaw, Cherokee, Creek.* New York: Garland, 1974.

Prucha, Francis Paul, ed. *Documents of United States Indian Policy,* 2d ed. Lincoln: University of Nebraska Press, 1990.

Tyler, Lyman S. *A History of Indian Policy.* Washington, D.C.: U.S. Government Printing Office, 1973.

Treaty with the Chickasaw (Treaty of Hopewell)

SIGNED: January 10, 1786, at Hopewell, on the Keowee

SIGNATORIES: United States vs. representatives of the Chickasaw Indians

IN FORCE: From signing

OVERVIEW: A treaty restoring peace with the Chickasaw Indians following the American Revolution.

DISCUSSION:

The treaty restores peace between the Chickasaws and the United States, lays down Chickasaw acknowledgment of United States authority over them, and establishes the boundaries of the Chickasaw territory. The principal text of this very brief treaty follows:

ARTICLE 1.

The Commissioners Plenipotentiary of the Chickasaw nation, shall restore all the prisoners, citizens of the United States, to their entire liberty, if any there be in the Chickasaw nation. They shall also restore all the negroes, and all other property taken during the late war, from the citizens, if any there be in the Chickasaw nation, to such person, and at such time and place, as the Commissioners of the United States of America shall appoint.

ARTICLE II.

The Commissioners Plenipotentiary of the Chickasaws, do hereby acknowledge the tribes and the towns of the Chickasaw nation, to be under the protection of the United States of America, and of no other sovereign whosoever.

REFERENCES:

Axelrod, Alan. *Chronicle of the Indian Wars: From Colonial Times to Wounded Knee.* New York: Macmillan General Reference, 1993.

Coupler, Charles J., ed. *Indian Treaties, 1778-1883.* New York: Interland, 1972.

Fairbanks, Charles H. *Chickasaw, Cherokee, Creek.* New York: Garland, 1974.

Prucha, Francis Paul, ed. *Documents of United States Indian Policy,* 2d ed. Lincoln: University of Nebraska Press, 1990.

Tyler, Lyman S. *A History of Indian Policy.* Washington, D.C.: U.S. Government Printing Office, 1973.

Treaty with the Shawnee

SIGNED: January 21, 1786, "at the Mouth of the Great Miami, on the North-western Bank of the Ohio"

SIGNATORIES: United States vs. "the Chiefs and Warriors of the Shawnee Nation"

IN FORCE: From signing

OVERVIEW: A treaty of peace with the Shawnee, following the American Revolution.

DISCUSSION:

Like most Indian tribes that did not manage to remain neutral during the American Revolution, the Shawnee sided with the

British and Loyalists in the belief that defeating the Americans would end incursions into their lands.

Like many of the post-Revolutionary treaties, this one begins by addressing the issue of prisoner return, but is unique among the early group of treaties in specifying that hostages are to be held as a guarantee of the safe return of prisoners. The use of hostages in this way was common at the time, but was not customarily incorporated into a formal treaty:

THREE hostages shall be immediately delivered to the Commissioners, to remain in the possession of the United States until all the prisoners, white and black, taken in the late war from among the citizens of the United States, by the Shawanee nation, or by any other Indian or Indians residing in their towns, shall be restored.

Article II takes note of a treaty concluded by Great Britain with the Shawnee and asserts the precedence of the sovereignty of the United States over the provisions of that treaty:

The Shawnee nation do acknowledge the United States to be the sole and absolute sovereigns of all the territory ceded to them by treaty of peace made between them and the King of Great Britain the fourteenth day of January, one thousand seven hundred and eighty-four.

The rest of the treaty deals with law enforcement and the definition of territories.

REFERENCES:
Axelrod, Alan. *Chronicle of the Indian Wars: From Colonial Times to Wounded Knee.* New York: Macmillan General Reference, 1993.
Coupler, Charles J., ed. *Indian Treaties, 1778-1883.* New York: Interland, 1972.
Prucha, Francis Paul, ed. *Documents of United States Indian Policy,* 2d ed. Lincoln: University of Nebraska Press, 1990.
Tyler, Lyman S. *A History of Indian Policy.* Washington, D.C.: U.S. Government Printing Office, 1973.

Treaty with the Six Nations (Treaty of Fort Harmar)

SIGNED: January 9, 1789
SIGNATORIES: United States vs. "the sachems and warriors of the Six Nations" (the Iroquois Confederation, consisting of the Mohawk, Oneida, Onondaga, Cayuga, Seneca, and Tuscarora tribes)
IN FORCE: From signing
OVERVIEW: The treaty confirms and elaborates on the territorial cessions made by the Iroquois in the **Treaty with the Six Nations (Treaty of Fort Stanwix)** of 1784.

DISCUSSION:
The Treaty of Fort Harmar sets as its purpose "removing all causes of controversy, regulating trade, and settling boundaries between the Indian nations in the northerly department and the . . . the United States." The treaty elaborates on the nature and extent of the territorial cessions made by the Iroquois in the Treaty of Fort Stanwix.

The present treaty makes note of the absence of the Mohawks, the most powerful and hostile of the Six Nations; nevertheless, the treaty represents a renewal and confirmation of the 1784 boundary line in return for a specified gift of "goods, to the value of three thousand dollars."

The Mohawks were invited to sign the treaty "within six months." They did not; however, the locus of white-Indian hostility moved westward by this time, out of Mohawk country and to the territories encompassed within the Old Northwest (see **Treaty of Fort Greenville**).

REFERENCES:
Axelrod, Alan. *Chronicle of the Indian Wars: From Colonial Times to Wounded Knee.* New York: Macmillan General Reference, 1993.
Kappler, Charles J., comp. and ed., *Indian Affairs: Laws and Treaties,* vol. 2. Washington, D.C.: Government Printing Office, 1904.

Treaty with the Creeks

SIGNED: August 7, 1790, at New York City
SIGNATORIES: United States vs. "the undersigned Kings, Chiefs, and Warriors of the Creek Nation of Indians, on the Part and Behalf of the said Nation"
IN FORCE: From signing
OVERVIEW: A post-Revolutionary War treaty establishing peace with the Creek Indians.

DISCUSSION:
The Creeks were a large tribe, closely allied with the Seminoles, and occupying vast tracts of the lower Southeast. Substantial factions of the Creek tribe sided with the British and Loyalists during the Revolutionary War, and, in many places, hostilities with the Creeks did not end with the conclusion of the Revolution.

After proclaiming peace in Article 1, the treaty specifies the following in Article 2: "The undersigned Kings, Chiefs and Warriors, for themselves and all parts of the Creek Nation within the limits of the United States, do acknowledge themselves, and the said parts of the Creek nation, to be under the protection of the United States of America, and of no other sovereign whosoever; and they also stipulate that the said Creek Nation will not hold any treaty with an individual State, or with individuals of any State."

During the Revolution—and later as well—runaway slaves would sometimes obtain asylum among the Creeks. Article 3 stipulated that the "Creek Nation shall deliver as soon as practicable to the commanding officer of the troops of the United States, stationed at the Rock-Landing on the Oconee river, all citizens of the United States, white inhabitants or negroes, who are now prisoners in any part of the said nation. And if any such prisoners or negroes should not be so delivered, on or before the first day of June ensuing, the governor of Georgia may empower three persons to repair to the said nation, in order to claim and receive such prisoners and negroes."

Articles 4 through 8 describe the territory of the Creeks and guarantee its security. Articles 9 and 10 deal with the administration of justice and enforcement of laws. In a provision that would become commonplace in U.S.-Indian treaties, Article 12 embodies a scheme of social engineering, whereby Indians were to be "civilized" by encouraging them to farm:

That the Creek nation may be led to a greater degree of civilization, and to become herdsmen and cultivators, instead of remaining in a state of hunters, the United States will from time to time furnish gratuitously the said nation with useful domestic animals and implements of husbandry. And further to assist the said nation in so desirable a pursuit, and at the same time to establish a certain mode of communication, the United States will send such, and so many persons to reside in said nation as they may judge proper, and not exceeding four in number, who shall qualify themselves to act as interpreters. These persons shall have lands assigned them by the Creeks for cultivation, for themselves and their successors in office; but they shall be precluded exercising any kind of traffic.

REFERENCES:

Axelrod, Alan. *Chronicle of the Indian Wars: From Colonial Times to Wounded Knee.* New York: Macmillan General Reference, 1993.

Coupler, Charles J., ed. *Indian Treaties, 1778-1883.* New York: Interland, 1972.

Fairbanks, Charles H. *Chickasaw, Cherokee, Creek.* New York: Garland, 1974.

Prucha, Francis Paul, ed. *Documents of United States Indian Policy,* 2d ed. Lincoln: University of Nebraska Press, 1990.

Tyler, Lyman S. *A History of Indian Policy.* Washington, D.C.: U.S. Government Printing Office, 1973.

Treaty of Peace with the Cherokee

SIGNED: July 2, 1791, "at the treaty ground on the bank of the Holston, near the mouth of the French Broad [River]"

SIGNATORIES: United States vs. "the undersigned Chiefs and Warriors, of the Cherokee Nation of Indians, on the part and Behalf of the said Nation"

IN FORCE: From signing

OVERVIEW: A peace treaty with the Cherokee, redefining the territorial boundaries laid down in **Treaty with the Cherokee** of 1785 and proposing a program of agricultural aid.

DISCUSSION:

The end of the American Revolution did not bring an end to frontier violence; indeed, despite the United States victory over British forces, the fighting on the western frontier had gone badly for the Patriots. From 1786 to 1784, war between white settlers and Indians was general in the western regions and is often referred to as Little Turtle's War, after a leading Miami chief. Hostilities with the Cherokee were renewed during this period and were brought to a temporary end by the present treaty.

Of particular significance is the redrawing of the boundaries of the Cherokee territory, which has contracted in extent since the 1785 treaty (Article IV):

The boundary between the citizens of the United States and the Cherokee nation, is and shall be as follows: Beginning at the top of the Currahee mountain, where the Creek line passes it; thence a direct line to Tugelo river; thence northeast to the Occunna mountain, and over the same along the South-Carolina Indian boundary to the North-Carolina boundary; thence north to a point from which a line is to be extended to the river Clinch, that shall pass the Holston at the ridge which divides the waters running into Little River from those running into the Tennessee; thence up the river Clinch to Campbell's line, and along the same to the top of Cumberland mountain; thence a direct line to the Cumberland river where the Kentucky road crosses it; thence down the Cumberland river to a point from which a south west line will strike the ridge which divides the waters of Cumberland from those of Duck river, forty miles above Nashville; thence down the said ridge to a point from whence a south west line will strike the mouth of Duck river.

And in order to preclude forever all disputes relative to the said boundary, the same shall be ascertained, and marked plainly by three persons appointed on the part of the United States, and three Cherokees on the part of their nation.

Moreover, provision is made to acquire from the Cherokee additional territory:

And in order to extinguish forever all claims of the Cherokee nation, or any part thereof, to any of the land lying to the right of the line above described. beginning as aforesaid at the Currahee mountain, it is hereby agreed, that in addition to the consideration heretofore made for the said land, the United States will cause certain valuable goods, to be immediately delivered to the undersigned Chiefs and Warriors, for the use of their nation; and the said United States will also cause the sum of one thousand dollars to be paid annually to the said Cherokee nation. And the undersigned Chiefs and Warriors, do hereby for themselves and the whole Cherokee nation, their heirs and descendants, for the considerations above-mentioned, release, quit-claim, relinquish and cede, all the land to the right of the line described, and beginning as aforesaid.

By Article VII, "The United States solemnly guarantee to the Cherokee nation, all their lands not hereby ceded." However, the federal government would never honor this guarantee and would, in fact, allow the state of Georgia and other jurisdiction to violate Cherokee territorial rights repeatedly. The ongoing conflict between Georgians (and others) and the Cherokee would motivate passage of the **Indian Removal Act** of 1830, which formally "removed" the Cherokee from their eastern lands.

In a theme that would be repeated in numerous subsequent Indian treaties, Article XIV proposed what today would be called a project of social engineering:

That the Cherokee nation may be led to a greater degree of civilization, and to become herdsmen and cultivators, instead of remaining in a state of hunters, the United States will from time to time furnish gratuitously the said nation with useful implements of husbandry, and further to assist the said nation in so desirable a pursuit, and at the same time to establish a certain mode of communication, the United States will send such, and so many persons to reside in said nation as they may judge proper, not exceeding four in number, who shall qualify themselves to act as interpreters. These persons shall have lands assigned by the Cherokees for cultivation for themselves and their successors in office; but they shall be precluded exercising any kind of traffic.

While some of this agricultural program was implemented, the Indian Removal Act of 1830 rendered the program moot, as the Cherokee were evicted from their farmlands in the East.

This treaty was modified by the **Treaty with the Cherokee** of 1794.

REFERENCES:
Axelrod, Alan. *Chronicle of the Indian Wars: From Colonial Times to Wounded Knee.* New York: Macmillan General Reference, 1993.
Coupler, Charles J., ed. *Indian Treaties, 1778-1883.* New York: Interland, 1972.
Fairbanks, Charles H. *Chickasaw, Cherokee, Creek.* New York: Garland, 1974.
Treaties between the United States of America and the Cherokee Nation, from 1785. Tahlequah, Cherokee Nation: National Printing Office, 1870.
Prucha, Francis Paul, ed. *Documents of United States Indian Policy,* 2d ed. Lincoln: University of Nebraska Press, 1990.
Tyler, Lyman S. *A History of Indian Policy.* Washington, D.C.: U.S. Government Printing Office, 1973.

Treaty with the Cherokee

SIGNED: June 26, 1794, at Philadelphia
SIGNATORIES: United States vs. "the undersigned Chiefs and Warriors, in their own names, and in behalf of the whole Cherokee nation"
IN FORCE: From signing
OVERVIEW: A treaty elaborating on the **Treaty of Peace with the Cherokee** of 1791.

DISCUSSION:
The 1791 **Treaty of Peace with the Cherokee** was "not . . . fully carried into execution by reason of some misunderstandings which have arisen." The "misunderstandings" related chiefly to the exact boundaries of the Cherokee territory, the extent of territory to be ceded by the Cherokee, and the compensation to be rendered for those cessions. The 1794 treaty seeks to resolve these issues, as follows:

ARTICLE II.
It is hereby stipulated that the boundaries mentioned in the fourth article of the said treaty, shall be actually ascertained and marked in the manner prescribed by the said article, whenever the Cherokee nation shall have ninety days notice of the time and place at which the commissioners of the United States intend to commence their operation.

ARTICLE III.
The United States, to evince their justice by amply compensating the said Cherokee nation of Indians for all relinquishments of land made either by the treaty of Hopewell upon the Keowee river, concluded on the twenty-eighth of November one thousand seven hundred and eighty-five, or the aforesaid treaty made upon Holston river, on the second of July, one thousand seven hundred and ninety-one, do hereby stipulate, in lieu of all former slims to be paid annually to furnish the Cherokee Indians with goods suitable for their use, to the amount of five thousand dollars yearly.

Additionally, Article IV lays down steps to be taken to curb horse theft:

ARTICLE IV.
And the said Cherokee nation, in order to evince the sincerity of their intentions in future, to prevent the practice of stealing horses, attended with the most pernicious consequences to the lives and peace of both parties, do hereby agree, that for every horse which shall be stolen from the white inhabitants by any Cherokee Indians, and not returned within three months, that the sum of fifty dollars shall be deducted from the said annuity of five thousand dollars.

REFERENCES:
Axelrod, Alan. *Chronicle of the Indian Wars: From Colonial Times to Wounded Knee.* New York: Macmillan General Reference, 1993.
Coupler, Charles J., ed. *Indian Treaties, 1778-1883.* New York: Interland, 1972.
Prucha, Francis Paul, ed. *Documents of United States Indian Policy,* 2d ed. Lincoln: University of Nebraska Press, 1990.
Tyler, Lyman S. *A History of Indian Policy.* Washington, D.C.: U.S. Government Printing Office, 1973.

Treaty with the Oneida, Tuscarora, and Stockbridge Indians

OFFICIAL TITLE: Treaty between the United States and the Oneida, Tuscarora and Stockbridge Indians, Dwelling in the Country of the Oneidas
SIGNED: December 2, 1794, at Philadelphia
SIGNATORIES: United States vs. Oneida, Tuscarora, and the Stockbridge Indians
IN FORCE: From signing
OVERVIEW: A treaty to reward and compensate "a body of the Oneida and Tuscarora and the Stockbridge Indians" for services rendered during the American Revolution.

DISCUSSION:
Whereas all other post-Revolutionary War U.S.-Indian treaties address the conclusion of hostilities with tribes allied with the British and Loyalists, this treaty was concluded with tribes and tribal factions allied with the Americans. The principal text follows:

ARTICLE I.
The United States will pay the sum of five thousand dollars, to be distributed among individuals of the Oneida and Tuscorora nations,

as a compensation for their individual losses and services during the late war between Great-Britain and the United States. The only man of the Kaughnawaugas now remaining in the Oneida country, as well as some few very meritorious persons of the Stockbridge Indians, will be considered in the distribution.

ARTICLE II.

For the general accommodation of these Indian nations, residing in the country of the Oneidas, the United States will cause to be erected a complete grist-mill and saw-mill, in a situation to serve the present principal settlements of these nations. Or if such one convenient situation cannot be found, then the United States will cause to be erected two such grist-mills and saw-mills, in places where it is now known the proposed accommodation may be effected. Of this the United States will judge.

ARTICLE III.

The United States will provide, during three years after the mills shall be completed, for the expense of employing one or two suitable persons to manage the mills, to keep them in repair, to instruct some young men of the three nations in the arts of the miller and sawyer, and to provide teams and utensils for carrying on the work of the mills.

ARTICLE IV.

The United States will pay one thousand dollars, to be applied in building a convenient church at Oneida, in the place of the one which was there burnt by the enemy, in the late war.

ARTICLE V.

In consideration of the above stipulations to be performed on the part of the United States, the Oneida, Tuscorora and Stockbridge Indians afore-mentioned, now acknowledge themselves satisfied, and relinquish all other claims of compensation and rewards for their losses and services in the late war. Excepting only the unsatisfied claims of such men of the said nations as bore commissions under the United States, for any arrears which may be due to them as officers.

REFERENCES:

Axelrod, Alan. *Chronicle of the Indian Wars: From Colonial Times to Wounded Knee.* New York: Macmillan General Reference, 1993.

Coupler, Charles J., ed. *Indian Treaties, 1778-1883.* New York: Interland, 1972.

Prucha, Francis Paul, ed. *Documents of United States Indian Policy,* 2d ed. Lincoln: University of Nebraska Press, 1990.

Tyler, Lyman S. *A History of Indian Policy.* Washington, D.C.: U.S. Government Printing Office, 1973.

Treaty of Fort Greenville

SIGNED: August 3, 1795, at Fort Greenville, Northwest Territory

IN FORCE: From execution

SIGNATORIES: United States vs. Wyandot, Delaware, Shawnee, Ottawa, Chippewa, Potawatomi, Miami, Kickapoo, Piankeshaw, and Kaskaskia Indian tribes, as well as two nontribal Indian groups known as the Eel River Indians and the Weeas Indians

OVERVIEW: The treaty ending Little Turtle's War.

DISCUSSION:

From 1786 to 1795, the Shawnee war chief Blue Jacket and the Miami war chief Little Turtle waged a long, determined, and destructive war against settlers of the Old Northwest (the Ohio River valley and the upper Midwest). After suffering two major military defeats in what came to be called Little Turtle's War, United States forces, now trained and led by the former Revolutionary general "Mad Anthony" Wayne, scored a decisive victory at the Battle of Fallen Timbers (August 20, 1794). Ninety representatives of the hostile tribes, most notably the war leaders Blue Jacket of the Shawnees and Little Turtle of the Miamis, signed the Treaty of Fort Greenville, which secured United States occupation of lands northwest of the Ohio River, established a "permanent" boundary to U.S. settlement west of the present state of Ohio, and instituted a program of compensation for Indian territory lost. The treaty brought stability to Ohio frontier for some 15 years, and, with the Indian threat subdued, British interests fully acknowledged U.S. sovereignty in the region as well.

Following the Revolution, the United States considered those Indians who had allied themselves with the British a conquered people. Nevertheless, the government attempted to purchase rather than simply appropriate lands from the "conquered" tribes. The Shawnee and a number of other "western" tribes shunned such negotiation. Although the British may have lost the Revolutionary War, the Shawnee and its allied tribes felt that they had repeatedly defeated the Americans west of the Ohio and were not, therefore, about to behave as a conquered people. Nevertheless, in January 1786, U.S. negotiators met with about 300 Shawnees and informed their leader, Tame Hawk, that the Ohio country was now United States territory. Threatened with war, Tame Hawk agreed to cede the entire Miami Valley. Many Shawnee and Miami bands immediately repudiated this agreement, and, led by the Shawnee Blue Jacket and the Miami Little Turtle, these bands staged violent raids throughout the Miami Valley. Little Turtle's War would rage for almost eight years, the Indians decisively defeating two major military expeditions sent against them. At last, on August 20, 1794, the dashing Revolutionary hero General "Mad Anthony" Wayne led his carefully trained troops into battle at Fallen Timbers (in present-day Ohio), achieving a victory that persuaded the leaders of the combatant tribes to sign the Treaty of Fort Greenville.

The central provisions of the treaty are the establishment of peace and "friendly intercourse" between the United States and the Indian tribes, and the demarcation of boundaries between white and Indian settlements.

As the Treaty of Easton (1758) had established the Allegheny Mountains as the limit of white settlement and the **Proclamation of 1763** set the Appalachians as the limit to westward expansion, so the Treaty of Greenville pushed the *absolute* limit of settlement farther west—west of the present state of Ohio. Moreover, the treaty set forth a schedule of compensation for Indian lands ceded: a lump sum of $20,000 in trade goods and an annual payment of $9,500, also in goods.

Unfortunately, as with the earlier Treaty of Easton and the Proclamation of 1763, the "absolute" limit of white settlement proved impossible to enforce permanently—although the treaty did bring some 15 years of relative peace to this violent territory. Finally, by neutralizing Indian resistance in the Ohio country, the Treaty of Greenville compelled British interests in the area—mostly traders—to bow to U.S. authority. Thus the Treaty of Greenville achieved *in fact* the territorial sovereignty over the frontier granted *in principle* by the **Treaty of Paris.**

REFERENCES:

Axelrod, Alan. *Chronicle of the Indian Wars: From Colonial Times to Wounded Knee.* New York: Macmillan General Reference, 1993.

Coupler, Charles J., ed. *Indian Treaties, 1778-1883.* New York: Interland, 1972.

Prucha, Francis Paul, ed. *Documents of United States Indian Policy,* 2d ed. Lincoln: University of Nebraska Press, 1990.

Tyler, Lyman S. *A History of Indian Policy.* Washington, D.C.: U.S. Government Printing Office, 1973.

Chickasaw Treaty

SIGNED: July 23, 1805, at Washington, D.C.

SIGNATORIES: United States vs. "the Mingo chiefs and warriors of the Chickasaw nation of Indians"

IN FORCE: From signing

OVERVIEW: A treaty of territorial cession from the Chickasaws to the United States.

DISCUSSION:

Most treaties by which Indians ceded land to the United States followed directly from wars. This treaty, however, is a land cession in return for debt relief. The brief principal text follows:

ARTICLE 1.

WHEREAS the Chickasaw nation of Indians have been for some time embarrassed by heavy debts due to their merchants and traders, and being destitute of funds to effect important improvements in their country, they have agreed and do hereby agree to cede to the United States, and forever quit claim to the tract of country included within the following bounds, to wit: beginning on the left bank of Ohio, at the point where the present Indian boundary adjoins the same, thence down the left bank of Ohio to the Tennessee river, thence up the main channel of the Tennessee river to the mouth of Duck river; thence up the left bank of Duck river to the Columbian highway or road leading from Nashville to Natchez, thence along the said road to the ridge dividing the waters running into Duck river from those running into Buffaloe river, thence easterly along the said ridge to the great ridge dividing the waters running into the main Tennessee river from those running into Buffaloe river near the main source of Buffaloe river, thence in a direct line to the Great Tennessee river near the Chickasaw old fields or eastern point of the Chickasaw claim on that river; thence northwardly to the great ridge dividing the waters running into the Tennessee from those running into Cumberland river, so as to include all the waters running into Elk river, thence along the top of the said great ridge to the place of beginning:

reserving a tract of one mile square adjoining to, and below the mouth of Duck river on the Tennessee, for the use of the chief O'Koy or Tishumastubbee.

REFERENCES:

Axelrod, Alan. *Chronicle of the Indian Wars: From Colonial Times to Wounded Knee.* New York: Macmillan General Reference, 1993.

Coupler, Charles J., ed. *Indian Treaties, 1778-1883.* New York: Interland, 1972.

Fairbanks, Charles H. *Chickasaw, Cherokee, Creek.* New York: Garland, 1974.

Prucha, Francis Paul, ed. *Documents of United States Indian Policy,* 2d ed. Lincoln: University of Nebraska Press, 1990.

Tyler, Lyman S. *A History of Indian Policy.* Washington, D.C.: U.S. Government Printing Office, 1973.

Treaty of Fort Jackson

SIGNED: August 9, 1814, Fort Jackson, Florida

IN FORCE: From signing

SIGNATORIES: United States vs. the Creek Nation

OVERVIEW: The Creek War (1813-1814), which may be considered a phase of the War of 1812, was fought between the "Red Stick" faction of the Creek Nation and the United States. Following Andrew Jackson's decisive victory at the Battle of Horseshoe Bend (March 27, 1814), the Treaty of Fort Jackson ended the war and extorted 23 million acres of land belonging not only to the Red Sticks, but also to the White Sticks, a Creek faction that had been allied with the United States.

DISCUSSION:

During the War of 1812, the Creek Indians of Georgia, Tennessee, and the Mississippi Territory, fought an intratribal war between those advocating cooperation with the whites, and those who were determined to drive white settlers out of their territory. The latter faction, known as the Upper Creeks, or Red Sticks, fought against the Americans in the war, while the tribe's peace faction, the Lower Creeks, or White Sticks, joined U.S. Army and local militia forces in fighting the Red Sticks. After Red Sticks under William Weatherford (Red Eagle) attacked Fort Mims on the lower Alabama River, killing about 400 settlers (August 30, 1813), the Tennessee legislature sent Andrew Jackson, at the head of a large militia force, into Red Stick country. On March 27, 1814, with his militiamen augmented by 600 regulars from the U.S. 39th Infantry, Jackson attacked Horseshoe Bend, a peninsula on the Tallapoosa River, killing about 750 of a Red Stick force of 900.

Immediately after this victory, Jackson personally concluded the preliminary Treaty of Horseshoe Bend, the provisions of which were substantially carried forward in the more formal Treaty of Fort Jackson.

A one-side document, blaming the Creeks for an "unprovoked, inhuman, and sanguinary war" and "numberless aggressions," the treaty stipulates the Creek cession of about 23 million acres, making no distinction whatsoever between the land of the Red Sticks, against whom the Creek War had been fought, and that of the White Sticks, who had sided with the forces of the United States. The territorial cession is demanded of the entire Creek Nation. In return, two concessions are made to the Creeks:

- a guarantee of the "integrity of [Creek] territory eastwardly and northwardly of [a] line ... described ... in the first article"
- a pledge to provide the Creeks ("reduced to extreme want, and not at present having the means of subsistence") "gratuitously the necessaries of life."

The first guarantee was almost immediately violated by the state of Georgia and, subsequently, by the **Indian Removal Act** (1830). The promised provisions were delivered irregularly through the federal government's inept, indifferent, inadequate, and corrupt Indian agency system.

REFERENCES:
Axelrod, Alan. *Chronicle of the Indian Wars: From Colonial Times to Wounded Knee.* New York: Macmillan General Reference, 1993.
Braund, Kathryn E. Holland. *Deerskins and Duffels: The Creek Indian Trade with Anglo-America, 1685-1815.* Lincoln: University of Nebraska Press, 1996.
Coupler, Charles J., ed. *Indian Treaties, 1778-1883.* New York: Interland, 1972.
Debo, Angie. *Road to Disappearance: A History of the Creek Indians.* Norman: University of Oklahoma Press, 1985.
Griffith, Benjamin W., Jr. *McIntosh and Weatherford, Creek Indian Leaders.* Tuscaloosa: University of Alabama Press, 1998.
Prucha, Francis Paul, ed. *Documents of United States Indian Policy,* 2d ed. Lincoln: University of Nebraska Press, 1990.
Swanton, John Reed. *Early History of the Creek Indians and Their Neighbors.* 1922; reprint ed., Tallahassee: University Press of Florida, 1998.
Tyler, Lyman S. *A History of Indian Policy.* Washington, D.C.: U.S. Government Printing Office, 1973.
Wright, J. Leitch. *Creeks and Seminoles: Destruction and Regeneration of the Muscogulge People.* Lincoln: University of Nebraska Press, 1990.

Treaty with the Chickasaw

SIGNED: September 20, 1816, "at the Chickasaw council house"
SIGNATORIES: United States vs. "the whole Chickasaw nation, in council assembled"
IN FORCE: From signing
OVERVIEW: A treaty restoring peace with Chickasaws following the War of 1812 and the Creek War and laying down the cession of certain Chickasaw lands to the United States.

DISCUSSION:
Like many Indian tribes, the Chickasaws sided with the British in the War of 1812, and hostilities continued even after that war had ended in 1814. This treaty not only restores peace, but lays

down a large cession of territory, as well as the compensation for that cession, as follows:

ARTICLE 1.
Peace and friendship are hereby firmly established, and perpetuated, between the United States of America and Chickasaw nation.

ARTICLE 2.
The Chickasaw nation cede to the United States (with the exception of such reservations as shall hereafter be specified) all right or title to lands on the north side of the Tennessee river, and relinquish all claim to territory on the south side of said river, and east of a line commencing at the mouth of Caney creek, running up said creek to its source, thence a due south course to the ridge path, or commonly called Gaines's road, along said road south westwardly to a point on the Tombigby river, well known by the name of the Cotton Gin port, and down the west bank of the Tombigby to the Chocktaw boundary.

ARTICLE 3.
In consideration of the relinquishment of claim, and cession of lands, made in the preceding article, the commissioners agree to allow the Chickasaw nation twelve thousand dollars per annum for ten successive years, and four thousand five hundred dollars to be paid in sixty days after the ratification of this treaty into the hands of Levi Colbert, as a compensation for any improvements which individuals of the Chickasaw nation may have had on the lands surrendered; that is to say, two thousand dollars for improvements on the east side of the Tombigby, and two thousand five hundred dollars for improvements on the north side of the Tennessee river.

REFERENCES:
Axelrod, Alan. *Chronicle of the Indian Wars: From Colonial Times to Wounded Knee.* New York: Macmillan General Reference, 1993.
Coupler, Charles J., ed. *Indian Treaties, 1778-1883.* New York: Interland, 1972.
Fairbanks, Charles H. *Chickasaw, Cherokee, Creek.* New York: Garland, 1974.
Prucha, Francis Paul, ed. *Documents of United States Indian Policy,* 2d ed. Lincoln: University of Nebraska Press, 1990.
Tyler, Lyman S. *A History of Indian Policy.* Washington, D.C.: U.S. Government Printing Office, 1973.

Treaty with the Chickasaw

SIGNED: October 19, 1818, "at the treaty ground east of Old Town"
SIGNATORIES: United States vs. "the whole Chickasaw nation, by their chiefs, head men, and warriors, in full council assembled"
In force: From signing
OVERVIEW: A treaty additional to the Treaty with the Chickasaw of 1816, laying down additional land cessions.

DISCUSSION:
The young American republic's hunger for Indian lands proved insatiable. Two years after a "definitive" treaty was concluded with the Chickasaw, in which land was traded for peace (and other compensation), the 1818 treaty exacted even vaster cessions and consigned the Chickasaw to a "reservation." In a

manner more direct than the treaty of 1816, the 1818 document lays down the nature of the exchange: peace is purchased with land. The full principal text of the brief treaty follows:

ARTICLE 1.

Peace and friendship are hereby firmly established and made perpetual, between the United States of America and the Chickesaw nation of Indians.

ARTICLE 2.

To obtain the object of the foregoing article, the Chickesaw nation of Indians cede to the United States of America, (with the exception of such reservation as shall be hereafter mentioned) all claim or title which the said nation has to the land lying north of the south boundary of the state of Tennessee, which is bounded south by the thirty-fifth degree of north latitude, and which lands, hereby ceded, lies within the following boundary, viz: Beginning on the Tennessee river, about thirty-five miles, by water, below colonel George Colbert's ferry, where the thirty-fifth degree of north latitude strikes the same; thence, due west, with said degree of north latitude, to where it cuts the Mississippi river at or near the Chickasaw Bluffs; thence, up the said Mississippi river, to the mouth of the Ohio; thence, up the Ohio river, to the mouth of Tennessee river; thence, up the Tennessee river, to the place of beginning.

ARTICLE 3.

In consideration of the relinquishment of claim and cession of lands in the preceding article, and to perpetuate the happiness of the Chickasaw nation of Indians, the commissioners of the United States, before named, agree to allow the said nation the sum of twenty thousand dollars per annum, for fifteen successive years, to be paid annually; and, as a farther consideration for the objects aforesaid, and at the request of the chiefs of the said nation, the commissioners agree to pay captain John Gordon, of Tennessee, the sum of one thousand one hundred and fifteen dollars, it being a debt due by general William Colbert, of said nation, to the aforesaid Gordon; and the further sum of two thousand dollars, due by said nation of Indians, to captain David Smith, now of Kentucky, for that sum by him expended, in supplying himself and forty-five soldiers from Tennessee, in the year one thousand seven hundred and ninety-five, when assisting them (at their request and invitation) in defending their towns against the invasion of the Creek Indians; both which sums, (on the application of the said nation) is to be paid, within sixty days after the ratification of this treaty, to the aforesaid Gordon and Smith.

REFERENCES:

Axelrod, Alan. *Chronicle of the Indian Wars: From Colonial Times to Wounded Knee.* New York: Macmillan General Reference, 1993.

Coupler, Charles J., ed. *Indian Treaties, 1778-1883.* New York: Interland, 1972.

Prucha, Francis Paul, ed. *Documents of United States Indian Policy,* 2d ed. Lincoln: University of Nebraska Press, 1990.

Tyler, Lyman S. *A History of Indian Policy.* Washington, D.C.: U.S. Government Printing Office, 1973.

Treaty with the Potawatomi

SIGNED: September 20, 1828, at "the Missionary Establishments upon the St. Joseph, of Lake Michigan, in the Territory of Michigan"

SIGNATORIES: United States vs. Potawatomi Tribe

IN FORCE: From signing

OVERVIEW: An early Indian-U.S. treaty of cession.

DISCUSSION:

Many early treaties by which Indian tribes ceded land to the United States were little more than simple instruments of exchange. Article 1 of this treaty specifies the cession:

The Potowatomi tribe of Indians cede to the United States the tract of land included within the following boundaries:

1st. Beginning at the mouth of the St. Joseph, of Lake Michigan and thence running up the said river to a point on the same river, half way between La-vache-qui-pisse and Macousin village: thence in a direct line, to the 19th mile tree, on the northern boundary line oft the State Indiana; thence, with the same, west, to Lake Michigan; and thence, with the shore of the said Lake, to the place of beginning.

2. Beginning at a point on the line run in 1817, due east from the southern extreme of Lake Michigan, which point is due south from the head of the most easterly branch of the Kankekee river, and from that point running south ten miles; thence, in a direct line, to the northeast corner of Flatbelly's reservation; thence, to the northwest corner of the reservation at Seek's village; thence, with the lines of the said reservation, and of former cessions, to the line between the States of Indiana and Ohio; thence, with the same to the former described line, running due east from the southern extreme of Lake Michigan; and thence, with the said line, to the place of beginning.

The remaining articles detail the payments to be made to the tribe as a whole and to individual members of the tribe.

REFERENCES:

Axelrod, Alan. *Chronicle of the Indian Wars: From Colonial Times to Wounded Knee.* New York: Macmillan General Reference, 1993.

Coupler, Charles J., ed. *Indian Treaties, 1778-1883.* New York: Interland, 1972.

Prucha, Francis Paul, ed. *Documents of United States Indian Policy,* 2d ed. Lincoln: University of Nebraska Press, 1990.

Tyler, Lyman S. *A History of Indian Policy.* Washington, D.C.: U.S. Government Printing Office, 1973.

Indian Removal Act

SIGNED: May 28, 1830, at Washington

SIGNATORIES: President Andrew Jackson (approving an act of Congress)

IN FORCE: From signing

OVERVIEW: An act of Congress authorizing the president to grant Indian tribes certain western lands in exchange for their territories within state borders (mainly in the Southeast), from which the tribes would be "removed."

DISCUSSION:

The nation's very first president, George Washington, had imagined what he called a "Chinese Wall" that might separate Indians and whites. President Thomas Jefferson was motivated to conclude the Louisiana Purchase in large part because he saw the new western territory as a place to put the Indians. President James Madison also had a desire to exchange newly acquired western lands for the Indians' eastern holdings. It was president James Monroe's secretary of war, John C. Calhoun, who first proposed an act of Congress to mandate removal, and Monroe's successor, President John Quincy Adams, further laid the groundwork for the removal legislation that was finally enacted during the administration of Andrew Jackson.

The legislation was officially titled "An Act to Provide for an Exchange of Lands with the Indians Residing in Any of the States or Territories, and for Their Removal West of the River Mississippi," and its key provisions follow:

Be it enacted . . . , That it shall and may be lawful for the President of the United States to cause so much of any territory belonging to the United States, west of the river Mississippi, not included in any state of organized territory, and to which the Indian title has been extinguished, as he may judge necessary, to be divided into a suitable number of districts, for the reception of such tribes or nations of Indians as may choose to exchange the lands where they now reside, and remove there . . .

SEC. 4. *And be it further enacted,* That if, upon any of the lands now occupied by the Indians, and to be exchanged for, there should be such improvements as add value to the land claimed by any individual or individuals of such tribes or nations, it shall and may be lawful for the President to cause such value to be ascertained by appraisement or otherwise, and to cause such ascertained value to be paid to the person or persons rightfully claiming such improvements. And upon the payment of such valuation, the improvements so valued and paid for, shall pass to the United States, and possession shall not afterwards be permitted to any of the same tribe.

SEC. 5. *And be it further enacted,* That upon the making of any such exchange as is contemplated by this act, it shall and may be lawful for the President to cause such aid and assistance to be furnished to the emigrants as may be necessary and proper to enable them to remove to, and settle in, the country for which they may have exchanged; and also, to give them such aid and assistance as may be necessary for their support and subsistence for the first year after their removal . . .

As embodied in the law, the process of Indian "removal" was to be a voluntary exchange of eastern lands for western lands. In actual practice, however, Indians were typically coerced or duped into making the exchange by government officials who would secure the agreement of compliant Indian leaders whom the government unilaterally deemed as representative of the tribe. With these individuals, the exchange was made and then declared binding all members of tribe, regardless of whether or not a majority of the tribe concurred. Once an agreement was concluded, the government claimed the right to move all of the Indians off the land, by force, if necessary.

Some northern tribes were peacefully resettled in western lands (dubbed "Indian Territory" and centered on present-day Oklahoma) considered undesirable for white settlement. In the Southeast, however, members of the so-called Five Civilized Tribes—Chickasaw, Choctaw, Seminole, Cherokee, and Creek— resisted removal. Under military coercion, approximately 100,000 of these people were compelled to march off to Indian Territory during the 1830s. Some 25 percent died en route. The most infamous removal was that of the Cherokee during 1838- 1839, which was referred to as the "Trail of Tears" and was characterized by great cruelty and high mortality. Most fiercely resistant to removal were the Seminoles (and closely allied members of the Creek tribe) who lived in or near Florida. The Second Seminole War (1835-42) was fought over the issue, and many Seminoles were never removed from Florida.

REFERENCES:

Axelrod, Alan, *Chronicle of the Indian Wars: From Colonial Times to Wounded Knee.* New York: Macmillan General Reference, 1993.
Prucha, Francis Paul, *Documents of United States Indian Policy,* 2d ed. Lincoln: University of Nebraska Press, 1990.

Treaty with the Chickasaw

SIGNED: August 31, 1830, at Franklin, Tennessee
SIGNATORIES: United States vs. "the chiefs and head men of the Chickasaw Nation of Indians, duly authorized, by the whole nation, to conclude a treaty"
IN FORCE: Not ratified and did not enter into force
OVERVIEW: A treaty of cession pursuant to the **Indian Removal Act** of 1830.

DISCUSSION:

The treaty lays down the following cession:

ARTICLE 1.

The Chickasaw Nation hereby cede to the United States all the lands owned and possessed by them, on the East side of the Mississippi River, where they at present reside, and which lie north of the following boundary, viz: beginning at the mouth of the Oacktibbyhaw (or Tibbee) creek; thence, up the same, to a point, being a marked tree, on the old Natchez road, about one mile Southwardly from Wall's old place; thence, with the Choctaw boundary, and along it, Westwardly, through the Tunicha old fields, to a point on the Mississippe river, about twenty-eight miles, by water, below where the St. Francis river enters said stream, on the West side. All the lands North, and North-East of said boundary, to latitude thirty-five North the South boundary of the State of Tennessee, being owned by the Chickasaws, are hereby ceded to the United States.

ARTICLE 2.

In consideration of said cession, the United States agree to furnish to the Chickasaw Nation of Indians, a country, West of the territory of Arkansaw, to lie South of latitude thirty-six degrees and a half, and of equal extent with the one ceded; and in all respects as to timber, water and soil, it shall be suited to the wants and condition of said Chickasaw people. It is agreed further, that the United States will send one or more commissioners to examine and select a country of the description stated, who shall be accompanied by an interpreter and not more than twelve persons of the Chickasaws, to be chosen by the nation, to examine said country; and who, for their expenses and services, shall be allowed two dollars a day each, while so engaged. If, after proper examination, a country suitable to their wants and condition can not be found; then, it is stipulated and agreed, that this treaty, and all its provisions, shall be considered null and void. But, if a country shall be found and approved, the President of the United States shall cause a grant in fee simple to be made out, to be signed by him as other grants are usually signed, conveying the country to the Chickasaw people, and to their children, so long as they shall continue to exist as a nation, and shall reside upon the same.

In addition, the following conditions are laid down:

ARTICLE 3.

The Chickasaws being a weak tribe, it is stipulated that the United States will, at all times, extend to them their protection and care against enemies of every description, but it is, at the same time, agreed, that they shall act peacably, and never make war, nor resort to arms, except with the consent and approval of the President, unless in cases where they may be invaded by some hostile power or tribe.

ARTICLE 4.

As further consideration, the United States agree, that each warrior and widow having a family, and each white man, having an Indian family, shall be entitled to a half section of land, and if they have no family, to half that quantity. The delegation present, having full knowledge of the population of their country, stipulate, that the first class of cases (those with families), shall not exceed five hundred, and that the other class shall not exceed one hundred persons. The reservations secured under this article, shall be granted in fee simple, to those who choose to remain, and become subject to the laws of the whites; and who, having recorded such intention with the agent, before the time of the first removal, shall continue to reside upon, and cultivate the same, for five years; at the expiration of which time, a grant shall be issued. But should they prefer to remove, and actually remove, then the United States, in lieu of such reservations, will pay for the same, at the rate of one dollar and a half per acre; the same to be paid in ten equal, annual instalments, to commence after the period of the ratification of this treaty, if, at that time, they shall have removed.

ARTICLE 5.

It is agreed, that the United States, as further consideration, will pay to said Nation of Indians, fifteen thousand dollars annually, for twenty years; the first payment to be made after their removal shall take place, and they be settled at their new homes, West of the Mississippi.

Articles 6 through 10 specify certain reservations to be granted to certain prominent Chickasaws. Article 11 specifies provisions to be made for assistance during the removal, and articles 12 through 14 specify provisions to be made to assist resettlement.

Article 15 makes the following special provision:

A desire having been expressed by Levi Colbert, that two of his younger sons, Abijah Jackson Colbert, and Andrew Morgan Colbert, aged seven and five years, might be educated under the direction and care of the President of the United States; and George Colbert having also expressed a wish that his grand-son, Andrew Frazier, aged about twelve years, might have a similar attention: It is consented, that at a proper age, as far as they may be found to have capacity, they shall receive a liberal education, at the expense of the United States, under the direction and control of the President.

The treaty is typical of those entered into pursuant to the **Indian Removal Act** of 1830. From the point of view of the United States, the terms extended were generous. Nevertheless, many Indians objected to and resisted removal. Those Chickasaw leaders denouncing this treaty addressed President Andrew Jackson in a letter, which reads, in part:

Father
You call us your children whom you profess to have the highest regard for, we know you are sincere in your profession and it creates in our bosoms the warmest feelings of affection towards you as the great Father protector of your white red children, but we humbly beg leave to represent to you that we now conceive that we have now arrived to the age of maturity and that we may continue to act in this important occasion as will be best calculated to obtain as desirable an object, Peace, Quietness, and a perpetual home—and at the same time, we feel a disposition to accommodate the views of our Father in exchange of country as you have proposed if you will let us examine your country and we can find one that you have not already disposed of that will be equal to the one we now occupy, we will then talk in fairness about exchange, candid towards you, and Justice to our selves compels us to say to you that we cannot consent to exchange the country where we now live for one that we never have seen.

The final sentence was the strongest Indian objection to removal: they were compelled to leave familiar, settled country for "one that we never have seen."

Even though the Senate failed to ratify this treaty, the forcible removal of the Chickasaw to "Indian Territory" west of the Mississippi was carried out. Some of the provisions of the unratified treaty were indeed complied with, at least partially. Some compensation was forthcoming, and some portion of promised provisions and annuities were delivered. However, the failure of the Senate to ratify the treaty illustrates the ambiguous position Indians occupied with regard to the United States government. On the one hand, the conclusion of treaties implied that the Indian tribes were to be accorded the status and rights of sovereign nations, yet, on the other, they were made subject to domestic laws that rendered treaties moot.

REFERENCES:

Axelrod, Alan. *Chronicle of the Indian Wars: From Colonial Times to Wounded Knee.* New York: Macmillan General Reference, 1993.

Coupler, Charles J., ed. *Indian Treaties, 1778-1883.* New York: Interland, 1972.

Prucha, Francis Paul, ed. *Documents of United States Indian Policy,* 2d ed. Lincoln: University of Nebraska Press, 1990.

Tyler, Lyman S. *A History of Indian Policy.* Washington, D.C.: U.S. Government Printing Office, 1973.

Treaty of Fort Armstrong

SIGNED: September 21, 1832, at Rock Island, Illinois

IN FORCE: From signing

SIGNATORIES: United States vs. Sac and Fox Indians

OVERVIEW: This treaty ended the Black Hawk War of 1832, the last major Indian-white conflict east of the Mississippi River.

DISCUSSION:

In 1804, representatives of the closely linked Sac and Fox tribes ceded to the United States all tribal lands in Illinois. The cession required that the Indians resettle in Iowa on the west bank of the Mississippi River; however, they were permitted to remain in Illinois until the ceded lands had been sold. Thus the tribal move across the river consumed many years, and before all of the tribe had left Illinois, a charismatic Sac chief, Black Hawk (1767-1838) declared his repudiation of the 1804 cession. He refused to remove to the west bank of the Mississippi, and he further resisted white settlement in Illinois by fighting on the British side during the War of 1812. Black Hawk believed that a British victory would block further settlement of the region.

Black Hawk and his followers were not finally ordered into Iowa until 1828. The chief responded to the order by attempting to create an alliance between the Sac and Fox and the Winnebago, Potawatomi, and Kickapoo. When he failed in this attempt, he led his followers—universally known as the "British Band"—into Iowa, but defiantly returned to Illinois for spring planting during 1829, 1830, and 1831. The seasonal return of the British Band created terror among white settlers, and in 1832 a military force was organized to push Black Hawk and his people out of Illinois. The resulting Black Hawk War lasted only 15 weeks, during which the chief and his British Band were pursued into Wisconsin and then westward toward the Mississippi. Again, Black Hawk sought to strike an alliance with other tribes, but to no avail.

On August 3, 1832, the surviving members of the British Band were making their way west across the Mississippi when they were attacked with heavy loss of life. Black Hawk himself escaped, but, refused aid by other tribes, he surrendered. Imprisoned for a short time, he was allowed to settle in a Sac village on the Des Moines River.

The Treaty of Fort Armstrong refers to "certain lawless and desperate leaders," who violated previous treaties and started an "unprovoked" war. Black Hawk is mentioned by name only once, in Article VII of the treaty, which mentions the release of most Sac and Fox prisoners, except for Black Hawk and other leaders of the war, who "shall be held as hostages for the future good conduct of the late hostile bands, during the pleasure of the President of the United States." Nor is Black Hawk a signatory to the treaty. It was common practice, in concluding Indian treaties, for United States officials to treat exclusively with friendly leaders, conveniently deeming them representatives of the tribe. It is for just such a reason that Black Hawk repudiated the 1804 land cession, arguing that it had not been made by persons truly representative of the Sac and Fox. General Winfield Scott and John Reynolds, on behalf of the United States, concluded the treaty with Keokuk, a Sac chief eager to cooperate with the government, and thirty-two other Sac and Fox Indians.

The preamble to the treaty not only justifies the cause of the war, but sets forth the principal terms of peace:

> WHEREAS, under certain lawless and desperate leaders, a formidable band, constituting a large portion of the Sac and Fox nation, left their country in April last, and, in violation of treaties, commenced an unprovoked war upon unsuspecting and defenseless citizens of the United States, sparing neither age nor sex; and whereas, the United States, at a great expense of treasure, have subdued the said hostile band, killing or capturing all its principal Chiefs and Warriors-the said States, partly as indemnity for the expense incurred, and partly to secure the future safety and tranquillity of the invaded frontier, demand of the said tribes, to the use of the United States, a cession of a tract of the Sac and Fox country, bordering on said frontier, more than proportional to the numbers of the hostile band who have been so conquered and subdued.

By this treaty, the Sac and Fox cede a vast portion of the Mississippi Valley and pledge to live within a reservation set aside for them. In return, the United States agrees to pay a modest annuity and to settle tribal debts to certain Indian traders. The treaty also promises that a "suitable present" will be given to the signatory tribes "on their pointing out to any United States agent . . . the position or positions of one or more mines, supposed by the said tribes to be of a metal more valuable than lead or iron." No such mines were ever revealed.

REFERENCES:

Axelrod, Alan. *Chronicle of the Indian Wars: From Colonial Times to Wounded Knee.* New York: Macmillan General Reference, 1993.

Israel, Fred L. *Major Peace Treaties of Modern History, 1648-1967,* vol. 1. New York: Chelsea House and McGraw-Hill, 1967.

Prucha, Francis Paul, ed., *Documents of United States Indian Policy,* 2d ed. Lincoln: University of Nebraska Press, 1990.

Treaty with the Potawatomi

SIGNED: October 26, 1832, "at Tippecanoe River, in the State of Indiana"

SIGNATORIES: United States vs. "Chiefs, Headmen and Warriors, of the Pottawatimie Indians"

IN FORCE: From signing

OVERVIEW: The second major cession treaty concluded by the Potawatomis.

DISCUSSION:

This treaty was made at the conclusion of the Blackhawk War, which resulted in the forced removal of Sac and Fox Indians from Illinois and Wisconsin to territory west of the Mississippi. During this period, the Potawatomi, who had already made major land cessions by the **Treaty with the Potawatomi** of 1828, relinquished most of the rest of their territory in Indiana.

REFERENCES:

Axelrod, Alan. *Chronicle of the Indian Wars: From Colonial Times to Wounded Knee.* New York: Macmillan General Reference, 1993.

Coupler, Charles J., ed. *Indian Treaties, 1778-1883.* New York: Interland, 1972.

Prucha, Francis Paul, ed. *Documents of United States Indian Policy,* 2d ed. Lincoln: University of Nebraska Press, 1990.

Tyler, Lyman S. *A History of Indian Policy.* Washington, D.C.: U.S. Government Printing Office, 1973.

Treaty of Fort Laramie

SIGNED: September 17, 1851, at Fort Laramie, Wyoming

SIGNATORIES: United States vs. "the chiefs, headmen, and braves of the following Indian nations, residing south of the Missouri River, east of the Rocky Mountains, and north of the lines of Texas and New Mexico, viz, the Sioux or Dahcotahs, Cheyennes, Arapahoes, Crows, Assinaboines, Gros-Ventre Mandans, and Arrickaras"

IN FORCE: From signing

OVERVIEW: A treaty intended to gain security for westward-bound emigrants.

DISCUSSION:

By the middle of the nineteenth century, the government of the United States was motivated to seek peace with the tribes of the western plains in order to secure the safety of western travelers and settlers. The Treaty of Fort Laramie calls for the following:

- Peace, both between whites and Indians and among the signatory tribes
- Indian recognition of the right of the United States to build roads and establish outposts and military forts within the territories of the signatory tribes
- A pledge of the United States to protect the signatory tribes "against the commission of all depredations by the people of the . . . United States"
- The Indian signatories' agreement to make restitution for "any wrongs committed after ratification of this treaty"
- A definition of the territories of the Indian signatories

For its part, the United States agrees to deliver an annual subsidy to the signatory tribes of $50,000 (in goods, livestock, and so on) for ten years, with an option of extension for five more years. The types of goods delivered is left to the discretion of the president of the United States "as may be deemed best adapted to [the Indians'] condition."

REFERENCES:

Axelrod, Alan. *Chronicle of the Indian Wars: From Colonial Times to Wounded Knee.* New York: Macmillan General Reference, 1993.

Prucha, Francis Paul. *Documents of United States Indian Policy,* 2d ed. Lincoln: University of Nebraska Press, 1990.

Treaty with the Apache

SIGNED: July 1, 1852, at Santa Fe, New Mexico

SIGNATORIES: Representatives of the Apache tribe vs. United States

IN FORCE: From signing

OVERVIEW: A treaty of peace with the most warlike of the Southwestern tribes.

DISCUSSION:

A typically one-sided treaty between the United States and a Native American tribal group, the 1852 document seeks to end hostilities between Apaches and white settlers that had begun in the days of the conquistadors. This treaty shares the flaws common to most U.S.-Indian treaties:

- Tribal government was such that the phrase "authorized Chiefs" (Article 1) had little meaning. Tribes were not the equivalent of nations, and many tribal members did not feel themselves bound by treaties signed by others.
- The federal government was typically unsuccessful in enforcing conditions it had agreed to. Local individuals, militias, and state authorities frequently acted without regard to federal treaties.

The treaty proved ineffectual in ending hostilities. With the outbreak of the Civil War in 1861 and the transfer of U.S. Army troops from southwestern outposts to the battlegrounds of the East, raiding by Apaches became widespread and especially fierce, continuing so through the early 1880s.

REFERENCES:

Axelrod, Alan. *Chronicle of the Indian Wars: From Colonial Times to Wounded Knee.* New York: Macmillan General Reference, 1993.

Prucha, Francis Paul. *Documents of United States Indian Policy,* 2d ed. Lincoln: University of Nebraska Press, 1990.

Treaty of Fort Atkinson

SIGNED: July 27, 1853, at Fort Atkinson, Indian Territory

SIGNATORIES: United States vs. "Camanche [sic], and Kiowa, and Apache tribes or nations of Indians, inhabiting [Indian Territory] south of the Arkansas River"

IN FORCE: July 21, 1854

OVERVIEW: An early peace treaty with these three warrior tribes, principally to secure safe passage of emigrants and other travelers through Indian lands.

DISCUSSION:

The warrior tribes of the Southwest, including the Apache, Comanche, and Kiowa, had a long tradition of warfare with white settlers, traders, and travelers, citizens of the United States as well as Mexican nationals, and an even longer tradition of warfare among themselves. As white settlement, trade, and travel became more frequent in the homelands of these Indians, a state of chronic warfare developed. Despite this and other treaties, the violence would continue well into the 1880s.

The Treaty of Fort Atkinson begins with an article proclaiming peace with the United States: "Peace, friendship, and amity shall hereafter exist between the United States and the Camanche and Kiowa, and Apache tribes of Indians, parties to this treaty, and the same shall be perpetual." It then continues with an article in which the Indians bind themselves to peaceful relations with one another: "The Camanche, Kiowa, and Apache tribes of Indians do hereby jointly and severally convenant that peaceful relations shall likewise be maintained amongst themselves in future; and that they will abstain from all hostilities whatsoever against each other, and cultivate mutual good-will and friendship." This was of special concern to government officials because inter-tribal warfare frequently expanded to general warfare, in which settlers and others were engulfed.

Article 3 binds the Indians to "acknowledge the right of the United States to lay off and mark out roads or highways—to make reservations of land necessary thereto—to locate depots—and to establish military and other posts within the territories inhabited by the said tribes; and also to prescribe and enforce, in such manner as the President or the Congress of the United States shall from time to time direct, rules and regulations to protect the rights of persons and property among the said Indian tribes." Article 4 calls for the Indians to make "restitution . . . for any injuries done by any band or any individuals of their respective tribes to the people of the United States who may be lawfully residing in or passing through their said territories; and to abstain hereafter from levying contributions from, or molesting them in any manner; and, so far as may be in their power, to render assistance to such as need relief, and to facilitate their safe passage."

Article 5 relates to a third party, Mexico:

The Camanche, and Kiowa, and Apache tribes of Indians, parties to this treaty, do hereby solemnly covenant and agree to refrain in future from warlike incursions into the Mexican provinces, and from all depredations upon the inhabitants thereof; and they do likewise bind themselves to restore all captives that may hereafter be taken by any of the bands, war-parties, or individuals of the said several tribes, from the Mexican provinces aforesaid, and to make proper and just compensation for any wrongs that may be inflicted upon the people thereof by them, either to the United States or to the Republic of Mexico, as the President of the United States may direct and require.

Transboundary "Indian depredations" were a frequent source of jurisdictional and border disputes between the United States and Mexico. The Mexican government held the United States responsible for the actions of Indians domiciled within the United States.

In return for compliance with the provisions of the treaty, the United States concludes an annuity agreement with the tribes, specified in articles 6 through 9. As with most annuity

and reservation agreements, corruption and inefficiency among the agencies responsible for Indian affairs compromised fulfillment of the conditions of the treaty, generated continued resentment, and sparked further violence.

The final article, Article 10, lays down the following: "It is agreed between the United States and the Camanche, Kiowa, and Apache tribes of Indians, that, should it at any time hereafter be considered by the United States as a proper policy to establish farms among and for the benefit of said Indians, it shall be discretionary with the President, by and with the advice and consent of the Senate, to change the annuities herein provided for, or any part thereof, into a fund for that purpose." From the earliest days of treaty making between the United States and various Indian tribes, the federal government periodically introduced schemes of social engineering. It was believed that warrior traditions could be curtailed and the Indians themselves more effectively contained if they were compelled to adopt sedentary patterns of agriculture rather than continue their hunting traditions. Many Indian treaties include provisions for establishing farms and agricultural programs.

REFERENCES:

Axelrod, Alan. *Chronicle of the Indian Wars: From Colonial Times to Wounded Knee.* New York: Macmillan General Reference, 1993.

Prucha, Francis Paul. *Documents of United States Indian Policy,* 2d ed. Lincoln: University of Nebraska Press, 1990.

Treaty of the Little Arkansas

SIGNED: October 14, 1865, Little Arkansas River, Kansas
IN FORCE: From signing
SIGNATORIES: United States vs. Cheyenne and Arapaho Indians
OVERVIEW: The treaty ended the Cheyenne-Arapaho War, which had been triggered by the Sand Creek Massacre of November 29, 1864.

DISCUSSION:
When John Evans, governor of Colorado Territory, failed to negotiate acquisition of mineral-rich lands belonging to the Cheyenne and Arapaho, he authorized Colonel John M. Chivington, military commander of the territory, to force the Indians off the land and onto reservations. Chivington, who advocated the extermination of all Indians (including infants; "Nits make lice!" he said), ignored the peaceful overtures of Cheyenne chief Black Kettle, and provoked a war. In November 1864, Evans and Chivington met with the Cheyennes and Arapahos, instructing those who desired peace to "submit to military authority" by laying down their arms at a local fort. The Indians left the meeting and camped at Sand Creek, Colorado, presumably to discuss the terms offered.

Chivington ordered his regiment of volunteers to surround Sand Creek and attack. On November 29, 1864, 200 Cheyennes, two-thirds of them women and children, and nine chiefs were killed, many of them hideously mutilated. The Sand Creek Massacre provoked general war with the Cheyenne and Arapaho during late 1864 and early 1865.

The Treaty of the Little Arkansas stipulated reparations for the Sand Creek Massacre (Article VI) in exchange for the pledge of the Cheyenne and Arapaho to retire to a reservation, the limits of which are defined by Article II of the treaty. Like most U.S.-Indian treaties, the Little Arkansas failed to maintain peace; nevertheless, it is unique among such documents in its admission of the injustice of the Sand Creek Massacre.

REFERENCES:
Axelrod, Alan. *Chronicle of the Indian Wars: From Colonial Times to Wounded Knee* (New York: Macmillan General Reference, 1993.
Cutler, Bruce. *The Massacre at Sand Creek: Narrative Voices.* Norman: University of Oklahoma Press, 1997.
Israel, Fred L. *Major Peace Treaties of Modern History, 1648-1967*, vol. 2. New York: Chelsea House and McGraw-Hill, 1967.
Scott, Bob. *Blood at Sand Creek: The Massacre Revisited.* Caldwell, ID: Caxton Press, 1994.

Treaty of Fort Sully

SIGNED: October 20, 1865, at Fort Sully, Dakota Territory

IN FORCE: From signing

SIGNATORIES: United States vs. Yanktonai band of Sioux Indians

OVERVIEW: This treaty is representative of those made with other Sioux bands in an effort to end the chronic warfare on the Plains.

DISCUSSION:

The Civil War exacerbated the Indian hostility in the West because many soldiers had been drawn away from the frontier regions to fight the Confederates in the eastern theater of war. This circumstance motivated the federal government to push for settlement with the tribes.

Six straightforward articles follow the treaty's preamble:

- By Article I the Yanktonai acknowledged "themselves to be subject to the exclusive jurisdiction and authority of the United States" and not only pledged peace but also promised "to use their influence, and, if requisite, physical force, to prevent other bands of Dakota Indians, or other adjacent tribes, from making hostile demonstrations against the Government or people of the United States."

- In Article II, the Yanktonai agreed to "to discontinue . . . attacks upon other tribes, unless first attacked by them." Intertribal hostility often spilled over into warfare between Indians and whites.

- Article III gave the president authority to arbitrate disputes.

- By Article IV, the Yanktonai agreed not to harass travelers on the western trails, in return for which the federal government would pay an annuity of thirty dollars (in goods) for each lodge or family, annually, for twenty years.

- Article V set out terms of Indian settlement on public land. Unlike many other treaty tribes, the Yanktonai were not to be confined to a reservation, but the conditions set forth for occupying federal land encouraged a settled agricultural life rather than the wider-ranging hunting and warrior existence that was part of Plains culture: "Should any individual or individuals, or portion of the band of the Yanktonai band of Dakota or Sioux Indians, represented in council, desire hereafter to locate permanently upon any land claimed by said band for the purposes of agricultural or other similar pursuits, it is hereby agreed by the parties to this treaty that such individuals shall be protected in such location against any annoyance or molestation on the part of whites or Indians; and whenever twenty lodges or families of the Yanktonai band shall have located on lands for agricultural purposes, and signified the same to their agents or superintendent, they, as well as other families so locating, shall receive the sum of twenty-five dollars, annually, for five years, for each family, in agricultural implements and improvements; and when one hundred lodges or families shall have so engaged in agricultural pursuits they shall be entitled to a farmer and blacksmith, at the expense of the Government, as also teachers, at the option of the Secretary of the Interior, whenever deemed necessary."

- Finally, Article VI allowed for amendment of the treaty by the Senate.

REFERENCES:
Israel, Fred L. *Major Peace Treaties of Modern History, 1648-1967*, vol. 2 (New York: Chelsea House and McGraw-Hill, 1967).
Josephy, Alvin M., Jr. *The Civil War in the American West.* New York: Vintage, 1993.
Prucha, Francis Paul. *American Indian Treaties: The History of a Political Anomaly.* Berkeley: University of California Press, 1997.

Treaty of Fort Laramie

SIGNED: April 29, 1868, at Fort Laramie, Wyoming

SIGNATORIES: United States vs. "the different bands of the Sioux Nation of Indians"

IN FORCE: From signing

OVERVIEW: The treaty that ended the so-called War for the Bozeman Trail and Hancock's War, giving to the Indians much of what they had fought for, including abandonment of forts along the Bozeman Trail.

DISCUSSION:

The brilliant Oglala Sioux leader Red Cloud led a successful resistance against the United States Army's efforts to defend the Bozeman Trail, an important route of white trade and migration through Montana and Wyoming. The treaty, which followed two futile and costly military actions, known as the War for the Bozeman Trail and Hancock's Campaign, gave to Red

Cloud most of what he had fought for:

- Designation of the Powder River country as "unceded Indian territory"
- Establishment of a "Great Sioux Reservation" in all of present-day South Dakota west of the Missouri
- Hunting privileges outside of the reservation "so long as the buffalo may range thereon"
- Government abandonment of the Bozeman Trail and its forts

Like most treaties concluded with the Indians, the Treaty of Fort Laramie promised much but delivered little. The closing of the Bozeman Trail was no great sacrifice for the government, because the trail was about to be rendered obsolete by the transcontinental railroad, nearing completion. In general, however, the treaty proved unenforceable. While the United States pledged to punish any "bad men" who violated the treaty or did injury to the Indians, it lacked both the power and the will to do so. For their part, the Indian signatories could not control certain warlike factions (especially among the younger warriors), who simply refused to acknowledge the treaty.

The 1868 Treaty of Fort Laramie is noteworthy and unusual for having conceded so much to the Indian signatories, but it is otherwise quite routine as a document that had depressingly little effect on the violent reality of white-Indian relations in the American West.

REFERENCES:

Axelrod, Alan. *Chronicle of the Indian Wars: From Colonial Times to Wounded Knee.* New York: Macmillan General Reference, 1993.

Prucha, Francis Paul. *Documents of United States Indian Policy,* 2d ed., expanded. Lincoln: University of Nebraska Press, 1990.

Treaty with the Kiowa, Comanche, and Apache

SIGNED: October 21, 1868, at Medicine Lodge Creek

SIGNATORIES: United States vs. "Kiowa, Comanche, and Apache Indians, represented by their chiefs and headmen duly authorized and empowered to act for the body of the people of said tribes"

IN FORCE: From signing

OVERVIEW: A treaty consigning the Indian signatories to a reservation.

DISCUSSION:

The first Indian reservation in North America was Edge Pillock, established in New Jersey in 1758 for about 100 Unamis. It was not until the nineteenth century, however, that the idea of domiciling Indians on special reservations generally caught on, and by 1817, the area encompassing present-day Oklahoma and part of Kansas and Nebraska was designated "Indian Territory." The **Indian Removal Act** of 1830 sent the tribes of the Southeast to this territory.

From roughly 1870 to 1920, many reservations were established and were administered by the Bureau of Indian Affairs, at times under the control of the Department of War and, later, under control of the Department of the Interior. Throughout this period, most reservations were poorly administered, subject to indifference and corruption, so that they were often little better than large concentration camps. The privations and outrages of reservation life sparked many Indian-government conflicts during the late nineteenth century, including outright warfare.

By the second half of the nineteenth century, most peace treaties concluded between the United States and Indian tribes included a central provision consigning the tribe to a reservation. Article 1 of the present treaty follows:

> The said Apache tribe of Indians agree to confederate and become incorporated with the said Kiowa and Comanche Indians, and to accept as their permanent home the reservation described in the aforesaid treaty with said Kiowa and Comanche tribes, concluded as aforesaid at this place, and they pledge themselves to make no permanent settlement at any place, nor on any lands, outside of said reservation.

The government agrees to provide the amenities of "civilization" for the benefit of the reservation, along with material compensation, and an annuity. For their part, the Indians agree "to keep the peace toward the whites and all other persons under the jurisdiction of the United States . . ."

Given the usually intolerable conditions of reservation life, it is little wonder that treaties such as this were violated almost immediately, and the 1870s saw the height of warfare between the U.S. government and the Indians, especially of the Plains and the Southwest.

REFERENCES:

Axelrod, Alan. *Chronicle of the Indian Wars: From Colonial Times to Wounded Knee.* New York: Macmillan General Reference, 1993.

Prucha, Francis Paul. *Documents of United States Indian Policy,* 2d ed. Lincoln: University of Nebraska Press, 1990.

Dawes Severalty Act (General Allotment Act)

SIGNED: February 8, 1887

SIGNATORIES: Act of Congress

IN FORCE: From passage until passage of the **Wheeler-Howard Indian Reorganization Act**, 1934

OVERVIEW: An act of Congress calling for the dissolution of tribal lands and the granting of land "allotments" to individual Indians, who became U.S. citizens when they received allotments.

DISCUSSION:

Sponsored by Massachusetts senator Henry L. Dawes, the act aimed to end the reservation system by dismantling it through a program of assimilating Indians into "mainstream" American society instead of segregating them within tribal groups. White reformers determined that by breaking up the tribes' communal lands—now reservation lands—Indian society could be restructured around individual families who, as individuals, owned their land.

The Dawes Act authorized the president to designate certain tribes as ready for allotment. Each adult family head in such a tribe would receive 160 acres of land (other tribal members received smaller allotments), which could not be sold for at least the twenty-five-year period in which the government held each parcel in trust. Despite this provision, the act was strongly favored by land-hungry white westerners, because it called for the sale of "surplus" tribal lands—the reformers arguing that the Indians had more land than they could use as individuals. Proceeds from the sale of this surplus would fund Indian education programs.

Rightly fearing that the Dawes Severalty Act threatened to destroy their cultures, most Indians opposed the legislation.

REFERENCES:

Hoxie, Frederick E. *A Final Promise: The Campaign to Assimilate the Indians, 1880-1920.* Lincoln: University of Nebraksa Press, 1984.

McDonnell, Janet. *The Dispossession of the American Indian.* Bloomington: Indiana University Press, 1991.

Wall, Wendy L., "Dawes Act," in Charles Phillips and Alan Axelrod, eds., *Encyclopedia of the American West,* vol. 2. New York: Simon and Schuster, 1996.

Wheeler-Howard Indian Reorganization Act

SIGNED: June 18, 1934

SIGNATORIES: act of Congress

IN FORCE: From passage

OVERVIEW: This act reversed the process of assimilation promoted by the **Dawes Severalty Act** and promoted tribal organization among Indians.

DISCUSSION:

The Indian Reorganization Act reduced future allotment (per the **Dawes Severalty Act**) of tribal communal lands and called for the return of "surplus lands" to the tribes. It promoted tribal self-government by encouraging tribes to write constitutions and manage their own internal affairs. The Indian Reorganization Act established a credit program for tribal land purchases, for educational assistance, and for aiding tribal government.

The act still serves as the basis of federal legislation concerning Indian affairs.

REFERENCES:

Hoxie, Frederick E. *A Final Promise: The Campaign to Assimilate the Indians, 1880-1920.* Lincoln: University of Nebraska Press, 1984.

McDonnell, Janet. *The Dispossession of the American Indian.*

Bloomington: Indiana University Press, 1991.

Prucha, Francis Paul. *Documents of United States Indian Policy,* 2d ed. Lincoln: University of Nebraska Press, 1990.

Government-to-Government Relations with Native American Tribal Governments

OFFICIAL TITLE: Memorandum for the Heads of Executive Departments and Agencies on Government-to-Government Relations with Native American Tribal Governments

ISSUED: April 29, 1994, at Washington

SIGNATORY: Executive branch memorandum signed by President Bill Clinton

IN FORCE: From issuance

OVERVIEW: Executive-branch guidelines "to ensure that the rights of sovereign tribal governments are fully respected."

DISCUSSION:

The following directive from President Bill Clinton effectively has the force of a treaty with Native American tribal governments and, indeed, supercedes many U.S.-Native American treaties with regard to the definition of U.S. government-Indian government relations.

The text, which is brief, follows:

The United States Government has a unique legal relationship with Native American tribal governments as set forth in the Constitution of the United States, treaties, statutes, and court decisions. As executive departments and agencies undertake activities affecting Native American tribal rights or trust resources, such activities should be implemented in a knowledgeable, sensitive manner respectful of tribal sovereignty.

Today, as part of an historic meeting, I am outlining principles that executive departments and agencies, including every component bureau and office, are to follow in their interactions with Native American tribal governments. The purpose of these principles is to clarify our responsibility to ensure that the Federal Government operates within a government-to-government relationship with federally recognized Native American tribes. I am strongly committed to building a more effective day-to-day working relationship reflecting respect for the rights of self-government due the sovereign tribal governments.

In order to ensure that the rights of sovereign tribal governments are fully respected, executive branch activities shall be guided by the following:

(a) The head of each executive department and agency shall be responsible for ensuring that the department or agency operates within a government-to-government relationship with federally recognized tribal governments.

(b) Each executive department and agency shall consult, to the greatest extent practicable and to the extent permitted by law, with tribal governments prior to taking actions that affect federally recognized tribal governments. All such consultations are to be open and candid so that all interested parties may evaluate for themselves the potential impact of relevant proposals.

(c) Each executive department and agency shall assess the impact of Federal Government plans, projects, programs, and activities on tribal trust resources and assure that tribal government rights and concerns are considered during the development of such plans, projects, programs, and activities.

(d) Each executive department and agency shall take appropriate steps to remove any procedural impediments to working directly and effectively with tribal governments on activities that affect the trust property and/or governmental rights of the tribes.

(e) Each executive department and agency shall work cooperatively with other Federal departments and agencies to enlist their interest and support in cooperative efforts, where appropriate, to accomplish the goals of this memorandum.

(f) Each executive department and agency shall apply the requirements of Executive Orders Nos. 12875 ("Enhancing the Intergovernmental Partnership") and 12866 ("Regulatory Planning and Review") to design solutions and tailor Federal programs, in appropriate circumstances, to address specific or unique needs of tribal communities.

The head of each executive department and agency shall ensure that the department or agency's bureaus and components are fully aware of this memorandum, through publication or other means, and that they are in compliance with its requirements.

This memorandum is intended only to improve the internal management of the executive branch and is not intended to, and does not, create any right to administrative or judicial review, or any other right or benefit or trust responsibility, substantive or procedural, enforceable by a party against the United States, its agencies or instrumentalities, its officers or employees, or any other person.

REFERENCES:

Prucha, Francis Paul, ed. *Documents of United States Indian Policy,* 2d ed. Lincoln: University of Nebraska Press, 1990.

Tyler, Lyman S. *A History of Indian Policy.* Washington, D.C.: U.S. Government Printing Office, 1973.

Wars and Military Alliances

French and Indian War

Overview of the Conflict

The French and Indian War (1754-1763) was the North American phase of what many historians have termed the "first world war," the Seven Years' War, which involved the Holy Roman Empire, Prussia, France, Britain, Spain, and Russia in battles fought in Europe, India, Cuba, and the Philippines, as well as North America. The American phase of the great conflict got under way almost three years before Europe erupted into war, and it may be seen as the culmination of a series of eighteenth-century wilderness wars between French and English colonial interests, together with various Indian allies and enemies, often collectively called the French and Indian *Wars*. The conclusion of one of these conflagrations—called, in North America, King George's War, and in Europe the War of the Austrian Succession—encouraged England's King George II to grant huge wilderness tracts to a group of entrepreneurs organized as the Ohio Company (March 27, 1749). The grant stipulated that, within seven years, the company had to plant a settlement of one hundred families and build a fort for their protection. This stipulation served to rekindle the hostility of the French and their Indian allies, who feared an English invasion.

Their fears, of course, were entirely justified. Throughout 1749, an influx of British traders penetrated territories that had been the exclusive trading province of the French. In response, on June 26, 1749, Roland-Michel Galissonière, marquis de La Galissonière, governor of New France, dispatched Captain Pierre-Joseph Céleron de Blainville with 213 men to the Ohio country. By November 20, 1749, Céleron had made a round trip of three thousand miles, burying at intervals lead plates inscribed with France's claim to sovereignty over the territory. By this time, La Galissonière had been replaced as governor by Jacques-Pierre de Jonquière, marquis de La Jonquière. The new governor believed that it would take more than buried lead plates to control North America. He therefore ordered the construction of a chain of wilderness forts, and he authorized attacks against the Shawnee, most powerful of the Ohio country tribes who traded with the English. In the meantime, an English trader named Christopher Gist negotiated agreements with the Six Iroquois Nations, as well as the Delawares, Shawnees, and Wyandots, securing thereby, for Virginia and for the Ohio Company, deeds to the vast Ohio lands. French-allied Indians drove the English out of this wilderness country by 1752, and yet another new governor of New France, Ange

Duquesne de Menneville, marquis Duquesne, quickly built more French forts through the Ohio country, a string of military outposts that stretched from New Orleans up to Montreal.

Duquesne's aggressiveness alarmed some Indians, who were prompted to make overtures of alliance with the English, but English colonial authorities responded to most of these with contempt and thereby threw away numerous opportunities to create important alliances. Even as the English alienated the Indians, Britain's prime minister, Lord Halifax, in London, remote from the American scene, pushed the cabinet toward a declaration of war. He argued that the French, by trading throughout the Ohio Valley, had invaded Virginia, whose ambiguously defined charter was interpreted to encompass far western lands.

With war fever rising, Governor Robert Dinwiddie of Virginia easily secured authority from the crown to "evict" the French from territory under his jurisdiction. For this, he commissioned twenty-one-year-old Virginia militia captain George Washington to carry an ultimatum to the French interlopers. Young Washington set out from Williamsburg, Virginia's capital, on October 31, 1753 and delivered the ultimatum to the commandant of Fort LeBoeuf (Waterford, Pennsylvania) on December 12, 1753. When Washington's ultimatum was politely but firmly rebuffed, Governor Dinwiddie ordered the construction of a fort at the strategically critical "forks of Ohio," the junction of the Monongahela and Allegheny rivers, the site of present-day Pittsburgh.

While this exchange took place in Virginia, up north, in Nova Scotia, British authorities were demanding that the Acadians—French-speaking Roman Catholic farmers and fishermen who freely intermarried with the local Micmac and Abnaki Indians—swear loyalty to the British crown. The Acadians were an unpretentious people whose doom, it turned out, lay in their having chosen to live in the midst of the most important fishery in the world, waters coveted by all the nations of Europe. Now they were helplessly caught between great opposing forces. While the British threatened them with expulsion from Nova Scotia, the French threatened to turn their Indian allies against any Acadians who took the loyalty oath.

While the conflict in Nova Scotia simmered to a boil, the French, back in Virginia, having patiently watched the construction of Dinwiddie's fort, attacked the newly completed stockade.

Badly outnumbered, the British garrison surrendered on April 17, 1754. The English stronghold, now christened Fort Duquesne, was occupied by the French. Unaware that the fort had been lost, Dinwiddie sent Washington (promoted to lieutenant colonel) with 150 men to reinforce it. En route, on May 28, Washington surprised a thirty-three-man French reconnaissance party. In the ensuing combat, ten of the Frenchmen were killed, including Ensign Joseph Coulon de Villiers de Jumonville, a French "ambassador." This was the first battle of the French and Indian War.

Realizing that the French would retaliate, Washington desperately sought reinforcement from his Indian allies. A grand total of forty warriors answered the call. It was too late to retreat, so, at Great Meadows, Pennsylvania, Washington built a makeshift stockade, which he grimly dubbed Fort Necessity. On July 3, Major Coulon de Villiers, brother of the man Washington's small detachment had killed, led nine hundred French soldiers, Delawares, Ottawas, Wyandots, Algonquins, Nipissings, Abnakis, and French-allied Iroquois against Fort Necessity. After losing half of his command, Washington surrendered—on the fourth of July.

With the loss of the strategic Ohio fort and the defeat of Washington, it was the English rather than the French who suffered eviction from the Ohio country. A desperate congress convened at Albany from June 19 to July 10, 1754, and produced an abortive plan for colonial unity (see **Albany Plan of Union**, in Section 1.1). While British colonial officials dithered, the French and their many Indian allies raided freely throughout Pennsylvania, Maryland, and Virginia, using Fort Duquesne as their chief base of operations. At last, in December 1754, the English crown authorized Massachusetts governor William Shirley to reactivate two colonial regiments. These two thousand men were joined by two regiments of British regulars commanded by a courageous but obtuse career officer, Major General Edward Braddock. When the French responded by sending more troops to North America, British forces were expanded to ten thousand men. On April 14, 1755, Braddock laid out his grand strategy at a council of war. His subordinate, Brigadier General Robert Monckton, would campaign against Nova Scotia, while Braddock himself would capture Forts Duquesne and Niagara. Governor Shirley would strengthen and reinforce Fort Oswego and then proceed to Fort Niagara—in what seemed the unlikely event that Braddock was somehow detained at Fort Duquesne. Another colonial commander, William Johnson, was assigned to take Fort Saint Frédéric at Crown Point (at the head of Lake Champlain).

Monckton and John Winslow (a colonial commander) achieved early success in Nova Scotia, delivering most of the province into British hands. Braddock, however, had great trouble getting his unwieldy expedition under way to Fort Duquesne. Like other British commanders, he contemptuously alienated prospective Indian allies as well as the so-called "pro-vincials," the colonial militia, so that it was with great difficulty that he secured cooperation from colonial governors, who resisted collecting war levies. At long last, the general led two regiments of British regulars and a provincial detachment (under George Washington) out of Fort Cumberland, Maryland. Along the westward march toward Fort Duquesne, French-allied Indians sniped at the slow-moving column. At last, Washington advised Braddock to detach a "flying column" of 1,500 men to make the initial attack on Fort Duquesne, which Braddock believed was defended by eight hundred French and Indians. By July 7, the flying column had set up a camp ten miles from their objective. Boldly, the French garrison commander responded by attacking Braddock with an inferior force—just 72 regulars of the French Marine, 146 Canadian militiamen, and 637 assorted Indian allies. The result of the fierce surprise attack on the morning of July 9, 1755 was total panic among the British. Troops fired wildly, and it was reported that many of the British regulars did no more than huddle in the road like so many sheep. Braddock valiantly tried to rally his troops, before he himself fell mortally wounded. Of 1,459 officers and men engaged in what would be called the Battle of the Wilderness, only 462 survived, among them George Washington and most of his Virginians. As for Braddock, his dying words expressed incomprehension to the last. "Who would have thought it?" he said.

The devastating defeat at the Battle of the Wilderness drove many more Indians into the camp of the French and laid English settlements along the length of the frontier open to attack. The French had also captured Braddock's private papers, including his war plan, which prompted the French to reinforce Forts Niagara and Saint Frédéric—using the very cannon abandoned by the routed English. With the Pennsylvania, Maryland, and Virginia frontiers racked by Indian raids, William Johnson successfully led a provincial force to victory at the Battle of Lake George and built the strategically important Fort William Henry on the south end of the lake. Washington, having returned from the Battle of the Wilderness, persuaded authorities to build more forts, extending from the Potomac and James and Roanoke rivers, down into South Carolina. These, Washington said, were the only effective means of combating the widespread Indian raids unleashed by the French. Despite Johnson's victory and the building of the forts, by June 1756, British settlers in Virginia had withdrawn 150 miles from the prewar frontier.

In the flush of its triumphs and with the Seven Years' War expanding, France poured more troops into North America and sent to command them the dashing and highly capable Louis Joseph, Marquis de Montcalm, who arrived in Canada on May 11, 1756. In contrast, having learned little from the disaster at Fort Duquesne, the British were still reluctant to make good use of provincial forces. Fort Oswego, ineptly defended by regulars, fell to Montcalm on August 14, 1756. By gaining Oswego, the French seized control of Lake Ontario, thereby strengthening French communication with Fort Duquesne and the West. There was now no opportunity for the British to attack Fort Niagara, and the mighty Iroquois tribes, still officially neutral, inclined more sharply to the French victors.

The desperate British situation brightened in December 1756, when William Pitt became British secretary of state for the southern department, a post that put him in charge of American colonial affairs. Among his first acts was to relieve unqualified officers, who had achieved command by virtue of political influence, and give command to men with genuine military skill, including, as appropriate, "provincial" officers. Although Montcalm next captured Fort William Henry, dealing British forces a stunning defeat on August 9, 1757, the crown's fortunes gradually improved. Pitt chose Brigadier General John Forbes, one of his best commanders, to attempt a new assault on Fort Duquesne. Despite many delays, mainly caused by the incompetence and corruption of the British quartermaster (supply) corps, an army of 5,000 provincials, 1,400 Highlanders, and an ever- diminishing number of Indian allies lumbered toward the stubborn objective at the forks of the Ohio. An initial—and premature—assault by the Highlanders resulted in disaster. But this would prove a pyrrhic victory for the French. Losses among their Indian allies were so heavy that most of them, after seizing plunder, deserted the French cause. Even worse for the French, the British negotiated (October 1758) a separate peace with the French-allied Delaware, and, on November 24, Forbes made his main advance on Fort Duquesne. The French, recognizing that their situation in the fort was hopeless, blew it up rather than allow it fall into British hands. But that mattered little. The fort could be rebuilt, and the British now had control of the forks of the Ohio, gateway to the West.

If the year 1758 marked the turning of the tide in favor of the British, 1759 was the year of outright French disaster, culminating in the siege, battle, and loss of Quebec on September 18, 1759, which effectively brought to an end French power in North America. Quebec fell after a brief battle (in which both commanders, British general James Wolfe and his French counterpart, Montcalm, died) that had been the short, sharp conclusion of a long and frustrating campaign. Even though the loss of Quebec for all practical purposes decided the war, fighting continued through 1763. Despite the fall of Indian-held Detroit to English forces led by Robert Rogers and his famed Rangers, the southern frontier was consumed by a full-scale Indian uprising that would require two armies and two years to put down. Just as the war was winding down, Spain entered the fray on the side of France. England declared war on the new combatant on January 2, 1762, then defeated the new adversary with sea power alone. As it became clear that the war in America and in Europe was about to end, France hurriedly concluded a secret Treaty of San Ildefonso with Spain (November 3, 1762; not represented in this collection), in which it ceded to that country all of its territory west of the Mississippi and the Isle of Orleans in Louisiana. This was intended as compensation for the loss of

Spain's Caribbean holdings to the British. (Spain returned this territory to France in 1800 by the **Secret Treaty on the Retrocession of Louisiana**, thereby paving the way to the Louisiana Purchase; see Section 1.1.)

The French and Indian War was formally ended on February 10, 1763, by the **Treaty of Paris**, by which France essentially relinquished its North American empire. Yet peace was not immediately restored to the continent. Within days of the Treaty of Paris, on April 27, 1763, Pontiac, war chief of the Ottawa Indians, called a grand council of Ottawa and other tribes—most notably the Delaware, Seneca (as well as elements of other Iroquois tribes), and the Shawnee—then launched an attack on Detroit. This ignited a series of bloody assaults on the western outposts that the French had surrendered to the English. Although many Indian war leaders participated in these operations, the conflict would be called Pontiac's Rebellion. Combat was ended largely as a result of King George III's **Proclamation of 1763** (Section 1.1), which decreed a western limit to British colonial expansion.

Treaty of Paris

SIGNED: February 10, 1763, at Paris

IN FORCE: From signing

SIGNATORIES: Great Britain vs. France, Spain, and Portugal

OVERVIEW: This document, together with the Treaty of Hubertsburg, ended the Seven Years' War, which, in its North American phase, was called the French and Indian War, the largest colonial conflict prior to the American Revolution; the Treaty of Paris did no less than reshape the colonial world.

DISCUSSION:

Historians often call the Seven Years' War the "first world war" because of its scope. Britain and Prussia were aligned against Austria, France, Russia, Saxony, Sweden, and (after 1762) Spain and Portugal, and it included combat in the colonial possessions of some of these countries. Commencement of the European phase of the war, in 1756, was preceded by the beginning of the French and Indian War in North America, in 1754. In North America, British and French colonial troops and militia forces, supported by regular army troops from each nation and by Indian warriors, fought bitterly through 1763—although the fall of Quebec to the British on September 12-13, 1759, effectively ended the military power of France in North America.

In Europe, the war opened on August 29, 1756, when Frederick II the Great of Prussia, in an effort to preempt an attack from Maria Theresa of Austria and Elizabeth of Russia, launched an audacious offensive through the electorate of Saxony, a minor Austrian ally. Despite early victories, Frederick was submerged in a struggle against multiple enemies: Sweden aligned itself against Prussia, and Frederick's advance into Bohemia led to a Prussian defeat at Kolin in June 1757. Russian forces marched into East Prussia in August, and Austrian troops overran Berlin, occupying it for several days in October. Frederick recovered with great victories at Rossbach (November 1757) and Leuthen (December 1757). For their part, the nations opposed to Prussia never adequately coordinated their efforts, failed to coordinate their forces adequately. Still, prolonged warfare weakened Frederick's armies, which were defeated by the Russians at Kunersdorf (August 12, 1759). By the end of 1761, the Austrians had moved into Saxony and Silesia, and Russians held Prussian Pomerania. Just when Frederick's position seemed most desperate, the Russian empress Elizabeth died (January 1762) and was succeeded by Peter III, a great admirer of Frederick. He withdrew from the war, leaving Austria to face Prussia alone. Austria concluded a separate peace with Prussia, the Treaty of Hubertsburg (February 15, 1763).

In the meantime, Britain and France had been fighting most of their war in their contested colonial possessions, especially those in North America and India. In 1762, the Spanish entered the war against Britain, but quickly succumbed to superior British sea power.

Drained of treasure and will, the combatant nations concluded the Treaty of Paris early in 1763. As the Seven Years' War/French and Indian War was of greater geographical scope than any previous conflict among European nations, so the Treaty of Paris was sweeping in scope and decisive in effect:

- France relinquished to Britain all of its North American possessions, except Louisiana, which it had earlier ceded to Spain
- French troops were excluded from Bengal, thereby ending the French imperial presence in India and laying the foundation for exclusive British dominion of the subcontinent
- In Africa, France ceded Senegal to the British
- Britain acquired all of North America east of the Mississippi River, including Canada and Florida

This latter acquisition would prove less a benefit to Britain than to Britain's North American colonists. Once France and Spain had been evicted from the frontiers, the Indians lost their support for resistance to the expansion of British settlement. As colonists migrated farther westward, connections with the mother country grew increasingly tenuous, and hunger for independence grew. In this way, the Treaty of Paris helped create the conditions that would foster the American Revolution.

France did retain a few colonies: Saint Pierre and Miquelon (in the Gulf of Saint Lawrence); Saint Lucia, Haiti, Guadeloupe, and Martinique (in the West Indies); and Pondichery and Chandernagor (in India). Spain recovered Cuba and the Philippines, which it had lost in the course of the war, but ceded Florida to Britain.

REFERENCES:

Corbett, Julian S. *England in the Seven Years' War, 1759-63,* 2 vols. London: Greenhill Press, 1993.

Granville, Arthur. *The Fight with France for North America*. New York: Ayer, 1971.

Israel, Fred L. *Major Peace Treaties of Modern History, 1648-1967*, vol. 1. New York: Chelsea House and McGraw-Hill, 1967.

Jennings, Francis. *Empire of Fortune: Crown, Colonies, and Tribes in the Seven Years' War in America.* New York: W. W. Norton, 1990.

American Revolution

Overview of the Conflict

The **Proclamation of 1763** (Section 1.1), an effort to end Pontiac's Rebellion, did much to alienate settlers of the North American frontier. Commanded to remain east of the Appalachian Mountains, they simultaneously fumed against and defied the king. Pushing settlement across the forbidden mountains, they found themselves exposed to Indian raiders, and when they appealed to royal authorities for aid, they were refused—precisely because of their violation of the Proclamation Line. Despite many pockets of strong Loyalist sentiment, the frontier region grew apart from the mother country, and the Tidewater (the more-established coastal settlements) was now torn between outcries of the frontier and demands for obedience issuing from England. As the frontier regions became more populous and powerful, the allegiance of many authorities in the Tidewater leaned westward rather than toward Europe.

Alienation from the crown was not confined to the frontier. During the French and Indian War, the English treasury had amassed a huge debt, and the government, led by Chancellor of the Exchequer George Grenville, decided that the colonies themselves should bear their fair share of the financial burden that had been incurred on their behalf. In fact, various duties and taxes authorized by the Acts of Trade and Navigation had been on the books since the 1650s, but, in the past, it had been crown practice to treat the colonies with what historians have called "salutary neglect"; the duties and taxes simply were not collected. Now Grenville resolved to enforce existing taxes, and he also pushed through Parliament new duties on numerous commodities imported into the colonies, most notably molasses and sugar. This set of laws, which became known collectively as the Sugar Act, was passed in 1764. At the same time, Parliament passed the Currency Act, which forbade the colonies from issuing paper money and required the use of gold in all business transactions, thereby guaranteeing that the colonies would be economically dependent on England. The colonists did not object so much to the idea of being taxed as to being taxed without the benefit of Parliamentary representation.

Over the next decade, the crown removed some taxes, but levied others. During the course of this period, it became clear to certain influential colonial radicals that true Parliamentary representation would never be possible for England's remote colonies, and yet it was also true that taxation without representation is tyranny; therefore, these rebels concluded, the basis of the colonies' relation to the mother country was inherently and inescapably tyrannical. The idea of revolution followed from this, took hold, and the colonies—especially Massachusetts—became increasingly defiant. The crown responded with alternate gestures of conciliation, backing down on all taxes except that on tea, and repression, including acts that removed crown officials from the jurisdiction of local courts and that required the maintenance and quartering of British and mercenary ("Hessian") soldiers. Following Boston's infamous protest against the tea tax—the Boston Tea Party of December 16, 1773, in which colonists boarded three ships in Boston Harbor and dumped their costly cargo of tea chests overboard—Lord North, George III's prime minister, engineered passage of what the colonists would call the Intolerable Acts. Included in this legislation was the Boston Port Act, which closed the harbor to commerce until Boston paid for the destroyed tea; the Massachusetts Government Act, which reserved for the crown the power to appoint members of the upper house of the legislature, increased the royal governor's patronage powers, provided that juries be summoned by sheriffs rather than elected by colonists, and—most onerous of all—banned town meetings not explicitly authorized by law or by the governor; and the Impartial Administration of Justice Act, which authorized a change of venue to another colony or even to England for crown officers charged with capital crimes while performing official duties. Intended to restore order to Massachusetts, the Intolerable Acts instead prompted the colonies to rally behind Massachusetts and to unite, as never before, in convening the First Continental Congress during September 1774. In response to the colonies' action, liberals in Parliament offered a plan of conciliation in 1775, but the hyper-conservative House of Lords rejected it, and Parliament as a whole declared Massachusetts to be in rebellion. It was a foolish declaration; for, in a real sense, it was the British Parliament itself that declared the American Revolution.

Massachusetts responded to the Parliamentary declaration by organizing the Minutemen, militia units that could be ready for battle on a minute's notice. General Thomas Gage, commander of British regulars in Massachusetts, dispatched Lieutenant Colonel Francis Smith with a column from Boston to seize the gunpowder stored at the Massachusetts Provincial Congress in the town of Concord. On the morning of April 19, 1775, Smith's troops dispersed a company of Minutemen at Lexington, unintentionally killing several with an unauthorized burst of musket fire. Smith reached Concord, but found only a small portion of the gunpowder. Paul Revere and other couriers in the service of the revolutionary organization popularly known as the Sons of Liberty had warned the populace of the approach of British troops. Although the battles of Lexington and Concord were not colonial victories, they were hardly British triumphs, and as Smith's column returned to Boston, it was harassed by continual Patriot gunfire, resulting in seventy-three British deaths and the wounding of an additional two hundred soldiers. The pattern would be typical of the war. British forces, trained to fight European-style open-field battles, would often win such engagements, only to be cut up piecemeal by colonial guerrilla groups firing from concealed ambush.

Soon after the battles at Lexington and Concord, colonial militia forces from all over New England converged on Boston and laid siege to the city. In May 1775, a Vermont landowner named Ethan Allen led a militia outfit he had organized, the Green Mountain Boys, against Fort Ticonderoga between Lake Champlain and Lake George in New York and seized it from British regulars. Next, Crown Point, on the western shore of Lake Champlain, fell to rebel forces.

In Charlestown, just outside Boston, a British force under General Thomas Gage attacked a fortified rebel position on Breed's Hill (adjacent to Bunker Hill, after which the battle is named), on June 17, 1775. Ultimately, the colonials were forced off the hill, but the cost to the British was devastating: the loss of almost a thousand men out of the 2,500 engaged. And, in nearby Boston, the British army remained under siege, finally evacuating by sea in March 1776, leaving the city to the rebels, and fleeing far to the north, where a new headquarters was established at Halifax, Nova Scotia.

British strategists abandoned radical New England in order to concentrate on regions with a high population of Tories, as those who remained loyal to the crown were called. Sir Henry Clinton bombarded the harbor fortifications of Charleston, South Carolina, but Patriot forces drove off the attack by June 28, 1776. For the next two years, British operations in the South were stalled. Indeed, the first year of the war had gone far better for the rebels than anyone could have predicted: the British had been forced out of New England and the South. But the Patriots faced many formidable problems. Hoping to persuade the French citizens of Quebec to make common cause with them against the British, American strategists ordered an invasion of Canada, which soon failed for lack of local support. Then, in the summer of 1776, British forces managed to wrest the initiative from the Americans.

British general Guy Carleton, the very able governor of Quebec, chased all American forces out of Canada. His plan was then to push southward through the region of Lake Champlain and the Hudson River in order to sever the far northern tier of colonies from the southern. At the same time, a larger army led by General William Howe (who had replaced Gage as supreme commander of Britain's North American forces), would take New York City and its strategically vital harbor. With this objective secured, the British would have a base from which to advance up the Hudson, unite with Carleton, and then overrun all of New England. New England was the head of the Revolution. Cut it off, and the body would die.

Although Carleton easily drove all remaining Patriot forces out of Canada, his offensive through the wilderness of upper New York bogged down, and, with advent of the winter of 1776, Carleton withdrew to Canada. Howe, in the meantime, succeeded in defeating Washington on Long Island and in New York City. Nevertheless, Washington fought a long and brilliant rearguard action that proved very costly to the British. The victory in New York took four months. And then Howe, who might have moved up the Hudson to attack New England, instead pursued Washington's retreating army across New Jersey. If he had hoped to corner and fight the Continental Army to a standstill, Howe was mistaken. The Americans escaped across the Delaware River into Pennsylvania on December 7, 1776.

Howe regarded Washington as defeated. Washington, however, encamped in Pennsylvania, saw an opportunity to attack. On December 26, 1776, the American commander surprised and overran a garrison of Hessian mercenaries at Trenton, New Jersey, and next went on to an even bigger victory at Princeton on January 3, 1777. The revolution would continue, then. With growing weariness, the British commanders laid out plans for a new assault on the northern colonies.

Major General John Burgoyne was in charge of Britain's Canadian-based army, but he and Howe failed to work out a plan for coordinating their two forces. As Burgoyne led his army down the customary Lake Champlain-Hudson River route, Howe dithered, at last deciding not to support Burgoyne's offensive at all, but to leave a garrison under Sir Henry Clinton in New York City and to transport the bulk of his army by sea to attack Philadelphia. True, as the Patriots' capital and seat of the Continental Congress, Philadelphia was an enticing objective, but Howe's failure to coordinate with Burgoyne would prove a fatal blunder. Unassisted, Burgoyne recaptured Fort Ticonderoga on July 5, 1777, but proceeded at such an unhurried pace that American forces had plenty of time to regroup for guerrilla combat in the adjacent wilderness of upstate New York. A portion of Burgoyne's army suffered defeat at Fort Stanwix in New York's Mohawk Valley. At Bennington, Vermont, a contingent of Burgoyne's Hessians was badly cut up by militia forces under Brigadier General John Stark. Then, when Burgoyne himself pulled up at Bemis Heights on the west bank of the Hudson River, he was met by the revitalized Northern forces of the Continental Army commanded by Horatio Gates and supported by Benedict Arnold and Daniel Morgan. At the opening of the Battle of Saratoga, Burgoyne charged the Americans twice, on September 19 and October 7, 1777, only to be beaten back with heavy losses both times. Blocked to the south and without receiving aid from Howe or Clinton, Burgoyne was compelled to surrender his 6,000-man army (plus various auxiliary forces) to Patriot forces on October 17, 1777.

Saratoga was a great Patriot victory, but, in the meantime, Washington suffered defeat in the defense of Philadelphia. He counterattacked valiantly from Germantown (today, a Philadelphia neighborhood), but was again defeated and forced to withdraw on October 4, 1777. Losing the capital had been a great blow, but the American forces remained intact, and the rebellion continued. Most important of all, the French, who had hitherto aided the Patriot cause furtively, were deeply impressed by the American victory at Saratoga and by Washington's audacity (despite his failure) at Germantown. The government of Louis XVI agreed to a Franco-American alliance. (See the treaties concluded with France in this section.)

Washington understood a great truth about the revolution he was fighting. The burden was upon the British to achieve a decisive victory. As for himself, his principal task was to keep his army together, keep it on the field, and keep fighting—in the hope that the British government would tire of prosecuting the war. But surviving the winter of 1778 and holding together an army of citizen soldiers committed to brief periods of enlistment, paid and provisioned poorly and irregularly, proved a Herculean task. Washington prevailed nonetheless. Come spring, Howe returned to London, and Sir Henry Clinton assumed principal command in North America. He evacuated his army from Philadelphia—which had proved a prize of no military value—and decided to concentrate forces at New York City and in the Caribbean, in anticipation of French naval action there. Washington harried and pursued Clinton through New Jersey, fighting him to a tactical draw at Monmouth Courthouse on June 28, 1778. Monmouth was not decisive, but, as Washington saw it, the drawn battled marked the third year of a war in which the British could show no results.

While the major portions of the American and British armies jockeyed and fought along the East Coast, the frontier regions roiled in bitter guerrilla warfare. Although a few tribes allied themselves with the Patriots, most made common cause with the British army and with Tory militia. A Patriot victory, the Indians correctly believed, would mean unrestricted white settlement: an invasion.

The entire frontier, including western New York, the Ohio country, and the Kentucky borderlands, as well as the interior of the lower South, was convulsed in combat. By late 1778, the British army again shifted much of its effort to the South, reasoning that the region had a higher percentage of Loyalists than any other part of America and also offered more of the raw materials—indigo, rice, cotton—valued by the British. In December 1778, British forces subdued Georgia, then, during 1779, fought inconclusively along the Georgia-South Carolina border. A combined French and American attempt to recapture British-held Savannah was defeated. In February 1780, Sir Henry Clinton arrived in South Carolina from New York with 8,700 fresh troops and laid siege to Charleston, which, in a stunning defeat, was surrendered on May 12 by American general Benjamin Lincoln, who gave up some 5,000 soldiers as prisoners. Quickly, Patriot general Horatio Gates led a force to Camden in upper South Carolina, but was badly defeated on August 16, 1780 by troops under Lord Charles Cornwallis, whom Clinton, returning to New York, had put in command of the Southern forces.

With the Tidewater towns now in British hands, it fell to the Piedmont, the southern frontier, to carry on the resistance. Such legendary guerrilla leaders as the "Swamp Fox" Francis Marion and Thomas Sumter cost the British dearly. Then, on October 7, 1780, a contingent of Patriot frontiersmen—mostly mainly from the Watauga settlements in present-day eastern Tennessee—engaged and destroyed a force of one thousand Loyalist troops at the Battle of King's Mountain on the border of the Carolinas.

Cornwallis found himself pinned down by frontier guerrillas, breaking free at the beginning of 1781, only to be fought to a bitter draw on March 15, 1781, at Guilford Courthouse, North Carolina. Undefeated but effectively neutralized, Cornwallis withdrew to Virginia, where he joined forces with a raiding unit led by the most notorious turncoat in American history, Benedict Arnold. Cornwallis reasoned that Virginia was the key to possession of the South, and, therefore, he established his headquarters at the port of Yorktown. While the British commander may have been correct in his strategic assumptions about the importance of Virginia, he had badly blundered in concentrating his army on a peninsula vulnerable to a land-and-sea blockade.

Washington recognized Cornwallis's error. He combined his Continental troops with the French army of the Comte de Rochambeau and laid siege to Yorktown on October 6, 1781. Simultaneously, a French fleet under Admiral de Grasse prevented a British evacuation by sea. On October 19, Cornwallis, bottled up at Yorktown, surrendered his eight thousand troops to the vastly superior forces of the Franco-American allies. Although fighting would not end until the conclusion of the **Declaration for Suspension of Arms and Cessation of Hostilities** on January 20, 1783, followed by the formal end to hostilities brought about by the **Treaty of Paris** on September 3, 1783, Yorktown, for all practical military purposes, decided the outcome of the Revolution.

Treaty of Alliance (with France)

SIGNED: February 6, 1778
SIGNATORIES: France vs. United States
IN FORCE: May 4, 1778
OVERVIEW: One of two major treaties concluded between France and the United States during the Revolution, the Treaty of Alliance created a military alliance between France and the United States, pending outbreak of war between France and Britain. (See also **Treaty of Amity and Commerce [with France].**)

DISCUSSION:

For a discussion of the background of the treaty, see **Treaty of Amity and Commerce (with France).**

The most important provision of the treaty is written in its first article:

> If War should break out between France and Great Britain, during the continuance of the present War between the United States and England, his Majesty and the said United States, shall make it a common cause, and aid each other mutually with their good Offices, their Counsels, and their forces, according to the exigence of Conjunctures as becomes good & faithful Allies.

In its second article, the treaty defines the objective of the alliance as a fight for the "liberty, Sovereignty, and independence" of the United States:

> The essential and direct End of the present defensive alliance is to maintain effectually the liberty, Sovereignty, and independence absolute and unlimited of the said united States, as well in Matters of Government as of commerce.

Articles 5 and 7 contemplate success in arms neither side would actually achieve in the course of the Revolution:

> Article 5: If the united States should think fit to attempt the Reduction of the British Power remaining in the Northern Parts of America, or the Islands of Bermudas, those Countries or Islands in case of Success, shall be confederated with or dependent upon the said united States.

> Article 7: If his Most Christian Majesty shall think proper to attack any of the Islands situated in the Gulph of Mexico, or near that Gulph, which are at present under the Power of Great Britain, all the said Isles, in case of success, shall appertain to the Crown of France.

Article 8 stipulates that "Neither of the two Parties shall conclude either Truce or Peace with Great Britain, without the formal consent of the other first obtain'd; and they mutually engage not to lay down their arms, until the Independence of the United States shall have been formally or tacitly assured by the Treaty or Treaties that shall terminate the War." In the intrigue surrounding the negotiation of the **Treaty of Paris** (1783), which ended the American Revolution, the treaty commissioners on behalf of the United States would violate this provision in negotiating with the British independently of the French.

REFERENCES:
Idzerda, Stanley J. *France and the American War for Independence.* New York: Scott Limited Editions, 1975.
McKown, Robin. *The American Revolution: French Allies.* New York: McGraw-Hill, 1969.
Perkins, James Breck. *France in the American Revolution.* Williamstown, MA: Corner House Publications, 1970.

Treaty of Amity and Commerce (with France)

SIGNED: February 6, 1778
SIGNATORIES: France vs. United States
IN FORCE: May 4, 1778
Overview: One of two major treaties concluded between France and the United States during the Revolution, the Treaty of Amity and Commerce conveys French recognition of United States independence. (See also **Treaty of Alliance [with France].**)

DISCUSSION:

As early as September 1775, the French government, always interested in ways to confound the British, sent a secret agent, Achard de Bonvouloir, to report on the situation in the colonies. Benjamin Franklin, with three other members of a five-man Committee of Correspondence set up by Congress in November 1775 to make contact with "our friends abroad," met with Achard de Bonvouloir. Congress was encouraged by the meeting to send Silas Deane, Congressman from Connecticut, to Paris in April 1776 for the purpose of purchasing (on credit) clothing and equipment for the Continental Army, as well as artillery and munitions. Deane was also instructed to open a dialogue on a possible alliance.

The French entered into the alliance at first cautiously and deviously. Charles Gravier, Comte de Vergennes, the French foreign minister, met with Pierre Augustin Caron de Beaumarchais, in 1775 best known as the author of *Le Barbier de Séville* (in 1784, he would revive the Figaro character in *Le Mariage de Figaro*), but also a creative and highly successful businessman. Vergennes authorized Beaumarchais to create a dummy company, christened Roderigue Hortalez & Cie, to launder money both France and Spain would secretly supply in support of the American Revolution.

On December 4, 1776, Benjamin Franklin arrived in Paris to begin negotiations for a full-scale treaty of alliance between the United States and France. On December 17, 1777, after learning of the American victory at Saratoga and impressed by George Washington's bold spirit at the Battle of Germantown—despite his defeat there—French authorities informed Franklin and the other American envoys in Paris that the government of Louis XVI would recognize American independence.

Two major treaties were concluded. The Treaty of Amity and Commerce formalized French recognition of American independence, and the Treaty of Alliance set up a military alliance pending the outbreak of war between France and England.

After the French ambassador to England informed the British government of the treaties, on May 13, the British ambassador was recalled from Paris, thereby severing diplomatic relations, and war between France and England followed a minor naval exchange on June 20.

The principal thrust of the Treaty of Amity and Commerce was to establish friendly relations between France and the United States and to lay down the regulations of free commerce between the signatories, essentially granting to one another most-favored nation status. Article 8 addressed the always-bothersome piracy of the Barbary States (see the treaties in Section 3.4):

> The most Christian King will employ his good Offices and Interposition with the King or Emperor of Morocco or Fez, the Regencies of Algier, Tunis and Tripoli, or with any of them, and also with every other Prince, State or Power of the Coast of Barbary in Africa, and the Subjects of the said King Emperor, States and Powers, and each of them; in order to provide as fully and efficaciously as possible for the Benefit, Conveniency and Safety of the said United States, and each of them, their Subjects, People, and Inhabitants, and their Vessels and Effects, against all Violence, Insult, Attacks, or Depredations on the Part of the said Princes and States of Barbary, or their Subjects.

But the most important consequence of the treaty was stated nowhere explicitly in the treaty. The very act of making a treaty with the "United States of America" meant that France became the first nation in the world to recognize the independence and sovereignty of the nation.

REFERENCES:

Idzerda, Stanley J. *France and the American War for Independence*. New York: Scott Limited Editions, 1975.

McKown, Robin. *The American Revolution: French Allies*. New York: McGraw-Hill, 1969.

Perkins, James Breck. *France in the American Revolution*. Williamstown, MA: Corner House Publications, 1970.

Act Separate and Secret (with France)

SIGNED: February 6, 1778

SIGNATORIES: France vs. United States

IN FORCE: May 4, 1778

OVERVIEW: A secret adjunct to the Treaty of Amity and Commerce (with France) and the Treaty of Alliance (with France), the Act Separate and Secret allowed for the eventual entry of Spain into the alliance between France and the United States.

DISCUSSION:

The Act Separate and Secret is as follows:

> The most Christian King (of France) declares in consequence of the intimate union which subsists between him and the King of Spain, that in concluding with the united states of America this Treaty of amity and commerce, and that of eventual and defensive alliance, his Majesty hath intended and intends to reserve expressly, as he reserves by this present separate and secret act, to his said Catholick Majesty (of Spain), the Power of acceding to the said Treatys, and to participate in their stipulations at such time as he shall judge proper. It being well understood nevertheless, that if any of the Stipulations of the said Treatys are not agreeable to the King of Spain, his Catholick Majesty may propose other conditions analogous to the principal aim of the alliance and conformable to the Rules of equality, reciprocity & friendship.

On April 12, 1779, by the Convention of Aranjuez, Spain and France concluded an alliance against Britain separate from that between France and the United States. Spain's objective was to win from Britain cession of Gibraltar, while France wanted to recover Senegal and Dominica, gain Newfoundland, and be returned to India. Although Spain supported the American fight against Britain (and effectively declared war on England on June 16, 1779), it did not acknowledge United States independence, for fear that an independent United States would begin to occupy Spanish possessions in Louisiana and Mexico. The Spanish crown also feared that independence would set a dangerous example for its own colonies in the Western Hemisphere.

REFERENCES:

Idzerda, Stanley J. *France and the American War for Independence*. New York: Scott Limited Editions, 1975.

McKown, Robin. *The American Revolution: French Allies*. New York: McGraw-Hill, 1969.

Perkins, James Breck. *France in the American Revolution*. Williamstown, MA: Corner House Publications, 1970.

Declaration for Suspension of Arms and Cessation of Hostilities

SIGNED: January 20, 1783, at Versailles

SIGNATORIES: Great Britain vs. United States

IN FORCE: From signing

OVERVIEW: The **Treaty of Paris,** signed on September 3, 1783, and in force from May 12, 1784, formally ended the American Revolution and acknowledged the independence of the United States, but it was this declaration that first brought an end to the shooting.

DISCUSSION:

The text of the brief declaration follows:

> We the underwritten Ministers Plenipotentiary of the United States of North America, having received from Mr Fitz-Herbert, Minister Plenipotentiary of his Britannic Majesty, a Declaration relative to a Suspension of Arms to be establish'd between his said Majesty and the said States, of which the following is a Copy. viz:
> Whereas the Preliminary Articles agreed to and signed this Day between his Majesty the King of Great Britain, and his most Christian Majesty on the one Part, and also between his said Britannic Majesty

and his Catholic Majesty on the other Part, stipulate a Cessation of Hostilities between those three Powers, which is to Commence upon the Exchange of the Ratifications of the said Preliminary Articles; And whereas by the Provisional Treaty signed the thirtieth of November last, between his Britannic Majesty and the United States of North America, it was stipulated that the said Treaty should have its Effect as soon as Peace between the said Crowns should be established; The underwritten Minister Plenipotentiary of his Britannic Majesty declares in the Name, and by the express, Order of the King his Master, that the said United States of North America, their Subjects and their Possessions, shall be comprised in the suspension of Arms above-mentioned, And that they shall consequently enjoy the Benefit of the Cessation of Hostilities, at the same Periods and in the same Manner as the three Crowns aforesaid and their Subjects and Possessions respectively On Condition however, that on the Part and in the Name of the Said United States of North America, there shall be deliver'd a similar Declaration expressing the Assent to the present Suspension of Arms, and containing an Assurance of the most perfect Reciprocity on their Part.

In faith whereof, we, the Minister Plenipotentiary of his Britannic Majesty, have signed this present Declaration, and have thereto caused the Seal of our Arms to be affixed, at Versailles this twentieth Day of January One Thousand seven hundred & Eighty three.

(signed)
ALLEYNE FITZ-HERBERT
(L.S.)

We have in the Name of the said United States of North America & in Virtue of the Powers we are vested with, received the above Declaration and do accept the same by these Presents, and we do reciprocally declare, that the said States shall cause to cease all Hostilities against his Britannic Majesty, his Subjects and Possessions at the Terms or Periods agreed to between his said Majesty the King of Great Britain, his Majesty the King of France, and his Majesty the King of Spain, in the same manner as is stipulated between these, three Crowns, and to have the same Effect.

In faith whereof, We Ministers Plenipotentiary from the United States of America, have signed the present Declaration and have hereunto affixed the Seals of our Arms. At Versailles the twentieth of January one thousand seven hundred and eighty three.

JOHN ADAMS.
B FRANKLIN.

REFERENCES:
Commanger, Henry Steele, and Richard B. Morris, eds. *The Spirit of Seventy-Six: The Story of the American Revolution as Told by Participants.* 1958; reprint ed., New York: Da Capo, 1995.
Greene, Jack P., and J. R. Pole, eds. *The Blackwell Encyclopedia of the American Revolution.* Cambridge, MA: Blackwell, 1994.
Israel, Fred L. *Major Peace Treaties of Modern History, 1648-1967,* vol. 1. New York: Chelsea House and McGraw-Hill, 1967.
Miller, Hunter, ed. *Treaties and Other International Act of the United States of America,* vol. 2. Washington: Government Printing Office, 1931.

Treaty of Paris

SIGNED: September 3, 1783, at Paris
IN FORCE: From May 12, 1784
SIGNATORIES: Great Britain vs. the United States
OVERVIEW: The Treaty of Paris ended the American Revolution and is the instrument by which Great Britain recognized the independence and sovereignty of the United States. The treaty further stipulates the boundaries between the United States and British Canada and reserves for the United States certain fishing rights off Newfoundland. Related documents guarantee freedom of navigation on the Mississippi River to the United States, Britain, France, Spain, and Holland, and restore Florida to Spain and Senegal to France.

DISCUSSION:

As early as 1759, disputes developed on a modest scale between the British mother country and its North American colonies over vetoes of measures enacted by colonial assemblies and other acts. The performance of the British army and the inept, often indifferent attitude of royal officials during the French and Indian War (1754-1763), followed by **The Proclamation of 1763,** issued by King George III, prohibiting settlement west of the Appalachian divide, greatly exacerbated anti-British sentiment, especially along the frontier. New taxes levied on colonial commerce, as well as the enforcement of existing taxes hitherto unenforced, hastened the decay in relations between the colonies and the mother country—especially because the colonies, though taxed by Parliament, were not represented in Parliament.

As colonial protest grew increasingly organized and militant, the crown responded by introducing increasingly restrictive and burdensome legislation and by garrisoning increased numbers of troops in colonial towns.

Following the Boston Tea Party (December 16, 1773), in which colonists, disguised as Indians, threw a cargo of boycotted tea into Boston Harbor, Parliament passed the so-called Intolerable Acts, which closed the port of Boston, interfered with town and provincial government, made royal officials and functionaries independent of colonial jurisdiction, and provided for the quartering of troops in Boston. This prompted the other colonies to rally to the defense of Massachusetts by forming a Continental Congress in September 1774 to denounce the acts. The British, in turn, sent more troops to Boston, and, at Lexington and Concord, the colonial militia and the British regulars clashed on April 19, 1775. The Revolution had begun—although a formal Declaration of Independence was not signed until July 4, 1776.

Although the Americans faced the mightiest military power of the age, the Patriot forces were led by George Washington, a commander of great skill, charisma, courage, and character. The revolutionary republic also benefitted from the services of extraordinary diplomats, most notably Benjamin Franklin, John Adams, and John Jay, who were able to secure aid from sympathetic foreign powers, especially France. If the Continental Army and the various colonial militias lost many of the war's formal "set" battles, they made the British victories costly. In wilderness warfare, colonial militia forces often outmaneuvered and outfought the redcoats. Moreover, while the Patriots enjoyed inspired leadership and all the advantages of fighting on familiar ground, the British government was politically divided, especially over the issue of American independence.

Until October 1781, the Revolution was essentially deadlocked, neither side scoring decisive victories. Then came the Battle of Yorktown (Virginia), in which Patriot forces, aided by a French naval fleet, defeated British General Charles Cornwallis, who surrendered nearly 8,000 troops on October 19, 1781. Although fighting continued for two more years, especially on the frontier, and although British armies continued to occupy some American cities, British leadership was reconciled to relinquishing the colonies, and American John Jay, Benjamin Franklin, and John Adams, the American peace negotiators in Paris, deftly exploited the rivalry between France and England by trading British recognition of colonial independence for an American promise to refrain from an alliance with France.

The brief treaty, remarkably plain in its language, consists of ten articles:

1. An acknowledgment that the colonies are "free sovereign and independent states"

2. A description of the boundaries of the United States

3. A stipulation of fishing rights "on the Grand Bank and on all the other banks of Newfoundland, also in the Gulf of Saint Lawrence and at all other places in the sea, where the inhabitants of both countries used at any time heretofore to fish."

4. An acknowledgment of debts incurred

5. A promise of congressional recommendation to the state legislatures that the property of "real British subjects" be restored to them

6. A pledge to refrain from reprisals "against any person or persons for, or by reason of, the part which he or they may have taken in the present war

7. A declaration of peace, including the withdrawal of all armies

8. A declaration of British and United States freedom to navigate the Mississippi River

9. An agreement to restore any territory conquered during the interval between executing and delivering the treaty

10. An assurance of speedy ratification of the treaty

It is significant that the Indians, deeply involved on both sides of the war, were not included in treaty negotiations, nor even mentioned in the treaty.

The full text of this seminal treaty in American history follows:

In the name of the most holy and undivided Trinity.

It having pleased the Divine Providence to dispose the hearts of the

most serene and most potent Prince George the Third, by the grace of God, king of Great Britain, France, and Ireland, defender of the faith, duke of Brunswick and Lunebourg, arch-treasurer and prince elector of the Holy Roman Empire etc., and of the United States of America, to forget all past misunderstandings and differences that have unhappily interrupted the good correspondence and friendship which they mutually wish to restore, and to establish such a beneficial and satisfactory intercourse, between the two countries upon the ground of reciprocal advantages and mutual convenience as may promote and secure to both perpetual peace and harmony; and having for this desirable end already laid the foundation of peace and reconciliation by the Provisional Articles signed at Paris on the 30th of November 1782, by the commissioners empowered on each part, which articles were agreed to be inserted in and constitute the Treaty of Peace proposed to be concluded between the Crown of Great Britain and the said United States, but which treaty was not to be concluded until terms of peace should be agreed upon between Great Britain and France and his Britannic Majesty should be ready to conclude such treaty accordingly; and the treaty between Great Britain and France having since been concluded, his Britannic Majesty and the United States of America, in order to carry into full effect the Provisional Articles above mentioned, according to the tenor thereof, have constituted and appointed, that is to say his Britannic Majesty on his part, David Hartley, Esqr., member of the Parliament of Great Britain, and the said United States on their part, John Adams, Esqr., late a commissioner of the United States of America at the court of Versailles, late delegate in Congress from the state of Massachusetts, and chief justice of the said state, and minister plenipotentiary of the said United States to their high mightinesses the States General of the United Netherlands; Benjamin Franklin, Esqr., late delegate in Congress from the state of Pennsylvania, president of the convention of the said state, and minister plenipotentiary from the United States of America at the court of Versailles; John Jay, Esqr., late president of Congress and chief justice of the state of New York, and minister plenipotentiary from the said United States at the court of Madrid; to be plenipotentiaries for the concluding and signing the present definitive treaty; who after having reciprocally communicated their respective full powers have agreed upon and confirmed the following articles.

Article 1:

His Brittanic Majesty acknowledges the said United States, viz., New Hampshire, Massachusetts Bay, Rhode Island and Providence Plantations, Connecticut, New York, New Jersey, Pennsylvania, Maryland, Virginia, North Carolina, South Carolina and Georgia, to be free sovereign and independent states, that he treats with them as such, and for himself, his heirs, and successors, relinquishes all claims to the government, propriety, and territorial rights of the same and every part thereof.

Article 2:

And that all disputes which might arise in future on the subject of the boundaries of the said United States may be prevented, it is hereby agreed and declared, that the following are and shall be their boundaries, viz.; from the northwest angle of Nova Scotia, viz., that angle which is formed by a line drawn due north from the source of St. Croix River to the highlands; along the said highlands which divide those rivers that empty themselves into the river St. Lawrence, from those which fall into the Atlantic Ocean, to the northwesternmost head of Connecticut River; thence down along the middle of that river to the forty-fifth degree of north latitude; from thence by a line due west on said latitude until it strikes the river Iroquois or Cataraquy; thence along the middle of said river into Lake Ontario; through the middle of said lake until it strikes the communication by water between that lake and Lake Erie; thence along the middle of said communication into Lake Erie, through the middle of said lake until it arrives at the water communication between that lake and Lake Huron; thence along the middle of said water communication into Lake Huron, thence through the middle of said lake to the water communication between that lake and Lake Superior; thence through Lake Superior northward of the Isles Royal and Phelipeaux to the Long Lake; thence through the middle of said Long Lake and the water communication between it and the Lake of the Woods, to the said Lake of the Woods; thence through the said lake to the most northwesternmost point thereof, and from thence on a due west course to the river Mississippi; thence by a line to be drawn along the middle of the said river Mississippi until it shall intersect the northernmost part of the thirty-first degree of north latitude, South, by a line to be drawn due east from the determination of the line last mentioned in the latitude of thirty-one degrees of the equator, to the middle of the river Apalachicola or Catahouche; thence along the middle thereof to its junction with the Flint River, thence straight to the head of Saint Mary's River; and thence down along the middle of Saint Mary's River to the Atlantic Ocean; east, by a line to be drawn along the middle of the river Saint Croix, from its mouth in the Bay of Fundy to its source, and from its source directly north to the aforesaid highlands which divide the rivers that fall into the Atlantic Ocean from those which fall into the river Saint Lawrence; comprehending all islands within twenty leagues of any part of the shores of the United States, and lying between lines to be drawn due east from the points where the aforesaid boundaries between Nova Scotia on the one part and East Florida on the other shall, respectively, touch the Bay of Fundy and the Atlantic Ocean, excepting such islands as now are or heretofore have been within the limits of the said province of Nova Scotia.

Article 3:

It is agreed that the people of the United States shall continue to enjoy unmolested the right to take fish of every kind on the Grand Bank and on all the other banks of Newfoundland, also in the Gulf of Saint Lawrence and at all other places in the sea, where the inhabitants of both countries used at any time heretofore to fish. And also that the inhabitants of the United States shall have liberty to take fish of every kind on such part of the coast of Newfoundland as British fishermen shall use, (but not to dry or cure the same on that island) and also on the coasts, bays and creeks of all other of his Brittanic Majesty's dominions in America; and that the American fishermen shall have liberty to dry and cure fish in any of the unsettled bays, harbors, and creeks of Nova Scotia, Magdalen Islands, and Labrador, so long as the same shall remain unsettled, but so soon as the same or either of them shall be settled, it shall not be lawful for the said fishermen to dry or cure fish at such settlement without a previous agreement for that purpose with the inhabitants, proprietors, or possessors of the ground.

Article 4:

It is agreed that creditors on either side shall meet with no lawful impediment to the recovery of the full value in sterling money of all bona fide debts heretofore contracted.

Article 5:

It is agreed that Congress shall earnestly recommend it to the legislatures of the respective states to provide for the restitution of all estates, rights, and properties, which have been confiscated belonging to real British subjects; and also of the estates, rights, and properties of persons resident in districts in the possession on his Majesty's arms and who have not borne arms against the said United States. And that persons of any other description shall have free liberty to go to any part or parts of any of the thirteen United States and therein to remain twelve months unmolested in their endeavors to obtain the restitution of such of their estates, rights, and properties as may have been confiscated; and that Congress shall also earnestly recommend to the several states a reconsideration and revision of all acts or laws regarding the premises, so as to render the said laws or acts perfectly consistent not only with justice and equity but with that spirit of conciliation which on the return of the blessings of peace should universally prevail. And that Congress shall also earnestly recommend to the several states that the estates, rights, and properties, of such last mentioned persons shall be restored to them, they refunding to any persons who may be now in possession the bona fide price (where any has been given) which such persons may have paid on purchasing any of the said lands, rights, or properties since the confiscation.

And it is agreed that all persons who have any interest in confiscated lands, either by debts, marriage settlements, or otherwise, shall meet with no lawful impediment in the prosecution of their just rights.

Article 6:

That there shall be no future confiscations made nor any prosecutions commenced against any person or persons for, or by reason of, the part which he or they may have taken in the present war, and that no person shall on that account suffer any future loss or damage, either in his person, liberty, or property; and that those who may be in confinement on such charges at the time of the ratification of the treaty in America shall be immediately set at liberty, and the prosecutions so commenced be discontinued.

Article 7:

There shall be a firm and perpetual peace between his Brittanic Majesty and the said states, and between the subjects of the one and the citizens of the other, wherefore all hostilities both by sea and land shall from henceforth cease. All prisoners on both sides shall be set at liberty, and his Brittanic Majesty shall with all convenient speed, and without causing any destruction, or carrying away any Negroes or other property of the American inhabitants, withdraw all his armies, garrisons, and fleets from the said United States, and from every post, place, and harbor within the same; leaving in all fortifications, the American artillery that may be therein; and shall also order and cause all archives, records, deeds, and papers belonging to any of the said states, or their citizens, which in the course of the war may have fallen into the hands of his officers, to be forthwith restored and delivered to the proper states and persons to whom they belong.

Article 8:

The navigation of the river Mississippi, from its source to the ocean, shall forever remain free and open to the subjects of Great Britain and the citizens of the United States.

Article 9:

In case it should so happen that any place or territory belonging to Great Britain or to the United States should have been conquered by the arms of either from the other before the arrival of the said

Provisional Articles in America, it is agreed that the same shall be restored without difficulty and without requiring any compensation.

Article 10:

The solemn ratifications of the present treaty expedited in good and due form shall be exchanged between the contracting parties in the space of six months or sooner, if possible, to be computed from the day of the signatures of the present treaty. In witness whereof we the undersigned, their ministers plenipotentiary, have in their name and in virtue of our full powers, signed with our hands the present definitive treaty and caused the seals of our arms to be affixed thereto.

Done at Paris, this third day of September in the year of our Lord, one thousand seven hundred and eighty-three.

D. HARTLEY (SEAL) JOHN ADAMS (SEAL)
B. FRANKLIN (SEAL) JOHN JAY (SEAL)

REFERENCES:

Commanger, Henry Steele, and Richard B. Morris, eds. *The Spirit of Seventy-Six: The Story of the American Revolution as Told by Participants.* 1958; reprint ed., New York: Da Capo, 1995.

Greene, Jack P., and J. R. Pole, eds. *The Blackwell Encyclopedia of the American Revolution.* Cambridge, MA: Blackwell, 1994.

Israel, Fred L. *Major Peace Treaties of Modern History, 1648-1967,* vol. 1. New York: Chelsea House and McGraw-Hill, 1967.

Exchange of Notes Referring to Articles 2 and 3 of the Treaty of Amity and Commerce (with France)

SIGNED: August 27, 1784, at Versailles

SIGNATORIES: France vs. United States

IN FORCE: From signing

OVERVIEW: An exchange of notes guaranteeing that the United States will maintain trade with France on a most favored nation basis.

DISCUSSION:

The **Treaty of Amity and Commerce (with France),** concluded before the United States had won its independence, was the nation's first trade and commerce treaty. Having achieved independence, the United States then agreed to guarantee France the status of most favored nation in matters of trade. This exchange of notes, modifying the Treaty of Amity and Commerce, is, therefore, the first most-favored-nation agreement concluded by the United States.

The exchange follows, first from the French minister, Gravier de Vergennes:

Versailles
27th August, 1784.

SIR:

You have communicated to me an extract from the instructions which Congress addressed to you the 11th May last, which imports that the United States will in no case treat any other nation, with respect to commerce, more advantageously than the French. This disposition is much the wisest, as it will prevent those misunderstandings which might arise from the equivocal terms in which the second article of the Treaty of Amity and Commerce signed 6th February, 1778, is conceived. But that the resolution of Congress on this subject may be clearly stated, it would be best, Sir, that you furnish me with it in the form of a declaration, or at least in an official note signed by yourself. I have no doubt, Sir, but that you will adopt one of these two forms.

I have the honor to be, etc.

GRAVIER DE VERGENNES
PASSY, Sept. 3, 1784

Then this reply from the United States' minister to France, Benjamin Franklin:

SIR,

I have the Honour to transmit to your Excellency by Order of Congress a Resolution of theirs, dated the 11th of May last, which is in the Words following, Viz,

"Resolved,

That Doctor Franklin be instructed to express to the Court of France the constant Desire of Congress to meet their Wishes; That these States are about to form a general System of Commerce by Treaties with other Nations: That at this Time they cannot foresee what Claim might be given to those Nations by the explanatory Propositions from the Count de Vergennes on the 2d & 3d Articles of our Treaty of Amity & Commerce with His most Christian Majesty; but that he may be assured it will be our constant Care to place no People on more advantageous Ground than the Subjects of his Majesty."

With great Respect I am. Sir, Your Excellency's, most obedient and most humble Servant.

VERSAILLES,
9th September, 1784
B. Franklin

To which the French minister replied:

SIR:

I have received the letter which you did me the honor to write me the third instant. You there declare in the name of Congress that the United States will be careful not to treat any other nation, in matters of commerce, more advantageously than the French nation. This declaration, founded on the treaty of the 6th February, 1778, has been very agreeable to the King; and you, Sir, can assure Congress that the United States shall constantly experience a perfect reciprocity in France.

I have the honor to be, etc.,

GRAVIER DE VERGENNES

REFERENCES:

Idzerda, Stanley J. *France and the American War for Independence.* New York: Scott Limited Editions, 1975.

McKown, Robin. *The American Revolution: French Allies.* New York: McGraw-Hill, 1969.

Perkins, James Breck. *France in the American Revolution.* Williamstown, MA: Corner House Publications, 1970.

U.S.-Barbary States Wars, Quasi-War with France, and War of 1812

Overview of the Conflicts

In the aftermath of the American Revolution, the most pressing military problems the young republic faced were internal: the ongoing guerilla warfare between the Indians and settlers of the frontier regions, especially in the Ohio country. But before the eighteenth century ended, the new nation found itself threatened from very far away.

The "Barbary pirates" were Muslim seafarers who had been operating from the so-called Barbary states (present-day Morocco, Algeria, Tunisia, and Libya) off the coast of North Africa since the seventeenth century. The pirates were not mere outlaws, but enjoyed the financial and political backing of wealthy merchants and national leaders. To avoid harassment, capture, and confiscation of cargoes, "Christian" nations plying North African waters routinely paid extortionary tribute money to the Barbary states. Initially, the United States, like other nations, paid the tributes demanded, but this situation was perceived as an insult and threat to American sovereignty, and the United States successfully fought a series of limited naval wars to win the right of free navigation of the North African waters.

The Barbary Wars spanned 1801 to 1815, with the most concentrated action occurring in the Tripolitan-American War of 1801-1805, which was successfully concluded by the **Treaty of Tripoli** (1805). United States warships routinely were employed to combat the resurgence of piracy and to enforce the various Barbary treaties, including **Treaty of Peace and Friendship (with Morocco)** of 1786, **Treaty of Peace and Amity (with Algiers)** of 1795, **Treaty of Peace and Friendship (with Tripoli)** of 1796, and **Treaty with Tunis** of 1797, in addition to the 1805 **Treaty of Tripoli;** however, during the War of 1812, the warships were withdrawn from North African waters, and some of the Barbary pirates became highly active again. This led to the Algerine War of March 3-June 30, 1815, in which the United States brought an end to Algerian piracy. General Barbary piracy did sporadically continue into the 1830s, however, and the final United States treaty relating to the issue was not concluded until 1836 (**Treaty of Peace [with Morocco]**).

The end of the eighteenth century also saw a breakdown in relations between the United States and its Revolutionary War ally, France. Friction between the two nations had begun during peace negotiations ending the Revolution, when it became apparent that France was more interested in checkmating Britain and furthering the North American territorial ambitions

of its anti-British ally Spain than it was committed to furthering the interests of the United States. The fall of the Bourbon monarchy in the French Revolution caused a further deterioration in Franco-American relations because the French believed that United States policy now favored the British. In particular, **Jay's Treaty** of 1794 (Section 1.1) was regarded as an outright betrayal. Seeking to heal the rift, President John Adams sent a special mission to Paris in 1797. French Prime Minister Talleyrand imperiously demanded a bribe before he would grant the American commissioners an audience, an outrage that came to light as the infamous XYZ Affair and nearly brought France and the United States to outright war. As it was, French naval operations against the British in the West Indies had begun to interfere with American shipping. The crisis intensified, George Washington was recalled from retirement to command the army, and a U.S. Navy department was created on May 3, 1798. In November of that year, a French warship captured an American schooner off Guadaloupe, and on February 9, 1799, an American frigate, the *Constellation*, captured the French frigate *Insurgente*. Although additional exchanges took place sporadically through 1800, a full-fledged war never developed, and the **Convention between the French Republic and the United States of America** (1800) brought an end to what historians call the Naval Quasi-War with France by ensuring freedom of navigation.

Far more serious than the situation with France was the deterioration of Anglo-American relations. Generations of American schoolchildren have been taught that the War of 1812 began because the British, at war with Napoleon and in need of sailors for the Royal Navy, made it a practice to intercept and board United States merchant vessels on the high seas in order to "impress"—that is, abduct—American sailors into His Majesty's service. While it is true that the Royal Navy did intercept ships and impress men (albeit only those judged, unilaterally and on the spot, to be British subjects), the United States' declaration of war on Britain was not made until June 19, 1812, three days after Britain had agreed to stop impressing seamen from American vessels. The true cause of the war was less an issue of freedom of navigation than it was a symptom of land hunger. In Congress, the trans-Appalachian West was represented by a group of so-called "War Hawks," led by Representative Henry Clay of Kentucky. They saw war with Britain as an opportunity to gain relief from British-backed hostile Indians and as a chance to acquire what was then called Spanish Florida, a vast tract extending from present-day Florida west to the Mississippi River. Spain, which nominally held this land, was currently allied with Britain against Napoleon. War with Britain would, perforce, mean war with Spain, and victory would mean the acquisition of Spanish Florida and the completion of an unbroken territorial link from the Atlantic, through the recently purchased Louisiana Territory, clear to the Pacific. In a stroke, the United States would become a truly continental nation.

The military prowess of the early republic may have sufficed to quell the Barbary pirates and to deal with French naval operations in the West Indies, but it was hardly adequate to go up against the might of Great Britain. At the commencement of the war, the United States Army consisted of twelve thousand regular troops broadcast over a vast territory and led by commanders whose rank was often the product of political connections rather than military training or achievement. The U.S. Navy was better led, but its handful of ships would count for little if Britain chose to pitch any considerable portion of the Royal Navy—biggest in the world—against it.

Despite all shortcomings, U.S. strategists developed a grandiose plan for a three-pronged invasion of Canada. Armies would penetrate Canada from Lake Champlain to Montreal; from across the Niagara frontier; and from Detroit into Upper Canada.

Planning was one thing; execution another. The ineptly led American forces north of the Ohio River—three hundred regulars and 1,200 militiamen—left Detroit and marched into Canada on July 12, 1812. After three weeks, with barely a fight, the force retreated to Fort Detroit, which was surrendered to the British on August 16. Not a shot had been fired in the fort's defense.

In the fall, New York militia general Stephen Van Rensselaer led 2,270 militiamen and 900 regulars in an assault on Queenston Heights, Canada, just across the Niagara River. Part of this force, mostly the regulars, got across the river before being pinned down by the British. The remainder of Van Rensselaer's army, state militiamen, refused to cross the international boundary and stood idly by as 600 British regulars and 400 Canadian militiamen mauled and defeated their countrymen.

The principal American force had yet to attack. But it never would. Major General Henry Dearborn led five thousand troops, mostly militia, down Lake Champlain and, on November 19, was poised to cross into Canada. At this point, the militiamen asserted their "constitutional rights" and refused to fight in a foreign country. Dearborn had no choice but to withdraw without engaging the enemy.

In the opening months of the war, Detroit, Fort Dearborn (present-day Chicago), and the Canadian campaign had all collapsed, leaving the West, which had hungered for war, thor-

oughly vulnerable to Indian raids and British invasion. Fortunately for the Americans, the British commanders in the western theater lacked the initiative of their great Indian warrior ally, Tecumseh, and failed to press their advantage. Nevertheless, by the fall of 1813, 4,000 American regulars and militiamen had been killed or captured in the West, whereas combined British and Indian losses amounted to no more than 500.

In contrast to the dismal American performance on land, the fledgling U.S. Navy performed brilliantly with fourteen commissioned ships and a ragtag flotilla of privateers against 1,048 Royal Navy vessels brought to blockade U.S. naval and commercial shipping. Despite a series of American naval victories, however, the blockade remained effective enough to bring the fragile U.S. economy to the verge of collapse.

In the fall of 1813, after so much disaster in the West, General William Henry Harrison assembled an army of 8,000 men while a dashing young naval officer named Oliver Hazard Perry hastily built an inland navy. On September 10, Perry engaged the British fleet on Lake Erie and, in an intense battle, destroyed the entire British squadron, thereby cutting off British supply lines and forcing the abandonment of Fort Malden (near Detroit), as well as prompting a general British retreat from the Detroit region. On October 5, 1813, Harrison overtook the retreating British and their Indian allies at the Battle of the Thames. There Tecumseh fell, and, with him, the Indians' last realistic hope of halting the northwestward rush of American settlement also died. This had been the basis of the Indian alliance with the British, and, with Tecumseh's death, this alliance began to fall apart as well.

The American victories in the West, so long in coming, might have turned the tide of the war had it not been for the defeat of Napoleon in Europe and his first exile, to Elba. With Napoleon neutralized, British forces could now concentrate on North America. More ships and fresh troops arrived to attack three principal targets: in New York, along Lake Champlain and the Hudson River, in order to sever New England from the rest of the union; at New Orleans, to block the vital Mississippi artery; and in Chesapeake Bay, a vast diversionary maneuver designed to draw off U.S. manpower. By the fall of 1814, the situation looked very bleak for the United States. The nation's economy was in shambles, and, in New England, bitter opponents of the war had even begun talking about seceding from the Union. Late in the summer of 1814, the British triumphed in Maryland at the Battle of Bladensburg (August 24), then invaded Washington, D.C., where they burned most of the public buildings, including the Capitol and the White House—as President James Madison and most of the government were sent fleeing into the countryside. The next objective was Baltimore, which, however, offered stiff resistance. A young Baltimore lawyer named Francis Scott Key (1779-1843), detained on a British warship in Baltimore Harbor, witnessed the British bombardment of Fort McHenry during the night of September 13-14,

1814. At dawn, the sight of the "Star-Spangled Banner" confirmed that the fort had not fallen. The British broke off the attack and withdrew.

As Washington burned and Baltimore reeled under attack, a force of 10,000 British veterans of the Napoleonic wars was advancing into the United States from Montreal. On September 11, 1814, Captain Thomas MacDonough, U.S. Navy, met and defeated the British fleet on Lake Champlain, a blow sufficiently stunning to send the advancing British army into retreat. The failure of this major offensive contributed to the war weariness of Britain, exhausted by years of combat against Napoleon and frustrated by what it regarded as a nasty little war in North America. American and British negotiators met in the Flemish city of Ghent and concluded the **Treaty of Ghent** (December 24, 1814), which restored the *"status quo antebellum"*—things as they had been before the war. Of course, in 1814, trans-Atlantic communication was hardly instantaneous. Word of the Treaty of Ghent did not reach General Andrew Jackson as he moved on to New Orleans to engage 7,500 British veterans sailing from Jamaica to attack the city.

Jackson's forces, consisting of 3,100 Tennessee and Kentucky volunteers, in addition to New Orleans militiamen and a ragtag mob of locals, triumphed against the British, who withdrew from the field on January 8, 1815. Although the War of 1812 had actually ended in December 1814, victory in the Battle of New Orleans made many Americans feel that the reckless, disastrous, and economically ruinous War of 1812 had been a triumph after all.

In addition to the **Treaty of Ghent**, this section includes the **Cartel for the Exchange of Prisoners of War between Great Britain and the United States of America** (1812), an early example of an agreement on prisoner exchange. Neither the British nor the Americans wished to repeat the situation that had prevailed during the American Revolution, in which prisoners of war were subjected to inhumane neglect, many of them perishing from disease and hunger.

Treaty of Peace and Friendship (with Morocco)

SIGNED: June 28, 1786 and July 15, 1786, at Morocco
SIGNATORIES: Morocco vs. United States
IN FORCE: From July 18, 1787
OVERVIEW: An early attempt to put an end to the piracy against American vessels in the waters off Morocco.

DISCUSSION:
Morocco, like the other Barbary States, routinely perpetrated acts of piracy against ships of the United States and other non-Muslim countries. Extortionary tribute money was paid to Morocco and the other states as protection against this practice, which nevertheless persisted. The treaty makes no mention of the tribute

money, but does specify that "Commerce with the United States shall be on the same footing as is the Commerce with Spain or as that with the most favored Nation for the time being and their Citizens shall be respected and esteemed and have full Liberty to pass and repass our Country and Sea Ports whenever they please without interruption."

Like the other early treaties with the Barbary States, this one was mostly ineffective, and Barbary States piracy was not curbed until the United States fought the Tripolitan War (1800-1805) and the Algerine War (1815).

REFERENCES:
Chidsey, Donald Barr. *The Wars in Barbary: Arab Piracy and the United States Navy.* New York: Crown, 1971.
Nash, Howard Prevear. *The Forgotten Wars: The Role of the U.S. Navy in the Quasi-War with France and the Barbary Wars, 1798-1805.* South Brunswick, NJ: A. S. Barnes, 1968.
United States Office of Naval Records and Library. *Naval Documents Related to the United States Wars with the Barbary Powers . . . Including Diplomatic Background.* Washington, D.C.: U.S. Government Printing Office, 1939-44.

Treaty of Peace and Amity (with Algiers)

SIGNED: September 5, 1795, at Algiers
SIGNATORIES: Algeria vs. United States
IN FORCE: From March 7, 1796
OVERVIEW: A treaty aimed at ending piracy along the Barbary coast.

DISCUSSION:
For many years, the Muslim pirates of the Barbary States—Tripoli, Tunis, Algiers, and Morocco—routinely extorted tribute payments from the ships of Christian nations, the United States included, plying the waters of the Mediterranean off North Africa. Sailors were always in danger of capture and enslavement in these waters. The 1795 treaty was aimed at ending the piracy, but not the tribute payment, which is alluded to only as "the usual duties . . . paid by all nations at Peace with this Regency."

The treaty reduced but did not end the Algerian piracy. See **Treaty of Peace (with Algiers)**, 1815.

REFERENCES:
Chidsey, Donald Barr. *The Wars in Barbary: Arab Piracy and the United States Navy.* New York: Crown, 1971.
Nash, Howard Prevear. *The Forgotten Wars: The Role of the U.S. Navy in the Quasi-War with France and the Barbary Wars, 1798-1805.* South Brunswick, NJ: A. S. Barnes, 1968.
United States Office of Naval Records and Library. *Naval Documents Related to the United States Wars with the Barbary Powers . . . Including Diplomatic Background.* Washington, D.C.: U.S. Government Printing Office, 1939-44.

Treaty of Peace and Friendship (with Tripoli)

SIGNED: November 4, 1796, at Tripoli, and, January 3, 1797, at Algiers

SIGNATORIES: Tripoli vs. United States

IN FORCE: From June 10, 1797

OVERVIEW: An early treaty with Tripoli, aimed at securing protection from piracy in return for a lump-sum tribute payment.

DISCUSSION:

Tripoli, like the other Barbary States, routinely demanded annual payments of tribute from non-Muslim nations as protection against state-sponsored piracy. This treaty was an American effort to resolve the issue of piracy and tribute with a lump-sum payment to the Bey of Tripoli, as stipulated in Article 10:

> The money and presents demanded by the Bey of Tripoli as a full and satisfactory consideration on his part and on the part of his subjects for this treaty of perpetual peace and friendship are acknowledged to have been received by him previous to his signing the same, according to a receipt which is hereto annexed, except such part as is promised on the part of the United States to be delivered and paid by them on the arrival of their Consul in Tripoli, of which part a note is likewise hereto annexed. And no presence of any periodical tribute or farther payment is ever to be made by either party.

The peace did not hold, and piracy, as well as tribute demands, persisted, culminating in the Tripolitan War of 1800-1805. As a result of the war, the United States discontinued all tribute payment to Tripoli, but continued to pay tribute to the other Barbary States until the conclusion of the Algerine War in 1815 (see **Treaty of Peace (with Algiers)**, 1815).

REFERENCES:

Chidsey, Donald Barr. *The Wars in Barbary: Arab Piracy and the United States Navy.* New York: Crown, 1971.

Nash, Howard Prevear. *The Forgotten Wars: The Role of the U.S. Navy in the Quasi-War with France and the Barbary Wars, 1798-1805.* South Brunswick, NJ: A. S. Barnes, 1968.

United States Office of Naval Records and Library. *Naval Documents Related to the United States Wars with the Barbary Powers...Including Diplomatic Background.* Washington, D.C.: U.S. Government Printing Office, 1939-44.

Treaty with Tunis

SIGNED: August 28, 1797, and, with alterations, March 26, 1799, at Tunis

SIGNATORIES: Tunis and the "Ottoman nation" vs. United States

IN FORCE: From January 10, 1800

OVERVIEW: An early attempt to put an end to the piracy against American vessels in the waters off Tunis.

DISCUSSION:

One of several treaties made with the Barbary States, the Treaty with Tunis specified duties and other taxes to be paid by American vessels entering the Tunisian port. Although the treaty was directed against acts of piracy and abduction, it specifically recognized the "corsairs" of Tunis as, in effect, military personnel. Article 11 stipulates the protocol of salutation for American vessels as well as those of the corsairs:

> When a vessel of war of the United States of America shall enter the port of Tunis, and the Consul shall request that the castle may salute her, the number of guns shall be fired which he may request; and if the said Consul does not want a salute, there shall be no question about it. But in case he shall desire the salute, and the number of guns shall be fired which he may have requested, they shall be counted and returned by the vessel in as many barrels of cannon powder.
>
> The same shall be done with respect to the Tunisian corsairs when they shall enter any port of the United States.

Like the other early treaties with the Barbary States, this one did not succeed in ending piracy or in curbing the increasing demand for extortionary payment of tribute and protection from piracy. Barbary State piracy was greatly reduced after the United States fought the Tripolitan War (1800-1805) and the Algerine War (1815).

REFERENCES:

Chidsey, Donald Barr. *The Wars in Barbary: Arab Piracy and the United States Navy.* New York: Crown, 1971.

Nash, Howard Prevear. *The Forgotten Wars: The Role of the U.S. Navy in the Quasi-War with France and the Barbary Wars, 1798-1805.* South Brunswick, NJ: A. S. Barnes, 1968.

United States Office of Naval Records and Library. *Naval Documents Related to the United States Wars with the Barbary Powers...Including Diplomatic Background.* Washington, D.C.: U.S. Government Printing Office, 1939-44.

Convention between the French Republic and the United States of America

SIGNED: September 30, 1800, at Paris

SIGNATORIES: France vs. United States

IN FORCE: From December 21, 1801

OVERVIEW: The treaty ended the "Quasi-War," a naval conflict between France and the United States (1798-1800).

DISCUSSION:

Friction between France and the United States, close allies during the Revolution, began in the course of the peace negotiations ending the Revolution, as it became clear that France was more interested in opposing Britain and furthering the territorial ambitions of its ally Spain than in truly upholding the cause of United States independence. With the fall of the Bourbon monarchy in the French Revolution and renewed warfare between France and

Britain in 1793, relations deteriorated further as United States policy was perceived to favor the British over the French. The French regarded **Jay's Treaty** with Britain (1794) as a betrayal. When President John Adams sent a special mission to Paris in 1797 with the object of patching up the relationship, Prime Minister Talleyrand imperiously demanded a bribe from the Americans, leading to the infamous XYZ Affair. After this, the two nations tottered on the brink of outright war as French naval operations in the West Indies interfered with American shipping. George Washington was recalled to command the army, and a navy department was established on May 3, 1798. In November of that year, a French warship captured an American schooner off Guadaloupe, and on February 9, 1799, an American frigate, the *Constellation*, captured the French frigate *Insurgente*. Additional sporadic exchanges took place through 1800.

The treaty of 1800 was intended specifically to ensure freedom of navigation. A list of contraband goods (war materiel, subject to confiscation by either side) was enumerated; however, except for this contraband, "it shall be lawful for the Citizens of either Country to sail with their ships and Merchandize . . . from any port whatever, to any port of the enemy of the other, and to sail, and trade with their ships, and Merchandize, with perfect security, and liberty, from the countries ports, and places, of those who are enemies of both, or of either party, without any opposition, or disturbance whatsoever, and to pass not only directly from the places and ports of the enemy aforementioned to neutral ports, and places, but also from one place belonging to an enemy, to another place belonging to an enemy, whether they be under the jurisdiction of the same power, or under several, unless such ports, or places shall be actually blockaded, besieged, or invested." This clause not only directly addressed the source of the "Quasi-War" conflict, but, while reinstating friendly relations, effectively ended any implied military alliance between France and the United States.

REFERENCE:
Palmer, Michael A. *Stoddert's War: Naval Operations During the Quasi-War with France, 1798-1801.* 1987; reprint ed., Annapolis, MD: United States Naval Institute, 1999.

Treaty of Tripoli

SIGNED: June 4, 1805, at Tripoli, Barbary (present-day Libya)
IN FORCE: Ratified April 17, 1806
SIGNATORIES: United States vs. Tripoli
OVERVIEW: This treaty ended the Tripolitan War (1801-05) between the United States and Tripoli (one of the so-called Barbary States); in so doing, it also ended extortion payments ("tribute") the United States had been obliged to make to the Barbary Coast pirates.

DISCUSSION:
Like other Western nations before 1801, the United States routinely negotiated extortionate ("tribute") treaties with the North African Barbary States (Tripoli, Algiers, Morocco, and Tunis) to secure unmolested passage of merchant vessels through the Mediterranean. In 1801, the bashaw of Tripoli repudiated his treaty with the United States and declared war. President Thomas Jefferson dispatched the navy's Mediterranean squadron in a show of force that discouraged the other Barbary States from backing Tripoli. With Tripoli thus isolated, Commodore Edward Preble bombarded and blockaded Tripoli during 1803-1805, and Lieutenant Stephen Decatur entered Tripoli harbor, where he burned the frigate *Philadelphia*, which had been taken by Tripoli as a prize. Simultaneously with these naval actions, William Eaton led U.S. marines in a land campaign. Under these combined assaults, the bashaw sued for peace, and the resulting treaty, while it set a ransom for American prisoners, ended the annual tribute payments.

The treaty established free and unhindered commerce between the United States and Tripoli, but made no mention of the tribute money previously paid. Such mention would have tended to legitimate an act of extortion, and the U.S. treaty negotiators were at pains to avoid imparting any air of legality to the repudiated practice. Instead, the treaty affirms free and unmolested commerce by sea. Article II of the treaty provides for a $60,000 ransom to be paid for the release of Americans (captured sailors) presently under Tripolitan control.

Article 14 of the treaty seeks to avoid conflict arising from religious issues:

> As the Government of the United States of America, has in itself no character of enmity against the Laws, Religion or Tranquility of Musselmen, and as the said States never have entered into any voluntary war or act of hostility against any Mahometan Nation, except in the defence of their just rights to freely navigate the High Seas: It is declared by the contracting parties that no pretext arising from Religious Opinions, shall ever produce an interruption of the Harmony existing between the two Nations; And the Consuls and Agents of both Nations respectively, shall have liberty to exercise his Religion in his own house; all slaves of the same Religion shall not be Impeded in going to said Consuls house at hours of Prayer.

(Article 11 of the earlier, extortionate, treaty of January 3, 1797 goes even further to distance the United States from a religious agenda: "As the government of the United States of America is not in any sense founded on the Christian Religion, as it has in itself no character of enmity against the laws, religion or tranquility of Musselmen, and as the said States never have entered into any war or act of hostility against any Mehomitan nation, it is declared by the parties that no pretext arising from religious opinions shall ever produce an interruption of the harmony existing between the two countries.")

Victory in the Tripolitan War enhanced the prestige of the young American republic; however, the Treaty of Tripoli did not put an end to all piracy on the Barbary Coast. In 1815, the United States declared war on Algiers over ongoing, state-sanctioned acts of piracy. This war resulted in the permanent establishment of a United States naval squadron in the Mediterranean to enforce an end to piracy.

REFERENCES:

Israel, Fred L. *Major Peace Treaties of Modern History, 1648-1967*, vol. 1. New York: Chelsea House and McGraw-Hill, 1967).

Kitzen, Michael L. S. *Tripoli and the United States at War: A History of American Relations with the Barbary States, 1785-1805.* Jefferson, NC: McFarland, 1993.

Wright, Louis B. *The First Americans in North Africa: William Eaton's Struggle for a Vigorous Policy Against the Barbary Pirates, 1799-1805.* 1945; reprint ed., Westport, CT: Greenwood Press, 1969.

Cartel for the Exchange of Prisoners of War between Great Britain and the United States of America

SIGNED: November 28, 1812, at Halifax, Nova Scotia

SIGNATORIES: Great Britain vs. United States

IN FORCE: From May 12, 1813

OVERVIEW: Concluded during the War of 1812, this "cartel" governed the treatment and exchange of naval prisoners of war.

DISCUSSION:

Article I is the heart of the treaty:

The Prisoners taken at sea or on land on both sides shall be treated with humanity conformable to the usage and practice of the most civilized nations during war; and such prisoners shall without delay, and as speedily as circumstances will admit, be exchanged on the following terms and conditions. That is to say—An admiral or a General commanding in chief shall be exchanged for officers of equal rank or for sixty men each: a vice admiral or a Lieutenant General for officers of equal rank or for forty men each, a Rear Admiral or a Major General, for officers of equal rank, or for thirty men each; a Commodore with a broad pendant and a Captain under him or a Brigadier General for officers of equal rank or for twenty men each; a Captain of a line of Battle ship or a Colonel for officers of equal rank or for fifteen men each; a Captain of a frigate, or Lieutenant Colonel for officers of equal rank or for ten men each; Commanders of sloops of war, Bomb Catches, fire ships, and Packets or a Major for officers of equal rank, or for eight men each; Lieutenants or masters in the navy, or Captains in the army, for officers of equal rank, or for six men each; Masters-Mates, or Lieutenants in the army for officers of equal rank, or for four men each; Midshipmen, warrant officers, Masters of merchant vessels, and Captains of private armed vessels, or sub Lieutenants and Ensigns for officers of equal rank, or for three Men each: Lieutenants and mates of private armed vessels Mates of merchant vessels and all petty officers of ships of war, or all non commissioned officers of the army, for officers of equal rank, or for two men each-seamen and private soldiers one for the other.

Article IV lays down the rules of parole, the practice of releasing (not exchanging) prisoners in return for their pledge not to rejoin the fight for the duration of the war. In some cases (Article V), parole is to be granted pending prisoner exchange; once the paroled prisoner has been exchanged, he is eligible to rejoin the fight.

Anticipating later conventions on the humane treatment of prisoners of war, Article VII lays down:

No prisoner shall be struck with the hand, whip, stick or any other weapon whatever, the complaints of the prisoners shall be attended to, and real grievances redressed; and if they behave disorderly, they may be closely confined, and kept on two thirds allowance for a reasonable time not exceeding ten days. They are to be furnished by the government in whose possession they may be, with a subsistence of sound and wholesome provisions, consisting of, one pound of beef, or twelve ounces of pork; one pound of wheaten bread, and a quarter of a pint of pease, or six ounces of rice, or a pound of potatoes, per day to each man; and of salt and vinegar in the proportion of two quarts of salt and four quarts of vinegar to every hundred days subsistence. Or the ration shall consist of such other meats and vegetables (not changing the proportion of meat to the vegetables, and the quantity of bread salt and vinegar always remaining the same) as may from time to time be agreed on, at the several stations, by the respective agents of the two governments, as of equal nutriment with the ration first described. Both Governments shall be at liberty, by means of their respective agents to supply their prisoners with clothing, and such other small allowances, as may be deemed reasonable, and to inspect at all times the quality and quantity of subsistence provided for the prisoners of their nations respectively as stipulated in this article.

REFERENCE:

Hickey, Donald R. T*he War of 1812: A Forgotten Conflict.* Urbana and Chicago: University of Illinois Press, 1989.

Treaty of Ghent

OFFICIAL TITLE: Treaty of Peace and Amity

SIGNED: December 24, 1814, at Ghent, Belgium

IN FORCE: From February 17, 1815

SIGNATORIES: United States vs. Great Britain

OVERVIEW: Ended the War of 1812 (1812-1814) by restoring the *status quo antebellum.*

DISCUSSION:

The War of 1812 has been called America's "second war of independence" and has been justified as a fight to enforce United States sovereignty, which was being violated by the British in three ways:

1. By the incursion of British interests (mainly fur trappers and traders) in the West.
2. By British inducement of Indian hostility in the West.
3. By the Royal Navy's impressment of American sailors.

The last point, often cited in grade-school and high-school history lessons as the main cause of the War of 1812, requires discussion. It is true that Britain was at war with Napoleon during this period and had an urgent need of sailors to man its warships. Royal Navy vessels did frequently intercept and board the ships of neutrals, including merchant vessels of the United States, seizing and impressing into the British service men arbitrarily deemed to be British subjects. However, the United States declared war on Great Britain on June 18, 1812, even though, on the 16th, Great Britain had agreed to end impressment on the high seas, effective June 23. That impressment was, in fact, a nonissue is evident from the Treaty of Ghent's silence on the subject.

The first two issues mentioned, relating to the sovereignty and peace of U.S. western territories, more nearly approximate the true causes of the war. However, the single most pressing origin of the conflict was young nation's hunger for land, the most attractive parcel of which was Spanish Florida, which extended (in 1812) as far west as the Mississippi River. Because Spain was an ally of Great Britain against Napoleon, American "War Hawks" (congressmen and others who favored war) reasoned that victory in a war against Britain would ultimately result in the acquisition of its ally's territory, which would be joined to the vast territories acquired by the Louisiana Purchase.

The War Hawks, led by Henry Clay of Kentucky, persuaded President James Madison to declare war, but it soon became apparent that contemplating the fruits of victory was much easier than actually achieving that victory. Most of the early battles and campaigns of the War of 1812 were disastrous for the United States, whose meager, poorly equipped, and often poorly led forces were no match for a combination of British regular troops and their Indian allies, including Indian forces led by the brilliant Tecumseh. Despite such bright spots as Commander Oliver Hazard Perry's astounding victory against the British fleet on Lake Erie (September 10, 1813) and William Henry Harrison's triumph over British and Indian forces at the Battle of the Thames (October 5, 1813), the British devastated much of the western frontier and, burned many of the public buildings in Washington, D.C. (August 24, 1814), sending President Madison and the War Hawk Congress running for their lives. Later in 1814, U.S. forces successfully defended Baltimore and repulsed invaders from Canada.

With both sides war weary, the Treaty of Ghent functioned more as an armistice than the decisive conclusion of a great struggle. Although the treaty declared a restoration of the *status quo antebellum*—the way things were before the war—it also acknowledged that the chief source of the dispute was territorial. Although the Treaty of Ghent did not set the final boundary between the United States and Canada, it did establish a joint U.S.-British commission to do just that. (In fact, the commission failed to resolve many of the most important disputed claims, and the boundary issues were not satisfactorily resolved until the **Webster-Ashburton Treaty** of August 9, 1842.)

In addition to declaring an armistice and establishing a boundary commission, the Treaty of Ghent (in Article IX) stip-

ulated that both the United States and Great Britain would "engage to put an end immediately after the Ratification of the present Treaty to hostilities with all the Tribes or Nations of Indians with whom they may be at war at the time of such Ratification, and forthwith to restore to such Tribes or Nations respectively all the possessions, rights, and privileges which they may have enjoyed or been entitled to in one thousand eight hundred and eleven previous to such hostilities." Article X added a clause concerning the slave trade: "Whereas the traffic in slaves is irreconcilable with the principles of humanity and justice, and whereas both His Majesty and the United States are desirous of continuing their efforts to promote its entire abolition, it is hereby agreed that both the contracting parties shall use their best endeavors to accomplish so desirable an object."

REFERENCES:
Hickey, Donald R. *The War of 1812: A Forgotten Conflict.* Urbana and Chicago: University of Illinois Press, 1989.
Israel, Fred L. *Major Peace Treaties of Modern History, 1648-1967*, vol. 1. New York: Chelsea House and McGraw-Hill, 1967.
Mahon, John K. *The War of 1812.* Gainesville: University of Florida Press, 1972.

Treaty of Peace (with Algiers)

SIGNED: June 30 and July 3, 1815, at Algiers
SIGNATORIES: Algeria vs. United States
IN FORCE: From December 26, 1815
OVERVIEW: The treaty brought to an end the brief Algerine War and, with it, an end to the American payment of extortionary tributes to the dey of Algiers as protection from piracy.

DISCUSSION:
Like other non-Muslim countries, the United States paid an extortionary tribute to Algiers (and the other Barbary States) in return for protection against Muslim pirates off the Barbary Coast. When, despite the 1795 **Treaty of Amity and Peace,** an outbreak of piracy occurred in 1815, U.S. Navy Commodore Stephen Decatur was sent with a fleet to put an end to the piracy. After capturing the Algerian flagship and winning a quick naval victory, Decatur sailed into Algiers and negotiated the present treaty whereby the practice of tribute payment was terminated, all Americans held captive in Algiers were released, and a substantial indemnity was levied on the government of the bey.

Victory in the Algerine War, secured by this treaty, was a great boon to the national sovereignty and prestige of the United States; however, Algerian piracy remained a threat until France captured Algiers in 1830.

REFERENCES:
Chidsey, Donald Barr. *The Wars in Barbary: Arab Piracy and the United States Navy.* New York: Crown, 1971.
Nash, Howard Prevear. *The Forgotten Wars: The Role of the U.S. Navy in the Quasi-War with France and the Barbary Wars, 1798-1805.* South Brunswick, NJ: A. S. Barnes, 1968.

United States Office of Naval Records and Library. *Naval Documents Related to the United States Wars with the Barbary Powers...Including Diplomatic Background.* Washington, D.C.: U.S. Government Printing Office, 1939-44.

Treaty of Peace and Amity (with Algiers)

SIGNED: December 22 and 23, 1816, at Algiers
SIGNATORIES: Algeria vs. United States
IN FORCE: From February 11, 1822
OVERVIEW: A treaty renewing and rendering more permanent the **Treaty of Peace (with Algiers, 1815)**.

DISCUSSION:

The 1815 treaty with Algiers was concluded hastily and under some duress to end the Algerine War. Both signatories felt the need for an additional document "to restore and maintain upon a stable and permanent footing."

Most important are the following:

ARTICLE 1st.

There shall be from the conclusion of this Treaty, a firm, perpetual, inviolable and universal peace and friendship between the President and Citizens of the United States of America on the one part, and the Dey and subjects of the Regency of Algiers in Barbary on the other, made by the free consent of both parties, and on the terms of the most favoured Nations; and if either party shall hereafter grant to any other Nation, any particular favor or privilege in Navigation, or (commerce, it shall immediately become common to the other party, freely, when freely it is granted to such other Nations, but when the grant is conditional, it shall be at the option of the contracting parties, to accept, alter, or reject such conditions in such manner as shall be most conducive to their respective interests.

ARTICLE 2d

It is distinctly understood between the contracting parties, that no tribute, either as biennial presents or under any other form, or name whatever, shall be required by the Dey and Regency of Algiers from the United States of America on any pretext whatever.

ARTICLE 5th.

If any goods belonging to any Nation with which either of the parties are at War, should be loaded on board vessels belonging to the other party, they shall pass free and unmolested and no attempt shall be made to take or detain them.

ARTICLE 6th.

If any citizens or subjects belonging to either party shall be found on board a prize-vessel taken from an enemy by the other party, such citizens or subjects shall be liberated immediately and in no case, or on any presence whatever shall any American citizen be kept in captivity or confinement, or the property of any American citizen found on board of any vessel belonging to any Nation with which Algiers may be at War, be detained from its lawful owners after the exhibition of sufficient proofs of American citizenship and American property by the Consul of the United States, residing at Algiers.

REFERENCES:
Chidsey, Donald Barr. *The Wars in Barbary: Arab Piracy and the United States Navy.* New York: Crown, 1971.
Nash, Howard Prevear. *The Forgotten Wars: The Role of the U.S. Navy in the Quasi-War with France and the Barbary Wars, 1798-1805.* South Brunswick, NJ: A. S. Barnes, 1968.
United States Office of Naval Records and Library. *Naval Documents Related to the United States Wars with the Barbary Powers . . . Including Diplomatic Background.* Washington, D.C.: U.S. Government Printing Office, 1939-44.

Rush-Bagot Convention

OFFICIAL TITLE: Exchange of Notes Relative to Naval Forces on the American Lakes
SIGNED: April 28 and 29, 1817, at Washington
SIGNATORIES: Great Britain vs. United States
IN FORCE: From April 28, 1818
OVERVIEW: An exchange of notes between Acting U.S. Secretary of State Richard Rush and Charles Bagot, British minister to the United States, limiting naval forces on the Great Lakes in the aftermath of the War of 1812.

DISCUSSION:

The agreement allowed each country no more than one vessel on Lake Champlain, one on Lake Ontario, and two on the upper lakes. Each vessel was restricted to a maximum weight of 100 tons and one 18-pound cannon.

The agreement, somewhat modified over the years, remains in force and has served as the enduring basis of peaceful border relations between the United States and Canada. The text of the exchange of notes follows:

The Undersigned, His Britannick Majesty's Envoy Extraordinary and Minister Plenipotentiary, has the honour to acquaint Mr Rush, that having laid before His Majesty's Government the correspondence which passed last year between the Secretary of the Department of State and the Undersigned upon the subject of a proposal to reduce the Naval Force of the respective Countries upon the American Lakes, he has received the Commands of His Royal Highness The Prince Regent to acquaint the Government of the United States, that His Royal Highness is willing to accede to the proposition made to the Undersigned by the Secretary of the Department of State in his note of the 2d of August last.

His Royal Highness, acting in the name and on the behalf of His Majesty, agrees, that the Naval Force to be maintained upon the American Lakes by His Majesty and the Government of the United States shall henceforth be confined to the following Vessels on each side—that is

On Lake Ontario to one Vessel not exceeding one hundred Tons burthen and armed with one eighteen pound cannon.

On the Upper Lakes to two Vessels not exceeding like burthen each and armed with like force.

On the Waters of Lake Champlain to one Vessel not exceeding like burthen and armed with like force.

And His Royal Highness agrees, that all other armed Vessels on these Lakes shall be forthwith dismantled, and that no other Vessels of War shall be there built or armed.

His Royal Highness further agrees, that if either Party should hereafter be desirous of annulling this Stipulation, and should give notice to that effect to the other Party, it shall cease to be binding after the expiration of six months from the date of such notice.

The Undersigned has it in command from His Royal Highness the Prince Regent to acquaint the American Government, that His Royal Highness has issued Orders to His Majesty's Officers on the Lakes directing, that the Naval Force so to be limited shall be restricted to such Services as will in no respect interfere with the proper duties of the armed Vessels of the other Party.

The Undersigned has the honour to renew to Mr Rush the assurances of his highest consideration.

Richard Rush replied in the affirmative on the behalf of the United States.

REFERENCES:

Fitzpatrick, Charles, Sir. *The Rush-Bagot Agreement.* New York: N. Pub., 1917.

Naval Forces on the American Lakes, Application and Interpretation of the Rush-Bagot Agreement. Washington, D.C.: U.S. Government Printing Office, 1949.

Treaty of Peace (with Morocco)

SIGNED: September 16, 1836, at Meccanez, Morocco
SIGNATORIES: Morocco vs. United States
IN FORCE: From January 28, 1837
OVERVIEW: Last of the treaties with Barbary States, ending the reign of piracy in the coastal waters there.

DISCUSSION:

The treaty is similar to the others made with the Barbary States, specifying an end to piracy and to the payment of extortionary tributes.

REFERENCES:

Chidsey, Donald Barr. *The Wars in Barbary: Arab Piracy and the United States Navy.* New York: Crown, 1971.

Nash, Howard Prevear. *The Forgotten Wars: The Role of the U.S. Navy in the Quasi-War with France and the Barbary Wars, 1798-1805.* South Brunswick, NJ: A. S. Barnes, 1968.

United States Office of Naval Records and Library. *Naval Documents Related to the United States Wars with the Barbary Powers . . . Including Diplomatic Background.* Washington, D.C.: U.S. Government Printing Office, 1939-44.

U.S.-Mexican War

Overview of the Conflict

After Texas won its independence from Mexico (**Treaty of Velasco**, 1836, in Section 1.1), the United States hesitated to act on the newborn republic's bid for annexation. Legislators were reluctant to add a slave state to the union and thereby upset the always delicate balance between slave states and free, and they were also concerned about igniting war with Mexico. But neither the United States nor Texas existed in a vacuum, and when France and England made overtures of alliance to Texas, outgoing President John Tyler urged Congress to adopt an annexation resolution. Tyler's successor, James K. Polk, endorsed the resolution, and Texas was admitted to the Union on December 29, 1845.

Thus Texas had been saved from the imperialist clutches of England and France, which now appeared to be casting a hungry eye on California, which was held but feebly by Mexico. Polk offered Mexico $40 million for California, but the Mexican president not only spurned the offer, he arrogantly refused even to see Polk's emissary. In response, Polk commissioned the U.S. consul at Monterey (California), Thomas O. Larkin, to organize California's small but powerful American community into a separatist movement sympathetic to annexation by the U.S. At this point, a California independence movement called the Bear Flag Rebellion quickly ousted Mexican officials from California.

The Bear Flag Rebellion would soon dissolve into the larger U.S.-Mexican War. For, as most Americans had predicted, the annexation of Texas outraged the Mexican government, which began to dispute over the boundary of the new state. As the dispute heated up, President Polk dispatched troops to Texas and, on May 13, 1846, declared war on Mexico. In fact, combat had begun before the official declaration, as Mexican forces had laid siege against Fort Texas (present-day Brownsville) on May 1. General Zachary Taylor, marching to the relief of the fort, faced 6,000 Mexican troops with a mere 2,000 Americans, but nevertheless emerged victorious in the May 8 Battle of Palo Alto.

Palo Alto set the pattern for the rest of the conflict. Almost always outnumbered, American forces nevertheless usually outmatched the ineptly led and poorly equipped Mexican forces. Palo Alto was followed on May 9 by the Battle of Resaca de la Palma, a dry riverbed just north of the Rio Grande. Achieving victory here, Taylor invaded Mexico.

In the meantime, early in June, Stephen Watts Kearny led a United States force from Fort Leavenworth, Kansas, to California via New Mexico. Near Santa Fe, at steep-walled Apache Canyon, New Mexico's Governor Manuel Armijo set up an ambush to destroy Kearny's column, but the governor's ill-disciplined and ill-equipped troops panicked and dispersed. Kearny passed through the canyon unopposed, Santa Fe was taken, and, on August 15, New Mexico was annexed to the United States, and, by January 1847, California was securely in American hands.

During this time, General Taylor pressed the American campaign deeper into Mexico, attacking Monterrey (Mexico) on September 20, 1846, and taking that city after a four-day siege. At this point Antonio López de Santa Anna, exiled to Cuba after an earlier rebellion had ended his dictatorship of Mexico, made a proposal to the government of the United States, pledging to help it win the war, to secure a Rio Grande boundary for Texas, and to secure a California boundary through San Francisco Bay. He asked $30 million and safe passage to Mexico. American officials were prudent enough not to pay him, but he was allowed to return to his homeland. No sooner had he arrived than he organized an army intended to defeat Zachary Taylor. By January 1847, Santa Anna had gathered eighteen thousand men, leading fifteen thousand of them against Taylor's 4,800-man force at Buena Vista. After two days of combat, the outnumbered Americans forced Santa Anna's withdrawal on February 23.

At this point, President Polk, fearful of making a military celebrity out of a potential political rival, replaced Taylor with General Winfield Scott, a hero of War of 1812, and a man without political ambition. Fortunately, Scott was also a daring, vigorous, and highly capable commander. On March 9, he launched an invasion of Vera Cruz, which began with the first amphibious assault in U.S. military history. He laid siege against the fortress at Vera Cruz for eighteen days, forcing Santa Anna to withdraw to the steep Cerro Gordo canyon with eight thousand of his best troops. Here Scott declined the frontal attack the Mexicans expected and, instead, sent part of his force to cut paths up either side of Cerro Gordo in order to make a pincers attack on Santa Anna. The Mexican troops, taken wholly by surprise, retreated all the way to Mexico City. Scott gave chase. On September 13, Chapultepec Palace, the seemingly impregnable fortress guarding Mexico City, fell, and, on September 17, Santa Anna surrendered.

The **Treaty of Guadalupe Hidalgo** (1848) required formal Mexican cession of New Mexico (which also included parts of the present states of Utah, Nevada, Arizona, and Colorado) and California, as well as renunciation of claims to Texas above the Rio Grande.

Treaty of Guadalupe Hidalgo

SIGNED: February 2, 1848, at Guadalupe Hidalgo, Mexico
IN FORCE: From May 30, 1848
SIGNATORIES: United States vs. Mexico
OVERVIEW: The United States enjoyed great success in the U.S.–Mexican War (1846-1848), which was formally ended by this treaty. By this treaty, Mexico ceded to the United States "New Mexico" (the present state of New Mexico and portions of the present states of Utah, Nevada, Arizona, and Colorado) and California, and renounced claims to Texas above the Rio Grande. In return, the United States agreed to pay $15 million and to assume all claims of U.S. citizens against Mexico.

DISCUSSION:
The 1846-1848 war between the United States and Mexico was caused by the following:

- The United States annexation (June 16, 1845) of the Republic of Texas, which had won its independence from Mexico in 1836; this provoked a boundary dispute with Mexico
- United States involvement in the Bear Flag Rebellion, whereby California gained independence from Mexico
- Mexico's refusal to negotiate a land purchase
- The desire of the United States for additional western territory

Although U.S. forces were outnumbered in every engagement of the war, Mexican forces were poorly led, poorly trained, and poorly equipped. Each major engagement ended in an American victory. On September 17, 1848, General Winfield Scott, a hero of the War of 1812, took Mexico City, whereupon the General Antonio Lopez de Santa Anna surrendered, and the fighting ceased.

Peace talks had actually begun on August 27, before the invasion of Mexico City. Broken off by the Mexicans on September 7, they were resumed on November 22. General Scott persuaded a dubious President James K. Polk that the political situation in Mexico was so unstable that it was necessary to conclude a treaty swiftly, while a semblance of government remained in place. Without time to assemble a formal board of treaty commissioners, the president appointed Nicholas P. Trist, a relatively junior State Department official, to negotiate the treaty.

Considering the scope of the American victory in the war, the terms of the treaty were generous. In return for the territorial cessions, the United States paid Mexico $15,000,000 and assumed all claims of U.S. citizens against Mexico, which (as subsequently determined by a specially appointed commission) amounted to an additional $3,250,000. Further, the United States made restitution to Mexico for customs duties it had been unable to collect because of the war.

The treaty meticulously delineated the boundary line separating Mexico and the United States, and both sides subscribed to pledges of "peace and friendship, which shall confer reciprocal benefits upon the citizens of both." This conventional treaty phraseology notwithstanding, Guadalupe Hidalgo anticipated the possibility of renewed hostilities and included a statement of rules to govern "humane" warfare. In this, the treaty foreshadowed a number of later international conventions and accords. (See the treaties in **3.1 Arms Limitation, the Rules of Warfare, and War Crimes**).

The Treaty of Guadalupe Hidalgo was modified by the **Gadsden Treaty** (1853), which formalized the United States acquisition by purchase of additional territory from Mexico, and which abrogated Article XI, in which the United States pledged to prevent Indians from leaving territory acquired by that treaty and settling (or raiding) in territory still held by Mexico. Enforcement of this provision was considered unfeasible and, perhaps, even unconstitutional.

REFERENCES:
Eisenhower, John D. D. *So Far From God.* New York: Random House, 1989.
Israel, Fred L. *Major Peace Treaties of Modern History, 1648-1967*, vol. 2. New York: Chelsea House and McGraw-Hill, 1967.

SECTION 2.5

Civil War

Overview of the Conflict

The issue of slavery poisoned the American republic from its inception. Over the years, the addition of each new state to the Union brought bitter debate over whether the state would be admitted with or without slavery. Political compromises in 1820 (the Missouri Compromise) and 1850 postponed but did not prevent armed conflict, which was precipitated by the election to the presidency, in 1860, of Abraham Lincoln. By no means a radical abolitionist (he believed the Constitution protected slavery where it already existed), Lincoln was a candidate who nevertheless had made clear his intention to stop the extension of slavery to new states and territories. During the months preceding the outbreak of war, most of the slaveholding states seceded from the Union. Deeming this a violation of the Constitution and federal sovereignty, the Lincoln administration prepared to wage war. The seceded states, in the meantime, called themselves the Confederate States of America and likewise girded for battle.

The first target was Fort Sumter, situated in Charleston Harbor and commanded by Major Robert Anderson. When Anderson refused to surrender to Confederate general P. G. T. Beauregard, Confederate artillery opened fire on the fort at 4:30 on the morning of April 12, 1861.

Few anticipated the cost in blood and materiel that the Civil War would exact. Few in the North thought that the South could offer much of a fight. In terms of population, industrial capability, and economics, the North greatly overmatched the Confederate states. Yet the cream of the U.S. Army officer corps were southerners, and they left the army of the United States to join the Confederate cause. Moreover, many in the North were less than committed to prosecuting a war to liberate black slaves. Thus, the Confederate strategy resembled that of the Patriots during the American Revolution. The South understood that it could not defeat the North decisively, any more than the Continental Army could have annihilated the forces of the British empire. But a series of brilliant victories against the North could sap the Union's will to fight and bring about peace on terms favorable to the Confederacy.

Indeed, the early battles were, for the most part, stunning humiliations for the forces of the North. The Confederates prevailed at Bull Run (Manassas; July 21, 1861), at the so-called Seven Days (during the Peninsular Campaign of Union commander George B. McClellan), at the Second Battle of Bull

Run (Second Manassas; August 29-30, 1862), at Fredericksburg (December 13, 1862), and at Chancellorsville (May 2-4, 1863). Not only was the Union dealt defeat in these battles, but at a cost—to both sides—that was horrible to contemplate.

With difficulty, Lincoln maintained the Union's will to fight until, at last, the outcome of Antietam (Sharpsburg; September 17, 1862), albeit ambiguous, could legitimately be deemed a Northern victory. This gave the Union military effort sufficient credibility to enable Lincoln to issue, from what he felt was a position of strength, the preliminary Emancipation Proclamation. Now the slavery issue was at the forefront of the conflict, giving the struggle a solid moral dimension, in the eyes of American abolitionists and in the eyes of world as well.

At this point, General Robert E. Lee, commanding the Confederacy's main force, the Army of Northern Virginia, took the offensive by invading Pennsylvania, once again in the hope of eroding the Northern resolve to continue the war. Union forces under the overall command of General George G. Meade beat back Lee's army at Gettysburg (July 1-3, 1863), the turning-point battle of the war.

With the invading army repulsed, Northern morale rose, and England and France, which had contemplated some form of alliance with the Confederacy, abandoned all idea of supporting the South. Nevertheless, the war ground on. Union General Ulysses S. Grant scored important triumphs in the war's western theater, at Shiloh (April 6-7, 1862), at Vicksburg (under siege from October 1862 to July 4, 1863), and at Chattanooga (November 23-25, 1863). The Union seized control of the lower Mississippi after Admiral David Farragut captured New Orleans in April 1862. In 1864, Lincoln replaced a series of mediocre commanding generals with Grant, who slowly, and at terrible cost, forced Lee's army back toward the Confederate capital of Richmond. Grant's chief lieutenant, General William Tecumseh Sherman, advanced, in the meantime, through Tennessee and Georgia to Atlanta, which he captured, occupied, and finally burned (September-November 1864) before embarking on his infamously destructive "march to the sea," aimed at visiting such destruction on the Southern heartland that popular support for the Confederacy would dissolve.

Yet the will of the South proved difficult to break, and the conflict continued. General Philip Sheridan defeated Confederate general George E. Pickett at Five Forts (April 1, 1865), and

Grant took heavily fortified Petersburg, Virginia, after a long siege campaign that stretched from June 1864 to April 2, 1865, the day that Grant marched into the Confederate capital of Richmond. A week later, at Appomattox Court House, Virginia, General Robert E. Lee surrendered his Army of Northern Virginia to General Grant, effectively ending the Civil War.

No treaties were concluded between the belligerents, because the government in Washington did not recognize the Confederate States of America as a legitimate national entity. Instead, the fighting was ended by a series of truce documents concluded by the field commanders (**Civil War Truce Documents**), and immediate postwar terms were laid down by presidential proclamation (for example, **Proclamation of Amnesty and Pardon for the Confederate States** and **Proclamation of Provisional Government for North Carolina**). The war was formally ended by presidential proclamation as well (**Presidential Proclamations Ending the Civil War**).

The Civil War did occasion one treaty with a foreign power, the **Treaty of Washington,** concluded with Great Britain in 1871 to settle the so-called *Alabama* claims, for losses inflicted on United States merchant shipping during the Civil War by Confederate vessels (notably the CSS *Alabama*), which had been constructed in British shipyards in violation of that nation's neutrality.

Civil War Truce Documents

SIGNED: April 7-9, 1865, Northern Virginia

IN FORCE: From April 9, 1865

SIGNATORIES: Ulysses S. Grant, general, United States Army, vs Robert E. Lee, general, commanding the Army of Northern Virginia of the Confederate States Army

OVERVIEW: Contrary to much popular belief, Robert E. Lee's surrender to Ulysses S. Grant at Appomattox Court House, Virginia, on April 9, 1865, did not formally end the Civil War, but the final defeat of the Confederacy's principal army and its leading commander has always been regarded as the symbolic end to the conflict.

DISCUSSION:

After a protracted siege campaign (June 1864-April 2, 1865), Gen. Grant took heavily fortified Petersburg, Virginia, and then marched into Richmond, the Confederate capital through most of the war. Within a week, Lee surrendered the Army of Northern Virginia to General Grant. The armistice was initiated by a note from Grant to Lee:

Headquarters Armies of the United States,

General R. E. Lee,
Commanding C. S. Army:

April 7, 1865—5 P.M.

General:

The result of the last week must convince you of the hopelessness of further resistance on the part of the Army of Northern Virginia in this struggle. I feel that it is so, and regard it as my duty to shift from myself the responsibility of any further effusion of blood by asking of you the surrender of that portion of the C. S. Army known as the Army of Northern Virginia.

Very respectfully, your obedient servant,
U.S. GRANT,
Lieutenant-General,
Commanding Armies of the United States.

Lee replied:

April 7, 1865.

Lieut. Gen. U.S. Grant,
Commanding Armies of the United States:

General:

I have received your note of this date. Though not entertaining the opinion you express of the hopelessness of further resistance on the part of the Army of Northern Virginia, I reciprocate your desire to avoid useless effusion of blood, and therefore, before considering your proposition, ask the terms you will offer on condition of its surrender.

R. E. LEE,
General.

Two days later, from Grant:

Headquarters Armies of the United States,

General R. E. Lee,
Commanding C. S. Army:

April 9, 1865.

General:

Your note of yesterday is received. As I have no authority to treat on the subject of peace the meeting proposed for 10 A.M. to-day could lead to no good. I will state, however, general, that I am equally anxious for peace with yourself, and the whole North entertain the same feeling. The terms upon which peace can be had are well understood. By the South laying down their arms they will hasten that most desirable event, save thousands of human lives, and hundreds of millions of property not yet destroyed. Sincerely hoping that all our difficulties may be settled without the loss of another life, I subscribe myself,

Very respectfully, your obedient servant,
U.S. GRANT, Lieutenant-General, U.S. Army.

Lee responded with a request for a ceasefire and a conference. Grant responded:

Headquarters Armies of the United States,

April 9, 1865.

General R. E. Lee,

Commanding C. S. Army:

Your note of this date is but this moment (11.50 a. m.) received. In consequence of my having passed from the Richmond and Lynchburg road to the Farmville and Lynchburg road I am at this writing about four miles west of Walker's Church, and will push forward to the front for the purpose of meeting you. Notice sent to me on this road where you wish the interview to take place will meet me.

> Very respectfully, your obedient servant,
> U.S. GRANT, Lieutenant-General.

The actual surrender was accomplished by letters exchanged after a conference at the McLean house, at Appomattox Court House:

Headquarters Armies of the United States,

Appomattox Court-House, Va., April 9, 1865.

General R. E. Lee,
Commanding C. S. Army:

General:

In accordance with the substance of my letter to you of the 8th instant, I propose to receive the surrender of the Army of Northern Virginia on the following terms, to wit: Rolls of all the officers and men to be made in duplicate—one copy to be given to an officer to be designated by me, the other to be retained by such officer or officers as you may designate; the officers to give their individual paroles not to take up arms against the Government of the United States until properly exchanged, and each company or regimental commander sign a like parole for the men of their commands. The arms, artillery, and public property to be parked and stacked, and turned over to the officers appointed by me to receive them. This will not embrace the side-arms of the officers, nor their private horses or baggage. This done, each officer and man will be allowed to return to their homes, not to be disturbed by United States authority so long as they observe their paroles and the laws in force where they may reside.

> Very respectfully,
> U.S. GRANT, Lieutenant-General.

Lee's response:

Headquarters Army of Northern Virginia,

Lieut. Gen. U.S. Grant,
Commanding Armies of the United States:

April 9, 1865.

General:

I have received your letter of this date containing the terms of surrender of the Army of Northern Virginia as proposed by you. As they are substantially the same as those expressed in your letter of the 8th instant, they are accepted. I will proceed to designate the proper officers to carry the stipulations into effect.

> Very respectfully, your obedient servant,
> R. E. LEE,
> General.

REFERENCES:
Cauble, Frank. *Surrender Proceedings, April 9, 1865, Appomattox Court House.* Lynchburg, VA: H. E. Howard, 1987.
Commanger, Henry Steele, ed. *Fifty Basic Civil War Documents.* Malabar, FL: Krieger Publishing Company, 1982.
Israel, Fred L. *Major Peace Treaties of Modern History, 1648-1967,* vol. 1 (New York: Chelsea House and McGraw-Hill, 1967).

Proclamation of Amnesty and Pardon for the Confederate States

PROCLAIMED: May 29, 1865, at Washington, D.C.
IN FORCE: On proclamation
SIGNATORY: Andrew Johnson, president of the United States
OVERVIEW: Almost immediately after the end of the Civil War, President Andrew Johnson issued a broad amnesty and pardon for citizens of the former Confederacy.

DISCUSSION:
During the war, on December 8, 1863, President Abraham Lincoln issued an amnesty proclamation as part of an effort to set up loyal governments in Southern states that were then Union control. At the time, these included Louisiana, Tennessee, and Arkansas. For these states, Lincoln appointed provisional governors and, as a gesture of amnesty, he authorized each governor to call a convention to create a new state government as soon as 10 percent of the voters in the 1860 presidential election had signed oaths of loyalty to the Union. Governments were duly formed pursuant to the oaths, but Congress refused to recognize them and, in 1864, enacted the Wade-Davis Reconstruction Bill, which would delay a state's readmission to Union until 50 percent of its 1860 voters had signed loyalty oaths. Lincoln responded with a "pocket veto." The bill had been presented for signature within ten days of the adjournment of Congress, and Lincoln held the bill unsigned until Congress had adjourned.

After Lincoln's assassination in April 1865, Vice-President Andrew Johnson assumed office and adopted a modified form of the Wade-Davis plan. With relatively few exceptions, Johnson granted amnesty to anyone who would take an oath to be loyal to the Union in the future. New state governments were rapidly created, Johnson's amnesty requiring
• That the state ratify the 13th Amendment, freeing the slaves
• That the state's constitution abolish slavery
• That the state repudiate debts incurred while in rebellion
• That the state declare secession null and void

By the end of 1865, all of the secessionist states but Texas had completely complied.

Amnesty was denied to the following classes of individuals:
• Members of the Confederate government
• "All who left judicial stations under the United States to aid the rebellion"

- Confederate military or naval officers "above the rank of colonel in the army or lieutenant in the navy"
- "All who left seats in the Congress of the United States to aid the rebellion"
- "All who resigned or tendered resignations of their commissions in the Army or Navy of the United States to evade duty in resisting the rebellion"
- Those who abused prisoners of war
- "All persons who have been or are absentees from the United States for the purpose of aiding the rebellion"
- Confederate military officers "who were educated by the government in the Military Academy at West Point or the United States Naval Academy"
- Defectors to the Confederate states
- "All persons who have been engaged in the destruction of the commerce of the United States upon the high seas and all persons who have made raids into the United States from Canada"
- Current prisoners of war
- "All persons who have voluntarily participated in said rebellion and the estimated value of whose taxable property is over $20,000"
- Violators of the amnesty oath of 1863

Unfortunately, the amnesty proclamation did not resolve the nation's bitter postwar problems. Johnson and Congress were continually embattled, resulting in Johnson's impeachment (he was saved from removal by a single Senate vote), and two decades of sometimes well-intended but harshly punitive Reconstruction, which impoverished the South and exacerbated rather than ameliorated the persecution of African Americans.

REFERENCES:

The Annals of America, vol. 9 (Chicago: Encyclopaedia Britannica, Inc., 1976).

Foner, Eric. *Reconstruction: America's Unfinished Revolution, 1863-1877.* New York: HarperCollins, 1989.

Richter, William L. *The ABC-Clio Companion to American Reconstruction, 1862-1877.* Santa Barbara, CA: ABC-Clio, 1997.

Proclamation of Provisional Government for North Carolina

PROCLAIMED: May 29, 1865, at Washington, D.C.

IN FORCE: On proclamation

SIGNATORY: Andrew Johnson, president of the United States

OVERVIEW: This proclamation is typical of the documents that created provisional governments for the states of the former Confederacy during the postwar Reconstruction period.

DISCUSSION:

A pressing task, once the Civil War had ended, was to create provisional state governments for the former Confederate states. Andrew Johnson did this in a series of proclamations for each state, embodying the moderate policies that had been formulated by or with the approval of Abraham Lincoln, who had been assassinated a month and a half earlier.

The proclamation for North Carolina begins by asserting as its basis and rationale the Constitutional requirement that "the United States shall guarantee to every state in the Union a republican form of government and shall protect each of them against invasion and domestic violence."

... in obedience to the high and solemn duties imposed upon me by the Constitution of the United States and for the purpose of enabling the loyal people of said state to organize a state government whereby justice may be established, domestic tranquillity insured, and loyal citizens protected in all their rights of life, liberty, and property, I, Andrew Johnson, President of the United States and commander in chief of the Army and Navy of the United States, do hereby appoint William W. Holden provisional governor of the state of North Carolina, whose duty it shall be, at the earliest practicable period, to prescribe such rules and regulations as may be necessary and proper for convening a convention composed of delegates to be chosen by that portion of the people of said state who are loyal to the United States, and no others, for the purpose of altering or amending the constitution thereof, and with authority to exercise within the limits of said state all the powers necessary and proper to enable such loyal people of the state of North Carolina to restore said state to its constitutional relations to the Federal government ...

The proclamation then goes on to direct "the military commander of the department and all officers and persons in the military and naval service aid and assist the said provisional governor in carrying into effect this proclamation." Although the proclamation specified that the military is "enjoined to abstain from in any way hindering, impeding, or discouraging the loyal people from the organization of a state government as herein authorized," this provision provided for the military occupation of the state until the conditions for creating a new civil government were judged appropriate.

The proclamation further directed:

- "... the secretary of state ... to put in force all laws of the United States the administration whereof belongs to the State Department ..."
- The secretary of the treasury to appoint tax assessors and collectors within the state
- The postmaster general "to establish post offices and post routes"
- "... the district judge for the judicial district in which North Carolina is included proceed to hold courts within said state"
- "... the secretary of the navy [to] take possession of all public property [within the state] belonging to the Navy Department"
- "... that the secretary of the interior put in force the laws relating to the Interior Department applicable to the" state

While Johnson's proclamations left leeway for a military government in the states of the former Confederacy, they by no means imposed such a government and, in fact, made it clear that the military was not to impede the legitimate creation of civil government. Congress, always embattled against Johnson's Reconstruction policies, passed a Reconstruction Act on March 2, 1867, putting all of the South, save Tennessee, under military government, the spirit of the presidential proclamations notwithstanding. Military rule could be terminated only after a state had ratified a constitution providing for the enfranchisement of African Americans and the disenfranchisement of ex-Confederate military officers and civil office holders, and had ratified the 14th Amendment, guaranteeing voting rights to all citizens, including former slaves, barring former Confederates from holding public office, and repudiating compensation for "the loss of emancipation of any slave."

REFERENCES:

Commanger, Henry Steele, ed. *Fifty Basic Civil War Documents.* Malabar, FL: Krieger Publishing Company, 1982.

Foner, Eric. *Reconstruction: America's Unfinished Revolution, 1863-1877.* New York: HarperCollins, 1989.

James D. Richardson, ed., *A Compilation of Messages and Papers of the Presidents 1789-1897.* Washington, D.C.: U.S. Government Printing Office, 1909.

Richter, William L. *The ABC-Clio Companion to American Reconstruction, 1862-1877.* Santa Barbara, CA: ABC-Clio, 1997.

Presidential Proclamations Ending the Civil War

PROCLAIMED: April 2, 1866 and August 20, 1866, at Washington, D.C.

IN FORCE: On proclamation

SIGNATORIES: Andrew Johnson, president of the United States, and William H. Seward, secretary of state

OVERVIEW: Robert E. Lee's surrender of the Army of Northern Virginia at Appomattox Court House on April 9, 1865 (*see* **Civil War Truce Documents**) is often seen as the symbolic end of the Civil War, even though the last Confederate units did not lay down arms until May 26, 1865. No formal treaty ended the Civil War, since the United States did not recognize the former Confederate States as a legitimately constituted sovereign nation; instead, hostilities were definitively concluded by two presidential proclamations.

DISCUSSION:

The proclamation of April 2, 1866 applied to those states "in rebellion" that had

- Ratified the 13th Amendment to the Constitution, freeing the slaves and abolishing slavery
- Banned slavery in their state constitutions
- Repudiated debts incurred during the rebellion
- Declared the secession null and void

Texas initially rejected the proclamation terms, but later agreed and was encompassed in a second proclamation of August 20, 1866.

The principal substance of both proclamations is well represented in the first, which clearly develops the rationale for proclaiming the rebellion concluded and restoring the former Confederate states to normal status within the Union. The document concludes:

Whereas there now exists no organized armed resistance of misguided citizens or others to the authority of the United States in the States of Georgia, South Carolina, Virginia, North Carolina, Tennessee, Alabama, Louisiana, Arkansas, Mississippi, and Florida, and the laws can be sustained and enforced therein by the proper civil authority, State or Federal, and the people of said States are well and loyally disposed and have conformed or will conform in their legislation to the condition of affairs growing out of the amendment to the Constitution of the United States prohibiting slavery within the limits and jurisdiction of the United States; and

Whereas in view of the before-recited premises, it is the manifest determination of the American people that no State of its own will will have the right or the power to go out of, or separate itself from, or be separated from, the American Union, and that therefore each State ought to remain and constitute an integral part of the United States; and

Whereas the people of the several before-mentioned States have, in the manner aforesaid, given satisfactory evidence that they acquiesce in this sovereign and important resolution of national unity; and

Whereas it is believed to be a fundamental principle of government that people who have revolted and who have been overcome and subdued must either be dealt with so as to induce them voluntarily to become friends or else they must be held by absolute military power or devastated so as to prevent them from ever again doing harm as enemies, which last-named policy is abhorrent to humanity and to freedom; and

Whereas the Constitution of the United States provides for constituent communities only as States, and not as Territories. dependencies, provinces, or protectorates; and

Whereas such constituent States must necessarily be, and by the Constitution and laws of the United States are, made equals and placed upon a like footing as to political rights, immunities, dignity, and power with the several States with which they are united; and

Whereas the observance of political equality, as a principle of right and justice, is well calculated to encourage the people of the aforesaid States to be and become more and more constant and persevering in their renewed allegiance; and

Whereas standing armies, military occupation, martial law, military tribunals, and the Suspension of the privilege of the writ of habeas corpus are in time of peace dangerous to public liberty, incompatible with the individual rights of the citizen, contrary to the genius and spirit of our free institutions, and exhaustive of the national resources, and ought not, therefore, to be sanctioned or allowed except in cases of actual necessity for repelling invasion or suppressing insurrection or rebellion; and

Whereas the policy of the Government of the United States from the beginning of the insurrection to its overthrow and final suppression has been in conformity with the principles herein set forth and enumerated:

Now, therefore, I, Andrew Johnson, President of the United States, do hereby proclaim and declare that the insurrection which heretofore existed in the States of Georgia, South Carolina, Virginia, North Carolina, Tennessee, Alabama, Louisiana, Arkansas, Mississippi, and Florida is at an end and is henceforth to be so regarded.

Tragically, these well-reasoned proclamations did little to heal the wounds of war. The process of Reconstruction, which may be said to have formally begun with these proclamations, became significantly tainted by a politically opportunistic agenda of retribution against the South.

REFERENCES:
Cauble, Frank. *Surrender Proceedings, April 9, 1865, Appomattox Court House.* Lynchburg, VA: H. E. Howard, 1987.
Commanger, Henry Steele, ed. *Fifty Basic Civil War Documents.* Malabar, FL: Krieger Publishing Company, 1982.
Israel, Fred L. *Major Peace Treaties of Modern History, 1648-1967,* vol. 1 (New York: Chelsea House and McGraw-Hill, 1967).

Treaty of Washington

SIGNED: May 8, 1871, at Washington, D.C.
IN FORCE: From signing
SIGNATORIES: United States vs. Great Britain
OVERVIEW: The treaty settled the "*Alabama* claims" for losses inflicted on United States merchant shipping during the Civil War by Confederate vessels (notably the CSS *Alabama*), which had been constructed in British shipyards in violation of that nation's neutrality.

DISCUSSION:
The government of Great Britain tended to sympathize with the Confederacy during the American Civil War, in large measure because of the strong economic ties between Britain and the Southern states, which supplied much of the cotton used by English cloth mills. Despite this sympathy Britain declared itself neutral in the conflict because it could not openly side with a nation committed to a policy of slavery. Britain's Neutrality Act forbade British manufacturers and shipyards from supplying any war materiel to either side, including ships. The law notwithstanding, however, British concerns enjoyed a profitable trade from selling arms and shipping to the Confederacy while officials of Her Majesty's government turned a blind eye.

Most celebrated of the British-built Confederate warships was the CSS *Alabama*, launched from the Liverpool shipyards in the summer of 1862. Under the command of the brilliant Raphael Semmes, it took as prizes almost seventy U.S. merchant ships. After the war, the United States and Great Britain bitterly wrangled over responsibility for damages caused by British-built vessels, and U.S. claims against Britain were collectively referred to as the *Alabama* claims.

The settlement of the *Alabama* claims was not embodied in the Treaty of Washington itself. Instead, the treaty called for the creation of an international panel to arbitrate settlement. Thus the primary significance of the Treaty of Washington is in its establishment of the principle of international arbitration to resolve peacefully disputes between nations. The treaty also laid the foundation for permanent international law governing such disputes in the future, and it outlined cardinal principles of neutrality in time of war.

In addition to creating the arbitration panel for resolution of the *Alabama* claims and setting out rules of conduct for neutral nations, the treaty also included articles governing U.S. fishing rights in Canadian waters, navigation of the St. Lawrence River, and an agreement to submit to international arbitration (in this case, the emperor of Germany) a dispute over the boundary off the Pacific Northwest coast. (This was resolved by a declaration of Kaiser Wilhelm I, May 8, 1871, awarding the United States the boundary it claimed.) As for the *Alabama* claims, a panel of United States, British, Brazilian, Swiss, and Italian arbitrators met in 1872 in Geneva and awarded the United States the sum of $15.5 million in damages, payable by the British government.

REFERENCES:
Davis, John Chandler Bancroft. *Mr. Fish and the Alabama Claims: A Chapter in Diplomatic History.* Freeport, NY: Books for Libraries Press, 1969.
Cook, Adrian. *The Alabama Claims: American Politics and Anglo-American Relations, 1865-1872.* Ithaca, NY.: Cornell University Press, 1975.
Israel, Fred L. *Major Peace Treaties of Modern History, 1648-1967,* vol. 2. New York: Chelsea House and McGraw-Hill, 1967.
Manning, J. F., comp. *Opinions of the Court of Commissioners of Alabama Claims.* Boston: Smith and Porter, 1884.
United States Department of State. *Correspondence Concerning Claims against Great Britain: Transmitted to the Senate of the United States.* Millwood, NY: Kraus Reprint, 1976.

Spanish-American War

Overview of the Conflict

Cuba, a Spanish colony, had long been seething with rebellion when, in February 1896, Spain sent General Valeriano Weyler to govern the island and restore order there. Among the general's first acts was to establish "reconcentration camps" for the incarceration of rebels as well as other citizens accused of supporting or even sympathizing with the rebels. Although both U.S. presidents Grover Cleveland and his successor William McKinley stoutly resisted United States intervention in Cuba, American popular sentiment, whipped up by atrocity stories published in the papers of Joseph Pulitzer and William Randolph Hearst, at last moved McKinley to order the battleship *Maine* into Havana Harbor to protect American citizens and property there.

United States war fever was not exclusively a symptom of popular sentiment. By the late nineteenth century, large United States business concerns had made major investments in the island, especially in sugar plantations. Revolutionary unrest posed a threat to those investments; however, a successful revolution, if properly supported by the United States, could create a pliant "independent" Cuban government, beholden to the United States. Alternatively, Cuba might even be annexed. Either outcome would be favorable to American business in Cuba.

On February 9, 1898, Hearst scored a journalistic coup by publishing a purloined private letter in which the Spanish minister to the United States insulted President McKinley. The American nation had been brought to the brink of war when, on February 15, an explosion suddenly rocked Havana Harbor. The battleship *U.S.S. Maine* blew up, killing 266 crewmen. The Hearst and Pulitzer papers vied with one another to fix blame on Spain, and cries of "Remember the *Maine* . . . to hell with Spain!" echoed throughout the nation. President McKinley, still reluctant to go to war, temporized until April before asking Congress to authorize an invasion of Cuba. The legislators not only complied, but went beyond the president's request, voting a resolution recognizing Cuban independence from Spain. In response to these acts, Spain declared war on the United States on April 24.

The first action of the war took place not in Cuba, but in the Spanish-occupied Philippine Islands, when U.S. Admiral George Dewey sailed his Asiatic Squadron from Hong Kong to Manila Bay and, on May 1, attacked the Spanish fleet there. Without incurring any losses, Dewey sank all ten Spanish vessels in the bay. Next came a landing of 11,000 U.S. troops, who, acting in concert with the guerrilla forces of Filipino rebel leader Emilio Aguinaldo, quickly defeated the Spanish army in the islands. In July, Spanish Guam also fell to the United States, which grabbed up previously unclaimed Wake Island as well. Driven by the imperialist momentum of these actions, Congress, during this time, passed the **Newlands Resolution (Annexation of Hawaii)**(Section 1.1).

Back on Cuba, the action also developed swiftly and decisively. On May 29, the American fleet blockaded the Spanish fleet at Santiago Harbor, and in June, 17,000 U.S. troops landed at Daiquiri for an assault on Santiago. The war's make-or-break land battle, at San Juan Hill on July 1, included a magnificent charge by the volunteer Rough Riders, led by Lieutenant Colonel Theodore Roosevelt. On July 3, after the American victory at San Juan Hill, the admiral commanding the Spanish fleet decided to run the naval blockade. Within a mere four hours, his fleet was almost completely destroyed, and on July 17, 24,000 Spanish troops surrendered. Madrid sued for peace nine days later.

The **Treaty of Paris** formally ended the war, with Spain agreeing to withdraw from Cuba and ceding to the United States Puerto Rico and Guam. Spain also agreed to sell the Philippines to the United States for $20 million. The United States quickly established a territorial government in Puerto Rico, but did not rush in to deprive Cuba of the independence for which it had fought. Instead, the U.S. established a military government on the island while Cuba drafted its own constitution, albeit under American supervision, which ensured that it included provisos granting the United States the right to establish American military bases on the island and to intervene in Cuban affairs, as necessary, "in order to preserve [Cuban] independence." The arrangements for U.S. military facilities in Cuba were formalized by **Agreement (with Cuba) for the Lease to the United States of Lands for Coaling and Naval Stations** and by **Treaty with Cuba**, both concluded in 1903.

In the meantime, Emilio Aguinaldo, leader of the Philippine independence movement, refused to accept the terms of the **Treaty of Paris** ceding the Philippines to the United States. He proclaimed an independent Philippine republic on January 20, 1899, and, the next month, hostilities broke out between Filipinos and American troops. The guerrilla warfare was not ended by the capture of Aguinaldo on March 23, 1901, even though he was compelled to swear allegiance to the United States and to issue a proclamation calling for peace. By early 1902, however, most of the guerrilla leaders had surrendered, and, on July 4, President Theodore Roosevelt issued **Proclamation Ending the Philippine-American War.**

Treaty of Paris (1898)

SIGNED: December 10, 1898, at Paris

IN FORCE: From April 11, 1899

SIGNATORIES: United States vs. Spain

OVERVIEW: The treaty ended the Spanish-American War. Spain granted Cuba its independence and ceded Puerto Rico, Guam, and the Philippine Islands to the United States. Historians regard the Treaty of Paris as the signal of U.S. emergence as an imperialist power.

DISCUSSION:

The "safety-valve theory" proposed by the American historian Frederick Jackson Turner at the end of the nineteenth century held that the vast American West served as an outlet—a safety valve—for the nation's expansionist impulses. After U.S. western expansion had been completed with the suppression of the Native Americans, the nation, lacking the western safety valve, would direct expansion outward, off shore. Certainly, this seemed to be the case when Cuban nationalists began a revolt against the repressive Spanish colonial government after 1895. After the island's military governor, General Valeriano Weyler, herded thousands of suspected Cuban radicals into squalid concentration camps, American imperialism found a compelling and apparently lofty reason to intervene on the island. The powerful publisher of the *New York Journal*, William Randolph Hearst, and others called for the annexation of Cuba by the United States. Mindful that a war would be good for circulation, Hearst obtained and published a private letter from the Spanish minister to the United States that was insultingly critical of President William McKinley.

With war fever running high, all that was needed for the commencement of hostilities was a provocative incident. That occurred on February 15, 1898, when the American battleship *Maine* exploded in Havana harbor, killing 266 sailors. A naval court of inquiry concluded that the ship had hit a Spanish mine (modern analysts believe that the ship's powder magazine spontaneously exploded through no hostile action), and, whipped up by Hearst and others, the public raised the battle cry of "Remember the *Maine*!"

Although Spain tried to avert war by accelerating its withdrawal from Cuba, President McKinley yielded to public pressure and requested a declaration of war, which Congress passed on April 25. Begun and ended in ten weeks, the war was swift and decisive. The Spanish army and navy proved less formidable adversaries than the Yellow Fever that was endemic to the island of Cuba. The 24,000 Spanish troops on

the island surrendered on July 17, 1898, and Spain sued for peace nine days later.

American victory was achieved not only in Cuba, but in the Spanish-held Phillippines as well, where Admiral George Dewey demolished the obsolescent Spanish fleet as it lay at anchor off Manila. That city fell on August 13, 1898. In the meantime, U.S. naval forces also seized Spanish Guam as well as previously unclaimed Wake Island. These acquisitions moved Congress to annex Hawaii as well.

A protocol embodying the terms for peace was concluded on August 12, 1898, and the Treaty of Paris was signed on December 10. Among U.S. lawmakers, moral objections to an act of bald expansionism had produced the Teller Amendment to the original declaration of war, which barred the annexation of Cuba. For this reason, U.S. negotiators did not seek to acquire the island. Instead, Article I of the treaty stipulates Spain's grant of independence for Cuba. The Teller Amendment did not extend to other Spanish possessions, however, and President McKinley pressed his negotiators to obtain cession of Puerto Rico, Guam, and the Philippine Islands. These acts of imperialism made the treaty controversial, and the fight over ratification was bitter, proponents arguing that it was America's duty to serve the world as the agent of civilization. On a more pragmatic level, the acquisitions in the Pacific would give the United States a crucial leg up in trade with China. In the end, the treaty was ratified by a margin of 57 to 27—just two votes more than the two-thirds majority required.

Secretary of State John Hay called the ten-week conflict a "splendid little war," and, despite the controversy it created, it established the United States as a major power in the Far East and the dominant power in the Caribbean. It also triggered a four-year guerrilla insurrection against American dominion in the Phillippines. In the 1930s, the United States granted the islands almost complete independence; full independence followed World War II. Puerto Rico and Guam became and remain U.S. territories, and Hawaii, in 1960, moved from territorial status to statehood. Cuba, made nominally independent by the Treaty of Paris, was, in fact, a U.S. client state, a condition that endured until Fidel Castro's revolution of 1959. Even today, the United States maintains Guantanamo Naval Base on Cuban land ceded by the 1898 treaty.

REFERENCES:

Bradford, James C., ed. *Crucible of Empire: The Spanish-American War and its Aftermath.* Annapolis, MD: Naval Institute Press, 1993.

Israel, Fred L. *Major Peace Treaties of Modern History, 1648-1967*, vol. 2. New York: Chelsea House and McGraw-Hill, 1967.

Marrin, Albert. *The Spanish-American War.* New York: Atheneum, 1991.

Musicant, Ivan. *Empire by Default: The Spanish-American War and the Dawn of the American Century.* New York: Henry Holt, 1998.

Proclamation Ending the Philippine-American War

PROCLAIMED: July 4, 1902, at Washington

SIGNATORY: Theodore Roosevelt, president of the United States

IN FORCE: On proclamation

OVERVIEW: A proclamation ending the Philippine Insurrection of 1899-1902 and granting amnesty to all those involved.

DISCUSSION:

The Philippines had declared independence from Spain on June 12, 1898, but Spain ceded the islands to the United States by the **Treaty of Paris** of December 10, 1898. Emilio Aguinaldo, leader of the independence movement, refused to accept the treaty and set up a republic on January 20, 1899. The next month, hostilities broke out between Filipinos and American troops. The guerrilla warfare was not ended by the capture of Aguinaldo on March 23, 1901, even though he was compelled to swear allegiance to the United States and to issue a proclamation calling for peace. By early 1902, however, most of the guerilla leaders had surrendered, and, on July 4, President Theodore Roosevelt issued the following proclamation:

Whereas many of the inhabitants of the Philippine Archipelago were in insurrection against the authority and sovereignty of the Kingdom of Spain at divers times from August, eighteen hundred and ninety-six, until the cession of the archipelago by that Kingdom to the United States of America, and since such cession many of the persons so engaged in insurrection have until recently resisted the authority and sovereignty of the United States; and

Whereas the insurrection against the authority and sovereignty of the United States is now at an end, and peace has been established in all parts of the archipelago except in the country inhabited by the Moro tribes, to which this proclamation does not apply; and

Whereas during the course of the insurrection against the Kingdom of Spain and against the Government of the United States, persons engaged therein, or those in sympathy with and abetting them, committed many acts in violation of the laws of civilized warfare, but it is believed that such acts were generally committed in ignorance of those laws, and under orders issued by the civil or insurrectionary leaders; and

Whereas it is deemed to be wise and humane, in accordance with the beneficent purposes of the Government of the United States towards the Filipino people, and conducive to peace, order, and loyalty among them, that the doers of such acts who have not already suffered punishment shall not be held criminally responsible, but shall be relieved from punishment for participation in these insurrections, and for unlawful acts committed during the course thereof, by a general amnesty and pardon:

Now, therefore, be it known that I, Theodore Roosevelt, President of the United States of America, by virtue of the power and authority vested in me by the Constitution, do hereby proclaim and declare, without reservation or condition, except as hereinafter provided, a full and complete pardon and amnesty to all persons in the Philippine Archipelago who have participated in the insurrections aforesaid, or who have given aid and comfort to persons participating in said insurrections, for the offenses of treason or sedition and for all offenses political in their character committed in the course of such insurrections pursuant to orders issued by the civil or military insurrectionary authorities, or which grew out of internal political feuds or dissensions between Filipinos and Spaniards or the Spanish authorities, or which resulted from internal political feuds or dissensions among the Filipinos themselves, during either of said insurrections:

Provided, however, That the pardon and amnesty hereby granted shall not include such persons committing crimes since May first, nineteen hundred and two, in any province of the archipelago in which at the time civil government was established, nor shall it include such persons as have been heretofore finally convicted of the crimes of murder, rape, arson, or robbery by any military or civil tribunal organized under the authority of Spain, or of the United States of America, but special application may be made to the proper authority for pardon by any person belonging to the exempted classes, and such clemency as is consistent with humanity and justice will be liberally extended; and

Further provided, That this amnesty and pardon shall not affect the title or right of the Government of the United States, or that of the Philippine Islands, to any property or property rights heretofore used or appropriated by the military or civil authorities of the Government of the United States, or that of the Philippine Islands, organized under authority of the United States, by way of confiscation or otherwise;

Provided further, That every person who shall seek to avail himself of this proclamation shall take and subscribe the following oath before any authority in the Philippine Archipelago authorized to administer oaths, namely:

"I, _____, solemnly swear (or affirm) that I recognize and accept the supreme authority of the United States of America in the Philippine Islands and will maintain true faith and allegiance thereto; that I impose upon myself this obligation voluntarily, without mental reservation or purpose of evasion. So help me God."

Given under my hand at the city of Washington this fourth day of July in the year of our Lord one thousand nine hundred and two, and in the one hundred and twenty-seventh year of the Independence of the United States.

The United States established a civil government for the islands (the first governor was William Howard Taft, who would succeed Roosevelt as president of the United States), which were not granted full independence until 1946.

REFERENCES:

Graff, Henry F., ed. *American Imperialism and the Philippine Insurrection: Testimony Taken from Hearings on Affairs in the Philippine Islands before the Senate Committee on the Philippines, 1902.* Boston: Little, Brown, 1969.

Marrin, Albert. *The Spanish-American War.* New York: Atheneum, 1991.

Taylor, John R. M. *The Philippine Insurrection against the United States: A Compilation of Documents with Notes and Introduction.* Pasay City, Philippines: Eugenio Lopez Foundation, 1971.

Walsh, John E. *The Philippine Insurrection, 1899-1902: America's Only Try for an Overseas Empire.* New York: Watts, 1973.

Agreement (with Cuba) for the Lease of Lands for Coaling and Naval Stations

SIGNED: February 23, 1903, at Havana

IN FORCE: From February 23, 1903

SIGNATORIES: Cuba vs. United States

OVERVIEW: An agreement to establish coaling stations—vital for naval operations in the days of steam-powered navies—in Cuba.

DISCUSSION:

This agreement for the establishment of coaling stations ensured the continuing presence of the United States military in Cuba and is the basis for the naval base maintained at Guantanamo Bay. The treaty was executed pursuant to "the provisions of Article VII of the Act of Congress approved March second, 1901, and of Article VII of the Appendix to the Constitution of the Republic of Cuba promulgated on the 20th of May, 1902."

Articles I and II define the lease:

The Republic of Cuba hereby leases to the United States, for the time required for the purposes of coaling and naval stations, the following described areas of land and water situated in the Island of Cuba:

1st. In Guantanamo (see Hydrographic Office Chart 1857). From a point on the south coast, 4.37 nautical miles to the eastward of Windward Point Light House, a line running north (true) a distance of 4.25 nautical miles;

From the northern extremity of this line, a line running west (true), a distance of 5.87 nautical miles;

From the western extremity of this last line, a line running southwest (true) 3.31 nautical miles;

From the southwestern extremity of this last line, a line running south (true) to the seacoast.

This lease shall be subject to all the conditions named in Article II of this agreement.

2nd. In Northwestern Cuba (see Hydrographic Office Chart 2036).

In Bahia Honda (see Hydrographic Office Chart 520b).

All that land included in the peninsula containing Cerro del Morrillo and Punta del Carenero situated to the westward of a line running south (true) from the north coast at a distance of thirteen hundred yards east (true) from the crest of Cerro del Morrillo, and all the adjacent waters touching upon the coast line of the above described peninsula and including the estuary south of Punta del Carenero with the control of the headwaters as necessary for sanitary and other purposes.

And in addition all that piece of land and its adjacent waters on the western side of the entrance to Bahia Honda including between the shore line and a line running north and south (true) to low water marks through a point which is west (true) distant one nautical mile from Pta. del Cayman.

ARTICLE II

The grant of the foregoing Article shall include the right to use and occupy the waters adjacent to said areas of land and water, and to improve and deepen the entrances thereto and the anchorages therein, and generally to do any and all things necessary to fit the premises for use as coaling or naval stations only, and for no other purpose.

Vessels engaged in the Cuban trade shall have free passage through the waters included within this grant.

REFERENCES:

Benjamin, Jules R. *The United States and the Origins of the Cuban Revolution: An Empire of Liberty in an Age of National Liberation.* Princeton, NJ: Princeton University Press, 1992.

Langley, Lester D. *The Cuban Policy of the United States: A Brief History.* New York: Wiley, 1968.

Malloy, William M., ed., *Treaties, Conventions, International Acts, Protocols and Agreements between the United States of America and other Powers 1776-1909* (Washington, D.C., 1902).

Marrin, Albert. *The Spanish-American War.* New York: Atheneum, 1991.

Treaty with Cuba

SIGNED: May 22, 1903, at Havana

IN FORCE: March 3, 1904

SIGNATORIES: United States vs. Cuba

OVERVIEW: Newly independent from Spain and from a U.S. military government, the republic of Cuba conceded to the United States the authority to intervene in its affairs in order to protect its independence, effectively acknowledging itself a U.S. protectorate.

DISCUSSION:

After achieving victory in the Spanish-American War in 1898 (see **Treaty of Paris**), the United States maintained a military occupation force in Cuba. The first constitution the island nation drafted in 1900 lacked clauses defining Cuban-U.S. relations. Wishing to maintain control over Cuba, the United States government conditioned military withdrawal on insertion of such clauses. Secretary of States Elihu Root drew up the desired provisions, attaching them to the Army Appropriations Bill of 1901. This so-called Platt Amendment (sponsored by Senator Orville H. Platt) effectively made Cuba a protectorate by

- Limiting Cuba's treaty-making capacity
- Limiting Cuba's authority to contract public debt
- Securing for the United States Cuban land for naval bases and naval coaling stations
- Reserving to the United States the authority to intervene in Cuban affairs to preserve Cuba's independence and maintain order

The provisions of the Platt Amendment were incorporated into the Cuban constitution of 1901, which the United State approved; troops were withdrawn the following year. In the 1903 treaty, relations as defined in the Platt Amendment and the Cuban constitution were additionally formalized. The most significant provisions include:

ARTICLE I

The government of Cuba shall never enter into any treaty or other compact with any foreign power or powers which will impair or tend to impair the independence of Cuba, nor in any manner authorize or permit any foreign power or powers to obtain by colonization or for military or naval purposes, or otherwise, lodgment in or control over any portion of said island.

ARTICLE II

The government of Cuba shall not assume or contract any public debt [that cannot be paid discharged by] the ordinary revenues of the island of Cuba . . .

ARTICLE III

The government of Cuba consents that the United States may exercise the right to intervene for the preservation of Cuban independence, the maintenance of a government adequate for the protection of life, property, and individual liberty, and for discharging the obligations with respect to Cuba imposed by the Treaty of Paris on the United States, now to be assumed and undertaken by the government of Cuba.

ARTICLE IV

All acts of the United States in Cuba during its military occupancy thereof are ratified and validated, and all lawful rights acquired thereunder shall be maintained and protected.

ARTICLE V

The government of Cuba will execute . . . plans to be mutually agreed upon . . . for the sanitation of the cities of the island, to the end that a recurrence of epidemic and infectious diseases may be prevented, thereby assuring protection to the people and commerce of Cuba, as well as to the commerce of the Southern ports of the United States and the people residing therein.

ARTICLE VII

To enable the United States to maintain the independence of Cuba, and to protect the people thereof, as well as for its own defense, the government of Cuba will sell or lease to the United States lands necessary for coaling or naval stations, at certain specified points to be agreed upon with the President of the United States.

The 1903 treaty is an illustrative product of the moderate imperialism that dominated American foreign policy at the turn of the 20th century. The treaty was superceded by the United States-Cuba Treaty of Relations (1934), which repudiated the Platt Amendment and acknowledged the full independence of Cuba; however, the naval lease endured, and, despite severely limited diplomatic relations that have existed between Cuba and the United States since the Communist revolution led by Fidel Castro in 1959, the United States has maintained and continues to maintain a naval base at Guantanamo Bay.

REFERENCES:

Benjamin, Jules R. *The United States and the Origins of the Cuban Revolution: An Empire of Liberty in an Age of National Liberation.* Princeton, NJ: Princeton University Press, 1992.

Langley, Lester D. *The Cuban Policy of the United States: A Brief History.* New York: Wiley, 1968.

Malloy, William M., ed., *Treaties, Conventions, International Acts, Protocols and Agreements between the United States of America and other Powers 1776-1909* (Washington, D.C., 1902).

Marrin, Albert. *The Spanish-American War.* New York: Atheneum, 1991.

SECTION 2.7

Boxer Rebellion

Overview of the Conflict

The United States' role in the so-called Boxer Rebellion in China was another aspect of the imperialist expansionism that guided American foreign policy at the end of the nineteenth century and beginning of the twentieth. The historical background of the **Boxer Protocol** is discussed in the entry on this document.

Boxer Protocol

SIGNED: September 7, 1901, at Peking (Beijing)

IN FORCE: From signing

SIGNATORIES: Germany, Austria-Hungary, Belgium, Spain, United States, France, Great Britain, Italy, Japan, Netherlands, Russia (the "Great Powers") vs. China

OVERVIEW: The protocol was forced on China after the "Great Powers" put down an antiforeign uprising there known as the Boxer Rebellion. The protocol assessed an exorbitant punitive indemnity to be paid by China, which also agreed to the stationing of foreign troops at the legations in Peking (Beijing) and along overland routes to the sea. With the Spanish-American War (1898), United States intervention in the Boxer Rebellion and the subsequent protocol marked America's entry into international politics as a world power with at least a moderately imperialist agenda.

DISCUSSION:

In 1899, U.S. Secretary of State John Hay communicated with the governments of France, Germany, Great Britain, Italy, Russia, and Japan, endorsing an "Open Door Policy" (first suggested by a British customs official, Alfred E. Hippisley) with regard to China, proposing that all should have equal access to Chinese trade.

The Open Door Policy met with almost universal approval among the nations of the West (Japan balked)—except that, in a high-handed manner, none of the nations involved consulted China on the matter. That ancient empire, racked by internal disturbances and tenuously held by Tz'u-hsi, the empress dowager, was in the throes of intense antiforeign feeling. In the spring of 1900, the empress dowager encouraged an uprising of units of a militant secret society called the Yihe Quang, loosely translated as the "righteous harmony of fists" and derisively called by Westerners "the Boxers." The Boxers rampaged throughout the country, killing foreigners as well as Christian Chinese, and in the capital city of Peking (Beijing), they attacked the legations of European nations and Japan. A German diplomat and a Japanese diplomat were slain.

An international coalition of British, French, German, Japanese, Russian, and U.S. troops was sent to the Chinese capital to put down the Boxer Rebellion. After this was readily accomplished, the coalition nations drew up the Boxer Protocol, imposing an exorbitant $333 million indemnity against China, which was also compelled to agree to the stationing of U.S. and other troops in the country.

Even before the troops had been dispatched, Secretary Hay, who feared that the other members of the coalition would use the Boxer Uprising as a pretext to abrogate the Open Door policy and dismember China, issued a "circular letter" (July 3), stating the policy of the United States "to seek a solution which may bring about permanent safety and peace to China, preserve Chinese territorial and administrative entity, protect all rights guaranteed to friendly powers by treaty and international law, and safeguard for the world the principle of equal and impartial trade with all parts of the Chinese Empire."

Hay's statement of policy notwithstanding, the United States not only endorsed the Boxer Protocol, but was to share in the indemnity to the tune of $24,500,000. In a fit of conscience, the United States subsequently reduced its share of the indemnity to $12 million, then, in 1924, forgave the unpaid balance due on that reduced amount. Although these gestures were calculated to demonstrate America's good faith, the United States itself would repeatedly acquiesce to violations of the Open Door Policy. The Taft-Katsura memorandum of 1905, between the United States and Japan, established a foundation for a Japanese protectorate in Korea, and the United States acknowledged Japan's "special interests" in China with the **Lansing-Ishii Agreement** of 1917. This helped set the stage for the 1932 Japanese invasion of Manchuria, a prelude to World War II.

The Boxer Protocol had even more immediate effects on China. It proved the final undoing of the Qing, or Manchu, dynasty, which had ruled since 1644 and would be overthrown in the Chinese Revolution of 1911.

In addition to the indemnity and the stationing of troops, the Boxer Protocol called for:

- Chinese funding of a monument to the German minister to China, killed by the Boxers
- An official apology to Japan for the assassination of the chancellor of the Japanese legation

- Prosecution and punishment of "the principal authors of the . . . crimes committed against the foreign Governments and their nationals"
- Erection of "expiatory monuments in each of the foreign or international cemeteries which were desecrated" during the Boxer Rebellion
- Prohibition of Chinese importation of arms and ammunition for at least two years, with optional extensions "in case of necessity recognized by the Powers"
- An area of Peking (Beijing) to be put under the "exclusive control" of the Great Powers for the purpose of maintaining their legations
- Chinese legislation forbidding membership in any antiforeign society ("under pain of death")

- Improvement of internal waterways to make them accessible to foreign commerce; expenses to be shared by China and the Great Powers

REFERENCES:

Bodin, Lynn. *The Boxer Rebellion.* Mechanicsburg, PA: Stackpole Books, 1979

Buck, David. ed., *Recent Chinese Studies of the Boxer Movement.* Armonk, NY, 1987.

Cohen, Paul A. *History in Three Keys: The Boxers as Event, Experience, and Myth.* New York: Columbia University Press, 1997.

Israel, Fred L. *Major Peace Treaties of Modern History, 1648-1967,* vol. 1. New York: Chelsea House and McGraw-Hill, 1967.

SECTION 2.8

World War I

Overview of the Conflict

On June 28, 1914, the Austro-Hungarian Archduke Franz Ferdinand and his wife, the Grand Duchess Sophie, were assassinated in Sarajevo by a young Serbian nationalist named Gavrilo Princip. Austria-Hungary responded by accusing Serbia of having plotted the assassination, and, through a tangled complex of alliances, most of Europe was suddenly plunged into a war that engulfed not only the continent, but the farflung colonial possessions of the belligerents as well. Of the major world powers, only the United States managed to remain aloof from what was being called the Great War and would later be called World War I. Anxious to preserve the rights of American neutrality, President Woodrow Wilson sternly warned Germany in February 1915 that the United States would hold it strictly accountable for the loss of American lives in the sinking of neutral or passenger ships. Just four months later, on May 7, 1915, a German U-boat torpedoed the British passenger liner *Lusitania*, killing 1,200 people, including 128 Americans. Many in the United States, among them former president Theodore Roosevelt, called for immediate entry into the war, but Wilson demurred, instead issuing a strong protest to Germany, demanding reparations and the cessation of unrestricted submarine warfare. For a time, Germany complied, but relations between the United States and Germany deteriorated steadily after the *Lusitania* sinking. A crisis occurred in February 1917, when Germany announced the resumption of unrestricted submarine warfare (a policy of striking without warning), and, on February 3, a U-boat torpedoed and sank the *U.S.S. Housatonic*. President Wilson responded by severing diplomatic relations with Germany. In the meantime, evidence of German espionage operations in the United States mounted. On March 1, the American public learned of the "Zimmerman Note" or "Zimmerman Telegram," a coded message, sent on January 19, 1917 from German foreign secretary Alfred Zimmermann to his nation's ambassador to Mexico, outlining the terms of a proposed German-Mexican alliance against the United States.

It was the last straw. On April 2, 1917, Wilson asked Congress for a declaration of war, which was voted on April 6.

America mobilized as never before. The U.S. Army, numbering only about 200,000 troops in 1917, would grow to four million men by the end of the war, about half of whom would serve overseas in the AEF (Allied Expeditionary Forces). The American commander, General John J. Pershing, arrived in Paris on June 14, 1917, at a low point in the fortunes of the Allies. Every French

offensive had failed, and the demoralized French army was plagued by mutinies. The British had made a major push in Flanders, which ended in a costly stalemate. The Russians, fighting on the Eastern Front, had collapsed and were rushing headlong toward a revolution that would not only end centuries of czarist rule and introduce communism into the world, but that would result in a "separate peace" between Russia and Germany, freeing up masses of German troops for service on the Western Front. Although the first AEF troops followed Pershing on June 26, it would be October 21, 1917, before units were committed to battle, and the spring of 1918 before large numbers of Americans actually made a difference in the fighting.

Between June 6 and July 1, 1918, American units recaptured for the allies Vaux, Bouresches, and Belleau Wood, while also managing to hold the critically important Allied position at Cantigny against a great German offensive during June 9–15. During the period from July 18 to August 6, 85,000 American troops broke the seemingly endless stalemate of the long war by decisively defeating the last major German offensive at the Second Battle of the Marne. This was followed by Allied offensives at the Somme, Oise-Aisne, and Ypres-Lys.

While Americans participated in each of the major August offensives, they took full responsibility for an attack on the St. Mihiel salient during September 12–16, the opening battle in a campaign involving 1.2 million U.S. troops, who pounded and then cut German supply lines between the Meuse River and the Argonne Forest. This campaign, which continued until the very day of armistice, November 11, 1918, was highly successful, but terribly costly, with American units suffering, on average, a casualty rate of 10 percent. The campaign made it clear to Germany that the Americans were both willing and able to press on with the war. Germany and its allies soon surrendered.

President Wilson took a leading role in negotiating the **Treaty of Versailles**, which formally ended the war, and which was linked to the creation of the League of Nations (**Covenant of the League of Nations**) as well as various subsidiary treaties (including the **Treaty of St. Germain** and the **Treaty of Trianon**, represented here). However, in the aftermath of the war, the United States was swept by a tide of isolationism, and President Wilson, chief architect of the Treaty of Versailles and the League of Nations, found himself unable to persuade the Republican-controlled Senate to ratify any of the agreements ending the war and seeking to prevent war in the future.

It was not until 1921 that the United States formally concluded brief peace treaties with Germany, Hungary, and Austria.

Treaty of Versailles

SIGNED: June 28, 1919, Versailles, France

IN FORCE: Not ratified by the United States Senate

SIGNATORIES: United States (failed to ratify), British Empire, France, Italy, and Japan ("Principal Allied and Associated Powers"), Belgium, Bolivia, Brazil, China, Cuba, Ecuador, Greece, Guatemala, Haiti, the Hedjaz, Honduras, Liberia, Nicaragua, Panama, Peru, Poland, Portugal, Romania, Serb-Croat-Slovene State, Siam, Czechoslovakia, and Uruguay ("The Allied and Associated Powers") vs. Germany

OVERVIEW: One of the most momentous treaties in history, the Treaty of Versailles ended World War I, but levied punitive conditions against Germany, which created the climate in which the outbreak of another world war was virtually assured.

DISCUSSION:

Hostilities in the "Great War," as it was then called—World War I, as it would come to be known—ended with the armistice of November 11, 1918. On November 17, 1918, under terms of the armistice, Allied troops began to reoccupy those portions of France and Belgium that had been held by the Germans since their first big push during the opening weeks of the war, in 1914. Allied and U.S. troops followed the withdrawing Germans into Germany itself, and, on December 9, the Allied armies crossed the Rhine, taking up positions at the bridgeheads agreed to in the armistice. A peace conference—among the Allies and excluding the "Central Powers" (Germany, Austria-Hungary, and its allies)—was convened at Paris on January 18, 1919.

Although twenty-seven Allied nations participated in the creation of the Treaty of Versailles, the four major Allied powers, Britain, France, Italy, and the United States, dominated the Paris Peace Conference. U.S. president Woodrow Wilson championed a conciliatory settlement based on his famous "Fourteen Points," which he had enumerated before a joint session of Congress on January 8, 1918, as the basis for a just peace:

- Point one called for "open covenants, openly arrived at," mandating an end to the kind of secret treaties and alliances that had dragged Europe into war.
- Point two, freedom of the seas
- Point three, removal of economic barriers to international trade
- Point four, radical reduction of armaments to the lowest point consistent with domestic security
- Point five, modification of all colonial claims on the basis of the self-determination of peoples

The eight points that followed these addressed specific postwar territorial settlements, and, most important, the fourteenth point called for a league of nations, an international body that would guarantee political independence and territorial integrity for all nations and would provide a forum for the peaceful resolution of conflict.

Opposed to Wilson's idealistically conciliatory position was French premier Georges Clemenceau. It was France that had made the greatest sacrifices in the war, and Clemenceau wanted not only to secure France against future German attack by destroying Germany's ability to make war, but also to exact vengeance. He favored a thoroughly punitive treaty.

The two other constituents of the "Big Four," British prime minister David Lloyd George and Italy's Premier Vittorio Orlando, also had their own aims. Lloyd George personally favored moderation, but had been elected on his promise that Germany would be punished. He was also concerned that Wilson's Fourteen Points would interfere with British colonial policy. As for Orlando, his principal concern was to ensure that Italy would receive the territories it had been promised in 1915 as inducement to join the Allied cause.

After much debate, Clemenceau abandoned his chief demand, that the left bank of the Rhine be detached from Germany and put under French military control, in exchange for British and American promises of future alliance and support. Yet most of the treaty by no means conformed to the Fourteen Points, either. It was both punitive and humiliating to Germany and its allies, collectively called the Central Powers. None of these nations were allowed to participate in the Versailles peace conference and had no part in hammering out terms.

The Treaty of Versailles is a complex document, the size of a small book. Its chief provisions include German territorial cessions, German admission of guilt for the war, German disarmament, and an assessment against Germany (and other Central Powers) of harsh monetary reparations. More specifically:

- The population and territory of Germany was reduced by about 10 percent by the treaty.
- Alsace and Lorraine were returned to France.
- The Saarland was placed under the supervision of the League of Nations until 1935.
- Three small northern areas were given to Belgium.
- Pursuant to a plebiscite in Schleswig, northern Schleswig was taken from Germany and returned to Denmark.
- A new Poland was created, given most of formerly German West Prussia and Poznán (Posen), as well as a "corridor" to the Baltic Sea; pursuant to a plebiscite, it also gained part of Upper Silesia.
- Danzig (Gdansk) was declared a free city.
- Germany's overseas colonies in China, the Pacific, and Africa were taken over by Britain, France, Japan, and other Allied nations.
- Germany was compelled to endorse a "war guilt clause," deeming itself the aggressor. This was not only spiritually

debilitating, it made Germany liable for all reparations to the Allied nations.

- Part VII of the treaty accused the German emperor, Kaiser Wilhelm II, of having committed war crimes. He was guaranteed a fair trial, and the Allies reserved the right to bring unspecified others before war crimes tribunals.(Ultimately, neither the kaiser nor anyone else was tried for war crimes following World War I. Wilhelm fled to Holland after the war, and the Dutch government declined to extradite him to the jurisdiction of the Allies. He remained in Dutch exile until his death, at the beginning of World War II, on June 8, 1941. He was an ardent supporter of Adolf Hitler and the Nazi party.)
- Reparations were called for, but had not been computed by the time the treaty was signed. In 1921, they were fixed at $33,000,000,000. Even though all of the signatories understood that payment of such a sum would destroy the German economy, which, in turn, would have a negative impact on international finances, the Allies insisted that Germany pay, and the treaty allowed for punitive actions if Germany failed to make the payments according to a specified schedule.
- The German army was limited to 100,000 men, and the general staff was abolished. (This provision would backfire on the Allies. German military authorities took advantage of the limitation to create an elite, all-volunteer Fuhrerheer, roughly translated as "army of leaders." It would form the core of the formidable army with which Adolf Hitler would terrorize Europe and prosecute World War II.)
- The manufacture of armored cars, tanks, submarines, airplanes, and poison gas was prohibited, and munitions production was drastically curtailed.
- Germany west of the Rhine and up to 30 miles east of that river was declared a demilitarized zone.
- Allied occupation of the Rhineland was set to continue for at least fifteen years, and possibly longer.

In fairness to the Allies, the disarmament of Germany was intended to spark voluntary disarmament by other nations. In this spirit, and in accordance with Wilson's fourteenth point, the Treaty of Versailles included the Covenant of the League of Nations (treated in a separate entry), creating an international body chiefly for the peaceful arbitration of international disputes.

On May 7, 1919, the treaty was presented to a German delegation headed by German foreign minister Graf Ulrich von Brockdorff-Rantzauthe. The delegation denounced it, protesting that it abrogated the Fourteen Points, which had been the basis of the armistice on November 11, 1918. Brockdorff-Rantzauthe further declared that Germany was unable to pay the reparations demanded. Germany's chancellor, Philipp Scheidemann, likewise denounced the treaty when it was presented to him. In response, the Allies initiated a naval blockade of Germany. Scheidemann and Brockdorff-Rantzau

resigned in protest on June 21, and, that same day, at Scapa Flow, German sailors scuttled all fifty warships of High Seas Fleet to keep the vessels from becoming Allied prizes. A new German chancellor, Gustav Bauer, sent another delegation to Versailles, and, on June 28, signed the document under protest, informing the Allies that the treaty was being accepted only to end the hardships caused by the "inhuman" blockade.

The Treaty of Versailles is one of history's great tragic documents. It created the political, economic, and emotional climate that promoted the rise of Adolf Hitler and Naziism, and that made a *second* world war inevitable. Almost immediately, Germany flouted the treaty and rearmed—at first covertly and then, under Adolf Hitler during the 1930s, openly. The war-weary Allies did nothing.

In a particularly pointed irony, the United States Senate failed to ratify the Treaty of Versailles or the Covenant of the League of Nations. President Wilson campaigned intensively for ratification, taking his case to the American people in a cross-country whistle-stop speaking tour. The desperate effort broke his health. After collapsing in Pueblo, Colorado, he suffered a debilitating stroke and served out the remainder of his term as a shadow of himself. Later, the United States arranged separate peace treaties with Germany, Austria, and Hungary.

REFERENCES:

Boemeke, Manfred F. *The Treaty of Versailles: A Reassessment after 75 Years.* London: Cambridge University Press, 1998.

Israel, Fred L. *Major Peace Treaties of Modern History, 1648-1967*, vol. 2. New York: Chelsea House and McGraw-Hill, 1967.

Kleine-Ahlbrandt, W. Laird. *The Burden of Victory: France, Britain, and the Enforcement of the Versailles Peace, 1919-1925.* Lanham, MD: University press of America, 1995.

United States Department of States Staff. *Treaty of Versailles and After: Annotation of the Text and Treaty.* Atlanta: Scholarly Press, 1968.

Covenant of the League of Nations

SIGNED: June 28, 1919, Versailles, France (with amendments adopted through December 1924)

IN FORCE: Not ratified by the United States Senate

SIGNATORIES: United States (failed to ratify), British Empire, France, Italy, and Japan ("Principal Allied and Associated Powers"), Belgium, Bolivia, Brazil, China, Cuba, Ecuador, Greece, Guatemala, Haiti, the Hedjaz, Honduras, Liberia, Nicaragua, Panama, Peru, Poland, Portugal, Romania, Serb-Croat-Slovene State, Siam, Czechoslovakia, and Uruguay ("The Allied and Associated Powers") vs. Germany

OVERVIEW: The Covenant of the League of Nations, an integral part of the **Treaty of Versailles** (as well as certain other treaties relating to the conclusion of World War I), created the League as a permanent organization to promote international peace, to achieve the pacific resolution of international disputes, and to define and protect the rights, sovereignty, and self-determination of all nations.

DISCUSSION:

The Hague conferences of 1899 and 1907 (see **Hague Convention [1899]** and **Hague Convention [1907]**) and the horrors of World War I (1914-1918) encouraged many diplomats and political leaders to consider international alternatives to war. Woodrow Wilson, Jan Smuts of South Africa, and Lord Robert Cecil of the British cabinet, advocated an international league to prevent future wars, and this idea was embodied in the last of Wilson's "Fourteen Points," which the president proposed in the final year of World War I as the basis for a just peace. It was largely at Wilson's insistence that the Covenant of the League of Nations became part and parcel of the Treaty of Versailles in 1919.

The twenty-six-article Covenant sets out three principal approaches to preventing war:
- arbitration in to resolve international disputes
- general disarmament
- establishment of collective security through guarantees of rights and sovereignty

The sixty-three nations that ultimately subscribed to the Covenant became members of the League and were represented in an assembly, which was to hold regular sessions annually and additional sessions as necessary. The Covenant gave each member one vote; however, unanimity was required for all decisions. This requirement doomed the League to chronic paralysis.

The general assembly of all member nations regulated matters of ways and means as well as membership, and it functioned as a forum for airing international issues. A more select body, the council, conducted the principal political work of the League, most importantly the resolution of international disputes. Permanent seats on the council were reserved for Britain, France, Japan, Italy, and, later, Germany and the Soviet Union. Had the United States Senate ratified the Treaty of Versailles and thereby consented to join the League, it, too, would have had a place on the council. Other nations were elected to temporary representation on the council. The administrative functions of the League were administered by a third body, the secretariat.

The League also administered the Permanent International Court of Justice, or World Court, which had evolved from the Permanent Court of Arbitration (popularly called the Hague Tribunal), established by the Hague Convention (1899). An International Labor Organization was also under the aegis of the League. The League of Nations first convened on January 10, 1920. A mandate system, whereby major Allied powers assigned governmental authority over former colonies and possessions of the Central Powers, was also established and administered by the League. Although never a League member, the United States partic-ipated in assigning mandates, while refusing any mandate roles for itself.

International sentiment, at first highly favorable to the League of Nations, became increasingly negative as the shortcomings of the institution became increasingly apparent.
- Making the Covenant part of the Treaty of Versailles compromised the League's impartiality, making it appear to be a tool of the victorious Allies.
- The failure of the United States to join the League crippled it.
- The requirement of unanimous often prevented the League from taking meaningful action; for example, the Geneva Protocol of 1924, which defined aggressive war as an international crime, failed because of British opposition.

Although the League successfully resolved a handful of minor disputes, it failed to meet its first major challenge. When the Japanese invaded Manchuria in September 1931, the League responded by sending a commission of inquiry in 1932, and Japan simply withdrew from the League the following year. The League of Nations was powerless to do anything to compel Japan to return the territory it had seized. Throughout the 1930s, the League failed to act effectively against the aggression of Nazi Germany and Fascist Italy. Ultimately, these aggressor nations made the League irrelevant by withdrawing from it.

REFERENCES:

Israel, Fred L. *Major Peace Treaties of Modern History, 1648-1967*, vol. 3. New York: Chelsea House and McGraw-Hill, 1967.

Kuehl, Warren F., and Lynne K. Dunn. *Keeping the Covenant: American Internationalists and the League of Nations, 1920-1939*. Kent, OH: Kent State University Press, 1997.

Ostrower, Gary B. *The League of Nations: From 1919 to 1929*. Wayne, NJ: Avery, 1996.

Treaty of St. Germain

SIGNED: September 10, 1919, at St. Germain-en-Laye

IN FORCE: Not ratified by the United States Senate

SIGNATORIES: United States (failed to ratify), British Empire, France, Italy, and Japan ("Principal Allied and Associated Powers"), Belgium, China, Cuba, Ecuador, Greece, Nicaragua, Panama, Poland, Portugal, Romania, Serb-Croat-Slovene State, Siam, and Czechoslovakia ("The Allied and Associated Powers") vs. Austria

OVERVIEW: With the **Treaty of Versailles** and the Treaty of Brest-Litovsk (the separate peace between the Soviet Union and Germany), the Treaty of St. Germain, dissolving the Austro-Hungarian Empire, is among the most important treaties ending World War I.

DISCUSSION:

World War I was formally concluded by several volumes of treaties, including the **Treaty of Versailles,** the central document; the Treaty of Neuilly (named for the Paris suburb where it was negotiated), between Bulgaria and the Allies; the **Treaty of Trianon**, which reduced the territory of Hungary from 109,000 square miles to less than 36,000 square miles and imposed other severe conditions; the Treaty of Sèvres (named for another Paris suburb), between the Allies and Turkey; and the Treaty of Lausanne, by which Turkey recognized the independence of the Arab Kingdom of Hejaz, the French mandate over Syria, and the British mandates over Palestine and Mesopotamia, as well as Greek and Italian occupation of most of its former Aegean islands.

Named for yet another Paris suburb, the Treaty of St. Germain formalized the dissolution of the Austro-Hungarian (Hapsburg) Empire, which had taken place, in fact, during October-November 1918. Austria, now a small republic, acceded to the following political dispositions made stipulated in the Treaty of Versailles:

- The independence of Czechoslovakia, Poland, Yugoslavia
- The award of Galicia to Poland and of the Trentino, South Tyrol, Trieste, and Istria to Italy
- The reduction of the Austrian to a maximum of 30,000 men
- The payment of reparations
- An acknowledgment of a ban on any union with Germany (a provision abrogated by the 1938 *Anschluss,* Nazi Germany's annexation of Austria)

As with the Treaty of Versailles, the Covenant of the League of Nations was an integral part of the treaty, constituting its "Part I." Part II defined the new, greatly contracted frontiers of Austria. Part III, "Political Clauses for Europe," stipulated Austria's acknowledgment of relevant cessions and awards made by the Treaty of Versailles and secured Austria's pledge to protect minorities within its borders, pursuant to one of Woodrow Wilson's Fourteen Points. In Part IV, Austria renounced all of its colonial possessions.

REFERENCES:
Boemeke, Manfred F. *The Treaty of Versailles: A Reassessment after 75 Years.* London: Cambridge University Press, 1998.
Israel, Fred L. *Major Peace Treaties of Modern History, 1648-1967,* vol. 2. New York: Chelsea House and McGraw-Hill, 1967.
Kleine-Ahlbrandt, W. Laird. *The Burden of Victory: France, Britain, and the Enforcement of the Versailles Peace, 1919-1925.* Lanham, MD: University press of America, 1995.
United States Department of States Staff. *Treaty of Versailles and After: Annotation of the Text and Treaty.* Atlanta: Scholarly Press, 1968.

Treaty of Trianon

SIGNED: June 4, 1920, Trianon, Versailles, France
IN FORCE: Not ratified by the United States Senate
SIGNATORIES: The "Principal Allied Powers" (United States [failed to ratify], British Empire [U.K.], France, Italy, and Japan) and the "Associated Powers" (Belgium, China, Cuba, Greece, Nicaragua, Panama, Poland, Portugal, Romania, the Serb-Croat-Slovene State, Siam, and Czechoslovakia) vs. Hungary
OVERVIEW: One of the numerous treaties related to **The Treaty of Versailles** and attendant upon the end of World War I, Trianon, together with the **Treaty of St. Germain**, brought an end to the Austro-Hungarian Empire.

DISCUSSION:
The defeat of the Central Powers in World War I brought an end to the Austro-Hungarian (Hapsburg) Empire. The Treaty of St. Germain broke up the dual empire, and the Treaty of Trianon subtracted three-quarters of what was left of Hungary.

Like the other World War I peace treaties associated with the Treaty of Versailles, the Treaty of Trianon begins with the Covenant of the League of Nations. Next, the treaty defines the contracted frontiers of Hungary:

- To Italy was ceded "all rights and title . . . [to] the territories of the former Austro-Hungarian Monarchy recognized as forming part of Italy in accordance with [the Treaty of St. Germain]."
- Similar cessions were made to the Serb-Croat-Slovene State created by the Treaty of Versailles, to Romania, and to Czechoslovakia.
- The ethnically Italian Adriatic port city of Fiume, formerly a part of Austria-Hungary, was renounced; however, its disposition was left undecided.
- In articles similar to those of the Allies' treaty with Bulgaria (Treaty of Neuilly), Hungary was bound to protect the civil and human rights of minorities living within its borders.

The break up of the Austro-Hungarian Empire and the reduction of Hungary (from 109,000 square miles to less 36,000 square miles in extent) created many problems of nationality, addressed in "Clauses Relating to Nationality" (treaty Articles 61-66), but which resurfaced throughout the twentieth century and which will likely continue to figure in the geopolitics of southeastern Europe into twenty-first century.

The Treaty of Trianon (Articles 102-160) reduced strength of the Hungarian armed forces to a maximum of 35,000 men, and obligated the nation to pay war reparations, but deferred fixing the amount to a later time, pending the work of a Reparation Commission.

Because the Treaty of Trianon required membership in the League of Nations, the United Senate declined to ratify the treaty, and a separate peace was made with Hungary (United States and Hungary Treaty of Peace) in 1921.

REFERENCES:
Israel, Fred L. *Major Peace Treaties of Modern History, 1648-1967,* vols. 2 and 3. New York: Chelsea House and McGraw-Hill, 1967.
United States Department of States Staff. *Treaty of Versailles and After: Annotation of the Text and Treaty.* Atlanta: Scholarly Press, 1968.

United States and Germany Treaty of Peace

SIGNED: August 25, 1921, at Berlin
IN FORCE: From signing
SIGNATORIES: United States vs. Germany
OVERVIEW: The Senate having declined to ratify the **Treaty of Versailles** (1919) definitively ending World War I, the United States made this separate peace with Germany.

DISCUSSION:

Whereas the Treaty of Versailles is a complex, book-length document, the United States and Germany Treaty of Peace is a mere four pages. The text of the treaty consists mainly of a citation of a Joint Resolution of Congress, approved by President Warren G. Harding on July 2, 1921, resolving that war between the United States and Germany had ended and selectively approving sections of the Treaty of Versailles (including all items of reparation, disarmament, and German admission of war guilt) as applying to the terms of peace prevailing between the two nations. In this way, the United States acknowledged the validity of the Treaty of Versailles without formally ratifying it (and without, therefore, accepting membership in the League of Nations). The treaty is similar to treaties concluded between the United States and Austria and Hungary.

REFERENCES:

Boemeke, Manfred F. *The Treaty of Versailles: A Reassessment after 75 Years.* London: Cambridge University Press, 1998.

Israel, Fred L. *Major Peace Treaties of Modern History, 1648-1967,* vol. 2. New York: Chelsea House and McGraw-Hill, 1967.

Kleine-Ahlbrandt, W. Laird. *The Burden of Victory: France, Britain, and the Enforcement of the Versailles Peace, 1919-1925.* Lanham, MD: University press of America, 1995.

United States Department of States Staff. *Treaty of Versailles and After: Annotation of the Text and Treaty.* Atlanta: Scholarly Press, 1968.

United States and Hungary Treaty of Peace

SIGNED: August 29, 1921, at Budapest
IN FORCE: From December 17, 1921
SIGNATORIES: United States vs. Hungary
OVERVIEW: The Armistice of November 11, 1918 ended hostilities between the United States and the Central Powers (including Hungary), but the U.S. Senate declined to ratify the **Treaty of Versailles** and the other major treaties of peace with the Central Powers (because these treaties required membership in the League of Nations, which the Senate rejected); therefore, the United State made a separate peace with Hungary, as it did with the other Central Powers.

DISCUSSION:

Concluded within days following the U.S. treaties with Austria (**United States and Austria Treaty of Peace**) and Germany (**United States and Germany Treaty of Peace**), the Hungarian treaty is identical in principle to those. It asserts the U.S. right to the benefits of the **Treaty of Trianon**, which the other Allies concluded with Hungary, but which the United States Senate declined to ratify because signature entailed membership in the League of Nations, which the Senate repudiated.

REFERENCES:

Boemeke, Manfred F. *The Treaty of Versailles: A Reassessment after 75 Years.* London: Cambridge University Press, 1998.

Israel, Fred L. *Major Peace Treaties of Modern History, 1648-1967,* vol. 2. New York: Chelsea House and McGraw-Hill, 1967.

Kleine-Ahlbrandt, W. Laird. *The Burden of Victory: France, Britain, and the Enforcement of the Versailles Peace, 1919-1925.* Lanham, MD: University press of America, 1995.

United States Department of States Staff. *Treaty of Versailles and After: Annotation of the Text and Treaty.* Atlanta: Scholarly Press, 1968.

United States and Austria Treaty of Peace

SIGNED: August 24, 1921, at Vienna
IN FORCE: From November 8, 1921
SIGNATORIES: United States vs. Austria
OVERVIEW: The Armistice of November 11, 1918 ended hostilities between the United States and the Central Powers (including Austria), but the U.S. Senate declined to ratify the **Treaty of Versailles** and the other major treaties of peace with the Central Powers (because these treaties required membership in the League of Nations, which the Senate rejected); therefore, the United State made a separate peace with Austria, as it did with the other Central Powers.

DISCUSSION:

As with the **United States and Germany Treaty of Peace** and the **United States and Hungary Treaty of Peace**, the treaty with Austria is little more than the statement of a joint resolution of the U.S. Congress. The treaty asserts the U.S. right to the benefits of the **Treaty of St. Germain**, which the other allies concluded with Austria, but which the United States Senate declined to ratify because signature entailed membership in the League of Nations, which the Senate repudiated.

REFERENCES:

Boemeke, Manfred F. *The Treaty of Versailles: A Reassessment after 75 Years.* London: Cambridge University Press, 1998.

Israel, Fred L. *Major Peace Treaties of Modern History, 1648-1967,* vol. 2. New York: Chelsea House and McGraw-Hill, 1967.

Kleine-Ahlbrandt, W. Laird. *The Burden of Victory: France, Britain, and the Enforcement of the Versailles Peace, 1919-1925.* Lanham, MD: University press of America, 1995.

United States Department of States Staff. *Treaty of Versailles and After: Annotation of the Text and Treaty.* Atlanta: Scholarly Press, 1968.

SECTION 2.9

World War II

Overview of the Conflict

During much of the 1930s, the United States nervously eyed Europe, which, driven by the bellicose dictators of Italy and Germany, seemed unalterably destined for war. Congress responded to the situation by enacting a policy of neutrality (**Neutrality Act of 1937, Neutrality Act of 1939**), but also by affirming **The Monroe Doctrine** of 1823 (Section 1.1) in such documents as **Act of Havana** (1940), **U.S. State Department Bulletin on Hemispheric Defense** (1940), and **Resolution Reaffirming the Monroe Doctrine** (1941). Toward Great Britain, at war with Germany since September 1939 and in imminent danger of invasion, the United States progressively relaxed its policy of neutrality, at first supplying Britain with munitions on a cash-and-carry basis, then on the more liberal basis of "Lend-Lease," which gave the president the authority to aid any nation whose defense he deemed critical to that of the United States, and further authorized the acceptance of repayment not necessarily in cash, but "in kind or property, or any other direct or indirect benefit which the President deems satisfactory" (**Lend-Lease Act**, 1941).

Although a military draft and other war preparations were set into motion, the United States held back from entering the European war until the morning of December 7, 1941, when the Japanese executed a massive surprise attack against the U.S. naval and army bases at Pearl Harbor, Hawaii. The nation declared war the next day and found itself called to fight on two fronts.

The blow at Pearl Harbor was just one of many Japanese assaults. Japanese forces attacked Wake Island and Guam (both U.S. possessions), British Malaya, Singapore, the Dutch East Indies, Burma, Thailand, and the Philippines (at the time a U.S. commonwealth territory). The U.S. garrison on Guam was overwhelmed and surrendered, and, on Wake Island, Marines repelled a first Japanese attack, but yielded to a second. Britain's crown colony of Hong Kong collapsed, soon followed by Singapore (another British possession), and then the Dutch East Indies and Burma. Worst of all was the loss of the Philippines, defended valiantly, but at last relinquished on May 6, 1942.

Desperate for a counterstrike against Japan, the Army Air Force approved the plan of Lieutenant Colonel James Doolittle to take sixteen twin-engine B-25 bombers aboard the aircraft carrier Hornet and launch, on April 18, 1942, a surprise raid on Tokyo. The raid created only minor physical damage to Tokyo, but its psychological effect was great. The attack profoundly shocked the Japanese, who were forced to tie up more fighter aircraft at home, and American morale was given a terrific boost.

But the principal American effort in the early years of the war was in the Atlantic theater. The British and Americans agreed to conduct a North African campaign, defeat the Germans there, and then use North Africa as stepping-off point to attack what Britain's great wartime prime minister, Winston Churchill, called the "soft underbelly of Europe." Forces under British Field Marshal Bernard Law Montgomery and American generals Dwight D. Eisenhower and George S. Patton decisively defeated the Germans and Italians in North Africa by May 1943, then launched an invasion of Sicily.

Now, as Africa was being pried from German hands, American forces began to turn the tide in the Pacific. During May 3-9, 1942, the navy sunk or disabled more than twenty-five Japanese ships, blocking Japan's extension to the south and preventing the Japanese from severing supply lines to Australia. However, the Japanese soon returned to the offensive by attacking the island of Midway, some 1,100 miles northwest of Hawaii. The great naval Battle of Midway commenced on June 3, 1942, and U.S. aircraft, launched from the *Hornet, Yorktown,* and *Enterprise,* sank four Japanese carriers. Reeling from this blow, the Imperial Navy withdrew its fleet, but the Americans gave chase, sinking or disabling two heavy cruisers and three destroyers, as well as destroying 322 Japanese planes. Despite heavy U.S. Navy losses, Midway was a victory for the United States, which prevented Japan from resuming the offensive in the Pacific.

After the defeat at Midway, the Japanese turned their attention to mounting a full-scale assault on Australia, which they began by building an airstrip on Guadalcanal in the southern Solomon Islands. Responding to this development, on August 7, 1942, U.S. Marines landed at Guadalcanal and fought a pitched battle against the Japanese for the next six months. The American victory at Guadalcanal was the beginning of a strategy of "island hopping," a plan to take all of the Japanese-held islands, gradually closing in for an invasion of the Japanese mainland itself.

As U.S. forces island hopped in the Pacific, British and American troops began the invasion of Europe via Sicily and thence, on September 3, 1943, to the Italian mainland. The Italian campaign was grindingly slow and costly, and it was not until June

4, 1944, that Rome fell to the Allies. From this point on, the Germans steadily retreated northward. Although U.S. forces entered Europe through Italy, fighting on the Continent was far more widespread. The Soviets, who suffered the heaviest casualties of the war and who had been devastated by a surprise German invasion begun on June 22, 1941, were fighting back with a vengeance. The Battle of Stalingrad (present-day Volgograd), fought from July 17 to November 18, 1942, resulted in the loss of 750,000 Soviet troops, but also 850,000 Nazis. It turned the grim tide of warfare on the Eastern Front in favor of the Soviets.

In the meantime, too, since May 1942, British Royal Air Force (RAF) bombers and (beginning in the summer of 1942) U.S. Army Air Corps bombers had been pummeling industrial targets throughout Germany. At sea, the Battle of the Atlantic had raged since early 1942. From January to June, German U-boats sunk three million tons of U.S. shipping. However, the development of longer-range aircraft and more advanced radar systems led to effective defenses against U-boats, and, by the spring of 1943, the U-boat threat had been greatly reduced.

With pressure applied from the south, from the east, from the air, and at sea, the time was at last right for a major Allied thrust from the west. For this, the Allies mounted in Britain the largest and most powerful invasion force in history. Officially christened Operation Overlord, the invasion of Normandy became popularly known by the military designation of the day of its commencement: D-Day, June 6, 1944. From France, the Allies launched an invasion into the German homeland itself. By early September, British forces liberated Brussels, Belgium, and American troops crossed the German frontier at Eupen. On October 21, the U.S. First Army captured Aachen—the first German city to fall to the Allies. Through the fall and winter, the Germans retreated, until December 16, 1944, when General Gerd von Rundstedt led a desperate counteroffensive, driving a wedge into Allied lines through the Ardennes on the Franco-Belgian frontier. With German forces distending the Allied line westward, the ensuing combat was called the Battle of the Bulge. The U.S. First and Third armies—the latter led brilliantly by General George S. Patton—pushed back the bulge, which was wholly contained by January 1945. It was the last great German offensive, and it was Germany's last chance to stop the Allies' advance into its homeland.

During February 1945, General Patton sped his armored units to the Rhine River and, after clearing the west bank, captured the bridge at Remagen, near Cologne, on March 7. Allied forces crossed this bridge, as well as at other points along the Rhine, and were now poised to make a run for Berlin. However, General Eisenhower, believing Hitler would make his last stand in the German south, chose to head for Leipzig. With U.S. troops just ninety-six miles west of Berlin, the Supreme Allied Commander sent a message to Soviet dictator Josef Stalin, telling him that he was leaving the German capital to the Red Army. While the British and Americans had been closing in from the West, the Soviets had executed a massive assault on the German's Eastern Front. By the end of January, the Red Army had pushed through Poland into Germany itself. On April 16, 1945, Soviet Marshal Georgy Zhukov moved his troops into Berlin. Westbound Soviet and eastbound American troops met at the river Elbe on April 25, 1945. Five days later, Adolf Hitler, holed up in a bunker beneath the shattered streets of Berlin, killed himself. On May 7, 1945, senior representatives of Germany's armed forces surrendered to the Allies at General Eisenhower's headquarters in Rheims, France (**Act of Military Surrender [at Rheims]**). The very next day came a formal unconditional surrender (**Act of Military Surrender [at Berlin]**).

The war in the Pacific raged on, and the Allies turned to planning the final invasion of Japan. By the **Yalta Agreement** (1945), the Soviet Union resolved to enter the war against Japan. But an invasion was made unnecessary when the United States unleashed its terrible new "secret weapon" on the Japanese cities of Hiroshima (August 6, 1945) and Nagasaki (August 9). These two "atomic bombs" abruptly ended World War II. On August 10, the day after the attack on Nagasaki, Japan sued for peace on condition that the emperor be allowed to remain as sovereign ruler. On August 11, the Allies replied that they and they alone would determine the future of Emperor Hirohito. At last, on August 14, the emperor personally accepted the Allied terms, a cease-fire was declared on August 15, and, on September 2, 1945, General MacArthur presided over the Japanese signing of the formal surrender document on the deck of the U.S. battleship *Missouri*, anchored in Tokyo Bay (**Japanese Surrender Documents**).

Neutrality Act of 1937

SIGNED: May 1, 1937, at Washington, D.C.
SIGNATORIES: Act of Congress
IN FORCE: From signing
OVERVIEW: The third of four neutrality acts of the late 1930s, which guided United States international policy on the eve of World War II and at its outbreak.

DISCUSSION:
The first neutrality act of the era was passed in August 1935 in response to Italy's attack on Ethiopia. It empowered the president to embargo arms shipments to belligerents and to warn United States citizens traveling on belligerents' ships that they did so at their own risk. A second act, passed in February 1936, added a prohibition on extending loans or credits to belligerents. Significantly, neither act distinguished between aggressor and victim.

The outbreak of the Spanish Civil War in July 1936 posed a problem because the existing acts applied only to wars between nations, not civil conflicts. A joint resolution of Congress of January 6, 1937, forbade supplying either side with arms, and when the 1936 Neutrality Act expired, the 1937 act not only included civil wars, but also authorized the president to expand the embargo list with the addition of strategic materials. Even more significantly, the 1937 act outlawed travel by United States nationals aboard ships of the belligerents.

As President Franklin Roosevelt increasingly saw the nation's interests as lying with the opponents of fascism, the Neutrality Act of 1937 became an obstacle to foreign policy, and the president enforced it selectively, especially in supplying aid to China, which had been invaded by Japan.

The 1937 act made these additional provisions:

- Section 4 excepted from the act "an American republic or republics engaged in war against a non-American state or states, provided the American republic is not cooperating with a non-American state or states in such a war." This was pursuant to the long-standing policies known as the **Monroe Doctrine** and the Roosevelt Corollary to the Monroe Doctrine.
- Section 5 created a National Munitions Control Board, charged with carrying out the provisions of the act.
- Section 6 prohibited American vessels from carrying arms to belligerent states.
- Section 7: "(a) Whenever, during any war in which the United States is neutral, the President, or any person thereunto authorized by him, shall have cause to believe that nay vessel, domestic or foreign, whether requiring clearance or not, is about to carry out of a port of the Untied States, fuel, men, arms, ammunition, implements of war, or other supplies to any warship, tender, or supply ship of a belligerent state, but the evidence is not deemed sufficient to justify forbidding the departure of the vessel as provided for by section 1, title V, chapter 30, of the Act approved June 15, 1917, and if, in the President's judgment, such action will serve to maintain peace between the United States and foreign states, or to protect the commercial interests of the United States and its citizens, or to promote the security or neutrality of the United States, he shall have the power and it shall be his duty to require the owner, master, or person in command thereof, before departing from a port of the United States, to give a bond to the United States, with sufficient sureties, in such amount as he shall deem proper, conditioned that the vessel will not deliver the men, or any part of the cargo, to any warship, tender, or supply ship of the belligerent state. (b) If the President, or any person thereunto authorized by him, shall find that a vessel, domestic or foreign, in a port of the United States, has previously cleared from a port of the United States during such war and delivered its cargo or any part thereof to a warship, tender, or supply ship of a belligerent state, he may prohibit the departure of such vessel during the duration of the war."
- Section 8: "Whenever, during any war in which the United States is neutral, the President shall find that special restrictions placed on the use of the ports and territorial waters of the United States by the submarines or armed merchant vessels of a foreign state, will serve to maintain peace between the United States and foreign states, or to protect the commercial interests of the United States and its citizens, or to promote the security of the United States, and shall make proclamation therefore, it shall thereafter be unlawful for any such submarine or armed merchant vessel to enter a port or the territorial waters of the United States or to depart therefrom, except under such conditions and subject to such limitations as the President may prescribe. Whenever, in his judgment, the conditions which have caused him to issue his proclamation have ceased to exist, he shall revoke his proclamation and the provisions of this section shall thereupon cease to apply."
- Section 9 prohibited the arming of American merchant vessels.

Also see **Neutrality Act of 1939.**

REFERENCES:
Drummond, Donald Francis. *The Passing of American Neutrality, 1937-1941.* 1955; reprint ed., New York: Greenwood Press, 1968.
United States Congress. *Neutrality Act of 1937.* Washington, D.C.: U.S. Government Printing Office, 1937.

Neutrality Act of 1939

SIGNED: November 4, 1939
SIGNATORIES: Act of Congress
IN FORCE: From signing
OVERVIEW: A neutrality act replacing the **Neutrality Act of 1937** and providing for the "cash-and-carry" purchase of arms by belligerents.

DISCUSSION:
The 1939 neutrality act was passed after the outbreak of war in Europe. While it substantially recapitulated the **Neutrality Act of 1937,** it permitted sales of arms and strategic materials to belligerents, except as might be prohibited by presidential proclamation. All sales were to be on a cash-and-carry basis only, so that the United States would not be drawn into a war by holding debt in some belligerent country or by violating a blockade in the delivery of goods. It is this provision that created an obstacle to the concept of lend-lease, and it was this obstacle that the **Lend-Lease Act** of 1940 overcame by permitting repayment for purchase of arms "in kind or property, or any other direct or indirect benefit which the President deems satisfactory."

Additionally the 1939 act gave the president the authority to designate "combat areas," through which travel by United States nationals and vessels would be prohibited. As originally passed, the act retained the earlier prohibition against the arming of merchant vessels; however, on November 17, 1941, after incidents with German submarines and the torpedoing of the

United States destroyer *Reuben James,* Congress amended the act to permit the arming of merchant vessels and additionally permitted those vessels to carry cargoes into belligerent ports. The amendment was soon rendered moot, however, by the entry of the United States into World War II on December 8, 1941, the day after the Japanese attack on Pearl Harbor.

REFERENCES:

Drummond, Donald Francis. *The Passing of American Neutrality, 1937-1941.* 1955; reprint ed., New York: Greenwood Press, 1968.

United States Congress. *Neutrality Act of 1937.* Washington, D.C.: U.S. Government Printing Office, 1937.

United States. Congress. *American Neutrality: Comparative Print of H. J. Res. 306, the Neutrality Act of 1939; Present Neutrality Law Approved May 1, 1937; Proposed Neutrality Act 1939 (H. J. Res. 306) as Passed by the House of Representatives, June 30, 1939; Proposed Substitute Neutrality Act of 1939 (H. J. Res. 306) as Reported to the Senate by the Senate Foreign Relations Committee, September 29, 1939.* Washington, D.C.: U.S. Government Printing Office, 1939.

Act of Havana

SIGNED: July 30, 1940, at Havana, Cuba
IN FORCE: From signing
SIGNATORIES: Argentina, Bolivia, Brazil, Chile, Colombia, Costa Rica, Cuba, Dominican Republic, Ecuador, El Salvador, Guatemala, Haiti, Honduras, Mexico, Nicaragua, Panama, Paraguay, Peru, United States, Uruguay, and Venezuela.
OVERVIEW: During the early days of World War II, before any American republic became involved in the conflict, the Act of Havana provided for the provisional administration of European colonies and possessions in the Americas should a change of sovereignty create a threat to the nations of the Americas. In practice, the Act of Havana acknowledged the United States as the guarantor of security in the region.

DISCUSSION:

The outbreak of World War II in Europe during September 1939 gave great impetus to inter-American solidarity. A meeting of the foreign ministers of the American republics was held in Panama during September 23-October 3, 1939, which produced a joint declaration of neutrality, the establishment of a neutral zone extending to three hundred miles off the shores of the American republics, and a resolution that if any region in the Americas belonging to a European state should change sovereignties and thereby imperil the security of the Americas, a consultive meeting would be urgently called.

After Germany had conquered the Netherlands and France, the perception of danger was heightened in the Americas, and a second meeting was called, this time in Havana, Cuba, from July 21 to July 30, 1940. This meeting produced the Act of Havana, which stated a more aggressive policy with regard to the status of European colonies and possessions in the Americas:

- Should a change of sovereignty create a threat, the nations of the Americas would collectively create a committee to administer the colony or possession.
- If such an emergency developed before collective committee action was possible, one signatory could take unilateral action.

The Act of Havana implied possession of the resources and willingness to back provisional administration militarily. In practice, the only republic in the Americas that possessed such resources and willingness was the United States, which, therefore, was identified as the guarantor of the security of the Americas during World War II. By providing for collective decision making, but allowing for unilateral action, the Act of Havana simultaneously confirmed inter-American solidarity while leaving the United States with a free hand in the region.

An additional document, Convention on the Provisional Administration of European Colonies and Possessions in the Americas, was signed on July 30, 1940, and entered into force on January 8, 1940; it amplified and formalized the principles of the Act of Havana. Although drafted specifically in response to the exigencies of World War II, both the Act and the Convention remain in force.

REFERENCES:

Bethell, Leslie, and Ian Roxborough, eds. *Latin America Between the Second World War and the Cold War, 1944-1948.* New York: Cambridge University Press, 1997.

Grenville, J. A. S. *The Major International Treaties 1914-1973: A History Guide with Texts.* New York: Stein and Day, 1974.

U.S. State Department Bulletin on Hemispheric Defense

ISSUED: August 18, 1940
PUBLISHED: August 24, 1940, as State Department Bulletin
OVERVIEW: Bulletin announcing United States-Canada cooperation in defense of the "north half of the Western Hemisphere."

DISCUSSION:

The brief bulletin was issued after an August 17, 1940, conference between President Franklin Delano Roosevelt and Prime Minister Mackenzie King of Canada at Odgensburg, New York, to discuss mutual defense concerns of the United States and Canada. The entire text follows:

The Prime Minister and the President have discussed the mutual problems of defense in relation to the safety of Canada and the United States. It has been agreed that a Permanent Joint Board on Defense shall be set up at once by the two countries. This Permanent Joint Board on Defense shall commence immediate studies relating to sea, land and air problems including personnel and materiel. It will consider in the broad sense the defense of the north half of the Western Hemisphere. The Permanent Joint Board on Defense will consist of four or five members from each country, most of them from the services. It will meet shortly.

REFERENCES:

Bethell, Leslie, and Ian Roxborough, eds. *Latin America Between the Second World War and the Cold War, 1944-1948*. New York: Cambridge University Press, 1997.

California, University of, Committee on International Relations. *Problems of Hemispheric Defense*. Berkeley and Los Angeles: University of California Press, 1942.

Laves, Walter Herman Carl, ed. *Inter-American Solidarity*. Chicago: University of Chicago Press, 1941.

Lend-Lease Act

OFFICIAL TITLE: An Act to Promote the Defense of the United States

SIGNED: March 11, 1941

SIGNATORIES: Act of Congress

IN FORCE: From signing

OVERVIEW: The act of Congress on which America's lend-lease agreements with its allies were based.

DISCUSSION:

Well before the United States entered World War II, and while it was nominally neutral in that war, President Franklin D. Roosevelt committed the nation to a course of aid to powers fighting fascism. United States law mandated that Great Britain, the first recipient of material aid, had to pay in cash for all arms purchased from the United States. By the summer of 1940, British prime minister Winston Churchill warned the United States that his nation would soon be unable to make such cash payments. On December 8, 1940, President Roosevelt suggested the concept of lend-lease as an alternative to cash for arms. The resulting legislation gave the president the authority to aid *any* nation whose defense he deemed critical to that of the United States; it further authorized the acceptance of repayment "in kind or property, or any other direct or indirect benefit which the President deems satisfactory."

Section 3 contains the essence of the act:

Section 3.

(a) Notwithstanding the provisions of any other law, the President may, from time to time, when he deems it in the interest of national defense, authorize the Secretary of War, the Secretary of the Navy, or the head of any other department or agency of the Government

(1) To manufacture in arsenals, factories, and shipyards under their jurisdiction, or otherwise procure, to the extent to which funds are made available therefor, or contracts are authorized from time to time by the Congress, or both, any defense article for the government of any country whose defense the President deems vital to the defense of the United States.

(2) To sell, transfer title to, exchange, lease, lend, or otherwise dispose of, to any such government any defense article, but no defense article not manufactured or procured under paragraph (1) shall in any way be disposed of under this paragraph, except after consultation with the Chief of Staff of the Army or the Chief of Naval Operations of the Navy, or both . . . .

Lend-lease was authorized in response to the needs of Great Britain, but it was soon extended to China and to the Soviet Union. By the end of the war, more than forty nations had participated in lend-lease, to a total of aid valued at $49,100,000,000. Also see: **Lend-Lease Agreement with United Kingdom.**

REFERENCES:

Dougherty, James J. *The Politics of Wartime Aid: American Economic Assistance to France and French Northwest Africa, 1940-1946*. Westport, CT: Greenwood Press, 1978.

Stettinius, Edward Reilly. *Lend-Lease, Weapon for Victory*. New York, Macmillan, 1944.

Whidden, Howard Primrose. *Reaching a Lend-Lease Settlement*. New York: Foreign Policy Association, 1944.

Resolution Reaffirming the Monroe Doctrine

SIGNED: April 10, 1941, in Congress

SIGNATORIES: Joint resolution of Congress

IN FORCE: From signing

OVERVIEW: A joint resolution of the U.S. Congress "affirming and approving non-recognition of the transfer of any geographic region in this hemisphere from one non-American power to another non-American power, and providing for consultation with other American republics in the event that such transfer should appear likely."

DISCUSSION:

With World War II raging in Europe, the United States Congress resolved to reassert the principles of the **Monroe Doctrine** as follows:

Whereas our traditional policy has been to consider any attempt on the part of non-American powers to extend their system to any portion of this hemisphere as dangerous to the peace and safety not only of this country but of the other American republics; and

Whereas the American republics agreed at the Inter-American Conference for the Maintenance of Peace held in Buenos Aires in 1936 and at the Eighth International Conference of American States held in Lima in 1938 to consult with one another in the event that the peace, security, or territorial integrity of any American republic should be threatened; and

Whereas the Meeting of the Foreign Ministers of the American Republics at Panama October 3, 1939, resolved "That in case any geographic region of America subject to the jurisdiction of any non-American state should be obliged to change its sovereignty and there should result therefrom a danger to the security of the American Continent, a consultative meeting such as the one now being held will be convoked with the urgency that the case may require": Therefore be it

Resolved by the Senate and House of Representatives of the United States of America in Congress assembled, (1) That the United States would not recognize any transfer, and would not acquiesce in any attempt to transfer, any geographic region of this hemisphere from one non-American power to another non-American power; and

(2) That if such transfer or attempt to transfer should appear likely, the United States shall, in addition to other measures, immediately consult with the other American republics to determine upon the steps which should be taken to safeguard their common interests.

REFERENCES:
Kirk, Grayson L. *The Monroe Doctrine Today*. New York, Toronto, Farrar & Rinehart, Inc., 1941.

Atlantic Charter

SIGNED: August 14, 1941, aboard the cruiser U.S.S. *Augusta*, in Placentia Bay, Newfoundland
IN FORCE: From signing
SIGNATORIES: United States and Great Britain
OVERVIEW: The product of the first wartime meeting of U.S. president Franklin D. Roosevelt and British prime minister Winston Churchill, the Atlantic Charter was an Anglo-American statement of common principles—made five months before the United States entered the war as Britain's military ally.

DISCUSSION:
Although the United States would not enter World War II until December 8, 1941, the day after the Japanese attack on Pearl Harbor, President Roosevelt had steadily moved the nation toward closer relations with England, culminating in March 1941 with the **Lend-Lease Act.** During August 9-12, President Roosevelt and Prime Minister Churchill met aboard the U.S. Navy cruiser *Augusta* in Placentia Bay, off the coast of Newfoundland and produced the Atlantic Charter, a statement of eight principles of American and British aims in war as well as peace:

The President of the United States of America and the Prime Minister, Mr. Churchill, representing His Majesty's Government in the United Kingdom, being met together, deem it right to make known certain common principles in the national policies of their respective countries on which they base their hopes for a better future for the world.

First, their countries seek no aggrandizement, territorial or other;

Second, they desire to see no territorial changes that do not accord with the freely expressed wishes of the peoples concerned;

Third, they respect the right of all peoples to choose the form of government under which they will live; and they wish to see sovereign rights and self government restored to those who have been forcibly deprived of them;

Fourth, they will endeavor, with due respect for their existing obligations, to further the enjoyment by all States, great or small, victor or vanquished, of access, on equal terms, to the trade and to the raw materials of the world which are needed for their economic prosperity;

Fifth, they desire to bring about the fullest collaboration between all nations in the economic field with the object of securing, for all, improved labor standards, economic advancement and social security;

Sixth, after the final destruction of the Nazi tyranny, they hope to see established a peace which will afford to all nations the means of dwelling in safety within their own boundaries, and which will afford assurance that all the men in all lands may live out their lives in freedom from fear and want;

Seventh, such a peace should enable all men to traverse the high seas and oceans without hindrance;

Eighth, they believe that all of the nations of the world, for realistic as well as spiritual reasons must come to the abandonment of the use of force. Since no future peace can be maintained if land, sea or air armaments continue to be employed by nations which threaten, or may threaten, aggression outside of their frontiers, they believe, pending the establishment of a wider and permanent system of general security, that the disarmament of such nations is essential. They will likewise aid and encourage all other practicable measure which will lighten for peace-loving peoples the crushing burden of armaments.

Franklin D. Roosevelt
Winston S. Churchill

The charter's principles were given broader scope when they were endorsed by twenty-six allied nations in the **United Nations Declaration** of January 1, 1942.

REFERENCES:
Brinkley, Douglas, and David R. Facey-Crowther, eds. *The Atlantic Charter*. New York: St. Martin's Press, 1994.
Drakidis, Philippe. *The Atlantic and United Nations Charters: Common Law Prevailing for World Peace and Security*. Besançon, France: Centre De Recherche et D'information Politique et Sociale, 1995.
Grenville, J. A. S. *The Major International Treaties 1914-1973: A History Guide with Texts*. (New York: Stein and Day, 1974.
Wilson, Theodore A. *The First Summit: Roosevelt and Churchill at Pladentia Bay, 1941*. Lawrence: University Press of Kansas, 1991.

United Nations Declaration

SIGNED: January 1, 1942, at Washington, D.C.
IN FORCE: From signature
SIGNATORIES: United States of America, the United Kingdom of Great Britain and Northern Ireland, the Union of Soviet Socialist Republics, China, Australia, Belgium, Canada, Costa Rica, Cuba, Czechoslovakia, Dominican Republic, El Salvador, Greece, Guatemala, Haiti, Honduras, India, Luxembourg, Netherlands, New Zealand, Nicaragua, Norway, Panama, Poland, South Africa, Yugoslavia. In addition, the following nations communicated adherence to the declaration: Mexico (June 5, 1942), Philippines (June 10, 1942), Ethiopia (July 28, 1942), Iraq (Jan. 16, 1943), Brazil (Feb. 8, 1943), Bolivia (Apr. 27, 1943), Iran (Sept. 10, 1943), Colombia (Dec. 22, 1943), Liberia (Feb. 26, 1944), France (Dec. 26, 1944), Ecuador (Feb. 7, 1945), Peru (Feb. 11, 1945), Chile (Feb. 12, 1945), Paraguay (Feb. 12,

1945), Venezuela (Feb. 16, 1945), Uruguay (Feb. 23, 1945), Turkey (Feb. 24, 1945), Egypt (Feb. 27, 1945), and Saudi Arabia (Mar. 1, 1945).

OVERVIEW: In a meeting at Washington. D.C., the twenty-six principal nations united against the Axis powers in World War II pledged their resources to achieving complete victory and adopted the principles of the **Atlantic Charter.**

DISCUSSION:

The United Nations Declaration is brief and straightforward:

The Governments signatory hereto,

Having subscribed to a common program of purposes and principles embodied in the Joint Declaration of the President of United States of America and the Prime Minister of the United Kingdom of Great Britain and Northern Ireland dated August 14, 1941, known as the Atlantic Charter.

Being convinced that complete victory over their enemies is essential to defend life, liberty, independence and religious freedom, and to preserve human rights and justice in their own lands as well as in other lands, and that they are now engaged in a common struggle against savage and brutal forces seeking to subjugate the world,

DECLARE:

(1) Each Government pledges itself to employ its full resources, military or economic, against those members of the Tripartite Pact and its adherents with which such government is at war.

(2) Each Government pledges itself to cooperate with the Governments signatory hereto and not to make a separate armistice or peace with the enemies.

The foregoing declaration may be adhered to by other nations which are, or which may be, rendering material assistance and contributions in the struggle for victory over Hitlerism.

The principles of the Atlantic Charter, jointly issued on August 14, 1941, by U.S. president Franklin D. Roosevelt and U.K. prime minister Winston Churchill, to which the signatories of the declaration here subscribed, are as follows:

- Renunciation of territorial aggression

- Prohibition of territorial changes without consent of the peoples concerned

- Restoration of sovereign rights and self-government access to raw materials for all nations

- World economic cooperation

- Freedom from fear

- Freedom from want

- Freedom of the seas

- Disarmament of aggressors

Much as Woodrow Wilson's "Fourteen Points" (1918) became the basis of the Covenant of the League of Nations, the Atlantic Charter principles would serve as the philosophical

foundation for the permanent postwar establishment of the United Nations (**United Nations Charter**, in Section 3.10).

REFERENCES:

Armstrong, David, Lorna Lloyd, and John Redmond. *From Versailles to Maastricht: International Organizations in the Twentieth Century.* New York: St. Martin's Press, 1996.

Army Information School. *Pillars of Peace: Documents Pertaining to American Interest in Establishing a Lasting World Peace.* Carlisle Barracks, PA: Book Department, Army Information School, 1946.

Grenville, J. A. S. *The Major International Treaties 1914-1973: A History Guide with Texts.* New York: Stein and Day, 1974.

Hoopes, Townsend, and Douglas Brinkley. *FDR and the Creation of the U.N.* New Haven, CT: Yale University Press, 1997.

Patterson, Charles. *The Oxford 50th Anniversary Book of the United Nations.* New York: Oxford University Press, 1995.

Lend-Lease Agreement with United Kingdom

OFFICIAL TITLE: Agreement Relating to the Principles Applying to the Provision of Aid in the Prosecution of the War
SIGNED: February 23, 1942
SIGNATORIES: United Kingdom vs. United States
IN FORCE: From signing
OVERVIEW: Concluded in accordance with the **Lend-Lease Act** of 1941, the agreement provided military supplies and equipment to Great Britain on a non-cash basis.

DISCUSSION:

The United States began aiding Great Britain and other allied nations with war materiel before entering World War II itself on December 8, 1941. In 1940, British prime minister Winston Churchill warned that his nation could not afford to pay cash for war materials much longer. Because United States law required cash payment, President Franklin D. Roosevelt moved to change the law. On Dec. 8, 1940, he proposed the idea of lend-lease, which Congress passed into law as the **Lend-Lease Act** on March 11, 1941. Roosevelt was now authorized to extend material aid to any nation whose defense he deemed vital to the United States in return for repayment "in kind or property, or any other direct or indirect benefit which the President deems satisfactory."

The present agreement codified and clarified the provisions of the Lend-Lease Act, including arrangements for payment of patent holders, if necessary, and incorporated, in its penultimate article, a statement on measures to promote worldwide economic betterment:

In the final determination of the benefits to be provided to the United States of America by the Government of the United Kingdom in return for aid furnished under the Act of Congress of March 11, 1941, the terms and conditions thereof shall be such as not to burden commerce between the two countries, but to promote mutually advantageous economic relations between them and the betterment of world-wide economic relations. To that end, they shall include provision for agreed action by the United States of America and the United Kingdom, open to participation by all other countries of like mind, directed to the expansion, by appropriate international and domestic measures, of production, employment, and the exchange and consumption of goods, which are the material foundations of the liberty and welfare of all peoples; to the elimination of all forms of discriminatory treatment in international commerce, and to the reduction of tariffs and other trade barriers; and, in general, to the attainment of all the economic objectives set forth in the Joint Declaration made on August 14, 1941, by the President of the United States of America and the Prime Minister of the United Kingdom.

REFERENCES:

Dougherty, James J. *The Politics of Wartime Aid: American Economic Assistance to France and French Northwest Africa, 1940-1946.* Westport, CT: Greenwood Press, 1978.

Stettinius, Edward Reilly. *Lend-Lease, Weapon for Victory.* New York, Macmillan, 1944.

Whidden, Howard Primrose. *Reaching a Lend-Lease Settlement.* New York: Foreign Policy Association, 1944.

Arrangement (with the United Kingdom) Relating to Apportioning African Asbestos

OFFICIAL TITLE: Exchange of Notes Constituting an Arrangement Relating to the Apportioning Supplies of African Asbestos
SIGNED: April 30, 1943, at London
SIGNATORIES: United Kingdom vs. United States
IN FORCE: From signing
OVERVIEW: A wartime agreement concerning allocation of a vital commodity between allies.

DISCUSSION:

The fire-retardant insulator asbestos was a vital World War II military commodity, which was mined in great quantity in Africa. The Allies made various agreements in an effort to equitably and efficiently apportion such vital, but scarce commodities. This agreement details importation and apportionment policies with the central purpose of insuring that each government will have a year's supply of the material for 1944.

REFERENCES:
None

Armistice with Italy

SIGNED: September 3, 1943, Fairfield Camp, Sicily
IN FORCE: From September 3, 1943
SIGNATORIES: Italy vs. Great Britain, United States, "and in the interest of the United Nations"
OVERVIEW: Document laying down "conditions of an Armis-

tice . . . presented by General Dwight D. Eisenhower, Commander-in-Chief of the Allied Forces, acting by authority of the Governments of the United States and Great Britain and in the interest of the United Nations, and . . . accepted by Marshal Pietro Badoglio, Head of the Italian Government."

DISCUSSION:
The twelve conditions of the armistice with Italy are as follows:

1. Immediate cessation of all hostile activity by the Italian armed forces.

2. Italy will use its best endeavors to deny, to the Germans, facilities that might be used against the United Nations.

3. All prisoners or internees of the United Nations to be immediately turned over to the Allied Commander in Chief, and none of these may now or at any time be evacuated to Germany.

4. Immediate transfer of the Italian Fleet and Italian aircraft to such points as may be designated by the Allied Commander in Chief, with details of disarmament to be prescribed by him.

5. Italian merchant shipping may be requisitioned by the Allied Commander in Chief to meet the needs of his military-naval program.

6. Immediate surrender of Corsica and of all Italian territory, both islands and mainland, to the Allies, for such use as operational bases and other purposes as the Allies may see fit.

7. Immediate guarantee of the free use by the Allies of all airfields and naval ports in Italian territory, regardless of the rate of evacuation of the Italian territory by the German forces. These ports and fields to be protected by Italian armed forces until this function is taken over by the Allies.

8. Immediate withdrawal to Italy of Italian armed forces from all participation in the current war from whatever areas in which they may be now engaged.

9. Guarantee by the Italian Government that if necessary it will employ all its available armed forces to insure prompt and exact compliance with all the provisions of this armistice.

10. The Commander in Chief of the Allied Forces reserves to himself the right to take any measure which in his opinion may be necessary for the protection of the interests of the Allied Forces for the prosecution of the war, and the Italian Government binds itself to take such administrative or other action as the Commander in Chief may require, and in particular the Commander in Chief will establish Allied Military Government over such parts of Italian territory as he may deem necessary in the military interests of the Allied Nations.

11. The Commander in Chief of the Allied Forces will have a full right to impose measures of disarmament, demobilization, and demilitarization.

12. Other conditions of a political, economic and financial nature with which Italy will be bound to comply will be transmitted at a later date.

Also see **Instrument of Surrender (Italy)**, **Amendment of Instrument of Surrender (Italy)**, **Cunningham-de Courten**

Agreement, and **Cunningham-de Courten Agreement, Amendment of November 17, 1943**.

REFERENCES:
Adams, Henry Hitch. *Italy at War*. Alexandria, VA.: Time-Life Books, 1982.
Leiss, Amelia C., ed. *European Peace Treaties after World War II: Negotiations and Texts of Treaties with Italy, Bulgaria, Hungary, Rumania, and Finland*. Boston: World Peace Foundation, 1954.
United Nations. *Surrender of Italy, Germany and Japan, World War II: Instruments of Surrender, Public Papers and Addresses of the President and of the Supreme Commanders*. Washington, D.C.: U.S. Government Printing Office, 1946.

Cunningham-de Courten Agreement

OFFICIAL TITLE: Armistice with Italy: Employment and Disposition of Italian Fleet and Merchant Marine
SIGNED: September 23, 1943, Taranto, Italy
SIGNATORIES: "Allied Naval Commander in Chief, Mediterranean" vs. "Italian Minister of Marine"
IN FORCE: From signing
OVERVIEW: An amendment to the **Armistice with Italy** of September 3, 1943, the agreement laid down how "the [Italian naval] Fleet and the Italian Mercantile Marine should be employed in the Allied effort to assist in the prosecution of the war against the Axis powers."

DISCUSSION:
This agreement detailing how the Allies were to use and control Italian vessels in the war effort was, in effect, a "gentlemen's agreement" inasmuch as no signed copy was ever registered. Admiral Rafaella de Courten, Italian Minister of Marine, later explained: "The agreement made at Taranto September 23, 1943, with Admiral [Sir Andrew] Cunningham [Allied Naval Commander in Chief, Mediterranean] is not registered in a document signed by the two parties." Assent to the agreement as drafted was "was communicated verbally."

The gist of the document is expressed in its opening paragraphs:

The armistice having been signed between the Head of the Italian Government and the Allied Commander-in-Chief under which all Italian warships and the Italian Mercantile Marine were placed unconditionally at the disposal of the United Nations, and H. M. The King of Italy and the Italian Government having since expressed the wish that the Fleet and the Italian Mercantile Manne should be employed in the Allied effort to assist in the prosecution of the war against the Axis powers, the following principles are established on which the Italian Navy and Mercantile Marine will be disposed.

(A) Such ships as can be employed to assist actively in the Allied effort will be kept in commission and will be used under the orders of the Commander-in-Chief, Mediterranean as may be arranged between the Allied Commander-in-Chief and the Italian Government.

(B) Ships which cannot be so employed will be reduced to a care and maintenance basis and be placed in designated ports, measures of disarmament being undertaken as may be necessary.

(C) The Government of Italy will declare the names and whereabouts of

(i) Warships

(ii) Merchant ships now in their possession which previously belonged to any of the United Nations. These vessels are to be returned forthwith as may be directed by the Allied Commander-in-Chief. This will be without prejudice to negotiations between the Governments which may subsequently be made in connection with replacing losses of ships of the United Nations caused by Italian action.

See also **Cunningham-de Courten Agreement, Amendment of November 17, 1943**

REFERENCES:
Adams, Henry Hitch. *Italy at War*. Alexandria, VA.: Time-Life Books, 1982.
Leiss, Amelia C., ed. *European Peace Treaties after World War II: Negotiations and Texts of Treaties with Italy, Bulgaria, Hungary, Rumania, and Finland*. Boston: World Peace Foundation, 1954.
United Nations. *Surrender of Italy, Germany and Japan, World War II: Instruments of Surrender, Public Papers and Addresses of the President and of the Supreme Commanders*. Washington, D.C.: U.S. Government Printing Office, 1946.

Instrument of Surrender of Italy

SIGNED: September 29, 1943, at Malta
SIGNATORIES: Italy vs. United Kingdom and United States (on behalf of the United Nations)
IN FORCE: From signing; terminated September 15, 1947, upon entry into force of **Peace Treaty between the Allies and Italy** of February 10, 1947
OVERVIEW: "The . . . terms on which the United States and United Kingdom Governments acting on behalf of the United Nations are prepared to suspend hostilities against Italy so long as their military operations against Germany and her Allies are not obstructed and Italy does not assist these Powers in any way and complies with the requirements of these Governments."

DISCUSSION:
"These terms have been presented by GENERAL DWIGHT D. EISENHOWER, Commander-in-Chief, Allied Forces, duly authorised to that effect; and have been accepted by MARSHAL PIETRO BADOGLIO, Head of the Italian Government." The surrender was unconditional. See also **Amendment of Instrument of Surrender**, November 9, 1943.

REFERENCES:
Adams, Henry Hitch. *Italy at War*. Alexandria, VA.: Time-Life Books, 1982.
Leiss, Amelia C., ed. *European Peace Treaties after World War II:*

Negotiations and Texts of Treaties with Italy, Bulgaria, Hungary, Rumania, and Finland. Boston: World Peace Foundation, 1954.

United Nations. *Surrender of Italy, Germany and Japan, World War II: Instruments of Surrender, Public Papers and Addresses of the President and of the Supreme Commanders.* Washington, D.C.: U.S. Government Printing Office, 1946.

Joint Four-Nation Declaration of the Moscow Conference

SIGNED: October 1943, at Moscow

SIGNATORIES: United States, United Kingdom, Union of Soviet Socialist Republics, and China

IN FORCE: From signing

OVERVIEW: A pledge to prosecute the war to victory, with joint agreement on war aims and policies, and a statement concerning atrocities.

DISCUSSION:

The signatories jointly declare the following:

1. That their united action, pledged for the prosecution of the war against their respective enemies, will be continued for the organization and maintenance of peace and security.

2. That those of them at war with a common enemy will act together in all matters relating to the surrender and disarmament of that enemy.

3. That they will take all measures deemed by them to be necessary to provide against any violation of the terms imposed upon the enemy.

4. That they recognize the necessity of establishing at the earliest practicable date a general international organization, based on the principle of the sovereign equality of all peace-loving states, and open to membership by all such states, large and small, for the maintenance of international peace and security.

5. That for the purpose of maintaining international peace and security pending the re-establishment of law and order and the inauguration of a system of general security they will consult with one another and as occasion requires with other members of the United Nations, with a view to joint action on behalf of the community of nations.

6. That after the termination of hostilities they will not employ their military forces within the territories of other states except for the purposes envisaged in this declaration and after joint consultation.

7. That they will confer and cooperate with one another and with other members of the United Nations to bring about a practicable general agreement with respect to the regulation of armaments in the post-war period.

Concerning Italy, the document declares agreement that "Allied policy toward Italy must be based upon the fundamental principle that Fascism and all its evil influence and configuration shall be completely destroyed and that the Italian people shall be given every opportunity to establish governmental and other institutions based on democratic principles." The docu-ment also declares agreement "that Austria, the first free country to fall a victim to Hitlerite aggression, shall be liberated from German domination."

The Moscow document concludes with a key declaration on war atrocities, signed by President Franklin Roosevelt, Prime Minister Winston Churchill and Premier Josef Stalin:

At the time of granting of any armistice to any government which may be set up in Germany, those German officers and men and members of the Nazi party who have been responsible for or have taken a consenting part in the above atrocities, massacres and executions will be sent back to the countries in which their abominable deeds were done in order that they may be judged and punished according to the laws of these liberated countries and of free governments which will be erected therein. Lists will be compiled in all possible detail from all these countries having regard especially to invaded parts of the Soviet Union, to Poland and Czechoslovakia, to Yugoslavia and Greece including Crete and other islands, to Norway, Denmark, Netherlands, Belgium, Luxembourg, France and Italy.

Thus, Germans who take part in wholesale shooting of Polish officers or in the execution of French, Dutch, Belgian or Norwegian hostages or Cretan peasants, or who have shared in slaughters inflicted on the people of Poland or in territories of the Soviet Union which are now being swept clear of the enemy, will know they will be brought back to the scene of their crimes and judged on the spot by the peoples whom they have outraged.

Let those who have hitherto not imbued their hands with innocent blood beware lest they join the ranks of the guilty, for most assuredly the three Allied powers will pursue them to the uttermost ends of the earth and will deliver them to their accusers in order that justice may be done.

The above declaration is without prejudice to the case of German criminals whose offenses have no particular geographical localization and who will be punished by joint decision of the government of the Allies.

The concluding paragraph of the declaration on atrocities became the basis for the postwar establishment of an international war crimes tribunal. (See **London Agreement [Nuremberg Tribunal Establishing Document]** and **Charter of the International Military Tribunal [Nuremberg Rules]**.)

REFERENCE:

United States Department of State. *War Conference at Moscow: Press Releases of the Department of State, Containing the Declaration Providing for the Prosecution of the Present War Which Was Signed by the Foreign Secretaries of the United States of America, the United Kingdom, and the Soviet Union and the Chinese Ambassador at Moscow, at the Conference Held at Moscow, Russia, Together with Other Papers Relating Thereto.* Washington, D.C.: U.S. Government Printing Office, 1943.

Amendment of Instrument of Surrender (of Italy)

SIGNED: November 9, 1943

SIGNATORIES: Italy vs. United States and United Kingdom (on behalf of the United Nations)

IN FORCE: On signing; terminated September 15, 1947, upon entry into force of treaty of peace of February 10, 1947

OVERVIEW: The key amendments to the **Instrument of Surrender of Italy** were the explicit inclusion of the Soviet Union in the document and a change regarding the disposition of Italian war criminals."

DISCUSSION:

Article 29 of the **Instrument of Surrender of Italy—**

Benito Mussolini, his Chief Fascist associates and all persons suspected of having committed war crimes or analogous offenses whose names appear on lists to be communicated by the United Nations will forthwith be apprehended and surrendered into the hands of the United Nations. Any instructions given by the United Nations for this purpose will be complied with.

—was modified as follows:

Benito Mussolini, his chief Fascist associates, and all persons suspected of having committed war crimes or analogous offenses whose names appear on lists to be communicated by the United Nations and who now or in the future are on territory controlled by the Allied Military Command or by the Italian Government, will forthwith be apprehended and surrendered into the hands of the United Nations. Any instructions given by the United Nations to this purpose will be complied with.

The article was rendered moot when Mussolini and his mistress, Clara Petacci, were captured by Italian partisans, who executed the couple on April 28, 1945.

REFERENCES:

Adams, Henry Hitch. *Italy at War.* Alexandria, VA.: Time-Life Books, 1982.

Leiss, Amelia C., ed. *European Peace Treaties after World War II: Negotiations and Texts of Treaties with Italy, Bulgaria, Hungary, Rumania, and Finland.* Boston: World Peace Foundation, 1954.

United Nations. *Surrender of Italy, Germany and Japan, World War II: Instruments of Surrender, Public Papers and Addresses of the President and of the Supreme Commanders.* Washington, D.C.: U.S. Government Printing Office, 1946.

Cunningham-de Courten Agreement, Amendment of November 17, 1943

OFFICIAL TITLE: Armistice with Italy: Employment and Disposition of Italian Fleet and Merchant Marine, Amendment of November 17, 1943

SIGNED: November 17, 1943, at Brindisi, Italy

SIGNATORIES: Statement by Admiral Rafaella de Courten, Italian Minister of Marine

IN FORCE: From November 17, 1943; terminated September 15, 1947, upon entry into force of **Peace Treaty between the Allies and Italy** of February 10, 1947

OVERVIEW: As a matter of national pride and sovereignty, the document amends the **Armistice with Italy** and the **Cunningham-de Courten Agreement** by stipulating that Italian vessels employed by the Allies in the war effort shall "be manned so far as possible by crews provided by Italian Ministry of Marine and will fly the Italian flag."

REFERENCES:

Adams, Henry Hitch. *Italy at War.* Alexandria, VA.: Time-Life Books, 1982.

Leiss, Amelia C., ed. *European Peace Treaties after World War II: Negotiations and Texts of Treaties with Italy, Bulgaria, Hungary, Rumania, and Finland.* Boston: World Peace Foundation, 1954.

United Nations. *Surrender of Italy, Germany and Japan, World War II: Instruments of Surrender, Public Papers and Addresses of the President and of the Supreme Commanders.* Washington, D.C.: U.S. Government Printing Office, 1946.

U.S. Department of State Bulletin on the Cairo Conference

RELEASED: December 1, 1943

SIGNATORIES: U.S. State Department on behalf of China, United Kingdom, and United States

IN FORCE: On release

OVERVIEW: Announcement of a three-way alliance against Japan with the goal of stripping Japan of all territories seized since 1914.

DISCUSSION:

The following bulletin was issued after the first of two Cairo conferences (November 22-26), between Winston Churchill and Franklin D. Roosevelt. The statement was issued also in behalf of China's Generalissimo Chiang Kai-shek, who had not been present at the conference:

The several military missions have agreed upon future military operations against Japan. The Three Great Allies expressed their resolve to bring unrelenting pressure against their brutal enemies by sea, land, and air. This pressure is already mounting.

The Three Great Allies are fighting this war to restrain and punish the aggression of Japan. They covet no gain for themselves and have no thought of territorial expansion. It is their purpose that Japan shall be stripped of all the islands in the Pacific which she has seized or occupied since the beginning of the first World War in 1914, and that all the territories Japan has stolen form the Chinese, such as Manchuria, Formosa, and the Pescadores, shall be restored to the Republic of China. Japan will also be expelled from all other territories which she has taken by violence and greed.

The aforesaid three great powers, mindful of the enslavement of the people of Korea, are determined that in due course Korea shall become free and independent.

With these objects in view the three Allies, in harmony with those of the United Nations at war with Japan, will continue to persevere in the serious and prolonged operations necessary to procure the unconditional surrender of Japan.

Following the first Cairo Conference, Churchill and Roosevelt traveled to the Tehran Conference with the Soviet Union's Joseph Stalin, then returned to Cairo for a second conference, during which they unsuccessfully attempted to persuade Turkey's president Ismet Inönü to join the war on the side of the Allies.

REFERENCE:

United States Department of State. *Conferences at Cairo and Tehran, 1943.* Washington, D.C.: U. S. Government Printing Office, 1961.

Armistice Agreement with Rumania

SIGNED: September 12, 1944, at Moscow

SIGNATORIES: Rumania vs. United States of America, the United Kingdom, and the Union of Soviet Socialist Republics

IN FORCE: From signing

OVERVIEW: "As from August 24, 1944, at four A.M., Rumania has entirely discontinued military operations against the Union of Soviet Socialist Republics on all theaters of war, has withdrawn from the war against the United Nations, has broken off relations with Germany and her satellites, has entered the war and will wage war on the side of the Allied Powers against Germany and Hungary for the purpose of restoring Rumanian independence and sovereignty, for which purpose she provides not less than twelve infantry divisions with corps troops.

"Military operations on the part of Rumanian armed forces, including naval and air forces, against Germany and Hungary will be conducted under the general leadership of the Allied (Soviet) High Command."

DISCUSSION:

In addition to agreeing to fight on the side of the Allies, Rumania also agreed to immediate restoration of "the state frontier between the Union of Soviet Socialist Republics and Rumania, established by the Soviet-Rumanian Agreement of June 8 1940."

Article 2 laid down the following:

The Government and High Command of Rumania undertake to take steps for the disarming and interning of the armed forces of Germany and Hungary on Rumanian territory and also for the interning of the citizens of both states mentioned who reside there.

However, an "Annex to Article Two" stated the following exception: "The measures provided for in Article 2 of the agreement regarding the internment of citizens of Germany and Hungary now in Rumanian territory do not extend to citizens of those countries of Jewish origin." Rumania had been among the German-allied or German-controlled nations that had perpetrated the Holocaust.

REFERENCE:

Leiss, Amelia C., ed. *European Peace Treaties after World War II: Negotiations and Texts of Treaties with Italy, Bulgaria, Hungary, Rumania, and Finland.* Boston: World Peace Foundation, 1954.

Armistice Agreement with Bulgaria

SIGNED: October 28, 1944, at Moscow

SIGNATORIES: Bulgaria vs. United Kingdom, United States, Union of Soviet Socialist Republics (all on behalf of the United Nations)

IN FORCE: From signing

OVERVIEW: An armistice and unconditional surrender.

DISCUSSION:

In addition to standard clauses concerning cessation of hostilities, severance of relations Germany, and submission to Allied occupation and control, the agreement specified the following:

ARTICLE ELEVEN.

The Government of Bulgaria undertakes to return to the Soviet Union, to Greece and Yugoslavia and to the other United Nations, by the dates specified by the Allied Control Commission and in a good state of preservation, all valuables and materials removed during the war by Germany or Bulgaria from United Nations territory and belonging to state, public or cooperative organizations, enterprises, institutions or individual citizens, such as factory and works equipment, locomotives, rolling-stock, tractors, motor vehicles, historic monuments, museum treasures and any other property.

ARTICLE TWELVE.

The Government of Bulgaria undertakes to hand over as booty to the Allied (Soviet) High Command all war material of Germany and her satellites located on Bulgarian territory, including vessels of the fleets of Germany and her satellites located in Bulgarian waters.

REFERENCE:

Leiss, Amelia C., ed. *European Peace Treaties after World War II: Negotiations and Texts of Treaties with Italy, Bulgaria, Hungary, Rumania, and Finland.* Boston: World Peace Foundation, 1954.

Armistice Agreement with Hungary

SIGNED: January 20, 1945, at Moscow

SIGNATORIES: Hungary vs. Union of Soviet Socialist Republics, United Kingdom, and the United States

IN FORCE: From January 20, 1945

OVERVIEW: "The Provisional National Government of Hungary, recognizing the fact of the defeat of Hungary in the war against the Soviet Union, the United Kingdom, the United States of America, and other United Nations, accepts the armistice terms presented by the Governments of the above-mentioned three powers, acting on behalf of all the United Nations which are in a state of war with Hungary."

DISCUSSION:

In addition to such standard conditions of armistice as immediate cessation of hostilities, severance of relations with Germany, disarming of all Axis soldiers within Hungary, and so on, the armistice specified the following in Article 5:

The Government of Hungary will immediately release, regardless of citizenship and nationality, all persons held in confinement in connection with their activities in favor of the United Nations or because of their sympathies with the United Nations' cause or for racial or religious reasons, and will repeal all discriminatory legislation and disabilities arising therefrom.

The Government of Hungary will take all necessary measures to ensure that all displaced persons or refugees within the limits of Hungarian territory, including Jews and stateless persons, are accorded at least the same measure of protection and security as its own nationals.

REFERENCE:

Leiss, Amelia C., ed. *European Peace Treaties after World War II: Negotiations and Texts of Treaties with Italy, Bulgaria, Hungary, Rumania, and Finland.* Boston: World Peace Foundation, 1954.

Yalta Agreement

SIGNED: February 11, 1945
IN FORCE: From signing
SIGNATORIES: Soviet Union, United States, and Great Britain
OVERVIEW: With the war in Europe coming to a successful close, this document outlined the endgame strategy against Japan, securing from the Soviet Union a pledge to join the war against Japan.

DISCUSSION:

In their "Report of the Yalta (Crimea) Conference," which accompanied the Yalta Agreement, the "Big Three"—Franklin D. Roosevelt, Winston Churchill, and Josef Stalin—concluded that "Nazi Germany [was] doomed." The same might have been said about Japan, except that, doomed or not, Japanese forces continued to fight at tremendous cost to themselves as well as to the Allies. Thus far, the Soviets had refrained from declaring war on Japan. Stalin could ill afford to fight a two-front war. At Yalta, however, an ailing Roosevelt persuaded Stalin to declare war on Japan "two or three months after Germany has surrendered," in return for Soviet acquisition of southern Sakhalin Island and the Kuril Islands (the territories lost in the Russo-Japanese War of 1904-05; see **Treaty of Portsmouth**, in Section

3.11) and Soviet dominance in Outer Mongolia and Manchuria. This was formalized in the Yalta Agreement.

As circumstances unfolded, the Yalta Agreement turned out to be an excellent bargain for the Soviet Union. The invasion of Japan, with its anticipated high rate of casualties, was rendered unnecessary by the atomic bombs the United States dropped on the Japanese cities of Hiroshima (August 6, 1945) and Nagasaki (August 9). The Soviets did not declare war on Japan until August 8, two days after Hiroshima. On August 10, the Japanese indicated acceptance of most of the Allied surrender terms, and five days later bowed to the final American demand, that Emperor Hirohito would be subject to the Supreme Allied Commander. Thus the Soviets reaped the benefits of the Yalta Agreement without having had to fight the Japanese.

REFERENCES:

Fenno, Richard F. *The Yalta Conference.* Lexington, MA: Heath, 1972.
Grenville, J. A. S. *The Major International Treaties 1914-1973: A History Guide with Texts.* New York: Stein and Day, 1974.
Stettinius, Edward R. *Roosevelt and the Russians: The Yalta Conference.* Westport, Conn.: Greenwood Press, 1970.

German Instrument of Surrender (Forces in Holland, Northwest Germany, and Denmark)

OFFICIAL TITLE: Instrument of Surrender of All German Armed Forces in Holland, in Northwest Germany Including All Islands, and in Denmark.
SIGNED: May 4, 1945, at Rheims, France
SIGNATORIES: Germany vs. United Kingdom (on behalf of all the Allies)
IN FORCE: From signing
OVERVIEW: The instrument of German surrender and cease-fire in the British-controlled theater of the European war.

DISCUSSION:

The document is brief and definitive, its object to secure immediate surrender and cessation of hostilities. Signed by British field marshal Bernard Law Montgomery, on behalf of the Allies, and by a group of German commanders on behalf of Germany, the surrender was authorized by Adm. Karl Dönitz, chosen by Adolf Hitler as head of state immediately before Hitler committed suicide.

The text follows:

1. The German Command agrees to the surrender of all armed forces in HOLLAND, in northwest GERMANY including the FRISLIAN ISLANDS and HELIGOLAND and all islands, in SCHLESWIG-HOLSTEIN, and in DENMARK, to the C.-in-C. 22 Army Group.

=This to include all naval ships in these areas=

These forces to lay down their arms and to surrender unconditionally.

2. All hostilities on land, on sea, or in the air by German forces in the above areas to cease at 0800 hrs. British Double Summer Time on Saturday 5 May 1945.

3. The German command to carry out at once, and without argument or comment, all further orders that will be issued by the Allied Powers on any subject.

4. Disobedience of orders, or failure to comply with them, will be regarded as a breach of these surrender terms and will be dealt with by the Allies in accordance with the laws and usages of war.

5. This instrument of surrender is independent of, without prejudice to, and will be superseded by any general instrument of surrender imposed by or on behalf of the Allied Powers and applicable to Germany and the German armed forces as a whole.

6. This instrument of surrender is written in English and in German.

The English version is the authentic text.

7. The decision of the Allied Powers will be final if any doubt or dispute arise as to the meaning or interpretation of the surrender terms.

REFERENCE:
United Nations. *Surrender of Italy, Germany and Japan, World War II: Instruments of Surrender, Public Papers and Addresses of the President and of the Supreme Commanders.* Washington, D.C.: U.S. Government Printing Office, 1946.

Orders Relating to Army and Air Forces under German Control

OFFICIAL TITLE: Orders by the Supreme Commander, Allied Expeditionary Force Relating to Army and Air Forces under German Control
SIGNED: May 7, 1945, at Rheims, France
SIGNATORIES: Supreme Allied Commander, acknowledged by the German High Command
IN FORCE: From signing
OVERVIEW: Detailed orders regarding the surrender and disposition of German military assets.

DISCUSSION:
As part of the German surrender in Europe, detailed orders were issued regarding the surrender, disposition, and control of all German military forces. Of special interest are the documents relating to the surrender of submarines (U-boats), which were widely dispersed at sea at the time of the German surrender:

To all "U" Boats at sea:

Carry out the following instructions forthwith which have been given by the Allied Representatives

(A) Surface immediately and remain surfaced.

(B) Report immediately in P/L your position in latitude and longitude and number of your "U" Boat to nearest British, US, Canadian or Soviet coast W/T station on 500 kc/s (600 metres) and to call sign GZZ 10 on one of the following high frequencies: 16845-12685 or 5970 kc/s.

(C) Fly a large black or blue flag by day.

(D) Burn navigation lights by night.

(E) Jettison all ammunition, remove breachblocks from guns and render torpedos safe by removing pistols. All mines are to be rendered safe.

(F) Make all signals in P/L.

(G) Follow strictly the instructions for proceeding to Allied ports from your present area given in immediately following message.

(H) Observe strictly the orders of Allied Representatives to refrain from scuttling or in any way damaging your "U" Boat.

2. These instructions will be repeated at two-hour intervals until further notice.

REFERENCE:
United Nations. *Surrender of Italy, Germany and Japan, World War II: Instruments of Surrender, Public Papers and Addresses of the President and of the Supreme Commanders.* Washington, D.C.: U.S. Government Printing Office, 1946.

Act of Military Surrender (at Rheims)

SIGNED: May 7, 1945, at Rheims, France
SIGNATORIES: Supreme Allied Commander (U.S. and Soviet commanders present, with French commander witnessing) vs. German High Command
IN FORCE: From signing
OVERVIEW: "We the undersigned, acting by authority of the German High Command, hereby surrender unconditionally to the Supreme Commander, Allied Expeditionary Forces and simultaneously to the Soviet High Command all forces on land, sea and in the air who are at this date under German control."

DISCUSSION:
This is the preliminary instrument of Germany's surrender and armistice. The text follows:

1. We the undersigned, acting by authority of the German High Command, hereby surrender unconditionally to the Supreme Commander, Allied Expeditionary Forces and simultaneously to the Soviet High Command all forces on land, sea and in the air who are at this date under German control.

2. The German High Command will at once issue orders to all German military, naval and air authorities and to all forces under German control to cease active operations at =2301= hours Central European time on =8 May= and to remain in the positions occupied at that time. No ship, vessel, or aircraft is to be scuttled, or any damage done to their hull, machinery or equipment.

3. The German High Command will at once issue to the appropriate commander, and ensure the carrying out of any further orders issued by the Supreme Commander, Allied Expeditionary Force and by the Soviet High Command.

4. This act of military surrender is without prejudice to, and will be superseded by any general instrument of surrender imposed by, or on behalf of the United Nations and applicable to GERMANY and the German armed forces as a whole.

5. In the event of the German High Command or any of the forces under their control failing to act in accordance with this Act of Surrender, the Supreme Commander, Allied Expeditionary Force and the Soviet High Command will take such punitive or other action as they deem appropriate.

On the following day, at the insistence of the Soviet Union, a definitive **Act of Surrender** was signed at Berlin.

REFERENCE:

United Nations. *Surrender of Italy, Germany and Japan, World War II: Instruments of Surrender, Public Papers and Addresses of the President and of the Supreme Commanders.* Washington, D.C.: U.S. Government Printing Office, 1946.

Act of Military Surrender (at Berlin)

SIGNED: May 8, 1945, at Berlin

SIGNATORIES: Supreme Commander, Allied Expeditionary Forces, and Supreme High Command of the Red Army vs. German High Command

IN FORCE: From signing

OVERVIEW: The definitive instrument of the military surrender of Germany in World War II.

DISCUSSION:

On May 7, an **Act of Military Surrender** was signed at Supreme Allied Headquarters in Rheims, France. Largely at the insistence of the Soviets, a second Act of Military Surrender was concluded the following day at Berlin. This is the document that definitively ended the war in Europe:

1. We the undersigned, acting by authority of the German High Command, hereby surrender unconditionally to the Supreme Commander, Allied Expeditionary Force and simultaneously to the Supreme High Command of the Red Army all forces on land, at sea, and in the air who are at this date under German control.

2. The German High Command will at once issue order to all German military, naval and air authorities and to all forces under German control to cease active operations at 2301 hours Central European time on 8th May 1945, to remain in all positions occupied at that time and to disarm completely, handing over their weapons and equipment to the local allied commanders or officers designated by Representatives of the Allied Supreme Commands. No ship, vessel, or aircraft is to be scuttled, or any damage done to their hull, machinery or equipment, and also to machines of all kinds, armament, appara-

tus, and all the technical means of prosecution of war in general.

3. The German High Command will at once issue to the appropriate commanders, and ensure the carrying out of any further orders issued by the Supreme Commander, Allied Expeditionary Force and by the Supreme Command of the Red Army.

4. This act of military surrender is without prejudice to, and will be superseded by any general instrument of surrender imposed by, or on behalf of the United Nations and applicable to GERMANY and the German armed forces as a whole.

5. In the event of the German High Command or any of the forces under their control failing to act in accordance with this Act of Surrender, the Supreme Commander, Allied Expeditionary Force and the Supreme High Command of the Red Army will take such punitive or other action as they deem appropriate.

6. This Act is drawn up in the English, Russian and German languages. The English and Russian are the only authentic texts.

REFERENCE:

United Nations. *Surrender of Italy, Germany and Japan, World War II: Instruments of Surrender, Public Papers and Addresses of the President and of the Supreme Commanders.* Washington, D.C.: U.S. Government Printing Office, 1946.

Proclamation on the End of the War in Europe

OFFICIAL TITLE: By the President of the United States of America: a Proclamation

PROCLAIMED: May 8, 1945, at Washington

SIGNATORY: President Harry S Truman

IN FORCE: On proclamation

OVERVIEW: The United States proclamation ending the war in Europe.

DISCUSSION:

Following execution of the **Act of Military Surrender (at Berlin)** on May 8, 1945, United States president Harry S Truman issued the following proclamation:

The Allied armies, through sacrifice and devotion and with God's help, have wrung from Germany a final and unconditional surrender. The western world has been freed of the evil forces which for five years and longer have imprisoned the bodies and broken the lives of millions upon millions of free-born men. They have violated their churches, destroyed their homes, corrupted their children, and murdered their loved ones. Our Armies of Liberation have restored freedom to these suffering peoples, whose spirit and will the oppressors could never enslave.

Much remains to be done. The victory won in the West must now be won in the East. The whole world must be cleansed of the evil from which half the world has been freed. United, the peace-loving nations have demonstrated in the West that their arms are stronger by far than the might of dictators or the tyranny of military cliques that once called us soft and weak. The power of our peoples to defend themselves against all enemies will be proved in the Pacific as it has been proved in Europe.

For the triumph of spirit and of arms which we have won, and of its promise to peoples everywhere who join us in the love of freedom, it is fitting that we, as a nation, give thanks to Almighty God, who has strengthened us and given us the victory.

NOW, THEREFORE, I, HARRY S TRUMAN, President of the United States of America, do hereby appoint Sunday, May 13, 1945 to be a day of prayer.

I call upon the people of the United States, whatever their faith, to unite in offering joyful thanks to God for the victory we have won and to pray that He will support us to the end of our present struggle and guide us into the way of peace.

I also call upon my countrymen to dedicate this day of prayer to the memory of those who have given their lives to make possible our victory.

IN WITNESS WHEREOF, I have hereunto set my hand and caused the seal of the United States of America to be affixed.

REFERENCE:
United Nations. *Surrender of Italy, Germany and Japan, World War II: Instruments of Surrender, Public Papers and Addresses of the President and of the Supreme Commanders.* Washington, D.C.: U.S. Government Printing Office, 1946.

Allied Declaration on Control of Germany

SIGNED: June 5, 1945, at Berlin, Germany
SIGNATORIES: France (Provisional Government), Union of Soviet Socialist Republics, United Kingdom, United States
IN FORCE: From signing
OVERVIEW: A "declaration regarding the defeat of Germany and the assumption of supreme authority with respect to Germany by the Governments of the United States of America, the Union of Soviet Socialist Republics, the United Kingdom and the Provisional Government of the French Republic."

DISCUSSION:
This document was the official instrument by which the Allies assumed control of the German government following Germany's unconditional surrender.

"The German armed forces on land, at sea and in the air have been completely defeated and have surrendered unconditionally and Germany, which bears responsibility for the war, is no longer capable of resisting the will of the victorious Powers," the declaration begins. "The unconditional surrender of Germany has thereby been effected, and Germany has become subject to such requirements as may now or hereafter be imposed upon her."

The declaration mandated immediate cessation of hostilities and the surrender and disarming of all German forces.

REFERENCE:
United Nations. *Surrender of Italy, Germany and Japan, World War II: Instruments of Surrender, Public Papers and Addresses of the President and of the Supreme Commanders.* Washington, D.C.: U.S. Government Printing Office, 1946.

Allied Statements on the Occupation of Germany

SIGNED: June 5, 1945 and November 30, 1945
IN FORCE: From signing
SIGNATORIES: United States, United Kingdom, Soviet Union, Provisional Government of the French Republic
OVERVIEW: With victory in Europe, the Allies divided Germany, giving most of eastern Germany to Poland and the Soviet Union and dividing the remainder into four provisional zones of occupation, each zone under the control of one of the signatories.

DISCUSSION:
Germany's defeat contracted its frontiers to their extent as of December 31, 1937, before the *Anschluss* (annexation of Austria), the acquisition of the Sudetanland in Czechslovakia, and the invasion of Poland. Thus contracted, Germany was then divided

for the purposes of occupation . . . into four zones, one to be allotted to each Power as follows:

an eastern zone to the Union of Soviet Socialist Republics;

a north-western zone to the United Kingdom;

a south-western zone to the United States of America;

a western zone to France.

Each of the four occupying nations was to designate a commander-in-chief with responsibility for its zone. Berlin was treated as a special case. Although it was deep within the Soviet zone, it, too, was to be divided into four zones of occupation: "An Inter-Allied Governing Authority (in Russian, Komendatura) consisting of four Commandants, appointed by their respective Commanders-in-Chief, will be established to direct jointly its administration."

The "control machinery" for Germany during the "period when Germany is carrying out the basic requirements of unconditional surrender" was established as follows:

Supreme authority in Germany will be exercised, on instructions from their Governments, by the British, United States, Soviet and French Commanders-in-Chief, each in his own zone of occupation, and also jointly, in matters affecting Germany as a whole. . . .

The administration of the "Greater Berlin" area will be directed by an Inter-Allied Governing Authority, which will operate under the general direction of the Control Council, and will consist of four Commandants, each of whom will serve in rotation as Chief Commandant. They will be assisted by a technical staff which will supervise and control the activities of the local German organs.

The arrangements outlined above will operate during the period of occupation following German surrender, when Germany is carrying out the basic requirements of unconditional surrender. Arrangements for the subsequent period will be the subject of a separate agreement.

The isolation of Berlin in the Soviet zone of occupation made it necessary to establish three air corridors into Berlin, which were recorded in minutes of the Thirteenth Meeting of the Control Council as Berlin-Hamburg, Berlin-Buckeburg, and Berlin-Frankfurt-on-Main. Soviet Marshal Zhukov "expressed himself confident that in due course . . . other air corridors would be opened."

A reading of the Allied statements on the occupation of Germany suggests a high degree of agreement among the four Allies. The climate of accord soon broke down, however, and the Western Allies ultimately failed to agree with the Soviets on whether (or how) to reunite the four occupied zones. During the long Cold War era that followed World War II, the temporary dividing lines between the Soviet zone in the east and the British, French, and U.S. zones became a permanent boundary. A crisis was not long in coming. On June 7, 1948, the Western nations announced their intention to create West Germany as a separate capitalist nation. The Soviets responded two weeks later with a blockade of West Berlin, protesting that Berlin, deep within Soviet-occupied territory, could not serve as the capital of West Germany. U.S. President Harry S Truman ordered the greatest airlift in history to keep West Berlin supplied with food and fuel. After some 272,000 airlift flights over 321 days, the Soviets relented and reopened access to West Berlin on May 12, 1949 (see **Lifting of the West Berlin Blockade,** Section 2.10). Later that month, East and West Germany became separate nations. Over the next several months and years, Soviet authorities directed the construction of a wall between East and West Berlin, designed to prevent those under communist control from escaping to the West. "The Wall" endured for more than forty years as a hateful symbol of Soviet oppression. Its fall—its political and physical destruction, beginning in 1989—marked the end of the Cold War and was a prelude to the collapse of the Soviet Union.

REFERENCES:
Giangreco, D. M., and Robert E. Griffin. *Airbridge to Berlin: The Berlin Crisis of 1948.* Novato, Calif.: Presidio Press, 1988.
Grenville, J. A. S. *The Major International Treaties 1914-1973: A History Guide with Texts* (New York: Stein and Day, 1974.
Haydock, Michael D. *City Under Siege: The Berlin Blockade and Airlift, 1948-49.* Washington, D.C.: Brasseys, 1999.

Agreement between the United States, British, and Yugoslav Governments on Venezia Giulia

SIGNED: June 9, 1945, at Belgrade, Yugoslavia
SIGNATORIES: United Kingdom and United States vs. Yugoslavia
IN FORCE: From signing
OVERVIEW: An agreement on the disposition of the Italian *regione* of Venezia Giulia.

DISCUSSION:
Venezia Giulia, long a region (*regione*) of northeastern Italy, bordering north and east on Austria and Slovenia, south on the Adriatic Sea, and west on Veneto, became a subject of dispute between Italy and Yugoslavia before World War II. By the present agreement, part of the region, including the Istrian Peninsula, the hinterland of Trieste, and the Karst plateau, was ceded to Yugoslavia. Trieste itself and the area surrounding it was declared a free territory divided into northern and southern zones—zones A and B—under U.S.-British (Zone A) and Yugoslavian administration (Zone B). The province (*provinzia*) of Udine was detached from Veneto and united with Gorizia *provincia* to form Friuli-Venezia Giulia. In 1954, an agreement concluded at London restored the city of Trieste and a portion of Zone A to Italy.

REFERENCE:
United Nations. *Surrender of Italy, Germany and Japan, World War II: Instruments of Surrender, Public Papers and Addresses of the President and of the Supreme Commanders.* Washington, D.C.: U.S. Government Printing Office, 1946.

Potsdam Protocol

SIGNED: August 2, 1945, at Potsdam, Germany
IN FORCE: From signature
SIGNATORIES: Union of Soviet Socialist Republics, United Kingdom, and United States
OVERVIEW: Hammered out by Soviet premier Josef Stalin, U.S. president Harry S Truman, and British prime minister Clement Atlee (replacing Winston Churchill, who was defeated in a reelection bid) in the Potsdam Conference (July 17-August 2, 1945), the Potsdam Protocol created the mechanism for concluding peace treaties with Italy and the minor Axis powers, finalized plans for the military occupation of Germany, formulated German disarmament, and resolved to try leading Nazis as war criminals.

DISCUSSION:
The final Allied conference of World War II followed the defeat of Germany and came on the eve of Japan's surrender.
- Article I created a Council of Foreign Ministers to conclude treaties with Italy and the lesser Axis powers.

- Article II outlined principles to govern the military occupation of Germany. The article established a policy popularly called "denazification," the removal of prominent Nazis from public office. In conjunction with Article VI, Article II calls for the arrest and punishment of war criminals and leading Nazis.
- A second part of Article II established the economic principles of the occupation, including a prohibition of arms production, development of agriculture and "peaceful domestic industries," and prompt repair of the essential infrastructure. In contrast to the **Treaty of Versailles** ending World War I, it was resolved that reparations should "leave enough resources to enable the German people to subsist without external assistance."
- Article III outlined the subject of German reparations, specifying that "reparation claims of the U.S.S.R. shall be met by removals from the zone of Germany occupied by the U.S.S.R., and from appropriate German external assets," and "the reparation claims of the United States, the United Kingdom and other countries entitled to reparations shall be met from the Western zones and from appropriate German external assets." Additionally, the U.S.S.R. was awarded certain percentages of "usable and complete industrial capital equipment" in the Western zone.
- Article IV divided the vessels of the German navy and merchant marine among the three signatory powers.
- Article V addressed the proposed western frontier of the Soviet Union.
- Article VI called for war crimes trials to begin at the earliest possible date. Articles VII and VIII addressed the disposition of Austria and Poland:
- Article VII called for an examination of a Soviet proposal to extend the authority of the Austrian Provisional Government to all of Austria. It was also "agreed that reparations should not be exacted from Austria."
- Article VIII is a declaration on Poland, recognizing the authority of the a Polish Provisional Government of National Unity and deferring determination of the western frontier of Poland until "the peace settlement."
- Article IX called for treaties with Italy and minor Axis powers, as provided for in the Report of the Yalta (Crimea) Conference. It also proposed opening the "United Nations Organization" to "all . . . peace-loving States who accept the obligations contained in the present Charter." The three signatories recorded their opposition to the membership of Spain, however, "in view of its origins, its nature, its record and its close association with the aggressor States, [it does not] possess the qualifications necessary to justify . . . membership."

Lesser issues addressed in the protocol include:
- Issues of territorial trusteeship
- Revision of Allied Control Commission procedures in Rumania, Bulgaria and Hungary

- The disposition of oil equipment in Rumania
- Provision for the withdrawal of Allied troops from Iran
- A pledge to create an International Zone in Tangier A resolution to revise an agreement on the Black Sea Straits.

The Potsdam Protocol concluded by touching on the "orderly transfer of German populations":

> The three Governments, having considered the question in all its aspects, recognize that the transfer to Germany of German populations, or elements thereof, remaining in Poland, Czechoslovakia and Hungary, will have to be undertaken. They agree that any transfers that take place should be effected in an orderly and humane manner . . . .

This statement hardly suggests the scope of the impending refugee crisis. Nor did the Protocol document begin to suggest the magnitude of the ideological differences that motivated the Western and Eastern allies at the end of the war.

REFERENCES:
Feis, Herbert. *Between War and Peace: The Potsdam Conference.* Westport, CT: Greenwood Publishing Group, Inc., 1983.
Grenville, J. A. S. *The Major International Treaties 1914-1973: A History Guide with Texts.* New York: Stein and Day, 1974.
Merrill, Dennis K. *Documentary History of the Truman Presidency: Planning for the Postwar World: Pres. Truman and the Potsdam Conference, July 17-August 2, 1945.* Bethesda, MD: University Publications of America, 1995.

Japanese Surrender Documents

SIGNED: September 2, 1945, at Tokyo Bay, Japan
SIGNATORIES: Australia, Canada, China, France (Provisional Government of the French Republic), Netherlands, New Zealand, Union of Soviet Socialist Republics, United Kingdom, United States vs. Japan
IN FORCE: From signing
OVERVIEW: Signed in a ceremony aboard the United States battleship *Missouri* in Tokyo Bay, Japan's instrument of unconditional surrender ended World War II.

DISCUSSION:
The Japanese proved an implacable enemy, who, despite one disastrous defeat after another and impending invasion of their homeland, refused to surrender. Then, on August 6, 1945, a United States Army Air Force B-29 bomber dropped the newly developed atomic bomb on the Japanese city of Hiroshima. Three days later, a second atomic bomb was dropped on Nagasaki. The loss of life in both cities was devastating. Against the protests of some in his government and many in the military, and even threatened with a *coup d'etat*, Japan's emperor, Hirohito, made an unprecedented radio broadcast to his nation on August 15. He announced that he had ordered "Our Government" to accept the terms laid down by the United States, Great Britain, China, and the Soviet Union in the **Potsdam**

Declaration of July 26, 1945, calling for the unconditional surrender of Japan as the only terms on which the war would be ended. The broadcast was the first time the people of Japan had heard their emperor's voice.

The instrument of surrender was prepared for signature by representatives of the Allied nations and those of the Japanese government and military in a ceremony, on September 2, aboard the United States battleship *Missouri*, which was anchored in Tokyo Bay.

The documents include the emperor's presentation of the credentials of his representatives, a foreign minister and a general:

HIROHITO,

By the Grace of Heaven, Emperor of Japan, seated on the Throne occupied by the same Dynasty changeless through ages eternal,

To all who these Presents shall come, Greeting!

We do hereby authorise Mamoru Shigemitsu, Zyosanmi, First Class of the Imperial Order of the Rising Sun to attach his signature by command and in behalf of Ourselves and Our Government unto the Instrument of Surrender which is required by the Supreme Commander for the Allied Powers to be signed. In witness whereof, We have hereunto set Our signature and caused the Great Seal of the Empire to be affixed. Given at Our Palace in Tokyo, this first day of the ninth month of the twentieth year of Syowa, being the two thousand six hundred and fifth year from the Accession of the Emperor Zinmu.

HIROHITO,

By the Grace of Heaven, Emperor of Japan, seated on the Throne occupied by the same Dynasty changeless through ages eternal,

To all who these Presents shall come, Greeting!

We do hereby authorise Yoshijiro Umezu, Zyosanmi, First Class of the Imperial Order of the Rising Sun to attach his signature by command and in behalf of Ourselves and Our Government unto the Instrument of Surrender which is required by the Supreme Commander for the Allied Powers to be signed. In witness whereof, We have hereunto set Our signature and caused the Great Seal of the Empire to be affixed. Given at Our Palace in Tokyo, this first day of the ninth month of the twentieth year of Syowa, being the two thousand six hundred and fifth year from the Accession of the Emperor Zinmu.

The Instrument of Surrender is a brief document, which begins with the Japanese acceptance of the provisions of the Potsdam Declaration and concludes by relinquishing to the Supreme Commander for the Allied Powers all government authority:

We, acting by command of and in behalf of the Emperor of Japan, the Japanese Government and the Japanese Imperial General Headquarters, hereby accept the provisions set forth in the declaration issued by the heads of the Governments of the United States, China, and Great Britain on 26 July 1945 at Potsdam, and subsequently adhered to by the Union of Soviet Socialist Repub-lics, which four powers are hereafter referred to as the Allied Powers.

We hereby proclaim the unconditional surrender to the Allied Powers of the Japanese Imperial General Headquarters and of all Japanese armed forces and all armed forces under the Japanese control wherever situated.

We hereby command all Japanese forces wherever situated and the Japanese people to cease hostilites forthwith, to preserve and save from damage all ships, aircraft, and military and civil property and to comply with all requirements which my be imposed by the Supreme Commander for the Allied Powers or by agencies of the Japanese Government at his direction.

We hereby command the Japanese Imperial Headquarters to issue at once orders to the Commanders of all Japanese forces and all forces under Japanese control wherever situated to surrender un-conditionally themselves and all forces under their control. We hereby command all civil, military and naval officials to obey and enforce all proclamations, and orders and directives deemed by the Supreme Commander for the Allied Powers to be proper to effectuate this surrender and issued by him or under his authority and we direct all such officials to remain at their posts and to continue to perform their non-combatant duties unless specifically relieved by him or under his authority.

We hereby undertake for the Emperor, the Japanese Government and their successors to carry out the provisions of the Potsdam Declaration in good faith, and to issue whatever orders and take whatever actions may be required by the Supreme Commander for the Allied Powers or by any other designated representative of the Allied Powers for the purpose of giving effect to that Declaration.

We hereby command the Japanese Imperial Government and the Japanese Imperial General Headquarters at once to liberate all allied prisoners of war and civilian internees now under Japanese control and to provide for their protection, care, maintenance and immediate transportation to places as directed.

The authority of the Emperor and the Japanese Government to rule the state shall be subject to the Supreme Commander for the Allied Powers who will take such steps as he deems proper to effectuate these terms of surrender.

The instrument of surrender was accepted, on behalf of the Allied powers, by Gen. Douglas McArthur, the supreme Allied commander in the Pacific.

On the same day the instrument was executed, Hirohito made a proclamation on receipt of the surrender documents:

Accepting the terms set forth in the Declaration issued by the heads of the Governments of the United States, Great Britain, and China on July 26th, 1945 at Potsdam and subsequently adhered to by the Union of Soviet Socialist Republics, We have commanded the Japanese Imperial Government and the Japanese Imperial General Headquarters to sign on Our behalf the Instrument of Surrender presented by the Supreme Commander for the Allied Powers and to issue General Orders to the Military and Naval Forces in accordance with the direction of the Supreme Commander for the Allied Powers. We command all Our people forthwith to cease hostilities, to lay down their arms and faithfully to carry out all the provisions of Instrument of Surrender and the General Orders issued by the Japanese Imperial General Headquarters hereunder. This second day of the ninth month of the twentieth year of Syowa.

On the following day, September 3, 1945, Gen. Tomoyuki Yamashita, commanding the Imperial Japanese Army in the Philippines, and Vice Adm. Denhici Okochi, commanding the Imperial Japanese Navy in the Philippines, signed an Instrument of Surrender of the Japanese and Japanese-Controlled Armed Forces in the Philippine Islands (*see* **Japanese Surrender in the Philippines**). Additional documents effected the surrender of Japanese forces in Korea (**Japanese Surrender in Korea**) and in Southeast Asia (**Japanese Surrender in Southeast Asia**).

REFERENCE:
United Nations. *Surrender by Japan: Terms Between the United States of America and the Other Allied Powers and Japan, Signed at Tokyo Bay September 2, 1945, Effective September 2, 1945, Together with Proclamation by the Emperor of Japan.* Washington, D.C.: U.S. Government Printing Office, 1946.

Japanese Surrender in the Philippines

OFFICIAL TITLE: Surrender of the Japanese and Japanese-Controlled Armed Forces in the Philippine Islands to the Commanding General United States Army Forces, Western Pacific
SIGNED: September 3, 1945, at Camp John Hay, Baquio, Mountain Province, Luzon, Philippine Islands
SIGNATORIES: Japan (Japanese Imperial General Headquarters) vs. United States (Commander-in-Chief, United States Army Forces, Pacific)
IN FORCE: From signing
OVERVIEW: Pursuant to the Instrument of Surrender of September 2, 1945, this document effected the unconditional surrender of all Japanese forces in the Philippines.

DISCUSSION:
Like the Instrument of Surrender concluded aboard the U.S. battleship *Missouri* in Tokyo Bay on September 2, 1945 (see **Japanese Surrender Documents**), the instrument by which Japanese commanders surrendered their forces in the Philippines was based on Emperor Hirohito's acceptance of the terms for unconditional surrender laid down in the **Potsdam Declaration** of July 26, 1945. Of particular urgency was the release of Allied prisoners of war (paragraph 3), many of whom had been held, in deplorable circumstances, since the earliest days of the war in the Pacific:

3. We hereby direct the commanders of all Japanese forces in the Philippine Islands to issue at once to all forces under their command to surrender unconditionally themselves and all forces under their control, as prisoners of war, to the nearest United States Force Commander.

Gen. Tomoyuki Yamashita, who, with Vice Adm. Denhici Okochi, signed the Instrument of Surrender, was subsequently tried for and convicted of war crimes relating to atrocities committed by Japanese troops defending Manila in early 1945. He was executed on February 23, 1946.

REFERENCE:
United Nations. *Surrender by Japan: Terms Between the United States of America and the Other Allied Powers and Japan, Signed at Tokyo Bay September 2, 1945, Effective September 2, 1945, Together with Proclamation by the Emperor of Japan.* Washington, D.C.: U.S. Government Printing Office, 1946.

Japanese Surrender in Korea

OFFICIAL TITLE: Formal Surrender by the Senior Japanese Ground, Sea, Air and Auxiliary Forces Commands Within Korea South of 38 North Latitude to the Commanding General, United States Army Forces in Korea, for and in Behalf of the Commander-in-Chief United States Army Forces, Pacific
SIGNED: September 9, 1945, at Seoul, Korea
SIGNATORIES: Japan (by commanders of Japanese ground, air, and naval forces in Korea, north and south of 38 degrees north latitude) vs. United States (by commanders of United States Army Forces in Korea and of the U.S. Navy); the Japanese governor-general of Korea signed a special acknowledgment of the document
IN FORCE: From signing
OVERVIEW: The formal unconditional surrender of Japanese forces in Korea

DISCUSSION:
The document formally surrendered Japanese forces south of the 38th parallel to the United States Army Forces in Korea; although territory north of the 38th parallel lay outside of U.S. Army authority, the Japanese commander of forces in that region also signed the surrender document.

REFERENCE:
United Nations. *Surrender by Japan: Terms Between the United States of America and the Other Allied Powers and Japan, Signed at Tokyo Bay September 2, 1945, Effective September 2, 1945, Together with Proclamation by the Emperor of Japan.* Washington, D.C.: U.S. Government Printing Office, 1946.

Japanese Surrender in Southeast Asia

OFFICIAL TITLE: Instrument of Surrender of Japanese Forces under the Command or Control of the Supreme Commander, Japanese Expeditionary Forces, Southern Regions, Within the Operational Theatre of the Supreme Allied Commander, South East Asia
SIGNED: September 12, 1945, at Singapore
SIGNATORIES: Allied Forces (by Supreme Allied Commander, Southeast Asia) vs. Japan (by Supreme Commander, Japanese Expeditionary Forces, Southern Regions)

IN FORCE: From signing

OVERVIEW: The instrument of the unconditional surrender of Japanese forces in Southeast Asia

DISCUSSION:

The signatory on behalf of the Allies was Britain's Lord Louis Mountbatten, Supreme Allied Commander, Southeast Asia. The entire document follows:

1. In pursuance of and in compliance with:

(a) the Instrument of Surrender signed by the Japanese plenipotentiaries by command and on behalf of the Emperor of Japan, the Japanese Government and the Japanese Imperial General Headquarters at Tokyo on 2 September, 1945;

(b) General Order No. 1, promulgated at the same place and on the same date;

(c) the Local Agreement made by the Supreme Commander, Japanese Expeditionary Forces, Southern Regions, with the Supreme Allied Commander, South East Asia at Rangoon on 27 August, 1945;

to all of which Instrument of Surrender, General Order and Local Agreement this present Instrument is complementary and which it in no way supersedes, the Supreme Commander, Japanese Expeditionary Forces, Southern Regions (Field Marshall Count Terauchi) does hereby surrender unconditionally to the Supreme Allied Commander, South East Asia (Admiral The Lord Louis Mountbatten) himself and all Japanese sea, ground, air and auxiliary forces under his command or control and within the operational theatre of the Supreme Allied Commander, South East Asia.

2. The Supreme Commander, Japanese Expeditionary Forces, Southern Regions, undertakes to ensure that all orders and instructions that may be issued from time to time by the Supreme Allied Commander, South East Asia, or by any of his subordinate Naval, Military, or AirForce Commanders of whatever rank acting in his name, are scrupulously and promptly obeyed by all Japanese sea, ground, air and auxiliary forces under the command or control of the Supreme Commander, Japanese Expeditionary Forces, Southern Regions, and within the operational theatre of the Supreme Allied Commander, South East Asia.

3. Any disobedience of, or delay or failure to comply with, orders or instructions issued by the Supreme Allied Commander, South East Asia, or issued on his behalf by any of his subordinate Naval, Military, or Air Force Commanders of whatever rank, and any action which the Supreme Allied Commander, South East Asia, or his subordinate Commanders action on his behalf, may determine to be detrimental to the Allied Powers, will be dealt with as the Supreme Allied Commander, South East Asia may decide.

4. This Instrument takes effect from the time and date of signing.

5. This Instrument is drawn up in the English Language, which is the only authentic version. In any case of doubt to intention or meaning, the decision of the Supreme Allied Commander, South East Asia is final. It is the responsibility of the Supreme Commander, Japanese Expeditionary Forces, Southern Regions, to make such translations into Japanese as he may require.

REFERENCE:

United Nations. *Surrender by Japan: Terms Between the United States of America and the Other Allied Powers and Japan, Signed at Tokyo Bay September 2, 1945, Effective September 2, 1945, Together with Proclamation by the Emperor of Japan.* Washington, D.C.: U.S. Government Printing Office, 1946.

Moscow Communiqué on Procedure for Peace Treaties

SIGNED: December 24, 1945, at Moscow

SIGNATORIES: Union of Soviet Socialist Republics, United Kingdom, United States

IN FORCE: From signing

OVERVIEW: A communiqué from the "Big Three" (Josef Stalin, Anthony Eden, and Harry S Truman) laying down procedures for concluding treaties ending World War II.

DISCUSSION:

The Big Three Allied leaders laid down the following procedures for concluding treaties with the defeated enemy nations:

1. In the drawing up of the peace treaties with Italy, Rumania, Bulgaria, Hungary and Finland by the Council of Foreign Ministers, only those members of the Council will take part who are, or—in accordance with the agreement on the institution of the Council of Foreign Ministers passed at the Berlin Conference—are considered to be parties who have signed the conditions of surrender, unless or until the Council decides in accordance with this agreement to invite other members to take part in the Council with regard to questions in which they are directly concerned, i.e.:

(A) The conditions of a peace treaty with Italy are to be drawn up by the Foreign Ministers of Great Britain, U. S. A., U.S.S.R. and France.

(B) The conditions of a peace treaty with Rumania, Bulgaria and Hungary by the Foreign Ministers of the U.S.S.R., U. S. A. and Great Britain.

(C) The conditions of a peace treaty with Finland by the Foreign Ministers of U.S.S.R. and Great Britain.

2. The deputies of the Foreign Ministers will immediately resume their work in London on the basis of an agreement reached on questions that had been discussed at the first session of the Council of Foreign Ministers in London.

As soon as the preparation of all these drafts is completed, the Council will call a conference to discuss peace treaties with Italy, Rumania, Bulgaria, Hungary and Finland. The conference will consist of the five members of the Council of Foreign Ministers and also of all those members of the United Nations which took an active part in the war against enemy states in Europe with substantial military contingents, to wit: U. S. A., U.S.S.R., Great Britain, China, France, Australia, Belgium, White Russian Soviet Socialist Republic, Brazil, Greece, the Netherlands, India, Canada, New Zealand, Norway, Poland, Ukrainian Soviet Socialist Republic, Czechoslovakia, Ethiopia, Yugoslavia and the South African Union. The conference will take place not later than May 1, 1946.

3. After the conference has concluded its work and its recommendations have been examined, the states which had signed the armistice terms with Italy, Rumania, Bulgaria, Hungary and Finland, and France-which is considered as one of the Allied signatory states as far as the peace treaty is concerned-will draw up, respectively, the final texts of peace treaties.

4. The final texts of the respective peace treaties thus drawn up will be signed by the representatives of the states represented at the conference and in a state of war with the respective enemy state. The texts of the respective peace treaties will then be submitted to other United Nations in a state of war against the respective enemy state.

5. The peace treaties will come into force immediately after their ratifications by Allied States who had signed the respective armistice terms and also by France (which is considered as one of them as far as Italy is concerned). The peace treaties are also subject to ratification by the respective enemy states.

The talks on other questions continue in a friendly spirit. There is hope that a communiqué embracing the work of the conference will be issued in one or two days.

REFERENCES:
None

Washington Agreement Relating to the Liquidation of German Property in Switzerland

SIGNED: May 25, 1946, at Washington, D.C.
SIGNATORIES: France, United Kingdom, and United States (also on behalf of Albania, Australia, Belgium, Canada, Czechoslovakia, Denmark, Egypt, Greece, India, Luxembourg, Netherlands, New Zealand, Norway, South Africa and Yugoslavia) vs. Switzerland
IN FORCE: From signing (implemented during 1946-1960)
OVERVIEW: An agreement for the liquidation, to satisfy Allied war claims, of German property (much of it gold) transferred to Switzerland during World War II.

DISCUSSION:
During World War II, the German government and many German citizens transferred their assets into bank accounts in neutral Switzerland in an effort to preserve them from seizure by the Allies. In some cases, this transferred property—much of it gold—had been looted from individuals as well as conquered nations. In other cases, it was arguably the rightful property of the German government or German citizens. Nevertheless, the Allies, even during the war, systematically laid a legal foundation for eventual seizure of all German assets and property transferred to neutral countries, the most important of which was Switzerland. During and immediately after the war, the Allies took the following steps to prepare for seizure of the assets in question:
- Issued warnings to all states against accepting German looted gold and did not recognize the legality of such transactions

- Announced an intention to find, seize, and restore to rightful owners assets illegally expropriated by Germany
- Announced the non-recognition of the legality of transfers to neutral states also
- Fixed the amount of German reparations $20 billion and announced the principle that all German assets abroad should be impounded for the purposes of reparations (Yalta Conference, 1945)
- Determined the division of reparations among the Western Allies and the U.S.S.R.; German assets in neutral west European states to go to the three Western Allies and fifteen other Allied states (Potsdam Conference, 1945)
- Enacted the Allied Control Commission Law No. 5 (October 30, 1945), depriving German owners of the right of disposal over their assets abroad, and assigned this to the Control Commission
- Held the Paris Conference on Reparations (November-December 1945), at which eighteen signatory states created an Inter-Allied Reparation Agency (IARA) in Brussels

After the war, the Allies took a hard line with Switzerland, blacklisting certain Swiss companies and imposing controls on Swiss private holdings in the United States. They pushed for an agreement to resolve the question of looted property in order to achieve two principal objectives:
- Discovery and seizure of German assets in neutral states (Europe, South America, Asia), to prevent the re-arming of the German Reich
- Confiscation of German assets abroad for purposes of reparation

For its part, Switzerland wanted to achieve the following:
- Put an end to international isolation
- Maintain respect for Swiss sovereignty
- Normalize its relations with the Allied state
- Abolish the blacklists against Swiss companies, and bring about the lifting of controls on Swiss private holdings in the United States

The agreement the parties hammered out provided for the following:
- Swiss agreement to trace and liquidate assets located in Switzerland belonging to Germans living in Germany
- Swiss agreement to pay 50 percent of the proceeds of liquidation to the Allies for purposes of reconstruction, with the Swiss Federal Council being free to dispose of the remaining 50 percent
- Agreement that owners of liquidated assets would receive compensation in German currency
- Joint commission (Switzerland, United States, United Kingdom and France) created as an organ of information and consultation to implement the agreement

- Disputes over the interpretation of the agreement to be resolved through a Swiss appeal court, and, if necessary, by an ad-hoc court of arbitration
- In settlement of the issue of looted gold, Switzerland to pay the Allies gold to the value of 250 million Swiss francs; in exchange for this payment, the Allies would renounce further claims against the Swiss government in connection with gold acquired by Germany during the war
- United States to release Swiss assets in the United States in accordance with a procedure to be negotiated jointly
- Allies to abolish blacklists affecting Swiss companies
- Swiss confirmation that it would take a favorable view of the Allied request to transfer holdings of Nazi victims who died without leaving heirs to the Allied governments for the benefit of refugee organizations

The complex and difficult agreement contained many loopholes and ambiguities. While some provisions were quickly implemented, some issues remained unresolved until a final Swiss-West German negotiation in 1960. Many questions involving the seized and transferred assets of Jews and others "deported" to death camps during the Holocaust surfaced in the late 1990s, and an embarrassed Swiss government agreed to work to restore these assets to the heirs of the rightful owners. The 1946 agreement served as a basis for the international pressure applied to Switzerland to restore the unclaimed assets.

REFERENCE:
Picard, Jacques. *Switzerland and the Assets of the Missing Victims of the Nazis: Assets in Switzerland Belonging to Victims of Racial, Religious and Political Persecution and Their Disposition Between 1946 and 1973.* Zürich: Bank Julius Bär, 1996.

Agreement Concerning the Status and Admission into Belgium of Displaced Persons

OFFICIAL TITLE: Agreement Concerning the Status and Admission into Belgium of Displaced Persons at Present in the American Zone of Germany
SIGNED: January 23, 1947, at Brussels
SIGNATORIES: Belgium vs. United States
IN FORCE: From March 10, 1947
OVERVIEW: An agreement to resettled displaced persons temporarily residing in the United States-occupied zone of Germany after World War II.

DISCUSSION:
In the aftermath of World War II, Europe faced a refugee problem of staggering proportions. By this agreement, the United States sought permanent residence for "displaced persons" (as the era's refugees were called) temporarily housed in the American-controlled sector of occupied Germany. The Belgian government agreed to accept certain of these displaced persons on the following conditions:
- The Belgian government would protect their safety and rights.
- The Belgian government would guarantee a contract (subjoined to the agreement) with the Federation of Coal Mines, insuring "regular and permanent employment" for the displaced persons.
- Acceptance was limited to "individuals who have never collaborated in any way with the Nazi regime"; these persons would be "offered an immediate opportunity to begin a normal and free life in Belgium."
- Heads of displaced families were to be admitted to Belgium and, after ninety days, could be "joined by members of their immediate family (wife and minor children)." Other dependants might be admitted "after individual arrangements with the Belgian Government." The ninety days was to be considered a probationary period.
- Relocation in Belgium would be strictly voluntary, the volunteers to be given free transport to the "Belgian frontier by the American authorities. Volunteers will be permitted to bring with them all their legal belongings."
- As workers, the relocated individuals would be granted "exactly the same working and living conditions and wages as Belgian workers performing the same job."
- Workers could cancel their labor contracts at will, whereupon the Belgian government will issue "documents necessary to leave Belgium."

REFERENCES:
Auerbach, Frank Ludwig. *The Admission and Resettlement of Displaced Persons in the United States.* New York: Common Council for American Unity, 1949.
Riggs, Fred Warren. *The World's Refugee Problem.* New York: Foreign Policy Association, 1951.

Peace Treaty between the Allies and Italy

SIGNED: February 10, 1947, at Paris
IN FORCE: From September 15, 1947
SIGNATORIES: Albania, Australia, Belgium, Brazil, Canada, China, Czechoslovakia, Ethiopia, France, Greece, India, Iraq, Mexico, Netherlands, New Zealand, Pakistan, Poland, Slovak Republic, South Africa, Union of Soviet Socialist Republics, United Kingdom, United States, and Yugoslavia vs. Italy
OVERVIEW: This treaty formally and definitively ended World War II hostilities between Italy and the Allies.

DISCUSSION:
The treaty begins by acknowledging that Italian fascism was overturned as a result of Allied victory and "with the assistance of the

democratic elements of the Italian people." For this reason, Italy was accorded privileged status among the defeated nations of the former Axis. The Allies recognized that while the government of Benito Mussolini bore responsibility for aggressive war, a significant portion of the Italian people opposed the government and its war.

The treaty reestablished Italy's frontiers as they had existed on January 1, 1938, except that the conquests of Albania and Ethiopia were annulled, the Dodecanese was ceded to Greece, and certain Adriatic islands were likewise ceded to Greece or Albania. The boundary between Italy and France was also subject to adjustment. Additional, lesser territorial adjustments were made as well.

Part II of the treaty is devoted to "Political Clauses," including provisions to enforce human rights and eliminate all vestiges of fascism:

Article 15
Italy shall take all measures necessary to secure to all persons under Italian jurisdiction . . . the enjoyment of human rights and of the fundamental freedoms, including freedom of expression, of press and publication, of religious worship, of political opinion, and of public meeting.

Article 17
Italy . . . shall not permit the resurgence on Italian territory of [Fascist] organizations, whether political, military, or semi-military, whose purpose it is to deprive the people of their democratic rights.

The Italian armed forces were very strictly limited, although such limitation was subject to modification "by agreement between the Allied and Associated Powers and Italy or, after Italy becomes a member of the United Nations, by agreement between the Security Council and Italy." Finally, a schedule for the withdrawal of Allied troops was established and reparations were fixed:

- The Soviet Union, $100 million
- Yugoslavia, $125 million
- Greece, $105 million
- Ethiopia, $25 million
- Albania, $5 million

France, Britain, and the United States renounced reparations claims.

REFERENCES:

Becker, Josef, ed. *Power in Europe? Great Britain, France, Italy, and Germany in a Postwar World, 1945-1950.* Berlin, Germany, and Hawthorn, NY: Walter De Gruyter, 1986.

Cooke, Philip. *The Italian Resistance: An Anthology.* Manchester, UK: Manchester University Press, 1998.

Grenville, J. A. S. *The Major International Treaties 1914-1973: A History Guide with Texts.* New York: Stein and Day, 1974.

Trusteeship Agreement for the Former Japanese Mandated Islands

SIGNED: April 2, 1947, at New York

SIGNATORIES: Former Japanese Mandate Islands, United Nations, United States

IN FORCE: From July 18, 1947

OVERVIEW: An agreement transferring the Japanese Mandate Islands to the Trusteeship System of the United Nations under the administering authority of the United States.

DISCUSSION:

Article 22 of the **Covenant of the League of Nations** (Section 2.8) assigned to Japan mandate the Pacific islands north of the equator formerly held by Germany. As a result of its defeat in World War II, Japan "ceased to exercise any authority in these islands"; therefore, the United Nations placed them under the Trusteeship System, designating them the Trust Territory and assigning to the United States "administering authority" over the islands.

The major provisions of the agreement assign full powers of administration of the Trust Territory to the United States, which was authorized to establish a military presence on the islands. Moreover, the United States was obligated to "foster the development of such political institutions as are suited to the Trust Territory" and, progressively, to promote "self-government or independence as may be appropriate to the particular circumstances of the Trust Territory." The United States also accepted responsibility for promoting economic advancement and self-sufficiency, social advancement, and educational advancement.

REFERENCE:

Army Library. *Pacific Islands and Trust Territories; a Select Bibliography.* Washington, D.C.: U.S. Government Printing Office, 1971.

Agreement (with France) Concerning Interment of American Soldiers

OFFICIAL TITLE: Agreement Concerning the Interment in France and in Territories of the French Union or the Removal to the United States of the Bodies of American Soldiers Killed in the War of 1939-1945

SIGNED: October 1, 1947, at Paris

SIGNATORIES: France vs. United States

IN FORCE: From signing

OVERVIEW: An agreement whereby France grants to the United States certain plots of land for the construction of military cemeteries and war monuments.

DISCUSSION:

The agreement provides as follows:

- Grants of land, gratis, "chosen and utilized either as permanent cemeteries for the burial of American victims of the war of 1939-1945, or for the construction of monuments commemorative of the exploits of the Armed forces of the United States . . ."

- The land granted to remain the property of the French state and their location to be subject to French approval
- Maintenance of cemeteries and monuments to be the responsibility of the United States government

The agreement also provides for facilitation of the burial of the remains of American victims of the war and for their exhumation, in cases where it is desired to return bodies to the United States for burial.

REFERENCES:
None

Protocol Relating to the Transfer to the Italian Government of Gold Captured by the Allied Military Forces at Fortezza

SIGNED: October 10, 1947, at London
SIGNATORIES: Italy, United Kingdom, United States
IN FORCE: From September 15, 1947
OVERVIEW: An agreement whereby the Allies agree to return captured gold to Italy.

DISCUSSION:
During World War II, Allied forces captured a cache of gold, in the custody of the Bank of Italy, at Fortezza, and was held by "Allied Military Authorities." Pursuant to the **Peace Treaty between the Allies and Italy** of 1947, this protocol to that treaty was concluded to effect the return of the gold to Italy.

See also **Agreement (with Spain) Relating to the Restitution of Monetary Gold Looted by Germany, Arbitration of Claims with Respect to Gold Looted by the Germans from Rome,** and **Washington Agreement Relating to the Liquidation of German Property in Switzerland.**

REFERENCE:
United States. *Restitution of Property, Monetary Gold Looted by Germany.* Washington, D.C.: U. S. Government Printing Office, 1951.

Agreement (with Spain) Relating to the Restitution of Monetary Gold Looted by Germany

SIGNED: April 30 and May 3, 1948, at Madrid, Spain
SIGNATORIES: Spain vs. United States
IN FORCE: From May 3, 1948
OVERVIEW: An agreement whereby Spain undertakes to restore to the Netherlands eight bars of gold looted by Germany during

World War II and deposited by them with Spain.

DISCUSSION:
Among the resolutions adopted at the Bretton Woods conference held among the Allies in 1944 was a resolve to locate and secure the restoration of gold looted by the Germans. When a quantity of gold—eight bars, 101.6 kilograms—was discovered in Spain and determined to have been looted by the Germans, the Spanish government agreed to restore the gold to the Netherlands. The agreement stipulates that the Spanish government "had not been aware of [the gold's] looted origin at the time of . . . acquisition."

The agreement stipulates that "no claims for any such additional gold presented after April 30, 1949, will be considered."

See also **Arbitration of Claims with Respect to Gold Looted by the Germans from Rome, Protocol Relating to the Transfer to the Italian Government of Gold Captured by the Allied Military Forces at Fortezza,** and **Washington Agreement Relating to the Liquidation of German Property in Switzerland.**

REFERENCE:
United States. *Restitution of Property, Monetary Gold Looted by Germany.* Washington, D.C.: U. S. Government Printing Office, 1951.

Agreements on Germany (France, U.K., U.S.)

SIGNED: April 8, 1949, at Washington
SIGNATORIES: France, United Kingdom, United States
IN FORCE: From signing
OVERVIEW: A collection of documents regarding the signatories' powers and responsibilities following establishment of the German Federal Republic.

DISCUSSION:
Following Germany's defeat in World War II, the wartime Allies, the United Kingdom, the Soviet Union, the United States, and France (which had been liberated late in the war) agreed on joint occupation of Germany (*see* **Allied Statements on the Occupation of Germany**). As the wartime alliance with the Soviet bloc was transformed into a Cold War between the powers of the West and the East, Germany was divided into a set of Western Zones, controlled by France, the United Kingdom, and the United States, and an Eastern Zone, controlled by the Soviets.

Early in 1948, the Western allies voiced their commitment to establish a separate capitalist, democratic state of West Germany. The Agreement on Germany, concluded in April of the following year, embodies the Western allies' statements of their role in the government of the new nation.

The Agreements on Germany consist of the following:

1. **Memorandum Regarding Germany (U.S., France, U.K)** (Official title: Agreed Memorandum Regarding the Principles Governing Exercise of Powers and Responsibilities of US-UK-French Governments following Establishment of German Federal Republic)

2. **Occupation Statute Defining the Powers to be Retained by the Occupation Authorities**

3. **Agreement as to Tripartite Controls (for West Germany)**

4. **Agreed Minute Respecting Berlin**

5. **Agreed Minute on Claims Against Germany**

6. **Agreed Minute on Wuerttemberg-Baden Plebiscite**

7. **Agreement Regarding Kehl**

8. **Message to the Military Governors from the Foreign Ministers of the U.S., U.K., and France**

9. **Message to the Bonn Parliamentary Council from the Foreign Ministers of the US, UK, and France**

Each of these documents is included in separate entries in this book.

Although it was well within the Soviet zone, Berlin was itself divided into Western and Eastern zones. On June 24, 1948, some two weeks after the Western allies officially announced their intention to establish West Germany, the Soviets responded by blockading West Berlin. The United States, in turn, initiated the Berlin Airlift, conducting almost a year of continuous, highly hazardous flights over Soviet-occupied territory to supply the beleaguered people of West Berlin. The Agreements on Germany were written and signed during the blockade and airlift. On May 12, 1949, a month after the documents were signed, the Soviets, effectively conceding that the blockade had failed, lifted it. Later that month, West and East Germany were formally created as separate nations.

REFERENCES:
Frederiksen, Oliver Jul. *The American Military Occupation of Germany, 1945-1953.* Darmstadt, Germany: Historical Division, Headquarters, U.S. Army, Europe, 1953.
Ruhm von Oppen, Beate. *Documents on Germany under Occupation, 1945-1954.* London and New York: Oxford University Press, 1955.

Memorandum Regarding Germany (France, U.K., U.S.)

OFFICIAL TITLE: Agreed Memorandum Regarding the Principles Governing Exercise of Powers and Responsibilities of US-UK-French Governments following Establishment of German Federal Republic

SIGNED: April 8, 1949, at Washington

SIGNATORIES: France, United Kingdom, United States

IN FORCE: From signing

OVERVIEW: A brief statement of the continued role of the three Western allies in governing the German Federal Republic.

DISCUSSION:

For the historical background of this document, see **Agreements on Germany (France, U.K., U.S.).**

The principal provision of the memorandum was the retention, by the United States, the United Kingdom, and France, of "supreme authority," including the "right to revoke or alter any legislative or administrative decisions in the three western zones of Germany." However: "The German governing authorities . . . shall be at liberty to take administrative and legislative action, and such action will have validity if not vetoed by the Allied Authority. This means that military government will disappear, and that the function of the Allies shall be mainly supervisory." The memorandum concludes by stating that "It is a major objective of the three Allied Governments to encourage and facilitate the closest integration, on a mutually beneficial basis, of the German people under a democratic federal state within the framework of a European association."

REFERENCES:
Frederiksen, Oliver Jul. *The American Military Occupation of Germany, 1945-1953.* Darmstadt, Germany: Historical Division, Headquarters, U.S. Army, Europe, 1953.
Ruhm von Oppen, Beate. *Documents on Germany under Occupation, 1945-1954.* London and New York: Oxford University Press, 1955.

Occupation Statute Defining the Powers to Be Retained by the Occupation Authorities

SIGNED: April 8, 1949, at Washington

SIGNATORIES: France, United Kingdom, United States

IN FORCE: From signing

OVERVIEW: A precise statement, by the Western allies occupying Germany, of the ongoing role of the United States, France, and the United Kingdom in governing the newly created Federal Republic of Germany (West Germany).

DISCUSSION:

For the historical background of this document, see **Agreements on Germany (France, U.K., U.S.).**

This document amplifies the principle set out in **Memorandum Regarding Germany (France, U.K., U.S.)** that, while the Western allies would continue to exercise "supreme authority" over German government, they also "desire and intend that the German people shall enjoy self-government to the maximum possible degree consistent with . . . occupation."

The Occupation Statute reserved to the Western allies the following powers:

- Authority in disarmament and demilitarization issues
- Controls in regard to the Ruhr River, restitution, reparations, claims against Germany
- Authority in foreign affairs

- Authority in matters relating to displaced persons and refugees
- Authority in matters relating to the Allied forces
- Respect for the Basic Law and Land cosntitutions
- Control over foreign trade
- "Control over internal action, only to the minimum extent necessary to ensure use of funds, food and other supplies in such manner as to reduce to a minimum the need for external assistance to Germany"
- Control of persons charged with war crimes

Beyond these areas, the Western allies expressed the "hope and expectation . . . that the occupation authorities will not have occasion to take action in [other] fields." In addition, the statute gives the German Federal Government power to "legislate and act in the fields reserved to [the occupation] authorities," subject to approval of the occupation authorities.

REFERENCES:

Frederiksen, Oliver Jul. *The American Military Occupation of Germany, 1945-1953.* Darmstadt, Germany: Historical Division, Headquarters, U.S. Army, Europe, 1953.

Ruhm von Oppen, Beate. *Documents on Germany under Occupation, 1945-1954.* London and New York: Oxford University Press, 1955.

Agreement as to Tripartite Controls (for West Germany)

SIGNED: April 8, 1949, at Washington
SIGNATORIES: France, United Kingdom, United States
IN FORCE: From signing
OVERVIEW: An agreement, "prior to entry into effect of the **Occupation Statute Defining the Powers to be Retained by the Occupation Authorities**, for "trizonal fusion" of the British, French, and American sectors of Germany into a single Western Zone.

DISCUSSION:

For the historical background of this document, see **Agreements on Germany (France, U.K., U.S.).**

This agreement created the machinery by which the three Western allies consolidated their occupation of western Germany into a single Western Zone governed by a single authoritative body, the Allied High Commission, composed of one High Commissioner from each occupying power. The function of the Allied High Commission was to carry out the provisions of the **Occupation Statute Defining the Powers to be Retained by the Occupation Authorities** after the establishment of the German Federal Republic (West Germany).

The most important provisions of the Agreement as to Tripartite Controls include the following:

- Personnel of the Allied High Commission were to be kept top

a minimum, to facilitate German federal exercise of responsibility for government.
- Approval of amendments to the Federal Constitution required unanimous agreement among the High Commissioners.
- The authority of each of the three occupying powers would be, in part, proportional to the funding provided by that power. (Thus, in some matters, the United States would have more influence than either France or the UK.)
- An apparatus for appeal of High Commission decisions was established.
- To the extent possible, all High Commission directives were to be addressed to German government authorities (not directly to the German people).

REFERENCES:

Frederiksen, Oliver Jul. *The American Military Occupation of Germany, 1945-1953.* Darmstadt, Germany: Historical Division, Headquarters, U.S. Army, Europe, 1953.

Ruhm von Oppen, Beate. *Documents on Germany under Occupation, 1945-1954.* London and New York: Oxford University Press, 1955.

Agreed Minute Respecting Berlin

SIGNED: April 8, 1949, at Washington
SIGNATORIES: France, United Kingdom, United States
IN FORCE: From signing
OVERVIEW: "It was agreed that the provisions of the **Agreement as to Tripartite Controls** shall be applied as far as practicable to the western sectors of Berlin."

DISCUSSION:

For the historical background of this document, see **Agreements on Germany (France, U.K., U.S.).**

REFERENCES:

Frederiksen, Oliver Jul. *The American Military Occupation of Germany, 1945-1953.* Darmstadt, Germany: Historical Division, Headquarters, U.S. Army, Europe, 1953.

Ruhm von Oppen, Beate. *Documents on Germany under Occupation, 1945-1954.* London and New York: Oxford University Press, 1955.

Agreed Minute on Claims Against Germany

SIGNED: April 8, 1949, at Washington
SIGNATORIES: France, United Kingdom, United States
IN FORCE: From signing
OVERVIEW: The three Western allies occupying Germany undertake "to develop proposals for the settlement of financial claims against Germany."

DISCUSSION:

For the historical background of this document, see **Agreements on Germany (France, U.K., U.S.).**

The entire text of the minute follows:

The governments of France, the United Kingdom and the United States will proceed, in consultation with other governments concerned, to develop proposals for the settlement of financial claims against Germany, claims arising out of the war which remain unsettled, claims with respect to Allied property in Germany, and other questions of an economic or legal character arising out of the existence of a state of war between Germany and the Allied Powers. There should also be appropriate consultations with the German Federal Republic. Prior to the relinquishment of reserved powers in the field of foreign exchange, the three governments will give consideration to the desirability of obtaining from the German Federal Government formal recognition of such claims.

REFERENCES:

Frederiksen, Oliver Jul. *The American Military Occupation of Germany, 1945-1953*. Darmstadt, Germany: Historical Division, Headquarters, U.S. Army, Europe, 1953.

Ruhm von Oppen, Beate. *Documents on Germany under Occupation, 1945-1954*. London and New York: Oxford University Press, 1955.

Agreed Minute on Wuerttemberg-Baden Plebiscite

SIGNED: April 8, 1949, at Washington
SIGNATORIES: France, United Kingdom, United States
IN FORCE: From signing
OVERVIEW: An agreement concerning the establishment of the German *Land* (state) of Baden-Wurtemberg.

DISCUSSION:

For the historical background of this document, see **Agreements on Germany (France, U.K., U.S.)**.

Most of the present *Land* (state) of Baden-Württemberg was occupied by American troops at the end of World War II, and it was during occupational rule after the war that the region was formed into a *Land*. This status was on the verge of confirmation by plebiscite when the Western allies decided to push ahead with the formation of an independent West Germany. The minute agreed on reads in full as follows:

It was agreed that the status quo in Wuerttemberg and Baden would be maintained for the time being and that the plebiscite recommended by the German Minister Presidents would be postponed in the interest of avoiding any possible delays in the establishment of the German Federal Government.

It was further agreed that the question of Wuerttenberg-Baden Land boundaries would be reexamined after the establishment of the German Federal Government.

The *Land* was created in 1951 and enlarged to its present extent the following year.

REFERENCES:

Frederiksen, Oliver Jul. *The American Military Occupation of Germany, 1945-1953*. Darmstadt, Germany: Historical Division, Headquarters, U.S. Army, Europe, 1953.

Ruhm von Oppen, Beate. *Documents on Germany under Occupation, 1945-1954*. London and New York: Oxford University Press, 1955.

Agreement Regarding Kehl

SIGNED: April 8, 1949, at Washington
SIGNATORIES: France, United Kingdom, United States
IN FORCE: From signing
OVERVIEW: An interim agreement on control of the Rhine port city of Kehl.

DISCUSSION:

For the historical background of this document, see **Agreements on Germany (France, U.K., U.S.)**.

Following the war, the Rhine city of Kehl was subject to dispute between Germany and France. In the face of Soviet aggression in the form of the blockade of West Berlin, the Western allies were eager to conclude the formation of the German Federal Republic. The Agreement Regarding Kehl, a temporary solution to the question of whether France or Germany should control the port zone, was intended to avoid a conflict that threatened to delay the creation of the West German state. The substance of the agreement follows:

It was agreed, on a proposal of the French Government, that the city of Kehl would gradually be returned to a German administration. It was foreseen that the French temporarily domiciled in Kehl might remain during a four-year period required for the preparation of additional housing in Strasbourg. Around one-third of the French inhabitants will be able to leave Kehl within several months, and the remainder progressively thereafter as housing becomes available.

The final decision with respect to the Kehl port zone will be made in the peace settlement. If the port authority develops harmoniously, the US and UK will be willing at the time of the peace settlement to bring an attitude of good will toward the establishment of permanent joint authority.

REFERENCES:

Frederiksen, Oliver Jul. *The American Military Occupation of Germany, 1945-1953*. Darmstadt, Germany: Historical Division, Headquarters, U.S. Army, Europe, 1953.

Ruhm von Oppen, Beate. *Documents on Germany under Occupation, 1945-1954*. London and New York: Oxford University Press, 1955.

Message to the Military Governors from the Foreign Ministers of the U.S., U.K., and France

SIGNED: April 8, 1949, at Washington
SIGNATORIES: France, United Kingdom, United States
IN FORCE: From signing
OVERVIEW: An interim message to the military governors of the western sectors of occupied Germany to guide their policies on the eve of the creation of the German Federal Republic.

DISCUSSION:

For the historical background of this document, see **Agreements on Germany (France, U.K., U.S.)**.

The message informed military governors that the policy of the civil governments of the Western allies occupying Germany called for encouraging both the German federal and state governments to move "in the direction of securing financial independence" and to encourage them in their progress toward self-government.

REFERENCES:

Frederiksen, Oliver Jul. *The American Military Occupation of Germany, 1945-1953*. Darmstadt, Germany: Historical Division, Headquarters, U.S. Army, Europe, 1953.

Ruhm von Oppen, Beate. *Documents on Germany under Occupation, 1945-1954*. London and New York: Oxford University Press, 1955.

Message to the Bonn Parliamentary Council from the Foreign Ministers of the U.S., U.K., and France

SIGNED: April 8, 1949, at Washington

SIGNATORIES: France, United Kingdom, United States

IN FORCE: From signing

OVERVIEW: The consensus message transmitted to the Bonn Parliamentary Council regarding the role of the Western allies in the government of West Germany.

DISCUSSION:

For the historical background of this document, see **Agreements on Germany (France, U.K., U.S.)**.

The foreign ministers of the Western allies requested that the military governors of occupied western Germany transmit the following to the Bonn Parliamentary Council:

The Foreign Ministers have considered the problem of a Federal German Republic in all its aspects in Washington and have come to a number of important decisions of policy in regard thereto. They have decided that, in general, the German authorities shall be at liberty to take administrative and legislative action, and that such action will have validity if not vetoed by Allied authorities. There will be certain limited fields in which the Allies will reserve the right to take direct action themselves and which are set out in the Occupation Statute . . .

With the establishment of the German Federal Republic, Military Government as such will terminate and the functions of the Allied Authorities will be divided—control functions being exercised by a High Commissioner and Military functions by a Commander-in-Chief. The three High Commissioners together will constitute an Allied High Commission, and it is the aim of the three governments to restrict to a minimum the size of the supervisory staffs attached to their respective High Commissioners.

The Foreign Ministers further affirm that it is a major objective of the three Allied Governments to encourage and facilitate the closest integration on a mutually beneficial basis of the German people under a democratic Federal State within the framework of a European association.

Nevertheless, before far-reaching developments which they contemplate can be put in hand, it is essential that an agreement should be reached by the Parliamentary Council upon a Basic Law [constitution] for the German Federal Republic.

REFERENCES:

Frederiksen, Oliver Jul. *The American Military Occupation of Germany, 1945-1953*. Darmstadt, Germany: Historical Division, Headquarters, U.S. Army, Europe, 1953.

Ruhm von Oppen, Beate. *Documents on Germany under Occupation, 1945-1954*. London and New York: Oxford University Press, 1955.

Agreement for the Establishment of an International Authority for the Ruhr

SIGNED: April 28, 1949, at London

SIGNATORIES: Belgium, France, Luxembourg, Netherlands, United Kingdom, United States

IN FORCE: From signing

OVERVIEW: An agreement for the administration of the coal-, coke-, and steel-rich resources of Germany's Ruhr Valley.

DISCUSSION:

The preamble to the agreement begins:

Whereas international security and general economic recovery require—

that the resources of the Ruhr shall not in the future be used for the purpose of aggression but shall be used in the interest of peace;

that access in the coal, coke and steel of Ruhr, which was previously subject to the exclusive control of Germany, be in the future assured on an equitable basis to the countries cooperating in the common economic good . . .

[the Allied nations hereby establish] an International Authority for the Ruhr . . .

Consisting of representatives of the signatory governments and Germany, the Authority is charged with the following principal functions:

• To make "a division of coal, coke and steel from the Ruhr as between German consumption and export" with the object of ensuring "adequate access to supplies of these products by countries cooperating in the common economic good, taking into consideration the essential needs of Germany"

• To ensure that the resources of Ruhr are used exclusively in the interests of peace

The body of the agreement lays down details of the composition, conduct, authority, and financing of the Authority.

REFERENCES:

Frederiksen, Oliver Jul. *The American Military Occupation of Germany, 1945-1953*. Darmstadt, Germany: Historical Division, Headquarters, U.S. Army, Europe, 1953.

Ruhm von Oppen, Beate. *Documents on Germany under Occupation, 1945-1954*. London and New York: Oxford University Press, 1955.

Treaty of Peace with Japan

SIGNED: September 8, 1951, at San Francisco

IN FORCE: From April 28, 1952

SIGNATORIES: Argentina, Australia, Belgium, Bolivia, Brazil, Cambodia, Canada, Chile, Costa Rica, Cuba, Dominican Republic, Ecuador, Egypt, El Salvador, Ethiopia, France, Greece, Guatemala, Haiti, Honduras, Iran, Iraq, Laos, Lebanon, Liberia, Mexico, Netherlands, New Zealand, Nicaragua, Norway, Pakistan, Panama, Paraguay, Peru, Philippines, Saudi Arabia, South Africa, Sri Lanka, Syrian Arab Republic, Turkey, United Kingdom, United States, Uruguay, Venezuela, and Vietnam vs Japan. Among the Allied and Associated powers, the Soviet Union, the People's Republic of China, and Taiwan did not sign the treaty.

OVERVIEW: Japan had surrendered unconditionally on September 2, 1945, by signing a "document of surrender" (see **Japanese Surrender Documents**) aboard the *U.S.S. Missouri*. The 1951 treaty formalized the original terms, stipulated and defined others, and included representatives of most of the Allied and Associated powers.

DISCUSSION:

The signing of the 1951 treaty recapitulated the terms outlined in the "document of surrender" of 1945, including Japanese affirmation of its renunciation of rights to all territories surrendered by the armistice. By the 1951 treaty, Japan additionally renounced any special rights with regard to China. However, the treaty did not convey to the Soviet Union any special title to the Kuril Islands or to southern Sakhalin, territories promised to the Soviet Union by the **Yalta Agreement**. Nor did the treaty convey Taiwan to the People's Republic of China. For these reasons, neither the Soviet Union nor the two Chinas signed the treaty. Because the vast majority of the Allies and Associated powers did sign, however, the treaty was considered universally valid.

Other important treaty provisions include:

- A stipulation that Japan should pay reparations, the amounts of which were deferred to bilateral negotiation
- A stipulation that Japan would adhere to the principles of the United Nations Charter
- A stipulation that Japan would adhere to internationally accepted fair trade and commerce practices

The treaty provided for a transition from a government of military occupation to full civil sovereignty within ninety days of the date on which the treaty came into force. Of great importance is the absence of military clauses reducing and restricting armed forces in Japan. Such clauses were made unnecessary by the Japanese constitution adopted in 1946, which forbade the maintenance of *any* Japanese armed forces. Ironically, only at the insistence of the United States did Japan subsequently create a small defense force.

On the day that the peace treaty was signed, Japan concluded the **Japanese-United States Security Treaty**, which permitted the United States to maintain military forces in Japan. This treaty was supplemented in 1954 by the **Mutual Defense Assistance Agreement with Japan** and superceded in 1960 by the **Treaty of Mutual Cooperation and Security between the United States and Japan**. (For these treaties, See Section 2.10.)

REFERENCES:

Ando, Nisuke. *Surrender, Occupation, and Private Property in International Law: An Evaluation of U.S. Practice in Japan*. Oxford, UK: Clarendon Press, 1991.

Butow, R. C. *Japan's Decision to Surrender*. Palo Alto, CA: Stanford University Press, 1954.

Finn, Richard B. *Winners in Peace: MacArthur, Yoshida, and Postwar Japan*. Berkeley: University of California Press, 1992.

Grenville, J. A. S. *The Major International Treaties 1914-1973: A History Guide with Texts*. New York: Stein and Day, 1974.

Agreement Concerning German Property in Switzerland

SIGNED: August 28, 1952, at Berne, Switzerland

SIGNATORIES: France, Switzerland, United Kingdom, United States

IN FORCE: From March 19, 1953

OVERVIEW: An agreement whereby Switzerland agrees to turn over to the three Allied signatories certain German assets in partial settlement of Germany's World War II reparations.

DISCUSSION:

With the **Washington Agreement Relating to the Liquidation of German Property in Switzerland**, this agreement settles the disposition of certain wartime German assets deposited in Switzerland. By terms of the agreement, the Swiss government is to turn over to the Allied governments 121,500,000 Swiss francs, a sum payable to Switzerland by Germany in accordance with a "Swiss-German Agreement."

REFERENCE:

Picard, Jacques. *Switzerland and the Assets of the Missing Victims of the Nazis: Assets in Switzerland Belonging to Victims of Racial, Religious and Political Persecution and Their Disposition Between 1946 and 1973*. Zürich: Bank Julius Bär, 1996.

Notification to the Japanese Government of Pre-War Treaties to Keep in Force or Revive

OFFICIAL TITLE: Note by which the Government of the United States of America, in Pursuance of Article 7 of the Treaty of Peace with Japan, signed at San Francisco on 8 September 1951, Notified the Japanese Government of those Pre-War Bilateral Treaties between the Two Countries which the United States of America Desires to Keep in Force or Revive

SIGNED: April 22, 1953, at Tokyo

SIGNATORIES: Japan vs. United States

IN FORCE: ". . . treaties listed in this note are considered to have been continued in force or revived on 22 July 1953"

OVERVIEW: A list of those pre-World War II U.S.-Japanese treaties that the United States wished to continue or reinstate.

DISCUSSION:

The **Treaty of Peace with Japan** of 1951 left it to the option of the United States to determine which prewar U.S.-Japan treaties it wished to continue or revive. This note lists the treaties the United States nominated. These include treaties in the following areas:

- Extradition
- Narcotic drug conventions
- Postal conventions
- Arrangement Relating to Perpetual Leaseholds (1937)
- Liquor smuggling convention
- Arrangement Relating to Reciprocal Exemption from Taxation of Income from the Operation of Merchant Vessels

"It is understood, of course," the note explains, "that either of the two Governments may propose revisions in any of the treaties or other agreements mentioned in the . . . list."

REFERENCES:
None

Agreement (with the Netherlands) Concerning the Return of Silver Supplied Under Lend-Lease

OFFICIAL TITLE: Exchange of Notes Constituting an Agreement Concerning the Return of Silver Supplied to the Government of the Kingdom of Netherlands under Lend-Lease

SIGNED: March 30 and May 25, 1955, at Washington

SIGNATORIES: Netherlands vs. United States

IN FORCE: From May 25, 1955

OVERVIEW: An agreement concerning the postwar return of silver supplied to the Netherlands under terms of lend-lease.

DISCUSSION:

For a background discussion of Lend-Lease, see the **Lend-Lease Act** (1941) and **Lend-Lease Agreement with United Kingdom** (1942). Although, it its typical form, Lend-Lease involved the delivery of weapons and other war materiel on a basis other than cash-and-carry, it could involve virtually any commodity of value. In the case of the Netherlands, an amount of silver bullion was delivered, to be returned to the United States Treasury within five years. The 1955 agreement specifies that the Netherlands will return the silver by April 27, 1957, and makes provision for accepting the return in the form of silver-copper bars and/or coins of a lesser fineness than that supplied under lend-lease. The agreement lays down a schedule for return and specifications as to the form and quality of the silver to being returned.

REFERENCE:
Picard, Jacques. *Switzerland and the Assets of the Missing Victims of the Nazis: Assets in Switzerland Belonging to Victims of Racial, Religious and Political Persecution and Their Disposition Between 1946 and 1973.* Zürich: Bank Julius Bär, 1996.

Agreement (with France) for the Creation of Permanent Military Cemeteries

OFFICIAL TITLE: Agreement Relative to the Grant of Plots of Land Located in France for the Creation of Permanent Military Cemeteries and the Construction of War Memorials

SIGNED: March 19, 1956, at Paris

SIGNATORIES: France vs. United States

IN FORCE: From signing

OVERVIEW: An agreement to create cemeteries "in calm and dignified sites, destined to receive the bodies of American nationals victims of the 1939-1945 war" and to erect "memorials to commemorate their sacrifice."

DISCUSSION:

The agreement grants to the United States certain tracts of land within France for the exclusive purpose of creating American military cemeteries and war memorials to bury and honor the dead of World War II. The agreement formalizes an initial agreement concluded on October 1, 1947, and specifies the plots of land granted, as well as the conditions pertaining to those grants.

REFERENCES:
None

Memorandum of Understanding (with Italy) Regarding War Damage Claims

SIGNED: March 29, 1957, at Rome
SIGNATORIES: Italy vs. United States
IN FORCE: From October 22, 1957
OVERVIEW: Settlement of war damage claims agreed to in Articles 78 and 83 of the **Peace Treaty between the Allies and Italy** of 1947.

DISCUSSION:

By this memorandum, the government of Italy agreed to deposit the sum of 950,000,000 lire into a special bank account pending final settlement of war-damage claims (resulting from Italian actions in World War II) by decision of the Italian-United States Conciliation Commission.

REFERENCE:

Reparations; Restitution and Liquidation of Confiscated Property Recovered in Italy from German Forces. Washington, D.C.: U. S. Government Printing Office, 1955.

Agreement (with U.S.S.R.) Regarding the Settlement of Lend-Lease Accounts

SIGNED: October 18, 1972, at Washington, D.C.
SIGNATORIES: Union of Soviet Socialist Republics vs. United States
IN FORCE: From signing
OVERVIEW: Belated settlement of open World War II lend-lease accounts.

DISCUSSION:

By this agreement, the United States and the Soviet Union agree to settle the U.S.S.R.'s unpaid lend-lease balance in return for the United States' extension of most-favored-nation trading status to the Soviet Union. The balance due is specified as $674,000,000.

REFERENCE:

Dawson, Raymond H. *The Decision to Aid Russia, 1941: Foreign Policy and Domestic Politics.* Chapel Hill: University of North Carolina Press, 1959.

Cold War, Korea, and Vietnam

Overview of the Conflicts

The great alliance between the Western powers and the Soviet Union, forged by the necessities of war, quickly disintegrated after Germany and Japan had been defeated. The Allies attempted to reach agreement on the division of occupied Germany (see **Allied Declaration on Control of Germany** and **Agreement as to Tripartite Controls** in Section 2.9) and on the political division of Europe (see **Potsdam Protocol** in Section 2.9), but it soon became chillingly clear that new battle lines were being drawn across the globe, dividing the "Free World" from the world of communist totalitarianism. Winston Churchill crystallized the postwar situation in a speech of March 5, 1946, to the graduation class of tiny Westminster College in Fulton, Missouri: "From Stettin in the Baltic to Trieste in the Adriatic, an iron curtain has descended across the continent."

President James Monroe had issued the **Monroe Doctrine** in 1823 (Section 1.1), warning European powers that the United States would act to halt any new attempts to colonize the Americas. In 1947, President Harry S Truman promulgated the "Truman Doctrine," warning the Soviet Union—which supported a threatened communist takeover of Greece and Turkey—that the United States would act to halt the spread of communism wherever in the world it threatened democracy. This policy had its basis in a proposal by State Department official George F. Kennan that the most effective way to combat communism was to *contain* it, confronting the Soviet Union whenever and wherever it sought to expand its ideological influence. The result was not a postwar world of peace, but of continual low-level combat, sometimes with shooting, sometimes without, but always a "Cold War."

During the Cold War period—from roughly 1947 until the fall of the Berlin Wall in 1989—the United States concluded a great number of defensive treaties throughout the "free world," all with the object either of "containing" communism or directly defending against possible Soviet thermonuclear attack. Most of the documents in this section are mutual defense agreements of these types. The agreements range from individual bilateral military aid arrangements and agreements to permit the installation of U.S. military bases on a nation's soil to such major multilateral defensive pacts as the **North Atlantic (NATO) Treaty** (1949), the **ANZUS Treaty** (1951), and the **South-East Asia Collective Defense Treaty (SEATO)** (1954). The principle of hemispheric defense was laid down by the **Pact of Rio** (1947)

and by several other multilateral and bilateral agreements, and Canada and the United States became close partners in continental defense against thermonuclear attack (see, for example, **Agreement [with Canada] Regarding the Extension and Coordination of the Continental Radar Defense System**, 1951; **Agreement [with Canada] Relating to North American Air Defense Command**, 1958; **Agreement Concerning Establishment of Canada-United States Ministerial Committee on Joint Defense**, 1958; **Agreement [with Canada] Relating to the DEW Line**, 1959; **Agreement [with Canada] on Civil Emergency Planning and Civil Defense**, 1963; **Agreement [with Canada] on Cooperation on Civil Emergency Planning**, 1967; **Agreement [with Canada] Concerning NORAD**, 1975; **Agreement Concerning the Test and Evaluation of U.S. Defense Systems in Canada**, 1983; and **Agreement [with Canada] on the Modernization of the North American Air Defense System**, 1985).

President Truman's policy of containment prompted the United States and its western allies to take a strong stand in Germany after the Soviet Union began detaining troop trains bound for West Berlin in March 1948. On June 7, the western allies announced their intention to create a separate, permanent capitalist state of West Germany. Two weeks later, the Soviet Union blockaded West Berlin, protesting that, because of its location in Soviet-controlled territory, it could not serve as the capital of West Germany. Instead of reacting to this with armed aggression, Truman ordered an airlift, a spectacular chain of round-the-clock supply flights into West Berlin—272,000 of them over 321 days, carrying tons of supplies to circumvent the blockade. The airlift was a political as well as logistical triumph, which caused the Soviet Union to lift the blockade (**Lifting of the West Berlin Blockade**, 1949). It was also a vindication of the policy of containment, and, in April 1949, it led to the creation of the North Atlantic Treaty Organization—NATO—a key defensive alliance of the western nations against the communist East (**North Atlantic [NATO] Treaty**).

The Cold War was a long, costly period of psychological and political tension, of rattling sabers, and of stockpiling weapons of mass—indeed, of total—destruction; and it was more. As eastern Europe had fallen behind an Iron Curtain, so China, the world's most populous nation, long the subject of a struggle between communist forces (led primarily by Mao Tse-tung) and capitalist-nationalist forces (whose strongest leader was U.S. World War II ally Chiang Kai-shek), became a communist nation in 1949. Elsewhere in Asia, communist factions were positioning themselves to take power. After World War II, Korea was divided along the 38th parallel between a Soviet occupation zone in the north and a U.S. zone in the south. In November 1947, the United Nations resolved to create a unified independent Korea, but the communists barred free elections in the north. Only in the U.S. southern zone were elections held, and, on August 15, 1948, the Republic of Korea was born. In North Korea, the communists created the Democratic People's Republic of Korea in September.

On June 25, 1950, communist-backed forces from the north invaded South Korea. The United States secured a United Nations sanction against the invasion and contributed the lion's share of troops to repel it.

At first, the war went badly for the United Nations forces, which were pushed back toward to the southern tip of the Korean peninsula. General Douglas MacArthur, who had served as supreme Allied commander in the Pacific during World War II, now in command of the U.N. troops, struggled to hold the critical southern port of Pusan in order to buy time until the arrival of reinforcements. Once these were available, he led a daring amphibious landing at Inchon, on the west coast of Korea, *behind* North Korean lines. The landing, by all accounts the single greatest tactical and strategic accomplishment of MacArthur's long career, turned the tide against the forces of the North. By October 1, 1950, the North Koreans had been pushed out of South Korea, and U.N. forces were now arrayed along the 38th parallel.

Within the Truman administration debate raged over whether to cross the 38th parallel and invade North Korea. President Truman compromised, by authorizing the crossing, but also by taking steps to avoid provoking the Chinese and the Soviets directly. No UN troops would enter Manchuria or the U.S.S.R., and only South Koreans would operate along international borders. Furthermore, the United States secured United Nations approval of the action. On October 19, the North Korean capital of P'yongyang fell, and the North Korean armies were pushed far north, to the Yalu River, the nation's border with Manchuria.

The war seemed to have been won. But then, between October 14 and November 1, an army of communist "volunteers" crossed the Yalu from China. Once again, U.N. troops were pushed back across the 38th parallel, and, in January 1951, the South Korean capital of Seoul fell to the communists. By March, however, U.N. forces had forced the communists out of Seoul and had reestablished a strong defensive position on the 38th parallel. In the meantime, however, General MacArthur demanded Truman's permission to retaliate against the Chinese by bombing Manchuria. Both the president and the United Nations, fearing that such a move would trigger World War III, turned MacArthur down. Refusing to subordinate himself

quietly to the president's policy, MacArthur publicly blamed his military setbacks in Korea on Truman. Worse, on March 25, 1951, just after Truman had completed preparation of a cease-fire plan, MacArthur broadcast an unauthorized and provocative ultimatum to the enemy commander. In response to this outright insubordination, the president relieved MacArthur of command in Korea on April 11, replacing him with Matthew B. Ridgway. Shortly after this transfer of command, the Chinese launched a second offensive that sent U.N. forces reeling, but a counterattack inflicted heavy casualties on the communists, who withdrew into the North. By the beginning of summer 1951, the war was deadlocked at the 38th parallel, and, for the next two years, both sides pounded one another fruitlessly as armistice negotiations, commencing in June 1951, dragged on.

The thorniest single issue proved to be the disposition of POWs. United Nations negotiators wanted prisoners to decide for themselves whether or not they would return to their homes in the North or the South; the communists, fearful of mass defection, held out for mandatory repatriation. In an effort to break the negotiation deadlock, General Mark Clark, who had succeeded Ridgway, stepped up bombing raids on North Korea. At last, during April 1953, the POW issue was resolved: a compromise permitted freed prisoners to choose sides, but under supervision of a neutral commission. South Korean president Syngman Rhee, unwilling to accept anything less than unification of Korea and wholly voluntary repatriation as conditions for cease-fire, attempted to sabotage the peace process by unilaterally ordering the release of 25,000 North Korean prisoners who wanted to live in the South. To regain Rhee's cooperation, the United States promised Rhee a mutual security pact and long-term economic aid. Nevertheless, the armistice signed on July 27, 1953, did not include South Korea. (See **Korean Armistice**, 1953, and **U.S-South Korea Mutual Defense Treaty**, 1953.)

The Korean War did not so much end as it was suspended. Although U.N.-U.S. action had succeeded in *containing* communism, in that it confined it to North Korea, the war surely did not feel to Americans like a victory. Inconclusive in most respects, it did provide a precedent for intervention in another Asian war, this time in divided Vietnam, at the beginning in the next decade.

Just as World War II had left Korea unstable and divided between communist and capitalist forces, so it destabilized much of Southeast Asia. During the nineteenth century, France had colonized Laos, Cambodia, and Vietnam, and when France caved in to Germany in 1940, the Japanese allowed French colonial officials puppet authority in Southeast Asia until the Allied liberation of France in 1945. Japan then seized full control, purging the French police agencies and soldiery that had kept various nationalist groups in check. In Vietnam, the popular communist leader Ho Chi Minh led the most powerful of these independence-seeking groups, the Viet Minh, which, aided by

U.S. Office of Strategic Services (OSS) personnel, fought a guerrilla war against the Japanese occupiers. At the conclusion of the war in Europe, Allied forces could turn more of their attention to Vietnam and the rest of Southeast Asia. Nationalist Chinese troops, under Chiang Kai-shek, occupied northern Vietnam, while the British secured southern Vietnam for eventual re-entry of the French. That re-entry, when it came, was met with stubborn resistance, and a state of low-level guerrilla warfare developed, then sharply intensified after Chiang Kai-shek, hoping to checkmate communist ambitions in the region, withdrew from northern Vietnam and turned that region over to French control.

Pursuant to its containment policy, the United States concluded an **Agreement for Mutual Defense Assistance in Indochina** in 1950 with Cambodia, France, Laos, and the colonial government of Vietnam to supply the French forces with funding, and military equipment. On August 3, 1950, the first contingent of U.S. military "advisors" was dispatched to Vietnam, and by 1953, the United States was funding 80 percent of the cost of France's war effort. After French planners directed General Henri Eugene Navarre to strike a decisive blow against the Viet Minh on the strategically located plain of Dien Bien Phu, near Laos, President Eisenhower stepped up military aid. Despite this, Navarre suffered a humiliating defeat, and Diem Bien Phu fell to the forces of Ho Chi Minh on May 7, 1954. A series of Viet Minh victories followed, and, in July, the French and the Viet Minh, agreeing to divide Vietnam along the 17th parallel, concluded a cease-fire (**Geneva Agreement on the Cessation of Hostilities in Viet-Nam**, 1954).

As a condition of the Geneva armistice, the divided Vietnam was to hold elections within two years to reunify. South Vietnam's President Ngo Dinh Diem assumed that Ho Chi Minh would win a popular election, and, therefore, reneged on this provision of the Geneva accords, refusing to hold the promised elections. The United States, more concerned to block communism than to honor an international agreement, backed Diem's position. Two key assistance agreements were concluded with South Vietnam in 1955, **Agreement (with Vietnam) Relating to Economic Assistance** and **Agreement Relating to Financial Assistance for Direct Support of Vietnamese Armed Forces**, and, through the early 1960s, the number of military "advisors" sent to Vietnam steadily rose. By the end of 1963, when Lyndon B. Johnson assumed the presidency following the assassination of John F. Kennedy, the United States was deeply involved in the Vietnam War and in South Vietnamese politics. During the Johnson administration, operations against North Vietnamese insurgents were stepped up, and the CIA was authorized to direct diversionary raids on the northern coast of Vietnam while the navy conducted electronic espionage in the Gulf of Tonkin. On August 7, 1964, the U.S. Senate passed the Gulf of Tonkin Resolution after the American destroyer *Maddox*, on a surveillance mission in the gulf, was

fired on by North Vietnamese torpedo boats. The resolution gave the president a free hand to expand the war in order to prevent further North Vietnamese "aggression."

Johnson embarked on a strategy of gradual escalation of a war of attrition intended to wear down the North Vietnamese without provoking the overt intervention of China or the Soviet Union. This proved, quite literally, to be a no-win strategy. While the cost exacted on the communists was terrible, they refused to give up, and it was, ineluctably, the will of the South Vietnamese and the United States to continue the fight that was worn down.

By the end of 1967, it was becoming clear that the Vietnam War was gruesomely deadlocked. President Johnson repeatedly went before the nation, assuring television viewers that there was "light at the end of the tunnel," but the increasing numbers of U.S. casualties created a "credibility gap" between what the administration claimed and what the public believed. On March 31, 1968, President Johnson made two surprise television announcements. He declared that he would restrict bombing above the 20th parallel, thereby opening the door to a negotiated settlement of the war, and he announced that he would not seek another term as president. He recognized that his advocacy of the war was tearing the United States apart, and he therefore stepped down.

Cease-fire negotiations began in May, only to stall over Hanoi's demands for a complete bombing halt and NLF (National Liberation Front) representation at the peace table. Johnson resisted, but in November agreed to these terms. In the meantime. Richard M. Nixon was elected president of the United States, and, despite a campaign pledge to end the war, he expanded the war into neighboring Laos and Cambodia, soon after entering office, in violation of the 1962 **Declaration on the Neutrality of Laos**. Nixon's overall foreign-relations objective was to improve relations with the Soviets (through trade and an arms-limitation agreement) in order to disengage Moscow from Hanoi and, for the same reason, to work toward normalization of relations with China. Once the Soviets and the Chinese had cut the North Vietnamese loose, Nixon reasoned, the United States, by applying increased military pressure to the North, could negotiate a "peace with honor" in Vietnam.

The grand American strategy failed. While relations with the Soviets did improved, that nation also announced its recognition of the Provisional Revolutionary Government (PRG) formed by the NLF in June 1969. With this, peace talks convened in Paris began to drift. With the failure of diplomacy, Nixon turned to force, striking at Communist supply and staging areas in Cambodia. This incursion intensified the antiwar protests on the American home front, a hundred thousand demonstrators marched on Washington, and Congress rescinded the Gulf of Tonkin Resolution. The president ordered the withdrawal of ground troops from Cambodia, but stepped up bombing raids. When communist infiltration continued unabated, the United

States supplied air support for a South Vietnamese invasion of Laos in February 1971—even as the U.S. steadily withdrew more of its troops from Vietnam.

On January 31, 1973, the United States and North Vietnam signed the **Paris Peace Accords**, which brought the complete withdrawal of the United States military and the return of the POWs, some of whom had been languishing in North Vietnamese prisons for nearly a decade. A four-party Joint Military Commission and an International Commission of Control and Supervision supervised the cease-fire. However, the Nixon administration continued to send massive amounts of aid to the government of South Vietnam, and both the North and South freely violated the Paris agreement. To pressure the North into abiding by them, the United States resumed bombing Cambodia and menaced North Vietnam with reconnaissance overflights, but a war-weary Congress, in November 1973, passed the War Powers Act, which effectively ended the president's power to make war without full congressional approval. By early 1975, with President Nixon out of office (he had resigned on August 9, 1974 rather than face impeachment as a result of the Watergate affair) and United States financial and military aid all but cut off, South Vietnam suffered one military defeat after another. When Congress rejected President Gerald Ford's request for $300 million in "supplemental aid" to South Vietnam, that nation's president, Nguyen Van Thieu, stepped down and turned over the presidency to Duong Van Minh, whose single official act was unconditional surrender to the North on April 30, 1975.

The long, bitter Vietnam experience caused many Americans to question the nation's Cold War role as self-proclaimed guardian of the Free World. Yet the most important anti-communist alliances endured, including, most significantly, NATO. Despite the lack of resolution in a still-divided Korea and the "loss" of Vietnam to communism, the Cold War did come to an end with the remarkable dissolution of communism throughout Eastern Europe and the break-up of the Soviet Union itself. China remained a communist power, but also evolved into a major trading partner with the United States and other Western nations.

Agreement (with the Philippines) Concerning Military Bases

SIGNED: March 14, 1947, at Manilla
SIGNATORIES: Philippines vs. United States
IN FORCE: March 26, 1947
OVERVIEW: Provides for the establishment of twenty-three United States military, naval, and air bases in the Philippines.

DISCUSSION:
In addition to providing for the establishment of twenty-three bases for a period of ninety-nine years, certain United States

bases established before the Philippines proclaimed independence from the United States on July 4, 1946, would continue to be maintained by the United States, while others would be transferred to Philippine control.

Subsequent agreements concerning U.S. bases in the Philippines include the following provisions:
- In 1956, the United States affirmed recognition of Philippine sovereignty over all U.S. bases on Philippine territory.
- In a memorandum of October 12, 1959, the leases granted in the 1947 agreement were shortened from 99 to 25 years. The United States also agreed to consult with the Philippine government on the operational use of the bases, particularly before setting up long-range missile sites on them.
- In an agreement of January 6, 1979, the lease on Clark Field was extended five years; however, Filipino commanders were to be appointed to the bases, and the land area of the bases was reduced. Military assistance funds were pledged by the United States.
- On June 1, 1983, access to Clark Field and to the Subic Bay Naval Base was extended five years. Cooperative defense plans were created, and more military aid pledged.
- On October 17, 1988, access to Clark Field and Subic Bay was extended to December 31, 1991, in return for $4.5 billion in export credits.

REFERENCES:
Castro, Pacifico A., ed. *Agreements on United States Military Facilities in Philippine Military Bases, 1947-1988.* Manila, Philippines: Foreign Service Institute, 1988.
Greene, Fred, ed. *The Philippine Bases: Negotiating for the Future American and Philippine Perspectives.* New York: Council on Foreign Relations, 1988.

Pact of Rio

SIGNED: September 2, 1947
IN FORCE: From December 3, 1948
SIGNATORIES: Argentina, Bolivia, Brazil, Chile, Colombia, Costa Rica, Cuba (withdrew in 1960), the Dominican Republic, El Salvador, Guatemala, Haiti, Honduras, Mexico, Panama, Paraguay, Peru, United States, Uruguay, and Venezuela
OVERVIEW: Pursuant to Article 51 of the **United Nations Charter** (see Section 3.10) and motivated by fears of Communist incursions in the Americas, the pact created an inter-American alliance against aggression.

DISCUSSION:
The Pact of Rio, also called the Inter-American Treaty of Reciprocal Assistance, resulted from the Ninth Inter-American Conference for the Maintenance of Continental Peace and Security, which met near Rio de Janeiro from August 15 through September 2, 1947. Article 4 of the document defined the regional scope of the agreement as encompassing all of North

and South America, including Canada, Greenland, and a portion of Antarctica, even though Canada was not a party to the agreement.

The pact defined hemispheric defense as the joint responsibility of all the American republics. Although the pact mandated two-thirds majority agreement on cooperative defensive action, each signatory was also permitted to act immediately on its own for its direct self-defense. Of particular importance in the context of the Cold War was the definition of "indirect aggression" as the support of insurrection or revolution in one state by another—a reference, in effect, to communist subversion. Collective response in this case called for a consensus among the signatories. In addition, pursuant to Article 53 of the United Nations Charter, any enforcement action decided upon in cases of indirect aggression called for authorization from the U.N. Security Council.

Premised in part on the World War II pan-American alliance known as the **Act of Chapultepec**, the Pact of Rio in turn would serve as a model for the **North Atlantic Treaty**, which established NATO. Other regional defense agreements were also based on the pact. In 1948, the Organization of American States (OAS) was established, in part as a permanent body to enforce the provisions of Pact of Rio (see **Charter of the Organization of American States** in Section 3.7).

REFERENCES:
Grenville, J. A. S. *The Major International Treaties 1914-1973: A History Guide with Texts* (New York: Stein and Day, 1974.

Sheinin, David. *The Organization of American States.* New Brunswick, NJ: Transaction Publishing, 1995.

Stoetzer, O. Carlos. *The Organization of American States,* 2d. ed. New York: Praeger Publishing, 1993.

Agreement (with France) Relating to an Aerial Mapping Project for Certain Areas of the Pacific

OFFICIAL TITLE: Exchange of Notes (with Annexes) Constituting an Agreement Relating to an Aerial Mapping Project for Certain Areas of the Pacific
SIGNED: November 27, 1948, at Paris
SIGNATORIES: France vs. United States
IN FORCE: From signing
OVERVIEW: An agreement to undertake a joint aerial mapping project of certain areas of the Pacific.

DISCUSSION:
As part of an extensive defense-mapping project, relating in part to nuclear weapons testing, the United States Army Mapping Service undertook various aerial photography series over the Pacific, including areas encompassing French Pacific possessions. In cooperation and coordination with this aerial effort, the French government, by this document, agrees to perform ground-survey work. Both nations are to share the resulting maps.

REFERENCE:
Aerial Mapping: Pacific Area Project. Washington, D.C.: U. S. Government Printing Office, 1952.

North Atlantic (NATO) Treaty

SIGNED: April 4, 1949, at Washington DC
IN FORCE: From August 24, 1949
SIGNATORIES: Belgium, Canada, Denmark, France, Iceland, Italy, Luxembourg, the Netherlands, Norway, Portugal, United Kingdom and United States; Greece and Turkey (joined in 1952), Federal Republic of Germany (1955), Spain (1982); Poland, the Czech Republic, and Hungary (all joined in 1999).
OVERVIEW: The North Atlantic Treaty established the North Atlantic Treaty Organization (NATO), a military alliance of Western nations to oppose Soviet aggression in Europe. NATO was the first peacetime military alliance in which the United States participated.

DISCUSSION:
Faced with the aggressive postwar expansion of the Soviet sphere of influence in Europe, the United States joined many of the nations of western Europe in a military alliance to counter the communist threat. The preamble to the treaty, together with Article 5, most succinctly express the purpose of the North Atlantic Treaty Organization:

The Parties to this Treaty reaffirm their faith in the purposes and principles of the Charter of the United Nations and their desire to live in peace with all peoples and all governments.

They are determined to safeguard the freedom, common heritage and civilisation of their peoples, founded on the principles of democracy, individual liberty and the rule of law.

They seek to promote stability and well-being in the North Atlantic area.

They are resolved to unite their efforts for collective defence and for the preservation of peace and security.

Article 5 explains:

The Parties agree that an armed attack against one or more of them in Europe or North America shall be considered an attack against them all, and consequently they agree that, if such an armed attack occurs, each of them, in exercise of the right of individual or collective self defence recognised by Article 51 of the Charter of the United Nations, will assist the Party or Parties so attacked by taking forthwith, individually, and in concert with the other Parties, such action as it deems necessary, including the use of armed force, to restore and maintain the security of the North Atlantic area ...

It is important to note that NATO was founded in conformity with Article 51 of the **United Nations Charter** (see Section

3.10), which grants nations the right of collective defense. It is also important to note that the NATO alliance extends beyond military matters and promotes political, social, and economic ties among the members, as stipulated in Article 2:

The Parties will contribute toward the further development of peaceful and friendly international relations by strengthening their free institutions, by bringing about a better understanding of the principles upon which these institutions are founded, and by promoting conditions of stability and well-being. They will seek to eliminate conflict in their international economic policies and will encourage economic collaboration between any or all of them.

The specific impetus for the treaty included such events as the Soviet-backed coup d'etat in Prague in February 1948 and the blockade of Berlin by Soviet forces beginning in June 1948. It was not until the outbreak of the Korean War, in June 1950, however, that the permanent military structure and apparatus of NATO were put into place, the principal element being Allied Command Europe, headquartered in Brussels, Belgium. Ongoing policy decision are made by the North Atlantic Council, which is also headquartered in Brussels.(The council met in Paris until 1967, a year after France withdrew from the military structure of NATO.)

The end of the Cold War and the dissolution of the Warsaw Treaty Organization (Warsaw Pact), which had been formed by the Soviet bloc to counter NATO, brought some calls for replacing NATO with a less exclusively military organization. Indeed, the United States reduced its military commitment to the organization, but, in 1999, NATO demonstrated its continued military viability by conducting operations to compel Serbia to accept settlement of a dispute over the political status of Kosovo. This was the first non-defensive action NATO had ever taken.

REFERENCES:
Clark, Ramsey, ed. *NATO in the Balkans: Voices of Opposition*. New York: International Action Center, 1998.
Gompert, David C., and F. Stephen Larrabee, eds. *America in Europe: A Partnership for a New Era*. New York: Cambridge University Press, 1997.
Grenville, J. A. S. *The Major International Treaties 1914-1973: A History Guide with Texts*. New York: Stein and Day, 1974.
Heller, Francis H., and John R. Gillingham, eds. *NATO: The Founding of the Atlantic Alliance and the Integration of Europe*. New York: St. Martin's Press, 1992.

Lifting of the West Berlin Blockade

OFFICIAL TITLE: Agreement Relating to the Removal of Restrictions on Communications, Transportation and Trade between Berlin and the Eastern and Western Zones of Germany
SIGNED ("INITIALED"): May 4, 1949, at New York
SIGNATORIES: France, Union of Soviet Socialist Republics, United Kingdom, United States

IN FORCE: From signing
OVERVIEW: The agreement officially ending the Soviet blockade of West Berlin.

DISCUSSION:
For the historical background of this document, see **Agreements on Germany (France, U.K., U.S.)** and **Quadripartite Agreement (on Berlin)**, both in Section 2.9.

After nearly a year, the Soviets lifted their blockade of West Berlin. Their plan—to prove the untenability of maintaining a Western enclave in the Soviet-controlled zone of Germany by effectively starving West Berlin—had been foiled by the great airlift of supplies and provisions continuously conducted by the United States during the long siege. The following brief agreement acknowledges the lifting of the blockade:

1. All the restrictions imposed since March 1, 1948, by the Government of the USSR on communications, transportation and trade between Berlin and the Western Zones of Germany and between the Eastern Zone and the Western Zones will be removed on May 12, 1949.

2. All the restrictions imposed since March 1, 1948, by the Governments of France, the United Kingdom and the United States, or any of them, on communications, transportation and trade between Berlin and the Eastern Zone and between the Western and Eastern Zones of Germany will also be removed.

3. Eleven days subsequent to the removal of the restrictions . . . a meeting of the Council of Froeign Ministers will be convened in Paris to consider questions relating to Germany and problems arising out of the situation in Berlin including also the question of currency in Berlin.

Note that the agreement was made reciprocal—both sides agreed to remove restrictions—although the Western allies had imposed no such restrictions. This fiction of a quid pro quo was a measure whereby the Soviets, compelled to back down from their blockade, were diplomatically allowed to save face.

REFERENCES:
Giangreco, D. M., and Robert E. Griffin. *Airbridge to Berlin: The Berlin Crisis of 1948*. Novato, Calif.: Presidio Press, 1988.
Grenville, J. A. S. *The Major International Treaties 1914-1973: A History Guide with Texts* (New York: Stein and Day, 1974).
Haydock, Michael D. *City Under Siege: The Berlin Blockade and Airlift, 1948-49*. Washington, D.C.: Brasseys, 1999.

Agreement Providing for the Services of a United States Air Force Mission to the Republic of Cuba

SIGNED: December 22, 1950, at Washington. D.C.
SIGNATORIES: Cuba vs. United States
IN FORCE: From signing

OVERVIEW: An agreement establishing a United States Air Force military advisory mission in Cuba.

DISCUSSION:

For discussion of the background of military assistance to Cuba, see **Military Assistance Agreement (with Cuba)** and **Agreement Providing for the Services of a United States Army Mission to the Republic of Cuba.**

On August 28, 1951, the United States and Cuba would conclude agreements to establish U.S. Army and Navy missions in Cuba, each of which to function in a tactical and technical advisory role to Cuban military forces. The Air Force mission, established the year before, was created to provide technical and tactical advice to the Cuban Air Force. As with the Army and Navy mission agreements, the precise staffing, extent, and duties of the mission are not specified or delimited, but remain open as required by circumstances.

REFERENCE:
Mutual Defense Assistance. Washington, D.C.: U.S. Government Printing Office, 1952.

Agreement for Mutual Defense Assistance in Indochina

SIGNED: December 23, 1950, at Saigon, Vietnam
SIGNATORIES: Cambodia, France, Laos, United States, Vietnam
IN FORCE: From signing
OVERVIEW: A defensive alliance with France and members of the French Union in Indochina.

DISCUSSION:

Following World War II, France was losing its grip on its colonies in Indochina, which were moving toward independence. In the Cold War atmosphere of the postwar years, however, this movement typically meant a headlong rush into communist domination. For this reason, the United States, pursuant to its foreign policy of "containment" of communism, first enunciated in 1948, concluded various alliances with colonial powers as well as emerging independent nations. The preamble to the agreement makes this clear in speaking of acting in "the common interest of free peoples of the world in the maintenance of the independence, peace, and security of nations devoted to the principles of freedom."

This agreement may be seen as the commencement of United States military involvement in Southeast Asia generally and in Vietnam specifically. Although "services" are specified in addition to "equipment and materials," the substance of the agreement deals exclusively with military supplies rather than troops or advisors.

The agreement lays down the principles of military assistance to Cambodia, France, Laos, and Vietnam as follows:
• The United States will make available equipment, material,

and services, and "each Government receiving [these] agrees to facilitate the production, transport ... and the transfer to ... the United States ... such quantities ... as may be agreed upon, of raw and semi-possessed materials as may be required by the United States ..."
• The governments receiving equipment and material shall use and maintain it efficiently
• The governments receiving equipment and material shall retain title to the equipment and material
• The French Union commander exercises control over aid intended for French Union forces

REFERENCE:
Mutual Defense Assistance in Indochina: Agreement Between the United States of America and Cambodia, France, Laos, and Viet-nam, Amending Annex to Agreement of December 23, 1950, Effected by Exchanges of Notes Between the United States of America and France, Dated at Saigon August 10 and September 8, 1951; Between the United States of America and Viet-nam, Dated at Saigon August 10 and September 17, 1951; Between the United States of America and Laos, Dated at Saigon August 16, 1951, and at Vientiane November 6, 1951; Between the United States of America and Cambodia, Dated at Saigon August 16, 1951, at Phnom-penh January 7, 1952, Entered into Force January 7, 1952, Operative Retroactively July 1, 1951. Washington, D.C.: U. S. Government Printing Office, 1955.

Agreement (with Denmark) on the Defense of Greenland

SIGNED: April 27, 1951, at Copenhagen
SIGNATORIES: Denmark vs. United States
IN FORCE: From June 8, 1951
OVERVIEW: An agreement allowing the United States to establish and maintain military facilities in the Danish protectorate Greenland.

DISCUSSION:

The location of Greenland, off the coast of the North American continent and directly within the Great Circle Route by which Soviet aircraft or missiles might be expected to reach Canada and the United States, made it strategically vital as a defensive base against strategic weapons. Pursuant to the **North Atlantic (NATO) Treaty**, this agreement provides for the United States to participate in the defense of Greenland. The Preamble expresses the spirit of the agreement:

The Government of the United States of America and the Government of the Kingdom of Denmark, being parties to the North Atlantic Treaty signed at Washington on April 4, 1949 having regard to their responsibilities thereunder for the defense of the North Atlantic Treaty area, desiring to contribute to such defense and thereby to their own defense in accordance with the principles of self-help and mutual aid, and having been requested by the North Atlantic Treaty Organization (NATO) to negotiate arrangements under which armed forces of the parties to the North Atlantic Treaty Organization may

make use of facilities in Greenland in defense of Greenland and the rest of the North Atlantic Treaty area, have entered into an Agreement for the benefit of the North Atlantic Treaty Organization . . .

REFERENCES:

Clark, Ramsey, ed. *NATO in the Balkans: Voices of Opposition.* New York: International Action Center, 1998.

Gompert, David C., and F. Stephen Larrabee, eds. *America in Europe: A Partnership for a New Era.* New York: Cambridge University Press, 1997.

Grenville, J. A. S. *The Major International Treaties 1914-1973: A History Guide with Texts.* New York: Stein and Day, 1974.

Heller, Francis H., and John R. Gillingham, eds. *NATO: The Founding of the Atlantic Alliance and the Integration of Europe.* New York: St. Martin's Press, 1992.

Agreement on the Defense of Iceland

SIGNED: May 5, 1951, at Reykjavik

SIGNATORIES: Iceland vs. United States

IN FORCE: From signing

OVERVIEW: Pursuant to the **North Atlantic (NATO) Treaty**, an agreement for United States' participation in the defense of Iceland.

DISCUSSION:

The location of Iceland at the top of the European continent makes it territory of great strategic importance in the defense of western Europe. For this reason, pursuant to the **North Atlantic (NATO) Treaty**, the United States concluded an agreement to participate in the ongoing defense of the nation. The preamble expresses the rationale for the agreement:

Having regard to the fact that the people of Iceland cannot themselves adequately secure their own defenses, and whereas experience has shown that a country's lack of defenses greatly endangers its security and that of its peaceful neighbors, the North Atlantic Treaty Organization has requested, because of the unsettled state of world affairs, that the United States and Iceland in view of the collective efforts of the parties to the North Atlantic Treaty to preserve peace and security in the North Atlantic Treaty area, make arrangements for the use of facilities in Iceland in defense of Iceland and thus also the North Atlantic Treaty area. In conformity with this proposal the following Agreement has been entered into.

REFERENCES:

Clark, Ramsey, ed. *NATO in the Balkans: Voices of Opposition.* New York: International Action Center, 1998.

Gompert, David C., and F. Stephen Larrabee, eds. *America in Europe: A Partnership for a New Era.* New York: Cambridge University Press, 1997.

Grenville, J. A. S. *The Major International Treaties 1914-1973: A History Guide with Texts.* New York: Stein and Day, 1974.

Heller, Francis H., and John R. Gillingham, eds. *NATO: The Founding of the Atlantic Alliance and the Integration of Europe.* New York: St. Martin's Press, 1992.

Agreement (with Canada) Regarding the Extension and Coordination of the Continental Radar Defense System

OFFICIAL TITLE: Exchange of Notes Constituting an Agreement Regarding the Extension and Coordination of the Continental Radar Defense System

SIGNED: August 1, 1951, at Washington, D.C.

SIGNATORIES: Canada vs. United States

IN FORCE: From signing

OVERVIEW: A joint agreement between Canada and the United States for the construction and operation within Canada of an extension of the continental radar defense system.

DISCUSSION:

Canada and the United States have long enjoyed neighborly relations and have been close allies in two world wars and throughout the Cold War era. North American air defense planners took for granted that the most likely route of an aerospace attack on the continent would be from the north, since incoming enemy aircraft or missiles from the either the Soviet Union or Communist China would use the Great Circle Route. For this reason, a network of defense radar stations was built in Canada through a cooperative defense program between Canada and the United States.

In essence, this is an agreement granting the United States leave to build and operate specialized military installations on Canadian soil for the purpose of mutual defense.

The agreement also specifies the cost sharing for constructing the extension of the radar system—one-third of the costs to be borne by Canada, two-thirds by the United States—and the disposition of titles to properties concerned (Canada to retain title to the sites, the United States to retain ownership of equipment it supplies).

REFERENCE:

Morenus, Richard. *Dew Line: Distant Early Warning, the Miracle of America's First Line of Defense.* New York, Rand McNally, 1957.

Agreement Providing for the Services of a United States Army Mission to the Republic of Cuba

SIGNED: August 28, 1951, at Washington, D.C.

SIGNATORIES: Cuba vs. United States

IN FORCE: From signing

OVERVIEW: An agreement establishing a United States Army military advisory mission in Cuba.

DISCUSSION:

For discussion of the background of military assistance to Cuba, see **Military Assistance Agreement (with Cuba)**.

"In conformity with the discussions held between the Governments of the United States of America and the Republic of Cuba on hemispheric military cooperation and a possible uniformity of military tactics and methods, the President of the United States of America has authorized the appointment of officers and enlisted men to constitute a United States Army Mission to the Republic of Cuba ..." The purpose of the mission is to serve as "tactical and technical advisors to the Cuban Army."

The agreement specifies that the mission is to continue for two years, renewable at the request of Cuba and with the approval of the United States, and terminable by either government on three months' notice. A general agreement in principle, the document does not specify the precise composition and numbers of the mission, nor does it stipulate duties other than those "as may be agreed upon by the Chief of Staff of the Army of the Republic of Cuba and the [U.S.] Chief of the Mission."

REFERENCE:
Mutual Defense Assistance. Washington, D.C.: U.S. Government Printing Office, 1952.

Agreement Providing for the Services of a United States Naval Mission to the Republic of Cuba

SIGNED: August 28, 1951, at Washington. D.C.
SIGNATORIES: Cuba vs. United States
IN FORCE: From signing
OVERVIEW: An agreement establishing a United States Navy military advisory mission in Cuba.

DISCUSSION:
For discussion of the background of military assistance to Cuba, see **Military Assistance Agreement (with Cuba)** and **Agreement Providing for the Services of a United States Army Mission to the Republic of Cuba.**

On this date, the United States and Cuba concluded agreements to establish U.S. Army and Navy missions in Cuba, each of which to function in a tactical and technical advisory role to the Cuban military forces. The previous year, the two nations had concluded an **Agreement Providing for the Services of a United States Air Force Mission to the Republic of Cuba.**

REFERENCE:
Mutual Defense Assistance. Washington, D.C.: U.S. Government Printing Office, 1952.

Mutual Defense Treaty (with the Philippines)

SIGNED: August 30, 1951, at Washington, D.C.
SIGNATORIES: Philippines vs. United States
IN FORCE: From August 27, 1952
OVERVIEW: A mutual defense treaty to help secure the strategically important Philippine Islands.

DISCUSSION:
The Philippines were granted full independence from the United States following World War II, but the United States retained a strong military presence in the islands, which assumed great strategic importance during the Cold War years. The Mutual Defense Treaty begins with a preamble evoking the common cause between the Philippines and the United States during World War II: "Recalling with mutual pride the historic relationship which brought their two peoples together in a common bond of sympathy and mutual ideals to fight side-by-side against imperialist aggression during the last war ..." The treaty itself ensures that the United States will maintain a significant military presence in the nation.

The text of the major articles follows:

ARTICLE I
The Parties undertake, as set forth in the Charter of the United Nations, to settle any international disputes in which they may be involved by peaceful means in such a manner that international peace and security and justice are not endangered and to refrain in their international relations from the threat or use of force in any manner inconsistent with the purposes of the United Nations.

ARTICLE II
In order more effectively to achieve the objective of this Treaty, the Parties separately and jointly by self-help and mutual aid will maintain and develop their individual and collective capacity to resist armed attack.

ARTICLE III
The Parties, through their Foreign Ministers or their deputies, will consult together from time to time regarding the implementation of this Treaty and whenever in the opinion of either of them the territorial integrity, political independence or security of either of the Parties is threatened by external armed attack in the Pacific.

ARTICLE IV
Each Party recognizes that an armed attack in the Pacific Area on either of the Parties would be dangerous to its own peace and safety and declares that it would act to meet the common dangers in accordance with its constitutional processes.

Any such armed attack and all measures taken as a result thereof shall be immediately reported to the Security Council of the United Nations. Such measures shall be terminated when the Security Council has taken the measures necessary to restore and maintain international peace and security.

ARTICLE V
For the purpose of Article IV, an armed attack on either of the

Parties is deemed to include an armed attack on the metropolitan territory of either of the Parties, or on the island territories under its jurisdiction in the Pacific or on its armed forces, public vessels or aircraft in the Pacific.

REFERENCES:

Castro, Pacifico A., ed. *Agreements on United States Military Facilities in Philippine Military Bases, 1947-1988.* Manila, Philippines: Foreign Service Institute, 1988.

Greene, Fred, ed. *The Philippine Bases: Negotiating for the Future American and Philippine Perspectives.* New York: Council on Foreign Relations, 1988.

ANZUS Treaty

SIGNED: September 1, 1951, at San Francisco
IN FORCE: From April 29, 1952; "as of September 17, 1986, the United States suspended obligations under the treaty as between the United States and New Zealand."
SIGNATORIES: Australia, New Zealand and United States
OVERVIEW: ANZUS is an acronym formed by the initial letters of the names of the signatory nations concluding a mutual-defense agreement.

DISCUSSION:

Concluded as one of a series of Cold War-era mutual defense treaties, the ANZUS pact was formed to defend the western Pacific. The treaty's defense clause (Article IV) binds each signatory to act against armed attack on any other signatory in the Pacific. Representatives of the signatories form the Anzus Council, which meets annually to discuss issues relating to defense in the Pacific area.

The United States suspended its ANZUS obligations to New Zealand in 1986 after that nation banned visits by nuclear-powered or nuclear-armed ships. Australia, which remains within ANZUS, maintains a defense link with New Zealand outside the ANZUS framework.

The text of the principal articles of the treaty follow:

ARTICLE I

The Parties undertake, as set forth in the Charter of the United Nations, to settle any international disputes in which they may be involved by peaceful means in such a manner that international peace and security and justice are not endangered and to refrain in their international relations from the threat or use of force in any manner inconsistent with the purposes of the United Nations.

ARTICLE II

In order more effectively to achieve the objective of this Treaty the Parties separately and jointly by means of continuous and effective self-help and mutual aid will maintain and develop their individual and collective capacity to resist armed attack.

ARTICLE III

The Parties will consult together whenever in the opinion of any of them the territorial integrity, political independence or security of any of the Parties is threatened in the Pacific.

ARTICLE IV

Each Party recognizes that an armed attack in the Pacific Area on any of the Parties would be dangerous to its own peace and safety and declares that it would act to meet the common danger in accordance with its constitutional processes.

Any such armed attack and all measures taken as a result thereof shall be immediately reported to the Security Council of the United Nations. Such measures shall be terminated when the Security Council has taken the measures necessary to restore and maintain international peace and security.

ARTICLE V

For the purpose of Article IV, an armed attack on any of the Parties is deemed to include an armed attack on the metropolitan territory of any of the Parties, or on the island territories under its jurisdiction in the Pacific or on its armed forces, public vessels or aircraft in the Pacific.

ARTICLE VI

This Treaty does not affect and shall not be interpreted as affecting in any way the rights and obligations of the Parties under the Charter of the United Nations or the responsibility of the United Nations for the maintenance of international peace and security.

ARTICLE VII

The Parties hereby establish a Council, consisting of their Foreign Ministers or their Deputies, to consider matters concerning the implementation of this Treaty. The Council should be so organized as to be able to meet at any time.

ARTICLE VIII

Pending the development of a more comprehensive system of regional security in the Pacific Area and the development by the United Nations of more effective means to maintain international peace and security, the Council, established by Article VII, is authorized to maintain a consultative relationship with States, Regional Organizations, Associations of States or other authorities in the Pacific Area in a position to further the purposes of this Treaty and to contribute to the security of that Area.

See also **North Atlantic Treaty** and **Southeast Asia Collective Defense Treaty.**

REFERENCES:

Albinski, Henry S. *ANZUS, the United States, and Pacific Security.* Lanham, MD: University Press of America, 1987.

Bercovitch, Jacob, ed. *ANZUS in Crisis: Alliance Management in International Affairs.* New York: St. Martin's Press, 1988.

Grenville, J. A. S. *The Major International Treaties 1914-1973: A History Guide with Texts.* New York: Stein and Day, 1974.

McIntyre, W. David. *Background to the ANZUS Pact: Policy-Making, Strategy, and Diplomacy, 1945-55.* New York: St. Martin's Press, 1995.

Pugh, Michael C. *The ANZUS Crisis, Nuclear Visiting, and Deterrence.* New York: Cambridge University Press, 1989.

Agreement (with Portugal) on Military Facilities in the Azores

SIGNED: September 6, 1951, at Lisbon, Portugal

SIGNATORIES: Portugal vs. United States

IN FORCE: From signing

OVERVIEW: An agreement, pursuant to the **North Atlantic (NATO) Treaty**, permitting the United States to use Azores-based military facilities it provides to Portugal.

DISCUSSION:

This agreement is typical of many concluded by the United States and its NATO (and other) allies during the Cold War. Through separate military assistance (sometimes called "technical assistance") agreements, the United States supplied military equipment and facilities to various allies. Subsequent agreements, such as this one with Portugal, stipulated that, in time of war, the United States would be given free access to use the equipment and facilities wherever they were based.

REFERENCES:

Clark, Ramsey, ed. *NATO in the Balkans: Voices of Opposition.* New York: International Action Center, 1998.

Gompert, David C., and F. Stephen Larrabee, eds. *America in Europe: A Partnership for a New Era.* New York: Cambridge University Press, 1997.

Grenville, J. A. S. *The Major International Treaties 1914-1973: A History Guide with Texts.* New York: Stein and Day, 1974.

Heller, Francis H., and John R. Gillingham, eds. *NATO: The Founding of the Atlantic Alliance and the Integration of Europe.* New York: St. Martin's Press, 1992.

Japanese-United States Security Treaty

SIGNED: September 8, 1951, at San Francisco

IN FORCE: From April 28, 1952

SIGNATORIES: Japan and the United States

OVERVIEW: Concluded simultaneously with the **Treaty of Peace with Japan**, this agreement provided for the provisional stationing of United States armed forces in Japan to maintain "international peace and security in the Far East."

DISCUSSION:

The preamble to the Security Treaty begins with a misleading statement, implying that the nation was disarmed by the Treaty of Peace with Japan:

Japan has this day signed a Treaty of Peace with the Allied Powers. On the coming into force of that Treaty, Japan will not have the effective means to exercise its inherent right of self-defense because it has been disarmed.

In fact, the Treaty of Peace contained no military clauses stipulating disarmament or arms reduction. The framers of the treaty felt such provisions were unnecessary because the Japanese constitution, adopted in 1946, barred Japan from maintaining armed forces of any kind. It was, therefore, the constitution, not the Treaty of Peace, that disarmed Japan. Nevertheless, an unarmed Japan required defense, which the United States agreed to provide, explicitly expanding the scope of the defensive mission beyond the borders of Japan and for the "maintenance of international peace and security in the Far East."

Additional articles prohibited Japan from allowing other nations to establish a military presence on its soil. The treaty was supplemented in 1954 by the **Mutual Defense Assistance Agreement with Japan** and superceded in 1960 by the **Treaty of Mutual Cooperation and Security between the United States and Japan.**

The text of the principal articles follows:

Japan has this day signed a Treaty of Peace with the Allied Powers. On the coming into force of that Treaty, Japan will not have the effective means to exercise its inherent right of self-defense because it has been disarmed.

There is danger to Japan in this situation because irresponsible militarism has not yet been driven from the world. Therefore Japan desires a Security Treaty with the United States of America to come into force simultaneously with the Treaty of Peace between the United States of America and Japan.

The Treaty of Peace recognizes that Japan as a sovereign nation has the right to enter into collective security arrangements, and further, the Charter of the United Nations recognizes that all nations possess an inherent right of individual and collective self-defense.

In exercise of these rights, Japan desires, as a provisional arrangement for its defense, that the United States of America should maintain armed forces of its own in and about Japan so as to deter armed attack upon Japan.

The United States of America, in the interest of peace and security, is presently willing to maintain certain of its armed forces in and about Japan, in the expectation, however, that Japan will itself increasingly assume responsibility for its own defense against direct and indirect aggression, always avoiding any armament which could be an offensive threat or serve other than to promote peace and security in accordance with the purposes and principles of the United Nations Charter.

Accordingly, the two countries have agreed as follows:

ARTICLE I

Japan grants, and the United States of America accepts, the right, upon the coming into force of the Treaty of Peace and of this Treaty, to dispose United States land, air and sea forces in and about Japan. Such forces may be utilized to contribute to the maintenance of international peace and security in the Far East and to the security of Japan against armed attack from without, including assistance given at the express request of the Japanese Government to put down largescale internal riots and disturbances in Japan, caused through instigation or intervention by an outside power or powers.

ARTICLE II

During the exercise of the right referred to in Article I, Japan will not grant, without the prior consent of the United States of America, any bases or any rights, powers or authority whatsoever, in or relating to bases or the right of garrison or of maneuver, or transit of ground, air or naval forces to any third power.

ARTICLE III

The conditions which shall govern the disposition of armed forces of the United States of America in and about Japan shall be determined by administrative agreements between the two Governments.

ARTICLE IV

This Treaty shall expire whenever in the opinion of the Governments of the United States of America and Japan there shall have come into force such United Nations arrangements or such alternative individual or collective security dispositions as will satisfactorily provide for the maintenance by the United Nations or otherwise of international peace and security in the Japan Area.

REFERENCES:

Ando, Nisuke. *Surrender, Occupation, and Private Property in International Law: An Evaluation of U.S. Practice in Japan.* Oxford, Eng.: Clarendon Press, 1991.

Butow, R. C. *Japan's Decision to Surrender.* Palo Alto, Calif.: Stanford University Press, 1954.

Finn, Richard B. *Winners in Peace: MacArthur, Yoshida, and Postwar Japan.* Berkeley: University of California Press, 1992.

Grenville, J. A. S. *The Major International Treaties 1914-1973: A History Guide with Texts.* New York: Stein and Day, 1974.

Military Assistance Agreement (with Cuba)

SIGNED: March 7, 1952, at Havana, Cuba
SIGNATORIES: Cuba vs. United States
IN FORCE: From signing
OVERVIEW: A military assistance agreement with pre-Castro Cuba.

DISCUSSION:

Beginning with the **Monroe Doctrine** (Section 1.1) in 1823 and reaching its height in the Spanish-American War of 1898, the United States has assumed a strong, at times even imperialist, policy of protecting the integrity of the Americas. During the Cold War, United States policy makers deemed it particularly important to discourage the spread of communism to typically volatile Latin American governments. Economic and political ties between the United States and Cuba, just ninety miles off the coast of Florida, were especially strong, and, pursuant to various Organization of American States agreements and other mutual defense agreements, a Military Assistance Agreement was concluded with Cuba in 1952.

Although framed as a bilateral agreement, by which the two nations would come to one another's aid in time of need, the practical value of the agreement was as a warning to Moscow and other potential aggressors that the United States stood ready to defend Cuba and that it considered the defense of Cuba vital to the defense of the Western Hemisphere.

The agreement is a general one and does not specify the extent or nature of ongoing assistance, but, rather, provides the basis for such assistance as may, from time to time, be deemed appropriate.

REFERENCES:

Mutual Defense Assistance. Washington, D.C.: U.S. Government Printing Office, 1952.

United States Department of State, *Treaties in Force: A List of Treaties and other International Agreements of the United States in Force on January 1, 1997.* Washington, D.C.: U.S. Government Printing Office, 1997.

Korean War Armistice

SIGNED: July 27, 1953, at Panmunjom, South Korea (on the 38th parallel)
IN FORCE: From signature
SIGNATORIES: United Nations Command (including the United States) vs. North Korea and China
OVERVIEW: This armistice, concluded between the United Nations Command (without the participation of South Korea) and North Korea and China, divided Korea along the 38th parallel.

DISCUSSION:

The Korean War began in June 1950 between the Democratic People's Republic of Korea (North Korea) and the Republic of Korea (South Korea). The United States, as chief participant in a United Nations force, soon joined the war on the side of the anti-Communist South. After suffering initial defeats, the United Nations forces pushed the invading North Koreans back to the Yalu River, the border between North Korea and Manchuria. This provoked Chinese forces to come to the aid of the North Koreans, and the United Nations forces retreated to the 38th parallel. Here the war was essentially deadlocked from the beginning of 1951 until the armistice.

Negotiations toward an armistice began late in June 1951, in response to a Soviet proposal of a conference. The U.N. Command nations wanted an immediate end to hostilities, with the resolution of political questions to be deferred to a postwar international conference. The Communists insisted that the political questions be resolved before declaring a cease-fire. As a result, armistice talks dragged on for two years.

Talks formally began on July 10, 1951. On July 26, a four-point agenda was agreed on:

- Establishment of a demarcation line and demilitarized zone between the North and South
- Supervision of the truce
- Prisoner exchange
- Recommendations to the belligerent governments

The talks were characterized by delays and deadlocks, the thorniest issues involving disposition of prisoners of war. The

United Nations wanted prisoners to be permitted to decide for themselves whether or not they would return home, whereas the Communists wanted forced repatriation. The deadlock was broken in April 1953 with a compromise permitting prisoners to choose sides under supervision of a neutral commission. No sooner was this resolved, however, than South Korean president Syngman Rhee, who would admit of no settlement that failed to bring about the reunification of Korea, attempted to sabotage the proceedings on June 18 by releasing some 25,000 North Korean prisoners who wanted to live in the South. To appease Rhee, the United States agreed to a **United States-South Korea Mutual Defense Treaty,** long-term economic aid, and other concessions to the South. Nevertheless, South Korea did not sign the July 27, 1953 armistice.

The most enduring feature of the armistice is the demarcation line and demilitarized zone, both of which continue to exist today:

A military demarcation line shall be fixed and both sides shall withdraw two (2) kilometres from this line so as to establish a demilitarized zone between the opposing forces. A demilitarized zone shall be established as a buffer zone to prevent the occurrence of incidents which might lead to a resumption of hostilities....

Among the "Recommendation to the Governments concerned on both sides" in Article VI was "a political conference of a higher level of both sides . . . to settle through negotiation the questions of the withdrawal of all foreign forces from Korea, the peaceful settlement of the Korean question, etc. . . ." Accordingly, discussions in Geneva, Switzerland, were set up to decide the political issues, but North and South Korean have yet to be reunified, and the military situation at the 38th parallel continued to be potentially explosive. No definitive peace treaty has been concluded.

REFERENCES:

Alexander, Bevin. *Korea: The First War We Lost.* New York: Hippocrene, 1997.

Edwards, Paul M., comp. *The Korean War.* Westport, CT: Greenwood Publishing Group, 1998.

Fehrenbach, T. R. *This Knid of War: The Classic Korean War History.* Washington, D.C.: Brasseys, 1998.

Grenville, J. A. S. *The Major International Treaties 1914-1973: A History Guide with Texts.* New York: Stein and Day, 1974.

Agreement on United States Military Facilities in Spain

SIGNED: September 26, 1953, at Madrid

SIGNATORIES: Spain vs. United States

IN FORCE: From signing

OVERVIEW: An agreement whereby Spain permits the United States to establish and maintain certain military facilities within its territory.

DISCUSSION:

The Cold War foreign policy of the United States revolved around the political and military strategy of "containing Communism"—that is, confronting Communist expansion wherever it occurred in the world—and providing global defense against nuclear aggression. To serve the purposes of this policy, the United States, through NATO and other alliances, established military bases and other facilities in many nations of the West. The 1953 agreement with Spain is typical of United States Cold War philosophy and policy. Note that this agreement predates Spain's entry into NATO, which did not come until 1982.

The text of the agreement's principal articles follows:

ARTICLE I

In consonance with the principles agreed upon in the Mutual Defense Assistance Agreement, the Governments of the United States and of Spain consider that the contingencies with which both countries may be faced indicate the advisability of developing their relations upon a basis of continued friendship, in support of the policy of strengthening the defense of the West. This policy shall include:

1. On the part of the United States, the support of Spanish defense efforts for agreed purposes by providing military end item assistance to Spain during a period of several years to contribute to the effective air defense of Spain and to improve the equipment of its military and naval forces, to the extent to be agreed upon in technical discussions in the light of the circumstances, and with the cooperation of the resources of Spanish industry to the extent possible. Such support will be conditioned as in the case of other friendly nations by the priorities and limitations due to the international commitments of the United States and the exigencies of the international situation and will be subject to Congressional appropriations.

2. In consequence of the above stated premises and for the same agreed purposes, the Government of Spain authorizes the Government of the United States, subject to terms and conditions to be agreed, to develop, maintain and utilize for military purposes, jointly with the Government of Spain, such areas and facilities in territory under Spanish jurisdiction as may be agreed upon by the competent authorities of both Governments as necessary for the purposes of this agreement.

3. In granting assistance to Spain within the policy outlined above, as the preparation of the agreed areas and facilities progresses, the Government of the United States will satisfy, subject to the provisions of paragraph one, the minimum requirements for equipment necessary for the defense of Spanish territory, to the end that should a moment requiring the wartime utilization of the areas and facilities arrive, from this moment, the requirements are covered to the extent possible as regards the air defense of the territory and the equipment of the naval units; and that the armament and equipment of the Army units be as far advanced as possible.

ARTICLE II

For the purposes of this agreement and in accordance with technical arrangements to be agreed upon between the competent authorities of both Governments, the Government of the United States is authorized to improve and fit agreed areas and facilities for military use, as well as to undertake necessary construction in this connection in cooperation with the Government of Spain; to station and house therein the necessary military and civilian personnel and to provide for their security, discipline and welfare; to store and maintain custody of provisions, supplies, equipment and material; and to maintain and operate the facilities and equipment necessary in support of such areas and personnel.

ARTICLE III

The areas which, by virtue of this Agreement, are prepared for joint utilization, will remain under Spanish flag and command, and Spain will assume the obligation of adopting the necessary measures for the external security. However, the United States may, in all cases, exercise the necessary supervision of United States personnel, facilities, and equipment.

The time and manner of wartime utilization of said areas and facilities will be as mutually agreed upon.

ARTICLE IV

The Government of Spain will acquire, free of all charge and servitude, the land which may be necessary for all military purposes and shall retain the ownership of the ground and of the permanent structures which may be constructed thereon. The United States Government reserves the right to remove all other constructions and facilities established at its own expense when it is deemed convenient by the Government of the United States or upon the termination of this Agreement; in both cases the Spanish Government may acquire them, after previous assessment, whenever they are not installations of a classified nature.

The Spanish state will be responsible for all claims made against the United States Government by a third party, in all cases referring to the ownership and utilization of the above-mentioned land.

REFERENCE:
Liedtke, Boris Nikolai. *Embracing a Dictatorship: U.S. Relations with Spain, 1945-53*. New York: St. Martin's Press, 1997.

United States-South Korea Mutual Defense Treaty

SIGNED: October 1, 1953, at Washington, D.C.
IN FORCE: November 15, 1954
SIGNATORIES: South Korea and the United States
OVERVIEW: This treaty followed the signing of the **Korean Armistice** (July 27, 1953) and pledged the United States to defend against future aggression and to preserve its sovereignty.

DISCUSSION:

The armistice that ended the Korean War on July 27, 1953, signaled America's abandonment of the objective of achieving reunification of Korea under democratic principles. To compensate the government of South Korea for this compromise of its stated policy, the United States concluded a Mutual Defense Treaty.

The "mutual" in the treaty's title serves the purpose of preserving South Korean sovereignty. In practice, the treaty is

America's guarantee to come to South Korea's aid in the event that it is attacked again.

The treaty stipulates that "neither party is obligated . . . to come to the aid of the other except in case of an external attack against such party; nor shall anything in the present Treaty be construed as requiring the United States to give assistance to Korea except in the event of an armed attack against territory which has been recognized by the United States as lawfully brought under the administrative control of the Republic of Korea." In this way, the United States sought to avoid entanglement in a civil war within South Korea or in a war initiated by South Korean aggression against the North. The treaty has been repeatedly amended to cover such issues as ongoing military assistance and training, equipment supply, cooperation in the development of military technology, and the stationing and operation of U.S. troops in the country.

REFERENCES:
Grenville, J. A. S. *The Major International Treaties 1914-1973: A History Guide with Texts*. New York: Stein and Day, 1974.
Hong, Yong-Pyo. *State Security and Regime Security: President Syngman Rhee and the Insecurity Dilemma in South Korea, 1953-60*. New York: St. Martin's Press, 1999.
Pollack, Jonathan D., et al. *A New Alliance for the Next Century: The Future of U.S.-Korean Security Cooperation*. Washington, D.C.: Rand Corporation, 1996.

Agreement (with Greece) on Use of Defense Facilities

SIGNED: October 12, 1953, at Athens
SIGNATORIES: Greece vs. United States
IN FORCE: From signing
OVERVIEW: An agreement, pursuant to Greece's entry into NATO, allowing the United States to establish, maintain, and use certain military facilities in Greece.

DISCUSSION:

In March 1946, after World War II, Greece held its first elections in a decade. Because the far left abstained in protest, however, the royalist right was overwhelmingly swept into power, but King George II, restored to his throne, died within six months and was succeeded by his brother Paul. In the meantime, Greek factionalism intensified, and the nation erupted into civil war. In December 1947, Greek communists established a Provisional Democratic Government and, although numbering in the minority, took control of a large portion of northern Greece through a combination of skilled guerrilla tactics and logistical support from Soviet satellite nations. By this time, however, President Harry S Truman had promulgated the Truman Doctrine and had embraced a global policy of "containing communism." The United States now provided military equipment and advice to the Greek right. Combined with the withdrawal of support from Tito's Yugoslavia, the splintering of the Greek communist party, and certain military blunders, the royalists defeated the communist guerrillas by the summer of 1949. The royalist regime brought Greece into NATO in 1952, and the following year concluded this military agreement with the United States. Article I contains the core of the agreement.

The Government of Greece hereby authorizes the Government of the United States of America, subject to the terms and conditions set forth in this Agreement and to technical arrangements between appropriate authorities of the two Governments, to utilize such roads, railways and areas, and to construct, develop, use and operate such military and supporting facilities in Greece as appropriate authorities of the two Governments shall from time to time agree to be necessary for the implementation of, or in furtherance of, approved NATO plans. The construction, development, use and operation of such facilities shall be consistent with recommendations, standards and directives from the North Atlantic Treaty Organization (NATO) where applicable . . . .

REFERENCES:
Clark, Ramsey, ed. *NATO in the Balkans: Voices of Opposition.* New York: International Action Center, 1998.
Gompert, David C., and F. Stephen Larrabee, eds. *America in Europe: A Partnership for a New Era.* New York: Cambridge University Press, 1997.
Grenville, J. A. S. *The Major International Treaties 1914-1973: A History Guide with Texts.* New York: Stein and Day, 1974.
Heller, Francis H., and John R. Gillingham, eds. *NATO: The Founding of the Atlantic Alliance and the Integration of Europe.* New York: St. Martin's Press, 1992.

Bilateral Military Assistance Agreement (with Nicaragua)

SIGNED: April 23, 1954, at Managua, Nicaragua
SIGNATORIES: Nicaragua vs. United States
IN FORCE: From signing
OVERVIEW: An agreement, pursuant to the **Rio Treaty of Reciprocal Assistance,** in which the signatories undertake to supply each other with military assistance "in accordance with such terms and conditions as may be agreed."

DISCUSSION:
Beginning in the nineteenth century, United States-based fruit companies exerted great influence in what came to be called the "banana republics" of Central America, including Nicaragua. From 1909 to 1925, U.S. Marines were stationed there to back a conservative government that was friendly to American business interests. No sooner were the Marines withdrawn than civil violence erupted, and the Marines returned. Before the Marines left once again in 1933, they trained the Nicaraguan National Guard and handpicked one Anastasio Somoza Garcia to command it. During this period, the radical guerrilla Cesar Augusto Sandino led the resistance movement against the Nicaraguan government and the United States presence in the country. Somoza Garcia sought to put an end to the uprising by inviting Sandino to a peace conference and there assassinating him. Next, in 1936, Somoza Garcia assumed the presidency of Nicaragua, thereby inaugurating the long Somoza dynasty, which exploited Nicaragua's meager wealth while continuing to serve the interests of American business. As President Franklin D. Roosevelt is said to have put it in 1936, "Somoza may be a son of a bitch, but he's our son of a bitch."

Maintaining the stability of Nicaragua became of increasing interest to the United States during the Cold War, when radical reform was inextricably linked to communism. Both in an effort to protect United States investment in Nicaragua and to block the spread of communism into this Central American nation, the United States concluded with the Somoza government a series of military assistance agreements.

The 1954 document is quite simple:
- The two signatories will assist each other as they deem necessary
- Any assistance "shall be consistent with the Charter of the United Nations"
- Nicaragua undertakes to "make effective use of assistance received from . . . the United States . . . for the purpose of implementing defense plans, accepted by the two governments, under which the two Governments will participate in missions important to the defense of the Western Hemisphere . . ."
- Nicaragua will not transfer military equipment to a third party
- The two signatories will maintain security to prevent the disclosure of classified information
- "Each government will take appropriate measures consistent with security to keep the public informed of operations under this Agreement."

The latter provision is particularly important, as is the registration of the agreement with the United Nations, since both signatories were anxious to avoid accusations of making covert agreements.

See also **Agreement Relating to a Military Assistance Advisory Group**.

REFERENCES:
Agreement between the United States of America and Nicaragua, signed at Managua April, 23, 1954, entered into force April, 23, 1954. Washington, D.C.: U. S. Government Printing Office, 1955.
Bell, Belden, ed. *Nicaragua, an Ally under Siege.* Washington, D.C.: Council on American Affairs, 1978.
United States Congress, Committee on Foreign Relations. *United States Policy Options with Respect to Nicaragua and Aid to the Contras: Hearings Before the Committee on Foreign Relations, United States Senate, One Hundredth Congress, First Session, January 28 and February 5, 1987.* Washington: U.S. Government Printing Office, 1987.

Geneva Agreement on the Cessation of Hostilities in Viet-Nam

SIGNED: July 20, 1954, at Geneva

SIGNATORIES: France vs. Viet Minh forces in Laos, Cambodia, and Vietnam

IN FORCE: From signing

OVERVIEW: The document ending the colonial war between France and the forces of the Viet Minh.

DISCUSSION:

Although neither the United States nor Vietnam are signatories to this agreement, the document is basic to eventual United States involvement in the Vietnam War.

The major provisions of the Geneva Agreement follow:

- Creation of provisional military demarcation line and demilitarized zone "temporarily" dividing Vietnam into North and South Vietnam approximately along the 17th parallel
- Implementation of a cease-fire, as follows: in northern Vietnam at 8:00 A.M. on July 27 1954; in central Vietnam at 8:00 A.M. on August 1, 1954; and in Southern Vietnam at 8:00 a. M. on August 11, 1954
- Detailed conditions of the cease-fire
- Ban on introduction of fresh troops, military personnel, arms and munitions, military bases
- Liberation and return of POWs and civilian internees
- Creation of a Joint Commission and an International Commission for Supervision and Control of Viet-Nam

The Geneva Agreement was intended to serve to maintain the peace until the divided Vietnams were reunified through "free elections" to be held by July 20, 1956. The South, with the covert support of the United States, blocked the elections, thereby triggering the long civil war in which the United States would ultimately intervene.

REFERENCES:

Agreement Between the United States of America and Cambodia, France, Laos, and Viet-nam, Amending Annex to Agreement of December 23, 1950, Effected by Exchanges of Notes Between the United States of America and France, Dated at Saigon August 10 and September 8, 1951; Between the United States of America and Viet-nam, Dated at Saigon August 10 and September 17, 1951; Between the United States of America and Laos, Dated at Saigon August 16, 1951, and at Vientiane November 6, 1951; Between the United States of America and Cambodia, Dated at Saigon August 16, 1951, at Phnom-penh January 7, 1952, Entered into Force January 7, 1952, Operative Retroactively July 1, 1951. Washington, D.C.: U. S. Government Printing Office, 1955.

Documents Related to the Implementation of the Geneva Agreements Concerning Viet-nam. Hanoi, Vietnam: N. Pub., 1956.

Lind, Michael. *Vietnam: The Necessary War.* New York: Free Press, 1999.

Logevall, Fredrik. *Choosing War: The Lost Chance for Peace and the Escalation of War.* Berkeley: University of California Press, 1999.

South-East Asia Collective Defense Treaty (SEATO)

SIGNED: September 8, 1954, at Manila, Philippines

IN FORCE: From February 19, 1955

SIGNATORIES: Australia, France, New Zealand, Pakistan, Philippines, Thailand, United Kingdom, and United States; Pakistan withdrew in 1972, and France discontinued financial support in 1974 after ceasing to participate in the organization's military activities.

OVERVIEW: The purpose of the Southeast Atlantic Treaty Organization (SEATO) was to provide mutual defense for the signatories. Under a special protocol, Cambodia, Laos, and South Vietnam were also protected. By decision of the SEATO Council (September 24, 1975) the organization ceased to exist as of June 30, 1977, but the collective defense treaty remains in force.

DISCUSSION:

After communist forces defeated the French in Indochina during the 1950s, U.S. Secretary of State John Foster Dulles advocated the creation of SEATO, the Asian equivalent of Europe's collective defense body, NATO (*see* **North Atlantic Treaty**). By the SEATO treaty, signatories pledged collective action in the event of external aggression or internal subversion against any one of them. Economic cooperation was also provided for, but the main purpose of the treaty was collective military defense against the inroads of communism.

The United States appended to the treaty a unilateral "Understanding" that "aggression" was to be defined specifically as "communist aggression"; however, the United States "affirms that in the event of other aggression or armed attack it will consult under the provisions of Article 4," which defined "aggression" in the main body of the treaty. In addition to a Protocol on Indo-China, which encompassed Cambodia, Laos, and South Vietnam (which were not signatories), the treaty included the **Pacific Charter**, signed by all treaty parties, which set forth general principles relating to the maintenance of "peace and security in South-East Asia." The signatories harmonized their objectives with those of the **United Nations Charter**, agreeing to "uphold the principle of equal rights and self-determination" and affirming their intention to "co-operate in the economic, social and cultural fields in order to promote higher living standards, economic progress and social well-being in this region."

Although it was modeled on NATO, SEATO failed to secure firm, long-term military commitments from its members. The United States' involvement in the Vietnam War severely crippled the alliance, since several SEATO members were reluctant to support the effort. Pakistan withdrew from SEATO in 1972, after the Indo-Pakistani War, and France withdrew its financial support and military participation in 1974. Three years later, in 1977, SEATO was formally dissolved, although the underlying mutual defense treaty remained in force.

REFERENCES:

Buszynski, Leszek. *SEATO: The Failure of an Alliance Strategy.* Singapore: Singapore University Press, 1984.

Grenville, J. A. S. *The Major International Treaties 1914-1973: A History Guide with Texts.* New York: Stein and Day, 1974.

Pacific Charter

SIGNED: September 8, 1954, at Manila, Philippines

IN FORCE: From February 19, 1955

SIGNATORIES: Australia, France, New Zealand, Pakistan, Philippines, Thailand, United Kingdom, and United States; Pakistan withdrew from SEATO in 1972, and France discontinued financial support of SEATO in 1974 after ceasing to participate in the organization's military activities.

OVERVIEW: A document associated with the **South-East Asia Collective Defense Treaty (SEATO),** the charter lays down general principles relating to the maintenance of "peace and security in South-East Asia."

DISCUSSION:

For a discussion of this charter and SEATO, see **South-East Asia Collective Defense Treaty (SEATO).**

The text of the charter follows:

The Delegates of Australia, France, New Zealand, Pakistan, the Republic of the Philippines, the Kingdom of Thailand, the United Kingdom of Great Britain and Northern Ireland, and the United States of America;

DESIRING to establish a firm basis for common action to maintain peace and security in Southeast Asia and the Southwest Pacific;

CONVINCED that common action to this end, in order to be worthy and effective, must be inspired by the highest principles of justice and liberty;

Do HEREBY PROCLAIM:

First, in accordance with the provisions of the United Nations Charter, they uphold the principle of equal rights and self-determination of peoples and they will earnestly strive by every peaceful means to promote self-government and to secure the independence of all countries whose peoples desire it and are able to undertake its responsibilities;

Second, they are each prepared to continue taking effective practical measures to ensure conditions favorable to the orderly achievement of the foregoing purposes in accordance with their constitutional processes;

Third, they will continue to cooperate in the economic, social and cultural fields in order to promote higher living standards, economic progress and social well-being in this region;

Fourth, as declared in the Southeast Asia Collective Defense Treaty, they are determined to prevent or counter by appropriate means any attempt in the treaty area to subvert their freedom or to destroy their sovereignty or territorial integrity.

PROCLAIMED at Manila, this eighth day of September, 1954.

REFERENCES:

Buszynski, Leszek. *SEATO: The Failure of an Alliance Strategy.* Singapore: Singapore University Press, 1984.

Grenville, J. A. S. *The Major International Treaties 1914-1973: A History Guide with Texts.* New York: Stein and Day, 1974.

Agreement (with El Salvador) for a United States Army Mission

SIGNED: September 23, 1954, at San Salvador, El Salvador

SIGNATORIES: El Salvador vs. United States

IN FORCE: From November 17, 1954

OVERVIEW: An agreement made "at the request of the Government of El Salvador" for the "appointment of officers and non-commissioned officers to constitute a United States Army Mission to the Republic of El Salvador."

DISCUSSION:

In conformity with United States' hemispherical policy, which introduced a U.S. economic and military presence into numerous Latin American countries, especially during the Cold War period, this agreement authorizes a U.S. Army mission in El Salvador, charged with "enhancing the technical efficiency of the Salvadoran Army."

The agreement stipulates a duration four years, renewable by proposal of El Salvador six months before its expiration. On three months' notice by either government, the agreement may be terminated prior to expiration.

The agreement lays down the composition of the mission only to the extent that it shall be commanded by a colonel or lieutenant colonel and shall consist of other personnel as the two nations agree on. The members of the mission "will go on active duty with the Salvadoran Army" and may perform functions agreed upon between the Salvadoran minister if defense and the U.S. chief of the mission, "except that they shall not have command functions." Members of the mission shall have "precedence over all Salvadoran personnel of the same rank." The size of the mission is not specified in the agreement.

REFERENCES:

None

United States-Nationalist China Mutual Defense Treaty

SIGNED: December 2, 1954, at Washington, D.C.

IN FORCE: From signing; terminated on January 1, 1979, when the United States recognized the People's Republic of China (Mainland China) as the "sole legal Government of China."

SIGNATORIES: United States and the Republic of China (Nationalist China)

OVERVIEW: After the forces of the People's Republic of China (Communist Mainland China) attacked the islands of Quemoy and Matsu, held by the Nationalist Chinese, in 1954, the United States entered into a treaty of "mutual defense" with the Nationalist government of Taiwan.

DISCUSSION:

In 1949, the island of Taiwan (also called Formosa) became the refuge for the government-in-exile of the Republic of China led by Chiang Kai-Shek and his Nationalist (Kuomintang) party following the final communist victory on the vast mainland and the proclamation of the Communist People's Republic of China. Pursuant to its Cold War policy of acting to "contain" communist aggression and expansion, the United States entered into a defensive alliance with the Taiwan government in 1954 after forces of the People's Republic attacked the strategically important, Nationalist-held islands of Quemoy and Matsu.

By the mutual defense treaty, the United States agreed to aid Taiwan in the event of armed attack; however, any action was to be subject to each nation's "constitutional processes." This proviso was intended primarily to insure that the president of the United States could not commit to a war footing without the approval of Congress. The treaty further stipulated that the United States absolutely obligated to defend Quemoy and Matsu, islands uncomfortably close to the Chinese mainland. Before ratifying the treaty, the U.S. Senate added three "understandings":

- The treaty would have no bearing on the ultimate legal title to Taiwan (Formosa). This "understanding" allowed the United States to avoid commitment to either side's claims in a civil war.
- United States intervention was to be strictly limited to instances of clear self-defense,
- The treaty would not automatically apply to the protection of any additional territory without the express consent of the Senate.

The treaty was set to remain in force indefinitely, although either party might "terminate it one year after notice [was] given to the other party."

Pursuant to the treaty, the United States redeployed the Seventh Fleet in response to a 1958 attack on Quemoy and Matsu. The tense international incident was resolved when the Communist Chinese called off the attack. Possession of the islands are still in dispute, but, after formally recognizing the People's Republic of China as the "sole legal Government of China," the United States terminated the defense treaty.

REFERENCES:

Christensen, Thomas J. *Useful Adversaries: Grand Strategy, Domestic Mobilization, and Sino-American Conflict, 1947-1958*. Princeton, NJ: Princeton University Press, 1997.

Garver, John W. *Face Off: China, the United States, and Taiwan's Democratization*. Seattle: University of Washington Press, 1997.

Grenville, J. A. S. *The Major International Treaties 1914-1973: A History Guide with Texts*. New York: Stein and Day, 1974.

Agreement (with Japan) Relating to the Settlement of Japanese Claims Resulting from Nuclear Tests

OFFICIAL TITLE: Exchange of Notes Constituting an Agreement Relating to the Settlement of Japanese Claims for Personal and Property Damages Resulting from Nuclear Tests in the Marshall Islands in 1954

SIGNED: January 4, 1955, at Tokyo

SIGNATORIES: Japan vs. United States

IN FORCE: From signing

OVERVIEW: An agreement settling damage claims for injuries and death caused by a United States hydrogen bomb test in the Bikini Atoll.

DISCUSSION:

Bikini Atoll, in the Marshall Islands, was a major testing area for the United States' nuclear arsenal. On March 1, 1954, a hydrogen bomb, code named Bravo, was detonated on the surface of the reef in the northwestern corner of Bikini Atoll. An hour and a half after the detonation, a Japanese fishing vessel, the *Lucky Dragon*, was showered by radioactive fallout. The twenty-three fishermen aboard the vessel soon fell ill, and one man died. In response to the mishap, the United States tendered, by this agreement, the sum of $2,000,000 in full and complete settlement of any and all Japanese claims against the United States. The United States ambassador also expressed the nation's "deep concern and sincere regret . . . over the injuries suffered by Japanese fishermen in the course of these tests" and further expressed "earnest hopes" for the recovery of the men.

REFERENCE:

Divine, Robert A. *Blowing on the Wind: The Nuclear Test Ban Debate, 1954-1960*. New York: Oxford University Press, 1978.

Agreement (with Vietnam) Relating to Economic Assistance

OFFICIAL TITLE: Exchange of Notes Constituting an Agreement Relating to Economic Assistance

SIGNED: February 21 and March 7, 1955, at Saigon

SIGNATORIES: United States vs. Vietnam

IN FORCE: From March 7, 1955

OVERVIEW: A general agreement with the government of Ngo Dinh Diem for the economic assistance.

DISCUSSION:

For a discussion of the background of United States financial and military assistance to the government of South Vietnam, see **Agreement Relating to Financial Assistance for Direct Support of Vietnamese Armed Forces.**

This agreement extends an agreement made with Vietnam in 1951, when it was still under full French colonial control. It provides for additional funds—amounts and terms unspecified—to the new government of Prime Minister (later President) Diem, who had declared himself a staunch anti-communist.

REFERENCES:
Lind, Michael. *Vietnam: The Necessary War.* New York: Free Press, 1999.
Logevall, Fredrik. *Choosing War: The Lost Chance for Peace and the Escalation of War.* Berkeley: University of California Press, 1999.

Agreement Relating to Financial Assistance for Direct Support of Vietnamese Armed Forces

SIGNED: April 22 and 23, 1955, at Saigon, Vietnam

SIGNATORIES: United States vs. Vietnam

IN FORCE: From April 23, 1955

OVERVIEW: An agreement to help finance the military of the newly formed government of South Vietnam.

DISCUSSION:

Following the defeat of French forces at Dien Bien Phu in 1954, France's colonial domination of Vietnam began rapidly to end. At the Geneva conference of 1955, Vietnam was divided—temporarily—into northern and southern segments, the north controlled by communist forces and the south by the French, a puppet emperor, Bao Dai, and a prime minister, Ngo Dinh Diem. Under the strongly anti-communist Diem, South Vietnam quickly achieved full independence from the last vestiges of French control, and the United States began a program of military and economic support to bolster what it perceived as a bastion of anti-communism in a region menaced by the political forces of China and the Soviet Union.

The 1955 agreement provides direct financial assistance to the Vietnamese Armed Forces and acknowledges the role of the United States Military Assistance Advisory Group (MAAG) "for assisting the Government of Vietnam in the organization and training of its armed forces." For its part, the government of Vietnam undertakes to provide the "maximum possible financial contribution to the support of its armed forces, to the extraordinary governmental expenses for refugee resettlement, and to other economic programs during calendar year 1955." The agreement lays down the expectation that Vietnam will contribute no less than $79.8 million and the United States, $223.4 million. Beyond this, the nature and extent of the military programs are not stipulated.

Also see **Agreement (with Vietnam) Relating to Economic Assistance.**

REFERENCES:
Lind, Michael. *Vietnam: The Necessary War.* New York: Free Press, 1999.
Logevall, Fredrik. *Choosing War: The Lost Chance for Peace and the Escalation of War.* Berkeley: University of California Press, 1999.

Agreement Relating to the Boundary between the United States Sector of Berlin and the Soviet Zone of Occupation

SIGNED: June 25, 1955, at Berlin

SIGNATORIES: Union of Soviet Socialist Republics vs. United States

IN FORCE: From signing

OVERVIEW: The definitive agreement on the boundary between West Berlin and East Berlin.

DISCUSSION:

Since the end of World War II, Berlin, like all of Germany, had been divided between occupation and control by the Western allies and by the Soviet Union. It was not, however, until 1955 that a formal agreement was concluded demarcating the precise boundary between the United States sector of Berlin and the Soviet zone of occupation. The agreement was accompanied by a map, and the boundary was described in this way: "the location of the boundary of Greater Berlin [lies] along the southern side of Koenigs Weg from the Autobahn (Avus Zubringer) southwesterly to Kurfuersten Weg (with the inclusion of the roadway in the American Sector)."

For additional historical background of this document, see **Agreements on Germany (France, U.K., U.S.).**

REFERENCES:
Giangreco, D. M., and Robert E. Griffin. *Airbridge to Berlin: The Berlin Crisis of 1948.* Novato, CA: Presidio Press, 1988.
Grenville, J. A. S. *The Major International Treaties 1914-1973: A History Guide with Texts* (New York: Stein and Day, 1974.
Haydock, Michael D. *City Under Siege: The Berlin Blockade and Airlift, 1948-49.* Washington, D.C.: Brasseys, 1999.

Agreement (with Cuba) Relating to a Military Assistance Advisory Group

OFFICIAL TITLE: Exchange of Notes Constituting an Agreement Relating to a Military Assistance Advisory Group
SIGNED: August 3, 1955, at Havana, Cuba
SIGNATORIES: Cuba vs. United States
IN FORCE: From August 10, 1955
OVERVIEW: A pre-Castro agreement amplifying the **Mutual Defense Assistance Agreement (with Cuba).**

DISCUSSION:

The principal provision of the agreement is the stipulation that members of the Military Assistance Advisory Group "may perform the functions specified in Article V of the **Mutual Defense Agreement** [(**with Cuba**)] of March 7, 1952, namely operating as part of the Embassy under the direction and control of the Chief of the Diplomatic Mission." Thus members of the U.S. military missions to Cuba would be accorded full diplomatic status.

REFERENCE:
Mutual Defense Assistance. Washington, D.C.: U.S. Government Printing Office, 1952.

Agreement (with Nicaragua) Relating to a Military Assistance Advisory Group

OFFICIAL TITLE: Exchange of Notes Constituting an Agreement Relating to a Military Assistance Advisory Group
SIGNED: January 17 and February 9, 1957, at Managua, Nicaragua
SIGNATORIES: Nicaragua vs. United States
IN FORCE: From February 9, 1957
OVERVIEW: An agreement confirming the establishment and presence of United States "military advisors" in Nicaragua.

DISCUSSION:

Whereas the **Bilateral Military Assistance Agreement (with Nicaragua)** of 1954 emphasized material military assistance to Nicaragua rather than the standing presence of U.S. military personnel, the Agreement Relating to a Military Assistance Advisory Group, an agreement made pursuant to the 1954 agreement, acknowledged and confirmed the presence of United States military personnel as "advisors," thereby sanctioning a standing U.S. military presence in the country.

REFERENCE:
Agreement Between the United States of America and Nicaragua Effected by Exchange of Notes Signed at Managua January 17 and February 9, 1957. Washington, D.C.: U.S. Government Printing Office, 1957.

Agreement (with Lebanon) Relating to Equipment, Materials Services, and Other Assistance

SIGNED: June 3 and 6, 1957, at Beirut, Lebanon
SIGNATORIES: Lebanon vs. United States
IN FORCE: From June 6, 1957
OVERVIEW: An agreement making available to Lebanon United States military assistance.

DISCUSSION:

During the Suez War of October-December 1956, between Egypt and Israel, the Lebanese government of Camille Chamoun incurred the enmity of Nasser's Egypt when it declined to sever diplomatic relations with Britain and France, which had allied themselves with Israel against Egypt. As the crisis in Lebanon intensified following the heated parliamentary elections of 1957 (allegedly manipulated to favor the reelection of Chamoun), the United States, also a supporter of Israel, came to Lebanon's aid with the program of military assistance laid down in this agreement.

The agreement is broadly general, specifying only that "the United States has agreed to make available to the Government of Lebanon such military assistance as the Government of Lebanon may request and the Government of the United States may authorize.

The following year, the United States did intervene in Lebanon. After Syria had created with Egypt the United Arab Republic, Muslim opposition to Chamoun agitated for Lebanon to join the UAR, while, in the meantime, an insurrection developed in Tripoli and then spread to Iraq. At this juncture, President Chamoun requested U.S. military intervention, which came in the form of the landing of a U.S. marine contingent outside Beirut. A shooting confrontation did not develop between the marines and the insurgents; however, the insurrection gradually dissolved.

REFERENCE:
Westwood, J. N. *The History of the Middle East Wars.* London and New York: Hamlyn, 1984.

Agreement for Mutual Assistance in Cartography between the Khmer Geographic Service and the Army Map Service

SIGNED: October 17, 1957, at Phnom-Penh, Cambodia
SIGNATORIES: Cambodia vs. United States
IN FORCE: From signing
OVERVIEW: An agreement to collaborate on the mapping of Cambodia.

DISCUSSION:

By the mid 1950s, Southeast Asia had become a hot spot of the Cold War. With the defeat of France in Vietnam, that nation was about to become the stage on which the next conflict between communism and democracy would be played out, and American military planners saw it as essential to create detailed maps of Vietnam's neighbor, Cambodia. It is significant that, whereas the Cambodian mapping agency was ostensibly civilian, the United States agency involved was frankly military.

REFERENCES:

Lind, Michael. *Vietnam: The Necessary War*. New York: Free Press, 1999.

Logevall, Fredrik. *Choosing War: The Lost Chance for Peace and the Escalation of War*. Berkeley: University of California Press, 1999.

Agreement (with Canada) Relating to North American Air Defense Command

OFFICIAL TITLE: Exchange of Notes Constituting an Agreement Relating to North American Air Defense Command

SIGNED: May 12, 1958, at Washington, D.C.

SIGNATORIES: Canada vs. United States

IN FORCE: From signing

OVERVIEW: An agreement on the principles governing the North American Air Defense Command (NORAD).

DISCUSSION:

The creation of NORAD, the North American Air Defense Command, a joint United States-Canadian military defense system, was announced in 1957. This agreement sets down the basic principles by which NORAD will operate:

• The commander-in-chief NORAD (CINCNORAD) is to be responsible to the Chiefs of Staff Committee of Canada and the Joint Chiefs of Staff of the United States.

• NORAD is to operate according to the objectives of NATO.

• NORAD is to include only the units assigned to it by the two governments.

• CINCNORAD is to have operational control over NORAD.

• The appointment of CINCNORAD and his deputy is to be approved by the United States and Canada.

• NORAD plans are to be reviewed and approved by national authorities of both nations.

• The financing of NORAD will be settled by mutual agreement of the two governments.

• NORAD will operated for ten years and may be renewed upon review by both governments.

REFERENCE:

Crosby, Ann Denholm. *Dilemmas in Defense Decision-Making: Constructing Canada's Role in NORAD, 1958-96*. New York: St. Martin's, 1998.

Agreement Concerning the Establishment of Canada-United States Ministerial Committee on Joint Defense

OFFICIAL TITLE: Exchange of Notes Constituting an Agreement Concerning the Establishment of Canada-United States Ministerial Committee on Joint Defense

SIGNED: August 29 and September 2, 1958, at Ottawa

SIGNATORIES: Canada vs. United States

IN FORCE: From September 2, 1958

OVERVIEW: An agreement establishing a Canada-United States Ministerial Committee to "consider periodically important matters affecting the joint defence of our two countries."

DISCUSSION:

In addition to establishing jointly the North American Air Defense Command (NORAD) (see **Agreement [with Canada] Relating to North American Air Defense Command**), the United States and Canada created a standing committee for the more effective integration of the two nations' air defenses. The committee is to consist of Canada's secretary of state of external affairs, minister of national defence, and minister of finance and the United States' secretary of state, secretary of defense, and secretary of the treasury. Functions of the committee include the following:

• To consult on any matters affecting the joint defense of Canada and the United States

• To resolve any problems that arise and to strengthen "further the close and intimate cooperation between the two Governments on joint defence matters"

• To report to the governments and make recommendations to improve joint defense

REFERENCE:

Crosby, Ann Denholm. *Dilemmas in Defense Decision-Making: Constructing Canada's Role in NORAD, 1958-96*. New York: St. Martin's, 1998.

Agreement (with Canada) Relating to the DEW Line

OFFICIAL TITLE: Exchange of Notes (with Annex) Constituting an Agreement Relating to the Augmentation of Communication Facilities at Cape Dyer, Baffin Island, to Support the Greenland Extension of the DEW Line

SIGNED: April 13, 1959, at Ottawa, Canada

SIGNATORIES: Canada vs. United States

IN FORCE: From signing

OVERVIEW: An agreement relating to an element of the Defense Early Warning System (the DEW Line) established in Canada.

DISCUSSION:

During the Cold War, under threat of a massive nuclear air strike, the United States and Canada cooperated in the defense of North America by jointly creating the Defense Early Warning System (the DEW Line). When elements of the system required the presence of United States military or construction personnel on Canadian territory, agreements such as this had to be concluded. This one addresses the construction of communications facilities to augment the DEW Line by linking it to new radar facilities constructed in Greenland.

REFERENCE:

Crosby, Ann Denholm. *Dilemmas in Defense Decision-Making: Constructing Canada's Role in NORAD, 1958-96.* New York: St. Martin's, 1998.

Agreement (with Turkey) Relating to the Introduction of Modern Weapons into NATO's Defense Forces

OFFICIAL TITLE: Exchange of Notes Constituting an Agreement Relating to the Introduction of Modern Weapons into NATO's Defense Forces

SIGNED: September 18 and October 28, 1959, at Ankara, Turkey

SIGNATORIES: Turkey vs. United States

IN FORCE: From October 28, 1959

OVERVIEW: An agreement in which NATO member Turkey allows the placement of United States "modern" (i.e., nuclear) weapons within Turkey.

DISCUSSION:

By this agreement, Turkey gives permission to the United States, as a fellow NATO member, to base "modern weapons, including nuclear weapons" within the territory of Turkey.

REFERENCES:

Athanassopolou, Ekavi. *Turkey: Anglo-American Security Interests, 1945-1952: The First Enlargement of NATO.* Ilford, UK: Frank Cass.

Kaplan, Lawrence. *The Long Entanglement: NATO's First Fifty Years.* New York: Praeger, 1999.

Treaty of Mutual Cooperation and Security between the United States and Japan

SIGNED: January 19, 1960, at Washington

IN FORCE: From June 23, 1960

SIGNATORIES: Japan and the United States

OVERVIEW: This treaty superceded the **Japanese-United States Security Treaty** of 1951, reducing the American military presence in Japan and removing derogations of Japanese sovereignty.

The treaty also recognized the existence of Japan's defense forces and acknowledged that they were to be used only in self-defense.

DISCUSSION:

With the postwar Japanese economic recovery, the Japanese government requested revision of the Japanese-United States Security Treaty of 1951. The reasons for the call to revise the earlier agreement included these two major motives:

- A desire to reestablish national sovereignty in full and to be treated by other nations as an equal
- A desire to obtain acknowledgment that the Japanese people had been the victims of nuclear attack

The 1960 treaty reduced the number of U.S. military personnel permanently stationed in Japan, but included a guarantee that the United States would continue to enjoy the right to operate bases for American naval, land, and air forces on Japanese soil. The treaty also explicitly affirmed Japan's sovereignty, removing all derogations of that sovereignty contained in or implied by the earlier treaty. The treaty also explicitly acknowledged that Japanese forces could be used only in self-defense. The earlier treaty had left this issue ambiguous by citing Japan's military obligations under the **United Nations Charter**. By virtue of the charter, Japan could be called upon to participate in a military action mandated by the United Nations, even if such action was not required directly for self defense.

REFERENCES:

Ando, Nisuke. *Surrender, Occupation, and Private Property in International Law: An Evaluation of U.S. Practice in Japan.* Oxford, UK: Clarendon Press, 1991.

Butow, R. C. *Japan's Decision to Surrender.* Palo Alto, CA: Stanford University Press, 1954.

Finn, Richard B. *Winners in Peace: MacArthur, Yoshida, and Postwar Japan.* Berkeley: University of California Press, 1992.

Grenville, J. A. S. *The Major International Treaties 1914-1973: A History Guide with Texts.* New York: Stein and Day, 1974.

Mutual Weapons Development Program (with Australia)

SIGNED: August 23, 1960, at Washington, D.C.

SIGNATORIES: Australia vs. United States

IN FORCE: From signing

OVERVIEW: An agreement with Australia to engage in a Mutual Weapons Development Program financed by the United States.

DISCUSSION:

Although the agreement inaugurates a "Mutual Weapons Development Program," the document is, first and foremost, a military assistance agreement in which the United States undertakes to provide "financial and technical assistance." Australia, on its part, undertakes to "accept and make effective use of any assistance received . . . in order to press forward with the agreed projects." All proprietary rights relating to military articles produced under the program shall be available to the United States without cost. Items that may be produced by Australia as a result of the program will be made "available for use by the Armed Forces of the United States and to such other countries of the free world as may be agreed upon . . . at reasonable prices and on equitable terms and conditions."

On its part, Australia undertakes the following:

- To "join in promoting international understanding . . . good will . . . and . . . world peace"
- To "take such action as may be mutually agreed upon to eliminate causes of international tension"
- To fulfill military obligations assumed under various treaties
- To make "the full contribution" possible to "the development and maintenance of its own defensive strength and the defensive strength of the free world"
- To maintain the "security of any article, service, or information furnished under this Agreement"
- To permit "continuous observation and review [by the United States] of this program"

REFERENCE:

U.S. Department of Defense: *Mutual Weapons Development Program.* Washington, D.C.: U.S. Government Printing Office, 1960.

Agreement (with France) Relating to a Weapons Production Program

OFFICIAL TITLE: Exchange of Notes Constituting an Agreement Relating to a Weapons Production Program

SIGNED: September 19, 1960, at Paris

SIGNATORIES: France vs. United States

IN FORCE: From signing

OVERVIEW: An agreement for French participation in producing, maintaining, repairing, and overhauling United States military equipment and articles used in fulfilment of U.S. NATO obligations.

DISCUSSION:

With a view to increasing the capacity of NATO "to produce, maintain, repair, and overhaul military material and equipment needed for . . . mutual defense," the United States concluded Weapons Production Program agreements with all NATO member nations, including this representative agreement with France.

The major principles of the agreement are as follows:

- The United States will furnish assistance (equipment, materials, and services) to France to increase its capacity to produce, maintain, repair, and overhaul military material and equipment.
- Projects for which assistance will be granted may include NATO projects as well as projects carried out exclusively by France.
- Projects may include "joint projects of coordinated production."
- France will make available to NATO members the military products and services it produces under this program "at fair and reasonable prices, and will not discriminate among such nations, especially as regards prices, quality, or time for delivery, manufacture or repair."
- With regard to its military products and services, France will grant NATO member nations other considerations, including customs and tax exemptions.
- France will not transfer to any third party military materials to which the United States has contributed either directly or indirectly.
- France will not transfer to any third party classified matter.
- To the extent possible, France will furnish to the United States, without cost, "technical information . . . arising out of the production, maintenance, repair or overhaul . . . of military items covered by the 'Weapons Production Program.'"
- France will grant the United States royalty-free license on inventions "made in connection with work carried out under the 'Weapons Production Program.'"

REFERENCE:

Young, John W. France, *The Cold War, and the Western Alliance, 1944-49: French Foreign Policy and Post-war Europe.* Leicester, UK: Leicester University Press, 1990.

Agreement Relating to a United States-Danish Committee on Greenland Projects

SIGNED: December 2, 1960, at Washington, D.C.

SIGNATORIES: Denmark vs. United States

IN FORCE: From singing

OVERVIEW: An agreement with Denmark creating a Consultative Committee to enable U.S.-Danish collaboration on mutual defense projects in Greenland.

DISCUSSION:

Greenland is a Danish dependency (granted home rule in 1979) whose location makes it a vital platform for hemispherical defense installations. As early as the middle 1950s, it played a part in the DEW (Defense Early Warning) Line, and in 1960, this agreement upgraded collaboration between Denmark and the United States by creating the Consultative Committee to extend and modernize DEW Line facilities and discuss additional defense-related projects for the territory on an ongoing basis.

REFERENCE:

Danish Institute of International Affairs. *Greenland During the Cold War: Danish and American Security Policy 1945-68.* Copenhagen: Danish Institute of International Affairs, 1997.

Declaration on the Neutrality of Laos

SIGNED: July 23, 1962, at Geneva, Switzerland

SIGNATORIES: Burma, Cambodia, Canada, Democratic Republic of Viet-Nam, France, India, People's Republic of China, Poland, Republic of Viet-Nam, Thailand, Union of Soviet Socialist Republics, United Kingdom, United States

IN FORCE: From signing

OVERVIEW: A declaration of Laotian neutrality as part of an agreement to end civil war in Laos and bring peace to Southeast Asia.

DISCUSSION:

After French rule in Indochina ended in 1954, a conference among nations including France, Great Britain, the United States, China, and the Soviet Union held at Geneva agreed that all of Laos should be governed by the royal Laotian government and not be partitioned (as Vietnam was, into North and South). Nevertheless, two so-called "regroupment zones" were allowed in Laotian provinces adjacent to North Vietnam to allow the communist Pathet Lao forces to assemble. The result was a de facto partition of the country into a communist north and royalist, pro-Western south. In 1959, these two factions went to war, and a new Geneva conference was called in May 1961. It produced, the following year, a Declaration on the Neutrality of Laos, calling for the neutralization of the nation, accompanied by a new tripartite division of government, consisting of elements from the left—the Pathet Lao (linked to North Vietnam), the right (linked to Thailand and friendly to the United States), and the true neutrals (led by Prince Souvanna Phouma).

The substance of the agreement is the neutrality declaration of the Royal Government of Laos and attested to by the signatory nations; however, the cease-fire created by the agreement was brief, as the uneasy tripartite coalition violently split apart in 1964, involving Laos, as well as Cambodia, in the escalating Vietnam War.

REFERENCES:

Lind, Michael. Vietnam: *The Necessary War.* New York: Free Press, 1999.

Logevall, Fredrik. *Choosing War: The Lost Chance for Peace and the Escalation of War.* Berkeley: University of California Press, 1999.

Polaris Sales Agreement (with United Kingdom)

SIGNED: April 6, 1963, at Washington, D.C.

SIGNATORIES: United Kingdom vs. United States

IN FORCE: From signing

OVERVIEW: The United States agrees to sell submarine-launched Polaris missiles (less nuclear warheads) to the United Kingdom.

DISCUSSION:

Introduced in 1960, the Polaris was the United States' first submarine-launched ballistic missile and, sold to the Royal Navy, became the principal component of the British nuclear deterrent force through the 1970s and well into the 1980s. The Polaris was designed to be launched from submerged nuclear-powered submarines, which carried sixteen missiles each. The earliest model, A-1, had a range of 1,400 miles and carried a one-megaton nuclear warhead. The range was increased to 1,700-miles in the model A-2, and to 2,800 miles in the A-3, which carried multiple (three) 200-kiloton warheads.

The agreement called for the United Kingdom to purchase an unspecified quantity of missiles and a full range of supporting equipment as well as advisory expertise.

REFERENCE:

DiCerto, J. J. *Missile Base Beneath the Sea; the Story of Polaris.* New York, St. Martin's, 1967.

Hot Line Memorandum

OFFICIAL TITLE: Memorandum of Understanding between the United States of America and the Union of Soviet Socialist Republics Regarding the Establishment of a Direct Communications Link

SIGNED: June 20, 1963, at Geneva

SIGNATORIES: U.S.S.R. vs United States

IN FORCE: From June 20, 1963

OVERVIEW: "For use in time of emergency the Government of the United States of America and the Government of the Union of Soviet Socialist Republics have agreed to establish as soon as technically feasible a direct communications link between the two Governments."

DISCUSSION:

The "Hot Line Memorandum" was the result of recognition that timely communication could reduce the danger that accident, miscalculation, or surprise attack might trigger a nuclear war. The Cuban Missile Crisis of October 1962, in which the United States and the Soviet Union met on the verge of thermonuclear war over the issue of Soviet missile bases erected in Cuba, emphasized the importance of efficient and direct communication between heads of state.

The 1963 memorandum detailed responsibility for a continuously available emergency link between the White House and the Kremlin. An annex to the memorandum set forth the technical details, specifying:

- Two terminal points with teletype equipment
- A full-time duplex wire telegraph circuit: Washington-London-Copenhagen-Stockholm-Helsinki-Moscow
- A full-time duplex radiotelegraph circuit: Washington-Tangier-Moscow

Not only has the "Hot Line" proved valuable in times of crisis (as in explaining United States deployments during the Arab-Israeli wars of 1967 and 1973), it was the first bilateral agreement between the United States and the Soviet Union to address and attempt to cope with the perils of the modern nuclear world.

The "Hot Line" agreement has been updated and modernized 1971, 1984, and 1988 to reflect technological improvements, including satellite communication and fax capability.

REFERENCE:
Fursenko, A. A. *One Hell of a Gamble: Khrushchev, Castro, and Kennedy, 1958-1964.* New York: Norton, 1997.

Agreement (with Canada) on Civil Emergency Planning and Civil Defense

OFFICIAL TITLE: Exchange of Notes Constituting an Agreement Relating to Civil Emergency Planning and Civil Defense Matters
SIGNED: November 15, 1963, at Ottawa
SIGNATORIES: Canada vs. United States
IN FORCE: From signing
OVERVIEW: An agreement to establish direct, ongoing liaison between the United States and Canada in matters of civil defense.

DISCUSSION:

This is one of several defense-related agreements during the Cold War period between the United States and its neighbor to the north. The agreement establishes a "Joint United States-Canada Civil Emergency Planning Committee with responsibility for making recommendations to the two Governments ... concerning plans and arrangements for cooperation and mutual assistance between the civil authorities of the two countries in the event of an attack on either country." The committee is to include, as ex officio members, the secretary of the Cabinet of Canada, the director of the Emergency Measures Organization of Canada, the director of the Office of Emergency Planning of the United States, the assistant secretary of Defense (Civil Defense) of the United States, in addition to others "as may be designated from time to time."

One of the chief tasks of the committee is to "arrange for direct communication between such national authorities of Canada and of the United States as the Committee considers to be concerned with aspects of civil emergency planning in either country likely to be directly affected by comparable planning in the other."

REFERENCE:
Crosby, Ann Denholm. *Dilemmas in Defense Decision-Making: Constructing Canada's Role in NORAD, 1958-96.* New York: St. Martin's, 1998.

NATO Agreement on Cooperation Regarding Atomic Information

OFFICIAL TITLE: Agreement between the Parties to the North Atlantic Treaty for Cooperation Regarding Atomic Information
SIGNED: June 18, 1964, at Paris
SIGNATORIES: Belgium, Canada, Denmark, France, Germany (Federal Republic), Greece, Iceland, Italy, Luxembourg, Netherlands, Norway, Portugal, Turkey, United Kingdom, United States
IN FORCE: From March 12, 1965
OVERVIEW: An agreement among NATO members to share atomic information "to make substantial and material contributions to the mutual defense and security."

DISCUSSION:

The United States, reciprocally with the other NATO members, agrees to communicate atomic information in the following areas:

- Development of defense plans
- Training of personnel in the employment of and defense against atomic weapons
- Evaluation of capabilities of potential enemies in the deployment of atomic weapons
- Development of new weapons delivery systems

The agreement concludes with provisions designed to maintain "full security protection" of atomic information.

REFERENCE:
Kaplan, Lawrence. *The Long Entanglement: NATO's First Fifty Years.* New York: Praeger, 1999.

Agreement (with Canada) on Cooperation on Civil Emergency Planning

OFFICIAL TITLE: Exchange of Notes Constituting an Agreement on Cooperation on Civil Emergency Planning (with Annex)
SIGNED: August 8, 1967, at Ottawa
SIGNATORIES: Canada vs. United States
IN FORCE: From signing
OVERVIEW: An agreement "improving" cooperation between Canada and the United States in civil emergency planning.

DISCUSSION:

This convention replaces **Agreement (with Canada) on Civil Emergency Planning and Civil Defense** of 1963 and provides more detailed guidance to assist the Joint United States-Canada Civil Emergency Planning Committee. An annex subjoined to the agreement lists specific principles to be observed by the Committee.

REFERENCE:
Crosby, Ann Denholm. *Dilemmas in Defense Decision-Making: Constructing Canada's Role in NORAD, 1958-96.* New York: St. Martin's, 1998.

Agreement for Disposal in Viet-Nam by the United States of Excess Personal Property in the Possession of Military Authorities

OFFICIAL TITLE: Exchange of Notes Constituting an Agreement for the Disposal in Viet-Nam by the United States of Excess Personal Property in the Possession of Military Authorities of the Government of the United States
SIGNED: November 9, 1968, at Saigon, Republic of Vietnam (South Vietnam)
SIGNATORIES: Republic of Vietnam vs. United States
IN FORCE: From signing
OVERVIEW: An agreement to "dispose of" (donate) excess personal property located in the Republic of Vietnam.

DISCUSSION:
This agreement, concluded in 1968, attests to the growing magnitude of the United States presence in South Vietnam. Recognizing that retrieval and return of the "excess" personal property of thousands of United States military personnel would be burdensome, American authorities concluded an agreement to dispose of property "which is or will become excess" by "sale, donation or abandonment." The government of the Republic of Vietnam would have the priority right to purchase property listed for sale as "prices and terms to be mutually agreed upon." Absent such purchase, the property would be auctioned. Funds from the sale of excess property may be used by the United States government for any and all purposes.

Property deemed not to have commercial value may be donated or abandoned, provided that such property is not harmful.

REFERENCES:
Lind, Michael. *Vietnam: The Necessary War.* New York: Free Press, 1999.
Logevall, Fredrik. *Choosing War: The Lost Chance for Peace and the Escalation of War.* Berkeley: University of California Press, 1999.

Understanding Relating to an M-16 Rifle Program in Korea

SIGNED: March 31, 1971, at Seoul, Republic of Korea, and April 22, 1971, at Washington, D.C.
SIGNATORIES: Republic of Korea vs. United States
IN FORCE: From April 22, 1971
OVERVIEW: An agreement to establish an M-16 rifle production facility in South Korea pursuant to the **Mutual Defense Agreement (with South Korea)** of 1950.

DISCUSSION:
The M-16 has long been the standard U.S. Army infantry rifle. The facility to be established in South Korea is to produce 600,000 M-16s over a six-year period for use by South Korean defense forces. The United States is to provide financing in the amount of $72,600,000 for construction and start-up of the facility.

REFERENCE:
Kim, Hyun-Dong. *Korea and the United States: The Evolving Transpacific Alliance in the 1960s.* Seoul, South Korea: Research Center for Peace and Unification of Korea, 1990.

Quadripartite Agreement (on Berlin)

SIGNED: September 3, 1971, "in the building formerly occupied by the Allied Control Council in the American Sector of Berlin"
SIGNATORIES: France, Union of Soviet Socialist Republics, United Kingdom, United States
IN FORCE: From June 3, 1972
OVERVIEW: An agreement to "strive to promote the elimination of tension and the prevention of complications in [divided Berlin]."

DISCUSSION:
For the historical background of this document, see **Agreements on Germany (France, U.K., U.S.)**.

Since its division in 1945 into sectors controlled by the Western allies and a zone controlled by the Soviets, the city of Berlin, which lay well within Soviet-controlled eastern Germany—and, later, the Soviet satellite nation, East Germany—was a postwar flashpoint. In 1948, after the Western allies announced their intention of supporting the creation of a democratic West Germany, the Soviets blockaded West Berlin, prompting the United States to initiate the great and greatly hazardous Berlin airlift.

During the 1950s and 1960s, as the barbed-wire barricades dividing West and East Berlin grew into a heavily guarded wall and an ugly symbol of the grim Cold War division between a "free world" and a communist world. Even more dangerously, through much of the Cold War period, tensions created by a divided Berlin threatened to explode into a larger war—perhaps a thermonuclear war. Yet it was not until 1971, at the beginning of the Cold War thaw known as detente, that the governments of the West and the Soviet Union made a concerted effort to reduce tensions in Berlin with the Quadripartite Agreement. Its chief "General Provisions" are as follows:

1. The four Government will strive to promote the elimination of tension and the prevention of complications in the relevant area.

2. The four Governments, taking into account their obligations under the Charter of the United Nations, agree that there shall be no use or threat of force in the area and that disputes shall be settled solely by peaceful means.

3. The four Governments will mutually respect their individual and joint rights and responsibilities, which remain unchanged.

4. The four Governments agree that, irrespective of the differences in legal views, the situation which has developed in the area, and as it is defined in this Agreement as well as in the other agreements referred to in this Agreement, shall not be changed unilaterally.

Part II of the Agreement includes "Provisions Relating to the Western Sectors of Berlin" and specifies that the Soviet Union would never again imposed a blockade. Annex I, subjoined to the agreement, specifies in detail "Arrangements concerning civilian traffic" to and from Western Berlin. On their part, the French, British, and American governments "declare that the ties between the Western Sectors of Berlin and the Federal Republic of Germany [West Germany] will be maintained and developed, taking into account that these Sectors continue not to be a constituent part of the Federal Republic of Germany and not to be governed by it." Annex II specifies "detailed arrangements concerning the relationship between the Western Sectors of Berlin and the Federal Republic of Germany."

Perhaps the most important provision of the agreement is the following:

The Government of the Union of Soviet Socialist Republics declares that communications between the Wester Sectors of Berlin and areas bordering on these Sectors and those areas of the German Democratic Republic [East Germany] which do no border on these Sectors will be improved. Permanent residents of the Western Sectors of Berlin will be able to travel to and visit such areas for compassionate, family, religious, cultural or commercial reasons, or as tourists, under conditions comparable to those applying to other persons entering these areas.

Although it was restricted to visits from the West to the East— East Berliners were still not permitted to corss into the West— this was the first relaxation of travel into East Berlin since the division of the city. It was a hopeful sign of an improvement in East-West relations.

REFERENCES:

Giangreco, D. M., and Robert E. Griffin. *Airbridge to Berlin: The Berlin Crisis of 1948.* Novato, CA: Presidio Press, 1988.

Grathwol, Robert P. *Berlin and the American Military: A Cold War Chronicle,* 2d ed. New York: New York University Press, 1999.

Grenville, J. A. S. *The Major International Treaties 1914-1973: A History Guide with Texts* (New York: Stein and Day, 1974.

Haydock, Michael D. City Under Siege: *The Berlin Blockade and Airlift, 1948-49.* Washington, D.C.: Brasseys, 1999.

Morris, Eric. *Blockade: Berlin and the Cold War.* New York: Stein and Day, 1973.

Agreement (with Nicaragua) Regarding Deposits for Military Assistance

OFFICIAL TITLE: Exchange of Notes Constituting an Agreement Regarding Deposits for Military Assistance under the Foreign Assistance Act of 1971
SIGNED: March 6 and April 10, 1972, at Managua, Nicaragua
SIGNATORIES: Nicaragua vs. United States
IN FORCE: Retroactively from February 7, 1972
OVERVIEW: An agreement whereby Nicaragua undertakes to pay to the United States 10 percent of the value of military assistance and defense articles provided by the United States.

DISCUSSION:

For the background of United States military aid to Nicaragua, see **Bilateral Military Assistance Agreement (with Nicaragua).** This agreement was made pursuant to United States legislation, the Foreign Assistance Act of 1971, which mandated payment of 10 percent of the value of military assistance and "defense articles" supplied by the United States to other nations. The agreement calls for the deposit of "no more than 20 million Nicaraguan *cordobas*" in a designated account "for deliveries in any one United States fiscal year."

REFERENCES:
None.

Paris Peace Accords

SIGNED: January 27, 1973, at Paris
IN FORCE: A cease-fire nominally came into force on January 28, 1973, but fighting continued.
SIGNATORIES: United States, Republic of Vietnam (South Vietnam), Democratic Republic of Vietnam (North Vietnam), Provisional Revolutionary Government of the Republic of South Vietnam
OVERVIEW: The Paris Peace Accords, result of a protracted series of peace conferences held in Paris, brought a nominal cease-fire in one of the longest, costliest, and most divisive wars in American history.

DISCUSSION:

United States involvement in what was essentially a civil war between North and South Vietnam began in the 1950s, when President Dwight Eisenhower sent military advisors to assist French forces in the region. The involvement deepened during the administration of John F. Kennedy and became a major military commitment under Lyndon B. Johnson after the Gulf of Tonkin Resolution was passed in 1964. In the fall of 1968, at the height of the U.S. presence in the war (approximately a half-million military personnel) and in the face of the war's growing unpopularity among increasing numbers of Americans, the Johnson administration agreed to meet representatives of the North Vietnamese in a series of peace talks in Paris. The talks dragged, were repeatedly stalemated, and broke down entirely in December 1972. President Richard M. Nixon—the fourth commander in chief to be burdened with the war—ordered intensive bombing of Hanoi and other North Vietnamese cities, a campaign that brought North Vietnamese negotiators back to the peace table. An agreement emerged on January 27, 1973, consisting of a preamble, twenty-three articles, and four protocols. The major points are these:

- Article 1 states, "The United States and all other countries respect the independence, sovereignty, unity and territorial integrity of Vietnam as recognized by the 1954 Geneva Agreements on Vietnam."

These Geneva agreements had ended the war between France and the independence-seeking Viet Minh, ending French colonial control over Vietnam. The agreements stipulated that free elections would be held throughout Vietnam in 1956 to reunify North and South Vietnam under a single popularly elected government. South Vietnamese president Ngo Dihm Diem, believing that the elections would make North Vietnam's leader Ho Chi Minh president of a unified Vietnam, refused to hold the scheduled elections. President Eisenhower, motivated by a desire to "contain" the spread of communism in Indochina, supported Diem's position. Guerilla warfare intensified into a full-scale war between the North and South.

- Articles 2 and 3 proclaim a cease-fire, "durable and without limit of time," to commence at midnight of January 27, 1973.
- Articles 4 through 6 pledge and detail United States withdrawal from South Vietnam.
- Article 8 deals with the return of prisoners of war and for cooperation in determining the status of those missing in action.
- All of Chapter IV addresses the exercise of the South Vietnamese people's right to self-determination, specifying that the "South Vietnamese people shall decide themselves the political future of South Vietnam through genuinely free and democratic general elections under international supervision."
- All of Chapter V addresses the reunification of Vietnam, specifying that it was to be "carried out ... through peaceful means on the basis of discussions and agreements between North and South Vietnam, without coercion or annexation by either part, and without foreign interference. The time for reunification will be agreed upon by North and South Vietnam."
- All of Chapter VI is devoted to setting up a four-party military commission, consisting of representatives of the signatories, to implement the cease-fire, troop withdrawal, dismantlement of bases, and return of prisoners of war. The military commission would work with an International

Commission of Control, consisting of representatives of nations not directly involved in the conflict, who would ensure that the provisions of the peace accords were carried out satisfactorily and faithfully.

- Articles in Chapter VII pledge an end to military activity in Laos and Cambodia, and affirmed the sovereignty and rights of those nations.
- In Chapter VIII, Articles 21 and 22 define the relationship between North Vietnam and the United States, which notes its "anticipation [of] an era of reconciliation" and declares that, "in pursuance of traditional policy, the United States will contribute to healing the wounds of war and to post-war reconstruction" of North Vietnam.
- The final chapter provides for the agreement's immediate entry into force.

Both the North Vietnamese and the South Vietnamese (still backed by American aid) repeatedly violated the cease-fire, and the United States continued to bomb Cambodia and resumed reconnaissance flights over North Vietnam. At home, however, President Nixon was in the throes of the Watergate Scandal, and, with the president weakened and preoccupied, Congress passed legislation requiring the cessation of all military operations in and over Indochina by August 15, 1973. In November 1973, Congress passed the War Powers Act, requiring the president to inform Congress within forty-eight hours of deployment of U.S. military forces abroad and, in the absence of Congressional approval, mandating the withdrawal of troops within sixty days. These two acts of Congress assured an end to American involvement in Indochina. Despite them, South Vietnam planned new offensives, which, without American aid, failed, and the North ultimately routed the unsupported South Vietnamese forces. South Vietnamese president Nguyen Van Thieu resigned office and fled, leaving Duong Van Minh to become president just long enough to surrender unconditionally to the North on April 30, 1975. The United States has concluded no definitive peace treaty with the reunified Vietnam.

REFERENCES:

Herring, George. *America's Longest War: The United States and Vietnam, 1950-1975*. New York: McGraw-Hill College Division, 1996.

McCormick, Thomas, et al, eds. *America in Vietnam: A Documentary History*. New York: W. W. Norton, 1989.

Rengger, N. J. *Treaties and Alliances of the World*, 5th ed. Harlow, UK: Longman Group, 1990.

Agreement (with United Kingdom) Concerning the Lease of Land to the U.S. Navy

OFFICIAL TITLE: Exchange of Notes Constituting an Agreement Concerning the Lease of a Parcel of Land in the British Virgin

Islands for Use by the United States Navy as a Drone Launching Facility

SIGNED: February 1, 1973, at Washington, D.C.

SIGNATORIES: British Virgin Islands and United Kingdom vs. United States

IN FORCE: From signing

OVERVIEW: An agreement to lease approximately six acres in the British Virgin Islands to the U.S. Navy for use as a drone launching facility.

DISCUSSION:

Under the aegis of the **North Atlantic Treaty**, the United States Navy leased, by this agreement, six acres on Anegada Island for use as a drone launching facility. Drones are pilotless aircraft used as aerial targets in target-practice exercises.

REFERENCES:
None

Agreement (with Canada) Relating to Liability for Loss or Damage from Certain Rocket Launches

OFFICIAL TITLE: Exchange of Notes Constituting an Agreement Relating to Liability for Loss or Damage from Certain Rocket Launches (with Enclosure)

SIGNED: December 31, 1974, at Ottawa

SIGNATORIES: Canada vs. United States

IN FORCE: From signing

OVERVIEW: A pledge by the United States to assume liability for any damage that might be caused from the launch of "two Black Brant rockets from the DEW [Defense Early Warning] Station at Cape Parry, Northwest Territory, Canada, in early January 1975."

DISCUSSION:

The agreement affirms the United States' intention to "comply fully with its obligation under the **Treaty of Principles Governing the Activities of States in the Exploration and Use of Outer Space**."

REFERENCE:
Crosby, Ann Denholm. *Dilemmas in Defense Decision-Making: Constructing Canada's Role in NORAD, 1958-96.* New York: St. Martin's, 1998.

Agreement (with Nicaragua) Relating to Military Assistance Payments under Foreign Assistance Act of 1973

Official title: Exchange of Notes Constituting an Agreement

Relating to Military Assistance Payments under Foreign Assistance Act of 1973

SIGNED: May 15 and June 28, 1974, at Managua, Nicaragua

SIGNATORIES: Nicaragua vs. United States

IN FORCE: From July 1, 1974

OVERVIEW: An agreement whereby Nicaragua undertakes to repay to the United States any net proceeds from the sale of defense supplies received from the United States.

DISCUSSION:

For the background of United States military aid to Nicaragua, see **Bilateral Military Assistance Agreement (with Nicaragua)**. This agreement was made pursuant to United States legislation, the Foreign Assistance Act of 1973, which required states receiving military aid from the United States to turn over to the United States net proceeds from any sale of surplus equipment supplied. Moreover, the agreement stipulates that such proceeds may be used to finance other, non-military, United States foreign aid programs to Nicaragua:

In accordance with the new statutory provision, it is proposed that the Government of Nicaragua agree that the net proceeds of sale received by the Government of Nicaragua in disposing of any weapon, weapons system, munition, aircraft, military boat, military vessel, or other defense article, including scrap from any such defense articles, received heretofore or hereafter under the Military Assistance Program of the United States Government will be paid to the United States Government and shall be available to pay all official costs of the United States Government payable in currency of the Government of Nicaragua, including all costs relating to the financing of international educational and cultural exchange activities in which the Government of Nicaragua participates.

REFERENCE:
Morley, Morris H. *Washington, Somoza, and the Sandinistas: State and Regime in U.S. Policy Toward Nicaragua, 1969-1981.* New York: Cambridge University Press, 1994.

U.S.-Kuwait Defense Agreement

SIGNED: February 24 and April 15, 1975

SIGNATORIES: Kuwait vs. United States

IN FORCE: From dates (above) of exchange of notes

OVERVIEW: An agreement by which Kuwait may procure from the United States defense articles and services.

DISCUSSION:

Although this exchange of notes does not obligate the United States to defend Kuwait, it did serve, in part, as a basis for the United States' defense of Kuwait against Iraqi aggression in the Gulf War of 1990-1991. The agreement made it possible for Kuwait to purchase equipment as well as limited defense-related services. It also established a United States military liaison office in Kuwait.

REFERENCE:
Joyce, Miriam. *Kuwait 1945-1996: An Anglo-American Perspective.* Ilford, UK: Frank Cass, 1998.

Agreement (with Canada) Concerning NORAD

OFFICIAL TITLE: Exchange of Notes Constituting an Agreement Concerning the Organization and Operation of the North American Air Defense Command (NORAD)
SIGNED: May 8, 1975, at Washington, D.C.
SIGNATORIES: Canada vs. United States
IN FORCE: From signing (with effect from May 12, 1975)
OVERVIEW: A revision of the 1958 **Agreement (with Canada) Relating to North American Air Defense Command** to reflect new weapon technologies.

DISCUSSION:
"In the years since the NORAD Agreement was first concluded [in 1958]," the introductory portion of the agreement declares, "there have been significant changes in the character of strategic weapons and in the nature of threat they pose to North America. The most important of these changes has been the major increase in the number and sophistication of strategic missiles.... [W]hile long-range bombers continue to pose a threat to North America, missiles now constitute the principal threat."

The 1975 agreement renews and revises the 1958 agreement, placing special emphasis on maintaining a close working relationship between Canada and the United States "to safeguard the sovereignty of [their] airspace."

REFERENCE:
Crosby, Ann Denholm. *Dilemmas in Defense Decision-Making: Constructing Canada's Role in NORAD, 1958-96.* New York: St. Martin's, 1998.

Memorandum of Mapping, Charting, and Geodesy Arrangements (with Mexico)

OFFICIAL TITLE: Memorandum of Mapping, Charting, and Geodesy Arrangements between the Defense Mapping Agency, the United States Department of Defense, and the Commission on Studies of the National Territory of Mexico
SIGNED: July 25, 1975, at Mexico City
SIGNATORIES: Mexico vs. United States
IN FORCE: From signing
OVERVIEW: An agreement between the Defense Mapping Agency (United States) and the Commission on Studies of the National Territory (Mexico) "concerning cooperation and mutual assistance in mapping, charting and geodesy, as well as the exchange of maps, charts, and related data."

DISCUSSION:
The cooperation agreed to in this document relates to the mutual defense requirements of Mexico and the United States; however, in contrast to the program of cooperation concluded in **Mapping, Charting and Geodesy Agreement (with Canada)**, the objective of cooperation also includes "the purpose of promoting better understanding between" Mexico and the United States.

REFERENCES:
None

Protocol of Amendment to the Rio Treaty

OFFICIAL TITLE: Protocol of Amendment to the Inter-American Treaty of Reciprocal Assistance (Rio Treaty)
SIGNED: July 26, 1975, at San Jose, Costa Rica
SIGNATORIES: Argentina, Bolivia, Brazil, Chile, Colombia, Costa Rica, Dominican Republic, Ecuador, El Salvador, Guatemala, Haiti, Honduras, Mexico, Nicaragua, Panama, Paraguay, Peru, Trinidad and Tobago, United States, Uruguay, Venezuela
IN FORCE: "When two thirds of the signatory states have deposited their instruments of ratification" (not yet in force)
OVERVIEW: An amendment to the OAS **Rio Treaty of Reciprocal Assistance** of 1947, emphasizing the principles of nonintervention and sovereignty.

DISCUSSION:
A substantial revision of the Rio Treaty of 1947, a hemispherical defense agreement, was opened to signature in 1975. It remains open to signature and ratification, but its entry into force is still pending ratification by two-thirds of the membership of the Organization of American States.

The proposed modifications to the original agreement emphasize the following:

- A condemnation, in principle, of war
- A pledge to "make every effort" to settle disputes within the hemisphere by peaceful means
- A reaffirmation that armed attack against any signatory shall be considered an attack against all signatories
- A reaffirmation that, in an emergency, signatory states may take immediate action, even in the absence of authorization by the Organ of Consultation provided for in the treaty
- A provision for coordinating action with that of the Security Council of the United Nations
- A precise definition of the territory to which the Rio Treaty applies
- An enumeration of acts constituting "aggression"

REFERENCES:
None

Memorandum of Understanding (with the United Kingdom) Relating to Defense Equipment

OFFICIAL TITLE: Memorandum of Understanding Relating to the Principles Governing Cooperation in Research and Development, Production, and Procurement of Defense Equipment

SIGNED: September 24, 1975, at London

SIGNATORIES: United Kingdom vs. United States

IN FORCE: From signing

OVERVIEW: In accordance with NATO regulations, an agreement setting out "the guiding principles governing mutual cooperation in defense equipment production and purchasing."

DISCUSSION:

The memorandum lays down principles to guide cooperation between the United Kingdom and the United States in developing, producing, and procuring defense equipment pursuant to the alliance of the two nations under NATO. The major principles are as follows:

- The governments will provide appropriate policy guidance and administrative procedures.
- The governments "will identify and nominate for consideration by each other items of defense equipment believed suitable to satisfy their respective requirements."
- Equitable and efficient procurement and bidding procedures will be established and maintained.
- The governments will exchange technical information, as necessary.
- The governments will coordinate the requirements of the agreement with industries in their countries.

An appendix lays down detailed procedures for securing and evaluating bids from suppliers.

REFERENCES:
None

Memorandum of Agreement (with Israel) Concerning Middle East Peace

OFFICIAL TITLE: Memorandum of Agreement Concerning Assurances, Consultations, and United States Policy on Matters Related to Middle East Peace

SIGNED: February 27, 1976, at Jerusalem and at Washington

SIGNATORIES: Israel vs. United States

IN FORCE: From signing

OVERVIEW: An agreement whereby the United States undertakes to provide confidence-building assistance to Israel in support of the Egypt-Israel Agreement initialed on September 1, 1975, initiating the Egyptian-Israeli peace process.

DISCUSSION:

For a discussion of the background of the United States role in the peace negotiations between Egypt and Israel, see **Egyptian-Israeli Peace Treaty**, and for a discussion of the United States' role in supporting Israel after signature of that 1979 treaty, see **Memorandum of Agreement (with Israel) Concerning Assurances Relating to Middle East Peace.**

In an effort to facilitate the Israeli-Egyptian peace process, the United States pledged ongoing support to Israel as a confidence-building measure to ensure that Israel would not be militarily vulnerable to violations of the preliminary Egypt-Israel Agreement. The United States undertook the following:

- To make "every effort to be fully responsive ...on an on-going and long-term basis to Israel's military equipment and other defense requirements, to its energy requirements and to its economic needs"
- To consult on Israel's long-term military needs
- To provide certain guarantees to ensure Israel's long-term supply of oil
- To formulate a joint military contingency plan
- To affirm support of the Egypt-Israel Agreement
- To help guarantee freedom of navigation
- To fulfill its role of military aid, even if the United Nations Emergency Force or any other United Nations organ in withdrawn from the region

The memorandum of agreement was partially terminated and superceded by **Memorandum of Agreement (with Israel) Concerning Assurances Relating to Middle East Peace** of 1979, following the conclusion of the definitive **Egyptian-Israeli Peace Treaty** of 1978.

REFERENCE:
Moore, John Norton. *The Arab-Israeli Conflict: The Difficult Search for Peace (1975-1988).* Princeton, NJ: Princeton University Press, 1992.

Agreement (with Indonesia) Relating to Military Assistance

OFFICIAL TITLE: Exchange of Notes Constituting an Agreement Relating to Military Assistance: Eligibility Requirements Pursuant to the International Security Assistance and Arms Export Control Act of 1976

SIGNED: August 3 and 24, 1976, at Jakarta, Indonesia

SIGNATORIES: Indonesia vs. Untied States

IN FORCE: From August 24, 1976

OVERVIEW: An agreement to bring military aid to Indonesia into conformity with United States law.

DISCUSSION:

The United States had been a longtime supplier of military aid to Indonesia when it concluded this agreement pursuant to passage of the International Security Assistance and Arms Export Control Act of 1976. In accordance with the act, the agreement lays down the following:

- That Indonesia will not transfer U.S.-supplied defense articles, services, or training to any third party individual, group, or nation without the permission of the United States
- That Indonesia will not use these for any purposes other than those for which they were furnished
- That Indonesia will maintain the security of all defense articles
- That Indonesia will permit United States observation and supervision of their use
- That, absent other explicit arrangement, Indonesia will return defense articles to the United States when no longer needed

REFERENCES:
None

Mapping, Charting and Geodesy Agreement (with Canada)

SIGNED: August 24, 1976, at Ottawa
SIGNATORIES: Canada vs. United States
IN FORCE: From signing
OVERVIEW: A cartography agreement to facilitate United States-Canada cooperative defense efforts.

DISCUSSION:

Since the years before World War II, the United States and Canada have agreed to coordinate efforts for mutual defense and the defense of the hemisphere. The present agreement outlines a program of cooperation in providing maps, charts, geodetic data, geophysical data, "and related products" to support the requirements of the Canada-United States Basic Security Plan "and other military requirements of agreed mutual concern."

A similar agreement, **Memorandum of Mapping, Charting, and Geodesy Arrangements (with Mexico),** had been concluded with Mexico in 1975.

REFERENCE:
Crosby, Ann Denholm. *Dilemmas in Defense Decision-Making: Constructing Canada's Role in NORAD, 1958-96.* New York: St. Martin's, 1998.

Memorandum of Agreement (with Thailand) Relating to Ammunition Storage

SIGNED: March 22, 1977, at Bangkok, Thailand

SIGNATORIES: Thailand vs. United States
IN FORCE: From signing
OVERVIEW: An agreement to store and to purchase United States ammunition stockpiled in Thailand during the Vietnam War.

DISCUSSION:

With United States involvement in the Vietnam War having ended in 1975, the United States Army and Air Force needed to dispose of "approximately 14,500 short tons" of ammunition stocks stored in Thailand. The Memorandum of Agreement provides for the ongoing storage of the ammunition until the Thai government should consummate purchase of these stocks, on a schedule specified in the memorandum as October 31 of 1977, 1978, and 1979.

REFERENCES:
Lind, Michael. *Vietnam: The Necessary War.* New York: Free Press, 1999.
Logevall, Fredrik. *Choosing War: The Lost Chance for Peace and the Escalation of War.* Berkeley: University of California Press, 1999.

United States-Somalia Defense Agreement

SIGNED: March 22-23 and April 19 and 29, 1978
SIGNATORIES: Somalia vs. United States
IN FORCE: From April 29, 1978
OVERVIEW: An "exchange of notes" concerning the furnishing of defense articles and services to Somalia.

DISCUSSION:

Somalia was one of many African nations once under the colonial control of Europe and now independent, but plagued by such dire poverty that independence had hardly served to set its people free. In 1960, the independent Republic of Somalia was created, but, after its president, Cabdirashiid Cali Sherma'arke, was assassinated in 1969, a military coup led by Major General Maxamed Siyaad Barre replaced parliamentary government with a dictatorial Supreme Revolutionary Council. The new military dictatorship allied itself with the Soviet Union and invaded the Ogaden region of Ethiopia in an attempt to annex the territory. The Soviets rapidly shifted support to Ethiopia, defeating Siyaad's armies and creating chaos in Somalia.

The 1978 exchange of notes between Somalia and the United States served as the immediate basis for emergency military aid (including rifles, ammunition, and communication equipment) sent in 1982 for use against Soviet-backed Ethiopia. Somalia had earlier ordered anti-aircraft guns and radar; delivery was accelerated during the 1982 crisis.

In 1982-1983, United States servicemen took part in joint military exercises with Somali forces, and in 1983 the United States funded and managed a project to improve military facilities at the Red Sea port of Berbera.

In 1991, Siyaad was ousted by an alliance of clan-based rebel groups, which, however, never succeeded in creating a new government. Instead, anarchy reigned in a country of eight million, now shattered into regions controlled by various clans. Warfare became a way of life, and agricultural production, already reeling under a protracted drought, ceased almost entirely. By the early 1990s, some 1.5 million Somalis were starving or close to starvation.

Beginning 1992, President Bill Clinton announced the U.S.-led and U.N.-sanctioned Operation Restore Hope, the purpose of which was to bring humanitarian aid and order to Somalia. By the end of March 1993, much food had been delivered, but U.S. and U.N. troops had not succeeded in disarming the militias of the various warlords. When the most prominent and intractable of them, Muhammad Farah Aydid, stepped up violence, which resulted in the deaths of eighteen U.S. soldiers and the capture of others, American politicians rethought the U.S. presence in the country. United States and United Nations troops withdrew from Somalia in 1995, sparking fears that civil war would be general throughout the land. But, unpredictably, Somalia seemed to return to some semblance of normality, especially after the death of General Aydid in a 1996 battle.

REFERENCE:
Tripodi, Paolo. *The Colonial Legacy in Somalia.* New York: St. Martin's Press, 1999.

Memorandum of Agreement (with Israel) Concerning Assurances Relating to Middle East Peace

SIGNED: March 26, 1979, at Washington, D.C.
SIGNATORIES: Israel vs. United States
IN FORCE: From signing
OVERVIEW: An agreement by which the United States, acknowledging the role it played in the conclusion of the **Egyptian-Israeli Peace Treaty,** undertakes to "take appropriate measures to promote full observation of the Treaty of Peace."

DISCUSSION:
For a discussion of the background of the United States role in the peace negotiations between Egypt and Israel, see **Egyptian-Israeli Peace Treaty** in Section 3.11.

By this memorandum of agreement, the United States undertakes the following:

- To "take appropriate measures to promote full observation of the Treaty of Peace"
- To consult with the parties to the Egyptian-Israeli Peace Treaty in the event of a "violation or threat of violation"
- To employ remedial measures the United States "deems appropriate"

- To support actions taken by Israel in the event of "demonstrated violations"
- To support the signatories' right to navigation and overflight over the Strait of Tiran and Gulf of Aqaba "pursuant to the Treaty of Peace"
- To endeavor "to be responsive to military and economic assistance requirements of Israel"
- To enforce restrictions on weapons supply to nations who threaten Israel

See also **Memorandum of Agreement (with Israel) Concerning Middle East Peace** of 1976, relating to United States support of Israel during negotiations with Egypt.

REFERENCE:
Moore, John Norton. *The Arab-Israeli Conflict: The Difficult Search for Peace (1975-1988).* Princeton, NJ: Princeton University Press, 1992.

Agreement Concerning the Acquisition by the United Kingdom of the Trident I Weapons System

OFFICIAL TITLE: Exchange of Notes Constituting an Agreement Concerning the Acquisition by the United Kingdom of the Trident I Weapons System under the **Polaris Sales Agreement**
SIGNED: September 30, 1980, at Washington, D.C.
SIGNATORIES: United Kingdom vs. United States
IN FORCE: From signing
OVERVIEW: An agreement to deem the **Polaris Sales Agreement (with United Kingdom)** applicable to sales of the Trident I to the U.K.

DISCUSSION:
The submarine-launched Trident I nuclear missile was deployed beginning in 1979 and replaced the Poseidon missile, which, in turn, had replaced the Polaris. The Trident I is a MIRV (multiple independent reentry vehicle) device, which delivers eight *independently targetable* 100-kiloton nuclear warheads to a range of 4,600 miles. Under terms identical to that which had regulated sales of the Polaris missiles to the United Kingdom, the United States sold Trident I missiles for deployment by the Royal Navy.

Also see **Agreement Concerning the Acquisition by the United Kingdom of the Trident II Weapons System.**

REFERENCES:
Paterson, Robert H. *Britain's Strategic Nuclear Deterrent: From Before the V-Bomber to Beyond Trident.* Ilford, UK: Frank Cass and Co., 1997.
Spinardi, Graham. *From Polaris to Trident: The Development of U.S. Fleet Ballistic Missile Technology.* New York: Cambridge University Press, 1994.

Agreement (with Egypt) Concerning Privileges and Immunities of United States Military and Related Personnel

OFFICIAL TITLE: Exchange of Notes Constituting an Agreement Concerning Privileges and Immunities of United States Military and Related Personnel

SIGNED: November 3 and 5, 1980, at Cairo, Egypt

SIGNATORIES: Egypt vs. United States

IN FORCE: From November 5, 1980

OVERVIEW: An agreement pursuant to a joint Egyptian-United States Army and Air Force training exercise.

DISCUSSION:

With the conclusion of the **Egyptian-Israeli Peace Treaty** in 1978, the United States and Egypt became, with Israel, allies with the common purpose of maintaining peace in the region. Accordingly, the United States engaged in military exercises with Egyptian forces. This exchange of notes establishes the legal status of U.S. Army and Air Force personnel while in Egypt, stipulating that these personnel be "accorded the same privileges, immunities and treatment as provided under the exchange of notes dated April 12 and 25, 1974 . . . related to the clearance of mines and unexploded ordnance from the Suez Canal."

REFERENCE:

Moore, John Norton. *The Arab-Israeli Conflict: The Difficult Search for Peace (1975-1988)*. Princeton, NJ: Princeton University Press, 1992.

Memorandum on United States-Israel Strategic Cooperation

OFFICIAL TITLE: Memorandum of Understanding between the Government of the United States and the Government of Israel on Strategic Cooperation

SIGNED: November 30, 1981, at Washington

SIGNATORIES: Israel vs. United States

IN FORCE: From signing

OVERVIEW: An agreement on military cooperation, primarily to deter Soviet threats in the Middle East.

DISCUSSION:

During late 1981, Israel's Defense Minister Ariel Sharon and U.S. Secretary of Defense Caspar Weinberger concluded this memorandum of understanding on strategic cooperation. Their principal objective was to counteract Soviet threats in the Middle East through a program of joint military exercises and planning for the establishment and maintenance of joint readiness activities. The main text of the memorandum follows:

ARTICLE I

United States-Israel strategic cooperation, as set forth in this memorandum, is designed against the threat to peace and security of the region caused by the Soviet Union or Soviet-controlled forces from outside the region introduced into the region. It has the following broad purposes:

A. To enable the parties to act cooperatively and in a timely manner to deal with the above-mentioned threat.

B. To provide each other with military assistance for operations of their forces in the area that may be required to cope with this threat.

C. The strategic cooperation between the parties is not directed at any state or group of states within the region. It is intended solely for defensive purposes against the above-mentioned threat.

ARTICLE II

The fields in which strategic cooperation will be carried out to prevent the above-mentioned threat from endangering the security of the region include:

Military cooperation between the parties, as may be agreed by the parties.

1. Joint military exercise, including naval and air exercises in the Eastern Mediterranean Sea, as agreed upon by the parties.

2. Cooperation for the establishment and maintenance of joint readiness activities, as agreed upon by the parties.

3. Other areas within the basic scope and purpose of this agreement, as may be jointly agreed.

Details of activities within these fields of cooperation shall be worked out by the parties in accordance with the provisions of Article III below. The cooperation will include, as appropriate, planning, preparations, and exercises.

ARTICLE III

The Secretary of Defense and the Minister of Defence shall establish a coordinating council to further the purpose of this memorandum.

To coordinate and provide guidance to joint working groups.

To monitor the implementation of cooperation in the fields agreed upon by the parties within the scope of this agreement.

To hold periodic meetings, in Israel and the United States, for the purposes of discussing and resolving outstanding issues and to further the objectives set forth in this memorandum. Special meetings can be held at the request of either party. The Secretary of Defense and Minister of Defence will chair these meetings whenever possible.

Joint working groups will address the following issues:

Military cooperation between the parties, including joint U.S.-Israel exercises in the Eastern Mediterranean Sea.

Cooperation for the establishment of joint readiness activities including access to maintenance facilities and other infrastructure, consistent with the basic purposes of this agreement.

Cooperation in research and development, building on past cooperation in this area.

Cooperation in defence trade.

Other fields within the basic scope and purpose of this agreement, such as questions of prepositioning, as agreed by the coordinating council.

The future agenda for the work of the joint working groups, their composition and procedures for reporting to the coordinating council shall be agreed upon by the parties.

REFERENCE:

Moore, John Norton. *The Arab-Israeli Conflict: The Difficult Search for Peace (1975-1988)*. Princeton, NJ: Princeton University Press, 1992.

Agreement Concerning the Acquisition by the United Kingdom of the Trident II Weapons System

OFFICIAL TITLE: Exchange of Notes Constituting an Agreement Concerning the Acquisition by the United Kingdom of the Trident II Weapons System under the **Polaris Sales Agreement**

SIGNED: October 19, 1982, at Washington, D.C.

SIGNATORIES: United Kingdom vs. United States

IN FORCE: From signing

OVERVIEW: An agreement to deem the **Polaris Sales Agreement (with United Kingdom)** applicable to sales of the Trident II to the U.K.

DISCUSSION:

The submarine-launched Trident I nuclear missile was deployed beginning in 1979 and replaced the Poseidon missile, which, in turn, had replaced the Polaris. Whereas the Trident I delivered eight *independently targetable* 100-kiloton nuclear warheads to a range of 4,600 miles, the Trident II is capable of carrying ten 475-kiloton warheads 7,000 miles. Under terms identical to that which had regulated sales of the Polaris missiles to the United Kingdom, the United States sold Trident II missiles for deployment by the Royal Navy.

Also see **Agreement Concerning the Acquisition by the United Kingdom of the Trident I Weapons System**.

REFERENCES:

Paterson, Robert H. *Britain's Strategic Nuclear Deterrent: From Before the V-Bomber to Beyond Trident*. Ilford, UK: Frank Cass and Co., 1997.

Spinardi, Graham. *From Polaris to Trident: The Development of U.S. Fleet Ballistic Missile Technology*. New York: Cambridge University Press, 1994.

Agreement Concerning the Test and Evaluation of U.S Defense Systems in Canada

OFFICIAL TITLE: Exchange of Notes Constituting an Agreement Concerning the Test and Evaluation of U.S. Defense Systems in Canada

SIGNED: February 2, 1983, at Washington, D.C.

SIGNATORIES: Canada vs. United States

IN FORCE: From signing

OVERVIEW: An agreement establishing "The Canada/US (CANUS) Test and Evaluation Program."

DISCUSSION:

Conducted under the aegis of NATO, the "T&E Program" established by the agreement was a large-scale test of United States defense systems installed in Canada. Although the agreement gives Canada the right to participate in the tests, the program outlined is essentially a U.S. operation carried out with the permission of Canada in the interest of North American defense. The agreement specifically bars nuclear, biological, and chemical weapons from being brought into Canada. Cruise missiles are to be unarmed. Canadian officials agreed to demarcate specified test areas.

REFERENCE:

Crosby, Ann Denholm. *Dilemmas in Defense Decision-Making: Constructing Canada's Role in NORAD, 1958-96*. New York: St. Martin's, 1998.

Agreement Concerning Possession of Privately Owned Weapons by U.S. Military Personnel in the Federal Republic of Germany

OFFICIAL TITLE: Agreement Concerning the Acquisition and Possession of Privately Owned Weapons by Personnel of the Armed Forces of the United States in the Federal Republic of Germany

SIGNED: November 29, 1984, at Bonn, Federal Republic of Germany

SIGNATORIES: Federal Republic of Germany (West Germany) vs. United States

IN FORCE: From August 18, 1986

OVERVIEW: An agreement to regulate the acquisition and possession of privately owned weapons by U.S. military personnel serving in West Germany.

DISCUSSION:

The agreement specifies that permits and registration certificates issued by the military authorities of the United States in the Federal Republic of Germany to U.S. military personnel "shall be equivalent to the permits which authorize the acquisition and possession of firearms according to the weapons law of the Federal Republic of Germany." The agreement stipulates that military personnel carrying personal weapons will carry their registration certificate and official identity card at all times. Moreover, "The military authorities shall comply with requests from German authorities for withdrawal of registration certificates in individual, well-founded cases." The agreement also includes an annex of excluded personal weapons.

REFERENCES:

Eisenberg, Carolyn Woods. *Drawing the Line: The American Decision to Divide Germany, 1944-1949.* New York: Cambridge University Press, 1996.

Trachtenberg, Marc. *A Constructed Peace: The Making of the European Settlement, 1945-1963.* Princeton, NJ: Princeton University Press, 1999.

Agreement (with Canada) on the Modernization of the North American Air Defense System

OFFICIAL TITLE: Exchange of Letters Constituting an Agreement on the Modernization of the North American Air Defense System (with Memorandum of Understanding)

SIGNED: March 18, 1985, at Quebec

SIGNATORIES: Canada vs. United States

IN FORCE: From signing

OVERVIEW: An agreement to undertake a collaborative program to modernize the North American early warning system.

DISCUSSION:

The agreement recognizes that "major elements of the existing North American Air Defense System . . . established jointly by Canada and the United States during the 1950s . . . are now in the final stages of obsolescence and are proving increasingly expensive to operate and maintain." Moreover, the agreement continues, "our potential adversaries" have increased and improved "their strategic inventory, . . . thereby requiring improved capabilities to detect and deter . . . an attack."

The modernization agreement, concluded pursuant to "mutual defence responsibilities within the North Atlantic Treaty Organization," included installation or upgrading of the following components:

- North Warning System (NWS): 12 long range radar and 39 short range radar stations deployed across northern Alaska and northern Canada
- Over-the-Horizon-Backscatter radar coverage provided from sites located within the United States
- Airborne radar coverage by USAF Airborne Warning and Control System (AWACS) aircraft
- Forward operating locations and dispersed operating bases for AWACS and fighter aircraft at existing airfields in Canada
- Communication upgrades

The agreement details the installation, upgrading, and cooperative operation of all of these defense-system components.

A section on "Financial Responsibilities" lays down the principle that "cost sharing will be effected by allocation of function rather than by reimbursement between the parties." The agreement goes on to detail the cost sharing for each component. Costs for the main fixed component, the North Warning System, are to be shared 60/40 by the United States and Canada, respectively.

REFERENCE:

Crosby, Ann Denholm. *Dilemmas in Defense Decision-Making: Constructing Canada's Role in NORAD, 1958-96.* New York: St. Martin's, 1998.

Diplomacy and International Organizations

SECTION 3.1

Arms Limitation

Overview of Treaties in This Category

Over many years of warfare, most nations of the world informally evolved certain principles of military practice that might loosely be termed the rules of warfare or, to risk oxymoron, the rules of "civilized" warfare (see Section 3.2). It was not until the very end of the nineteenth century, however, that the rules of warfare, together with issues of arms limitation, became the subject of formal multilateral agreements.

In 1899, at the behest of Czar Nicholas II of Russia, an international conference was convened at the Hague, Netherlands, with the object of instituting arms limitations as a first step toward eventual international disarmament. Although the **Hague Conventions (1899)**, which resulted from the conference, did not finally address arms limitation, let alone disarmament, they did include provisions for impartial arbitration as an alternative to war, and they provided declarations against the use of asphyxiating gases and expanding ("dum-dum") bullets as inhumane weapons. A second conference in 1907 produced the **Hague Conventions (1907)**, which did not renew the declarations against gas warfare and expanding bullets, but did more fully define the procedures, institutions, and apparatus for peaceful international arbitration and also produced a *Convention on Prisoners of War*, which codified rules of treatment already generally accepted and in practice. It was not until the 1925 **Protocol for the Prohibition of the Use in War of Asphyxiating, Poisonous or Other Gases, and of Bacteriological Methods of Warfare** that a comprehensive international ban on poison gas and "germ warfare" was concluded, the nations of the world having experienced the horrors of gas weapons during World War I.

The experience of World War I also occasioned the Washington Conference of November 1921-February 1922, which produced the **Washington Naval Treaty**, setting limits to the naval strength of the five signatory nations, the United States, British Empire, France, Italy, and Japan. A **Convention on Maritime Neutrality**, concluded six years later, in 1928, sought to make political-military neutrality a more viable international option by carefully defining the rights and obligations of neutrals on the high seas. Two years after this, the **London Naval Treaty** (1930), expanded on the Washington Naval Treaty by further attempting to create a balance of naval strength among the world's major powers. The treaty included provisions addressing the operation of submarines and other war vessels

with respect to unarmed merchant vessels. Most ambitiously idealistic of all the interwar agreements was the **Kellogg-Briand Pact** of 1928, an agreement to renounce war altogether as an instrument of national policy. The **Saavedra Lamas Treaty** (1933) was a Pan-American treaty likewise condemning and disavowing warfare.

The outbreak, scope, and inhumanity of World War II constitute ample testimony to the ineffectiveness of the various interwar attempts to limit, rationalize, humanize, and altogether avoid warfare. (That poison gas was almost never used in combat during that war is due less to considerations of humanity than it is to the unreliability of gas as a weapon.)

During the postwar years, the development and proliferation of nuclear and thermonuclear weapons gave greatly added urgency of motive to agreements on arms limitation. The most important of these agreements are those between the United States and the Soviet Union (especially the SALT and START agreements) and the **Nuclear Test Ban Treaty** of 1963, which, in banning atmospheric (as well as underwater and outer space) testing of nuclear weapons, was regarded not only as an act to protect the environment from nuclear contamination, but as a gesture toward eventual nuclear disarmament. A **Comprehensive Test Ban Treaty,** prohibiting all testing of nuclear weapons—including underground tests, not banned by the 1963 treaty—and providing for extensive international inspection to ensure compliance, was opened for signature in 1996 and entered into force in 1999. Although President Bill Clinton had been the first head of state to sign the treaty in 1996, the United States Senate refused to ratify the document in 1999.

During the post-World War II era, nuclear weapons have not been the only focus of agreements aimed at arms control. **Convention on the Prohibition of Military or Any Other Hostile Use of Environmental Modification Techniques** (1976) bars weapons that modify the environment. Certain classes of conventional (non-nuclear) weapons considered inhumane or excessively destructive are prohibited by the **Conventional Weapons Convention** of 1980, and chemical weapons are regulated by the **Chemical Weapons Convention** of 1993. In 1995, a **Draft Protocol on Blinding Laser Weapons** was proposed for addition to the **Conventional Weapons Convention.**

Among the cruelest of modern conventional weapons are anti-personnel mines, which, cheap and plentiful, are widely used and typically remain behind after battles, often injuring or killing non-combatants. The United States signed the 1980 **Protocol on Prohibitions or Restrictions on the Use of Mines, Booby-Traps and Other Devices (Protocol II)**, but declined to sign the much more comprehensive **Convention on the Prohibition of the Use, Stockpiling, Production and Transfer of Anti-Personnel Mines and on Their Destruction** of 1997.

In 1999, the **Inter-American Convention on Transparency in Conventional Weapons Acquisition** was opened for signature. Whereas "transparency" (the principle of openness backed by practical, confidence-building inspection provisions) has been a feature of many agreements limiting nuclear weapons, similar provisions have not always applied to the area of non-nuclear arms. The 1999 convention is intended (in the words of its preamble) "to contribute more fully to regional openness and transparency in the acquisition of conventional weapons by exchanging information regarding such acquisitions, for the purpose of promoting confidence among States in the Americas."

Hague Conventions (1899)

SIGNED: July 29, 1899, at the Hague, Netherlands
IN FORCE: From September 4, 1900; for the United States, from April 9, 1902. Replaced by the **Hague Conventions (1907)**
SIGNATORIES: Austria-Hungary, Belgium, Bulgaria, China, Denmark, France, Germany, Great Britain, Greece, Italy, Japan, Luxemburg, Mexico, Montenegro, Netherlands, Persia, Portugal, Romania, Russia, Serbia, Siam, Spain, Switzerland, Turkey, United Kingdoms of Sweden and Norway, and the United States
OVERVIEW: The Hague conference was called by Czar Nicholas II of Russia as a step toward general disarmament. The Convention of 1899, which resulted from the conference, did not accomplish this purpose, but did formulate rules for mediation and international arbitration of disputes as an alternative to war. (A second conference produced another **Hague Conventions (1907)**, which extended the principles of international arbitration.)

DISCUSSION:
This "Convention for the Pacific Settlement of International Disputes" was signed by most of the great powers. They failed to reach an agreement even on basic guidelines for arms control or arms reduction, but, in Title I, they did subscribe to peace as a controlling principle of international relations.

- Title II of the convention provided for informal mediation of disputes through the "good offices" of "one or more friendly Powers."
- Title III extended the principle of arbitration by defining international commissions of inquiry to investigate and resolve disputes in specific areas, such as boundaries, commercial rights, and so on. These would not be standing

bodies, however, but were to be constituted from time to time, as circumstances might require.

- Title IV did introduce one important standing body for the peaceful resolution of international disputes: the Permanent Court of Arbitration. Popularly called the Hague Tribunal, it was the modern world's first permanent international body designed to achieve the peaceful resolution of conflicts among nations.

The Hague Convention concluded with an article providing an "out" for signatories who wished to "denounce" (withdraw from) the convention. A signatory could withdraw effective one year period from the announcement of the denunciation.

REFERENCES:
International Peace Conference. *The Hague Convention of 1899 (I) and 1907 (I) for the Pacific Settlement of International Disputes.* N.p.: International Peace Conference, 1915.
Israel, Fred L. *Major Peace Treaties of Modern History, 1648-1967,* vol. 2. New York: Chelsea House and McGraw-Hill, 1967)

Hague Conventions (1907)

SIGNED: October 18, 1907
SIGNATORIES: Australia, Austria, Belgium, Bolivia, Brazil, Canada, China, Denmark, El Salvador, Ethiopia, Finland, France, Germany, Guatemala, Haiti, Hungary, India, Ireland, Japan, Laos, Liberia, Luxembourg, Mexico, Netherlands, New Zealand, Nicaragua, Norway, Pakistan, Panama, Philippines, Poland, Portugal, Romania, South Africa, Spain, Sri Lanka, Sweden, Switzerland, Thailand, Union of Soviet Socialist Republics, United Kingdom, United States
IN FORCE: From January 26, 1910
OVERVIEW: Revised and renewed the **Hague Conventions** of 1899 concerning the rules of war.

DISCUSSION:
The 1907 international conference at the Hague was attended by representatives from 44 nations. Conventions adopted by the conference revised and renewed the 1899 conventions, but did not renew the declarations barring the use of asphyxiating gases and expanding bullets.

Like the 1899 conference, the second Hague meeting had as a prime object the formulation of an international program of disarmament or, at least, arms reduction. And, like the earlier conference, it failed to achieve this object. Instead, the 1907 convention reaffirmed the principles and procedures for peacefully arbitrating international disputes set out in 1899. Seventeen additional nations—all South and Central American, except for Haiti—subscribed to the 1907 convention. The 1907 document more fully defined the constitution and operation of the international commissions of inquiry, which were enumerated in 1899. The nature of the Permanent Court of Arbitration was also more fully developed and a procedure for summary arbitration was established in an effort to achieve rapid resolution of particularly dangerous situations.

As it emerged in the 1907 convention, the Permanent Court of Arbitration was a precursor of the League of Nations, which, in turn, was the model on which the United Nations built and improved. In 1921, the Permanent Court of Arbitration was supplanted by the Permanent Court of International Justice, which was created under the League of Nations. In 1945, the International Court of Justice, a United Nations body, replaced the 1921 institution.

The most important of the new conventions included in the 1907 documents is the *Convention on Prisoners of War*, which codified rules of treatment already generally accepted and in practice. Prisoners of war were to be subject to the following:

- Humane treatment
- Protection from violence
- Freedom from reprisal
- Supplied with reasonable nourishment, medical, and sanitary facilities
- Regarded as being in the power of the government of the captors, not in the power of the captors themselves
- Permitted to retain their personal belongings
- Not to be detained in a convict prison
- May be used as laborers, provided that they be paid according to rank and ability and not be subject to excessive work or compelled to work on any task relating to military operations; officers are to be exempted from labor

Prisoners of war were not to be required to give any information other than their true name and rank. The convention also specified procedures for prisoner of war exchanges.

The 1907 conference produced ten other important conventions, addressing the following issues:

1. The limitation of force for the recovery of contract debts
2. The need for aggressive action to be preceded by a declaration of war, either "a reasoned declaration . . . or . . . an ultimatum with a conditional declaration"
3. The rights and duties of neutral nations in land wars
4. The status of enemy merchant vessels at the outbreak of war
5. The conversion of merchant vessels into warships
6. The laying of submarine contact mines
7. Bombardment by naval forces
8. The right of capture in maritime war
9. The establishment of an international prize court
10. The rights and duties of neutral nations in maritime war

REFERENCES:
International Peace Conference. *The Hague Convention of 1899 (I) and 1907 (I) for the Pacific Settlement of International Disputes.* N.p.: International Peace Conference, 1915.
Israel, Fred L. *Major Peace Treaties of Modern History, 1648-1967*, vol. 2. New York: Chelsea House and McGraw-Hill, 1967)

Washington Naval Treaty

SIGNED: February 6, 1922, at Washington, D.C.

IN FORCE: From August 21, 1923

SIGNATORIES: United States, British Empire, France, Italy, and Japan

OVERVIEW: One of three major treaties resulting from the Washington Conference of November 1921-February 1922, the Naval Treaty promoted disarmament after World War I by setting limits to the naval strength of the five signatories.

DISCUSSION:

The thorniest problem in disarmament negotiations after World War I was reducing naval strength while maintaining a balance of power among the major powers. The Washington Naval Treaty not only limited the size of the signatories' navies, it also set proportions of capital warships, primarily battleships, as follows:

> Britain: 5
> United States: 5
> Japan: 3
> France: 1.7
> Italy: 1.7

Furthermore, construction of most capital ships was subject to a ten-year "naval holiday," and then was to be strictly limited until 1936. The proportion formula was only part of the story. In the Pacific, the treaty put Japan at an apparent proportionate disadvantage, but this was compensated for by the European powers' agreement to limit construction of new naval bases in the Pacific and to limit the expansion of those already existing. The U.S. territory of Hawaii was explicitly excluded from such limitation.

The major article limiting tonnage is Article IV:

The total capital ship replacement tonnage of each of the Contracting Powers shall not exceed in standard displacement, for the United States 525,000 tons (533,400 metric tons); for the British Empire 525,000 tons (533,400 metric tons); for France 175,000 tons (177,800 metric tons); for Italy 175,000 tons (177,800 metric tons); for Japan 315,000 tons (320,040 metric tons).

From a technological point of view, the Naval Treaty was quite forward looking. Naval aviation, a topic unknown before World War I and in its infancy during the 1920s, is treated explicitly in the agreement. Article IX stipulates limited construction of aircraft carriers, a ship type that had appeared as recently as 1918, when the British Royal Navy converted the cruiser *Furious* into the first carrier; H.M.S. *Argus,* the first carrier with a true flight deck, followed soon afterward. The first American carrier, *Langley,* converted from a collier, entered service in 1922, the same year that Japan launched the *Hosho,* the first ship actually constructed from the keel up as an aircraft carrier. In World War II, aircraft carriers would supplant battleships as key operational vessels.

REFERENCES:
Goldstein, Erik, and John Maurer. *The Washington Conference, 1921-22: Naval Rivalry, East Asian Stability and the Road to Pearl Harbor.* Ilford, Essex, UK: Frank Cass, 1994.
Grenville, J. A. S. *The Major International Treaties 1914-1973: A History Guide with Texts.* New York: Stein and Day, 1974.
League of Nations. *Reduction of Armaments: Report of the Third Committee to the Fourth Assembly.* Genève: Imp. Jent, s.a., 1923.
Latimer, Hugh. *Naval Disarmament: A Brief Record from the Washington Conference to Date.* London: Royal Institute of International Affairs, 1930.

Protocol for the Prohibition of the Use in War of Asphyxiating, Poisonous or Other Gases, and of Bacteriological Methods of Warfare

SIGNED: June 17, 1925, at Geneva

SIGNATORIES: Afghanistan, Angola, Antigua and Barbuda, Argentina, Australia, Austria, Bahamas, Bahrain, Bangladesh, Barbados, Belgium, Belize, Benin, Bhutan, Bolivia, Botswana, Brazil, Bulgaria, Burkina Faso (Upper Volta), Burma, Cambodia, Cameroon, Canada, Cape Verde, Central African Republic, Chile, China (People's Republic of), China (Taiwan), Comoros, Cuba, Cyprus, Czechoslovakia, Denmark, Djibouti, Dominica, Dominican Republic, Ecuador, Egypt, Estonia, Ethiopia, Equatorial Guinea, Fiji, Finland, France, Gambia, Germany (GDR/FRG), Ghana, Greece, Grenada, Guatemala, Guinea-Bissau, Guyana, Holy See, Hungary, Iceland, India, Indonesia, Iran, Iraq, Ireland, Jordan, Kenya, Kiribati, Korea (North), Korea (South), Kuwait, Laos, Latvia, Lebanon, Lesotho, Liberia, Libya, Liechtenstein, Lithuania, Luxembourg, Madagascar, Malawi, Malaysia, Maldives (Islands), Mali, Malta, Mauritius, Mexico, Monaco, Mongolia, Morocco, Nepal, Netherlands, New Zealand, Nicaragua, Niger, Nigeria, Norway, Pakistan, Panama, Papua New Guinea, Paraguay, Peru, Philippines, Poland, Portugal, Qatar, Romania, Rwanda, St. Kitts and Nevis, St. Lucia, St. Vincent and the Grenadines, Saudi Arabia, Seychelles, Sierra Leone, Singapore, Solomon Islands, South Africa, Spain, Sri Lanka, Sudan Suriname, Swaziland, Sweden, Switzerland, Syrian Arab Republic, Tanzania, Thailand, Togo, Tonga, Trinidad and Tobago, Tunisia, Turkey, Tuvalu, Uganda, Union of Soviet Socialist Republics, United Kingdom, United States, Uruguay

IN FORCE: From February 8, 1928 (United States ratification January 22, 1975; proclaimed by U.S. president, April 29, 1975)

OVERVIEW: The treaty bans the use of poison gas in war.

DISCUSSION:

The **Treaty of Versailles**, ending World War I, includes provisions prohibiting the use of poison gases in war and specifically prohibits Germany from manufacturing such gases. The present treaty was meant as a worldwide extension of the prohibition. It was drawn up as a result of the 1925 Geneva Conference for the Supervision of the International Traffic in Arms. The United States sought to prohibit the export of gases for use in war. It was the French who suggested a protocol prohibiting the use of poisonous gases, and it was a Polish suggestion that the ban be extended to bacteriological weapons.

Before World War II, the protocol was ratified by all the great powers except the United States and Japan. Some nations, including the United Kingdom, France, and the U.S.S.R., declared that the ban would cease to be binding on them if their enemies violated the ban. Italy, a party to the protocol, did, in fact, use poison gas in its war of conquest against Ethiopia, but the ban was generally observed in World War II.

In 1966 the Communist-bloc nations criticized the United States for using tear gas and chemical herbicides in the Vietnam War. In the United Nations General Assembly, Hungary charged that the use in war of these agents was a violation of the Geneva Protocol. Although the United States denied that the protocol applied to non-lethal agents, it was not until 1975 that the Geneva Protocol was ratified by the Senate and proclaimed by the president.

REFERENCE:
Price, Richard M. *The Chemical Weapons Taboo.* Ithaca, NY: Cornell University Press, 1997.

Convention on Maritime Neutrality

SIGNED: February 20, 1928, at Havana

SIGNATORIES: Antigua and Barbuda, Argentina, Bahamas, Bolivia, Brazil, Chile, Colombia, Costa Rica, Cuba, Dominica, the Dominican Republic, Ecuador, El Salvador, Grenada, Guatemala, Haiti, Honduras, Jamaica, Mexico, Nicaragua, Panama, Paraguay, Peru, St. Kitts-Nevis, Saint Lucia, Saint Vincent and the Grenadines, Suriname, United States, Uruguay, Venezuela

IN FORCE: From January 21, 1931

OVERVIEW: A convention defining the rules of maritime neutrality in times of war, including the rights and duties of belligerents and neutrals.

DISCUSSION:

This product of the Sixth International Conference of American States established the following:

- Rules governing freedom of seagoing commerce in times of war
- Maritime duties and rights of belligerents
- Maritime rights and duties of neutrals
- Indemnification of neutrals and their vessels by belligerents

Principal duties and rights of belligerents include the following:

- Belligerents have the right to stop and inspect neutral vessels on the high seas.
- Belligerents may enter neutral waters and neutral ports, but are to be governed by certain rules thereon, which severely limit the military usefulness of such entry.
- Airships (dirigibles) belonging to belligerents are to be governed by essentially the same rules as seagoing vessels.
- Neutrals must, in essence, remain neutral; they cannot supply munitions to belligerents or grant them loans of any kind.
- Neutral ports cannot be used for directly military purposes, but may be used in certain cases of emergency.
- "Neutral states shall not oppose the voluntary departure of nationals of belligerent states even though they leave simultaneously in great numbers; but they may oppose the voluntary departure of their own nationals going to enlist in the armed forces."
- "The use by the belligerents of the means of communication of neutral states or which cross or touch their territory is subject to the measures dictated by the local authority."
- "If as the result of naval operations beyond the territorial waters of neutral states there should be dead or wounded on board belligerent vessels, said states may send hospital ships under the vigilance of the neutral government to the scene of the disaster. These ships shall enjoy complete immunity during the discharge of their mission."

REFERENCE:

Petrie, John N. *American Neutrality in the 20th Century: The Impossible Dream.* Washington, D.C.: Institute for National Strategic Studies, National Defense University, 1995.

Kellogg-Briand Pact

SIGNED: August 27, 1928, at Paris

IN FORCE: From January 17, 1929

SIGNATORIES: (*Original signatories:*) Australia, Dominion of Canada, Czechoslovakia, Germany, Great Britain, India, Irish Free State, Italy, New Zealand, Union of South Africa, and the United States; (*Subsequent signatories:*) Afghanistan, Albania, Austria, Bulgaria, Chile, China, Costa Rica, Cuba, Danzig, Denmark, Dominican Republic, Egypt, Estonia, Ethiopia, Finland, Greece, Guatemala, Honduras, Hungary, Iceland, Latvia, Liberia, Lithuania, Luxembourg, Netherlands, Nicaragua, Norway, Panama, Persia, Peru, Portugal, Rumania, Russia, Kingdom of the Serbs, Croats and Slovenes, Siam, Spain, Sweden, Turkey, Venezuela

OVERVIEW: Drafted under authority of the governments of France and the United States on the initiative of French foreign minister Aristide Briand and with the sponsorship of U.S. Secretary of State Frank B. Kellogg, the Kellogg-Briand Pact (also called the Pact of Paris) was an idealistic international agreement to renounce war as an instrument of national policy.

DISCUSSION:

When French foreign minister Aristide Briand proposed that his nation and the United States conclude an exemplary pact permanently renouncing war as a means of settling disputes with one another, Secretary of State Frank B. Kellogg enthusiastically assented, but suggested that the agreement be opened to other signatories as well. On August 27, 1928, the document was signed by fifteen nations. Subsequently, many other nations subscribed as well.

Hailed as a profound step toward making the ideal of universal peace a reality, the pact was flawless in spirit, but fatally flawed in letter. Its substance was contained in two brief articles:

ARTICLE I

The High Contracting Parties solemnly declare in the names of their respective peoples that they condemn recourse to war for the solution of international controversies, and renounce it, as an instrument of national policy in their relations with one another.

ARTICLE II

The High Contracting Parties agree that the settlement or solution of all disputes or conflicts of whatever nature or of whatever origin they may be, which may arise among them, shall never be sought except by pacific means.

The fatal flaw here was that the pact, naive and even simpleminded, made no provisions for enforcement. The pact also left a gaping loophole in that it was silent on the subject of undeclared wars. For example, the 1931 Japanese invasion of Manchuria could not be deemed a violation of the agreement because it was not a declared war. Even if it had been judged a violation, the agreement did not provide for sanctions.

The pact was also subject to three reservations:

- Each signatory retained the right to defend itself.
- If a single nation violated the pact, all other nations were thereby released from it.
- The pact was not to interfere with French military obligations under the League of Nations or the Locarno Pact, a series of agreements concluded on December 1, 1925, whereby Germany, France, Belgium, Great Britain, and Italy mutually guaranteed peace in western Europe.

Although noble in its aspiration, the Kellogg-Briand Pact was self-defeating as well as self-denying. It was a war-weary expression of hope more than it was a viable instrument of policy.

REFERENCES:

Ferrell, Robert H. *Peace in Their Time: The Origins of the Kellogg-Briand Pact.* Hamden, CT: Archon, 1968.
Grenville, J. A. S., *The Major International Treaties 1914-1973: A History Guide with Texts.* New York: Stein and Day, 1974.
Kneeshaw, Stephen J. *In Pursuit of Peace: The American Reaction to the Kellogg-Briand Pact, 1928-1929.* New York: Garland, 1991.
Myers, Denys P. *Origin and Conclusion of the Paris Pact.* New York: Garland, 1972.
Shotwell, James Thomson. *War as an Instrument of National Policy, and its Renunciation in the Pact of Paris.* New York: N. pub., 1929.

London Naval Treaty

OFFICIAL TITLE: Treaty for the Limitation and Reduction of Naval Armaments

SIGNED: April 22, 1930, at London

SIGNATORIES (TO PART IV): Afghanistan, Albania, Australia, Austria, Belgium, Brazil, Bulgaria, Canada, Costa Rica, Czechoslovakia, Denmark, Egypt, El Salvador, Estonia, Finland, France, Germany, Greece, Guatemala, Haiti, Holy See, Hungary, India, Indonesia, Iran. Ireland, Italy, Japan, Latvia, Lithuania, Mexico, Nepal, Netherlands (including Curaçao), New Zealand, Norway, Panama, Peru, Poland, Saudi Arabia, Slovak Republic, South Africa, Sweden, Switzerland, Thailand, Turkey, Union of Soviet Socialist Republics, United Kingdom, United States, Yugoslavia

IN FORCE: From December 31, 1930; all provisions of the treaty expired on December 31, 1936, except for Part IV , which was to "remain in force without limit of time"

OVERVIEW: A treaty attempting to create a balance of naval strength among the major powers; the most important part, Part IV, addresses the operation of submarines and other war vessels with respect to merchant vessels.

DISCUSSION:

The primary purpose of the London Naval Treaty was the revision of earlier agreements, including the **Treaty of Versailles** (Section 2.8) and the **Washington Naval Treaty**, in attempting to create a balance of strength among the navies of the world. The duration of the London Naval Treaty was limited, and, except for the provisions of Part IV, went out of force in 1936. Part IV continues in force. The most important article relates to submarine warfare:

Art. 22. The following are accepted as established rules of international law: (1) In their action with regard to merchant ships, submarines must conform to the rules of international law to which surface vessels are subject. (2) In particular, except in the case of persistent refusal to stop on being duly summoned, or of active resistance to visit or search, a warship, whether surface vessel or submarine, may not sink or render incapable of navigation a merchant vessel without having first placed passengers, crew and ship's papers in a place of safety. For this purpose the ship's boats are not regarded as a place of safety unless the safety of the passengers and crew is assured, in the existing sea and weather conditions, by the proximity of land, or the presence of another vessel which is in a position to take them on board.

None of the signatories adhered to this provision during World War II.

REFERENCES:

Grenville, J. A. S. The Major International Treaties 1914-1973: A History Guide with Texts. New York: Stein and Day, 1974.

League of Nations. Reduction of Armaments: Report of the Third Committee to the Fourth Assembly. Genève: Imp. Jent, s.a., 1923.

Latimer, Hugh. Naval Disarmament: A Brief Record from the Washington Conference to Date. London: Royal Institute of International Affairs, 1930.

Saavedra Lamas Treaty

OFFICIAL TITLE: Antiwar Treaty of Non-aggression and Conciliation

SIGNED: October 10, 1933, at Rio de Janeiro

SIGNATORIES: Argentina, Brazil, Chile, Mexico, Paraguay, Uruguay. The United States did not sign, but did acknowledge adherence to, the treaty.

IN FORCE: From November 13, 1935

OVERVIEW: A Pan-American treaty condemning and disavowing warfare.

DISCUSSION:

As war clouds began to gather over Europe with the rise of Italian and German Fascism in the early and mid 1930s, some of the nations of the Americas, at the instigation of Carlos Saavedra Lamas, Brazil's minister of Foreign Relations and Worship, concluded a multilateral treaty condemning war and espousing non-aggression. That the United States chose not to sign the treaty, but did acknowledge adherence to it, albeit with reservations, indicates the uneasy and ambivalent mood of isolationism prevailing in the nation during the 1930s.

The United States' reservation is stated as follows: "In adhering to this Treaty the United States does not thereby waive any rights it may have under other treaties or conventions or under international law." The key articles follow:

ARTICLE I

The high contracting parties solemnly declare that they condemn wars of aggression in their mutual relations or in those with other states, and that the settlement of disputes or controversies of any kind that may arise among them shall be effected only by the pacific means which have the sanction of international law.

ARTICLE II

They declare that as between the high contracting parties territorial questions must not be settled by violence, and that they will not recognize any territorial arrangement which is not obtained by pacific means, nor the validity of the occupation or acquisition of territories that may be brought about by force of arms.

ARTICLE III

In case of noncompliance, by any state engaged in a dispute, with the obligations contained in the foregoing articles, the contracting states undertake to make every effort for the maintenance of peace. To that end they will adopt in their character as neutrals a common and solidary attitude; they will exercise the political, juridical, or economic means authorized by international law; they will bring the influence of public opinion to bear, but will in no case resort to intervention, either diplomatic or armed; subject to the attitude that may be incumbent on them by virtue of other collective treaties to which such states are signatories.

ARTICLE IV

The high contracting parties obligate themselves to submit to the conciliation procedure established by this treaty the disputes specially mentioned and any others that may arise in their reciprocal relations, without further limitations than those enumerated in the following article, in all controversies which it has not been possible to settle by diplomatic means within a reasonable period of time.

REFERENCES:

Argentina, Ministerio de Relaciones Exteriores y Culto. *Draft of an Anti-war Treaty.* Washington, D.C.: Embassy of Argentina, 1932.

Guinsburg, Thomas N. *the Pursuit of Isolationism in the United States Senate from Versailles to Pearl Harbor.* New York: Garland, 1982.

Nuclear Test Ban Treaty

OFFICIAL TITLE: Treaty Banning Nuclear Weapon Tests in the Atmosphere, in Outer Space and Under Water

SIGNED: August 5, 1963, at Moscow

IN FORCE: From October 10, 1963

SIGNATORIES: Soviet Union, United Kingdom, and the United States, original signatories; opened for signature to all nations; as of 1999, a total of 124 additional nations have signed

OVERVIEW: The official name of what is popularly called the Nuclear Test Ban Treaty defines its scope: "Treaty Banning Nuclear Weapon Tests in the Atmosphere, in Outer Space and Under Water." The treaty permits underground testing.

DISCUSSION:

An international movement to ban nuclear weapons got under way in January 1946, just six months after the bombing of Hiroshima and Nagasaki, when the United Nations General Assembly created the Atomic Energy Commission. Among the chief functions of this agency was promoting nuclear disarmament. By June of 1946, the commission had devised an ambitious plan to outlaw all atomic weapons. Debate on the plan was cut off by a veto from the Soviets, who not only rejected the presence of U.N.-mandated inspectors inside its borders, but refused to relinquish its veto power over atomic matters in the Security Council by entrusting the regulation of such matters to the Atomic Energy Commission.

After the failure of the Atomic Energy Commission proposal, a ten-power Disarmament Committee, consisting of five Eastern-bloc and five Western-bloc nations, was set up in Geneva, Switzerland, independently of the U.N. in September 1959. It disbanded in June 1960. On December 20, 1961, searching for some aspect of nuclear policy on which they could agree, the United States and the Soviet Union issued a joint resolution in the U.N. General Assembly to form a new, eighteen-nation Disarmament Committee. Consisting of five NATO countries, five Warsaw Pact countries, and eight non-aligned nations (Brazil, Burma, Ethiopia, India, Mexico, Nigeria, Egypt, and Sweden), it met in almost continuous session in Geneva and was later enlarged to twenty-six members. (France, although it was a member of the committee from the beginning, boycotted the entire process.)

The first product of the reconstituted Disarmament Committee was the Nuclear Test Ban Treaty. Its purpose was as much environmental as it was political; for, in the years following World War II, the United States, the Soviet Union, and China (as each developed nuclear capability) detonated numerous nuclear and thermonuclear devices. The tests were always carried out in remote locations, but radioactive fallout was nevertheless carried into populated regions, where it was detected in water, in the atmosphere, and in the food chain (in the United States and Great Britain, milk was routinely monitored for radioactivity). Few nations were willing to take a stand against keeping safe the milk children drink, and the treaty, banning all nuclear tests except those underground, was readily agreed to.

As valuable as the Test Ban Treaty is for the environment, its symbolic significance as a first, small step toward disarmament is perhaps even more important. Beginning on August 8, 1963, the treaty was held open for signature in Washington, Moscow, and London, the capitals of the three original signatories. While 124 nations have signed since that time, significant holdouts remain the People's Republic of China and France, both of which have nuclear arsenals. Albania, Cuba, Guinea, Kampuchea, North Korea, and Saudi Arabia, non-nuclear nations, also declined to subscribe.

See also **Comprehensive Nuclear Test Ban Treaty (CTBT)** of 1996.

REFERENCES:

Grenville, J. A. S., *The Major International Treaties 1914-1973: A History Guide with Texts.* New York: Stein and Day, 1974.

Oliver, Kendrick. *Kennedy, MacMillan, and the Nuclear Test-Ban Debate, 1961-63.* New York: St. Martin's Press, 1998.

United Nations. *In Pursuit of a Nuclear Test Ban Treaty: A Guide to Debate in the Conference on Disarmament.* New York: United Nations Publications, 1991.

Treaty on the Non-Proliferation of Nuclear Weapons (TNP or NPT)

SIGNED: July 1, 1968, at London, Moscow and Washington

IN FORCE: March 5, 1970

SIGNATORIES: The principal signatories are the United States, the U.S.S.R., and the United Kingdom, with China and France joining the principals in 1992. As of 1999, 188 nations have subscribed to the treaty; the majority of signatory nations are non-nuclear powers. The treaty remains open for additional signatures.

OVERVIEW: This multilateral treaty, administered by the International Atomic Energy Commission (an agency of the United Nations), requires signatory nations that did not possess nuclear weapons prior to 1967 to refrain from developing such weapons as a condition for receiving assistance from the nuclear powers in planning and developing their own peaceful nuclear industries (primarily reactors for the generation of electricity).

DISCUSSION:

No sooner was the nuclear genie released from its bottle with the August 1945 atomic bombings of Hiroshima and Nagasaki, Japan, than United States military commanders and civilian policy makers began agonizing over the prospect of other nations developing nuclear weapons. In 1949, the Soviet Union did develop its own atomic bomb, and, in 1955, a hydrogen (thermonuclear) weapon as well. The United Kingdom developed atomic weapons in 1952, France in 1960, and China in 1964. India, one of a minority of nations that has not signed TNP, tested its first atomic weapon in 1974. (In 1998, India's implacable foe, Pakistan, another nonsignatory, created international anxiety by conducting tests of its newly developed nuclear weapons.)

TNP began as a result of negotiations between the two principal nuclear powers, the United States and the Soviet Union, and was intended to prevent or at least curb the spread of nuclear weapons to other states. The initial signatories included 62 states. The three principals, the United States, the U.S.S.R., and the United Kingdom, agreed to refrain from assisting other nations in obtaining or producing nuclear weapons. The 59 non-nuclear signatories (and the others that have followed), in turn, agreed not to obtain or develop such weapons. In exchange for these pledges, the three principal signatories agreed to offer assistance in the development of the peaceful application of nuclear energy. Most of the states that have subscribed to TNP have agreed to the full provisions of the treaty, which include the right of safeguard inspections under United Nations supervision. Some signatories, however, have not agreed to such inspections.

The treaty went into force in March 1970 and was to remain in effect for 25 years. In 1995, TNP was extended indefinitely by a consensus vote in the United Nations of 174 countries.

The essential provisions of the treaty include:

- The principal signatories' pledge not "to transfer to any recipient whatsoever nuclear weapons or other nuclear explosive devices or control over such weapons or explosive devices directly, or indirectly; and not in any way to assist, encourage, or induce any non-nuclear-weapon State to manufacture or otherwise acquire nuclear weapons or other nuclear explosive devices, or control over such weapons or explosive devices."
- The non-nuclear signatories' pledge "not to . . . acquire . . . nuclear weapons" from any other state, nor to manufacture such weapons.

In addition, Article III provides for the acceptance by "each non-nuclear-weapon State Party to the Treaty" of inspection safeguards by the International Atomic Energy Agency, a United Nations agency. The treaty specifies that such safeguards will not abridge "the inalienable right of all the Parties to the Treaty to develop research, production and use of nuclear energy for peaceful purposes." Not all non-nuclear signatories have agreed to the safeguard provisions of Article III.

Additional provisions of the TNP include:

- An agreement among signatories "to pursue negotiations in good faith on effective measures relating to cessation of the nuclear arms race at an early date and to nuclear disarmament, and on a treaty on general and complete disarmament under strict and effective international control."
- A call for a conference 25 years after the treaty enters into force "to decide whether the Treaty shall continue in force indefinitely, or shall be extended for an additional fixed period or periods." The conference was held in 1995 and the treaty extended indefinitely.

REFERENCES:

Grenville, J. A. S. *The Major International Treaties 1914-1973: A History Guide with Texts.* New York: Stein and Day, 1974.

Isaacs, Jeremy, and Taylor Downing, *Cold War: An Illustrated History, 1945-1991.* Boston: Little, Brown, 1998.

Rengger, Nicholas, ed., *Treaties and Alliances of the World,* 5th ed. Essex, UK: Longman Current Affairs, 1990.

Nuclear Seabed Ban

OFFICIAL TITLE: Treaty on the Prohibition of the Emplacement of Nuclear Weapons and Other Weapons of Mass Destruction on the Sea Bed and the Ocean Floor and in the Subsoil Thereof

SIGNED: February 11, 1971, at London

IN FORCE: From May 18, 1972

SIGNATORIES: Afghanistan, Antigua and Barbuda, Argentina, Australia, Austria, Belgium, Benin, Bolivia, Brazil, Bulgaria, Burma, Canada, China, Cyprus, Czechoslovakia, Denmark, Ethiopia, Finland, Gambia, Germany, Ghana, Greece, Hungary, Iceland, India, Iran (Islamic Republic of), Ireland, Italy, Jamaica, Japan, Jordan, Korea, Lao People's Democratic Republic, Latvia, Lebanon, Liechtenstein, Luxembourg, Malaysia, Malta, Mauritius, Mexico, Mongolia, Morocco, Nepal, Netherlands (in respect of the Kingdom in Europe, Netherlands Antilles and Aruba), New Zealand, Norway, Poland, Portugal, Qatar, Romania, Russian Federation, Rwanda, Seychelles, Sierra Leone, Singapore, Slovenia, Solomon Islands, South Africa, Spain, Sudan, Sweden, Switzerland, Tunisia, Turkey, United Kingdom, United States, Yugoslavia, Zambia.

OVERVIEW: The purpose of the treaty is to exclude the seabed, the ocean floor, and the subsoil thereof from the arms race as a step toward disarmament, the reduction of international tensions, and the maintenance of world peace.

DISCUSSION:

Signatories to the treaty agree not to place on the sea bed, on the ocean floor or in the subsoil thereof, nuclear weapons or other weapons of mass destruction, or structures for launching, storing, testing or using such weapons. The treaty specifies that the outer limit of the seabed zone is the twelve-mile limit referred to in the **Convention on the Territorial Sea and the Contiguous Zone** (1958).

Signatories agree that observers from any party may observe and verify the activities of any other party on the seabed. In case of doubt, the signatories are to consult and cooperate to remove such doubt by means of inspection and any other agreed procedures. If a serious question remains concerning the fulfillment of the obligations under the treaty, a signatory may refer the matter directly to the United Nations Security Council.

The treaty remains open to all states for signature.

REFERENCE:

Segal, Gerald, et al. *Nuclear War and Nuclear Peace,* 2d ed. New York: St. Martin's Press, 1988.

Agreement (with U.S.S.R.) to Reduce the Risk of Nuclear War

OFFICIAL TITLE: Agreement on Measures to Reduce the Risk of Outbreak of Nuclear War between the United States of America and the Union of Soviet Socialist Republics
SIGNED: September 30, 1971, at Washington, D.C.
SIGNATORIES: Union of Soviet Socialist Republics vs. United States
IN FORCE: From September 30, 1971
OVERVIEW: An agreement on steps to prevent the accidental outbreak of nuclear war.

DISCUSSION:
Recognizing that highly technical weapons systems are subject to malfunction and may trigger catastrophic misunderstanding, the United States and the Soviet Union concluded, in the course of the Strategic Arms Limitation Talks (SALT), an agreement on safeguards to reduce uncertainties and prevent misunderstandings in the event of a nuclear incident. Three principal areas are addressed in the agreement:

1. Each party pledged continually to maintain and improve its organizational and technical safeguards against accidental or unauthorized use of nuclear weapons.

2. Each party agreed to arrangements for immediate notification should a risk of nuclear war arise from detection of unidentified objects on early warning systems or from accidental, unauthorized, or other unexplained incidents.

3. Each party agreed to notify the other of any planned missile launches beyond its territory and in the direction of the other party.

REFERENCES:

Garthoff, Raymond L. *Detente and Confrontation: American-Soviet Relations from Nixon to Reagan.* Washington, D.C.: Brookings Institution, 1994.
Nelson, Keith L. *The Making of Detente: Soviet-American Relations in the Shadow of Vietnam.* Baltimore: Johns Hopkins University Press, 1995.
Van Oudenaren, John. *Detente in Europe: The Soviet Union and the West Since 1953.* Durham, NC: Duke University Press, 1991.

SALT I Treaty on the Limitation of Anti-Ballistic Missile Systems

OFFICIAL TITLE: Treaty between the United States of America and the Soviet Union and the Union of Soviet Socialist Republics on the Limitation of Anti-Ballistic Missile Systems
SIGNED: May 26, 1972, at Moscow
SIGNATORIES: Union of Soviet Socialist Republics vs. United States
IN FORCE: From October 3, 1972
OVERVIEW: A treaty limiting the number and scope of anti-ballistic missile (ABM) systems in order to maintain the principle of "mutually assured destruction" as a deterrent to nuclear war.

DISCUSSION:
Treaties rarely limit the purely defensive measures a nation may take, but in the dangerous world of nuclear warfare, such a limitation was deemed necessary. Throughout the Cold War period, the single most important deterrent to the outbreak of nuclear war was the concept of mutually assured destruction, known by the fitting acronym "MAD." As long as each of the two nuclear superpowers, the United States and the Soviet Union, were convinced that using nuclear weapons would trigger immediate retaliation in kind, against which there was no viable defense, both sides would refrain from using such weapons. The development of anti-ballistic missiles, defensive weapons capable of intercepting and destroying incoming ballistic missiles bearing nuclear warheads, threatened to undermine the MAD concept. If one side believed a nuclear war was survivable, the temptation to initiate a first or preemptive nuclear strike would be increased. Therefore, this treaty, popularly called "The ABM Treaty," limited deployment of ABM systems:

• Each party was limited to two ABM deployment areas, purposely restricted and located so that they could not provide a nationwide ABM defense.
• Each party agreed to deploy its two sites such that one defended the capital and the other an ICBM (intercontinental ballistic missile) launch area.
• Each party limited the number of ABM interceptor missiles at each site to no more than 100.
• Each party agreed to limit "qualitative improvement" of ABM technology in specific ways.
• Each party agreed to prohibit testing or development of sea-based, air-based, or space-based ABM systems.

The treaty weathered a major crisis beginning in March 1983, when President Ronald Reagan backed development of the Strategic Defense Initiative (SDI)—derisively dubbed the "Star Wars defense" in reference to the popular George Lucas

Star Wars science fiction movie—a space-based system intended to shoot down incoming ICBMs.

REFERENCES:

Garthoff, Raymond L. *Detente and Confrontation: American-Soviet Relations from Nixon to Reagan.* Washington, D.C.: Brookings Institution, 1994.

Nelson, Keith L. *The Making of Detente: Soviet-American Relations in the Shadow of Vietnam.* Baltimore: Johns Hopkins University Press, 1995.

Van Oudenaren, John. *Detente in Europe: The Soviet Union and the West Since 1953.* Durham, NC: Duke University Press, 1991.

Biological Weapons Ban

OFFICIAL TITLE: Convention on the Prohibition of the Development, Production, and Stockpiling of Bacteriological (Biological) and Toxin Weapons and on Their Destruction

SIGNED: April 10, 1972, at Washington, London, and Moscow

SIGNATORIES: Afghanistan, Albania, Argentina, Armenia, Australia, Austria, Bahamas, Bahrain, Bangladesh, Barbados, Belarus, Belgium, Belize, Bhutan, Bolivia, Bosnia Herzegovina, Botswana, Brazil, Brunei Darussalam, Bulgaria, Burkina Faso, Burundi, Cambodia (Kampuchea), Canada, Cape Verde, Central African Republic, Chile, China (People's Republic of), Colombia, Congo, Costa Rica, Côte d'Ivoire, Croatia, Cuba, Cyprus, Czech Republic, Denmark, Dominica, Dominican Republic, Ecuador, Egypt, El Salvador, Equatorial Guinea, Estonia, Ethiopia, Fiji, Finland, France, Gabon, Gambia, The, Georgia, Germany, Ghana, Greece, Grenada, Guatemala, Guinea-Bissau, Guyana, Haiti, Honduras, Hungary, Iceland, India, Indonesia, Iran, Iraq, Ireland, Italy, Jamaica, Japan, Jordan, Kenya, Korea (Democratic People's Republic of), Korea (Republic of), Kuwait, Laos, Latvia, Lebanon, Lesotho, Liberia, Libya, Liechtenstein, Luxembourg, Macedonia (Former Yugoslav Republic of), Madagascar, Malawi, Malaysia, Maldives, Mali, Malta, Mauritius, Mexico, Mongolia, Morocco, Myanmar (Burma), Nepal, Netherlands, New Zealand, Nicaragua, Niger, Nigeria, Norway, Oman, Pakistan, Panama, Papua New Guinea, Paraguay, Peru, Philippines, Poland, Portugal, Qatar, Romania, Russian Federation, Rwanda, San Marino Sao Tome and Principe, Saudi Arabia, Senegal, Serbia-Montenegro (Formerly Yugoslavia), Seychelles, Sierra Leone, Singapore, Slovak Republic, Slovenia, Solomon Islands, Somalia, South Africa, Spain, Sri Lanka, St. Lucia, St. Kitts and Nevis, Suriname, Swaziland, Sweden, Switzerland, Syria, Tanzania, Thailand, Togo, Tonga, Tunisia, Turkey, Turkmenistan, Uganda, Ukraine, United Kingdom, United States, United Arab Emirates, Uruguay, Uzbekistan, Vanuatu, Venezuela, Vietnam, Yemen, Zaire, Zimbabwe

IN FORCE: From March 26, 1975

OVERVIEW: A comprehensive ban on the development, storage, and use of biological weapons and "toxins" (chemical poisons produced by biological processes).

DISCUSSION:

The use of biological and chemical weapons has been generally repugnant to "civilized warfare," and after poison gas was used in World War I, the **Geneva Protocol** of 1925 prohibited the use of chemical poisons as well as bacteriological substances in warfare. This notwithstanding, many nations, including the United States, continued to develop chemical and biological weapons. On November 26, 1969, President Richard Nixon declared that the United States unilaterally renounced first use of chemical agents and renounced all methods of biological warfare. On February 14, 1970, the ban was extended to toxin weapons (chemical poisons produced by biological processes). Applauded by most of the world, the United States action prompted development of the present convention, which President Nixon hailed as "the first international agreement since World War II to provide for the actual elimination of an entire class of weapons."

Parties to the convention agreed not to develop, produce, stockpile, or acquire biological agents or toxins "of types and in quantities that have no justification for prophylactic, protective, and other peaceful purposes." They further agreed to destroy all such existing weapons and agents within nine months of the convention's entry into force.

REFERENCES:

Garthoff, Raymond L. *Detente and Confrontation: American-Soviet Relations from Nixon to Reagan.* Washington, D.C.: Brookings Institution, 1994.

Nelson, Keith L. *The Making of Detente: Soviet-American Relations in the Shadow of Vietnam.* Baltimore: Johns Hopkins University Press, 1995.

Price, Richard M. *The Chemical Weapons Taboo.* Ithaca, NY: Cornell University Press, 1997.

Van Oudenaren, John. *Detente in Europe: The Soviet Union and the West Since 1953.* Durham, NC: Duke University Press, 1991.

Agreement on the Prevention of Nuclear War

SIGNED: June 22, 1973, at Washington, D.C.

IN FORCE: From signing

SIGNATORIES: Union of Soviet Socialist Republics vs. United States

OVERVIEW: The document pledges the two nations to work toward removing "the danger of nuclear war and . . . the use of nuclear weapons."

DISCUSSION:

United States president Richard Nixon and Soviet premier Leonid Brezhnev had both earned reputations as ideological hardliners and confirmed "Cold Warriors"; they therefore surprised the world by opening a dialogue aimed at achieving "detente" and concluded a **SALT I Treaty on the Limitation of Anti-Ballistic Missile Systems**, which was followed by an agreement to adopt policies designed to prevent nuclear war: "the parties agree that they will act in such a manner as to prevent the development of situations capable of causing a dangerous exacerbation of their relations, as to avoid military confrontations, and as to exclude the outbreak of nuclear war between them and between either of the parties and other countries."

- Article II specifies "that each party will refrain from the threat or use of force against the other party."
- Article IV states that, "If at any time relations between the parties or between either party and other countries appear to involve the risk of a nuclear conflict . . . the United States and the Soviet Union, acting in accordance with the provisions of this Agreement, shall immediately enter into urgent consultations with each other and make every effort to avert this risk."

As a repudiation of the nuclear policy that had guided the two nations throughout the Cold War period, the agreement was profound in its implications; however, it offered few specifics and no prescription or mechanism for averting nuclear war.

REFERENCES:

Gaddis, John, Philip Gordon, and Ernest May, eds. *Cold War Statesmen Confront the Bomb: Nuclear Diplomacy Since 1945.* New York: Oxford University Press, 1999.

Grenville, J. A. S., *The Major International Treaties 1914-1973: A History Guide with Texts.* New York: Stein and Day, 1974.

Nation, Joseph E. *The De-Escalation of Nuclear Crises.* New York: St. Martin's Press, 1992.

Convention on the Prohibition of Military or Any Other Hostile Use of Environmental Modification Techniques

SIGNED: May 18, 1977, at Geneva

SIGNATORIES: Afghanistan, Algeria, Antigua and Barbuda, Argentina, Australia, Austria, Bangladesh, Belgium, Benin, Bolivia, Brazil, Brunei, Bulgaria, Byelorussian S.S.R., Canada, Cape Verde, Chile, Cuba, Cyprus, Czechoslovakia, Czech Republic, Denmark, Dominica, Egypt, Ethiopia, Finland, German Democratic Republic, Germany (Federal Republic of), Ghana, Greece, Guatemala, Holy See, Hungary, Iceland, India, Iran, Iraq, Ireland, Italy, Japan, Korea (Democratic People's Republic of), Korea (Republic of), Kuwait, Laos, Lebanon, Liberia, Luxembourg, Malawi, Mauritius, Mongolia, Morocco, Netherlands, New Zealand, Nicaragua, Niger, Norway, Pakistan, Papua New Guinea, Poland, Portugal, Romania, St. Christopher-Nevis, St. Lucia, St. Vincent and the Grenadines, Sao Tome and Principe, Sierra Leone, Solomon Islands, Spain, Sri Lanka, Sweden, Switzerland, Syria, Tunisia, Turkey, Uganda, Ukrainian S.S.R., Union of Soviet Socialist Republics, United Kingdom,

United States, Uruguay, Uzbekistan, Vietnam, Yemen Arab Republic (Sanaa), Yemen (Aden), Zaire

IN FORCE: From October 5, 1978 (for the United States, December 13, 1979)

OVERVIEW: A convention prohibiting the use of environmental modification techniques for hostile purposes.

DISCUSSION:

This forward-looking convention addresses a class of weapon that plays no major role in military planning at present: large-scale environmental modification. The Convention defines environmental modification techniques as changing, through the deliberate manipulation of natural processes, the dynamics, composition or structure of the earth, including its biota, lithosphere, hydrosphere, and atmosphere, or of outer space. Changes in weather or climate patterns, in ocean currents, or in the state of the ozone layer or ionosphere, or an upset in the ecological balance of a region are some possible forms of environmental modification.

Article I presents the basic commitment: "Each State Party to this Convention undertakes not to engage in military or any other hostile use of environmental modification techniques having widespread, long-lasting or severe effects as the means of destruction, damage or injury to any other State Party." The terms of this statement are broadly defined: "widespread" as "encompassing an area on the scale of several hundred square kilometers"; "long-lasting" as "lasting for a period of months, or approximately a season"; and "severe" as "involving serious or significant disruption or harm to human life, natural and economic resources or other assets."

The convention provides for mutual consultation to address any complaints arising from the agreement and establishes a program of periodic conferences.

REFERENCE:

Lanier-Graham, Susan D. *the Ecology of War: Environmental Impacts of Weaponry and Warfare.* New York: Walker, 1993.

Geneva Protocol I

OFFICIAL TITLE: Protocol Additional to the Geneva Conventions of 12 August 1949, and relating to the Protection of Victims of International Armed Conflicts

SIGNED: June 8, 1977, at Geneva

SIGNATORIES: Australia, Austria, Belgium, Benin, Botswana, Bulgaria, Byelorussian Soviet Socialist Republic, Canada, Chile, Côte d'Ivoire, Cyprus, Czechoslovakia, Denmark, Ecuador, Egypt, El Salvador, Finland, German Democratic Republic, Germany (Federal Republic), Ghana, Guatemala, Holy See, Honduras, Hungary, Iceland, Iran, Ireland, Italy, Jordan, Korea (Republic), Lao People's Democratic Republic, Libyan Arab Jamahiriya, Liechtenstein, Luxembourg, Madagascar, Mongolia, Morocco, Netherlands, New Zealand, Nicaragua, Niger, Norway,

Pakistan, Panama, Peru, Philippines, Poland, Portugal, Romania, San Marino, Senegal, Spain, Sweden, Switzerland, Togo, Tunisia, Ukrainian Soviet Socialist Republic, Union of Soviet Socialist Republics, United Kingdom, United States, Upper Volta, Vietnam, Yemen, Yugoslavia

IN FORCE: From December 7, 1978

OVERVIEW: The protocol extends and amplifies the Geneva Conventions of 1949 as they apply to the protection of all people involved armed conflicts, combatants, non-combatants, and military as well as civilian medical personnel.

DISCUSSION:

In addition to defining the scope of the application of the protocol, the document lays down rules concerning belligerents' responsibilities regarding the following:

• The wounded, sick and shipwrecked
• Medical transportation
• Missing and dead persons
• Method and means of warfare
• Civilian populations
• Specific protection of women and children
• Civilian objects
• The natural environment

Protocol I modifies the 1949 conventions in the following ways:

• Article 1 provides that armed conflicts in which peoples are fighting against colonial domination, alien occupation, or racist regimes are to be considered international conflicts.
• Part II expands the rules of the earlier conventions concerning the wounded, the sick, and the shipwrecked. Protection of the conventions is extended to civilian medical personnel, equipment, and supplies and to civilian units and transports. The protocol includes detailed provisions on medical transportation.
• Part III and portions of Part IV reaffirm and, to some degree, elaborate on provisions relating to the conduct of hostilities laid down in the Hague Convention of 1899 and Hague Convention of 1907 as well as by customary international law. Articles in these parts extend the rules of warfare to the protection of the civilian population. A definition of military objectives is provided, and prohibitions of attack on civilian persons and objects are made explicit. Also exempt from deliberate attack are civil defense organizations. Articles in these parts address the conduct of relief actions and the treatment of persons in the power of a party to a conflict.
• Part V addresses problems relating to the execution of the conventions as well as the protocol.

This protocol, together with **Geneva Protocol II,** is the most comprehensive and detailed convention regarding the rules of warfare as they relate to combatant and non-combatant populations.

REFERENCE:

Pilloud, Claude, et al., eds. *Commentary on the Additional Protocols of 8 June 1977 to the Geneva Conventions of 12 August 1949.* Dordrecht, Netherlands, and Boston: M. Nijhoff, 1987.

Geneva Protocol II

OFFICIAL TITLE: Protocol Additional to the Geneva Conventions of 12 August 1949, and relating to the Protection of Victims of Non-International Armed Conflicts

SIGNED: June 8, 1977, at Geneva

SIGNATORIES: Australia, Austria, Belgium, Botswana, Bulgaria, Byelorussian Soviet Socialist Republic, Canada, Chile, Côte d'Ivoire, Cyprus, Czechoslovakia, Denmark, Ecuador, Egypt, El Salvador, Finland, German Democratic Republic, Germany (Federal Republic), Ghana, Guatemala, Holy See, Honduras, Hungary, Iceland, Iran, Ireland, Italy, Jordan, Korea (Republic), Lao People's Democratic Republic, Libyan Arab Jamahiriya, Liechtenstein, Luxembourg, Madagascar, Mongolia, Morocco, Netherlands, New Zealand, Nicaragua, Niger, Norway, Pakistan, Panama, Peru, Philippines, Poland, Portugal, Romania, San Marino, Senegal, Spain, Sweden, Switzerland, Togo, Tunisia, Ukrainian Soviet Socialist Republic, Union of Soviet Socialist Republics, United Kingdom, United States, Upper Volta, Vietnam, Yemen, Yugoslavia

IN FORCE: From December 7, 1978

OVERVIEW: The second of two protocols extending and amplifying the Geneva Conventions of 1949 as they apply to the protection of all people involved armed conflicts, combatants, non-combatants, and military as well as civilian medical personnel.

DISCUSSION:

The second protocol specifically applies to civil conflicts, which "take place in the territory of a High Contracting Party between its armed forces and dissident armed forces or other organized armed groups which, under responsible command, exercise such control over a part of its territory as to enable them to carry out sustained and concerted military operations and to implement this Protocol." The protocol distinguishes between armed civil conflict and riot and applies exclusively to the former.

Signatories undertake the following:

• To guarantee humane treatment of dissidents and others
• To refrain from ordering "that there shall be no survivors"
• To provide adequate care to children
• To treat prisoners ("persons whose liberty has been restricted") humanely, according to standards analogous to the treatment accorded prisoners of war
• To ensure justice in all penal prosecutions arising from the civil conflict, such that "no sentence shall be passed and no penalty shall be executed on a person found guilty of an offence except pursuant to a conviction pronounced by a

court offering the essential guarantes of independence and impartiality"

- To provide aid to the wounded or the shipwrecked
- To protect medical and religious personnel
- Generally to protect civilian persons and civilian objects

Before the adoption of Protocol II, only Article 3, common to all four Geneva Conventions of 1949, pertained to non-international conflicts. Because some 80 percent of the victims of armed conflicts since 1945 have been victims of non-international conflicts, the single article was felt to be inadequate. Moreover, non-international conflicts—that is, civil war—tend to be fought with greater cruelty and less regard to the accepted rules of warfare than international conflicts. Protocol II, therefore, extends the essential rules of the law of armed conflicts to internal wars.

The protocol was controversial in that it threatens to encroach on state sovereignty. Originally, an extensive protocol of 47 articles was proposed. To avoid questions of conflict with state sovereignty, the final protocol was shortened and simplified to 28 articles. The thrust of the final document is mainly humanitarian, and it is careful to distinguish between civil insurrection and genuine civil war: "This Protocol shall not apply to situations of internal disturbances and tensions, such as riots, isolated and sporadic acts of violence and other acts of a similar nature, as not being armed conflicts." Although the protocol generally expands on Article 3, it defines a narrower range of applicable internal conflicts than does Article 3 common to the conventions of 1949, specifying the following: that the internal conflict must "take place in the territory of a High Contracting Party between its armed forces and *dissident armed forces* or *other organized armed groups* which, *under responsible command, exercise such control over a part of its territory as to enable them to carry out sustained and concerted military operations*" (emphasis added).

REFERENCES:
Levie, Howard S., ed. *The Law of Non-international Armed Conflict: Protocol II to the 1949 Geneva Conventions.* Dordrecht, Netherlands, and Boston: M. Nijhoff, 1987.
Pilloud, Claude, et al., eds. *Commentary on the Additional Protocols of 8 June 1977 to the Geneva Conventions of 12 August 1949.* Dordrecht, Netherlands, and Boston: M. Nijhoff, 1987.

SALT II Treaty

SIGNED: June 18, 1979, at Vienna
SIGNATORIES: Union of Soviet Socialist Republics vs. United States
IN FORCE: Did not enter into force; see **START II Treaty**
OVERVIEW: The product of years of negotiation, the treaty focused on limiting the number of strategic launchers in the U.S.

and U.S.S.R. nuclear arsenals.

DISCUSSION:
A complex treaty reflecting the technological complexity of modern nuclear weapons systems, the SALT II document set limits on the number of strategic launchers to be employed by the United States and the U.S.S.R. Strategic launchers may be land based or submarine based and are capable of launching MIRVs—multiple independently targetable reentry vehicles. MIRVed missiles are capable of targeting several targets, thereby rendering the enemy's ICBM (intercontinental ballistic missile) sites particularly vulnerable. Each side was to be limited to 2,400 ICBM, SLBM (submarine-launched ballistic missile), and ASBM (air-to-surface ballistic missile) launchers. "Launchers" included land-based sites, submarines, and heavy bombers (capable of carrying ASBMs).

A protocol to the SALT II treaty was also signed, specifying the following:

- That neither the U.S. nor U.S.S.R. would deploy mobile ICBM launchers
- That neither would deploy cruise missiles "capable of a range in excess of 600 kilometers on se-based launchers or land-based launchers"
- That neither would deploy ASBMs

On January 3, 1980, President Jimmy Carter formally requested that the United States Senate delay consideration of ratification of the SALT II Treaty because of the Soviet invasion of Afghanistan in December 1979. This notwithstanding, however, the United States and the Soviet Union voluntarily observed the arms limits agreed upon in SALT II while negotiations were reopened between the two superpowers. By 1982, these negotiations, conducted in Geneva, were now known as the Strategic Arms Reduction Talks, or START.

REFERENCE:
Panofsky, Wolfgang Kurt Hermann. *Arms Control and SALT II.* Seattle: University of Washington Press, 1979.

Conventional Weapons Convention

OFFICIAL TITLE: Convention on Prohibitions or Restrictions on the Use of Certain Conventional Weapons Which May Be Deemed to Be Excessively Injurious or to Have Indiscriminate Effects
SIGNED: October 10, 1980, at Geneva
SIGNATORIES: Argentina, Australia, Austria, Belarus, Belgium, Benin, Bosnia-Herzegovina, Brazil, Bulgaria, Canada, China, Croatia, Cuba, Cyprus, Czech Republic, Denmark, Ecuador, Finland, Former Yugoslav Republic of Macedonia, France, Georgia, Germany, Greece, Guatemala, Hungary, Iceland, India,

Ireland, Israel, Italy, Japan, Jordan, Laos, Latvia, Liechtenstein, Luxembourg, Malta, Mauritius, Mexico, Mongolia, Netherlands, New Zealand, Niger, Norway, Pakistan, Philippines, Poland, Romania, Russian Federation, Slovak Republic, Slovenia, South Africa, Spain, Sweden, Switzerland Togo, Tunisia, Uganda, Ukraine, United Kingdom, United States, Uruguay, Yugoslavia

IN FORCE: From December 2, 1983 (in force for the United States from September 24, 1995)

OVERVIEW: The convention extended 1949 Geneva conventions and their protocols in prohibiting or restricting certain conventional (non-nuclear) weapons.

DISCUSSION:

The convention prohibits or restricts the use of non-nuclear weapons that are deemed to be excessively or indiscriminately injurious. Protocols specifically address weapons that produce non-detectable fragments, mines, booby traps, and incendiary weapons. Although the United States is a signatory to this treaty, it has declined to sign the **Convention on the Prohibition of the Use, Stockpiling, Production and Transfer of Anti-Personnel Mines and on Their Destruction** (1997), which nevertheless has been widely supported by private American citizens.

REFERENCE:
Pierre, Andrew J., ed. *Cascade of Arms: Managing Conventional Weapons Proliferation.* Washington, D.C.: Brookings Institute, 1997.

Protocol on Prohibitions or Restrictions on the Use of Mines, Booby-Traps and Other Devices (Protocol II)

SIGNED: October 10, 1980, at Geneva

SIGNATORIES: Argentina, Australia, Austria, Belarus, Belgium, Benin, Bosnia-Herzegovina, Brazil, Bulgaria, Canada, China, Croatia, Cuba, Cyprus, Czech Republic, Denmark, Ecuador, Finland, Former Yugoslav Republic of Macedonia, France, Georgia, Germany, Greece, Guatemala, Hungary, Iceland, India, Ireland, Israel, Italy, Japan, Jordan, Laos, Latvia, Liechtenstein, Luxembourg, Malta, Mauritius, Mexico, Mongolia, Netherlands, New Zealand, Niger, Norway, Pakistan, Philippines, Poland, Romania, Russian Federation, Slovak Republic, Slovenia, South Africa, Spain, Sweden, Switzerland Togo, Tunisia, Uganda, Ukraine, United Kingdom, United States, Uruguay, Yugoslavia

IN FORCE: From December 2, 1983 (in force for the United States from September 24, 1995)

OVERVIEW: The protocol to the Geneva Conventions regulates and restricts the deployment of land-based and certain water-based (but not anti-ship) mines and restricts and regulates the use of booby traps.

DISCUSSION:
Signatories to the protocol undertake to refrain from the following:

- Purposely use mines and booby traps against civilians
- Deploy these devices indiscriminately
- Remotely deploy mines in civilian, non-combat areas

The use of booby traps is addressed in Article 6:

1. Without prejudice to the rules of international law applicable in armed conflict relating to treachery and perfidy, it is prohibited in all circumstances to use: (a) any booby-trap in the form of an apparently harmless portable object which is specifically designed and constructed to contain explosive material and to detonate when it is disturbed or approached, or (b) booby-traps which are in any way attached to or associated with: (i) internationally recognized protective emblems, signs or signals; (ii) sick, wounded or dead persons; (iii) burial or cremation sites or graves; (iv) medical facilities, medical equipment, medical supplies or medical transportation; (v) children's toys or other portable objects or products specially designed for the feeding, health, hygiene, clothing or education of children; (vi) food or drink; (vii) kitchen utensils or appliances except in military establishments, military locations or military supply depots; (viii) objects clearly of a religious nature; (ix) historic monuments, works of art or places or worship which constitute the cultural or spiritual heritage of peoples; (x) animals or their carcasses.

2. It is prohibited in all circumstances to use any booby-trap which is designed to cause superfluous injury or unnecessary suffering.

Signatories agree to record the location of all mines and to assist in their safe removal at the conclusion of hostilities.

While the United States is a signatory to this protocol, it has declined to ratify the 1997 **Convention on the Prohibition of the Use, Stockpiling, Production and Transfer of Anti-Personnel Mines and on Their Destruction**.

REFERENCE:
Pierre, Andrew J., ed. *Cascade of Arms: Managing Conventional Weapons Proliferation.* Washington, D.C.: Brookings Institute, 1997.

Treaty on the Elimination of Intermediate-Range and Shorter-Range Missiles (INF Treaty)

SIGNED: December 8, 1987, at Washington, D.C.

SIGNATORIES: Union of Soviet Socialist Republics vs. United States

IN FORCE: From June 1, 1988

OVERVIEW: The product of months of negotiation, the treaty called for each party to eliminate from its nuclear arsenal all intermediate and shorter-range missiles.

DISCUSSION:
The so-called INF Treaty (*INF*: Intermediate-range Nuclear Forces) was the first arms-control treaty to dismantle, destroy,

and otherwise abolish an entire category of weapon systems. Equally ground-breaking were the two protocols attached to the treaty, which created unprecedented procedures for observers from both nations to verify the other nation's adherence to the treaty by destruction of its missiles.

Intermediate-range ballistic missiles (IRBMs) and ground-launched cruise missiles (GLCMs) were defined by the treaty as having ranges of 620 to 3,400 miles; shorter-range ballistic missiles (SRBMs), also covered by the treaty, were defined as having ranges from 300 to 619 miles. The treaty thus applied directly to the deployment of missiles in Europe, as opposed to missiles of inter-continental range. The United States, under the auspices of NATO, had IRBM and SRBMs in Europe, and the Soviet Union had such missiles deployed within territory under its control.

After protracted negotiation, the Soviet Union agreed to elimination (not mere reduction) of all land-based IRBMs and SRBMs. This entitled dismantling, over a three-year period, 2,619 missiles. Two-thirds of the missiles affected were Soviet, the rest were American. Although the missiles, launchers, and support apparatus were all to be destroyed, each nation was allowed to keep intact the warheads and guidance systems of the destroyed missiles. Each nation was accorded the right, for a period of thirteen years, to conduct periodic inspections.

REFERENCES:

Sigel, Leon. *Nuclear Forces in Europe: Enduring Dilemmas, Present Prospects.* Washington, D.C.: Brookings Institute, 1984.

Sur, Serge. *Verification Problems of the Washington Treaty on the Elimination of Intermediate Range Missiles.* New York: United Nations Publications, 1989.

Thies, Wallace J. *Atlantic Alliance, Nuclear Weapons, and European Attitudes: Reexamining the Conventional Wisdom,* Berkeley: University of California Press, 1983.

Treaty on Conventional Armed Forces in Europe

SIGNED: November 19, 1990, at Paris

SIGNATORIES: Belgium, Bulgaria, Canada, Czech and Slovak Federal Republic, Denmark, France, Germany (Federal Republic), Greece, Hungary, Iceland, Italy, Luxembourg, Netherlands, Norway, Poland, Portugal, Romania, Spain, Turkey, Union of Soviet Socialist Republics, United Kingdom, United States

IN FORCE: From November 9, 1992

OVERVIEW: An international treaty limiting the deployment of conventional armed forces and equipment in Europe.

DISCUSSION:

In the Cold War era, arms control, arms limitation, and disarmament treaties focused mainly on strategic—nuclear and thermonuclear—weapons. The present treaty addresses the limitation of tactical—non-nuclear, or conventional—forces

and weapons. The preamble to the treaty sets down its chief objectives:

- To "prevent any military conflict in Europe"
- To "achieve greater stability and security in Europe"
- To "replace military confrontation with a new pattern of security relations among all the States Parties based on peaceful cooperation and thereby to contribute to overcoming the division of Europe"
- To establish "a secure and stable balance of conventional armed forces in Europe at lower levels than heretofore"
- To eliminate "disparities prejudicial to stability and security"
- To eliminate "the capability for launching surprise attack and for initiating large-scale offensive action in Europe"

Overall, the signatories committed themselves "to the objective of ensuring that the numbers of conventional armaments and equipment limited by the Treaty within the area of application of this Treaty do not exceed 40,000 battle tanks, 60,000 armoured combat vehicles, 40,000 pieces of artillery, 13,600 combat aircraft and 4,000 attack helicopters." The body of the treaty defines in detail the conventional forces covered by the treaty and the areas governed by the treaty. The treaty also lays down timetables for the reduction of forces and designates what equipment is to be withdrawn entirely from the treaty area, what equipment is to be permanently stored in designated areas, and what equipment is to be dismantled or destroyed.

Article 14 provides for procedures to verify compliance with the treaty, granting "each State Party . . . the right to conduct, and the obligation to accept, within the area of application, inspections in accordance with the provisions of the Protocol on Inspection," which is subjoined to the treaty.

Article 16 establishes a Joint Consultative Group, within which the signatory parties may do the following:

(A) address questions relating to compliance with or possible circumvention of the provisions of this Treaty;

(B) seek to resolve ambiguities and differences of interpretation that may become apparent in the way this Treaty is implemented;

(C) consider and, if possible, agree on measures to enhance the viability and effectiveness of this Treaty;

(D) update the lists [of equipment] contained in the Protocol on Existing Types . . .;

(E) resolve technical questions in order to seek common practices among the States Parties in the way this Treaty is implemented;

(F) work out or revise, as necessary, rules of procedure, working methods, the scale of distribution of expenses of the Joint Consultative Group and of conferences convened under this Treaty and the distribution of costs of inspections between or among States Parties;

(G) consider and work out appropriate measures to ensure that information obtained through exchanges of information among the States Parties or as a result of inspections pursuant to this Treaty is used solely for the purposes of this Treaty, taking into account the particular requirements of each State Party in respect of safeguarding information which that State Party specifies as being sensitive;

(H) consider, upon the request of any State Party, any matter that a State Party wishes to propose for examination . . .; and

(I) consider matters of dispute arising out of the implementation of this Treaty.

Although the treaty is of unlimited duration, a signatory may withdraw upon 150 days' notice. Moreover, "Each State Party shall, in particular, in exercising its national sovereignty, have the right to withdraw from this Treaty if another State Party increases its holdings in battle tanks, armoured combat vehicles, artillery, combat aircraft or attack helicopters, as defined in Article II, which are outside the scope of the limitations of this Treaty, in such proportions as to pose an obvious threat to the balance of forces within the area of application."

The treaty was successfully renegotiated in 1996 and 1999, with each new version further reducing conventional arms stocks and deployment in Europe.

REFERENCE:

Bellany, Ian, and Tim Huxley, eds. *New Conventional Weapons and Western Defense.* Ilford, UK: Frank Cass and CO., 1987.

START II Treaty

OFFICIAL TITLE: Treaty between the United States of America and the Russian Federation on Further Reduction and Limitation of Strategic Offensive Arms

SIGNED: January 3, 1993, at Moscow

SIGNATORIES: Russian Federation vs. United States

IN FORCE: Not in force as of 1999 (ratified by the U.S. Senate; not yet ratified by the Russian Federation)

OVERVIEW: A reaffirmation and substantial extension of SALT I strategic arms reduction, pending ratification by the Russian Federation as of 1999.

DISCUSSION:

The START negotiations—Strategic Arms Reduction Talks—between the United States and the Soviet Union had as their object the reduction of the two superpowers' nuclear arsenals. START was the successor to SALT (Strategic Arms Limitation Talks), a series of negotiations that began in 1969 and extended into the 1970s. START began in 1982, was suspended during 1983-1985, and resumed late in 1985, culminating in July 1991 with a comprehensive strategic arms-reduction agreement agreed to by U.S. President George Bush and Soviet leader Mikhail Gorbachev.

The START II Treaty is in part a reaffirmation by the Russian Federation of obligations under the START Treaty, concluded before the dissolution of the Soviet Union. But START II mandates reductions in the arsenals of the two nations that go far beyond those agreed to in START I. Whereas START I had cut U.S. and Soviet warheads by about 25 percent to 30 percent, START II calls for the destruction of about 70 percent of pre-START nuclear warheads.

The bulk of the treaty specifies reductions and limits in numbers of nuclear-capable bombers, missiles, and missile installations.

The United States Senate ratified the START II Treaty, but the Russian Federal Assembly refused to take up the issue of ratification, many legislators expressing fears that Russia had been overly hasty in concluding a disadvantageous agreement. Although both the United States and the Russian Federation have continued to cut their strategic nuclear forces in conformity with the START I Treaty, START II is not yet in force.

REFERENCES:

Meiers, Franz-Josef. *From Start I to Start II: Arms Control under Uncertainty.* Geneva, Switzerland: Programme for Strategic and International Security Studies, 1994.

United States Senate, Committee on Foreign Relations. *Treaty Between U.S. and the Russian Federation on Further Reduction and Limitation of Strategic Offensive Arms (The Start II Treaty) Treaty Doc. 103-1: Hearings Before the Committee on Foreign Relations, United States Senate, One Hundred Third Congress, First Session, May 11, 18; June 17 and 24, 1993.* Washington, D.C.: U.S. Government Printing Office, 1994.

United States Senate, Committee on Armed Services. *National Security Implications of U.S. Ratification of the Strategic Arms Reduction Treaty—Start II: Hearing Before the Committee on Armed Services, United States Senate, One Hundred Fourth Congress, First Session, May 17, 1995.* Washington, D.C.: U.S. Government Printing Office, 1996.

Chemical Weapons Convention

OFFICIAL TITLE: Convention on the Prohibition of the Development, Production, Stockpiling and Use of Chemical Weapons and on Their Destruction

SIGNED: January 13, 1993, at Paris

SIGNATORIES: Afghanistan, Albania, Algeria, Argentina, Armenia, Australia, Austria, Azerbaijan, Bahamas, Bahrain, Bangladesh, Belarus, Belgium, Benin, Bhutan, Bolivia, Bosnia-Herzegovina, Botswana, Brazil, Brunei Darussalam, Bulgaria, Burkina Faso, Burma (Myanmar), Burundi, Cambodia, Cameroon, Canada, Cape Verde, Central African Rep., Chad, Chile, China, Colombia, Comoros, Congo, Cook Islands, Costa Rica, Côte d'Ivoire, Croatia, Cuba, Cyprus, Czech Republic, Denmark, Djibouti, Dominica, Dominican Republic, Ecuador, El Salvador, Equatorial Guinea, Estonia, Ethiopia, Fiji, Finland, France, Gabon, Gambia, Georgia, Germany, Ghana, Greece, Grenada, Guatemala, Guinea, Guinea-Bissau, Guyana, Haiti, Holy See, Honduras, Hungary, Iceland, India, Indonesia, Iran, Ireland, Israel, Italy, Jamaica, Japan, Jordan, Kazakhstan, Kenya, Korea (Republic of), Kuwait, Kyrgyzstan, Laos (P.D.R.), Latvia,

Lesotho, Liberia, Liechtenstein, Lithuania, Luxembourg, Macedonia, Madagascar, Malawi, Malaysia, Maldives, Mali, Malta, Marshall Islands, Mauritania, Mauritius, Mexico, Micronesia, Moldova (Republic of), Monaco, Mongolia, Morocco, Namibia, Nauru (Republic of), Nepal, Netherlands, New Zealand, Nicaragua, Niger, Nigeria, Norway, Oman, Pakistan, Panama, Papua New Guinea, Paraguay, Peru, Philippines, Poland, Portugal, Qatar, Romania, Russian Federation, Rwanda, Samoa, San Marino, Saudi Arabia, Senegal, Seychelles, Sierra Leone, Singapore, Slovak Republic, Slovenia, South Africa, Spain, Sri Lanka, St. Kitts and Nevis, St. Lucia, St. Vincent and the Grenadines, Sudan, Suriname, Swaziland, Sweden, Switzerland, Tajikistan, Tanzania, Thailand, Togo, Trinidad and Tobago, Tunisia, Turkey, Turkmenistan, Uganda, Ukraine, United Arab Emirates, United Kingdom, United States, Uruguay, Uzbekistan, Venezuela, Vietnam, Yemen, Zaire, Zambia, Zimbabwe

IN FORCE: From April 29, 1997

OVERVIEW: A global treaty that bans an entire class of weapons of mass destruction: chemical weapons.

DISCUSSION:

The CWC bans the production, acquisition, stockpiling, transfer and use of chemical weapons. The signatories undertake to refrain from

- Developing, producing, acquiring, stockpiling or retaining chemical weapons, or transferring them to anyone
- Using chemical weapons
- Engaging in any military preparation to use chemical weapons
- Assisting, encouraging, or inducing anyone to use chemical weapons

Signatory parties agreed to destroy all weapons currently stockpiled.

The CWC contains highly detailed provisions regarding the operation and monitoring of the chemical industry to ensure that substances manufactured for legitimate, peaceful purposes are not appropriated for the production of chemical weapons. The CWC is the first arms control and arms limitation treaty that directly affects the private sector.

REFERENCE:

Price, Richard M. *The Chemical Weapons Taboo*. Ithaca, NY: Cornell University Press, 1997.

Draft Protocol on Blinding Laser Weapons

DRAFTED AND REVISED: September 25-October 12, 1995, at Vienna

SIGNATORIES: Draft protocol; not yet open for signature

IN FORCE: Not yet in force

OVERVIEW: A proposed protocol to the **Conventional Weapons Agreement** prohibiting laser weapons intended solely to cause permanent blindness.

DISCUSSION:

Lasers have a wide variety of uses in military applications. One proposed use is as a weapon intended to blind enemy personnel. The proposed protocol to the Conventional Weapons Agreement deems such laser weapons "excessively injurious" and inhumane and prohibits their military use; however, "blinding as an incidental or collateral effect of the legitimate military employment of laser systems . . . is not covered."

The protocol has yet to be opened for signature.

REFERENCES:
None

Comprehensive Nuclear Test Ban Treaty (CTBT)

SIGNED: September 10, 1996, at New York

SIGNATORIES: Albania, Algeria, Andorra, Angola, Antigua and Barbuda, Argentina, Armenia, Australia, Austria, Azerbaijan, Bahrain, Bangladesh, Belarus, Belgium, Benin, Bolivia, Bosnia and Herzegovina, Brazil, Brunei Darussalam, Bulgaria, Burkina Faso, Burundi, Cambodia, Canada, Cape Verde, Chad, Chile, China, Colombia, Comoros, Congo (Republic of [Brazzaville]), Congo (Democratic Republic of [Kinshasa]), Cook Islands, Costa Rica, Côte d'Ivoire, Croatia, Cyprus, Czech Republic, Denmark, Djibouti, Dominican Republic, Ecuador, Egypt, El Salvador, Equatorial Guinea, Estonia, Ethiopia, Fiji, Finland, Former Yugoslav Republic of Macedonia, France, Gabon, Georgia, Germany, Ghana, Greece, Grenada, Guinea, Guinea-Bissau, Haiti, Holy See, Honduras, Hungary, Iceland, India, Indonesia, Iran (Islamic Republic), Ireland, Israel, Italy, Jamaica, Japan, Jordan, Kazakhstan, Kenya, Kuwait, Kyrgyzstan, Lao People's Democratic Republic, Latvia, Lesotho, Liberia, Liechtenstein, Lithuania, Luxembourg, Madagascar, Malawi, Malaysia, Maldives, Mali, Malta, Marshall Islands, Mauritania, Mexico, Micronesia (Federated States of), Moldova, Monaco, Mongolia, Morocco, Mozambique, Myanmar, Namibia, Nepal, Netherlands, New Zealand, Nicaragua, Niger, North Korea, Norway, Pakistan, Panama, Papua New Guinea, Paraguay, Peru, Philippines, Poland, Portugal, Qatar, Republic of Korea, Romania, Russian Federation, Saint Lucia, Samoa, San Marino, Sao Tome and Principe, Senegal, Seychelles, Singapore, Slovakia, Slovenia, Solomon Islands, South Africa, Spain, Sri Lanka, Suriname, Swaziland, Sweden, Switzerland, Tajikistan, Thailand, Togo, Tunisia, Turkey, Turkmenistan, Uganda, Ukraine, United Arab Emirates, United Kingdom, United States (signed but failed to ratify), Uruguay, Uzbekistan, Vanuatu, Venezuela, Vietnam, Yemen, Zambia

IN FORCE: Not yet in force

OVERVIEW: From Article 1: "Each State Party undertakes not to carry out any nuclear weapon test explosion or any other nuclear explosion, and to prohibit and prevent any such nuclear explosion at any place under its jurisdiction or control."

DISCUSSION:

A comprehensive ban on all nuclear weapons testing was first proposed during the 1950s but failed to become a reality during the long chill of the Cold War. It was finally adopted by the United Nations General Assembly in 1996, but will not enter into force until it is ratified by the 44 states listed in Annex 2 of the treaty; these are states that formally participated in the 1996 session of the Conference on Disarmament.

The treaty was motivated by the recognition among the signatories that "an end to all such nuclear explosions will . . . constitute a meaningful step in the realization of a systematic process to achieve nuclear disarmament." It is comprehensive in that it bans all forms of nuclear explosion—atmospheric, on or under water, and underground—and in its detail, particularly with regard to monitoring for compliance. The text of the treaty runs to more than 60 densely printed pages.

Article 1 is the heart of the treaty:

1. Each State Party undertakes not to carry out any nuclear weapon test explosion or any other nuclear explosion, and to prohibit and prevent any such nuclear explosion at any place under its jurisdiction or control. 2. Each State party undertakes, furthermore, to refrain from causing, encouraging, or in any way participating in the carrying out of any nuclear weapon test explosion or any other nuclear explosion.

Although the treaty has not yet entered into force, on November 19 1996, a Preparatory Commission for the Comprehensive Nuclear Test Ban Treaty Organization was established, charged with creating the global verification regime of the treaty and to prepare for its entry into force. Such preparation was made necessary by the treaty's elaborate provisions for an International Monitoring System (IMS) and an International Data Centre (IDC), key elements of a verification regime that will consist of a global network of 321 monitoring stations, as well as 16 laboratories, capable of detecting nuclear explosions worldwide. This network of 170 seismic, 80 radionuclide, 60 infrasound and 11 hydroacoustic stations, as well as 16 radionuclide laboratories—comprising a total of 337 facilities—will supply data for processing and analysis to IDC. Both the raw and processed data will be available to all the signatories. If a suspicious occurrence cannot be resolved through consultation and clarification, each signatory will have right to request an on-site inspection.

The treaty consists of a preamble, 17 articles, two annexes and a protocol. The Protocol describes verification procedures and contains two annexes, one of which lists the 337 facilities comprising the International Monitoring System (IMS) and the other describes parameters for standard event screening by the International Data Centre (IDC).

Article II establishes the Comprehensive Nuclear Test Ban Treaty Organization. Charged with ensuring the full and adequate implementation of the treaty, the organization, to be based in Vienna, will also provide a forum for consultation and cooperation.

Article III requires each signatory to take necessary measures to implement its obligations under the treaty, including the establishment of a national authority for liaison with the Organization and other States parties.

Article IV and the protocol establish the verification regime, which consists of monitoring through IMS and IDC, consultation and clarification, and on-site inspections and confidence-building measures. Verification activities are carefully defined and specified:

- They are to be based on objective information, limited to the subject matter of the treaty
- They are to be carried out on the basis of full respect for the sovereignty of signatories
- They are to be as non-intrusive as possible

Confidence-building measures include the following:

- To reduce the likelihood that verification data may be misinterpreted, each signatory is to notify the Technical Secretariat of any single chemical explosion using 300 ton or more of TNT-equivalent blasting material on its territory.
- Each signatory is to cooperate in calibrating the stations of IMS by carrying out chemical calibration explosions.

Article V addresses measures of redress and to ensure compliance. Under the treaty, the Conference may revoke a state's rights under the Treaty, may recommend to signatorie collective measures in conformity with international law, or, if the case is urgent, may bring the issue to the attention of the United Nations.

Article VI describes the mechanisms by which disputes concerning the application or interpretation of the treaty may be settled; subject to certain conditions, the International Court of Justice may be requested to give an advisory opinion.

Articles VII and VIII provides for amendment and review of the treaty, and the remaining articles deal with implementation, reservations, despositary, and authentic texts.

The protocol consists of the following three parts:

- Part I describes the International Monitoring System (IMS) and outlines the functions of the International Data Centre (IDC).
- Part II sets up the procedures for on-site inspections, specifying them in detail.
- Part III elaborates on the confidence-building measures listed under Article IV (Verification) of the treaty.

Although U.S. President Bill Clinton was the first head of state to sign the treaty, the Republican-controlled Senate refused to ratify the document in a vote on October 13, 1999, which many compared to the Senate's rebuff of President Woodrow Wilson in its rejection of the **Treaty of Versailles** and the **Covenant of the League of Nations**. If the treaty does come into force, it will stand as the most inclusive and ambitious nuclear test ban ever enacted. Yet, without the participation of the United States, it is doubtful that CTBT will realize the aspiration expressed in the preamble and serve as a first step toward international nuclear disarmament.

REFERENCES:

McKinzie, Matthew, ed. *The Comprehensive Test Ban Treaty: Issues and Answers.* Ithaca, NY: Cornell University, Peace Studies Program, 1997.

Panel on Basic Research Requirements in Support of Comprehensive Test Ban Monitoring, Committee on Seismology, Board on Earth Sciences and Resources, Commission on Geosciences, Environment, and Resources, National Research Council. *Research Required to Support Comprehensive Nuclear Test Ban Treaty Monitoring.* Washington, DC: National Academy Press, 1997.

United States Congress, Committee on Armed Services, Intelligence and Military Application of Nuclear Energy Subcommittee, Panel on the Strategic Arms Limitation Talks and the Comprehensive Test Ban Treaty. *Effects of a Comprehensive Test Ban Treaty on United States National Security Interests: Hearings Before the Panel on the Strategic Arms Limitations Talks and the Comprehensive Test Ban Treaty of the Intelligence and Military Application of Nuclear Energy Subcommittee of the Committee on Armed Services, House of Representatives, Ninety-fifth Congress, Second Session, August 14, 15, 1978.* Washington, D.C.: U.S. Government Printing Office, 1978.

Convention on the Prohibition of the Use, Stockpiling, Production and Transfer of Anti-Personnel Mines and on Their Destruction

SIGNED: September 18, 1997; the United States is not a signatory

SIGNATORIES (AS OF 1999): Albania, Algeria, Andorra, Angola, Antigua and Barbuda, Argentina, Australia, Austria, Bahamas, Bangladesh, Barbados, Belgium, Belize, Benin, Bolivia, Bosnia-Herzegovina, Botswana, brazil, Brunei Darussalam, Bulgaria, Burkina Faso, Burundi, Cambodia, Cameroon, Canada, Cape Verde, Chad, Chile, Colombia, Cook Islands, Costa Rica, Côte d'Ivoire, Croatia, Cyprus, Czech Republic, Denmark, Djibouti, Dominica, Dominican Republic, Ecuador, El Salvador, Equatorial Guinea, Ethiopia, Fiji, Former Yugoslav Republic of Macedonia, France, Gabon, Gambia, Germany, Ghana, Greece, Grenada, Guatemala, Guinea, Guinea-Bissau, Guyana, Haiti, Holy See, Honduras, Hungary, Iceland, Indonesia, Ireland. Italy, Jamaica, Japan, Jordan, Kenya, Lesotho, Liechtenstein, Lithuania, Luxembourg, Madagascar, Malawi, Malaysia, Maldives, Mali, Malta, Marshall Islands, Mauritania, Mauritius, Mexico, Moldova (Republic of), Monaco, Mozambique, Namibia, Netherlands, New Zealand, Nicaragua, Niger, Niue, Norway, Panama, Paraguay, Peru, Philippines, Poland, Portugal, Qatar, Romania, Rwanda, St. Kitts and Nevis, St. Lucia, St. Vincent and the Grenadines, Samoa, San Marino, Sao Tome, Senegal, Seychelles, Sierra Leone, Slovak Republic, Slovenia, Solomon Islands, South Africa, Spain, Sudan, Suriname, Swaziland, Sween, Switzerland, Tanzania (United Republic of) Thailand, Togo, Trinidad and Tobago, Tunisia, Turkmenistan, Uganda, Ukraine, United Kingdom, Uruguay, Vanatu, Venezuela, Yemen, Zambia, Zimbabwe

IN FORCE: From March 1, 1999 (after ratification by 40 nations)

OVERVIEW: An international convention to ban the use of anti-personnel mines, to destroy present stockpiles of these weapons, and to locate and remove currently deployed mines.

DISCUSSION:

The **Protocol on Prohibitions or Restrictions on the Use of Mines, Booby-Traps and Other Devices (Protocol II)** of 1980 is an international agreement regulating and restricting the use of anti-personnel weapons; however, by the early 1990s, a number of non-governmental organizations and individuals began an international movement for an outright and total ban on antipersonnel landmines. In October 1992, the International Campaign to Ban Landmines (ICBL) was formed and, by 1999, grew into a network representing more than 1,100 human rights, demining, humanitarian, children's, veterans', medical, development, arms control, religious, environmental, and women's groups in over 60 countries. The coordinator of ICBL, Jody Williams, an American, received the Nobel Peace Prize for her work in 1997.

The principal thrust of the treaty is contained in its opening article:

1. Each State Party undertakes never under any circumstances:

   a) To use anti-personnel mines;

   b) To develop, produce, otherwise acquire, stockpile, retain or transfer to anyone, directly or indirectly, anti-personnel mines;

   c) To assist, encourage or induce, in any way, anyone to engage in any activity prohibited to a State Party under this Convention.

2. Each State Party undertakes to destroy or ensure the destruction of all anti-personnel mines in accordance with the provisions of this Convention.

The rest of the treaty details procedures for carrying out these principal provisions, including guidelines for international cooperation and assistance.

Despite support for the anti-mine movement from many United States non-governmental organizations and individuals, the United States government, as of 1999, opposes the treaty and has not signed it, citing the security needs of United States troops stationed along the demilitarized zone dividing North and South Korea. Although the United States has pledged voluntarily to limit the deployment of anti-personnel mines and to seek alternatives to them specifically for application on the South Korean frontier, the nation has placed itself in ideologically unfamiliar company by opposing the ban. Other opposing nations include Belarus, China, Cuba ("Cuba cannot be attached to any international agreement prohibiting the use of AP mines whilst she is under the threats and hostility of the United States of America"—statement of the Directorate of Multilateral Affairs of the Cuban Ministry of Foreign Affairs), Egypt, India, Iran, Libya, Pakistan, Russian Federation, Sri Lanka, and Syria.

REFERENCE:

Human Rights Watch. *Landmine Monitor Report 1999: Toward a Mine-Free World: International Campaign to Ban Landmines.* Washington, D.C.: Human Rights Watch, 1999.

Inter-American Convention on Transparency in Conventional Weapons Acquisitions

SIGNED: June 7, 1999, at Guatemala City, Guatemala

SIGNATORIES: Argentina, Bolivia, Brazil, Canada, Chile, Colombia, Costa Rica, Dominica, Ecuador, El Salvador, Guatemala, Haiti, Mexico, Nicaragua, Paraguay, Peru, United States, Uruguay, Venezuela

IN FORCE: Not yet in force

OVERVIEW: "The objective of this Convention is to contribute more fully to regional openness and transparency in the acquisition of conventional weapons by exchanging information regarding such acquisitions, for the purpose of promoting confidence among States in the Americas."

DISCUSSION:

Signatories to the convention undertake to "report annually to the depositary on their imports and exports of conventional weapons during the preceding calendar year, providing information, with respect to imports, on the exporting State, and the quantity and type of conventional weapons imported; and information, with respect to exports, on the importing State, and the quantity and type of conventional weapons exported." They also undertake to report on "acquisition through national production" and to report even if no arms have been acquired during the previous calendar year. Reports are to be made to the convention depositary, the General Secretariat of the Organization of American States. Annexes to the convention specify weapons categories to be reported and furnish model forms for reporting.

The rationale for the convention is as a confidence-building measure that constitutes "an important step towards achieving one of the essential purposes established in the Charter of the Organization of American States, which is "to achieve an effective limitation of conventional weapons that will make it possible to devote the largest amount of resources to the economic and social development of the Member States."

REFERENCE:

Pierre, Andrew J., ed. *Cascade of Arms: Managing Conventional Weapons Proliferation.* Washington, D.C.: Brookings Institute, 1997.

SECTION 3.2

War Crimes and Rules of Warfare

Overview of Treaties in This Category

In addition to international agreements seeking to regulate or limit arms—or to abolish war itself—the twentieth century saw a series of agreements seeking to define (and punish) war crimes and to establish the rules of "civilized" warfare.

The year 1929 witnessed the international adoption of important "Geneva Conventions" on warfare, including **Convention Relative to the Treatment of Prisoners of War** and **Convention for the Amelioration of the Condition of the Wounded and Sick in Armies in the Field**. Both of these conventions would be renewed and expanded in 1949. The Hague and Geneva conventions were used, in part, as the basis for prosecuting war crimes and crimes against humanity that had been committed by the Germans and Japanese during World War II. (See **London Agreement [Nuremberg Tribunal Establishing Document]**, 1945; **Charter of the International Military Tribunal [Nuremberg Rules]**, 1945; **Control Council Law No. 10, Punishment of Persons Guilty of War Crimes, Crimes Against Peace and Against Humanity**, 1945; and **Charter of the International Military Tribunal for the Far East**, 1946.)

Human beings are not the only targets of war. The **Roerich Pact** (1935) sought to exempt historic monuments, museums, scientific, artistic, educational and cultural institutions from attack during war. The concept of protecting cultural property in war was expanded in **Convention for the Protection of Cultural Property in the Event of Armed Conflict** of 1954.

Convention Relative to the Treatment of Prisoners of War

SIGNED: July 27, 1929, at Geneva
SIGNATORIES: Afghanistan, Angola, Antigua and Barbuda, Argentina, Australia, Austria, Bahamas, Bahrain, Bangladesh, Barbados, Belgium, Belize, Benin, Bhutan, Bolivia, Botswana, Brazil, Bulgaria, Burkina Faso (Upper Volta), Burma, Cambodia, Cameroon, Canada, Cape Verde, Central African Republic, Chile, China (People's Republic), China (Taiwan), Comoros, Cuba, Cyprus, Czechoslovakia, Denmark, Djibouti, Dominica, Dominican Republic, Ecuador, Egypt, Estonia, Ethiopia, Equatorial Guinea, Fiji, Finland, France, Gambia, Germany (GDR/FRG), Ghana, Greece, Grenada, Guatemala, Guinea-Bissau, Guyana, Holy See, Hungary, Iceland, India, Indonesia, Iran, Iraq, Ireland, Jordan, Kenya, Kiribati, Korea (North), Korea (South), Kuwait, Laos, Latvia, Lebanon, Lesotho, Liberia, Libya, Liechtenstein, Lithuania, Luxembourg, Madagascar, Malawi, Malaysia, Maldives (Islands), Mali, Malta, Mauritius, Mexico, Monaco, Mongolia, Morocco, Nepal, Netherlands, New Zealand, Nicaragua, Niger, Nigeria, Norway, Pakistan, Panama, Papua New Guinea, Paraguay, Peru, Philippines, Poland, Portugal, Qatar, Romania, Rwanda, St. Kitts and Nevis, St. Lucia, St. Vincent and the Grenadines, Saudi Arabia, Seychelles, Sierra Leone, Singapore, Solomon Islands, South Africa, Spain, Sri Lanka, Sudan Suriname, Swaziland, Sweden, Switzerland, Syrian Arab Republic, Tanzania, Thailand, Togo, Tonga, Trinidad and Tobago, Tunisia, Turkey, Tuvalu, Uganda, Union of Soviet Socialist Republics, United Kingdom, United States, Uruguay
IN FORCE: From August 4, 1932
OVERVIEW: "... in the extreme event of a war, it will be the duty of every Power to mitigate as far as possible the inevitable rigors thereof and to alleviate the condition of prisoners of war."

DISCUSSION:

The convention extends and amplifies the **Geneva Conventions** of 1907, detailing rules of humane treatment of prisoners of war. The key provisions are stated in Article 2: "Prisoners of war are in the power of the hostile Government, but not of the individuals or formation which captured them. They shall at all times be humanely treated and protected, particularly against acts of violence, from insults and from public curiosity. Measures of reprisal against them are forbidden." Beyond this, the convention lays down minimum requirements concerning:

- Conditions of capture
- Evacuation of POWs from the combat zone
- Requirements for POW camps
- POW labor rules
- The right of communication with family, etc.
- Discipline, punishment, and prisoners' relations with authorities
- Release
- Application to certain civilians ("Persons who follow the armed forces without directly belonging thereto, such as correspondents, newspaper reporters, sutlers, or contractors, who fall into the hands of the enemy, and whom the latter think fit to detain, shall be entitled to be treated as prisoners of war, provided they are in possession of an authorization from the military authorities of the armed forces which they were following.")

The convention was updated and revised in 1949; see **Convention Relative to the Treatment of Prisoners of War**, 1949.

REFERENCE:

Grenville, J. A. S. *The Major International Treaties 1914-1973: A History Guide with Texts.* New York: Stein and Day, 1974.

Convention for the Amelioration of the Condition of the Wounded and Sick in Armies in the Field

SIGNED: July 27, 1929, at Geneva

SIGNATORIES: Afghanistan, Angola, Antigua and Barbuda, Argentina, Australia, Austria, Bahamas, Bahrain, Bangladesh, Barbados, Belgium, Belize, Benin, Bhutan, Bolivia, Botswana, Brazil, Bulgaria, Burkina Faso (Upper Volta), Burma, Cambodia, Cameroon, Canada, Cape Verde, Central African Republic, Chile, China (People's Republic), China (Taiwan), Comoros, Cuba, Cyprus, Czechoslovakia, Denmark, Djibouti, Dominica, Dominican Republic, Ecuador, Egypt, Estonia, Ethiopia, Equatorial Guinea, Fiji, Finland, France, Gambia, Germany (GDR/FRG), Ghana, Greece, Grenada, Guatemala, Guinea-Bissau, Guyana, Holy See, Hungary, Iceland, India, Indonesia, Iran, Iraq, Ireland, Jordan, Kenya, Kiribati, Korea (North), Korea (South), Kuwait, Laos, Latvia, Lebanon, Lesotho, Liberia, Libya, Liechtenstein, Lithuania, Luxembourg, Madagascar, Malawi, Malaysia, Maldives (Islands), Mali, Malta, Mauritius, Mexico, Monaco, Mongolia, Morocco, Nepal, Netherlands, New Zealand, Nicaragua, Niger, Nigeria, Norway, Pakistan, Panama, Papua New Guinea, Paraguay, Peru, Philippines, Poland, Portugal, Qatar, Romania, Rwanda, St. Kitts and Nevis, St. Lucia, St. Vincent and the Grenadines, Saudi Arabia, Seychelles, Sierra Leone, Singapore, Solomon Islands, South Africa, Spain, Sri Lanka, Sudan Suriname, Swaziland, Sweden, Switzerland, Syrian Arab Republic, Tanzania, Thailand, Togo, Tonga, Trinidad and Tobago, Tunisia, Turkey, Tuvalu, Uganda, Union of Soviet Socialist Republics, United Kingdom, United States, Uruguay

IN FORCE: From August 4, 1932

OVERVIEW: "Being equally animated by the desire to lessen, so far as lies in their power, the evils inseparable from war and desiring, for this purpose, to perfect and complete the provisions agreed to at Geneva on 22 August 1864, and 6 July 1906, for the amelioration of the condition of the wounded and sick in armies in the field, have resolved to conclude a new Convention for that purpose ..."

DISCUSSION:

The 1929 convention addressed provisions for the treatment of wounded and sick prisoners of war, issues that were not addressed in detail by earlier documents, such as the **Geneva Convention** of 1907. Signatories to the convention also under-

took to provide for burial of the enemy dead and to provide lists of wounded and dead to officials on the opposite side. A key section of the convention laid down rules concerning the noncombatant status of "medical formations and establishments," which were not to be subject to attack. Medical personnel, including medical-corps troops and civilian volunteers, were to be considered immune from attack, and, in the case of military medical personnel, were to be allowed to function as medical personnel in the event of their capture. Although military medical buildings and vehicles were to be considered subject to capture, they were also to be clearly marked and, therefore, immune from attack. The familiar red cross marking was specifically prescribed:

As compliment to Switzerland, the heraldic emblem of the red cross on a white ground, formed by reversing the Federal colors, is retained as the emblem and distinctive sign of the medical service of armed forces.

Nevertheless, in the case of countries which already use, in place of the red cross, the red crescent or the red lion and sun on a white ground as a distinctive sign, these emblems are also recognized by the terms of the present Convention.

REFERENCE:

Grenville, J. A. S. *The Major International Treaties 1914-1973: A History Guide with Texts.* New York: Stein and Day, 1974.

Roerich Pact

OFFICIAL TITLE: Treaty on the Protection of Artistic and Scientific Institutions and Historic Monuments

SIGNED: April 15, 1935, at Washington

SIGNATORIES: Argentina, Bolivia, Brazil, Chile, Colombia, Costa Rica, Cuba, Dominican Republic, Ecuador, El Salvador, Guatemala, Haiti, Honduras, Mexico, Nicaragua, Panama, Paraguay, Peru, United States, Uruguay, Venezuela

IN FORCE: From August 26, 1935

OVERVIEW: "The historic monuments, museums, scientific, artistic, educational and cultural institutions shall be considered as neutral and as such respected and protected by belligerents. The same respect and protection shall be due to the personnel of the institutions mentioned above. The same respect and protection shall be accorded to the historic monuments, museums, scientific, artistic, educational and cultural institutions in time of peace as well as in war."

DISCUSSION:

The preamble to the agreement briefly summarizes its background:

The High Contracting Parties, animated by the purpose of giving conventional form to the postulates of the resolution approved on 16 December 1933, by all the States represented at the Seventh International Conference of American States, held at Montevideo, which recommended to "the Governments of America which have not yet done so that they sign the 'Roerich Pact,' initiated by the 'Roerich Museum' in the United States, and which has as its object the universal adoption of a flag, already designed and generally known, in order thereby to preserve in any time of danger all nationally and privately owned immovable monuments which form the cultural treasure of peoples . . ."

The flagged monuments would be considered neutral and immune from attack or destruction. The provisions of the pact were not observed in World War II, and the principles laid down here were clarified in **Convention for the Protection of Cultural Property in the Event of Armed Conflict** of 1954.

REFERENCE:

International Convention for the Roerich Pact and Banner of Peace. *Roerich Pact, Banner of Peace: Proceedings.* Washington, D.C.: International Convention for the Roerich Pact and Banner of Peace, 1933.

London Agreement (Nuremberg Tribunal Establishing Document)

SIGNED: August 8, 1945, at London

SIGNATORIES: United States, Provisional Government of the French Republic, United Kingdom, and Union of Soviet Socialist Republics

IN FORCE: From signing

OVERVIEW: "Agreement . . . for the Prosecution and Punishment of the Major War Criminals of the European Axis."

DISCUSSION:

Pursuant to the **Joint Four-Nation Declaration of the Moscow Conference** of 1943, "there shall be established after consultation with the Control Council for Germany an International Military Tribunal for the trial of war criminals whose offenses have no particular geographical location whether they be accused individually or in their capacity as members of the organizations or groups or in both capacities." The result was the establishment of the International Military Tribunal, which met in Nuremberg, Germany, during 1945-1946 to try certain Nazi military and political leaders on charges of war crimes and crimes against humanity.

The tribunal was given authority to bring to justice any individual guilty of the commission of war crimes and to declare any group or organization to be criminal in character. Defendants would be entitled to receive a copy of the indictment, to offer defense, to be represented by counsel, and to confront and cross-examine the witnesses.

The first session took place not in Nuremberg, but in Berlin, on October 18, 1945. Twenty-four former Nazi leaders were charged with the perpetration of war crimes, and certain groups (such as the Gestapo) were charged with being criminal in character. From November 20, 1945, trial sessions were moved to Nuremberg. A total of 216 court sessions were held, and, on October 1, 1946, the verdicts on 22 of the original 24 defendants

was handed down. (Two defendants were not tried: Robert Ley committed suicide, and arms magnate Gustav Krupp von Bohlen und Halbachs was deemed mentally incompetent and physically unable to stand trial.) Three of the original defendants were acquitted, four were sentenced to terms of imprisonment from ten to twenty years, three were sentenced to life imprisonment, and twelve were sentenced to execution by hanging. Ten of these men were hanged on October 16, 1946. Two of the most infamous of the condemned escaped the noose: Martin Bormann, tried and convicted in absentia, was never apprehended, and Hermann Göring committed suicide before he could be executed.

The Nuremberg trials were not merely revenge or punishment for heinous acts, but firmly established the principle that crimes of international law are committed by persons, not states, and that individuals were liable to punishment. (For additional discussion of the mission and scope of the tribunal, see **Charter of the International Military Tribunal [Nuremberg Rules]**).

REFERENCES:

Ball, Howard. *Persecuting War Crimes and Genocide: The Twentieth-Century Experience.* Lawrence: University Press of Kansas, 1999.

Buscher, Frank M. *The U.S. War Crimes Trial Program in Germany, 1946-1955.* Westport, CT: Greenwood, 1989.

Persico, Joseph E. *Nuremberg: Infamy on Trial.* New York: Viking, 1994.

Charter of the International Military Tribunal (Nuremberg Rules)

SIGNED: October 6, 1945, at Berlin

SIGNATORIES: United States of America, the Provisional Government of the French Republic, the United Kingdom, and Union of Soviet Socialist Republics

IN FORCE: From signing

OVERVIEW: Pursuant to the **London Agreement (Nuremberg Tribunal Establishing Document)**, the document laid down the mission, scope, and rules of procedure of the Nuremberg War Crimes Tribunal.

DISCUSSION:

For the background of the Nuremberg Tribunal, see **London Agreement (Nuremberg Tribunal Establishing Document)**.

Article 6 of the charter defines punishable war crimes:

(a) CRIMES AGAINST PEACE: namely, planning, preparation, initiation or waging of a war of aggression, or a war in violation of international treaties, agreements or assurances, or participation in a common plan or conspiracy for the accomplishment of any of the foregoing;

(b) WAR CRIMES: namely, violations of the laws or customs of war. Such violations shall include, but not be limited to, murder, ill-treatment or deportation to slave labor or for any other purpose of civilian population of or in occupied territory, murder or ill-treatment of prisoners of war or persons on the seas, killing of hostages, plunder of public or private property, wanton destruction of cities, towns or villages, or devastation not justified by military necessity;

(c) CRIMES AGAINST HUMANITY: namely, murder, extermination, enslavement, deportation, and other inhumane acts committed against any civilian population, before or during the war; or persecutions on political, racial or religious grounds in execution of or in connection with any crime within the jurisdiction of the Tribunal, whether or not in violation of the domestic law of the country where perpetrated.

Leaders, organizers, instigators and accomplices participating in the formulation or execution of a common plan or conspiracy to commit any of the foregoing crimes are responsible for all acts performed by any persons in execution of such plan.

The **Charter of the International Military Tribunal** (**Nuremberg Rules**) permitted latitude on the important question of ultimate responsibility for particular acts: "The fact that the Defendant acted pursuant to order of his Government or of a superior shall not free him from responsibility, but may be considered in mitigation of punishment if the Tribunal determines that justice so requires." In contrast, the later **Charter of the International Military Tribunal for the Far East**, which addressed war crimes in the Pacific theater, permitted no such latitude; obedience to orders was not to be considered a mitigation.

REFERENCES:
Ball, Howard. *Persecuting War Crimes and Genocide: The Twentieth-Century Experience*. Lawrence: University Press of Kansas, 1999.
Buscher, Frank M. *The U.S. War Crimes Trial Program in Germany, 1946-1955*. Westport, CT: Greenwood, 1989.
Persico, Joseph E. *Nuremberg: Infamy on Trial*. New York: Viking, 1994.

Control Council Law No. 10, Punishment of Persons Guilty of War Crimes, Crimes Against Peace and Against Humanity

SIGNED: December 20, 1945, at London
SIGNATORIES: Union of Soviet Socialist Republics, United Kingdom, United States
IN FORCE: From signing
OVERVIEW: A definition of war crimes pursuant to the **London Agreement** (**Nuremberg Tribunal Establishing Document**).

DISCUSSION:
Following the surrender of Germany in World War II, the Allied occupation authority, known as the Control Council for Germany, enacted the following definitions of punishable war crimes, atrocities, and crimes against humanity:

a) *Crimes against Peace*. Initiation of invasions of other countries and wars of aggression in violation of international laws and treaties,

including but not limited to planning, preparation, initiation or waging a war of aggression, or a war in violation of international treaties, agreements, or assurances, or participation in a common plan or conspiracy for the accomplishment of any of the foregoing.

b) *War Crimes*. Atrocities or offences against persons or property, constituting violations of the laws or customs of war, including but not limited to, murder, ill treatment or deportation to slave labour or for any other purpose of civilian population from occupied territory, murder or ill treatment of prisoners of war or persons on the seas, killing of hostages, plunder of public or private property, wanton destruction of cities, towns or villages, or devastation not justified by military necessity.

c) *Crimes against Humanity*. Atrocities and offences, including but not limited to murder, extermination, enslavement, deportation, imprisonment, torture, rape, or other inhumane acts committed against any civilian population, or persecutions on political, racial or religious grounds whether or not in violation of the domestic laws of the country where perpetrated.

These definitions not only became the basis for the trials of World War II war criminals in Europe, but also in Asia, and also served to guide procedures against war criminals in subsequent conflicts.

REFERENCES:
Ball, Howard. *Persecuting War Crimes and Genocide: The Twentieth-Century Experience*. Lawrence: University Press of Kansas, 1999.
Buscher, Frank M. *The U.S. War Crimes Trial Program in Germany, 1946-1955*. Westport, CT: Greenwood, 1989.
Persico, Joseph E. *Nuremberg: Infamy on Trial*. New York: Viking, 1994.

Charter of the International Military Tribunal for the Far East

SIGNED: May 3, 1946
SIGNATORIES: "By command of General [Douglas] MacArthur"
IN FORCE: From signing
OVERVIEW: The document laying down the mission and rules of the tribunal established to investigate and try war crimes in the Pacific theater of World War II.

DISCUSSION:
In addition to establishing the constitution of the tribunal and setting its meeting place in Tokyo, the charter laid down its mission, scope, and procedures, as follows:

II JURISDICTION AND GENERAL PROVISIONS

Article 5.... The following acts, or any of them, are crimes coming within the jurisdiction of the Tribunal for which there shall be individual responsibility:

(a) *Crimes against Peace*: Namely, the planning, preparation, initiation or waging of a declared or undeclared war of aggression, or a war in violation of international law, treaties, agreements or assurances, or participation in a common plan or conspiracy for the accomplishment of any of the foregoing;

(b) *Conventional War Crimes:* Namely, violations of the laws or customs of war;

(c) *Crimes against Humanity:* Namely, murder, extermination, enslavement, deportation, and other inhumane acts committed against any civilian population, before or during the war, or persecutions on political or racial grounds in execution of or in connection with any crime within the jurisdiction of the Tribunal, whether or not in violation of the domestic law of the country where perpetrated. Leaders, organizers, instigators and accomplices participating in the formulation or execution of a common plan or conspiracy to commit any of the foregoing crimes are responsible for all acts performed by any person in execution of such plan.

Article 6. Responsibility of Accused. Neither the official position, at any time, of an accused, nor the fact that an accused acted pursuant to order of his government or of a superior shall, of itself, be sufficient to free such accused from responsibility for any crime with which he is charged, but such circumstances may be considered in mitigation of punishment if the Tribunal determines that justice so requires.

Although most of the tribunal's rules of procedure were modeled on traditional Anglo-American jurisprudence, the rules of evidence were liberalized: "The Tribunal shall not be bound by technical rules of evidence. It shall adopt and apply to the greatest possible extent expeditious and non-technical procedure, and shall admit any evidence which it deems to have probative value. All purported admissions or statements of the accused are admissible."

Under section V, "Judgment and Sentence," the tribunal was given "the power to impose upon an accused, on conviction, death or such other punishment as shall be determined by it to be just." Execution and review of the sentence was to be on authority of the Supreme Commander for the Allied Powers, "who may at any time reduce or otherwise alter the sentence except to increase its severity."

REFERENCES:
Ball, Howard. *Persecuting War Crimes and Genocide: The Twentieth-Century Experience.* Lawrence: University Press of Kansas, 1999.
Tanaka, Yuki. *Hidden Horrors: Japanese War Crimes in World War II.* Los Angeles: Westview Press, 1998.

Convention for the Amelioration of the Condition of the Wounded and Sick in Armed Forces in the Field

SIGNED: August 12, 1949, at Geneva
SIGNATORIES: Afghanistan, Albania, Algeria, Andorra, Angola, Antigua and Barbuda, Argentina, Australia, Austria, Bahamas, Bahrain, Bangladesh, Barbados, Belarus, Belgium, Belize, Benin, Bolivia, Botswana, Brazil, Brunei, Bulgaria, Burkina Faso, Burma, Burundi, Cambodia, Cameroon, Canada, Cape Verde, Central African Republic, Chad, Chile, China, Colombia,

Comoros, Congo, Costa Rica, Côte d'Ivoire, Croatia, Cuba, Cyprus, Czechoslovakia, Denmark, Djibouti, Dominica, Dominican Republic, Ecuador, Egypt, El Salvador, Equatorial Guinea, Ethiopia, Fiji, Finland, Former Yugoslav Republic of Macedonia, France, Gabon, Gambia, Georgia, German Democratic Republic, Germany (Federal Republic), Ghana, Greece, Grenada, Guatemala, Guinea, Guinea-Bissau, Guyana, Haiti, Holy See, Honduras, Hungary, Iceland, India, Indonesia, Iran, Iraq, Ireland, Israel, Italy, Jamaica, Japan, Jordan, Kazakstan, Kenya, Kirbati, Korea (Democratic People's Republic), Korea (Republic), Kuwait, Kyrgyz Republic, Laos, Latvia, Lebanon, Lesotho, Liberia, Libya, Liechtenstein, Luxembourg, Madagascar, Malawi, Malaysia, Maldives, Mali, Malta, Mauritania, Mauritius, Mexico, Micronesia, Monaco, Mongolia, Morocco, Mozambique, Namibia (U.N. Council for), Nepal, Netherlands, New Zealand, Nicaragua, Niger, Nigeria, Norway, Oman, Pakistan, Palau, Panama, Papua New Guinea, Paraguay, Peru, Philippines, Poland, Portugal, Qatar, Romania, Russian Federation, Rwanda, St. Kitts and Nevis, St. Lucia, St. Vincent and the Grenadines, San Marino, Sao Tome and Principe, Saudi Arabia, Senegal, Seychelles, Sierra Leone, Singapore, Slovak Republic, Slovenia, Solomon Islands, Somalia, South Africa, Spain, Sri Lanka, Sudan, Suriname, Swaziland, Sweden, Switzerland, Syrian Arab Republic, Tajikistan, Tanzania, Thailand, Togo, Tonga, Trinidad and Tobago, Tunisia, Turkey, Turkmenistan, Tuvalu, Uganda, Ukraine, Union of Soviet Socialist Republics, United Arab Emirates, United Kingdom, United States, Uruguay, Uzbekistan, Vanuatu, Venezuela, Vietnam (Socialist Republic), Western Samoa, Yemen (Aden), Yemen (Sanaa), Yugoslavia, Zaire, Zambia, Zimbabwe
IN FORCE: From October 21, 1950
OVERVIEW: The fourth version of the Geneva Convention on the wounded and sick, after those adopted in 1864, 1906, and 1929.

DISCUSSION:
The 1949 version is largely the same as that of 1929, except for the following:
• A new introductory chapter on general provisions
• Changes were introduced into Chapter IV, covering personnel. In the 1929 convention, medical personnel and chaplains falling into enemy hands were to be immediately repatriated. The 1949 convention provides that they may, in certain circumstances, be retained to care for prisoners of war.
• Medical aircraft were permitted to fly over neutral territory in some circumstances.

See **Convention for the Amelioration of the Condition of the Wounded and Sick in Armies in the Field** of 1929.

REFERENCE:
Grenville, J. A. S. *The Major International Treaties 1914-1973: A History Guide with Texts.* New York: Stein and Day, 1974.

Convention Relative to the Treatment of Prisoners of War

SIGNED: August 12, 1949, at Geneva

SIGNATORIES: Afghanistan, Albania, Algeria, Andorra, Angola, Antigua and Barbuda, Argentina, Australia, Austria, Bahamas, Bahrain, Bangladesh, Barbados, Belarus, Belgium, Belize, Benin, Bolivia, Botswana, Brazil, Brunei, Bulgaria, Burkina Faso, Burma, Burundi, Cambodia, Cameroon, Canada, Cape Verde, Central African Republic, Chad, Chile, China, Colombia, Comoros, Congo, Costa Rica, Côte d'Ivoire, Croatia, Cuba, Cyprus, Czechoslovakia, Denmark, Djibouti, Dominica, Dominican Republic, Ecuador, Egypt, El Salvador, Equatorial Guinea, Ethiopia, Fiji, Finland, Former Yugoslav Republic of Macedonia, France, Gabon, Gambia, Georgia, German Democratic Republic, Germany (Federal Republic), Ghana, Greece, Grenada, Guatemala, Guinea, Guinea-Bissau, Guyana, Haiti, Holy See, Honduras, Hungary, Iceland, India, Indonesia, Iran, Iraq, Ireland, Israel, Italy, Jamaica, Japan, Jordan, Kazakstan, Kenya, Kirbati, Korea (Democratic People's Republic), Korea (Republic), Kuwait, Kyrgyz Republic, Laos, Latvia, Lebanon, Lesotho, Liberia, Libya, Liechtenstein, Luxembourg, Madagascar, Malawi, Malaysia, Maldives, Mali, Malta, Mauritania, Mauritius, Mexico, Micronesia, Monaco, Mongolia, Morocco, Mozambique, Namibia (U.N. Council for), Nepal, Netherlands, New Zealand, Nicaragua, Niger, Nigeria, Norway, Oman, Pakistan, Palau, Panama, Papua New Guinea, Paraguay, Peru, Philippines, Poland, Portugal, Qatar, Romania, Russian Federation, Rwanda, St. Kitts and Nevis, St. Lucia, St. Vincent and the Grenadines, San Marino, Sao Tome and Principe, Saudi Arabia, Senegal, Seychelles, Sierra Leone, Singapore, Slovak Republic, Slovenia, Solomon Islands, Somalia, South Africa, Spain, Sri Lanka, Sudan, Suriname, Swaziland, Sweden, Switzerland, Syrian Arab Republic, Tajikistan, Tanzania, Thailand, Togo, Tonga, Trinidad and Tobago, Tunisia, Turkey, Turkmenistan, Tuvalu, Uganda, Ukraine, Union of Soviet Socialist Republics, United Arab Emirates, United Kingdom, United States, Uruguay, Uzbekistan, Vanuatu, Venezuela, Vietnam (Socialist Republic), Western Samoa, Yemen (Aden), Yemen (Sanaa), Yugoslavia, Zaire, Zambia, Zimbabwe

IN FORCE: From October 21, 1950

OVERVIEW: A convention replacing the **Convention Relative to the Treatment of Prisoners of War** of 1929.

DISCUSSION:

The 1949 convention on prisoners of war expanded that of 1929, from 97 to 143 articles. The revisions reflected changes in the conduct of warfare and in the general living condition of peoples. Because it was felt that the welfare of POWs was highly dependent on individual interpretation given to the general regulations, the revised convention was more specific than the 1929 document. Key revisions include the following:

- Because the convention was to be posted in all POW camps, the revision attempts to render the language of the convention readily comprehensible to general readers.
- The categories of persons entitled to prisoner of war status (with the rights and protections that status confers) were broadened.
- Conditions and places of captivity were more precisely defined.
- Use of prisoners for labor was more precisely defined.
- Certain aspects of treatment (especially relating to financial resources, relief received, and judicial proceedings) were clarified.
- The principle that prisoners are to be released and repatriated without delay after the cessation of active hostilities was made explicit and emphatic.

REFERENCE:

Grenville, J. A. S. *The Major International Treaties 1914-1973: A History Guide with Texts.* New York: Stein and Day, 1974.

Convention for the Protection of Cultural Property in the Event of Armed Conflict

SIGNED: May 14, 1954, at The Hague

SIGNATORIES: Burma, Ecuador, Egypt, Hungary, Mexico, San Marino, Yugoslavia

IN FORCE: From August 7, 1956

OVERVIEW: Inspired by the **Treaty on the Protection of Artistic and Scientific Institutions and Historic Monuments (Roerich Pact)** of 1935, the convention lays down more comprehensive rules for the protection of monuments and works of art in time of war.

DISCUSSION:

As with the **Roerich Pact,** this convention seeks to designate certain monuments, cultural institutions, and works of art as "neutral" in wartime and, therefore, immune from attack. In 1939, a draft convention was created under the auspices of the International Museums Office to improve upon the Roerich Pact. The document was presented internationally by the Netherlands, but was soon rendered moot by the outbreak of World War II. Shortly after the war, the project was revived and, in 1948, a new proposal was submitted to UNESCO, again by the Netherlands. In 1951, UNESCO drew upon the services of experts to draft a definitive convention. The 1954 document, submitted to the governments for advice, was the result. The United States did not sign the new pact—indeed, few major nations did—electing to stand by the original Roerich Pact, which was framed in more general terms and is a statement of principle rather than an agreement binding in detail.

REFERENCE:
International Convention for the Roerich Pact and Banner of Peace. *Roerich Pact, Banner of Peace: Proceedings.* Washington, D.C.: International Convention for the Roerich Pact and Banner of Peace, 1933.

Convention on the Non-Applicability of Statutory Limitations to War Crimes and Crimes Against Humanity

SIGNED: November 26, 1968, at New York

SIGNATORIES: Bulgaria, Byelorussian Soviet Socialist Republic, Czechoslovakia, Hungary, Mexico, Mongolia, Nigeria, Poland, Romania, Ukrainian Soviet Socialist Republic, Union of Soviet Socialist Republics, Yugoslavia

IN FORCE: From November 11, 1970

OVERVIEW: A convention barring statutory limitations on war crimes.

DISCUSSION:

The principal provision of the convention is contained in Article 1:

No statutory limitation shall apply to the following crimes, irrespective of the date of their commission:

(a) War crimes as they are defined in the Charter of the International Military Tribunal, Nurnberg, of 8 August 1945 and confirmed by resolutions 3 (1) of 13 February 1946 and 95 (I) of 11 December 1946 of the General Assembly of the United Nations, particularly the "grave breaches" enumerated in the Geneva Conventions of 12 August 1949 for the protection of war victims;

(b) Crimes against humanity whether committed in time of war or in time of peace as they are defined in the Charter of the International Military Tribunal, Nurnberg, of 8 August 1945 and confirmed by resolutions 3 (I) of 13 February 1946 and 95 (I) of 11 December 1946 of the General Assembly of the United Nations, eviction by armed attack or occupation and inhuman acts resulting from the policy of apartheid, and the crime of genocide as defined in the 1948 Convention on the Prevention and Punishment of the Crime of Genocide, even if such acts do not constitute a violation of the domestic law of the country in which they were committed.

Although the United States pursued war crime prosecution vigorously following World War II, the nation is not a signatory of this convention. With the exception of Mexico, all of the signatories were, at the time of signing, members of the so-called "Soviet bloc."

REFERENCES:
None

War Crimes Convention

OFFICIAL TITLE: Principles of International Cooperation in the Detection, Arrest, Extradition and Punishment of Persons Guilty of War Crimes and Crimes Against Humanity

SIGNED: December 3, 1973 as United Nations General Assembly resolution 3074

SIGNATORIES: United Nations General Assembly

IN FORCE: On passage

OVERVIEW: A General Assembly resolution outlining principles of cooperation among nations in locating, apprehending, extraditing, and punishing war criminals.

DISCUSSION:

The resolution is a brief statement of the following principles:

1. War crimes and crimes against humanity, wherever they are committed, shall be subject to investigation and the persons against whom there is evidence that they have committed such crimes shall be subject to tracing, arrest, trial and, if found guilty, to punishment.

2. Every State has the right to try its own nationals for war crimes against humanity.

3. States shall co-operate with each other on a bilateral and multilateral basis with a view to halting and preventing war crimes and crimes against humanity, and shall take the domestic and international measures necessary for that purpose.

4. States shall assist each other in detecting, arresting and bringing to trial persons suspected of having committed such crimes and, if they are found guilty, in punishing them.

5. Persons against whom there is evidence that they have committed war crimes and crimes against humanity shall be subject to trial and, if found guilty, to punishment, as a general rule in the countries in which they committed those crimes. In that connection, States shall co-operate on questions of extraditing such persons.

6. States shall co-operate with each other in the collection of information and evidence which would help to bring to trial the persons indicated in paragraph 5 above and shall exchange such information.

7. In accordance with article 1 of the Declaration on Territorial Asylum of 14 December 1967, States shall not grant asylum to any person with respect to whom there are serious reasons for considering that he has committed a crime against peace, a war crime or a crime against humanity.

8. States shall not take any legislative or other measures which may be prejudicial to the international obligations they have assumed in regard to the detection, arrest, extradition and punishment-of persons guilty of war crimes and crimes against humanity.

9. In co-operating with a view to the detection, arrest and extradition of persons against whom there is evidence that they have committed war crimes and crimes against humanity and, if found guilty, their punishment, States shall act in conformity with the provisions of the Charter of the United Nations and of the Declaration on

Principles of International Law concerning Friendly Relations and Co-operation among States in accordance with the Charter of the United Nations.

REFERENCES:
None

Rome Statute of the International Criminal Court

SIGNED: July 17, 1998, at Rome

SIGNATORIES: (As of September 1998, the following nations had signed the Rome Statute; only four of these had ratified it.) Albania, Andorra, Angola, Antigua and Barbuda, Argentina, Australia, Austria, Belgium, Bolivia, Burkina Faso, Burundi, Bulgaria, Cameroon, Canada, Chile, Colombia, Congo, Costa Rica, Côte d'Ivoire, Croatia, Cyprus, Czech Republic, Denmark, Djibouti, Ecuador, Eritrea, Finland, France, Gabon, Gambia, Georgia, Germany, Ghana, Greece, Haiti, Honduras, Hungary, Iceland, Ireland, Italy , Jordan, Kenya, Kyrgyzstan, Latvia, Lesotho, Liberia, Liechtenstein, Lithuania, Luxembourg, Madagascar, Malawi, Mali, Malta, Mauritius, Monaco, Namibia, Netherlands, New Zealand, Niger, Norway, Panama, Paraguay, Poland, Portugal, Romania, Samoa, San Marino, Senegal, Sierra Leone, Slovakia, Slovenia, Solomon Islands, South Africa, Spain, Sweden, Switzerland, Tajikistan, Trinidad and Tobago, Uganda, The former Yugoslav Republic of Macedonia, United Kingdom, Venezuela, Zambia, Zimbabwe

IN FORCE: Not yet in force

OVERVIEW: Primarily an international statue giving the International Criminal Court the power to try those accused of genocide, crimes against humanity, and war crimes where national courts are unable or unwilling to do so.

DISCUSSION:

The statute creates a permanent international tribunal to try those accused of war crimes and genocide received. The International Criminal Court would be based in the Hague and would have jurisdiction over persons charged with genocide, crimes against humanity, aggression, and other war crimes. Cases could be initiated by the court's independent prosecutor, by a nation, or by the United Nations Security Council. Proceedings would require the permission either of the nation where the crime was allegedly committed or the suspect's home country.

REFERENCES:
None

SECTION 3.3
Criminal Law, Civil Law, and Extradition

Overview of Treaties in This Category

In no area have nations more jealously guarded their sovereignty than in domestic criminal and civil law; nevertheless, most nations have also realized that, issues of sovereignty aside, international cooperation and coordination are indispensable to the execution of justice. The most basic form of international cooperation in law enforcement is extradition, the surrender of a fugitive to the jurisdiction of another country. While the United States concluded extradition treaties as early as the nineteenth century, the importance of extradition increased greatly during the twentieth century, with greater accessibility to rapid international travel. The art of creating an extradition treaty resides in balancing issues of sovereignty with the exigencies of law enforcement, and in writing the treaty such that crimes of a political nature are exempted from extradition, lest one nation find itself being used as the political tool of another.

By the twentieth century, the trade in illicit narcotics had become a widespread international law-enforcement problem. A number of agreements, both bilateral as well as multilateral documents, address issues of international cooperation in the interdiction of illegal narcotics and in the prosecution of drug cases. Related to the international trade in narcotics is the expansion of organized crime on a global scale. The **Draft United Nations Convention Against Transnational Organized Crime** (1999) promises to be a groundbreaking multilateral agreement for international cooperation in law enforcement.

The later twentieth century also saw the rapid expansion of international business and, with it, a need for various conventions creating standards for international contracts, monetary transfers, and international investment. A number of such international civil law agreements are found in this section.

Convention for the Surrender of Criminals between the United States and France

SIGNED: November 9, 1843, at Washington
SIGNATORIES: France vs. United States
IN FORCE: Six months from signing
OVERVIEW: The first extradition convention concluded by the United States.

DISCUSSION:
The substantive articles of the brief treaty, the first extradition agreement into which the United States entered, follow:

ARTICLE I.
It is agreed that the High Contracting Parties shall, on requisitions made in their name, through the medium of their respective Diplomatic Agents, deliver up to justice persons who, being accused of the crimes enumerated in the next following article, committed within the jurisdiction of the requiring party, shall seek an asylum, or shall be found within the territories of the other: Provided, That this shall be done only when the fact of the commission of the crime shall be so established as that the laws of the country in which the fugitive or the person so accused shall be found would justify his or her apprehension and commitment for trial, if the crime had been there committed.

ARTICLE II.
Persons shall be so delivered up who shall be charged, according to the provisions of this Convention, with any of the following crimes, to wit: murder, (comprehending the crimes designated in the French Penal Code by the terms, assassination, parricide, infanticide, and poisoning,) or with an attempt to commit murder, or with rape, or with forgery, or with arson, or with embezzlement by public officers, when the same is punishable with infamous punishment.

ARTICLE III.
On the part of the French Government, the surrender shall be made only by authority of the Keeper of the Seals, Minister of Justice; and on the part of the Government of the United States, the surrender shall be made only by authority of the Executive thereof.

ARTICLE IV.
The expenses of any detention and delivery effected in virtue of the preceding provisions, shall be borne and defrayed by the Government in whose name the requisition shall have been made.

ARTICLE V.
The provisions of the present Convention shall not be applied in any manner to the crimes enumerated in the second article, committed anterior to the date thereof, nor to any crime or offence of a purely political character.

On November 9, 1843, an "Additional Article" was appended to the convention to redress the omission from the convention of robbery and burglary as extraditable crimes.

REFERENCES:
Bassiouni, M. Cherif, and Edward M. Wise. *Aut Dedere Aut Judicare: The Duty to Extradite or Prosecute in International Law.* Dordrecht, Netherlands, and Boston: M. Nijhoff, 1995.
___. *International Extradition: United States Law and Practice,* 3d ed. Dobbs Ferry, NY: Oceana Publications, 1996.
Yarnold, Barbara M. *International Fugitives.* New York: Praeger, 1991.

Extradition Convention between the United States and Austria-Hungary

SIGNED: July 3, 1856, at Washington
SIGNATORIES: Austria-Hungary vs. United States
IN FORCE: From December 15, 1856
OVERVIEW: An early brief example of a United States extradition treaty with a foreign power.

DISCUSSION:
The principal text of the brief treaty follows:

ARTICLE I

It is agreed that the United States and Austria shall, upon mutual requisitions by them or their ministers, officers or authorities, respectively made, deliver up to justice all persons who, being charged with the crime of murder, or assault with intent to commit murder, or piracy, or arson, or robbery, or forgery, or the fabrication or circulation of counterfeit money, whether coin or paper money, or the embezzlement of public moneys, committed within the jurisdiction of either party, shall seek an asylum or shall be found within the territories of the other: Provided, That this shall only be done upon such evidence of criminality as, according to the laws of the place where the fugitive or person so charged shall be found, would justify his apprehension and commitment for trial if the crime or offense had there been committed; and the respective judges and other magistrates of the two Governments shall have power, jurisdiction and authority, upon complaint made under oath, to issue a warrant for the apprehension of the fugitive or person so charged, that he may be brought before such judges or other magistrates, respectively, to the end that the evidence of criminality may be heard and considered; and if, on such hearing, the evidence be deemed sufficient to sustain the charge, it shall be the duty of the examining judge or magistrate to certify the same to the proper executive authority, that a warrant may issue for the surrender of such fugitive. The expense of such apprehension and delivery shall be borne and defrayed by the party who makes the requisition and receives the fugitive. The provisions of the present convention shall not be applied, in any manner, to the crimes enumerated in the first article committed anterior to the date thereof nor to any crime or offense of a political character.

ARTICLE II

Neither of the contracting parties shall be bound to deliver up its own citizens or subjects under the stipulations of this convention.

ARTICLE III

Whenever any person accused of any of the crimes enumerated in this convention shall have committed a new crime in the territories of the State where he has sought an asylum or shall be found, such person shall not be delivered up, under the stipulations of this convention, until he shall have been tried and shall have received the punishment due to such new crime, or shall have been acquitted thereof.

ARTICLE IV

The present convention shall continue in force until the first of January, eighteen hundred and fifty-eight; and if neither party shall have given to the other six months' previous notice of its intention then to terminate the same, it shall further remain in force until the end of twelve months after either of the high contracting parties shall have given notice to the other of such intention; each of the high contracting parties reserving to itself the right of giving such notice to the other at any time after the expiration of the said first day of January, 1858.

REFERENCES:
Bassiouni, M. Cherif, and Edward M. Wise. *Aut Dedere Aut Judicare: The Duty to Extradite or Prosecute in International Law.* Dordrecht, Netherlands, and Boston: M. Nijhoff, 1995.
___. *International Extradition: United States Law and Practice,* 3d ed. Dobbs Ferry, NY: Oceana Publications, 1996.
Yarnold, Barbara M. *International Fugitives.* New York: Praeger, 1991.

Treaty between the United States of America and the Republic of Mexico for the Extradition of Criminals

SIGNED: December 11, 1861
SIGNATORIES: Mexico vs. United States
IN FORCE: From June 20, 1862
OVERVIEW: A treaty of international extradition with a bordering nation and in time of civil war.

DISCUSSION:

Like other extradition treaties, the 1861 document lays down procedures for extradition of persons accused of any of a number of enumerated crimes, excluding crimes or offenses "of a purely political character" and excluding "fugitive slaves, nor the delivery of criminals who, when the offense was committed, shall have been held in the place where the offense was committed in the condition of slaves, the same being expressly forbidden by the Constitution of Mexico." The government of the United States, now torn by the Civil War, was doubtless pleased to grant Mexico the concession of fugitive slaves. The United States also made the following provision for extradition in time of civil war (emphasis added):

In the ease of crimes committed in the frontier States or Territories of the two contracting parties, requisitions may be made through their respective diplomatic agents, or through the chief civil authority of said States or Territories, or through such chief civil or judicial authority of the districts or counties bordering on the frontier as may for this purpose be duly authorized by the said chief civil authority of the said frontier States or Territories, *or when, from any cause, the civil authority of such State or Territory shall be suspended, through the chief military officer in command of such State or Territory.*

REFERENCES:
Bassiouni, M. Cherif, and Edward M. Wise. *Aut Dedere Aut Judicare: The Duty to Extradite or Prosecute in International Law.* Dordrecht, Netherlands, and Boston: M. Nijhoff, 1995.
___. *International Extradition: United States Law and Practice,* 3d ed. Dobbs Ferry, NY: Oceana Publications, 1996.
Yarnold, Barbara M. *International Fugitives.* New York: Praeger, 1991.

Extradition Convention between the United States and Argentina

SIGNED: September 26, 1896

SIGNATORIES: Argentina vs. United States

IN FORCE: From June 5, 1900

OVERVIEW: A treaty of extradition.

DISCUSSION:

The treaty enumerates the crimes for which extradition may be sought and explicitly excludes any "crime or offense of a political character."

REFERENCES:

Bassiouni, M. Cherif, and Edward M. Wise. *Aut Dedere Aut Judicare: The Duty to Extradite or Prosecute in International Law.* Dordrecht, Netherlands, and Boston: M. Nijhoff, 1995.

___. *International Extradition: United States Law and Practice,* 3d ed. Dobbs Ferry, NY: Oceana Publications, 1996.

Yarnold, Barbara M. *International Fugitives.* New York: Praeger, 1991.

Protocol for Limiting and Regulating the Cultivation of the Poppy Plant

OFFICIAL TITLE: Protocol for Limiting and Regulating the Cultivation of the Poppy Plant, the Production of, International and Wholesale Trade in, and Use of Opium

SIGNED: June 23, 1953, at New York

SIGNATORIES: Argentina, Australia, Belgian Congo, Belgium, Brazil, Cambodia, Cameroon, Canada, Central African Republic, Ceylon, Chile, China, Congo, Cook Islands, Costa Rica, Côte d'Ivoire, Cuba, Denmark, Dominican Republic, Ecuador, Egypt, El Salvador, France, French Whole Territory, Germany (Federal Republic), Greece, Guatemala, Guinea, India, Indonesia, Iran, Iraq, Israel, Italy, Japan, Jordan, Korea (Republic), Land Berlin, Lebanon, Liechtenstein, Luxembourg, Madagascar, Monaco, Nauru, Netherlands, New Zealand, Nicaragua, Niue Island, Norfolk Island, Pakistan, Panama, Papua New Guinea, Philippines, Rwanda, Senegal, South Africa, Southwest Africa (Namibia), Spain, Sweden, Switzerland, Tokelau Islands, Turkey, United Arab Republic, United Kingdom, United States, United States Territories, Venezuela, Western Samoa, Yugoslavia

IN FORCE: From March 8, 1963

OVERVIEW: A convention to strengthen international narcotics control by regulating the production of, trade in, and use of opium.

DISCUSSION:

The convention renews, reaffirms, and strengthens earlier international agreements, including the International Opium Convention (1912), Agreement Concerning the Suppression of the Manufacture of, Internal Trade in, and Use of, Prepared Opium and the International Opium Convention (1925), Convention for Limiting the Manufacture and Regulating the Distribution of Narcotic Drugs (1931), Agreement Concerning the Suppression of Opium Smoking (1931), Convention of 1936 for the Suppression of the Illicit Traffic in Dangerous Drugs (1936), and Protocol Bringing under International Control Drugs (1946).

Underpinning the convention is the single provision of Article 2: "The Parties shall limit the use of opium exclusively to medical and scientific needs." States that produce opium agreed to establish government agencies to regulate and license poppy cultivation, opium production, and opium export. Furthermore, the protocol laid down maximum limits of production for each producing country.

To enforce the regulations of the protocol, signatories agreed to import opium only from producing nations that were party to the protocol. Regulations for accounting for opium stocks and exports were included in the protocol, together with the creation of a central regulatory board to which all statistics would be reported. Enforcement measures included a variety of notification procedures and economic sanctions.

REFERENCES:

Bewley-Taylor, David R. *The United States and International Drug Control, 1909-1997.* London: Cassell Academic, 1999.

Chepesiuk, Ron. *Hard Target: The United States War Against International Drug Trafficking, 1982-1997.* Jefferson, NC: McFarland and Company, 1998.

Protocol on the Exercise of Criminal Jurisdiction over United Nations Forces in Japan

SIGNED: October 26, 1953, at Tokyo

SIGNATORIES: Australia, Belgium, Canada, France, Italy, Japan, Netherlands, New Zealand, Union of South Africa, United Kingdom, United States

IN FORCE: From October 29, 1953

OVERVIEW: A protocol governing criminal jurisdiction over the military forces serving in postwar Japan.

DISCUSSION:

This agreement governs criminal jurisdiction over military personnel serving in Japan in the years following World War II. The major provisions, set down in an Annex subjoined to the agreement, are as follows:

- The military authorities of the sending state have the right to exercise within Japan all criminal and disciplinary jurisdiction conferred on them by the law of the sending state over all persons subject to the military law of that state.
- The authorities of Japan have jurisdiction over the members of the United Nations forces or of the civilian components thereof, and their dependents with respect to offenses

committed within the territory of Japan and punishable by the law of Japan.

- The military authorities of the sending state have the right to exercise exclusive jurisdiction over persons subject to the military law of that state with respect to offenses punishable by the law of that sending state but not by the law of Japan.
- Japanese authorities have the right to exercise exclusive jurisdiction over members of the United Nations forces with respect to offenses punishable by Japanese law but not by the law of the sending state.

The Annex also details liaison procedures between Japanese authorities and military authorities.

REFERENCES:
Burkman, Thomas W., ed. *The Occupation of Japan: The International Context: the Proceedings of the Fifth Symposium Sponsored by the MacArthur Memorial, Old Dominion University, the MacArthur Memorial Foundation, 21-22 October 1982.* Norfolk, VA: The Foundation, 1984.
Passin, Herbert. *The Legacy of the Occupation—Japan.* New York: East Asian Institute, Columbia University, 1968.
Ward, Robert Edward, and Frank J. Shulman. *The Allied Occupation of Japan, 1945-1952: an Annotated Bibliography of Western-language Materials.* Chicago, American Library Association, 1974.

Agreement Constituting an International Commission for the International Tracing Service

SIGNED: June 6, 1955, at Bonn, West Germany
SIGNATORIES: Belgium, France Germany (Federal Republic), Israel, Italy, Luxembourg, Netherlands, United Kingdom, United States
IN FORCE: Retroactively, from May 5, 1955
OVERVIEW: An agreement creating an International Tracing Service to trace missing persons and relevant documents "relating to Germans and non-Germans who were interned in National-Socialist concentration or labor camps or to non-Germans who were displaced as a result of the Second World War."

DISCUSSION:
The international commission created by this agreement was charged with "ensuring cooperation between the Governments represented on the Commission in matters relating to the International Tracing Service" and ensuring cooperation with the International Committee of the Red Cross.

REFERENCES:
International Tracing Service. *ITS: International Tracing Service, 1945-1965.* Geneva: International Committee of the Red Cross, 1965.
Johnstone, Michael. *Reunited!: Loved Ones Traced by the British Red Cross.* Henley on Thames, UK: Aidan Ellis, 1995.

Convention on Consent to Marriage, Minimum Age for Marriage and Registration of Marriages

SIGNED: December 10, 1962, at New York
SIGNATORIES: Ceylon, Chile, Cuba, Czechoslovakia, Denmark, Dominican Republic, Finland, France, Greece, Guinea, Israel, Italy, Mali, Netherlands, New Zealand, Niger, Norway, Philippines, Poland, Romania, Sweden, United States, Upper Volta, Western Samoa, Yugoslavia
IN FORCE: From December 9, 1964
OVERVIEW: An international convention to affirm and ensure that marriages are entered into by persons of legal age and only with their full and free consent.

DISCUSSION:
The convention is an agreement in principle rather than in detail. It lays down three substantive provisions:

- "No marriage shall be legally entered into without the full and free consent of both panties, such consent to be expressed by them in person after due publicity and in the presence of the authority competent to solemnize the marriage and of witnesses, as prescribed by law."
- "States parties to the present Convention shall take legislative action to specify a minimum age for marriage. . . ."
- "All marriages shall be registered in an appropriate official register by the competent authority."

The most significant effect of the convention is to proscribe either forced marriages or marriages arranged by families or others without the consent of those who are to be married. Such practices are common in some countries, regions, and cultures.

REFERENCES:
None

Convention on the Taking of Evidence Abroad in Civil or Commercial Matters

SIGNED: March 18, 1970, at the Hague
SIGNATORIES: Denmark, Norway, United States
IN FORCE: From October 7, 1972
OVERVIEW: An agreement to facilitate obtaining evidence in international civil and commercial matters of litigation.

DISCUSSION:
The principal object of the agreement is the facilitation of the transmission and execution of Letters of Request, by which a

judicial authority of one contracting state may request from that of another contracting state the service of obtaining evidence or of performing some other judicial act. This avoids the necessity of officials from one state traveling to and functioning in another.

The agreement details the form of Letters of Request and lays down rules for taking evidence.

REFERENCES:

Bassiouni, M. Cherif, and Edward M. Wise. *Aut Dedere Aut Judicare: The Duty to Extradite or Prosecute in International Law.* Dordrecht, Netherlands, and Boston: M. Nijhoff, 1995.

___. *International Extradition: United States Law and Practice,* 3d ed. Dobbs Ferry, NY: Oceana Publications, 1996.

Yarnold, Barbara M. *International Fugitives.* New York: Praeger, 1991.

Supplementary Convention to the Extradition Convention (with France) of January 1909

SIGNED: February 12, 1970, at Paris
SIGNATORIES: France vs. United States
IN FORCE: From April 3, 1971
OVERVIEW: A convention updating and revising the basic Extradition Convention of 1909.

DISCUSSION:

The Supplementary Convention enlarges the list of offenses for which extradition may be secured, most significantly including offense relating to tax matters. Even more important, it bars extradition in the following cases:

- When the person whose surrender is sought is being proceeded against or has been tried and discharged or punished in the territory of the requested party for the acts for which his extradition is requested
- When the person whose extradition is sought establishes that he has been tried and acquitted or had undergone punishment in a third state for the acts for which extradition is requested
- When the person claimed has become immune, according to the law of either the requesting or requested state, by the reason of lapse of time from prosecution or punishment
- If the offense is of a political character
- If the offense is purely military

REFERENCES:

Bassiouni, M. Cherif, and Edward M. Wise. *Aut Dedere Aut Judicare: The Duty to Extradite or Prosecute in International Law.* Dordrecht, Netherlands, and Boston: M. Nijhoff, 1995.

___. *International Extradition: United States Law and Practice,* 3d ed. Dobbs Ferry, NY: Oceana Publications, 1996.

Yarnold, Barbara M. *International Fugitives.* New York: Praeger, 1991.

Convention on Psychotropic Substances

SIGNED: February 21, 1971, at Vienna
SIGNATORIES: Afghanistan, Algeria, Antigua and Barbuda, Argentina, Armenia, Australia, Austria, Azerbaijan, Bahrain, Bahamas, Bangladesh, Barbados, Belarus, Belgium, Benin, Bolivia, Bosnia and Herzegovina,Brazil, Botswana, Brunei Darussalam, Bulgaria, Burkina Faso, Burundi, Cameroon, Canada, Cape Verde, Chad, Chile, China, Colombia, Costa Rica, Côte d'Ivoire, Croatia, Cuba, Cyprus, Czech Republic, Democratic Republic of the Congo, Denmark, Dominica, Dominican Republic, Ecuador, Egypt, El Salvador, Estonia, Ethiopia, Fiji, Finland, Former Yugoslav Republic of Macedonia, France, Gabon, Gambia, Georgia, Germany, Ghana, Greece, Grenada, Guatemala, Guinea, Guinea-Bissau, Guyana, Holy See, Hungary, Iceland, India, Indonesia, Iran (Islamic Republic), Iraq, Ireland, Israel, Italy, Jamaica, Japan, Jordan, Kazakhstan, Korea (Republic), Kyrgyzstan, Kuwait, Lao People's Democratic Republic, Latvia, Lebanon, Lesotho, Liberia, Libyan Arab Jamahiriya, Lithuania, Luxembourg, Madagascar, Malawi, Malaysia, Mali, Malta, Marshall Islands, Mauritania, Mauritius, Mexico, Micronesia (Federated States), Monaco, Morocco, Mozambique, Myanmar, Netherlands, Namibia, New Zealand, Nicaragua, Niger, Nigeria, Norway, Oman, Pakistan, Palau, Panama, Papua New Guinea, Paraguay, Peru, Philippines, Poland, Portugal, Qatar, Moldova, Romania, Russian Federation, Rwanda, Saint Kitts and Nevis, Saudi Arabia, Sao Tome and Principe, Senegal, Seychelles, Sierra Leone, Singapore, Slovakia, Slovenia, Somalia, South Africa, Spain, Sri Lanka, Sudan, Suriname, Swaziland, Sweden, Switzerland, Syrian Arab Republic, Tajikistan, Thailand, Togo, Tonga, Trinidad and Tobago, Tunisia, Turkey, Turkmenistan, Uganda, Ukraine, United Arab Emirates, United Kingdom, United States, Uruguay, Uzbekistan, Venezuela, Vietnam, Yemen, Yugoslavia, Zambia, Zimbabwe
IN FORCE: From August 16, 1976
OVERVIEW: An international convention to control the production, trade in, and use of psychotropic substances.

DISCUSSION:

As early as the International Opium Convention of 1912 and in several subsequent international agreements, of which the **Single Convention on Narcotic Drugs** (as amended, 1975) is the most important, the world's nations have concluded cooperative conventions with the aim of controlling the traffic in illicit drugs. All of these agreements have applied to narcotic drugs and to cannabis-based drugs (chiefly marijuana). The 1971 Vienna convention applies to psychotropic substances—substances, such as LSD (lysergic acid diethylamide), that have an altering effect on perception or behavior. Because the deleterious effects of psychotropic substances may be more difficult to assess than those of narcotic drugs, the convention provides a set of criteria for deciding whether a given psychotropic substance should be subject to international control. If the substance meets any of the following criteria, it should be regulated according to the convention:

- Creates a state of dependence
- Causes central nervous system stimulation or depression, resulting in hallucinations or disturbances in motor function or thinking or behavior or perception or mood
- There is sufficient evidence that the substance is being or is likely to be abused so as to constitute a public health and social problem

Much of the convention provides for the controls on the legitimate production of psychotropic substances for scientific and medical use. The convention provides guidelines for licensing and monitoring at the national level and develops safeguards and standards for international trade in such substances.

Enforcement provisions are similar to those included in the **Single Convention on Narcotic Drugs** (as amended, 1975).

REFERENCES:
Bewley-Taylor, David R. *The United States and International Drug Control, 1909-1997.* London: Cassell Academic, 1999.
Chepesiuk, Ron. *Hard Target: The United States War Against International Drug Trafficking, 1982-1997.* Jefferson, NC: McFarland and Company, 1998.

Treaty on Extradition (with Canada)

SIGNED: December 3, 1971, at Washington, D.C.
SIGNATORIES: Canada vs. United States
IN FORCE: From March 22, 1976
OVERVIEW: A treaty of extradition with the Canada.

DISCUSSION:
Given the close, neighborly relations between the United States and Canada and the ease with which the border is crossed, issues of extradition are of particular importance to "the cooperation of the two countries in the repression of crime."

The treaty includes a schedule of extraditable offenses, but also stipulates the general provision that "Extradition shall also be granted for any offense against a federal law of the United States in which one of the offenses listed in the annexed Schedule . . . is a substantial element." Thus, from the point of view of the United States, the treaty encompasses a very broad range of offenses for which extradition may be requested.

A special provision is made regarding offenses "punishable by death under the laws of the requesting State and the laws of the requested State do not permit such punishment for that offense." In such cases, "extradition may be refused unless the requesting State provides such assurances as the requested State considers sufficient that the death penalty shall not be imposed,

or, if imposed, shall not be executed." Pursuant to this provision, Canadian authorities have refused to extradite certain offenders because United States authorities would not provide the required assurances.

As with other modern extradition treaties, the document lays down specific procedures for requesting extradition and for complying with such requests.

REFERENCES:
Bassiouni, M. Cherif, and Edward M. Wise. *Aut Dedere Aut Judicare: The Duty to Extradite or Prosecute in International Law.* Dordrecht, Netherlands, and Boston: M. Nijhoff, 1995.
___. *International Extradition: United States Law and Practice,* 3d ed. Dobbs Ferry, NY: Oceana Publications, 1996.
Yarnold, Barbara M. *International Fugitives.* New York: Praeger, 1991.

Extradition Treaty (with United Kingdom)

SIGNED: June 8, 1972, at London
SIGNATORIES: United Kingdom vs. United States
IN FORCE: From January 21, 1977
OVERVIEW: The basic extradition agreement between the United Kingdom and the United States.

DISCUSSION:
This is a standard extradition treaty, which provides for extradition in the following general cases:

- The offense is punishable under the laws of both parties by imprisonment or other form of detention for more than one year or by the death penalty.
- The Offense is extraditable under the law of the United Kingdom.
- The offense constitutes a felony under United States law.

Extradition is barred in the following general cases:

- If the person sought would, if proceeded against in the territory of the requested party, be entitled to be discharged on the grounds of a previous acquittal or conviction
- If the prosecution has become barred by lapse of time according to the law of the requesting or requested party
- If the offense is political

REFERENCES:
Bassiouni, M. Cherif, and Edward M. Wise. *Aut Dedere Aut Judicare: The Duty to Extradite or Prosecute in International Law.* Dordrecht, Netherlands, and Boston: M. Nijhoff, 1995.
___. *International Extradition: United States Law and Practice,* 3d ed. Dobbs Ferry, NY: Oceana Publications, 1996.
Yarnold, Barbara M. *International Fugitives.* New York: Praeger, 1991.

Treaty on Extradition (with Paraguay)

SIGNED: May 24, 1973, at Asuncion, Paraguay
SIGNATORIES: Paraguay vs. United States
IN FORCE: From May 7, 1974
OVERVIEW: A treaty of extradition between Paraguay and the United States.

DISCUSSION:

In contrast to many other extradition treaties to which the United States is a party, the treaty with Paraguay does not provide for extradition for crimes punishable under the laws of both parties or either party, but instead enumerates a list of specific extraditable offenses. Specifically barred is extradition for crimes of a political character.

The treaty also outlines and specifies the procedure for requesting extradition.

REFERENCES:

Bassiouni, M. Cherif, and Edward M. Wise. *Aut Dedere Aut Judicare: The Duty to Extradite or Prosecute in International Law.* Dordrecht, Netherlands, and Boston: M. Nijhoff, 1995.

___. *International Extradition: United States Law and Practice,* 3d ed. Dobbs Ferry, NY: Oceana Publications, 1996.

Yarnold, Barbara M. *International Fugitives.* New York: Praeger, 1991.

Convention Providing a Uniform Law on the Form of an International Will

SIGNED: October 26, 1973, at Washington
SIGNATORIES: Belgium, Belgium, Bosnia-Herzegovina, Canada, Cyprus, Czechoslovakia, Ecuador, France, Holy See, Iran, Italy, Laos, Libyan Arab Jamahiriya, Niger, Portugal, Sierra Leone, Slovenia, Union of Soviet Socialist Republics, United States, United Kingdom, Yugoslavia
IN FORCE: From February 9, 1978; not yet in force for the United States
OVERVIEW: A convention "to provide to a greater extent for the respecting of last wills by establishing an additional form of will hereinafter to be called an 'international will' which, if employed, would dispense to some extent with the search for the applicable law."

DISCUSSION:

Signatories agree to recognize the validity of an "international will," the form of which is described in an annex to the convention.

REFERENCES:
None

Agreement with Mexico Relating to the Detection of Opium Poppy Cultivation

SIGNED: June 10 and June 24, 1974, at Mexico City
SIGNATORIES: Mexico vs. United States
IN FORCE: From June 24, 1974
OVERVIEW: An agreement by which the United States undertakes to supply Mexico with a "multi-spectral aerial photographic system capable of detecting opium poppy cultivation."

DISCUSSION:

In a cooperative program of illegal drug interdiction, the United States agrees to supply an advanced photographic detecting system (at a cost of $459,002) and technical support services necessary to the operation of the equipment (at a cost not to exceed $598,702). In return, the Mexican government agrees to operate the equipment for at least ten months each year "to detect and map the locations in Mexico where opium poppy is being cultivated and harvested in order that it more effectively can carry out its eradication efforts."

REFERENCES:

Bewley-Taylor, David R. *The United States and International Drug Control, 1909-1997.* London: Cassell Academic, 1999.

Chepesiuk, Ron. *Hard Target: The United States War Against International Drug Trafficking, 1982-1997.* Jefferson, NC: McFarland and Company, 1998.

Inter-American Convention on Letters Rogatory

SIGNED: January 30, 1975, at Panama City, Panama
SIGNATORIES: Argentina, Bolivia, Brazil, Chile, Colombia, Costa Rica, Ecuador, El Salvador, Guatemala, Honduras, Mexico, Nicaragua, Panama, Paraguay, Peru, Spain, United States, Uruguay, Venezuela
IN FORCE: From January 16, 1976
OVERVIEW: An Organization of American States convention laying down uniform procedure for letters rogatory.

DISCUSSION:

As used in the convention, letters rogatory (Spanish, *exhortos* or *cartas rogatorias*) are documents by which a court or legal authority in one nation requests from a court or legal authority in another nation information or aid in obtaining information. The convention prescribes uniform transnational procedures for creating and executing letters rogatory. The scope of the convention is limited by Article 2 to the following:

Letters rogatory, issued in conjunction with proceedings in civil and commercial matters held before the appropriate authority of one of the States Parties to this Convention, that have as their purpose:

a. The performance of procedural acts of a merely formal nature, such as service of process, summonses or subpoenas abroad;

b. The taking of evidence and the obtaining of information abroad, unless a reservation is made in this respect.

Article 3 lays down that "This Convention shall not apply to letters rogatory relating to procedural acts other than those specified in the preceding article; and in particular it shall not apply to acts involving measures of compulsion."

An **Additional Protocol to the Inter American Convention on Letters Rogatory** of 1979 lays down more formal and procedural specifics relating to letters rogatory.

REFERENCES:

Bassiouni, M. Cherif, and Edward M. Wise. *Aut Dedere Aut Judicare: The Duty to Extradite or Prosecute in International Law.* Dordrecht, Netherlands, and Boston: M. Nijhoff, 1995.

___. *International Extradition: United States Law and Practice,* 3d ed. Dobbs Ferry, NY: Oceana Publications, 1996.

Yarnold, Barbara M. *International Fugitives.* New York: Praeger, 1991.

Understanding on the Drug Enforcement Administration Representative to the American Embassy in Jakarta

OFFICIAL TITLE: Exchange of Letters Constituting Understandings Relating to the Designation of the Drug Enforcement Administration Representative to the American Embassy in Jakarta to Advance the U.S.-Indonesian Common Interest in Preventing Illegal Traffic and Narcotic Drugs

SIGNED: April 1, 1975, at Djakarta, Indonesia

SIGNATORIES: Indonesia vs. United States

IN FORCE: From signing

OVERVIEW: An agreement on the designation and diplomatic status of a United States Drug Enforcement Administration (DEA) agent to be stationed in Djakarta.

DISCUSSION:

Beginning mainly in the 1970s, the United States increasingly adopted a policy of countering the influx of illegal drugs into the country by working with authorities in the nations that produced these substances. This agreement designates a United States drug enforcement representative to be attached to the United States embassy in Djakarta. The agreement stipulates that "all activities of the DEA representative will be determined by the United States Ambassador and the Chairman of BAKO-LAK," the Indonesian drug-enforcement authority. An annex to the agreement enumerates the "possible functions of the DEA representative" as follows:

• To assist in training Indonesian law enforcement personnel

• To assist Indonesian law enforcement personnel in conducting criminal investigations

• To work with Indonesian law enforcement personnel to collect intelligence

• To serve as a channel for information exchange between the DEA and Indonesian law enforcement personnel

• To carry out various liaison activities as determined by the U.S. ambassador and the chairman of BAKOLAK

REFERENCES:

Bewley-Taylor, David R. *The United States and International Drug Control, 1909-1997.* London: Cassell Academic, 1999.

Chepesiuk, Ron. *Hard Target: The United States War Against International Drug Trafficking, 1982-1997.* Jefferson, NC: McFarland and Company, 1998.

Single Convention on Narcotic Drugs

OFFICIAL TITLE: Single Convention on Narcotic Drugs, 1961, as Amended by the Protocol Amending the Single Convention on Narcotic Drugs, 1961

SIGNED: August 8, 1975, at New York

SIGNATORIES: Argentina, Australia, Berlin (territorial application), Brazil, Chile, Colombia, Costa Rica, Côte d'Ivoire, Cyprus, Dahomey, Denmark, Ecuador, Egypt, Fiji, Finland, France, Germany (Federal Republic), Guatemala, Haiti, Iceland, Israel, Italy, Japan, Jordan, Kenya, Korea (Republic), Kuwait, Lesotho, Madagascar, Malawi, Monaco, Niger, Norway, Panama, Paraguay, Philippines, Romania, Senegal, Singapore, South Africa, Sweden, Syrian Arab Republic, Thailand, Tonga, United Republic of Cameroon, United States, Uruguay

IN FORCE: From signing

OVERVIEW: " . . . a generally acceptable international convention replacing existing treaties on narcotic drugs, limiting such drugs to medical and scientific use, and providing for continuous international co-operation and control . . ."

DISCUSSION:

The preamble states the principal objective of this international convention: to replace existing treaties on narcotic drugs in order to limit such drugs to "medical and scientific use" and to provide for "continuous international co-operation and control" in the field of narcotics.

After defining key terms, the convention enumerates the substances under control, which are specifically listed, by their chemical names, in schedules appended to the convention. The controlled substances include opium-based (such as heroin) and coca-based narcotics (such as cocaine), as well as cannabis-based substances (such as marijuana). The inclusion or exclusion of substances from the schedules is determined by a commission under authority of the World Health Organization.

The basic obligations of signatories are laid down in Article 4 as follows:

The Parties shall take such legislative and administrative measures as may be necessary:

a. To give effect to and carry out the provisions of this Convention within their own territories;

b. To co-operate with other States in the execution of the provisions of this Convention; and

c. Subject to the provisions of this Convention, to limit exclusively to medical and scientific purposes the production, manufacture, export, import, distribution of, trade in, use and possession of drugs.

Beyond this, the balance of the convention deals with methods and procedures for reporting legitimate drug needs (so that production can be appropriately monitored), with measures to limit the cultivation and production of opium and coca, and to control cannabis production. Enforcement is addressed with provisions concerning the following:

• Action against illicit traffic
• Penal provisions
• Seizure and confiscation
• Measures against drug abuse

All of these are the responsibility of the individual state signatories; however, the convention provides a framework for international cooperation and sets minimum standards for enforcement.

REFERENCES:

Bewley-Taylor, David R. *The United States and International Drug Control, 1909-1997*. London: Cassell Academic, 1999.
Chepesiuk, Ron. *Hard Target: The United States War Against International Drug Trafficking, 1982-1997*. Jefferson, NC: McFarland and Company, 1998.

Agreement (with Mexico) Relating to Narcotic Drugs: Indemnification for Flight Operations

OFFICIAL TITLE: Exchange of Letters Constituting an Agreement Relating to Narcotic Drugs: Indemnification for Flight Operations
SIGNED: September 12, 1975, at Mexico City
SIGNATORIES: Mexico vs. United States
IN FORCE: From September 12, 1975
OVERVIEW: An agreement barring U.S. liability for loss of life or property in connection with cooperative drug-enforcement aircraft operations.

DISCUSSION:

Over the years, the United States and Mexico have concluded numerous agreements concerning drug-law enforcement and the interdiction of the illegal narcotics trade between the two nations. This document addresses an issue of liability in connection with one aspect of the cooperative effort: training of Mexican law-enforcement pilots by United States personnel. An exchange of brief letters constitutes an agreement on the subject of indemnification:

We propose [writes United States Ambassador Joseph John Jova to the attorney general of Mexico] that the Mexican Government indemnify and safeguard the United States Government, its personnel and its contractors, who perform flight operations in support of the cooperative program for the . . . liabilities.

The Mexican attorney general's affirmative reply entered the agreement into force.

REFERENCES:

Bewley-Taylor, David R. *The United States and International Drug Control, 1909-1997*. London: Cassell Academic, 1999.
Chepesiuk, Ron. *Hard Target: The United States War Against International Drug Trafficking, 1982-1997*. Jefferson, NC: McFarland and Company, 1998.

Treaty (with Mexico) on the Execution of Penal Sentences

SIGNED: November 25, 1975, at Mexico City
SIGNATORIES: Mexico vs. United States
IN FORCE: From November 20, 1977
OVERVIEW: A treaty allowing nationals of the two parties to serve most penal sentences in their home country.

DISCUSSION:

Article I of the treaty provides as follows:

(1) Sentences imposed in the United Mexican States on nationals of the United States of America may be served in penal institutions or subject to the supervision of the authorities of the United States of America in accordance with the provisions of this Treaty.

(2) Sentences imposed in the United States of America on nationals of the United Mexican States may be served in penal institutions or subject to the supervision of the authorities of the United Mexican States in accordance with the provisions of this Treaty.

As with treaties on extradition, crimes of a political character are excluded. The balance of the treaty lays down procedures for effecting transfer of execution.

REFERENCES:

Bassiouni, M. Cherif, and Edward M. Wise. *Aut Dedere Aut Judicare: The Duty to Extradite or Prosecute in International Law*. Dordrecht, Netherlands, and Boston: M. Nijhoff, 1995.
___. *International Extradition: United States Law and Practice*, 3d ed. Dobbs Ferry, NY: Oceana Publications, 1996.
Yarnold, Barbara M. *International Fugitives*. New York: Praeger, 1991.

Treaty on Extradition (with Japan)

SIGNED: March 3, 1978, at Tokyo
SIGNATORIES: Japan vs. United States
IN FORCE: From March 26, 1980
OVERVIEW: A treaty of extradition with Japan.

DISCUSSION:

This is a standard extradition treaty, whereby each signatory undertakes to grant extradition of persons charged with "an offense punishable by the laws of both Contracting Parties by death, by life imprisonment, or by deprivation of liberty for a period of more than one year; or for any other offense when such offense is punishable by the federal laws of the United States and by the laws of Japan ..." As with other extradition treaties, offenses of a political nature are generally excluded from extradition.

A schedule of forty-seven specifically extraditable offenses is subjoined to the treaty.

REFERENCES:

Bassiouni, M. Cherif, and Edward M. Wise. *Aut Dedere Aut Judicare: The Duty to Extradite or Prosecute in International Law.* Dordrecht, Netherlands, and Boston: M. Nijhoff, 1995.

___. *International Extradition: United States Law and Practice,* 3d ed. Dobbs Ferry, NY: Oceana Publications, 1996.

Yarnold, Barbara M. *International Fugitives.* New York: Praeger, 1991.

Agreement (with Malaysia) Relating to Heroin Addiction

OFFICIAL TITLE: Exchange of Notes Constituting an Agreement Relating to Heroin Addiction and Other Forms of Drug Abuse
SIGNED: November 16 and December 8, 1978, at Kuala Lumpur, Malaysia
SIGNATORIES: Malaysia vs. United States
IN FORCE: From December 8, 1978
OVERVIEW: An agreement to engage in a cooperative program to combat the spread of heroin addiction and other forms of drug abuse in Malaysia.

DISCUSSION:

By this agreement, the United States is to furnish technical advice and equipment for the program, the objective of which is to "develop and field test a training model that can be used ... for ongoing training of welfare officers assigned to work in drug abuse rehabilitation."

The project outlined is in two phases: a design phase and an implementation phase, both of which are laid down in detail by the agreement.

REFERENCES:

Bewley-Taylor, David R. *The United States and International Drug Control, 1909-1997.* London: Cassell Academic, 1999.

Chepesiuk, Ron. *Hard Target: The United States War Against International Drug Trafficking, 1982-1997.* Jefferson, NC: McFarland and Company, 1998.

Extradition Treaty (with Mexico)

SIGNED: May 4, 1978, at Mexico City
SIGNATORIES: Mexico vs. United States
IN FORCE: From January 25, 1980
OVERVIEW: A treaty of extradition with Mexico.

DISCUSSION:

Thorough, unambiguous treaties of extradition are especially important in the case of bordering nations. The 1978 Extradition Treaty with Mexico is part of a series of treaties and agreements intended to promote the coordination of law-enforcement activities between Mexico and the United States.

The extradition treaty is standard, straightforward, and broad in its application, laying down the following principal provisions:

- "The Contracting Parties agree to mutually extradite ... persons who the competent authorities of the requesting Party have charged with an offense or found guilty of committing an offense, or are wanted by said authorities to complete a judicially pronounced penalty of deprivation of liberty for an offense committed within the territory of the requesting Party."
- Reference is also made to a schedule of specific offenses for which extradition is always applicable.
- Political and military offenses are excluded from extradition.

Special treatment is accorded capital offenses: "When the offense for which extradition is requested is punishable by death under the laws of the requesting Party and the laws of the requested Party do not permit such punishment for that offense, extradition may be refused, unless the requesting Party furnishes such assurances as the requested Party considers sufficient that the death penalty shall not be imposed, or, if imposed, shall not be executed."

REFERENCES:

Bassiouni, M. Cherif, and Edward M. Wise. *Aut Dedere Aut Judicare: The Duty to Extradite or Prosecute in International Law.* Dordrecht, Netherlands, and Boston: M. Nijhoff, 1995.

___. *International Extradition: United States Law and Practice,* 3d ed. Dobbs Ferry, NY: Oceana Publications, 1996.

Yarnold, Barbara M. *International Fugitives.* New York: Praeger, 1991.

Treaty (with Turkey) on Extradition and Mutual Assistance in Criminal Matters

SIGNED: June 7, 1979, at Ankara, Turkey
SIGNATORIES: Turkey vs. United States
IN FORCE: From January 1, 1981
OVERVIEW: A treaty governing extradition with Turkey.

DISCUSSION:

The treaty lays down the general obligation of extradition and includes an appendix of extraditable offenses, but also stipulates that "Offenses, regardless of whether listed in the appendix . . . or not, which are punishable under both the federal laws of the United States and the laws of Turkey by deprivation of liberty at least for a period exceeding one year or by a more severe penalty" are extraditable. As with other extradition treaties, offenses of a political character are excluded.

REFERENCES:

Bassiouni, M. Cherif, and Edward M. Wise. *Aut Dedere Aut Judicare: The Duty to Extradite or Prosecute in International Law.* Dordrecht, Netherlands, and Boston: M. Nijhoff, 1995.

___. *International Extradition: United States Law and Practice,* 3d ed. Dobbs Ferry, NY: Oceana Publications, 1996.

Yarnold, Barbara M. *International Fugitives.* New York: Praeger, 1991.

Agreement (with Colombia) Concerning Cooperation to Curb Illegal Traffic in Narcotic Drugs

OFFICIAL TITLE: Exchange of Notes Constituting an Agreement Concerning Cooperation to Curb Illegal Traffic in Narcotic Drugs

SIGNED: July 21 and August 6, 1980, at Bogota

SIGNATORIES: Columbia vs. United States

IN FORCE: From August 6, 1980

OVERVIEW: An agreement by which the United States undertakes to supply Colombia with funding for drug-enforcement policing equipment.

DISCUSSION:

By the late 1970s, United States law enforcement officials charged with combating the epidemic rise in the trade in and use of illegal narcotic drugs increasingly turned their attention to the ultimate sources of those drugs rather than merely attempting to suppress street dealers and addicts. It was recognized that Colombia was a principal source of narcotics flowing into the United States, and a series of cooperative law-enforcement programs were initiated between the United States and Colombia. In the 1980 agreement, the United States undertakes to grant $13,225,000 "for supplying and maintaining helicopters, patrol vessels, fixed radar equipment, transport vehicles, and fuel, which will be used exclusively in interdicting drug traffic, and for whatever other purposes the United States Congress may authorize."

REFERENCES:

Bewley-Taylor, David R. *The United States and International Drug Control, 1909-1997.* London: Cassell Academic, 1999.

Chepesiuk, Ron. *Hard Target: The United States War Against International Drug Trafficking, 1982-1997.* Jefferson, NC: McFarland and Company, 1998.

United States Department of State, *Treaties in Force: A List of Treaties and other International Agreements of the United States in Force on January 1, 1997.* Washington, D.C.: U.S. Government Printing Office, 1997.

Extradition Treaty (with the Netherlands)

SIGNED: June 24, 1980, at the Hague

SIGNATORIES: Netherlands vs. United States

IN FORCE: From September 15, 1983

OVERVIEW: A typical extradition treaty.

DISCUSSION:

The Extradition Treaty between the United States and the Netherlands is typical of extradition agreements made by the United States. It includes the following major provisions:

- An undertaking by the parties to extradite
- A statement of extraditable offenses, with reference to a schedule of specific offenses
- Conditions allowing extradition
- Application of the treaty to territories of the signatory states
- Exclusion of extradition in the case of political and military offenses
- Exclusion of extradition in cases of double jeopardy
- Exclusion of extradition in instances of the lapse of the statute of limitations according to the law of the requested state
- Capital punishment: "When the offense for which extradition is requested is punishable by death under the laws of the Requesting State and the laws of the Requested State do not permit such punishment for that offense, extradition may be refused unless the Requesting State furnishes such assurances as the Requested States considers sufficient that the death penalty shall not be imposed, or, if imposed, shall not be executed."
- Special circumstances: "In special circumstances, having particular regard to the age, health or other personal condition of the person sought, the Executive Authority of the Requested State may refuse extradition if it has reason to believe that extradition will be incompatible with humanitarian considerations."
- Extradition of nationals: neither party may refuse extradition of its own nationals solely on the basis of their nationality

The treaty concludes by laying down the procedures and documents required for requesting extradition and for responding to the request, executing it, or refusing it.

REFERENCES:

Bassiouni, M. Cherif, and Edward M. Wise. *Aut Dedere Aut Judicare: The Duty to Extradite or Prosecute in International Law.* Dordrecht, Netherlands, and Boston: M. Nijhoff, 1995.

___. *International Extradition: United States Law and Practice,* 3d ed. Dobbs Ferry, NY: Oceana Publications, 1996.

Yarnold, Barbara M. *International Fugitives.* New York: Praeger, 1991.

Agreement (with United Kingdom) Concerning Cooperation in the Suppression of Narcotics

OFFICIAL TITLE: Exchange of Notes Constituting an Agreement Concerning Cooperation in the Suppression of the Unlawful Importation of Narcotic Drugs into the United States

SIGNED: November 12, 1981, at London

SIGNATORIES: United Kingdom vs. United States

IN FORCE: From signing

OVERVIEW: An agreement by which the United Kingdom agrees to the boarding of British-flagged private vessels for purposes of search and seizure of illegal drugs.

DISCUSSION:

Pursuant to the **Single Convention on Narcotic Drugs** of 1961, this agreement promotes international cooperation in the interdiction of illegal drugs by allowing United States authorities to board, search, and, if necessary, to seize private vessels flying the British flag, provided that the authorities "reasonably believe the vessel has on board a cargo of drugs for importation into the United States."

REFERENCES:

Bewley-Taylor, David R. *The United States and International Drug Control, 1909-1997.* London: Cassell Academic, 1999.

Chepesiuk, Ron. *Hard Target: The United States War Against International Drug Trafficking, 1982-1997.* Jefferson, NC: McFarland and Company, 1998.

Agreement (with United Kingdom) Concerning Narcotics Activity in the Cayman Islands

OFFICIAL TITLE: Exchange of Letters Constituting an Agreement Concerning the Cayman Islands and Matters Connected with, Arising from, Related to, or Resulting from any Narcotics Activity Referred to in the **Single Convention on Narcotic Drugs**, 1961, as Amended by the Protocol Amending the Single Convention on Narcotic Drugs, 1961

SIGNED: July 26, 1984, at London

SIGNATORIES: United Kingdom vs. United States

IN FORCE: From August 29, 1984

OVERVIEW: An agreement to prevent narcotics traffickers from using the banking confidentially laws of the Cayman Islands to protect their activities.

DISCUSSION:

The Cayman Islands, located northwest of Jamaica, are administered by the United Kingdom, but have long had a reputation as a shelter for sometimes criminal financial transactions due to the nature of the island's confidential banking laws. The 1984 agreement provides the means by which prosecutors in the United States may, on demonstrating good cause, pierce the veil of confidentiality for the purpose of criminal investigation or prosecution.

The agreement concludes with the parties undertaking to negotiate a comprehensive law-enforcement treaty relating to the Cayman Islands.

REFERENCES:

Bewley-Taylor, David R. *The United States and International Drug Control, 1909-1997.* London: Cassell Academic, 1999.

Chepesiuk, Ron. *Hard Target: The United States War Against International Drug Trafficking, 1982-1997.* Jefferson, NC: McFarland and Company, 1998.

Convention Against Illicit Traffic in Drugs

OFFICIAL TITLE: United Nations Convention Against Illicit Traffic in Narcotic Drugs and Psychotropic Substances

SIGNED: December 20, 1988, at Vienna

SIGNATORIES: Afghanistan, Algeria, Andorra, Antigua and Barbuda, Argentina, Armenia, Australia, Austria, Azerbaijan, Bahamas, Bahrain, Bangladesh, Barbados, Belarus, Belize, Belgium, Benin, Bhutan, Bolivia, Bosnia and Herzegovina, Botswana, Brazil, Brunei Darussalam, Bulgaria, Burkina Faso, Burundi, Cameroon, Canada, Cape Verde, Chad, Chile, China, Colombia, Costa Rica, Côte d'Ivoire, Cuba, Cyprus, Czech Republic, Democratic Republic of the Congo, Denmark, Dominica, Dominican Republic, Ecuador, Egypt, El Salvador, Ethiopia, European Community, Fiji, Finland, Former Yugoslav Republic of Macedonia, France, Gabon, Gambia, Georgia, Germany, Ghana, Greece, Grenada Guatemala, Guinea, Guinea-Bissau, Guyana, Haiti, Holy See, Honduras, Hungary, Iceland, India, Indonesia, Iran (Islamic Republic), Iraq, Israel, Italy, Jamaica, Japan, Jordan, Kazakhstan, Kenya, Korea (Republic), Kuwait, Kyrgyzstan, Latvia, Lebanon, Lesotho, Libyan Arab Jamahiriya, Lithuania, Luxembourg, Madagascar, Malawi, Malaysia, Maldives, Mali, Malta, Mauritania, Mauritius, Mexico, Monaco, Morocco, Mozambique, Myanmar, Nepal, Netherlands, New Zealand, Nicaragua, Niger, Nigeria, Norway, Oman, Pakistan, Panama, Paraguay, Peru, Philippines, Poland, Portugal, Qatar, Republic of Moldova, Romania, Russian Federation Saint Kitts and Nevis, Saint Lucia, Saint Vincent and the Grenadines, Sao Tome and Principe, Saudi Arabia, Senegal, Seychelles, Sierra Leone, Singapore, Slovakia, Slovenia, South Africa, Spain, Sri Lanka, Sudan, Suriname, Swaziland, Sweden, Switzerland,

Syrian Arab Republic, Tajikistan, Tanzania, Togo, Tonga, Trinidad and Tobago, Tunisia, Turkey, Turkmenistan, Uganda, Ukraine, United Arab Emirates, United Kingdom, United States, Uruguay, Uzbekistan, Vatican, Vietnam, Yemen, Yugoslavia, Zambia, Zimbabwe

IN FORCE: From November 11, 1990

OVERVIEW: "The purpose of this Convention is to promote cooperation among the Parties so that they may address more effectively the various aspects of illicit traffic in narcotic drugs and psychotropic substances having an international dimension."

DISCUSSION:

More than any previous multilateral drug-control convention, the Vienna document takes a worldwide, long-term view, declaring in its preamble deep concern over "the magnitude of and rising trend in the illicit production of, demand for and traffic in narcotic drugs and psychotropic substances, which pose a serious threat to the health and welfare of human beings and adversely affect the economic, cultural an political foundations of society." The preamble calls the problem a matter of the "highest priority," and, in contrast to earlier conventions, which seek mainly to monitor and regulate production of narcotic and psychotropic substances, this document calls for eliminating "the root causes of the problem of abuse of narcotic drugs and psychotropic substances, including the illicit demand for such drugs and substances and the enormous profits derived from illicit traffic."

As in earlier conventions, the signatories undertake to enforce drug laws and to prosecute and punish offenders; however, in laying down standards for such prosecution and punishment, the present convention broadens the focus to include action against funds used to finance illicit drug activity and the profits derived from that activity. The convention specifies such law-enforcement response as seizure of assets and property. More than earlier conventions, the present document also emphasizes international law-enforcement cooperation, including expedited extradition procedures, sharing of information, and joint enforcement actions. Also to a greater degree than in earlier conventions, the Vienna convention addresses regulation and monitoring of the raw materials used in the production of narcotics and psychotropic drugs, not just trafficking in the finished products. Guidelines for monitoring transportation, freight operations, and mails, with the purpose of curbing smuggling, are laid down.

REFERENCES:

Bewley-Taylor, David R. *The United States and International Drug Control, 1909-1997.* London: Cassell Academic, 1999.

Chepesiuk, Ron. *Hard Target: The United States War Against International Drug Trafficking, 1982-1997.* Jefferson, NC: McFarland and Company, 1998.

Model Treaty on Extradition

SIGNED: Adopted by the Eighth Crime Congress, Havana, August 27-September 7, 1990

SIGNATORIES: Model treaty; no signatories

IN FORCE: Model treaty; not in force

OVERVIEW: A United Nations-sanctioned model treaty for use by parties desiring to conclude extradition treaties.

DISCUSSION:

In addition to a **Model Treaty on the Transfer of Proceedings in Criminal Matters,** the United Nations or its agencies produced **Model Treaty on the Transfer of Supervision of Offenders Who Have Been Conditionally Sentenced or Conditionally Released** and this Model Extradition Treaty.

Extradition is among the most basic forms of international cooperation and, particularly in an age of easy and rapid air travel, is critical to law enforcement. For this reason, the entire model treaty is reproduced here:

ARTICLE 1
Obligation to extradite

Each Party agrees to extradite to the other any person who is wanted in the requesting State for prosecution for an extraditable offence or for the imposition or enforcement of a sentence in respect of such an offence.

ARTICLE 2
Extraditable offences

Extraditable offences are those punishable under the laws of both Parties by imprisonment or deprivation of liberty for a maximum period of at least [one/two] year(s), or by a more severe penalty. Where request for extradition relates to a person wanted for enforcement of a sentence, extradition shall be granted only if a period of at least [four/six] months remains to be served.

In determining whether or an offence is punishable under the laws of both Parties, it shall not matter whether:

a) The laws of both Parties place the acts or omissions constituting the offence within the same category of offence or denominate the offence by the same terminology;

b) Under the laws of the Parties the constituent elements of the offence differ, it is the totality of the acts or omissions that shall betaken into account.

Where extradition is sought for an offence against a law relating to taxation, customs duties or other revenue matters, extradition may not be refused on the ground that the law of the requesting State does not impose the same kind of tax or duty.

If the request for extradition includes several separate offences each of which is punishable under the laws of both Parties, but some of which do not fulfil other conditions set out in paragraph 1 of this article, the requested Party may grant extradition for the latter offences provided the persons is to be extradited for at least one extraditable offence.

ARTICLE 3

Mandatory grounds for refusal

Extradition shall not be granted in any of the following circumstances:

a) If the offence for which extradition is requested is regarded as a political offence;

b) If there are grounds to believe the request has been made to prosecute or punish a person on account of that person's race, religion, nationality, ethnic origin, political opinions, sex or status, or that the person's position may be prejudiced for any of these reasons;

c) If the offence is an offence under military law and not also an offence under criminal law;

d) If final judgement has been rendered against the person in the requested State in respect of the offence for which the person's extradition is requested;

e) If the person whose extradition has been requested has, under the law of either Party, become immune from prosecution or punishment for any reason, including lapse of time or amnesty;

f) If the person would be subjected to torture or cruel, inhuman treatment or degrading punishment or if that person has not or would not receive the minimum guarantees in criminal proceedings as contained in the International Covenant on Civil and Political Rights, article 14.

g) If the judgement of the requesting State has been rendered in absentia, the convicted person has not had sufficient notice of the trial nor opportunity to arrange for a defence and has not or will not have the opportunity to have the case retried.

ARTICLE 4

Optional grounds for refusal

Extradition may be refused in any of the following circumstances:

a) If the person whose extradition is requested is a national of the requested State;

b) If the competent authorities of the requested State have decided either not to institute or to terminate proceedings against the person for the offence for which extradition is requested;

c) f prosecution in the requested State is pending for the same offence;

d) If the offence carries the death penalty under the law of the requesting State;

e) If the offence has been committed outside the territory of either Party and the law of the requested State does not provide for jurisdiction over such an offence committed outside its territory;

f) If the offence is regarded under the law of the requested State as having been committed in whole or in part within that State;

g) If the person whose extradition has been requested has been sentenced or would be liable to be tried in the requesting State by an extraordinary or ad hoc court or tribunal;

h) If extradition would be incompatible with humanitarian considerations in view of age, health or other personal circumstances of that person.

ARTICLE 5

Channels of communication and required documents

A request for extradition shall be made in writing and transmitted, along with supporting documents, through diplomatic channels directly between the ministries of justice or other designated authorities.

A request shall be accompanied by the following:

a) In all cases,

i) As accurate a description as possible of the person sought and information to help establish that person's identity, nationality and location;

ii) The text of the relevant provision of the law creating the offence and a statement of the penalty that can be imposed;

b) If a warrant for arrest has been issued, by a certified copy of that warrant, a statement of the offence for which extradition is requested and a description of the acts or omissions constituting the alleged offence;

c) If the person has been convicted, by a statement of the offence and a description of the acts or omissions constituting the offence and by the original or certified copy of the judgement;

d) If the person has been convicted in his or her absence, in addition to the documents set out in paragraph 2 c), by a statement as to the legal means available to the person to prepare a defence or have the case retried;

e) If the person has been convicted but no sentence imposed, by a statement of the offence, a document setting out the conviction and a statement affirming intent to impose a sentence.

The documents shall be accompanied by a translation into the language of the requested State or another language acceptable to that State.

ARTICLE 6

Simplified extradition procedure

The requested State may grant extradition after receipt of a request for provisional arrest, provided that the person sought explicitly consents before a competent authority.

ARTICLE 7

Certification and authentication

Except as provided by this Treaty, a request for extradition and the supporting documents thereto shall not require certification or authentication.

ARTICLE 8

Additional information

If the requested State considers that the information provided in a request for extradition is not sufficient, it may request additional information to be furnished within such reasonable time as it specifies.

ARTICLE 9
Provisional arrest

In case of urgency, the requesting State may apply for the provisional arrest of the person sought pending presentation of the request for extradition.

The application for provisional arrest shall contain a description of the person sought, a statement of the existence of one of the documents mentioned in paragraph 2 of article 5, a statement of the punishment that has or can be imposed and a concise statement of the facts of the case and the location, where known, of the person.

The requested State shall decide on the application and communicate its decision without delay.

The person arrested shall be set at liberty upon the expiration of [40] days if a request for extradition supported by the relevant documents has not been received.

Such release shall not prevent rearrest and institution of extradition proceedings if the request is subsequently received.

ARTICLE 10
Decision on the request

The requested State shall promptly communicate its decision on the request for extradition to the requesting State.

Reasons shall be given for any complete or partial refusal of the request.

ARTICLE 11
Surrender of the person

Upon being informed that extradition has been granted, the Parties shall without undue delay arrange for the surrender of the person sought and the requested State shall inform the requesting State of the length of time for which the person was detained with a view to surrender.

The person shall be removed from the territory of the requested State within such reasonable time as the requested State specifies and, if the person is not removed by then, the requested State may release the person and may refuse extradition for the same offence.

If circumstances beyond its control prevent a Party from surrendering or removing the person to be extradited it shall notify the other Party and a new date of surrender will be agreed upon.

ARTICLE 12
Postponed or conditional surrender

The requested State may postpone the surrender of a person sought in order to proceed against that person or enforce a sentence imposed for an offence other than that for which extradition is sought.

The requested State may, instead of postponing surrender, temporarily surrender the person sought to the requesting State in accord with conditions determined between the Parties.

ARTICLE 13
Surrender of property

To the extent permitted under the law of the requested State and subject to the rights of third parties, all property found in the requested State that has been acquired as a result of the offence or that may be required as evidence shall, upon request, be surrendered if extradition is granted.

Said property may, on request, be surrendered to the requesting State even if the extradition having been agreed to cannot be carried out.

When said property is liable to seizure or confiscation in the requested State, it may retain it or temporarily hand it over.

Where the law of the requested State or protection of the rights of third parties so require, any property so surrendered shall be returned to the requested State free of charge after completion of proceedings, if that State so requests.

ARTICLE 14
Rule of speciality

A person extradited under this Treaty shall not be proceeded against, sentenced, detained, re-extradited to a third State, or subjected to any other restriction of personal liberty in the territory of the requesting State for any offence committed before surrender other than:

a) An offence for which extradition was granted;

b) Any other offence in respect of which the requested State consents.

A request for the consent of the requested State under this article shall be accompanied by the documents mentioned in paragraph 2 of article 5 and a legal record of any statement made by the extradited person with respect to the offence.

Paragraph 1 of this article shall not apply if the person has had an opportunity to leave the requesting State and has not done so within [30/45] days of final discharge in respect of the offence for which that person was extradited or if the person has voluntarily returned to the territory of the requesting State after leaving it.

ARTICLE 15
Transit

Where a person is to be extradited to a Party from a third State through the territory of the other Party, the Party to which the person is to be extradited shall request the other Party to permit transit through its territory.

The requested State shall grant such a request expeditiously unless its essential interests would be prejudiced thereby.

The State of transit shall ensure legal provisions enabling the person to be held in custody during transit.

In the event of an unscheduled landing, the Party to be requested to permit transit may, at the request of the escorting officer, hold the person in custody for [48 hours] pending receipt of the transit request.

ARTICLE 16
Concurrent requests

If a party receives requests for extradition for the same person from both the other Party and a third State it shall, at its discretion, determine to which of those States the person is to be extradited.

ARTICLE 17
Costs

The requested State shall meet the cost of any proceedings in its jurisdiction arising out of a request for extradition.

The requested State shall also bear the costs incurred in its territory with the seizure and handing over of property or the arrest and detention of the person sought.

The requesting State shall bear the costs incurred in conveying the person from the territory of the requested State, including transit costs.

ARTICLE 18
Final provisions

This Treaty is subject to (ratification, acceptance or approval).

This Treaty shall enter into force on the thirtieth day after the day on which the instruments of (ratification, acceptance or approval) are exchanged.

This Treaty shall apply to requests made after its entry into force, even if the relevant acts or omissions occurred prior to that date.

Either Party may denounce this Treaty by giving notice in writing to the other Party. Such denunciation shall take effect six months following the date on which notice is received by the other Party.

REFERENCES:
Bassiouni, M. Cherif, and Edward M. Wise. *Aut Dedere Aut Judicare: The Duty to Extradite or Prosecute in International Law.* Dordrecht, Netherlands, and Boston: M. Nijhoff, 1995.
___. *International Extradition: United States Law and Practice,* 3d ed. Dobbs Ferry, NY: Oceana Publications, 1996.
Yarnold, Barbara M. *International Fugitives.* New York: Praeger, 1991.

Model Treaty on the Transfer of Proceedings in Criminal Matters

SIGNED: Adopted by U.N General Assembly, December 14, 1990, at New York
SIGNATORIES: Model treaty; no signatories
IN FORCE: Model treaty; not in force
OVERVIEW: A United Nations-sanctioned model treaty for use by parties desiring to conclude bilateral transfer of proceedings agreements.

DISCUSSION:

In addition to a **Model Extradition Treaty**, the United Nations produced **Model Treaty on the Transfer of Supervision of Offenders Who Have Been Conditionally Sentenced or Conditionally Released** and this Model Treaty on the Transfer of Proceedings in Criminal Matters. The transfer of proceedings from one nation to another is the reverse of the more familiar extradition process. In the case of extradition, one state requests

from another state the return of a prisoner apprehended in that other state so that the prisoner may be prosecuted for crimes alleged to have been committed in the requesting state. In the case of transfer of proceedings, it is the apprehending state that initiates a request for transfer; that is, as stated in Article 1 of the model agreement, "When a person is suspected of having committed an offence under the law of a State which is a Contracting Party, that State may, if the interests of the proper administration of justice so require, request another State which is a Contracting Party to take proceedings in respect of this offence."

The model treaty lays down provisions in the following areas to ensure that transfers of proceedings are efficient and just:
- Establishing channels through diplomatic means
- Presentation of required documentation, including the authority presenting the request; description of the act for which transfer of proceedings is being requested (with specific time and place of the offense); statement on the results of investigations that substantiate the suspicion of an offence; legal provisions of the requesting state on the basis of which the act is considered to be an offense; reasonably exact statement on the identity, nationality, and residence of the suspected person
- Dual criminality: "A request to take proceedings can be complied with only if the act on which the request is based would be an offence if committed in the territory of the requested State."
- Grounds for refusal, including: the suspected person is not a national of or ordinarily resident in the requested state; the act is an offence under military law, which is not also an offence under ordinary criminal law; the offense is in connection with taxes, duties, customs or exchange; the offense is regarded by the requested state as being of a political nature.

The model treaty provides protection for the rights of the suspected person, as follows:

The position of the suspected person

1. The suspected person may express to either State his or her interest in the transfer of the proceedings. Similarly, such interest may be expressed by the legal representative or close relatives of the suspected person.

2. Before a request for transfer of proceedings is made, the requesting State shall, if practicable, allow the suspected person to present his or her views on the alleged offence and the intended transfer, unless that person has absconded or otherwise obstructed the course of justice.

It also provides for protection of the rights of victims:

The requesting and requested States shall ensure in the transfer of proceedings that the rights of the victim of the offence, in particular his or her right to restitution or compensation, shall not be affected as a result of the transfer. If a settlement of the claim of the victim has not been reached before the transfer, the requested State shall permit the representation of the claim in the transferred proceedings, if its law provides for such a possibility. In the event of the death of the victim, these provisions shall apply to his or her dependants accordingly.

Finally, as to costs, barring additional agreement, each party is to bear responsibility for whatever costs are incurred.

REFERENCES:

Bassiouni, M. Cherif, and Edward M. Wise. *Aut Dedere Aut Judicare: The Duty to Extradite or Prosecute in International Law.* Dordrecht, Netherlands, and Boston: M. Nijhoff, 1995.

___. *International Extradition: United States Law and Practice,* 3d ed. Dobbs Ferry, NY: Oceana Publications, 1996.

Yarnold, Barbara M. *International Fugitives.* New York: Praeger, 1991.

Model Treaty on the Transfer of Supervision of Offenders Conditionally Sentenced or Conditionally Released

SIGNED: Adopted by General Assembly resolution 45/119 of December 14, 1990, at New York

SIGNATORIES: Model treaty; no signatories

IN FORCE: Model treaty; not in force

OVERVIEW: A United Nations-sanctioned model treaty between states desiring to allow offenders to serve certain types of sentences in their home country.

DISCUSSION:

In addition to a **Model Treaty on the Transfer of Proceedings in Criminal Matters** and **Model Extradition Treaty**, the United Nations or its agencies also produced this Model Treaty on the Transfer of Supervision of Offenders Who Have Been Conditionally Sentenced or Conditionally Released.

The chief principle governing this type of treaty is a belief that "supervision in the home country of the offender rather than enforcement of the sentence in a country where the offender has no roots . . . contributes to an earlier and more effective reintegration into society." The transfer to the home country of supervision of an offender found guilty in another nation applies only to persons under conditional sentences or conditional releases.

REFERENCES:

Bassiouni, M. Cherif, and Edward M. Wise. *Aut Dedere Aut Judicare: The Duty to Extradite or Prosecute in International Law.* Dordrecht, Netherlands, and Boston: M. Nijhoff, 1995.

___. *International Extradition: United States Law and Practice,* 3d ed. Dobbs Ferry, NY: Oceana Publications, 1996.

Yarnold, Barbara M. *International Fugitives.* New York: Praeger, 1991.

Inter-American Convention on Mutual Assistance in Criminal Matters

SIGNED: May 23, 1992, at Nassau, Bahamas

SIGNATORIES: Brazil, Canada, Chile, Ecuador, Grenada, Nicaragua, Paraguay, Peru, Suriname, United States, Uruguay, Venezuela

IN FORCE: From April 14, 1996

OVERVIEW: An agreement among Organization of American States member nations "to render to one another mutual assistance in criminal matters."

DISCUSSION:

The convention is a multilateral treaty of cooperation in criminal matters, as laid down in Article 2:

The states parties shall render to one another mutual assistance in investigations, prosecutions, and proceedings that pertain to crimes over which the requesting state has jurisdiction at the time the assistance is requested.

This convention does not authorize any state party to undertake, in the territory of another state party, the exercise of jurisdiction or the performance of functions that are placed within the exclusive purview of the authorities of that other party by its domestic law.

This convention applies solely to the provision of mutual assistance among states parties. Its provisions shall not create any right on the part of any private person to obtain or exclude any evidence or to impede execution of any request for assistance.

Article 5 relates to the issue of "double criminality":

The assistance shall be rendered even if the act that gives rise to it is not punishable under the legislation of the requested state.

When the request for assistance pertains to the following measures: (a) immobilization and sequestration of property and (b) searches and seizures, including house searches, the requested state may decline to render the assistance if the act that gives rise to the request is not punishable under its legislation.

And Article 6 further stipulates that "the act that gives rise to the request must be punishable by one year or more of imprisonment in the requesting state."

Under Article 9, the requested state may decline the request for assistance under the following circumstances:

a. The request for assistance is being used in order to prosecute a person on a charge with respect to which that person has already been sentenced or acquitted in a trial in the requesting or requested state;

b. The investigation has been initiated for the purpose of prosecuting, punishing, or discriminating in any way against an individual or group of persons for reason of sex, race, social status, nationality, religion, or ideology;

c. The request refers to a crime that is political or related to a political crime, or to a common crime prosecuted for political reasons;

d. The request has been issued at the request of a special or ad hoc tribunal;

e. Public policy *(ordre public)*, sovereignty, security, or basic public interests are prejudiced; and

f. The request pertains to a tax crime. Nevertheless, the assistance shall be granted if the offense is committed by way of an intentionally incorrect statement, whether oral or written, or by way of an intentional failure to declare income derived from any other offense covered by this convention for the purpose of concealing such income.

The balance of the convention addresses procedures by which legal assistance is to be carried out.

REFERENCES:

Bassiouni, M. Cherif, and Edward M. Wise. *Aut Dedere Aut Judicare: The Duty to Extradite or Prosecute in International Law.* Dordrecht, Netherlands, and Boston: M. Nijhoff, 1995.
___. *International Extradition: United States Law and Practice,* 3d ed. Dobbs Ferry, NY: Oceana Publications, 1996.
Yarnold, Barbara M. *International Fugitives.* New York: Praeger, 1991.

Inter-American Convention on Serving Criminal Sentences Abroad

SIGNED: June 9, 1993, at Managua, Nicaragua

SIGNATORIES: Brazil, Canada, Chile, Costa Rica, Ecuador, Mexico, Panama, Paraguay, United States, Venezuela

IN FORCE: From April 12, 1996

OVERVIEW: A convention among certain member states of the Organization of American States permitting, under most conditions, nationals of one state party to serve a prison sentence in the "state of which he or she is a national."

DISCUSSION:

The "General Principles" of the convention are stated in Article 2 as follows:

a. a sentence imposed in one state party upon a national of another state party may be served by the sentenced person in the state of which he or she is a national; and

b. the states parties undertake to afford each other the fullest cooperation in connection with the transfer of sentenced persons

Article 3 lays down the conditions for application of the convention, which encompass seven points:

1. The sentence must be final . . .

2. The sentenced person must consent to the transfer, having been previously informed of the legal consequences thereof.

3. The act for which the person has been sentenced must also constitute a crime in the receiving state. . . .

4. The sentenced person must be a national of the receiving state.

5. The sentence to be served must not be the death penalty.

6. At least six months of the sentence must remain to be served at the time the request is made.

7. The administration of the sentence must not be contrary to domestic law in the receiving state.

Article 4 provides that the signatories "shall inform any sentenced person covered by the provisions of this convention as to its content." Article 5 lays down the procedure for transfer, and Article 6 lays down the procedure for refusal of a transfer request. Article 7 addresses the rights of the sentenced person who is transferred:

1. A sentenced person who is transferred under the provisions of this convention shall not be arrested, tried, or sentenced again in the receiving state for the same offense . . .

2. . . . the sentence . . . shall be served in accordance with the laws and procedures of the receiving state, including application of any provisions relating to reduction of time of imprisonment or of alternative service of the sentence.

No sentence may be enforced by a receiving state in such fashion as to lengthen the sentence beyond the date on which it would expire under the terms of the sentence of the court of the sentencing state.

REFERENCES:

Bassiouni, M. Cherif, and Edward M. Wise. *Aut Dedere Aut Judicare: The Duty to Extradite or Prosecute in International Law.* Dordrecht, Netherlands, and Boston: M. Nijhoff, 1995.
___. *International Extradition: United States Law and Practice,* 3d ed. Dobbs Ferry, NY: Oceana Publications, 1996.
Yarnold, Barbara M. *International Fugitives.* New York: Praeger, 1991.

Optional Protocol on Inter-American Convention on Mutual Assistance in Criminal Matters

SIGNED: June 11, 1993, at Managua, Nicaragua

SIGNATORIES: Brazil, Chile, Ecuador, Paraguay, United States

IN FORCE: Not yet in force

OVERVIEW: An optional protocol to **Inter-American Convention on Mutual Assistance in Criminal Matters** of 1992 applying to assistance in the case of tax crimes.

DISCUSSION:

Signatories to the optional protocol agree not to "exercise the right provided for . . . [in] the Convention to refuse a request for assistance solely on the ground that the request concerns a tax crime." The object of the protocol is to prevent attempted evasion of prosecution for tax crimes by flight to nations that may not render extradition or other legal assistance in the case of such crimes.

REFERENCES:
Bassiouni, M. Cherif, and Edward M. Wise. *Aut Dedere Aut Judicare: The Duty to Extradite or Prosecute in International Law.* Dordrecht, Netherlands, and Boston: M. Nijhoff, 1995.
___. *International Extradition: United States Law and Practice,* 3d ed. Dobbs Ferry, NY: Oceana Publications, 1996.
Yarnold, Barbara M. *International Fugitives.* New York: Praeger, 1991.

Inter-American Convention Against Corruption

SIGNED: March 29, 1996, at Caracas, Venezuela
SIGNATORIES: Argentina, Bahamas, Bolivia, Brazil, Canada, Chile, Colombia, Costa Rica, Dominican Republic, Ecuador, El Salvador, Guatemala, Guyana, Haiti, Honduras, Jamaica, Mexico, Nicaragua, Panama, Paraguay, Peru, Suriname, Trinidad and Tobago, United States, Uruguay, Venezuela
IN FORCE: From March 6, 1997
OVERVIEW: A convention among members of the Organization of American States to "to promote and strengthen the development by each of the States Parties of the mechanisms needed to prevent, detect, punish and eradicate corruption and . . . to promote, facilitate and regulate cooperation among the States Parties to ensure the effectiveness of measures and actions to prevent, detect, punish and eradicate corruption in the performance of public functions and acts of corruption specifically related to such performance."

DISCUSSION:
Signatory states undertake to establish the following:

1. Standards of conduct for the correct, honorable, and proper fulfillment of public functions. These standards shall be intended to prevent conflicts of interest and mandate the proper conservation and use of resources entrusted to government officials in the performance of their functions. These standards shall also establish measures and systems requiring government officials to report to appropriate authorities acts of corruption in the performance of public functions. Such measures should help preserve the public's confidence in the integrity of public servants and government processes.

2. Mechanisms to enforce these standards of conduct.

3. Instruction to government personnel to ensure proper understanding of their responsibilities and the ethical rules governing their activities.

4. Systems for registering the income, assets and liabilities of persons who perform public functions in certain posts as specified by law and, where appropriate, for making such registrations public.

5. Systems of government hiring and procurement of goods and services that assure the openness, equity and efficiency of such systems.

6. Government revenue collection and control systems that deter corruption.

7. Laws that deny favorable tax treatment for any individual or corporation for expenditures made in violation of the anticorruption laws of the States Parties.

8. Systems for protecting public servants and private citizens who, in good faith, report acts of corruption, including protection of their identities, in accordance with their Constitutions and the basic principles of their domestic legal systems.

9. Oversight bodies with a view to implementing modern mechanisms for preventing, detecting, punishing and eradicating corrupt acts.

10. Deterrents to the bribery of domestic and foreign government officials, such as mechanisms to ensure that publicly held companies and other types of associations maintain books and records which, in reasonable detail, accurately reflect the acquisition and disposition of assets, and have sufficient internal accounting controls to enable their officers to detect corrupt acts.

11. Mechanisms to encourage participation by civil society and nongovernmental organizations in efforts to prevent corruption.

12. The study of further preventive measures that take into account the relationship between equitable compensation and probity in public service.

The convention is especially significant in that it recognizes corruption as a transnational problem—because criminals in one nation may use the laws of another to evade prosecution—requiring a transnational solution.

REFERENCES:
Elliott, Kimberly Ann, ed. *Corruption and the Global Economy.* Washington, DC: Institute for International Economics, 1996.
Jordan, David C. *Drug Politics: Dirty Money and Democracies.* Norman: University of Oklahoma Press, 1999.

Inter-American Convention Against the Illicit Manufacturing of and Trafficking in Firearms

OFFICIAL TITLE: Inter-American Convention Against the Illicit Manufacturing of and Trafficking in Firearms, Ammunition, Explosives, and Other Related Materials
SIGNED: November 14, 1997, at Washington
SIGNATORIES: Antigua and Barbuda, Argentina, Bahamas, Belize, Bolivia, Brazil, Canada, Chile, Colombia, Costa Rica, Dominican Republic, Ecuador, El Salvador, Grenada, Guatemala, Guyana, Haiti, Honduras, Jamaica, Mexico, Nicaragua, Panama, Paraguay, Peru, Saint Lucia, Saint Vincent and the Grenadines, St. Kitts and Nevis, Suriname, Trinidad and Tobago, United States, Uruguay, Venezuela
IN FORCE: From July 1, 1998
OVERVIEW: "The purpose of this Convention is to prevent, combat, and eradicate the illicit manufacturing of and trafficking in firearms, ammunition, explosives, and other related materials."

DISCUSSION:

The principal provision of the convention is contained in Article 4:

States Parties that have not yet done so shall adopt the necessary legislative or other measures to establish as criminal offenses under their domestic law the illicit manufacturing of and trafficking in firearms, ammunition, explosives, and other related materials.

Following articles that outline prosecution and enforcement measures that should be available to signatories, Article 10 addresses "Strengthening of Controls at Export Points":

Each State Party shall adopt such measures as may be necessary to detect and prevent illicit trafficking in firearms, ammunition, explosives, and other related materials between its territory and that of other States Parties, by strengthening controls at export points.

Additional articles outline a program of cooperation among signatories. The concluding articles of the convention create a Consultative Committee to coordinate the cooperative endeavor among the signatory states.

REFERENCE:

Rathjen, Heidi, and Charles Montpetit. *December 6th: From the Montreal Massacre to Gun Control: The Inside Story.* Toronto: McClelland and Stewart, 1999.

Draft United Nations Convention Against Transnational Organized Crime

REVISION DRAFTED: October 4-15, 1999, at Vienna
SIGNATORIES: Draft treaty, not yet open for signature
IN FORCE: Not yet in force
OVERVIEW: A draft (in progress as of November 1999) of a convention to promote international cooperation to prevent and combat transnational organized crime more effectively.

DISCUSSION:

While nations have long cooperated in combating various forms of crime and in tracking international fugitives, the draft convention is the first to recognize the special problems presented by serious crimes involving transnational organized criminal groups.

The draft convention includes provisions affecting the domestic law of the signatories, each of which will undertake to establish the following as criminal offenses:

- Organizing, directing, aiding, abetting, facilitating or counseling the commission of a serious crime involving an organized criminal group
- Agreeing with one or more persons to commit a serious crime involving an organized criminal group
- Participation in criminal activities of an organized crime group

Two major organized crimes enumerated in the convention include the following, together with measures to combat them:

- International money laundering
- International corruption, including bribery of officials

Prosecution under the convention applies to natural persons as well as legal persons (that is, corporate entities), and the convention includes guidelines for prosecution and punishment, including the use of confiscation of assets and property, in which action the signatories agree to cooperate.

Additional articles address issues of jurisdiction and extradition, as well as mutual legal assistance and mutual assistance using special investigative techniques, such as controlled delivery of suspected or incriminating goods for the purposes of investigating offenders, electronic surveillance, and undercover operations. Signatories also agree to cooperate in protecting law-enforcement officials (often the targets of intimidation and reprisal) as well as witnesses and victims.

The convention sets up mechanisms for direct cooperation among national law-enforcement agencies and for sharing and exchanging information on an ongoing basis. A program of training and technical assistance is also created.

Also see **Draft United Nations Protocol Against Illicit Manufacturing of and Trafficking in Firearms.**

REFERENCES:

Bassiouni, M. Cherif, and Edward M. Wise. *Aut Dedere Aut Judicare: The Duty to Extradite or Prosecute in International Law.* Dordrecht, Netherlands, and Boston: M. Nijhoff, 1995.
___. *International Extradition: United States Law and Practice,* 3d ed. Dobbs Ferry, NY: Oceana Publications, 1996.
Yarnold, Barbara M. *International Fugitives.* New York: Praeger, 1991.

Draft United Nations Protocol Against Illicit Manufacturing of and Trafficking in Firearms

OFFICIAL TITLE: Revised Draft Protocol against Illicit Manufacturing of and Trafficking in Firearms, Ammunition, and Other Related Materials, Supplementary to the United Nations Convention Against Transnational Organized Crime
REVISION DRAFTED: October 4-15, 1999, at Vienna
SIGNATORIES: Draft treaty, not yet open for signature
IN FORCE: Not yet in force
OVERVIEW: A draft (in progress as of November 1999) of a protocol to promote international cooperation in combating the illegal manufacture, exportation, and importation of firearms.

DISCUSSION:

A draft protocol supplementary to the **Draft United Nations Convention Against Transnational Organized Crime,** the document is directed at stopping the illegal manufacture, exportation, and importation of firearms and ammunition. The protocol is intended specifically to combat "the illegal activities carried out by criminal organizations in the areas of illicit manufacturing of and trafficking in firearms ... as well as their use for the purpose of facilitating their unlawful enterprises."

The draft protocol faces a serious challenge in harmonizing a wide variation among national laws with regard to firearms: some nations regulate firearms very stringently, while others, including the United States, allow great latitude where firearms are concerned—and much firearms regulation takes place at the subnational (state and provincial) level. The major thrust of the protocol, therefore, is directed at control of the transnational movement of firearms.

REFERENCE:
Rathjen, Heidi, and Charles Montpetit. *December 6th: From the Montreal Massacre to Gun Control: The Inside Story.* Toronto: McClelland and Stewart, 1999.

Cultural Property and Cultural Relations

Overview of Treaties in This Category

Military and trade relations have been subjects of treaty making since the earliest agreements concluded in the ancient world. Beginning in the later twentieth century, however, nations, including the United States, have recognized that the terms of international cultural relations may also be beneficially defined by treaty. Some of the treaties in this section deal with cultural exchange, accepting the premise that such exchange is inherently valuable for promoting peaceful and productive relations among nations. Other treaties are intended to aid in the protection and preservation of national cultural heritage, especially by preventing the removal, theft, or illegal exportation of national archaeological, cultural, and historical properties.

Convention for the Promotion of Inter-American Cultural Relations

SIGNED: March 28, 1954, at Caracas, Venezuela

SIGNATORIES: Argentina, Bolivia, Brazil, Chile, Colombia, Costa Rica, Cuba, Dominican Republic, Ecuador, El Salvador, Guatemala, Haiti, Honduras, Mexico, Nicaragua, Panama, Paraguay, Peru, United States, Uruguay, Venezuela

IN FORCE: "For each country on the date of its instrument of ratification depository"; for the United States, November 3, 1957

OVERVIEW: A convention "to revise the text and strengthen the spirit of the Convention for the Promotion of Inter-American Cultural Relations, concluded at Buenos Aires in 1936."

DISCUSSION:

The convention is a practical agreement on programs of cultural exchange among the signatory states, all members of the Organization of American States. The principal articles of the convention follow:

Article 1

Every year each government shall award one or more fellowships, insofar as it may be able to do so, for the ensuing scholastic year, which may be granted to graduate students or to teachers or to other persons with equivalent qualifications from each of the other Member States. The recipients shall be chosen in accordance with the procedure established in Article 4 of this Convention. Notwithstanding the foregoing, each government may award a greater number of fellowships for study if this has been provided in other international agreements or otherwise.

Article 2

Each fellowship shall include, through such agency as may be deemed appropriate, tuition in an institution of higher learning designated by the country awarding the fellowship, as well as textbooks, working materials, and, in addition, a monthly allowance to cover lodging, subsistence, and other necessary additional expenses. The expenses of traveling to the designated institution and those of returning to the country of origin and, in addition, an amount for incidental travel expenses during the journey shall be borne by the recipient or by the nominating government.

Article 7

The High Contracting Parties will encourage, in other ways, especially during vacation periods, the exchange, for cultural purposes, of teachers, artists, students, and other persons engaged in the professions, between their respective countries.

Article 11

The High Contracting Parties declare that this Convention is motivated by the highest principles of cooperation, the extent of the interchange depending upon the circumstances peculiar to each country.

REFERENCE:

United States Department of State, *Treaties in Force: A List of Treaties and other International Agreements of the United States in Force on January 1, 1997.* Washington, D.C.: U.S. Government Printing Office, 1997.

Statutes of the International Centre for the Study of the Preservation and Restoration of Cultural Property (ICCROM)

SIGNED: December 5, 1956, at Rome

SIGNATORIES: Albania, Algeria, Australia, Austria, Belgium, Brazil, Bulgaria, Canada, Chile, Colombia, Cuba, Cyprus, Democratic Kampuchea, Denmark, Dominican Republic, Ecuador, Egypt, Ethiopia, Finland, France, Gabon, Germany (Federal Republic), Ghana, Guatemala, Guinea, Honduras, India, Iran, Iraq, Israel, Italy, Japan, Jordan, Kuwait, Lebanon, Libyan Arab Jamahiriyya, Luxembourg, Madagascar, Malaysia, Malta, Mexico, Morocco, Nepal, Netherlands, Nicaragua, Nigeria, Norway, Pakistan, Paraguay, Peru, Poland, Portugal, Republic of Korea, Republic of Vietnam, Romania, Somalia, Spain, Sri Lanka, Sudan Sweden, Switzerland, Syrian Arab Republic, Thailand, Tunisia, Turkey, Union of Soviet Socialist Republics, United Kingdom, United States, Yugoslavia

IN FORCE: From May 10, 1958

OVERVIEW: The constitution of an international center devoted to the study of the preservation and restoration of cultural property.

DISCUSSION:

The principal purposes of the International Centre for the Study of the Preservation and Restoration of Cultural Property (ICCROM) are the following:

- To collect, study, and circulate documentation concerning the scientific and technical problems of the preservation and restoration of cultural property

- To coordinate, stimulate, or institute research in this field

- To advise on general or specific points concerning preservation and restoration

- To assist in training research workers and technicians

The statutes relate to issues of membership, organization, financing, and management of the ICCROM.

REFERENCE:

King, Thomas F. *Cultural Resource Laws and Practice: An Introductory Guide.* Walnut Creek, CA: Altamira Press, 1998.

Treaty of Cooperation (with Mexico) in Providing for the Recovery and Return of Stolen Archaeological, Historical and Cultural Properties

SIGNED: July 17, 1970, at Mexico City

SIGNATORIES: Mexico vs. United States

IN FORCE: From March 24, 1971

OVERVIEW: A treaty to cooperate in the recovery and return of stolen artifacts and items of cultural heritage.

DISCUSSION:

During much of the nineteenth and twentieth centuries, the pre-Columbian heritage of Mexico has been freely looted by tourists as well as dealers in antiquities. The 1970 Treaty of Cooperation was intended to help bring an end to this practice—and to preserve and protect all items of archaeological and cultural value in both countries. The principal provision of the treaty is an undertaking by each signatory to "employ the legal means at its disposal to recover and return from its territory stolen archaeological, historical and cultural properties that are removed after the date of entry into force of this Treaty."

REFERENCE:

Messenger, Phyllis Mauch, ed. *The Ethics of Collecting Cultural Property: Whose Culture? Whose Property?* Albuquerque: University of New Mexico Press, 1999.

Convention Concerning the Protection of the World Cultural and Natural Heritage

SIGNED: November 23, 1972, at Paris, France

SIGNATORIES: Albania, Algeria, Antigua and Barbuda, Argentina, Australia, Bahrain, Bangladesh, Belarus, Belize, Benin, Bolivia, Brazil, Bulgaria, Burkina Faso, Burundi, Cambodia, Cameroon, Canada, Cape Verde, Central African Republic, Chile, China, Colombia, Congo, Costa Rica, Côte d'Ivoire, Cuba, Cyprus, Czech and Slovak (Federal Republic), Denmark, Dominican Republic, Ecuador, Egypt, El Salvador, Ethiopia, Finland, France, Gabon, Gambia, Fiji, Germany, Ghana, Greece, Guatemala, Guinea, Guyana, Haiti, Holy See, Honduras, Hungary, India, Indonesia, Iran (Islamic Republic), Iraq, Ireland, Italy, Jamaica, Japan, Jordan, Kenya, Korea (Republic), Lao People's Democratic Republic, Lebanon, Libyan Arab Jamahiriya, Lithuania, Luxembourg, Madagascar, Malawi, Malaysia, Maldives, Mali, Malta, Mauritania, Mexico, Monaco, Mongolia, Morocco, Mozambique, Nepal, New Zealand, Nicaragua, Niger, Nigeria, Norway, Oman, Pakistan, Panama, Paraguay, Peru, Philippines, Poland, Portugal, Qatar, Romania, Russian Federation, San Marino, Solomon Islands, St. Christopher and Nevis, St. Lucia, Saudi Arabia, Senegal, Seychelles, Spain, Sri Lanka, Sudan, Sweden, Switzerland, Syrian Arab Republic, Thailand, Tunisia, Turkey, Uganda, Ukraine, United Kingdom, United Republic of Tanzania, United States, Uruguay, Venezuela, Vietnam, Yemen, Yugoslavia, Zaire, Zambia, Zimbabwe

IN FORCE: From December 17, 1975

OVERVIEW: An international convention to create a system of collective protection of the cultural and natural heritage of outstanding universal value, organized on a permanent basis and in accordance with modern scientific methods.

DISCUSSION:

Each signatory acknowledges a duty to identify, protect, conserve, and transmit to future generations the cultural and natural heritage belonging to the signatory state. Toward this end, the signatories undertake the following:

- To integrate the protection of their heritage into comprehensive planning programs

- To set up services for the protection of their heritage

- To develop scientific and technical studies and to take necessary legal, scientific, administrative and financial steps to protect their heritage

- To assist other signatory states in the protection of the world's cultural and natural heritage

- To establish a World Heritage Committee, and to submit to it an inventory of the state's national heritage; the committee will then publish a "World Heritage List" and a "List of World Heritage in Danger"

- To participate in financing a World Heritage Fund

REFERENCE:
King, Thomas F. *Cultural Resource Laws and Practice: An Introductory Guide.* Walnut Creek, CA: Altamira Press, 1998.

Convention of San Salvador

OFFICIAL TITLE: Convention on the Protection of the Archeological, Historical, and Artistic Heritage of the American Nations

SIGNED: June 16, 1976, at San Salvador

SIGNATORIES: Antigua and Barbuda, Argentina, Bahamas, Barbados, Bolivia, Brazil, Chile, Colombia, Costa Rica, Dominica, the Dominican Republic, Ecuador, El Salvador, Grenada, Guatemala, Haiti, Honduras, Jamaica, Mexico, Nicaragua, Panama, Paraguay, Peru, St. Kitts-Nevis, Saint Lucia, Saint Vincent and the Grenadines, Suriname, Trinidad and Tobago, United States, Uruguay, Venezuela

IN FORCE: Not yet in force, pending ratification by signatories

OVERVIEW: A convention to combat the "continuous looting and plundering of the native cultural heritage suffered by the countries of the hemisphere, particularly the Latin American countries."

DISCUSSION:

The convention calls for the signatory parties "to identify, register, protect, and safeguard the property making up the cultural heritage of the American nations in order: (a) to prevent illegal exportation or importation of cultural property, and (b) to promote cooperation among the American states for mutual awareness and appreciation of their cultural property." Article 2 enumerates the categories of cultural property to be protected as follows:

a. Monuments, objects, fragments of ruined buildings, and archeological materials belonging to American cultures existing prior to contact with European culture, as well as remains of human beings, fauna, and flora related to such cultures;

b. Monuments, buildings, objects of an artistic, utilitarian, and ethnological nature, whole or in fragments, from the colonial era and the Nineteenth Century;

c. Libraries and archives; incunabula and manuscripts; books and other publications, iconographies, maps and documents published before 1850;

d. All objects originating after 1850 that the States Parties have recorded as cultural property, provided that they have given notice of such registration to the other parties to the treaty;

e. All cultural property that any of the States Parties specifically declares to be included within the scope of this convention.

Article 3 prohibits exportation and importation of protected cultural property "except when the state owning it authorizes its exportation for purposes of promoting knowledge of national cultures."

REFERENCES:
King, Thomas F. *Cultural Resource Laws and Practice: An Introductory Guide.* Walnut Creek, CA: Altamira Press, 1998.
Messenger, Phyllis Mauch, ed. *The Ethics of Collecting Cultural Property: Whose Culture? Whose Property?* Albuquerque: University of New Mexico Press, 1999.

Cultural Agreement (with China)

SIGNED: January 31, 1979, at Washington, D.C.

SIGNATORIES: China vs. United States

IN FORCE: From signing

OVERVIEW: An agreement in principle to undertake programs of cultural exchange between China and the United States.

DISCUSSION:

Following the breakthroughs in Chinese-United States relations during the administrations of President Richard M. Nixon and, later, Jimmy Carter, various trade, technical, scientific, and cultural agreements were concluded between the nations. In the 1979 Cultural Agreement, the signatories undertake to "encourage a deeper knowledge of their respective histories, cultures, literatures, arts, languages, sports and other areas . . . through cooperative programs as well as exchanges." Furthermore, the two governments undertake to encourage "interchanges between representatives of professional groups, cultural organizations, news and public information organizations, radio and television organizations and academic institutions." Programs of publication and broadcasting are also encouraged.

The document is signed by President Jimmy Carter and by Chinese premier Deng Xiaoping.

REFERENCES:
Mann, James. *About Face: A History of America's Curious Relationship with China from Nixon to Clinton.* New York: Knopf, 1999.
Tyler, Patrick. *A Great Wall: Six Presidents and China.* Washington,. D.C.: Public Affairs, 1999.

Unidroit Convention on Stolen or Illegally Exported Cultural Objects

SIGNED: June 24, 1995, at Rome

SIGNATORIES: Bolivia, Burkina Faso, Cambodia, Côte d'Ivoire, Croatia, Finland, France, Georgia, Guinea, Hungary, Italy, Lithuania, Netherlands, Pakistan, Paraguay, Peru, Portugal, Romania, Russian Federation, Senegal, Switzerland, Zambia; the following have acceded to the convention: Brazil, China, Ecuador; as of September 1999, the United States has neither signed or acceded to the convention.

IN FORCE: Not in force for the United States

OVERVIEW: A convention "intended to facilitate the restitution and return of cultural objects" illegally taken or exported from a state.

DISCUSSION:

Article 3 includes a simple statement of the underlying principle of the convention: "The possessor of a cultural object which has been stolen shall return it." The balance of the convention includes provisions addressing the following issues:

- Restitution of stolen cultural objects
- Compensation to "the possessor of a cultural object who acquired the object after it was illegally exported shall be entitled, at the time of its return, to payment by the requesting State of fair and reason compensation, provided that the possessor neither knew nor ought reasonably to have known at the time of acquisition that the object had been illegally exported."
- Return of illegally exported cultural objects
- Resolution of disputes

REFERENCES:

King, Thomas F. *Cultural Resource Laws and Practice: An Introductory Guide.* Walnut Creek, CA: Altamira Press, 1998.

Messenger, Phyllis Mauch, ed. *The Ethics of Collecting Cultural Property: Whose Culture? Whose Property?* Albuquerque: University of New Mexico Press, 1999.

Final Communiqué of the NATO Partnership for Peace Conference on Cultural Heritage Protection in Wartime and in State of Emergency

SIGNED: June 21, 1996 at Cracow, Poland

SIGNATORIES: Albania, Armenia, Austria, Azerbaijan, Belarus, Belgium, Bulgaria, Canada, Czech Republic, Denmark, Estonia, Finland, Former Yugoslav Republic of Macedonia, France, Georgia, Germany, Greece, Hungary, Iceland, Italy, Kazakhstan, Kyrghyz Republic, Latvia, Lithuania, Luxembourg, Moldova, Netherlands, Norway, Poland, Portugal, Romania, Russia, Slovakia, Slovenia, Spain, Sweden, Switzerland, Turkey, Turkmenistan, Ukraine, United Kingdom, United States, Uzbekistan

IN FORCE: From signing

OVERVIEW: A statement of recommendations for international cooperation in the protection of cultural heritage during war or state of emergency.

DISCUSSION:

The Partnership for Peace (PfP) was introduced by NATO at a January 1994 summit held in Brussels. The aim of PfP is to enhance stability and security throughout Europe by focusing on defense-related cooperation. The PfP reaches beyond the NATO member nations to all European states able and willing to contribute to a program intended to expand and intensify political and military cooperation throughout Europe, increase stability, and diminish threats to peace. One outgrowth of PfP was a conference devoted to "Cultural Heritage Protection in Wartime and in State of Emergency," held in Cracow, Poland, during June 18-21, 1996. The following recommendations resulted from the conference:

1. States' laws, regulations and normative documents relevant to the protection of cultural property should be published, and widely distributed to serve as a common basis for the education of governments, armed forces, institutions and populations.

2. International co-operation and exchange of experiences should be developed on the implementation of the **Hague Convention on the Protection of Cultural Property in the Event of Armed Conflicts** (1954) and other existing instruments such as the **Convention concerning the Protection of the World Cultural and Natural Heritage** (1972), including initiatives under the International Committee of the Blue Shield.

3. The Hague Convention and its Protocol and their implementation could be improved on the following points:

3.1 Precise definition of the term "military necessity" and the conditions under which it may be invoked;

3.2 Extension of the term "armed conflict" to include internal civil and armed conflicts, in particular ethnic ones, and provision for the laws and mechanisms for the protection of cultural property also be applied in such cases;

3.3 Inclusion of the concept of a minimum distance of separation of military operations from a cultural property under protection;

3.4 Use of new technology for internationally recognised marking and signals for cultural properties;

3.5 Inclusion of specific topographic symbols on maps for areas containing of protected cultural properties.

4. The willful damaging or destruction of cultural property during military operations in violation of the Hague Convention of 1954 should be recognised as a war crime subject to international and states' tribunals.

The conference also recognised the need for improved mechanisms for the return of cultural properties taken in violation of international law. Accordingly, the Conference recommends that NATO and its PfP partners, following the Cracow Conference, explore the possibility of further co-operation with UNESCO and with the International Committee of the Blue Shield to improve and promote the implementation of existing instruments, to improve national and local preparedness and response capability through, among others, training, adequate risk analysis taking into account heritage and cultural values, and better communication between responsible authorities, in order to reduce the losses of cultural heritage in the event of emergencies of human or natural origin.

The Final Communiqué of the NATO Partnership for Peace Conference on Cultural Heritage Protection in Wartime and in State of Emergency is an example of an international document type that has appeared with increasing frequency in recent years. A communiqué of this kind is an official announcement by a duly constituted international organization, which, however, carries very little legal weight under international law.

Such documents often become the basis for binding agreements, but are themselves generally non-binding.

REFERENCES:

King, Thomas F. *Cultural Resource Laws and Practice: An Introductory Guide.* Walnut Creek, CA: Altamira Press, 1998.

United States Department of State, *Treaties in Force: A List of Treaties and other International Agreements of the United States in Force on January 1, 1997.* Washington, D.C.: U.S. Government Printing Office, 1997.

SECTION 3.5

Diplomatic Relations

Overview of Treaties in This Category

"Diplomatic relations" encompasses the ground rules that govern the routine relations of one nation with another and international relations generally. Relating as they do to an area so broad, it may be appreciated that the treaties and agreements in this section are of an especially varied nature.

The **Clayton-Bulwer Treaty** (1850), between Great Britain and the United States, focuses on issues anticipated in connection with the construction and operation of the planned Panama Canal.

Relations with Asian nations is the subject of six early treaties in this section. **Empire of Japan Treaty (Kanagawa Treaty, Perry Convention)** of 1854 opened diplomatic and trade relations with Japan, and **Kingdom of Chosen Treaty** (1882) did the same with Korea. With Japan, the United States concluded the **Root-Takahira Agreement** of 1908, mutually affirming the wish of both nations to maintain the status quo in the Pacific and to defend the Open Door Policy—giving all nations equal access to trade—with regard to China. This was modified and amplified by the 1917 **Lansing-Ishii Agreement**, in which the United States recognized Japan's special interests in China in return for Japan's reaffirmation of the Open Door policy. While the **Four Power Treaty** of 1921 sought to define a balance among the United States, British Empire, France, and Japan with regard to their respective possessions and interests in the Pacific, the **Nine Power Treaty Concerning China** (1922) was intended more specifically to preserve Chinese sovereignty in order to limit Japanese expansion in China, a development that threatened European and American interests in the Pacific and, therefore, also threatened the stability of the region.

Global diplomatic maneuvering was not confined to Asia and the Pacific during the early twentieth century. The **Algeciras Convention** of 1906 was aimed at resolving imperialist power politics in North Africa and is an important document in the development of the United States as a genuine *world* power.

Many diplomatic treaties have less to do with political maneuvering and the preservation of a balance of power and influence than they do with simply establishing and defining diplomatic relations between one country and another. **Treaty of Friendship, Commerce and Consular Rights with Estonia** (1925) is an example of a bilateral diplomatic treaty establishing basic relations, whereas **Vienna Convention on Diplomatic Relations** (1961) and **Vienna Convention on Consular**

Relations (1963) are multilateral conventions defining general rules governing diplomatic relations, while **Vienna Convention on the Law of Treaties** (1969) establishes common standards for treaty making. In 1961, after the Congo achieved independence from Belgium, the United States concluded **Agreement (with Republic of the Congo) Relating to the Continued Application of Certain Treaties**, which defined which treaties, originally made with the Belgian Congo, would remain in force with the new republic. The issue of the succession of states in respect of treaties was deemed of sufficient importance to merit the creation of a multilateral convention on the subject, **Vienna Convention on Succession of States in Respect of Treaties** (1978). Since the creation of the United Nations, an increasing number of international agreements include organizations as well as states, a situation addressed by **Vienna Convention on the Law of Treaties between States and International Organizations or between International Organizations** (1986).

In 1960, the United States broke off diplomatic relations with Cuba, but both Cuba and the United States came to recognize that some means of diplomatic communication was still required between them. Accordingly, the nations drew up the **U.S.-Cuba Agreement to Establish Interest Sections** in 1977. Diplomatic relations with communist China did not exist at all, because, after the success of the communist revolution in China, the United States recognized the Nationalist government in exile on Taiwan, not the mainland communist government, as the legitimate government of China. In 1972, however, the United States and mainland China announced the limited resumption of diplomatic relations between them in the first (a second was issued in 1978) **United States-People's Republic of China Joint Communiqué**, a major step toward ultimate full normalization of relations.

Clayton-Bulwer Treaty

OFFICIAL TITLE: Convention between the United States of America and Her Britannic Majesty
SIGNED: April 19, 1850, at Washington
SIGNATORIES: Great Britain vs. United States
IN FORCE: Six months from signing
OVERVIEW: An equivocal and therefore problematic treaty

providing for Britain and the United States to share control and protection of the anticipated Panama Canal.

DISCUSSION:

Negotiated between Sir Henry Lytton Bulwer, British minister to Washington, and John M. Clayton, U.S. secretary of state, the Clayton-Bulwer Treaty was intended to establish the principle of Anglo-American joint control and protection of a canal planned to be built across the Isthmus of Panama. The treaty's first article proved highly controversial:

The governments of the United States and Great Britain hereby declare, that neither the one nor the other will ever obtain or maintain for itself any exclusive control over the said ship canal; agreeing that neither will ever erect or maintain any fortifications commanding the same or in the vicinity thereof, or occupy, or fortify, or colonize, or assume or exercise any dominion over Nicaragua, Costa Rica, the Mosquito coast, or any part of Central America; nor will either make use of any protection which either affords or may afford, or any alliance which either teas or may have, to or with any State or people, for the purpose of erecting or maintaining any such fortifications, or of occupying, fortifying, or colonizing Nicaragua, Costa Rica, the Mosquito coast, or any part of Central America, or of assuming or exercising dominion over the same; nor will the United States or Great Britain take advantage of any intimacy, or use any alliance, connection, or influence that either may possess, with any State or government through whose territory the said canal may pass, for the purpose of acquiring or holding, directly or indirectly, for the citizens or subjects of the one, any rights or advantages in regard to commerce or navigation through the said canal which shall not be offered on the same terms to the citizens or subjects of the other.

Interpretation of this pledge of neutrality in Central America sparked a long and rancorous dispute. The United States held that the article obliged Britain to renounce its protectorate over the Mosquito Coast, the British Honduras, and the Bay Islands. Britain countered that the treaty upheld the status quo on these matters. Difficulties in building the canal delayed its construction and provided plenty of time for wrangling. As the nineteenth century drew to a close, imperialist sentiment in the United States increased, and there was widespread demand for abrogation of Clayton-Bulwer so that the United States could build the canal on its own. The **Hay-Pauncefote Treaty** of 1901, in which Britain agreed that the United States should construct and control the canal, superseded Clayton-Bulwer.

REFERENCES:

McCullough, David. *Path Between the Seas: The Creation of the Panama Canal, 1870-1914.* New York: Simon and Schuster, 1999.

Olney, Richard. *The Clayton-Bulwer Treaty; Memorandum.* Washington, D.C.: 1900.

Travis, Ira Dudley. *The History of the Clayton-Bulwer Treaty.* Ann Arbor, MI: The Association, 1900.

United States Department of State. *The Clayton-Bulwer Treaty and the Monroe Doctrine.* Washington, D.C.: U.S. Government Printing Office, 1882.

Empire of Japan Treaty (Kanagawa Treaty, Perry Convention)

SIGNED: March 31, 1854, at Kanagawa, Japan

IN FORCE: From signing

SIGNATORIES: United States vs. Japan

OVERVIEW: Japan's first treaty with a Western nation, the agreement ended the long period (beginning in 1639) of Japan's self-imposed seclusion from the Western world. Japan agreed to admit U.S. ships to the ports of Shimoda and Hakodate and to accept a U.S. consul at Shimoda. The treaty was, therefore, the foundation of a trade relationship between Japan and the United States—and, ultimately, between Japan and the West.

DISCUSSION:

President Millard Fillmore, desirous of opening Japan to U.S. commerce, dispatched to Japan Matthew Calbraith Perry, a distinguished naval officer and brother of War of 1812 hero Oliver Hazard Perry, to negotiate a treaty. Perry brought with him the entire Eastern Squadron, the firepower of which was intended to intimidate the Japanese and ensure that President Fillmore's overtures were conveyed to the highest authorities. The strategy was highly effective.

The brief treaty stipulates the following:

- The establishment of a "perfect, permanent, and universal peace" as well as a "cordial amity" between the United States and Japan
- The opening of designated ports to vessels of the United States
- The establishment of a policy of assistance to shipwrecked American sailors and other citizens of the United States in need
- The extension to the United States of any rights and privileges that may be granted to other nations in the future
- The establishment of a U.S. consulate in the port town of Shimoda

The treaty commenced the commercial, cultural, and political opening of Japan to the West and was a first step in Japan's rise to the position of a world power.

REFERENCES:

Icenhower, Joseph Bryan. *Perry and the Open Door to Japan.* New York: Franklin Watts, 1973.

Israel, Fred L. *Major Peace Treaties of Modern History, 1648-1967,* vol. 2. New York: Chelsea House and McGraw-Hill, 1967.

Palmer, Aaron Haight. *Documents and Facts Illustrating the Origin of the Mission to Japan.* Wilmington, DE: Scholarly Resources, 1973.

Perry, Matthew C. *The Japan Expedition, 1852-1854.* Washington, D.C.: Smithsonian Institution Press, 1968.

Wiley, Peter Booth. *Yankees in the Land of the Gods: Commodore Perry and the Opening of Japan.* New York: Viking, 1990.

Kingdom of Chosen Treaty

SIGNED: May 22, 1882, at Yin Chuen, Chosen [Korea]
IN FORCE: From November 20, 1882
SIGNATORIES: United States vs. Kingdom of Chosen [Korea]
OVERVIEW: Korea, long known as the "hermit kingdom," was the last of the three major Asian empires, after China and Japan, to establish commercial relations with the United States.

DISCUSSION:

The treaty establishes trade and diplomatic relations between the United States and Korea. It is the first step in a trading and diplomatic relationship that would, in the twentieth century, develop into a military alliance for mutual security and, among other things, result in the United States taking a leading role in a civil war between North and South Korea (the Korean War, 1950-1953).

Of special interest are the articles prohibiting trade in opium, regulating Korean export of foodstuffs in time of famine, regulating trade in arms and munitions, and providing for educational exchange between the nations:

Article VII

The Governments of the United States and of Chosen mutually agree and undertake that subjects of Chosen shall not be permitted to import opium into any of the ports of the United States, and citizens of the United States shall not be permitted to import opium into any of the open ports of Chosen, to transport it from one open port to another open port, or to traffic in it in Chosen. This absolute prohibition, which extends to vessels owned by the citizens or subjects of either Power, to foreign vessels employed by them, and to vessels owned by the citizens or subjects of either Power, and employed by other persons for the transportation of opium, shall be enforced by appropriate legislation on the part of the United States and of Chosen, and offenders against it shall be severely punished.

Article VIII

Whenever the Government of Chosen shall have reason to apprehend a scarcity of food within the limits of the kingdom, His Majesty may by Decree temporarily prohibit the export of all breadstuffs ...

Chosen having of old prohibited the exportation of red ginseng, if citizens of the United States clandestinely purchase it for export, it shall be confiscated and the offenders punished.

Article IX

Purchase of cannon, small arms, swords, gunpowder, shot, and all munitions of war is permitted only to officials of the Government of Chosen, and they may be imported by citizens of the United States only under a written permit from the authorities of Chosen....

Article XI

Students of either nationality, who may proceed to the country of the other, in order to study the language, literature, law, or arts, shall be given all possible protection and assistance in evidence of cordial goodwill.

The provision for educational exchange is unique among the first wave of United States-Asian trade treaties.

REFERENCES:
Israel, Fred L. *Major Peace Treaties of Modern History, 1648-1967,* vol. 2 (New York: Chelsea House and McGraw-Hill, 1967).
McNamara, Dennis L. *Trade and Transformation in Korea, 1876-1945.* Boulder, CO: Westview Press, 1996.
Moskowitz, Karl, ed. *From Patron to Partner: The Development of U.S.-Korean Business and Trade Relations.* Lexington, MA: Lexington Books, 1984.
Scalapino, Robert A., and Hongkoo Lee, eds. *Korea-U.S. Relations: The politics of Trade and Security.* Berkeley, CA: Institute of Asian Studies, 1989.

Algeciras Convention

SIGNED: April 7, 1906, Algeciras, Spain
IN FORCE: From signing
SIGNATORIES: Germany, Austria-Hungary, Belgium, Spain, France, Great Britain, Italy, Morocco, Netherlands, Portugal, Russia, Sweden, United States
OVERVIEW: With the aim of dissolving the Anglo-French Entente of 1904, Germany challenged the impending partition of Morocco by France and Spain. The Algeciras Convention was the product of a conference of European and American diplomats called to settle the challenge. United States participation in this treaty is a measure of the degree to which the nation was now regarded as a world power.

DISCUSSION:

By the start of the twentieth century, North Africa was the focus of intense European power politics. The French had unsuccessfully attempted to gain control in the Egyptian Sudan in 1898 and now sought to strengthen their hold on Saharan Africa. Through agreements with Spain, Italy, and England, France closed in on the Sultanate of Morocco and proposed to establish a protectorate there. The German Kaiser Wilhelm II moved to preempt this by paying a personal and ostentatious visit to the sultan of Morocco in 1905. The kaiser gambled that this demonstration would move England to back down from its recently concluded Entente Cordiale with France. Wilhelm's stratagem backfired, drawing traditional rivals England and France closer together.

Caught in the middle, the sultan of Morocco requested an international conference at Algeciras, Spain, during January 16-April 7, 1906, to resolve peacefully what was developing into an explosive crisis. The Algeciras Convention includes:

- Affirmation of the independence of Morocco—which pleased Germany
- Award to France of control over much of this "independent" country, including regulation of the Moroccan police and finances; this, of course, was contrary to the German interest

Pursuant to what amounted to a French protectorate of Morocco, the Algeciras Convention provides detailed "chapters" on such topics as the establishment of a paramilitary police force; the creation of a substantially French-controlled state bank; reform of tax laws, customs, antismuggling controls, and public works and services administration.

For its part, the United States added an addendum to the convention, clarifying and limiting its role in the agreement:

Resolved . . . That the Senate, as a part of this act of ratification, understands that the participation of the United States in the Algeciras conference and in the formation and adoption of the general act and protocol which resulted therefrom, was with the sole purpose of preserving and increasing its commerce in Morocco, the protection as to life, liberty, and property of its citizens residing or traveling therein, and of aiding by its friendly offices and efforts, in removing friction and controversy which seemed to menace the peace between powers signatory with the United States to the treaty of 1880, all of which are on terms of amity with this Government; and without purpose to depart from the traditional American foreign policy which forbids participation by the United States in the settlement of political questions which are entirely European in their scope.

The addendum is an incisive gloss on just how ambivalent American legislators were concerning the nation's role in world politics. During this pre–World War I period, strong imperialist and isolationist impulses coexisted uneasily in American politics and foreign policy.

Kaiser Wilhelm II, displeased with the convention, intervened in the region again, in 1911, sending a gunboat to Agadir after French forces punitively occupied the Moroccan capital of Fez. The kaiser backed down during this crisis, however, and recognized French rights in Morocco. In 1912, most of the area became a formal French protectorate.

REFERENCES:

Cohen, Mark I. *Morocco: Old Land, New Nation.* New York: Praeger, 1966.

Israel, Fred L. *Major Peace Treaties of Modern History, 1648-1967,* vol. 2. New York: Chelsea House and McGraw-Hill, 1967.

Rolo, P. J. V. *Entente Cordiale: The Origins and Negotiation of the Anglo-French Agreements of 8 April 1904.* London: Macmillan, 1969.

Root-Takahira Agreement

SIGNED: November 30, 1908, at Washington, D.C.

SIGNATORIES: Japan vs. United States

IN FORCE: From signing

OVERVIEW: An agreement whereby the signatories mutually affirm their wish to maintain the status quo in the Pacific and to defend the Open Door Policy with regard to China.

DISCUSSION:

During the late nineteenth century, imperial China, rife with corruption and torn by internal strife, was in steep decline as a sovereign nation. The European powers and Japan, followed by the United States, rushed in to fill the power vacuum that had been created in China, carving the country up into so many so-called "spheres of influence," regions in which each foreign power held economic sway. A British customs official stationed in China, Alfred E, Hippisley, proposed that the foreign powers put an end to this divisive economic policy, which was likely, sooner or later, to provoke war. He proposed that the nations adopt an Open Door Policy toward China, in which all nations would enjoy equal trading and development rights in the country. United States Secretary of State John Hay enthusiastically advocated the Open Door idea and, in 1899, communicated it in a Circular Letter sent to France, Germany, Great Britain, Italy, Russia, and Japan. Of these nations, only Japan openly challenged the policy. The others gave lip service to it, though, in fact, none of the nations strictly adhered to it in practice.

In the case of Japanese policy toward China, the United States made several concessions, the most important of which is embodied in the Root-Takahira Agreement. Pursuant to President Theodore Roosevelt's foreign-policy cornerstone of maintaining good relations with Japan, Secretary of State Elihu Root met with Japan's ambassador to the United States, Takahira Kogoro, and formulated an agreement whereby both governments pledged to uphold the status quo in Asia (effectively, this meant that Japan would forsake imperialist designs in the region), to uphold and defend the Open Door Policy, and to respect the integrity, independence, and sovereignty of China. Furthermore, Japan and the United States agreed to develop their commerce in East Asia and to respect each other's territorial possessions in that region.

It is important to note that while maintaining the "status quo" in Asia primarily meant that Japan would refrain from wars of conquest and other acquisitive moves against Asian nations and territories, it also meant that the United States agreed to acknowledge Japan's right to annex Korea and that it enjoyed a special administrative and economic position in the vast Chinese province of Manchuria. Although the Root-Takahira Agreement must be counted a United States diplomatic triumph inasmuch as it averted open conflict with Japan and did, for a time, discourage Japanese imperialist aggression, it also allowed Japan a key foothold in Korea and China, which would give it an economic and military advantage at the outbreak of World War II.

REFERENCES:

Carnegie Endowment for International Peace, Division of Intercourse and Education. *The Imperial Japanese Mission, 1917.* Washington, D.C.: Press of B. S. Adams, 1918.

Mamot, Patricio R. *Asian Americans: The Filipino, Chinese, and Japanese Immigration to the United States.* Bloomington, IN: Philippine Heritage Publications, 1984.

McClatchy, Valentine Stuart, ed. *Four Anti-Japanese Pamphlets.* New York: Arno, 1978.

Lansing-Ishii Agreement

SIGNED: November 2, 1917, at Washington, D.C.

SIGNATORIES: Japan vs. United States

IN FORCE: From signing

OVERVIEW: An agreement concluded by U.S. Secretary of State Robert Lansing and Japanese Imperial Commissioner Kikujiro Ishii, by which the United States recognized Japan's special interests in China in return for Japan's reaffirmation of the Open Door policy.

DISCUSSION:

For background on the Open Door Policy with regard to China and Japan's special interests in China, see **Root-Takahira Agreement.**

The **Lansing-Ishii Agreement** was intended to ease growing tensions between the United States and Japan over Japan's aggressive imperialism in Asia and, in particular, its assertion of economic dominion over certain parts of China. The agreement is in the form of a brief exchange of diplomatic notes, as follows:

Note from the Secretary of State to the Japanese Ambassador

DEPARTMENT OF STATE, Washington, NOV. 2, 1917.

Excellency:

I have the honor to communicate herein my understanding of the agreement reached by us in our recent conversations touching the questions of mutual interest to our governments relating to the republic of China.

In order to silence mischievous reports that have from time to time been circulated it is believed by us that a public announcement once more of the desires and intentions shared by our two governments with regard to China is advisable.

The governments of the United States and Japan recognize that territorial propinquity creates special relations between countries, and, consequently, the government of the United. States recognizes that Japan has special interests in China, particularly in the part to which her possessions are contiguous.

The territorial sovereignty of China, nevertheless, remains unimpaired, and the government of the United States has every confidence in the repeated assurances of the Imperial Japanese government that while geographical position gives Japan such special interests they have no desire to discriminate against the trade of other nations or to disregard the commercial rights heretofore granted by China in treaties with other powers.

The governments of the United States and Japan deny that they have any purpose to infringe in any way the independence or territorial integrity of China, and they declare, furthermore, that they always adhere to the principle of the so-called "open door" or equal opportunity for commerce and industry in China.

Moreover, they mutually declare that they are opposed to the acquisition by any government of any special rights or privileges that would affect the independence or territorial integrity of China or that would deny to the subjects or citizens of any country the full enjoyment of equal opportunity in the commerce and industry of China.

I shall be glad to have Your Excellency confirm this understanding of the agreement reached by us.

Accept, Excellency, the renewed assurance of my highest consideration.

(Signed) ROBERT LANSING.

The Japanese reply follows:

Sir:

I have the honor to acknowledge the receipt of your note today, communicating to me your understanding of the agreement reached by us in our recent conversations touching the questions of mutual interests to our governments relating to the republic of China.

I am happy to be able to confirm to you, under authorization of my government, the understanding in question set forth in the following terms: [Here the special Ambassador repeats the language of the agreement as given in Secretary Lansing's note].

(Signed) K. ISHII, Ambassador Extraordinary and Plenipotentiary of Japan on Special Mission.

REFERENCE:

Carnegie Endowment for International Peace, Division of Intercourse and Education. *The Imperial Japanese Mission, 1917.* Washington, D.C.: Press of B. S. Adams, 1918.

Four Power Treaty

SIGNED: December 13, 1921, at Washington, D.C.

IN FORCE: From August 23, 1923

SIGNATORIES: British Empire, France, Japan, United States,

OVERVIEW: One of three treaties resulting from the Washington Conference of November 1921-February 1922, the Four Power Treaty was intended to define and maintain the post-World War I balance of power in the Pacific. (*See also* **Nine Power Treaty Concerning China.**)

DISCUSSION:

Article I of the treaty expresses the essence of the document:

The High Contracting Parties agree as between themselves to respect their rights in relation to their insular possessions and insular dominions in the region of the Pacific Ocean.

If there should develop between any of the High Contracting Parties a controversy arising out of any Pacific question and involving their said rights which is not satisfactorily settled by diplomacy and is likely to affect the harmonious accord now happily subsisting between them, they shall invite the other High Contracting Parties to a joint conference to which the whole subject will be referred for consideration and adjustment.

The signatories took pains to avoid entanglement in the kind of interlocking alliance that had pulled so many nations into World War I. Article II specified that the signatories would "arrive at an understanding as to the most efficient measures to be taken, jointly or separately, to meet the exigencies of the particular situation." The phrase "jointly or separately" allowed a high degree of flexibility, and, in subsequently ratifying the treaty, the United States underscored this reservation, adding in Article IV the proviso that "The United States understands that . . . there is no commitment to armed force, no alliance, no obligation to join in any defense."

American negotiators crafted reserved approaches to two more issues. Reservation is expressed in the very preamble to the treaty: "With a view to the preservation of the general peace and the maintenance of their rights in relation to their insular possessions and insular dominions in the region of the Pacific Ocean, [the signatories] have determined to conclude a Treaty . . . ." The phrases "insular possessions" and "insular dominions" skirted recognition of Japan's expansionist claims in China and Siberia. A "Supplementary Agreement" subjoined to the treaty specifically defined "insular possessions and insular dominions" to "include only Karafuto (or the southern portion of the island of Sakhalin), Formosa and the Pescadores, and the islands under the mandate of Japan . . . ."

United States negotiators were also careful to avoid making the treaty an implicit U.S. endorsement of the authority of the League of Nations. The League had assigned to the European powers various "mandates" with regard to the postwar status of what had been prewar colonial possessions of the Central Powers. A United States "Declaration Accompanying the Treaty" stipulated "that the making of the Treaty shall not be deemed to be an assent on the part of the United States of America to the mandates and shall not preclude agreements between the United States of America and the Mandatory Powers respectively in relation to the mandated islands."

While treaty was motivated by a rational desire to circumvent potential causes of war, the document contained so many reservations that it was, ultimately, binding only in spirit. As such, it is typical of the temporizing tenure of many of the multilateral agreements of the early interwar years.

REFERENCES:

Grenville, J. A. S., *The Major International Treaties 1914-1973: A History Guide with Texts.* New York: Stein and Day, 1974.

Lynch, Cecelia. *Beyond Appeasement: Interpreting Interwar Peace Movements in World Politics.* Ithaca, NY: Cornell University Press, 1999.

Stirk, Peter M. R. *European Unity in Context: The Interwar Period.* London: Pinter Publishing, Ltd., 1989.

Nine Power Treaty Concerning China

SIGNED: February 6, 1922, at Washington, D.C.

IN FORCE: From August 5, 1925

SIGNATORIES: Belgium, British Empire, China, France, Italy, Japan, Netherlands, Portugal, United States

OVERVIEW: The Nine Power Treaty was intended to defend territorial integrity and independence of China against post-World War I Japanese expansionism.

DISCUSSION:

After World War I, the victorious Allied and Associated nations assigned to Japan mandates over what had been Germany's island colonies in the Pacific north of the equator. Japan was also awarded Germany's rights in the province of Shantung. Left unresolved by immediate postwar conferences were the relationships among the Allied and Associated powers relative to China and the Pacific. The Washington Conference was convened in 1921-1922 to define these relationships. The two most important agreements it produced were the **Four Power Treaty** and the Nine Power Treaty.

In the Nine Power Treaty, Japan made certain concessions with regard to its mandate in Shantung, and all of the signatories pledged to respect Chinese sovereignty and integrity and the "Open Door Policy" as enunciated by U.S. Secretary of State John M. Hay in 1899 and 1900 (*see* **Boxer Protocol**). However, the treaty did not call for the withdrawal of Japanese troops from Manchuria, nor did it recognize Chinese sovereignty over Manchuria. Japan and the European signatories also retained their special trading and political rights in China, although they pledged not to attempt to extend those rights. In sum, the Nine Power Treaty acknowledged the rights and integrity of China without offending Japan and without significantly sacrificing the exploitive trade advantages the European powers had enjoyed in China since the conclusion of the Opium Wars in the mid nineteenth century.

The major principles relating to Chinese sovereignty are embodied in Article I:

The Contracting Powers, other than China, agree:

1. To respect the sovereignty, the independence, and the territorial and administrative integrity of China;

2. To provide the fullest and most unembarrassed opportunity to China to develop and maintain for herself an effective and stable government;

3. To use their influence for the purpose of effectually establishing and maintaining the principle of equal opportunity for the commerce and industry of all nations throughout the territory of China;

4. To refrain from taking advantage of conditions in China in order to seek special rights or privileges which would abridge the rights of subjects or citizens of friendly States, and from countenancing action inimical to the security of such States.

Most of the rest of the treaty is an agreement among all of the nations to maintain equal and unimpeded access to Chinese trade.

By allowing Japanese troops to continue to occupy Manchuria, and by declining to recognize Chinese sovereignty over Manchuria, the Nine Power Treaty failed in the purpose stated in the treaty's introductory paragraph: to "stabilize conditions in the Far East." In 1931, Japanese military officers orchestrated the "Mukden Incident," the bombing of the Japanese-controlled South Manchurian Railroad. Japan exploited this incident as a pretext for invading Manchuria and setting up the puppet state of Manchukuo. In July 1937, full-scale war between Japan and China broke out—a conflict that was subsumed into World War II.

REFERENCES:

Goldstein, Erik, and John Maurer, eds. *The Washington Conference, 1921-22: Naval Rivalry, East Asian Stability and the Road to Pearl Harbor.* Ilford, UK: Frank Cass, 1994.

Grenville, J. A. S., *The Major International Treaties 1914-1973: A History Guide with Texts.* New York: Stein and Day, 1974.

Willoughby, Westel Woodbury. *China at the Conference: A Report.* Westport, CT: Greenwood Press, 1974.

Yoshihas, Takehiko. *Conspiracy at Mukden.* Westport, CT: Greenwood Publishing Group, 1980.

Young, Louise. *Japan's Total Empire: Manchuria and the Culture of Wartime Imperialism.* Berkeley: University of California Press, 1998.

Treaty of Friendship, Commerce, and Consular Rights with Estonia

SIGNED: December 23, 1925, at Washington

SIGNATORIES: Estonia vs. United States

IN FORCE: From May 22, 1926 (modified, July 10 and 16, 1951)

OVERVIEW: A typical bilateral treaty establishing friendly and commercial relations between the United States and another nation.

DISCUSSION:

Estonia obtained independence from Russia in 1918, in the aftermath of World War I. In the years following the war, the United States concluded treaties of friendship, commerce, and consular rights with numerous newly independent nations, including Estonia.

The most basic provisions of the relationship established by the treaty are laid down in Article 1:

The nationals of each of the High Contracting Parties shall be permitted to enter, travel and reside in the territories of the other; to exercise liberty of conscience and freedom of worship; to engage in scientific, religious, philanthropic, manufacturing and commercial work of every kind without interference; to carry on every form of commercial activity which is not forbidden by the local law; to engage in every trade, vocation and profession not reserved exclusively to nationals of the country; to own, erect or lease and occupy appropriate buildings and to lease lands for residential, scientific, religious, philanthropic, manufacturing, commercial and mortuary purposes; to employ agents of their choice, and generally to do anything incidental to or necessary for the enjoyment of any of the foregoing priv-

ileges upon the same terms as nationals of the state of residence or as nationals of the nation hereafter to be most favored by it, submitting themselves to all local laws and regulations duly established. The nationals of either High Contracting Party within the territories of the other shall not be subjected to the payment of any internal charges or taxes other or higher than those that are exacted of and paid by its nationals. The nationals of each High Contracting Party shall enjoy freedom of access to the courts of justice of the other on conforming to the local laws, as well for the prosecution as for the defense of their rights, and in all degrees of jurisdiction established by law. The nationals of each High Contracting Party shall receive within the territories of the other, upon submitting to conditions imposed upon its nationals, the most constant protection and security for their persons and property, and shall enjoy in this respect that degree of protection that is required by international law. Their property shall not be taken without due process of law and without payment of just compensation. Nothing contained in this Treaty shall be construed to affect existing statutes of either of the High Contracting Parties in relation to the immigration of aliens or the right of either of the High Contracting Parties to enact such statutes.

In addition, all forms of private property, including real property, personal property, monetary property, and investment interests, owned by nationals of the signatory nations, are to be respected and protected by both signatories. Religious freedom and freedom of worship are similarly guaranteed.

Commercial relations are established on a broad footing:

Between the territories of the High Contracting Parties there shall be freedom of commerce and navigation. The nationals of each of the High Contracting Parties equally with those of the most favored nation, shall have liberty freely to come with their vessels and cargoes to all places, ports and waters of every kind within the territorial limits of the other which are or may be open to foreign commerce and navigation. Nothing in this treaty shall be construed to restrict the right of either High Contracting Party to impose, on such terms as it may see fit, prohibitions or restrictions of a sanitary character designed to protect human, animal, or plant life, or regulations for the enforcement of police or revenue laws. Each of the High Contracting Parties binds itself unconditionally to impose no higher or other duties or conditions and no prohibition on the importation of any article, the growth, produce or manufacture, of the territories of the other than are or shall be imposed on the importation of any like article, the growth, produce or manufacture of any other foreign country. Each of the High Contracting Parties also binds itself unconditionally to impose no higher or other charges or other restrictions or prohibitions on goods exported to the territories of the other High Contracting Party than are imposed on goods exported to any other foreign country. Any advantage of whatsoever kind which either High Contracting Party may extend to any article, the growth, produce, or manufacture of any other foreign country shall simultaneously and unconditionally, without request and without compensation, be extended to the like article the growth, produce or manufacture of the other High Contracting Party. All articles which are or may be legally imported from foreign countries into ports of the United States or are or may be legally exported therefrom in vessels of the United States may likewise be imported into those ports or exported therefrom in Estonian vessels, without being liable to any other or higher duties or charges whatsoever than if such articles were imported or exported in vessels of the United States; and, reciprocally, all articles which are or may be legally imported from foreign countries into the ports of Estonia or are or may be legally exported therefrom in Estonian vessels may likewise be imported into these ports or exported therefrom in vessels of the United States without being liable to any other or higher duties or charges whatsoever than if such articles were imported or exported in Estonian vessels. With respect to the amount and collection of duties on imports and exports of every kind, each of the two High Contracting Parties binds itself to give to the nationals, vessels and goods of the other the advantage of every favor, privilege or immunity which it shall have accorded to the nationals, vessels and goods of a third State, whether such favored State shall have been accorded such treatment gratuitously or in return for reciprocal compensatory treatment. Every such favor, privilege or immunity which shall hereafter be granted the nationals, vessels or goods of a third State shall simultaneously and unconditionally, without request and without compensation, be extended to the other High Contracting Party, for the benefit of itself, its nationals and vessels....

Subsequent articles bar special or discriminatory taxes on or handling of the merchandise of the signatories. This is the equivalent of establishing most-favored-nation status; the signatories undertake to grant one another the best trade terms granted to any other trading-partner nation.

Having established full commercial relations on a most-favored-nation basis, the treaty concludes by establishing full consular relations with all diplomatic privileges and immunities.

REFERENCES:
None

U.S.-Cuba Treaty of Relations

SIGNED: May 29, 1934, at Washington
IN FORCE: From March 23, 1935
SIGNATORIES: Cuba vs. United States
OVERVIEW:By this treaty the United States acknowledged full Cuban independence while retaining the perpetual right to lease land at Guantanamo Bay for the purpose of maintaining a naval base.

DISCUSSION:
The **Treaty of Paris (1898)** ending the Spanish-American War won Cuba's independence from Spain, but the United States assumed the role as effective protector of the island nation. The Cuban constitution of 1901 acknowledged substantial U.S. authority in Cuban affairs, pursuant to the Platt Amendment, and the **Treaty with Cuba (1903)** formalized Cuba's status as a quasi-protectorate of the United States. The significance of the key provisions in the Cuban constitution, the Platt Amendment, and the 1903 treaty may be summed up in this way:
- Cuba's treaty-making capacity was limited.
- Cuba's authority to contract public debt was limited.
- The United States secured Cuban land for naval bases and naval coaling stations.

- The United States reserved the authority to intervene in Cuban affairs to preserve Cuba's independence and maintain order.

The 1934 treaty formally abrogated the 1903 treaty and repealed the Platt Amendment, thereby granting Cuba full independence from the United States. The most important reservation of the 1934 treaty, however, relates to the U.S. right to retain the naval base at Guantanamo:

Until the two contracting parties agree to the modification or abrogation of the stipulations of the agreement in regard to the lease to the United States of America of lands in Cuba for coaling and naval stations signed by the President of the Republic of Cuba on February 16, 1903, and by the President of the United States of America on the 23d day of the same month and year, the stipulations of that agreement with regard to the naval station of Guantanamo shall continue in effect. The supplementary agreement in regard to naval and coaling stations signed between the two Governments on July 2, 1903, also shall continue in effect in the same form and on the same conditions with respect to the naval station at Guantanamo. So long as the United States of America shall not abandon the said naval station of Guantanamo or the two Governments shall not agree to a modification of its present limits, the station shall continue to have the territorial area that it now has, with the limits that it has on the date of the signature of the present Treaty.

Following the breakdown of U.S.-Cuban relations after the Communist revolution led by Fidel Castro in 1959, the Cuban government has repeatedly attempted to terminate the Guantanamo lease. The United States' position has been (in the words of an official State Department statement on the matter) that its "presence in Guantanamo rests upon international agreements containing no termination date and making no provision for unilateral termination." Furthermore, all of the relevant treaties give the United States "complete jurisdiction and control" of the defined base area.

REFERENCES:
Benjamin, Jules R. *The United States and the Origins of the Cuban Revolution: An Empire of Liberty in an Age of National Liberation.* Princeton, NJ: Princeton University Press, 1992.
Langley, Lester D. *The Cuban Policy of the United States: A Brief History* New York: Wiley, 1968.
Malloy, William M., ed., *Treaties, Conventions, International Acts, Protocols and Agreements between the United States of America and other Powers 1776-1909.* Washington, D.C., 1902.

Agreement (with Republic of Congo) Relating to the Continued Application of Certain Treaties

OFFICIAL TITLE: Exchange of Notes Constituting an Agreement Relating to the Continued Application to the Republic of the Congo of Certain Treaties and Agreements Concluded between the United States of America and France Prior to the Independence of the Republic of the Congo

SIGNED: May 12 and August 5, 1961, at Brazzaville

SIGNATORIES: Republic of Congo vs. United States

IN FORCE: From August 5, 1961

OVERVIEW: An exchange of notes affirming the continuation of U.S.-Congo treaties made before the creation of a Republic of the Congo independent from France.

DISCUSSION:

International law generally holds that treaties concluded by or on behalf of a colony continue in force after the colony achieves independence unless the newly created government explicitly denounces a treaty. This agreement affirms that principle. The agreement is in the form of an exchange of notes, beginning with a United States inquiry and concluding with the Congolese reply:

The Ambassador of the United States of America presents his compliments to His Excellency the Minister of Foreign Affairs of the Republic of Congo and has the honor to request the views of the Ministry on the present applicability of international agreements concluded by the Government of France on behalf of the Congo territory prior to the independence of the Republic of Congo.

The minister replied:

In accordance with the practices of international law and because of the circumstances under which the Republic of Congo attained international sovereignty, the latter considers itself to be a party to the treaties and agreements signed prior to its independence ... provided that such treaties or agreements have not been expressly denounced by it or tacitly abrogated by a text replacing them.

REFERENCE:

O'Ballance, Edgar. *The Congo-Zaire Experience, 1960-98.* New York: St. Martin's, 2000.

Vienna Convention on Diplomatic Relations

SIGNED: April 18, 1961

SIGNATORIES: Afghanistan, Albania, Algeria, Andorra, Angola, Argentina, Armenia, Australia, Austria, Azerbaijan, Bahamas, Bahrain, Bangladesh, Barbados, Belarus, Belgium, Benin, Bhutan, Bolivia, Bosnia-Herzegovina, Botswana, Brazil, Bulgaria, Burkina Faso, Burma, Burundi, Cambodia, Cameroon, Canada, Cape Verde, Central African Republic, Chad, Chile, China, Colombia, Congo, Costa Rica, Côte d'Ivoire, Croatia, Cuba, Cyprus, Czech Republic, Czechoslovakia, Denmark, Djibouti, Dominica, Dominican Republic, Ecuador, Egypt, El Salvador, Equatorial Guinea, Estonia, Ethiopia, Fiji, Finland, Former Yugoslav Republic of Macedonia, France, Gabon, Georgia, German Democratic Republic, Germany (Federal Republic), Ghana, Greece, Grenada, Guatemala, Guinea,

Guinea-Bissau, Guyana, Haiti, Holy See, Honduras, Hungary, Iceland, India, Indonesia, Iran, Iraq, Ireland, Israel, Italy, Jamaica, Japan, Jordan, Kazakstan, Kenya, Kiribati, Korea (Democratic People's Republic), Korea (Republic), Kuwait, Kyrgyz Republic, Laos, Latvia, Lebanon, Lesotho, Liberia, Libya, Liechtenstein, Lithuania, Luxembourg, Madagascar, Malawi, Malaysia, Mali, Malta, Marshall Islands, Mauritania, Mauritius, Mexico, Micronesia, Moldova, Mongolia, Morocco, Mozambique, Namibia, Nauru, Nepal, Netherlands, New Zealand, Nicaragua, Niger, Nigeria, Norway, Oman, Pakistan, Panama, Papua New Guinea, Paraguay, Peru, Philippines, Poland, Portugal, Qatar, Rumania, Russian Federation, Rwanda, St. Lucia, San Marino, Sao Tome and Principe, Saudi Arabia, Senegal, Seychelles, Sierra Leone, Slovak Republic, Slovenia, Somalia, South Africa, Spain, Sri Lanka, Sudan, Suriname, Swaziland, Sweden, Switzerland, Syrian Arab Republic, Tajikistan, Tanzania, Thailand, Togo, Tonga, Trinidad and Tobago, Tunisia, Turkey, Turkmenistan, Tuvalu, Uganda, Ukraine, Union of Soviet Socialist Republics, United Arab Emirates, United Kingdom, United States, Uruguay, Uzbekistan, Venezuela, Vietnam (Socialist Republic), Western Samoa, Yemen (Aden), Yemen (Sanaa), Yugoslavia, Zaire, Zambia

IN FORCE: From April 24, 1964

OVERVIEW: The convention sets out definitions relevant to diplomatic relations among nations.

DISCUSSION:

The convention defines key diplomatic issues relating to diplomatic personnel and the buildings of diplomatic missions. It defines the tasks of diplomatic missions, the procedures for establishing such missions, the rights and the duties of mission personnel, the right of the host country to declare any member of a mission persona non grata without stating any reason, the conditions of diplomatic immunity, and the guarantee of uncontrolled communications for official purposes.

REFERENCES:

Denza, Eileen. *Diplomatic Law: A Commentary on the Vienna Convention on Diplomatic Relations,* 2d ed. Oxford and New York: Oxford University Press, 1998.

United Nations Conference on Diplomatic Intercourse and Immunities. *Vienna Convention on Diplomatic Relations and Optional Protocol Concerning the Compulsory Settlement of Disputes.* London, H. M. Stationery Office, 1965.

Vienna Convention on Consular Relations and Optional Protocols

SIGNED: April 24, 1963, at Vienna

SIGNATORIES: Albania, Algeria, Andorra, Angola, Antigua and Barbuda, Argentina, Armenia, Australia, Austria, Azerbaijan, Bahamas, Bahrain, Bangladesh, Barbados, Belarus, Belgium, Benin, Bhutan, Bolivia, Bosnia-Herzegovina, Brazil, Bulgaria,

Burkina Faso, Cameroon, Canada, Cape Verde, Chile, China, Colombia, Costa Rica, Croatia, Cuba, Cyprus, Czech Republic, Czechoslovakia, Denmark, Djibouti, Dominica, Dominican Republic, Ecuador, Egypt, El Salvador, Equatorial Guinea, Estonia, Fiji, Finland, Former Yugoslav Republic of Macedonia, France, Gabon, Georgia, German Democratic Republic Germany (Federal Republic), Ghana, Greece, Grenada, Guatemala, Guinea, Guyana, Haiti, Holy See, Honduras, Hungary, Iceland, India, Indonesia, Iran, Iraq, Ireland, Italy, Jamaica, Japan, Jordan, Kazakstan, Kenya, Kiribati, Korea (Democratic People's Republic), Korea (Republic), Kuwait, Kyrgyz Republic, Laos, Latvia, Lebanon, Lesotho, Liberia, Liechtenstein, Lithuania, Luxembourg, Madagascar, Malawi, Malaysia, Maldives, Mali, Marshall Islands, Mauritius, Mexico, Micronesia, Moldova, Mongolia, Morocco, Mozambique, Namibia, Nepal, Netherlands, New Zealand, Nicaragua, Niger, Nigeria, Norway, Oman, Pakistan, Panama, Papua New Guinea, Paraguay, Peru, Philippines, Poland, Portugal, Romania, Russian Federation, Rwanda, St. Kitts and Nevis, St. Lucia, St. Vincent and the Grenadines, Sao Tome and Principe, Saudi Arabia, Senegal, Seychelles, Slovak Republic, Slovenia, Solomon Islands, Somalia, South Africa, Spain, Sudan, Suriname, Sweden, Switzerland, Syrian Arab Republic, Tajikistan, Tanzania, Togo, Tonga, Trinidad and Tobago, Tunisia, Turkey, Turkmenistan, Tuvalu, Ukraine, Union of Soviet Socialist Republics, United Arab Emirates, United Kingdom, United States, Uruguay, Uzbekistan, Vanuatu, Venezuela, Vietnam (Socialist Republic), Vietnam (Republic), Western Samoa, Yemen (Sanaa), Yugoslavia, Zaire; Signatories to the Optional Protocol to the Convention on Consular Relations Concerning the Compulsory Settlement of Disputes Antigua and Barbuda, Australia, Austria, Belgium, Bosnia-Herzegovina, Bulgaria, Burkina Faso, Denmark, Dominica, Dominican Republic, Estonia, Finland, France, Gabon, Germany (Federal Republic), Grenada, Hungary, Iceland, India, Iran, Italy, Japan, Kenya, Korea (Republic), Laos, Liechtenstein, Luxembourg, Madagascar, Malawi, Mauritius, Nepal, Netherlands, New Zealand, Nicaragua, Niger, Norway, Oman, Pakistan, Panama, Paraguay, Philippines, St. Kitts and Nevis, St. Lucia, St. Vincent and the Grenadines, Senegal, Seychelles, Solomon Islands, Suriname, Sweden, Switzerland, United Kingdom, United States, Vietnam (Republic)

IN FORCE: From March 19, 1967; for the United States, December 24, 1969

OVERVIEW: A product of the United Nations Conference on Diplomatic Intercourse and Immunities adopted the Vienna Convention on Diplomatic Relations, the convention lays down rules for consular relations.

DISCUSSION:

After defining the key terms relating to consular relations, the convention lays down three major principles governing consular relations:

1. The establishment of consular relations between States takes place by mutual consent.

2. The consent given to the establishment of diplomatic relations between to States implies, unless otherwise stated, consent to the establishment of consular relations.

3. The severance of diplomatic relations shall not ipso facto involve the severance of consular relations.

The convention also lays down provisions regarding the following:

- Establishment of a consular post
- Consular functions
- Exercise of consular functions on behalf of a third state
- Heads of consular posts
- The exequatur ("The head of a consular post is admitted to the exercise of his functions by an authorization from the receiving State termed an exequatur . . .")
- Performance of diplomatic acts by consular officers
- Consular staff
- Regulations regarding size of the consular staff
- Declaration of persona non grata
- "Protection of consular premises and archives and of the interests of the sending state in exceptional circumstances"
- Facilities, privileges and immunities relating to consular posts, career consular officers and other members of a consular post (including the concept of "diplomatic immunity")

REFERENCES:

Denza, Eileen. *Diplomatic Law: A Commentary on the Vienna Convention on Diplomatic Relations,* 2d ed. Oxford and New York: Oxford University Press, 1998.

United Nations Conference on Diplomatic Intercourse and Immunities. *Vienna Convention on Diplomatic Relations and Optional Protocol Concerning the Compulsory Settlement of Disputes.* London, H. M. Stationery Office, 1965.

Vienna Convention on the Law of Treaties

SIGNED: May 23, 1969, at Vienna

SIGNATORIES: Albania, Algeria, Andorra, Angola, Antigua and Barbuda, Argentina, Armenia, Australia, Austria, Azerbaijan, Bahamas, Bahrain, Bangladesh, Barbados, Belarus, Belgium, Benin, Bhutan, Bolivia, Bosnia-Herzegovina, Brazil, Bulgaria, Burkina Faso, Cameroon, Canada, Cape Verde, Chile, China, Colombia, Costa Rica, Croatia, Cuba, Cyprus, Czech Republic, Czechoslovakia, Denmark, Djibouti, Dominica, Dominican Republic, Ecuador, Egypt, El Salvador, Equatorial Guinea, Estonia, Fiji, Finland, Former Yugoslav Republic of Macedonia, France, Gabon, Georgia, German Democratic Republic Germany (Federal Republic), Ghana, Greece, Grenada,

Guatemala, Guinea, Guyana, Haiti, Holy See, Honduras, Hungary, Iceland, India, Indonesia, Iran, Iraq, Ireland, Italy, Jamaica, Japan, Jordan, Kazakstan, Kenya, Kiribati, Korea (Democratic People's Republic), Korea (Republic), Kuwait, Kyrgyz Republic, Laos, Latvia, Lebanon, Lesotho, Liberia, Liechtenstein, Lithuania, Luxembourg, Madagascar, Malawi, Malaysia, Maldives, Mali, Marshall Islands, Mauritius, Mexico, Micronesia, Moldova, Mongolia, Morocco, Mozambique, Namibia, Nepal, Netherlands, New Zealand, Nicaragua, Niger, Nigeria, Norway, Oman, Pakistan, Panama, Papua New Guinea, Paraguay, Peru, Philippines, Poland, Portugal, Romania, Russian Federation, Rwanda, St. Kitts and Nevis, St. Lucia, St. Vincent and the Grenadines, Sao Tome and Principe, Saudi Arabia, Senegal, Seychelles, Slovak Republic, Slovenia, Solomon Islands, Somalia, South Africa, Spain, Sudan, Suriname, Sweden, Switzerland, Syrian Arab Republic, Tajikistan, Tanzania, Togo, Tonga, Trinidad and Tobago, Tunisia, Turkey, Turkmenistan, Tuvalu, Ukraine, Union of Soviet Socialist Republics, United Arab Emirates, United Kingdom, United States, Uruguay, Uzbekistan, Vanuatu, Venezuela, Vietnam (Socialist Republic), Vietnam (Republic), Western Samoa, Yemen (Sanaa), Yugoslavia, Zaire

IN FORCE: From January 27, 1980

OVERVIEW: A non-retroactive convention laying down the law of treaties.

DISCUSSION:

The "law of treaties" is a set of conventions governing the following:

- Conclusion and entry into force of treaties
- The concept and function of reservations
- Entry into force and provisional application of treaties
- Observance, application and interpretation of treaties
- Treaties and third states
- Amendment and modification
- Invalidity, termination, and suspension of the operation of treaties

The convention was drafted in the belief (as stated in the preamble) "that the codification and progressive development of the law of treaties achieved in the present Convention will promote the purposes of the United Nations set forth in the Charter, namely, the maintenance of international peace and security, the development of friendly relations and the achievement of co-operation among nations." The convention is essentially an effort to standardize and render uniform treaty form and treaty making. The convention does not apply retroactively to existing treaties, nor is it intended necessarily to render invalid any international agreements, past, present, or future (in relation to the convention) that do not adhere to the provisions of the convention.

REFERENCE:
Denza, Eileen. *Diplomatic Law: A Commentary on the Vienna Convention on Diplomatic Relations,* 2d ed. Oxford and New York: Oxford University Press, 1998.

United States-People's Republic of China Joint Communiqué

SIGNED: February 27, 1972, at Shanghai
SIGNATORIES: People's Republic of China vs. United States
IN FORCE: From signing
OVERVIEW: The first step in normalizing relations between the United States and Communist China.

DISCUSSION:

This joint communiqué was a product of President Richard M. Nixon's ground-breaking visit to China and series of meetings with Chinese officials, including Mao Tse-tung. The communiqué specified the following:

- That "neither side should seek hegemony in the Asia-Pacific region"
- That "neither [country] is prepared to negotiate on behalf of any third party or to enter into agreements or understanding with the other directed at other states"

The communiqué was thus an agreement that neither side would use the Asia-Pacific region as an arena in which to fight the kind of economic and ideological battles that produced the Korean War and the Vietnam War.

REFERENCES:
Mann, James. *About Face: A History of America's Curious Relationship with China from Nixon to Clinton.* New York: Knopf, 1999.
Tyler, Patrick. *A Great Wall: Six Presidents and China.* Washington, D.C.: Public Affairs, 1999.

Convention on the Prevention and Punishment of Crimes Against Internationally Protected Persons, Including Diplomatic Agents

SIGNED: December 14, 1973, at New York
SIGNATORIES: Australia, Austria, Berlin (West), Bulgaria, Byelorussian Soviet Republic, Canada, Chile, Costa Rica, Cyprus, Czechoslovakia, Denmark, Dominican Republic, Ecuador, Faeroe Islands, Federal Republic of Germany, Finland, France, German Democratic Republic, Ghana, Greenland, Guatemala, Hungary, Iceland, Italy, Liberia, Malawi, Mongolia, Nicaragua, Norway, Pakistan, Paraguay, Philippines, Poland, Romania, Rwanda, Sweden, Tunisia, Ukrainian Soviet Socialist Republic, Union of Soviet Socialist Republics, United Kingdom, United States, Yugoslavia, Zaire

IN FORCE: From February 20, 1977

OVERVIEW: A multilateral convention to "adopt appropriate and effective measures for the prevention and punishment of . . . crimes" against internationally protected persons.

DISCUSSION:

"Internationally protected persons" include heads of state, representatives or officials of states, and agents of international or intergovernmental organizations. The crimes addressed by the convention include murder, kidnapping, or other attacks against the person or liberty of the person; attack against the official premises or private accommodation of the protected person; threat of attack; attempted attack; and participation in an attack. Each signatory state undertakes to "take such measures as may be necessary to establish its jurisdiction over . . . crimes against protected persons" and to apprehend, prosecute, and punish offenders.

REFERENCE:

Denza, Eileen. *Diplomatic Law: A Commentary on the Vienna Convention on Diplomatic Relations,* 2d ed. Oxford and New York: Oxford University Press, 1998.

U.S.-Cuba Agreement to Establish Interest Sections

OFFICIAL TITLE: Agreement Relating to the Establishment of Interest Sections of the United States and Cuba in the Embassy of Switzerland in Havana and the Embassy of Czechoslovakia in Washington, Respectively.

SIGNED: May 30, 1977 at New York

SIGNATORIES: Cuba vs. United States

IN FORCE: From signing

OVERVIEW: An agreement reestablishing limited diplomatic relations between the United States and Cuba.

DISCUSSION:

When Fidel Castro, an idealistic young lawyer turned guerrilla, led the revolution that toppled the corrupt regime of Cuba's president Fulgencio Batista in 1959, the United States at first greeted the prospect of reform on the island nation, a mere ninety miles from Miami. Within the first six months of the new regime, however, Castro increasingly aligned his government with the Soviet Union, and he took frequent opportunity to vent outrage at the United States, for having maintained and exploited Cuba as a virtual puppet since the Spanish-American War of 1898. In 1960, President Dwight D. Eisenhower responded to increasing hostility from Cuba by severing diplomatic relations—and by approving plans for an invasion, which was abortively and disastrously executed in April 1961, during the early part of John F. Kennedy's presidency.

From this point on, relations between Cuba and the United States entered a deep freeze, punctuated by the 1965 **Agreement**

(with Cuba) Concerning the Movement of Cuban Refugees to the United States. It was not until 1977 that the two nations reestablished diplomatic relations to a very limited degree by the present agreement.

Although neither nation reopened an embassy in the capital of the other nation, both agreed to establish "interest sections" in third-party embassies in order to facilitate communication and rudimentary diplomacy. The United States established its interest section within the Swiss embassy in Havana, and Cuba established its within the Czech embassy in Washington.

REFERENCE:

Schwab, Peter. *Cuba: Confronting the U.S. Embargo.* New York: St. Martin's, 1999.

Vienna Convention on Succession of States in Respect of Treaties

SIGNED: August 23, 1978, at Vienna

SIGNATORIES: Angola, Bosnia and Herzegovina, Brazil, Chile, Côte d'Ivoire, Croatia, Czech Republic, Democratic Republic of the Congo, Dominica, Egypt, Estonia, Ethiopia, Former Yugoslav Republic of Macedonia Holy See, Iraq, Madagascar, Morocco, Niger, Pakistan, Paraguay, Peru, Poland, Saint Vincent and the Grenadines, Senegal, Seychelles, Slovakia, Slovenia, Sudan, Tunisia, Ukraine, Uruguay, Yugoslavia

IN FORCE: From November 6, 1996

OVERVIEW: A convention to render uniform (especially "considering the profound transformation of the international community brought about by the decolonization process") the succession of states in respect of treaties and treaty obligations.

DISCUSSION:

This convention addresses the sometimes thorny issue of the status of the status of treaty obligations in cases where one state succeeds another, as in instances of decolonization or other succession.

The convention applies to treaties between states, not between states and international organizations. By Article 6, it is understood that the convention "applies only to the effects of a succession of States occurring in conformity with international law and, in particular, the principles of international law embodied in the Charter of the United Nations."

The detailed provisions of the convention are complex, but the general principles are laid down as follows:

• Successor states are not automatically bound by treaty obligations entered into by predecessor states.

• Other parties to a treaty are not automatically bound by obligations entered into with the predecessor state.

• "A successor State may, at the time of expressing its consent to be bound by the present convention or at any time thereafter, make a declaration that it will apply the provisions of the Convention in respect of its own succession of States which has occurred before the entry into force of the Convention in relation to any other contracting State or State Party to the Convention which makes a declaration accepting the declaration of the successor State. Upon the entry into force of the Convention as between the States making the declarations or upon the making of the declaration of acceptance, whichever occurs later, the provisions of the Convention shall apply to the effects of the succession of States as from the date of that succession of States."

- "A successor State may at the time of signing or of expressing its consent to be bound by the present Convention make a declaration that it will apply the provisions of the Convention provisionally in respect of its own succession of States which has occurred before the entry into force of the Convention in relation to any other signatory or contracting State which makes a declaration accepting the declaration of the successor State; upon the making of the declaration of acceptance, those provisions shall apply provisionally to the effects of the succession of States as between those two States as from the date of that succession of States."

Article 8 addresses agreements for the devolution of treaty obligations or rights from a predecessor State to a successor State:

The obligations or rights of a predecessor State under treaties in force in respect of a territory at the date of a succession of States do not become the obligations or rights of the successor State towards other States parties to those treaties by reason only of the fact that the predecessor State and the successor State have concluded an agreement providing that such obligations or rights shall devolve upon the successor State.

Article 9 covers unilateral declaration by a successor State regarding treaties of the predecessor State:

Obligations or rights under treaties in force in respect of a territory at the date of a succession of States do not become the obligations or rights of the successor State or of other States parties to those treaties by reason only of the fact that the successor State has made a unilateral declaration providing for the continuance in force of the treaties in respect of its territory.

Article 11 lays down the important principles that "boundary regimes" are not affected by a succession of states. That is, succession does not affect "(a) a boundary established by a treaty; or (b) obligations and rights established by a treaty and relating to the regime of a boundary."

Article 16 lays down the principle that a "newly independent State is not bound to maintain in force, or to become a party to, any treaty by reason only of the fact that at the date of the succession of States the treaty was in force in respect of the territory to which the succession of States relates." Article 17 main-

tains that "a newly independent State may, by a notification of succession, establish its status as a party to any multilateral treaty which at the date of the succession of States was in force in respect of the territory to which the succession of States relates." However, this "does not apply if it appears from the treaty or is otherwise established that the application of the treaty in respect of the newly independent State would be incompatible with the object and purpose of the treaty or would radically change the conditions for its operation."

The convention was a long time in coming into force. As of December 1999, the United States, like many major nations, had not signed.

REFERENCE:

Denza, Eileen. *Diplomatic Law: A Commentary on the Vienna Convention on Diplomatic Relations,* 2d ed. Oxford and New York: Oxford University Press, 1998.

United States-People's Republic of China Joint Communiqué

SIGNED: December 15-16, 1978, at Shanghai
SIGNATORIES: United Stats vs. People's Republic of China
IN FORCE: January 1, 1979
OVERVIEW: Established diplomatic relations between the nations.

DISCUSSION:

The communiqué reaffirmed the principles laid down in the **United States-People's Republic of China Joint Communiqué** of February 27, 1972 and announced the establishment of diplomatic relations between the two nations, effective from January 1, 1979. Less than a month after this, on January 31, 1979, additional agreements were signed to establish consular relations and to initiate programs of cultural exchange and cooperation in science and technology.

A series of agreements followed, relating to the settlement of United States claims against China and the release of Chinese assets frozen in the United States since the Korean War, establishing trade relations (including a grant of most-favored nation status), initiating the sale of certain military equipment to China, establishing a program of U.S. assistance and cooperation in hydroelectric operations and in industry and technology, including nuclear technology.

REFERENCES:

Mann, James. *About Face: A History of America's Curious Relationship with China from Nixon to Clinton.* New York: Knopf, 1999.
Tyler, Patrick. *A Great Wall: Six Presidents and China.* Washington,. D.C.: Public Affairs, 1999.

Vienna Convention on the Law of Treaties between States and International Organizations or between International Organizations

SIGNED: March 21, 1986, at Vienna

SIGNATORIES: Argentina, Australia, Austria, Belgium, Benin, Bosnia and Herzegovina, Brazil, Bulgaria, Burkina Faso, Côte d'Ivoire, Council of Europe, Croatia, Cyprus, Czech Republic, Democratic Republic of the Congo, Denmark, Egypt, Estonia, Food and Agriculture Organisation of the United Nations, Germany, Greece, Hungary, International Civil Aviation Organization, International Labour Organisation, International Maritime Organisation, International Telecommunications Union, Italy, Japan, Liechtenstein, Malawi, Mexico, Morocco, Netherlands, Senegal, Slovakia, Spain, Sudan, Sweden, Switzerland, Republic of Korea, Republic of Moldava, United Kingdom, United Nations, United Nations Educational, Scientific and Cultural Organisation, United States, Uruguay, World Health Organisation, World Meteorological Organisation, Yugoslavia, Zambia

IN FORCE: Not yet in force

OVERVIEW: Whereas the **Vienna Convention on the Law of Treaties** of 1969 primarily addressed international agreements among nations, the 1986 agreement addressed the specific issues of the law of treaties between states and international organizations or between international organizations.

DISCUSSION:

Recognizing that "the specific features of treaties to which international organizations are parties as subjects of international law distinct from states" and acknowledging the growing importance of international organizations in international relations, the convention lays down provisions governing "treaties between one or more States and one or more international organizations, and . . . treaties between international organizations."

The principal areas addressed are as follows:

- Conclusion and entry into force of treaties
- The concept and function of reservations
- Entry into force and provisional application of treaties
- Observance, application and interpretation of treaties
- Treaties and third states
- Amendment and modification
- Invalidity, termination, and suspension of the operation of treaties
- Depositaries, notifications, corrections, and registration

A detailed annex to the convention provides guidelines for arbitration and conciliation procedures in the event of disuputes arising from treaties.

REFERENCE:

Denza, Eileen. *Diplomatic Law: A Commentary on the Vienna Convention on Diplomatic Relations,* 2d ed. Oxford and New York: Oxford University Press, 1998.

International Dispute Resolution

Overview of Treaties in This Category

Nations have long sought alternatives to war or other punitive actions in the resolution of international disputes. Such organizations as the League of Nations and the United Nations were founded in pursuit of this global aspiration. Among the treaties included here are one multilateral agreement on the general principle of pacific settlement (**Pact of Bogota [American Treaty on Pacific Settlement]**) and a set of important bilateral agreements concerning the resolution of specific disputes.

Pact of Bogota

OFFICIAL TITLE: American Treaty on Pacific Settlement
SIGNED: April 30, 1948, at Bogota, Colombia
SIGNATORIES: Argentina, Bolivia, Brazil, Chile, Colombia, Costa Rica, Cuba, Dominican Republic, Ecuador, El Salvador, Guatemala, Haiti, Honduras, Mexico, Nicaragua, Panama, Paraguay, Peru, United States, Uruguay, Venezuela
IN FORCE: From May 6, 1948
OVERVIEW: A convention laying down principles and procedures for the pacific settlement of disputes among the members of the Organization of American States.

DISCUSSION:
Among the many steps the OAS took toward hemispheric solidarity was the creation of a comprehensive convention on the pacific settlement of disputes. Not only does the convention articulate the principle of the peaceful settlement of disputes, it establishes procedures and mechanisms for arbitration and adjudication.
  Issues addressed include the following:
• Obligation to settle disputes by pacific means
• Procedures of good offices and mediation
• Procedure of investigation and conciliation
• Judicial procedure
• Procedure of arbitration
• Fulfillment of decisions
• Advisory opinions

REFERENCES:
Grenville, J. A. S., *The Major International Treaties 1914-1973: A History Guide with Texts.* New York: Stein and Day, 1974.
Oceana Publications. *Inter-American System: Treaties, Conventions, and Other Documents.* Dobbs Ferry, NY: Oceana Publications, 1983.

Organization of American States. *OAS and the Evolution of the Inter-American System.* Washington, D.C.: Organization of American States Bookshop, 1982.
Thomas, Christopher R. *The Organization of American States in its 50th Year: Overview of a Regional Commitment.* Washington, D.C.: Organization of American States Bookshop, 1998.

Agreement Relating to the Italian-United States Conciliation Commission

OFFICIAL TITLE: Exchange of Notes Constituting an Agreement Relating to the Designation of the Third Permanent Member of the Italian-United States Conciliation Commission
SIGNED: February 12 and 13, 1951, at Rome
SIGNATORIES: Italy vs. United States
IN FORCE: From February 13, 1951
OVERVIEW: An agreement to designate a third member to the commission charged with settling claims of United States nationals against Italy and Italian nationals against the United States arising from World War II.

REFERENCE:
Italian-United States Conciliation Commission. *Collection of Decisions of the Italian-United States Conciliation Commission.* N.p.: N. pub., n.d.

Arbitration of Claims with Respect to Gold Looted by the Germans from Rome

OFFICIAL TITLE: Agreement for the Submission to an Arbitrator of Certain Claims with Respect to Gold Looted by the Germans from Rome in 1943
SIGNED: April 25, 1951, at Washington, D.C.
SIGNATORIES: France, United Kingdom, and United States
IN FORCE: From signing
OVERVIEW: An agreement to arbitrate an international dispute over the disposition of certain amounts of gold looted during World War II.

DISCUSSION:
By the Final Act of the Paris Conference on Reparation, the Allied governments agreed to the principle of restoring mone-

tary gold looted by the Germans. Where the sources of the gold could be identified, the looted gold was to be restored to them. Other recovered gold was to be allocated to a pool and distributed to nations that had subscribed to the reparation agreement. In the case of 2,338.7565 kilograms of gold looted by the Germans from Italy, however, Albania and Italy made conflicting claims. Accordingly, the three principal Allied government, France, United Kingdom, and United States, established an arbitrator to render an opinion as to whether Albania or Italy has proven that 2338.7565 kilograms of monetary gold was looted by the Germans. Per the Final Act of the Paris Conference on Reparation, both Italy and Albania were bound to accept the decision of the arbitrator.

REFERENCE:
Protocol Between the Governments of the United Kingdom and the United States and France and Italy Relating to the Restitution to Italy of Monetary Gold Looted by Germany. London: H. M. Stationery Office, 1947.

Agreement (with Canada) Concerning an Arbitral Tribunal to Dispose of United States Claims Relating to Gut Dam

OFFICIAL TITLE: Agreement Concerning the Establishment of an International Arbitral Tribunal to Dispose of United States Claims Relating to Gut Dam.
SIGNED: March 25, 1965, at Ottawa, Canada
SIGNATORIES: Canada vs. United States
IN FORCE: From October 11, 1966
OVERVIEW: An agreement creating a tribunal to arbitrate claims made against Canada for damages in the United States.

DISCUSSION:
In 1965, various individuals in the United States lodged claims against the Canadian government for damages incurred as a result of high water levels in Lake Ontario and the St. Lawrence River created by the Gut Dam Canada had built in the international section of the St. Lawrence River. Although the dam was Canadian, its location in the international section of the river created special problems relating to liability for damage claims. This agreement created the Lake Ontario Claims Tribunal United States and Canada "for the purpose of hearing and finally disposing of claims of nationals of the United States of America including judicial persons [that is, corporations] that are presented to the Tribunal." The agreement establishes the tribunal, lays down its membership, and outlines its authority as ultimate arbitrator in these cases.

REFERENCE:
Establishment of International Arbitral Tribunal to Dispose of United States Claims Relating to Gut Dam. Washington, D..C.: U.S. Government Printing Office, 1966.

Compromis (with France) of Arbitration

SIGNED: July 11, 1978, at Washington, D.C.
SIGNATORIES: France vs. United States
IN FORCE: From signing
OVERVIEW: An agreement to submit to nonbinding arbitration certain disputes over international commercial aviation.

DISCUSSION:
The United States and France were unable to resolve, through consultation, the following dispute with regard to international law and the Air Services Agreement between the United States and France of 1946:

Does a United States-designated carrier have the right to operate West Coast-Paris service under the Air Services Agreement with a "change of gauge" (transshipment to a smaller aircraft on the outward journey and to a larger aircraft on the return journey)?

Under the terms of the agreement, the arbitral tribunal is to submit a report of its opinion, which shall be nonbinding. In addition to putting the question to the tribunal, the agreement creates the tribunal and sets forth its composition.

Related to this agreement is **Agreement (with Switzerland) Regarding the Status, Privileges and Immunities in Switzerland of the Tribunal of Arbitration**, which deals with aspects of the conduct of the tribunal in Switzerland.

REFERENCES:
None

Agreement (with France and Switzerland) on the Tribunal of Arbitration

OFFICIAL TITLE: Agreement Regarding the Status, Privileges and Immunities in Switzerland of the Tribunal of Arbitration Established Pursuant to the Compromise Signed at Washington on 11 July 1978 between the United States of America and France, and of the Persons Participating in the Work of the Tribunal
SIGNED: December 12, 1978, at Berne, Switzerland
SIGNATORIES: France and the United States vs Switzerland
IN FORCE: From signing
OVERVIEW: An agreement between the United States and France, of the one part, and Switzerland, of the other part, concerning the establishment, in Geneva, of a Tribunal of Arbitration.

DISCUSSION:
This agreement is typical of a special type of agreement relating to the establishment and function of an impartial body in a neutral country. In this instance, the United States and France wished to lay down rules governing the status of a Tribunal of Arbitration the two nations created to rule on various matters relating to measures adopted by them bearing on the air traffic

between the two countries. In order to preserve the disinterested status of the tribunal, it was thought expedient to establish it in Geneva, Switzerland. Accordingly, the present agreement was drawn up among the three parties to "fix the status, privileges and immunities of the Tribunal of Arbitration and the persons participating in its work." These items include the following:

- Facilities furnished by the Swiss government
- Swiss government assistance in securing suitable premises for the tribunal
- Exemption of the tribunal from taxation
- A guarantee of the inviolability of the premises
- A guarantee of the inviolability of archives and documents
- A guarantee of freedom of movement for tribunal personnel
- A guarantee of freedom of communication
- A guarantee of personal inviolability and diplomatic immunity for members of the tribunal
- Exemption from taxation for members of the tribunal

REFERENCES:
None

Agreement (with Canada) to Submit a Boundary Dispute to the International Court of Justice

OFFICIAL TITLE: Special Agreement to Submit to a Chamber of the International Court of Justice the Delimitation of the Maritime Boundary in the Gulf of Maine Area

SIGNED: March 29, 1979, at Washington, D.C.

SIGNATORIES: Canada vs. United States

IN FORCE: From November 20, 1981

OVERVIEW: An agreement to submit a maritime boundary dispute to the International Court of Justice in the interest of reaching "an early and amicable settlement."

DISCUSSION:

From time to time, portions of the international boundary between the United States and Canada have been in dispute. Particularly thorny is the issue of the delimitation of the continental shelf and the fisheries zones of Canada and the United States in the Gulf of Maine area. After negotiation failed to resolve the issues of determining the maritime boundary in this region, Canada and the United States agreed to submit the issue to a Chamber of the International Court of Justice. The agreement details the following:

- The constitution of the chamber—five persons chosen in consultation with the parties
- The issue to be resolved: "What is the course of the single maritime boundary that divides the continental shelf and fisheries zones of Canada and the United States" in the Maine Gulf area
- A specification that the Chamber describe the boundary in terms of geodetic lines connecting geographic coordinates of points
- A request that the Chamber appoint a technical expert to assist the parties in respect to technical matters
- An undertaking by the parties to "accept as final and binding . . . the decision of the Chamber"

Also see **Treaty (with Canada) to Submit to Binding Dispute Settlement the Delimitation of the Maritime Boundary in the Gulf of Maine Area**.

REFERENCES:
None

Treaty (with Canada) to Submit to Binding Dispute Settlement the Delimitation of the Maritime Boundary in the Gulf of Maine Area

SIGNED: March 29, 1979, at Washington, D.C.

SIGNATORIES: Canada vs. United States

IN FORCE: From November 20, 1981

OVERVIEW: A treaty accompanying **Agreement (with Canada) to Submit a Boundary Dispute to the International Court of Justice**, in which the signatories undertake to notify the Court of International Justice of the Agreement.

DISCUSSION:

To give full legal force to the **Agreement (with Canada) to Submit a Boundary Dispute to the International Court of Justice**, the United States and Canada concluded a treaty in which they undertook to notify the Court of the Agreement. The brief treaty also addresses issues of the interim state of the disputed region prior to the decision of the Court of Justice.

REFERENCES:
None

Organization of American States and Other Pan-American Matters

Overview of Treaties in This Category

The **Monroe Doctrine** of 1823 (Section 1.1) was, for better or worse, a unilateral declaration of hemispheric solidarity, proclaiming a United States policy of regarding any foreign incursion into any American state an attack on the United States. Throughout the nineteenth century and well into the twentieth, United States relations with the nations of South and Central America and the Carribean were chronically strained, marked by often well-founded distrust of United States imperialism. When Herbert Hoover was elected to the presidency in 1928, relations with Latin America were at perhaps their lowest point, largely the result of interventions in Haiti and Nicaragua during the administration of Calvin Coolidge. Directly after his election and even before his inauguration, Hoover made a goodwill tour of Latin American capitals, declaring in Honduras that the United States had a "desire to maintain not only the cordial relations of governments with each other but also the relations of good neighbors."

Although Hoover did introduce a number of initiatives to improve relations—including the repudiation of the Roosevelt Corollary to the Monroe Doctrine (which had declared that only the United States could enforce the collection of debts owed to foreigners by countries of the Western Hemisphere), the withdrawal of troops from Nicaragua, and a plan to withdraw them from Haiti—it was Hoover's successor, Franklin D. Roosevelt, who most vigorously advanced what became known as the Good Neighbor Policy. During the 1930s, the United States advocated a far-reaching policy of nonintervention in Latin American affairs and introduced low tariff policies to liberalize trade with the region. The Platt Amendment, which gave the United States broad authority to intervene in Cuban affairs, was repealed in 1934, and, two years later, terms governing United States control of the Panama Canal were liberalized.

The Good Neighbor Policy was of tremendous benefit to the United States as World War II engulfed Europe, and Germany made overtures of alliance to various Latin American states. Such documents as **Act of Havana** (1940), **U.S. State Department Bulletin on Hemispheric Defense** (1940), and **Resolution Reaffirming the Monroe Doctrine** (1941) (see Section 2.9) affirmed the solidarity of the Americas against foreign aggression, and the 1945 **Act of Chapultepec,** in this section, formalized the principles of the Good Neighbor Policy by defining friendly relations between the United States and Latin America, especially in the context of cooperation in collective defense.

The combined effects of the Good Neighbor Policy and the experience of the principle of collective defense in World War II created conditions favorable to the establishment of the Organization of American States in 1948 (**Charter of the Organization of American States**, 1948, **Protocol of Buenos Aires**, 1967, and **Protocol of Managua Amending the Charter of the OAS**, 1993).

Despite improvement in U.S.-Latin American relations, much distrust, ambiguity, and friction has periodically persisted, and, in pursuit of its Cold War policy of "containing" communism, the United States has several times intervened militarily in Latin American affairs, both covertly and openly. In 1961, the administration of John F. Kennedy sought to improve relations through the **Alliance for Progress** (and **Agreement Concerning Certain Funds to Be Made Available under the Alliance for Progress**, 1961), a program of aid to Latin America inspired by the success of the Marshall Plan in postwar Europe.

Act of Chapultepec

SIGNED: March 6, 1945, at Chapultepec (Mexico City), Mexico
In force: From March 8, 1945
SIGNATORIES: Argentina, Bolivia, Brazil, Chile, Colombia, Costa Rica, Cuba, the Dominican Republic, Ecuador, El Salvador, Guatemala Haiti, Honduras, Mexico, Nicaragua, Panama, Paraguay, Peru, the United States, Uruguay, Venezuela
OVERVIEW: This act formalized the principles of President Franklin D. Roosevelt's "Good Neighbor Policy," defining friendly relations between the United States and Latin America, especially in the context of U.S.-Latin American cooperation in World War II.

DISCUSSION:

A statement of the "Good Neighbor Policy" was included in FDR's inaugural address of 1933, and, at the end of that year, at the Pan American Conference in Montevideo, Uruguay, the United States signed a convention forbidding intervention by one state in the affairs of another. In 1934, the U.S. Marines withdrew from a two-decade occupation of Haiti, and the Roosevelt administration formally abrogated the Platt

Amendment, thereby acknowledging the full independence of Cuba (see **U.S.-Cuba Treaty of Relations**). The exigencies of World War II prompted the United States to sponsor the Act of Chapultepec, with the object of formally affirming the unity and commonality of interest of the nations of the Americas. The document established the first multinational collective security system in the Western Hemisphere.

The following is central to the document:

THE GOVERNMENTS represented at the Inter-American Conference on War and Peace declare:

1. That all sovereign states are juridically equal amongst themselves.

2. That every state has the right to the respect of its individuality and independence on the part of the other members of the international community.

3. That every attack of a state against the integrity or the inviolability of the territory, or against the sovereignty or political independence of an American state, shall . . . be considered as an act of aggression against the other states which sign this act. In any case, invasion by armed forces of one state into the territory of another, trespassing boundaries established by treaty and demarcated in accordance therewith, shall constitute an act of aggression.

4. That in case acts of aggression occur or there may be reasons to believe that an aggression is being prepared by any other state against the integrity and inviolability of the territory, or against the sovereignty or political independence of an American state, the states signatory to this act will consult amongst themselves in order to agree upon the measures it may be advisable to take.

5. That during the war . . . the signatories of this act recognize that such threats and acts of aggression, as indicated in paragraphs 3 and 4 above, constitute an interference with the war effort of the United Nations, calling for such procedures, within the scope of their constitutional powers of a general nature and for war, as may be found necessary, including recall of chiefs of diplomatic missions; breaking of diplomatic relations; breaking of consular relations; breaking of postal, telegraphic, telephonic, radiotelephonic rela tions; interruption of economic, commercial, and financial relations; use of armed force to prevent or repel aggression.

REFERENCES:

Annals of America, vol. 16. Chicago: Encyclopaedia Britannica, Inc., 1978.

Bethell, Leslie, and Ian Roxborough, eds. *Latin America between the Second World War and the Cold War, 1944-1948.* Cambridge: Cambridge University Press, 1993.

Humphreys, R.A. *Latin America and the Second World War: 1942-1945.* Atlantic Highlands, NJ: Athlone Press, 1983.

Charter of the Organization of American States

SIGNED: April 30, 1948, at Bogota, Colombia
IN FORCE: From December 13, 1951

SIGNATORIES: Antigua and Barbuda, Argentina, Bahamas, Barbados (joined 1967), Bolivia, Brazil, Chile, Colombia, Costa Rica, Cuba (expelled 1962), Dominica, the Dominican Republic, Ecuador, El Salvador, Grenada, Guatemala, Haiti, Honduras, Jamaica, Mexico, Nicaragua, Panama, Paraguay, Peru, St. Kitts-Nevis, Saint Lucia, Saint Vincent and the Grenadines, Suriname, Trinidad and Tobago(joined 1967), the United States, Uruguay, and Venezuela

OVERVIEW: The Organization of American States, created by this charter, is the principal regional political body of the Americas.

DISCUSSION:

The origin of the OAS is found as early 1889-1890 and the First International Conference of American States held in Washington, which created an International Union of American Republics. In 1910, this body became the Pan-American Union, an organization of limited scope, which functioned mainly as a clearinghouse for the exchange of information and for consultation on issues of common interest. Gradually, however, the scope of the Pan-American Union broadened until World War II brought a sharp sense of urgency to the need for solidarity among the republics of the Americas (*see* **Act of Havana**). After the war, the Ninth International Conference of American States held in Bogota, Colombia, in 1948, established the Organization of American States, the most broadly based Pan-American union yet created. The principal goals of the OAS include:

- The prevention of aggression from outside of the Western Hemisphere
- The maintenance of peace among the states of the Americas

At bottom, the OAS is based on the **Monroe Doctrine**, issued in 1823 by President James Monroe and proclaiming the intention of the United States to regard an outside attack on any American state an attack on itself. The OAS charter "continentalized" this principle, creating obligations for the other states without restricting the right of the United States to take immediate action in self-defense (as self-defense is broadly defined by the Monroe Doctrine). In addition to establishing the framework for collective defense of the hemisphere and implementing the mutual-security **Pact of Rio**, the OAS charter also defines a mission of economic cooperation for the organization.

The charter defines the structure of the Organization of American States, which is loosely modeled on that of the United Nations:

- Administration of the OAS is the responsibility of a General Secretariat, headed by a secretary-general elected to a five-year term.
- Policy is made by the General Assembly, which meets annually and at which member states are represented by their foreign ministers or chiefs of state.
- The Permanent Council, consisting of an ambassador from each member state, acts in cases of attack or aggression

within or between member states. The Permanent Council serves as a provisional body of consultation until all the ministers of the member states can assemble. Action by the Permanent Council requires approval of two-thirds of the foreign ministers present.

The OAS has frequently proved effective in its hemispherical peacemaking and peacekeeping roles, successfully intervening in numerous border disputes, providing the structure in which the Soccer War (1969) between Honduras and El Salvador was resolved, and supporting the U.S. quarantine of Cuba during the Cuban Missile Crisis of 1962. The OAS has been especially active in responding to Cuban attempts to subvert neighboring countries.

REFERENCES:

Grenville, J. A. S., *The Major International Treaties 1914-1973: A History Guide with Texts.* New York: Stein and Day, 1974.

Oceana Publications. *Inter-American System: Treaties, Conventions, and Other Documents.* Dobbs Ferry, NY: Oceana Publications, 1983.

Organization of American States. *OAS and the Evolution of the Inter-American System.* Washington, D.C.: Organization of American States Bookshop, 1982.

Thomas, Christopher R. *The Organization of American States in its 50th Year: Overview of a Regional Commitment.* Washington, D.C.: Organization of American States Bookshop, 1998.

Alliance for Progress

SIGNED: August 17, 1961

IN FORCE: On signing

SIGNATORIES: Antigua and Barbuda, Argentina, Bahamas, Barbados, Bolivia, Brazil, Chile, Colombia, Costa Rica, Dominica, the Dominican Republic, Ecuador, El Salvador, Grenada, Guatemala, Haiti, Honduras, Jamaica, Mexico, Nicaragua, Panama, Paraguay, Peru, St. Kitts-Nevis, Saint Lucia, Saint Vincent and the Grenadines, Suriname, Trinidad and Tobago, the United States, Uruguay, and Venezuela

OVERVIEW: The Charter of Punta Del Este (Uruguay) established a $100 billion U.S. aid program for the economic and social development of Latin America. The "Alliance for Progress" had been proposed by President John F. Kennedy (message to Congress, March 14, 1961)—from the point of view of the United States, as a means of keeping the nations of Latin America out of the communist camp.

DISCUSSION:

The "Declaration to the Peoples of America," which preceded the Charter proper, set out the goals of the Alliance for Progress:

This Alliance is established on the basic principle that free men working through the institution of representative democracy can best satisfy man's aspirations, including those for work, home and land, health and schools. No system can guarantee true progress unless it affirms the dignity of the individual which is the foundation of our civilization.

Therefore the countries signing this Declaration in the exercise of their sovereignty have agreed to work toward the following goals during the coming years:

To improve and strengthen democratic institutions through application of the principle of self-determination by the people.

To accelerate economic and social development, thus rapidly bringing about a substantial and steady increase in the average income in order to narrow the gap between the standard of living in Latin American countries and that enjoyed in the industrialized countries.

To carry out urban and rural housing programs to provide decent homes for all our people.

To encourage, in accordance with the characteristics of each country, programs of comprehensive agrarian reform, leading to the effective transformation, where required, of unjust structures and systems of land tenure and use; with a view to replacing latifundia and dwarf holdings by an equitable system of property so that, supplemented by timely and adequate credit, technical assistance and improved marketing arrangements, the land will become for the man who works it the basis of his economic stability, the foundation of his increasing welfare, and the guarantee of his freedom and dignity.

To assure fair wages and satisfactory working conditions to all our workers; to establish effective systems of labor-management relations and procedures for consultation and cooperation among government authorities, employers' associations, and trade unions in the interests of social and economic development.

To wipe out illiteracy; to extend, as quickly as possible, the benefits of primary education to all Latin Americans; and to provide broader facilities, on a vast scale, for secondary and technical training and for higher education.

To press forward with programs of health and sanitation in order to prevent sickness, combat contagious disease, and strengthen our human potential.

To reform tax laws, demanding more from those who have most, to punish tax evasion severely, and to redistribute the national income in order to benefit those who are most in need, while, at the same time, promoting savings and investment and reinvestment of capital.

To maintain monetary and fiscal policies which, while avoiding the disastrous effects of inflation or deflation, will protect the purchasing power of the many, guarantee the greatest possible price stability, and form an adequate basis for economic development.

To stimulate private enterprise in order to encourage the development of Latin American countries at a rate which will help them to provide jobs for their growing populations, to eliminate unemployment, and to take their place among the modern industrialized nations of the world.

To find a quick and lasting solution to the grave problem created by excessive price fluctuations in the basic exports of Latin American countries on which their prosperity so heavily depends.

To accelerate the integration of Latin America so as to stimulate the economic and social development of the continent. This process has already begun through he General Treaty of Economic Integration of Central America and, in other countries, through the Latin American Free Trade Association.

The Declaration goes on to assert that "profound economic, social, and cultural changes can come about only through the self-help efforts of each country...reinforced by essential contributions of external assistance....The United States, for its part, pledges its efforts to supply financial and technical cooperation in order to achieve the aims of the Alliance for Progress."

The Declaration the outlines certain programs of financial assistance from the Untied States. In turn, the Declaration includes a pledge from "the countries of Latin America . . . to devote a steadily increasing share of their own resources to economic and social development, and to make the reforms necessary to assure that all share fully in the fruits of the Alliance for Progress."

By addressing the chronic poverty and political oppression that long plagued the peoples of Latin America, the United States hoped not only to improve the quality of life in the hemisphere, but to maintain Latin America in the U.S. sphere of influence. The Alliance for Progress was an ambitious program for using massive economic "weapons" to fight the ongoing Cold War in the Americas.

REFERENCES:

Bierck, Harold Alfred. *The United States and Latin America, 1933-1968: from the Good Neighbor to the Alliance for Progress.* New York: Macmillan, 1969.

Grenville, J. A. S., *The Major International Treaties 1914-1973: A History Guide with Texts.* New York: Stein and Day, 1974.

Krause, Walter. *The United States and Latin America: the Alliance for Progress Program.* Austin: Bureau of Business Research, University of Texas, 1963.

May, Herbert K. *Problems and Prospects of the Alliance for Progress; a Critical Examination.* New York, Praeger, 1968.

Perloff, Harvey S. *Alliance for Progress: A Social Invention in the Making.* Baltimore: Johns Hopkins Press, 1969.

Agreement Concerning Certain Funds to Be Made Available under the Alliance for Progress

SIGNED: November 29, 1961, at Washington, D.C.

SIGNATORIES: United States vs. Pan American Union

IN FORCE: From signature

OVERVIEW: Pursuant to agreements establishing the **Alliance for Progress**, an agreement funding programs of cooperation between the United States and the Pan American Union.

DISCUSSION:

This agreement, concluded under President John F. Kennedy's **Alliance for Progress**, a cooperative alliance with the nations of Latin America aimed at discouraging the spread of communism

in Central and South America, governed disbursement of moneys in the Special Inter-American Fund for Social Progress, an aid fund created by the United States. The agreement directed that the $6,000,000 of the Special Inter-American Fund and "any additional funds which the United States may subsequently agree to use" should be administered by the Pan American Union for the following purposes:

- Field investigations relating to social and economic development
- Meetings of experts and officials
- Payment of technical experts

The agreement established reporting and accounting procedures.

REFERENCES:

Bierck, Harold Alfred. *The United States and Latin America, 1933-1968: from the Good Neighbor to the Alliance for Progress.* New York: Macmillan, 1969.

Grenville, J. A. S., *The Major International Treaties 1914-1973: A History Guide with Texts.* New York: Stein and Day, 1974.

Krause, Walter. *The United States and Latin America: the Alliance for Progress Program.* Austin: Bureau of Business Research, University of Texas, 1963.

May, Herbert K. *Problems and Prospects of the Alliance for Progress; a Critical Examination* . New York, Praeger, 1968.

Perloff, Harvey S. *Alliance for Progress: A Social Invention in the Making.* Baltimore: Johns Hopkins Press, 1969.

Protocol of Buenos Aires

OFFICIAL TITLE: Protocol of Amendment to the Charter of the Organization of American States

SIGNED: February 27, 1967, at Buenos Aires, Argentina

SIGNATORIES: Antigua and Barbuda, Argentina, Bahamas, Barbados, Bolivia, Brazil, Chile, Colombia, Costa Rica, Dominica, Dominican Republic, Ecuador, El Salvador, Grenada, Guatemala, Haiti, Honduras, Jamaica, Mexico, Nicaragua, Panama, Paraguay, Peru, Saint Lucia, Saint Vincent and the_Grenadines, St. Kitts and Nevis, Suriname, Trinidad and Tobago, United States, Uruguay, Venezuela

IN FORCE: From February 27, 1970

OVERVIEW: An amendment to the **Charter of the Organization of American States** intended to "forge a new dynamism for the inter-American system and imperative to modify the working structure of the Organization of American, States, as well as to establish in the Charter new objectives and standards for the promotion of the economic, social, and cultural development of the peoples of the Hemisphere, and to speed up the process of economic integration."

DISCUSSION:

The major revisions in the original charter emphasize human rights and the right of development. Increased levels of general cooperation are called for, and an increased level of economic cooperation is mandated. The charter's original provisions concerning "Social Standards" are expanded and amplified. The original charter's provisions concerning "Cultural Standards" are also expanded and amplified.

REFERENCES:

Grenville, J. A. S., *The Major International Treaties 1914-1973: A History Guide with Texts*. New York: Stein and Day, 1974.

Oceana Publications. *Inter-American System: Treaties, Conventions, and Other Documents*. Dobbs Ferry, NY: Oceana Publications, 1983.

Organization of American States. *OAS and the Evolution of the Inter-American System*. Washington, D.C.: Organization of American States Bookshop, 1982.

Thomas, Christopher R. *The Organization of American States in its 50th Year: Overview of a Regional Commitment*. Washington, D.C.: Organization of American States Bookshop, 1998.

Protocol of Managua Amending the Charter of the OAS

OFFICIAL TITLE: Protocol of Amendment to the Charter of the Organization of American States ("Protocol of Managua")

SIGNED: June 10, 1993, at Managua, Nicaragua

SIGNATORIES: Antigua and Barbuda, Argentina, Bahamas, Barbados, Belize, Bolivia, Brazil, Canada, Chile, Colombia, Costa Rica, Dominica, Dominican Republic, Ecuador, El Salvador, Grenada, Guatemala, Guyana, Haiti, Honduras, Jamaica, Mexico Nicaragua, Panama, Paraguay, Peru, Saint Lucia, Saint Vincent and the Grenadines, St. Kitts and Nevis, Suriname, Trinidad and Tobago, United States, Uruguay, Venezuela

IN FORCE: From January 29, 1996_

OVERVIEW: An amendment to the **Charter of the Organization of American States** of 1948 expanding technical cooperation among the signatory states.

DISCUSSION:

The protocol defines the mission of the Inter-American Council for Integral Development, which is charged with the following responsibilities:

- To formulate a strategic plan in matters of cooperation for integral development
- To formulate guidelines for budgeting a program for technical cooperation
- To promote progress is such areas as trade, tourism, integration, and the environment
- To promote improvement and extension of education
- To strengthen the "civic conscience of the American peoples"

REFERENCES:

Grenville, J. A. S., *The Major International Treaties 1914-1973: A History Guide with Texts*. New York: Stein and Day, 1974.

Oceana Publications. *Inter-American System: Treaties, Conventions, and Other Documents*. Dobbs Ferry, NY: Oceana Publications, 1983.

Organization of American States. *OAS and the Evolution of the Inter-American System*. Washington, D.C.: Organization of American States Bookshop, 1982.

Thomas, Christopher R. *The Organization of American States in its 50th Year: Overview of a Regional Commitment*. Washington, D.C.: Organization of American States Bookshop, 1998.

Rights and Duties of States

Overview of Treaties in This Category

Questions of where individual sovereignty ends and international law begins are, by nature, difficult. The small group of treaties in this section represent attempts to define and standardize concepts of the rights and duties of states, both in the limited context of times of civil strife and as a matter of general principle. **Convention on the Rights and Duties of States in the Event of Civil Strife** (1928) and **Protocol to the Convention on the Rights and Duties of States in the Event of Civil Strife** (1957) exist in part to safeguard human rights and individual political rights and in part to define when international intervention may and may not be appropriate in nations undergoing civil strife.

The suspended fate of the more general **Draft Declaration on the Rights and Duties of States** is testimony to the difficulties inherent in defining such issues in any general, enduring, and enforceable manner. The International Law Commission, a commission of the United Nations, drafted the document in 1949 and submitted to the General Assembly later that year. The draft has yet to be approved and opened for signature.

Convention on Duties and Rights of States in the Event of Civil Strife

SIGNED: February 20, 1928, at Havana
SIGNATORIES: Argentina, Brazil, Costa Rica, Cuba, Dominican Republic, El Salvador, Haiti, Honduras, Peru, United States
IN FORCE: From signing
OVERVIEW: The original Pan-American Union document addressing conduct of state in case of civil strife.

DISCUSSION:

The provisions of the 1928 document are, in all principal respects, substantively the same as those of the **Protocol to the Convention on Duties and Rights of States in the Event of Civil Strife** of 1957.

REFERENCE:

United States Department of State, *Treaties in Force: A List of Treaties and other International Agreements of the United States in Force on January 1, 1997.* Washington, D.C.: U.S. Government Printing Office, 1997

Draft Declaration on Rights and Duties of States

SIGNED: Text adopted by the Commission at its first session, in 1949.
SIGNATORIES: Draft declaration not yet open for signature
IN FORCE: Draft declaration not in force
OVERVIEW: An attempt to establish a foundation of agreement on the rights and duties of states.

DISCUSSION:

In 1949, the International Law Commission, a commission of the United Nations, drafted a statement of the rights and duties of states. Submitted to the General Assembly in 1949, the draft has yet to be approved and opened for signature. A declaration of principles so basic to issues of sovereignty and international morality has proved to be highly controversial and remains an unapproved draft. The articles follow:

Article 1
Every State has the right to independence and hence to exercise freely, without dictation by any other State, all its legal powers, including the choice of its own form of government.

Article 2
Every State has the right to exercise jurisdiction over its territory and over all persons and things therein, subject to the immunities recognized by international law.

Article 3
Every State has the duty to refrain from intervention in the internal or external affairs of any other State.

Article 4
Every State has the duty to refrain from fomenting civil strife in the territory of another State, and to prevent the organization within its territory of activities calculated to foment such civil strife.

Article 5
Every State has the right to equality in law with every other State.

Article 6
Every State has the duty to treat all persons under its jurisdiction with respect for human rights and fundamental freedoms, without distinction as to race, sex, language, or religion.

Article 7
Every State has the duty to ensure that conditions prevailing in its territory do not menace international peace and order.

Article 8

Every State has the duty to settle its disputes with other States by peaceful means in such a manner that international peace and security, and justice, are not endangered.

Article 9

Every State has the duty to refrain from resorting to war as an instrument of national policy, and to refrain from the threat or use of force against the territorial integrity or political independence of another State in any other manner inconsistent with international law and order.

Article 10

Every State has the duty to refrain from giving assistance to any State which is acting in violation of article 9, or against which the United Nations is taking preventive or enforcement action.

Article 11

Every State has the duty to refrain from recognizing any territorial acquisition by another State acting in violation of article 9.

Article 12

Every State has the right of individual or collective self-defence against armed attack.

Article 13

Every State has the duty to carry out in good faith its obligations arising from treaties and other sources of international law, and it may not invoke provisions in its constitution or its laws as an excuse for failure to perform this duty.

Article 14

Every State has the duty to conduct its relations with other States in accordance with international law and with the principle that the sovereignty of each State is subject to the supremacy of international law.

REFERENCES:
None

Protocol to the Convention on Duties and Rights of States in the Event of Civil Strife

SIGNED: May 1, 1957, at Washington
SIGNATORIES: Argentina, Brazil, Costa Rica, Cuba, Dominican Republic, El Salvador, Haiti, Honduras, Peru, United States
IN FORCE: From December 9, 1957
OVERVIEW: A protocol "clarifying, supplementing, and strengthening the principles and rules stipulated in the **Convention on Duties and Rights of States in the Event of Civil Strife**" (1928).

DISCUSSION:
The major provision of the protocol is laid down in Article 1:

Each Contracting State shall, in areas subject to its jurisdiction:

a) Keep under surveillance the traffic in arms and war material that it has reason to believe is intended for starting, promoting, or supporting civil strife in another American State;

b) Suspend the exportation or importation of any shipment of arms and war material during the period of its investigation of the circumstances relating to the shipment, when it has reason to believe that such arms and war material may be intended for starting, promoting, or supporting civil strife in another American State; and

c) Prohibit the exportation or importation of any shipment of arms and war material intended for starting, promoting, or supporting civil strife in another American State.

Article 5 lays down the following:

Each Contracting State shall, in areas subject to its jurisdiction and within the powers granted by its Constitution, use all appropriate means to prevent any person, national or alien, from deliberately participating in the preparation, organization, or carrying out of a military enterprise that has as its purpose the starting, promoting or supporting of civil strife in another Contracting State, whether or not the government of the latter has been recognized. For the purposes of this article, participation in the preparation, organization, or carrying out of a military enterprise includes, among other acts:

a) The contribution, supply or provision of arms and war material;

b) The equipment, training, collection, or transportation of members of a military expedition; or

c) The provision or receipt of money, by any method, intended for the military enterprise.

REFERENCES:
None

Terrorism

Overview of Treaties in This Category

In the years following World War II, global politics was dominated by the so-called rival "superpowers," the United States and the Soviet Union, with many nations aligned as allies of one or the other. Yet an unaligned group of smaller, much less powerful, and, typically, impoverished (or "developing") nations also emerged during this period. This "Third World" was often marked by an instability born of combinations of extreme political idealism (from some perspectives, fanaticism), desperation, and, sometimes, religious zeal. Unable to compete politically, economically, or militarily with the superpowers and their allies, Third World states, as well as factions within them, sometimes asserted themselves through acts of terrorism in an effort to coerce and extort desired actions from conventionally more powerful nations.

The 1970s and 1980s saw a rash of terrorist acts, ranging from the hijacking of civilian commercial aircraft ("skyjacking"), to hostage taking, to bombings. The United States responded by participating in a range of multilateral and bilateral anti-terrorist agreements, the most important of which are represented in this section.

Convention for the Suppression of Unlawful Acts Against the Safety of Civil Aviation

SIGNED: September 23, 1971, at Montreal

SIGNATORIES: Afghanistan, Algeria, Antigua and Barbuda, Argentina, Australia, Austria, Bahamas, Bahrain, Bangladesh, Barbados, Belarus, Belgium, Bhutan, Bolivia, Bosnia-Herzegovina, Botswana, Brazil, Brunei, Bulgaria, Burkina Faso, Burma, Cambodia, Cameroon, Canada, Cape Verde, Central African Republic, Chad, Chile, China, Colombia, Comoros, Costa Rica, Côte d'Ivoire, Croatia, Cyprus, Czech Republic, Czechoslovakia, Denmark, Djibouti, Dominican Republic, Ecuador, Egypt, El Salvador, Equatorial Guinea, Estonia, Ethiopia, Fiji, Finland, Former Yugoslav Republic of Macedonia, France, Gabon, Gambia, Georgia, German Democratic Republic, Germany (Federal Republic), Ghana, Greece, Grenada, Guatemala, Guinea, Guinea-Bissau, Guyana, Haiti, Honduras, Hungary, Iceland, India, Indonesia, Iran, Iraq, Ireland, Israel, Italy, Jamaica, Japan, Jordan, Kenya, Korea (Democratic People's Republic), Korea (Republic), Kuwait, Laos, Lebanon, Lesotho, Liberia, Libya, Lithuania, Luxembourg, Madagascar, Malawi, Malaysia, Maldives, Mali, Marshall Islands, Mauritania, Mauritius, Mexico, Monaco, Mongolia, Morocco, Nauru, Nepal, Netherlands, New Zealand, Nicaragua, Niger, Nigeria, Norway, Oman, Pakistan, Palau, Panama, Papua New Guinea, Paraguay, Peru, Philippines, Poland, Portugal, Qatar, Romania, Rwanda, St. Lucia, Saudi Arabia, Senegal, Seychelles, Sierra Leone, Singapore, Slovak Republic, Slovenia, Solomon Islands, South Africa, Spain, Sri Lanka, Sudan, Suriname, Sweden, Switzerland, Syrian Arab Republic, Tajikistan, Tanzania, Thailand, Togo, Tonga, Trinidad and Tobago, Tunisia, Turkey, Uganda, Ukraine, Union of Soviet Socialist Republics, United Arab Emirates, United Kingdom, United States, Uruguay, Vanuatu, Venezuela, Vietnam (Socialist Republic), Yemen (Aden), Yemen (Sanaa), Yugoslavia, Zaire, Zambia, Zimbabwe

IN FORCE: January 26, 1973

OVERVIEW: "For the purpose of deterring . . . [unlawful] acts [against civil aviation]," the convention provides "appropriate measures for punishment of offenders."

DISCUSSION:

This agreement is similar to the Convention on the Suppression of Unlawful Seizures of Aircraft of 1971, but extends the scope of coverage beyond "skyjacking" to cover any person who commits any unlawful act against civil aviation, including (as defined by Article 1), any person who:

(a) performs an act of violence against a person on board an aircraft in flight if that act is likely to endanger the safety of that aircraft; or

(b) destroys an aircraft in service or causes damage to such an aircraft which renders it incapable of flight or which is likely to endanger its safety in flight; or

(c) places or causes to be placed on an aircraft in service, by any means whatsoever, a device or substance which is likely to destroy that aircraft, or to cause damage to it which renders it incapable of flight, or to cause damage to it which is likely to endanger its safety in flight; or

(d) destroys or damages air navigation facilities or interferes with their operation, if any such act is likely to endanger the safety of aircraft in flight; or

(e) communicates information which he knows to be false, thereby endangering the safety of an aircraft in flight.

As provided for in Article 3, "Each Contracting State undertakes to make the offences mentioned in Article 1 punishable by severe penalties." And, per Article 10, "Contracting States shall, in accordance with international and national law, endeavour to take all practicable measure for the purpose of preventing the offences mentioned in Article 1."

REFERENCES:
Clyne, Peter. *An Anatomy of Skyjacking.* London: Abelard-Schumann, 1973.
Rubin, Barry, ed. *The Politics of Counterterrorism: The Ordeal of Democratic States.* Washington, D.C.: Foreign Policy Institute, Paul H. Nitze School of Advanced International Studies, Johns Hopkins University, 1990.

Convention to Prevent and Punish Acts of Terrorism Against Persons of International Significance

OFFICIAL TITLE: Convention to Prevent and Punish Acts of Terrorism Taking the Form of Crimes Against Persons and Related Extortion That Are of International Significance

SIGNED: February 2, 1971, at Washington

SIGNATORIES: Brazil, Chile, Colombia, Costa Rica, Dominican Republic, Ecuador, El Salvador, Guatemala, Honduras, Jamaica, Mexico, Nicaragua, Panama, Peru, Trinidad and Tobago, United States, Uruguay, Venezuela

IN FORCE: "For each state on the date of deposit of its instrument of ratification"; for the United States, October 20, 1976

OVERVIEW: A convention "to prevent and punish acts of terrorism, especially kidnaping, murder, and other assaults against the life or physical integrity of those persons to whom the state has the duty according to international law to give special protection, as well as extortion in connection with those crimes."

DISCUSSION:

The late 1960s and early 1970s saw a rash of terrorist assaults against diplomats and other government officials, including kidnaping for the purpose of extorting ransom money or other objectives, such as forcing the release of putative political prisoners. As the preamble to the convention explains, "criminal acts against persons entitled to special protection under international law are occurring frequently, and those acts are of international significance because of the consequences that may flow from them for relations among states." For this reason, the preamble continues, it "is advisable to adopt general standards that will progressively develop international law as regards cooperation in the prevention and punishment of such acts." However, "in the application of those standards the institution of asylum should be maintained and, likewise the principle of nonintervention should not be impaired."

Article 1 lays down: "The contracting states undertake to cooperate among themselves by taking all the measures that they may consider effective, under their own laws, and especially those established in this convention, to prevent and punish acts of terrorism, especially kidnaping, murder, and other assaults against the life or physical integrity of those persons to whom the state has the duty according to international law to give special protection, as well as extortion in connection with those crimes." Article 2 defines the special scope of the convention: "For the purposes of this convention, kidnaping, murder, and other assaults against the life or personal integrity of those persons to whom the state has the duty to give special protection according to international law, as well as extortion in connection with those crimes, shall be considered common crimes of international significance, regardless of motive." The concluding phrase is of critical importance, because it excludes claims to such motives as political or military action as legitimation of terrorist acts. The convention defines the acts as criminal, motive notwithstanding. Article 3 lays down as explicit that persons guilty of terrorist kidnaping and related crimes are subject to extradition; this provision is intended to ensure that governments do not evade their obligations under extradition agreements and that defendants may not assert, in order to evade extradition, that they are being prosecuted for a political act.

Article 8 emphasizes international cooperation to prevent terrorist kidnaping:

To cooperate in preventing and punishing the crimes contemplated in Article 2 of this convention, the contracting states accept the following obligations:

a. To take all measures within their power, and in conformity with their own laws, to prevent and impede the preparation in their respective territories of the crimes mentioned in Article 2 that are to be carried out in the territory of another contracting state.

b. To exchange information and consider effective administrative measures for the purpose of protecting the persons to whom Article 2 of this convention refers.

c. To guarantee to every person deprived of his freedom through the application of this convention every right to defend himself.

d. To endeavor to have the criminal acts contemplated in this convention included in their penal laws, if not already so included.

e. To comply most expeditiously with the requests for extradition concerning the criminal acts contemplated in this convention.

REFERENCE:
Rubin, Barry, ed. *The Politics of Counterterrorism: The Ordeal of Democratic States.* Washington, D.C.: Foreign Policy Institute, Paul H. Nitze School of Advanced International Studies, Johns Hopkins University, 1990.

Exchange of Notes (with Cuba) Relating to Hijacking of Aircraft and Vessels

OFFICIAL TITLE: Exchange of Notes Constituting and Agreement Relating to Hijacking of Aircraft and Vessels and Other Offenses (with Memorandum of Understanding)

SIGNED: February 15, 1973, at Washington and Havana

SIGNATORIES: Cuba vs. United States

IN FORCE: From signing

OVERVIEW: An agreement to punish hijackers, primarily directed at radicals who "skyjack" aircraft from the United States to Cuba.

DISCUSSION:

Fidel Castro deposed the pro-United States Cuban president Fulgencio Batista on New Year's Day 1959 and soon after aligned himself, as a Marxist, with the Soviet Union. Relations between Cuba and the United States quickly deteriorated. In January of 1961, President Dwight Eisenhower severed diplomatic relations with the Castro government, and trade as well as travel to the island nation was prohibited. On May 1, 1961, the first hijacking of an airliner within the United States occurred when a man forced a commercial aircraft en route from Miami to Key West, Florida, to detour to Cuba. By the end of 1961, four planes had been hijacked to Cuba. During the remainder of the decade and into the 1970s, Cuban expatriates, leftists, and others occasionally "skyjacked" American planes to Havana.

Neither nation approved of the practice, but the lack of diplomatic relations made it difficult to conclude a cooperative agreement to combat skyjacking. In fact, not all diplomatic interchange between Cuba and the United States had been cut off. The two nations used intermediaries to communicate with each other, and the present exchange of notes was made on behalf of the United States through the Swiss embassy in Havana and on behalf of Cuba through the Czech embassy in Washington.

The agreement is simple:

- Both nations agree that skyjacking is a severely punishable offense. Offenders are to be arrested and either extradited to the "party of registry of the aircraft or vessel" or "brought before the courts of the party whose territory he reached for trial in conformity with its laws for the offense punishable by the most severe penalty according to the circumstances and the seriousness of the acts."
- Both nations agree to "take all necessary steps to facilitate without delay the continuation of the journey of the passengers and crew innocent of the hijacking."
- Both nations agree to restore to the rightful owners any money or property taken from the innocent passengers and crew.
- Both nations agree to "protect the physical integrity of the aircraft or vessel."

The agreement adds that, "In the event that offenses referred to above are not punishable under the laws existing in the country to which the persons committing them arrived, the party in question shall be obligated" to extradite the offenders.

The agreement prohibits the use of a hijacked aircraft or vessel as a means of obtaining illegal entry into the country: "Each party shall apply strictly its own laws to any national of the other party who, coming from the territory of the other party, enters its territory, violating laws as well as national and international requirements pertaining to immigration, health, customs and the like."

The final substantive paragraph of the agreement addresses the issue of "extenuating and mitigating circumstances in those cases in which the persons responsible for the acts were being sought for strictly political reasons and were in real and imminent danger of death without a viable alternative for leaving the country, provided there was no financial extortion or physical injury to the members of the crew, passengers, or other persons in connection with the hijacking." Thus the agreement leaves open the possibility of a victim of political persecution, in extraordinary circumstances, hijacking a plane or ship with impunity.

REFERENCES:

Clyne, Peter. *An Anatomy of Skyjacking.* London: Abelard-Schumann, 1973.

Rubin, Barry, ed. *The Politics of Counterterrorism: The Ordeal of Democratic States.* Washington, D.C.: Foreign Policy Institute, Paul H. Nitze School of Advanced International Studies, Johns Hopkins University, 1990.

International Convention Against the Taking of Hostages

SIGNED: December 17, 1979, at New York

SIGNATORIES: Antigua and Barbuda, Argentina, Australia, Austria, Bahamas, Barbados, Belarus, Bhutan, Bosnia-Herzegovina, Brunei, Bulgaria, Cameroon, Canada, Chile, China, Côte d'Ivoire, Cyprus, Czech Republic, Czechoslovakia, Denmark, Dominica, Ecuador, Egypt, El Salvador, Finland, German Democratic Republic, Germany (Federal Republic), Ghana, Greece, Grenada, Guatemala, Haiti, Honduras, Hungary, Iceland, India, Italy, Japan, Jordan, Kazakstan, Kenya, Korea, Kuwait, Lesotho, Liechtenstein, Luxembourg, Malawi, Mali, Mauritius, Mexico, Mongolia, Nepal, Netherlands, New Zealand, Norway, Oman, Panama, Philippines, Portugal, Romania, Saudi Arabia, Slovak Republic, Slovenia, Spain, Sudan, Surname, Sweden, Switzerland, Togo, Trinidad and Tobago, Turkey, Ukraine, Union of Soviet Socialist Republics, United Kingdom, United States, Venezuela, Yugoslavia

IN FORCE: From June 3, 1983 (in force for the United States from January 6, 1985)

OVERVIEW: The convention requires signatory states to make the taking of hostages a punishable offense.

DISCUSSION:

The convention is aimed against the terrorism in the specific form of hostage taking. Signatories disavow hostage-taking as a state-sanctioned action by pledging to punish all instances. The convention specifies procedures for extradition of offenders, where appropriate, but Article 9 notes that states may withhold requests for extradition in the presences of "substantial grounds for believing that the alleged offender would be punished on account of his race, religion, nationality, ethnic origin or political opinion." Objecting to this provision, the U.S.S.R. ratified the convention with a reservation as to Article 9.

REFERENCES:

Antokol, Norman. *No One a Neutral: Political Hostage-taking in the Modern World*. Medina, Ohio: Alpha Publications of Ohio, 1990.

Crelinsten, Ronald D., and Denis Szabo. *Hostage-Taking*. Lexington, MA: Lexington Books, 1979.

Poland, James M., and Michael J. McCrystle. *Practical, Tactical, and Legal Perspectives of Terrorism and Hostage-taking*. Lewiston, NY: Edwin Mellon Press, 1999.

Counterterrorism Accord (with Israel)

SIGNED: April 30, 1996, at Washington, D.C.
SIGNATORIES: Israel vs. United States
IN FORCE: From July 29, 1996
OVERVIEW: An agreement to cooperate in "enhancing . . . capabilities to deter, prevent, respond to and investigate international terrorist acts or threats of international terrorist acts against Israel or the United States."

DISCUSSION:

The agreement calls for cooperation in the following areas of counterterrorism:

- Sharing of information and analyses regarding terrorists and terrorist organizations
- Training
- Exchange of experts
- Exchange of experience in dealing with terrorist incidents, including crisis management
- Exchange of information regarding terrorism-related investigation
- Exchange of information on transfers of funds to organizations involved in international terrorism
- Extradition, prosecution and other legal mechanisms
- Research and development
- Consulting closely on counterterrorism policy, including regional and global counterterrorism initiatives
- Enhancing the counterterrorism capabilities of others

To achieve these objectives, the agreement establishes the Israel-United States Joint Counterterrorism Group (JCG).

REFERENCE:

Rubin, Barry, ed. *The Politics of Counterterrorism: The Ordeal of Democratic States*. Washington, D.C.: Foreign Policy Institute, Paul H. Nitze School of Advanced International Studies, Johns Hopkins University, 1990.

International Convention for the Suppression of Terrorist Bombings

SIGNED: January 12, 1998, at New York
SIGNATORIES: Algeria, Argentina, Belarus, Austria, Belgium, Brazil, Burundi, Canada, Comoros, Costa Rica, Côte d'Ivoire, Cyprus, Czech Republic, Finland, Former Yugoslav Republic of Macedonia, France, Germany, Greece, Iceland, India, Ireland, Israel, Italy, Japan, Lithuania, Luxembourg, Madagascar, Monaco, Nepal, Netherlands, Norway, Panama, Philippines, Poland, Romania, Russian Federation, Slovakia, Slovenia, Spain, Sri Lanka, Sudan, Sweden, Togo, Turkey, Turkemnistan, Uganda, United Kingdom, United States, Uruguay, Uzbekistan, Venezuela
IN FORCE: Not yet in force
OVERVIEW: A convention of international cooperation to counteract terrorism.

DISCUSSION:

The convention defines crimes related to terrorist bombing in Article 2:

1. Any person commits an offence within the meaning of this Convention if that person unlawfully and intentionally delivers, places, discharges or detonates an explosive or other lethal device in, into or against a place of public use, a State or government facility, a public transportation system or an infrastructure facility:

    (a) With the intent to cause death or serious bodily injury; or

    (b) With the intent to cause extensive destruction of such a place, facility or system, where such destruction results in or is likely to result in major economic loss.

2. Any person also commits an offence if that person attempts to commit an offence as set forth in paragraph 1 of the present article.

3. Any person also commits an offence if that person:

    (a) Participates as an accomplice in an offence as set forth in paragraph 1 or 2 of the present article; or

    (b) Organizes or directs others to commit an offence as set forth in paragraph 1 or 2 of the present article; or

    (c) In any other way contributes to the commission of one or more offences as set forth in paragraph 1 or 2 of the present article by a group of persons acting with a common purpose; such contribution shall be intentional and either be made with the aim of furthering the general criminal activity or purpose of the group or be made in the knowledge of the intention of the group to commit the offence or offences concerned.

The convention applies to terrorist bombing only in an international context; that is, per Article 3: "This Convention shall not apply where the offence is committed within a single State, the alleged offender and the victims are nationals of that State, the alleged offender is found in the territory of that State . . ." Such an offence is strictly a matter of domestic law under national sovereignty.

Signatories not only undertake to enact and enforce laws to punish acts defined in Article 2, but to cooperate with one another in apprehending and prosecuting persons who commit such acts. Critical to the convention are provisions on extradition. Since most extradition treaties explicitly exclude automatic extradition in the case of offenses of a political nature, the convention defines terrorist bombing as a criminal activity, not a form of political protest or expression.

REFERENCE:

Rubin, Barry, ed. *The Politics of Counterterrorism: The Ordeal of Democratic States.* Washington, D.C.: Foreign Policy Institute, Paul H. Nitze School of Advanced International Studies, Johns Hopkins University, 1990.

UN Establishing Document

Overview

The nations allied against Germany and Japan during World War II referred to themselves as the "United Nations." As the war drew to its conclusion, it was the hope of Franklin Roosevelt and Winston Churchill—and, albeit to a far lesser degree, the hope even of Josef Stalin—to perpetuate after the war, if not an outright alliance, at least cooperation. Toward this end, from August to October 1944, representatives of the United States, Great Britain, the U.S.S.R., and China met at a Washington, D.C. estate called Dumbarton Oaks to sketch out plans for a new world deliberative and legislative body. As planned at Dumbarton Oaks, the wartime allies—with the addition of France—would constitute a peacekeeping ("security") council, while the other nations of the world, although fully represented, and their rights respected and protected, would play secondary roles. This would be the basic structure of the United Nations: At its core, a Security Council of the greatest powers; surrounding it, a General Assembly of all nations.

The climate of the Dumbarton Oaks Conference was far more promising than what had prevailed at the creation of the League of Nations. Nevertheless, two major issues were darkly vexing: Should United Nations action require the unanimous agreement of the Security Council members? And should the Western powers agree to the Soviet demand for separate membership for each of the sixteen "republics" that made up the U.S.S.R.? Left open at the conclusion of Dumbarton Oaks, these issues were resolved the Yalta conference in February 1945. By the **Yalta Agreement** (Section 2.9), Roosevelt, Stalin, and Churchill agreed to uphold the principle of unanimity; any permanent member of the Security Council could veto enforcement actions, but no member could veto discussion and debate. Stalin compromised on his demand for separate memberships for sixteen republics to membership for just three: Russia, Ukraine, and Byelorussia. The **United Nations Charter** was drawn up and adopted by 50 nations at a conference in San Francisco.

United Nations Charter

SIGNED: June 25, 1945, at San Francisco

IN FORCE: From October 24, 1945

SIGNATORIES: Fifty-one original member nations

OVERVIEW: The establishing document of the United Nations, the international peacemaking and peacekeeping organization established at the end of World War II to replace the ineffectual League of Nations.

DISCUSSION:

Pursuant to the **United Nations Declaration** of January 1, 1942, and subsequent meetings and discussion, two sets of conferences were held at Dumbarton Oaks, in Washington, D.C., from August 21 to September 28, 1944 and from September 29 to October 7, 1944, and produced *Proposals for the Establishment of a General International Organization*, which outlined the main structure of the United Nations. The proposals, while comprehensive, left unresolved three major issues:

- The voting procedures of the Security Council (principal peace-keeping arm of the organization)
- The membership of the organization
- The question of trusteeship over and disposition of colonial territories

The Yalta Conference (*see* **Yalta Agreement**) partially resolved the voting procedures question, giving each permanent member of the council the right to veto any military enforcement action, and resolved membership questions, agreeing, among other things, that the three Soviet states, Russia, Ukraine, and Byelorussia, would each be admitted and that China and France would be invited to membership along with the Big Three.

During April 25-June 26, 1945, the San Francisco Conference established important Security Council procedures, and established the key right of nations to defend themselves singly or in alliance in the event that the Security Council, through lack of agreement, did not act. This right, embodied in Article 51 of the United Nations Charter, became the basis for the formation of NATO (*see* **North Atlantic (NATO) Treaty** and other regional alliances.

The eloquent Preamble to the Charter, which owes much of its inspiration to the Preamble of the United States Constitution, sets forth the primary motives, goals, and mission of the organization:

WE THE PEOPLES OF THE UNITED NATIONS DETERMINED
to save succeeding generations from the scourge of war, which twice in our lifetime has brought untold sorrow to mankind, and to reaffirm faith in fundamental human rights, in the dignity and worth of the human person, in the equal rights of men and women and of nations large and small, and to establish conditions under which justice and respect for the obligations arising from treaties and other

sources of international law can be maintained, and to promote social progress and better standards of life in larger freedom,

AND FOR THESE ENDS

to practice tolerance and live together in peace with one another as good neighbors, and to unite our strength to maintain international peace and security, and to ensure by the acceptance of principles and the institution of methods, that armed force shall not be used, save in the common interest, and to employ international machinery for the promotion of the economic and social advancement of all peoples, HAVE RESOLVED TO COMBINE OUR EFFORTS TO ACCOMPLISH THESE AIMS.

Accordingly, our respective Governments, through representatives assembled in the city of San Francisco, who have exhibited their full powers found to be in good and due form, have agreed to the present Charter of the United Nations and do hereby establish an international organization to be known as the United Nations.

The politically and morally idealistic Preamble made a dramatic contrast to the tenor of the **Covenant of the League of Nations,** which was judicial and legalistic in tenor.

Article 1 of Chapter 1 of the Charter defines the purposes of the United Nations:

- To maintain international peace and security
- To develop friendly relations among nations
- To achieve international cooperation in solving international problems "of an economic, social, cultural or humanitarian character" and to promote basic human rights
- "To be a center for harmonizing the actions of nations in the attainment of . . . common ends"

Article 2 sets forth the principles of the organization, including sovereign equality for all members, a commitment on the part of members to solve disputes peacefully, and a commitment from members to assist the United Nations and not to work against it.

Membership in the United Nations was made "open to all . . . peace-loving States which accept the obligations contained in the present Charter and, in the judgement of the Organization, are able and willing to carry out these obligations" (Chapter II, Article 4). Chapter III establishes the "principal organs of the United Nations": the Security Council, the General Assembly, the Economic and Social Council, the Trusteeship Council, the International Court of Justice, and a Secretariat. The Charter also allowed for the subsequent creation of "subsidiary organs" as required.

Chapters 6 and 7 define procedures for the "pacific settlement of disputes" and action that may be taken "with respect to threats to the peace, breaches of the peace, and acts of aggression." Article 51 in Chapter 7 and all of Chapter 8 address "regional arrangements or agencies for dealing with . . . matters relating to . . . international peace." Membership in the United Nations was not to preclude membership in regional defensive alliances.

Chapter 9 of the charter outlines the U.N. role in promoting international economic and social cooperation. Chapters 11 and 12 deal with "non self-governing territories" and establish an international trusteeship system for the governance of such territories.

The core of the United Nations as a peacekeeping organization is the Security Council. Its operation was based on a dubious and naive assumption that the "Big Five" allies of World War II—the United States, the Soviet Union, Great Britain, France, and China—would remain essentially allied and could therefore reach unanimity on issues of war and peace in the postwar world. The General Assembly, in which all member nations participated, was set up as a forum for debating world issues. The grounding assumption here was a belief that free discussion of disputes among nations would promote their peaceful resolution.

Other major standing bodies and agencies included:

- The Economic and Social Council was founded in the conviction that much international conflict was rooted in poverty and want and that, therefore, international efforts to raise standards of living worldwide would promote peace worldwide.
- The Trusteeship Council was established to promote the peaceful independence of colonial states
- The International Court of Justice, carried over from the League of Nations, was established as a legally binding forum for resolving international differences peacefully.
- The Secretariat was established to administer the day-to-day workings and programs of the organization. This body would be operated by personnel who did not answer primarily to their nation of citizenship, but to the international community.

Since its founding, the United Nations has been the source of much controversy, but has endured and has never suffered the wholesale withdrawal of members that afflicted the League of Nations. Many diplomats, political leaders, and ordinary citizens measure the effectiveness of the United Nations by pointing out that, despite many local and regional conflicts since World War II, the world has not exploded into a major nuclear war.

REFERENCES:

Goodrich, Leland M., et al. *Charter of the United Nations: Commentary and Documents.* New York: Columbia University Press, 1969.

Halderman, John W. *The United Nations and the Rule of Law: Charter Development through the Handling of International Disputes and Stipulations.* Dobbs Ferry, NY: Oceana Publications, 1966.

Lauterpacht, Hersch, Sir. *Human Rights, the Charter of the United Nations, and the International Bill of Rights of Man: Preliminary Report.* Lake Success, NY: N. pub., 1948.

Rengger, N. J. Treaties and Alliances of the World, 5th ed. Essex, UK: Longman Group, 1990.

United States Senate Committee on Foreign Relations. *Review of the United Nations Charter.* Westport, CT: Greenwood Press, 1970.

U.S. as Peacemaker

Overview of Treaties in This Category

The warning George Washington issued in his Farewell Address, as he stepped down from the presidency in the last decade of the eighteenth century, dominated American foreign policy through most of the nineteenth century. The first president had enjoined his countrymen to "avoid foreign entanglements," and so the nation pursued a largely isolationist foreign policy until its 1898 intervention in the Cuban war for independence. From that point forward, despite periodic reemergent spasms of isolationist sentiment, the United States became, increasingly, a world power. This status did not always involve military or economic intervention, but was often a diplomatic role.

The United States stepped onto the stage of international diplomacy as intermediary in the bloody Russo-Japanese War. Through the efforts of Theodore Roosevelt, Russia and Japan were brought to the peace table to negotiate an end to a conflict that not only cost many lives, but—because of Japan's imperial expansionism—threatened world stability in general and America's Asian interests in particular. The belligerents met in the quiet New England town of Portsmouth, New Hampshire, and concluded the **Treaty of Portsmouth (between Japan and Russia)** in 1905. Roosevelt, often criticized for his bellicose bluster, was subsequently awarded a Nobel Peace Prize for his role in the treaty.

The next great era of American peacemaking did not come until the 1970s, as President Jimmy Carter played an instrumental role in reconciling two seemingly implacable enemies, Egypt and Israel, bringing Egyptian president Muhammad Anwar al-Sadat and Israeli prime minister Menachem Begin to the presidential retreat at Camp David, Maryland, to hammer out an enduring peace, backed by United States security guarantees. (See **Camp David Accords [between Egypt and Israel]**, 1978; **Egyptian-Israeli Peace Treaty**, 1979; **Agreement [with Israel and Egypt] Concerning the U.S. Role in Establishing the Multinational Force and Observers**, 1981; and **Agreement Concerning Air Surveillance**, 1981.)

The 1990s saw another era of American peace making. The United States served as intermediary in creating treaties and accords between Israel and the Palestine Liberation Organization (PLO): **Israel-PLO Recognition** (1993), **PLO-Israel Accord** (1993), **Agreement on Preparatory Transfer of Powers and Responsibilities** (1994), and **Israeli-Palestinian Interim Agreement on the West Bank and the Gaza Strip** (1995), and the **Wye River Memorandum** (1998). Between Israel and Jordan, the United States helped to negotiate **Israel-Jordan Common Agenda** (1993), **Washington Declaration (of Israel, Jordan, and the United States)**(1994), and the **Israel-Jordan Peace Treaty** (1994). The United States also participated in the conclusion of the **Israel-Lebanon Ceasefire Understanding** of 1996.

The dissolution of the Soviet Union and Soviet-controlled communism throughout Eastern Europe during the 1980s and 1990s ushered into the region democracy—as well as, in some cases, violent instability. Nowhere was post-communist-era warfare fiercer than in the Balkan states that had been forcibly united under communist Yugoslavia. The **Dayton Peace Accord**, negotiated among the Republic of Bosnia and Herzegovina, Republic of Croatia, and the Federal Republic of Yugoslavia in a series of meetings at Wright-Patterson Air Force Base, outside of Dayton, Ohio, ended a bitter war in Bosnia and Herzegovina. The **Kosovo Military Technical Agreement** and the **Rambouillet Accords (Interim Agreement for Peace and Self-Government in Kosovo)** were concluded in 1999, after NATO (led by the United States) militarily intervened to bring peace in a civil war between the province of Kosovo, on the one hand, and the Federal Republic of Yugoslavia and Federal Republic of Serbia, on the other.

Treaty of Portsmouth (between Japan and Russia)

SIGNED: September 5, 1905, at Portsmouth, New Hampshire
IN FORCE: From signature
SIGNATORY ENTITIES: Japan vs. Russia
OVERVIEW: President Theodore Roosevelt brokered this peace in the Russo-Japanese War (1904-1905).

DISCUSSION:
The Russo-Japanese War stunned the world in part because of the great cost to both sides in men and materiel and in part because it was the first modern war in which an Asian nation was victorious over a European empire. The principal issue of the war was a contest to gain control of Manchuria and Korea. The war commenced on February 8, 1904 with a Japanese attack and blockade of the Russian fleet at Port Arthur (present-day

Lushun, China) after Czar Nicholas II refused to withdraw Russian troops occupying Manchuria. (They had come as a result of the Boxer Uprising—see **Boxer Protocol**—and, having thereby gained a foothold in Manchuria, the Russian government did want to leave.). Although both sides suffered heavily, the war was an unmitigated disaster for Russia, which lost Port Arthur (January 1905), suffered terrible losses at the Battle of Mukden (February-March 1905), and lost most of its Baltic fleet at the Battle of Tsushima (May 27-28, 1905). The warring nations accepted an offer of mediation from President Theodore Roosevelt, who brokered the peace treaty signed at Portsmouth. Roosevelt's efforts later earned him the Nobel Peace Prize.

By the Treaty of Portsmouth, Russia acknowledged Japanese control of Korea and also transferred to Japan its lease of Port Arthur and the Liaodong (Liaotung) Peninsula. Russia also ceded to Japan the southern half of Sakhalin, consisting of Sakhalin Island and the Kuril Island chain. The treaty also outlined conditions for how the two nations would conduct commerce in Manchuria. Rail lines built by Japan and Russia in the region were barred from military use and reserved exclusively for commerce.

The Treaty of Portsmouth brought an immediate end to a most bitter war, which had demonstrated the efficacy of modern artillery and battleships and which had taught the world that an Asian nation could fight—and win—a modern war. The treaty also underscored the abject humiliation of Russia at the hands of the Japanese. The defeat dealt a severe undercutting blow to the already tottering government of Nicholas II. It helped precipitate the abortive Russian Revolution of 1905; that, in turn, a prelude to the Russian Revolution of 1917, which brought an end to the reign of the czars. As for the United States, its international prestige was greatly enhanced by the brokering of the Treaty of Portsmouth.

REFERENCES:

Esthus, Raymond A. *Double Eagle and Rising Sun: The Russians and Japanese at Portsmouth in 1905.* Durham, N.C.: Duke University Press, 1995.

Israel, Fred L. *Major Peace Treaties of Modern History, 1648-1967*, vol. 2. New York: Chelsea House and McGraw-Hill, 1967.

Nish, Ian Hill. *The Origins of the Russo-Japanese War.* New York: Addison-Wesley, 1986.

Takshaahi, Sakuyé. *International Law Applied to the Russo-Japanese War, with the Decisions of the Japanese Prize Courts.* London, Stevens, 1908.

Camp David Accords (between Egypt and Israel)

SIGNED: September 17, 1978, at Camp David, Maryland
IN FORCE: From signing
SIGNATORIES: United Arab Republic of Egypt vs. Israel; witnessed by Jimmy Carter, president of the United States

OVERVIEW: The accords, concluded under the aegis of U.S. president Jimmy Carter, are two agreements creating the "framework for peace" between Egypt and Israel, technically and sometimes actually in a state of war since 1948.

DISCUSSION:

"After four wars during 30 years," paragraph 2 of the Preamble to the Accords begins, "despite intensive human efforts, the Middle East, which is the cradle of civilization and the birthplace of three great religions, does not enjoy the blessings of peace. The people of the Middle East yearn for peace so that the vast human and natural resources of the region can be turned to the pursuits of peace and so that this area can become a model for coexistence and cooperation among nations."

Having fought four wars, Egypt and Israel had been in a continuous technical state of war since Israel's founding in 1948. Israel had occupied the Sinai Peninsula since capturing it from Egypt in the Six-Day War of 1967. The long stalemate was broken on November 19-21, 1977, when Egypt's president Anwar Sadat made an unprecedented visit to Jerusalem to address the Knesset (Israeli parliament). Within weeks, peace negotiations began. In 1978, having reached a deadlock, Sadat and Israeli prime minister Menachem Begin accepted President Jimmy Carter's invitation to a U.S.-Israeli-Egyptian summit at Camp David.

The two agreements concluded at Camp David provided (1) a broad framework for achieving peace in the Middle East, and (2) a more specific framework for a peace treaty between Egypt and Israel.

The broad framework called for Israel gradually to grant self government to the Palestinians in the Israeli-occupied West Bank and Gaza Strip and to partially withdraw its forces from those areas as prelude to negotiations on their final status. The more specific framework called for a phased withdrawal of Israeli forces from the Sinai, specifying the return of that region to Egypt within three years of the signing of a peace treaty. The right of passage for Israeli ships through the Suez Canal was also guaranteed by the specific framework.

On March 26, 1979, a peace treaty closely adhering to the Accords was signed. It formally ended the state of war, Israel agreed to the phased withdraw from the Sinai Peninsula, and normal diplomatic relations were established between the signatories. Although these provisions were all carried out, Israel (as of 1999) has not implemented Palestinian self-rule in the West Bank and Gaza areas.

REFERENCES:

Moore, John Norton. *The Arab-Israeli Conflict: The Difficult Search for Peace (1975-1988).* Princeton, NJ: Princeton University Press, 1992.

Quandt, William B. *Camp David: Peacemaking and Politics.* Washington, D.C.: Brookings Institute, 1986.

Segev, Samuel. *Crossing the Jordan: Israel's Hard Road to Peace.* New York: St. Martin's, 1998.

Egyptian-Israeli Peace Treaty

SIGNED: March 26, 1979, at Washington

SIGNATORIES: Egypt vs. Israel (in the presence of U.S. President Jimmy Carter)

IN FORCE: From April 25, 1979 (instruments of ratification exchanged at the U.S. surveillance post in the Sinai Desert)

OVERVIEW: An outgrowth of the **Camp David Accords**, this U.S.-brokered treaty ended the state of war that had existed between Egypt and Israel since the founding of Israel in 1948.

DISCUSSION:

Through the intervention of President Jimmy Carter, Egyptian president Anwar Sadat and Israeli prime minister Menachem Begin met at the presidential retreat, Camp David, Maryland, and agreed on a framework for peace and for a peace treaty (**Camp David Accords**). The treaty that resulted includes the following principal points:

- The state of war between Egypt and Israel was ended.
- Israel agreed to withdraw its armed forces and civilians from the Sinai, over which Egypt assumed sovereignty.
- Normal and friendly relations were decreed between the signatories.
- The signatories agreed to recognize and respect each other's independence and sovereignty.
- The signatories agreed to refrain from acts of violence toward one another.
- The signatories agreed to the establishment of "limited-force zones" in Egypt and Israel and to the stationing of United Nations observers in certain areas.
- The Suez Canal was opened to the free passage of Israeli ships.

In letters addressed to Egypt and Israel, the United States government pledged that, in the event of actual or threatened violation of the treaty, it would, at the request of one or both signatories, "take such ... action as it may deem appropriate and helpful to achieve compliance with the treaty." In a separate Memorandum of Understanding of March 26, 1979, between the United States and Israel, the United States pledged to "provide support it deems appropriate for proper actions taken by Israel in response to ... demonstrated violations of the treaty of peace"—especially "if a violation ... is deemed to threaten the security of Israel . . ." The Egyptian government refused to recognize the legality of this memorandum.

In connection with the treaty, the United States pledged financial assistance to Israel totaling $3 billion and to Egypt in the amount of $1.5 billion.

REFERENCES:

Moore, John Norton. *The Arab-Israeli Conflict: The Difficult Search for Peace (1975-1988)*. Princeton, NJ: Princeton University Press, 1992.

Quandt, William B. *Camp David: Peacemaking and Politics*. Washington, D.C.: Brookings Institution, 1986.

Segev, Samuel. *Crossing the Jordan: Israel's Hard Road to Peace*. New York: St. Martin's, 1998.

Agreement (with Israel and Egypt) Concerning the U.S. Role in Establishing the Multinational Force and Observers

OFFICIAL TITLE: Exchanges of Letters Constituting an Agreement Concerning the United States of America's Role in the Establishment and Maintenance of the Multinational Force and Observers

SIGNED: August 3, 1981, at Washington, D.C.

SIGNATORIES: Egypt, Israel, and the United States

IN FORCE: From signing

OVERVIEW: An agreement relating to the United States' peacekeeping role in the Middle East, pursuant to the **Camp David Accords**.

DISCUSSION:

On March 26, 1979, Israel and Egypt signed the United States-brokered **Camp David Accords,** which ended the technical—and sometimes actual—state of war that had existed between the two countries for three decades. Under terms of the agreement, Israel returned the entire Sinai Peninsula to Egypt, and, for its part, Egypt recognized Israel's right to exist. To enforce the peace, and as a confidence-building measure, a Multinational Force and Observers were established to oversee return of the Sinai. This agreement establishes the United States' role in that force.

The main provisions of the agreement are as follows:

- The United States will contribute to the Multinational Force and Observers (MFO) an infantry battalion and a logistics support unit as well as civilian observers.
- The United States will contribute one-third of the annual operating expenses of the MFO and will also contribute funds to satisfy other costs.
- The United States will use its best effort to find acceptable replacements for contingents from other nations that withdraw from the MFO.
- The United States will take "those steps necessary to ensure the maintenance of an acceptable MFO."

REFERENCES:

Moore, John Norton. *The Arab-Israeli Conflict: The Difficult Search for Peace (1975-1988)*. Princeton, NJ: Princeton University Press, 1992.

Agreement Concerning Air Surveillance

OFFICIAL TITLE: Exchange of Notes Constituting an Agreement Concerning Air Surveillance Flights Provided by the United

States of America

SIGNED: July 23 and 25, 1981, at Cairo; July 23 and 31, 1981 at Tel Aviv

SIGNATORIES: Egypt, Israel, United States

IN FORCE: From July 31, 1981

OVERVIEW: An agreement among Egypt, Israel, and the United States providing for the United States to fly surveillance missions over the Sinai following Israeli withdrawal from the region.

DISCUSSION:

On March 26, 1979, Israel and Egypt concluded the U.S.-brokered **Egyptian-Israeli Peace Treaty** formally ending the state of war that had existed between the two countries for some thirty years. The treaty, pursuant to the **Camp David Accords**, called for Israel to return the entire Sinai Peninsula to Egypt in return for Egypt's recognition of Israel's right to exist. Israel agreed to a scheduled withdrawal of the Sinai, with the United States assigned to provide aerial surveillance of the region as a confidence-building measure not only to certify Israeli compliance with the withdrawal provisions, but ensure that there would be no build-up of Egyptian forces in the region. The exchange of diplomatic notes arranging for the surveillance was made pursuant to the **Agreement Concerning United States Participation in the Multinational Force and Observers Established by Egypt and Israel** of 1981.

REFERENCES:

Moore, John Norton. *The Arab-Israeli Conflict: The Difficult Search for Peace (1975-1988)*. Princeton, NJ: Princeton University Press, 1992.

Quandt, William B. *Camp David: Peacemaking and Politics*. Washington, D.C.: Brookings Institution, 1986.

Segev, Samuel. *Crossing the Jordan: Israel's Hard Road to Peace*. New York: St. Martin's, 1998.

Israel-PLO Recognition

SIGNED: Exchange of letters, September 9, 1993

SIGNATORIES: Yasser Arafat (for the PLO) vs. Itzhak Rabin (for Israel)

IN FORCE: On exchange

OVERVIEW: A historic exchange of letters, in which the PLO and Israel acknowledged their mutual legitimacy and right to exist, that formed the basis for the **PLO-Israel Accord**, culmination of a U.S.-brokered peace process.

DISCUSSION:

The United States brokered secret negotiations between Yasir Arafat, leader of the Palestine Liberation Organization, and Prime Minister Itzhak Rabin of Israel, which led to the following exchange of letters between leaders of people who had long regarded one another as implacable enemies:

From Arafat to Rabin:

September 9, 1993

Mr. Prime Minister,

The signing of the Declaration of Principles marks a new era in the history of the Middle East. In firm conviction thereof, I would like to confirm the following PLO commitments:

The PLO recognizes the right of the State of Israel to exist in peace and security.

The PLO accepts United Nations Security Council Resolutions 242 and 338 [laying down principles for ultimate Palestinian self-government].

The PLO commits itself to the Middle East peace process, and to a peaceful resolution of the conflict between the two sides and declares that all outstanding issues relating to permanent status will be resolved through negotiations.

The PLO considers that the signing of the Declaration of Principles constitutes a historic event, inaugurating a new epoch of peaceful coexistence, free from violence and all other acts which endanger peace and stability. Accordingly, the PLO renounces the use of terrorism and other acts of violence and will assume responsibility over all PLO elements and personnel in order to assure their compliance, prevent violations and discipline violators

In view of the promise of a new era and the signing of the Declaration of Principles and based on Palestinian acceptance of Security Council Resolutions 242 and 338, the PLO affirms that those which deny Israel's right to exist, and the provisions of the Covenant which are inconsistent with the commitments of this letter are now inoperative and no longer valid. Consequently, the PLO undertakes to submit to the Palestinian National Council for formal approval the necessary changes in regard to the Palestinian Covenant.

Sincerely,

Yasser Arafat Chairman The Palestine Liberation Organization

From Rabin to Arafat:

September 9, 1993

Mr. Chairman,

In response to your letter of September 9, 1993, I wish to confirm to you that, in light of the PLO commitments included in your letter, the Government of Israel has decided to recognize the PLO as the representative of the Palestinian people and commence negotiations with the PLO within the Middle East peace process.

Yitzhak Rabin Prime Minister of Israel

REFERENCES:

Moore, John Norton. *The Arab-Israeli Conflict: The Difficult Search for Peace (1975-1988)*. Princeton, NJ: Princeton University Press, 1992.

Quandt, William B. *Camp David: Peacemaking and Politics*. Washington, D.C.: Brookings Institution, 1986.

Segev, Samuel. *Crossing the Jordan: Israel's Hard Road to Peace*. New York: St. Martin's, 1998.

PLO-Israel Accord

OFFICIAL TITLE: Declaration of Principles on Interim Self-Government Arrangements
SIGNED: September 13, 1993, at Washington, D.C.
SIGNATORIES: Israel vs. Palestine Liberation Organization
IN FORCE: From signing
OVERVIEW: A U.S.-brokered framework for peace between Israel and the PLO.

DISCUSSION:

Palestinians—and their descendants—without a homeland. In 1964, the Palestine Liberation Organization was formed to consolidate leadership of dispersed Palestinian resistance groups. Its goal was the creation of a "democratic and secular" Palestinian state. After the defeat of the Arabs in the "Six-Day War" against Israel in 1967, the PLO gained recognition among Arab interests as genuinely representative of the Palestinian cause. From this point on, despite the presence of moderate factions within the PLO, a state of chronic terrorist warfare existed between the PLO and Israel, with, apparently, no room for negotiation.

Through the intermediation of the United States, Yasir Arafat, who had led the PLO since 1969, entered into secret negotiations with Israel beginning in April 1993, with the object of, at long last, negotiating peace. An exchange of letters on September 9, 1993 (**Israel-PLO Recognition**) made possible the signing of the groundbreaking **PLO-Israel Accords**, which were signed, in the presence of President Bill Clinton, at Washington.

The accords constitute a "Declaration of Principles on Interim Self-Government Arrangements" for the Palestinians. These principles are as follows:

- Article 1: "The aim of the Israeli-Palestinian negotiations within the current Middle East peace process is, among other things, to establish a Palestinian Interim Self-Government Authority, the elected Council (the "Council"), for the Palestinian people in the West Bank and the Gaza Strip, for a transitional period not exceeding five years, leading to a permanent settlement . . ."
- Article 3: "In order that the Palestinian people in the West Bank and Gaza Strip may govern themselves according to democratic principles, direct, free and general political elections will be held for the Council under agreed supervision and international observation, while the Palestinian police will ensure public order. . . ."
- Article 4: "Jurisdiction of the Council will cover West Bank and Gaza Strip territory, except for issues that will be negotiated in the permanent status negotiations. The two sides view the West Bank and the Gaza Strip as a single territorial unit, whose integrity will be preserved during the interim period."
- Article 5:

"1. The five-year transitional period will begin upon the withdrawal from the Gaza Strip and Jericho area.
"2. Permanent status negotiations will commence as soon as possible, but not later than the beginning of the third year of the interim period, between the Government of Israel and the Palestinian people representatives.
"3. It is understood that these negotiations shall cover remaining issues, including: Jerusalem, refugees, settlements, security arrangements, borders, relations and cooperation with other neighbors, and other issues of common interest.
"4. The two parties agree that the outcome of the permanent status negotiations should not be prejudiced or preempted by agreements reached for the interim period."

- Article 6 provides for the transfer of authority in the West Bank-Gaza Strip region from Israel to the authorized Palestinians.
- Article 7 mandates the conclusion of an interim agreement governing the period of transition from Israeli to Palestinian governance of the West Bank-Gaza Strip.
- Article 8: "In order to guarantee public order and internal security for the Palestinians of the West Bank and the Gaza Strip, the Council will establish a strong police force, while Israel will continue to carry the responsibility for defending against external threats, as well as the responsibility for overall security of Israelis for the purpose of safeguarding their internal security and public order."
- Articles 9 through 12 address Israeli-Palestinian administrative cooperation and liaison.
- Article 13 stipulates the "redeployment of Israeli military forces:
  "1. After the entry into force of this Declaration of Principles, and not later than the eve of elections for the Council, a redeployment of Israeli military forces in the West Bank and the Gaza Strip will take place, in addition to withdrawal of Israeli forces carried out in accordance with Article XIV.
  "2. In redeploying its military forces, Israel will be guided by the principle that its military forces should be redeployed outside populated areas.
  "3. Further redeployments to specified locations will be gradually implemented commensurate with the assumption of responsibility for public order and internal security by the Palestinian police force pursuant to Article VIII above."
- Article 14 mandates the ultimate withdrawal of Israel from the Gaza Strip and Jericho area.

Additional articles and protocols address procedures for elections, withdrawal of Israeli troops, and economic and developmental cooperation.

By any measure, the U.S.-brokered accords were a break-through in turbulent, often seemingly hopeless Middle East politics. As of the close of the twentieth century, however, the peace process has not been completed. Dissension among the Palestinians and the election of a right-wing government is Israel in 1996 has threatened, slowed, but not halted progress toward an enduring resolution that would bring peaceful coexistence between Israelis and Palestinians.

REFERENCES:

Moore, John Norton. *The Arab-Israeli Conflict: The Difficult Search for Peace (1975-1988)*. Princeton, NJ: Princeton University Press, 1992.

Quandt, William B. *Camp David: Peacemaking and Politics*. Washington, D.C.: Brookings Institution, 1986.

Segev, Samuel. *Crossing the Jordan: Israel's Hard Road to Peace*. New York: St. Martin's, 1998.

Israel-Jordan Common Agenda

SIGNED: September 14, 1993, at Washington

SIGNATORIES: Israel vs. Jordan

IN FORCE: From signing

OVERVIEW: U.S.-brokered breakthrough in Israel-Jordan relations.

DISCUSSION:

For the first decade of Israel's existence, from 1948 until the end of the 1950s, relations between Jordan and Israel were unfriendly, but tolerable, in contrast to the outright hostility that existed between Israel and the other Arab nations. In the mid 1960s, Jordan became the staging area for terrorist raids into Israel. Israel responded with raids into the Jordanian-controlled West Bank in an effort to force that nation to put a stop to the terrorist actions. Jordan's King Hussein had been, in fact, seeking to improve relations with Israel, and even broke diplomatic ties with Syria, chief sponsor of the terrorist raids. Nevertheless, as tensions rose between Israel and Egypt and Syria during early 1967, King Hussein suddenly reversed his position and, on May 30, concluded a defense pact with Egypt and Syria. During the Arab-Israeli War of 1967, Jordan and Israel clashed, resulting in Jordan's loss of the West Bank to Israel.

Following the 1967 war, King Hussein resumed secret talks with Israel, and he did not commit Jordan to the 1973 war against Israel. Despite Hussein's inclination to come to terms with Israel, the Israeli elections of 1977 brought the right-wing Likud Party into power, and relations with Jordan deteriorated as Prime Minister Menachem Begin announced his intention of formally annexing all of the West Bank. From the end of 1977 until 1984, Jordan broke off contact with Israel. Then, by the 1980s, Hussein began to work toward the goal of creating a Jordanian-Palestinian-Israeli administration of the West Bank, which would make that territory independent of the PLO while enabling Jordan to reach a settlement with Israel. However, in 1987, the *intifada*, a Palestinian uprising on the West Bank,

prompted Hussein to renounce Jordanian claims to sovereignty of the West Bank in favor of the PLO's claims. As Israel and the PLO achieved accord (**PLO-Israel Accord**) in 1993, the time became ripe for the conclusion of an **Israel-Jordan Treaty of Peace**. The first formal step toward this was the formulation of a Common Agenda.

The document, which follows, was concluded at Washington:

Components of Israel-Jordan Peace Negotiations:

1. Searching for steps to arrive at a state of peace based on Security Council Resolutions 242 and 338 in all their aspects.

UN Security Council Resolution 242 was passed on November 22, 1967 and calls for the following:

1. Withdrawal of Israeli armed forces from territories occupied in the recent conflict;

2. Termination of all claims or states of belligerency and respect for and acknowledgment of the sovereignty, territorial integrity and political independence of every State in the area and their right to live in peace within secure and recognized boundaries free from threats or acts of force.

Resolution 338, of October 22, 1973, called for "negotiations . . . between the parties concerned under appropriate auspices aimed at establishing a just and durable peace in the Middle East."

The Common Agenda continues:

2. Security:

Refraining from actions or activities by either side that may adversely affect the security of the other or may prejudge the final outcome of negotiations.

3. Threats to security resulting from all kinds of terrorism:

Mutual commitment not to threaten each other by any use of force and not to use weapons by one side against the other including conventional and non-conventional mass destruction weapons.

4. Mutual commitment, as a matter of priority and as soon as possible, to work towards a Middle East free from weapons of mass destruction, conventional and non-conventional weapons; this goal is to be achieved in the context of a comprehensive, lasting and stable peace characterized by the renunciation of the use of force, reconciliation and openness . . . .

Mutually agreed upon security arrangements and security confidence building measures.

5. Water:

Securing the rightful water shares of the two sides.

Searching for ways to alleviate water shortage.

6. Refugees and Displaced Persons:

Achieving an agreed just solution to the bilateral aspects of the problem of refugees and displaced persons in accordance with international law.

7. Borders and Territorial Matters:

Settlement of territorial matters and agreed definitive delimitation and demarcation of the international boundary between Israel and Jordan with reference to the boundary definition under the Mandate, without prejudice to the status of any territories that came under Israeli Military Government control in 1967. Both parties will respect and comply with the above international boundary.

8. Exploring the potentials of future bilateral cooperation, within a regional context where appropriate, in the following:

Natural Resources . . .

Human Resources . . .

Infrastructure . . .

Economic areas including tourism.

. . . It is anticipated that the above endeavor will ultimately, following the attainment of mutually satisfactory solutions to the elements of this agenda, culminate in a peace treaty.

REFERENCES:

Moore, John Norton. *The Arab-Israeli Conflict: The Difficult Search for Peace (1975-1988).* Princeton, NJ: Princeton University Press, 1992.

Quandt, William B. *Camp David: Peacemaking and Politics.* Washington, D.C.: Brookings Institution, 1986.

Segev, Samuel. *Crossing the Jordan: Israel's Hard Road to Peace.* New York: St. Martin's, 1998.

Washington Declaration (of Israel, Jordan, and the United States)

SIGNED: July 25, 1994, at Washington

SIGNATORIES: Israel, Jordan, United States

IN FORCE: From signing

OVERVIEW: Product of a meeting arranged by U.S. president Bill Clinton, the document is a declaration of Israel and Jordan's desire to achieve peace.

DISCUSSION:

Encouraged by the United States, and, in particular, by the personal diplomacy of President Bill Clinton, Israeli prime minister Yitzhak Rabin and Jordan's King Hussein met in Washington in 1993 to formulate the **Israel-Jordan Common Agenda**. From this developed the Trilateral United States-Jordan-Israel Economic Committee, established by President Clinton, Jordan's Crown Prince Hassan, and Israeli foreign minister Shimon Peres at Washington on October 1, 1993. In parallel with the work of this committee, King Hussein and Prime Minister Rabin continued negotiations. In the summer of 1994, President Clinton invited the two leaders to Washington for a definitive and culminating conference. The Washington Declaration was the document that conference produced. It provided a solid foundation of principle on which the subsequent **Israel-Jordan Peace Treaty** of October 26, 1994, was

built. The text follows:

A. After generations of hostility, blood and tears and in the wake of years of pain and wars, His Majesty King Hussein and Prime Minister Yitzhak Rabin are determined to bring an end to bloodshed and sorrow. It is in this spirit that His Majesty King Hussein of the Hashemite Kingdom of Jordan and Prime Minister and Minister of Defense, Mr. Yitzhak Rabin of Israel, met in Washington today at the invitation of President William J. Clinton of the United States of America. This initiative of President William J. Clinton constitutes an historic landmark in the United States' untiring efforts in promoting peace and stability in the Middle East. The personal involvement of the President has made it possible to realise agreement on the content of this historic declaration.

The signing of this declaration bears testimony to the President's vision and devotion to the cause of peace.

B. In their meeting, His Majesty King Hussein and Prime Minister Yitzhak Rabin have jointly reaffirmed the five underlying principles of their understanding on an Agreed Common Agenda designed to reach the goal of a just, lasting and comprehensive peace between the Arab States and the Palestinians, with Israel.

C. Jordan and Israel aim at the achievement of just, lasting and comprehensive peace between Israel and its neighbours and at the conclusion of a Treaty of Peace between both countries.

D. The two countries will vigorously continue their negotiations to arrive at a state of peace, based on Security Council Resolutions 242 and 338 in all their aspects, and founded on freedom, equality and justice.

E. Israel respects the present special role of the Hashemite Kingdom of Jordan in Muslim Holy shrines in Jerusalem. When negotiations on the permanent status will take place, Israel will give high priority to the Jordanian historic role in these shrines. In addition the two sides have agreed to act together to promote interfaith relations among the three monotheistic religions.

F. The two countries recognise their right and obligation to live in peace with each other as well as with all states within secure and recognised boundaries. The two states affirmed their respect for and acknowledgment of the sovereignty, territorial integrity and political independence of every state in the area.

G. The two countries desire to develop good neighbourly relations of cooperation between them to ensure lasting security and to avoid threats and the use of force between them.

H. The long conflict between the two states is now coming to an end. In this spirit the state of belligerency between Jordan and Israel has been terminated.

I. Following this declaration and in keeping with the Agreed Common Agenda, both countries will refrain from actions or activities by either side that may adversely affect the security of the other or may prejudice the final outcome of negotiations. Neither side will threaten the other by use of force, weapons, or any other means, against each otherm and both sides will thwart threats to security resulting from all kinds of terrorism.

J. His Majesty King Hussein and Prime Minister Yitzhak Rabin took note of the progress made in the bilateral negotiations within the Jordan-Israel track last week on the steps decided to implement the sub-agendas on borders, territorial matters, security, water, energy, environment and the Jordan Rift Valley.

In this framework, mindful of items of the Agreed Common Agenda (borders and territorial matters) they noted that the boundary sub-commission has reached agreement in July 1994 in fulfillment of part of the role entrusted to it in the sub-agenda. They also noted that the sub-commission for water, environment and energy agreed to mutually recognise, as the role of their negotiations, the rightful allocations of the two sides in Jordan River and Yarmouk River waters and to fully respect and comply with the negotiated rightful allocations, in accordance with agreed acceptable principles with mutually acceptable quality. Similarly, His Majesty King Hussein and Prime Minister Yitzhak Rabin expressed their deep satisfaction and pride in the work of the trilateral commission in its meeting held in Jordan on Wednesday, July 20th 1994, hosted by the Jordanian Prime Minister, Dr. Abdessalam al-Majali, and attended by Secretary of State Warren Christopher and Foreign Minister Shimon Peres. They voiced their pleasure at the association and commitment of the United States in this endeavour.

K. His Majesty King Hussein and Prime Minister Yitzhak Rabin believe that steps must be taken both to overcome psychological barriers and to break with the legacy of war. By working with optimism towards the dividends of peace for all the people in the region, Jordan and Israel are determined to shoulder their responsibilities towards the human dimension of peace making. They recognise imbalances and disparities are a root cause of extremism which thrives on poverty and unemployment and the degradation of human dignity. In this spirit His Majesty King Hussein and Prime Minister Yitzhak Rabin have today approved a series of steps to symbolise the new era which is now at hand:

L. Direct telephone links will be opened between Jordan and Israel.

M. The electricity grids of Jordan and Israel will be linked as part of a regional concept.

N. Two new border crossings will be opened between Jordan and Israel—one at the southern tip of Aqaba-Eilat and the other at a mutually agreed point in the north.

O. In principle free access will be given to third country tourists traveling between Jordan and Israel.

P. Negotiations will be accelerated on opening an international air corridor between both countries.

Q. The police forces of Jordan and Israel will cooperate in combating crime with emphasis on smuggling and particularly drug smuggling. The United States will be invited to participate in this joint endeavour.

R. Negotiations on economic matters will continue in order to prepare for future bilateral cooperation including the abolition of all economic boycotts.

All these steps are being implemented within the framework of regional infrastructural development plans and in conjunction with the Jordan-Israel bilaterals on boundaries, security, water and related issues and without prejudice to the final outcome of the negotiations on the items included in the Agreed Common Agenda between Jordan and Israel.

S. His Majesty King Hussein and Prime Minister Yitzhak Rabin have agreed to meet periodically or whenever they feel necessary to review the progress of the negotiations and express their firm intention to shepherd and direct the process in its entirety.

T. In conclusion, His Majesty King Hussein and Prime Minister Yitzhak Rabin wish to express once again their profound thanks and appreciation to President William J. Clinton and his Administration for their untiring efforts in furthering the cause of peace, justice and prosperity for all the peoples of the region. They wish to thank the President personally for his warm welcome and hospitality. In recognition of their appreciation to the President, His Majesty King Hussein and Prime Minister Yitzhak Rabin have asked President William J. Clinton to sign this document as a witness and as a host to their meeting.

His Majesty King Hussein Prime Minister Yitzhak Rabin President William J. Clinton

REFERENCES:

Moore, John Norton. *The Arab-Israeli Conflict: The Difficult Search for Peace (1975-1988).* Princeton, NJ: Princeton University Press, 1992.

Quandt, William B. *Camp David: Peacemaking and Politics.* Washington, D.C.: Brookings Institution, 1986.

Segev, Samuel. *Crossing the Jordan: Israel's Hard Road to Peace.* New York: St. Martin's Press, 1998.

Agreement on Preparatory Transfer of Powers and Responsibilities

SIGNED: August 29, 1994, at Erez, Israel

SIGNATORIES: Israel vs. Palestine Liberation Organization

IN FORCE: From signing

OVERVIEW: An agreement pursuant to the U.S.-brokered **PLO-Israel Accord** of 1993 and preparatory to the U.S.-brokered **Israeli-Palestinian Interim Agreement on the West Bank and the Gaza Strip** of 1995.

DISCUSSION:

The transfer of authority, from Israel to the Palestinians, over the West Bank and the Gaza Strip figured as the cornerstone of an enduring peace between the PLO and Israel. This agreement was an intermediate step toward that transfer. It provides as follows:

- "Israel shall transfer and the Palestinian Authority shall assume powers and responsibilities from the Israeli military government and its Civil Administration in the West Bank in the following spheres: education and culture, health, social welfare, tourism, direct taxation and Value Added Tax on local production (hereinafter 'VAT'), as specified in this Agreement (hereinafter 'the Spheres')."

• "In accordance with the Declaration of Principles, the jurisdiction of the Palestinian Authority with regard to the powers and responsibilities transferred by this Agreement will not apply to Jerusalem, settlements, military locations and, unless otherwise provided in this Agreement, Israelis."

Additionally, the agreement specifies the nature and scope of the authority of the "Palestinian Authority," relations between Israeli authorities and the Palestinian Authority, the procedure for the transfer of power, and procedures for administering civil laws and maintaining public safety and order. Budgetary issues are also addressed. Finally, Article XII stipulates that "With regard to each of the Spheres, Israel and the Palestinian Authority will ensure that their respective systems contribute to the peace between the Israeli and Palestinian peoples and to peace in the entire region, and will refrain from the introduction of any motifs that could adversely affect the process of reconciliation."

Subjoined to the agreement are annexes addressing the following issues:

• Schedule 1 -Six-month Budget for the Spheres
• Annex I -Protocol Concerning Preparatory Transfer of Powers and Responsibilities in the Sphere of Education and Culture
• Annex II -Protocol Concerning Preparatory Transfer of Powers and Responsibilities in the Sphere of Health
• Annex III -Protocol Concerning Preparatory Transfer of Powers and Responsibilities in the Sphere of Social Welfare
• Annex IV -Protocol Concerning Preparatory Transfer of Powers and Responsibilities in the Sphere of Tourism
• Annex V -Protocol Concerning Preparatory Transfer of Powers and Responsibilities in the Sphere of Direct Taxation
• Annex VI -Protocol Concerning Preparatory Transfer of Powers and Responsibilities in the Sphere of VAT on Local Production

REFERENCES:
Moore, John Norton. *The Arab-Israeli Conflict: The Difficult Search for Peace (1975-1988)*. Princeton, NJ: Princeton University Press, 1992.
Quandt, William B. *Camp David: Peacemaking and Politics*. Washington, D.C.: Brookings Institution, 1986.
Segev, Samuel. *Crossing the Jordan: Israel's Hard Road to Peace*. New York: St. Martin's, 1998.

Israel-Jordan Peace Treaty

SIGNED: October 26, 1994, at the Arava/Araba Crossing Point on the Israel-Jordan border
SIGNATORIES: Israel vs. Jordan; United States as witness
IN FORCE: From November 27, 1994
OVERVIEW: Groundbreaking, U.S.-brokered treaty between Israel and a key Arab state.

DISCUSSION:
With the encouragement and personal diplomacy of President Bill Clinton, Israel's Prime Minister Yitzhak Rabin and Jordan's King Hussein held talks over a two-year period in Washington, D.C., finally issuing the **Israel-Jordan Common Agenda** of 1993 and, after another meeting in Washington, the **Washington Declaration** of 1994, which set out the principles on which a definitive peace treaty would be written.

Following directly from the Washington Declaration, the treaty included provisions addressing:

• Establishment of full diplomatic relations
• Agreement on the international boundary, with minor modifications
• Agreement to an immediate end to belligerency
• Agreement to cooperate in the prevention of terrorism
• Agreement on allocations of water and the development of new water resources
• Agreement on freedom of access to religious sites
• Recognition of the special role of the Hashemite Kingdom over Muslim holy shrines in Jerusalem
• Agreement to permit full freedom of passage by land, sea, and air
• Agreement to cooperate in such areas as the economy, transportation, telecommunications, tourism, environment, energy, health, agriculture, and the war against crime and drugs
• Commitment to resolve the problem of refugees and displaced persons through agreed-upon negotiating frameworks

Five annexes subjoined to the treaty specify details concerning the international boundary between Israel and Jordan, water policy, crime and drug policy, environmental policy, and interim measures to be taken on an immediate basis pending the conclusion of various definitive agreements pursuant to the treaty.

REFERENCES:
Moore, John Norton. *The Arab-Israeli Conflict: The Difficult Search for Peace (1975-1988)*. Princeton, NJ: Princeton University Press, 1992.
Quandt, William B. *Camp David: Peacemaking and Politics*. Washington, D.C.: Brookings Institution, 1986.
Segev, Samuel. *Crossing the Jordan: Israel's Hard Road to Peace*. New York: St. Martin's, 1998.

Dayton Peace Accords

SIGNED: November 21, 1995, at Wright-Patterson air Force Base, Dayton, Ohio
SIGNATORIES: Republic of Bosnia and Herzegovina, Republic of Croatia, Federal Republic of Yugoslavia
IN FORCE: From signing
OVERVIEW: A United States-brokered peace for the war-torn republics of the former Yugoslavia.

DISCUSSION:

During 1989-90, in the general collapse of Communism throughout eastern Europe, Bosnia and Herzegovina, formerly a part of Yugoslavia, was caught up in a tide of nationalism that swept the region. After Croatia quit the Yugoslav federation in 1991, Bosnian Croats and Muslims approved referenda calling for an independent, multinational republic. The Bosnian Serbs, however, refused to secede from Yugoslavia, which was now dominated by Serbia. The result of this refusal was a civil war, which erupted in 1992 and tore apart Bosnia and Herzegovina. Serbs managed to take much of the north and east, "ethnically cleansing" these regions of non-Serbian populations, while the Croats seized the west, and Muslims managed to hold onto cities in the central and and northwestern regions.

The United States played a major role in brokering a peace by the end of 1995, producing a set of accords that were the product of conferences held at Wright-Patterson Air Force Base, outside of Dayton, Ohio. The major provision of the Dayton Accord was the creation of a federalized Bosnia and Herzegovina, which was divided between a Bosnian-Muslim-Bosnian-Croat federation, and a Bosnian-Serb republic.

In greater detail, the key provisions are as follows:

- Bosnia would be preserved as a single state within its present borders, but would consist of two parts: the Bosnian-Croat Federation and the Bosnian Serb Republic.
- The capital city of Sarajevo would remain united as the seat of a central government, to include a national parliament, the presidency, and a constitutional court with responsibility for foreign policy, foreign trade, monetary policy, citizenship, immigration and other important functions.
- The president and parliament would be chosen through free, democratic elections held under international supervision.
- Refugees would be allowed to return to their homes.
- People would be permitted to move freely throughout Bosnia, and the human rights "of every Bosnian citizen" would be monitored by an independent commission and an internationally trained civilian police force.
- Individuals found guilty of war crimes would be excluded from political life.
- A "strong international force" would be constituted to supervise the separation of forces and to give them confidence that each side would live up to the agreements made.

REFERENCES:

Bildt, Carl. *Peace Journey: The Struggle for Peace in Bosnia.* New York: Orion, 1999.

Burg, Steven L., and Paul S. Shoup. *The War in Bosnia-Herzegovina: Ethnic Conflict and International Intervention.* Armonk, NY: M. E. Sharpe, 1999.

Holbrooke, Richard. *To End a War.* New York: Modern Library, 1999.

Israeli-Palestinian Interim Agreement on the West Bank and the Gaza Strip

SIGNED: September 28, 1995, at Washington

SIGNATORIES: Israel vs. Palestine Liberation Organization; with Egypt, European Union, Jordan, Norway, and United States signing as witnesses

IN FORCE: From signing

OVERVIEW: Pursuant to the U.S.-brokered peace process, an agreement governing the transfer of control of the West Bank and Gaza Strip from Israel to the Palestinians.

DISCUSSION:

The culmination of a long peace process, the final stages of which were brokered by the United States, the agreement transfers control of the West Bank and the Gaza Strip from Israel to a "Palestinian Authority" also known as the Council. The objective of the agreement is to bring peace between Israel and the PLO (and other Middle Eastern factions and interests) by "restoring" to the Palestinians a significant portion of the homeland given to Israel when the state of Israel was created in 1948.

The agreement lays down provisions relating to the following:

- The constitution of the Council
- Elections
- Establishment of open government for the Palestinians
- Judicial review authority for Palestinian courts
- Powers and responsibilities of the Council
- Redeployment of Israeli military forces (essentially, the staged withdrawal of forces from the West Bank and Gaza Strip)
- Definition of the territory to be transferred
- Provisions for public security and order
- Constitution of the Palestinian police
- Prevention of terrorism
- Provision of confidence-building measures
- Human rights provisions, obligations, and guarantees
- Definition of relations between Israel and the Council
- Definition of economic relations between Israel and the Palestinians
- Agreement to create cooperative programs
- Establishment of a Joint Israeli-Palestinian Liaison Committee
- Provisions relating to Liaison and Cooperation with Jordan and Egypt
- An agreement to cooperate in the location of missing persons

REFERENCES:

Moore, John Norton. *The Arab-Israeli Conflict: The Difficult Search for Peace (1975-1988).* Princeton, NJ: Princeton University Press, 1992.

Quandt, William B. *Camp David: Peacemaking and Politics.* Washington, D.C.: Brookings Institution, 1986.

Segev, Samuel. *Crossing the Jordan: Israel's Hard Road to Peace.* New York: St. Martin's, 1998.

Israel-Lebanon Ceasefire Understanding

SIGNED: April 26, 1996, at Washington

SIGNATORIES: United States: an "understanding" based on talks with Israel and Lebanon and in consultation with Syria

IN FORCE: From April 27, 1996

OVERVIEW: A ceasefire following Israeli military action ("Operation Grapes of Wrath") in Lebanon.

DISCUSSION:

During the 1970s, the government of Lebanon largely disintegrated, and the nation became a haven for Syrian-backed terrorist activity directed primarily against Israel. On July 17, 1981, Israeli forces bombed PLO headquarters in West Beirut, killing, in the process, some 300 civilians. This prompted the United States to arrange a cease-fire between the Israelis and the PLO. Despite this, on June 6, 1982, some 60,000 Israeli troops invaded Lebanon. The stated goal of this action was to stop PLO raids into Israeli territory, but it was also clear that the Israelis intended to to destroy the PLO in their power base and to establish a Lebanese government that would conclude a peace treaty with Israel along the lines of the **Egyptian-Israeli Peace Treaty** of 1979. Indeed, on May 17, 1983, Israel and Lebanon did conclude a peace treaty, which called for the withdrawal of Israeli forces, the creation of a special security zone in the south, and the establishment of bilateral relations. This official rapprochement with Lebanon, however, incited various Lebanese factions to attack Israel. As the Israeli withdrawal proceeded, the attacks turned against the international peacekeeping force in Lebanon. When that force left Beirut in February 1984, Syria and Lebanese Muslims and leftists compelled the Lebanese government to abrogate the 1983 Lebanon-Israel treaty.

It was not until the United States-backed Washington talks, between Israel and certain of its Arab neighbors, of 1993-1994 that Israel and Lebanon resumed negotiations. However, despite the success of these talks in the case of Jordan (see **Washington Declaration [of Israel, Jordan, and the United States]**), negotiations between Lebanon and Israel broke down in February 1994.

In the absence of negotiations, tensions between Israel and Lebanon mounted. Israel asserted that, while it made no claims to Lebanese land or resources, it was determined to ensure the security of its northern border. Accordingly, Israel proposed the following principles for a permanent settlement of the Israeli-Lebanese crisis:

- Deployment of the Lebanese Army north of a security zone and, for a period of six months, to prevent any terror activities against the security zone and Israel
- Conclusion of a peace agreement with Lebanon three months after the deployment begins.

- Israeli forces to remain deployed on the Lebanese front until Israel is convinced that the military organs of all terrorist groups currently operating out of Lebanon will be irreversibly disbanded
- Guarantees that no harm will be inflicted upon Lebanese citizens and Southern Lebanese Army personnel currently residing in the security zone and that they will be absorbed in the governmental and societal fabric of Lebanon

With these principles on the table, Lebanon continued to serve as a staging area for anti-Israeli terrorism. In April 1996, after months of operations by Iranian-backed Hizbullah terrorists based in Lebanon, Israel launched a military incursion into Lebanon labeled Operation Grapes of Wrath. Through the intervention of the United States, this incursion was ended by means of the Israel-Lebanon Ceasefire Understanding, the text of which follows:

The United States understands that after discussions with the governments of Israel and Lebanon, and in consultation with Syria, Lebanon and Israel will ensure the following:

Armed groups in Lebanon will not carry out attacks by Katyusha rockets or by any kind of weapon into Israel.

Israel and those cooperating with it will not fire any kind of weapon at civilians or civilian targets in Lebanon.

Beyond this, the two parties commit to ensuring that under no circumstances will civilians be the target of attack and that civilian populated areas and industrial and electrical installations will not be used as launching grounds for attacks.

Without violating this understanding, nothing herein shall preclude any party from exercising the right of self-defense.

A Monitoring Group is established consisting of the United States, France, Syria, Lebanon and Israel. Its task will be to monitor the application of the understanding stated above. Complaints will be submitted to the Monitoring Group.

In the event of a claimed violation of the understanding, the party submitting the complaint will do so within 24 hours. Procedures for dealing with the complaints will be set by the Monitoring Group.

The United States will also organize a Consultative Group, to consist of France, the European Union, Russia and other interested parties, for the purpose of assisting in the reconstruction needs of Lebanon.

It is recognized that the understanding to bring the current crisis between Lebanon and Israel to an end cannot substitute for a permanent solution. The United States understands the importance of achieving a comprehensive peace in the region.

Toward this end, the United States proposes the resumption of negotiations between Syria and Israel and between Lebanon and Israel at a time to be agreed upon, with the objective of reaching comprehensive peace.

The United states understands that it is desirable that these negotiations be conducted in a climate of stability and tranquility.

This understanding will be announced simultaneously at 1800 hours, April 26, 1996, in all countries concerned.

The time set for implementation is 0400 hours, April 27, 1996.

REFERENCES:

Moore, John Norton. *The Arab-Israeli Conflict: The Difficult Search for Peace (1975-1988)*. Princeton, NJ: Princeton University Press, 1992.

Quandt, William B. *Camp David: Peacemaking and Politics*. Washington, D.C.: Brookings Institution, 1986.

Segev, Samuel. *Crossing the Jordan: Israel's Hard Road to Peace*. New York: St. Martin's, 1998.

Joint Statement of the U.S.-Israeli Interparliamentary Commission on National Security

ISSUED: September 17, 1998, at Washington

SIGNATORIES: Israel and United States

IN FORCE: From issuance

OVERVIEW: Creates the U.S.-Israeli Interparliamentary Commission on National Security, the first joint institution ever of the U.S. Congress and Israeli Knesset (parliament).

DISCUSSION:

The main purpose of this joint statement was to announce the creation of the Interparliamentary Commission on National Security, a permanently constituted body charged with consulting on strategic issues of common interest to both nations. On the date of issuance of the joint statement, the Interparliamentary Commission also published the following "findings":

- With the Cold War's end, longstanding expectations—"rules of the road"—regarding international affairs have been overtaken by the rise of aggressive regional powers hostile to the West and active in pursuit of nonconventional weapons and missiles to deliver them. This requires countries like the United States and Israel to reconsider venerable assumptions regarding strategy, diplomacy and international law, There is a need for updated rules of the road and the political will on the part of governments of responsible powers to enforce such rules. The flouting of international norms by states such as Iran, Iraq, Syria and North Korea represents a dangerous challenge to world order.

- In particular, the missile threat from hostile states is grave, immediate and growing more serious over time. It is in the interests of both countries to deploy effective defenses against this threat.

- These states already have missiles and among them chemical, biological and nuclear weapons programs that threaten U.S. forces in the Middle East (and elsewhere) and U.S. allies and friends, including Israel, Turkey, Jordan, South Korea and Japan.

- Hostile states are investing in programs to improve the range, accuracy, reliability and penetrability of their missiles and to develop additional weapons of mass destruction including nuclear weapons. The time lines for such programs are short and within a few years such states will enhance substantially their capabilities

in this field. Our intelligence agencies may not be able to ensure enough warning time of threatening developments regarding missiles and non-conventional weapons to allow our policy makers, in a timely fashion, to deploy necessary defenses.

- To deal properly with these threats, a range of measures is necessary, including (i) military capability to deter and to punish aggression, (ii) sensible international cooperation to restrict the flow of technology and goods that might contribute to the development in hostile countries of missiles and weapons of mass destruction and (iii) systems that can be relied upon to intercept ballistic missiles.

- There are affordable technologies and programs under development to defend against theater ballistic missiles. The threat from such missiles, however, is developing more rapidly than are the programs to build missile defenses.

- The gap between the maturity of theater missile threats and the maturity of defense systems subjects our countries to serious risk. It is in the interests of the United States and Israel to narrow that gap as completely and as quickly as possible. Arrow is helping to narrow the gap, but unless higher priority and greater urgency attach to our missile defense efforts generally, the gap is more likely to widen than close.

- Accelerating the development and deployment of theater missile defense programs of either country serves the common interest in peace, security, deterrence and defense.

- U.S.-Israeli cooperation in all aspects of missile defense has borne fruit. The jointly-funded and -developed Arrow missile defense system is scheduled for deployment in 1999. The most recent test of the Arrow, conducted earlier this week, was a success. Continued U.S. support for Arrow is of great importance to both countries. A relatively small investment has been made by the two countries in a joint project ("IBIS") on boost-phase interception of ballistic missiles. Another relatively small investment has been made in a joint project ("THEL") to use lasers to defend against rockets. Important work has been done by the United States and Israel to ensure interoperability of U.S. missile defense systems, including for early warning, and Israeli systems.

- The United States and Israel have a strong common interest in additional and expanded cooperation between them in the missile defense field. Both countries have something to gain from sharing technology, operational concepts and the fruits of actual experience in confronting missile threats and attacks.

- The key to effective protection against missiles is multiple layers of defense that permit a defender, if necessary, to get multiple shots at intercepting a given missile. Accordingly, it would be valuable for our two countries to intensify efforts—jointly or separately—to develop the capability to intercept missiles in the boost (or ascent) phase. Boost-phase interception ("BPI") is advantageous for it targets missiles at the beginning of the trajectory, before they can deploy any multiple warheads, Early interception of a missile could cause debris to fall on the attacker, not the defender, thereby contributing to the deterrence and punishment of aggression. Deployment of an effective BPI system would free other defense systems—those designed to intercept missiles in mid-course or in the descent phase (e.g., the Israeli Arrow—to target only those warheads that managed to get through the BPI layer of defense.

- The threat posed by missiles and weapons of mass destruction in the hands of rogue states is a danger not only to Israel and the United States. It is in the interest of all responsible states to cooperate in countering and defending against this threat. Israel and the United States should work to enlist from other countries, such as Turkey and Jordan, appropriate types of cooperation in the field of missile defense.

REFERENCES:

Moore, John Norton. *The Arab-Israeli Conflict: The Difficult Search for Peace (1975-1988)*. Princeton, NJ: Princeton University Press, 1992.

Quandt, William B. *Camp David: Peacemaking and Politics*. Washington, D.C.: Brookings Institution, 1986.

Segev, Samuel. *Crossing the Jordan: Israel's Hard Road to Peace*. New York: St. Martin's, 1998.

U.S.-Israel Security Memorandum of Agreement

SIGNED: October 31, 1998, at Jerusalem and Washington, D.C.

SIGNATORIES: Israel vs. United States

IN FORCE: From signing

OVERVIEW: An agreement in principle to collaborate on enhancing Israel's defensive and deterrent capabilities and on upgrading the framework of the U.S.-Israeli strategic, military, and technological relationships.

DISCUSSION:

The text of the brief memorandum follows:

In view of the long-standing security relationship between the United States and Israel and the long-term commitment by the United States to the maintenance of Israel's qualitative edge, and considering the developing regional threats emanating from the acquisition of ballistic missile capabilities and the proliferation of weapons of mass destruction, the governments of the United States and Israel have decided to work jointly consistent with their long-standing policies towards the attainment of the following objectives:

- Enhancing Israel's defensive and deterrent capabilities.

- Upgrading the framework of the U.S.-Israeli strategic and military relationships, as well as the technological cooperation between them.

The two governments will forthwith designate representatives to a joint strategic planning committee which will formulate specific recommendations on steps that can be implemented as quickly as possible to advance the foregoing objectives.

The United States Government would view with particular gravity direct threats to Israel's security arising from the regional deployment of ballistic missiles of intermediate range or greater. In the event of such a threat, the United States Government would consult promptly with the Government of Israel with respect to what support, diplomatic or otherwise, or assistance, it can lend to Israel.

REFERENCES:

Moore, John Norton. *The Arab-Israeli Conflict: The Difficult Search for Peace (1975-1988)*. Princeton, NJ: Princeton University Press, 1992.

Quandt, William B. *Camp David: Peacemaking and Politics*. Washington, D.C.: Brookings Institution, 1986.

Segev, Samuel. *Crossing the Jordan: Israel's Hard Road to Peace*. New York: St. Martin's, 1998.

Wye River Memorandum

SIGNED: October 28, 1998, at Washington, D.C.

SIGNATORIES: Israel vs. PLO; witnessed by President Bill Clinton, United States

IN FORCE: From signing

OVERVIEW: "Steps to facilitate implementation of the **Interim Agreement on the West Bank and Gaza Strip** of September 28, 1995 . . . and other related agreements."

DISCUSSION:

In October 1998, U.S. president Bill Clinton hosted a summit of Israeli and Palestinian leaders at Wye River, Maryland. The objective was to formulate precise steps for the implementation of the transfer of authority over the West Bank and Gaza Strip from Israel to the Palestinians, as specified in the **Interim Agreement on the West Bank and Gaza Strip** of September 28, 1995.

The summit produced a detailed memorandum, the main provisions of which follow:

- Israel will transfer to the Palestinian side certain specified percentages of the West Bank and Gaza Strip in exchange for various security guarantees.

- The Palestinian side agrees to make known a policy of zero tolerance for terror and violence against both sides.

- A security work plan will be developed by the Palestinians and shared with the United States.

- In addition to bilateral Israeli-Palestinian security cooperation, a U.S.-Palestinian committee will meet weekly to review the steps being taken to eliminate terrorism.

- The Palestinian side will apprehend specific individuals suspected of perpetrating acts of violence and terror for the purpose of further investigation, prosecution and punishment.

- The Palestinian side will establish and implement a program for the collection and appropriate handling of illegal firearms.

- The two sides agree that their security cooperation will be based on a spirit of partnership and will include:

Bilateral cooperation

An exchange of forensic expertise, training and other assistance

The establishment of a high-ranking U.S.-Palestinian-Israeli committee, which will meet frequently to assess current threats and deal with any impediments to security cooperation

- The Palestinian side will issue a decree prohibiting all forms of incitement to violence and terror, and will establish mechanisms for acting systematically against all expressions or threats of violence or terror.

- A U.S.-Palestinian-Israeli committee will monitor cases of possible incitement to violence or terror and make recommendations and reports on how to prevent such incitement.

- The Palestinian side will provide a list of its policemen to the Israeli side in conformity with the prior agreements.

- The executive committee of the PLO and the Palestinian Central Council will reaffirm the nullification of the Palestinian National Charter provisions that call for the destruction of Israel.

- Both the Israeli and Palestinian sides will launch a strategic economic dialogue to enhance their economic relationship.

- The Israeli and Palestinian sides have agreed on arrangements to permit the timely opening of the Gaza Industrial Estate, a cooperative project.

- The Israeli and Palestinian sides have also concluded a protocol on the operation of the international airport in the Gaza Strip during the interim period.

- Both sides will renew negotiations on "safe passage" of people and goods.

- Recognizing the importance of the port of Gaza, both sides commit themselves to proceeding without delay to conclude an agreement to allow the construction and operation of the port in accordance with the prior agreements.

- The two sides will immediately resume permanent status negotiation on an accelerated basis and will make a determined effort to reach agreement by May 4, 1999.

- Neither side shall initiate or take any step that will change the status of the West Bank and the Gaza Strip in accordance with the Interim Agreement.

REFERENCES:

Moore, John Norton. *The Arab-Israeli Conflict: The Difficult Search for Peace (1975-1988)*. Princeton, NJ: Princeton University Press, 1992.
Quandt, William B. *Camp David: Peacemaking and Politics*. Washington, D.C.: Brookings Institution, 1986.
Segev, Samuel. *Crossing the Jordan: Israel's Hard Road to Peace.* New York: St. Martin's, 1998.

Kosovo Military Technical Agreement

OFFICIAL TITLE: Military Technical Agreement between the International Security Force (KFOR) and the Governments of Federal Republic of Yugoslavia and the Republic of Serbia.
SIGNED: June 9, 1999, at Belgrade, Federal Republic of Yugoslavia
SIGNATORIES: International Security Force (KFOR) [which included United States forces] vs. Federal Republic of Yugoslavia and Republic of Serbia

IN FORCE: From signing
OVERVIEW: The cease-fire that ended the NATO bombing of Yugoslavia and brought about the withdrawal of Serb forces from Kosovo

DISCUSSION:
For a discussion of the background the Kosovo conflict, see **Rambouillet Accords (Interim Agreement for Peace and Self-Government in Kosovo)**.

As set out in Article 1, the purposes of the agreement are as follows:

a. To establish a durable cessation of hostilities, under no circumstances shall any forces of the FRY [Federal Republic of Yuogslavia] and the Republic of Serbia enter into, re-enter, or remain within the territory of Kosovo or the Ground Safety Zone (GSZ) and the Air Safety Zone (ASZ) described in paragraph 3, Article I without the prior express consent of the international security force (KFOR) commander. Local police will be allowed to remain in the GSZ....

b. To provide for the support and authorization of the international security force (KFOR) and in particular to authorize the international security force (KFOR) to take such actions as are required, including the use of necessary force, to ensure compliance with this agreement and protection of the international security force (KFOR), and to contribute to a secure environment for the international civil implementation presence, and other international organizations, agencies, and nongovernmental organizations....

The body of the agreement sets out a detailed schedule and procedures for the phased withdrawal of Serbian forces from Kosovo and the ground and air zones defined by the agreement.

REFERENCES:
Bildt, Carl. *Peace Journey: The Struggle for Peace in Bosnia*. New York: Orion, 1999.
Burg, Steven L., and Paul S. Shoup. *The War in Bosnia-Herzegovina: Ethnic Conflict and International Intervention*. Armonk, NY: M. E. Sharpe, 1999.
Holbrooke, Richard. *To End a War.* New York: Modern Library, 1999.
Malcolm, Noel. *Kosovo: A Short History.* New York: New York University Press, 1998.

Rambouillet Accords (Interim Agreement for Peace and Self-Government in Kosovo)

SIGNED: Opened for signature February 23, 1999, at Rambouillet, France
SIGNATORIES: Kosovo Liberation Army; witness signatures by European Union, Russian Federation, United States. Awaiting signature by Federal Republic of Yugoslavia and Federal Republic of Serbia to enter into force
IN FORCE: Not in force
OVERVIEW: A three-year interim agreement to end conflict

between Yugoslavia and Serbia, on the one hand, and Kosovo, on the other, as a transition to permanent peace.

DISCUSSION:

Historically, the Balkans have been torn by ethnic and nationalist violence. As a result of the **Treaty of Versailles**, ending World War I, the Kingdom of the Serbs, Croats, and Slovenes was formed from what had part of the fallen Austro-Hungarian Empire and two independent states, Serbia and Montenegro. In 1929, the name of this collection of states was changed to Yugoslavia, and, following World War II, the monarchy become a communist republic under the leadership of a strongman prime minister, Josep Broz Tito. As constituted after the war, Yugoslavia consisted of six republics, Serbia, Croatia, Bosnia and Herzegovina, Macedonia, Slovenia, and Montenegro. In addition, two provinces were attached to Yugoslavia, Kosovo and Vojvodina.

Tito almost singlehandedly kept Yugoslavia's jarring ethnic factions together during his long tenure as prime minister. With his death in 1980, however, the nation, cobbled together to begin with, began to fall apart. Slovenia and Croatia each declared independence, followed by Macedonia and then Bosnia and Herzegovina. Bosnia erupted into a war that spanned 1992 to 1995 (see **Dayton Peace Accord**), when an uneasy peace was achieved by dividing the small country into three ethnically homogenous, self-governed areas. In the meantime, Serbia and Montenegro joined to form the Federal Republic of Yugoslavia, under the leadership of Slobodan Milosevic.

Less than a year after peace had been established in Bosnia, violent civil unrest began in the southern Yugoslavian province of Kosovo as the Kosovo Liberation Army (KLA) launched guerrilla attacks on Serbian police forces. Early in 1998, Milosevic dispatched troops to Kosovo to crush its bid for independence, and full-scale civil war was under way. NATO and the United Nations repeatedly attempted to broker a peace, but peace talks in Rambouillet, France, dissolved in March 1999, with only the KLA finally accepting the settlement. At last, on March 24, NATO, spearheaded by the United States, launched air strikes on Serbian Yugoslavia. On June 10, 1999, the Milosevic government agreed to a military withdrawal from Kosovo and signed the **Kosovo Military Technical Agreement**, effectively a full withdrawal and cease-fire, albeit a document without the political dimensions of Rambouillet.

The future of the Rambouillet Accords is certainly in doubt. As they presently stand, they are a proposed three-year interim agreement, largely dictated by the United States and NATO, intended to provide democratic self-government, peace, and security for everyone, of all ethnicity, living in Kosovo.

Principal provisions address the following:

- Democratic self-government: to encompass all matters of daily importance to people in Kosovo, including education, health care, and economic development; the agreement provides for a president, an assembly, courts, strong local government, and national community institutions for Kosovo

- Security: to be guaranteed by international troops deployed on the ground throughout Kosovo; local police, representative of all national communities in Kosovo, to provide routine law enforcement; Federal and Republic security forces to leave Kosovo, except for a limited border protection presence

- Mechanism for final settlement: An international meeting to be convened after three years to determine a mechanism for a final settlement for Kosovo, in large part according to the will of the people

REFERENCES:

Bildt, Carl. *Peace Journey: The Struggle for Peace in Bosnia.* New York: Orion, 1999.

Burg, Steven L., and Paul S. Shoup. *The War in Bosnia-Herzegovina: Ethnic Conflict and International Intervention.* Armonk, NY: M. E. Sharpe, 1999.

Holbrooke, Richard. *To End a War.* New York: Modern Library, 1999.

Malcolm, Noel. *Kosovo: A Short History.* New York: New York University Press, 1998.

Trade, Commerce, and Transportation

Aviation and Space Exploration

Overview of Treaties in This Category

Throughout the twentieth century, advances in science and technology necessitated the conclusion of international agreements governing activities enabled by such advances. By their nature, aviation and, later, space exploration, involve transnational issues, which are best resolved through international agreements.

Among the earliest conventions relating to commercial aviation is the **Warsaw Convention**, which aimed to standardize specifications for passenger tickets, specifications for luggage tickets, and specifications for air consignment notes relating to international carriage of persons and goods by air. Of particular importance to the development of international aviation were rules and limits relating to liability for loss of life and property as a result of mishap in international air travel. The Warsaw Convention was amended in 1955 by the **Hague Protocol to the Warsaw Convention**, which increased liability limits, and has been modified by other important commercial aviation conventions (including **Guatemala City Protocol of 1971** and **Montreal Protocol Number 4** of 1975).

Whereas the Warsaw Convention and subsequent documents address the rights of air passengers, the **International Air Transport Agreement** (1944) and the **Convention on International Civil Aviation** (1944) concern the rights and privileges of air carriers and the home nations of air carriers. The most basic privilege guaranteed is that of flying across the territory of each signatory without landing.

Other issues relating to international commercial aviation include "sanitary" (health) measures to prevent the international spread of disease (**International Sanitary Convention for Aerial Navigation**, 1933 and **International Sanitary Convention for Aerial Navigation**, 1944); international law governing aircraft ownership issues (**Convention on the International Recognition of Rights in Aircraft**, 1948); and agreements establishing facilities to aid international aerial navigation (**Agreement on North Atlantic Stations**, 1954 and **Agreement on Air Navigation Services in Greenland and Faroe Islands**, 1956). The **Tokyo Convention** of 1963 defines international law as it applies to offenses against penal law and other acts that jeopardize safety on board aircraft in international flight. (See also Section 3.9, which includes conventions specifically relating to "skyjacking.")

Agreements establishing facilities to track space vehicles and communicate with them are among the first international agreements relating to space exploration. See, for example, **Agreement (with the United Kingdom) Concerning the Establishment in Canton Island of a Space Vehicle Tracking and Communications Station**, 1961). The launching and operation of communication satellites was also an early subject of international agreement (**Agreement on Cooperation in Intercontinental Testing in Connection with Experimental Communications Satellites**, 1961) and has been the subject of many subsequent agreements. In 1967, the landmark **Outer Space Treaty** barred the use of outer space and celestial bodies for military purposes. The demilitarization of outer space was amplified and expanded by later agreements, including, most importantly, **Agreement Governing the Activities of States on the Moon and Other Celestial Bodies** of 1979.

In 1968, a large number of nations undertook to provide for the "safe and prompt return" of astronauts and space objects in the event of unplanned landing (**Agreement on the Rescue of Astronauts, the Return of Astronauts and the Return of Objects Launched into Outer Space**) and, in 1972, many of these signatories concluded **Convention on International Liability for Damage Caused by Space Objects** and, two years later, further agreed to register any object launched into space (**Convention on Registration of Objects Launched into Outer Space**).

This section includes two additional types of international space- and aviation-related treaties.

The **Treaty on Open Skies**, opened for signature in 1992, but not yet entered into force, is a comprehensive agreement providing for aerial surveillance of all signatory nations to ensure compliance with various arms control and disarmament agreements.

A second type of agreement has assumed great commercial importance in recent years. With the end of the Cold War and the consequent improvement of relations among former East-West adversaries, nations such as China, Russia, and the Ukraine have sought to turn their space vehicle launching facilities and expertise from military to commercial purposes. This section contains a number of "commercial launch service" trade agreements concluded between the United States and other nations.

Warsaw Convention

OFFICIAL TITLE: Convention for the Unification of Certain Rules Relating to International Carriage by Air

SIGNED: October 12, 1929, at Warsaw, Poland

SIGNATORIES: Afghanistan, Algeria, Argentina, Australia, Austria, Bahamas, Bangladesh, Barbados, Belarus, Belgium, Benin, Botswana, Brazil, Brunei, Bulgaria, Burkina Faso, Burma, Cameroon. Canada, Chile, China, Colombia, Congo, Costa Rica, Côte d'Ivoire, Cuba, Cyprus, Czechoslovakia, Denmark (not including Greenland), Dominican Republic, Ecuador, Egypt, Ethiopia, Fiji, Finland, France (including French colonies), Gabon, German Democratic Republic, Germany (Federal Republic), Greece, Guinea, Hungary, Iceland, India, Indonesia, Iran, Iraq, Ireland, Israel, Italy, Japan, Jordan, Kenya, Korea (Democratic People's Republic), Kuwait, Laos, Latvia, Lebanon, Lesotho, Liberia, Libya, Liechtenstein, Luxembourg, Madagascar, Malaysia, Mali, Malta, Mauritania, Mexico, Mongolia, Morocco, Nauru, Nepal, Netherlands, New Zealand, Niger, Nigeria, Norway, Oman, Pakistan, Papua New Guinea, Paraguay, Philippines, Poland, Portugal, Qatar, Romania, Rwanda, Saudi Arabia, Senegal, Seychelles, Sierra Leone, Slovak Republic, Solomon Islands, South Africa, Spain, Sri Lanka, Sudan, Sweden, Switzerland, Syrian Arab Republic, Tanzania, Togo, Tonga, Trinidad and Tobago, Tunisia, Turkey, Uganda, Ukraine, Union of Soviet Socialist Republics, United Arab Emirates. United Kingdom, United States, Uruguay, Vanuatu, Venezuela, Vietnam (Socialist Republic), Western Samoa, Yemen (Sanaa), Yugoslavia, Zaire, Zambia, Zimbabwe

IN FORCE: From February 12, 1933; for the United States, from October 29, 1934

OVERVIEW: The first international convention governing "all international carriage of persons, luggage or goods performed by aircraft for reward."

DISCUSSION:

The Warsaw Convention aimed to standardize the following procedures relating to international carriage of persons and goods by air:

- Specifications for passenger tickets
- Specifications for luggage tickets
- Specifications for air consignment notes

Most important are the provisions relating to the liability of the air carrier. The convention provides for presumptive liability of an air carrier for personal injury or death of a passenger or damage to or loss of goods in international air carriage. While liability for goods is to be determined according to the value of the goods and the extent of the loss, liability for death or personal injury was originally limited to $8300. The low limit of liability discouraged the United States from adhering to the Warsaw Convention until 1934. The **Hague Protocol to the Warsaw Convention** of 1955 doubled the liability limit.

Although the United States signed the convention, the Senate failed to ratify it because it considered that the liability limit was still too low. The 1955 agreement was finally ratified in 1999.

REFERENCE:

Goldhirsch, Lawrence. *The Warsaw Convention Annotated: A Legal Handbook.* Dordrecht, Netherlands, and Boston: Martinus Nijihoff, 1988.

International Sanitary Convention for Aerial Navigation

SIGNED: April 12, 1933, at the Hague

SIGNATORIES: Australia, Belgian Congo, Belgium, Bolivia, British Guiana, British Honduras, British Virgin Islands, Canada, China, Cuba, Cyprus, Dominica, Dominican Republic, Ecuador, Egypt, France, Greece, Grenada, Haiti, Honduras, India, Italy, Jamaica, Luxembourg, Mauritius, Netherlands, New Zealand, Nicaragua, Peru, Poland, Syria, Trinidad and Tobago, Union of South Africa, United Kingdom, United States

IN FORCE: From August 1, 1935

OVERVIEW: A convention for the "regulation of the sanitary control of aerial navigation."

DISCUSSION:

Early in the history of international aviation, it was recognized that the freedom of flight posed challenges to health, particularly regarding the prevention and control of epidemic disease. The 1933 convention specified that sanitary services at "aerodromes" open to international traffic would offer:

(a) An organised medical service with one medical officer at least and one or more sanitary inspectors, it being understood that this staff will not necessarily be in permanent attendance at the aerodrome;

(b) A place for medical inspection;

(c) Equipment for taking and despatching suspected material for examination in a laboratory, if such examination cannot be made on the spot;

(d) Facilities, in the case of necessity for the isolation, transport and care of the sick, for the isolation of contacts separately from the sick and for carrying out any other prophylactic measure in suitable premises either within the aerodrome or in proximity to it;

(e) Apparatus necessary for carrying out disinfection, disinsectisation and deratisation if required, as well as any other measures laid down in the present Convention.

The aerodrome shall be provided with a sufficient supply of wholesome drinking water, and with a proper and safe system for the disposal of excreta and refuse, and for the removal of waste water. The aerodrome shall, as far as possible, be protected from rats.

The convention was updated by the 1944 **International Sanitary Convention for Aerial Navigation.**

REFERENCE:
United States Senate, Committee on Foreign Relations. *International Sanitary Convention for Aerial Navigation.* Washington, D.C.: U.S. Government Printing Office, 1935.

International Air Transport Agreement

SIGNED: December 7, 1944, at Chicago

SIGNATORIES: Afghanistan, Bolivia, China, Dominican Republic, El Salvador, Ethiopia, Greece, Honduras, Liberia, Netherlands, Nicaragua, Paraguay, Sweden, Thailand, Turkey, United States, Venezuela

IN FORCE: From February 8, 1945

OVERVIEW: With the **Convention on International Civil Aviation**, one of two major and basic civil aviation agreements signed in Chicago during World War II.

DISCUSSION:

In part to reinforce the bonds that connected friendly nations during World War II, the International Civil Aviation Organization held a conference in Chicago during 1944 to arrive at basic agreements regulating civil air transport internationally.

The International Air Transport Agreement provided for the following basic freedoms of scheduled international air services:

- The privilege to fly across the territory of each signatory without landing
- The privilege to land for non-traffic purposes
- The privilege to put down passengers, mail, and cargo taken on in the territory of the state whose nationality the aircraft possesses

Key restrictions on scheduled international air service were also specified in the agreement, including the following:

- The right of each contracting state to refuse permission to the aircraft of other contracting states to take on its territory passengers, mail, or cargo for flight to another point within the state
- The right to designate the air route to be followed within the state's territory and to designate which airports may be used
- The right to charge reasonable fees for the use of airports within the state

The agreement also provided for resolution of disputes arising from the terms laid down.

REFERENCES:
None

Convention on International Civil Aviation

SIGNED: December 7, 1944, at Chicago

SIGNATORIES: Argentina, Australia, Brazil, Canada, China, Czechoslovakia, Denmark, Dominican Republic, Ethiopia, India, Ireland, Liberia, Mexico, Nicaragua, Paraguay, Peru, Philippines, Poland, Portugal, Spain, Sweden, Switzerland, Turkey, Union of South Africa, United Kingdom, United States

IN FORCE: From April 4, 1947

OVERVIEW: An important early convention on international civil aviation concluded during World War II in the belief that "the future development of international civil aviation can greatly help to create and preserve friendship and understanding among the nations and peoples of the world."

DISCUSSION:

While the preamble to the convention emphasizes the role of civil aviation in promoting "friendship and understanding among the nations of the world," it also mentions that the abuse of civil aviation "can become a threat to the general security." The convention, the first extensive and detailed international agreement on civil aviation, sets as its object the development of international civil aviation "in a safe and orderly manner" and "on the basis of equality of opportunity."

Article 1 states the most basic principle of the convention: "every State has complete and exclusive sovereignty over the airspace above its territory." Article 2 defines "territory" to include the land areas and territorial waters.

After defining civil aircraft (in contrast to state and military aircraft) in Article 3, the convention goes on in Article 4 to prohibit the use of civil aviation for purposes "inconsistent with the aims of this Convention."

Principal provisions of the convention include the following:
- The right of non-scheduled flight to transit the territory of signatories and to make non-traffic stops, provided that safety and other regulations are observed
- The principle that schedule international air service requires "special permission or other authorization of [the contracting] State"
- The right of the contracting State to refuse permission to foreign aircraft to transport passengers, mail, or cargo domestically from point to point
- The right of the contracting State to refuse permission for pilotless aircraft to overfly its territory
- The right of the contracting State to designate areas in which overflight is prohibited or otherwise restricted
- The right of the contracting State to designate airports authorized to receive international flights
- The obligation of aircraft and aircrews to obey the laws and regulations of the contracting States over which they are flying

- The obligation of the contracting State to enforce clear and uniform rules of the air
- The obligation of aircraft, aircrews, and passengers to obey the contracting State's laws and regulations relating to entry, clearance, immigration, passports, customs, and so on
- The obligation of the contracting State to "take effective measures to prevent the spread by means of air navigation of . . . communicable diseases"
- The obligation of the contracting State to provide uniform access to airports for the aircraft of all contracting States
- The right of the contracting State to charge reasonable, uniform fees for the use of airports and air navigation facilities
- The right of the contracting State to search aircraft on landing or departure

The convention also addresses the issue of the nationality of aircraft, specifying that "Aircraft have the nationality of the State in which they are registered," that they must not be simultaneously registered in more than one state, and that they must "bear . . . appropriate nationality and registration marks."

In a chapter devoted to "Measures to Facilitate Air Navigation," signatories undertake to "adopt all practicable measures . . . to facilitate and expedite navigation by aircraft . . . and to prevent unnecessary delays." Special attention is given to aircraft in distress, with each contracting State undertaking to provide aid to aircraft in distress. In the event of a serious accident, the contracting State in which the accident occurred undertakes to invite observers from the state in which the aircraft was registered to participate in the investigation of the accident.

The contracting States undertake to provide airport, navigation, and meteorological services, and to cooperate in adopting standard and uniform communication, lighting, signaling, and other procedures.

A chapter devoted to "Conditions to Be Fulfilled with Respect to Aircraft" lists documents to be carried in aircraft, radio equipment requirements, certificates of airworthiness, licenses of personnel, and log books. Civil aircraft in international flight must not carry munitions or implements of war, and a contracting State may "prohibit or regulate the use of photographic apparatus in aircraft over its territory."

The penultimate chapter of the convention addresses "International Standards and Recommended Practices," which includes articles of an advisory rather than a mandatory character concerning the following:
- Communications systems
- Navigation aids
- Characteristics of airports and landing areas
- Rules of the air and air-traffic control practices
- Licensing of operating and mechanical personnel
- Airworthiness of aircraft

- Registration and identification of aircraft
- Collection and exchange of meteorological information
- Log books
- Aeronautical maps and charts
- Customs and immigration procedures
- Aircraft in distress and investigation of accidents

Part II of the convention, containing the final chapter, establishes the International Civil Aviation Organization, which has as its objectives the following:
- To insure the safe and orderly growth of international civil aviation
- To encourage the arts of aircraft design and operation for peaceful purposes
- To encourage the development of airways, airports, and air navigation facilities
- To meet the needs of the peoples of the world for safe, regular, efficient, and economical air transport
- To "prevent economic waste caused by unreasonable competition"
- To "insure that the rights of the contracting States are fully respected and that every contracting State has a fair opportunity to operate international airlines"
- To avoid discrimination between contracting states
- To promote safety
- To promote the development of all aspects of international civil aeronautics

REFERENCES:
None

International Sanitary Convention for Aerial Navigation

SIGNED: December 15, 1944, at Washington
SIGNATORIES: Antigua, Ashanti, Australia, Barbados, Basutoland, Bechuanaland, Belgian Congo, Belgium, Bolivia, British Guiana, British Honduras, British Virgin Islands, Canada, China, Colony of Aden, Cuba, Cyprus, Dominica, Dominican Republic, Ecuador, Egypt, Falkland Islands and Dependencies, Federation of Malaya, Fiji, France, Gambia Colony, Gambia Protectorate, Gibraltar, Gilbert and Ellice Islands, Gold Coast Colony, Greece, Grenada, Haiti, Honduras, Hong Kong, India, Italy, Jamaica, Kenya Colony, Kenya Protectorate, Leeward Islands, Luxembourg, Mauritius, Montserrat, Netherlands, New Zealand, Newfoundland, Nicaragua, Nigeria Colony, Nigeria Protectorate, Northern Rhodesia, Nyasaland, Palestine-Mandated Territory, Peru, Poland, Ruanda-Urundi, Saint Christopher and Nevis, Sierra Leone Colony, Sierra Leone Protectorate, Singapore, Solomon Islands, Southern Rhodesia. St. Lucia, St. Vincent, Swaziland, Syria, Taganyika, Territory of the Cameroons under British Administration, Transjordan,

Trinidad and Tobago, Uganda Protectorate, Union of South Africa, United Kingdom, United States, Western Samoa, Windward Islands, Zanzibar Protectorate

IN FORCE: From January 15, 1945

OVERVIEW: A wartime revision and modernization of the 1933 **International Sanitary Convention for Aerial Navigation**.

DISCUSSION:

The main purposes of the 1944 convention were to update the 1933 convention and to vest administration of the convention in the United Nations Relief and Rehabilitation Administration because the International Office of Public Health was unable to administer the convention due to the exigencies of World War II. The 1944 convention includes stricter and more sweeping anti-epidemic measures "in the light of the present-day conditions which call for special measures to prevent the spread by air across frontiers of epidemic or other communicable diseases."

REFERENCES:

None

Convention on the International Recognition of Rights in Aircraft

SIGNED: June 19, 1948, at Geneva

SIGNATORIES: Argentina, Australia, Belgium, Brazil, Chile, China, Colombia, Cuba, Denmark, Dominican Republic, Ecuador, El Salvador, France, Greece, Iceland, Iran, Ireland, Italy, Laos, Mexico, Netherlands, Norway, Pakistan, Peru, Portugal, Sweden, Switzerland, United Kingdom, United States, Venezuela

IN FORCE: From September 17, 1953

OVERVIEW: An international convention governing the transfer of title to aircraft.

DISCUSSION:

Pursuant to the **International Air Transport Agreement** of 1944, this convention governs, among the signatory states, the following issues:

- Rights of property in aircraft
- Rights to acquire aircraft by pruchase coupled with possession of the aircraft
- Rights to possession of aircraft under leases of six months or more
- Mortgages and similar rights in aircraft

REFERENCE:

United States Department of State, *Treaties in Force: A List of Treaties and other International Agreements of the United States in Force on January 1, 1997*. Washington, D.C.: U.S. Government Printing Office, 1997.

Agreement on North Atlantic Stations

SIGNED: February 25, 1954, at Paris

SIGNATORIES: Canada, Denmark, Ireland, Israel, Norway, Sweden, United Kingdom, United States

IN FORCE: From February 2, 1954

OVERVIEW: An international agreement concerning the establishment and operation of weather stations in the North Atlantic for purposes of air navigation.

REFERENCE:

International Civil Aviation Organization. *North Atlantic Weather Stations*. Washington, D.C.: U. S. Government Printing Office, 1953.

Hague Protocol to the Warsaw Convention

OFFICIAL TITLE: Protocol to Amend the Convention for the Unification of Certain Rules Relating to International Carriage by Air, Signed at Warsaw on 12 October 1929

SIGNED: September 28, 1955, at the Hague

SIGNATORIES: Australia, Belgium, Brazil, Byelorussian Soviet Socialist Republic, Cameroon, Canada, Congo (Brazzaville), Côte d'Ivoire, Czechoslovakia, Dahomey, Denmark, Egypt, El Salvador, France, German Democratic Republic, Germany (Federal Republic of), Greece, Hungary, Iceland, Ireland, Israel, Italy, Laos, Liechtenstein, Luxembourg, Madagascar, Mali, Mexico, Morocco, Netherlands, New Zealand, Niger, Norway, Pakistan, Philippines, Poland, Portugal, Romania, Sweden, Switzerland, Ukrainian Soviet Socialist Republic, Union of Soviet Socialist Republics, United Kingdom, United States (signed, but did not ratify until 1999), Venezuela

IN FORCE: From January 8, 1963

OVERVIEW: A revision updating and rationalizing provisions of the **Warsaw Convention** of 1929.

DISCUSSION:

The most important provision of the 1955 **Hague Protocol to the Warsaw Convention** doubles the air carriers' maximum liability for death or injury of passengers, raising the limit from the 1929 level of $8300 to about $16,600. Although the United States signed the protocol, the Senate refused to ratify it, arguing that the liability limit was still too low. In 1969, air-carrier members of the International Air Transport Association (IATA), a trade association, agreed to raise the liability limit to $75,000 for passengers traveling to or from or passing through the United States. In 1971, the **Guatemala City Protocol to the Warsaw Convention** raised the limit to $100,000, stipulating, however, that this limit was to be unbreakable. The Guatemala Protocol was subsequently amended by **Montreal Protocol No. 4,** which changed the limit from $100,000 to "100,000 Special Drawing Rights," units of international monetary exchange administered by the International Monetary Fund. After the lapse of years, the 1955 protocol was finally ratified by the U.S. Senate in September 1999.

REFERENCE:
Goldhirsch, Lawrence. *The Warsaw Convention Annotated: A Legal Handbook.* Dordrecht, Netherlands, and Boston: Martinus Nijihoff, 1988.

Agreement on Air Navigation Services in Greenland and Faroe Islands

OFFICIAL TITLE: Agreement on the Joint Financing of Certain Air Navigation Services in Greenland and the Faroe Islands
SIGNED: September 25, 1956, at Geneva
SIGNATORIES: Australia, Belgium, Canada, Denmark, France. Germany (Federal Republic), France, Iceland, Israel, Italy, Netherlands, Norway, Sweden, Switzerland, United Kingdom, United States
IN FORCE: From June 6, 1958
OVERVIEW: An agreement among member states of the International Civil Aviation Organization to finance air navigation services provided by the government of Denmark in Greenland and the Faroe Islands.

DISCUSSION:

As an essential aid to international air navigation, the government of Denmark agreed to provide and maintain navigational and meteorological equipment, stations, and personnel in Greenland and the Faroe Islands in return for joint financing of these services by member states of the International Civil Aviation Organization. The agreement lays down a full schedule of contributions from each state and, in annexes, specifies the nature of the services to be provided.

REFERENCES:
None

Agreement (with the United Kingdom) Concerning the Establishment in Canton Island of a Space Vehicle Tracking and Communications Station

SIGNED: April 6, 1961, at London
SIGNATORIES: United Kingdom vs. United States
IN FORCE: From signing
OVERVIEW: An agreement whereby the United Kingdom undertakes to permit the United States to establish a tracking communications station for use in Project Mercury, the "manned satellite program."

DISCUSSION:
The agreement secures permission to build the station on the British-controlled island for the purposes of tracking and communicating with Project Mercury spacecraft.

REFERENCES:
None

Agreement (with West Germany) on Cooperation in Intercontinental Testing in Connection with Experimental Communications Satellites

SIGNED: September 5 and 29, 1961, at Bonn/Bad Godesberg
SIGNATORIES: Federal Republic of Germany vs. Untied States
IN FORCE: From September 29, 1961
OVERVIEW: An agreement between NASA and the Deutsche Bundespost for cooperative testing of experimental communication satellites.

DISCUSSION:

An agreement to test intercontinental communications using United States satellites launched under Project Relay and Project Rebound, both pioneering programs and satellite communications. The United States also concluded similar agreements with other friendly countries to secure assistance in testing the satellites.

REFERENCE:
Morgan, Walter L., and Gary D. Gordon. *Communications Satellite Handbook.* New York: Wiley, 1989.

Tokyo Convention

OFFICIAL TITLE: Convention on Offences and Certain Other Acts Committed on Board Aircraft
SIGNED: September 14, 1963, at Tokyo
SIGNATORIES: Afghanistan, Algeria, Antigua and Barbuda, Argentina, Australia, Austria, Bahamas, Bahrain, Bangladesh, Barbados, Belarus, Belgium, Bhutan, Bolivia, Botswana, Brazil, Brunei, Bulgaria, Burkina Faso, Burundi, Cameroon, Canada, Cape Verde, Central African Republic, Chad, Chile, China, Colombia, Comoros, Congo, Costa Rica, Côte d'Ivoire, Croatia, Cyprus, Czech Republic, Czechoslovakia, Denmark, Djibouti, Dominican Republic, Ecuador, Egypt, El Salvador, Equatorial Guinea, Estonia, Ethiopia, Fiji, Finland, France, Gabon, Gambia, German Democratic Republic, Germany (Federal Republic), Ghana, Greece, Grenada, Guatemala, Guyana, Haiti, Honduras, Hungary, Iceland, India, Indonesia, Iran, Iraq, Ireland, Israel, Italy, Jamaica, Japan, Jordan, Kenya, Korea (Democratic People's Republic), Korea (Republic), Kuwait, Laos, Lebanon, Lesotho,

Libya, Luxembourg, Madagascar, Malawi, Malaysia, Maldives, Mali, Malta, Marshall Islands, Mauritania, Mauritius, Mexico, Monaco, Mongolia, Morocco, Nauru, Nepal, Netherlands, New Zealand, Nicaragua, Niger, Nigeria, Norway, Oman, Pakistan, Panama, Papua New Guinea, Paraguay, Peru, Philippines, Poland, Portugal, Qatar, Romania, Russian Federation, Rwanda, St. Lucia, St. Vincent and the Grenadines, Saudi Arabia, Senegal, Seychelles, Sierra Leone, Singapore, Slovenia, Solomon Islands, South Africa, Spain, Sri Lanka, Suriname, Sweden, Switzerland, Syrian Arab Republic, Tanzania, Thailand, Togo, Trinidad and Tobago, Tunisia, Turkey, Uganda, Ukraine, Union of Soviet Socialist Republics, United Arab Emirates, United Kingdom, United States, Uruguay, Vanuatu, Venezuela, Vietnam (Socialist Republic), Yemen (Sanaa), Yugoslavia, Zaire, Zambia, Zimbabwe
IN FORCE: From December 4, 1969
OVERVIEW: An international convention addressing offenses against penal law and other acts that jeopardize safety on board aircraft in international flight.

DISCUSSION:

This comprehensive convention addresses many issues relating to criminal offenses on board aircraft in international flight. The principal areas covered by the convention include the following:

- Powers of the aircraft commander. These include measures, such as restraint of the offender, "to protect the safety of the aircraft, or of persons or property therein," "to maintain good order and discipline on board," and to enable delivery of the offender "to competent authorities."

- Actions in cases of unlawful seizure of the aircraft. "Skyjacking" is not addressed in detail in this convention; however, Article 11 lays down that "Contracting States shall take all appropriate measures to restore control of the aircraft to its lawful commander or to preserve his control of the aircraft."

- Powers and duties of states. These primarily concern the obligation to "take delivery of any person whom the aircraft commander delivers" pursuant to his judgment that the person has committed an offense or poses a danger. The provisions also concern subsequent handling and disposition of the offender.

REFERENCE:
United States Congress, Committee on Interstate and Foreign Commerce, Subcommittee on Transportation and Aeronautics. *Implementation of Tokyo Convention. Hearing, Ninety-first Congress, First Session ... November 4, 1969.* Washington, D.C.: U.S. Government Printing Office, 1969.

Agreement (with ESRO) on the Establishment and Operation of a Satellite Telemetry/Telecommand Station Near Fairbanks

OFFICIAL TITLE: Exchange of Notes Constituting an Agreement Concerning the Establishment and Operation of a Satellite Telemetry/Telecommand Station near Fairbanks, Alaska
SIGNED: November 28, 1966, at Paris
SIGNATORIES: European Space Research Organization (ESRO) vs. United States
IN FORCE: From signing
OVERVIEW: An agreement to allow the ESRO to establish a satellite telemetry/telecommand station in Alaska.

DISCUSSION:

This example of a treaty concluded not with another state, but with an intergovernmental organization, gives the ESRO permission to establish "an earth station on United States territory for space telemetering and telecommand purposes." The United States agrees to the following:

- To facilitate the acquisition of an appropriate lease of land
- An understanding that construction costs will be borne by the ESRO, but that the National Aeronautics and Space Administration (NASA) will cooperate in design and construction
- To allow construction of a station exclusively for the purpose of satellite telemetry and telecommand
- To take precautionary measures to eliminate or minimize harmful radio interference, which would compromise operations of the station
- To grant ESRO certain immunities with regard to customs duties, searches, and judicial immunity

In return, ESRO agrees to share its telemetry and other data on request of the United States.

REFERENCES:
None

Outer Space Treaty

OFFICIAL TITLE: Treaty on Principles Governing the Activities of States in the Exploration and Use of Outer Space, Including the Moon and other Celestial Bodies
SIGNED: January 27, 1967, at Washington, London, and Moscow
SIGNATORIES: Afghanistan, Algeria, Antigua and Barbuda, Argentina, Australia, Austria, Bahamas, Bangladesh, Barbados, Belarus, Belgium, that mean, Brazil, Brunei, Bulgaria, Burkina Faso, Burma, Canada, Chile, China, Cuba, Cyprus, Czech Republic, Czechoslovakia, Denmark, Dominica, Dominican Republic, Ecuador, Egypt, El Salvador, Fiji, Finland, France,

German Democratic Republic, German Federal Republic, Greece, Grenada, Guinea-Bissau, Hungary, Iceland, India, Iraq, Ireland, Israel, Italy, Jamaica, Japan, Kenya, Korea, Kuwait, Laos, Lebanon, Libya, Madagascar, Mali, Mauritius, Mexico, Mongolia, Morocco, Nepal, Netherlands, New Zealand, Niger, Nigeria, Norway, Pakistan, Papua New Guinea, Peru, Poland, Romania, Russian Federation, St. Kitts and Nevis, St. Lucia, San Marino, Saudi Arabia, Seychelles, Sierra Leone, Singapore, Slovak Republic, Solomon Islands, South Africa, Spain, Sri Lanka, Swaziland, Sweden, Switzerland, Syrian Arab Republic, Thailand, Togo, Tonga, Tunisia, Turkey, Uganda, Ukraine, Union of Soviet Socialist Republics, United Kingdom, United States, Uruguay, Venezuela, Vietnam, Socialist Republic, Yemen(Aden), Zambia

IN FORCE: From October 10, 1967

OVERVIEW: Bars the use of space and celestial bodies for military purposes.

DISCUSSION:

The so-called "Outer Space Treaty" was modeled on the **Antarctic Treaty**, which barred the use of Antarctica for military purposes. Between 1959 and 1962, the Western powers made a series of proposals to bar the use of outer space for military purposes, but the Soviet Union insisted on linking such proposals to broader issues of disarmament, including the removal of United States ICBMs from various locations in the world. This created a deadlock until 1963, when the United States and the Soviet Union both issued statements expressing their intention never to use space for military purposes and calling upon all states to refrain from introducing weapons of mass destruction into outer space. On June 16, 1966, both the United States and the Soviet Union submitted draft treaties addressing the demilitarization of outer space. The U.S. draft dealt only with celestial bodies; the Soviet draft covered the whole outer space environment. The United States subsequently accepted the Soviet position on the scope of the treaty.

Article IV contains the crux of the treaty's arms control provisions:

- Signatories undertake not to place in orbit around the earth, install on the moon or any other celestial body, or otherwise station in outer space, nuclear or any other weapons of mass destruction.
- Signatories agree that the moon and other celestial bodies shall be used exclusively for peaceful purposes.

REFERENCE:

Goldman, Nathan C. *American Space Law: International and Domestic.* San Diego, CA: Univelt, 1996.

Agreement on the Rescue of Astronauts, the Return of Astronauts, and the Return of Objects Launched into Outer Space

SIGNED: April 22, 1968

SIGNATORIES: Antigua and Barbuda, Argentina, Australia, Austria, Bahamas, Barbados, Belarus, Belgium, Bosnia-Herzegovina, Botswana, Brazil, Brunei, Bulgaria, Cameroon, Canada, Chile, China, Cuba, Cyprus, Czech Republic, Czechoslovakia, Denmark, Dominica, Ecuador, Egypt, El Salvador, European Space Agency, Fiji, Finland, France, Gabon, Gambia, German Democratic Republic, Germany (Federal Republic), Greece, Grenada, Guinea-Bissau, Guyana, Hungary, Iceland, India, Iran, Iraq, Ireland, Israel, Italy, Japan, Korea, Kuwait, Laos, Lebanon, Madagascar, Maldives, Mauritius, Mexico, Mongolia, Morocco, Nepal, Netherlands, New Zealand, Niger, Nigeria, Norway, Pakistan, Papua New Guinea, Peru, Poland, Portugal, Romania, Russian Federation, St. Kitts and Nevis, St. Lucia, San Marino, Seychelles, Singapore, Slovak Republic, Slovenia, Solomon Islands, South Africa, Swaziland, Sweden, Switzerland, Syrian Arab Republic, Thailand, Tonga, Tunisia, Ukraine, Union of Soviet Socialist Republics, United Kingdom, United States, Uruguay, Yugoslavia, Zambia

IN FORCE: From December 3, 1968

OVERVIEW: The convention provides for the "safe and prompt return" of astronauts and space objects in the event of unplanned landing.

DISCUSSION:

The signatories of the agreement bind themselves to render "all possible assistance to astronauts in the event of accident, distress, emergency or unintended landing." They also agree to return astronauts and space objects safely and promptly to the state of origin. Details of the agreement include provisions for reimbursement of expenses incurred as a result of rendering assistance and returning objects. To the extent possible, launching states must notify other states of impending or actual unplanned landings by astronauts or spacecraft.

REFERENCE:

Goldman, Nathan C. *American Space Law: International and Domestic.* San Diego, CA: Univelt, 1996.

Guatemala City Protocol

OFFICIAL TITLE: Protocol to Amend the Convention for the Unification of Certain Rules Relating to International Carriage by Air, Signed at Warsaw on 12 October 1929, as Amended by the Protocol Done at the Hague on 28 September 1955

SIGNED: March 8, 1971, at Guatemala City

SIGNATORIES: Algeria, Argentina, Australia, Austria, Bahrain, Barbados, Belgium, Brazil, Bulgaria, Burma, Canada, Chile, Cuba, Czechoslovakia, Dahomey, Democratic Yemen, Denmark, Ecuador, Egypt, Ethiopia, Finland, France, Germany (Federal Republic), Ghana, Greece, Guyana, Hungary, Iceland, India, Indonesia, Iran, Ireland, Jamaica, Japan, Jordan, Kenya, Korea (Republic), Kuwait, Laos, Lebanon, Libyan Arab Republic, Luxembourg, Madagascar, Malawi, Malaysia, Mali, Mauritius, Mexico, Morocco, Netherlands, New Zealand, Nicaragua, Niger, Nigeria, Norway, Pakistan, Panama, Philippines, Poland, Portugal, Romania, Rwanda, Saudi Arabia, Senegal, Singapore, South Africa, Spain, Sri Lanka, Sweden, Switzerland, Syrian Arab Republic, Thailand, Togo, Trinidad and Tobago, Tunisia, Uganda, Union of Soviet Socialist Republics, United Kingdom, United Republic of Tanzania, United States, Yugoslavia, Zaire, Zambia

IN FORCE: From June 8, 1975

OVERVIEW: A revision of the **Warsaw Convention** (1929) and of the **Hague Protocol to the Warsaw Convention** (1955) updating specifications for tickets and shipping documents and raising the limit of carrier liability for death and personal injury.

DISCUSSION:

The most important provision of the Guatemala City Protocol is establishing an "unbreakable" maximum liability limit of $100,000 for each instance of death or injury in an international aviation transportation accident. The protocol was itself revised by **Montreal Protocol Number 4**.

REFERENCE:

Goldhirsch, Lawrence. *The Warsaw Convention Annotated: A Legal Handbook.* Dordrecht, Netherlands, and Boston: Martinus Nijihoff, 1988.

Convention on International Liability for Damage Caused by Space Objects

SIGNED: March 29, 1972, at Washington, London, and Moscow

SIGNATORIES: Antigua and Barbuda, Argentina, Australia, Austria, Belarus, Belgium, Benin, Bosnia-Herzegovina, Botswana, Brazil, Bulgaria, Canada, Chile, China, Cuba, Cyprus, Czech Republic, Czechoslovakia, Denmark, Dominica, Dominican Republic, Ecuador, European Space Agency, European Telecommunications Satellite Organization, Fiji, Finland, France, Gabon, German Democratic Republic, German Federal Republic, Greece, Granada, Hungary, India, Indonesia, Iran, Iraq, Ireland, Israel, Italy, Japan, Kenya, Korean Republic, Kuwait, Laos, Liechtenstein, Luxembourg, Mali, Malta, Mexico, Mongolia, Morocco, Netherlands, New Zealand, Niger, Pakistan, Panama, Papua New Guinea, Poland, Qatar, Romania, Russian Federation, St. Kitts and Nevis, St. Lucia, St. Vincent and the

Grenadines, Saudi Arabia, Senegal, Seychelles, Singapore, Slovak Republic, Slovenia, Solomon Islands, Spain, Sri Lanka, Sweden, Switzerland, Syrian Arab Republic, Togo, Trinidad and Tobago, Tunisia, Ukraine, U.S.S.R., United Kingdom, United States, Uruguay, Venezuela, Yugoslavia, Zambia

IN FORCE: From July 1, 1975

OVERVIEW: A convention to "elaborate effective international rules and procedures concerning liability for damage caused by space objects and to ensure . . . prompt payment . . . to victims of such damage."

DISCUSSION:

The crux of the international convention is Article II: "A launching State shall be absolutely liable to pay compensation for damage caused by its space object on the surface of the earth of to aircraft in flight." In addition to specifying the terms of liability, the convention provides for the establishment of an ad-hoc Claims Commission to arbitrate and adjudicate the matter.

REFERENCE:

Goldman, Nathan C. *American Space Law: International and Domestic.* San Diego, CA: Univelt, 1996.

Convention on Registration of Objects Launched into Outer Space

SIGNED: November 12, 1974

SIGNATORIES: Antigua and Barbuda, Argentina, Australia, Austria, Belarus, Belgium, Brunei, Bulgaria, Canada, Chile, China, Cuba, Cyprus, Czech Republic, Czechoslovakia, Denmark, Dominica, European Space Agency, France, German Democratic Republic, Germany (Federal Republic), Hungary, India, Japan, Korea (Republic), Mexico, Mongolia, Netherlands, Niger, Norway, Pakistan, Peru, Poland, Russian Federation, St. Kitts and Nevis, St. Lucia, St. Vincent and the Grenadines, Seychelles, Slovak Republic, Solomon Islands, Spain, Sweden, Switzerland, Ukraine, Union of Soviet Socialist Republics, United Kingdom, United States, Uruguay, Yugoslavia

IN FORCE: From January 19, 1976

OVERVIEW: A convention extending the **Treaties on Principles Governing the Activities of States in the Exploration and use of Outer Space** and requiring each launching state to keep a registry showing details of each space object launched into earth orbit or beyond.

DISCUSSION:

All registration information is to be deposited with the United Nations Secretary General and be available on a basis of "full and open access" to all nations.

REFERENCE:

Goldman, Nathan C. *American Space Law: International and Domestic.* San Diego, CA: Univelt, 1996.

Montreal Protocol Number 4

OFFICIAL TITLE: Montreal Protocol No.4 to Amend the Convention for the Unification of Certain Rules Relating to International Carriage by Air, Signed at Warsaw on 12 October 1929, as Amended by the Protocol Done at the Hague on 28 September 1955

SIGNED: September 25, 1975, at Montreal

SIGNATORIES: Algeria, Argentina, Australia, Austria, Bahrain, Barbados, Belgium, Brazil, Bulgaria, Canada, Cape Verde, Chile, China, Colombia, Cuba, Czechoslovakia, Democratic Yemen, Denmark, Dominican Republic, Ecuador, Egypt, El Salvador, Ethiopia, Fiji, Finland, France, Gambia, Germany (Federal Republic), Ghana, Greece, Guyana, Hungary, Iceland, India, Indonesia, Iran, Iraq, Ireland, Jamaica, Jordan, Kenya, Korea (Democratic People's Republic), Korea (Republic), Kuwait, Lebanon, Libyan Arab Jamahiriya, Luxembourg, Madagascar, Malawi, Maldives, Mali, Malta, Mauritania, Mauritius, Mexico, Morocco, Netherlands, New Zealand, Nicaragua, Niger, Norway, Oman, Pakistan, Peru, Poland, Qatar, Romania, Singapore, Spain, Sudan, Swaziland, Sweden, Switzerland, Syrian Arab Republic, Togo, Tunisia, Uganda, Union of Soviet Socialist Republics, United Kingdom, United Republic of Tanzania, United States, Uruguay, Venezuela, Yemen, Yugoslavia

IN FORCE: From February 15, 1980

OVERVIEW: The latest revision of the principal convention regulating international air transportation of passengers, luggage, and cargo.

DISCUSSION:

The 1971 protocol revises the **Warsaw Convention** (1929), the **Hague Protocol to the Warsaw Convention** (1955), and the **Guatemala City Protocol** (1971) as follows:

- It allows air-freight forwarders to use paperless (electronic) air waybills (with the shipper's consent).
- It establishes a stricter system of liability for cargo carriers.
- It specifies circumstances under which the air carrier may be exonerated from liability, as when destruction, loss, or damage to cargo results solely from an inherent defect, quality, or vice of the cargo; defective packing of the cargo by a person other than the carrier or its agents; an act of war or armed conflict; an act of public authority carried out in connection with entry, exit, or transit of cargo.
- The protocol also provides that, if a carrier proves that any loss or damage was caused by or contributed to by the negligence or wrongful act or omission of the claimant, the carrier's liability can be wholly or partially exonerated.

The protocol came before the United States Senate in 1983, but ratification was delayed until September 1999.

REFERENCE:

Goldhirsch, Lawrence. *The Warsaw Convention Annotated: A Legal Handbook*. Dordrecht, Netherlands, and Boston: Martinus Nijihoff, 1988.

Convention on the International Maritime Satellite Organization (INMARSAT)

OFFICIAL TITLE: Convention on the International Maritime Satellite Organization (INMARSAT) with Annex and Operating Agreement

SIGNED: September 3, 1976, at London

SIGNATORIES: Algeria, Argentina, Australia, Bahrain, Belarus, Belgium, Brazil, Bulgaria, Cameroon, Canada, Chile, China, Colombia, Croatia, Cuba, Cyprus, Czechoslovakia, Denmark, Egypt, Finland, France, Gabon, German Democratic Republic, Germany (Federal Republic), Greece, Iceland, India, Indonesia, Iran, Iraq, Israel, Italy, Japan, Korea, Kuwait, Liberia, Malaysia, Malta, Mauritius, Monaco, Mozambique, Netherlands, New Zealand, Nigeria, Norway, Oman, Pakistan, Panama, Peru, Philippines, Qatar, Romania, Saudi Arabia, Singapore, Slovak Republic, Spain, Sri Lanka, Sweden, Switzerland, Tunisia, Turkey, Ukraine, Union of Soviet Socialist Republics, United Arab Emirates, United Kingdom, United States, Yugoslavia

IN FORCE: From July 16, 1979

OVERVIEW: A convention creating INMARSAT pursuant to a "principle set forth in Resolution 1721 (XVI) of the General Assembly of the United Nations that communication by means of satellites should be available to the nations of the world as soon as practicable on a global and nondiscriminatory basis."

DISCUSSION:

The principal provision of the agreement is the creation of INMARSAT, an organization to promote and manage "improvements to the maritime distress and safety systems and to the communication link between ships and between ships and their management as well as between crew or passengers on board and persons on shore . . . by using satellites." The purpose of INMARSAT is "to make provision for the benefit of ships of all nations through the most advanced suitable space technology available, for the most efficient and economic facilities possible consistent with the most efficient and equitable use of the radio frequency spectrum and of satellite orbits."

The main agreement deals with the constitution of INMARSAT, its scope, its mission, its governance, and its sources of finance. An Annex details Procedures for the Settlement of Disputes, and supplementary documents include the following:

- Operating Agreement on the International Maritime Satellite Organization, which details the financing and investment structure of the organization
- Protocol on the Privileges and Immunities of the International Maritime Satellite Organization (INMARSAT), which elaborates on the legal and diplomatic status of the organization
- An Amendment to the Operating Agreement on the International Maritime Satellite Organization (INMARSAT)

modifies the investment structure of the organization detailed in Article V of the Operating Agreement

REFERENCE:
Morgan, Walter L., and Gary D. Gordon. *Communications Satellite Handbook.* New York: Wiley, 1989.

Agreement Governing the Activities of States on the Moon and other Celestial Bodies

SIGNED: December 18, 1979

SIGNATORIES: Afghanistan, Algeria, Antigua and Barbuda, Argentina, Australia, Austria, Bahamas, Bangladesh, Barbados, Belarus, Belgium, Benin, Brazil, Brunei, Bulgaria, Burkina Faso, Burma, Canada, Chile, China, Cuba, Cyprus, Czech Republic, Czechoslovakia, Denmark, Dominica, Dominican Republic, Ecuador, Egypt, El Salvador, Fiji, Finland, France, German Democratic Republic, Germany (Federal Republic), Greece, Grenada, the Guinea-Bissau, Hungary, Iceland, India, Iraq, Ireland, Israel, Italy, Jamaica, Japan, Kenya, Korea, Kuwait, Laos, Lebanon, Libya, Madagascar, Mali, Mauritius, Mexico, Mongolia, Morocco, Nepal, Netherlands, New Zealand Niger, Nigeria, Norway, Pakistan, Papua New Guinea, Peru, Poland, Romania, Russian Federation, St. Kitts and Nevis, St. Lucia, San Marino, Saudi Arabia, Seychelles, Sierra Leone, Singapore, Slovak Republic, Solomon Islands, South Africa, Spain, Sri Lanka, Swaziland, Sweden, Switzerland, Syrian Arab Republic, Thailand, Togo, Congo, Tunisia, Turkey, Uganda, Ukraine, U.S.S.R., United Kingdom, United States, Uruguay, Venezuela, Vietnam, Yemen, Zambia

IN FORCE: July 11, 1984

OVERVIEW: The signatories agree that all activities on the moon or other celestial bodies are to be carried out in accordance with international law, and that these bodies are to be used exclusively for peaceful purposes.

DISCUSSION:

In addition to agreeing to abide by international law and to use celestial bodies exclusively for peaceful purposes, the signatories pledge to carry out exploration for the benefit and in the interest of all nations. The signatories also agree to supply detailed information about their activities to the United Nations Secretary-General and to the public. Measures are to be taken to prevent the disruption of the existing balance of the environment of the celestial bodies.

REFERENCES:
Goldman, Nathan C. *American Space Law: International and Domestic.* San Diego, CA: Univelt, 1996.
Rengger, N. J. *Treaties and Alliances of the World,* 5th ed. London: Longman Group, 1990.

Agreement (with Botswana) Concerning a Space Vehicle Communications Facility

OFFICIAL TITLE: Exchange of Notes Constituting an Agreement Concerning the Establishment and Operation of a Space Vehicle Communications Facility

SIGNED: December 4, 1980, at Houston, Texas

SIGNATORIES: Botswana vs. United States

IN FORCE: From signing

OVERVIEW: An agreement to establish in Botswana a space vehicle communications station as part of a worldwide tracking network in connection with the United States Space Transportation System based on the Space Shuttle.

DISCUSSION:

To provide voice communication support to the astronauts and other Space Shuttle crew members, a global network of communications stations was required. The agreement with Botswana is typical of agreements secured from other nations allowing the establishment of a communications facility. The agreement lays down the following:

- Description of the facility
- Botswana's agreement to make a site available
- The United States' agreement to provide technical training for a certain number of Botswana nationals
- The United States' agreement to bear all costs connected with the project
- The United States' agreement to make maximum use of telecommunications facilities available in Botswana
- Tax exemption for the facility
- The site to remain the property of Botswana, the equipment the property of the United States
- Botswana's agreement to facilitate travel and customs for NASA personnel

REFERENCES:
None

Agreement Concerning the Furnishing of Launch and Associated Services for Australia's National Satellite System

SIGNED: March 7, 1985, at Washington, D.C.

SIGNATORIES: Australia vs. United States

IN FORCE: From signing

OVERVIEW: An agreement concerning the use of the United States Space Transportation System (that is, the Space Shuttle) to launch geostationary communication satellites for Australia.

DISCUSSION:

One of the major political "selling points" of NASA's space shuttle program was the prospect of using the vehicle to carry satellites into orbit—an economical and more reliable alternative to launching them as the payload of conventional, unmanned rocket boosters.

The document lays down the broad principles of a launch agreement in the following areas:

- U.S. launch policy as established by the president of the United States
- Description of the payload
- Responsibilities of the U.S. and Australian authorities to exchange relevant technical data
- Specification of reimbursement for the launch service—amount and terms to be agreed on
- Liability provisions to be agreed on
- Mutual guarantee of security of proprietary data
- Australia's agreement to register any space object launched
- Agreement that Australia will retain jurisdiction over the launched object

REFERENCE:

Morgan, Walter L., and Gary D. Gordon. *Communications Satellite Handbook.* New York: Wiley, 1989.

Memorandum of Agreement (with China) Regarding International Trade in Commercial Launch Services

SIGNED: January 26, 1989

SIGNATORIES: China vs. United States

IN FORCE: From March 16, 1989

OVERVIEW: A bilateral trade agreement on Chinese provision of commercial launch services.

DISCUSSION:

While the United States is still the dominant provider of launch services for commercial satellites, other nations, including China, have entered the market. The 1989 memorandum, which expired on 31 December 1994, allowed China to launch nine commercial satellites into geostationary earth orbit (GEO) for "international customers." Major projects successfully launched included the Apstar II, AsiaSat II, Intelsat 708, and Echostar I satellites. Chinese launch operations depend heavily on cooperation with American technology suppliers.

On March 3 1995, the two nations concluded a new **Agreement on International Trade in Commercial Launch Services.**

REFERENCES:

Owen, Harrison. *Expanding Our Now: The Story of Open Space Technology.* Berkeley, CA: North Atlantic Books, 1997.

Stine, G. Harry. *The Manna Project: Business Opportunities in Outer Space.* New York: M. Evans, 1998.

Treaty on Open Skies

SIGNED: March 24, 1992

SIGNATORIES: Belarus, Belgium, Bulgaria, Canada, the Czech Republic, Denmark, France, Georgia, Germany, Greece, Hungary, Iceland, Italy, Kyrgyzstan, Luxembourg, the Netherlands, Norway, Poland, Portugal, Romania, Russia, Slovakia, Spain, Turkey, Ukraine, United Kingdom, United States

IN FORCE: Not yet in force

OVERVIEW: A multilateral "security-building" treaty, permitting signatories to conduct a limited number of unarmed flights over the territory of other participants for the purposes of monitoring compliance with arms-control and arms-limitation agreements.

DISCUSSION:

Monitoring and verification have always been the weak links in efforts at arms control, arms limitation, and disarmament. In 1955, President Dwight D. Eisenhower proposed the concept of "open skies," whereby a program of overflights would be permitted in order to observe and verify compliance with arms agreements. In the Cold War chill of the 1950s, the Eisenhower proposal was never acted upon. It was revived by President George Bush in 1989, and the present treaty was signed by twenty-five nations on March 24, 1992.

The treaty prescribes a regime of monitoring flights over the signatory's entire territory, without limitation other than those necessitated by safety considerations and by international law. The overflights would be allotted on a quota system derived from the geographic size of the participating countries: a prescribed number of flights of a prescribed duration would be allowed over a prescribed period. Regardless of size, each participant would be obliged to accept one overflight per quarter. Aircraft would carry observers from the host nation as well as the observing nation, and would be equipped only with sensing devices approved by the signatories.

Although a number of nations have signed the treaty, it still awaits full ratification to be put into force.

REFERENCE:

Krepon, Michael. *Open Skies, Arms Control, and Cooperative Security.* New York: St. Martin's, 1992.

Agreement (with the Russian Federation) on International Trade in Commercial Space Launch Services

OFFICIAL TITLE: Agreement Between the Government of the United States of America and the Government of the Russian Federation Regarding International Trade in Commercial Space Launch Services

SIGNED: September 2, 1993, at Washington

SIGNATORIES: Russian Federation vs. United States

IN FORCE: From signing

OVERVIEW: An agreement allowing the Russian Federation to enter the international commercial space launch market in a manner intended to prevent disruption of normal competition during the country's transition to a free-market economy.

DISCUSSION:

Like the **Memorandum of Agreement (with China) Regarding International Trade in Commercial Launch Services** (1989) and the **Agreement (with China) Regarding International Trade in Commercial Launch Services** (1995), this is an agreement intended to foster national transition from a non-market economy to a free-market economy, by allowing a nation to enter the potentially profitable but highly cost intensive launch services market without distorting normal international free-market competition.

The origin of the agreement is a June 1992 Summit between President George Bush and Russian President Boris Yeltsin, at which the United States announced that it was granting a one-time exception to its policy of prohibiting the export of U.S.-made satellites or satellites incorporating U.S. technology (essentially all Western satellites) to Russia for launch on Russian vehicles. The purpose of the exception was to allow the International Maritime Satellite Organization (INMARSAT) to select a Russian launcher to launch an INMARSAT 3 satellite. Although the United States stated that no further exceptions would be granted, it also announced willingness to negotiate Russian entry into the international commercial space launch services market. The result was the present agreement.

The agreement establishes rules for avoiding market distortion resulting from government involvement in the commercial space launch market. To this end, it prohibits certain government subsidies, government-backed marketing inducements, and corrupt business practices. Moreover, the agreement includes the following:

- The agreement permits launching up to eight payloads, in addition to the INMARSAT-3 satellite, to geosynchronous earth orbit (GEO) or geosynchronous transfer orbit (GTO), through December 31, 2000. Not more than two of these launches may be conducted in any twelve-month period.
- Three low earth orbit (LEO) launches are permitted.

- Certain other additional launches are to be considered on a case-by-case basis.
- The agreement stipulates that prices, terms, and conditions offered by Russian space launch service providers must be comparable to those offered by commercial launch service providers operating in market economy countries.
- The agreement requires that the United States and Russia hold annual consultations to "review and examine implementation of the Agreement and market developments."

In response to the terms of the **Agreement (with China) Regarding International Trade in Commercial Launch Services** (1995), the Russian agreement was renegotiated and liberalized by an agreement of amendment concluded on January 30, 1996. Additional launches and more liberal pricing terms were granted.

REFERENCES:
Owen, Harrison. *Expanding Our Now: The Story of Open Space Technology.* Berkeley, CA: North Atlantic Books, 1997.
Stine, G. Harry. *The Manna Project: Business Opportunities in Outer Space.* New York: M. Evans, 1998.

Agreement (with China) Regarding International Trade in Commercial Launch Services

SIGNED: March 3, 1995, at Washington

SIGNATORIES: China vs. United States

IN FORCE: From signing

OVERVIEW: A second agreement authorizing China to provide launch services for international customers.

DISCUSSION:

The original **Memorandum of Agreement Regarding International Trade in Commercial Launch Services** expired on December 31, 1994 and was immediately followed by the present agreement.

Whereas the first agreement allowed the launching of nine satellites into geostationary earth orbit, the new agreement permits eleven commercial GEO launches through 31 December 2001, provided that prices offered by China are "on a par" with those offered by Western launch-service providers. The agreement stipulates that, if the Chinese offer is more than 15 percent less than the price for a comparable Western launch, China must consult with the United States before concluding a launch contract.

The new agreement additionally allows China an unspecified number of commercial launches to low earth orbit (LEO), subject to United States review. If the United States determines that China is conducting a disproportionate number of LEO launches, it will enter into consultations with China.

REFERENCES:

Owen, Harrison. *Expanding Our Now: The Story of Open Space Technology.* Berkeley, CA: North Atlantic Books, 1997.

Stine, G. Harry. *The Manna Project: Business Opportunities in Outer Space.* New York: M. Evans, 1998.

U.S.-Russia Commercial Space Launch Agreement Amendment

OFFICIAL TITLE: The Agreement between the Government of the United States of America and the Government of the Russian Federation Regarding International Trade in Commercial Space Launch Services

SIGNED: January 30, 1996, at Washington, D.C.

SIGNATORIES: Russian Federation vs. United States

IN FORCE: From signing

OVERVIEW: The amendment extends the **Agreement (with the Russian Federation) on International Trade in Commercial Space Launch Services** of 1993.

DISCUSSION:

The amended agreement applies to commercial space launch services provided by the Russian Federation for international customers to geo-synchronous earth orbit (GEO), to geosynchronous transfer orbit (GTO), and to other orbits and suborbital launches. By the 1996 agreement, Russia is allowed up to fifteen launch contracts (in addition to the INMARSAT 3 satellite) for launches to GEO; however, if the market for commercial space launch services improves significantly beyond current expectations, Russia will be allowed up to four additional contracts for launches to GEO.

In the case of low-earth orbit (LEO) launches, the United States will assess whether the participation by Russia, China, and Ukraine in the deployment of any single LEO constellation of satellites is greater than the participation of market-economy launch providers.

Contractual terms and conditions, including the price, for both GEO and LEO, offered by Russian space launch service providers must be comparable to the terms and conditions offered by market economy countries. The following provisions apply:

- When a Russian bid for GEO space launch services is greater than 15 percent below the price offered by market economy countries, the U.S. may request special consultations.

- In the case of a Russian bid which is more than 15 percent below the price offered by market economy countries, U.S. and Russian analyses of the reasons for the low price will be guided by a specific set of price comparability factors.

In any event, the United States and Russia are to consult annually regarding the agreement and developments in the international market for commercial launch services. The expiration of the amended agreement is December 31, 2000.

U.S.-Ukraine Agreement Regarding International Trade in Commercial Space Launch Services

SIGNED: February 21, 1996, at Washington, D.C.

SIGNATORIES: Ukraine vs. United States

IN FORCE: From signing

OVERVIEW: An agreement allowing Ukraine to enter the space launch services market.

DISCUSSION:

Like China and Russia, Ukraine possesses space-launch capabilities, which it desires to commercialize by providing space-launch services to international customers. For background on the economic rationale motivating space-launch agreements, see **Memorandum of Agreement (with China) Regarding International Trade in Commercial Launch Services** (1989), **Agreement (with the Russian Federation) on International Trade in Commercial Space Launch Services** (1993), **Agreement (with China) Regarding International Trade in Commercial Launch Services** (1995), and **U.S.-Russia Commercial Space Launch Agreement Amendment** (1996).

The agreement with Ukraine provides for the following:

- Allows Ukraine to enter the international space launch market in a fashion that will not disrupt the marketplace

- Allows commercial Space launches to geosynchronous earth orbit (GEO)—currently the most frequently used orbit for commercial satellites—as well as to low earth orbit (LEO), a rapidly growing market

- Allows five launches to GEO, in addition to up to eleven more GEO launches for use by a contemplated U.S.-Ukrainian joint venture

- Under certain circumstances, provides the possibility of winning up to four additional launch contracts, three of which would be reserved for a U.S.-Ukrainian joint venture

- Establishes guidelines for Ukraine's participation in the market for launching commercial satellites to low earth orbit

- Stipulates that prices provided by Ukrainian space launch services will be comparable to those offered by the United States or other market economy countries

REFERENCES:

Owen, Harrison. *Expanding Our Now: The Story of Open Space Technology.* Berkeley, CA: North Atlantic Books, 1997.

Stine, G. Harry. *The Manna Project: Business Opportunities in Outer Space.* New York: M. Evans, 1998.

Commerce, Trade, and Standardization Issues

Overview of Treaties in This Category

For most nations, including the United States, only one broad category of treaty is more voluminous than that of war and defense. Commerce, trade, and trade-related issues of standardization have occasioned perhaps the single most extensive category of American treaties, which range from basic bilateral agreements establishing trade with a partner nation to detailed multilaterals, such as the **North American Free Trade Agreement (NAFTA)** of 1992. This section contains the most important historical and current United States trade and trade-related treaties, as well as a sampling of minor documents that, nevertheless, are highly representative of the general run of United States commercial agreements.

International trade is, in and of itself, a necessary component of any market economy, but it is also a basis for peaceful, "normal" relations between nations. The **Convention to Regulate the Commerce between the Territories of the United States and of His Britannick Majesty** of 1815 is an early example of a reciprocal treaty of free trade between the United States and another nation, and, drawn up in the aftermath of the War of 1812, it is also an example of a trade treaty functioning to reestablish normal relations between two nations. The concept of free trade—trade without undue tariff or other barriers—is at the core of most general trade treaties.

If "free trade" may be blocked by protective tariffs and other national legal restrictions, it may also be impeded by restrictions on navigation and transport; for the essence of international commerce is movement. Two treaties with Argentina, from 1853, serve as examples of trade treaties wedded to agreements of free navigation: **Treaty (with Argentina) for the Free Navigation of the Rivers Parana and Uruguay** and **Treaty (with Argentina) of Friendship, Commerce and Navigation.** While international freedom of the high seas is a long-accepted principle (although one that has proved difficult to define in detail; see Section 4.8), nations enjoy sovereignty and exclusivity with regard to their territorial and internal waterways. Special agreements may be required to secure freedom of navigation of these bodies for trade purposes.

In the name of trade, internal waterways have been opened to international commerce and great artificial waterways created. The Suez Canal was opened in 1869 across the Isthmus of Suez and linking the Red Sea and the Gulf of Suez with the Mediterranean Sea. After 1875, it came under British control, which lasted until 1956, when Britain turned the canal over to Egypt. Although the United States was not a signatory to the **Constantinople Convention of the Suez Canal** (1888), it, like all other nations of the world, was and continues to be a beneficiary of the guarantee of freedom of navigation of the canal. Moreover, the treaty served as a model for the key agreements relating to the Panama Canal, in which the United States played a primary role.

The main provisions of the Suez treaty and the early treaties relating to the Panama Canal (**Hay-Pauncefote Treaty, Hay-Herrán Treaty,** and **Hay-Bunau-Varilla Treaty;** see also **Clayton-Bulwer Treaty** [1850] in Section 3.5) is the simultaneous assertion of administrative and military control over the canal and a guarantee that the canal is to be open to shipping of all nations, both merchant and military. The United States' role in the ongoing administration of the Panama Canal gradually created enmity with Panama (and other Latin American countries) over issues of United States imperialism. In the interest of international justice, hemispheric stability, and general economic well-being, the United States negotiated an orderly transfer of control of the canal to Panama by the **Panama Canal Treaty (Torrijos-Carter Treaty)** and **the Panama Canal Neutrality Treaty,** both of 1977.

The exigencies of World War II occasioned another United States transportation project in a foreign country. The Alaska Highway, most of which traverses Canadian territory, was rapidly constructed during the war as a means of supplying and defending Alaska and of transporting oil drilled there. Three wartime agreements are typical of those relating to the highway project: **Agreement on Workmen's Compensation and Unemployment Insurance in Connection with Construction of the Alaska Highway** (1942), **Agreement Relating to Access to the Alaska Highway** (1943), and **Agreement Designating the Official Name of the Alaska Highway** (1943). After the war, the highway was turned over to Canada, and, in 1977, the United States agreed to fund some work on the highway: **Agreement (with Canada) on Reconstruction of Canadian Portions of the Alaska Highway.** (Another war-related commercial treaty is **Agreement [with Canada] Relating to the Patent Rights in Connection with RDX and other Explosives**, of 1946, which settles questions of patent rights arising from products jointly created by the two nations during the war.)

The greatest public works transportation project on which the United States and Canada collaborated was the St. Lawrence Seaway, an international waterway, some 2,350 miles long, incorporating an extensive system of canals, dams, and locks in the St. Lawrence River and connecting channels through the Great Lakes and giving the interior of eastern Canada and the U.S. Midwest access to the Atlantic Ocean. The basic agreements include: **Agreement (with Canada) Relating to the St. Lawrence Seaway Project** (1952), **Agreement Relating to the Establishment of the St. Lawrence River Joint Board of Engineers** (1953), **Agreement of 30 June 1952 Relating to the St. Lawrence Seaway Project** (1954), and **Agreement (with Canada) on the Relocation of Part of Roosevelt Bridge** (1956). In the 1970s, construction of the great Alaska Pipeline, transporting natural gas from the Alaska oilfields to Canada and the lower forty-eight United States, was another major U.S.-Canada cooperative public works project. The basic agreement relating to the enterprise is **Agreement (with Canada) on Principles Applicable to a Northern Natural Gas Pipeline**.

Another important class of bilateral commercial treaty establishes most-favored-nation trade with a particular trading partner. Treaties such as **Treaty of Friendship, Commerce, and Navigation with Republic of China (Taiwan)** of 1945 and **Treaty of Friendship, Commerce and Navigation with Japan** (1953), for example, provide mutual guarantees that the two nations will grant one another the trade terms granted to the "most favored" trading partners. Often, however, the exigencies of domestic and international markets require additional trade agreements between countries, typically setting equitable quotas for imports versus exports of certain goods or categories of goods. In a free-market economy, such agreements may be necessary to protect domestic industries by preventing distortions of the market. Examples of this class of bilateral treaty include **Auto Pact (with Canada)** (1965), **Agreement Concerning Brazilian Exports of Soluble Coffee to United States** (1971), **Agreement with the European Economic Community on Wine** (1983), **Textile Agreement with Haiti** (1986), and others.

Two other bilateral trade agreement types should also be noted.

To facilitate trade between two nations, it is sometimes advantageous to resolve certain differences as regards standards of measurement, safety, or product specifications. The **Memorandum of Understanding (with Mexico) Relating to the Exchange of Information on FDA-Regulated Products** (1974) is an example of such an agreement.

Trade is a principal means of establishing friendly, productive relations among nations. The United States has frequently used trade to influence the development of friendly ideologies throughout the world. Such documents as **Loan Agreement (with Bangladesh) for the Ashuganj Fertilizer Plant** (1975) and **Project Grant Agreement (with Bangladesh) for Agricultural Inputs Project** (1977), for example, provide economic aid for humanitarian as well political purposes. As communist Poland began to show interest in achieving a degree of economic independence from the Soviet bloc, the United States concluded **Agreement (with Poland) on Economic and Industrial Cooperation** (1978).

While bilateral trade agreements will always be important, the trend over the past half century has been toward development of multilateral trade agreements, which reflect even as they enable and enhance the globalization of trade.

For the United States, the single most important agreement governing international trade is the **General Agreement on Tariffs and Trade (GATT)**, first created in 1947 and amended many times since. The **North American Free Trade Agreement (NAFTA)**, concluded among the United States, Canada, and Mexico, in 1992 is the most important regional trade agreement, establishing a free trade area for the continent and laying down detailed rules to maintain free trade on an equitable basis. Other multilateral treaties address such subjects as standardization of measurement (for example, **Convention Establishing an International Organization of Legal Metrology**, 1955, and **International Convention on Tonnage Measurement of Ships**, 1969), standardization of contracts (**Convention on Contracts**, 1964), provision of arbitration procedures and apparatus (**Inter-American Convention on International Commercial Arbitration**, 1975), standardization of factoring (**Unidroit Convention on International Factoring**, 1988), standardization of leasing (**Unidroit Convention on International Financial Leasing**, 1988), stabilization of important raw materials and commodities (**International Natural Rubber Agreement**, 1979 and 1995), and agreements on the exploitation of certain international natural resources (**Provisional Understanding Regarding Deep Seabed Matters**, 1984).

NAFTA, as just observed, was a momentous step toward regionalization of American trade. The creation of NAFTA was prompted in large part by the development of the European Community, an effort to unite the disparate national markets and producers of Europe into a single entity at once more efficient and more powerful in the global marketplace. In 1997, the United States and the European Community concluded **Agreement on Mutual Recognition between the United States and the European Community**, to facilitate trade between the United States and the European transnational entity. Recent years have seen the creation of an increasing number of agreements not among states, but among states and organizations or other non-state entities, such as the European Community.

Convention to Regulate the Commerce between the Territories of the United States and of His Britannick Majesty

SIGNED: July 3, 1815

SIGNATORIES: Great Britain vs. United States

IN FORCE: Six months from signing

OVERVIEW: A reciprocal treaty of free trade between the United States and Great Britain, made in the aftermath of the War of 1812.

DISCUSSION:

The substance of the treaty is encompassed within its first article:

There shall be between the Territories of the United States of America and all the Territories of His Britannick Majesty in Europe a reciprocal liberty of Commerce. The Inhabitants of the two Countries respectively shall have liberty freely and securely to come with their ships and cargoes to all such places Ports and Rivers in the Territories aforesaid to which other Foreigners are permitted to come, to enter into the same, and to remain and reside in any parts of the said Territories respectively, also to hire and occupy Houses and warehouses for the purposes of their commerce, and generally the Merchants and Traders of each Nation respectively shall enjoy the most complete protection and security for their Commerce but subject always to the Laws and Statutes of the two countries respectively

Establishing a friendly relationship of reciprocal free trade between Britain and the United States was intended, in part, to heal the wounds of the recently concluded War of 1812. (*See* **Treaty of Ghent**).

REFERENCE:

Hickey, Donald R. *The War of 1812: A Forgotten Conflict*. Urbana and Chicago: University of Illinois Press, 1990.

Treaty (with Argentina) for the Free Navigation of the Rivers Parana and Uruguay

SIGNED: July 10, 1853, at San Jose de Flores, Argentina

SIGNATORIES: Argentina vs. United States

IN FORCE: From April 9, 1855

OVERVIEW: A treaty to facilitate trading by United States interests in Argentina through free navigation of the principal rivers, Parana and Uruguay.

DISCUSSION:

By the mid nineteenth century, the United States was taking substantial steps to extend its sphere of influence throughout the hemisphere, particularly in Central and South America, where American business interests had a firm foothold. This treaty is an early example of a commercial agreement with a South American nation. It opens up Argentina's principal internal waterways to the ships of all nations. In effect, the treaty institutes an "open door" policy for Argentina.

REFERENCE:

Rock, David. *Argentina, 1516-1987: From Spanish Colonization to Alfonsin*. Berkeley: University of California Press, 1989

Treaty (with Argentina) of Friendship, Commerce and Navigation

SIGNED: July 27, 1853, at San Jose de Flores, Argentina

SIGNATORIES: Argentina vs. United States

IN FORCE: From April 9, 1855

OVERVIEW: "Commercial intercourse having been for some time established between the United States and the Argentine Confederation, it seems good for the security as well as the encouragement of such commercial intercourse, and for the maintenance of good understanding between the two Governments, that the relations now subsisting between them should be regularly acknowledged and confirmed by the signing to a treaty of friendship, commerce and navigation."

DISCUSSION:

Concluded immediately after the **Treaty (with Argentina) for the Free Navigation of the Rivers Parana and Uruguay**, the Treaty of Friendship, Commerce, and Navigation expands the scope of the first treaty by fully establishing "normal" commercial relations between Argentina and the United States.

REFERENCE:

Rock, David. *Argentina, 1516-1987: From Spanish Colonization to Alfonsin*. Berkeley: University of California Press, 1989.

Constantinople Convention of the Suez Canal

SIGNED: October 29, 1888, at Constantinople

SIGNATORIES: Great Britain, Germany, Austria-Hungary, Spain, France, Italy, the Netherlands, Russia and Turkey

IN FORCE: Not in force for the United States

OVERVIEW: A convention guaranteeing the freedom of navigation of the Suez Canal.

DISCUSSION:

Although the United States is not a signatory to this convention, it, like all other nations of the world, is a beneficiary of the guarantee of freedom of navigation of the canal. Moreover, the treaty served as a model for the key United States agreements relating to the Panama Canal.

The principal text of the treaty articles follows:

ARTICLE I

The Suez Maritime Canal shall always be free and of commerce or of war, without distinction of flag. Consequently, the High Contracting Parties agree not in any way to interfere with the free use of the Canal, in time of war as in time of peace. The Canal shall never be subjected to the exercise of the right of blockade.

ARTICLE II

The High Contracting Parties, recognising that the Fresh-Water Canal is indispensable to the Maritime Canal, take note of the engagements of His Highness the Khedive towards the Universal Suez Canal Company as regards the Fresh-Water Canal; which engagements are stipulated in a Convention bearing the date of 18th March, 1863, containing an expose and four Articles.

They undertake not to interfere in any way with the security of that Canal and its branches, the working of which shall not be exposed to any attempt at obstruction.

ARTICLE III

The High Contracting Parties likewise undertake to respect the plant, establishments, buildings, and works of the Maritime Canal and of the Fresh-Water-Canal.

ARTICLE IV

The Maritime Canal remaining open in time of war as a free passage, even to ships of war of belligerents, according to the terms of Article I of the present Treaty, the High Contracting Parties agree that no right of war, no act of hostility, nor any act having for its object to obstruct the free navigating of the Canal, shall be committed in the Canal and its ports, even though the Ottoman Empire should be one of the belligerent Powers.

Vessels of war of belligerents shall not revictual or take in stores in the Canal and its ports of access, except in so far may be strictly necessary. The transit of the aforesaid vessels through the Canal shall be effected with the least possible delay, in accordance with the Regulations in force, and without any intermission than the resulting from the necessities of the service. Their stay at Port Said and in the roadstead of Suez shall not exceed twenty-four hours, except in case if distress. In such case they shall be bound to leave as soon as possible. An interval of twenty-four hours shall always elapse between the sailing of a belligerent ship from one of the ports of access and the depasture of a ship belonging to the hostile Power.

ARTICLE V

In time of war belligerent Powers shall not disembark nor embark within the Canal and its ports of access either troops, munitions, or materials of war. But in case of an accidental hindrance in the Canal, men may be embarked or disembarked at the ports of access by detachments not exceeding 1,000 men, with a corresponding amount of war material.

ARTICLE VI

Prizes shall be subjected, in all respects, to the same rules as the vessels of war of belligerents.

ARTICLE VII

The Powers shall not keep any vessel of war in the waters of the Canal (including Lake Timsah and the Bitter Lakes). Nevertheless, they may station vessel of war in the ports of access of Port Said and Suez, the number of which shall not exceed two for each power. This right shall not be exercised by belligerents.

ARTICLE VIII

The agents in Egypt of the Signatory Powers of the present Treaty shall be charged to watch over its execution. In case of any event threatening the security or the free passage of the Canal, they shall meet on the summons of three of their number under the presidency of their Doyen, in order to proceed to the necessary verifications. They shall inform the Khedivial Government of the danger which they may have perceived, in order that that Government may take proper steps to insure the protection and the free use of the Canal. Under any circumstances, they shall meet once a year to take note of the due execution of the Treaty. The last mentioned meetings shall take place under the presidency of a Special Commissioner nominated for that purpose by the Imperial Ottoman Government. A Commissioner of the Khedive may also take part in the meeting, and may preside over it in case of the absence of the Ottoman Commissioner. They shall especially demand the suppression of any work or the dispersion of any assemblage on either bank of the Canal, the object or effect of which might be to interfere with the liberty and the entire security of the navigation.

ARTICLE XI

The Egyptian Government shall, within the limit of its powers resulting from the Firmans, and under the conditions provided for in the present Treaty, take the necessary measures for insuring the execution of the said Treaty. In case the Egyptian Government shall not have sufficient means at its disposal, it shall call upon the Imperial Ottoman Government, which shall take the necessary measures to respond to such appeal, shall give notice thereof to the Signatory Powers of the Declaration of London of the 17th March, 1885, and shall, if necessary, concert with them on the subject. The provisions of Articles IV, V, VII and VIII shall not interfere with the measures which shall be taken in virtue of the present Article.

ARTICLE X

Similarly, the provisions of Articles IV, V, VII and VIII shall not interfere with the measures which His Majesty the Sultan and His Highness the Khedive, in the name of His Imperial Majesty, and within the limits of the Firmans granted, might find it necessary to take for securing by their own forces the defence of Egypt and the maintenance of public order. In case His Imperial Majesty the Sultan, or His Highness the Khedive, would find it necessary to avail themselves of the exceptions for which this article provides, the Signatory Powers of the Declaration of London shall be notified thereof by the Imperial Ottoman Government. It is likewise understood that the provisions of the four Articles aforesaid shall in no case occasion any obstacle to the measures which the Imperial Ottoman Government may think it necessary to take in order to insure by its own forces the defence of its other possessions situated on the eastern coast of the Red Sea.

ARTICLE XI

The measures which shall be taken in the cases provided for by Article IX and X of the present Treaty shall not interfere with the free use of the Canal. In the same cases, the erection of permanent fortifications contrary to the provisions of Article VIII is prohibited.

ARTICLE XII

The High Contracting Parties, by application of the principle of equality as regards the free use of the Canal, a principle which forms one of the bases of the present Treaty, agree that none of them shall endeavour to obtain with respect to the Canal territorial or commercial advantages or privileges in any international arrangements which may be concluded. Moreover, the rights of Turkey as the territorial Power are reserved.

ARTICLE XII

With the exception of the obligations provided for in this treaty, no encroachment is legalised on the rights of sovereignty or prerogatives deriving from the firmans.

ARTICLE XIV

The High Contracting Parties agree that the engagements resulting from present Treaty shall not be limited by the duration of the Acts of Concession of the Universal Suez Canal Company.

ARTICLE XV

The stipulations of the present Treaty shall not interfere with the sanitary measures in force in Egypt.

ARTICLE XVI

The High Contracting Parties undertake to bring the present Treaty to the knowledge of the States which have not signed it, inviting them to accede to it.

REFERENCES:
None

Hay-Pauncefote Treaty

OFFICIAL TITLE: Treaty to Facilitate the Construction of a Ship Canal
SIGNED: November 18, 1901, at Washington
SIGNATORIES: Great Britain vs. United States
IN FORCE: From February 21, 1902
OVERVIEW: A treaty superseding the controversial **Clayton-Bulwer Treaty (Convention Between the United States of America and Her Britannic Majesty)** of 1850 as an agreement on Anglo-American policy concerning the proposed Panama Canal.

DISCUSSION:

Negotiated between John Hay, U.S. secretary of state, and Lord Julian Pauncefote, British ambassador to the United States, the treaty resolved the troublesome Clayton-Bulwer Treaty, which had created bitter controversy over Britain's interests in Central America. The United States insisted that the Clayton-Bulwer document called for complete neutrality in Central America, which meant a British renunciation of a protectorate in the British Honduras, Mosquito Coast, and Bay Islands. The British insisted that the treaty did not affect the status quo. Following the Spanish-American War (1898), popular sentiment in the United was decidedly imperialist, and there was a call for abrogation of the 1850 treaty, so that the United States could build the canal without British participation.

By 1900, Great Britain was indeed amenable to a canal built solely by the United States, provided that the canal zone itself would remain neutral. This new consensus was embodied in the first draft of the Hay-Pauncefote Treaty, which provided for the following:

- The United States would direct construction of the Panama Canal.
- The canal zone would be permanently neutral
- The canal zone would not be fortified.
- Other nations would be invited to join in guarantees of neutrality.

The United States Senate refused to ratify the draft, however, but amended it to permit the United States to take whatever measures it saw fit for its own defense in the canal zone, and the Senate deleted the invitation to other nations to participate in the treaty. When Great Britain objected to these amendments, negotiations were resumed, and the document was again revised. The revision provided for the following:

- The United States retained full control of the construction and management of the canal.
- The U.S. was to be sole guarantor of the neutrality of the canal and was permitted to build fortifications for the purpose of defending its neutrality only.
- The canal was to be open to ships of all nations equally, except that the United States could bar passage in times of war.

The newly revised treaty was ratified, and the Panama Canal was built and operated according to its provisions. In 1911 Great Britain lodged a complaint that the United States had vioalted the provision opening the canal to ships of all nations under equal terms by passage of the Panama Canal Act, which exempted American coastal shipping from paying canal tolls. President Woodrow Wilson prevailed on Congress to repeal the act in 1914.

The basic provisions of Hay-Pauncefote were superceded in 1977 by two new treaties with Panama, providing for the gradual transfer of control of the canal and of the Panama Canal Zone to the nation of Panama. (See **Panama Canal Basic Treaty** and **Panama Canal Neutrality Treaty**; also see **Hay-Herrán Treaty** and **Hay-Bunau-Varilla Treaty**).

REFERENCES:
Canal Treaties. Washington, D.C.: U.S. Government Printing Office, 1914.
Nesbitt, Wallace. *The Panama Canal and its Treaty Obligations.* Toronto: Rous and Mann, Ltd., 1912.
Parrish, Samuel L. *The Hay-Paunceforte Treaty and the Panama Canal,* New York: N. Pub., 1913).

Hay-Herrán Treaty

SIGNED: January 22, 1903, at Washington, D.C.
SIGNATORIES: Colombia vs. United States
IN FORCE: Ratified by the U.S. Senate, March 14, 1903; rejected by the Colombian Senate; did not enter into force
OVERVIEW: Treaty negotiated by U.S. Secretary of State John

Hay with Colombian foreign minister Tomás Herrán, providing for U.S. control of the prospective Panama Canal and for U.S. acquisition of a canal zone; rejected by the Colombian Senate.

DISCUSSION:

The principal provisions of the treaty include the following:

- The right of the New Panama Canal Company, which held an option on the canal route, to sell its properties to the United States
- An agreement by Colombia, of which Panama was a province, to lease a strip of land across the Isthmus of Panama to the United States for construction of a canal
- An agreement by the United States to pay Colombia $10 million and, after nine years, an annuity of $250,000.

United States president Theodore Roosevelt had wanted a treaty that would give the United States complete governmental control over the proposed canal zone. The treaty, as negotiated, did not provide this, but did offer enough to the United States to prompt the U.S. Senate to ratify the agreement. The Colombian Senate, however, delayed ratification in the hope of increasing the price offered by the United States. Finally, however, it refused to ratify the treaty, in part because of dissatisfaction with the financial terms, but also from a popular push to resist "Yankee imperialism" and to relinquish a significant measure of national sovereignty.

President Roosevelt responded to the rejection of the treaty by lending support to Panamanian insurgents for a bloodless coup by which Panama gained independence from Colombia. In return for this support, Panama quickly concluded with the United States a new canal and canal zone agreement, the **Hay-Bunau-Varilla Treaty.**

REFERENCES:

Canal Treaties. Washington, D.C.: U.S. Government Printing Office, 1914.

Nesbitt, Wallace. *The Panama Canal and its Treaty Obligations.* Toronto: Rous and Mann, Ltd., 1912.

Parrish, Samuel L. *The Hay-Pauncefore Treaty and the Panama Canal,* New York: N. Pub., 1913).

Hay-Bunau-Varilla Treaty

OFFICIAL TITLE: Convention for the Construction of a Ship Canal

SIGNED: November 18, 1903, at Washington, D.C.

SIGNATORIES: Panama vs. United States

IN FORCE: From February 26, 1904

OVERVIEW: Treaty negotiated by U.S. Secretary of State John Hay with Panama's minister plenipotentiary Philippe Bunau-Varilla, providing for U.S. control of the prospective Panama Canal and for U.S. acquisition of a canal zone.

DISCUSSION:

For background to this treaty, see **Hay-Herrán Treaty.**

Philippe Bunau-Varilla was a French engineer who had been employed by the Compagnie Universelle du Canal Interocéanique, the French Panama Canal Company, in 1884. When the French canal project failed in 1889, Bunau-Varilla approached the United States and was commissioned by American government to negotiate a treaty with Colombia, of which Panama was a part. This resulted in the **Hay-Herrán Treaty.** When that treaty was rejected by the Colombian Senate, Bunau-Varilla, supported by the Roosevelt government, helped foment the bloodless coup that brought about Panamanian independence. The provisional government of the newly independent Panama named Bunau-Varilla minister plenipotentiary, and he quickly signed a canal treaty with Secretary of State John Hay.

The treaty, one of the most significant in American history, is reproduced at length as follows:

The United States of America and the Republic of Panama being desirous to insure the construction of a ship canal across the Isthmus of Panama to connect the Atlantic and Pacific oceans, and the Congress of the United States of America having passed an act approved June 28, 1902, in furtherance of that object, by which the President of the United States is authorized to acquire within a reasonable time the control of the necessary territory of the Republic of Colombia, and the sovereignty of such territory being actually vested in the Republic of Panama, the high contracting parties have resolved for that purpose to conclude a convention and have accordingly appointed as their plenipotentiaries,—

The President of the United States of America, John Hay, Secretary of State, and The Government of the Republic of Panama, Philippe Bunau-Varilla, Envoy Extraordinary and Minister Plenipotentiary of the Republic of Panama, thereunto specially empowered by said government, who after communicating with each other their respective full powers, found to be in good and due form, have agreed upon and concluded the following articles:

ARTICLE I

The United States guarantees and will maintain the independence of the Republic of Panama.

ARTICLE II

The Republic of Panama grants to the United States in perpetuity the use, occupation and control of a zone of land and land under water for the construction maintenance, operation, sanitation and protection of said Canal of the width of ten miles extending to the distance of five miles on each side of the center line of the route of the Canal to be constructed; the said zone beginning in the Caribbean Sea three marine miles from mean low water mark and extending to and across the Isthmus of Panama into the Pacific ocean to a distance of three marine miles from mean low water mark with the proviso that the cities of Panama and Colon and the harbors adjacent to said cities, which are included within the boundaries of the zone above described, shall not be included within this grant. The Republic of Panama further grants to the United States in perpetuity the use, occupation and control of any other lands and waters outside of the zone above described which may be necessary and convenient for the construction, maintenance, operation, sanitation and protection of the said Canal or of any auxiliary canals or other works necessary and convenient for the construction, maintenance, operation, sanitation and protection of the said enterprise.

The Republic of Panama further grants in like manner to the United States in perpetuity all islands within the limits of the zone above described and in addition thereto the group of small islands in the Bay of Panama, named, Perico, Naos. Culebra and Flamenco.

ARTICLE III

The Republic of Panama grants to the United States all the rights, power and authority within the zone mentioned and described in Article II of this agreement and within the limits of all auxiliary lands and waters mentioned and described in said Article II which the United States would possess and exercise if it were the sovereign of the territory within which said lands and waters are located to the entire exclusion of the exercise by the Republic of Panama of any such sovereign rights, power or authority.

ARTICLE IV

As rights subsidiary to the above grants the Republic of Panama grants in perpetuity to the United States the right to use the rivers, streams, lakes and other bodies of water within its limits for navigation, the supply of water or water-power or other purposes, so far as the use of said rivers, streams, lakes and bodies of water and the waters thereof may be necessary and convenient for the construction, maintenance, operation, sanitation and protection of the said Canal.

ARTICLE V

The Republic of Panama grants to the United States in perpetuity a monopoly for the construction, maintenance and operation of any system of communication by means of canal or railroad across its territory between the Caribbean Sea and the Pacific ocean.

ARTICLE VI

The grants herein contained shall in no manner invalidate the titles or rights of private land holders or owners of private property in the said zone or in or to any of the lands or waters granted to the United States by the provisions of any Article of this treaty, nor shall they interfere with the rights of way over the public roads passing through the said zone or over any of the said lands or waters unless said rights of way or private rights shall conflict with rights herein granted to the United States in which case. the rights of the United States shall be superior. All damages caused to the owners of private lands or private property of any kind by reason of the grants contained in this treaty or by reason of the operations of the United States, its agents or employees, or by reason of the construction, maintenance, operation, sanitation and protection of the said Canal or of the works of sanitation and protection herein provided for, shall be appraised and settled by a joint Commission appointed by the Governments of the United States and the Republic of Panama, whose decisions as to such damages shall be final and whose awards as to such damages shall be paid solely by the United States. No part of the work on said Canal or the Panama railroad or on any auxiliary works relating thereto and authorized by the terms of this treaty shall be prevented, delayed or impeded by or pending such proceedings to ascertain such damages. The appraisal of said private lands and private property and the assessment of damages to them shall be based upon their value before the date of this convention.

ARTICLE VII

The Republic of Panama grants to the United States within the limits of the cities of Panama and Colon and their adjacent harbors and within the territory adjacent thereto the right to acquire by purchase or by the exercise of the right of eminent domain, any lands, buildings, water rights or other properties necessary and convenient for the construction, maintenance, operation and protection of the Canal and of any works of sanitation, such as the collection and disposition of sewage and the distribution of water in the said cities of Panama and Colon, which in the discretion of the United States may be necessary and convenient for the construction, maintenance, operation, sanitation and protection of the said Canal and railroad. All such works of sanitation, collection and disposition of sewage and distribution of water in the cities of Panama and Colon shall be made at the expense of the United States, and the Government of the United States, its agents or nominees shall be authorized to impose and collect water rates and sewerage rates which shall be sufficient to provide for the payment of interest and the amortization of the principal of the cost of said works within a period of fifty years and upon the expiration of said term of fifty years the system of sewers and water works shall revert to and become the properties of the cities of Panama and Colon respectively, and the use of the water shall be free to the inhabitants of Panama and Colon, except to the extent that water rates may be necessary for the operation and maintenance of said system of sewers and water.

The Republic of Panama agrees that the cities of Panama and Colon shall comply in perpetuity with the sanitary ordinances whether of a preventive or curative character prescribed by the United States and in case the Government of Panama is unable or fails in its duty to enforce this compliance by the cities of Panama and Colon with the sanitary ordinances of the United States the Republic of Panama grants to the United States the right and authority to enforce the same.

The same right and authority are granted to the United States for the maintenance of public order in the cities of Panama and Colon and the territories and harbors adjacent thereto in case the Republic of Panama should not be, in the judgment of the United States, able to maintain such order.

ARTICLE VIII

The Republic of Panama grants to the United States all rights which it now has or hereafter may acquire to bee property of the New Panama Canal Company and the Panama Railroad Company as a result of the transfer of sovereignty from the Republic of Colombia to the Republic of Panama over the Isthmus of Panama and authorizes the New Panama Canal Company to sell and transfer to the United States its rights, privileges, properties and concessions as well as the Panama Railroad and all the shares or part of the shares of that company; lot the public lands situated outside of the zone described in Article II of this treaty now included in the concessions to both said enterprises and not required in the construction or operation of the Canal shall revert to the Republic of Panama except any property now owned by or in the possession of said companies within Panama or Colon or the ports or terminals thereof.

ARTICLE IX

The United States agrees that the ports at either entrance of the Canal and the waters thereof, and the Republic of Panama agrees that the towns of Panama and Colon shall be free for all time so that there shall not be imposed or collected custom house tolls, tonnage, anchorage, lighthouse, wharf, pilot, or quarantine dues or any other charges or taxes of any kind upon any vessel using or passing through the Canal or belonging to or employed by the United States, directly or indirectly, in connection with the construction, maintenance, operation, sanitation and protection of the main Canal, or auxiliary works, or upon the cargo, officers, crew, or passengers of any such vessels, except such tolls and charges as may be imposed by the United States for the use of the Canal and other works, and except tolls and charges imposed by the Republic of Panama upon merchandise destined to be introduced for the consumption of the rest of the Republic of Panama, and upon vessels touching at the ports of Colon and Panama and which do not cross the Canal.

The Government of the Republic of Panama shall have the right to establish in such ports and in the towns of Panama and Colon such houses and guards as it may deem necessary to collect duties on importations destined to other portions of Panama and to prevent contraband trade.

The United Skates Shall have the right to make use of the towns and harbors of Panama and Colon as places of anchorage, and for making repairs, for loading, unloading, depositing, or transshipping cargoes either in transit or destined for the service of the Canal and for other works pertaining to the Canal.

ARTICLE X

The Republic of Panama agrees that there shall not be imposed any taxes, national, municipal, departmental, or of any other class, upon the Canal, the railways and auxiliary works, tugs and other vessels employed in bye service of the Canal, store houses, work shops, offices, quarters for laborers, factories of all kinds, warehouses, wharves, machinery and other works, property, and effects appertaining to the Canal or railroad and auxiliary works, or their officers or employees, situated within the cities of Panama and Colon, and that there shall not be imposed contributions or charges of a personal character of any kind upon officers, employees, laborers, and other individuals in the service of the Canal and railroad and auxiliary works.

ARTICLE XI

The United States agrees that the official dispatches of the Government of the Republic of Panama shall be transmitted over any telegraph and telephone lines established for canal purposes and used for public and private business at rates not higher than those required from officials in the service of the United States.

ARTICLE XII

The Government of the Republic of Panama shall permit the immigration and free access to the lands and workshops of the Canal and its auxiliary works of all employees and workmen of whatever nationality under contract to work upon or seeking employment upon or in any wise connected with the said Canal and its auxiliary works, with their respective families, and all such persons shall be free and exempt from the military service of the Republic of Panama.

ARTICLE XIII

The United States may import at any time into the said zone and auxiliary lands, free of custom duties, imposts, taxes, or other charges, and without any restrictions, any and all vessels, dredges, engines, cars, machinery, tools, explosives, materials, supplies, and other articles necessary and convenient in the construction, maintenance, opera-

tion, sanitation and protection of the Canal and auxiliary works, and all provisions, medicines, clothing, supplies and other things necessary and convenient for the officers, employees, workmen and laborers in the service and employ of the United States and for their families. If any such articles are disposed of for use outside of the zone and auxiliary lands granted to the United States and within the territory of the Republic, they shall be subject to the same import or other duties as like articles imported under the laws of the Republic of Panama.

ARTICLE XIV

As the price or compensation for the rights, powers and privileges granted in this convention by the Republic of Panama to the United States, the Government of the United States agrees to pay to the Republic of Panama the sum of ten million dollars ($10,000,000) in gold coin of the United States on the exchange of the ratification of this convention and also an annual payment during the life of this convention of two hundred and fifty thousand dollars ($250,000) in like gold coin, beginning nine years after the date aforesaid.

The provisions of this Article shall be in addition to all other benefits assured to the Republic of Panama under this convention. But no delay or difference opinion under this Article or any other provisions of this treaty shall affect or interrupt the full operation and effect of this convention in all other respects.

ARTICLE XV

The joint commission referred to in Article VI shall be established as follows:

The President of the United States shall nominate two persons and the President of the Republic of Panama shall nominate two persons and they shall proceed to a decision; but in case of disagreement of the Commission (by reason of their being equally divided in conclusion) an umpire shall be appointed by tire two Governments who shall render the decision. In the event of the death, absence, or incapacity of a Commissioner or Umpire, or of his omitting, declining or ceasing to act, his place shall be filled by the appointment of another person in the manner above indicated. All decisions by a majority of the Commission or by the Umpire shall be final.

ARTICLE XVI

The two Governments shall make adequate provision by future agreement for the pursuit, capture, imprisonment, detention and delivery within said zone and auxiliary lands to the authorities of the Republic of Panama of persons charged with the commitment of crimes, felonies or misdemeanors without said zone and for the pursuit, capture, imprisonment, detention and delivery without said zone to the authorities of the United States of persons charged with the commitment of crimes, felonies and misdemeanors within said zone and auxiliary lands.

ARTICLE XVII

The Republic of Panama grants to the United States the use of all the ports of the Republic open to commerce as places of refuge for any vessels employed in the Canal enterprise, and for all vessels passing or bound to pass through the Canal which may be in distress and be driven to seek refuge in said ports. Such vessels shall be exempt from anchorage and tonnage dues on the part of the Republic of Panama.

ARTICLE XVIII

The Canal, when constructed, and the entrances thereto shall be neutral in perpetuity, and shall be opened upon the terms provided for by Section I of Article three of, and in conformity with all the stipulations of, the treaty entered into by the Governments of the United States and Great Britain on November 18,1901.

ARTICLE XIX

The Government of the Republic of Panama shall have the right to transport over the Canal its vessels and its troops and munitions of war in such vessels at all times without paying charges of any kind. The exemption is to be extended to the auxiliary railway for the transportation of persons in the service of the Republic of Panama, or of the police force charged with the preservation of public order outside of said zone, as well as to their baggage, munitions of war and supplies.

ARTICLE XX

If by virtue of any existing treaty in relation to the territory of the Isthmus of Panama, whereof the obligations shall descend or be assumed by the Republic of Panama, there may be any privilege or concession in favor the Government or the citizens and subjects of a third power relative to an interoceanic means of communication which in any of its terms may be incompatible with the terms of the present convention, the Republic of Panama agrees to cancel or modify such treaty in due form, for which purpose it shall give to the said third power the requisite notification within the term of four months from the date of the present convention, and in case the existing treaty contains no clause permitting its modification or annulment, the Republic of Panama agrees to procure its modification or annulment in such form that there shall not exist any conflict with the stipulations of the present convention.

ARTICLE XXI

The rights and privileges granted by the Republic of Panama to the United States in the preceding Articles are understood to be free of all anterior debts, liens, trusts, or liabilities, or concessions or privileges to other Governments, corporations, syndicates or individuals, and consequently, if there should arise any claims on account of the present concessions and privileges or otherwise, the claimants shall resort to the Government of the Republic of Panama and not to the United States for any indemnity or compromise which may be required.

ARTICLE XXII

The Republic of Panama renounces and grants to the United States the participation to which it might be entitled in the future earnings of the Canal under Article XV of the concessionary contract with Lucien N. B. Wyse now owned by the New Panama Canal Company and any and all other rights or claims of a pecuniary nature arising under or relating to said concession, or arising under or relating to the concessions to the Panama Railroad Company or any extension or modification thereof; and it likewise renounces, confirms and grants to the United States, now and hereafter, all the rights and property reserved in the said concessions which otherwise would belong to Panama at or before the expiration of the terms of ninety-nine years of the concessions granted to or held by the above mentioned party and companies, and all right, title and interest which it now has or many hereafter have, in and to the lands, canal, works, property and rights held by the said companies under said concessions or otherwise, and acquired or to be acquired by the United States from or through the New Panama Canal Company, including any property and rights which might or may in the future either by lapse of time, forfeiture or otherwise, revert to the Republic of Panama, under any contracts or concessions, with said Wyse, the Universal Panama Canal Company, the Panama Railroad Company and the New Panama Canal Company.

The aforesaid rights and property shall be and are free and released from any present or reversionary interest in or claims of Panama and the title of the United States thereto upon consummation of the contemplated purchase by the United States from the New Panama Canal (company, shall be absolute, so far as concerns the Republic of Panama, excepting always the rights of the Republic specifically secured under this treaty.

ARTICLE XXIII

If it should become necessary at any time to employ armed forces for the safety or protection of the Canal, or of the ships that make use of the same, or the railways and auxiliary works, the United States shall have the right, at all times and in its discretion, to use its police and its land and naval forces or to establish fortifications for these purposes.

ARTICLE XXIV

No change either in the Government or in the laws and treaties of the Republic of Panama shall, without the consent of the United States, affect any right of the United States under the present convention, or under any treaty stipulation between the two countries that now exists or may hereafter exist touching the subject matter of this convention.

If the Republic of Panama shall hereafter enter as a constituent into any other Government or into any union or confederation of states, so as to merge her sovereignty or independence in such Government, union or confederation, the rights of the United States under this convention shall not be in any respect lessened or impaired.

ARTICLE XXV

For the better performance of the engagements of this convention and to the end of the efficient protection of the Canal and the preservation of its neutrality, the Government of the Republic of Panama will sell or lease to the United States lands adequate and necessary for naval or coaling stations on the Pacific coast and on the western Caribbean coast of the Republic at certain points to be agreed upon with the President of the United States.

ARTICLE XXVI

This convention when signed by the Plenipotentiaries of the Contracting Parties shall be ratified by the respective Governments and the ratifications shall be exchanged at Washington at the earliest date possible.

The treaty was superceded by two 1977 agreements, the **Panama Canal Basic Treaty** and the **Panama Canal Neutrality Treaty.**

REFERENCES:
Canal Treaties. Washington, D.C.: U.S. Government Printing Office, 1914.
Nesbitt, Wallace. *The Panama Canal and its Treaty Obligations.* Toronto: Rous and Mann, Ltd., 1912.
Parrish, Samuel L. *The Hay-Paunceforte Treaty and the Panama Canal,* New York: N. Pub., 1913.

Agreement on Workmen's Compensation and Unemployment Insurance in Connection with Construction of the Alaska Highway

OFFICIAL TITLE: Exchange of Notes Constituting an Agreement Relating to Workmen's Compensation and Unemployment Insurance in Connexion with the Construction of the Military Highway to Alaska and other American Projects in Canada

SIGNED: November 2 and 4, 1942, at Ottawa

SIGNATORIES: Canada vs. United States

IN FORCE: From November 4, 1942

OVERVIEW: An agreement relating to wartime construction of the Alaska Highway (then called the Military Highway to Alaska).

DISCUSSION:

For background on the Alaska Highway, see **Agreement Designating the Official Name of the Alaska Highway**. The agreement sorts out which nation's laws govern nationals of Canada and nationals of the United States who work on construction of the Alaska Highway. In particular, the agreement addresses issues of unemployment insurance coverage and workmen's compensation. These issues became complex in a project that not only involved workers from two nations, but nationals of one nation who might be employees of nationals of the other nation.

REFERENCE:

Coates, Kenneth, and W.R. Morrison. *The Alaska Highway in World War II: The U.S. Army of Occupation in Canada's Northwest.* Toronto: University of Toronto Press. 1992.

Agreement Relating to Access to the Alaska Highway

SIGNED: April 10, 1943, at Ottawa

SIGNATORIES: Canada vs. United States

IN FORCE: From signing

OVERVIEW: An agreement clarifying free access by United States nationals to the Alaska Highway via other highways in the Canadian system.

DISCUSSION:

For background information on the Alaska Highway, see **Agreement Designating the Official Name of the Alaska Highway.**

The agreement makes explicit the understanding that, after the Canadian portion of the Alaska Highway reverts to Canadian authority following the conclusion of World War II, United States nationals will have free access to it via the Canadian highway system.

REFERENCE:

Coates, Kenneth, and W.R. Morrison. *The Alaska Highway in World War II: The U.S. Army of Occupation in Canada's Northwest.* Toronto: University of Toronto Press. 1992.

Agreement Designating the Official Name of the Alaska Highway

OFFICIAL TITLE: Exchange of Notes Constituting an Agreement Relating to the Designation of Alaska Highway as the Official Name for the Highway from Dawson Creek, British Columbia, to Fairbanks, Alaska

SIGNED: July 19, 1943, at Washington

SIGNATORIES: Canada vs. United States

IN FORCE: From signing

OVERVIEW: An agreement on the official designation of the Alaska Highway.

DISCUSSION:

The 1,523-mile-long Alaska Highway was built by U.S. Army engineers during March to November 1942 as an emergency war measure to provide an overland military supply route to Alaska. It was first called the Alaskan International Highway, the Alaska Military Highway, and the Alcan Highway. In July 1943, Secretary of State Cordell Hull sent the following to Leighton McCarthy, minister of Canada:

I have the honor to inform you that the Honorable Anthony J. Dimond, Delegate of Alaska, United States House of Representatives. has proposed that the highway from Dawson Creek, British Columbia, to Fairbanks, Alaska, be given the official name "Alaska Highway."

The Government of the United States believes that the name . . . is usitable and in harmony with popular usage. It is of the further opinion that the highway should be jointly named by the Governments of the United States and Canada in view of the location of the greater part of the highway within Canada and in veiw of the friendly cooperation which has made possible its construction.

In accordance with the foregoing, I have the honor to propose that the highway . . . be designated the "Alaska Highway." If the Canadian Government is agreeable to this proposal, it is suggested that this note and your reply in that sense shall be considered as placing on record the agreement of the two Governments in this matter.

The Canadian reply conveyed concurrence, and the highway was so designated. In 1946, the Canadian portion of the highway, 1,200 miles long, was turned over to Canada.

REFERENCE:

Coates, Kenneth, and W.R. Morrison. *The Alaska Highway in World War II: The U.S. Army of Occupation in Canada's Northwest.* Toronto: University of Toronto Press. 1992.

Agreement (with Canada) Relating to the Patent Rights in Connection with RDX and Other Explosives

OFFICIAL TITLE: Exchange of Notes Constituting an Agreement Relating to the Patent Rights in Connection with RDX and Other Explosives

SIGNED: September 3 and 27, 1946, at Washington, D.C.

SIGNATORIES: Canada vs. United States

IN FORCE: From September 27, 1946

OVERVIEW: An agreement on the disposition of patent rights to certain explosives created jointly by Canada and the United States as allies during World War II.

DISCUSSION:

The exigencies of war do not always allow for the formal conclusion of agreements in various areas, including those of intellectual and industrial property. Like the **Agreement (with United Kingdom) on the Exchange of Information on Penicillin**, the RDX agreement retroactively addresses issues in these areas.

The agreement lists various inventions in the area of explosives, identifying certain items as having been developed under United States auspices and others as having been developed under Canadian auspices. Each country is to be responsible for registering the patents of inventions assigned to it; however, "each Government grants to the other a non-exclusive, royalty-free license to have the inventions . . . used or manufactured by or for the Governments of the respective countries, said license to extend throughout the world."

REFERENCE:

Perras, Galen Roger. *Franklin Roosevelt and the Origins of the Canadian-American Security Alliance, 1933-1945.* New York: Praeger, 1998.

Treaty of Friendship, Commerce, and Navigation with Republic of China (Taiwan)

SIGNED: November 4, 1946, at Nanking

SIGNATORIES: Republic of China vs. United States

IN FORCE: From November 30, 1948

OVERVIEW: The foundation United States trade treaty with Nationalist China.

DISCUSSION:

This treaty was concluded with the non-communist government of the Republic of China (Nationalist China) while it was engaged in the long civil war with communist forces. In October 1949, less than a year after the treaty entered into force, the nationalist government, defeated by Mao Tse-tung, was compelled to withdraw to Taiwan. There it proclaimed itself, in effect, the rightful Chinese government in exile. The Treaty of Friendship, Commerce, and Navigation remained in force.

As with other such treaties, the principal purpose of this document is to establish friendly relations through trade, and to define that trade in terms of "national treatment" and most-favored-nation status. *National treatment* is treatment accorded within the territories of a signatory nation upon terms no less favorable than the treatment accorded to nationals, companies, products, vessels or other objects of the signatory nation itself. *Most-favored-nation treatment* is treatment granted on terms no less favorable than the treatment accorded to nationals, companies, products, vessels or other objects of any third country.

On January 1, 1979, the United States recognized the People's Republic of China—the communist government of mainland China—as the sole legal government of China, thereby rendering the status of Taiwan ambiguous with respect to the United States. Nevertheless, this treaty, and the **United States-Nationalist Chinese Mutual Defense Treaty** of 1954 remain in force.

REFERENCE:

Gibert, Stephen P., and William M. Carpenter, eds. *America and Island China: A Documentary History.* Lanham, MD: University Press of America, 1989.

General Agreement on Tariffs and Trade (GATT)

SIGNED: October 30, 1947, at Geneva, and amended through 1966

SIGNATORIES IN 1947: Australia, Belgium, Brazil, Burma, Canada, Ceylon, Chile, China, Cuba, Czechoslovakia, France, India, Lebanon, Luxemburg, Netherlands, New Zealand, Norway, Pakistan, Southern Rhodesia, Syria, South Africa, United Kingdom, United States

IN FORCE: From January 1, 1948

OVERVIEW: An international agreement to liberalize world trade by eliminating or reduce protectionist tariffs; in 1995, GATT was replaced and superseded by the World Trade Organization (WTO).

DISCUSSION:

GATT was concluded after World War II as an interim trade liberalization agreement pending the formation of a United Nations agency. As it turned out, that agency—the World Trade Organization—was not established until 1995, and GATT, repeatedly amended, continued to serve as an effective instrument of world trade liberalization. Thanks in large part to GATT, the postwar world saw dramatic expansion of international trade. By the time it was superseded, GATT had been signed by 125 nations and controlled about 90 percent of international trade.

GATT is essentially a code of conduct covering the practice of world trade. As amended, it is a complex document of 125 pages, but it rests upon a single, simple principle: trade without discrimination. Each signatory nation undertakes to open its markets equally to every other. GATT presents this as more than a mere statement of principle. At its core is an unconditional "most-favoured nation clause," which has this effect: Once a signatory nation and its largest trading partners agree to reduce a tariff, that reduction is automatically extended to every other GATT member. Much of the GATT document consists of schedules of tariff concessions for each contracting nation; these are the tariff rates that each country agrees to extend to others.

While operating to reduce and equalize tariffs, GATT also sought to eliminate such trade barriers as import quotas and other quantitative trade restrictions by replacing these exclusively with tariffs. Although each signatory agreed to negotiate for tariff cuts upon the request of another, GATT did not lock signatories into self-destructive trade concessions. Contracting states were allowed to modify agreement if domestic producers suffered excessive losses.

Beyond addressing tariffs and eliminating quota and quota-like trade barriers, GATT also laid down uniform customs regulations intended to facilitate international trade.

Under the aegis and authority of GATT, specific trade issues were routinely negotiated. Seven times, between 1947 and 1993, major trade conferences (informally called "rounds") were held, all of which with the general object of reducing tariffs.

As a result of the final round—the "Uruguay Round," held from 1986 to 1994—GATT, which had slashed average tariffs from 40 percent of a good's market value in 1947 to 5 percent in 1993, further liberalized itself out of existence by creating the World Trade Organization—the United Nations agency that, finally, supplanted what had been conceived as a provisional instrument of agreement. *See* **Marakesh Agreement Establishing the World Trade Organization**.

REFERENCES:

Kirshner, Orin, and Edward M. Bernstein, eds. *The Bretton Woods-GATT System: Retrospect and Prospect after Fifty Years.* Armonk, NY: M. E. Sharpe, 1995.

Zeiler, Thomas W. *Free Trade, Free World: The Advent of the GATT.* Chapel Hill: University of North Carolina Press, 1999.

Convention (with Belgium) for the Avoidance of Double Taxation

OFFICIAL TITLE: Convention for the Avoidance of Double Taxation and the Prevention of Fiscal Evasion with Respect to Taxes on Income

SIGNED: October 28, 1948, at Washington, D.C.

SIGNATORIES: Belgium vs. United States

IN FORCE: From January 1, 1953

OVERVIEW: A convention for the avoidance of double taxation and the prevention of evasion of income taxes.

DISCUSSION:

The United States has concluded with many nations reciprocal agreements on income taxes with the purpose of avoiding the double taxation of individuals and corporations and of preventing individuals and corporations from evading income taxes.

The agreement lays down regulations for the taxation of various types of income earned by a national of one signatory who resides in the territory of the other signatory. The principal provisions include the following:

- Compensation paid by one of the contracting states to citizens of that state residing in the other state shall be exempt from taxation in the latter state.
- A resident of the United States is exempt from Belgian tax if he resides in Belgium for no more than 90 days during each calendar year and receives no more than $3,000 compensation in Belgium, or if he resides in Belgium for no more than 183 days during the year and is paid by a United States natural or judicial person or corporation. In these cases, the United States reserves the right to collect income tax on the full income for the calendar year.
- A resident of Belgium is exempt from United States income taxes on terms precisely reciprocal to those just outlined. In these cases, Belgium reserves the right to collect income tax on the full income for the calendar year.

Special consideration is given to professors or teachers, who may teach for a period of two years without being taxed by the host state. The stipends and scholarships received by students are also exempt from taxation by the host state.

In addition to the reciprocal arrangement with regard to income tax, Belgium and the United States agree to "lend assistance and support to each other in the collection of the taxes to which the ... Convention relates."

REFERENCE:

United States Department of State, *Treaties in Force: A List of Treaties and other International Agreements of the United States in Force on January 1, 1997.* Washington, D.C.: U.S. Government Printing Office, 1997.

Agreement (with Canada) Relating to the St. Lawrence Seaway Project

SIGNED: June 30, 1952, at Washington, D.C.

SIGNATORIES: Canada vs. United States

IN FORCE: From signing

OVERVIEW: An agreement preparatory to commencement of construction of the St. Lawrence Seaway.

DISCUSSION:

The St. Lawrence Seaway is an international waterway, some 2,350 miles long, incorporating an extensive system of canals, dams, and locks in the St. Lawrence River and connecting channels through the Great Lakes and giving the interior of eastern Canada and the U.S. Midwest access to the Atlantic Ocean. The massive engineering project was jointly developed by the United States and Canada and was opened in 1959.

This agreement establishes several key points, including the following:

- Canadian emphasis on hydroelectric facilities as part of the project
- Canadian responsibility for constructing locks and canals on its side of the boundary

REFERENCE:

Baxter, Richard Reeve. *Documents on the St. Lawrence Seaway*. New York, Praeger, 1960.

Treaty of Friendship, Commerce and Navigation with Japan

SIGNED: April 9, 1953, at Tokyo
SIGNATORIES: Japan vs. United States
IN FORCE: From October 30, 1953
OVERVIEW: A treaty definitively normalizing relations between Japan and the United States.

DISCUSSION:

In general, treaties framed as embracing "friendship, commerce, and navigation" are, in fact, trade treaties—the presumption being that trade relations define "friendly" relations. The core of any modern trade treaty is an agreement to establish trade on a most-favored-nation basis. As developed in this treaty, this means that the signatory parties undertake to grant one another "national treatment" in all activities related to trade, commerce, and navigation. That is, as the treaty defines it, "treatment accorded within the territories of a Party upon terms no less favorable than the treatment accorded therein, in like situations, to nationals, companies, products, vessels or other objects, as the case may be, of such Party." Moreover, the signatories agree to extend to one another most-favored-nation treatment—"treatment accorded within the territories of a Party upon terms no less favorable than the treatment accorded therein, in like situations, to nationals, companies, products, vessels or other objects, as the case may be, of any third country."

REFERENCES:

Forsberg, Aaron. *America and the Japanese Miracle: The Cold War Context of Japan's Postwar Economic Revival, 1950-1960*. Chapel Hill: University of North Carolina Press, 2000.
Sato, Ryuzo. *Beyond Trade Friction: Japan-U.S. Economic Relations*. New York: Cambridge University Press, 1989.

Agreement Relating to the Establishment of the St. Lawrence River Joint Board of Engineers

OFFICIAL TITLE: Exchange of Notes Constituting an Agreement Relating to the Establishment of the St. Lawrence River Joint Board of Engineers
SIGNED: November 12, 1953, at Washington, D.C.
SIGNATORIES: Canada vs. United States
IN FORCE: From signing
OVERVIEW: An agreement establishing a Joint Board of Engineers to oversee construction of the St. Lawrence Seaway.

DISCUSSION:

This document established a technical administrative body to direct and oversee construction of the St. Lawrence Seaway project. For background on the Seaway, see **Agreement (with Canada) Relating to the St. Lawrence Seaway Project**.

REFERENCE:

Baxter, Richard Reeve. *Documents on the St. Lawrence Seaway*. New York, Praeger, 1960.

Agreement between the United States and Canada Modifying the Agreement of 30 June 1952 Relating to the St. Lawrence Seaway Project

OFFICIAL TITLE: Exchange of Notes Constituting an Agreement between the United States of America and Canada Modifying and Supplementing the Agreement of 30 June 1952 Relating to the St. Lawrence Seaway Project
SIGNED: August 17, 1954, at Ottawa
SIGNATORIES: Canada vs. United States
IN FORCE: From signing
OVERVIEW: An agreement reassigning some of the responsibility for construction of the St. Lawrence Seaway

DISCUSSION:

Pursuant to discussions, this agreement modifies the **Agreement (with Canada) Relating to the St. Lawrence Seaway Project** of 1952, reassigning responsibility for the construction of certain locks and canals near the international boundary. The object of the agreement is to ensure that an uninterrupted 27-foot standard of navigation is maintained throughout the seaway in order to accommodate the largest ocean-going freighters.

REFERENCE:

Baxter, Richard Reeve. *Documents on the St. Lawrence Seaway*. New York, Praeger, 1960.

Convention on Establishing an International Organisation of Legal Metrology

SIGNED: October 12, 1955, at Paris
SIGNATORIES: Australia, Austria, Belgium, Bulgaria, Cuba, Czechoslovakia, Denmark, Dominican Republic, Finland, France Germany (Federal Republic), Guinea, Hungary, India, Indonesia, Iran, Italy, Japan, Lebanon, Monaco, Morocco, Netherlands, New Sealand, Norway, Pakistan, Poland, Romania, Spain, Sweden Switzerland, Turkey, Union of Soviet Socialist Republics, United Arab Republic, United Kingdom, Venezuela, Yugoslavia
IN FORCE: From May 28, 1958; not in force for the United States
OVERVIEW: A convention establishing an international organization to resolve technical and administrative problems raised by the use of measuring instruments.

DISCUSSION:
Metrology is the science of measurement, and legal metrology is the application of that science to matters of law, trade, and commerce. The purpose of this ambitious agreement is to create an organization to accomplish the following:

- Set up a documentation and information center—largely in an effort to catalogue and harmonize various national systems of metrology
- Translate and edit relevant legal texts
- Determine the principles of legal metrology
- Study the problems of legal metrology
- Establish model draft laws and regulations for measuring instruments and their use
- Draw up a draft plan for an international inspection service to check measuring instruments
- Determine standards for measuring instruments

It might be expected that an international organization for legal metrology would readily win universal international approval. However, many nations, most notably the United States, declined to sign the agreement and thereby declined to join the organization. In areas as basic as instruments of measurement, principles of measurement, and submission to international inspection of instruments of measurement, numerous strongly nationalist countries offer significant resistance. The United States prefers to establish measurement standards, where necessary, as part of individual commercial agreements.

REFERENCE:
Convention establishing an International Organisation of Legal Metrology. London, H. M. Stationery Office, 1972.

Agreement (with Canada) on the Relocation of Part of Roosevelt Bridge

OFFICIAL TITLE: Exchange of Notes Constituting an Agreement Relating to the Relocation of That Part of Roosevelt Bridge which Crosses the Cornwall South Channel
SIGNED: October 24, 1956, at Washington, D.C.
SIGNATORIES: Canada vs. United States
IN FORCE: From signing
OVERVIEW: Agreement relating to the construction of a new international bridge between Canada and the United States

DISCUSSION:
The construction of the St. Lawrence Seaway (see **Agreement [with Canada] Relating to the St. Lawrence Seaway Project for the Construction of Certain Navigation Facilities**) was a massive project of international cooperation between the United States and Canada. Under the aegis of two agencies created to administer St. Lawrence Seaway development, St. Lawrence Seaway Authority (United States) and the St. Lawrence Seaway Development Corporation (Canada), the United States proposed international cooperation in the construction, maintenance, and operation of a new highway bridge over the South Channel of the Cornwall River, from the United States mainland to Cornwall, Ontario. "Contracts for the construction of the new bridge shall be shared between Canadian and United States contractors, by agreement between the two Seaway entities." For purposes of the work, the two nations would grant mutual waivers of customs and immigration regulations.

REFERENCE:
Baxter, Richard Reeve. *Documents on the St. Lawrence Seaway.* New York, Praeger, 1960.

International Convention for the Protection of New Varieties of Plants

SIGNED: December 2, 1961, at Paris; amended November 10, 1972, at Paris, and October 23, 1978, at Geneva
SIGNATORIES: Australia, Belgium, Canada, Czechoslovakia, Denmark, France, Germany, Hungary (1978 revision only), Ireland (12978 revision only), Israel, Japan (1978 revision only), Netherlands, New Zealand, Poland, South Africa, Spain (1961 version only), Sweden, Switzerland, United Kingdom, United States (1978 revision only)
IN FORCE: From August 10, 1968; for the United States, from November 11, 1981
OVERVIEW: A convention to recognize and protect the rights of breeders of new varieties of plants and their successors in title.

DISCUSSION:

The principal provision of the agreement is the creation among the signatories of a Union for the Protection of New Varieties of Plants (UPOV). The members of the union agree upon the following:

- That the breeder has a right to authorize any production or commercial marketing of the new variety
- That the breeder's rights must not be restricted unless the breeder receives sufficient remuneration
- That titles of protection are to be issued by member states after official examination of the variety
- That titles may be granted for a limited period
- That nationals of member states of the union shall enjoy the same treatment
- That, under certain circumstances, the rights granted may be annulled and forfeited

REFERENCE:

Beier, Friedrich-Karl, R. S. Crespi, and J. Straus. *Biotechnology and Patent Protection : an International Review.* Paris: Organisation for Economic Co-operation and Development,1985.

Convention of Mar Del Plata on Waterborne Transportation

OFFICIAL TITLE: Inter-American Convention on Facilitation of International Waterborne Transportation (Convention of Mar Del Plata)

SIGNED: June 7, 1963, at Mar Del Plata, Argentina

SIGNATORIES: Argentina, Bolivia, Chile, Colombia, Costa Rica, Dominican Republic, Ecuador, Guatemala, Haiti, Honduras, Mexico, Panama, Paraguay, Peru, United States, Uruguay

IN FORCE: From January 11, 1981

OVERVIEW: A convention among Organization of American States members "facilitating international waterborne transportation in the Western Hemisphere by reducing to a minimum the formalities, documentary requirements and procedures for the entry and clearance of vessels and the treatment of their passengers, crews, cargo and baggage."

DISCUSSION:

The substance of this international convention is contained within the first four articles:

Article 1

Each Contracting State agrees to adopt all practicable measures, through the issuance of special regulations or otherwise, to facilitate and expedite waterborne transportation between the territories of the Contracting States, and to prevent unnecessary delays to vessels, passengers, crews, cargo and baggage in the administration of the laws relating to immigration, public health, customs, and other provisions relative to arrivals and departures of vessels.

Article 2

Each Contracting State undertakes, so far as it may find practicable,-to establish appropriate procedures and legal provisions on im-migration, public health, customs and other matters relative to arrivals and departures of vessels, in accordance with the standards and recommended practices which may be established from time to time, pursuant to this Convention. Nothing in this Convention shall be construed as preventing the establishment of customs-free ports or free zones.

Article 3

Each Contracting State undertakes to collaborate in securing the highest practicable degree of uniformity in appropriate procedures and legal provisions in relation to the entry and clearance of vessels and the treatment of passengers, crews, cargo and baggage in all matters in which such uniformity will facilitate and improve international waterborne transportation.

Article 4

(a) To these ends, the Inter-American Port and Harbor Conference of the Organization of American States shall, from time to time, when necessary, adopt and amend inter-American standards and recommended practices dealing with all matters relating to formalities, requirements and procedures relevant to the efficient and economic entry and clear-ance of vessels, and the expeditious and appropriate treatment of their passengers, crews, cargo and baggage.

REFERENCE:

Inter-American Port and Harbor Conference. *Message from the President of the United States, transmitting the Inter-American convention on facilitation of international waterborne transportation (Convention of Mar del Plata), signed for the United States on June 7, 1963.* Washington, D.C.: U.S. Government Printing Office, 1966.

Agreement (with Canada) Relating to the Establishment of the Roosevelt Campobello International Park

SIGNED: January 22, 1964, at Washington, D.C.

SIGNATORIES: Canada vs. United States

IN FORCE: From August 14, 1964

OVERVIEW: An agreement to establish and maintain a United States-Canadian international park in memory of Franklin Delano Roosevelt.

DISCUSSION:

Campobello is an island at the entrance to Passamaquoddy Bay in southwestern New Brunswick, Canada. It is the site of President Franklin D. Roosevelt's summer home. (The future president was stricken there with polio in 1921.) Subsequent owners of the property, the Hammer family, deeded the property jointly to the governments of the Untied States and Canada on condition that it be opened to the general public as a memorial museum. The 1964 agreement formalizes the creation of the 2,721-acre Roosevelt Campobello International Park to be jointly operated by the United States and Canada. The agreement details the mechanism of that joint administration by means of a Roosevelt Campobello International Park Commission, which the agreement creates.

Of particular interest is the spirit of the agreement, conveyed in the desire "to take advantage of the unique opportunity to symbolize the close and neighborly relations between the peoples of the United States of America and Canada by the utilization of the gift to establish a United States-Canadian memorial park."

REFERENCES:
None

Convention on Contracts

OFFICIAL TITLE: Convention Relating to a Uniform Law on the Formation of Contracts for the International Sale of Goods
SIGNED: July 1, 1964, at the Hague
SIGNATORIES: Argentina, Austria, Belgium, Bulgaria, Colombia, Denmark, Finland, France, Germany (Federal Republic), Greece, Hungary, Ireland, Israel, Italy, Japan, Mexico, Netherlands, Norway, Portugal, San Marino, South Africa, Spain, Sweden, Switzerland, Turkey, United Arab Emirates, United Kingdom, United States, Vatican City State, Venezuela, Yugoslavia
IN FORCE: From August 23, 1972
OVERVIEW: An international convention creating a uniform law on the formation of contracts for the international sale of goods.

DISCUSSION:
As with many other conventions seeking to standardize international practices in trade and commerce, the Convention on Contracts met with considerable resistance and hesitation, protracting the period from signature to entry into forces from 1964 to 1972. The convention requires each contracting state to incorporate the Uniform Law into its own legislation, a requirement that also contributed to delays in entry into force.

The Uniform Law, a set of practices and procedures governing the form and content of international trade contracts, is set forth in two annexes subjoined to the convention proper. The main part of the convention deals with incorporation of the Uniform Law into national law and allowable exceptions to adherence to the Uniform Law.

REFERENCE:
Boggiano, Antonio. *International Standard Contracts : the Price of Fairness.* Boston: Graham & Trotman/Martinus Nijhoff, 1991.

Auto Pact (with Canada)

OFFICIAL TITLE: Agreement Concerning Automotive Products (with Annexes and Exchange of Notes)
SIGNED: January 16, 1965, at Johnson City, Texas
SIGNATORIES: Canada vs. United States
IN FORCE: Provisionally from signing; definitively, September 16, 1966
OVERVIEW: An agreement to liberalize trade regulations between Canada and the United States with respect to automotive products.

DISCUSSION:
The agreement has three objectives:
1. To create broader markets for automotive products
2. To reduce trade restrictions, especially tariffs in order to create a more equitable marketplace with respect to automotive products
3. To improve the trade pattern in automotive products generally
The agreement seeks to achieve these objectives by a quid-pro-quo program of duty relief and reductions enumerated in an annex subjoined to the main document.

REFERENCES:
None

International Convention on Tonnage Measurement of Ships, 1969

SIGNED: June 23, 1969, at London
SIGNATORIES: Algeria, Argentina, Australia, Austria, Bahmas, Bangladesh, Belgium, Berlin (West), Brazil, China, Colombia, Czechoslovakia, Denmark, Egypt, Fiji, Finland, France, German Democratic Republic, Germany (Federal Republic), Ghana, Greece, Guinea, Hungary, Iceland, India, Iran, Iraq, Israel, Italy, Japan, Korea (Republic) Kuwait, Liberia, Malaysia, Mexico, Monaco, Netherlands, New Zealand, Norway, Pakistan, Panama, Peru, Philippines, Poland, Romania, Saudi Arabia, Spain, Sweden, Switzerland, Syrian Arab Republic, Tonga, Trinidad and Tobago, Turkey, Union of Soviet Socialist Republics, United Kingdom, United States, Venezuela, Yemen, Yugoslavia
IN FORCE: From July 18, 1982
OVERVIEW: An international convention to establish uniform principles and rules with respect to the determination of tonnage of ships engaged on international voyages.

DISCUSSION:
Standardization of methods and practices used to determine the tonnage of ships engaged in international voyages bears directly on matters of navigation, commerce, and taxation, and is therefore highly important to the facilitation of international trade. Nevertheless, as with other conventions calling for international regulation, standardization, and oversight of measurement issues (see **Convention on Establishing an International Organisation of Legal Metrology**), many nations were resistant to and slow to adopt the convention. Signed in 1969, it was 1982 before it received the requisite number of ratifications to carry it into force.

The principal provision of the convention is an undertaking by the signatory states to entrust the determination of gross and net tonanges to an Administration created by the convention.

The Administration then issues an International Tonnage Certificate to every ship covered by the convention (warships and certain other vessels are excluded from coverage). Signatory governments have the right to inspect the ships of other signatories, in port, to verify the presence of the International Tonnage Certificate and conformity therewith.

REFERENCES:
None

Agreement for the Protection of Names of Bourbon Whiskey and Certain French Brandies

OFFICIAL TITLE: Exchange of Notes Constituting an Agreement for the Protection of Names of Bourbon Whiskey and Certain French Brandies
SIGNED: December 2, 1970, at Paris
SIGNATORIES: France vs. United States
IN FORCE: From March 20, 1971
OVERVIEW: A mutual agreement to protect the appellations of characteristic products of the Untied States and France.

DISCUSSION:
The substance of the agreement follows:

The Government of the United States has requested that the French Government, taking into consideration the fact that "Bourbon Whiskey" is a distinctive American product the characteristics of which are defined by Federal regulation, prohibit the use in France of the names "Bourbon" and "Bourbon Whiskey" for the designation of any whiskey or mixture of whiskeys produced in France, and that it prohibit the sale in France or the export from France of any whiskey labeled or described in such a manner, unless produced in the United States in conformity with American legislation regulating the manufacture of the spirit.

In support of its request, the United States Government has noted that certain appellations of origin for French brandies, in particular the names "Cognac" and "Armagnac," are, in fact, protected in the United States. However, the United States Government has thus far undertaken no obligation to France to continue the protection of these appellations in the territory of the United States. Under these circumstances, the Government of the French Republic proposes that the Government of the United States undertake to reserve the use, in the interstate and foreign commerce of the United States, of the names "Cognac," "Armagnac," and "Calvados" to the French products entitled by virtue of existing French legislation to use those names and to prohibit and repress the use of thise names for nay other product, even if modified by such terms as "kind," "type," "fashion," or similar expressions, or by an indication of the true place of origin.

In return, the French Government will reserve the use in French territory of the names "Borubon" and "Bourbon Whiskey" exclusively to whiskey produced in the territory of the United States ...

REFERENCES:
None

Agreement Concerning the Question of Brazilian Exports of Soluble Coffee to the United States

OFFICIAL TITLE: Exchange of Notes Constituting an Agreement Concerning the Question of Brazilian Exports of Soluble Coffee to the United States
SIGNED: April 2, 1971, at Brasilia
SIGNATORIES: Brazil vs. United States
IN FORCE: From signing
OVERVIEW: An agreement relating to the supply of coffee to United States manufacturers and suppliers.

DISCUSSION:
The agreement sets out quotas of coffee Brazil agrees to make available to United States manufacturers and suppliers and distinguishes between soluble coffee exports and exports of green coffee, which must be processed into soluble coffee. The agreement further stipulates the removal of a 13-cent-per-pound export tax imposed by Brazil on soluble coffee exports to the United States.

The purpose of commodity export-import agreements such as this is generally to stabilize prices of the commodity, both for the exporting and for the importing nation, and to ensure a reliable supply of the commodity.

REFERENCE:
Bates, Robert H. *Open-Economy Politics: The Political Economy of the World Coffee Trade.* Princeton, NJ: Princeton University Press, 1999.

Agreement (with the International Atomic Energy Agency and Republic of China) for the Application of Safeguards

SIGNED: December 6, 1971, at Vienna
SIGNATORIES: International Atomic Energy Agency, Republic of China (Taiwan), United States
IN FORCE: From signing
OVERVIEW: An agreement to ensure the security of nuclear materials transferred to the Republic of China (Taiwan) for civil use.

DISCUSSION:
The International Atomic Energy Agency, a United Nations specialized agency, is charged with overseeing the security of "special fissionable material" transferred from one nation to another for use in reactors, nuclear power plants, and for other civil purposes. This agreement is typical of those concluded

under the agency's auspices between the United States and a country to which it is transferring fissionable material. The principal provisions of the agreement follow:

- Both nations undertake not to use the material "in such a way as to further any military purpose."
- Both nations undertake to apply safeguards to all equipment and fissionable material to ensure its security.
- The state parties and the agency undertake to maintain accurate inventories of the fissionable material and to issue notifications of any transfers. (The agreement also specifies other inventory-control measures to be taken.)
- The state parties agree to allow agency inspection of all facilities in which the fissionable material is used.
- The state parties agree to bear the financial cost of implementing the agreement.

REFERENCES:
None

Master Agreement Governing Sales of Source, By-Product, and Special Nuclear Materials for Research Purposes

SIGNED: June 14, 1974, at Vienna

SIGNATORIES: International Atomic Energy Commission vs. United States

IN FORCE: From signing

OVERVIEW: An agreement on the terms and conditions governing the sale of nuclear materials for research purposes.

DISCUSSION:

This Master Agreement is intended to regulate the sale of nuclear materials supplied by the United States to other nations for research purposes. General principles laid down include the following:

- Condition of sale
- Condition of delivery and transportation
- Disposition of title
- Costs of transportation
- Liability
- Return of material
- Pricing policy
- Payment terms
- Disallowance of financial interest on the part of U.S. officials in sale or purchase
- Resolution of disputes

REFERENCE:
International Nuclear Safeguards, 1994: Vision for the Future. Vienna: International Atonic Energy Agency., 1995.

Memorandum of Understanding (with Mexico) Relating to the Exchange of Information on FDA-Regulated Products

OFFICIAL TITLE: Memorandum of Understanding Relating to the Exchange of Information on Food and Drug Administration Regulated Products

SIGNED: August 13, 1974, at Mazatlan, Mexico

SIGNATORIES: Mexico vs. United States

IN FORCE: From signing

OVERVIEW: An agreement governing the interchange of information between U.S. and Mexican authorities on FDA-regulated products.

DISCUSSION:

The agreement, signed by the directors of the Food and Drug Administration (United States) and the National Commission of Quality for Export Products (Mexico), is intended to help ensure that FDA-regulated products traded between the two countries meet FDA standards of quality and safety. By exchanging information, the standards applied by the U.S. and Mexican authorities may be harmonized. The information to be exchanged relates to the following:

- Methods and procedures for sampling
- Methods of analysis
- Methods of confirmation
- Specifications and tolerances
- Reference Standards
- Procedures for check analysis
- Routine inspectional procedures
- Laws
- Regulations

The agreement also outlines procedures for detaining noncomplying products in the importing country.

REFERENCES:
None

Inter-American Convention on International Commercial Arbitration

SIGNED: January 30, 1975, at Panama City, Panama

SIGNATORIES: Argentina, Bolivia, Brazil, Chile, Colombia, Costa Rica, Dominican Republic, Ecuador, El Salvador, Guatemala, Honduras, Mexico, Nicaragua, Panama, Paraguay, Peru, United States, Uruguay, Venezuela

IN FORCE: From June 16, 1976

OVERVIEW: A convention in which signatories agree to arbitration of disputes relating to commercial transactions.

DISCUSSION:

Signatories, certain member states of the Organization of American States, agree to submit commercial disputes to arbitration "appointed in the manner agreed upon by the parties." In default of an express agreement, the arbitration is to be conducted by the Inter-American Commercial Arbitration Commission, a standing agency of the OAS. Except under certain circumstances enumerated under Article 5 of the convention, "an arbitral decision or award . . . shall have the force of a final judicial judgment."

REFERENCE:

Dezalay, Yves, et al. *Dealing in Virtue: International Commercial Arbitration and the Construction of a Transnational Legal Order.* Chicago: University of Chicago Press, 1998.

Loan Agreement (with Bangladesh) for the Ashuganj Fertilizer Project

SIGNED: February 12, 1975, at Dacca, Bangladesh
SIGNATORIES: Bangladesh vs. United States
IN FORCE: From signing
OVERVIEW: A loan agreement with a nation in severe economic and human crisis.

DISCUSSION:

Beginning in the mid 1970s, years of civil strife, the destruction of war, and endemic grinding poverty combined with a drought to produce a devastating famine throughout the densely populated Asian nation of Bangladesh. The very name of this country became a byword for Third World economic collapse. The United States, through the United Nations Agency for International Development (AID), conveyed various forms of aid to the beleaguered country. In addition to the present agreement, the following are important—and typical of aid agreements made between the United States and developing nations during the 1970s and 1980s:

• **Loan Agreement (with Bangladesh) for Fertilizer Storage**
• **Project Grant Agreement (with Bangladesh) for Agricultural Inputs Project**, 1977, 1979
• **Amendment to the Loan Agreement (with Bangladesh) for the Ashuganj Fertilizer Project**

The loan agreement is typical of United States aid during this period in that its objective is to foster self-sufficiency. It is not simply a one-time gift of food or supplies, but a loan to help enable the nation to better produce its own food.

The loan amount in this case is $30,000,000, which is to be combined with other funds loaned by the International Development Association, the Federal Republic of Germany, Switzerland, the United Kingdom, Iran, and the Asian Development Bank. Interest is set at 2 percent for ten years, and 3 percent thereafter on the unpaid balance only, with the principal to be repaid within forty years.

REFERENCE:

Ahmed, Raisuddin, and Steven Haggblade, eds. *Out of the Shadow of Famine: Evolving Food Markets and Food Policy in Bangladesh.* Baltimore: Johns Hopkins University, 2000.

Agreement (with Japan) Concerning Specialty Steel Imports

SIGNED: June 11, 1976, at Washington, D.C.
SIGNATORIES: Japan vs. United States
IN FORCE: From signing
OVERVIEW: An agreement to regulate and limit specialty steel imports from Japan.

DISCUSSION:

Nations engaged in international trade often introduce measures to protect domestic industries from harmful competition with foreign producers. By the 1970s, the American steel industry, once virtually unchallenged in the world marketplace, was being seriously threatened by imported steel from Japan. Trade agreements such as that concluded in 1976 were intended to protect certain sectors of the American industry without unduly damaging trade relations with Japan.

The agreement sets quotas and conditional quotas for the importation of certain Japanese speciality steels, which are enumerated in annexes subjoined to the main agreement. The specialty steels regulates include stainless steel sheet and strip, stainless steel plate, stainless steel bar, and stainless steel rod.

REFERENCES:

Forsberg, Aaron. *America and the Japanese Miracle: The Cold War Context of Japan's Postwar Economic Revival, 1950-1960.* Chapel Hill: University of North Carolina Press, 2000.
Sato, Ryuzo. *Beyond Trade Friction: Japan-U.S. Economic Relations.* New York: Cambridge University Press, 1989.

Grant Agreement for the Senegal River Basin Survey and Mapping

SIGNED: August 31, 1976, at Dakar, Senegal
SIGNATORIES: Organization for the Development of the Senegal River vs. United States
IN FORCE: From signing
OVERVIEW: An agreement to implement U.S. funding of a mapping project in Senegal for the purpose of developing irrigation and other projects.

DISCUSSION:

By this agreement, the United States acts through the Agency for International Development, a United Nations entity, to fund "a geodetic network and precise leveling in the Valley of the Senegal River Basin. These are necessary for the [eventual construction of] planned irrigation, dams and ports projects and for studies of forestry and natural resources." The large-scale mapping project is to be funded by a $1,200,000 grant to be administered by the Organization for the Development of the Senegal River.

REFERENCES:

Donald, Gordon, Jr. *U.S. Foreign Aid and the National Interest.* New York: National Policy Association, 1983.
Eberstadt, Nicholas. *U.S. Foreign Aid Policy: A Critique.* New York: Foreign Policy Association, 1990.

Loan Agreement (with Bangladesh) for Fertilizer Storage

SIGNED: December 8, 1976, at Dacca, Bangladesh
SIGNATORIES: Bangladesh vs. United States
IN FORCE: From signing
OVERVIEW: A loan agreement, through the United Nations Agency for International Development (AID) to Bangladesh for construction of a 50,000-metric-ton fertilizer warehouse.

DISCUSSION:

For a discussion of the background of this agreement, see **Loan Agreement (with Bangladesh) for the Ashuganj Fertilizer Project.**

REFERENCE:

Ahmed, Raisuddin, and Steven Haggblade, eds. *Out of the Shadow of Famine: Evolving Food Markets and Food Policy in Bangladesh.* Baltimore: Johns Hopkins University, 2000.

Agreement (with Canada) on Reconstruction of Canadian Portions of the Alaska Highway

OFFICIAL TITLE: Exchange of Notes Constituting an Agreement on Reconstruction of Canadian Portions of the Alaska Highway (with Annex)
SIGNED: January 11 and February 11, 1977, at Ottawa
SIGNATORIES: Canada vs. United States
IN FORCE: From February 11, 1977
OVERVIEW: An agreement for joint financing of maintenance and reconstruction of the Canadian portion of the Alaska Highway.

DISCUSSION:

For background on the Alaska Highway, see **Agreement Designating the Official Name of the Alaska Highway.**

Although the highway was originally built by the United States as an emergency wartime measure during World War II, the Canadian portions were returned to Canada in 1946. Because the highway is heavily trafficked by vehicles going to an from Alaska, maintenance and reconstruction costs of the Canadian portion of the highway are shared by the two nations. In the case of this agreement, reconstruction costs are to be funded entirely by the United States.

REFERENCE:

Coates, Kenneth, and W.R. Morrison. *The Alaska Highway in World War II: The U.S. Army of Occupation in Canada's Northwest.* Toronto: University of Toronto Press. 1992.

Loan Agreement (with Pakistan) for the Fauji-Agrico Fertilizer Project

SIGNED: April 1, 1977, at Islamabad, Pakistan
SIGNATORIES: Pakistan vs. United States
IN FORCE: From signing
OVERVIEW: A typical United States loan agreement through the Agency for International Development (AID).

DISCUSSION:

The United States has long had a extensive program of foreign aid, motivated in part by humanitarian objectives, and also by a desire to maintain a strong positive influence in the Third World in order to discourage the spread of communism there. The loan agreement funds, on very liberal terms, the building of a massive fertilizer plant in Pakistan. The agreement addresses the following issues:

• The amount and terms of the loan itself
• Conditions precedent to disbursement
• Rules governing equitable procurement of materials to build the plant
• Rules governing disbursement of funds
• Rules governing the marketing of the finished fertilizer product
• Rules governing investment in the fertilizer corporation

REFERENCES:

Donald, Gordon, Jr. *U.S. Foreign Aid and the National Interest.* New York: National Policy Association, 1983.
Eberstadt, Nicholas. *U.S. Foreign Aid Policy: A Critique.* New York: Foreign Policy Association, 1990.

Panama Canal Treaty (Torrijos-Carter Treaty)

SIGNED: September 7, 1977, at Washington, D.C.
SIGNATORIES: Panama vs. United States

IN FORCE: From October 1, 1979

OVERVIEW: Treaty laying down the transition to Panama of full authority to operate the Panama Canal and the restoration to Panama of sovereignty over the former Canal Zone.

DISCUSSION:

For the historical background of the Panama Canal and the United States' role in its construction and operation, see **Hay-Pauncefote Treaty**, **Hay-Herrán Treaty**, and **Hay-Bunau-Varilla Treaty** in this section, and **Clayton-Bulwer Treaty** in Section 3.5.

It was the **Hay-Bunau-Varilla Treaty** of 1903 that made it possible for the United States to build and operate the Panama Canal and that granted to the United States, in perpetuity, the use, occupation and control of a Canal Zone, approximately ten miles wide, in which the United States would possess full sovereign rights "to the entire exclusion of the exercise by the Republic of Panama of any such sovereign rights, power or authority." In return for this concession, the United States guaranteed the independence of Panama and agreed to a payment of $10 million in addition to an annuity of $250,000. The United States then purchased the rights and properties of the French, who had worked from 1879 to 1889 to build a canal, for $40 million and also paid private landholders within what would be the Canal Zone a mutually agreeable price for their properties.

In 1936, a new treaty was negotiated, increasing the annuity to $430,000 and, at the request of Panama, withdrawing the guarantee of independence. The annuity was increased to $1.93 million in 1955, and the Panama Canal Company, responsible for operating the canal, was turned over to the Panamanian Republic. In 1962, the United States completed the construction of a high-level bridge over the Pacific entrance to the canal, and the flags of Panama and the United States were flown jointly over areas of the Canal Zone for the first time. In 1972 and 1973, the annuity was adjusted in proportion to the devaluation of the U.S. dollar, to $2.1 million and $2.33 million, respectively.

The present treaty, negotiated between U.S. president Jimmy Carter and Panamanian president Omar Torrijos Herrera, provided for the operation of the canal until December 31, 1999, at which point the Panama Canal was turned over to Panama. Major provisions of the treaty include the following:

- The Republic of Panama receives a fixed annuity of $10 million for the provision of certain public services and an additional amount per net ton for each transiting vessel.
- Six months after ratification, Panama assumed general territorial jurisdiction over the former Canal Zone and was permitted to use portions of the area not needed for the operation and defense of the Canal.
- Within the Canal Zone, Panamanian penal and civil codes replaced United States codes.
- Six months after ratification, Panama assumed responsibility for commercial ship repairs and supplies, railway and pier operations, passengers, police and courts, all of which had been administered by the Panama Canal Company and the Canal Zone Government.
- The United States undertook to maintain operational control, until noon on December 31, 1999, over all lands, waters, and installations, including military bases, necessary to manage, operate and defend the Panama Canal.
- The treaty created a United States agency, the Panama Canal Commission, to operate the Canal during the transition period.
- The treaty created a policy making board of five U.S. citizens and four Panamanians as directors. During the first ten years of the treaty transition period, until 1990, the Canal's chief executive officer, called the administrator, was a United States citizen and the deputy administrator was Panamanian. Since 1990, the positions have been reversed, with a Panamanian serving as administrator and a United States citizen serving as deputy. (This is the first time in history that a United States government agency was headed by a non-U.S. citizen.)

Despite controversy and objections among some in the United States that the transition constituted a "giveaway," the treaty was ratified, and the two-decade transition process proceeded smoothly. The turnover of the canal took place, as scheduled, on December 31, 1999.

See also **Treaty Concerning the Permanent Neutrality and Operation of the Panama Canal**.

REFERENCES:

Canal Treaties. Washington, D.C.: U.S. Government Printing Office, 1914.

Nesbitt, Wallace. *The Panama Canal and its Treaty Obligations*. Toronto: Rous and Mann, Ltd., 1912.

Parrish, Samuel L. *The Hay-Pauncefforte Treaty and the Panama Canal*, New York: N. Pub., 1913).

Treaty Concerning the Permanent Neutrality and Operation of the Panama Canal

SIGNED: September 7, 1977, at Washington, D.C.

SIGNATORIES: Panama vs. United States

IN FORCE: From October 1, 1979

OVERVIEW: Signed in conjunction with **Panama Canal Treaty (Torrijos-Carter Treaty)**, the treaty lays down Panama's guarantee that the Panama Canal shall forever remain neutral.

DISCUSSION:

For the historical background of the Panama Canal and the United States' role in its construction and operation, see **Hay-Pauncefote Treaty**, **Hay-Herrán Treaty**, **Hay-Bunau-Varilla Treaty**, and **Panama Canal Treaty (Torrijos-Carter Treaty)** in this section, and **Clayton-Bulwer Treaty** in Section 3.5.

An absolute condition for the turnover of the Panama Canal to Panama is a guarantee of the canal's perpetual neutrality. The condition was felt to be so important that it was made the subject of a treaty separate from the main canal treaty. The text of the principal articles follows:

Article I

The Republic of Panama declares that the Canal, as an international transit waterway, shall be permanently neutral in accordance with the regime established in this Treaty. The same regime of neutrality shall apply to any other international waterway that may be built either partially or wholly in the territory of the Republic of Panama.

Article II

The Republic of Panama declares the neutrality of the Canal in order that both in time of peace and in time of war it shall remain secure and open to peaceful transit by the vessels of all nations on terms of entire equality, so that there will be no discrimination against any nation, or its citizens or subjects, concerning the conditions or charges of transit, or for any other reason, and so that the Canal, and therefore the Isthmus of Panama, shall not be the target of reprisals in any armed conflict between other nations of the world. The foregoing shall be subject to the following requirements:

(a) Payment of tolls and other charges for transit and ancillary services, provided they have been fixed in conformity with the provisions of Article III (c);

(b) Compliance with applicable rules and regulations, provided such rules and regulations are applied in conformity with the provisions of Article III;

(c) The requirement that transiting vessels commit no acts of hostility while in the Canal; and

(d) Such other conditions and restrictions as are established by this Treaty.

Article III

1. For purposes of the security, efficiency and proper maintenance of the Canal the following rules shall apply:

(a) The Canal shall be operated efficiently in accordance with conditions of transit through the Canal, and rules and regulations that shall be just, equitable and reasonable, and limited to those necessary for safe navigation and efficient, sanitary operation of the Canal;

(b) Ancillary services necessary for transit through the Canal shall be provided;

(c) Tolls and other charges for transit and ancillary services shall be just, reasonable, equitable and consistent with the principles of international law;

(d) As a pre-condition of transit, vessels may be required to establish clearly the financial responsibility and guarantees for payment of reasonable and adequate indemnification, consistent with international practice and standards, for damages resulting from acts or omissions of such vessels when passing through the Canal.

In the case of vessels owned or operated by a State or for which it has acknowledged responsibility, a certification by that State that it shall observe its obligations under international law to pay for damages resulting from the act or omission of such vessels when passing through the Canal shall be deemed sufficient to establish such financial responsibility;

(e) Vessels of war and auxiliary vessels of all nations shall at all times be entitled to transit the Canal, irrespective of their internal operation, means of propulsion, origin, destination or armament, without being subjected, as a condition of transit, to inspection, search for surveillance. However, such vessels may be required to certify that they have complied with all applicable health, sanitation and quarantine regulations. In addition, such vessels shall be entitled to refuse to disclose their internal operation, origin, armament, cargo or destination. However, auxiliary vessels may be required to present written assurances, certified by an official at a high level of the government of the State requesting the exemption, that they are owned or operated by that government and in this case are being used only on government non-commercial service.

2. For the purposes of this Treaty, the terms "Canal," "vessel of war," "auxiliary vessel," "internal operation," "armament" and "inspection" shall have the meanings assigned them in Annex A to this Treaty.

Article IV

The United States of America and the Republic of Panama agree to maintain the regime of neutrality established in this Treaty, which shall be maintained in order that the Canal shall remain permanently neutral notwithstanding the termination of any other treaties entered into by the two Contracting Parties.

Article V

After the termination of the Panama Canal Treaty, only the Republic of Panama shall operate the Canal and maintain military forces, defense sites and military installations within its national territory.

Article VI

1. In recognition of the important contributions of the United States of America and of the Republic of Panama to the construction, operation, maintenance, and protection and defense of the Canal, vessels of war and auxiliary vessels of those nations shall notwithstanding any other provisions of this Treaty, be entitled to transit the Canal irrespective of their internal operation, means of propulsion, origin, destination, armament or cargo carried. Such vessels of war and auxiliary vessels will be entitled to transit the Canal expeditiously.

2. The United States of America, so long as it has responsibility for the operation of the Canal, may continue to provide the Republic of Colombia toll-free transit through the Canal for its troops, vessels and materials of war. Thereafter, the Republic of Panama may provide the Republic of Colombia and the Republic of Costa Rica with the right of toll-free transit.

REFERENCES:

Canal Treaties. Washington, D.C.: U.S. Government Printing Office, 1914.

Nesbitt, Wallace. *The Panama Canal and its Treaty Obligations.* Toronto: Rous and Mann, Ltd., 1912.

Parrish, Samuel L. *The Hay-Paunceforte Treaty and the Panama Canal,* New York: N. Pub., 1913).

Agreement (with Canada) on Principles Applicable to a Northern Natural Gas Pipeline

SIGNED: September 20, 1977, at Ottawa

SIGNATORIES: Canada vs. United States

IN FORCE: From signing (except for provisions requiring legislative approval, which entered into force on July 24, 1978)

OVERVIEW: The basic agreement between Canada and the United States on cooperation in the construction and operation of a pipeline for the transportation of Alaskan natural gas from Alaska through Canada.

DISCUSSION:

The agreement outlines the principles to be adhered to in this large international project. Issues addressed include the following:

- The pipeline route
- Undertakings by both signatories to expedite necessary permits, licenses, etc., for expeditious construction
- An outline of the construction timetable
- Specifications of capacity of the line
- Financing principles (which are detailed in a separate annex)
- Taxation principles, including guaranteed rates and caps on a special Yukon Property Tax
- Tariffs and cost allocation principles governing the assignment of costs to each shipper
- Supply of goods and services (also addressed separately in **Agreement on Procurement of Certain Items for the Alaska Highway Gas Pipeline** of 1980)
- Principles of coordination and consultation, including among regulatory authorities
- Agreement to establish a Technical Study Group on Pipe for ongoing evaluation of various pipe designs and materials

REFERENCE:

Coates, Peter A. The *Trans-Alaska Pipeline Controversy: Technology, Conservation and the Frontier.* Allentown, PA: Lehigh University Press, 1991.

Project Grant Agreement (with Bangladesh) for Agricultural Inputs Project

OFFICIAL TITLE: Project Grant Agreement for Agricultural Inputs Project III Relating to Fertilizer Distribution and Marketing (with Annexes)

SIGNED: August 31, 1977, at Dacca, Bangladesh

SIGNATORIES: Bangladesh vs. United States

IN FORCE: From signing

OVERVIEW: A grant to Bangladesh for the improvement of its fertilizer distribution and marketing system.

DISCUSSION:

For a discussion of the background of this agreement, see **Loan Agreement (with Bangladesh) for the Ashuganj Fertilizer Project.**

Having entered into agreements to finance construction of a fertilizer plant and fertilizer warehouse facilities in famine-stricken Bangladesh, the United States concluded, through the United Nations Agency for International Development (AID), a grant agreement to finance improvements in Bangladesh's distribution and marketing of the fertilizer product. The amount fo the grant provided is $27,500,000.

REFERENCES:

Donald, Gordon, Jr. *U.S. Foreign Aid and the National Interest.* New York: National Policy Association, 1983.

Eberstadt, Nicholas. *U.S. Foreign Aid Policy: A Critique.* New York: Foreign Policy Association, 1990.

Tourism Agreement (with Mexico)

SIGNED: May 4, 1978, at Mexico City

SIGNATORIES: Mexico vs. United States

IN FORCE: Frm February 20, 1979

OVERVIEW: The first of two agreements to develop tourism between the United States and Mexico.

DISCUSSION:

This agreement was superceded in 1983 by **Agreement (with Mexico) on the Development and Facilitation of Tourism.** The 1978 agreement introduced many of the provisions included in the alter agreement, which, however, proposed several more programs. The 1978 agreement included one provision—for the development of tourism from third countries—dropped from the 1983 agreement.

REFERENCES:

None

Amendment to Loan Agreement (with Bangladesh) for the Ashuganj Fertilizer Project

SIGNED: August 31, 1978, at Dacca, Bangladesh

SIGNATORIES: Bangladesh vs. United States

IN FORCE: From signing

OVERVIEW: An amendment to the 1975 **Loan Agreement (with Bangladesh) for the Ashuganj Fertilizer Project** increasing the loan amount from $30,000,000 to $53,000,000.

DISCUSSION:

For a discussion of the background of this agreement, see **Loan Agreement (with Bangladesh) for the Ashuganj Fertilizer Project.**

REFERENCES:

Donald, Gordon, Jr. *U.S. Foreign Aid and the National Interest.* New York: National Policy Association, 1983.

Eberstadt, Nicholas. *U.S. Foreign Aid Policy: A Critique.* New York: Foreign Policy Association, 1990.

Agreement (with Poland) on Economic and Industrial Cooperation

OFFICIAL TITLE: Agreement (with Poland) on the Participation of Small and Medium-sized Firms and Economic Organizations in Trade and in Economic and Industrial Cooperation

SIGNED: November 9, 1978, at Washington, D.C.

SIGNATORIES: Poland vs. United States

IN FORCE: From signing

OVERVIEW: An agreement whereby Poland and the United States jointly undertake to "support the development of economic and industrial cooperation and trade involving small and medium-sized firms and economic organizations, in particular by facilitating the establishment of contacts and the negotiation of contracts."

DISCUSSION:

By the late 1970s, Poland, under Soviet domination since the end of World War II, was progressively moving toward increasing degrees of independence and, with this, away from a state-controlled demand economy and closer to the capitalist model. The United States, wishing to encourage this development and to exploit a growing weakness in the Iron Curtain, concluded an agreement to foster free enterprise in Poland.

The agreement provides as follows:

- The signatories jointly undertake to "support the development of economic and industrial cooperation and trade involving small and medium-sized firms and economic organizations, in particular by facilitating the establishment of contacts and the negotiation of contracts."

- The signatories "shall support direct cooperation between organizations and institutions of both countries for the purpose of exchanging information and developing procedures useful to small and medium-sized firms . . ."

- The United States Small Business Administration, the Polish Chamber of Foreign Trade, and the Central Union of Cooperative Work will collaborate on cooperative trade-development programs.

REFERENCE:

Zloch-Christy, Illiana. *East-West Financial Relations: Current Problems and Future Prospects.* New York: Cambridge University Press, 1991.

Convention on the Physical Protection of Nuclear Material

SIGNED: March 3, 1980, at New York

SIGNATORIES: Argentina, Australia, Austria, Belgium, Brazil, Bulgaria, Canada, China, Czechoslovakia, Denmark, Dominican Republic, Ecuador, EURATOM, Finland, France, German Democratic Republic, Germany (Federal Republic), Greece, Guatemala, Haiti, Hungary, Indonesia, Ireland, Israel, Italy, Japan, Korea (Republic of), Liechtenstein, Luxembourg, Mexico, Mongolia, Morocco, Netherlands, Niger, Norway, Panama, Paraguay, Philippines, Poland, Portugal, Romania, South Africa, Spain, Sweden, Switzerland, Turkey, Union of Soviet Socialist Republics, United Kingdom, United States, Yugoslavia

IN FORCE: February 8, 1987

OVERVIEW: "Each State Party shall take appropriate steps within the framework of its national law and consistent with international law to ensure as far as practicable that, during international nuclear transport, nuclear material within its territory, or on board a ship or aircraft under its jurisdiction insofar as such ship or aircraft is engaged in the transport to or from that State, is protected . . ."

DISCUSSION:

The convention lays down provisions for the safe transportation, including importation and exportation, of nuclear materials for peaceful use. Annexes to the convention classify nuclear materials into standard categories and, according to these, provide for levels of physical protection to be applied in international transport.

REFERENCE:

International Nuclear Safeguards, 1994: Vision for the Future. Vienna: International Atonic Energy Agency., 1995.

Amendment to Project Grant Agreement (with Bangladesh) for Agricultural Inputs Project

SIGNED: July 25, 1979, at Dacca, Bangladesh

SIGNATORIES: Bangladesh vs. United States

IN FORCE: From signing

OVERVIEW: An amendment amplifying terms of financing the project.

DISCUSSION:

For a discussion of the background of this agreement, see **Loan Agreement (with Bangladesh) for the Ashuganj Fertilizer Project.**

The amendment established a system of incremental financing of the project for which a grant was made in the 1978 **Project Grant Agreement (with Bangladesh) for Agricultural Inputs Project.** The purpose of the incremental mechanism was to provide a means by which "both Parties" may assess how well the project achieved its "basic purpose of assisting small farmer access to fertilizer."

REFERENCES:
Donald, Gordon, Jr. *U.S. Foreign Aid and the National Interest*. New York: National Policy Association, 1983.
Eberstadt, Nicholas. *U.S. Foreign Aid Policy: A Critique*. New York: Foreign Policy Association, 1990.

International Natural Rubber Agreement, 1979

SIGNED: October 6, 1979, at Geneva

SIGNATORIES: Australia, Belgium, Brazil, Canada, China, Czechoslovakia, Denmark, European Economic Community, Finland, France, Germany (Federal Republic), Indonesia, Ireland, Italy, Japan, Liberia, Luxembourg, Malaysia, Mexico, Morocco, Netherlands, Norway, Papua New Guinea, Peru, Philippines, Sri Lanka, Sweden, Thailand, Union of Soviet Socialist Republics, United Kingdom, United States

IN FORCE: Provisionally, from October 23, 1980; definitively, from April 15, 1982

OVERVIEW: An international agreement to stabilize prices of natural rubber "in the interests of consumers and natural rubber markets."

DISCUSSION:

The chief objectives of the agreement are as follows:

- To achieve balanced growth between the supply of and demand for natural rubber
- To achieve stable conditions in natural rubber trade through avoiding excessive natural rubber price fluctuations
- To help stabilize export earning from natural rubber of exporting members, and to increase their earnings based on expanding natural rubber export volumes at fair and remunerative prices, thereby helping to provide the necessary incentives for a dynamic and rising rate of production and the resources for accelerated economic growth and social development
- To seek to ensure adequate supplies of natural rubber
- To take feasible steps in the event of a surplus or shortage of natural rubber to mitigate the economic difficulties that members might encounter
- To expand international trade in natural rubber
- To improve the competitiveness of natural rubber by encouraging research and development
- To encourage the efficient development of the natural rubber economy by seeking to facilitate and promote improvements in the processing, marketing and distribution of raw natural rubber
- To further international cooperation and consultations on natural rubber matters

REFERENCES:
None

Agreement (with Canada) on Procurement of Certain Items for the Alaska Highway Gas Pipeline

OFFICIAL TITLE: Exchange of Notes Constituting an Agreement on Procedures Governing the Procurement in Canada and the United States of America of Certain Designated Items for the Alaska Highway Gas Pipeline (with Annexed Procedures)

SIGNED: June 10, 1980, at Washington, D.C.

SIGNATORIES: Canada vs. United States

IN FORCE: From signing

OVERVIEW: An agreement on procedures for procuring supplies for construction and maintenance of the Northern Natural Gas Pipeline, which traverses Canada and Alaska.

DISCUSSION:

This agreement was concluded pursuant to **Agreement on Principles Applicable to a Northern Natural Gas Pipeline** of 1977 and addresses the equitable and economical procurement of material for construction and maintenance of the pipeline. Issues addressed include the following:

- Agreement on qualification of bidders
- Agreement on technical specification and tendering documents
- Agreement on decision recommendations
- Agreement on procedures for final award of contracts

REFERENCE:
Coates, Peter A. *The Trans-Alaska Pipeline Controversy: Technology, Conservation and the Frontier*. Allentown, PA: Lehigh University Press, 1991.

Agreement (with Malaysia) Relating to Trade in Textile and Textile Products

SIGNED: December 5, 1980 and February 27, 1981, at Kuala Lumpur, Malaysia

SIGNATORIES: Malaysia vs. United States

IN FORCE: From February 27, 1981

OVERVIEW: An agreement setting limits on Malaysian textile exports to the United States.

DISCUSSION:

This agreement regulates textile exports from Malaysia to the United States, setting limits to exports in three broad categories:

1. Yarns, fabrics, made-up goods, and miscellaneous products of cotton and manmade fibers
2. Apparel of cotton and manmade fibers
3. Wool textiles and textile products

The agreement lays down annual limits for exports to the United States in each group, as well as formulas for adjustment of these limits in certain cases. An annex breaks down the categories into specific items and classes of items, providing "conversion factors" for each item or class, by which each may be figured into the agreed-upon export limits.

REFERENCE:
Blokker, Niels. *International Regulation of World Trade in Textiles: Lessons for Practice.* Dornstadt, Netherlands: Matinus Nijihoff, 1989.

Agreement (with Mexico) on the Development and Facilitation of Tourism

SIGNED: April 18, 1983, at Mexico City
SIGNATORIES: Mexico vs. United States
IN FORCE: From January 25, 1984
OVERVIEW: A cooperative agreement to develop tourism between the United States and Mexico

DISCUSSION:

The agreement incorporates the following:

- Facilitation of travel promotion offices in each country
- Facilitation and encouragement of the activities of travel agents, tour operators, and so on
- Facilitation of the promotional activities of carriers, including airlines, rail operators, bus operators, cruise operators, and so on
- Facilitation of tourist procedures, including the elimination of most documentary requirements
- Encouragement of courteous official treatment to tourists
- Programs to encourage tourist and cultural activities
- Programs to facilitate the training of tourism professionals
- Compilation and exchange of tourism statistics
- Inauguration of joint marketing of tourism

The agreement supercedes the **Tourism Agreement (with Mexico)** of 1978.

REFERENCE:
None

Agreement with the European Economic Community on Wine

SIGNED: July 26, 1983, at Washington, D.C.
SIGNATORIES: European Economic Community vs. United States
IN FORCE: From signing
OVERVIEW: An agreement relating to standardization of the wine trade between the EEC and the United States.

DISCUSSION:

The agreement sets down standards for wine culture and the wine trade in the following areas:

- Enological practices
- Agreement on permitted additives and preservatives
- EEC certification requirements
- Geographic designations of origin for wine
- Harmonization of EEC and U.S. labeling requirements
- EEC-U.S. collaboration in investigations in the wine sector

REFERENCE:
Lundestad, Geir. *Empire by Integration: The United States and European Integration, 1945-1997.* London and New York: Oxford University Press, 1998.

Provisional Understanding Regarding Deep Seabed Matters

SIGNED: August 3, 1984, at Geneva
SIGNATORIES: Belgium, France, Germany (Federal Republic), Italy, Japan, Netherlands, United Kingdom, United States
IN FORCE: From September 2, 1984
OVERVIEW: A agreement to forestall dispute over rights to mining of the seabed.

DISCUSSION:

This agreement sets up mechanisms to resolve conflicting claims among the signatories over deep seabed mining rights in certain areas. Hard mineral mining of the deep seabed continues to evolve as a commercially feasible enterprise, and, in the 1980s, the parties believed the agreement was necessary to forestall any preemptive claims on a potentially highly profitable industry.

REFERENCES:
Barkenbus, Jack N. *Deep Seabed Resources: Politics and Technology.* New York: Free Press, 1979.
Kronmiller, Theodore G. *Lawfulness of Deep Seabed Mining.* Dobbs Ferry, NY: Oceana, 1980.

Agreement (with Israel) on the Establishment of a Free Trade Area

SIGNED: April 22, 1985, at Washington
SIGNATORIES: Israel vs. United States
IN FORCE: From August 19, 1985
OVERVIEW: An agreement establishing "a Free Trade Area . . . [without] duties and other restrictive regulations of commerce on trade between the two nations in products originating therein."

DISCUSSION:

A free-trade area or free-trade zone is a defined geographical area within which goods may be landed, handled, manufactured (or reconfigured), and re-exported without being subjected to customs formalities. Such zones are typically set up at seaports, international airports, and national frontiers. Their effect is to remove from the seaport, airport, or border impediments to trade created by high tariffs and complex customs regulations. With expenses and delays reduced, trade is stimulated. The agreement with Israel is representative of free-trade zone agreements the United States has concluded with numerous nations.

The principal provision of the agreement, set down in Article 2, is as follows:

1. Products of Israel shall, when imported into the customs territory of the United States, be governed by the provisions of Annex 1.

2. Products of the United States shall, when imported into Israel, be governed by the provisions of Annex 2.

The rest of the agreement details certain exceptions to free-trade status for certain goods under certain economic conditions.

Effective January 1, 1995 all duties on the vast majority of Israeli exports into the United States were eliminated, as were duties on United States imports into Israel, effectively rendering the entire territory of both nations free-trade zones.

REFERENCE:
Trade Policy Review—Israel. Lanham, MD: Bernan Associates, 1999.

Investment Treaty with Bangladesh

OFFICIAL TITLE: Treaty between the United States of America and the People's Republic of Bangladesh Concerning the Reciprocal Encouragement and Protection of Investment
SIGNED: March 12, 1986, at Washington, D.C.
SIGNATORIES: Bangladesh vs. United States
IN FORCE: From July 25, 1989
OVERVIEW: A representative bilateral investment treaty ("BIT") with a developing nation.

DISCUSSION:
This treaty was concluded as part of a "BIT program," an ongoing series of agreements designed to promote and to protect United States investment in developing countries. The treaty is intended "to encourage Bangladesh . . . to adopt macroeconomic and structural policies that will promote economic growth." At the same time, the treaty secures the following:

- Treatment of investors in accordance with international law
- Treatment of foreign investors on terms no less favorable than investors of the host country and no less favorably than investors of third countries
- Application of international law standards to the expropriation of investments and to the payment of compensation for expropriation
- Free transfers of funds associated with an investment into and out of the host country
- Establishment of procedures to allow an investor to take disputes directly to binding third-party arbitration.

REFERENCE:
Dolzer, Rudolf, and Margrete Stevens. *Bilateral Investment Treaties.* The Hague: Kluwer Law International, 1995.

Textile Agreement with Haiti

OFFICIAL TITLE: Agreement Relating to Trade in Cotton, Wool, and Man-made Fiber Textiles and Textile Products, with Annexes.
SIGNED: September 26 and 30, 1986, at Port-au-Prince, Haiti
SIGNATORIES: Haiti vs. United States
IN FORCE: From September 30, 1986 (with amendments and extensions, June 9 and 23, 1987, and July 18 and November 19 and 28, 1990)
OVERVIEW: An agreement establishing permissible quantities of textile products that Haiti may export to the United States.

DISCUSSION:
This agreement, typical of trade agreements made with developing nations in which labor costs are substantially less than those in the United States, establishes monthly limits to the quantity of textile products that may be exported to the United States. The object of such limits is to prevent, minimize, or control distortion of the labor market that would result from the unregulated influx into the United States of cheaply assembled clothing. Such an influx would almost certainly result in the loss of United States textile-and clothing-industry jobs.

REFERENCES:
None

Inter-American Amateur Radio Service Convention ("Lima Convention")

SIGNED: August 14, 1987, at Lima, Peru
SIGNATORIES: Argentina, Bolivia, Brazil, Canada, Chile, Colombia, Guatemala, Haiti, Mexico, Paraguay, Peru, Suriname, United States, Uruguay, Venezuela
IN FORCE: From February 21, 1990
OVERVIEW: "The provisions of this Convention shall apply to the issuance of authorizations allowing temporary operation of appropriate Amateur Radio Service to citizens of one State Party in the territory of another State Party, as long as such persons are duly authorized by the competent authority of a State Party to operate such Amateur Radio Service." (Article 1)

DISCUSSION:
This is one of very few international communications agreements that apply to amateur radio, in contrast to commercial broadcasting. It applies to persons who are citizens of member states of the Inter-American Telecommunication Commission

(CITEL). Also see **Inter-American Convention on an International Amateur Radio Permit**.

REFERENCES:
None

Unidroit Convention on International Factoring

SIGNED: May 28, 1988, at Ottawa, Canada
SIGNATORIES: Belgium, Czechoslovakia, Finland, France, Germany, Ghana, Guinea, Hungary, Italy, Latvia, Morocco, Nigeria, Philippines, United Kingdom, United Republic of Tanzania, United States
IN FORCE: Not yet in force for the United States
OVERVIEW: A convention "adopting uniform rules to provide a legal framework that will facilitate international factoring, while maintaining a fair balance of interests between the different parties involved in factoring transactions."

DISCUSSION:
Generally speaking, a factor is a person or firm that accepts accounts receivable as security against short-term loans. Factors figure frequently in international trade, performing (as described by the convention) "at least two of the following functions":

• Finance for the supplier, including loans and advance payments
• Maintenance of accounts (ledgering) relating to the receivables
• Collection of receivables
• Protection against default in payment by debtors

The present "Convention applies whenever the receivables assigned pursuant to a factoring contract arise from a contract of sale of goods between a supplier and a debtor whose places of business are in different States and: (a) those States and the State in which the factor has its place of business are Contracting States; or (b) both the contract of sale of goods and the factoring contract are governed by the law of a Contracting State."

The convention succinctly defines the rights and duties of the parties (that is, supplier vs. factor) to a "factoring contract."

REFERENCE:
Bonell, Michael Joachim. *An International Restatement of Contract Law: The Unidroit Principle of International Commercial Contracts.* New York: Transnational Publishers, 1998.

Unidroit Convention on International Financial Leasing

SIGNED: May 20, 1988, at Ottawa, Canada
SIGNATORIES: Belarus, Belgium, Czechoslovakia, Finland, France, Ghana, Guinea, Hungary, Italy, Latvia, Morocco, Nigeria,

Panama, Philippines, Russian Federation, United Republic of Tanzania, United States
IN FORCE: From May 28, 1988; for the United States, December 28, 1990
OVERVIEW: A convention to remove "certain legal impediments to the international financial leasing of equipment, while maintaining a fair balance of interests between the different parties to the transaction."

DISCUSSION:
The convention defines the rights and duties of lessees and lessors in an international context. The convention "applies when the lessor and the lessee have their places of business in different States and: (a) those States and the State in which the supplier has its place of business are Contracting States; or (b) both the supply agreement and the leasing agreement are governed by the law of a Contracting State." The document is intended specifically to govern "a transaction which includes the following characteristics: (a) the lessee specifies the equipment and selects the supplier without relying primarily on the skill and judgment of the lessor; (b) the equipment is acquired by the lessor in connection with a leasing agreement which, to the knowledge of the supplier, either has been made or is to be made between the lessor and the lessee; and (c) the rentals payable under the leasing agreement are calculated so as to take into account in particular the amortization of the whole or a substantial part of the cost of the equipment."

REFERENCE:
Bonell, Michael Joachim. *An International Restatement of Contract Law: The Unidroit Principle of International Commercial Contracts.* New York: Transnational Publishers, 1998.

Agreement (with the Russian Federation) on Trade Relations

SIGNED: June 1, 1990, at Washington, D.C.
SIGNATORIES: Russian Federation vs. United States
IN FORCE: From June 17, 1992
OVERVIEW: An agreement providing for reciprocal most favored nation (MFN) tariff treatment to the products of each country.

DISCUSSION:
This agreement was signed with the Soviet Union, but came into force after the dissolution of the U.S.S.R. and is therefore deemed an agreement with the Russian Federation.

The agreement permits Russia to export goods to the United States while receiving non-discriminatory treatment of its goods. The intention is to create commercial opportunities for Russian enterprises and to promote the development of a market-based economy in Russia. At the same time, the agreement lays the groundwork for enhanced trade opportunities in Russia for U.S. business. The main provisions of the agreement include the following:

- Improved market access and non-discriminatory treatment for U.S. goods and services in Russia
- Step-by-step provision of national treatment for U.S. products and services
- Facilitation of business by allowing free operation of commercial representations in each country and by permitting companies to engage and serve as agents and consultants and to conduct market studies
- Establishment of strong intellectual property rights protection through reaffirmation of existing multilateral patent, trademark, and copyright conventions

REFERENCE:

Davydov, Oleg D. *Inside Out: The Radical Transformation of Russian Foreign Trade, 1992-1997.* New York: Fordham University Press, 1998.

Agreement (with the CEC) Regarding the Application of Competition Laws

SIGNED: September 23, 1991, at Washington, D.C.

SIGNATORIES: Commission of the European Communities vs. United States

IN FORCE: From signing

OVERVIEW: Agreement "to promote cooperation and coordination and lessen the possibility or impact of differences between the Parties in the application of their competition laws."

DISCUSSION:

The agreement sets up procedures for exchanging information between the CEC and the United States on laws relating to competition and for harmonizing United States and CEC laws and regulations. Issue areas addressed include the following:

- Exchange of information
- Cooperation and coordination of enforcement action
- Cooperation regarding anticompetitive activities in the territory of one party that adversely affect the interests of the other party
- Avoidance of conflict in enforcement activities
- Procedures governing consultation and confidentiality

Recent years have seen numerous agreements between the United States and the CEC, signaling the United States' full recognition of the European Communities as a diplomatic and economic entity.

REFERENCES:
None

The Tokyo Declaration on the U.S.-Japan Global Partnership

SIGNED: January 9, 1992, at Tokyo

SIGNATORIES: Japan vs. United States

IN FORCE: From signing

OVERVIEW: A comprehensive joint statement creating and acknowledging a collaborative "global partnership" between the two nations.

DISCUSSION:

The Tokyo Declaration is not a formal treaty, but a statement of cooperation and common cause on trade-related issues, as well as a broad spectrum of other issues. The major resolves contained in the Tokyo Declaration are as follows:

- "Together, both nations pledge to: work together to maintain world peace and security; promote development of the world economy; support the world-wide trend toward democratization and market-oriented economies; and meet new transnational challenges. To achieve these goals, the two countries will cooperate to strengthen the GATT multilateral trading system; reinvigorate the U.N. organization; advance arms control and the non-proliferation of weapons of mass destruction; assist the-developing world to promote growth and stability; and protect and improve the global environment. The United States and Japan recommit their resources and the talents of their peoples to the purposes of the United Nations Charter. ..."
- "The U.S. and Japan reaffirm their commitments to the 1960 Treaty of Mutual Cooperation and Security, which is central to the U.S.-Japan Alliance."
- "... the two governments are resolved to enhance openness and oppose protectionism in their commercial, financial, and investment markets. To this end, Japan and the United States will strengthen policy initiatives to reduce structural impediments.... Japan and the United States further pledge to make their economies the most open, productive, and competitive in the world ..."
- "... the two governments undertake to expand scientific and technical cooperation, including basic research, based on reciprocal access, for the benefit of both societies and the human community. They pledge to increase research on global environmental issues and will take a leadership role in fostering an international consensus on measures to meet this challenge."
- "... the United States and Japan pledge to undertake and support programs which will advance the rich and diverse intellectual, cultural, and public interaction between their two peoples. ..."

Beyond agreeing to cooperation according to these general principles, Japan and the United States agreed to work together in the following more specific areas:

- Arms control and arms reduction
- Cooperate in policies designed to bring stability to Asia and the Pacific, as well Latin America, the Carribean, central and eastern Europe, and the Middle East
- Cooperate in countering terrorism
- Take specific steps to enhance mutual security through strengthening the defensive alliance between the two nations
- Embark upon a specified list of environmental projects to safeguard and enhance the natural environment
- Cooperate in the area of improving human life through programs related to health, narcotics control, refugee relief, and emergency (disaster) response
- Cooperate upon a specified list of scientific and technological projects

Finally, the two nations declare their joint commitment to "identify and solve economic and trade issues for a smooth and sound management of Japan-U.S. economic relations, which are vital not only for the two countries but for the world economy as a whole." The concluding portions of the Tokyo Declaration inventory specific economic and trade issues to be resolved, most of them revolving around the reduction of protectionist Japanese trade policies, which create and perpetuate a deep American trade deficit with regard to Japan.

REFERENCES:
Forsberg, Aaron. *America and the Japanese Miracle: The Cold War Context of Japan's Postwar Economic Revival, 1950-1960.* Chapel Hill: University of North Carolina Press, 2000.
Sato, Ryuzo. *Beyond Trade Friction: Japan-U.S. Economic Relations.* New York: Cambridge University Press, 1989.

Japan Agreement on Computer Products and Services

SIGNED: January 22, 1992, at Washington
SIGNATORIES: Japan vs. United States
IN FORCE: From signing
OVERVIEW: An agreement opening Japan's public-sector markets to computers manufactured by United States and other non-domestic) manufacturers.

DISCUSSION:
In the years since World War II, Japan, bitter foe of the United States, rapidly became a key U.S. trading partner. The postwar rise of Japanese industry was fueled, in part, by strongly protectionist legislation, which placed heavy restrictions on import goods that compete with those domestically produced. In the case of trade with the United States, Japanese protectionism contributed to an extremely lopsided balance of trade, as the United States imported from Japan far more than it exported to it. The reduction of Japan's protectionist policies has been the subject of much trade negotiation between Japan and the

United States. Japan Agreement on Computer Products and Services is one product of such negotiation. It relaxes certain restrictions on public-sector (that is, government) procurement of computer products and service, an area in which both United States and Japanese manufacturers are very active. Before the present agreement liberalized policy, American computer products were virtually barred from the public-sector marketplace.

The heart of the agreement is this from the section on "General Policies":

In the interest of expanding trade opportunities based on the principles of non-discrimination, transparency, and fair and open competition in public sector procurements of computer products (including peripherals and packaged software) and computer services (operation and maintenance of computers input of data into computers; development of computer systems, including development of software and systems integration, maintenance of computer software and other related services) (collectively referred to as "computer products and services") the Government of Japan ("the Government") will strive actively to further improve its public sector procurement procedures. Accordingly, the Government will initiate these "Measures Related to Japanese Public Sector Procurements of Computer Products and Services" ("the Measures") set forth herein, with the aim of expanding procurements of competitive foreign computer products and services.

The conclusion of this agreement represents an economically modest but symbolically important step toward establishing a more equitable balance of trade between the United States and Japan.

REFERENCES:
Forsberg, Aaron. *America and the Japanese Miracle: The Cold War Context of Japan's Postwar Economic Revival, 1950-1960.* Chapel Hill: University of North Carolina Press, 2000.
Sato, Ryuzo. *Beyond Trade Friction: Japan-U.S. Economic Relations.* New York: Cambridge University Press, 1989.

Agreement (with Albania) on Trade Relations

SIGNED: May 14, 1992, at Washington, D.C.
SIGNATORIES: Albania vs. United States
IN FORCE: From November 2, 1992
OVERVIEW: An agreement establishing trade relations with a former member of the Soviet bloc.

DISCUSSION:
As the Soviet Union crumbled in the early 1990s and its satellite nations left the orbit of its political and economic domination, the United States eagerly moved to conclude trade agreements intended to foster the development of market economies in these nations. The transition to market economies was considered critical to the transition from communist domination to democratic government friendly to the West.

The principal thrust of the agreement is to establish trade relations between Albania and the United States on an open, non-discriminatory basis. The signatories agree to extend to one another the better of national treatment or most-favored-nation treatment. *National treatment* is treatment accorded within the territories of a signatory party on terms no less favorable than the treatment accorded to nationals, companies, products, vessels or other objects, as the case may be, of that party. *Most-favored-nation treatment* is treatment accorded within the territories of a signatory party on terms no less favorable than the treatment accorded to nationals, companies, products, vessels or other objects, as the case may be, of any third country.

The agreement also includes provisions on the following:

• Protection of intellectual property (copyrights, patents, and trademarks)
• Safeguards to prevent market disruptions: Consultative steps in the event that Albanian government subsidy of some industry should create unfair international competition within that industry

REFERENCE:
United States Congress, Subcommittee on Trade of the Committee on Ways and Means. *Written Comments on Trade Agreements Between the United States and Albania and the United States and Romania.* Washington, D.C. : U.S. Government Printing Office. 1992.

Agreement (with the EEC) on Trade in Large Civil Aircraft

OFFICIAL TITLE: Agreement between the Government of the United States of America and the European Economic Community Concerning the Application of the GATT Agreement on Trade in Large Civil Aircraft
SIGNED: July 17, 1992, at Washington, D.C., and Brussels
SIGNATORIES: European Economic Community vs. United States
IN FORCE: From signing
OVERVIEW: A fair-trade agreement regulating direct or indirect government support of trade in large civil aircraft.

DISCUSSION:
As the opening of the agreement explains, the objective of the document is to prevent "trade distortions resulting from direct or indirect government support for the development and production of Large Civil aircraft and of introducing greater disciplines on such support." The agreement seeks to reduce the effect of government subsidies in creating unfair competition in the market for large civil aircraft. By placing restrictions on such government support, the agreement seeks to maintain an open market in which American aircraft manufacturers can compete more equitably with subsidized European manufacturers.

REFERENCE:
United States Department of State, *Treaties in Force: A List of Treaties and other International Agreements of the United States in Force on January 1, 1997.* Washington, D.C.: U.S. Government Printing Office, 1997.

North American Free Trade Agreement (NAFTA)

OFFICIAL TITLE: North American Free Trade Agreement, with Notes and Annexes
SIGNED: December 8, 11, 14, and 17, 1992, at Washington, Ottawa, and Mexico City
SIGNATORIES: Canada, Mexico, United States
IN FORCE: From January 1, 1994
OVERVIEW: A document establishing comprehensively a free trade area among the signatories.

DISCUSSION:
After years of discussion, controversy, and debate, the three principal nations of North America created a comprehensive agreement on trade, the main purpose of which is the establishment of free trade among the three nations through the elimination of trade barriers.

The Preamble affirms the signatories' commitment to promoting employment and economic growth in each country through the expansion of trade and investment opportunities in the free trade area and by enhancing the competitiveness of Canadian, Mexican and U.S. firms in global markets—and doing so in a manner consistent with protection of the environment. The Preamble confirms the resolve of the signatories to promote sustainable development, to protect, enhance and enforce workers' rights, and to improve working conditions in each country.

Following the Preamble is a statement of objectives and other opening provisions. The substantive portion of the NAFTA begins by formally establishing a free trade area between Canada, Mexico and the United States, consistent with the **General Agreement on Tariffs and Trade (GATT).** The following objectives are then laid down:

• To eliminate barriers to trade
• To promote conditions of fair competition
• To increase investment opportunities
• To provide adequate protection for intellectual property rights
• To establish effective procedures for the implementation and application of the NAFTA and for the resolution of disputes and to further trilateral, regional and multilateral cooperation

To meet these objectives, the NAFTA signatories undertake to observe the principles and rules of the Agreement, including, most importantly, national treatment (treating business interests of other nations as domestic business interests are treated), most-favored-nation treatment (trading with all signatories on the best terms offered any signatory), and procedural "transparency" (openness to inspection and audit among the signatories).

While each signatory affirms its respective rights and obligations under the GATT and other international agreements, NAFTA is established as taking priority over other agreements to the extent that there is any conflict. The agreement also provides for exceptions to this general rule, however; for example, the trade provisions of certain environmental agreements take precedence over NAFTA, subject to a requirement to minimize inconsistencies with the NAFTA.

NAFTA eliminates all tariffs on goods originating in Canada, Mexico and the United States over a "transition period," and lays down "Rules of Origin" to define which goods are eligible for this preferential tariff treatment. The object of the Rules of Origin are as follows:

- To ensure that NAFTA benefits are accorded only to goods produced in the North American region—not goods made wholly or in large part in other countries
- To provide clear rules and predictable results
- To minimize administrative burdens for exporters, importers, and producers trading under NAFTA

The rules of origin specify that goods originate in North America if they are wholly North American. Goods containing non-regional materials are also considered to be North American if the non-regional materials are sufficiently transformed in the NAFTA region so as to undergo a specified change in tariff classification. In some cases, goods must include a specified percentage of North American content in addition to meeting the tariff classification requirement.

To ensure that only goods satisfying the rules of origin are accorded preferential tariff treatment, and to provide certainty to and streamlined procedures for importers, exporters, and producers of the three countries, NAFTA includes special provisions on customs administration, including the following:

- Uniform regulations to ensure consistent interpretation, application, and administration of the rules of origin
- A uniform Certificate of Origin as well as certification requirements and procedures for importers and exporters that claim preferential tariff treatment
- Common record-keeping requirements in the three countries for such goods
- Rules for both traders and customs authorities with respect to verifying the origin of such goods
- A provision that importers, exporters, and producers will obtain advance rulings on the origin of goods from the customs authority of the country into which the goods are to be imported

- A provision that the importing country is to give exporters and producers in other NAFTA countries substantially the same rights of review and appeal of its origin determinations and advance rulings as it provides to importers in its territory
- The creation of a trilateral working group to address future modifications of the rules of origin and the uniform regulations
- Establishment of specific time periods to ensure the expeditious resolution of disputes regarding the rules of origin between NAFTA partners

Concerning trade in goods, NAFTA incorporates the fundamental national treatment obligation of the GATT. That is, once goods have been imported into one NAFTA country from another NAFTA country, they must not be the object of discrimination. Accordingly, NAFTA lays down provisions regarding the following:

- Market Access: Rules governing trade in goods with respect to customs duties and other charges, quantitative restrictions, such as quotas, licenses and permits, and import and export price requirements.
- Elimination of tariffs: NAFTA provides for the progressive elimination of all tariffs on goods qualifying as North American under its rules of origin. For most goods, existing customs duties will either be eliminated immediately or phased out in five or ten equal annual stages.
- Drawback: NAFTA establishes rules on the use of "drawback" or similar programs that provide for the refund or waiver of customs duties on materials used in the production of goods subsequently exported to another NAFTA country.
- Customs User Fees: The signatories agree not to impose new customs user fees similar to the U.S. merchandise processing fee or the Mexican customs processing fee, and to eliminate such existing fees.
- Waiver of Customs Duties: NAFTA prohibits any new performance-based customs duty waiver or duty remission programs.
- Export Taxes: NAFTA prohibits all three countries from applying export taxes unless such taxes are also applied on goods to be consumed domestically.

A section devoted to Textiles and Apparel provides special rules for trade in fibers, yarns, textiles and clothing in the North American market, including the following:

- Elimination of tariff and non-tariff barriers over a maximum period of 10 years
- Specific rules of origin to define when imported textile or apparel goods qualify for preferential treatment
- Labeling requirements: to eliminate unnecessary obstacles to textile trade resulting from different labelling requirements in the three countries

In the area of automotive goods, NAFTA eliminates barriers to trade and investment in North American automobiles, trucks, buses, and parts ("automotive goods") over a ten-year transition period. In connection with this, standards of manufacture and safety are to be universalized.

A section of NAFTA sets out the rights and obligations of the three countries regarding crude oil, gas, refined products, basic petrochemicals, coal, electricity and nuclear energy.

While the three countries confirm their full respect for their constitutions, they also recognize the desirability of strengthening the important role that trade in energy and basic petrochemical goods plays in the North American region and of enhancing this role through sustained and gradual liberalization.

The NAFTA's energy provisions incorporate and build on GATT disciplines regarding quantitative restrictions on imports and exports as they apply to energy and basic petrochemical trade. The NAFTA provides that under these disciplines a country may not impose minimum or maximum import or export price requirements, subject to the same exceptions that apply to quantitative restrictions. The NAFTA also makes clear that each country may administer export and import licensing systems, provided that they are operated in a manner consistent with the provisions of the Agreement. In addition, no country may impose a tax, duty or charge on the export of energy or basic petrochemical goods unless the same tax, duty or charge is applied to such goods when consumed domestically.

In the area of agriculture, NAFTA sets out separate bilateral undertakings on cross-border trade in agricultural products, one between Canada and Mexico, and the other between Mexico and the United States. Both include a special transitional safeguard mechanism. Between Canada and the United States, NAFTA generally maintains current fair-trade agreements on tariff and non-tariff barriers. Mexico and the United States agree to eliminate immediately all non-tariff barriers to their agricultural trade. Mexico and the United States also agree to eliminate immediately tariffs on a broad range of agricultural products. Special safeguard provisions and provisions for domestic support of agricultural products are included to protect domestic producers without distorting international trade.

Associated with the agricultural provisions is a section devoted to the development, adoption and enforcement of sanitary and phytosanitary measures for the protection of human, animal or plant life or health from risks arising from animal or plant pests or diseases, food additives or contaminants. Sanitary measures of each signatory must adhere to the following rules:

• Basis on scientific principles and a risk assessment
• Application only to the extent necessary to provide a country's chosen level of protection
• Do not constitute unfair discrimination or disguised restrictions on trade

The three signatories also undertake to work toward harmonization and equivalence of sanitary standards and practices.

Related to the section on sanitary measures is one on Technical Standards, which applies to standards-related measures, namely standards, governmental technical regulations, and the procedures used to determine that these standards and regulations are met.

NAFTA provides safeguards available to each signatory to provide temporary relief to industries adversely affected by surges in imports. A transitional bilateral safeguard mechanism applies to emergency actions taken against import surges that result from tariff reductions under the NAFTA. A global safeguard applies to import surges from all countries.

A section on Government Procurement opens a significant portion of the government procurement market in each NAFTA country on a non-discriminatory basis to suppliers from the other NAFTA countries for goods, services and construction services.

NAFTA expands on various existing trade agreements to create internationally agreed disciplines on government regulation of trade in services. The cross-border trade in services provisions establish a set of basic rules and obligations to facilitate trade in services between the three countries. Major provisions address the following:

• National treatment: Under NAFTA's national treatment rule, each NAFTA country must treat service providers of the other NAFTA countries no less favorably than it treats its own service providers in like circumstances.
• Most-favored-nation treatment: This rule requires each NAFTA country to treat service providers of the other NAFTA countries no less favorably than it treats service providers of any other country in like circumstances.
• Local presence: A NAFTA country may not require a service provider of another NAFTA country to establish or maintain a residence, representative office, branch or any other form of enterprise in its territory as a condition for the provision of a service.

Under NAFTA, barriers to the provision of land transportation services between the NAFTA countries are to be removed according to a specified timetable. Restrictions on cross-border land transportation services among the three countries are to be phased out in order to create equal opportunities in the North American international land transportation market. This applies to bus, truck, and rail services.

In a similar vein, NAFTA provides that public telecommunications transport networks (public networks) and services are to be available on reasonable and nondiscriminatory terms and conditions for firms or individuals who use those networks for the conduct of their business. These uses include the provision of enhanced or valueadded telecommunications services and intracorporate communications. However, the operation and provision of public networks and services have not been made subject to the NAFTA.

NAFTA removes significant investment barriers, ensures basic protections for NAFTA investors, and it further provides a mechanism for the settlement of disputes between such investors and a NAFTA country. Investment covers all forms of ownership and interests in a business enterprise, tangible and intangible property and contractual investment interests.

The NAFTA includes provisions on anticompetitive government and private business practices, in recognition that disciplines in this area will help fulfill the objectives of the Agreement. General areas addressed include competition policy and rules governing monopolies and state enterprises. A related section of NAFTA establishes a comprehensive principles-based approach to disciplining government measures regulating financial services. This section covers measures affecting the provision of financial services by financial institutions in the banking, insurance and securities sectors as well as other financial services. The section also sets out certain country-specific liberalization commitments, transition periods for compliance with the agreed principles and certain reservations listed by each country.

Building on the GATT and various international intellectual property treaties, NAFTA establishes a high level of obligations respecting intellectual property. Each country undertakes to provide adequate and effective protection of intellectual property rights on the basis of national treatment and will provide effective enforcement of these rights against infringement, both internally and at the border.

NAFTA sets out specific commitments regarding the protection of:

- Copyrights, including sound recordings
- Patents
- Trademarks
- Plant breeders' rights
- Industrial designs
- Trade secrets
- Integrated circuits (semiconductor chips and
- Geographical indications

To promote trade, NAFTA signatories commit themselves to facilitating on a reciprocal basis temporary entry into their respective territories of business persons who are citizens of Canada, Mexico or the United States. However, NAFTA does not create a common market for the movement of labor; each signatory maintains its rights to protect the permanent employment base of its domestic labor force, to implement its own immigration policies and to protect the security of its borders.

A large portion of the complex NAFTA agreement is devoted to the establishment of institutions responsible for implementing the Agreement, ensuring its joint management, and for avoiding and settling any disputes between the NAFTA countries

regarding its interpretation and application. Institutions established by NAFTA include a Trade Commission and a Secretariat. The agreement also lays down a specific body of Dispute Settlement Procedures.

REFERENCES:
Audley, John Joseph. *Green Politics and Global Trade: NAFTA and the Future of Environmental Politics.* Washington, D.C.: Georgetown University Press, 1997.

Mayer, Frederick. *Interpreting NAFTA: The Science and Art of Political Analysis.* New York: Columbia University Press, 1998.

Orme, William A. *Understanding NAFTA: Mexico, Free Trade, and the New North America.* Austin: University of Texas Press, 1996.

Agreement on Trade Relations with Azerbaijan

SIGNED: April 12, 1993, at Washington, D.C.
SIGNATORIES: Azerbaijan vs. United States
IN FORCE: Not yet in force
OVERVIEW: An agreement establishing trade relations with a former Soviet republic making a transition from a non-market to a market economy.

DISCUSSION:

After the final break-up of the Soviet Union in 1991, the United States began concluding trade agreements with various former Soviet republics and other former communist nations. The agreement with Azerbaijan is typical. The rationale for the treaty is set out in its preamble—to develop bilateral trade in order to promote "better mutual understanding and cooperation," and to promote the successful "economic restructuring and the development of a market-based economy in Azerbaijan."

Principal provisions include the following:

- Trade on the basis of non-discrimination and most-favored-nation status
- Mutual undertaking to improve market access for products and services
- Affirmation of a mutual desire to expand trade in products and services
- Unfettered operation of government commercial offices in each country
- A pledge of the best efforts of each country to facilitate business
- A promise to provide transparency of access to information pertaining to all laws and regulations related to commercial activity, including trade, investment, taxation, banking, insurance and other financial services, transport and labor
- An agreement to transact business in U.S. currency "or any other freely convertible currency that may be mutually agreed upon by such nationals and companies"
- Guarantees of the protection of intellectual property

- An undertaking by each nation to facilitate transit of goods through its territory
- A pledge to take steps to foster further economic cooperation
- An agreement to undertake consultation in the event of market disruption caused by some aspect of trade
- Provisions for the settlement of disputes

REFERENCE:
None

Treaty (with Albania) Concerning the Encouragement and Reciprocal Protection of Investment

OFFICIAL TITLE: Treaty between the Government of the United States of America and the Government of the Republic of Albania Concerning the Encouragement and Reciprocal Protection of Investment, with Annex and Protocol
SIGNED: January 11, 1995, at Washington
SIGNATORIES: Albania vs. United States
IN FORCE: From February 14, 1997
OVERVIEW: A trade treaty with a former communist country in process of converting from a non-market to a market economy.

DISCUSSION:
This bilateral investment treaty with Albania is intended to assist this former communist country make a transition from a non-market to a market economy. Provisions of the treaty are designed to protect (and therefore promote)United States investment in Albania and to assist the Albania in its efforts to develop a viable market economy by creating conditions more favorable for United States private investment.

Principal provisions include the following:
- All forms of United States investment in Albania are covered by the treaty.
- Covered investments receive the better of national treatment or most-favored-nation (MFN) treatment
- Performance requirements may not be imposed upon or enforced against covered investments.
- Expropriation can occur only in accordance with international law standards, namely, for a public purpose, in a nondiscriminatory manner, in accordance with due process of law, and only upon payment of prompt, adequate, and effective compensation.
- The unrestricted transfer, in a freely usable currency, of funds related to a covered investment is guaranteed.
- Investment disputes with the host government may be brought by investors, or by their subsidiaries, to binding international arbitration as an alternative to domestic courts.

The treaty with Albania, as of 1999 awaiting ratification by the United States Senate, is uniform with a 1994 BIT (bilateral investment treaty) prototype and, on ratification, will join the 21 BITs in force. (The BITs in force were concluded with Argentina, Bangladesh, Bulgaria, Cameroon, the Congo, the Czech Republic, Egypt, Grenada, Kazakhstan, Kyrgyzstan, Moldova, Morocco, Panama, Poland, Romania, Senegal, Slovakia, Sri Lanka, Tunisia, Turkey, and Zaire. As of the end of 1999, BITs with Armenia, Belarus, Ecuador, Estonia, Georgia, Haiti, Jamaica, Latvia, Mongolia, Russia, Trinidad and Tobago, Ukraine, and Uzbekistan, in addition to that with Albania, await ratification and entry into force.)

REFERENCE:
United States Congress, Subcommittee on Trade of the Committee on Ways and Means. *Written Comments on Trade Agreements Between the United States and Albania and the United States and Romania.* Washington, D.C.: U.S. Government Printing Office. 1992.

Inter-American Convention on an International Amateur Radio Permit

SIGNED: June 8, 1995, at Montrouis, Haiti
SIGNATORIES: Argentina, Brazil, Canada, El Salvador, Peru, United States, Uruguay, Venezuela
IN FORCE: From March 23, 1996
OVERVIEW: A convention whereby "each State Party agrees to permit temporary operation of amateur stations under authority of persons holding an IARP [International Amateur Radio Permit] issued by another State Party without further examination."

DISCUSSION:
The convention creates the International Amateur Radio Permit, issuable to citizens of signatories to the convention, and lays down requirements for the IARP. The present convention is the second inter-American convention relating to amateur radio; see **Inter-American Amateur Radio Service Convention ("Lima Convention")**.

REFERENCES:
None

International Natural Rubber Agreement

SIGNED: April 3, 1995, at Geneva
SIGNATORIES: Australia, Belgium, Brazil, Canada, China, Czechoslovakia, Denmark, European Economic Community, Germany, Finland, France, Indonesia, Ireland, Italy, Japan, Liberia, Luxembourg, Malaysia, Mexico, Morocco, Netherlands, Norway, Papua New Guinea, Peru, Philippines, Russian Federation, Sri Lanka, Sweden, Thailand, United Kingdom, United States

IN FORCE: Not yet in force
OVERVIEW: A revision of the International Rubber Agreement of 1979 and of 1987.

DISCUSSION:

The principal purpose of this major international trade agreement is to stabilize natural rubber prices and to achieve a balanced growth between demand and supply. Measures laid down in the agreement include the following:

- Stabilization of rubber prices through the operations of an international natural rubber Buffer Stock of 550,000 tons as the sole instrument of market intervention
- Governments of importing countries to share the cost of the Buffer Stock equally with exporting countries
- Periodic review of price regulations
- The Buffer Stock to be the only instrument for market intervention, thereby excluding export quotas or production controls

Like the 1979 and 1987 agreements, the 1995 agreement reference prices and trigger prices to regulate use of the Buffer Stock. The agreement provides detailed guidelines for use of this stock. These guidelines constitute the bulk of the agreement.

REFERENCE:
None

Agreement on Export of Firearms and Ammunition from the Russian Federation

SIGNED: April 3, 1996, at Washington, D.C.
SIGNATORIES: Russian Federation vs. United States
IN FORCE: From signing
OVERVIEW: An agreement both to encourage and to regulate Russian exportation of small firearms to the United States.

DISCUSSION:
The preamble to the agreement states the rationale of the document in these ways:

- To remove "a number of existing restrictions on the importation into the United States of firearms and ammunition from the Russian Federation"
- To expand "trade in firearms and ammunition between the United States and the Russian Federation in a manner compatible with domestic security"
- To grant the Russian Federation the same access to the United States market for firearms and ammunition as the United States grants all of its trading partners
- "To promote trade and cooperation on an equal and mutually beneficial basis between the United States and the Russian Federation and to expand economic opportunities in the two countries"

Annexes to the agreement list permitted and prohibited Russian-import firearms, and Article 6 reserves to the United States the right to impose emergency prohibitions if the U.S. security situation so requires.

REFERENCE:
Davydov, Oleg D. *Inside Out: The Radical Transformation of Russian Foreign Trade, 1992-1997.* New York: Fordham University Press, 1998.

Agreement on Mutual Recognition between the United States and the European Community

SIGNED: June 13, 1997, at Brussels
SIGNATORIES: European Community vs. United States
IN FORCE: From signing, with implementation over a two-to-three-year period
OVERVIEW: A Mutual Recognition Agreement (MRA) recognizes the results of product testing or certification requirements set by the signatory governments, so that the need for duplicative testing, inspection, or certification requirements for products from each signatory is eliminated.

DISCUSSION:
This document is a package of mutual recognition agreements designed to reduce trade barriers between the European Community and the United States in six industry sectors, accounting for approximately $50 billion in two-way trade. The agreements will recognize the results of product testing or certification requirements set by both governments and will, therefore, eliminate the need for duplicative testing, inspection, or certification requirements for products from each side of the Atlantic. The MRAs making up the package address products and issues relating to telecommunications, medical devices, electromagnetic compatibility, electrical safety, recreational craft, and pharmaceuticals. Each of these MRAs allow products or processes to be assessed for conformity in the United States to European Union standards, and vice versa.

After entry into force, the MRAs applying to electronic products will be phased in and fully implemented in two years; those for health products are subject to a three-year phase-in.

REFERENCES:
Craig, Paul, and Grainne De Burca, eds. *The Evolution of EU Law.* London and New York: Oxford University Press, 1999.
Urwin, Derek W. *The Community of Europe: A History of European Integration Since 1945.* New York: Addison-Wesley, 1995.

Agreed Minute (with the EU) on Humane Trapping of Animals

SIGNED: December 18, 1997, at Brussels

SIGNATORIES: European Union vs. United States

IN FORCE: From signing

OVERVIEW: An agreement on humane standards for trapping fur-bearing animals.

DISCUSSION:

The Agreed Minute includes technical specifications for trap performance, suggests guidelines for further research into trap design, and envisions phasing out certain trapping devices currently in use. An annex subjoined to the document lays down detailed "standards for the humane trapping of specified terrestrial and semi-aquatic mammals."

REFERENCES:

Craig, Paul, and Grainne De Burca, eds. *The Evolution of EU Law.* London and New York: Oxford University Press, 1999.

Thompson, Paul B. *Agricultural Ethics: Research, Teaching and Public Policy.* Ames: Iowa State University Press, 1998.

Urwin, Derek W. *The Community of Europe: A History of European Integration Since 1945.* New York: Addison-Wesley, 1995.

SECTION 4.3
Communication and Postal Agreements and Conventions

Overview of Treaties in This Category

The earliest international postal agreements were concluded bilaterally, between one country and another, and typically addressed issues of reciprocity and the disposition of postal fees. The **Postal Convention with Great Britain** (1848) and **Postal Convention between the United States of America and the Republic of Mexico** (1861) are typical of the early bilateral treaties.

In 1863, an international conference in Paris attempted to cut through the welter of bilateral postal agreements by establishing uniformity of principles governing international postal service. In 1874, at the first International Postal Congress, meeting in Bern, Switzerland, a General Postal Union was created, consisting of twenty-two countries, including the United States. Three years later, at a second congress, the union was formally renamed the Universal Postal Union. The 1877 document was repeatedly revised, until it emerged as the **Convention on Universal Postal Union, Revision of July 5, 1947**, signed in 1948. In this form, the Universal Postal Union was made a specialized agency of the United Nations and has been subject to many revisions, often reflecting advances in technology. As satellite communications increased in importance during the 1960s and 1970s, INTELSAT was established by **Agreement Relating to the International Telecommunications Satellite Organization "INTELSAT"** (1971).

Postal Convention with Great Britain

SIGNED: December 15, 1848
SIGNATORIES: Great Britain vs. United Stats
IN FORCE: Three months from signing
OVERVIEW: An early international postal convention.

DISCUSSION:

This convention distinguished between a port-to-port postal rate and an inland rate:

> There shall be charged upon all letters not exceeding half an ounce in weight, conveyed either by United States or by British packets, between a port in the United States and a port in the United Kingdom, an uniform sea rate of eight pence, or sixteen cents; and such postage shall belong to the country by which the packet conveying the letters is furnished.

In addition:

> There shall be charged by the post-office of the United Kingdom, upon all letters not exceeding half an ounce in weight, posted in the United Kingdom, and forwarded to the United States, or brought from the United States and delivered in the United Kingdom, whether such letters shall be conveyed by British or by United States packets, an inland postage rate of one penny halfpenny.

> There shall be charged by the post-office of the United States, upon all letters not exceeding half an ounce in weight, posted in the United States, and forwarded to the United Kingdom, or brought from the United Kingdom and delivered in the United States, whether such letters shall be conveyed by United States or by British packets, an inland postage rate of five cents.

Most later postal conventions stipulated a single rate, prepaid in the originating country and due exclusively to the originating country.

REFERENCE:
Crew, Michael A. *Regulation and Nature of Postal and Delivery Services.* The Hague: Kluwer Academic Publishers, 1993.

Postal Convention between the United States of America and the Republic of Mexico

SIGNED: December 11, 1861, at Mexico City
SIGNATORIES: Mexico vs. United States
IN FORCE: From June 20, 1862
OVERVIEW: "The United States of America and the United Mexican States, being desirous of drawing more closely the friendly relations existing between the two countries and of facilitating the prompt and regular transmission of correspondence between their respective territories, have resolved to conclude a Postal Convention..."

DISCUSSION:
The convention stipulates a schedule of rates and the principle that postage paid belongs to the nation in which the mail originates.

REFERENCE:
Crew, Michael A. *Regulation and Nature of Postal and Delivery Services.* The Hague: Kluwer Academic Publishers, 1993.

Convention on Universal Postal Union, Revision of July 5, 1947

SIGNED: July 5, 1948, at Bern, Switzerland

SIGNATORIES: Afghanistan, Albania, Germany, Algeria, Argentina, Australia, Austria, Belgian Congo, Belgium, Bolivia, Brazil, British Overseas Territories, Bulgaria, Byelorussian Soviet Socialist Republic, Canada, Chile, China, Colombia, Costa Rica, Cuba, Curaçao and Surinam, Czechoslovakia, Denmark, Dominican Republic, Ecuador, Egypt, El Salvador, Ethiopia, Finland, France, French Overseas Territories, Greece, Guatemala, Haiti, Honduras, Hungary, Iceland, India, Indochina, Iran, Iraq, Ireland, Italy, Japan, Korea, Lebanon, Liberia, Luxembourg, Mexico, Morocco (Exclusive of the Spanish Zone), Morocco (Spanish Zone), Netherlands Indies, Netherlands, New Zealand, Nicaragua, Norway, Panama, Paraguay, Peru, Philippines, Poland, Portugal, Portuguese Colonies in East Africa, Asia and Oceania, Portuguese Colonies in West Africa, Rumania, San Marino, Saudi Arabia, Siam, Spain, Spanish Colonies, Sweden, Swiss Confederation, Syria, Transjordania, Tunisia, Turkey, Ukrainian Soviet Socialist Republic, Union of Soviet Socialist Republics, Union of South Africa, United States, United States possessions, United Kingdom, Uruguay, Vatican City State, Venezuela, Yemen, Yugoslavia

IN FORCE: From July 1, 1948

OVERVIEW: The most thorough revision of the Universal Postal Union.

DISCUSSION:

The first attempt to establish uniformity of principles governing international postal service was made at an international conference in Paris in 1863. Before this, international postal exchange had been regulated by a bewildering and inconsistent assortment of bilateral agreements, treaties, and convention. It wasn't until the meeting of the first International Postal Congress in 1874, at Bern, Switzerland, that a true General Postal Union was created, consisting of twenty-two countries, including the United States. This union came into effect on July 1, 1875. Three years later, at a second congress, the union was formally renamed the Universal Postal Union.

The 1947 convention put the union in the form it would assume the following year, when it became a specialized agency of the United Nations. Throughout each revision, the main purpose of the Universal Postal Union has remained the same: to organize and improve postal service throughout the world and to ensure international collaboration in this area. Toward this end, the two most important principles laid down by the Universal Postal Convention are the following:

- The formation of a single territory by all signatory nations for the purposes of postal communication
- Adoption of uniform postal rates and units of weight

While the 1875 agreement applied exclusively to letter mail, subsequent revisions have encompassed many other postal services, including parcel post and international money orders.

REFERENCE:

Crew, Michael A. *Regulation and Nature of Postal and Delivery Services.* The Hague: Kluwer Academic Publishers, 1993.

Universal Postal Convention

SIGNED: October 3, 1957, at Ottawa, Canada

SIGNATORIES: Afghanistan, Albania, Algeria, Argentina, Australia, Australian Antarctic Territory, Austria, Belgian Congo, Belgium, Brazil, British Overseas Territories, Bulgaria, Burma, Byelorussian Soviet Socialist Republic, Cambodia, Cameroon, Canada, Central African Republic, Ceylon, Chad, Channel Islands, Chile, China, Christmas Island and the Cocos (Keeling) Islands, Colombia, Cook Islands, Costa Rica, Côte d'Ivoire, Cuba, Czechoslovakia, Dahomey, Democratic Republic of Vietnam, Denmark, Dominican Republic, Ecuador, El Salvador, Ethiopia, Federal Republic of Germany, Federation of Malaya, Finland, France, French Polynesia, French Somaliland, French Whole Territory, Gabon, Ghana, Greece, Guatemala, Haiti, Honduras, Hungary, Iceland, India, Indonesia, Iraq, Ireland, Isle of Man, Israel, Italian Somaliland, Italy, Japan, Jordan, Laos, Lebanon, Liberia, Libya, Luxembourg, Madagascar, Mauritania, Mexico, Monaco, Morocco, Nauru, Nepal, Netherlands, Netherlands Antilles, New Caledonia and Dependencies, New Hebrides, New Zealand, Nicaragua, Niger, Niue Island, Norfolk Island, Norway, Pakistan, Panama. Panama Canal Zone, Papua New Guinea, Paraguay, Peru, Philippines, Poland, Portugal, Portuguese Provinces in Asia, Portuguese Provinces in East Africa, Portuguese Provinces in Oceania, Portuguese Provinces in West Africa, Republic of China, Republic of Korea, Republic of the Congo, Romania, Ruanda-Urundi, Saint Pierre and Miquelon, San Marino, Saudi Arabia, Senegal, Spain, Spanish Territory in Africa, Sudan, Suriname, Sweden, Switzerland, Territory of Heard Island and McDonald Islands, Territory of New Guinea, Thailand, Togo, Trust Territory of the Pacific Islands, Tunisia, Turkey, Ukrainian Soviet Socialist Republic, Union of South Africa, Union of Soviet Socialist Republics, United Arab Republic (Egyptian Province), United Arab Republic (Syrian Province), United Kingdom, United States, United States Territories, Upper Volta, Uruguay, Vatican City State, Venezula, Vietnam, Western Samoa, Yemen, Yugoslavia

IN FORCE: From April 1, 1959

OVERVIEW: A convention affirming membership in the Universal Postal Union, "a single postal territory for the reciprocal exchange of correspondence."

DISCUSSION:

The Universal Postal Convention of 1957 is a complex and detailed document with a simple purpose: the creation and maintenance of a Universal Postal Union "to secure the organisation and improvement of the postal services and to promote in this sphere the development of international collaboration."

Areas addressed by the convention include the following:

- The constitution of the International Postal Union
- The organization of the International Postal Union
- A set of provisions defining the relationship of the International Postal Union to the United Nations
- Provisions relating to acts of the International Postal Union
- Procedures for amending and interpreting acts of the International Postal Union
- Procedures for arbitration of disputes
- Rules concerning the international postal service
- Establishment of the principle of freedom of transit
- Penal measures
- Detailed provisions regarding the letter post
- Detailed provisions regarding registered mail
- Provisions regarding allocation of transit charges

A Final Protocol to the Convention addresses various special issues, including issues involving free postage for literature for the blind, various exceptions to general regulations, special transit regulations in special cases, and other issues.

REFERENCE:
Crew, Michael A. *Regulation and Nature of Postal and Delivery Services.* The Hague: Kluwer Academic Publishers, 1993.

Universal Postal Convention

SIGNED: July 10, 1964, at Vienna

SIGNATORIES: Afghanistan, Albania, Algeria, Argentina, Australia, Australian Antarctic Territory, Austria, Belgium, Bolivia, Brazil, British Overseas Territories, Bulgaria, Burma, Birundi, Byelorussian Soviet Socialist Republic, Cambodia, Cameroon, Canada, Central African Republic, Ceylon, Chad, Chile, China, Christmas Island and the Cocos (Keeling) Islands, Colombia, Congo (Leopoldville), Cook Islands, Costa Rica, Côte d'Ivoire, Cuba, Cyprus, Czechoslovakia, Dahomey, Denmark, Dominican Republic, Ecuador, Ethiopia, Federal Republic of Germany, Federation of Malaya, Finland, France, French Whole Territory, Gabon, Ghana, Greece, Guatemala, Guinea, Guyana, Haiti, Honduras, Hungary, Iceland, India, Indonesia, Iran, Iraq, Ireland, Israel, Italy, Jamaica, Japan, Jordan, Kuwait, Land Berlin, Laos, Lebanon, Lesotho, Liberia, Libya, Liechtenstein, Luxembourg, Madagascar, Malawi, Maldives, Mali, Mauritania, Mexico, Monaco, Mongolia, Morocco, Nauru, Nepal, Netherlands, Netherlands Antilles, New Zealand, Nicaragua, Niger, Nigeria, Niue Island, Norfolk Island, Norway, Pakistan, Panama, Papua New Guinea, Paraguay, Peru, Philippines, Poland, Portugal, Republic of Korea, Republic of the Congo, Republic of Vietnam, Romania, Rwanda, San Marino, Saudi Arabia, Senegal, Sierra Leone, Singapore, Somalia, South Africa, Spain, Spanish Territory in Africa, Sudan, Suriname, Sweden, Switzerland, Syria, Territory of Heard Island and McDonald Islands, Territory of New Guinea, Thailand, Togo, Tokelau Islands, Trinidad and Tobago, Tunisia, Turkey, Uganda, Ukrainian Soviet Socialist Republic, Union of Soviet Socialist Republics, United Arab Republic, United Kingdom, United Republic of Tanganyika and Zanzibar, United Republic of Tanzania, United States, United States Overseas Territories, United States Territories, Upper Volta, Uruguay, Vatican City State, Venezuela, Yemen, Yugoslavia, Zambia

IN FORCE: From January 1, 1966

OVERVIEW: A revision of the 1957 **Universal Postal Convention**.

DISCUSSION:

The 1964 convention modifies some of the rules of the 1957 convention, making the most significant changes as follows:

- The 1964 convention puts special emphasis on the principal of freedom of transit, underscoring the obligation to forward international correspondence always by the "quickest routes which it uses for its own items." Additional clauses relate to permitted exceptions to this principle, as, for example, among member countries that do not participate in the exchange of letters containing perishable, biological substances, or radioactive substances.
- The 1964 convention devotes an entire chapter to the subject of responsibility: as it relates to postal administrations and to the sender.

REFERENCE:
Crew, Michael A. *Regulation and Nature of Postal and Delivery Services.* The Hague: Kluwer Academic Publishers, 1993.

Agreement Relating to the International Telecommunications Satellite Organization "INTELSAT"

SIGNED: August 20, 1971, at Washington, D.C.

SIGNATORIES: Afghanistan, Algeria, Angola, Argentina, Armenia, Australia, Austria, Azerbaijan, Bahamas, Bahrain, Bangladesh, Barbados, Belgium, Benin, Bhutan, Bolivia, Bosnia-Herzegovina, Botswana, Brazil, Brunei, Bulgaria, Burkina Faso, Cameroon, Canada, Cape Verde, Central African Republic, Chad, Chile, China, Colombia, Congo, Costa Rica, Côte d'Ivoire, Croatia, Cyprus, Czechoslovakia, Denmark, Dominican Republic, Ecuador, Egypt, El Salvador, Equatorial Guinea, Ethiopia, Fiji, Finland, France, Gabon, Germany (Federal Republic), Ghana, Greece, Guatemala, Guinea, Haiti, Honduras, Hungary, Iceland, India, Indonesia, Iran, Iraq, Ireland, Israel, Italy, Jamaica, Japan, Jordan, Kazakstan, Kenya, Korea, Kuwait, Kyrgyz Republic, Lebanon, Libya, Liechtenstein, Luxembourg,

Madagascar, Malawi, Malaysia, Mali, Malta, Mauritania, Mauritius, Mexico, Micronesia, Monaco, Morocco, Mozambique, Namibia, Nepal, Netherlands, New Zealand, Nicaragua, Niger, Nigeria, Norway, Oman, Pakistan, Panama, Papua New Guinea, Paraguay, Peru, Philippines, Poland, Portugal, Qatar, Romania, Russian Federation, Rwanda, Saudi Arabia, Senegal, Singapore, Slovak Republic, Somalia, South Africa, Spain, Sri Lanka, Sudan, Swaziland, Sweden, Switzerland, Syrian Arab Republic, Tajikistan, Tanzania, Thailand, Togo, Trinidad and Tobago, Tunisia, Turkey, Uganda, Union of Soviet Socialist Republics, United Arab Emirates, United Kingdom, United States, Uruguay, Vatican City, Venezuela, Vietnam (Socialist Republic), Yemen (Sanaa), Yugoslavia, Zaire, Zambia, Zimbabwe

IN FORCE: From February 12, 1973

OVERVIEW: A convention creating INTELSAT pursuant to a "principle set forth in Resolution 1721 (XVI) of the General Assembly of the United Nations that communication by means of satellites should be available to the nations of the world as soon as practicable on a global and nondiscriminatory basis."

DISCUSSION:

The agreement includes provisions establishing INTELSAT, an Operating Agreement, and annexes relating to the routine operations of the organization. The major provisions include the following:

- The establishment of INTELSAT
- Definition of the mission and scope of INTELSAT: "INTELSAT shall have as its prime objective the provision, on a commercial basis, of the space segment required for international public telecommunications services of high quality and reliability to be available on a non-discriminatory basis to all areas of the world."
- Establishment of legal and financial status for INTELSAT
- Constitution of the organization

REFERENCE:

Morgan, Walter L., and Gary D. Gordon. *Communications Satellite Handbook.* New York: Wiley, 1989.

SECTION 4.4
Copyrights, Patents, Industrial Property, and Intellectual Property

Overview of Treaties in This Category

The domestic laws of most nations recognize the importance of providing legal protection for copyrights and patents, as well as rights in industrial and intellectual property. Without such protection, individuals and corporate entities have little incentive to create, to invent, and to innovate. Well before the end of the nineteenth century, the United States began to extend the reach of intellectual property law beyond the domestic sphere by concluding bilateral trademark and patent treaties with numerous nations (for example, **Trade-Mark Convention between the United States and Austria-Hungary**, 1871). But a welter of bilateral agreements quickly becomes cumbersome. Recognizing this, the United States joined other nations in establishing the **Berne Copyright Convention** of 1886 (which has been revised numerous times), the first large-scale multilateral convention on international copyright protection.

Over the years, the United States has participated in many other multilateral agreements and conventions to protect not only copyrights, but patents and trademarks. As technology advanced, concepts of intellectual property and its protection have frequently required revision (see, for example, **Convention for the Protection of Producers of Phonograms**, 1971; **Budapest Treaty on the Deposit of Microorganisms**, 1977; and **Treaty on Intellectual Property in Respect of Integrated Circuits**, 1989).

In 1967, the World Intellectual Property Organization (**Convention Establishing the World Intellectual Property Organization**, 1967) was created as a specialized agency of the United Nations for the purpose of providing uniform protection of copyrights, patents, and trademarks. In 1996, the **WIPO Copyright Treaty** was opened for signature. When it enters into force, it will be the most comprehensive multilateral treaty on copyright protection in history.

Trade-Mark Convention Between the United States and Austria-Hungary

SIGNED: November 25, 1871, at Vienna
SIGNATORIES: Austria-Hungary vs. United States
IN FORCE: From June 1, 1871

OVERVIEW: An early bilateral agreement to "secure [international] guarantee of property in trade marks."

DISCUSSION:
This treaty is an early, bilateral attempt to secure international property rights in trademarks. The text of the principal articles follows:

ARTICLE I.

Every reproduction of trade-marks which in the countries or territories of the one of the contracting parties are affixed to certain merchandize to prove its origin and quality is forbidden in the countries or territories of the other of the contracting parties, and shall give to the injured party ground for such action or proceedings to prevent such reproduction, and to recover damages for the same, as may be authorized by the laws of the country in which the counterfeit is proven, just as if the plaintiff were a citizen of that country.

The exclusive right to use a trade-mark for the benefit of citizens of the United States in the Austro-Hungarian Empire, or of citizens of the Austro-Hungarian Monarchy in the territory of the United States, cannot exist for a longer period than that fixed by the law of the country for its own citizens. If the trade-mark has become public property in the country of its origin, it shall be equally free to all in the countries or territories of the other of the two contracting parties.

ARTICLE II.

If the owners of trade marks, residing in the countries or territories of the one of the contracting parties, wish to secure their rights in the countries or territories of the other of the contracting parties, they must deposit duplicate copies of those marks in the Patent Once at Washington and in the Chambers of Commerce and Trade in Vienna and Pesth.

ARTICLE III.

The present arrangement shall take effect ninety days after the exchange of ratifications, and shall continue in force for ten years from this date.

In case neither of the high contracting parties gives notice of its intention to discontinue this Convention twelve months before its expiration, it shall remain in force one year from the time that either of the high contracting parties announces its discontinuance.

REFERENCES:
Hepp, François. *Evolution of International Copyright Law.* The Hague: M. Nijhoff, 1950.
Ladas, Stephen P. *the International Protection of Literary and Artistic Property.* New York: Macmillan, 1938.
Wallerstein, Michael B., et al, eds. *Global Dimensions of Intellectual Property Rights.* Washington, D.C.: National Academy Press, 1993.

Berne Copyright Convention

SIGNED: September 9, 1886, at Bern, Switzerland, "completed at PARIS on May 4, 1896, revised at BERLIN on November 13, 1908, completed at BERNE on March 20, 1914, revised at ROME on June 2, 1928, at BRUSSELS on June 26, 1948, at STOCKHOLM on July 14, 1967, and at PARIS on July 24, 1971, and amended on September 28, 1979"

SIGNATORIES: Albania, Algeria, Argentina, Australia, Austria, Azerbaijan, Bahamas, Bahrain, Bangladesh, Barbados, Belarus, Belgium, Benin, Bolivia, Bosnia and Herzegovina, Botswana, Brazil, Bulgaria, Burkina Faso, Cameroon, Canada, Cape Verde, Central African Republic, Chad, Chile, China, Colombia, Congo, Costa Rica, Côte d'Ivoire, Croatia, Cuba, Cyprus, Czech Republic, Democratic Republic of the Congo, Denmark, Dominica, Dominican Republic, Ecuador, Egypt, El Salvador, Equatorial Guinea, Estonia, Fiji, Finland, Former Yugoslav Republic of Macedonia, France, Gabon, Gambia, Georgia, Germany, Ghana, Greece, Grenada, Guatemala, Guinea, Guinea-Bissau, Guyana, Haiti, Holy See, Honduras, Hungary, Iceland, India, Indonesia, Ireland, Israel, Italy, Jamaica, Japan, Jordan, Kazakhstan, Kenya, Korea (Republic), Korea Kyrgyzstan, Latvia, Lebanon, Lesotho, Liberia, Libyan Arab Jamahiriya, Liechtenstein, Lithuania, Luxembourg, Madagascar, Malawi, Malaysia, Mali, Malta, Mauritania, Mauritius, Mexico, Monaco, Mongolia, Morocco, Namibia, Netherlands, New Zealand, Niger, Nigeria, Norway, Oman, Pakistan, Stockholm, Panama, Paraguay, Peru, Philippines, Poland, Portugal, Republic of Moldova, Romania, Russian Federation, Rwanda, Saint Kitts and Nevis, Saint Lucia, Saint Vincent and the Grenadines, Senegal, Singapore, Slovakia, Slovenia, South Africa, Spain, Sri Lanka, Suriname, Swaziland, Sweden, Switzerland, Thailand, Togo, Trinidad and Tobago, Tunisia, Turkey, Ukraine, United Kingdom, United Republic of Tanzania, United States, Uruguay, Venezuela, Yugoslavia, Zambia, Zimbabwe

IN FORCE: For the United States, from March 1, 1989

OVERVIEW: The first and most important multilateral, international copyright convention.

DISCUSSION:

Originally called the International Convention for the Protection of Literary and Artistic Works, the core agreement was adopted by an international conference in Bern (Berne), Switzerland, in 1886 and repeatedly modified at Paris in 1896, in Berlin in 1908, again at Bern in 1914, at Rome in 1928, Brussels in 1948, Stockholm in 1967, and Paris in 1971. The convention was amended in 1979. A major provision of the convention is the formation of the Berne Copyright Union, to which all of the signatories belong.

The central agreement of the convention is the provision that each signatory will provide automatic protection for works first published in other countries of the Berne Union and for unpublished works whose authors are citizens of or resident in Union countries. Each country of the Berne Union guarantees to authors who are nationals of other member countries the rights that its own laws grant to its nationals.

The 1928 revision extended the convention to include every production in the literary, scientific, and artistic domain, regardless of the mode of expression, so that it encompassed

- Books, pamphlets, and other writings
- Lectures, addresses, sermons, etc.
- Dramatic or dramatic-musical works
- Choreographic works and entertainments in dumb show
- Musical compositions
- Drawings, paintings, works of architecture, sculpture, engraving, and lithography
- Illustrations, geographical charts, plans, sketches, and plastic works relative to geography, topography, architecture, or science
- Translations, adaptations, arrangements of music, and other reproductions in an altered form of a literary or artistic work
- Collections or anthologies of different works

The revision of 1948 added cinematographic works and photographic works to those granted international copyright protection. Also, both the 1928 and 1948 revisions extended protection to works of art applied to industrial purposes so far as consonant with the legislation of each member country.

In 1928, the term of copyright (for most works) was fixed at the duration of the author's life plus fifty years; however, it was recognized that some countries might grant a shorter term.

The Stockholm Protocol of 1967 and the Paris revision of 1971 granted more liberalized the rights of translation, with the object of promoting publication in developing countries.

REFERENCES:

Hepp, François. *Evolution of International Copyright Law.* The Hague: M. Nijhoff, 1950.

Ladas, Stephen P. *the International Protection of Literary and Artistic Property.* New York: Macmillan, 1938.

Wallerstein, Michael B., et al, eds. *Global Dimensions of Intellectual Property Rights.* Washington, D.C.: National Academy Press, 1993.

Nice Agreement Concerning the International Classification of Goods and Services

OFFICIAL TITLE: Nice Agreement Concerning the International Classification of Goods and Services for the Purposes of the Registration of Marks

SIGNED: June 15, 1957, at Nice, France; revised at Stockholm on July 14, 1967, and at Geneva on May 13, 1977, and amended on September 28, 1979

SIGNATORIES: Algeria, Australia, Austria, Barbados, Belarus,

Belgium, Benin, Bosnia and Herzegovina, China, Croatia, Cuba, Czech Republic, Denmark, Estonia, Finland, Former Yugoslav Republic of Macedonia, France, Germany, Greece, Guinea, Hungary, Iceland, Ireland, Israel, Italy, Kyrgyzstan, Japan, Korea (Democratic People's Republic), Korea (Republic), Latvia, Lebanon, Liechtenstein, Lithuania, Malawi, Monaco, Morocco, Netherlands, Norway, Poland, Portugal, Republic of Moldova, Romania, Russian Federation, Singapore, Slovakia, Slovenia, Spain, Suriname, Sweden, Switzerland, Tajikistan, Trinidad and Tobago, Tunisia, Turkey, United Kingdom, United States, Yugoslavia

IN FORCE: As amended, from September 28, 1979

OVERVIEW: "The countries to which this Agreement applies constitute a Special Union [the "Nice Union"] and adopt a common classification of goods and services for the purposes of the registration of marks . . ."

DISCUSSION:

The convention standardizes and renders uniform the classification categories for goods and services for the purpose of the international registration and protection of "marks" (trademarks). The classification consists of the following:

- A list of classes, together with, as the case may be, explanatory notes
- An alphabetical list of goods and services, with an indication of the class into which each of the goods or services falls

The classification, in the amended agreement, is based on that published in 1971 by the International Bureau of Intellectual Property of the World Intellectual Property Organization (WIPO).

REFERENCES:
Hepp, François. *Evolution of International Copyright Law*. The Hague: M. Nijhoff, 1950.
Ladas, Stephen P. *The International Protection of Literary and Artistic Property*. New York: Macmillan, 1938.
___. *Patents, Trademarks and Related Rights*. Cambridge, MA: Harvard University Press, 1975.
Wallerstein, Michael B., et al, eds. *Global Dimensions of Intellectual Property Rights*. Washington, D.C.: National Academy Press, 1993.

Convention Revising the Paris Convention of March 20, 1883, as Revised, for the Protection of Industrial Property

SIGNED: July 14, 1967, at Stockholm
IN FORCE: From April 26, 1970 (in force for the United States, September 5, 1970), except for articles 1-12, which entered into force on May 19, 1970 (for the United States, August 25, 1973)
SIGNATORIES: Albania, Algeria, Argentina, Armenia, Australia, Austria, Azerbaijan, Bangladesh, Barbados, Belarus, Belgium,

Benin, Bolivia, Bosnia-Herzegovina, Brazil, Bulgaria, Burkina Faso, Burundi, Cameroon, Canada, Central African Republic, Chad, Chile, China, Colombia, Congo, Costa Rica, Côte d'Ivoire, Croatia, Cuba, Cyprus, Czech Republic, Czechoslovakia, Denmark, Egypt, El Salvador, Estonia, Finland, Former Yugoslav Republic of Macedonia, France, Gabon, Gambia, Georgia, German Democratic Republic, Germany (Federal Republic), Ghana, Greece, Guinea, Guinea-Bissau, Guyana, Haiti, Honduras, Hungary, Iceland, Indonesia, Iraq, Ireland, Israel, Italy, Japan, Jordan, Kazakstan, Kenya, Korea (Democratic People's Republic of), Korea (Republic of), Kyrgyz Republic, Latvia, Lebanon, Lesotho, Liberia, Libya, Liechtenstein, Lithuania, Luxembourg, Madagascar, Malawi, Malaysia, Mali, Malta, Mauritania, Mauritius, Mexico, Moldova, Monaco, Mongolia, Morocco, Netherlands, New Zealand, Nicaragua, Niger, Norway, Panama, Paraguay, Peru, Philippines, Poland, Portugal, Romania, Russian Federation, Rwanda, St. Kitts and Nevis, St. Lucia, St. Vincent and the Grenadines, San Marino, Senegal, Singapore, Slovak Republic, Slovenia, South Africa, Spain, Sri Lanka, Sudan, Suriname, Swaziland, Sweden, Switzerland, Tajikistan, Tanzania, Togo, Trinidad and Tobago, Tunisia, Turkey, Turkmenistan, Uganda, Ukraine, Union of Soviet Socialist Republics, United Arab Emirates, United Kingdom, United States, Uruguay, Uzbekistan, Vatican City, Venezuela, Vietnam, Yugoslavia, Zaire, Zambia, Zimbabwe

OVERVIEW: A convention intended to secure and extend international patent protections.

DISCUSSION:

This convention is the culmination of a convention first approved in Paris in 1883, revised in conferences at Brussels in 1900, at Washington in 1911, at the Hague in 1925, at London in 1934, at Lisbon in 1958, and finally at Stockholm in 1967. Its principal thrust is to protect inventors' patents by providing that patent applications in the other member countries should apply from the same date as the patent application in the inventor's home country.

REFERENCES:
Ladas, Stephen. *Patents, Trademarks and Related Rights*. Cambridge, MA: Harvard University Press, 1975.
Wallerstein, Michael B., et al, eds. *Global Dimensions of Intellectual Property Rights*. Washington, D.C.: National Academy Press, 1993.

Convention Establishing the World Intellectual Property Organization

SIGNED: July 14, 1967, Stockholm; amended, September 28, 1979
SIGNATORIES: Argentina, Austria, Belarus, Belgium, Bolivia, Burkina Faso, Canada, Chile, Colombia, Costa Rica, Croatia, Denmark, Ecuador, El Salvador, Estonia, European Community, Finland, France, Germany, Ghana, Greece, Hungary, Indonesia,

Ireland, Israel, Italy, Kazakhstan, Kenya, Kyrgyzstan, Luxembourg, Mexico, Monaco, Mongolia, Namibia, Netherlands, Nigeria, Panama, Portugal, Republic of Moldova, Romania, Senegal, Slovakia, Slovenia, South Africa, Spain, Sweden, Switzerland, Togo, United Kingdom, United States, Uruguay, Venezuela

IN FORCE: From April 26, 1970

OVERVIEW: A convention establishing the World Intellectual Property Organization, intended "to modernize and render more efficient the administration of the Unions established in the fields of the protection of industrial property and the protection of literary and artistic works, while fully respecting the independence of each of the Unions."

DISCUSSION:

Article 1 establishes WIPO. Article 3 sets down the objectives of WIPO: to "promote the protection of intellectual property throughout the world through cooperation among States and, where appropriate, in collaboration with any other international organization," and "to perform the administrative tasks of the Paris Union, the Special Unions established in relation with that Union, and the Berne Union." WIPO also "may agree to assume, or participate in, the administration of any other international agreement designed to promote the protection of intellectual property." Reflecting modern thought on the nature and scope of copyright and patent rights, the WIPO convention defines "intellectual property" as broadly as possible, such that it includes the rights to the following:

- literary, artistic and scientific works
- performances of performing artists, phonograms (sound recordings), and broadcasts
- inventions in all fields of human endeavor
- scientific discoveries
- industrial designs
- trademarks, service marks, and commercial names and designations
- protection against unfair competition
- all other rights resulting from intellectual activity in the industrial, scientific, literary or artistic fields

Article 4 enumerates the basic functions of WIPO with regard to intellectual property. In addition to the functions just mentioned, WIPO:

- shall promote the development of measures designed to facilitate the efficient protection of intellectual property throughout the world and to harmonize national legislation in this field
- shall encourage the conclusion of international agreements designed to promote the protection of intellectual property
- shall offer its cooperation to States requesting legal-technical assistance in the field of intellectual property
- shall assemble and disseminate information concerning the

protection of intellectual property, carry out and promote studies in this field, and publish the results of such studies
- shall maintain services facilitating the international protection of intellectual property and, where appropriate, provide for registration in this field and the publication of the data concerning the registrations

The convention establishes a "General Assembly consisting of the States party to this Convention which are members of any of the Unions." Its chief functions are to appoint a director general for WIPO and to review and approve reports made by the WIPO Coordination Committee, which is responsible for creating the "draft agenda and the draft program and budget of the Conference. Among other functions, the Conference, consisting of delegates from all the signatory states, is charged with discussing "matters of general interest in the field of intellectual property and may adopt recommendations relating to such matters, having regard for the competence and autonomy of the Unions."

An International Bureau, under the direction of the director general, functions as the secretariat of WIPO, charged with the day-to-day functions of the organization. The convention establishes WIPO headquarters in at Geneva.

REFERENCES:
Hepp, François. *Evolution of International Copyright Law.* The Hague: M. Nijhoff, 1950.
Ladas, Stephen P. *The International Protection of Literary and Artistic Property.* New York: Macmillan, 1938.
___. *Patents, Trademarks and Related Rights.* Cambridge, MA: Harvard University Press, 1975.
Wallerstein, Michael B., et al, eds. *Global Dimensions of Intellectual Property Rights.* Washington, D.C.: National Academy Press, 1993.

Patent Cooperation Treaty

SIGNED: June 19, 1970, at Washington; amended, 1979 and modified, 1984

SIGNATORIES: Albania, Armenia, Australia, Austria, Azerbaijan, Barbados, Belarus, Belgium, Benin, Bosnia and Herzegovina, Brazil, Bulgaria, Burkina Faso, Cameroon, Canada, Central African Republic, Chad, China, Congo, Costa Rica, Côte d'Ivoire, Croatia, Cuba, Cyprus, Czech Republic, Denmark, Dominica, Estonia, Finland, Former Yugoslav Republic of Macedonia, France, Gabon, Gambia, Georgia, Germany, Ghana, Greece, Grenada, Guinea, Guinea-Bissau, Hungary, Iceland, India, Indonesia, Ireland, Israel, Italy, Japan, Kazakhstan, Kenya, Korea (Democratic People's Republic), Korea (Republic), Kyrgyzstan, Latvia, Lesotho, Liberia, Liechtenstein, Lithuania, Luxembourg, Madagascar, Malawi, Mali, Mauritania, Mexico, Monaco, Mongolia, Morocco, Netherlands, New Zealand, Niger, Norway, Poland, Portugal, Republic of Moldova, Romania, Russian Federation, Saint Lucia, Senegal, Sierra Leone, Singapore, Slovakia, Slovenia, South Africa, Spain, Sri Lanka, Sudan, Swaziland, Sweden, Switzerland, Tajikistan, Togo, Trinidad and Tobago, Turkey, Turkmenistan, Uganda, Ukraine, United Arab Emirates, United Kingdom, United Republic of Tanzania, United States, Uzbekistan, Vietnam, Yugoslavia, Zimbabwe

IN FORCE: From January 24, 1978

OVERVIEW: The treaty enables applicants to seek patent protection for an invention simultaneously in each of a large number of countries by filing an "international" patent application.

DISCUSSION:

Administered by the World Intellectual Property Organization (WIPO), the treaty is open to states party to the **Paris Convention for the Protection of Industrial Property** (1883). The treaty enables applicants to seek patent protection for an invention simultaneously in each of the signatory states by filing a single "international" patent application. The applicant must be a national or resident of a contracting state, and the application may be filed with the national patent office of the contracting state of which the applicant is a national or resident, or it may be filed directly with the International Bureau of WIPO in Geneva, Switzerland. In some cases, other patent filing options are also available.

The bulk of the treaty details the application procedure and the "international search" process, whereby a listing of the citations of such published documents that might affect the patentability of the invention is generated and communicated to the applicant. The applicant may then decide to withdraw his application, if the report of the international search makes the granting of patents unlikely. If the report is favorable, however, the application and the report are communicated to the patent offices of all the signatory nations the applicant designates as countries in which he desires patent protection.

The signatories are not bound by the decisions of other signatories; however, signatories may be guided by those decisions. The principal purpose of the treaty is to expedite the process of securing patent protection in multiple countries and to obtain the legal protection of priority by applying for patent protection with many countries simultaneously.

REFERENCE:
Ladas, Stephen. *Patents, Trademarks and Related Rights.* Cambridge, MA: Harvard University Press, 1975.

Strasbourg Agreement Concerning the International Patent Classification

SIGNED: March 24, 1971, at Strasbourg, and amended on September 28, 1979

SIGNATORIES: Australia, Austria, Belarus, Belgium, Brazil, Canada, China, Cuba, Czech Republic, Denmark, Egypt,

Estonia, Finland, France, Germany, Greece, Guinea, Ireland, Israel, Italy, Japan, Korea (Republic), Kyrgyzstan, Luxembourg, Malawi, Monaco, Netherlands, Norway, Poland, Portugal, Republic of Moldova, Romania, Russian Federation, Slovakia, Spain, Suriname, Sweden, Switzerland, Tajikistan, Trinidad and Tobago, Turkey, United Kingdom, United States

IN FORCE: From September 28, 1979, as amended

OVERVIEW: A convention creating "a Special Union . . . [to] adopt a common classification for patents for invention, inventors' certificates, utility models and utility certificates, to be known as the 'International Patent Classification.'"

DISCUSSION:

The convention was created in the belief that "the universal adoption of a uniform system of classification of patents, inventors' certificates, utility models and utility certificates is in the general interest and is likely to establish closer international cooperation in the industrial property field, and to contribute to the harmonization of national legislation in that field." Furthermore, a system of uniform classification will give developing countries "easier access to the ever-expanding volume of modern technology."

The purpose of the classification, which is based on the European Convention on the International Classification of Patents for Invention of December 19, 1954 (coming into force on September 1, 1968), is to clarify and expedite claims to international patent protection by ensuring that all signatories work from a common system of classification.

REFERENCE:
Ladas, Stephen. *Patents, Trademarks and Related Rights.* Cambridge, MA: Harvard University Press, 1975.

Convention for the Protection of Producers of Phonograms

OFFICIAL TITLE: Convention for the Protection of Producers of Phonograms Against Unauthorized Duplication of Their Phonograms

SIGNED: October 29, 1971, at Geneva

SIGNATORIES: Argentina, Australia, Austria, Barbados, Brazil, Bulgaria, Burkina Faso, Chile, China, Colombia, Costa Rica, Cyprus, Czech Republic, Democratic Republic of the Congo, Denmark, Ecuador, Egypt, El Salvador, Fiji, Finland, Former Yugoslav Republic of Macedonia, France, Germany, Greece, Guatemala, Holy See, Honduras, Hungary, India, Israel, Italy, Jamaica, Japan, Kenya, Korea (Republic), Latvia, Luxembourg, Mexico, Monaco, Netherlands, New Zealand, Norway, Panama, Paraguay, Peru, Romania, Russian Federation, Slovakia, Slovenia, Spain, Sweden, Switzerland, Trinidad and Tobago, United Kingdom, United States, Uruguay, Venezuela

IN FORCE: April 18, 1973

OVERVIEW: "Each Contracting State shall protect producers of phonograms who are nationals of other Contracting States against the making of duplicates without the consent of the producer and against the importation of such duplicates, provided that any such making or importation is for the purpose of distribution to the public, and against the distribution of such duplicates to the public."

DISCUSSION:

"Phonograms" are sound recordings in any medium. Each signatory to this convention undertakes to provide phonograms produced by nationals or residents of any other signatory state the same copyright protection provided to phonograms produced by its own nationals or residents. "The means by which this Convention is implemented shall be a matter for the domestic law of each Contracting State and shall include one or more of the following: protection by means of the grant of a copyright or other specific right; protection by means of the law relating to unfair competition; protection by means of penal sanctions." Duration" of the protection given shall be a matter for the domestic law of each Contracting State. However, if the domestic law prescribes a specific duration for the protection, that duration shall not be less than twenty years from the end either of the year in which the sounds embodied in the phonogram were first fixed or of the year in which the phonogram was first published."

REFERENCES:

Hepp, François. *Evolution of International Copyright Law.* The Hague: M. Nijhoff, 1950.

Ladas, Stephen P. *The International Protection of Literary and Artistic Property.* New York: Macmillan, 1938.

___. *Patents, Trademarks and Related Rights.* Cambridge, MA: Harvard University Press, 1975.

Wallerstein, Michael B., et al, eds. *Global Dimensions of Intellectual Property Rights.* Washington, D.C.: National Academy Press, 1993.

Universal and Berne Copyright Conventions as Revised at Paris

SIGNED: July 24, 1971, at Paris

SIGNATORIES: Algeria, Berlin (West), British Virgin Islands, Cameroon, France, Germany (Federal Republic), Gibraltar, Grenada, Guam, Hong Kong, Hungary, Isle of Man, Kenya, Monaco, Norway, Panama Canal Zone, Puerto Rico, Saint Helena, Senegal, Seychelles, Spain, St. Lucia, St. Vincent, Sweden, United Kingdom, United States, United States Virgin Islands, Yugoslavia

IN FORCE: From July 10, 1974

OVERVIEW: The most important revision of a series of conventions beginning with the 1866 Berne Convention.

DISCUSSION:

The 1866 Berne Convention extended copyright protection internationally to authors of works of literature, art, and music. The convention was variously renewed and revised in Paris (1896), in Berlin (1908), in Berne (1914), in Rome (1928 and 1941), and in Brussels (1948). The 1948 Brussels revision extended copyright protection to the areas of film, radio, television, and arts allied to these. It also laid down the principle that international disputes arising from the copyright convention should be submitted to the International Court of Justice.

The **Convention Revising the Paris Convention of March 20, 1883, as Revised, for the Protection of Industrial Property**, concluded in 1967 in Stockholm, included an additional amendment to the Berne Copyright Convention in the form of a protocol giving preferential rights to those developing countries that are members of the Berne Copyright Convention, namely:

- The right to translate and publish without permission any book to be used for teaching, study, and research in the field of education

- To translate and publish (but not publish in the original language) literary and artistic works without permission three years or more after their original publication

- To pay royalties in the cases mentioned according to rates prevailing in the developing country
  In 1952, under auspices of UNESCO, a conference was held in Geneva, which resulted in the **Universal Copyright Convention.** The principal provisions included:

- Each signatory agrees to give foreign works the same copyright protection given to works of its own nationals. The terms of such protection will be not less than the life of the author and 25 years after his or her death.

- All formalities of registration and legal deposit were replaced by the simple requirement that the letter "C" be imprinted within a circle on each copy of the work protected, followed by the author's name and date of first publication.

- During a seven-year period from publication, the author was granted the exclusive right to publish or authorize translations.

To the provisions of the Berne and Universal conventions, the 1971 Paris revisions added three new articles:

1. Definition of "non-industrialized countries" and a specification of the period of preferential treatment granted them

2. Reduction of the seven-year exclusive translation period to three years for works used for teaching, scholarship, and research; in the case of little-used languages, the period is reduced to one year

3. Enablement of any national of a contracting country to obtain a licence for reproduction of a work for "purpose of systematic instructional activities" if that work has not been distributed within a specified period

REFERENCES:

Hepp, François. *Evolution of International Copyright Law.* The Hague: M. Nijhoff, 1950.

Ladas, Stephen P. *The International Protection of Literary and Artistic Property.* New York: Macmillan, 1938.

___. *Patents, Trademarks and Related Rights.* Cambridge, MA: Harvard University Press, 1975.

Wallerstein, Michael B., et al, eds. *Global Dimensions of Intellectual Property Rights.* Washington, D.C.: National Academy Press, 1993.

Convention Relating to the Distribution of Programme-Carrying Signals Transmitted by Satellite

SIGNED: May 21, 1974, at Brussels

SIGNATORIES: Armenia, Australia, Austria, Bosnia and Herzegovina, Costa Rica, Croatia, Former Yugoslav Republic of Macedonia, Germany, Greece, Kenya, Mexico, Morocco, Nicaragua, Panama, Peru, Portugal, Russian Federation, Slovenia, Switzerland, Trinidad and Tobago, United States, Yugoslavia

IN FORCE: From August 25, 1979

OVERVIEW: An international convention "to prevent distributors from distributing programme-carrying signals transmitted by satellite which were not intended for those distributors."

DISCUSSION:

"Each Contracting State undertakes to take adequate measures to prevent the distribution on or from its territory of any programme-carrying signal by any distributor for whom the signal emitted to or passing through the satellite is not intended. This obligation shall apply where the originating organization is a national of another Contracting State and where the signal distributed is a derived signal."

REFERENCES:

Hepp, François. *Evolution of International Copyright Law.* The Hague: M. Nijhoff, 1950.

Ladas, Stephen P. *The International Protection of Literary and Artistic Property.* New York: Macmillan, 1938.

___. *Patents, Trademarks and Related Rights.* Cambridge, MA: Harvard University Press, 1975.

Morgan, Walter L., and Gary D. Gordon. *Communications Satellite Handbook.* New York: Wiley, 1989.

Geneva Act to the Nice Agreement

OFFICIAL TITLE: Geneva Act to the Nice Agreement Concerning the International Classification of Goods and Services for the Purposes of the Registration of Marks of June 15, 1957 as revised at Stockholm on July 14, 1967

SIGNED: May 13, 1977, at Geneva, Switzerland

SIGNATORIES: Australia, Austria, Belgium, Benin, Czechoslovakia, Finland, France, German Democratic Republic, Germany (Federal Republic), Hungary, Ireland, Italy, Luxembourg, Monaco, Netherlands, Norway, Portugal, Spain, Sweden, Switzerland, Tunisia, Union of Soviet Socialist Republics, United Kingdom, United States

IN FORCE: From February 6, 1979

OVERVIEW: An international act updating and revising the **Nice Agreement** of 1957.

DISCUSSION:

The Geneva Act updates the Nice Agreement, including its 1967 Stockholm revision, primarily in administrative details, including the designation of the Director General of the World Intellectual Property Organization (WIPO) as the official depository of the "authentic copy" of the current agreement and of future changes and modifications to the agreement.

The Act also establishes a Committee of Experts charged with the following:

- Deciding on changes in the classification
- Addressing recommendations of member nations
- Facilitating application of the classification by developing nations

REFERENCES:

Hepp, François. *Evolution of International Copyright Law.* The Hague: M. Nijhoff, 1950.

Ladas, Stephen P. *The International Protection of Literary and Artistic Property.* New York: Macmillan, 1938.

___. *Patents, Trademarks and Related Rights.* Cambridge, MA: Harvard University Press, 1975.

Wallerstein, Michael B., et al, eds. *Global Dimensions of Intellectual Property Rights.* Washington, D.C.: National Academy Press, 1993.

Budapest Treaty on the Deposit of Microorganisms

OFFICIAL TITLE: Budapest Treaty on the International Recognition of the Deposit of Microorganisms for the Purposes of Patent Procedure

SIGNED: April 28, 1977, at Budapest; amended September 26, 1980

SIGNATORIES: Australia, Austria, Belgium, Bulgaria, Canada, China, Cuba, Czech Republic, Denmark, Estonia, Finland, France, Germany, Greece, Hungary, Iceland, Ireland, Israel, Italy, Japan, Korea (Republic), Latvia, Liechtenstein, Lithuania, Monaco, Netherlands, Norway, Philippines, Poland, Portugal, Republic of Moldova, Romania, Russian Federation, Singapore, Slovakia, Slovenia, South Africa, Spain, Sweden, Switzerland, Tajikistan, Trinidad and Tobago, Turkey, Ukraine, United Kingdom, United States, Yugoslavia

IN FORCE: From August 19, 1980, for the United States

OVERVIEW: A convention establishing a union for the international recognition of the deposit of microorganisms for the purposes of patent procedure, such that "Contracting States which allow or require the deposit of microorganisms for the purposes of patent procedure shall recognize, for such purposes, the deposit of a microorganism with any international depositary authority. Such recognition shall include the recognition of the fact and date of the deposit as indicated by the international depositary authority as well as the recognition of the fact that what is furnished as a sample is a sample of the deposited microorganism."

DISCUSSION:

This convention recognizes that, in certain cases, microorganisms may be subject to patent protection (protection as industrial property), as when such microorganisms are the products of genetic engineering or other scientific or technological process. The convention creates a union of states that agree, for purposes of securing patent protection, to "recognize the deposit of a microorganism with any international depositary authority. Such recognition shall include the recognition of the fact and date of the deposit as indicated by the international depositary authority as well as the recognition of the fact that what is furnished as a sample is a sample of the deposited microorganism." The creation of this union is intended to reduce the necessity of importing and exporting microorganisms, which might present a threat to "national security or . . . health or the environment."

The convention does not constitute a general agreement on the protection of microorganisms as industrial property, nor does it define criteria for extending protection to microorganisms (contrast, for example, **Treaty on Intellectual Property in Respect of Integrated Circuits**); however, by creating a union to recognize deposit of microorganisms for purposes of securing a patent, the convention implies that microorganisms may, under certain circumstances—left undefined by the convention—merit patent protection.

REFERENCE:

Beier, Friedrich-Karl, R. S. Crespi, and J. Straus. *Biotechnology and Patent Protection : an International Review*. Paris: Organisation for Economic Co-operation and Development, 1985.

Treaty on Intellectual Property in Respect of Integrated Circuits

SIGNED: May 26, 1989, at Washington, D.C.

SIGNATORIES: China, Egypt, Ghana, Guatemala, India, Liberia, Yugoslavia, Zambia

IN FORCE: Not yet in force

OVERVIEW: A convention creating a union for the purposes of granting international protection to integrated electronic circuits.

DISCUSSION:

International copyright protection began with the **Berne Convention** of 1886, which was modified several times, in part to extend protection to new forms of intellectual property, such as recorded music and film. Modern electronic circuits, which are printed or engraved on circuit boards or semiconductor "chips," have an ambiguous status between industrial property and intellectual property. This convention seeks to define them chiefly as intellectual property, more closely analogous to, say, a book than to a mechanical device. As such, the convention would secure broad intellectual property protection for integrated circuits.

Because the convention ventures into technical territory, it begins with careful definitions of key terms:

- "Integrated circuit" means a product, in its final form or an intermediate form, in which the elements, at least one of which is an active element, and some or all of the interconnections are integrally formed in and/or on a piece of material and which is intended to perform an electronic function."
- "Layout-design (topography)" means the three-dimensional disposition, however expressed, of the elements, at least one of which is an active element, and of some or all of the interconnections of an integrated circuit, or such a three-dimensional disposition prepared for an integrated circuit intended for manufacture."

The basic provisions of the convention are as follows:

Each Contracting Party shall have the obligation to secure, throughout its territory, intellectual property protection in respect of layout-designs (topographies) in accordance with this Treaty. It shall, in particular, secure adequate measures to ensure the prevention of acts considered unlawful under Article 6 and appropriate legal remedies where such acts have been committed.

The right of the holder of the right in respect of an integrated circuit applies whether or not the integrated circuit is incorporated in an article.

To merit protection, integrated circuits must be original "in the sense that they are the result of their creators' own intellectual effort and are not commonplace among creators of layout-designs (topographies) and manufacturers of integrated circuits at the time of their creation." In Article 6, the convention lays down as unlawful, reproducing, "whether by incorporation in an integrated circuit or otherwise, a protected layout-design (topography) in its entirety or any part thereof" and "the act of importing, selling or otherwise distributing for commercial purposes a protected layout-design (topography) or an integrated circuit in which a protected layout-design (topography) is incorporated." Protection shall last at least eight years.

REFERENCES:

Hepp, François. *Evolution of International Copyright Law*. The Hague: M. Nijhoff, 1950.

Ladas, Stephen P. *The International Protection of Literary and Artistic Property*. New York: Macmillan, 1938.

___. *Patents, Trademarks and Related Rights*. Cambridge, MA: Harvard University Press, 1975.

Wallerstein, Michael B., et al, eds. *Global Dimensions of Intellectual Property Rights.* Washington, D.C.: National Academy Press, 1993.

Agreement (with Ecuador) Concerning the Protection and Enforcement of Intellectual Property Rights

SIGNED: October 15, 1993, at Washington, D.C.
SIGNATORIES: Ecuador vs. United States
IN FORCE: From signing
OVERVIEW: An agreement "to provide adequate and effective protection and enforcement of all intellectual property rights, while ensuring that measures to enforce intellectual property rights do not themselves become barriers to legitimate trade."

DISCUSSION:

This agreement is typical of recent bilateral agreements protecting intellectual property. Such bilateral agreements complement and reinforce the multilateral conventions protecting intellectual property, while serving to enhance the trade relations between the two countries.

Principal provisions of the agreement include the following:

- An agreement to adhere at minimum to the **Geneva Convention for the Protection of Producers of Phonograms Against Unauthorized Duplications of their Phonograms** (1971), the **Berne Convention for the Protection of Literary and Artistic Works** (1971), and the **Convention Revising the Paris Convention of March 20, 1883, as revised, for the Protection of Industrial Property** (1967).
- Protection of copyright
- Protection of encrypted satellite signals
- Protection of trademarks
- Protection of patents
- Protection of layout-designs of semiconductor Integrated circuits
- Protection from acts contrary to honest commercial practice
- Protection of trade secrets

Also addressed are the subjects of enforcement and civil as well as criminal procedures applicable in intellectual property cases.

REFERENCES:
Hepp, François. *Evolution of International Copyright Law.* The Hague: M. Nijhoff, 1950.
Ladas, Stephen P. *The International Protection of Literary and Artistic Property.* New York: Macmillan, 1938.
___. *Patents, Trademarks and Related Rights.* Cambridge, MA: Harvard University Press, 1975.
Wallerstein, Michael B., et al, eds. *Global Dimensions of Intellectual Property Rights.* Washington, D.C.: National Academy Press, 1993.

Mutual Understanding (with Japan) on Patents

SIGNED: January 20, 1994, at Tokyo and Washington
SIGNATORIES: Japan vs. United States
IN FORCE: From signing
OVERVIEW: A "mutual understanding" between the Japanese Patent Office and the United States Patent and Trademark Office.

DISCUSSION:

The "mutual understanding" was concluded directly between the patent agencies of the two countries and consists, simply, of a list of actions to be taken by Japan, on the one hand, and the United States, on the other. Japanese actions are as follows:

1. By July 1, 1995, the Japanese Patent Office (JPO) will permit foreign nationals to file patent applications in the English language, with a translation into Japanese to follow within two months. 2. Prior to the grant of a patent, the JPO will permit the correction of translation errors up to the time allowed for the reply to the first substantive communication from the JPO. 3. After the grant of a patent, the JPO will permit the correction of translation errors to the extent that the correction does not substantially extend the scope of protection. 4. Appropriate fees may be charged by the JPO for the above procedures

United States actions are as follows:

1. By June 1, 1994, the United States Patent and Trademark Office (USPTO) will introduce legislation to amend U.S. patent law to change the term of patents from 17 years from the date of grant of a patent for an invention to 20 years from the date of filing of the first complete application. 2. The legislation that the USPTO will introduce shall take effect six months from the date of enactment and shall apply to all applications filed in the United States thereafter.

REFERENCES:
Hepp, François. *Evolution of International Copyright Law.* The Hague: M. Nijhoff, 1950.
Ladas, Stephen P. *The International Protection of Literary and Artistic Property.* New York: Macmillan, 1938.
___. *Patents, Trademarks and Related Rights.* Cambridge, MA: Harvard University Press, 1975.
Wallerstein, Michael B., et al, eds. *Global Dimensions of Intellectual Property Rights.* Washington, D.C.: National Academy Press, 1993.

WIPO Copyright Treaty

SIGNED: December 20, 1996, at Geneva
SIGNATORIES: Argentina, Austria, Belarus, Belgium, Bolivia, Burkina Faso, Canada, Chile, Colombia, Costa Rica, Croatia, Denmark, Ecuador, El Salvador Estonia, European Community Finland, France, Germany, Ghana, Greece, Hungary, Indonesia, Ireland, Israel, Italy, Kazakhstan, Kenya, Kyrgyzstan, Luxembourg, Mexico, Monaco, Mongolia, Namibia, Netherlands, Nigeria, Panama, Portugal, Republic of Moldova, Romania, Senegal, Slovakia, Slovenia, South Africa, Spain, Sweden,

Switzerland, Togo, United Kingdom, United States, Uruguay, Venezuela

IN FORCE: Not yet in force

OVERVIEW: A convention intended to complement and to interpret the **Berne Copyright Convention** with "new international rules . . . to provide adequate solutions to the questions raised by new economic, social, cultural, and technological developments."

DISCUSSION:

The WIPO Copyright Treaty aims to extend uniform international copyright protection to all traditional forms of expression as well as forms enabled by and affected by new technologies. For example:

- Article 4 lays down that computer programs are protected as literary works within the meaning of Article 2 of the Berne Convention. The protection applies to computer programs, whatever may be the mode or form of their expression.

- Article 5 protects databases, "which by reason of the selection or arrangement of their contents constitute intellectual creations . . . . This protection does not extend to the data or the material itself and is without prejudice to any copyright subsisting in the data or material contained in the compilation."

The treaty recognizes the challenges posed by new distribution technologies, which tend to facilitate unauthorized duplication and distribution of copyrighted works. The treaty reaffirms the author's right of distribution and rental and, in Article 11, lays down the following: "Contracting Parties shall provide adequate legal protection and effective legal remedies against the circumvention of effective technological measures that are used by authors in connection with the exercise of their rights under this Treaty or the Berne Convention and that restrict acts, in respect of their works, which are not authorized by the authors concerned or permitted by law." Article 12 elaborates on signatories' obligations:

Obligations concerning Rights Management Information

(1) Contracting Parties shall provide adequate and effective legal remedies against any person knowingly performing any of the following acts knowing, or with respect to civil remedies having reasonable grounds to know, that it will induce, enable, facilitate or conceal an infringement of any right covered by this Treaty or the Berne Convention:

(i) to remove or alter any electronic rights management information without authority;

(ii) to distribute, import for distribution, broadcast or communicate to the public, without authority, works or copies of works knowing that electronic rights management information has been removed or altered without authority.

(2) As used in this Article, "rights management information" means information which identifies the work, the author of the work, the owner of any right in the work, or information about the terms and conditions of use of the work, and any numbers or codes that represent such information, when any of these items of information is attached to a copy of a work or appears in connection with the communication of a work to the public.

REFERENCES:

Hepp, François. *Evolution of International Copyright Law.* The Hague: M. Nijhoff, 1950.

Ladas, Stephen P. *The International Protection of Literary and Artistic Property.* New York: Macmillan, 1938.

___. *Patents, Trademarks and Related Rights.* Cambridge, MA: Harvard University Press, 1975.

Wallerstein, Michael B., et al, eds. *Global Dimensions of Intellectual Property Rights.* Washington, D.C.: National Academy Press, 1993.

WIPO Performances and Phonograms Treaty

SIGNED: December 20, 1996, at Geneva

SIGNATORIES: Argentina, Austria, Belarus, Belgium, Bolivia, Burkina Faso, Canada, Chile, Colombia, Costa Rica, Croatia, Denmark, Ecuador, El Salvador, Estonia, European Communities, Finland, France, Germany, Ghana, Greece, Hungary, Indonesia, Ireland, Israel, Italy, Kazakhstan, Kenya, Luxembourg, Mexico, Monaco, Mongolia, Namibia, Netherlands, Nigeria, Panama, Portugal, Republic of Moldova, Romania, Senegal, Slovakia, Slovenia, South Africa, Spain, Sweden, Switzerland, Togo, United Kingdom, United States, Uruguay, Venezuela

IN FORCE: Not yet in force

OVERVIEW: A convention updating and complementing the 1961 **Convention for the Protection of Performers, Producers of Phonograms and Broadcasting Organizations.**

DISCUSSION:

The World Intellectual Property Organization (WIPO) recognized "a the need to introduce new international rules in order to provide adequate solutions to the questions raised by economic, social, cultural and technological developments," especially in light of "the profound impact of the development and convergence of information and communication technologies on the production and use of performances and phonograms." In the context of the treaty, *phonogram* "means the fixation of the sounds of a performance or of other sounds, or of a representation of sounds, other than in the form of a fixation incorporated in a cinematographic or other audiovisual work," and *performers* "are actors, singers, musicians, dancers, and other persons who act, sing, deliver, declaim, play in, interpret, or otherwise perform literary or artistic works or expressions of folklore." As in other international copyright agreements, the crux of this treaty is the commitment of "each Contracting Party [to] accord to nationals of other Contracting Parties . . . the treatment [and protections] it accords to its own nationals."

The treaty explicitly extends the concepts of publication,

broadcasting, and reproduction to all contemporary media, and it calls on the signatories to "provide adequate legal protection and effective legal remedies against the circumvention of effective technological measures that are used by performers or producers of phonograms in connection with the exercise of their rights under this Treaty and that restrict acts, in respect of their performances or phonograms, which are not authorized by the performers or the producers of phonograms concerned or permitted by law" (Article 18). Furthermore, Article 19, lays down the following:

(1) Contracting Parties shall provide adequate and effective legal remedies against any person knowingly performing any of the following acts knowing, or with respect to civil remedies having reasonable grounds to know, that it will induce, enable, facilitate or conceal an infringement of any right covered by this Treaty:

(i) to remove or alter any electronic rights management information without authority;

(ii) to distribute, import for distribution, broadcast, communicate or make available to the public, without authority, performances, copies of fixed performances or phonograms knowing that electronic rights management information has been removed or altered without authority.

(2) As used in this Article, "rights management information" means information which identifies the performer, the performance of the performer, the producer of the phonogram, the phonogram, the owner of any right in the performance or phonogram, or information about the terms and conditions of use of the performance or phonogram, and any numbers or codes that represent such information, when any of these items of information is attached to a copy of a fixed performance or a phonogram or appears in connection with the communication or making available of a fixed performance or a phonogram to the public.

REFERENCES:

Hepp, François. *Evolution of International Copyright Law.* The Hague: M. Nijhoff, 1950.

Ladas, Stephen P. *The International Protection of Literary and Artistic Property.* New York: Macmillan, 1938.

__. *Patents, Trademarks and Related Rights.* Cambridge, MA: Harvard University Press, 1975.

Wallerstein, Michael B., et al, eds. *Global Dimensions of Intellectual Property Rights.* Washington, D.C.: National Academy Press, 1993.

Agreement (with Vietnam) on Establishment of Copyright Relations

SIGNED: April 16, 1997, at Washington, D.C.
SIGNATORIES: United States vs. Vietnam
IN FORCE: From December 23, 1998
OVERVIEW: A bilateral copyright agreement obligating the signatories to afford equal protection under their respective copyright laws to works of the other's authors first published in one of the contracting states.

DISCUSSION:

For many years following the end of the Vietnam War, the United States refused to establish relations of any kind with the Hanoi government. Gradually, limited relations were reestablished. The copyright treaty of 1997 is one step in this process.

Major provisions of the agreement include the following:

- Copyright protection to be extended to works of nationals and domiciliaries of the contracting state
- Protected works to include literary, musical, dramatic and choreographic works, motion pictures and other audiovisual work
- Copyright owners to be afforded a right to authorize or prohibit the public performance of certain works
- Vietnam to undertake to implement enforcement measures, including civil enforcement provisions (injunctive relief and damages, as well as seizure and destruction of infringing goods and their means of production), criminal penalties (including fines and imprisonment for copyright infringement on a commercial scale), effective customs procedures

In addition to its significance as a step toward fully normalizing relations between Vietnam and the United States, the agreement is immediately important for reciprocal protection of United States and Vietnamese copyrights, because Vietnam is not a member of either the Berne Convention for the Protection of Artistic and Literary Works or the Universal Copyright Convention. Despite the agreement, copyright attorneys and others in the United States have reported the continued blatant abuse of U.S. copyrights in Vietnam.

REFERENCES:
None

Customs, Transport, and Immigration Issues

Overview of Treaties in This Category

The United States has concluded few immigration treaties with other nations, and those in this section were concluded under extraordinary circumstances. The infamous **Gentleman's Agreement (with Japan)** of 1907 was a quasi-official measure to restrict the immigration of working-class Japanese, who, some Americans felt, deprived citizens of employment. It was concluded at the height of American xenophobia and, in particular, of a prejudice against Asian immigration.

Another set of immigration documents created under the pressure of extraordinary circumstances are the agreements with Cuba intended to normalize migration procedures with a communist dictatorship from which a significant number of citizens wished to flee. See **Agreement (with Cuba) Concerning the Movement of Cuban Refugees to the United States** (1965), **Joint Communiqué (with Cuba) on Immigration Matters** (1984), **Joint Communiqué (with Cuba) Concerning Normalizing Migration Procedures** (1994), and **Joint Statement (with Cuba) Further Normalizing Migration Procedures** (1995). These documents are most usefully read in chronological order.

The customs and transport issues in this section are of a somewhat miscellaneous character, dealing mainly with issues of standardization and/or facilitation and streamlining of customs formalities. Perhaps the single most significant multilateral agreement here respecting transport is the **Final Act of the United Nations Conference on Transit Trade of Land-Locked Countries** (1965), which lays down the principle of "the right of each land-locked State [to] free access to the sea." Coastal signatories to the Final Act undertake to allow, on a reciprocal basis, land-locked neighbors free transit to the sea.

Gentleman's Agreement (with Japan)

SIGNED: February 24, 1907, at Washington, D.C.
SIGNATORIES: Japan vs. United States
IN FORCE: From February 18, 1908
OVERVIEW: A quasi-official understanding by which Japan agreed not to issue passports to emigrants to the United States, except to certain categories of business and professional men.

DISCUSSION:
During the nineteenth century and into the twentieth, Asian immigrants were often the targets of discrimination and prejudice in the United States. An 1894 treaty with Japan had guaranteed free immigration, but as the numbers of Japanese laborers immigrating to California increased, hostility toward these people also grew. In 1900, Japan agreed to deny passports to laborers seeking emigration to the United States, but this policy was easily circumvented by intermediate immigration to Mexico, Canada, or Hawaii, followed by ultimate immigration to the United States.

During the first few years of the twentieth century, various community organizations were formed to fight Asian immigration, and on October 11, 1906, the city of San Francisco voted to place all Asian children in a wholly segregated school. Although Japan was willing to cooperate with the United States on immigration policy, it was deeply offended by the naked discrimination practiced against its people in San Francisco and elsewhere. At this juncture, President Theodore Roosevelt persuaded San Francisco's mayor to rescind the segregation order in return for a promise that the federal government would act to restrict Japanese immigration. The result was the 1907 Gentleman's Agreement, by which Japan formalized its policy of denying passports to Japanese emigrants who intended to settle in the United States (the policy applied to laborers and not to certain classes of business persons and professionals) and closed the loophole left in 1900 by recognizing that the United States had the right to exclude Japanese immigrants holding passports originally issued for other countries.

REFERENCES:
Ichioka, Yuji. *The Issei: The World of the First Generation Japanese Immigrants, 1885-1924*. New York: Free Press, 1990.

Gulick, Sidney L. *American Democracy and Asiatic Citizenship*. North Stratford, NH: Ayer Company Publishers, 1979.

Niiya, Brian. *Japanese American History: An A-to-Z Reference from 1868 to the Present*. New York: Facts on File, 1993.

Constitution of the Intergovernmental Committee for European Migration

SIGNED: October 19, 1953, at Venice, Italy

SIGNATORIES: Argentina, Australia, Austria, Canada, Chile, Denmark, Germany (Federal Republic), Greece, Israel, Italy, Netherlands, Norway, Paraguay, Philippines, Sweden, Switzerland, United States

IN FORCE: From November 30, 1954

OVERVIEW: The constitution of an international committee charged with fostering orderly migration from Europe.

DISCUSSION:

The Intergovernmental Committee for European Migration was established to achieve two chief purposes:

1. To make arrangements for the transport of migrants, for whom existing facilities are inadequate and who could not otherwise be moved, from European countries having surplus population to countries overseas which offer opportunities for orderly immigration

2. To promote the increase of the volume of migration from Europe by providing services in the processing, reception, first placement and settlement of migrants which other international organizations are not in a position to supply

The constitution establishes the committee and lays down its structure and authority, specifying the necessity of working within the domestic laws of nations taking in immigrants.

REFERENCES:

Desipio, Louis, et al. *Making Americans, Remaking America: Immigration and Immigrant Policy.* Boulder, CO: Westview Press, 1998.

Duignan, Peter, et al., eds. *The Debate in the United States over Immigration.* Palo Alto, CA: Hoover Institution Press, 1997.

Mills, Nicolaus, ed. *Arguing Immigration: The Debate over the Changing Face of America.* New York: Touchstone, 1994.

Customs Convention on the Temporary Importation of Private Road Vehicles

SIGNED: June 4, 1954, at New York

SIGNATORIES: Alaska (territorial application), Argentina, Austria, Belgian Congo, Belgium, Cambodia, Canada, Ceylon, Costa Rica, Cuba, Cyprus, Denmark, Dominican Republic, Ecuador, Egypt, Federation of Malaya, Fiji, France, Germany, Germany (Federal Republic), Guatemala, Haiti, Hawaii, Honduras, India, Israel, Italy, Jamaica, Japan, Jordan, Land Berlin, Luxembourg, Malta, Mexico, Monaco, Morocco, Netherlands, North Borneo, Panama, Philippines, Portugal, Puerto Rico, Ruanda-Urundi, Seychelles, Sierra, Leone, Singapore, Somali Protectorate, Spain, Sri Lanka, Sweden, Switzerland, Tonga, United Kingdom, United States, United States Virgin Islands, Uruguay, Vietnam, Zanzibar

IN FORCE: From December 15, 1957

OVERVIEW: A convention intended to facilitate the development of international touring by exempting from import taxes the automobiles of non-residents.

DISCUSSION:

Each signatory party undertakes to "grant temporary admission without payment of import duties and import taxes . . . to vehicles owned by persons normally resident outside its territory." Likewise, "the fuel contained in the ordinary supply tanks of vehicles temporarily imported shall be admitted without payment of import duties."

The body of the agreement provides details as to documentation and definition of the conditions and duration of "temporary importation" of vehicles.

REFERENCES:

None

Agreement (with Cyprus) Relating to the Waiver of Fingerprinting Requirements for Non-Immigrant Visas

SIGNED: July 11 1962 and January 11, 1963, at Nicosia, Cyprus

SIGNATORIES: Cyprus vs. United States

IN FORCE: From January 11, 1963

OVERVIEW: An agreement to waive fingerprinting for Americans seeking visas to Cyprus and for Cypriots seeking visas to the United States.

DISCUSSION:

This exchange of notes is an example of the kinds of goodwill gestures nations extend to one another from time to time. In this case, both nations agree to waive fingerprinting as a requirement for securing non-immigrant visas.

REFERENCE:

None

Agreement (with Cuba) Concerning the Movement of Cuban Refugees to the United States

OFFICIAL TITLE: Exchange of Notes (with Related Notes) Constituting an Agreement Concerning the Movement of Cuban Refugees to the United States

SIGNED: November 6, 1965, at Havana

SIGNATORIES: Cuba vs. United States

IN FORCE: From signing

OVERVIEW: An understanding whereby the Cuban government permits certain persons to emigrate to the United States.

DISCUSSION:

Traditionally, communist nations have been obliged to use varying degrees of coercion and force to control emigration and, in particular, flight to democratic nations. The case of Cuba under Fidel Castro was no different; however, in 1965, after negotiating through the Embassy of Switzerland in Havana (which represented United States interest in the Republic of Cuba since President Dwight Eisenhower had severed diplomatic relations in 1960), a Memorandum of Understanding was concluded on the subject of emigration to the United States. The key points are as follows:

- Cuba agrees to permit the departure from Cuba, and the United States agrees to permit entry into the United States, of Cubans who wish to leave Cuba for the United States.

The substance of the memorandum qualifies this permission as follows:

- Families who wish to emigrate are to be given priority.
- Cubans with immediate family members living in the United States are also to be given priority.
- Cuba and the United States will prepare and present to the Swiss embassy in Havana lists of persons with family in Cuba and the United States.
- Those whose names appear on both countries' lists will be permitted to leave Cuba and will be granted entry into the United States.
- Those whose names appear on only one list, will be subject to further examination to determine priority eligibility for emigration.
- Of those appearing on both lists, priority for departure will be assigned in the following order: parents and unmarried brothers and sisters under the age of 21 living in Cuba of children living in the United States; unmarried children under the age of 21 living in Cuba of parents living in the United States; spouses of persons living in Cuba of persons living in the United States.
- After the highest-priority emigrants have been transported, other persons will be granted permission to leave, especially those Cubans with non-immediate relatives in the United States.

The memorandum includes procedures for the assembly and departure of those granted permission to leave, with the United States to supply air transportation from Varadero airport. The volume of air transportation to be supplied will be sufficient to transport 3,000 to 4,000 persons per month, beginning no later than December 1, 1965.

Forming part of the exchange of notes constituting the agreement on emigration are Cuban reservations concerning the departure of certain classes of people:

- Technicians, skilled workers, and others deemed vital to Cuba's interests may be authorized to leave, but their leaving may be postponed indefinitely
- Young men between 17 and 26 years of age subject to compulsory military service, as well as those 15 and 16 years old, subject o military call up within two years, "do not have

the right to leave Cuba, and therefore will not be authorized to leave."

In reply to these reservations, the United States expresses regret as well as "the hope that the Government of Cuba is prepared to reconsider this position, The Government of the United States would like to emphasize the special importance such reconsideration would have in permitting many families to be reunited."

On the subject of the emigration of "persons who are prisoners in Cuba for political offenses," the United States expresses a desire that these persons be permitted to emigrate. The Cuban reply, forming part of the 1965 agreement, is a reaffirmation of its refusal to allow such prisoners to emigrate.

REFERENCE:
Masud-Pilato, Felix Roberto. *From Welcomed Exiles to Illegal Immigrants: Cuban Migration to the U.S., 1959-1995.* New York: Rowman and Littlefield, 1996.

Final Act of the United Nations Conference on Transit Trade of Land-Locked Countries

SIGNED: July 8, 1965, at New York

SIGNATORIES: Afghanistan, Argentina, Belgium, Bolivia, Brazil, Cameroon, Central African Republic, Chad, Chile, Czechoslovakia, Germany (Federal Republic), Holy See, Hungary, Italy, Laos, Luxembourg, Malawi, Mali, Mongolia, Nepal, Netherlands, Niger, Nigeria, Paraguay, Rwanda, San Marino, Sudan, Switzerland, Uganda, Union of Soviet Socialist Republics, United States, Yugoslavia, Zambia

IN FORCE: From June 9, 1967

OVERVIEW: A convention acting on the recognition of "the right of each land-locked State [to] free access to the sea."

DISCUSSION:
Pursuant to a General Assembly resolution (1028[XI]) on the rights of land-locked countries, a Conference on the Facilitation of Maritime Trade of Land-Locked Countries was held in 1965 and produced as its Final Act a Convention on Transit Trade of Land-Locked States.

The major provisions of the convention are as follows:

- Signatories recognize that the "right of each land-locked State of free access to the sea is an essential principle for the expansion of international trade and economic development."
- The vessels of land-locked states have identical rights to those of other states.
- "In order to enjoy the freedom of the seas on equal terms with coastal States, States having no sea coast should have free access to the sea. To this end, States situated between the sea

and a State having no sea coast shall by common agreement with the latter … accord to ships flying the flag of that State treatment equal to that accorded to their own ships or to the ships of any other State as regards access to seaports and the use of such ports."

- "In order to promote fully the economic development of the land-locked countries, the said countries should be afforded by all States, on the basis of reciprocity, free and unrestricted transit, in such a manner that they have free access to regional and international trade in all circumstances and for every type of goods."
- Good in transit should be exempted from customs duty.
- Regional agreements are encouraged to promote the economic growth of land-locked states.

REFERENCES:
None

Convention of the Facilitation of International Maritime Traffic

SIGNED: April 9, 1965, at London

SIGNATORIES: Algeria, Argentina, Belgium. Brazil, Canada, China, Côte d'Ivoire, Czechoslovakia, Denmark, Dominican Republic, Ecuador, Federation of Malaya, Finland, France, Germany (Federal Republic), Ghana, Greece, Hungary, Iceland, Israel, Italy, Japan, Korea, Land Berlin, Lebanon, Madagascar, Monaco, Netherlands, Netherlands Antilles, Nicaragua, Nigeria, Norway, Philippines, Poland, Senegal, Singapore, Spain, Suriname, Sweden, Switzerland, Trinidad and Tobago, Ukrainian Soviet Socialist Republic, Union of Soviet Socialist Republics, United Arab Republic, United Kingdom, United States, Yugoslavia, Zambia

IN FORCE: From March 5, 1967

OVERVIEW: An international convention to reduce and render uniform the formalities, documentary requirements, and procedures required on the arrival, stay, and departure of ships engaged in international voyages.

DISCUSSION:

The object of the convention is to reduce the documentation and formalities attendant on the arrival, stay, and departure of international vessels. The signatory governments undertake to cooperate in the formulation and application of measures for the facilitation of international commerce, including rendering formalities internationally uniform and reducing required formalities and documentation to an acceptable minimum.

REFERENCE:
None

Customs Convention on Containers

SIGNED: December 2, 1972, at Geneva

SIGNATORIES: Australia, Austria, Bulgaria, Byelorussian Soviet Socialist Republic, Canada, Cook Islands, Czechoslovakia, Finland, German Democratic Republic, Greece, Hungary, Korea (Republic), New Zealand, Niue Island, Poland, Romania, Spain, Switzerland, Tokelau Islands, Turkey, Ukrainian Soviet Socialist Republic, Union of Soviet Socialist Republics, United States

IN FORCE: From December 6, 1975

OVERVIEW: A convention to allow duty-free temporary admission to transportation containers.

DISCUSSION:

Beginning in the 1950s and growing rapidly by the 1970s, the shipping industry underwent a revolution based on the use of containers to consolidate shipments. As defined by the convention, "containers" are special structures for containing goods in transit or may be any article of transport equipment. The principal thrust of the convention is to exempt such items from taxation, provided that they are re-exported within three months of importation.

The convention includes provisions relating to approval of containers for transport under customs seal.

REFERENCES:
None

International Convention for Safe Containers (CSC)

SIGNED: December 2, 1972, at Geneva

SIGNATORIES: Austria, Berlin (West), Bulgaria, Byelorussian Soviet Socialist Republic, Canada, Cook Islands, Czechoslovakia, Finland, France, German Democratic Republic, Germany (Federal Republic), Hungary, India, Japan, Korea (Republic), Liberia, New Zealand, Niue Island, Poland, Romania, Spain, Switzerland, Tokelau Islands, Turkey, Ukrainian Soviet Socialist Republic, Union of Soviet Socialist Republics, United Kingdom, United States, Yugoslavia

IN FORCE: From September 6, 1977

OVERVIEW: A convention formalizing structural requirements to ensure safety in the handling, stacking and transporting of shipping containers.

DISCUSSION:

This convention was concluded at the same time as the **Customs Convention on Containers,** the entry for which provides a brief definition of the containers in question. The CSC lays down specifications for the safety approval of containers, including procedures for testing and inspection, as well as the issuance of official approval.

REFERENCES:
None

Agreement (with Iran) Relating to Multiple-Entry Non-Immigrant Visas

OFFICIAL TITLE: Exchange of Letters Constituting an Agreement Relating to Multiple-Entry Non-Immigrant Visas
SIGNED: December 13 and 16, 1976, at Tehran, Iran
SIGNATORIES: Iran vs. Untied States
IN FORCE: From January 1, 1977
OVERVIEW: An agreement with prerevolutionary Iran to allow multiple-entry visas.

DISCUSSION:

Before the Islamic fundamentalist revolution of 1979, Iran was a close strategic ally of the United States, As such, the two nations deemed it expedient to create a multiple-entry visa, which would allow the multiple entry of Iranians into the United States and Americans into Iran without the necessity of securing a new visa for each entry. The duration of the multiple-entry visa was four years.

Although the agreement remains officially in force, in practice visas are now issued a per-entry basis, and, since the fundamentalist revolution, they are issued on a highly irregular and exceptional basis.

REFERENCES:
None

Protocol of 1978 Relating to the International Convention for the Prevention of Pollution from Ships

SIGNED: February 17, 1978, at London
SIGNATORIES: Algeria, Antigua and Barbuda, Australia, Austria, Bahamas, Belgium, Brazil, Brunei Darussalam, Bulgaria, China, Colombia, Côte d'Ivoire, Cyprus, Czechoslovakia, Denmark, Djibouti, Ecuador, Egypt, Estonia, Finland, France, Gabon, Gambia, Germany, Ghana, Greece, Hungary, Iceland, India, Indonesia, Israel, Italy, Jamaica, Japan, Korea (Democratic People's Republic) Korea (Republic), Latvia, Lebanon, Liberia, Lithuania, Luxembourg, Malta, Marshall Islands, Mexico, Myanmar, Netherlands, Norway, Oman, Panama, Peru, Poland, Portugal, Russian Federation, Saint Vincent and the Grenadines, Seychelles, Singapore, South Africa, Spain, Suriname, Sweden, Switzerland, Syrian Arab Republic, Togo, Tunisia, Turkey, Tuvalu, United Kingdom, United States, Uruguay, Vanuatu, Vietnam, Yugoslavia
IN FORCE: From October 2, 1983

OVERVIEW: The 1978 Protocol modifies various provisions of the **International Convention for the Prevention of Pollution from Ships** of 1973, and in particular of its annex I, and it also postpones the entry into force of annex II of the Convention for a period of at least three years.

REFERENCE:
International Convention for the Prevention of Pollution of Sea by Oil: Message from the President of the United States. Washington, D.C. U.S. Government Printing Office, 1960.

Joint Communiqué (with Cuba) on Immigration Matters

SIGNED: December 14, 1984, at New York
SIGNATORIES: Cuba vs. United States
IN FORCE: From December 14, 1984
OVERVIEW: The chief provision of the communiqué is an agreement by Cuba to accept the return of the so-called *Marielitos.*

DISCUSSION:

During the waning days of the administration of Dwight David Eisenhower, diplomatic relations between the United States and Cuba, under the revolutionary Communist regime of Fidel Castro, were severed, and it was not until the **U.S.-Cuba Agreement to Establish Interest Sections** of May 30, 1977 that limited diplomatic relations were reestablished. Three years after this, beginning after April 1, 1980, emigration from Cuba to the United increased dramatically when Castro issued a response to the granting of asylum to would-be refugees by the Peruvian embassy in Havana. Up to this point, emigration from the island had been strictly limited, and legal emigration to the United States and other noncommunist nations almost unheard of. Now Castro announced that all Cubans who wanted to leave Cuba could do so freely. Within minutes of the announcement, some 10,000 Cubans swarmed onto the grounds of the Peruvian embassy. An airlift to Costa Rica was hastily organized, and Castro opened the port of Mariel to a "freedom flotilla" of ships and yachts sent from the United States—many owned or chartered by Cuban-Americans to bring out relatives.

The euphoria of the "Mariel Boat Lift" soon ended, as it became apparent that Castro had opened prisons and mental hospitals to permit criminals, the mentally ill, homosexuals, and others deemed undesirable by the Cuban government to join the refugees. In response to this, the United States interned large numbers of the "*Marielitos,*" pending determination of their background and their immigrant status, and the United States essentially froze relations with Cuba.

Not until December 14, 1984, with the signing of the Joint Communiqué, were relations partially restored. By the terms of the communiqué, Cuba agreed to take back more than 2,700 Cubans who had come to the United States in the Mariel exodus but were deemed ineligible to stay in the country under U.S. immigration law because of criminal or psychiatric disqualification.

On May 20, 1985, another crisis was precipitated when Castro canceled the agreement in response to United States propaganda broadcasts over the newly established Radio Marti. At this, on August 8, 1986, President Ronald Reagan issued an executive order suspending "entry into the United States as immigrants by all Cuban nationals" (except for those with immediate relatives in the United States) "in light of the continuing failure of the Government of Cuba to resume normal migration procedures with the United States while at the same time facilitating illicit migration to the United States."

On November 19, 1987, the United States and Cuba reinstated the provisions of the 1984 agreement. The **Joint Communiqué on U.S.-Cuba Immigration** superceded both the 1984 agreement and the 1987 restatement of it.

REFERENCES:

Masud-Pilato, Felix Roberto. *From Welcomed Exiles to Illegal Immigrants: Cuban Migration to the U.S., 1959-1995.* New York: Rowman and Littlefield, 1996.

Schwab, Peter. *Cuba: Confronting the U.S. Embargo.* New York: St. Martin's, 1999.

Joint Communiqué (with Cuba) Concerning Normalizing Migration Procedures

SIGNED: September 9, 1994, at New York

SIGNATORIES: Cuba vs. United States

IN FORCE: From signing

OVERVIEW: The most comprehensive agreement on U.S.-Cuban immigration matters since the 1959 Cuban revolution.

DISCUSSION:

For background on Cuban immigration to the United States, see **Joint Communiqué (with Cuba) on Immigration Matters** of 1984.

In 1994, representatives of the United States and Cuba conducted talks aimed at normalizing migration procedures between the two countries with the goal of ensuring that migration between the two countries is safe, legal, and orderly. The issues addressed include the following:

- Safety of life at sea: The signatories recognize their common interest in preventing unsafe departures from Cuba, which risk loss of human life, and the United States underscored its recent decisions to discourage unsafe voyages. Pursuant to the policy of both nations, migrants rescued at sea attempting to enter the United States will not be permitted to enter the United States, but instead will be taken to safe haven facilities outside of the United States.
- The United States discontinues its practice of granting parole to all Cuban migrants who reach U.S. territory in irregular ways.
- Cuba will take effective measures to prevent unsafe departures, using mainly "persuasive methods."
- Alien smuggling: The United States and Cuba reaffirm their support for the United Nations General Assembly resolution on alien smuggling. The two countries undertake to cooperate in acting promptly and effectively to prevent the transport of persons to the United States illegally.
- The signatories will take effective measures to oppose and prevent the use of violence by any persons seeking to reach, or who arrive in, the United States from Cuba by forcible diversions of aircraft and vessels.
- Legal migration: The signatories affirm their commitment to directing Cuban migration into safe, legal, and orderly channels consistent with strict implementation of the Joint Communiqué (with Cuba) on Immigration Matters of 1984.
- The United States will continue to issue, in conformity with United States law, immediate relative and preference immigrant visas to Cuban nationals who apply at the U.S. Interests Section and are eligible to immigrate to the United States.
- The United States also commits to authorize and facilitate additional lawful migration to the United States from Cuba.
- The United States ensures that total legal migration to the United States from Cuba will be a minimum of 20,000 Cubans each year, not including immediate relatives of United States citizens.
- As an additional, extraordinary measure, the United States will facilitate in a one-year period the issuance of documentation to permit the migration to the United States of those qualified Cuban nationals in Cuba currently on the immigrant visa waiting list. To this end, both signatories undertake to work together to facilitate the procedures necessary to implement this measure.
- Voluntary return: The signatories agree that the voluntary return of Cuban nationals who arrived in the United States or in safe havens outside the United States on or after August 19, 1994, will continue to be arranged through diplomatic channels.
- Excludables: The signatories agree to continue to discuss the return of Cuban nationals excludable from the United States.

The 1994 agreement was jeopardized late in 1999, when controversy erupted over the fate of Elian Gonzalez, a six-year-old refugee rescued on Thanksgiving Day by American fishermen after the boat that carried him, his mother, stepfather, and others sank. The boy was the only survivor, and while relatives in Florida petitioned for custody, the boy's natural father, a Cuban citizen, called for his return to Cuba. Fidel Castro orchestrated mass demonstrations protesting the "kidnaping" of

Gonzalez in violation of the 1994 agreement. As 1999 came to a close, the matter was still unresolved.

REFERENCES:

Masud-Pilato, Felix Roberto. *From Welcomed Exiles to Illegal Immigrants: Cuban Migration to the U.S., 1959-1995*. New York: Rowman and Littlefield, 1996.

Schwab, Peter. *Cuba: Confronting the U.S. Embargo*. New York: St. Martin's, 1999.

Joint Statement (with Cuba) Further Normalizing Migration Procedures

SIGNED: May 2, 1995, at Washington, D.C.

SIGNATORIES: Cuba vs. United States

IN FORCE: From signing

OVERVIEW: An elaboration of the **Joint Communiqué (with Cuba) Concerning Normalizing Migration Procedures** of 1994, to address safety and humanitarian concerns and to ensure that migration between the countries is safe, legal, and orderly.

DISCUSSION:

By this agreement, the following steps were taken to normalize further the migration relationship between Cuba and the United States:

- Humanitarian parole: The signatories recognize the special circumstances of Cuban migrants currently at Guantanamo Bay, the United States naval base established by treaty in Cuba, at which certain would-be immigrants have been detained. The signatories agree that a process of humanitarian parole into the United States should continue beyond those eligible for parole under existing criteria. The signatories agree that if the United States carries out such paroles, it may count them toward meeting the minimum number of Cubans it is committed to admit every year pursuant to the September 9, 1994, agreement. Up to 5,000 such paroles may be counted toward meeting the minimum number in any one year period beginning September 9, 1995, regardless of when the migrants are paroled into the United States.

- Safety of life at sea: The signatories reaffirm their common interest in preventing unsafe departures from Cuba. Accordingly, Cuban migrants intercepted at sea by the United States and attempting to enter the United States will be taken to Cuba. Similarly, migrants found to have entered Guantanamo illegally will also be returned to Cuba. The United States and Cuba will cooperate jointly in this effort. Migrants taken to Cuba will be informed by the United States officials about procedures to apply for legal admission to the United States at the U.S. Interests Section in Havana, and the signatories undertake to ensure that no action is taken against those migrants returned to Cuba as a consequence of their attempt to immigrate illegally.

REFERENCES:

Masud-Pilato, Felix Roberto. *From Welcomed Exiles to Illegal Immigrants: Cuban Migration to the U.S., 1959-1995*. New York: Rowman and Littlefield, 1996.

Schwab, Peter. *Cuba: Confronting the U.S. Embargo*. New York: St. Martin's, 1999.

SECTION 4.6
Finance

Overview of Treaties in This Category

Except for two bilateral agreements (**Loan Agreement [with Turkey] Relating to Balance-of-Payments Financing**, 1978, and **Agreement [with China] Relating to Investment Guaranties**, 1980), the treaties in this category are multilateral. Several establish major international financial institutions and funds: **Articles of Agreement of the International Monetary Fund** (1945), **Articles of Agreement of the International Bank for Reconstruction and Development** (1945), **Agreement Establishing the Inter-American Development Bank** (1959), **Convention on the Organisation for Economic Co-operation and Development** (1960), **Agreement Establishing the Asian Development Bank (with Annexes)** (1965), and **Agreement Establishing the African Development Fund** (1972). Others deal with issues of regulation and standardization: **Convention on a Settlement of Investment Disputes between States and Nationals of other States** (1965) and **Universal Postal Money Orders and Postal Travellers' Cheques Agreement (with Detailed Regulations)** (1969).

Articles of Agreement of the International Monetary Fund

SIGNED: December 27, 1945, at Washington, D.C.
SIGNATORIES: Belgium, Bolivia, Canada, China, Colombia, Czechoslovakia, Egypt, Ethiopia, France, Greece, Honduras, Iceland, India, Iraq, Luxembourg, Netherlands, Norway, Philippines, South Africa, United Kingdom, United States, Yugoslavia
IN FORCE: From signing
OVERVIEW: An agreement to create the IMF in order to secure international monetary cooperation, stabilize exchange rates, and expand international liquidity.

DISCUSSION:
The IMF was founded during the Bretton Woods Conference, which created the United Nations, even before World War II had ended. Members of the IMF undertake the following:

- To make orderly currency exchange arrangements
- To act to reduce the role of gold in international monetary transactions
- To expand the capability of the IMF to carry out its goals.
The IMF is also to function as an instrument of consultative

cooperation and a resource for research and statistical information on international monetary questions. The agreement specifies how member governments subscribe to the IMF, based on the volume of their international trade, their national income, and their international reserve holdings.

REFERENCES:
Harper, Richard H. R. *Inside the IMF: An Ethnography of Documents, Technology and Organizational Action.* Lanham, MD: Academic Press, 1998.
Khan, Shahrukh Rafi. *Do World Bank and IMF Policies Work?* New York: St. Martin's, 1999.

Articles of Agreement of the International Bank for Reconstruction and Development

SIGNED: December 27, 1945, at Washington
IN FORCE: From signing
SIGNATORIES: Belgium, Bolivia, Canada, China, Czechoslovakia, Egypt, Ethiopia, France, Greece, Honduras, Iceland, India, Iraq, Luxembourg, Netherlands, Norway, Philippines, South Africa, United Kingdom, United States, Yugoslavia
OVERVIEW: Under the auspices of the United Nations, the agreement established the International Bank for Reconstruction and Development, more commonly known as the World Bank, which provides finance for projects to aid the economic development of member nations.

DISCUSSION:
The World Bank had its origins in the United Nations Monetary and Financial (Bretton Woods) Conference of July 1944 and officially began operations in June 1946, shortly after World War II ended. The first loans were made exclusively to finance post–World War II recovery and reconstruction, but, by the 1950s, the focus of the World Bank had shifted to the Third World, and it was providing finance for economic development chiefly in Africa, Asia, the Middle East, and Latin America. The bank may make loans directly to governments or to private enterprises guaranteed by the appropriate government.

The mission of the World Bank is outlined in the "Introductory Article":

(i) **To assist in the reconstruction and development of territories of members by facilitating the investment of capital for productive purposes, including the res toration of economies destroyed or** disrupted by war, the reconversion of productive facilities to peace-time needs and the encouragement of the development of productive facilities and resources in less developed countries.

(ii) To promote private foreign investment by means of guarantees or participation in loans and other investments made by private investors; and when private capital is not available on reasonable terms, to supplement private investment by providing, on suitable conditions, finance for productive purposes out of its own capital, funds raised by it and its other resources.

(iii) To promote the long-range balanced growth of international trade and the maintenance of equilibrium in balances of payments by encouraging international investment for the development of the productive resources of members, thereby assisting in raising productivity, the standard of living and conditions of labour in their territories.

(iv) To arrange the loans made or guaranteed by it in relation to international loans through other channels so that the more useful and urgent projects, large and small alike, will be dealt with first.

(v) To conduct its operations with due regard to the effect of international investment on business conditions in the territories of members and, in the immediate post-war years, to assist in bringing about a smooth transition from a war-time to a peacetime economy.

REFERENCES:

Acheson, A. L. K., J. F. Chant, and M F. J. Prachowny, eds. *Bretton Woods Revisited: Evaluations of the International Monetary Fund and the International Bank for Reconstruction and Development.* Toronto: University of Toronto Press, 1972.

Grenville, J. A. S. *The Major International Treaties 1914-1973: A History Guide with Texts.* New York: Stein and Day, 1974.

Mason, Edward Sagendorph. *The World Bank Since Bretton Woods: The Origins, Policies, Operations, and Impact of the International Bank for Reconstruction and Development and the other Members of the World Bank Group.* Washington, D.C.: Brookings Institution, 1973.

Agreement Establishing the Inter-American Development Bank

SIGNED: April 8, 1959, at Washington, D.C.

SIGNATORIES: Argentina, Austria, Bahamas, Barbados, Belgium, Belize, Bolivia, Brazil, Canada, Chile, Colombia, Costa Rica, Denmark, Dominican Republic, Ecuador, El Salvador, Finland, France, Germany, Guatemala, Guyana, Haiti, Honduras, Israel, Italy, Jamaica, Japan, Mexico, Netherlands, Nicaragua, Norway, Panama, Paraguay, Peru, Spain, Suriname, Sweden, Switzerland, Trinidad and Tobago, United Kingdom, United States, Uruguay Venezuela, Yugoslavia

IN FORCE: From December 30, 1959

OVERVIEW: A convention creating the Inter-American Development Bank for the purpose of contributing "to the acceleration of the process of economic development of the member countries, individually and collectively."

DISCUSSION:

The mission of the bank is set out in the first section of the convention as follows:

i)   to promote the investment of public and private capital for development purposes;

ii) to utilize its own capital, funds raised by it in financial markets, and other available resources, for financing the development of the member countries, giving priority to those loans and guarantees that will contribute most effectively to their economic growth;

iii) to encourage private investment in projects, enterprises, and activities contributing to economic development and to supplement private investment when private capital is not available on reasonable terms and conditions;

iv) to cooperate with the member countries to orient their development policies toward a better utilization of their resources, in a manner consistent with the objectives of making their economies more complementary and of fostering the orderly growth of their foreign trade; and

v)   to provide technical assistance for the preparation, financing, and implementation of development plans and projects, including the study of priorities and the formulation of specific project proposals.

To carry out "its functions, the Bank shall cooperate as far as possible with national and international institutions and with private sources supplying investment capital." Membership in the bank is open to member states of the Organization of American States, who may subscribe to shares in the bank. The bank may make direct loans or may guarantee loans from other sources for the purpose of financing development among the member states. The convention fully outlines the structure and governance of the bank, which is by a Board of Governors and a Board of Executive Directors.

REFERENCE:

United States Department of State, *Treaties in Force: A List of Treaties and other International Agreements of the United States in Force on January 1, 1997.* Washington, D.C.: U.S. Government Printing Office, 1997.

Convention on the Organisation for Economic Co-operation and Development

SIGNED: December 14, 1960, at Paris

SIGNATORIES: Australia, Austria, Belgium, Canada, Denmark, Federal Republic of Germany, Finland, France, Greece, Iceland, Ireland, Italy, Japan, Luxembourg, Netherlands, New Zealand, Norway, Portugal, Spain, Sweden, Switzerland, Turkey, United Kingdom, United States

IN FORCE: From September 30, 1961

OVERVIEW: Convention creating the Organisation for Economic Co-operation and Development.

DISCUSSION:

As laid down by the convention, the objectives of the OECD, consisting of the signatories to the convention, are as follows:

- To achieve the highest sustainable economic growth and employment and a rising standard of living in member countries, while maintaining financial stability, and thus to contribute to the development of the world economy
- To contribute to sound economic expansion in member as well as non-member countries in the process of economic development
- To contribute to the expansion of world trade on a multilateral, non-discriminatory basis in accordance with international obligations

Per Article 2, "in the pursuit of these aims, the Members agree that they will, both individually and jointly" undertake the following:

- Promote the efficient use of their economic resources
- In the scientific and technological field, promote the development of their resources, encourage research and promote vocational training
- Pursue policies designed to achieve economic growth and internal and external financial stability and to avoid developments which might endanger their economies or those of other countries
- Pursue their efforts to reduce or abolish obstacles to the exchange of goods and services and current payments and maintain and extend the liberalization of capital movements
- Contribute to the economic development of both Member and non-member countries in the process of economic development by appropriate means and, in particular, by the flow of capital to those countries, having regard to the importance to their economies of receiving technical assistance and of securing expanding export markets

The function of the OECD is to guide and assist members in achieving the objectives just outlined by coordinating the economic policies and actions of the signatories.

REFERENCES:
None

Convention on a Settlement of Investment Disputes between States and Nationals of Other States

SIGNED: March 18, 1965, at Washington, D.C.
SIGNATORIES: Afghanistan, Austria, Belgium, Cameroon, Central

African Republic, Chad, China (Republic), Congo (Brazzaville), Côte d'Ivoire, Cyprus, Dahomey, Denmark, Ethiopia, Federation of Malaya, France, Gabon, Germany (Federal Republic), Ghana, Greece, Iceland, International Bank for Reconstruction and Redevelopment, Ireland, Italy, Jamaica, Japan, Kenya, Korea (Republic), Liberia, Luxembourg, Madagascar, Malawi, Mauritania, Morocco, Nepal, Netherlands, Niger, Nigeria, Norway, Pakistan, Senegal, Sierra Leone, Somalia, Sweden, Togo, Trinidad and Tobago, Tunisia, Uganda, United Kingdom, United States, Upper Volta

IN FORCE: From October 14, 1966
OVERVIEW: The convention establishes the International Centre for Settlement of Investment Disputes.

DISCUSSION:

The purpose of the center established by this convention is "to provide facilities for conciliation and arbitration of investment disputes between Contracting States and nationals of other Contracting States." The center is to be established at the principal office of the International Bank for Reconstruction and Development and is to consist of the following elements:

- An Administrative Council
- A Secretariat
- A Panel of Conciliators
- A Panel of Arbitrators

The key elements are the two panels, each of which consists of qualified persons "of high moral character and recognized competence in the fields of law, commerce, industry or finance, who may be relied upon to exercise independent judgment." It is to these panels that questions and issues of conciliation and arbitration are to be brought.

REFERENCE:
Sornarajah, M. *The International Law on Foreign Investment.* London and New York: Cambridge University Press, 1994.

Agreement Establishing the Asian Development Bank (with Annexes)

OFFICIAL TITLE: Final Act of the Conference of Plenipotentiaries on the Asian Development Bank and Agreement Establishing the Asian Development Bank (with Annexes)
SIGNED: December 12, 1965, at Manila, Philippines
SIGNATORIES: Afghanistan, Australia, Austria, Belgium, Cambodia, Canada, Ceylon, China (Republic), Denmark, Federation of Malaysia, Finland, Germany (Federal Republic), India, Iran, Italy, Japan, Korea (Republic), Lao People's Democratic Republic, Laos, Malaysia, Nepal, Netherlands, New Zealand, Norway, Pakistan, Philippines, Samoa, Singapore, Sweden, Thailand, United Kingdom, United States, Vietnam, Western Samoa

IN FORCE: From August 22, 1966

OVERVIEW: The Final Act of the 1965 conference establishes the Asian Development Bank.

DISCUSSION:

The agreement establishes a bank to foster economic growth and cooperation in the region of Asia and the Far East. To this end, the bank, as established in this document, performs the following functions:

- Promotes investment in the region
- Finances developing member countries in the region
- Assists members in coordinating their development policies
- Provides members with technical assistance
- Cooperates, as appropriate, with the United Nations and its organs

The agreement authorizes initial capitalization of $1 billion and lays down procedures by which member nations may acquire shares.

REFERENCES:
None

Universal Postal Union Money Orders and Postal Travellers' Cheques Agreement (with Detailed Regulations)

SIGNED: November 14, 1969, at Tokyo

SIGNATORIES: Afghanistan, Albania, Algeria, Argentina, Australia, Austria, Barbados, Belgium, Bhutan, Bolivia, Botswana, Brazil, Bulgaria, Burma, Burundi, Byelorussian Soviet Socialist Republic, Cameroon, Chad, Channel Islands, Chile, China (Republic), Colombia, Congo, Congo (Brazaville), Costa Rica, Côte d'Ivoire, Cuba, Cyprus, Czechoslovakia, Dahomey, Denmark, Dominican Republic, Ecuador, Egypt, El Salvador, Ethiopia, Finland, France, French Whole Territory, Gabon, Germany (Federal Republic), Ghana, Greece, Guatemala, Guinea, Haiti, Honduras, Hungary, Iceland, India, Indonesia, Iran, Iraq, Ireland, Isle of Man, Israel, Italy, Jamaica, Japan, Jordan, Kenya, Khmer Republic, Korea (Republic), (Kuwait, Land Berlin, Laos, Lebanon, Lesotho, Liberia, Libyan Arab Republic, Liechtenstein, Luxembourg, Malawi, Malaysia, Maldives, Mali, Mauritania, Mauritius, Monaco, Mongolia, Morocco, Nauru, Netherlands, Netherlands Antilles, New Zealand, Nicaragua, Nigeria, Norway, Pakistan, Panama, Paraguay, Peru, Philippines, Poland, Portugal, Portuguese Provinces in Asia, Portugese Provinces in East Africa, Portuguese Provinces in Oceania, Portuguese Provinces in West Africa, Qatar, Romania, Rwanda, San Marino, Senegal, Sierra Leone, Singapore, Somalia, South Africa, Spain, Spanish Territory in Africa, Sudan, Suriname, Sweden, Switzerland, Syrian Arab Republic, Tanzania, Thailand, Togo, Trinidad and Tobago, Trust Territory of the Pacific Islands, Tunisia, Turkey, Uganda, Ukrainian Soviet Socialist Republic, Union of Soviet Socialist Republics, United Arab Republic, United Kingdom, United Kingdom Territories, United States, United States Overseas Territories, Upper Volta, Uruguay, Vatican City State, Venezuela, Vietnam, Yemen, Yugoslavia, Zambia

IN FORCE: From July 1, 1971

OVERVIEW: A convention to standardize international money orders and postal travelers' cheques.

DISCUSSION:

The major provisions of the convention address the following issues:

- Currency conversion issues relating to the issuance of money orders
- Maximum amount issues
- Payment of funds and issuance of receipt
- Exemption from charges
- Issues relating to telegraph money orders
- Advice of payment service
- Express and special delivery options
- Redirection
- Endorsement issues
- Payment of money orders
- Liability issues
- Inpayment money orders
- Postal travelers' cheques rules and regualtions
- Payment of cheques
- Validity issues
- Claims and liability
- Allocation of charges

REFERENCES:
None

Agreement Establishing the African Development Fund

SIGNED: November 29, 1972, at Abidjan

SIGNATORIES: African Development Bank, Argentina, Belgium, Brazil, Canada, Denmark, Finland, France, Germany (Federal Republic), Italy, Japan, Korea (Republic), Kuwait, Netherlands, Norway, Saudi Arabia, Spain, Sweden, Switzerland, United Arab Emirates, United Kingdom, United States, Yugoslavia

IN FORCE: From May 30, 1973

OVERVIEW: An agreement creating a fund to assist the African Development Bank in "making an increasingly effective contribution to the economic and social development of the Bank's members and to the promotion of cooperation ... and increased international trade."

DISCUSSION:

The fund, created primarily by subscription of states signatory to this agreement, is intended to promote the development of nations in Africa. The agreement lays down rules for the following:

- Subscriptions: initial and subsequent
- Currency rules, including valuation of currencies used
- Fund operations, including use of resources and the condition, form, and terms of financing
- Provision of technical assistance
- Prohibition of funding of political activity
- Organization and management of the fund
- Interpretation and arbitration provisions

REFERENCE:
Muriithi, Samuel M. *African Development Dilemma: The Big Debate.* Lanham, MD: University Press of America, 1996.

IMF Compensation Study Agreement

OFFICIAL TITLE: Agreement Concerning a Study of Compensation Systems for the International Monetary Fund (IMF) and the International Bank for Reconstruction and Development (IBRD)
SIGNED: December 15, 1977, at Washington, D.C.
SIGNATORIES: France, Germany (Federal Republic), Japan, Land Berlin, United Kingdom, United States
IN FORCE: From signing
OVERVIEW: An agreement among the signatory governments to sponsor an independent study of compensation principles and structure for the IMF and IBRD.

DISCUSSION:

The signatories, concerned about the conduct of these two United Nations financial bodies, concluded an agreement to sponsor a study in order to "obtain a fresh, independent, expert and businesslike opinion on how the compensation systems of the International Monetary Fund (IMF) and World Bank (IBRD) should be structured, enabling them to recruit and retain adequate and highly qualified personnel." The agreement sets out the assumptions as well as the methods of the study, as well as the composition of the study committee.

REFERENCES:
Harper, Richard H. R. *Inside the IMF: An Ethnography of Documents, Technology and Organizational Action.* Lanham, MD: Academic Press, 1998.
Khan, Shahrukh Rafi. *Do World Bank and IMF Policies Work?* New York: St. Martin's, 1999.

Loan Agreement (with Turkey) Relating to Balance-of-Payments Financing

SIGNED: December 5, 1978, at Ankara
SIGNATORIES: Turkey vs. United States
IN FORCE: From signing
OVERVIEW: A $50,000,000 loan agreement to aid Turkey in stabilizing its economy by paying down its balance of payments deficit.

DISCUSSION:

The "balance of payments" is the record of all economic transactions between residents of one country and residents of other countries (including the governments). Lopsided balance of payment scenarios significantly destabilize a nation's economy. The loan set forth in this agreement is intended to help Turkey finance its balance of payments deficit in order to stabilize the Turkish economy and promote economic recovery.

The agreement states the amount of the loan as $50,000,000 and sets out the terms of repayment at 8.77 percent per annum.

REFERENCE:
None

Agreement (with China) Relating to Investment Guarantees

OFFICIAL TITLE: Exchange of Notes Constituting an Agreement Relating to Investment Guarantees
SIGNED: October 7 and October 30, 1980, at Beijing
SIGNATORIES: China vs. United States
IN FORCE: From October 30, 1980
OVERVIEW: An agreement on investment insurance and investment guarantees, to be administered by the Overseas Private Investment Corporation, relating to United States investment in Chinese enterprises.

DISCUSSION:

The agreement sets out rules for the provision of investment guarantees and investment insurance for United States investments relating to projects and activities approved by the government of the People's Republic of China. The agreement also provides for dispute resolution, if necessary, by an arbitral tribunal to be created on an ad hoc basis.

REFERENCE:
Wu, Yanrui. *Foreign Direct Investment and Economic Growth in China.* Northampton, MA: Edward Elgar Publishing, 1999.

Labor Matters

Overview of Treaties in This Category

The United States has concluded very few international labor agreements and has refrained from signing or acceding to most of the major multilateral accords, finding them incompatible with a free labor market. For example, the **International Convention on the Protection of the Rights of All Migrant Workers and Members of Their Families** (1990) has yet to be signed by the United States, which, however, did conclude a workers' rights/human rights bilateral labor agreement with Honduras (**Memorandum of Understanding [with Honduras] on Workers' Rights,** 1995).

Convention Concerning the Liability of the Shipowner in Case of Sickness, Injury or Death of Seamen

SIGNED: October 24, 1936, at Geneva
SIGNATORIES: Belgium, Mexico, United States
IN FORCE: From May 24, 1947 (as modified in 1946)
OVERVIEW: A convention setting forth the liability of the shipowner in case of sickness, injury, or death of seamen.

DISCUSSION:
Although concluded under the aegis of the International Labor Organization, the convention is subscribed by only three nations. It lays down the shipowner's liability as follows:

- The shipowner is liable in respect of "sickness and injury occurring between the date specified in the articles of agreement for reporting for duty and the termination of the engagement."
- The shipowner is also liable "for death resulting from such sickness or injury." ·

National laws may make certain exceptions to these general rules of liability, as, for example, if the injury was incurred otherwise than in the service of the ship, if the injury or sickness was due to the wilful act or misbehavior of the seaman, or if a sickness was intentionally concealed when the engagement was entered into. Generally, however, the shipowner is liable for the expense of medical care and maintenance until the sick or injured person has been cured or until the sickness or incapac-ity has been declared of a permanent character. As long as the sick or injured person remains on board the ship, he is entitled to full wages. In case of death, the shipowner is liable for burial costs.

REFERENCE:
Compa, Lance A. *Human Rights, Labor Rights, and International Trade.* Philadelphia: University of Pennsylvania Press, 1996.

Agreement (with France) Relating to Principles Governing French Recruitment of German Labor in the United States Zone of Germany

OFFICIAL TITLE: Exchange of Notes Constituting an Agreement Relating to Principles Governing French Recruitment of German Labor in the United States Zone of Germany
SIGNED: October 25, 1947, at Paris
SIGNATORIES: France vs. United States
IN FORCE: From signing
OVERVIEW: An agreement whereby France secures the right to recruit voluntary labor from among the population in the United States zone of occupied Germany.

DISCUSSION:
The agreement clears the way for French authorities to recruit labor at a fair wage from among Germans living the United States zone of occupation in Germany. Such labor, in all cases, is to be strictly voluntary.

REFERENCE:
None

Convention Concerning Freedom of Association and Protection of the Right to Organize

SIGNING: July 9, 1948
SIGNATORIES: Afghanistan, Algeria, Angola, Antigua and Barbuda, Argentina, Armenia, Australia, Austria, Azerbaijan, Bahamas, Bahrain, Bangladesh, Barbados, Belarus, Belgium, Belize, Benin, Bolivia, Bosnia-Herzegovina, Botswana, Brazil,

Bulgaria, Burkina Faso, Burma, Burundi, Cambodia, Cameroon, Canada, Cape Verde, Central African Republic, Chad, Chile, China, Colombia, Comoros, Congo, Costa Rica, Côte d'Ivoire, Croatia, Cuba, Cyprus, Czech Republic, Czechoslovakia, Denmark, Djibouti, Dominica, Dominican Republic, Ecuador, Egypt, El Salvador, Equatorial Guinea, Eritrea, Estonia, Ethiopia, Fiji, Finland, Former Yugoslav Republic of Macedonia, France, Gabon, Georgia, German Democratic Republic, Germany (Federal Republic), Ghana, Greece, Grenada, Guatemala, Guinea, Guinea-Bissau, Guyana, Haiti, Honduras, Hungary, Iceland, India, Indonesia, Iran, Iraq, Ireland, Israel, Italy, Jamaica, Japan, Jordan, Kazakstan, Kenya, Korea, Kuwait, Kyrgyz Republic, Laos, Latvia, Lebanon, Lesotho, Liberia, Libya, Lithuania, Luxembourg, Madagascar, Malawi, Malaysia, Mali, Malta, Mauritania, Mexico, Moldova, Mongolia, Morocco, Mozambique Namibia, Nepal, Netherlands, New Zealand, Nicaragua, Niger, Nigeria, Norway, Oman, Pakistan, Panama, Papua New Guinea, Paraguay, Peru, Philippines, Poland, Portugal, Qatar, Romania, Rwanda, St. Lucia, San Marino, Sao Tome and Principe, Saudi Arabia, Senegal, Seychelles, Sierra Leone, Singapore, Slovak Republic, Slovenia, Solomon Islands, Somalia, South Africa, Spain, Sri Lanka, Sudan, Suriname, Swaziland, Sweden, Switzerland, Syrian Arab Republic, Tajikistan, Tanzania, Thailand, Togo, Trinidad and Tobago, Tunisia, Turkey, Turkmenistan, Uganda, Ukraine, Union of Soviet Socialist Republics, United Arab Emirates, United Kingdom, United States, Uruguay, Uzbekistan, Venezuela, Vietnam (Socialist Republic), Yemen (Aden), Yemen (Sanaa), Yugoslavia, Zaire, Zambia, Zimbabwe

IN FORCE: From July 4, 1950

OVERVIEW: A convention guaranteeing in signatory nations the right to organize for labor purposes.

DISCUSSION:

Enacted under the aegis of the International Labor Conference, the convention guaranteed to "workers and employers, without distinction whatsoever … the right to establish and, subject only to the rules of the organisation concerned, to join organisations of their own choosing without previous authorisation." Moreover, "each Member of the International Labour Organisation for which this Convention is in force undertakes to take all necessary and appropriate measures to ensure that workers and employers may exercise freely the right to organise."

REFERENCE:

Compa, Lance A. *Human Rights, Labor Rights, and International Trade.* Philadelphia: University of Pennsylvania Press, 1996.

Agreement (with Mexico) Relating to Employment in the United States of America of Mexican Agricultural Workers

OFFICIAL TITLE: Exchange of Notes Constituting an Agreement Relating to Employment in the United States of America of Mexican Agricultural Workers

SIGNED: August 11, 1951, at Mexico City

SIGNATORIES: Mexico vs. United States

IN FORCE: From signing

OVERVIEW: An agreement embodying the U.S.-Mexican "Migrant Labor Agreement of 1951."

DISCUSSION:

The 1951 agreement addresses procedures by which the United States may secure migrant agricultural from Mexico. The agreement includes articles relating to the following issues:

- Presenting Requests for workers: communication is to originate from the U.S. Secretary of Labor to the Mexican government
- The Mexican government agrees to establish migratory stations at Guadalajara, Irapuato, Monterrey, Chihuahua, and elsewhere, if necessary.
- The United States government agrees to establish reception centers at Brownsville, Texas; Laredo, Texas; El Paso, Texas; Nogales, Arizona; and Calexico, California, as well as other places, if necessary.
- Operation of the migratory stations, including selection and assembly of workers, as well as health inspection
- Transportation from the migratory stations—to be provided by the United States Department of Labor
- Provision for declaring certain employers ineligible for contracting labor due to violations of various existing agreements
- Prohibition against discrimination because of nationality or ancestry
- Preference in employment for United States workers: "Mexican workers shall not be employed in the United States in any jobs for which domestic workers can be reasonably obtained …"
- Guidelines and requisites for contracting labor
- Limitation of employment: migrants to be employed in agriculture only
- Issues of contracts and wages: wages to be paid "in the manner prevailing in the area"
- Guarantee of work "for at least three-fourths of the work days of the total period during which the Work Contract [is] in effect"
- Transportation from the reception center to the place of employment to be at the expense of the employer
- Employment records to be maintained by employer

- Employer to be held liable for treatment of occupational injury and disease
- The migrant works shall enjoy the right of representation
- "In the event of strike or lockout . . . the Secretary of Labor shall make special effort to transfer such Workers to other agricultural employment"; failing this, their work contract shall be terminated.
- Migrant labor operations to be subject to inspection by U.S. officials as well as by "the appropriate Mexican Consul"
- U.S. and Mexican officials to have the right to verify payments due to Mexican workers
- Remedial and enforcement procedures: both governments to have rights relating to verification of compliance with the agreement, as well as with work contracts

Subjoined to the agreement is a "Standard Work Contract."

REFERENCE:
Zahniser, Steven. *Mexican Migration to the United States: The Role of Migration Networks and Human Capital Accumulation.* Detroit: Garland, 1999.

Agreement (with Mexico) Relating to the Illegal Entry of Migratory Workers

OFFICIAL TITLE: Joint Statement Constituting an Agreement Relating to the Illegal Entry of Migratory Workers
SIGNED: July 18, 1973, at Washington, D.C.
SIGNATORIES: Mexico vs. United States
IN FORCE: From signing
OVERVIEW: A brief action plan for cooperation in stemming the tide of the illegal immigration of migrant workers from Mexico into the United States.

DISCUSSION:
The joint statement was the product of a meeting in Washington between representatives of the Mexican government and that of the United States. For its part, the Mexican government detailed new policies directed toward the reorganization of agricultural productivity, which would create more opportunity in Mexico and, therefore, help reduce the flow of illegal immigrants. For its part, the United States presented a report on the problem of illegal immigration. The United States also proposed measures to alleviate the administrative and personal inconvenience attendant on the detention of illegal immigrants. Beyond this, the two governments agreed that a program of bilateral measures needed to be developed in a spirit of full cooperation, a program that would take into account the many and complex economic structures, cultural patterns, and historical and other factors that come into play.

REFERENCE:
Zahniser, Steven. *Mexican Migration to the United States: The Role of Migration Networks and Human Capital Accumulation.* Detroit: Garland, 1999.

International Convention on the Protection of the Rights of all Migrant Workers and Members of Their Families

ADOPTED BY THE U.N. GENERAL ASSEMBLY: December 18, 1990, at New York
SIGNATORIES: Azerbaijan, Bangladesh, Bosnia and Herzegovina, Cape Verde, Colombia, Chile, Egypt, Mexico, Morocco, Philippines, Senegal, Seychelles, Sri Lanka, Turkey, Uganda
IN FORCE: Not yet in force
OVERVIEW: A convention to apply established United Nations human rights precepts to explicitly to migrant workers.

DISCUSSION:
As of September 1999, the United States had yet to sign this ground-breaking convention, which was still short of the twenty ratifications required for it to come into force. The instrument remains open for signature.

The objects of the convention include the following:

- Ensuring that all United Nations conventions concerning human rights and the rights of labor are applied to migrant workers
- Harmonizing various international and national policies on migrant workers
- Managing the impact of the flows of migrant workers on states
- Reducing the vulnerability of migrant workers

The convention begins by defining international migrant workers, including:

- The migrant worker proper
- The frontier worker ("who retains his or her habitual residence in a neighbouring State to which he or she normally returns every day or at least once a week")
- The seasonal worker
- The seafarer ("employed on board a vessel registered in a State of which he or she is not a national"),
- The worker on an offshore installation ("employed on an offshore installation that is under the jurisdiction of a State of which he or she is not a national")
- The project-tied worker ("admitted to a State employment for a defined period to work solely on a specific project being carried out in that State by his or her employer")
- The specified-employment worker ("sent by his or her

employer for a restricted and defined period of time to a State of employment to undertake a specific assignment or duty")

- The self-employed worker ("who is engaged in a remunerated activity otherwise than under a contract of employment and who earns his or her living through this activity normally working alone or together with members of his or her family, and to any other migrant worker recognized as self-employed by applicable legislation of the State of employment or bilateral or multilateral agreements")

Signatories to the convention undertake to protect the migrant worker's human, political, and labor rights in a non-discriminatory manner. Essentially, signatories agree to afford migrants the same protections and basic rights enjoyed by citizens. They also agree not to engage in the collective expulsion of migrants.

Although migrants are to be subject to the laws of the host state, they are guaranteed the "right to have recourse to the protection and assistance of the consular or diplomatic authorities of their State of origin." The convention specifies the migrant's responsibility to pay required taxes to the host jurisdictions and to obey the laws of those jurisdictions.

The convention consists of 93 detailed articles, which may in part account for the length and difficulty of the ratification process. Few nations would argue with the objectives and principles of this convention, but, in many areas, its provisions threaten to encroach on national laws and sovereignty. The International Convention on the Protection of the Rights of All Migrant Workers and Members of Their Families exemplifies the difficulties of enacting complex multilateral treaties. The United States has yet to sign the treaty, let alone ratify it.

REFERENCE:
Cholewinski, Ryszard. *Migrant Workers in International Human Rights Law: Their Protection in Countries of Employment.* Oxford, UK: Clarendon Press, 1997.

Memorandum of Understanding (with Honduras) on Workers' Rights

SIGNED: November 15, 1995, at Tegucigalpa, Honduras,
SIGNATORIES: Honduras vs. United States
IN FORCE: From signing
OVERVIEW: An understanding reached concerning the rights of workers, including inspection of factories and guarantee of the right to organize.

DISCUSSION:

In recent years, the United States has sought to promote improvement of working conditions in certain developing nations by requiring that nations exporting goods to the United States maintain certain minimum standards in the areas of working conditions and workers' rights. Failure to meet these standards might result in a reduction of permitted imports. Pursuant to this policy, a memorandum was drawn up between United States officials and the minister of labor and social welfare of Honduras and other officials specifying minimum working regulations and allowing for periodic inspections.

REFERENCE:
Cholewinski, Ryszard. *Migrant Workers in International Human Rights Law: Their Protection in Countries of Employment.* Oxford, UK: Clarendon Press, 1997.

Navigation and Law of the Sea

Overview of Treaties in This Category

Like aviation and outer space activities, navigating, fishing, or otherwise exploiting the high seas is inherently an international activity, subject, therefore, to international agreement and regulation. Historically, nations have distinguished between territorial waters, over which the coastal state has sovereignty, and international waters—the high seas—to which all states have equal and free access. Defining the limits of territorial waters has, however, proved a thorny problem, as evidenced by the fact that the **United Nations Convention on the Law of the Sea** was opened for signature in 1982 but did not enter into force until 1994, when a sufficient number of signatories had ratified the agreement. Other agreements relating to territorial versus international waters include **Convention on the High Seas** (1958), **Convention on the Continental Shelf** (1958), and **Convention on the Territorial Sea and the Contiguous Zone** (1958).

The most basic international law relating to navigation of the high seas deals with rescue and salvage (for example, **Convention on Assistance and Salvage at Sea**, 1910; **International Convention for the Safety of Life at Sea**, 1974; and **International Convention on Salvage**, 1989). Fishing rights is another major area in which important agreements have been concluded, and many of the more recent agreements include a strong element of conservation in treaties dealing with the exploitation of the living resources of the sea. Examples of fishing conventions include **International Convention for the Regulation of Whaling** (1946), **International Convention for the Northwest Atlantic Fisheries** (1949), **Convention for the Establishment of an Inter-American Tropical Tuna Commission** (1949), **International Convention for the High Seas Fisheries of the Pacific Ocean** (1952), **Convention on Fishing and Conservation of the Living Resources of the High Seas** (1958), **International Convention for the Conservation of Atlantic Tunas** (1966), **Convention for the Conservation of Salmon in the North Atlantic Area** (1982), **Convention for the Protection and Development of the Marine Environment of the Wider Caribbean Region** (1983), **Convention for the Prohibition of Fishing with Long Drift Nets in the South Pacific (and Protocols)** (1989), and **Law of the Sea Relating to the Conservation and Management of Fish Stocks** (1995). **Convention (with Canada) on Great Lakes Fisheries** (1954) addresses fishing issues on the inland bodies of water on which the United States and Canada border.

Another group of treaties is of particular historical interest. **Agreement (with the Netherlands) on Public Liability for Damage Caused by the Private Operation of N.S. *Savannah*, Agreement (with Netherlands) on Public Liability for Damage Caused by the N.S. *Savannah*, and Operational Agreement (with the Netherlands) for a Visit of the N.S. *Savannah*,** all concluded in 1963, are representative of a large number of special agreements drawn up between the United States and ports of call of the first nuclear-powered merchant vessel, N.S. *Savannah*, indemnifying the port-of-call nations against liability for any damage that the experimental ship might cause.

Convention on Assistance and Salvage at Sea

OFFICIAL TITLE: Convention for the Unification of Certain Rules with Respect to Assistance and Salvage at Sea
SIGNED: September 23, 1910, at Brussels
SIGNATORIES: Algeria, Antigua and Barbuda, Argentina, Australia, Austria, Bahamas, Barbados, Belgium, Belize, Brazil, Canada, Croatia, Cyprus, Dominica, Dominican Republic, Egypt, Estonia, Fiji, Finland, France, Gambia, German Democratic Republic, Germany (Federal Republic), Ghana, Greece, Grenada, Guyana, Haiti, Hungary, India, Iran, Italy, Jamaica, Japan, Kiribati, Latvia, Luxembourg, Madagascar, Malaysia, Malta, Mauritius, Mexico, Netherlands, New Zealand, Nigeria, Norway, Oman, Papua New Guinea, Paraguay, Poland, Portugal, Romania, St. Kitts and Nevis, St. Vincent and the Grenadines, Seychelles, Sierra Leone, Singapore, Solomon Islands, Spain, Sri Lanka, Switzerland, Syrian Arab Republic, Tonga, Trinidad and Tobago, Turkey, Tuvalu, Union of Soviet Socialist Republics, United Kingdom, United States, Uruguay, Yugoslavia, Zaire
IN FORCE: From March 1, 1913
OVERVIEW: A convention governing "assistance and salvage of seagoing vessels in danger, of any things on board, of freight and passage money, and also services of the same nature rendered to each other by seagoing vessels and vessels of inland navigation."

DISCUSSION:

The convention is straightforward and has stood the test of time as an agreement that continues in force into the twenty-first century. Its major provisions follow:

Article 2

Every act of assistance or salvage which has had a useful result gives a right to equitable remuneration.

No remuneration is due if the services rendered have no beneficial result. In no case shall the sum to be paid exceed the value of the property salved.

Article 3 disallows remuneration for salvage if a vessel declines salvage services. Article 4 lays down that "a tug has no right to remuneration for assistance to or salvage of the vessel she is towing or of the vessel's cargo except where she has rendered exceptional services which can not be considered as rendered in fulfilment of the contract of towage."

Articles 5 and 6 deal further with remuneration, Article 5 providing that "remuneration is due notwithstanding that the salvage services have been rendered by or to vessels belonging to the same owner," and Article 6 laying down the principle that "the amount of remuneration is fixed by agreement between the parties, and, failing agreement, by the court. The proportion in which the remuneration is to be distributed among the salvors is fixed in the same manner." Article 7 provides that "Every agreement as to assistance or salvage entered into at the moment and under the influence of danger can, at the request of either party, be annulled or modified by the court if it considers that the conditions agreed upon are not equitable." Article 8 lays down criteria for court decisions on the level of remuneration.

Article 9 lays down the principle that "No remuneration is due from the persons whose lives are saved." Article 10 fixes a limit of "two years from the day on which the operations of assistance or salvage are terminated" for the introduction of claims to remuneration. Article 11 lays down the key principle that "Every master is bound, so far as he can do so without serious danger to his vessel, her crew and passengers, to render assistance to everybody even though an enemy, found at sea in danger of being lost."

REFERENCE:
Sebenius, James K. *Negotiating the Law of the Sea*. Cambridge, MA: Harvard University Pres, 1984.

International Convention for the Regulation of Whaling

SIGNED: December 2, 1946; amendment, November 19, 1956
IN FORCE: From November 10, 1948; amendment, May 4, 1959
SIGNATORIES: Antigua and Barbuda, Argentina, Australia, Belize, Brazil, Canada, Chile, China, Costa Rica, Denmark, Dominica, Dominican Republic, Ecuador, Egypt, Finland, France, Germany, Iceland, India, Italy, Ireland, Jamaica, Japan, Kenya, Korea (Republic of), Mauritius, Mexico, Monaco, Netherlands (extended to the Netherlands Antilles), New Zealand, Norway, Oman, Panama, Peru, Philippines, Russian Federation, Saint Kitts and Nevis, Saint Lucia, Saint Vincent and the Grenadines,

Senegal, Seychelles, Solomon Islands, South Africa, Spain, Sweden, Switzerland, United Kingdom, United States, Uruguay, and Venezuela

OVERVIEW: The convention protects all species of whales from overfishing and safeguards for future generations the great natural resources represented by whale stocks.

DISCUSSION:
The convention establishes a system of international regulation for the whale fisheries with the purpose of ensuring the conservation and development of whale stocks. Toward that end, the convention created an International Whaling Commission, charged with the following:

- Encouraging research and investigation
- Collecting and analyzing statistical information
- Appraising and disseminating information concerning whaling and whale stocks

Per Article 5 of the convention, the Whaling Commission is to meet annually to adopt regulations for the conservation and utilization of whale stocks. It is to designate protected and unprotected species, open and closed seasons, open and closed areas, size limits for species, maximum catches for any one season, types of gear and apparatus to be used. Appended to the convention is a schedule containing detailed regulations for whaling. The signatories agree to take measures to enforce these regulations, and to report any infraction to them to the Whaling Commission. The adherence of all governments is invited.

REFERENCE:
Stoett, Peter J. *The International Politics of Whaling*. Vancouver: University of British Columbia, 1997.

International Convention for the Northwest Atlantic Fisheries

SIGNED: February 8, 1949, at Washington, D.C.
SIGNATORIES: Canada, France, Iceland, Newfoundland, United Kingdom, United States
IN FORCE: From July 3, 1950
OVERVIEW: A multilateral convention for the investigation, protection, and conservation of the fisheries of the Northwest Atlantic Ocean to make possible the maintenance of a maximum sustained catch from these fisheries.

DISCUSSION:
Article 1 defines the area to which the convention applies, in terms of precise longitude and latitude, as the northwest Atlantic, off the coasts of Greenland, the northern United States, and the Canadian coasts of Quebec, New Brunswick, Nova Scotia, and Cape Breton Island. The convention creates an International Commission to regulate fishing in this area and specifically to monitor, study, and review the level of population of certain commercially significant fish species, making recom-

mendations and enacting rules governing the taking of these species. The convention also allows for the creation of various expert panels and of advisory groups, made up of scientists, fishermen, and others with practical expertise in the field of the commercial fishing industry.

The recommendations and guidance of the International Commission is not to be binding on the signatories, but the signatories agree to meet to discuss and potentially adopt action based on the work of the commission.

REFERENCE:

Vicuna, Francisco Orrego. *The Changing International Law of High Seas Fisheries.* London and New York: Cambridge University Press, 1999.

Convention for the Establishment of an Inter-American Tropical Tuna Commission

SIGNED: May 31, 1949, at Washington, D.C.

SIGNATORIES: Canada, Costa Rica, Ecuador, France, Japan, Mexico, Nicaragua, Panama, United States, Vanuatu

IN FORCE: March 3, 1950

OVERVIEW: A convention intended to maintain populations of yellow fin and skipjack tuna in the eastern Pacific Ocean such that maximum sustained catches are consistently yielded.

DISCUSSION:

The principal provision of the convention is the creation of an Inter-American Tropical Tuna Commission, which is charged with investigating the abundance, biology, and ecology of the tuna, as well as of fishes used as bait in the tuna fisheries. The commission is to collect, analyze, and publish information useful to the signatories and to make recommendations for joint, cooperative action by the signatories to maintain tuna stocks.

REFERENCE:

Vicuna, Francisco Orrego. *The Changing International Law of High Seas Fisheries.* London and New York: Cambridge University Press, 1999.

International Convention for the High Seas Fisheries of the North Pacific Ocean

SIGNED: May 9, 1952, at Tokyo

SIGNATORIES: Canada, Japan, United States

IN FORCE: From June 12, 1953

OVERVIEW: A convention establishing the International North Pacific Fisheries Commission, with the objective of ensuring "the maximum sustained productivity of the fishery resources of the North Pacific Ocean."

DISCUSSION:

The International North Pacific Fisheries Commission, established by the convention and consisting of representatives from the three signatory nations, is charged with the following functions:

- Study fish stocks enumerated in an annex subjoined to the convention.
- Determine which, if any, stocks should be subject to "abstention" from harvest.
- Permit other species to be added to the annex of resources subject to study and protection.
- Study other fish stocks to determine conservation needs.
- Recommend joint conservation measures as appropriate.
- Monitor compliance with conservation measures taken.
- Enact appropriate regulations and penalties.

Much of the convention details procedures and standards for study and for basing recommendations on study. The convention also addresses composition and financing of the Commission, as well as procedures for arbitration and the resolution of disputes.

REFERENCE:

Vicuna, Francisco Orrego. *The Changing International Law of High Seas Fisheries.* London and New York: Cambridge University Press, 1999.

Convention (with Canada) on Great Lakes Fisheries

SIGNED: September 10, 1954, at Washington, D.C.

SIGNATORIES: Canada vs. United States

IN FORCE: From October 11, 1955

OVERVIEW: A convention to inaugurate a program of joint and coordinated efforts to "determine the need for and the type of measures which will make possible the maximum sustained productivity in Great Lakes fisheries."

DISCUSSION:

Both the United States and Canada extensively fish the Great Lakes, and, by the mid 1950s, it was apparent that some of the Great Lakes fisheries were in decline, in part the result of damage caused by the parasitic sea lamprey. By this convention, Canada and the United States agree to establish the Great Lakes Fishery Commission, composed equally of Canadian and American representatives. All decisions and recommendations of the commission are to be the result of agreement by both nations.

The commission is charged with the following:

- Formulation of research programs to promote maximum sustained productivity of the fisheries
- Coordinate any subsequent research
- Recommend appropriate national and international measures

- Formulate a program to eradicate or minimize the sea lamprey populations in the convention area
- Publish scientific and other information as appropriate

REFERENCES:
None

Convention on the Continental Shelf

SIGNED: April 29, 1958, at Geneva, Switzerland
IN FORCE: From June 10, 1964
SIGNATORIES: Afghanistan, Albania, Argentina, Australia, Belarus, Bolivia, Bulgaria, Cambodia, Canada, Chile, China, Colombia, Costa Rica, Cuba, Cyprus, Czechoslovakia, Denmark, Dominican Republic, Ecuador, Fiji, Finland, France, Germany, Ghana, Greece, Guatemala, Haiti, Iceland, Indonesia, Iran, Ireland, Israel, Jamaica, Kenya, Lebanon, Lesotho, Liberia, Madagascar, Malawi, Malaysia, Malta, Mauritius, Mexico, Nepal, Netherlands, New Zealand, Nigeria, Norway, Pakistan, Panama, Peru, Poland, Portugal, Romania, Russian Federation, Senegal, Sierra Leone, Solomon Islands, South Africa, Spain, Sri Lanka, Swaziland, Sweden, Switzerland, Thailand, Tonga, Trinidad and Tobago, Tunisia, Uganda, Ukraine, United Kingdom, United States, Uruguay, Venezuela, and Yugoslavia
OVERVIEW: The objective of the convention is to define and delimit the rights of signatory states to explore and exploit the natural resources of the continental shelf (the ocean environment adjacent to coastal areas).

DISCUSSION:
The convention acknowledges the sovereign and exclusive rights of coastal states over the continental shelf for the purpose of exploration and exploitation, but specifies that such exploration or exploitation must not cause unjustifiable interference with navigation, fishing, or the conservation of the living resources of the sea, or with oceanographic or other scientific research. The convention remains open for signature by all member states of the United Nations and by members of U.N. specialized agencies.

REFERENCES:
ACCIS Guide to United Nations Information Sources on the Environment. New York: United Nations Publications, 1989.
Nelson. Brent F. *The State Offshore.* New York: Praeger, 1991.

Convention on Fishing and Conservation of the Living Resources of the High Seas

SIGNED: April 29, 1958, at Geneva
IN FORCE: From March 20, 1966

SIGNATORIES: Afghanistan, Argentina, Australia, Belgium, Bolivia, Burkina Faso, Cambodia, Canada, Colombia, Costa Rica, Cuba, Denmark, Dominican Republic, Fiji, Finland, France, Ghana, Haiti, Iceland, Indonesia, Iran (Islamic republic of), Ireland, Israel, Jamaica, Kenya, Lebanon, Lesotho, Liberia, Madagascar, Malawi, Malaysia, Mauritius, Mexico, Nepal, Netherlands (for all parts of the Kingdom), New Zealand, Nigeria, Pakistan, Panama, Portugal, Senegal, Sierra Leone, Solomon Islands, South Africa, Spain, Sri Lanka, Switzerland, Thailand, Tonga, Trinidad and Tobago, Tunisia, Uganda, United Kingdom, United States, Uruguay, Venezuela, and Yugoslavia
OVERVIEW: Through international cooperation, the convention seeks to solve the problems involved in the conservation of the living resources of the high seas, especially considering that through the development of modern techniques some of these resources are in danger of being over-exploited.

DISCUSSION:
Article 1 begins by affirming that all states have a duty to adopt, or cooperate with other states in adopting, measures necessary for the conservation of the living resources of the high seas. These measures should be formulated with a view to securing a supply of food for human consumption. Coastal states have special interests in the high seas adjacent to their territorial seas and may unilaterally adopt conservation measures for such areas. Such measures are to be valid for other states if there is an urgent need for them, and if the measures are based on scientific findings and do not discriminate against foreign fishermen.

The convention provides for resolution of disputes by a special commission of five members, whose decision is binding on the states concerned.

REFERENCES:
Platzoder, Renate. *The 1994 United Nations Convention on the Law of the Sea: Basic Documents.* Amsterdam: Kluwer Law International, 1995.
United Nations, *The Law of the Sea: Official Text of the United Nations Convention on the Law of the Sea, with Annexes and Index.* New York: St. Martin's, 1983.

Convention on the High Seas

SIGNED: April 29, 1958, at Geneva
IN FORCE: From September 30, 1962
SIGNATORIES: Afghanistan, Albania, Argentina, Australia, Austria, Belarus, Belgium, Bolivia, Burkina Faso, Canada, Central African Republic, Colombia, Costa Rica, Cuba, Cyprus, Czechoslovakia, Cambodia, Denmark, Dominican Republic, Fiji, Finland, France, Germany, Ghana, Guatemala, Haiti, Holy See, Hungary, Iceland, Indonesia, Iran (Islamic Republic of), Ireland, Israel, Italy, Jamaica, Japan, Kenya, Lebanon, Lesotho, Liberia, Madagascar, Malawi, Malaysia, Mauritius, Mexico, Mongolia, Nepal, Netherlands (for all the parts of the

Kingdom), New Zealand, Nigeria, Pakistan, Panama, Poland, Portugal, Romania, Russian Federation, Senegal, Sierra Leone, Slovenia, Solomon Islands, South Africa, Spain, Sri Lanka, Swaziland, Switzerland, Thailand, Tonga, Trinidad and Tobago, Tunisia, Uganda, Ukraine, United Kingdom, United States, Uruguay, Venezuela, and Yugoslavia

OVERVIEW: The convention codifies the rules of international law relating to the high seas.

DISCUSSION:

The 1958 convention was an attempt to codify a doctrine first articulated by the Dutch jurist Hugo Grotius as early as 1609. Freedom of the high seas became a principle of international law in the nineteenth century and was of a piece with the laissez-faire economic theory then prevailing. Today, freedom of the high seas encompasses freedom of navigation, fishing, the laying of submarine cables and pipelines, and overflight of aircraft. However, by the second half of the twentieth century, the doctrine of freedom of the high seas often came into conflict with demands some coastal states made for increased security and customs zones, for exclusive offshore-fishing rights, for conservation of maritime resources, and for exploitation of resources, especially oil, found in continental shelves. The first United Nations Conference on the Law of the Sea, meeting at Geneva in 1958, was convened to resolve these conflicts.

The conference, with its resulting convention, succeeded to a significant degree in codifying the long-held principle of freedom of the high seas, but left unresolved a number of issues, most importantly the maximum permissible breadth of the territorial sea subject to national sovereignty.

A second conference was convened at Geneva in 1960, and a third in Caracas, in 1973, later convening in Geneva and New York City. Ultimately, this series of conferences resulted in the **United Nations Convention on the Law of the Sea** (1982), which resolved most of the issues, including that of territorial waters.

Perhaps the most important aspects of the 1958 convention concern principles of pollution avoidance and management on the high seas, including provisions that

• States will draw up regulations to prevent pollution of the sea by oil from ships and pipelines or resulting from the exploration and exploitation of the sea-bed

• States will take measures to prevent pollution of the sea by dumping of radioactive waste and to cooperate with international agencies in taking such measures to prevent pollution of the seas or airspace above them resulting from radioactive materials or other harmful agents

REFERENCES:

Platzoder, Renate. *The 1994 United Nations Convention on the Law of the Sea: Basic Documents.* Amsterdam: Kluwer Law International, 1995.

United Nations, *The Law of the Sea: Official Text of the United Nations Convention on the Law of the Sea, with Annexes and Index.* New York: St. Martin's, 1983.

Convention on the Territorial Sea and the Contiguous Zone

SIGNED: April 29, 1958, at Geneva

SIGNATORIES: Australia, Belarus, Belgium, Bosnia-Herzegovina, Bulgaria, Cambodia, Croatia, Czech Republic, Czechoslovakia, Denmark, Dominican Republic, Fiji, Finland, German Democratic Republic, Haiti, Hungary, Israel, Italy, Jamaica, Japan, Kenya, Latvia, Lesotho, Lithuania, Madagascar, Malawi, Malaysia, Malta, Mauritius, Mexico, Netherlands, Nigeria, Portugal, Romania, Sierra Leone, Slovak Republic, Slovenia, Solomon Islands, South Africa, Spain, Swaziland, Switzerland, Thailand, Tonga, Trinidad and Tobago, Uganda, Ukraine, Union of Soviet Socialist Republics, United Kingdom, United States, Venezuela, Yugoslavia

IN FORCE: From September 30, 1962

OVERVIEW: A convention defining the "territorial sea" and "contiguous zone" of the the high seas.

DISCUSSION:

The first two articles of the convention established that the coastal state's sovereignty extends over its territorial sea and to the airspace and seabed and subsoil of the seabed. A coastal state may exclude foreign nationals and vessels from fishing and from coastal trading ("cabotage") in these territorial waters. The right of "innocent passage" for merchant ships (but not warships) is established by the convention. It is the coastal state's responsibility to publish any dangers to navigation in its coastal waters.

Although innocent passage may be suspended for security reasons, the right of innocent passage through international straits may not be suspended. On the subject of the passage of warships through such straits the convention is silent.

Article 3 of the convention established rules for determining the width of the territorial sea relative to the coast. Article 7 dealt with bays and "historic bays," which present special problems for determining the extent of coastal waters.

REFERENCES:

Platzoder, Renate. *The 1994 United Nations Convention on the Law of the Sea: Basic Documents.* Amsterdam: Kluwer Law International, 1995.

United Nations, *The Law of the Sea: Official Text of the United Nations Convention on the Law of the Sea, with Annexes and Index.* New York: St. Martin's, 1983.

Agreement (with the Netherlands) on Public Liability for Damage Caused by the N.S. *Savannah*

SIGNED: February 6, 1963, at the Hague

SIGNATORIES: Netherlands vs. United States

IN FORCE: From May 22, 1963

OVERVIEW: A United States guarantee of indemnification for damage caused by the operation of the experimental nuclear-powered ship *Savannah*.

DISCUSSION:

Savannah, launched in 1959, was the world's first nuclear-powered cargo ship. Built experimentally by the United States government in an effort to demonstrate the potential of the peaceful use of nuclear power for nonmilitary shipping, *Savannah* displaced 22,000 tons, could accommodate sixty passengers, and could carry 9,400 tons of cargo. During the 1960s, *Savannah* sailed on many demonstration cruises in the Atlantic and elsewhere, but proved a financial failure, its high costs of operation discouraging commercial shippers. A special problem was the demand many governments made regarding guarantees of indemnity for any public liability resulting from damage that might be caused by *Savannah*. Some nations were reluctant to admit the ship into their ports.

Prior to sailing on a round of demonstration voyages, numerous agreements were concluded with various port-of-call countries by which the United States guaranteed indemnification for liability.

See also **Operational Agreement (with the Netherlands) for a Visit of the N.S. *Savannah*** and **Agreement (with the Netherlands) on Public Liability for Damage caused by the Private Operation of N.S. *Savannah*.**

REFERENCES:
None

Operational Agreement (with the Netherlands) for a Visit of the N.S. *Savannah*

OFFICIAL TITLE: Operational Agreement between the Kingdom of the Netherlands and the United States of America on Arrangements for a Visit of the N.S. *Savannah* to the Netherlands
SIGNED: May 20, 1963, at the Hague
SIGNATORIES: Netherlands vs. United States
IN FORCE: From May 22, 1963
OVERVIEW: An agreement on conditions for the entry of N.S. *Savannah* into the Netherlands.

DISCUSSION:

For background on this agreement see **Agreement (with Netherlands) on Public Liability for Damage Caused by the N.S. *Savannah*.**

The agreement, typical of numerous agreements with other port-of-call countries relating to the *Savannah*, is an invitation to bring the ship into Netherlands waters and also an agreement on safety and other procedures relating to the entry of the ship into these waters.

Provisions include:
- Advance notification of arrival of *Savannah* in Netherlands waters
- Provision of a safety assessment and operations manual in advance of entry into Netherlands waters
- A guarantee that the ship will be operated in accordance with the safety assessment and operations manual
- A set of agreements on the use of the Rotterdam port area
- An undertaking to allow full and free inspection of the ship
- A guarantee that no radioactive waste would be dumped in Netherlands waters or on Netherlands territory
- A guarantee of advance warning of potential environmental hazard

See also **Agreement (with the Netherlands) on Public Liability for Damage caused by the N.S. *Savannah*** and **Agreement (with the Netherlands) on Public Liability for Damage caused by the Private Operation of N.S. *Savannah*.**

REFERENCES:
None

Agreement (with the Netherlands) on Public Liability for Damage Caused by the Private Operation of N.S. *Savannah*

OFFICIAL TITLE: Exchange of Notes Constituting an Agreement Regarding the Applicability of Agreement between the Government of the Kingdom of the Netherlands and the Government of the United States of America on Public Liability for Damage Caused by the N.S. *Savannah*
SIGNED: February 6, 1963, at the Hague
SIGNATORIES: Netherlands vs. United States
IN FORCE: September 8, 1965
OVERVIEW: A revision of **Agreement (with Netherlands) on Public Liability for Damage Caused by the N.S. *Savannah*** to reflect the transfer of operation of the vessel to private hands.

DISCUSSION:

For background on this agreement see **Agreement (with Netherlands) on Public Liability for Damage Caused by the N.S. *Savannah*.** This agreement, with the Netherlands, is typical of numerous agreements the United States concluded guaranteeing indemnification of any mishaps that might occur when the experimental nuclear-powered *Savannah* visited foreign ports. After operation of the ship was transferred from the United States Atomic Energy Commission to a private company, many governments required explicit guarantees that the United States would continue to accept public liability.

REFERENCES:
None

Convention for the International Council for the Exploration of the Sea

SIGNED: September 12, 1964, at Copenhagen, Denmark

SIGNATORIES: Canada, Denmark, Finland, France, Germany, Iceland, Ireland, Netherlands, Norway, Poland, Portugal, Russian Federation, Spain, Sweden, United Kingdom, United States

IN FORCE: From July 22, 1968

OVERVIEW: Provides a new and updated constitution for the International Council for the Exploration of the Sea, which was established in 1902.

DISCUSSION:

The principal provision of the convention is the definition of the scope and constitution of the International Council, with emphasis on its mission to promote and encourage research and investigations for the study of the sea, especially with regard its living resources. The convention specifies that the scope of the Council is the Atlantic Ocean and its adjacent seas, with emphasis on the north Atlantic. The convention further specified that the Council is to maintain working arrangements with other international organizations.

REFERENCES:

Platzoder, Renate. *The 1994 United Nations Convention on the Law of the Sea: Basic Documents.* Amsterdam: Kluwer Law International, 1995.

United Nations, *The Law of the Sea: Official Text of the United Nations Convention on the Law of the Sea, with Annexes and Index.* New York: St. Martin's, 1983.

International Convention for the Conservation of Atlantic Tunas

SIGNED: May 14, 1966, Rio de Janeiro

SIGNATORIES: Angola, Benin, Brazil, Canada, Cape Verde, Côte d'Ivoire, Cuba, Equatorial Guinea, France, Gabon, Ghana, Guinea, Japan, Korea (Republic), Morocco, Portugal, Russian Federation, Sao Tome and Principe, Senegal, South Africa, Spain, United States, Uruguay, Venezuela

IN FORCE: From March 21, 1969

OVERVIEW: A convention intended to maintain populations of tuna and tuna-like fish in the Atlantic Ocean at levels permitting the maximum sustainable catch for food and other purposes.

DISCUSSION:

The scope of the convention is the Atlantic Ocean and seas adjacent. The principal provision is the establishment of an International Commission for the Conservation of Atlantic Tunas, which is responsible for the following:

- Research into the abundance, ecology, and biometry of tunas, as well as the oceanography of their environment and the effects of human and natural factors on their abundance

- Making recommendations for the maintenance of the populations of tuna and tuna-like fish

REFERENCE:

Vicuna, Francisco Orrego. *The Changing International Law of High Seas Fisheries.* London and New York: Cambridge University Press, 1999.

International Convention for the Safety of Life at Sea

SIGNED: November 1, 1974, at London

SIGNATORIES: Argentina, Bahamas, Belgium, Berlin (West), Brazil, Canada, Cape Verde, Chile, China, Colombia, Czechoslovakia, Denmark, Dominican Republic, France, German Democratic Republic, Germany (Federal Republic), Greece, Hong Kong, Hungary, India, Israel, Italy, Japan, Kuwait, Liberia, Mexico, Netherlands, Netherlands Antilles, Norway, Panama, Peru, Romania, South Africa, Spain, Sweden, Tonga, Trinidad and Tobago, Tunisia, Turkey, Ukrainian Soviet Socialist Republic, Union of Soviet Socialist Republics, United Kingdom, United States, Uruguay, Yemen, Yugoslavia

IN FORCE: May 25, 1980

OVERVIEW: A "common agreement [on] uniform principles and rules" to promote safety of life at sea.

DISCUSSION:

The convention integrates existing national laws and regulations relating to the safety of life at sea and sets minimum international safety standards based on them. Each contracting state undertakes to "promulgate all laws, decrees, orders and regulations and to take all other steps which may be necessary to give the . . . Convention full and complete effect."

REFERENCES:
None

United Nations Convention on the Law of the Sea

SIGNED: December 10, 1982, at Montego Bay

SIGNATORIES: Algeria, Angola, Antigua and Barbuda, Argentina, Australia, Austria, Bahamas, Bahrain, Barbados, Belgium, Belize, Benin, Bolivia, Bosnia and Herzegovina, Botswana, Brazil, Brunei Darussalam, Bulgaria, Burkina Faso, Cameroon, Canada, Cape Verde, Chile, China, Comoros, Cook Islands, Costa Rica, Côte d'Ivoire, Croatia, Cuba, Cyprus, Czech Republic, Democratic Republic of the Congo, Denmark, Djibouti, Dominica, Egypt, Equatorial Guinea, European Community, Fiji, Finland, Former Yugoslav Republic of Macedonia, France, Gabon, Gambia, Georgia, Germany, Ghana, Greece, Grenada, Guatemala, Guinea, Guinea-Bissau, Guyana, Haiti, Holy See, Honduras, Iceland, India, Indonesia, Iraq, Ireland, Italy, Jamaica, Japan, Jordan, Kenya, Korea (Republic), Kuwait, Lao People's

Democratic Republic, Lebanon, Luxembourg, Malaysia, Maldives, Mali, Malta, Marshall Islands, Mauritania, Mauritius, Mexico, Micronesia (Federated States of), Monaco, Mongolia, Morocco, Mozambique, Myanmar, Namibia, Nauru, Nepal, Netherlands, New Zealand, Nicaragua, Nigeria, Norway, Oman, Pakistan, Palau, Panama, Papua New Guinea, Paraguay, Philippines, Poland, Portugal, Romania, Russian Federation, Saint Kitts and Nevis, Saint Lucia, Saint Vincent and the Grenadines, Samoa, Sao Tome and Principe, Saudi Arabia, Senegal, Seychelles, Sierra Leone, Singapore, Slovakia, Slovenia, Solomon Islands, Somalia, South Africa, Spain, Sri Lanka, Sudan, Suriname, Swaziland, Sweden, Switzerland, Togo, Tonga, Trinidad and Tobago, Tunisia, Uganda, Ukraine, United Kingdom, United Republic of Tanzania, United States, Uruguay, Vanuatu, Vietnam, Yemen, Yugoslavia, Zambia, Zimbabwe

IN FORCE: From November 16, 1994

OVERVIEW: A comprehensive international treaty consisting of 320 articles and nine annexes, governing all aspects of ocean space, such as delimitation, environmental control, marine scientific research, economic and commercial activities, transfer of technology and the settlement of disputes relating to ocean matters.

DISCUSSION:

This ambitious agreement, which is intended to unify and standardize an old and diverse body of international law governing the sea, was subject to much controversy and revision. It awaited coming into force for a dozen years.

The principal features are as follows:

- Coastal states exercise sovereignty over their territorial sea, the limit of which is not to exceed twelve nautical miles.
- Foreign vessels are allowed "innocent passage" through territorial waters.
- Ships and aircraft of all countries are allowed "transit passage" through straits used for international navigation; however, states bordering the straits can regulate aspects of passage.
- Archipelagic states, made up of a group or groups of closely related islands and interconnecting waters, have sovereignty over a sea area enclosed by straight lines drawn between the outermost points of the islands; however, all other states enjoy the right of archipelagic passage through such designated sea lanes.
- Coastal states have sovereign rights in a 200-nautical mile exclusive economic zone (EEZ) with respect to natural resources and certain economic activities, and they exercise jurisdiction over marine science research and environmental protection.
- All other states have freedom of navigation and overflight in the EEZ, as well as freedom to lay submarine cables and pipelines in these zones.
- Land-locked and geographically disadvantaged states have the right to participate on an equitable basis in exploitation of an appropriate part of the surplus of the living resources

of the EEZs of coastal states of the same region or sub-region.

- Highly migratory species of fish and marine mammals are accorded special protection in EEZs.
- Coastal states have sovereign rights over the continental shelf (the national area of the seabed) for exploring and exploiting it. The shelf can extend at least 200 nautical miles from the shore—even more under specified circumstances.
- Coastal states share with the international community part of the revenue derived from exploiting resources from any part of their shelf beyond the 200-mile limit.
- The Commission on the Limits of the Continental Shelf shall make recommendations to states on the shelf's outer boundaries when it extends beyond 200 miles
- All states enjoy the traditional freedoms of navigation, overflight, scientific research and fishing on the high seas.
- All states are obliged to adopt, or cooperate with other states in adopting, measures to manage and conserve living resources.
- The limits of the territorial sea, the exclusive economic zone, and continental shelf of islands are determined in accordance with rules applicable to land territory; however, rocks that could not sustain human habitation or economic life of their own have no economic zone or continental shelf.
- States bordering enclosed or semi-enclosed seas are expected to cooperate in managing living resources, environmental and research policies and activities
- Land-locked states have the right of access to and from the sea and enjoy freedom of transit through the territory of transit states.
- States are bound to prevent and control marine pollution and are liable for damage caused by violation of their international obligations to combat such pollution.
- All marine scientific research in the EEZ and on the continental shelf is subject to the consent of the coastal state; however, in most cases, the coastal state is obliged to grant consent to other states when the research is to be conducted for peaceful purposes and fulfills specified criteria.
- States are bound to promote the development and transfer of marine technology "on fair and reasonable terms and conditions," with proper regard for all legitimate interests.
- Signatory states are obliged to settle by peaceful means their disputes concerning the interpretation or application of this convention. Disputes may be submitted to the International Tribunal for the Law of the Sea (established by the convention), to the International Court of Justice, or to arbitration. Conciliation is also available.

REFERENCES:

Platzoder, Renate. *The 1994 United Nations Convention on the Law of the Sea: Basic Documents.* Amsterdam: Kluwer Law International, 1995.
United Nations, *The Law of the Sea: Official Text of the United Nations Convention on the Law of the Sea, with Annexes and Index.* New York: St. Martin's, 1983.

Convention for the Conservation of Salmon in the North Atlantic Ocean

SIGNED: March 2, 1982, at Reykjavik, Iceland

SIGNATORIES: Canada, Denmark, European Economic Community, Finland, Iceland, Norway, Sweden, United States

IN FORCE: From October 1, 1983

OVERVIEW: An international convention to promote the conservation, restoration, enhancement, and rational management of salmon stock in the North Atlantic Ocean through a program of international cooperation, including the acquisition, analysis, and dissemination of scientific information.

DISCUSSION:

The convention prohibits the fishing of salmon in certain areas, and it establishes the North Atlantic Salmon Conservation Organization to regulate salmon fishing. The signatories undertake to ensure that the provisions of the convention, including any regulatory measures pursuant to the convention, are enforced and made effective. All of the signatories undertake to to provide information on statistical, scientific, legal, and regulatory measures and programs relating to the conservation, restoration, and enhancement of salmon stocks. This includes the preparation of annual reports relating to the abundance of salmon stocks.

REFERENCE:

Vicuna, Francisco Orrego. *The Changing International Law of High Seas Fisheries.* London and New York: Cambridge University Press, 1999.

Convention for the Protection and Development of the Marine Environment of the Wider Caribbean Region

SIGNED: March 24, 1983, at Cartagena de Indias, Colombia

SIGNATORIES: Antigua and Barbuda, Barbados, Colombia, Cuba, France, Grenada, Guatemala, Jamaica, Mexico, Netherlands, Panama, St. Lucia, Saint Vincent and Grenadines, Trinidad and Tobago, United Kingdom, United States, Venezuela

IN FORCE: From October 11, 1986

OVERVIEW: A convention to protect and manage the marine environment and coastal areas of the Wider Caribbean region.

DISCUSSION:

Signatories agree to the following provisions:

- To take all necessary measures to prevent, reduce, and control pollution of the area covered by the convention, especially pollution from ships, from dumping, from land-based sources, from activities relating to exploration and exploitation of the sea bed, and from airborne pollution

- To protect and preserve rare or fragile ecosystems as well as the habitat of depleted, threatened, or endangered species and other marine life in specially designated protected areas

- To cooperate in handling pollution emergencies in the convention area

- To cooperate in assessing environmental impacts in the convention area, as well as in exchanging data and scientific and technical information

- To establish rules and procedures for the determination for liability and compensation for damage resulting from pollution of the convention area

REFERENCES:
None

Agreement (with China) Concerning Fisheries of the Coasts of the United States

SIGNED: July 23, 1985, at Washington, D.C.

SIGNATORIES: China vs. United States

IN FORCE: From November 19, 1985

OVERVIEW: An agreement regulating Chinese commercial fishing in the waters of the United States economic zone.

DISCUSSION:

By presidential proclamation of March 10, 1983, the United States declared an exclusive economic zone within 200 nautical miles of its coasts, within which the United States has sovereign rights to explore, exploit, conserve and manage all fish and other resources. In consideration of this, the present agreement was concluded "to promote effective conservation, rational management and the achievement of optimum yield in the fisheries of mutual interest off the coasts of the United States . . . and to establish a common understanding of the principles and procedures under which fishing may be conducted by nationals and vessels of the People's Republic of China for the living resources over which the United States has sovereign rights."

The substance of the agreement lays down the terms and conditions under which foreign vessels may harvest "that portion of the total allowable catch for a specific fishery that will not be harvested by United States fishing vessels." In return for permission to fish within the United States economic zone, China undertakes to "cooperate with and assist the United States in the development of the United States fishing industry and the increase of United States fishery exports by taking such measures as reducing or removing impediments to the importation and sale of United States fishery products."

REFERENCE:

Vicuna, Francisco Orrego. *The Changing International Law of High Seas Fisheries.* London and New York: Cambridge University Press, 1999.

International Convention on Salvage

SIGNED: April 28, 1989, at London

SIGNATORIES: Canada, Denmark, Finland, Germany, Ireland, Italy, Mexico, Netherlands, Nigeria, Norway, Poland, Russian Federation, Spain, Sweden, Switzerland, United Kingdom, United States

IN FORCE: Not yet in force

OVERVIEW: An international convention laying down uniform rules regarding salvage operations in the light of the need for timely operations and to protect the environment.

DISCUSSION:

The convention applies principally to the salvage of commercial vessels in navigable waters and provides for the rights and duties of a salvor and the contents of contracts of salvage. Of particular importance is Article 9, which recognizes the right of a coastal state to take measures in accordance with international law to protect its coastline from pollution or threat of pollution from a casualty or acts related to a casualty. Such a state may give directions regarding salvage operations, provided that the state takes into account the need to ensure the success of the salvage operation in order to save life or property and to prevent damage to the environment. Articles 13 and 14 lay down that special compensation is payable by the owner of the vessel to a salvor if a casualty vessel or its cargo threatens environmental damage and if the compensation has not been paid under the normal criteria for fixing reward.

REFERENCES:

Platzoder, Renate. *The 1994 United Nations Convention on the Law of the Sea: Basic Documents.* Amsterdam: Kluwer Law International, 1995.

United Nations, *The Law of the Sea: Official Text of the United Nations Convention on the Law of the Sea, with Annexes and Index.* New York: St. Martin's, 1983.

Convention for the Prohibition of Fishing with Long Drift Nets in the South Pacific

SIGNED: November 24, 1989, at Wellington, New Zealand

SIGNATORIES: Australia, Cook Islands, Federated States of Micronesia, France, Kiribati, Marshall Islands, Nauru, New Zealand, Niue, Palau, Solomon Islands, Tokelau, Tuvalu, United States, Vanuatu

IN FORCE: From May 17, 1991

OVERVIEW: The convention restricts and prohibits the use of drift nets in the South Pacific in order to conserve marine living resources.

DISCUSSION:

Drift-net fishing is a method by which large numbers of fish may be taken, using an array of large nets that are dragged by drift-ing vessels. After the nets are hauled, the fish are shaken out with special shaking machines. In the South Pacific, drift-net fishing threatens the abundance of fish stocks and is an ecological menace; therefore, the signatories to the convention agree to the following:

- To take measures to discourage the use of drift nets by prohibiting their use and by restricting the transhipment of drift-net catches, the importation of such catches, and by restricting access of vessels using drift nets to ports
- To take appropriate measures to ensure the application of the convention and to cooperate in surveillance and enforcement measures
- To cooperate with signatories and non-signatories to implement the convention
- To participate in the establishment of the South Pacific Forum Fisheries Agency, charged with coordinating the implementation of the convention

REFERENCE:

Vicuna, Francisco Orrego. *The Changing International Law of High Seas Fisheries.* London and New York: Cambridge University Press, 1999.

Law of the Sea Relating to the Conservation and Management of Fish Stocks

OFFICIAL TITLE: United Nations Agreement for the Implementation of the Provisions of the United Nations Convention on the Law of the Sea of 10 December 1982 relating to the Conservation and Management of Straddling Fish Stocks and Highly Migratory Fish Stocks

SIGNED: August 4, 1995, at New York

SIGNATORIES: Algeria, Argentina, Australia, Austria, Bhamas, Barbados, Belgium, Belize, Benin, Bolivia, Brunei Darussalam, Bulgaria, Chile, China, Cook Islands, Côte d'Ivoire, Croatia, Cyprus, Czech Republic, Equatorial Guinea, European Community, Fiji, Finland, Former Yugoslav Republic of Macedonia, France, Gabon, Georgia, Germany, Greece, Grenada, Guatemala, Guinea, Haiti, Iceland, India, Ireland, Italy, Jamaica, Japan, Jordan, Kenya, Korea (Republic), Lao People's Democratic Republic, Lebanon, Malaysia, Malta, Mauritania, Mauritius, Micronesia (Federated States), Monaco, Mongolia, Mozambique, Myanmar, Namibia, Nauru, Nepal, Netherlands, New Zealand, Nigeria, Norway, Oman, Pakistan, Palau, Panama, Papua New Guinea, Paraguay, Peru, Philippines, Poland, Portugal, Romania, Russian Federation, Samoa, Saudi Arabia, Senegal, Seychelles, Sierra Leone, Singapore, Slovakia, Slovenia, Solomon Islands, Somalia, South Africa, Spain, Sri Lanka, Suriname, Sweden, Togo, Tonga, Trinidad and Tobago, Uganda, Ukraine, United Republic of Tanzania, Vanuatu, Yugoslavia, Zambia, Zimbabwe

IN FORCE: Not yet in force

OVERVIEW: A convention that sets out principles for the conservation and management of fish stocks that straddle territorial waters of more than one state or that migrate from one territorial water to another.

DISCUSSION:

This agreement elaborates on the fundamental principle established in the **United Nations Convention on the Law of the Sea**, which lays down that states should cooperate to ensure conservation and promote the objective of the optimum utilization of fisheries resources both within and beyond the exclusive economic zone (EEZ). To achieve this objective, the agreement establishes a framework for cooperation in the conservation and management of those resources. It promotes good order in the oceans through the effective management and conservation of high seas resources by establishing, among other things, the following:

- Detailed minimum international standards for the conservation and management of straddling fish stocks and highly migratory fish stocks
- Means for ensuring that measures taken for the conservation and management of straddling and migratory fish stocks in areas under national jurisdiction and in the adjacent high seas are compatible and coherent
- Means for ensuring that there are effective mechanisms for compliance and enforcement of conservation measures on the high seas
- Recognition of the special requirements of developing signatory nations in relation to conservation and management as well as the development and participation in fisheries for the two types of fish stocks

Although the United States has signed the **United Nations Convention on the Law of the Sea**, it has yet to sign this supplementary convention.

REFERENCE:

Vicuna, Francisco Orrego. *The Changing International Law of High Seas Fisheries.* London and New York: Cambridge University Press, 1999.

International Convention on Arrest of Ships

SIGNED: Adopted March 12, 1999, at Geneva

SIGNATORIES: Opened for signature from September 1, 1999 to August 31, 2000.

IN FORCE: Not yet in force

OVERVIEW: ". . . a legal instrument establishing international uniformity in the field of arrest of ships which takes account of recent developments in related fields . . ."

DISCUSSION:

As used in this convention, *arrest* "means any detention or restriction on removal of a ship by order of a Court to secure a maritime claim, but does not include the seizure of a ship in execution or satisfaction of a judgment or other enforceable instrument."

The principal provisions are found in articles 2 and 3:

Article 2
Powers of Arrest

1. A ship may be arrested or released from arrest only under the authority of a Court of the State Party in which the arrest is effected.

2. A ship may only be arrested in respect of a maritime claim but in respect of no other claim.

3. A ship may be arrested for the purpose of obtaining security notwithstanding that, by virtue of a jurisdiction clause or arbitration clause in any relevant contract, or otherwise, the maritime claim in respect of which the arrest is effected is to be adjudicated in a State other than the State where the arrest is effected, or is to be arbitrated, or is to be adjudicated subject to the law of another State.

4. Subject to the provisions of this Convention, the procedure relating to the arrest of a ship or its release shall be governed by the law of the State in which the arrest was effected or applied for.

Article 3
Exercise of right of arrest

1. Arrest is permissible of any ship in respect of which a maritime claim is asserted if:

(a) the person who owned the ship at the time when the maritime claim arose is liable for the claim and is owner of the ship when the arrest is effected; or

(b) the demise charterer of the ship at the time when the maritime claim arose is liable for the claim and is demise charterer or owner of the ship when the arrest is effected; or

(c) the claim is based upon a mortgage or a "hypothèque" or a charge of the same nature on the ship; or

(d) the claim relates to the ownership or possession of the ship; or

(e) the claim is against the owner, demise charterer, manager or operator of the ship and is secured by a maritime lien which is granted or arises under the law of the State where the arrest is applied for.

2. Arrest is also permissible of any other ship or ships which, when the arrest is effected, is or are owned by the person who is liable for the maritime claim and who was, when the claim arose:

(a) owner of the ship in respect of which the maritime claim arose; or

(b) demise charterer, time charterer or voyage charterer of that ship.

This provision does not apply to claims in respect of ownership or possession of a ship.

3. Notwithstanding the provisions of paragraphs 1 and 2 of this article, the arrest of a ship which is not owned by the person liable for

the claim shall be permissible only if, under the law of the State where the arrest is applied for, a judgment in respect of that claim can be enforced against that ship by judicial or forced sale of that ship.

Subsequent articles address uniform procedures for release from arrest, the right of rearrest, and the rights of owners and charterers.

REFERENCES:

Platzoder, Renate. *The 1994 United Nations Convention on the Law of the Sea: Basic Documents.* Amsterdam: Kluwer Law International, 1995.

United Nations, *The Law of the Sea: Official Text of the United Nations Convention on the Law of the Sea, with Annexes and Index.* New York: St. Martin's, 1983.

Human and Political Rights

General Assistance and Disaster Relief Cooperation

Overview of Treaties in This Category

The United States compiled a long history in the post-World War II years of providing general economic assistance to developing nations and disaster relief assistance to various countries in times of emergency.

In addition to agreements specifying the type, amount, and terms of financial assistance, this section includes agreements securing exemption from duties and internal taxation for disaster-relief and aid personnel, as well as equipment and supplies (see, for example, **Agreement [with Chile] on Relief Supplies and Equipment** of 1955).

Non-emergency aid programs addressed by the agreements in this section include general programs of aid (for example, **Agreement [with Senegal] Relating to Economic, Financial, Technical and Related Assistance**, 1961) and programs directly involving the Peace Corps (for example, **Agreement [with El Salvador] Relating to the Peace Corps Program**, 1961).

Another class of agreement includes multilateral conventions on procedures in case of disaster or emergency. See, for example, **Convention on Assistance in the Case of a Nuclear Accident** (1986), **Convention on Early Notification of a Nuclear Accident** (1986), **Convention on the Transboundary Effects of Industrial Accidents** (1992), and **Tampere Convention on Emergency Telecommunications** (1998).

Agreement (with Chile) on Relief Supplies and Equipment

OFFICIAL TITLE: Exchange of Notes Constituting an Agreement Relating to Duty-Free Entry and Exemption from Internal Taxation of Relief Supplies and Equipment

SIGNED: April 5, 1955, at Santiago, Chile

SIGNATORIES: Chile vs. United States

IN FORCE: From signing

OVERVIEW: An agreement to facilitate entry of disaster relief supplies and equipment.

DISCUSSION:

To satisfy requirements of national as well as international law, the United States concludes duty- and internal tax-exemption agreements with countries to which it extends emergency disaster assistance. In this case, the United States government is securing such exemption for "supplies and goods approved by the Government of the United States, donated to or purchased by United States voluntary, non-profit relief and rehabilitation agencies, and consigned to such organizations, including branches of these agencies in Chile, for distribution in Chile."

Additionally:

• Personal items used by relief personnel (such as tobacco, cigars, cigarettes, alcoholic beverages) are not included in the exemption.

• The cost of internal transportation of relief supplies within Chile are to be borne by Chile.

REFERENCES:
Leaning, Jennifer, et al, eds. *Humanitarian Crises: The Medical and Public Health Response.* Cambridge, MA: Harvard University Press, 1999.
Middleton, Neil, and Phil O'Keefe. *Disaster and Development: The Politics of Humanitarian Aid.* Annandale, Australia: Pluto Press, 1998.

Agreement (with Senegal) Relating to Economic, Financial, Technical and Related Assistance

SIGNED: May 13, 1961, at Washington, D.C.

SIGNATORIES: Senegal vs. United States

IN FORCE: From signing

OVERVIEW: An agreement whereby the United States undertakes to furnish economic, financial, technical and related assistance "as may be requested by . . . Senegal and approved by . . . the United States."

DISCUSSION:

This open-ended agreement for United States assistance is limited only by the following general provisions:

• That the assistance furnished must be requested by Senegal and approved by the United States

• That Senegal contribute to projects for which assistance is requested as much as it is capable of contributing

• That the United States be permitted to observe and review assistance programs

• That funds and supplies be afforded adequate security

• That supplies and equipment furnished for assistance to Senegal be accorded tax- and duty-free status

REFERENCE:
Knight, Derrick. *A Burning Hunger: Three Decades of Personal Struggles Against Poverty—A West African Experience.* London: Panos/Christian Aid, 1994.

Agreement (with El Salvador) Relating to the Peace Corps Program

OFFICIAL TITLE: Exchange of Notes Constituting an Agreement Relating to the Peace Corps Program
SIGNED: August 11 and 13 and November 20, 1961, at San Salvador
SIGNATORIES: El Salvador vs. United States
IN FORCE: From November 13, 1961
OVERVIEW: An early agreement for placing Peace Corps volunteers in a host country.

DISCUSSION:

The Peace Corps was created by executive order of John F. Kennedy early in 1961. El Salvador was among the first nations to receive volunteers. under the program. The agreement with El Salvador established the model for subsequent agreement with other hosts:

- Peace Corps volunteers were to receive "equitable treatment" from the host nation and would receive the same protection and aid as nationals of that nation.
- El Salvador would receive a "Peace Corps representative and such staff and other personnel as they are acceptable to the Government of El Salvador."
- Peace Corps personnel and equipment would be exempt from taxation.

REFERENCES:
Fischer, Fritz. *Making Them Like Us: Peace Corps Volunteers in the 1960s.* Washington, D.C.: Smithsonian Institution Press, 1998.
Hoffman, Elizabeth Cobbs. *All You Need Is Love: The Peace Corps and the Spirit of the 1960s.* Cambridge, MA: Harvard University Press, 1998.
Schwarz, Karen. *What You Can Do for Your Country: Inside the Peace Corps: A Thirty-Year History.* New York: Anchor, 1993.
Searles, P. David. *The Peace Corps Experience: Challenge and Change, 1969-1976.* Lexington: University of Kentucky Press, 1997.

General Agreement (with Jamaica) for Economic, Technical and Related Assistance

SIGNED: October 24, 1963, at Kingston, Jamaica
SIGNATORIES: Jamaica vs. United States
IN FORCE: From signing
OVERVIEW: An agreement whereby the United States undertakes to furnish economic, financial, technical and related assistance "as may be requested by . . . Jamaica and approved by . . . the United States."

DISCUSSION:

This general agreement is based on concurrence between Jamaica and the United States "upon the need for specific plans of action designed to foster economic progress and improvements in the welfare and level of living of the people of Jamaica."

To the end of supplying this need, the United States agrees to furnish "economic, financial, technical and related assistance "as may be requested by . . . Jamaica and approved by . . . the United States."

Major provisions of the agreement include the following:

- Assistance is for the purpose of aiding Jamaica "in its national development through the effective use of its own resources
- An undertaking by Jamaica to contribute to projects for which assistance is requested as much as it is capable of contributing
- An undertaking by Jamaica to permit the United States to observe and review assistance programs
- An undertaking by Jamaica to afford adequate security to funds and supplies
- An undertaking by Jamaica to exempt from taxation all supplies and equipment furnished for assistance

REFERENCE:
Kirton, Claremont. *Jamaica: Debt and Poverty.* Amherst, NY: Prometheus Books, 1992.

Agreement (with the Philippines) on the Use of the Special Fund for Education for an Agrarian Reform Program

OFFICIAL TITLE: Exchange of Notes Constituting an Agreement on the Use of the Special Fund for Education for the Project for Assistance to the Philippine Agrarian Reform Education Program
SIGNED: March 21, 1972, at Manila, Philippines
SIGNATORIES: Philippines vs. United States
IN FORCE: From signing
OVERVIEW: An agreement establishing a special trust fund, using the Special Fund for Education, to finance agrarian reform education programs.

DISCUSSION:

By this agreement the United States approves the use of $1,281,935 remaining in the Special Fund for Education to establish a permanent trust fund, earnings from which shall be used for agrarian reform education programs. The thrust of United States grants-in-aid programs has always been to assist governments to develop their own resources.

REFERENCES:
Putzel, James. *A Captive Land: the Politics of Agrarian Reform in the Philippines.* London: Catholic Institute for International Relations; New York: Monthly Review Press, 1992.
Putzel, James, and John Cunnington. *Gaining Ground: Agrarian Reform in the Philippines.* London: War on Want, 1989.
Riedinger, Jeffrey M. *Agrarian Reform in the Philippines. Democratic Transitions and Redistributive Reform.* Palo Alto, CA: Stanford University Press, 1995.

Understanding (with Japan) Relating to Final Settlement of Obligations under the Postwar Economic Assistance Agreement

OFFICIAL TITLE: Exchange of Notes Constituting an Understanding Relating to Final Settlement of Obligations under the Postwar Economic Assistance Agreement and Certain Agricultural Commodity Agreements

SIGNED: April 30, 1973, at Washington, D.C.

SIGNATORIES: Japan vs. United States

IN FORCE: From signing

OVERVIEW: An agreement for final repayment of a United States assistance loan to Japan.

DISCUSSION:

At the conclusion of World War II, United States policy makers were concerned lest, having won the war, the Allies should "lose the peace," creating devastating economic conditions that would inevitably spawn yet another conflict, as the dire post-World War I conditions contributed to the rise of totalitarian regimes and, ultimately, a second world war. To avert this, the United States contributed enormous grants in aid and made liberal loans to the nations of Europe as well as to Japan. The 1973 agreement addresses the final repayment of a 1956 loan agreement, fixing the final repayment amount as $175,074,998, payable in full on May 1, 1793.

REFERENCE:

Milly, Deborah J. *Poverty, Equality, and Growth: The Politics of Economic Need in Postwar Japan.* Cambridge, MA: Harvard University Press, 1999.

Economic, Technical and Related Assistance Agreement (with Yemen)

SIGNED: April 20, 1974, at San'a, Yemen

SIGNATORIES: Yemen vs. United States

IN FORCE: From signing

OVERVIEW: An agreement whereby the United States undertakes to furnish economic, financial, technical and related assistance "as may be requested by . . . Yemen and approved by . . . the United States."

DISCUSSION:

This open-ended agreement for United States assistance is limited only by the following general provisions:

- That the assistance furnished must be requested by Yemen and approved by the United States
- That Yemen contribute to projects for which assistance is requested as much as it is capable of contributing

- That the United States be permitted to observe and review assistance programs
- That funds and supplies be afforded adequate security
- That supplies and equipment furnished for assistance to Yemen be accorded tax- and duty-free status

REFERENCES:

Leaning, Jennifer, et al, eds. *Humanitarian Crises: The Medical and Public Health Response.* Cambridge, MA: Harvard University Press, 1999.

Middleton, Neil, and Phil O'Keefe. *Disaster and Development: The Politics of Humanitarian Aid.* Annandale, Australia: Pluto Press, 1998.

Economic, Technical and Related Assistance Agreement (with Bangladesh)

SIGNED: May 21, 1974, at Dacca, Bangladesh

SIGNATORIES: Bangladesh vs. United States

IN FORCE: From signing

OVERVIEW: A general agreement whereby the United States undertakes to "furnish such economic, technical, and related assistance . . . as my be requested by . . . Bangladesh and approved by . . . the United States.

DISCUSSION:

This general agreement does not specify sums or terms of aid, but enables assistance on an ongoing basis, subject to the request of Bangladesh and the approval of the United States and its representatives in the field. Such enabling agreements are common between the United States and nations eligible to receive assistance.

Also see **Trust Account Agreement (with Bangladesh)**, concluded in July of 1974, which provides a means for disbursing immediate aid during the devastating famine crisis that gripped Bangladesh at this time.

REFERENCES:

Leaning, Jennifer, et al, eds. *Humanitarian Crises: The Medical and Public Health Response.* Cambridge, MA: Harvard University Press, 1999.

Middleton, Neil, and Phil O'Keefe. *Disaster and Development: The Politics of Humanitarian Aid.* Annandale, Australia: Pluto Press, 1998.

Trust Account Agreement (with Bangladesh)

SIGNED: July 1, 1974, at Dacca, Bangladesh

SIGNATORIES: Bangladesh vs. United States

IN FORCE: From signing

OVERVIEW: An agreement whereby the government of Bangladesh will deposit certain sums into a trust account to be administered by the U.S. Agency for International Development (AID) for the purposes of partial financing of an ongoing assistance program.

DISCUSSION:

During the devastating famine of the 1970s, the United States contributed large sums to the relief of Bangladesh. To facilitate day-to-day assistance, it was deemed necessary for the government of Bangladesh to advance certain relief monies, in the form of local currency, which were then held in trust by AID. This arrangement made possible the immediate disbursement of funds in relatively small amounts.

REFERENCES:

Leaning, Jennifer, et al, eds. *Humanitarian Crises: The Medical and Public Health Response*. Cambridge, MA: Harvard University Press, 1999.

Middleton, Neil, and Phil O'Keefe. *Disaster and Development: The Politics of Humanitarian Aid*. Annandale, Australia: Pluto Press, 1998.

Loan Agreement (with Egypt) for the Foreign Exchange Costs of Commodities and Commodity-Related Services

SIGNED: February 12, 1975, at Cairo, Egypt

SIGNATORIES: Egypt vs. United States

IN FORCE: From signing

OVERVIEW: An agreement whereby the United States undertakes to loan Egypt $80,000,000 to defray foreign exchange costs of commodities and commodity-related services.

DISCUSSION:

The loan, made through the Agency for International Development, is to be a low-interest loan, at 2 percent per annum for ten years, and 3 percent thereafter. The use of funds is restricted to certain commodities, such as enumerated foodstuffs, classified as eligible by AID.

REFERENCES:

Leaning, Jennifer, et al, eds. *Humanitarian Crises: The Medical and Public Health Response*. Cambridge, MA: Harvard University Press, 1999.

Middleton, Neil, and Phil O'Keefe. *Disaster and Development: The Politics of Humanitarian Aid*. Annandale, Australia: Pluto Press, 1998.

Agreement (with Italy) Relating to Earthquake Assistance

OFFICIAL TITLE: Exchange of Notes Constituting an Agreement Relating to Earthquake Assistance

SIGNED: June 9, 1976, at Rome

SIGNATORIES: Italy vs. United States

IN FORCE: From signing

OVERVIEW: An agreement to "permit and facilitate the effective use of United States assistance in the afflicted areas of Italy" following earthquakes.

DISCUSSION:

United States international policy has long dictated extending aid to nations in time of crisis produced by natural disaster. After a series of devastating earthquakes hit Italy in 1976, the agreement was quickly concluded a general assistance agreement, addressing the following broad points:

- The United States undertakes to make available assistance to the Italian government, its agencies, and to regional, provincial, and municipal governments.
- The purpose, amounts, and other terms and conditions of the assistance are to be "detailed by common accord . . . between the United States" and Italy.
- All aid furnished is to be exempt from Italian taxation

REFERENCES:

Leaning, Jennifer, et al, eds. *Humanitarian Crises: The Medical and Public Health Response*. Cambridge, MA: Harvard University Press, 1999.

Middleton, Neil, and Phil O'Keefe. *Disaster and Development: The Politics of Humanitarian Aid*. Annandale, Australia: Pluto Press, 1998.

Agreement Concerning the Establishment of a Peace Corps Program in Bangladesh

SIGNED: July 13, 1978, at Washington, D.C.

SIGNATORIES: Bangladesh vs. United States

IN FORCE: From signing

OVERVIEW: An agreement to establish a Peace Corps presence in Bangladesh.

DISCUSSION:

During the 1970s, the chronically impoverished nation of Bangladesh suffered catastrophic famine, resulting in widespread starvation. Dispatching Peace Corps volunteers was one among the several foreign-aid steps the United States took to help Bangladesh. This document is typical of other Peace Corps agreements. The United States agrees to "furnish such Peace Corps volunteers as may be requested by the Government of Bangladesh . . . to perform mutually agreed tasks . . . under the immediate supervision of government or private organizations designated by our two Governments." In turn, Bangladesh undertakes to "accord equitable treatment to Peace Corps volunteers" and to "afford them . . . full aid and protection." All volunteers are exempted from taxation by Bangladesh.

REFERENCES:

Fischer, Fritz. *Making Them Like Us: Peace Corps Volunteers in the 1960s*. Washington, D.C.: Smithsonian Institution Press, 1998.

Hoffman, Elizabeth Cobbs. *All You Need Is Love: The Peace Corps and the Spirit of the 1960s*. Cambridge, MA: Harvard University Press, 1998.

Schwarz, Karen. *What You Can Do for Your Country: Inside the Peace Corps: A Thirty-Year History*. New York: Anchor, 1993.

Searles, P. David. *The Peace Corps Experience: Challenge and Change, 1969-1976*. Lexington: University of Kentucky Press, 1997.

Convention on Assistance in the Case of a Nuclear Accident

OFFICIAL TITLE: Convention on Assistance in the Case of a Nuclear Accident or Radiological Emergency

SIGNED: September 26, 1986, at Vienna

SIGNATORIES: Afghanistan, Australia, Austria, Belgium, Brazil, Bulgaria, Byelorussian Soviet Socialist Republic, Canada, Chile, China, Costa Rica, Cuba, Czechoslovakia, Denmark, Egypt, Finland, France, German Democratic Republic, Germany (Federal Republic) Greece, Guatemala, Holy See, Hungary, Iceland, India, Indonesia, Iran (Islamic Republic), Ireland, Israel, Italy, Ivory Coast, Japan, Jordan, Korea (Democratic People's Republic), Lebanon, Liechtenstein, Mali, Mexico, Monaco, Mongolia, Morocco, Netherlands, New Zealand, Niger, Nigeria, Norway, Panama, Paraguay, Poland, Portugal, Spain, Sudan, Sweden, Switzerland, Tunisia, Turkey, Ukrainian Soviet Socialist Republic, Union of Soviet Socialist Republics, United Kingdom, United States, Zaire, Zimbabwe

IN FORCE: From February 26, 1987

OVERVIEW: A convention "to facilitate prompt assistance in the event of a nuclear accident or radiological emergency to minimize its consequences and to protect life, property and the environment from the effects of radioactive releases."

DISCUSSION:

Article 2 contains the core of the convention:

If a State Party needs assistance in the event of a nuclear accident or radiological emergency, whether or not such accident or emergency originates within its territory, jurisdiction or control, it may call for such assistance from any other State Party, directly or through the Agency, and from the Agency, or, where appropriate, from other international intergovernmental organizations . . .

The requesting party is obliged to furnish information on the nature and scope of the emergency, and the responding party "shall promptly decide and notify the requesting State Party, directly or through the Agency, whether it is in a position to render the assistance requested, and the scope and terms of the assistance that might be rendered."

REFERENCES:

International Atomic Energy Agency. *Handling Radiation Accidents 1977: Proceedings of a Symposium on the Handling of Radiation Accidents.* Lanham, MD: Unipub, 1978.

Sagan, Scott D. *The Limits of Safety: Organizations, Accidents, and Nuclear Weapons.* Princeton, NJ: Princeton University Press, 1995.

Convention on Early Notification of a Nuclear Accident

SIGNED: September 26, 1986, at Vienna

SIGNATORIES: Afghanistan, Australia, Austria, Belgium, Brazil, Bulgaria, Byelorussian Soviet Socialist Republic, Canada, Chile, China, Costa Rica, Côte d'Ivoire, Cuba, Czechoslovakia, Denmark, Egypt, Finland, France, German Democratic Republic, Germany (Federal Republic), Greece, Guatemala, Holy See, Hungary, Iceland, India, Indonesia, Iran (Islamic Republic), Ireland, Israel, Italy, Jordan, Korea (Democratic People's Republic), Lebanon, Liechtenstein, Luxembourg, Mali, Mexico, Monaco, Morocco, Netherlands, Niger, Norway, Panama, Paraguay, Poland, Portugal, Spain, Sudan, Sweden, Switzerland, Tunisia, Turkey, Ukrainian Soviet Socialist Republic, Union of Soviet Socialist Republics, United Kingdom of Great Britain, United States, Yugoslavia, Zaire, Zimbabwe

IN FORCE: From October 27, 1986

OVERVIEW: A convention binding signatory states "to provide relevant information about nuclear accidents as early as possible in order that transboundary radiological consequences can be minimized."

DISCUSSION:

Article 2 constitutes the core obligation of the convention:

In the event of an accident specified in article 1 (hereinafter referred to as a "nuclear accident"), the State Party referred to in that article shall:

(a) forthwith notify, directly or through the International Atomic Energy Agency (hereinafter referred to as the "Agency"), those States which are or may be physically affected as specified in article 1 and the Agency of the nuclear accident, its nature, the time of its occurrence and its exact location where appropriate; and

(b) promptly provide the States referred to in sub-paragraph (a) directly or through the Agency, and the Agency with such available information relevant to minimizing the radiological consequences . .

REFERENCES:

International Atomic Energy Agency. *Handling Radiation Accidents 1977: Proceedings of a Symposium on the Handling of Radiation Accidents.* Lanham, MD: Unipub, 1978.

Sagan, Scott D. *The Limits of Safety: Organizations, Accidents, and Nuclear Weapons.* Princeton, NJ: Princeton University Press, 1995.

Convention on the Transboundary Effects of Industrial Accidents

SIGNED: March 17, 1992, at Helsinki, Finland

SIGNATORIES: Albania, Austria, Belgium, Bulgaria, Canada, Denmark, Estonia, European Economic Community, Finland, France, Germany, Greece, Hungary, Italy, Latvia, Lithuania, Luxembourg, Netherlands, Poland, Portugal, Russian Federation, Spain, Sweden, Switzerland, United Kingdom, United States

IN FORCE: Not yet in force

OVERVIEW: A convention addressing issues of individual and collective national responsibility and capacity in the prevention and control of industrial accidents, as well as the transboundary effects of such accidents.

DISCUSSION:

This comprehensive international convention begins by defining the term *industrial accident*, as well as such ancillary key terms as *hazardous activity* and *transboundary effects*, then goes on to a statement of matters excluded from coverage by the convention, including nuclear accidents, radiological emergencies, accidents at military installations, dam failures, accidental release of genetically modified organisms, and spills of oil and other harmful substances at sea.

Signatories agree to the following:

- To take measures to protect human beings and the environment from the effects of industrial accidents
- To take appropriate legal and policy measures to prevent industrial accidents
- To consult with, inform, cooperate with, and share in assistance for the purpose of enhancing preparedness for coping with industrial accidents that have transboundary effects
- To cooperate in managing the tasks set out in the convention
- To cooperate in the settlement of disputes

REFERENCES:

Davis, Lee A. *Environmental Disasters: A Chronicle of Individual, Industrial, and Governmental Carelessness.* New York: Facts on File, 1998.

Sagan, Scott D. *The Limits of Safety: Organizations, Accidents, and Nuclear Weapons.* Princeton, NJ: Princeton University Press, 1995.

Tampere Convention on Emergency Telecommunications

OFFICIAL TITLE: Tampere Convention on the Provision of Telecommunications Resources for Disaster Investigation and Relief Operations

SIGNED: June 18, 1998, at Tampere, Finland

SIGNATORIES: Benin, Bosnia and Herzegovina, Burundi, Chile, Croatia, Cyprus, Denmark, Finland, Gabon, Germany, Ghana, Haiti, Italy, Jamaica, Kenya, Kuwait, Lebanon, Liberia, Mali, Malta, Mauritania, Mongolia, Nepal, Nicaragua, Niger, Poland, Portugal, Republic of the Congo, Romania, Sudan, Switzerland, Tajikistan, Usbekistan (The United States has not yet signed.)

IN FORCE: Not yet in force

OVERVIEW: A convention addressing the provision of telecommunication assistance in times of disaster relief.

DISCUSSION:

The convention recognizes that, in the event of a large-scale disaster, telecommunications equipment is urgently required; however, complex national legislation covering the importation, licensing, and use of such equipment often means its transit through customs is severely hampered or even prohibited. The principal objective of the Tampere Convention is to overcome such obstacles without compromising national sovereignty or control over the use of telecommunications equipment.

The convention text comprises sixteen articles covering the provision of telecommunication assistance in times of disaster relief. The articles provide for the protection of representatives of aid agencies and other organizations and, in particular, safeguard their right to possess and use various types of communications equipment.

- Aid workers and others associated with disaster clean-up operations are to be immune from prosecution for the use of telecommunications equipment.
- Telecommunications equipment used in relief operations will not be liable to seizure.
- Signatories undertake to reduce or remove regulatory barriers to the use of telecommunication resources for disaster mitigation and relief.
- Parties to the Convention will be obliged to recognize foreign equipment type-approvals and operating licences, and to facilitate the transit of personnel, equipment, materials and information involved in the use of telecommunication resources for disaster mitigation and relief.

Coordination of the provisions of the convention is assigned the United Nations, in cooperation with the International Telecommunication Union.

REFERENCES:

Davis, Lee A. *Environmental Disasters: A Chronicle of Individual, Industrial, and Governmental Carelessness.* New York: Facts on File, 1998.

Sagan, Scott D. *The Limits of Safety: Organizations, Accidents, and Nuclear Weapons.* Princeton, NJ: Princeton University Press, 1995.

Health

Overview of Treaties in This Category

The United States is a signatory to the **Constitution of the World Health Organization** (1946), the principal international health agency of the United Nations, and to the other multilateral agreements in this section, all of which were created under the authority of WHO.

Constitution of the World Health Organization

SIGNED: July 22, 1946, at New York

SIGNATORIES: Afghanistan, Albania, Argentina, Australia, Austria, Belgium, Bolivia, Brazil, Bulgaria, Burma, Byelorussian Soviet Socialist Republic, Canada, Ceylon, Chile, China, Colombia, Costa Rica, Cuba, Czechoslovakia, Denmark, Dominican Republic, Ecuador, Egypt, El Salvador, Ethiopia, Finland, France, Greece, Guatemala, Haiti, Honduras, Hungary, Iceland, India, Iran, Iraq, Ireland, Islamic Republic of Iran, Italy, Jordan, Lebanon, Liberia, Luxembourg, Mexico, Netherlands, New Zealand, Nicaragua, Norway, Pakistan, Panama, Paraguay, Peru, Philippines, Poland, Portugal, Romania, Saudi Arabia, South Africa, Sweden, Switzerland, Syria, Syrian Arab Republic, Thailand, Turkey, Ukrainian Soviet Socialist Republic, Union of South Africa, Union of Soviet Socialist Republics, United Kingdom, United States, Uruguay, Venezuela, Yugoslavia

IN FORCE: From April 7, 1948

OVERVIEW: The constitution of this specialized agency of the United Nations.

DISCUSSION:

The document begins with a definition of health as a "state of complete physical, mental and social well-being and not merely the absence of diseases or infirmity." From this assumption, it follows that "health" is a basic human right and therefore comes under the purview of the **Charter of the United Nations**. The constitution states the objective of WHO as nothing less than "the attainment by all peoples of the highest possible level of health." It sets forth the agency's functions as follows:

- To act as the directing and coordinating authority on international health work
- To establish and maintain effective collaboration with the United Nations and its agencies
- To assist governments in strengthening health services

- To furnish technical assistance in emergencies
- To provide health services to special groups, such as peoples of trust territories
- To establish and maintain administrative and technical services, including epidemiological and statistical services
- To stimulate advance work to eradicate epidemic and endemic disease
- To promote cooperation with other agencies to prevent accidental injuries
- To promote improvement of nutrition, housing, sanitation, and so on
- To promote cooperation among scientific groups for the advancement of health
- To propose conventions and agreements with respect to health matters
- To promote maternal and child health
- To foster activities in the area of mental health
- To promote and conduct research in the field of health
- To promote improved standards of teaching and training in health fields
- To study and report on administrative and social techniques affecting public health
- To provide information and counsel in the field of health
- To assist in developing informed public opinion on matters of health
- To establish and revise as necessary international nomenclatures of diseases; see **World Health Organization Regulations Regarding Nomenclature with Respect to Diseases and Causes of Death**
- To standardize diagnostic practices as necessary
- To develop, establish, and promote international standards with respect to food, biological, pharmaceutical, and similar products

REFERENCES:

Siddiqi, Javed. *World Health and World Politics: The World Health Organization and the UN System.* Columbia: University of South Carolina Press, 1995.

Beigbeder, Yves, et al. *The World Health Organization.* Amsterdam, Netherlands: Kluwer Academic Publishers, 1999.

International Sanitary Regulations

SIGNED: May 25, 1951, at Geneva

SIGNATORIES: Afghanistan, Argentina, Austria, Belgium, Bolivia, Brazil, British Overseas Territories, Cambodia, Canada, Ceylon, China, Costa Rica, Cuba, Denmark, Dominican Republic, Ecuador, El Salvador, Ethiopia, Faeroe Islands, Finland, France, French Overseas Territories, Greece, Greenland, Guatemala, Haiti, Honduras, Iceland, India, Indonesia, Iran, Iraq, Ireland, Israel, Italy, Japan, Jordan, Korea, Laos, Lebanon, Liberia, Libya, Luxembourg, Mexico, Monaco, Netherlands, New Zealand, New Zealand Territories, Nicaragua, Norway, Pakistan, Panama, Paraguay, Peru, Philippines, Portugal, Portuguese Overseas Territories, Saudi Arabia, Southwest Africa (Namibia), Spain, Sweden, Switzerland, Syria, Thailand, Turkey, Union of South Africa, United Kingdom, United States, Uruguay, Vatican City States, Venezuela, Yugoslavia

IN FORCE: From October 1, 1952

OVERVIEW: A set of international health regulations produced under the auspices of the World Health Organization.

DISCUSSION:

The material addressed in this agreement is essentially the same as that addressed in **International Health Regulations** of 1969, which updates and revises the regulations in light of developments in the state of the art of public health.

REFERENCES:

Siddiqi, Javed. *World Health and World Politics: The World Health Organization and the UN System.* Columbia: University of South Carolina Press, 1995.

Beigbeder, Yves, et al. *The World Health Organization.* Amsterdam, Netherlands: Kluwer Academic Publishers, 1999.

World Health Organization Regulations Regarding Nomenclature with Respect to Diseases and Causes of Death

SIGNED: May 22, 1967, at Geneva

SIGNATORIES: Afghanistan, Albania, Algeria, Angola, Argentina, Australia, Austria, Bahamas, Bahrain, Bangladesh, Barbados, Belgium, Benin, Bolivia, Botswana, Brazil, Bulgaria, Burma, Burundi, Byelorussian Soviet Socialist Republic, Canada, Cape Verde, Central African Republic, Chad, Chile, China, Colombia, Comoros, Congo, Costa Rica, Côte d'Ivoire, Cuba, Cyprus, Czechoslovakia, Democratic Kampuchea, Democratic People's Republic of Korea, Democratic Republic of Viet-Nam, Democratic Yemen, Denmark, Djibouti, Dominican Republic, Ecuador, Egypt, El Salvador, Ethiopia, Federal Republic of Germany, Fiji, Finland, France, Gabon, Gambia, German Democratic Republic, Ghana, Greece, Grenada, Guatemala, Guinea, Guinea-Bissau, Guyana, Haiti, Honduras, Hungary, Iceland, India, Indonesia, Iran, Iraq, Ireland, Israel, Italy, Jamaica, Japan, Jordan, Kenya, Kuwait, Lao People's Democratic Republic, Lebanon, Lesotho, Liberia, Libyan Arab Jamahiriya, Luxembourg, Madagascar, Malawi, Malaysia, Maldives, Mali, Malta, Mauritania, Mauritius, Mexico, Monaco, Mongolia, Morocco, Mozambique, Nepal, Netherlands, New Zealand, Nicaragua, Niger, Nigeria, Norway, Oman, Pakistan, Panama, Papua New Guinea, Paraguay, Peru, Philippines, Poland, Portugal, Qatar, Republic of Korea, Romania, Samoa, Sao Tome and Principe, Saudi Arabia, Senegal, Seychelles, Sierra Leone, Somalia, South Africa, Spain, Sri Lanka, Sudan, Suriname, Swaziland, Sweden, Switzerland, Syrian Arab Republic, Thailand, Togo, Tonga, Trinidad and Tobago, Tunisia, Turkey, Uganda, Ukrainian Soviet Socialist Republic, Union of Soviet Socialist Republics, United Arab Emirates, United Kingdom, United Republic of Cameroon, United Republic of Tanzania, United States, Upper Volta, Uruguay, Venezuela, Vietnam, Yemen, Yugoslavia, Zaire, Zambia

IN FORCE: From January 1, 1968

OVERVIEW: A WHO convention to standardize the nomenclature applied to diseases in order to enable the compilation and publication of statistics of mortality and morbidity in comparable form.

DISCUSSION:

The convention lays down specifications for the compilation and publication of statistics on mortality and morbidity, including standardization of the names of diseases and causes of death. The object is to render these specifications uniform, so that international health issues can be more accurately and meaningfully studied and evaluated.

REFERENCES:

Siddiqi, Javed. *World Health and World Politics: The World Health Organization and the UN System.* Columbia: University of South Carolina Press, 1995.

Beigbeder, Yves, et al. *The World Health Organization.* Amsterdam, Netherlands: Kluwer Academic Publishers, 1999.

International Health Regulations

SIGNED: January 20, 1969, at Boston, Massachusetts

SIGNATORIES: Afghanistan, Albania, Algeria, Argentina, Austria, Bahrain, Barbados, Belgium, Bolivia, Brazil, Bulgaria, Burma, Burundi, Byelorussian Soviet Socialist Republic, Cambodia, Cameroon, Canada, Central African Republic, Ceylon, Chad, Chile, China, Colombia, Congo, Congo People's Republic, Costa Rica, Côte d'Ivoire, Cuba, Cyprus, Czechoslovakia, Dahomey, Denmark, Dominican Republic, Ecuador, El Salvador, Equatorial Guinea, Ethiopia, Federal Republic of Germany, Finland, France, Gabon, Ghana, Greece, Guatemala, Guinea, Guyana, Haiti, Honduras, Hungary, Iceland, India, Indonesia, Iran, Iraq, Ireland, Israel, Italy, Jamaica, Japan, Jordan, Kenya,

Kuwait, Laos, Lebanon, Lesotho, Liberia, Libya, Luxembourg, Madagascar, Malawi, Malaysia, Maldives, Mali, Malta, Mauritania, Mauritius, Mexico, Monaco, Mongolia, Morocco, Nepal, Netherlands, New Zealand, Nicaragua, Niger, Nigeria, Norway, Panama, Paraguay, People's Democratic Republic of Yemen, Peru, Philippines, Poland, Portugal, Qatar, Republic of Korea, Romania, Rwanda, Saudi Arabia, Senegal, Sierra Leone, Somalia, Spain, Sudan, Suriname, Sweden, Switzerland, Syria, Thailand, Togo, Trinidad and Tobago, Tunisia, Turkey, Uganda, Ukrainian Soviet Socialist Republic, Union of Soviet Socialist Republics, United Kingdom, United Republic of Tanzania, United States, Upper Volta, Uruguay, Venezuela, Vietnam, Yemen, Yugoslavia, Zambia

IN FORCE: From January 1, 1971

OVERVIEW: A set of standard WHO health regulations, which updates and replaces the **International Sanitary Regulations** of 1951.

DISCUSSION:

The document begins by defining common terms relevant to public health, then lays down regulations in the following areas:

- Notifications and epidemiological information: communicating on issues of international health, especially in cases of epidemic or potentially epidemic disease
- Regulations and guidelines for national health organizations, especially as these must function in port and airport areas
- Required health measures and procedures
- Required health measures upon international departure from ports or airports
- Health measures applicable between ports or airports of departure and arrival
- Required health measures on arrival
- Measures concerning the international transport of cargo, goods, baggage, and mail
- Special provisions relating to the following epidemic and endemic diseases: plague, cholera, yellow fever, and smallpox
- Requirements relating to health documents

REFERENCES:

Siddiqi, Javed. *World Health and World Politics: The World Health Organization and the UN System.* Columbia: University of South Carolina Press, 1995.

Beigbeder, Yves, et al. *The World Health Organization.* Amsterdam, Netherlands: Kluwer Academic Publishers, 1999.

Human Rights, Equality, Slavery, and Genocide Issues

Overview of Treaties in This Category

The year 1948 saw the promulgation of two major declarations on human rights, to which the United States is signatory: **American Declaration of the Rights and Duties of Man** and **Universal Declaration of Human Rights**. Prior to this, "human rights" conventions were mainly limited to the issue of slavery (see **Treaty between United States and Great Britain for the Suppression of the Slave Trade,** 1862; **Additional Article to the Treaty for the Suppression of the African Slave Trade,** 1862; and **Convention to Suppress the Slave Trade and Slavery,** 1926).

It was the genocidal violations of human rights during World War II that prompted, in the second half of the twentieth century, a series of comprehensive multilateral conventions on human rights in general as well as, more particularly, conventions on racial and ethnic discrimination and issues of genocide: for example, **Convention on the Prevention and Punishment of the Crime of Genocide** (1948), **International Convention on the Elimination of all Forms of Racial Discrimination** (1965), **International Covenant on Civil and Political Rights** (1966), **International Covenant on Economic, Social and Cultural Rights** (1966) **Optional Protocol to the International Covenant on Civil and Political Rights** (1966), and the **Apartheid Convention** (1973). The protection of "minority" groups other than racial and ethnic minorities has also been addressed in international human rights conventions, including, for example, the rights of the mentally retarded (**Declaration on the Rights of Mentally Retarded Persons,** 1971), of prisoners (for example, **Convention Against Torture and Other Cruel, Inhuman or Degrading Treatment or Punishment** [1984], **Body of Principles for the Protection of All Persons under Any Form of Detention or Imprisonment** [1988], and **Basic Principles for the Treatment of Prisoners,** 1990), of children (see Section 5.4, Rights and Welfare of Children), and of women (see Section 5.5, Rights of Women), and of refugees (for example, **Convention Relating to the Status of Refugees** of 1951).

In recent years, a number of multilateral declarations have defined hunger as an offense against basic human rights: for example, **Universal Declaration on the Eradication of Hunger and Malnutrition** (1974) and **Food Aid Convention** (1999). The international community has increasingly sought to create rights documents that mandate and enable practical action; the **Vienna Declaration and Program of Action** (1993), for example, was a major effort to "rationalize and enhance" the United Nations position on and programs for human rights in order to bring them to efficient action. Another recent development is in the area of biomedical ethics. In response to significant innovations in such areas as genetic engineering, a **Convention on Human Rights and Biomedicine** was opened for signature in 1997.

Treaty between United States and Great Britain for the Suppression of the Slave Trade

SIGNED: April 7, 1862, at Washington
SIGNATORIES: Great Britain vs. United States
IN FORCE: From July 7, 1862
OVERVIEW: A treaty of Anglo-American cooperation in the suppression of the slave trade.

DISCUSSION:
By the **Webster-Ashburton Treaty** (Section 1.1) of 1842 Great Britain and the United States agreed to cooperate in the suppression of the slave trade. To the United States, engaged in a Civil War in large part over slavery issues, cooperation in suppressing the slave trade became particularly important in helping to cement friendly relations between Great Britain and the United States at a time when much British political and popular sentiment favored the Confederate cause.

By the present treaty, the signatories reciprocally agreed to permit inspection of their vessels at sea (within a defined area) suspected of transporting slaves. The agreement also established three courts, "one at Sierra Leone, one at the Cape of Good Hope, and one at New York," to adjudicate cases arising from enforcement of the provisions of the treaty, which included seizure of slave-trading vessels. By Article VI of the treaty, ships could be seized on suspicion of transporting slaves, even if no slaves were found on the vessel.

REFERENCES:
DuBois, W. E. B. *Suppression of the African Slave-Trade to the United States of America, 1638-1870.* Reprint ed., New York: Dover, 1999.
Eltis, David. *The Abolition of the Atlantic Slave Trade: Origins and Effects on Europe, Africa, and the Americas.* Madison: University of Wisconsin Press, 1982.
Hogg, Peter C. *the African Slave Trade and its Suppression, a Classified and Annotated Bibliography of Books, Pamphlets and Periodical Articles.* London, Frank Cass, 1973.

LeVeen, E. Phillip. *British Slave Trade Suppression Policies, 1821-1865.* New York : Arno Press, 1977.

Spears, John Randolph. *The American Slave-trade: an Account of its Origin, Growth and Suppression.* New York: Scribner, 1907.

Additional Article to the Treaty for the Suppression of the African Slave Trade

SIGNED: February 17, 1863

SIGNATORIES: Great Britain vs. United States

IN FORCE: From April 22, 1863

OVERVIEW: The document expanded the extent of the territory within which British and American vessels might be boarded for inspection on suspicion of engaging in the slave trade.

DISCUSSION:

The **Treaty Between United States and Great Britain for the Suppression of the Slave Trade** stipulated that "the reciprocal right of search and detention shall be exercised only within the distance of two hundred miles from the coast of Africa, and to the southward of the thirty-second parallel of north latitude, and within thirty leagues from the coast of the Island of Cuba." The Additional Article expanded this zone to include the area "within thirty leagues of the island of Madagascar, within thirty leagues of the island of Puerto Rico, and within thirty leagues of the island of San Domingo."

REFERENCES:

DuBois, W. E. B. *Suppression of the African Slave-Trade to the United States of America, 1638-1870.* Reprint ed., New York: Dover, 1999.

Eltis, David. *The Abolition of the Atlantic Slave Trade: Origins and Effects on Europe, Africa, and the Americas.* Madison: University of Wisconsin Press, 1982.

Hogg, Peter C. *the African Slave Trade and its Suppression, a Classified and Annotated Bibliography of Books, Pamphlets and Periodical Articles.* London, Frank Cass, 1973.

LeVeen, E. Phillip. *British Slave Trade Suppression Policies, 1821-1865.* New York : Arno Press, 1977.

Spears, John Randolph. *The American Slave-trade: an Account of its Origin, Growth and Suppression.* New York: Scribner, 1907.

Convention to Suppress the Slave Trade and Slavery

SIGNED: September 25, 1926, at Geneva; Protocol signed, December 7, 1953, at New York

SIGNATORIES: Afghanistan, Albania, Algeria, Antigua and Barbuda, Argentina, Australia, Austria, Azerbaijan, Bahamas, Bahrain, Bangladesh, Barbados, Belarus, Belgium, Belize, Benin, Bolivia, Bosnia-Herzegovina, Botswana, Brazil, Brunei, Bulgaria, Burma, Cambodia, Cameroon, Canada, Central African Republic, Chile, China (Taiwan), Congo, Côte d'Ivoire, Croatia, Cuba, Cyprus, Czech Republic, Czechoslovakia, Denmark, Djibouti, Dominica, Dominican Republic, Ecuador, Egypt, Estonia, Ethiopia, Fiji, Finland, Former Yugoslav Republic of Macedonia, France, Gambia, German Democratic Republic, Germany (Federal Republic), Ghana, Greece, Grenada, Guatemala, Guinea, Guyana, Haiti, Hungary, Iceland, India, Iran, Iraq, Ireland, Israel, Italy, Jamaica, Jordan, Kiribati, Kuwait, Laos, Latvia, Lebanon, Lesotho, Liberia, Libya, Luxembourg, Madagascar, Malawi, Malaysia, Mali, Malta, Mauritania, Mauritius, Mexico, Monaco, Mongolia, Morocco, Nauru, Nepal, Netherlands, New Zealand, Nicaragua, Niger, Nigeria, Norway, Pakistan, Papua New Guinea, Philippines, Poland, Portugal, Romania, Russian Federation, St. Kitts and Nevis, St. Lucia, St. Vincent and the Grenadines, San Marino, Saudi Arabia, Senegal, Seychelles, Sierra Leone, Singapore, Slovak Republic, Slovenia, Solomon Islands, South Africa, Spain, Sri Lanka, Sudan, Suriname, Swaziland, Sweden, Switzerland, Syrian Arab Republic, Tanzania, Togo, Tonga, Trinidad and Tobago, Tunisia, Turkey, Tuvalu, Uganda, Ukraine, Union of Soviet Socialist Republics, United Kingdom, United States, Vietnam, Yemen (Aden), Yugoslavia, Zaire, Zambia, Zimbabwe

IN FORCE: From March 9, 1927; for the United States, March 21, 1929; Protocol, from signing; for the United States, March 7, 1956

OVERVIEW: The convention aimed to "complete and extend the work accomplished under" the **General Act on the Suppression of the African Slave Trade** of 1890-1892 and other international agreements to abolish slavery and to suppress the slave trade.

DISCUSSION:

Besides agreeing to ban slavery and the slave trade within their own territories, the signatories undertook to work toward the abolition of slavery and the slave trade throughout the world. In addition:

> The High Contracting Parties recognise that recourse to compulsory or forced labour may have grave consequences and undertake, each in respect of the territories placed under its sovereignty, jurisdiction, protection, suzerainty or tutelage, to take all necessary measures to prevent compulsory or forced labour from developing into conditions analogous to slavery.

The Protocol of 1953 served mainly to bring the 1926 document, concluded under the League of Nations, under the aegis of the United Nations. The protocol reaffirmed the convention and reopened it to signature.

REFERENCES:

Eltis, David. *The Abolition of the Atlantic Slave Trade: Origins and Effects on Europe, Africa, and the Americas.* Madison: University of Wisconsin Press, 1982.

Hogg, Peter C. *the African Slave Trade and its Suppression, a Classified and Annotated Bibliography of Books, Pamphlets and Periodical Articles.* London, Frank Cass, 1973.

Convention Concerning Forced or Compulsory Labor

SIGNED: June 28, 1930, at Geneva

SIGNATORIES: Members of the International Labor Organization

IN FORCE: From May 1, 1932; revised, 1946; revision in force from August 31, 1948

OVERVIEW: "Each Member of the International Labor Organisation which ratifies this Convention undertakes to suppress the use of forced or compulsory labor in all its forms within the shortest possible period."

DISCUSSION:

The convention defined "forced or compulsory labor" as "all work or service which is exacted from any person under the menace of any penalty and for which the said person has not offered himself voluntarily," excluding the following:

(a) any work or service exacted in virtue of compulsory military service laws for work of a purely military character;

(b) any work or service which forms part of the normal civic obligations of the citizens of a fully self-governing country;

(c) any work or service exacted from any person as a consequence of a conviction in a court of law ... ;

(d) any work or service exacted in cases of emergency, that is to say, in the event of war or of a calamity or threatened calamity, such as fire, flood, famine, earthquake, violent epidemic or epizootic diseases, invasion by animal, insect or vegetable pests ... ;

(e) minor communal services of a kind which, being performed by the members of the community in the direct interest of the said community, can therefore be considered as normal civic obligations incumbent upon the members of the community ....

Articles 1 and 2 define the scope of the convention:

Article 1

1. Each Member of the International Labour Organisation which ratifies this Convention undertakes to suppress the use of forced or compulsory labour in all its forms within the shortest possible period ...

Article 2

1. For the purposes of this Convention the term "forced or compulsory labour" shall mean all work or service which is exacted from any person under the menace of any penalty and for which the said person has not offered himself voluntarily ...

REFERENCE:

Brass, Tom, and Marcel van der Linden, eds. *Free and Unfree Labour: the Debate Continues.* Bern, Switzerland, and New York: Peter Lang, 1997.

American Declaration of the Rights and Duties of Man

SIGNED: May 2, 1948, at Bogota, Colombia

SIGNATORIES: Antigua and Barbuda, Argentina, Bahamas, Bolivia, Brazil, Chile, Colombia, Costa Rica, Cuba, Dominica, Dominican Republic, Ecuador, El Salvador, Grenada, Guatemala, Haiti, Honduras, Jamaica, Mexico, Nicaragua, Panama, Paraguay, Peru, St. Kitts-Nevis, Saint Lucia, Saint Vincent and the Grenadines, Suriname, the United States, Uruguay, Venezuela

IN FORCE: From signing

OVERVIEW: An OAS declaration of the the basic rights and duties of humankind.

DISCUSSION:

The declaration, reviewed and revised in 1991, constitutes a kind of hemispherical bill of rights, with the addition of basic duties. The rights enumerated are as follows:

Article I.

Every human being has the right to life, liberty and the security of his person. Right to life, liberty and personal security.

Article II.

All persons are equal before the law and have the rights and duties established in this Declaration, without distinction as to race, sex, language, creed or any other factor. Right to equality before law.

Article III.

Every person has the right freely to profess a religious faith, and to manifest and practice it both in public and in private. Right to religious freedom and worship.

Article IV.

Every person has the right to freedom of investigation, of opinion, and of the expression and dissemination of ideas, by any medium whatsoever. Right to freedom of investigation, opinion, expression and dissemination.

Article V.

Every person has the right to the protection of the law against abusive attacks upon his honor, his reputation, and his private and family life. Right to protection of honor, personal reputation, and private and family life.

Article VI.

Every person has the right to establish a family, the basic element of society, and to receive protection therefor. Right to a family and to protection thereof.

Article VII.

All women, during pregnancy and the nursing period, and all children have the right to special protection, care and aid. Right to protection for mothers and children.

Article VIII.

Every person has the right to fix his residence within the territory of the state of which he is a national, to move about freely within such territory, and not to leave it except by his own will. Right to residence and movement.

Article IX.

Every person has the right to the inviolability of his home. Right to inviolability of the home.

Article X.

Every person has the right to the inviolability and transmission of his correspondence. Right to the inviolability and transmission of correspondence

Article XI.

Every person has the right to the preservation of his health through sanitary and social measures relating to food, clothing, housing and medical care, to the extent permitted by public and community resources. Right to the preservation of health and to well-being.

Article XII.

Every person has the right to an education, which should be based on the principles of liberty, morality and human solidarity. Right to education. Likewise every person has the right to an education that will prepare him to attain a decent life, to raise his standard of living, and to be a useful member of society. The right to an education includes the right to equality of opportunity in every case, in accordance with natural talents, merit and the desire to utilize the resources that the state or the community is in a position to provide. Every person has the right to receive, free, at least a primary education.

Article XIII.

Every person has the right to take part in the cultural life of the community, to enjoy the arts, and to participate in the benefits that result from intellectual progress, especially scientific discoveries. Right to the benefits of culture. He likewise has the right to the protection of his moral and material interests as regards his inventions or any literary, scientific or artistic works of which he is the author.

Article XIV.

Every person has the right to work, under proper conditions, and to follow his vocation freely, in sofar as existing conditions of employment permit. Right to work and to fair remuneration. Every person who works has the right to receive such remuneration as will, in proportion to his capacity and skill, assure him a standard of living suitable for himself and for his family.

Article XV.

Every person has the right to leisure time, to wholesome recreation, and to the opportunity for advantageous use of his free time to his spiritual, cultural and physical benefit. Right to leisure time and to the use thereof.

Article XVI.

Every person has the right to social security which will protect him from the consequences of unemployment, old age, and any disabilities arising from causes beyond his control that make it physically or mentally impossible for him to earn a living. Right to social security.

Article XVII.

Every person has the right to be recognized everywhere as a person having rights and obligations, and to enjoy the basic civil rights. Right to recognition of juridical personality and civil rights.

Article XVIII.

Every person may resort to the courts to ensure respect for his legal rights. There should likewise be available to him a simple, brief procedure whereby the courts will protect him from acts of authority that, to his prejudice, violate any fundamental constitutional rights. Right to a fair trial.

Article XIX.

Every person has the right to the nationality to which he is entitled by law and to change it, if he so wishes, for the nationality of any other country that is willing to grant it to him. Right to nationality.

Article XX.

Every person having legal capacity is entitled to participate in the government of his country, directly or through his representatives, and to take part in popular elections, which shall be by secret ballot, and shall be honest, periodic and free. Right to vote and to participate in government.

Article XXI.

Every person has the right to assemble peaceably with others in a formal public meeting or an informal gathering, in connection with matters of common interest of any nature. Right of assembly.

Article XXII.

Every person has the right to associate with others to promote, exercise and protect his legitimate interests of a political, economic, religious, social, cultural, professional, labor union or other nature. Right of association.

Article XXIII.

Every person has a right to own such private property as meets the essential needs of decent living and helps to maintain the dignity of the individual and of the home. Right to property.

Article XXIV.

Every person has the right to submit respectful petitions to any competent authority, for reasons of either general or private interest, and the right to obtain a prompt decision thereon. Right of petition.

Article XXV.

No person may be deprived of his liberty except in the cases and according to the procedures established by pre-existing law. Right of protection from arbitrary arrest. No person may be deprived of liberty for nonfulfillment of obligations of a purely civil character. Every individual who has been deprived of his liberty has the right to have the legality of his detention ascertained without delay by a court, and the right to be tried without undue delay or, otherwise, to be released. He also has the right to humane treatment during the time he is in custody.

Article XXVI.

Every accused person is presumed to be innocent until proved guilty. Right to due process of law. Every person accused of an offense has the right to be given an impartial and public hearing, and to be tried by courts previously established in accordance with pre-existing laws, and not to receive cruel, infamous or unusual punishment.

Article XXVII.

Every person has the right, in case of pursuit not resulting from ordinary crimes, to seek and receive asylum in foreign territory, in accordance with the laws of each country and with international agreements. Right of asylum.

Article XXVIII.

The rights of man are limited by the rights of others, by the security of all, and by the just demands of the general welfare and the advancement of democracy. Scope of the rights of man.

The corresponding duties of humankind follow:

Article XXIX.

It is the duty of the individual so to conduct himself in relation to others that each and every one may fully form and develop his personality. Duties to society.

Article XXX.

It is the duty of every person to aid, support, educate and protect his minor children, and it is the duty of children to honor their parents always and to aid, support and protect them when they need it. Duties toward children and parents.

Article XXXI.

It is the duty of every person to acquire at least an elementary education. Duty to receive instruction.

Article XXXII.

It is the duty of every person to vote in the popular elections of the country of which he is a national, when he is legally capable of doing so. Duty to vote.

Article XXXIII.

It is the duty of every person to obey the law and other legitimate commands of the authorities of his country and those of the country in which he may be. Duty to obey the law.

Article XXXIV.

It is the duty of every able-bodied person to render whatever civil and military service his country may require for its defense and preservation, and, in case of public disaster, to render such services as may be in his power. Duty to serve the community and the nation. It is likewise his duty to hold any public office to which he may be elected by popular vote in the state of which he is a national.

Article XXXV.

It is the duty of every person to cooperate with the state and the community with respect to social security and welfare, in accordance with his ability and with existing circumstances. Duties with respect to social security and welfare.

Article XXXVI.

It is the duty of every person to pay the taxes established by law for the support of public services.

Article XXXVII.

It is the duty of every person to work, as far as his capacity and possibilities permit, in order to obtain the means of livelihood or to benefit his community. Duty to work.

Article XXXVIII.

It is the duty of every person to refrain from taking part in political activities that, according to law, are reserved exclusively to the citizens of the state in which he is an alien. Duty to refrain from political activities in a foreign country.

REFERENCES:
None

Convention on the Prevention and Punishment of the Crime of Genocide

SIGNED: December 9, 1948, at Paris

SIGNATORIES: Afghanistan, Albania, Algeria, Antigua and Barbuda, Argentina, Armenia, Australia, Austria, Azerbaijan, Bahamas, Bahrain, Barbados, Belarus, Belgium, Bosnia-Herzegovina, Brazil, Bulgaria, Burkina Faso, Burma, Cambodia, Canada, Chile, China, Colombia, Costa Rica, Côte d'Ivoire, Croatia, Cuba, Cyprus, Czech Republic, Czechoslovakia, Denmark, Ecuador, Egypt, El Salvador, Estonia, Ethiopia, Fiji, Finland, Former Yugoslav Republic of Macedonia, France, Gabon, Gambia, Georgia, German Democratic Republic, Germany (Federal Republic), Ghana, Greece, Guatemala, Haiti, Honduras, Hungary, Iceland, India, Iran, Iraq, Ireland, Israel, Italy, Jamaica, Jordan, Korea (Democratic People's Republic), Korea (Republic), Kuwait, Laos, Latvia, Lebanon, Lesotho, Liberia, Libya, Liechtenstein, Lithuania, Luxembourg, Malaysia, Maldives, Mali, Mexico, Moldova, Monaco, Mongolia, Morocco, Mozambique, Namibia, Nepal, Netherlands, New Zealand, Nicaragua, Norway, Pakistan, Panama, Papua New Guinea, Peru, Philippines, Poland, Romania, Russian Federation, Rwanda, St. Vincent and the Grenadines, Saudi Arabia, Senegal, Seychelles, Singapore, Slovak Republic, Slovenia, Spain, Sri Lanka, Sweden, Syria, Tanzania, Togo, Tonga, Tunisia, Turkey, Uganda, Ukraine, Union of Soviet Socialist Republics, United Kingdom, United States, Uruguay, Venezuela, Vietnam, Yemen (Aden), Yemen (Sanaa), Yugoslavia, Zaire, Zimbabwe

IN FORCE: From January 12, 1951 (in force for the United States from February 23, 1989)

OVERVIEW: Parties to the convention agree that genocide, in time of peace or war, is a crime under international law and they undertake to prevent and punish it.

DISCUSSION:

Article 2 of the convention defines genocide as "acts committed with intent to destroy, in whole or part, a national, ethical, racial or religious group." Genocide includes killing members of the group, causing serious bodily or mental harm to members of the group, deliberately inflicting on the group conditions of life calculated to bring about its physical destruction in whole or part, imposing measures intended to prevent births within the group, or forcibly transferring children of the group to another group. Article 3 enumerates the acts punishable under international law, including genocide itself, conspiracy to commit genocide, direct and public incitement to commit genocide, attempted genocide, and complicity in genocide. The convention calls for the indictment, trial, and punishment of "persons committing genocide or any of the other acts enumerated in Article 3 . . . whether they are constitutionally responsible rulers, public officials or private individuals." The convention calls for the formation of a "competent tribunal" to try cases of genocide and related acts.

REFERENCES:

Dobkowski, Michael N., and Isidor Walliman, eds. *The Coming Age of Scarcity: Preventing Mass Death and Genoicde in the Twenty-First Century.* Syracuse, NY: Syracuse University Press, 1998.

Lerner, Richard M., et al. *Final Solutions: Biology, Prejudice, and Genocide.* College Park: Pennsylvania State University Press, 1992.

Summers, Craig, and Eric Markusen, eds. *Collective Violence: Harmful Behavior in Groups and Governments.* Lanham, MD: Rowman & Littlefield, 1998.

Universal Declaration of Human Rights

SIGNED: December 10, 1948, at San Francisco

SIGNATORIES: Afghanistan, Argentina, Australia, Belgium, Bolivia, Brazil, Burma, Canada, Chile, China, Colombia, Costa Rica, Cuba, Denmark, the Dominican Republic, Ecuador, Egypt, El Salvador, Ethiopia, France, Greece, Guatemala, Haiti, Iceland, India, Iran, Iraq, Lebanon, Liberia, Luxembourg, Mexico, Netherlands, New Zealand, Nicaragua, Norway, Pakistan, Panama, Paraguay, Peru, Philippines, Siam, Sweden, Syria, Turkey, United Kingdom, United States, Uruguay, Venezuela

IN FORCE: From signing

OVERVIEW: The first United Nations declaration on human rights, intended to protect the "inherent dignity and . . . the equal and inalienable rights of all members of the human family [as] the foundation of freedom, justice and peace in the world."

DISCUSSION:

The declaration lays down the following general principles:

- "All human beings are born free and equal in dignity and rights. They are endowed with reason and conscience and should act towards one another in a spirit of brotherhood."
- All people, without exception, are entitled to basic human rights.
- "Everyone has the right to life, liberty and security of person."
- No one may be enslaved.
- No one may be subject to torture or inhumane punishment or treatment.
- "Everyone has the right to recognition everywhere as a person before the law."
- "All are equal before the law . . ."
- All people must have access to effective legal remedy.
- All must be free from arbitrary arrest.
- All people have the right to fair trial.
- A person is presumed innocent until proven guilty.
- No one is to be subject to ex-post facto prosecution.
- All people have the right to privacy.
- All must enjoy freedom of movement.

- "Everyone has the right to seek and to enjoy in other countries asylum from [political] persecution."
- "Everyone has the right to a nationality."
- Everyone is entitled to marriage and family rights.
- "Everyone has the right to own property alone as well as in association with others."
- "Everyone has the right to freedom of thought, conscience and religion . . ."
- "Everyone has the right to freedom of opinion and expression . . ."
- "Everyone has the right to freedom of peaceful assembly and association."
- All people have the right to participate in government.
- "Everyone, as a member of society, has the right to social security and is entitled to realization, through national effort and international co-operation and in accordance with the organization and resources of each State, of the economic, social and cultural rights indispensable for his dignity and the free development of his personality."
- "Everyone has the right to work, to free choice of employment, to just and favourable conditions of work and to protection against unemployment."
- "Everyone has the right to rest and leisure, including reasonable limitation of working hours and periodic holidays with pay."
- "Everyone has the right to a standard of living adequate for the health and well-being of himself and of his family . . ."
- "Everyone has the right to education. Education shall be free, at least in the elementary and fundamental stages. Elementary education shall be compulsory."
- "Everyone has the right freely to participate in the cultural life of the community . . ."
- "Everyone has duties to the community in which alone the free and full development of his personality is possible."

Subsequently to the 1948 declaration, the United Nations has produced many conventions, declarations, and other documents relating to aspects of human rights. The most recent general document is the **Vienna Declaration of the World Conference on Human Rights** of 1993.

REFERENCE:

Morsink, Johannes. *The Universal Declaration of Human Rights: Origins, Drafting, and Intent.* Philadelphia: University of Pennsylvania Press, 1999.

Convention for the Suppression of the Traffic in Persons and of the Exploitation of the Prostitution of Others

SIGNED: March 21, 1950

SIGNATORIES: Brazil, Denmark, Ecuador, Finland, Honduras, India, Islamic Republic of Iran, Israel, Liberia, Luxembourg, Myanmar, Pakistan, Philippines, South Africa, Yugoslavia

IN FORCE: From July 25, 1951

OVERVIEW: The signatories "agree to punish any person who, to gratify the passions of another . . . Procures, entices or leads away, for purposes of prostitution, another person, even with the consent of that person; Exploits the prostitution of another person, even with the consent of that person."

DISCUSSION:

The convention reaffirms and amplifies earlier conventions, including International Agreement of 18 May 1904 for the Suppression of the White Slave Traffic (1904), as amended by the Protocol of 1948; International Convention for the Suppression of the White Slave Traffic (1910), as amended by the 1948 Protocol; International Convention of for the Suppression of the Traffic in Women and Children (1921), as amended by the Protocol of 1947; International Convention Suppression of the Traffic in Women of Full Age (1933). The United States has not signed this agreement.

REFERENCE:

Sakhrobanek, Siriphon, et al. *The Traffic in Women: Human Realities of the International Sex Trade.* London: Zed Books, 1997.

Convention Relating to the Status of Refugees

SIGNED: July 28, 1951, at Geneva

SIGNATORIES: Albania, Algeria, Angola, Antigua and Barbuda, Argentina, Armenia, Australia, Austria, Azerbaijan, Bahamas, Belgium, Belize, Benin, Bolivia, Bosnia-Herzegovina, Botswana, Brazil, Bulgaria, Burkina Faso, Burundi, Cambodia, Cameroon, Canada, Cape Verde, Central African Republic, Chad, Chile, China, Colombia, Congo, Costa Rica, Côte d'Ivoire, Croatia, Cyprus, Czech Republic, Czechoslovakia, Denmark, Djibouti, Dominica, Dominican Republic, Ecuador, Egypt, El Salvador, Equatorial Guinea, Ethiopia, Fiji, Finland, Former Yugoslav Republic of Macedonia, France, Gabon, Gambia, Germany (Federal Republic), Ghana, Greece, Guatemala, Guinea, Guinea-Bissau, Haiti, Holy See, Honduras, Hungary, Iceland, Iran, Ireland, Israel, Italy, Jamaica, Japan, Kenya, Kiribati, Korea, Kyrgyz Republic, Lesotho, Liberia, Liechtenstein, Luxembourg, Madagascar, Malawi, Mali, Malta, Mauritania, Monaco, Morocco, Mozambique, Netherlands, New Zealand, Nicaragua, Niger, Nigeria, Norway, Panama, Papua New Guinea, Paraguay, Peru, Philippines, Poland, Portugal, Romania, Russian Federation, Rwanda, St. Lucia, Samoa, Sao Tome and Principe, Senegal, Seychelles, Sierra Leone, Slovak Republic, Slovenia, Somalia, South Africa, Spain, Sudan, Suriname, Swaziland, Sweden, Switzerland, Tajikistan, Tanzania, Togo, Tunisia, Turkey, Tuvalu, Uganda, United Kingdom, United States, Uruguay, Venezuela, Yemen (Sanaa), Yugoslavia, Zaire, Zambia, Zimbabwe

IN FORCE: From April 22, 1954

OVERVIEW: A convention defining the status of refugee, as well as the rights and obligations of refugees and of states with regard to refugees.

DISCUSSION:

This convention revises and consolidates previous international agreements relating to the status of refugees, extending the scope of coverage and the protection accorded. Article 1 is a detailed definition of refugee status. Article 2 is a simple statement of the refugee's "duties to the country in which he finds himself, which require in particular that he conform to its laws and regulations as well as to measures taken for the maintenance of public order." The rest of the convention addresses the following issues:

- Non-discrimination: "The Contracting States shall apply the provisions of this Convention to refugees without discrimination as to race, religion or country of origin."
- Freedom of religion—not to be withheld by contracting states
- Exceptional measures—refugees to be exempt from "exceptional measures" taken by the host state
- Juridical status of the refugee, including the right to property, the right to protection of copyright and patent rights, the right of association, and access to courts
- Labor issues—the refugee has the right to work
- Non-discrimination with regard to rationing, housing, public relief, public education, social security
- Freedom of movement
- Identity documents
- Expulsion: "The Contracting States shall not expel a refugee lawfully in their territory save on grounds of national security or public order."
- Naturalization: "The Contracting States shall as far as possible facilitate the assimilation and naturalisation of refugees. They shall in particular make every effort to expedite naturalisation proceedings and to reduce as far as possible the charges and costs of such proceedings."

In 1967, the convention was renewed by **Protocol I Relating to the Status of Refugees,** in which signatories undertake to cooperate fully with the United Nations High Commissioner for Refugees.

REFERENCE:
Bernstein, Ann, and Myron Weiner, eds. *Migration and Refugee Policies: An Overview.* London: Pinter, 1999.

Supplementary Convention on the Abolition of Slavery, the Slave Trade, and Institutions and Practices Similar to Slavery

SIGNED: September 7, 1956, at Geneva

SIGNATORIES: Afghanistan, Albania, Algeria, Antigua and Barbuda, Argentina, Australia, Austria, Azerbaijan, Bahamas, Bahrain, Bangladesh, Barbados, Belarus, Belgium, Belize, Benin, Bolivia, Bosnia-Herzegovina, Botswana, Brazil, Brunei, Bulgaria, Burma, Cambodia, Cameroon, Canada, Central African Republic, Chile, China (Taiwan), Congo, Côte d'Ivoire, Croatia, Cuba, Cyprus, Czech Republic, Czechoslovakia, Denmark, Djibouti, Dominica, Dominican Republic, Ecuador, Egypt, Estonia, Ethiopia, Fiji, Finland, Former Yugoslav Republic of Macedonia, France, Gambia, German Democratic Republic, Germany (Federal Republic), Ghana, Greece, Grenada, Guatemala, Guinea, Guyana, Haiti, Hungary, Iceland, India, Iran, Iraq, Ireland, Israel, Italy, Jamaica, Jordan, Kiribati, Kuwait, Laos, Latvia, Lebanon, Lesotho, Liberia, Libya, Luxembourg, Madagascar, Malawi, Malaysia, Mali, Malta, Mauritania, Mauritius, Mexico, Monaco, Mongolia, Morocco, Nauru, Nepal, Netherlands, New Zealand, Nicaragua, Niger, Nigeria, Norway, Pakistan, Papua New Guinea, Philippines, Poland, Portugal, Romania, Russian Federation, St. Kitts and Nevis, St. Lucia, St. Vincent and the Grenadines, San Marino, Saudi Arabia, Senegal, Seychelles, Sierra Leone, Singapore, Slovak Republic, Slovenia, Solomon Islands, South Africa, Spain, Sri Lanka, Sudan, Suriname, Swaziland, Sweden, Switzerland, Syrian Arab Republic, Tanzania, Togo, Tonga, Trinidad and Tobago, Tunisia, Turkey, Tuvalu, Uganda, Ukraine, Union of Soviet Socialist Republics, United Kingdom, United States, Vietnam, Yemen (Aden), Yugoslavia, Zaire, Zambia, Zimbabwe

IN FORCE: From April 30, 1957; for the United States, December 6, 1967

OVERVIEW: The present documents "augments" the **Convention to Suppress the Slave Trade and Slavery** (1926) to the end of intensifying "national as well as international efforts towards the abolition of slavery, the slave trade and institutions and practices similar to slavery."

DISCUSSION:

The chief amplification of the 1926 document is the recognition of "institutions and practices similar to slavery," including debt bondage, serfdom, and:

Any institution or practice whereby:

(i) A woman, without the right to refuse, is promised or given in marriage on payment of a consideration in money or in kind to her parents, guardian, family or any other person or group; or

(ii) The husband of a woman, his family, or his clan, has the right to transfer her to another person for value received or otherwise; or

(iii) A woman on the death of her husband is liable to be inherited by another person;

(d) Any institution or practice whereby a child or young person under the age of 18 years is delivered by either or both of his natural parents or by his guardian to another person, whether for reward or not, with a view to the exploitation of the child or young person or of his labour.

Signatories to the Supplementary Convention undertake to deem all forms of slavery and practices similar to slavery criminal offenses and to cooperate with one another and with United Nations authorities to abolish slavery and similar practices.

REFERENCES:
Eltis, David. *The Abolition of the Atlantic Slave Trade: Origins and Effects on Europe, Africa, and the Americas.* Madison: University of Wisconsin Press, 1982.
Hogg, Peter C. *the African Slave Trade and its Suppression, a Classified and Annotated Bibliography of Books, Pamphlets and Periodical Articles.* London, Frank Cass, 1973.

Convention Concerning the Abolition of Forced Labor

SIGNED: June 25, 1957, at Geneva

SIGNATORIES: Antigua, Austria, Bahamas, Barbados, Basutoland, Bechuanaland, Bermuda, British Guiana, British Somaliland, British Virgin Islands, Brunei, Canada, China, Colony of Aden, Costa Rica, Cuba, Denmark, Dominica, Dominican Republic, El Salvador, Faeroe Islands, Falkland Islands, Federation of Malaya, Germany (Federal Republic), Ghana, Gibraltar, Gilbert and Ellice Islands, Grenada, Guernsey, Haiti, Honduras, Hong Kong, Iran, Iraq, Ireland, Isle of Man, Israel, Jamaica, Jersey, Jordan, Malta, Mauritius, Mexico, Montserrat, Netherlands, Netherlands Antilles, North Borneo, Norway, Poland, Portugal, Saint Helena, Sarawak, Seychelles, Sierra Leone, Singapore, Southern Rhodesia, St. Kitts-Nevis-Anguilla, St. Lucia, St. Vincent, Suriname, Swaziland, Sweden, Switzerland, Trinidad and Tobago, Tunisia, United Arab Republic, United Kingdom of Great Britain and Northern Ireland, Zanzibar

IN FORCE: From January 17, 1959

OVERVIEW: A convention adopted by members of the International Labor Organization to abolish forced or compulsory labor. The United States has declined to sign this convention.

DISCUSSION:

Article 1 embodies the substance of the convention as follows:

Each Member of the International Labour Organisation which

ratifies this Convention undertakes to suppress and not to make use of any form of forced or compulsory labor—

(a) as a means of political coercion or education or as a punishment for holding or expressing political views or views ideologically opposed to the established political, social or economic system;

(b) as a method of mobilizing and using labor for purposes of economic development;

(c) as a means of labor discipline;

(d) as a punishment for having participated in strikes;

(e) as a means of racial, social, national or religious discrimination.

REFERENCE:
Brass, Tom, and Marcel van der Linden, eds. *Free and Unfree Labour: the Debate Continues.* Bern, Switzerland, and New York: Peter Lang, 1997.

Declaration on the Granting of Independence to Colonial Countries and Peoples

ADOPTION: December 14, 1960, at New York
SIGNATORIES: United Nations General Assembly
IN FORCE: From adoption
OVERVIEW: A declaration denouncing "colonialism in all its forms and manifestations."

DISCUSSION:
The declaration denounces colonialism and lays down seven tenets in regard to it:

1. The subjection of peoples to alien subjugation, domination and exploitation constitutes a denial of fundamental human rights, is contrary to the Charter of the United Nations and is an impediment to the promotion of world peace and co-operation.

2. All peoples have the right to self-determination; by virtue of that right they freely determine their political status and freely pursue their economic, social and cultural development.

3. Inadequacy of political, economic, social or educational preparedness should never serve as a pretext for delaying independence.

4. All armed action or repressive measures of all kinds directed against dependent peoples shall cease in order to enable them to exercise peacefully and freely their right to complete independence, and the integrity of their national territory shall be respected.

5. Immediate steps shall be taken, in Trust and Non-Self-Governing Territories or all other territories which have not yet attained independence, to transfer all powers to the peoples of those territories, without any conditions or reservations, in accordance with their freely expressed will and desire, without any distinction as to race, creed or colour, in order to enable them to enjoy complete independence and freedom.

6. Any attempt aimed at the partial or total disruption of the national unity and the territorial integrity of a country is incompatible with the purposes and principles of the Charter of the United Nations.

7. All States shall observe faithfully and strictly the provisions of the Charter of the United Nations, the Universal Declaration of Human Rights and the present Declaration on the basis of equality, non-interference in the internal affairs of all States, and respect for the sovereign rights of all peoples and their territorial integrity.

REFERENCES:
Chalterjee, Partha. *The Nation and its Fragments: Colonial and Postcolonial Histories.* Princeton, NJ: Princeton University Press, 1993.
Prakash, Gyan, ed. *After Colonialism: Imperial Histories and Postcolonial Displacements.* Princeton, NJ: Princeton University Press, 1995.

International Convention on the Elimination of All Forms of Racial Discrimination

SIGNED: December 21, 1965, at New York
SIGNATORIES: Afghanistan, Albania, Algeria, Antigua and Barbuda, Argentina, Armenia, Australia, Austria, Azerbaijan, Bahamas, Bahrain, Bangladesh, Barbados, Belarus, Belgium, Benin, Bhutan, Bolivia, Bosnia Herzegovina, Botswana, Brazil, Bulgaria, Burkina Faso, Burundi, Cambodia, Cameroon, Canada, Cape Verde, Central African Republic, Chad, Chile, China, Colombia, Congo, Costa Rica, Côte d'Ivoire, Croatia, Cuba, Cyprus, Czech Republic, Denmark, Dominican Republic, Ecuador, Egypt, El Salvador, Estonia, Ethiopia, Fiji, Finland, Former Yugoslav Republic of Macedonia, France, Gabon, Gambia, Germany, Ghana, Greece, Grenada, Guatemala, Guinea, Guyana, Haiti, Holy See, Hungary, Iceland, India, Iran, Iraq, Ireland, Israel, Italy, Jamaica, Japan, Jordan, Korea, Kuwait, Laos, Latvia, Lebanon, Lesotho, Liberia, Libya, Luxembourg, Madagascar, Malawi, Maldives, Mali, Malta, Mauritania, Mauritius, Mexico, Moldova, Monaco, Mongolia, Morocco, Mozambique, Namibia, Nepal, Netherlands, New Zealand, Nicaragua, Niger, Nigeria, Norway, Pakistan, Panama, Papua New Guinea, Peru, Philippines, Poland, Portugal, Qatar, Romania, Russian Federation, Rwanda, St. Lucia, St. Vincent and the Grenadines, Senegal, Seychelles, Sierra Leone, Slovak Republic, Slovenia, Solomon Islands, Somalia, Spain, Sri Lanka, Sudan, Suriname, Swaziland, Sweden, Switzerland, Syria, Tajikistan, Tanzania, Togo, Tonga, Trinidad and Tobago, Tunisia, Turkey, Turkmenistan, Uganda, Ukraine, United Arab Emirates, United Kingdom, United States, Uruguay, Uzbekistan, Venezuela, Vietnam, Yemen, Yugoslavia, Zaire, Zambia, Zimbabwe
IN FORCE: From January 4, 1969 (in force for the United States from November 20, 1994)

OVERVIEW: A comprehensive convention defining and prohibiting racial discrimination that "has the purpose or effect of nullifying or impairing the recognition, enjoyment, or exercise, on an equal footing, of human rights and fundamental freedoms in the political, economic, social, cultural or any other field of public life."

DISCUSSION:
To eliminate racial discrimination, the convention calls for the following:
- Punishment of "all dissemination of ideas based on racial superiority or hatred, or incitement to racial discrimination, as well as all acts of violence or incitement to such acts against any group of persons of another color or ethnic origin"
- Prohibition of "Organizations, and also all propaganda activities, which promote and incite racial discrimination"
- Prohibition of public authorities and institutions from promoting discrimination

Basic human rights are to be guaranteed by each signatory, including political, civil, economic, social, and cultural rights, and "the right of access to any place or service intended for use by the general public."

REFERENCE:
Banton, Michael P. *International Action against Racial Discrimination.* Oxford, UK: Clarendon Press, 1996.

International Covenant on Civil and Political Rights

SIGNED: December 16, 1966, at New York
SIGNATORIES: Afghanistan, Albania, Algeria, Angola, Argentina, Armenia, Australia, Austria, Azerbaijan, Barbados, Belarus, Belgium, Belize, Benin, Bolivia, Bosnia-Herzegovina, Brazil, Bulgaria, Burundi, Cambodia, Cameroon, Canada, Cape Verde, Central African Republic, Chad, Chile, Colombia, Congo, Costa Rica, Côte d'Ivoire, Croatia, Cyprus, Czech Republic, Czechoslovakia, Denmark, Dominica, Dominican Republic, Ecuador, Egypt, El Salvador, Equatorial Guinea, Estonia, Ethiopia, Finland, Former Yugoslav Republic of Macedonia, France, Gabon, Gambia, Georgia, German Democratic Republic, Germany (Federal Republic), Grenada, Guatemala, Guinea, Guyana, Haiti, Hungary, Iceland, India, Iran, Iraq, Ireland, Israel, Italy, Jamaica, Japan, Jordan, Kenya, Korea (Democratic People's Republic), Korea (Republic), Kuwait, Kyrgyz Republic, Latvia, Lebanon, Lesotho, Libya, Lithuania, Luxembourg, Madagascar, Malawi, Mali, Malta, Mauritius, Mexico, Moldova, Mongolia, Morocco, Mozambique, Namibia, Nepal, Netherlands, New Zealand, Nicaragua, Niger, Nigeria, Norway, Panama, Paraguay, Peru, Philippines, Poland, Portugal, Romania, Russian Federation, Rwanda, St. Vincent and the Grenadines, San

Marino, Senegal, Seychelles, Sierra Leone, Slovak Republic, Slovenia, Somalia, Spain, Sri Lanka, Sudan, Suriname, Sweden, Switzerland, Syria, Tanzania, Thailand, Togo, Trinidad and Tobago, Tunisia, Uganda, Ukraine, Union of Soviet Socialist Republics, United Kingdom, United States, Uruguay, Uzbekistan, Venezuela, Vietnam, Yemen (Aden), Yugoslavia, Zaire, Zambia, Zimbabwe

IN FORCE: From March 23, 1976
OVERVIEW: An international covenant guaranteeing civil and political rights to all people.

DISCUSSION:
The signatories undertook to guarantee civil and political rights to all people within their territories. Principal rights include the following:
- Self-determination
- Freedom from discrimination on account of "race, color, sex, language, religion, political or other opinion, national or social origin, property, birth or other status"
- "Inherent right to life"
- Freedom from "torture or . . . cruel, inhuman or degrading treatment or punishment"
- Freedom from slavery
- Freedom from "arbitrary arrest or detention"
- Humane incarceration pursuant to due process of law
- "Freedom of thought, conscience and religion"
- "Freedom of association with others, including the right to form and join trade unions"
- State protection of families and of children

In addition to enumerating the rights signatories undertake to guarantee, the covenant set up apparatus for monitoring the rights situation worldwide and addressing rights violations.

REFERENCES:
Shue, Henry. *Basic RIghts: Subsistence, Affluence, and U.S. Foreign Policy.* Princeton, NJ: Princeton University Press, 1996.
Spinner, Jeff. *The Boundaries of Citizenship: Race, Ethnicity, and Nationality in the Liberal State.* Baltimore: Johns Hopkins University Press, 1995.

International Covenant on Economic, Social, and Cultural Rights

SIGNED: December 16, 1966, at New York
SIGNATORIES: Afghanistan, Albania, Algeria, Angola, Argentina, Armenia, Australia, Austria, Azerbaijan, Bangladesh, Barbados, Belarus, Belgium, Benin, Bolivia, Bosnia and Herzegovina, Brazil, Bulgaria, Burkina Faso, Burundi, Cambodia, Cameroon, Canada, Cape Verde, Central African Republic, Chad, Chile, China, Colombia, Congo, Costa Rica, Côte d'Ivoire, Croatia, Cyprus, Czech Republic, Democratic Republic of the Congo, Denmark,

Dominica, Dominican Republic, Ecuador, Egypt, El Salvador, Equatorial Guinea, Estonia, Ethiopia, Finland, France, Gabon, Gambia, Georgia, Germany, Greece, Grenada, Guatemala, Guinea, Guinea-Bissau, Guyana, Honduras, Hungary, Iceland, India, Iran (Islamic Republic of), Iraq, Ireland, Israel, Italy, Jamaica, Japan, Jordan, Kenya, Korea (Democratic People's Republic), Korea (Republic), Kuwait, Kyrgyzstan, Latvia, Lebanon, Lesotho, Liberia, Libyan Arab Jamahiriya, Liechtenstein, Lithuania, Luxembourg, Madagascar, Malawi, Mali, Malta, Mauritius, Mexico, Monaco, Mongolia, Morocco, Namibia, Nepal, Netherlands, New Zealand, Nicaragua, Niger, Nigeria, Norway, Panama, Paraguay, Peru, Philippines, Poland, Portugal, Republic of Moldova, Romania, Russian Federation, Rwanda, Saint Vincent and the Grenadines, San Marino, Sao Tome and Principe, Senegal, Seychelles, Sierra Leone, Slovakia, Slovenia, Solomon Islands, Somalia, South Africa, Spain, Sri Lanka, Sudan, Suriname, Sweden, Switzerland, Syrian Arab Republic, Tajikistan, Former Yugoslav Republic of Macedonia, Togo, Trinidad and Tobago, Tunisia, Turkmenistan, Uganda, Ukraine, United Kingdom, United Republic of Tanzania, United States, Uruguay, Uzbekistan, Venezuela, Vietnam, Yemen, Yugoslavia, Zambia, Zimbabwe

IN FORCE: From January 3, 1976

OVERVIEW: A convention that enumerates the basic economic, social, and cultural rights of individuals and nations.

DISCUSSION:

This document expands earlier United Nations human rights covenants more deeply into the economic sphere. The rights described here include:

- Right to self-determination
- Right to wages sufficient to support a minimum standard of living
- Right to equal pay for equal work
- Right to equal opportunity for advancement
- Right to form trade unions
- Right to strike
- Right to paid or otherwise compensated maternity leave
- Right to free primary education and accessible education at all levels
- Right to copyright, patent, and trademark protection for intellectual property

The convention also forbids exploitation of children, and requires signatories to undertake action to end world hunger. Nations ratifying the covenant are required to submit annual reports to the Secretary General on progress in providing for the rights enumerated to the Secretary General.

REFERENCES:

Shue, Henry. *Basic Rights: Subsistence, Affluence, and U.S. Foreign Policy.* Princeton, NJ: Princeton University Press, 1996.

Spinner, Jeff. *The Boundaries of Citizenship: Race, Ethnicity, and Nationality in the Liberal State.* Baltimore: Johns Hopkins University Press, 1995.

Optional Protocol to the International Covenant on Civil and Political Rights

SIGNED: December 16, 1966, at New York

SIGNATORIES: Algeria, Angola, Argentina, Armenia, Australia, Austria, Barbados, Belarus, Belgium, Benin, Bolivia, Bosnia and Herzegovina, Bulgaria, Burkina Faso, Cameroon, Canada, Central African Republic, Chad, Chile, China, Colombia, Congo, Costa Rica, Côte d'Ivoire, Croatia, Cyprus, Czech Republic, Democratic Republic of the Congo, Denmark, Dominican Republic, Ecuador, El Salvador, Equatorial Guinea, Estonia, Finland, Former Yugoslav Republic of Macedonia, France, Gambia, Georgia, Germany, Greece, Guinea, Guyana, Honduras, Hungary, Iceland, Ireland, Italy, Jamaica, Kyrgyzstan, Latvia, Libyan Arab Jamahiriya, Liechtenstein, Lithuania, Luxembourg, Madagascar, Malawi, Malta, Mauritius, Mongolia, Namibia, Netherlands, Nepal, New Zealand, Nicaragua, Niger, Norway, Panama, Paraguay, Peru, Philippines, Poland, Portugal, Republic of Korea, Romania, Russian Federation, Saint Vincent and the Grenadines, San Marino, Senegal, Seychelles, Sierra Leone, Slovakia, Slovenia, Somalia, Spain, Sri Lanka, Suriname, Sweden, Tajikistan, Trinidad and Tobago, Togo, Turkmenistan, Uganda, Ukraine, Uruguay, Uzbekistan, Venezuela, Yugoslavia, Zambia

IN FORCE: From March 23, 1976

OVERVIEW: An optional protocol to the 1966 **International Covenant on Civil and Political Rights** providing procedures for victims of rights violations to appeal directly to the United Nations Human Rights Committee.

DISCUSSION:

The United States is among a minority of United Nations member states that have not endorsed the optional protocol to the 1966 **International Covenant on Civil and Political Rights.** The protocol provides for individuals who believe themselves to be victims of a rights violation to appeal directly to the United Nations Human Rights Committee:

Article 1

A State Party to the Covenant that becomes a Party to the present Protocol recognizes the competence of the Committee to receive and consider communications from individuals subject to its jurisdiction who claim to be victims of a violation by that State Party of any of the rights set forth in the Covenant. No communication shall be received by the Committee if it concerns a State Party to the Covenant which is not a Party to the present Protocol.

Article 2

Subject to the provisions of Article 1, individuals who claim that any of their rights enumerated in the Covenant have been violated and who have exhausted all available domestic remedies may submit a written communication to the Committee for consideration.

REFERENCES:

Shue, Henry. *Basic Rights: Subsistence, Affluence, and U.S. Foreign Policy.* Princeton, NJ: Princeton University Press, 1996.

Spinner, Jeff. *The Boundaries of Citizenship: Race, Ethnicity, and Nationality in the Liberal State.* Baltimore: Johns Hopkins University Press, 1995.

Protocol I Relating to the Status of Refugees

SIGNED: January 31, 1967, at New York

SIGNATORIES: Albania, Algeria, Angola, Antigua and Barbuda, Argentina, Armenia, Australia, Austria, Azerbaijan, Bahamas, Belgium, Belize, Benin, Bolivia, Bosnia-Herzegovina, Botswana, Brazil, Bulgaria, Burkina Faso, Burundi, Cambodia, Cameroon, Canada, Cape Verde, Central African Republic, Chad, Chile, China, Colombia, Congo, Costa Rica, Côte d'Ivoire, Croatia, Cyprus, Czech Republic, Czechoslovakia, Denmark, Djibouti, Dominica, Dominican Republic, Ecuador, Egypt, El Salvador, Equatorial Guinea, Ethiopia, Fiji, Finland, Former Yugoslav Republic of Macedonia, France, Gabon, Gambia, Germany (Federal Republic), Ghana, Greece, Guatemala, Guinea, Guinea-Bissau, Haiti, Holy See, Honduras, Hungary, Iceland, Iran, Ireland, Israel, Italy, Jamaica, Japan, Kenya, Kinbati, Korea, Kyrgyz Republic, Lesotho, Liberia, Liechtenstein, Luxembourg, Malawi, Mali, Malta, Mauritania, Morocco, Mozambique, New Zealand, Nicaragua, Niger, Nigeria, Norway, Panama, Papua New Guinea, Paraguay, Peru, Philippines, Poland, Portugal, Romania, Russian Federation, Rwanda, St. Lucia, Samoa, Sao Tome and Principe, Senegal, Seychelles, Sierra Leone, Slovak Republic, Slovenia, Somalia, South Africa, Spain, Sudan, Suriname, Swaziland, Sweden, Switzerland, Tajikistan, Tanzania, Togo, Tunisia, Turkey, Tuvalu, Uganda, United Kingdom, United States, Uruguay, Venezuela, Yemen (Sanaa), Yugoslavia, Zaire, Zambia, Zimbabwe

IN FORCE: From October 4, 1967; for the United States, November 1, 1968

OVERVIEW: The protocol renews the **Convention Relating to the Status of Refugees** (1951), and signatories undertake to cooperate fully with the United Nations High Commissioner for Refugees.

REFERENCE:

Bernstein, Ann, and Myron Weiner, eds. *Migration and Refugee Policies: An Overview.* London: Pinter, 1999.

American Convention on Human Rights (Pact of San José, Costa Rica)

SIGNED: November 22, 1969, at San José, Costa Rica

SIGNATORIES: Barbados, Bolivia, Chile, Colombia, Costa Rica, Domincan Republic, Ecuador, El Salvador, Grenada, Guatemala, Haiti, Honduras, Jamaica, Nicaragua, Panama, Paraguay, Peru, United States, Uruguay, Venezuela

In force: From July 18, 1978

OVERVIEW: "... a convention reinforcing or complementing the protection provided by the domestic law of the American states ..."

DISCUSSION:

Enacted under the auspices of the Organization of American States, the convention seeks to guarantee the following basic human rights:

- "RIGHT TO JURIDICAL PERSONALITY. Every person has the right to recognition as a person before the law."
- Right to life
- Right to humane treatment
- Freedom from slavery
- Right to personal liberty
- Right to a fair trial
- "FREEDOM FROM 'EX POST FACTO' LAWS. No one shall be convicted of any act or omission that did not constitute a criminal offense, under the applicable law, at the time it was committed."
- "RIGHT TO COMPENSATION. Every person has the right to be compensated in accordance with the law in the event he has been sentenced by a final judgment through a miscarriage of justice."
- Right to privacy
- Freedom of conscience and religion
- Freedom of thought and expression
- "RIGHT OF REPLY. ... Anyone injured by inaccurate or offensive statements or ideas disseminated to the public in general by a legally regulated medium of communication has the right to reply or to make a correction using the same communications outlet, under such conditions as the law may establish."
- Right of assembly
- "RIGHTS OF THE FAMILY. ... The family is the natural and fundamental group unit of society and is entitled to protection by society and the state.
- "RIGHT TO A NAME. Every person has the right to a given name and to the surnames of his parents or that of one of them. The law shall regulate the manner in which this right shall be ensured for all, by the use of assumed names if necessary."
- "RIGHTS OF THE CHILD. Every minor child has the right to the measures of protection required by his condition as a minor on the part of his family, society, and the state."
- Right to nationality
- Right to property
- Freedom of movement and residence
- Right to participate in government

- "RIGHT TO EQUAL PROTECTION. All persons are equal before the law. Consequently, they are entitled, without discrimination, to equal protection of the law."
- Right to judicial protection

The convention established "The Inter-American Commission on Human Rights . . . composed of seven members who shall be persons of high moral character and recognized competence in the field of human rights. . . . The main function of the Commission shall be to promote respect for and defense of human rights." The commission was to report annually on the state of human rights to the General Assembly of the Organization of American States, which might take action accordingly.

REFERENCE:
Morsink, Johannes. *The Universal Declaration of Human Rights: Origins, Drafting, and Intent.* Philadelphia: University of Pennsylvania Press, 1999.

Declaration on the Rights of Mentally Retarded Persons

ADOPTED: December 20, 1971, at New York
SIGNATORIES: United Nations General Assembly resolution
IN FORCE: From adoption
OVERVIEW: A United Nations General Assembly resolution affirming the human rights of mentally retarded persons.

DISCUSSION:
The declaration affirms the following seven basic human rights of mentally retarded persons:

1. The mentally retarded person has, to the maximum degree of feasibility, the same rights as other human beings.
2. The mentally retarded person has a right to proper medical care and physical therapy and to such education, training, rehabilitation and guidance as will enable him to develop his ability and maximum potential.
3. The mentally retarded person has a right to economic security and to a decent standard of living. He has a right to perform productive work or to engage in any other meaningful occupation to the fullest possible extent of his capabilities.
4. Whenever possible, the mentally retarded person should live with his own family or with foster parents and participate in different forms of community life. The family with which he lives should receive assistance. If care in an institution becomes necessary, it should be provided in surroundings and other circumstances as close as possible to those of normal life.
5. The mentally retarded person has a right to a qualified guardian when this is required to protect his personal well-being and interests.

6. The mentally retarded person has a right to protection from exploitation, abuse and degrading treatment. If prosecuted for any offence, he shall have a right to due process of law with full recognition being given to his degree of mental responsibility.
7. Whenever mentally retarded persons are unable, because of the severity of their handicap, to exercise all their rights in a meaningful way or it should become necessary to restrict or deny some or all of these rights, the procedure used for that restriction or denial of rights must contain proper legal safeguards against every form of abuse. This procedure must be based on an evaluation of the social capability of the mentally retarded person by qualified experts and must be subject to periodic review and to the right of appeal to higher authorities.

REFERENCE:
Herr, Stanley S. *Rights and Advocacy for Retarded People.* Lexington, MA: Lexington Books, 1983.

Apartheid Convention

OFFICIAL TITLE: International Convention on the Suppression and Punishment of the International Crime of Apartheid
SIGNED: November 30, 1973, at New York
SIGNATORIES: Afghanistan, Algeria, Antigua and Barbuda, Argentina, Armenia, Azerbaijan, Bahamas, Bahrain, Bangladesh, Barbados, Belarus, Benin, Bolivia, Bosnia and Herzegovina, Bulgaria, Burkina Faso, Burundi, Cambodia, Cameroon, Cape Verde, Central African Republic, Chad, China, Colombia, Congo, Costa Rica, Croatia, Cuba, Czech Republic, Democratic Republic of the Congo, Ecuador, Egypt, El Salvador, Estonia, Ethiopia, Former Yugoslav Republic of Macedonia, Gabon, Gambia, Ghana, Guinea, Guyana, Haiti, Hungary, India, Iran (Islamic Republic of), Iraq, Jamaica, Jordan, Kenya, Kuwait, Kyrgyzstan, Lao People's Democratic Republic, Latvia, Lesotho, Liberia, Libyan Arab Jamahiriya, Madagascar, Maldives, Mali, Mauritania, Mexico, Mongolia, Mozambique, Namibia, Nepal, Nicaragua, Niger, Nigeria, Oman, Pakistan, Panama, Peru, Philippines, Poland, Qatar, Romania, Russian Federation, Rwanda, Saint Vincent and the Grenadines, Sao Tome and Principe, Senegal, Seychelles, Slovakia, Slovenia, Somalia, Sri Lanka, Sudan, Suriname, Syrian Arab Republic, Togo, Trinidad and Tobago, Tunisia, Uganda, Ukraine, United Arab Emirates, United Republic of Tanzania, Venezuela. Vietnam, Yemen, Yugoslavia, Zambia, Zimbabwe
IN FORCE: From July 18, 1976
OVERVIEW: "The States Parties to the present Convention declare that apartheid is a crime against humanity and that inhuman acts resulting from the policies and practices of apartheid and similar policies and practices of racial segregation and discrimination, as defined in Article II of the Convention, are crimes

violating the principles of international law, in particular the purposes and principles of the Charter of the United Nations, and constituting a serious threat to international peace and security."

DISCUSSION:

The failure of the United States to sign this convention caused great controversy at home and abroad, especially since an overwhelming majority of United Nations member nations both signed and ratified the document, which was directed primarily against South Africa, where apartheid—strict racial segregation—was a cornerstone of law and society. In part as a result of the moral suasion represented by this convention, and as a result of the pressure of international economic sanctions (in which the United States and many U.S.-based corporations participated), as well as internal protest, the policy of apartheid, which had been officially instituted in 1950, was brought to an end by legislation enacted by President F. W. de Klerk. In 1993, a new South African constitution fully enfranchised blacks and other racial groups, and the national elections of 1994 produced a coalition government with a black majority. As a legal force, apartheid was totally ended.

The scope of the convention is contained in the first two articles:

Article 1

1. The States Parties to the present Convention declare that apartheid is a crime against humanity and that inhuman acts resulting from the policies and practices of apartheid and similar policies and practices of racial segregation and discrimination, as defined in Article II of the Convention, are crimes violating the principles of international law, in particular the purposes and principles of the Charter of the United Nations, and constituting a serious threat to international peace and security.

2. The States Parties to the present Convention declare criminal those organizations, institutions and individuals committing the crime of apartheid.

Article 2

For the purpose of the present Convention, the term "the crime of apartheid," which shall include similar policies and practices of racial segregation and discrimination as practised in southern Africa, shall apply to the following inhuman acts committed for the purpose of establishing and maintaining domination by one racial group of persons over any other racial group of persons and systematically oppressing them:

(a) Denial to a member or members of a racial group or groups of the right to life and liberty of person:

(i) By murder of members of a racial group or groups;

(ii) By the infliction upon the members of a racial group or groups of serious bodily or mental harm, by the infringement of their freedom or dignity, or by subjecting them to torture or to cruel, inhuman or degrading treatment or punishment;

(iii) By arbitrary arrest and illegal imprisonment of the members of a racial group or groups;

(b) Deliberate imposition on a racial group or groups of living conditions calculated to cause its or their physical destruction in whole or in part;

(c) Any legislative measures and other measures calculated to prevent a racial group or groups from participation in the political, social, economic and cultural life of the country and the deliberate creation of conditions preventing the full development of such a group or groups, in particular by denying to members of a racial group or groups basic human rights and freedoms, including the right to work, the right to form recognized trade unions, the right to education, the right to leave and to return to their country, the right to a nationality, the right to freedom of movement and residence, the right to freedom of opinion and expression, and the right to freedom of peaceful assembly and association;

(d) Any measures, including legislative measures, designed to divide the population along racial lines by the creation of separate reserves and ghettos for the members of a racial group or groups, the prohibition of mixed marriages among members of various racial groups, the expropriation of landed property belonging to a racial group or groups or to members thereof;

(e) Exploitation of the labour of the members of a racial group or groups, in particular by submitting them to forced labour;

(f) Persecution of organizations and persons, by depriving them of fundamental rights and freedoms, because they oppose apartheid.

REFERENCE:

United Nations. *The United Nations and Apartheid, 1948-1994.* New York: United Nations Publications, 1994.

Universal Declaration on the Eradication of Hunger and Malnutrition

SIGNED: November 16, 1974, at Rome
SIGNATORIES: United Nations General Assembly resolution
IN FORCE: From General Assembly adoption, November 17, 1974
OVERVIEW: A declaration of policy against world hunger adopted by the United Nations World Food Conference.

DISCUSSION:

The declaration begins by recognizing the existence of a "grave food crisis that is afflicting the peoples of the developing countries where most of the world's hungry and ill-nourished live and where more than two thirds of the world's population produce about one third of the world's food." This "imbalance . . . threatens to increase in the next ten years," creating a situation that "is not only fraught with grave economic and social implications, but also acutely jeopardizes the most fundamental principles and values associated with the right to life and human dignity as enshrined in the **Universal Declaration of Human Rights.**"

The declaration continues with the following statements:

1. Every man, woman and child has the inalienable right to be free from hunger and malnutrition in order to develop fully and maintain their physical and mental faculties. Society today already possesses sufficient resources, organizational ability and technology and hence the competence to achieve this objective. Accordingly, the eradication of hunger is a common objective of all the countries of the international community, especially of the developed countries and others in a position to help.

2. It is a fundamental responsibility of Governments to work together for higher food production and a more equitable and efficient distribution of food between countries and within countries. Governments should initiate immediately a greater concerted attack on chronic malnutrition and deficiency diseases among the vulnerable and lower income groups. In order to ensure adequate nutrition for all, Governments should formulate appropriate food and nutrition policies integrated in overall socio-economic and agricultural development plans based on adequate knowledge of available as well as potential food resources. The importance of human milk in this connection should be stressed on nutritional grounds.

3. Food problems must be tackled during the preparation and implementation of national plans and programmes for economic and social development, with emphasis on their humanitarian aspects.

REFERENCE:
Young, Liz. *World Hunger.* New York: Routledge, 1997.

Convention Against Torture and Other Cruel, Inhuman or Degrading Treatment or Punishment

SIGNED: December 10, 1984
SIGNATORIES: Afghanistan, Albania, Algeria, Antigua and Barbuda, Argentina, Australia, Austria, Azerbaijan, Belarus, Belize, Benin, Bosnia-Herzegovina, Brazil, Bulgaria, Burundi, Cambodia, Cameroon, Canada, Cape Verde, Chad, Chile, China, Colombia, Costa Rica, Côte d'Ivoire, Croatia, Cuba, Cyprus, Czech Republic, Czechoslovakia, Denmark, Ecuador, Egypt, El Salvador, Estonia, Ethiopia, Finland, Former Yugoslav Republic of Macedonia, France, Georgia, Germany, Greece, Guatemala, Guinea, Guyana, Honduras, Hungary, Iceland, Israel, Italy, Jordan Korea, Kuwait, Latvia, Libya, Liechtenstein, Lithuania, Luxembourg, Malawi, Malta, Mauritius, Mexico, Moldova, Monaco, Namibia, Nepal, Netherlands, New Zealand, Norway, Panama, Paraguay, Peru, Philippines, Poland, Portugal, Romania, Russian Federation, Senegal, Seychelles, Slovak Republic, Slovenia, Somalia, South Africa, Spain, Sri Lanka, Sweden, Switzerland, Tajikistan, Togo, Tunisia, Turkey, Uganda,

Ukraine, United Kingdom, United States, Uruguay, Venezuela, Yemen, Yugoslavia, Zaire
IN FORCE: June 26, 1987; for the United States, November 20, 1994
OVERVIEW: A United Nations convention pursuant to the desire (in the words of the opening of the convention) "to make more effective the struggle against torture and other cruel, inhuman or degrading treatment or punishment throughout the world."

DISCUSSION:
The convention begins with a definition of torture, encompassing the infliction of pain or suffering, "whether physical or mental," and goes on to prohibit torture absolutely. Each signatory is enjoined to "take effective ... measures to prevent acts of torture in any territory under its jurisdiction," and "no exceptional circumstances whatsoever" may be used to justify torture, nor can an "order from a superior officer or public authority" be used to justify torture.

Part II of the convention establishes a Committee against Torture, consisting of 10 expert authorities in the field of human rights, elected by the member states of the United Nations, which functions to investigate and report on programs undertaken to eliminate torture and to investigate incidents of reported torture.

REFERENCE:
Duner, Bertil, ed. *An End to Torture: Strategies for its Eradication.* London: Zed Books, 1999.

Body of Principles for the Protection of All Persons under Any Form of Detention or Imprisonment

ADOPTED: December 9, 1988, at New York
SIGNATORIES: United Nations General Assembly resolution
IN FORCE: From adoption
OVERVIEW: Thirty-nine principles intended as a set of universal minimum standards for the treatment of arrested and detained persons as well as prisoners.

DISCUSSION:
Whereas the 1990 **Basic Principles for the Treatment of Prisoners** applies exclusively to prisoners and is an enumeration of basic rights, the 1988 document applies to all persons arrested or detained, in addition to those officially held as prisoners. The document specifies treatment "in a humane manner and with respect for the inherent dignity of the human person," moreover, "arrest, detention or imprisonment shall only be carried out strictly in accordance with the provisions of the law and by competent officials or persons authorized for that purpose."

REFERENCES:

Matthews, Roger, and Peter Francis, eds. *Prisons 2000: An International Perspective on the Current State and Future of Imprisonment*. New York: St. Martin's, 1996

Smit, Van Zyl. *Imprisonment Today and Tomorrow: International Perspectives on Prisoners' Rights and Prison Conditions*. Amsterdam, Netherlands: Kluwer Law International, 1991.

Second Optional Protocol to the International Covenant on Civil and Political Rights

OFFICIAL TITLE: Second Optional Protocol to the International Covenant on Civil and Political Rights, aiming at the Abolition of the Death Penalty

SIGNED: December 15, 1989, at New York

SIGNATORIES: Australia, Austria, Azerbaijan, Belgium, Bulgaria, Colombia, Costa Rica, Croatia, Denmark, Ecuador, Finland, Former Yugoslav Republic of Macedonia, Germany, Georgia, Greece, Honduras, Hungary, Iceland, Ireland, Italy, Liechtenstein, Luxembourg, Malta, Mozambique, Namibia, Nepal, Netherlands, New Zealand, Nicaragua, Norway, Panama, Portugal, Romania, Seychelles, Slovakia, Slovenia, Spain, Sweden, Switzerland, United Kingdom, Uruguay, Venezuela

IN FORCE: From July 11, 1991

OVERVIEW: "No one within the jurisdiction of a State Party to the present Protocol shall be executed.... Each State Party shall take all necessary measures to abolish the death penalty within its jurisdiction."

DISCUSSION:

The United States is not a signatory to this second optional protocol to the **International Covenant on Civil and Political Rights**, because the death penalty remains in force on the federal level and is a legal penalty in many U.S. state jurisdictions. To abolish the death penalty throughout the United States would require a constitutional amendment and would raise grave issues of state rights versus federal jurisdiction.

REFERENCE:

Schabas, William A. *The Abolition of the Death Penalty in International Law*. Cambridge, UK, and New York: Cambridge University Press, 1997.

Basic Principles for the Treatment of Prisoners

ADOPTION: December 14, 1990, at New York

SIGNATORIES: United Nations General Assembly resolution

IN FORCE: From adoption

OVERVIEW: A statement of eleven principles basic to the treatment of prisoners.

DISCUSSION:

The General Assembly adopted the following eleven statements on the minimum standards for the treatment of prisoners:

1. All prisoners shall be treated with the respect due to their inherent dignity and value as human beings.

2. There shall be no discrimination on the grounds of race, colour, sex, language, religion, political or other opinion, national or social origin, property, birth or other status.

3. It is, however, desirable to respect the religious beliefs and cultural precepts of the group to which prisoners belong, whenever local conditions so require.

4. The responsibility of prisons for the custody of prisoners and for the protection of society against crime shall be discharged in keeping with a State's other social objectives and its fundamental responsibilities for promoting the well-being and development of all members of society.

5. Except for those limitations that are demonstrably necessitated by the fact of incarceration, all prisoners shall retain the human rights and fundamental freedoms set out in the Universal Declaration of Human Rights, and, where the State concerned is a party, the International Covenant on Economic, Social and Cultural Rights, and the International Covenant on Civil and Political Rights and the Optional Protocol thereto, as well as such other rights as are set out in other United Nations covenants.

6. All prisoners shall have the right to take part in cultural activities and education aimed at the full development of the human personality.

7. Efforts addressed to the abolition of solitary confinement as a punishment, or to the restriction of its use, should be undertaken and encouraged.

8. Conditions shall be created enabling prisoners to undertake meaningful remunerated employment which will facilitate their reintegration into the country's labour market and permit them to contribute to their own financial support and to that of their families.

9. Prisoners shall have access to the health services available in the country without discrimination on the grounds of their legal situation.

10. With the participation and help of the community and social institutions, and with due regard to the interests of victims, favourable conditions shall be created for the reintegration of the ex-prisoner into society under the best possible conditions.

11. The above Principles shall be applied impartially.

REFERENCES:

Matthews, Roger, and Peter Francis, eds. *Prisons 2000: An International Perspective on the Current State and Future of Imprisonment*. New York: St. Martin's, 1996

Smit, Van Zyl. *Imprisonment Today and Tomorrow: International Perspectives on Prisoners' Rights and Prison Conditions*. Amsterdam, Netherlands: Kluwer Law International, 1991.

Vienna Declaration and Program of Action

DRAFTED: June 25, 1993, at Vienna

SIGNATORIES: Currently under review

IN FORCE: Not yet in force

OVERVIEW: A monumental effort to "rationalize and enhance" the United Nations position on and programs for human rights.

DISCUSSION:

The 28-page Vienna Declaration was the product of what has been described as a "less-than-successful" world conference on human rights, attended by 171 states. The conference failed to reach agreement on such basic matters as the appointment of a U.N. commissioner for human rights and, even more seriously, revealed critical divergences on human rights issues between developed and less developed nations. In the end, the Vienna Declaration mainly reaffirmed and restated human rights concepts developed in many earlier documents. No new rights were created by the declaration, although the principle of universality—the concept that fundamental human rights transcend cultural peculiarities—was affirmed by the declaration, as was a right to development, which, for the first time in U.N. history, was the subject of consensus.

While critics of the declaration complain that the language of the document is often "ambiguous" and even "grudging," others have pointed out that the declaration gives welcome support to women's rights groups and organizations supporting the rights of indigenous peoples.

REFERENCE:

Morsink, Johannes. *The Universal Declaration of Human Rights: Origins, Drafting, and Intent.* Philadelphia: University of Pennsylvania Press, 1999.

Convention on Human Rights and Biomedicine

SIGNED: April 4, 1997, Oviedo, Spain

SIGNATORIES: Member states of the Council of Europe: Croatia, Cyprus, Czech Republic, Denmark, Estonia, Finland, France, Greece, Hungary, Iceland, Italy, Latvia, Lithuania, Luxembourg, Moldova, Netherlands, Norway, Poland, Portugal, Romania, San Marino, Slovakia, Slovenia, Spain, Sweden, Switzerland, Former Yugoslav Republic of Macedonia, Turkey. The convention is open for signature by the following non-member states (which have not signed as of 1999): Australia, Canada, Holy See, Japan, United States

IN FORCE: Not yet in force as of 1999 (requires ratification by five signatory nations)

OVERVIEW: An international agreement to preserve human dignity, rights, and freedoms through prohibitions against the misuse of biological and medical advances.

DISCUSSION:

The convention puts the interests of human beings before those of science or society and lays down certain principles and prohibitions concerning bioethics, medical research, informed consent, the right to privacy, rules governing organ transplantation, and so on. The convention also bans all forms of discrimination based on genetic make-up, and it allows predictive genetic tests exclusively for medical purposes. The treaty restricts genetic engineering to preventive, diagnostic, and therapeutic applications, in which the object is not changing the genetic make-up of a person's descendants. Medically assisted procreation with the object of choosing the sex of the child is prohibited, except to avoid a serious hereditary condition.

The convention also includes the following:

- Rules for medical research, especially in the case of persons who cannot give their consent
- A prohibition on the creation of human embryos for research purposes
- Rules for providing protection of embryos where countries allow in-vitro research
- Rules for informed consent
- Stipulation that patients have a right to be informed about their health, including the results of predictive genetic tests
- Prohibition of the removal of organs and other tissues that cannot be regenerated from people not able to give consent

REFERENCE:

Brody, Baruch A. *Biomedical Ethics: An International Perspective.* Oxford, UK, and New York: Oxford University Press, 1998.

Food Aid Convention

SIGNED: April 13, 1999, at London

SIGNATORIES: Argentina, Australia, Canada, European Community, Japan, Norway, Switzerland, United States

IN FORCE: Not yet in force

OVERVIEW: The major objective of the convention is to ensure that "appropriate levels of food aid [are] available on a predictable basis."

DISCUSSION:

In addition to ensuring that "appropriate levels of food aid [are] available on a predictable basis," the convention sets the following as additional objectives:

- encouraging members to ensure that the food aid provided is aimed particularly at the alleviation of poverty and hunger of the most vulnerable groups, and is consistent with agricultural development in those countries;
- including principles for maximising the impact, the effectiveness and quality of the food aid provided as a tool in support of food security; and,
- providing a framework for co-operation, co-ordination and information-sharing among members on food aid related

matters to achieve greater efficiency in all aspects of food aid operations and better coherence between food aid and other policy instruments.

In Article 3, "members agree to provide food aid to developing countries or the cash equivalent thereof in [specified] the minimum annual amounts . . . (hereinafter referred to as 'the commitment'). The basic commitments follow:

Member	Tonnage (wheat equivalent)	Value (millions)	Total indicative value (millions)
Argentina	35,000	–	A$90
Australia	250,000	–	C$150
EC and member states	1,320,000	€130	€422
Japan	300,000		–
Norway	30,000		NOK 59
Switzerland	40,000	–	–
United States	2,500,000	–	US$900–1000

Article 4 specifies appropriate products to be furnished in aid, and Article 7 defines "eligible recipients" as follows:

(i) least-developed countries;

(ii) low-income countries;

(iii) lower middle-income countries, and other countries included in the WTO list of Net Food-Importing Developing Countries at the time of negotiation of this Convention, when experiencing food emergencies or internationally recognised financial crises leading to food shortage emergencies, or when food aid operations are targeted on vulnerable groups.

Article 8 provides guidelines relating to "needs," specifying the following:

(a) Food aid should only be provided when it is the most effective and appropriate means of assistance.

(b) Food aid should be based on an evaluation of needs by the recipient and the members, within their own respective policies, and should be aimed at enhancing food security in recipient countries. In responding to those needs, members shall pay attention to meeting the particular nutritional needs of women and children.

(c) Food aid for free distribution should be targeted on vulnerable groups.

(d) The provision of food aid in emergency situations should take particular account of longer-term rehabilitation and development objectives in the recipient countries and should respect basic humanitarian principles. Members shall aim to ensure that the food aid provided reaches the intended recipients in a timely manner.

(e) To the maximum extent possible, non-emergency food aid shall be provided by members on a forward planning basis, so that recipient countries may be able to take account, in their development programmes, of the likely flow of food aid they will receive during each year of this Convention.

(f) If it appears that, because of a substantial production shortfall or other circumstances, a particular country, region or regions is faced with exceptional food needs, the matter shall be considered by the Committee. The Committee may recommend that members should respond to the situation by increasing the amount of food aid provided.

(g) At the time of the identification of food aid needs, members or their partners shall endeavour to consult with each other at the regional and recipient country level, with a view to developing a common approach to needs analysis.

(h) Members agree, where appropriate, to identify priority countries and regions under their food aid programmes. Members will ensure transparency as to their priorities, policies and programmes, by providing information for other donors.

(i) Members will consult with each other, directly or through their relevant partners, on the possibilities for the establishment of common action plans for priority countries, if possible on a multi-annual basis.

Additional articles address means of delivery and coordination and cooperation among donor nations and between donor nations and recipient nations. The convention names the Food Aid Committee (established in 1967) to administer the convention.

REFERENCE:
Young, Liz. *World Hunger*. New York: Routledge, 1997.

SECTION 5.4

Rights and Welfare of Children

Overview of Treaties in This Category

Just as early national legislation concerning the welfare of children focused on regulating or eliminating child labor, so pioneering multilateral conventions in this area focused on the issue of labor. In 1936, Belgium, Brazil, France, Norway, Sweden, and the United States concluded the modest **Convention Fixing the Minimum Age for the Admission of Children to Employment at Sea**, but it was not until 1973 that the United States participated in the more general child-labor agreement, **Convention Concerning Minimum Age for Admission to Employment** (1973). Such international conventions on child labor are deceptively difficult to formulate because of the sharply differing cultural, family, and economic conditions prevailing in various countries.

In 1980, the United Nations addressed the problem of international child abduction—typically by an estranged spouse—in **Convention on the Civil Aspects of International Child Abduction**. Related, broader conventions came later: **Convention on the Protection of Children and Cooperation in Respect of Intercountry Adoption** (1993) and **Convention on Parental Responsibility** (1996). The UN proclaimed 1989 the International Year of the Child, and member states opened for signature a basic human rights convention relating to children: **United Nations Convention on the Rights of the Child.**

In addition to participating in major multilateral agreements on children's rights and welfare, the United States has, from time to time, concluded bilateral aid agreements with individual nations (for example, **Exchange of Notes [with Israel] Constituting an Agreement Relating to a School Feeding Program**, 1963) and with agencies of the United Nations, most notably UNICEF: **Letter of Agreement (with the United Nations Children's Fund) Relating to Assistance for Children and Mothers** (1974) and **Letter of Agreement (with the United Nation's Children's Fund) Amending the Letter Agreement of 26 December 1974 and 30 December 1974** (1975).

Convention Fixing the Minimum Age for the Admission of Children to Employment at Sea

SIGNED: October 24, 1936, at Geneva

SIGNATORIES: Belgium, Brazil, France, Norway, Sweden, United States

IN FORCE: From May 28, 1947 ("as modified by the Final Articles Revision Convention, 1946")

OVERVIEW: A convention specifying that "children under the age of fifteen years shall not be employed or work on vessels, other than vessels upon which only members of the same family are employed."

DISCUSSION:
The convention allows an exception for "work done by children on school-ships or training-ships, provided that such work is approved and supervised by public authority."

REFERENCE:
Hobbs, Sandy, et al. *Child Labor: A World History Companion.* Santa Barbara, CA: ABC-Clio, 1999.

Exchange of Notes (with Israel) Constituting an Agreement Relating to a School Feeding Program

SIGNED: February 28, 1963, at Tel Aviv, and March 21, 1963, at Jerusalem

SIGNATORIES: Israel vs. United States

IN FORCE: From March 21, 1963

OVERVIEW: An agreement whereby the United States undertakes to assist in the expansion of a school feeding program carried out by the Israeli Ministry of Education.

DISCUSSION:
By this agreement, the United States undertakes to help Israeli authorities "improve the quantity and quality of food being given to approximately 164,000 needy school children and to expand this number to a maximum of 200,000 individual recipients. The United States undertakes to supply certain foods over a two-year period up to a dollar value of $1,350,000, plus ocean transportation up to $145,000. The food is to be used to feed

"school children who are needy by reason of their economic status and whose diet is deficient when tested against accepted standards of health."

REFERENCES:
None

Convention Concerning Minimum Age for Admission to Employment

SIGNED: June 26, 1973, at Geneva

SIGNATORIES: Afghanistan, Algeria, Angola, Antigua and Barbuda, Argentina, Armenia, Australia, Austria, Azerbaijan, Bahamas, Bahrain, Bangladesh, Barbados, Belarus, Belgium, Belize, Benin, Bolivia, Bosnia-Herzegovina, Botswana, Brazil, Bulgaria, Burkina Faso, Burma, Burundi, Cambodia, Cameroon, Canada, Cape Verde, Central African Republic, Chad, Chile, China, Colombia, Comoros, Congo, Costa Rica, Côte d'Ivoire, Croatia, Cuba, Cyprus, Czech Republic, Czechoslovakia, Denmark, Djibouti, Dominica, Dominican Republic, Ecuador, Egypt, El Salvador, Equatorial Guinea, Eritrea, Estonia, Ethiopia, Fiji, Finland, Former Yugoslav Republic of Macedonia, France, Gabon, Georgia, German Democratic Republic, Germany (Federal Republic), Ghana, Greece, Grenada, Guatemala, Guinea, Guinea-Bissau, Guyana, Haiti, Honduras, Hungary, Iceland, India, Indonesia, Iran, Iraq, Ireland, Israel, Italy, Jamaica, Japan, Jordan, Kazakstan, Kenya, Korea, Kuwait, Kyrgyz Republic, Laos, Latvia, Lebanon, Lesotho, Liberia, Libya, Lithuania, Luxembourg, Madagascar, Malawi, Malaysia, Mali, Malta, Mauritania, Mexico, Moldova, Mongolia, Morocco, Mozambique Namibia, Nepal, Netherlands, New Zealand, Nicaragua, Niger, Nigeria, Norway, Oman, Pakistan, Panama, Papua New Guinea, Paraguay, Peru, Philippines, Poland, Portugal, Qatar, Romania, Rwanda, St. Lucia, San Marino, Sao Tome and Principe, Saudi Arabia, Senegal, Seychelles, Sierra Leone, Singapore, Slovak Republic, Slovenia, Solomon Islands, Somalia, South Africa, Spain, Sri Lanka, Sudan, Suriname, Swaziland, Sweden, Switzerland, Syrian Arab Republic, Tajikistan, Tanzania, Thailand, Togo, Trinidad and Tobago, Tunisia, Turkey, Turkmenistan, Uganda, Ukraine, Union of Soviet Socialist Republics, United Arab Emirates, United Kingdom, United States, Uruguay, Uzbekistan, Venezuela, Vietnam (Socialist Republic), Yemen (Aden), Yemen (Sanaa), Yugoslavia, Zaire, Zambia, Zimbabwe

IN FORCE: From June 19, 1976

OVERVIEW: "Each Member for which this Convention is in force undertakes to pursue a national policy designed to ensure the effective abolition of child labor and to raise progressively the minimum age for admission to employment or work to a level consistent with the fullest physical and mental development of young persons."

DISCUSSION:

Concluded by the International Labour Organisation, a United Nations entity, the convention was intended as "a general instrument . . . which would gradually replace the existing ones applicable to limited economic sectors, with a view to achieving the total abolition of child labour." Articles 3 and 4 established the general guideline that the minimum age for eligibility for labor "shall not be less than the age of completion of compulsory schooling and, in any case, shall not be less than 15 years," except in cases where the "economy and educational facilities [of a signatory nation] are insufficiently developed"; these states may "initially specify a minimum age of 14 years."

REFERENCE:
Hobbs, Sandy, et al. *Child Labor: A World History Companion.* Santa Barbara, CA: ABC-Clio, 1999.

Letter of Agreement (with the United Nation's Children's Fund) Relating to Assistance for Children and Mothers

SIGNED: December 26, 1974, at Washington, D.C., and December 30, 1974, at New York

SIGNATORIES: United Nations (United Nations Children's Fund) vs. United States

IN FORCE: From December 30, 1974

OVERVIEW: An agreement whereby the United States undertakes to make a contribution of $500,000 to the United Nations Children's Fund (UNICEF) "to be used for UNICEF assistance activities for children and mothers in South Vietnam, in Cambodia and in Laos."

DISCUSSION:

The agreement stipulates that the funds are to be used to upgrade health facilities and services, to reconstruct schools, to provide educational materials, and to improve sanitation facilities. The agreement further stipulates that "Funds contributed hereunder may be used by UNICEF for assistance in the area of South Vietnam nominally controlled by the Provisional Revolutionary Government [that is, the Communists] only if such assistance is channeled other than to or through the Provisional Revolutionary Government." The agreement was amended (**Letter Agreement (with the United Nation's Children's Fund) Amending the Letter Agreement of 26 December 1974 and 30 December 1974**) on February 10, 1975 to increase the amount of the contribution to $1.5 million.

REFERENCE:
Black, Maggie. *Children First: The Story of UNICEF, Past and Present.* New York: Oxford University Press, 1996.

Letter of Agreement (with the United Nation's Children's Fund) Amending the Letter Agreement of 26 December 1974 and 30 December 1974

OFFICIAL TITLE: Letter Agreement Amending the Letter Agreement of 26 December 1974 and 30 December 1974 Relating to Assistance for Children and Mothers

SIGNED: February 10, 1975, at New York

SIGNATORIES: United Nations (United Nations Children's Fund) vs. United States

IN FORCE: From February 14, 1975

OVERVIEW: An amendment to **Letter Agreement (with the United Nation's Children's Fund) Relating to Assistance for Children and Mothers,** increasing the United States' contribution from $500,000 to $1,500,000.

REFERENCE:

Black, Maggie. *Children First: The Story of UNICEF, Past and Present.* New York: Oxford University Press, 1996.

Convention on the Civil Aspects of International Child Abduction

SIGNED: October 25, 1980, at the Hague

SIGNATORIES: Belgium, Canada, France, Greece, Portugal, Switzerland, United States

IN FORCE: From December 1, 1983

OVERVIEW: A convention intended "to protect children internationally from the harmful effects of their wrongful removal or retention and to establish procedures to ensure their prompt return to the State of their habitual residence."

DISCUSSION:

Custody of children is often a bitterly contested issue in divorce, and abduction of children in defiance of a legal custody settlement is not uncommon. In some cases, this becomes a matter of international law, as when the estranged husband and wife are nationals of different countries, and one parent, in defiance of a legal custody settlement, removes the child or children to another country. This convention is intended primarily to address such situations, as well as to protect children generally from international abduction.

The convention provides for the following:

- That children wrongfully removed to or retained in any signatory state shall be promptly returned
- That the rights of custody and of access under the law of one signatory state are effectively respected in the other signatory state

Accordingly, the convention defines wrongful removal and/or retention of children and enumerates the steps the signatory state shall take to restore the child. Such "appropriate measures" include the following:

- Discovering the whereabouts of the child
- Preventing further harm to the child
- Securing the voluntary return of the child
- Exchange information as appropriate
- Initiate appropriate judicial proceedings to obtain the return of the child
- Facilitate legal aid, as appropriate
- Provide administrative arrangements to secure the safe return of the child

The convention also lays down procedures for application for the return of a child, as well as conditions and circumstances under which the application may be granted or denied.

REFERENCE:

McEleavy, Peter E., ed. *The Hague Convention on International Child Abduction.* New York and London: Oxford University Press, 1999.

United Nations Convention on the Rights of the Child

SIGNED: November 20, 1989, at New York

SIGNATORIES: Afghanistan, Albania, Algeria, Andorra, Angola, Antigua and Barbuda, Argentina, Armenia, Australia, Austria, Azerbaijan, Bahamas, Bahrain, Bangladesh, Barbados, Belarus, Belgium, Belize, Benin, Bhutan, Bolivia, Bosnia and Herzegovina, Botswana, Brazil, Brunei Darussalam, Bulgaria, Burkina Faso, Burundi, Cambodia, Cameroon, Canada, Cape Verde, Central African Republic, Chad, Chile, China, Colombia, Comoros, Congo, Cook Islands, Costa Rica, Côte d'Ivoire, Croatia, Cuba, Cyprus, Czech Republic, Democratic Republic of the Congo, Denmark, Djibouti, Dominica, Dominican Republic, Ecuador, Egypt, El Salvador, Equatorial Guinea, Eritrea, Estonia, Ethiopia, Fiji, Finland, Former Yugoslav Republic of Macedonia, France, Gabon, Gambia, Georgia, Germany, Ghana, Greece, Grenada, Guatemala, Guinea, Guinea-Bissau, Guyana, Haiti, Holy See, Honduras, Hungary, Iceland, India, Indonesia, Iran (Islamic Republic), Iraq, Ireland, Israel, Italy, Jamaica, Japan, Jordan, Kazakhstan, Kenya, Kiribati, Korea (Democratic People's Republic), Korea (Republic), Kuwait, Kyrgyzstan, Lao People's Democratic Republic, Latvia, Lebanon, Lesotho, Liberia, Libyan Arab Jamnahiriya, Liechtenstein, Lithuania, Luxembourg, Madagascar, Malawi, Malaysia, Maldives, Mali, Malta, Marshall Islands, Mauritania, Mauritius, Mexico, Micronesia (Federated States), Monaco, Mongolia, Morocco, Mozambique, Myanmar, Namibia, Nauru, Nepal, Netherlands, New Zealand, Nicaragua, Niger, Nigeria, Niue, Norway, Oman, Palau, Pakistan, Panama, Papua New Guinea, Paraguay, Peru, Philippines, Poland, Portugal, Qatar, Republic of Moldova, Romania, Russian Federation, Rwanda, Saint Kitts and Nevis, Saint Lucia, Saint Vincent and the Grenadines, Samoa, San Marino, Sao Tome and Principe, Saudi Arabia, Senegal, Seychelles, Sierra Leone, Singapore, Slovakia, Slovenia, Solomon Islands, South Africa, Spain, Sri Lanka, Sudan, Suriname, Swaziland, Sweden, Switzerland, Syrian Arab Republic, Tajikistan, Thailand, Togo, Tonga, Trinidad and Tobago, Tunisia, Turkey, Turkmenistan, Tuvalu, Uganda, Ukraine, United Arab Emirates, United Kingdom, United Republic of Tanzania, United States, Uruguay, Uzbekistan, Vanuatu, Venezuela, Vietnam, Yemen, Yugoslavia, Zambia, Zimbabwe

IN FORCE: From September 2, 1990

OVERVIEW: The third major international convention on the rights of the child.

DISCUSSION:

The 1989 convention is the third major international agreement addressing the rights of the child, after the Geneva Declaration of the Rights of the Child of 1924 and the **Declaration of the Rights of the Child** of 1959. The 1989 convention is the most detailed and comprehensive of these documents. Essentially, it extends and adapts specifically to the child the basic human rights defined in such international conventions as the **Universal Declaration of Human Rights** (1948), **International Covenant on Civil and Political Rights** (1966), **International Covenant on Economic, Social and Cultural Rights** (1966), and others.

Although the convention generally defines the child as a person under eighteen years of age, Article 38 gives surprising leeway to states in the matter of service in the armed forces: "States Parties shall refrain from recruiting any person who has not attained the age of fifteen years into their armed forces. In recruiting among those persons who have attained the age of fifteen years but who have not attained the age of eighteen years, States Parties shall endeavour to give priority to those who are oldest." This provision was the subject of reservation for several signatories.

REFERENCE:
Black, Maggie. *Children First: The Story of UNICEF, Past and Present.* New York: Oxford University Press, 1996.

Convention on Protection of Children and Co-operation in Respect of Intercountry Adoption

SIGNED: May 29, 1993

SIGNATORIES: Brazil, Burkina Faso, Canada, Costa Rica, Colombia, Cyprus, Ecuador, Finland, Israel, Mexico, Netherlands, Peru, Romania, Sri Lanka, Switzerland, United Kingdom, United States, Uruguay

IN FORCE: Not yet in force

OVERVIEW: A convention to establish a rational, uniform system of intercountry adoption.

DISCUSSION:

The objects of the convention are set forth in Article 1:

a. to establish safeguards to ensure that intercountry adoptions take place in the best interests of·the child and with respect for his or her fundamental rights as recognized in international law;

b. to establish a system of co-operation amongst Contracting States to ensure that those safeguards are respected and thereby prevent the abduction, the sale of, or traffic in children;

c. to secure the recognition in Contracting States of adoptions made in accordance with the Convention.

The convention applies in cases "where a child habitually resident in one Contracting State ('the State of origin') has been, is being, or is to be moved to another Contracting State ('the receiving State') either after his or her adoption in the State of origin by spouses or a person habitually resident in the receiving State, or for the purposes of such an adoption in the receiving State or in the State of origin.

REFERENCES:
Altstein, Howard. *Intercountry Adoption.* New York: Praeger, 1991.
Jaffe, Eliezer D., ed. *Intercountry Adoptions: Laws and Perspectives of "Sending" Countries.* Dordrecht, Netherlands, and Boston: Matimus Nijihoff, 1995.

Convention on Parental Responsibility

OFFICIAL TITLE: Convention on Jurisdiction, Applicable Law, Recognition, Enforcement and Co-operation in Respect of Parental Responsibility and Measures for the Protection of Children

SIGNED: October 19, 1996, at the Hague

SIGNATORIES: Andorra, Australia, Austria, Belarus (not yet ratified), Belgium (not yet ratified), Brazil, Burkina Faso, Burundi, Canada, Chile, Colombia, Costa Rica, Cyprus, Czech Republic (not yet ratified), Denmark, Ecuador, El Salvador, Finland, France, Georgia, Germany (not yet ratified), Ireland (not yet ratified), Israel, Italy (not yet ratified), Lithuania, Luxembourg (not yet ratified), Mauritius, Mexico, Moldova, Monaco, Netherlands, New Zealand, Norway, Panama, Paraguay, Peru, Philippines, Poland, Portugal (not yet ratified), Romania, Slovakia (not yet ratified), Spain, Sri Lanka, Sweden, Switzerland (not yet ratified), United Kingdom (not yet ratified), United States (not yet ratified), Uruguay (not yet ratified), Venezuela

IN FORCE: Not yet in force

OVERVIEW: A convention establishing the powers of state authorities and the law applicable in respect of the protection of minors.

DISCUSSION:

Article 1 begins:

1 The objects of the present Convention are—

a. to determine the State whose authorities have jurisdiction to take measures directed to the protection of the person or property of the child;

b. to determine which law is to be applied by such authorities in exercising their jurisdiction;

c. to determine the law applicable to parental responsibility;

d. to provide for the recognition and enforcement of such measures of protection in all Contracting States;

e. to establish such co-operation between the authorities of the Contracting States as may be necessary in order to achieve the purposes of this Convention.

To ensure that children ("from the moment of their birth until they reach the age of 18 years") are subject to protection of a competent government authority, Article 5 lays down the following:

1 The judicial or administrative authorities of the Contracting State of the habitual residence of the child have jurisdiction to take measures directed to the protection of the child's person or property.

2 Subject to Article 7, in case of a change of the child's habitual residence to another Contracting State, the authorities of the State of the new habitual residence have jurisdiction.

Refugee children are to be protected by the host state.

In addition to ensuring that the child is protected by competent authorities, the convention also asserts the state's role in custody disputes and specifically provides safeguards against parental abduction (as in divorce) involving the unlawful removal of the child from one nation to another.

REFERENCE:

McEleavy, Peter E., ed. *The Hague Convention on International Child Abduction.* New York and London: Oxford University Press, 1999.

Worst Forms of Child Labour Convention

SIGNED: June 17, 1999, at Geneva

SIGNATORIES: Afghanistan, Albania, Algeria, Angola, Antigua and Barbuda, Argentina, Armenia, Australia, Austria, Azerbaijan, Bahamas, Bahrain, Bangladesh, Barbados, Belarus, Belgium, Belize, Benin, Bolivia, Bosnia and Herzegovina, Botswana, Brazil, Bulgaria, Burkina Faso, Burundi, Cambodia, Cameroon, Canada, Cape Verde, Central African Republic, Chad, Chile, China, Colombia, Comoros, Congo, Costa Rica, Côte d'Ivoire, Croatia, Cuba, Cyprus, Czech Republic, Democratic Republic of the Congo, Denmark, Djibouti, Dominica, Dominican Republic, Ecuador, Egypt, El Salvador, Equatorial Guinea, Eritrea, Estonia, Ethiopia, Fiji, Finland, Former Yugoslav Republic of Macedonia, France, Gabon, Gambia, Georgia, Germany, Ghana, Greece, Grenada, Guatemala, Guinea, Guinea-Bissau, Guyana, Haiti, Honduras, Hungary, Iceland, India, Indonesia, Iran, Iraq, Ireland, Israel, Italy, Jamaica, Japan, Jordan, Kazakhstan, Kenya, Korea (Republic), Kuwait, Kyrgyzstan, Lao People's Democratic Republic, Latvia, Lebanon, Lesotho, Liberia, Libyan Arab Jamahiriya, Lithuania, Luxembourg, Madagascar, Malawi, Malaysia, Mali, Malta, Mauritania, Mauritius, Mexico, Moldova, Mongolia, Morocco, Mozambique, Myanmar, Namibia, Nepal, Netherlands, New Zealand, Nicaragua, Niger, Nigeria, Norway, Oman, Pakistan, Panama, Papua New Guinea, Paraguay, Peru, Philippines, Poland, Portugal, Qatar, Romania, Russian Federation, Rwanda, Saint Kitts and Nevis, Saint Lucia, Saint Vincent and the Grenadines, San Marino, Sao Tome and Principe, Saudi Arabia, Senegal, Seychelles, Sierra Leone, Singapore, Slovakia, Slovenia, Solomon Islands, Somalia, South Africa, Spain, Sri Lanka, Sudan, Suriname, Swaziland, Sweden, Switzerland, Syrian Arab Republic, Tajikistan, Tanzania, Thailand, Togo, Trinidad and Tobago, Tunisia, Turkey, Turkmenistan, Uganda, Ukraine, United Arab Emirates, United Kingdom, United States, Uruguay, Uzbekistan, Venezuela, Vietnam, Yemen, Yugoslavia, Zambia

IN FORCE: Not yet in force (As of January 2000, six signatories, including the United States, have ratified the treaty)

OVERVIEW: An international convention sponsored by the International Labour Organisation calling for steps to be taken toward the effective and immediate elimination of the worst forms of child labor.

DISCUSSION:

The convention protects those under eighteen years of age (with special emphasis on girls and on children under twelve) from the following:

- All forms of slavery or practices similar to slavery, such as the sale and trafficking of children, debt bondage and serfdom, and forced or compulsory labor, including forced or compulsory recruitment of children for use in armed conflict

- The use, procuring, or offering of a child for prostitution, for the production of pornography or for pornographic performances

- The use, procuring or offering of a child for illicit activities, in particular for the production and trafficking of drugs as defined in relevant international treaties

- Work that, by its nature or the circumstances in which it is carried out, is likely to jeopardize the health, safety or morals of child

REFERENCE:

Hobbs, Sandy, et al. *Child Labor: A World History Companion.* Santa Barbara, CA: ABC-Clio, 1999.

Rights of Women

Overview of Treaties in This Category

This section includes two important multilateral conventions to which the United States is party. The **Inter-American Convention on the Granting of Political Rights to Women** (1948) was concluded by a coalition of American states, whereas the **Convention on the Political Rights of Women** (1953) is a United Nations document. In addition, the United States has financed several foreign aid programs with the object of improving the social and economic opportunities of women in certain developing nations. Examples included in this section are **Project Grant Agreement (with Morocco) for Nonformal Education for Women** (1978), **Project Grant (with Morocco) for Industrial and Commercial Job Training for Women** (1978), and **Project Grant Agreement (with the Philippines) for Economic and Social Impact Analysis/Women in Development** (1978).

Inter-American Convention on the Granting of Political Rights to Women

SIGNED: May 2, 1948, at Bogota, Colombia
SIGNATORIES: Argentina, Bolivia, brazil, Chile, Colombia, Costa Rica, Cuba, Dominica, Dominican Republic, Ecuador, El Salvador, Guatemala, Haiti, Honduras, Mexico, Nicaragua, Panama, Paraguay, Peru, Suriname, United States, Uruguay, Venezuela
IN FORCE: From March 17, 1949
OVERVIEW: A hemispherical convention affirming the political rights of women.

DISCUSSION:
The substance of the convention is contained in a single, one-sentence article: "The High Contracting Parties agree that the right to vote and to be elected to national office shall not be denied or abridged by reason of sex."

REFERENCES:
Afkhami, Mahnaz, ed. *Faith and Freedom: Women's Human Rights in the Muslim World.* Syracuse, NY: Syracuse University Press, 1995.
Cook, Rebecca J., ed. *Human Rights of Women: National and International Perspectives.* Philadelphia: University of Pennsylvania Press, 1994.
D'Itri, Patricia Ward. *Cross Currents in the International Women's Movement, 1848-1948.* Bowling Green, OH: Bowling Green State University Press, 1999.

Convention on the Political Rights of Women

SIGNED: March 31, 1953
SIGNATORIES: Afghanistan, Albania, Angola, Antigua and Barbuda, Argentina, Australia, Austria, Bahamas, Barbados, Belarus, Belgium, Belize, Bolivia, Bosnia-Herzegovina, Brazil, Brunei, Bulgaria, Burundi, Canada, Central African Republic, Chile, China (Taiwan), Colombia, Congo, Costa Rica, Côte d'Ivoire, Croatia, Cuba, Cyprus, Czech Republic, Czechoslovakia, Denmark, Dominica, Dominican Republic, Ecuador, Egypt, Ethiopia, Fiji, Finland, Former Yugoslav Republic of Macedonia, France, Gabon, German Democratic Republic, Germany (Federal Republic), Ghana, Greece, Grenada, Guatemala, Guinea, Haiti, Hungary, Iceland, India, Indonesia, Ireland, Israel, Italy, Jamaica, Japan, Jordan, Kiribati, Korea, Laos, Latvia, Lebanon, Lesotho, Libya, Luxembourg, Madagascar, Malawi, Mali, Malta, Mauritania, Mauritius, Mexico, Moldova, Mongolia, Morocco, Nepal, Netherlands, New Zealand, Nicaragua, Niger, Nigeria, Norway, Pakistan, Papua New Guinea, Paraguay, Peru, Philippines, Poland, Romania, Russian Federations, St. Kitts and Nevis, St. Lucia, St. Vincent and the Grenadines, Senegal, Seychelles, Sierra Leone, Slovak Republic, Slovenia, Solomon Islands, Spain, Suriname, Swaziland, Tanzania, Thailand, Tonga, Trinidad and Tobago, Tunisia, Turkey, Tuvalu, Uganda, Ukraine, Union of Soviet Socialist Republics, United Kingdom, United States, Venezuela, Yemen (Aden), Yugoslavia, Zaire, Zambia, Zimbabwe
IN FORCE: From July 7, 1954
OVERVIEW: A convention guaranteeing political rights to women on an equal footing with those of men.

DISCUSSION:
The first three articles of the convention contain its substance:

Article I
Women shall be entitled to vote in all elections on equal terms with men without any discrimination.

Article II
Women shall be eligible for election to all publicly elected bodies, established by national law, on equal terms with men, without any discrimination.

Article III
Women shall be entitled to hold public office and to exercise all public functions, established by national law, on equal terms with men, without any discrimination.

REFERENCES:

Afkhami, Mahnaz, ed. *Faith and Freedom: Women's Human Rights in the Muslim World*. Syracuse, NY: Syracuse University Press, 1995.

Cook, Rebecca J., ed. *Human Rights of Women: National and International Perspectives*. Philadelphia: University of Pennsylvania Press, 1994.

D'Itri, Patricia Ward. *Cross Currents in the International Women's Movement, 1848-1948*. Bowling Green, OH: Bowling Green State University Press, 1999.

Project Grant Agreement (with Morocco) for Nonformal Education for Women

SIGNED: August 14, 1978, at Rabat, Morocco

SIGNATORIES: Morocco vs. United States

IN FORCE: From signing

OVERVIEW: A grant to Morocco's Ministry of Youth and Sports for its Promotion Féminine program to "foster new training and employment opportunities for women throughout Morocco."

DISCUSSION:

Through the Agency for International Development (AID), the United States granted Morocco $2,291,000 to strengthen the infrastructure of the Promotion Féminine program in the following ways:

- Financing training of program managers
- Financing teacher training and retraining
- Creating a job development unit to increase employment opportunities for women
- Train the advanced personnel of Promotion Féminine

Also see **Project Grant (with Morocco) for Industrial and Commercial Job Training for Women**.

REFERENCE:

Afkhami, Mahnaz, ed. *Faith and Freedom: Women's Human Rights in the Muslim World*. Syracuse, NY: Syracuse University Press, 1995.

Project Grant (with Morocco) for Industrial and Commercial Job Training for Women

SIGNED: August 14, 1978, at Rabat, Morocco

SIGNATORIES: Morocco vs. United States

IN FORCE: From signing

OVERVIEW: A grant to Morocco to improve employment opportunities for women in Morocco.

DISCUSSION:

Through the Agency for International Development (AID), the United States grants to Morocco's Ministry of Labor and Professional Training $2,400,000 for the purpose of integrating "women trainees into the Labor Ministry's industrial and commercial training centers (OFPPT), to prepare them with marketable skills, and to assist them in job placement appropriate to their training.

Also see **Project Grant Agreement (with Morocco) for Nonformal Education for Women**.

REFERENCE:

Afkhami, Mahnaz, ed. *Faith and Freedom: Women's Human Rights in the Muslim World*. Syracuse, NY: Syracuse University Press, 1995.

Project Grant Agreement (with the Philippines) for Economic and Social Impact Analysis/Women in Development

SIGNED: April 19, 1978, at Manila, Philippines

SIGNATORIES: Philippines vs. United States

IN FORCE: From signing

OVERVIEW: An agreement granting to the Philippines funds to study the impact on Filipino women of development projects.

DISCUSSION:

The United States grants to the government of the Philippines a sum not to exceed $1,000,000 for the purpose of carrying out a "series of studies, experiments, field tests, and training workshops aimed at developing, testing, and institutionalizing various methodologies and indicators for defining and measuring economic progress, social change, and the impact of development projects, with emphasis on the effects on Filipino women. The goal is to "help improve the economic and social well-being of the Philippine population, particularly the rural poor."

REFERENCES:

Cook, Rebecca J., ed. *Human Rights of Women: National and International Perspectives*. Philadelphia: University of Pennsylvania Press, 1994.

D'Itri, Patricia Ward. *Cross Currents in the International Women's Movement, 1848-1948*. Bowling Green, OH: Bowling Green State University Press, 1999.

Science and Environment

Conservation and Environment

Overview of Treaties in This Category

It is, of course, a platitude to observe that matters of conservation of living resources and of the environment transcend political boundaries. International organizations, especially the United Nations, have recognized the regional and global scope of environmental issues and have, accordingly, participated in the creation of a large number of agreements addressing environmental issues. Indeed, beginning in the 1970s, conventions and declarations relating to the environment have constituted a major "growth area" in the work of the United Nations, and the United States has been a key participant in many important multilateral agreements.

For the United States, domestically, the great pioneering era of environmentalism was inaugurated early in the twentieth century during the administration of President Theodore Roosevelt. At that time, "environmentalism" was called "conservation," and the term aptly defined the focus of the early movement: an attempt to conserve, to preserve, and generally to husband certain natural resources. Many of the early international multilateral agreements on the environment were similarly focused on conservation (for example, **Convention on Nature Protection and Wild Life Preservation in the Western Hemisphere,** 1940; **International Plant Protection Convention,** 1951; and **Convention on Conservation of North Pacific Fur Seals,** 1957). In addition, early agreements addressed specifically defined pollution problems, especially oil pollution: **International Convention for the Prevention of Pollution of the Sea by Oil** (1954) and **International Convention Relating to Intervention on the High Seas in Cases of Oil Pollution Casualties** (1969).

By the 1970s, interest in conservation had simultaneously broadened into a more comprehensive approach to issues of the environment and had sharpened in focus and increased in urgency to target the protection of certain "endangered species." The **Antarctic Treaty** of 1959 may be regarded as an early genuinely *environmental* treaty in that it addresses an entire ecosystem, and the same may be said of the 1971 **Convention on Wetlands of International Importance** or **Convention on the Conservation of Antarctic Marine Living Resources** (1980). Environmentally responsible exploitation of the sea's mineral resources is addressed in **Provisional Understanding Regarding Deep Seabed Matters** (1984). By the 1980s, the loss of rain forest environments had become of great concern, giving rise to the **International Tropical Timber Agreement** of 1983. Agreements such as these define entire ecosystems and lay down procedures and programs to protect them. **Convention on International Trade in Endangered Species of Wild Fauna and Flora (CITES)** (1973) is an important basic agreement addressing what was, in the 1970s, a newfound concern to preserve specifically endangered species. Another approach to "conservation" of the natural environment is represented in the 1972 **Convention for the Protection of the World Cultural and Natural Heritage,** which deliberately blurs the distinction between the natural and human-made environment, defining aspects of both as valuable elements in the heritage of the world.

The 1970s saw both a broadening and a rationalization of global approaches to reducing pollution. During the 1970s, the developed nations of the world experienced, in varying degrees, an "energy crisis," in part resulting from price increases and supply restrictions imposed by the Organization of Petroleum Exporting Countries (OPEC) cartel. This spurred creation of **Agreement on an International Energy Program** (1974), which viewed the pollution issue as an aspect of the greater issue of energy exploitation, conservation, and general management. In 1979, the **Convention on Long-Range Transboundary Air Pollution** addressed control of global pollution on the largest scale. Also of planetary concern, by the 1980s, was the depletion of the ozone layer, a part of the earth's atmosphere that is critical in protecting the global environment from overexposure to cosmic as well as infrared radiation. The **Vienna Convention for the Protection of the Ozone Layer** (1985), the 1987 **Montreal Protocol on Substances That Deplete the Ozone Layer,** and **London Amendment to the Montreal Protocol on Substances That Deplete the Ozone Layer** (1990) were landmark international agreements aimed at reversing a transnational problem vast in scope.

On a somewhat smaller, but still vast, scale is the issue of acid rain. In many instances, the industrial and automotive emissions of one country may travel in the atmosphere to acidify precipitation in another country, posing a serious threat to food crops, water quality, and the environment generally. **Convention on Long-Range Transboundary Air Pollution** of 1979 addressed this issue, which was more extensively dealt with in the 1988 **Protocol to the 1979 Convention on Long-range Transboundary Air Pollution Concerning the Control of Emissions of Nitrogen Oxides or Their Transboundary Fluxes.**

Beginning in the late 1980s, approaches to pollution turned increasingly toward strategies for ongoing management rather than cleaning up after crises and disasters. The **Basel Convention on the Control of Transboundary Movement of Hazardous Wastes and Their Disposal** (1989), **International Convention on Oil Pollution Preparedness, Response, and Cooperation** (1990), and **Convention on Environmental Impact Assessment in a Transboundary Context** (1990) are all examples of the proactive approach. During the 1990s, the proactive orientation was broadened by ambitious multilateral agreements that sought to integrate environmental issues into all political and economic aspects of international policy. The 1992 global conference on the environment, held in Rio, produced several documents of sweeping scope, including, most importantly, **United Nations Framework Convention on Climate Change** (subsequently modified and enlarged by the **Kyoto Protocol to the United Nations Framework Convention on Climate Change** of 1997), **Convention on Biological Diversity**, **Agenda 21**, and the **Rio Declaration on Environment and Development**.

Since the 1992 Rio conference, the trend in major environmental agreements has continued to be integrative. For example the **North American Agreement on Environmental Cooperation** (1993) is linked to and interlocked with the **North American Free Trade Agreement (NAFTA)** of 1992 (see Section 4.2). From its inception, NAFTA wedded the concept of regional free trade to regional environmental protection and responsibility. Several recent United Nations initiatives have linked the environment to the area of human rights (**Draft Declaration of Principles of Human Rights and the Environment**, 1994) and to individual political rights (**Convention on Access to Information and Justice in Environmental Matters** and **Rotterdam Convention on Prior Informed Consent**, both 1998).

Convention on Nature Protection and Wild Life Preservation in the Western Hemisphere

SIGNED: October 12, 1940, at Washington

SIGNATORIES: Argentina, Dominican Republic, Ecuador, El Salvador, Guatemala, Haiti, Mexico, Nicaragua, Peru, United States, Venezuela

IN FORCE: From April 3, 1942

OVERVIEW: An agreement, under the auspices of the Organization of American States, to preserve all species and genera of native American fauna and flora from extinction, and to preserve areas of extraordinary beauty, striking geological formations, or aesthetic, historic or scientific value.

DISCUSSION:

The preamble to the convention expresses its intent:

The Governments of the American Republics, wishing to protect and preserve in their natural habitat representatives of all species and genera of their native flora and fauna, including migratory birds, in sufficient numbers and over areas extensive enough to assure them from becoming extinct through any agency within man's control; and

Wishing to protect and preserve scenery of extraordinary beauty, unusual and striking geologic formations, regions and natural objects of aesthetic, historic or scientific value, and areas characterized by primitive conditions in those cases covered by this Convention; and

Wishing to conclude a convention on the protection of nature and the preservation of flora and fauna to effectuate the foregoing purposes have agreed upon the following Articles . . .

The principal means by which the signatories hoped to preserve the natural heritage was through the creation of national parks and preserves (Article 2). In addition, per Article 5, "the Contracting Governments agree to adopt, or to propose such adoption to their respective appropriate law-making bodies, suitable laws and regulations for the protection and preservation of flora and fauna within their national boundaries . . . ."

Beyond these main provisions, the following were agreed to:

- Enter into cooperative research programs (Article 6)
- Enter into cooperative programs to protect migratory species (Article 7)
- Afford special protection to endangered species enumerated in an annex to the convention (Articles 8 and 9)

REFERENCES:

Lipschutz, Ronnie D., ed. *Global Civil Society and Global Environmental Governance: The Politics of Nature from Place to Planet.* Albany: State University of New York Press, 1996.

Sachs, Wolfgang. *Global Ecology: A New Arena of Political Conflict.* London: Zed Books, 1993.

Shabecoff, Philip. *A New Name for Peace: International Environmentalism, Sustainable Development, and Democracy.* Hanover, NH: University Press of New England, 1996.

Wapner, Paul Kevin. *Environmental Activism and World Civic Politics.* Albany: State University of New York Press, 1996.

International Plant Protection Convention

SIGNED: December 6, 1951, at Rome

SIGNATORIES: Algeria, Argentina, Australia, Austria, Bahrain, Bangladesh, Barbados, Belgium, Belize, Bolivia, Brazil, Cambodia, Canada, Cape Verde, Chile, Colombia, Costa Rica, Cuba, Czechoslovakia, Denmark, Dominican Republic, Ecuador, Egypt, El Salvador, Ethiopia, Finland, France, Germany, Ghana, Greece, Grenada, Guatemala, Guinea, Guyana, Haiti, Hungary, India, Indonesia, Iran (Islamic Republic), Iraq, Ireland, Israel, Italy, Jamaica, Japan, Jordan, Kenya, Korea (Republic), Lao People's Democratic Republic, Lebanon,

Liberia, Libyan Arab Jamahiriya, Luxembourg, Malawi, Malaysia, Mali, Malta, Mauritius, Mexico, Morocco, Netherlands, New Zealand, Nicaragua, Niger, Norway, Oman, Pakistan, Panama, Papua New Guinea, Paraguay, Peru, Philippines, Portugal, Romania, Russian Federation, Senegal, Sierra Leone, Solomon Islands, South Africa, Spain, Sri Lanka, Saint Kitts and Nevis, Sudan, Suriname, Sweden, Thailand, Togo, Trinidad and Tobago, Tunisia, Turkey, United Kingdom, United States, Venezuela, Yemen, Yugoslavia, Zambia

IN FORCE: From April 3, 1952

OVERVIEW: A convention to maintain and increase international cooperation in controlling pests and diseases of plants and plant products, and in preventing their introduction and spread across national boundaries.

DISCUSSION:

The convention's first article lays down specific legislative, technical, and administrative measures for the protection of plants, to which all signatories agree. In addition, signatories agree to the following:

- To make specific and regional agreements in conjunction with the Food and Agriculture Organization of the United Nations
- To set up within each jurisdiction an official plant protection organization charged with inspecting areas under cultivation and consignments of plants in international traffic for existence or outbreak of plant pests or diseases; issuing certificates relating to the phytosanitary condition and origin of plants and plant products; researching plant protection
- To regulate the import and export of plants and plant products, by means, where necessary, of prohibitions, inspections, and destruction of consignments

REFERENCES:

Lipschutz, Ronnie D., ed. *Global Civil Society and Global Environmental Governance: The Politics of Nature from Place to Planet.* Albany: State University of New York Press, 1996.

Sachs, Wolfgang. *Global Ecology: A New Arena of Political Conflict.* London: Zed Books, 1993.

Shabecoff, Philip. *A New Name for Peace: International Environmentalism, Sustainable Development, and Democracy.* Hanover, NH: University Press of New England, 1996.

Wapner, Paul Kevin. *Environmental Activism and World Civic Politics.* Albany: State University of New York Press, 1996.

International Convention for the Prevention of Pollution of the Sea by Oil

SIGNED: May 12, 1954, at London

SIGNATORIES: Algeria, Argentina, Austria, Bahamas, Bahrain, Bangladesh, Belgium, Canada, Chile, Congo, Côte d'Ivoire, Cyprus, Denmark, Djibouti, Dominican Republic, Egypt, Fiji, Finland, France, Ghana, Greece, Guinea, Iceland, India, Ireland, Israel, Italy, Japan, Jordan, Kenya, Korea (Republic), Kuwait, Lebanon, Liberia, Libyan Arab Jamahiriya, Madagascar, Maldives, Malta, Mexico, Monaco, Morocco, Netherlands, New Zealand, Nigeria, Norway, Panama, Papua New Guinea, Philippines, Poland, Portugal, Qatar, Russian Federation, Saudi Arabia, Senegal, Spain, Sri Lanka, Suriname, Sweden, Switzerland, Syrian Arab Republic, Tunisia, United Arab Emirates, United Kingdom, United States, Uruguay, Vanuatu, Venezuela, Yemen, Yugoslavia,

IN FORCE: July 26, 1958

OVERVIEW: The convention includes provisions prescribing action to prevent pollution of the sea by oil discharged from ships.

DISCUSSION:

The convention applies to all ships registered to a signatory, except tankers of under 150 tons gross tonnage and other ships of under 500 tons gross tonnage as well as naval ships and ships engaged in whaling. The major provision is a prohibition of discharges, except when a ship is proceeding en route or when the instantaneous rate of discharge does not exceed 60 liters per mile. Under certain conditions, the prohibition is not applicable: in the case of a ship, when the oil content of the discharge is less than 100 parts per million parts of the mixture, or the discharge is made as far as practicable from land; in the case of a tanker, when the total quantity of oil discharged on a ballast voyage does not exceed one fifteen-thousandth of the total cargo-carrying capacity, or the tanker is more than fifty miles from the nearest land. Also excepted are "cases of necessity to secure safety of ships, save life or prevent damage to cargo, or where leakage is unavoidable and all measures have been taken to minimize it."

Signatories undertake to fit their ships within twelve months of the convention's entry into force to prevent escape of oil into the bilges. Furthermore, signatory parties agree to provide appropriate facilities at ports and oil-loading terminals and to ensure that all ships covered by the convention carry an oil record book (in a form specified by the annex to the convention).

REFERENCE:

Inter-Governmental Maritime Consultive Organization. *International Convention for the Prevention of Pollution of the Sea by Oil, 1954: As Amended in 1962 and 1969.* London: Inter-Governmental Maritime Consultive Organization, 1983.

Convention on Conservation of North Pacific Fur Seals

SIGNED: February 9, 1957; revised May 7, 1976 at Washington

SIGNATORIES: Canada, Japan, the Union of Soviet Socialist Republics, and the United States of America

IN FORCE: From October 14, 1957

OVERVIEW: A convention to promote "effective measures towards achieving the maximum sustainable productivity of the fur seal resources of the North Pacific Ocean so that the fur seal populations can be brought to and maintained at the levels which will provide the greatest harvest year after year."

DISCUSSION:

Signatories agreed to conduct coordinated and cooperative research on North Pacific fur seals and to restrict sealing in the Pacific Ocean north of the 30th parallel of north latitude, including the seas of Bering, Okhotsk, and Japan.

The convention established the North Pacific Fur Seal Commission, composed of one member from each signatory, to perform the following tasks:

- Formulate and coordinate research programs.
- Study data obtained from research programs.
- Recommend appropriate measures.
- "Study whether or not pelagic sealing ["the killing, taking, or hunting in any manner whatsoever of fur seals at sea"] in conjunction with land sealing could be permitted in certain circumstances without adversely affecting achievement of the objectives of this Convention."

The convention also set quotas on harvest and export of seals hunted on land and on sea, and signatories undertook "to ensure the utilization of those methods for the capture and killing and marking of fur seals on land or at sea which will spare the fur seals pain and suffering to the greatest extent practicable."

REFERENCE:

Scheffer, Victor B. *The Year of the Seal.* New York: Lyons, 1991.

Antarctic Treaty

SIGNED: December 1, 1959, Washington, D.C.

IN FORCE: From June 23, 1961

SIGNATORIES: Argentina, Australia, Austria, Belgium, Brazil, Bulgaria, Chile, China, Colombia, Cuba, Czechoslovakia, Denmark, Finland, France, Germany, Greece, Guatemala, Hungary, India, Italy, Japan, Korea (Democratic People's Republic of), Korea (Republic of), Netherlands (extended to the Netherlands Antilles and Suriname), New Zealand, Norway, Papua New Guinea, Peru, Poland, Romania, Russian Federation, South Africa, Spain, Sweden, Switzerland, United Kingdom, United States, Uruguay

OVERVIEW: Antarctica, unclaimed by any nation, is an international continent. The treaty is intended to ensure that Antarctica is used for peaceful purposes, for international cooperation in scientific research, and does not become the scene or object of international discord.

DISCUSSION:

The Antarctic Treaty was the culmination of a twelve-nation conference on peaceful international scientific cooperation in Antarctica. Its chief provisions are as follows:

- The continent is to be demilitarized. No military bases, military manoeuvres, or weapon testing is permitted.
- The continent is to be the scene of free scientific investigation and cooperation in the exchange of information regarding plans for such investigation, personnel engaged in research, and information resulting from research.
- Observers to inspect stations, installations, and equipment will be appointed by each signatory.
- Meetings of the signatories will be held for consultation and to formulate and recommend measures to further the objectives of the treaty.
- The treaty includes measures for the conservation of Antarctic fauna and flora.

The Antarctic Treaty led to later agreements, most notably the 1972 **Convention for the Conservation of Antarctic Seals** and, in 1979, conventions on the exploitation of Antarctic minerals, regulation of hunting, and international cooperation in telecommunications. In 1980, the Living Resources Convention was signed—and came into force on April 7, 1981—relating to the conservation of Antarctic species, especially krill (a protein-rich crustacean that is crucial in the marine food chain). The 1959 treaty remains open for signature by any United Nations member.

REFERENCES:

Jorgensen-Dahl, Arnfinn, and Willy Ostreng, eds. *The Antarctic Treaty System in World Politics.* New York; St. Martin's Press, 1991.

National Academy. *Antarctic Treaty System: An Assessment.* Washington, D.C.: National Academy Press, 1986.

Rengger, N. J. Treaties and Alliances of the World, 5th ed. Essex, UK: Longman Group, 1990.

Stokke, Olva Schram, and Davor Vidas, eds. *Governing the Antarctic: The Effectiveness and Legitimacy of the Antarctic Treaty System.* New York: Cambridge University Press, 1997.

International Convention Relating to Intervention on the High Seas in Cases of Oil Pollution Casualties

SIGNED: November 29, 1969, at Brussels, Belgium

SIGNATORIES: Argentina, Australia, Bahamas, Bangladesh, Belgium, Benin, Bulgaria, Cameroon, China, Côte d'Ivoire, Cuba, Denmark, Djibouti, Dominican Republic, Ecuador, Egypt, Fiji, Finland, France, Gabon, Germany, Ghana, Iceland, Ireland, Italy, Japan, Kuwait, Lebanon, Liberia, Mexico, Monaco, Morocco, Netherlands, New Zealand, Norway, Oman, Panama, Papua New Guinea, Poland, Portugal, Qatar, Russian Federation, Senegal, South Africa, Spain, Sri Lanka, Suriname, Sweden,

Switzerland, Syrian Arab Republic, Tunisia, United Arab Emirates, United Kingdom, United States, Yemen, Yugoslavia

IN FORCE: From May 6, 1975

OVERVIEW: Without violating the principle of freedom of the high seas, the convention enables countries to take action on the high seas in cases of a maritime casualty resulting in danger of oil pollution of sea and coastlines.

DISCUSSION:

The chief provision of the convention is the general principle that signatory parties may in all instances take such measures on the high seas as necessary to prevent, mitigate, or eliminate grave and imminent danger to their coastline or related interests from pollution or threat of pollution of the sea by oil; however, before taking action, a coastal state should notify the flag state of the ship, consult independent experts, and notify any person whose interests may be expected to be affected by such action. Recognizing that, in cases of extreme urgency, such preliminary steps may be impractical or impossible, the convention allows for immediate action.

In all cases, it is the duty of the coastal state to protect human life and assist persons in distress.

The convention includes the principle that any actions taken by the coastal state should conform to what is reasonably necessary only and should be proportionate to the damage, actual or threatened.

REFERENCE:
Burger, Joanna. *Oil Spills*. New Brunswick, NJ: Rutgers University Press, 1997.

Convention on Wetlands of International Importance

OFFICIAL TITLE: Convention on Wetlands of International Importance, Especially as Waterfowl Habitat (RAMSAR)

SIGNED: February 2, 1971, Ramsar, Iran

SIGNATORIES: Algeria, Australia, Austria, Belgium, Bolivia, Bulgaria, Burkina Faso, Canada, Chad, Chile, Czechoslovakia, Ecuador, Egypt, Denmark, Finland, France, Gabon, Germany, Ghana, Greece, Guatemala, Guinea Bissau, Hungary, Iceland, India, Iran (Islamic Republic), Ireland, Italy, Japan, Jordan, Kenya, Mali, Malta, Mauritania, Mexico, Morocco, Nepal, Netherlands, New Zealand, Niger, Norway, Pakistan, Panama, Poland, Portugal, Russian Federation, Senegal, South Africa, Spain, Sri Lanka, Suriname, Sweden, Switzerland, Tunisia, Uganda, United Kingdom, United States, Uruguay, Venezuela, Vietnam, Yugoslavia

IN FORCE: From December 21, 1975

OVERVIEW: The purpose of the convention is to stem the loss of wetlands and to recognize the fundamental ecological functions of wetlands and their economic, cultural, scientific, and recreational value.

DISCUSSION:

Each signatory undertakes to designate at least one national wetland for inclusion in a United Nations-sanctioned List of Wetlands of International Importance. All signatories acknowledge their international responsibilities for the conservation, management, and wise use of migratory stocks of wildfowl. Toward the end of preservation and management, the signatories agree to establish wetland nature reserves with their nations and to cooperate in the exchange of information and train personnel for wetland management. The convention provides for periodic conferences on wetlands and water-fowl conservation.

REFERENCE:
Mitsch, William J. *Wetlands*. New York: Wiley, 1997.

Convention for the Conservation of Antarctic Seals

SIGNED: June 1, 1972, at London

IN FORCE: March 11, 1978

SIGNATORIES: Argentina, Australia, Belgium, Brazil, Canada, Chile, France, Germany, Italy, Japan, New Zealand, Norway, Poland, Russian Federation, South Africa, United Kingdom, United States

OVERVIEW: The convention is intended to promote and achieve the protection, scientific study, and rational use of Antarctic seals, and to maintain a satisfactory balance within the ecological system of the Antarctic.

DISCUSSION:

Article 1 defines the region to which the convention applies—seas south of latitude 60 degrees south—and specifies application to the five species of seals and all southern fur seals. A list of specific measures adopted by the signatories is given in an Annex to the convention; however, the document also specifies that the signatories may also take measures relating to permissible catch, protected and unprotected species, open and closed areas and seasons, designated areas where seals are not to be disturbed, types of gear that may be employed in hunting, and so on.

The signatories pledged to exchange information among themselves and through the Scientific Committee on Antarctic Research of ICSU. The convention remains open for signature at the invitation of all contracting parties.

REFERENCES:
ACCIS Guide to United Nations Information Sources on the Environment. New York: United Nations Publications, 1989.
Laws, R. M. *Antarctic Seals: Research Methods and Techniques*. Cambridge, UK, and New York: Cambridge University Press, 1993.

Convention Concerning the Protection of the World Cultural and Natural Heritage

SIGNED: November 23, 1972, at Paris

IN FORCE: From December 17, 1975

SIGNATORIES: Afghanistan, Albania, Algeria, Antigua and Barbuda, Argentina, Australia, Bahrain, Bangladesh, Belarus, Belize, Benin, Bolivia, Brazil, Bulgaria, Burkina Faso, Burundi, Cambodia, Cameroon, Canada, Cape Verde, Central African Republic, Chile, China, Colombia, Congo, Costa Rica, Côte d'Ivoire, Cuba, Cyprus, Czech and Slovak (Federal Republic of), Denmark, Dominican Republic, Ecuador, Egypt, El Salvador, Ethiopia, Finland, France, Gabon, Gambia, Fiji, Germany, Ghana, Greece, Guatemala, Guinea, Guyana, Haiti, Holy See, Honduras, Hungary, India, Indonesia, Iran (Islamic Republic of), Iraq, Ireland, Italy, Jamaica, Japan, Jordan, Kenya, Korea (Republic of), Lao People's Democratic Republic, Lebanon, Libyan Arab Jamahiriya, Lithuania, Luxembourg, Madagascar, Malawi, Malaysia, Maldives, Mali, Malta, Mauritania, Mexico, Monaco, Mongolia, Morocco, Mozambique, Nepal, New Zealand (extended to Cook Islands and Niue), Nicaragua, Niger, Nigeria, Norway, Oman, Pakistan, Panama, Paraguay, Peru, Philippines, Poland, Portugal, Qatar, Romania, Russian Federation, San Marino, Solomon Islands, St. Christopher and Nevis, St. Lucia, Saudi Arabia, Senegal, Seychelles, Spain, Sri Lanka, Sudan, Sweden, Switzerland, Syrian Arab Republic, Thailand, Tunisia, Turkey, Uganda, Ukraine, United Kingdom, United Republic of Tanzania, United States, Uruguay, Venezuela, Vietnam, Yemen, Yugoslavia, Zaire, Zambia, Zimbabwe

OVERVIEW: This broad international convention establishes an effective system of collective protection of the cultural and natural heritage of outstanding universal value, organized on a permanent basis and in accordance with modern scientific methods.

DISCUSSION:

Each party to this convention recognizes that the duty of identification, protection, conservation, and transmission to future generations of the cultural and natural heritage belongs primarily to each signatory. Accordingly, the signatory parties agree to the following:

- To integrate the protection of their heritage into comprehensive planning programs
- To set up services for the protection of their heritage
- To develop scientific and technical studies and to take necessary legal, scientific, administrative and financial steps to protect their heritage
- To assist each other in the protection of the cultural and natural heritage

Articles 8 through 11 establishes a World Heritage Committee, to which each signatory agrees to submit an inventory of its national heritage. Using these inventories, the committee is to compile and publish a "World Heritage List" and a "List of World Heritage in Danger." Additionally, by Article 15, a World Heritage Fund was established, to be financed by the parties and other interested bodies. Any signatory may request assistance for property forming part of its listed heritage, and, per Articles 19 through 22, such assistance may be granted by the World Heritage Fund in the form of studies, provision of experts, training of staff, supply of equipment, loans, or subsidies. (arts. 19-22).

The convention remains open for ratification or acceptance by all members of UNESCO and by other states upon invitation of the signatories.

REFERENCES:

ACCIS Guide to United Nations Information Sources on the Environment. New York: United Nations Publications, 1989.

Hutter, Michael, and Ilde Rizzo, eds. *Economic Perspectives on Cultural Heritage.* New York: St. Martin's Press, 1997.

King, Thomas F. *Cultural Laws and Practice: An Introductory Guide.* Walnut Creek, CA: Altamira Press, 1998.

Convention on the Prevention of Marine Pollution by Dumping of Wastes and Other Matter

SIGNED: December 29, 1972, at London, Mexico City, Moscow, and Washington

SIGNATORIES: Afghanistan, Antigua and Barbuda, Argentina, Australia, Belgium, Brazil, Canada, China, Chile, Côte d'Ivoire, Cuba, Cyprus, Denmark, Egypt, Finland, France, Gabon, Germany, Greece, Hungary, Iceland, Ireland, Italy, Jamaica, Japan, Jordan, Khmer Republic, Kiribati, Kenya, Kuwait, Lebanon, Liberia, Libyan Arab Jamahiriya, Luxembourg, Malta, Mexico, Monaco, Nauru, Nepal, Netherlands, New Zealand, Nigeria, Norway, Oman, Papua New Guinea, Poland, Philippines, Portugal, Russian Federation, Seychelles, Slovenia, Solomon Islands, South Africa, Spain, Suriname, Sweden, Switzerland, Togo, Tunisia, United Arab Emirates, United Kingdom, United States, Yugoslavia, Zaire

IN FORCE: From August 30, 1975

OVERVIEW: The convention includes measures of direct control of pollution of the sea by dumping, as well as measures to encourage supplementary regional agreements.

DISCUSSION:

The scope of the convention encompasses all seas and all deliberate disposal of wastes other than that incidental to the normal operation of ships and aircraft. Annex I to the convention lists matter that must not be dumped; Annex II lists matter that may be dumped only by special permit; and Annex III lists matter that may be dumped by general permit. The convention also defines situations of extreme emergency or "force majeure," in which dumping of prohibited or restricted matter is unavoidable.

Signatories to the convention agree to the following:

- To establish authorities to issue permits, keep records, and monitor the condition of the seas
- To enforce anti-dumping measures on all flag aircraft and ships, as well as ships and aircraft loading within the signatory's territories or territorial seas
- To collaborate in training personnel, in supplying equipment for research and monitoring, and in disposing of and treating wastes
- To cooperate in developing procedures for assessment of liability and settlement of disputes
- To promote measures to prevent pollution by hydrocarbons, other matter transported other than for dumping, wastes generated during operation of ships, radioactive pollutants, and matter originating from exploration of the sea bed

Signatories with particular interests in certain areas of the sea further agree to enter into regional conventions to prevent marine pollution

REFERENCE:

Gorman, Martha. *Environmental Hazards: Marine Pollution*. Santa Barbara, CA: ABC-Clio, 1993.

Convention on International Trade in Endangered Species of Wild Fauna and Flora

SIGNED: March 3, 1973, at Washington, D.C.

IN FORCE: From July 1, 1975

SIGNATORIES: Afghanistan, Algeria, Argentina, Australia, Austria, Bahamas, Bangladesh, Barbados, Belgium, Belize, Benin, Bolivia, Botswana, Brazil, Brunei Darussalam, Bulgaria, Burkina Faso, Burundi, Cameroon, Canada, Central African Republic, Chad, Chile, China, Colombia, Congo, Costa Rica, Cuba, Cyprus, Czech Republic, Denmark, Djibouti, Dominican Republic, Ecuador, Egypt, El Salvador, Equatorial Guinea, Estonia, Ethiopia, Finland, France, Gabon, Gambia, Germany, Ghana, Greece, Guatemala, Guinea, Guinea Bissau, Guyana, Honduras, Hungary, India, Indonesia, Iran (Islamic Republic of), Israel, Italy, Japan, Jordan, Kenya, Liberia, Liechtenstein, Luxembourg, Madagascar, Malawi, Malaysia, Malta, Mauritius, Mexico, Monaco, Morocco, Mozambique, Namibia, Nepal, Netherlands, New Zealand, Nicaragua, Niger, Nigeria, Panama, Papua New Guinea, Paraguay, Peru, Philippines, Poland, Portugal, Russian Federation, Rwanda, Saint Lucia, Saint Vincent and the Grenadines, Senegal, Seychelles, Singapore, Slovakia, Somalia, South Africa, Spain, Sri Lanka, Sudan, Suriname, Sweden, Switzerland, Thailand, Togo, Trinidad and Tobago, Tunisia,

Uganda, United Arab Emirates, United Kingdom, United Republic of Tanzania, United States, Uruguay, Vanuatu, Venezuela, Zaire, Zambia, Zimbabwe

OVERVIEW: The convention is designed to protect certain endangered species from over-exploitation by means of an international system of import/export permits.

DISCUSSION:

Article 1 defines the scope of the convention to include animals and plants whether dead or alive, as well as any recognizable parts or derivatives thereof. A series of three appendixes enumerate the species to which the convention applies, as follows:

- Appendix I covers endangered species, trade in which is to be tightly controlled.
- Appendix II covers species that may become endangered unless trade is regulated.
- Appendix III covers species that any party wishes to regulate and requires international cooperation to control trade.

A fourth appendix contains model permits. Articles 3 and 4 specify that import/export permits are required for species listed in Appendixes I and II; these permits must certify that export/import will not be detrimental to the survival of the species.

Membership in the convention remains open to any state.

REFERENCES:

ACCIS Guide to United Nations Information Sources on the Environment. New York: United Nations Publications, 1989.

Burton, John A., ed. *The Atlas of Endangered Species.* New York: Macmillan, 1998.

Fitzgerald, Sarah. *International Wildlife Trade: Whose Business Is It?* Washington, D.C.: World Wildlife Fund, 1990.

Hemley, Ginette, and Kathryn S. Fuller, eds. *International Wildlife Trade: A Cites Sourcebook.* Washington, D.C.: Island Press, 1994.

Sherry, Clifford J. *Endangered Species: A Reference Handbook.* Santa Barbara, CA: ABC-Clio, 1998.

Agreement on Conservation of Polar Bears

SIGNED: November 15, 1973, Oslo, Norway

SIGNATORIES: Canada, Denmark, Norway, Union of Soviet Socialist Republics, United States

IN FORCE: From May 26, 1976; for the United States, November 1, 1976

OVERVIEW: An agreement to protect the polar bear as a significant resource of the Arctic region through conservation and management measures.

DISCUSSION:

The principal provisions of the agreement include the following:

- Prohibition of the taking of polar bears, except for approved scientific or conservation purposes, or to prevent disturbance of the management of other living resources, or by local people using traditional methods in accordance with the laws of the signatory parties
- An agreement among the signatories to take action to preserve the ecosystems of which the polar bears are part
- An agreement among the signatories to cooperate in researching techniques for the management and conservation of polar bears

REFERENCES:

ACCIS Guide to United Nations Information Sources on the Environment. New York: United Nations Publications, 1989.

Burton, John A., ed. *The Atlas of Endangered Species.* New York: Macmillan, 1998.

Fitzgerald, Sarah. *International Wildlife Trade: Whose Business Is It?* Washington, D.C.: World Wildlife Fund, 1990.

Hemley, Ginette, and Kathryn S. Fuller, eds. *International Wildlife Trade: A Cites Sourcebook.* Washington, D.C.: Island Press, 1994.

Sherry, Clifford J. *Endangered Species: A Reference Handbook.* Santa Barbara, CA: ABC-Clio, 1998.

Agreement on an International Energy Program

SIGNED: November 18, 1974, at Paris

SIGNATORIES: Australia, Austria, Belgium, Canada, Denmark, Germany, Greece, Ireland, Italy, Japan, Luxembourg, Netherlands, New Zealand, Portugal, Spain, Sweden, Switzerland, Turkey, United Kingdom, United States

IN FORCE: From January 19, 1976

OVERVIEW: A comprehensive program of energy cooperation within the framework of the United Nations International Energy Agency.

DISCUSSION:

The principal provisions of this international cooperative agreement are as follows:

- Creation of an allocation scheme to be used in times of energy emergency
- A program for maintaining emergency energy reserves
- A program of demand restraint measures
- Institution of an extensive information system on the international oil market
- A framework for consultation with oil companies
- A program for long-term cooperation in the areas of energy conservation, development of alternative sources of energy, and research and development of nuclear energy
- An agreement to promote cooperative relations with oil-producing and other oil-consuming countries, including developing countries

REFERENCE:

Clark, John G. *Political Economy of World Energy: A Twentieth Century Perspective.* Chapel Hill: University of North Carolina Press, 1991.

North American Plant Protection Agreement

SIGNED: October 13, 1976, at Yosemite, California

SIGNATORIES: Canada, Mexico, United States

IN FORCE: From October 13, 1976

OVERVIEW: A convention to strengthen "intergovernmental cooperation on plant quarantine and plant protection in North America."

DISCUSSION:

The major thrust of the agreement is to prevent the introduction and spread of "plant pests and noxious weeds." The signatories agree to the following:

- To record and review plant pest outbreaks
- To monitor the movement and spread of established plant pests
- To review progress in the "detection, eradication and control of plant pests"
- To review, consult, and cooperate on quarantine measures

REFERENCES:

Lipschutz, Ronnie D., ed. *Global Civil Society and Global Environmental Governance: The Politics of Nature from Place to Planet.* Albany: State University of New York Press, 1996.

Sachs, Wolfgang. *Global Ecology: A New Arena of Political Conflict.* London: Zed Books, 1993.

Shabecoff, Philip. *A New Name for Peace: International Environmentalism, Sustainable Development, and Democracy.* Hanover, NH: University Press of New England, 1996.

Wapner, Paul Kevin. *Environmental Activism and World Civic Politics.* Albany: State University of New York Press, 1996.

Memorandum of Understanding (with Guatemala) Relating to Cooperative Efforts to Protect Crops

OFFICIAL TITLE: Memorandum of Understanding Relating to Cooperative Efforts to Protect Crops from Plant Pest Damage and Plant Diseases

SIGNED: February 21, 1977, at Guatemala City

SIGNATORIES: Guatemala vs. United States

IN FORCE: From signing

OVERVIEW: An agreement "to plan and execute measures directed toward detecting, preventing, controlling, and/or eradicating plant pests and diseases of economic importance which affect or threaten crops and harvests in Guatemala and the United States."

DISCUSSION:

This agreement is typical of many cooperative agreements between the United States and other countries for the purpose of controlling plant pests. The principal provision of the agreement is to allow the United States Department of Agriculture, Animal Plant Health Inspection Service, Plant Protection and Quarantine to cooperate with Guatemala's Ministerio de Agricultura in programs to control and eradicate pests. Specifically, the agreement gives U.S. authorities certain latitude in operating within Guatemala for the purpose of "detecting, preventing, controlling, and/or eradicating pests and diseases."

REFERENCES:
None

Convention on the Conservation of Migratory Species of Wild Animals

SIGNED: June 23, 1979, at Bonn, Germany

SIGNATORIES: Argentina, Australia, Belgium, Benin, Bulgaria, Burkina Faso, Cameroon, Chad, Chile, Czech Republic, Democratic Republic of Congo, Denmark, Egypt, European Community, Finland, Former Yugoslav Republic of Macedonia, France, Germany, Ghana, Greece, Guinea, Guinea-Bissau, Hungary, India, Ireland, Israel, Italy, Kenya, Latvia, Liechtenstein, Luxembourg, Mali, Mauritania, Monaco, Mongolia, Morocco, Netherlands, Niger, Nigeria, Norway, Pakistan, Panama, Paraguay, Peru, Philippines, Poland, Portugal, Romania, Saudi Arabia, Senegal, Slovakia, Slovenia, Somalia, South Africa, Spain, Sri Lanka, Sweden, Switzerland, Tanzania, Togo, Tunisia, Ukraine, United Kingdom, Uruguay, Uzbekistan

IN FORCE: From November 1, 1983

OVERVIEW: "The Parties acknowledge the importance of migratory species being conserved and of Range States agreeing to take action to this end whenever possible and appropriate, paying special attention to migratory species the conservation status of which is unfavourable, and taking individually or in co-operation appropriate and necessary steps to conserve such species and their habitat."

DISCUSSION:

As laid down in Article 2, the signatories to this important environmental convention agree that they:

a) should promote, co-operate in and support research relating to migratory species;

b) shall endeavour to provide immediate protection for migratory species included in Appendix I; and

c) shall endeavour to conclude Agreements covering the conservation and management of migratory species included in Appendix II.

Appendix I of the convention lists migratory species that are endangered. Appendix II lists migratory species that have an unfavorable conservation status and that require international agreements for their conservation and management, as well as those that have a conservation status that would significantly benefit from the international cooperation that could be achieved by an international agreement.

Parties that are "Range States" of the migratory species listed in Appendix II agree to attempt to conclude agreements with one another to protect those species in an unfavorable conservation status. The convention provides a full set of guidelines for these agreements, noting that "the object of each Agreement shall be to restore the migratory species concerned to a favourable conservation status or to maintain it in such a status. Each Agreement should deal with those aspects of the conservation and management of the migratory species concerned which serve to achieve that object."

For reasons of sovereignty, the United States has not signed this agreement.

REFERENCES:
Lipschutz, Ronnie D., ed. *Global Civil Society and Global Environmental Governance: The Politics of Nature from Place to Planet.* Albany: State University of New York Press, 1996.
Sachs, Wolfgang. *Global Ecology: A New Arena of Political Conflict.* London: Zed Books, 1993.
Shabecoff, Philip. *A New Name for Peace: International Environmentalism, Sustainable Development, and Democracy.* Hanover, NH: University Press of New England, 1996.
Wapner, Paul Kevin. *Environmental Activism and World Civic Politics.* Albany: State University of New York Press, 1996.

Convention on Long-Range Transboundary Air Pollution

SIGNED: November 13, 1979, at Geneva

IN FORCE: From March 16, 1983

SIGNATORIES: Austria, Belarus, Belgium, Bulgaria, Canada, Cyprus, Czechoslovakia, Denmark, European Economic Community, Finland, France, Germany, Greece, Holy See, Hungary, Iceland, Ireland, Italy, Liechtenstein, Luxembourg, Netherlands, Norway, Poland, Portugal, Romania, Russian Federation, San Marino, Slovenia, Spain, Sweden, Switzerland, Turkey, Ukraine, United Kingdom, United States, Yugoslavia

OVERVIEW: The intent of the convention is to protect humankind and its environment against air pollution and to endeavor to limit and, as far as possible, gradually reduce and prevent air pollution, including long-range transboundary air pollution.

DISCUSSION:

The convention provides for limiting and reducing international air pollution by the following means:

• Exchanges of information, consultation, research and monitoring

- Developing cooperative policies and strategies to serve as a means of combating the discharge of air pollutants

In addition, the convention calls for cooperation in the conduct of research into and/or development of the following:

- Existing and proposed technologies for reducing emissions of sulphur compounds and other major air pollutants, including technical and economic feasibility, and their environmental consequences
- Development and implementation of instrumentation and other techniques for monitoring and measuring emission rates and ambient concentrations of air pollutants
- Development of improved models for better understanding of the transmission of long-range transboundary air pollutants
- Studies of the effects of sulphur compounds and other major air pollutants on human health and the environment, including agriculture, forestry, materials, aquatic and other natural ecosystems and visibility, with a view to establishing a scientific basis for dose/effect relationships designed to protect the environment
- Development and implementation of education and training programs related to the environmental aspects of pollution by sulphur compounds and other major air pollutants

The convention established an Executive Body to perform the following functions:

- Review the implementation of the convention
- Establish, as appropriate, working groups to consider matters related to the implementation and development of the convention, and, to this end, to prepare appropriate studies and other documentation and submit recommendations to be considered by the Executive Body
- To fulfil other functions as may be appropriate under the provisions of the convention

The convention remains open for signature by the member states of the Economic Commission for Europe, as well as States having consultative status with the ECE and by regional economic integration organizations constituted by sovereign states members of the ECE.

REFERENCES:

ACCIS Guide to United Nations Information Sources on the Environment. New York: United Nations Publications, 1989.

Assessment of Long-Range Transboundary Air Pollution: Report Prepared within the Framework of the Convention on long-Range Transboundary Air Pollution. New York: United Nations Publications, 1991.

Flinterman, Cees, Barbara Kwiatkowska, and Johan G. Lammers, eds. Transboundary Air Pollution: International Legal Aspects of the Cooperation of States. Dordrecht, Netherlands, Martinus Nijoff, 1986.

Knapp, Anthony H., and Mary-Scott Kaiser. The Long-Range Atmospheric Transport of Natural and Contaminant Substances. Amsterdam: Kluwer Academic Publications, 1990.

Convention on the Conservation of Antarctic Marine Living Resources

SIGNED: May 20, 1980, at Canberra, Australia

SIGNATORIES: Argentina, Australia, Belgium, Brazil, Canada, Chile, European Economic Community, Finland, France, Germany, Greece, India, Italy, Japan, Korea (Republic), Netherlands, New Zealand, Norway, Peru, Poland, Russian Federation, South Africa, Spain, Sweden, United Kingdom, United States, Uruguay

IN FORCE: From April 7, 1982

OVERVIEW: An international convention to safeguard the environment and protect the integrity of the ecosystem of the seas surrounding Antarctica, and to conserve Antarctic marine living resources.

DISCUSSION:

The principal provision of the convention is the establishment of a Commission for the Conservation of Antarctic Marine Living Resources, which is charged with the following responsibilities:

- The facilitation of research into Antarctic marine living resources and the Antarctic marine ecosystems
- The compilation of data on the status of and changes in populations of Antarctic marine living resources, and on factors affecting the distribution, abundance, and productivity of harvested species and dependent or related species or populations
- The acquisition of catch and effort statistics on harvested populations
- The analysis and publication of all information gathered
- Identification of conservation needs and assessment of the effectiveness of conservation measures
- The formulation, adoption, and revision of conservation measures
- The creation and implementation of a system of observation and inspection

REFERENCES:

Jorgensen-Dahl, Arnfinn, and Willy Ostreng, eds. The Antarctic Treaty System in World Politics. New York; St. Martin's Press, 1991.

National Academy. Antarctic Treaty System: An Assessment. Washington, D.C.: National Academy Press, 1986.

Rengger, N. J. Treaties and Alliances of the World, 5th ed. Essex, UK: Longman Group, 1990.

Stokke, Olva Schram, and Davor Vidas, eds. Governing the Antarctic: The Effectiveness and Legitimacy of the Antarctic Treaty System. New York: Cambridge University Press, 1997.

Agreement of Cooperation (with Mexico) Regarding Pollution of the Marine Environment

OFFICIAL TITLE: Agreement of Cooperation Regarding Pollution of the Marine Environment by Discharge of Hydrocarbons and other Hazardous Substances

SIGNED: July 24, 1980, at Mexico City

SIGNATORIES: Mexico vs. United States

IN FORCE: Provisionally from signing; definitively, March 30, 1981

OVERVIEW: An agreement to establish a "Mexico-United States joint contingency plan regarding pollution of the marine environment by discharges of hydrocarbons and other hazardous substances."

DISCUSSION:

The main part of the agreement is devoted to laying down the principles of the commitment to cooperation, which includes an undertaking by each nation to develop "nationally operative systems . . . that permit detection of the existence or imminent possibility of the occurrence of polluting incidents, as well as providing adequate means within their power to eliminate the threat . . ." Annexes subjoined to the agreement address the technical aspects of the cooperative plan.

REFERENCE:

Gorman, Martha. *Environmental Hazards: Marine Pollution.* Santa Barbara, CA: ABC-Clio, 1993.

Cooperative Agreement (with Mexico) Concerning Plant Protection Against the Mediterranean Fruit Fly

SIGNED: August 26, 1980, at Mexico City; September 17, 1980, at Washington

SIGNATORIES: Mexico vs. United States

IN FORCE: From September 17, 1980

OVERVIEW: An agreement of cooperation to control the spread of the agriculturally destructive Mediterranean fruit fly (medfly).

DISCUSSION:

Ceratitis capitata, the Mediterranean fruit fly, popularly called the medfly, lays its eggs (as many as 500 at a time) in all citrus fruits, except for lemons and sour limes. The larvae, which tunnel into the flesh of the fruit, render the crop unfit for human consumption. The pest was first discovered in the United States in Florida, in 1929, but was believed to have been eradicated in this country by 1930. It reappeared in 1956 and in the early 1960s, then, devastatingly, in California, during the late 1970s and early 1980s. Laws and international agreements were enacted worldwide to quarantine and eradicate the pest. The

agreement between Mexico and the United States was among these. Not only does it set up a cooperative program of quarantine and control, it also finances a program of eradication. Subjoined to the main agreement is a patent provision, establishing the disposition of rights to any processes or techniques for control or eradication that may be developed as a result of the cooperative program.

REFERENCES:
None

World Charter for Nature

ADOPTED: October 28, 1982, at New York

SIGNATORIES: All state members of the United Nations General Assembly, except for the United States

IN FORCE: From adoption

OVERVIEW: A collective statement on the duty of nations and individuals toward nature: "Nature shall be respected and its essential processes shall not be impaired."

DISCUSSION:

The World Charter for Nature is a statement of principles rather than a formal agreement on policy and action. Of particular significance is the fact that the charter directly addresses the rights and responsibilities of individuals, not exclusively states, in relation to nature. The main text is brief, general, and eloquent:

I. GENERAL PRINCIPLES

1. Nature shall be respected and its essential processes shall not be impaired.

2. The genetic viability on the earth shall not be compromised; the population levels of all life forms, wild and domesticated, must be at least sufficient for their survival, and to this end necessary habitat shall be safeguarded.

3. All areas of the earth, both land and sea, shall be subject to these principles of conservation; special protection shall be given to unique areas, to representative samples of all the different types of ecosystems and to the habitat of rare or endangered species.

4. Ecosystems and organisms, as well as the land, marine and atmospheric resources that are utilized by man, shall be managed to achieve and maintain optimum sustainable productivity, but not in such a way as to endanger the integrity of those other ecosystems or species with which they coexist.

5. Nature shall be secured against degradation caused by warfare or other hostile activities.

II. FUNCTIONS

6. In the decision-making process it shall be recognized that man's needs can be met only by ensuring the proper functioning of natural systems and by respecting the principles set forth in the present Charter.

7. In the planning and implementation of social and economic development activities, due account shall be taken of the fact that the conservation of nature is an integral part of those activities.

8. In formulating long-term plans for economic development, population growth and the improvement of standards of living, due account shall be taken of the long-term capacity of natural systems to ensure the subsistence and settlement of the populations concerned, recognizing that this capacity may be enhanced through science and technology.

9. The allocation of areas of the earth to various uses shall be planned and due account shall be taken of physical constraints, the biological productivity and diversity and the natural beauty of the areas concerned.

10. Natural resources shall not be wasted, but used with a restraint appropriate to the principles set forth in the present Charter, in accordance with the following rules:

(a) Living resources shall not be utilized in excess of their natural capacity for regeneration;

(b) The productivity of soils shall be maintained or enhanced through measures which safeguard their long-term fertility and the process of organic decomposition, and prevent erosion and all other forms of degradation;

(c) Resources, including water, which are not consumed as they are used shall be reused or recycled;

(d) Non-renewable resources which are consumed as they are used shall be exploited with restraint, taking into account their abundance, their rational possibilities of converting them for consumption, and the compatibility of their exploitation with the functioning of natural systems.

11. Activities which might have an impact on nature shall be controlled, and the best available technologies that minimize significant risks to nature or other adverse effects shall be used; in particular:

(a) Activities which are likely to cause irreversible damage to nature shall be avoided;

(b) Activities which are likely to pose a significant risk to nature shall be preceded by an exhaustive examination; their proponents shall demonstrate that expected benefits outweigh potential damage to nature, and where potential adverse effects are not fully understood, the activities should not proceed;

(c) Activities which may disturb nature shall be preceded by assessment of their consequences, and environmental impact studies of development projects shall be conducted sufficiently in advance, and if they are to be undertaken, such activities shall be planned and carried out so as to minimize potential adverse effects;

(d) Agriculture, grazing, forestry and fisheries practices shall be adapted to the natural characteristics and constraints of given areas;

(e) Areas degraded by human activities shall be rehabilitated for purposes in accord with their natural potential and compatible with the well-being of affected populations.

12. Discharge of pollutants into natural systems shall be avoided and:

(a) Where this is not feasible, such pollutants shall be treated at the source, using the best practicable means available;

(b) Special precautions shall be taken to prevent discharge of radioactive or toxic wastes.

13. Measures intended to prevent, control or limit natural disasters, infestations and diseases shall be specifically directed to the causes of these scourges and shall avoid averse side-effects on nature.

III. IMPLEMENTATION

14. The principles set forth in the present Charter shall be reflected in the law and practice of each State, as well as at the international level.

15. Knowledge of nature shall be broadly disseminated by all possible means, particularly by ecological education as an integral part of general education.

16. All planning shall include, among its essential elements, the formulation of strategies for the conservation of nature, the establishment of inventories of ecosystems and assessments of the effects on nature of proposed policies and activities; all of these elements shall be disclosed to the public by appropriate means in time to permit effective consultation and participation.

17. Funds, programmes and administrative structures necessary to achieve the objective of the conservation of nature shall be provided.

18. Constant efforts shall be made to increase knowledge of nature by scientific research and to disseminate such knowledge unimpeded by restrictions of any kind.

19. The status of natural processes, ecosystems and species shall be closely monitored to enable early detection of degradation or threat, ensure timely intervention and facilitate the evaluation of conservation policies and methods.

20. Military activities damaging to nature shall be avoided.

21. States and, to the extent they are able, other public authorities, international organizations, individuals, groups and corporations shall:

(a) Co-operate in the task of conserving nature through common activities and other relevant actions, including information exchange and consultations;

(b) Establish standards for products and other manufacturing processes that may have adverse effects on nature, as well as agreed methodologies for assessing these effects;

(c) Implement the applicable international legal provisions for the conservation of nature and the protection of the environment;

(d) Ensure that activities within their jurisdictions or control do not cause damage to the natural systems located within other States or in the areas beyond the limits of national jurisdiction;

(e) Safeguard and conserve nature in areas beyond national jurisdiction.

22. Taking fully into account the sovereignty of States over their natural resources, each State shall give effect to the provisions of the present Charter through its competent organs and in co-operation with other States.

23. All persons, in accordance with their national legislation, shall have the opportunity to participate, individually or with others, in the formulation of decisions of direct concern to their environment, and shall have access to means of redress when their environment has suffered damage or degradation.

24. Each person has a duty to act in accordance with the provisions of the present Charter, acting individually, in association with others or through participation in the political process, each person shall strive to ensure that the objectives and requirements of the present Charter are met.

The United States, alone among the state members of the U.N. General Assembly, has declined to sign the charter.

REFERENCE:
Burhenne, W. E., and Will A. Irwin. *The World Charter for Nature: A Background Paper*. Berlin: E. Schmidt, 1983.

Protocol to Amend the Convention on Wetlands of International Importance Especially as Waterfowl Habitat

SIGNED: December 3, 1982, at Paris
SIGNATORIES: Australia, Bulgaria, Canada, Chile, Denmark, Finland, France, Germany, Hungary, Iceland, India, Iran, Ireland, Italy, Japan, Jordan, Mali, Malta, Mexico, Morocco, Netherlands, Norway, New Zealand, Niger, Pakistan, Poland, Portugal, Senegal, South Africa, Spain, Sweden, Switzerland, Tunisia, United Kingdom, United States, Venezuela, Vietnam
IN FORCE: From October 1, 1986
OVERVIEW: An amendment to **Convention on Wetlands of International Importance Especially as Waterfowl Habitat (RAMSAR)** of 1971, which is intended to render the convention more effective by providing a mechanism for regularly amending it.

REFERENCE:
Mitsch, William J. *Wetlands*. New York: Wiley, 1997.

Protocol Concerning Cooperation in Combating Oil Spills in the Wider Caribbean Region

SIGNED: March 24, 1983, at Cartagena de Indias, Colombia
SIGNATORIES: Antigua and Barbuda, Barbados, Colombia, Cuba, France, Grenada, Guatemala, Jamaica, Mexico, Netherlands, Panama, Saint Lucia, Saint Vincent and the Grenadines,

Trinidad and Tobago, United Kingdom, United States, Venezuela
IN FORCE: From October 11, 1986
OVERVIEW: A convention concerning regional cooperation and assistance in coping with oil spills in the Caribbean region.

DISCUSSION:
Signatories agree to unite in taking all necessary measures to protect the marine environment of the Caribbean region against pollution from oil spills, and to cooperate in maintaining and promoting contingency plans and means of combating pollution. Toward these ends, the signatory parties agree to exchange information regarding their competent national authorities for combating pollution and information on laws, institutions, and procedures aimed at combating marine pollution by oil.

In the event of an emergency, each signatory agrees to take appropriate measures to combat pollution, to inform other states of the measures it has taken or intends to take, to assess the nature and extent of the marine emergency, and to determine the necessary and appropriate action to be taken. Any signatory may call on the others for assistance.

The convention calls on signatories to conclude whatever bilateral or multilateral subregional arrangements may be appropriate to facilitate fulfilment of the obligations under the present convention.

REFERENCE:
Burger, Joanna. *Oil Spills*. New Brunswick, NJ: Rutgers University Press, 1997.

Agreement (with Mexico) on Cooperation for the Protection and Improvement of the Environment in the Border Area

SIGNED: August 14, 1983, at La Paz, Mexico
SIGNATORIES: Mexico vs. United States
IN FORCE: From February 16, 1984
OVERVIEW: An agreement "to cooperate in the field of environmental protection in the border area on the basis of equality, reciprocity, and mutual benefit."

DISCUSSION:
This is an agreement in principle, rather than in detail, to cooperate in addressing problems of pollution in the border region. The agreement defines the border area as 100 kilometers on either side of the inland and maritime boundaries between the countries, and it sets up the coordinating agencies, with a mandate for annual meetings to formulate policy and action.

REFERENCES:
None

International Tropical Timber Agreement

SIGNED: November 11, 1983, at Geneva

SIGNATORIES: Australia, Austria, Belgium, Bolivia, Brazil, Cameroon, Canada, China, Colombia, Congo, Côte d'Ivoire, Denmark, Ecuador, Egypt, European Economic Community, Finland, France, Gabon, Germany, Ghana, Greece, Honduras, India, Indonesia, Ireland, Italy, Japan, Korea (Republic), Liberia, Luxembourg, Malaysia, Nepal, Netherlands, Norway, Panama, Papua New Guinea, Peru, Philippines, Portugal, Russian Federation, Spain, Sweden, Switzerland, Thailand, Togo, Trinidad and Tobago, United Kingdom, United States, Zaire

IN FORCE: From April 1, 1985

OVERVIEW: A convention to promote cooperation and consultation among countries producing and consuming tropical timber, to promote the expansion and diversification of international trade in tropical timber and the improvement of structural conditions in the tropical timber market, to promote and support research and development with a view to improving forest management and wood utilization, and to encourage the development of national policies aimed at sustainable utilization and conservation of tropical forests and their genetic resources, and at maintaining the ecological balance in the regions concerned.

DISCUSSION:

The principal provision of the convention is the creation of the International Tropical Timber Organization, which, functioning through the International Tropical Timber Council, is charged with achieving the objectives mentioned in the "Overview." The council also functions to create programs of consultation or cooperation with appropriate organs and agencies of the United Nations, as well as intergovernmental, governmental and non-governmental organizations. Under the aegis of the council, the convention established three permanent committees:

- Committee on Economic Information and Market Intelligence
- Committee on Reforestation and Forest Management
- Committee on Forest Industry

REFERENCES:

Gale, Fred P. *The Tropical Timber Regime.* New York: St. Martin's Press, 1998.

Panayotou, Theodore. *Not by Timber Alone: Economics and Ecology for Sustaining Tropical Forests.* Washington, D.C.: Island Press, 1992.

Provisional Understanding Regarding Deep Seabed Matters

SIGNED: August 3, 1984, at Geneva

SIGNATORIES: Belgium, France, Germany (Federal Republic),

Italy, Japan, Netherlands, United Kingdom, United States

IN FORCE: From September 2, 1984

OVERVIEW: A agreement to forestall dispute over rights to mining of the seabed.

DISCUSSION:

This agreement sets up mechanisms to resolve conflicting claims among the signatories over deep seabed mining rights in certain areas. Although hard mineral mining of the deep seabed was not commercially feasible when the understanding was concluded, the parties believed the agreement was necessary to forestall any preemptive claims.

REFERENCES:

Barkenbus, Jack N. *Deep Seabed Resources: Politics and Technology.* New York: Free Press, 1979.

Kronmiller, Theodore G., ed., *Lawfullness of Deep Seabed Mining.* Dobbs Ferry, NY: Oceana Publications, 1980.

Protocol to the 1979 Convention on Long-Range Transboundary Air Pollution

OFFICIAL TITLE: Protocol to the 1979 Convention on Long-range Transboundary Air Pollution on Long-term Financing of the Cooperative Programme For Monitoring and Evaluation of the Long-range Transmission of Air Pollutants in Europe (EMEP)

SIGNED: September, 28, 1984, at Geneva

SIGNATORIES: Austria, Belarus, Belgium, Bulgaria, Canada, Cyprus, Czechoslovakia, Denmark, European Economic Community, Finland, France, Germany, Greece, Hungary, Ireland, Italy, Liechtenstein, Luxembourg, Netherlands, Norway, Poland, Portugal, Slovenia, Russian Federation, Spain, Sweden, Switzerland, Turkey, United Kingdom, United States, Yugoslavia

IN FORCE: From January 28, 1988

OVERVIEW: Pursuant to the **Convention on Long-Range Transboundary Air Pollution** of 1979, the protocol provides for long-term funding after 1984 for the implementation of the Cooperative Programme for the Monitoring and Evaluation of the Long-range Transmission of Air Pollutants in Europe (EMEP).

DISCUSSION:

Signatories of this instrument agreed to finance EMEP by covering the annual costs of the international centers cooperating within EMEP. Financing is divided into mandatory and voluntary contributions. The mandatory contributions are made annually by all signatories within the geographical scope of EMEP, whereas the voluntary contributions may be made by signatories (such as the United States) that lie outside the geographical scope. The protocol also mandates the creation of an annual budget to be drawn up by the Steering Body of EMEP, and to be adopted by the Executive Body not later than one year in advance of the financial year to which it applies.

REFERENCE:

Flinterman, Cees, et al. *Transboundary Air Pollution: International Legal Aspects of the Cooperation of States.* Dordrecht, Netherlands: Martinus Nijihoff, 1986.

Vienna Convention for the Protection of the Ozone Layer

SIGNED: March 22, 1985, at Vienna

IN FORCE: From September 9, 1988

SIGNATORIES: Algeria, Antigua and Barbuda, Argentina, Australia, Austria, Bahamas, Bahrain, Bangladesh, Barbados, Belarus, Belgium, Botswana, Brazil, Brunei Darussalam, Bulgaria, Burkina Faso, Cameroon, Canada, Central African Republic, Chad, Chile, China, Colombia, Costa Rica, Côte d'Ivoire, Croatia, Cuba, Cyprus, Czech Republic, Denmark (except Faeroe Islands and Greenland), Dominica, Ecuador, Egypt, El Salvador, Equatorial Guinea, European Economic Community, Fiji, Finland, France, Gambia, Germany, Ghana, Greece, Grenada, Guatemala, Guinea, Hungary, Iceland, India, Indonesia, Iran (Islamic Republic of), Ireland, Israel, Italy, Jamaica, Japan, Jordan, Kenya, Kiribati, Korea (Republic of), Kuwait, Lebanon, Libyan Arab Jamahiriya, Liechtenstein, Luxembourg, Malawi, Malaysia, Maldives, Malta, Marshall Islands, Mauritius, Mexico, Morocco, Netherlands (for the Kingdom in Europe, the Netherlands, Antilles and Aruba), New Zealand (Does not apply to the Cook Islands and Niue.), Nicaragua, Niger, Nigeria, Norway, Pakistan, Panama, Papua New Guinea, Paraguay, Peru, Philippines, Poland, Portugal, Romania, Russian Federation, Saint Kitts and Nevis, Samoa, Saudi Arabia, Senegal, Seychelles, Singapore, Slovakia, Slovenia, Solomon Islands, South Africa, Spain, Sri Lanka, Sudan, Swaziland, Sweden, Switzerland, Syrian Arab Republic, Thailand, Togo, Trinidad and Tobago, Tunisia, Turkey, Uganda, Ukraine, United Arab Emirates, United Kingdom (on behalf of the United Kingdom of Great Britain and Northern Ireland, the Bailiwick of Jersey, the Isle of Man, Anguilla, Bermuda, British Antarctic Territory, British Indian Ocean Territory, British Virgin Islands, Cayman Islands, Falkland Islands, Gibraltar, Hong Kong, Montserrat, Pitcairn, Henderson, Ducie and Oeno Islands, Saint Helena, Saint Helena Dependencies, South Georgia and the South Sandwich Islands, Turks and Caicos Islands), United Republic of Tanzania, United States, Uruguay, Uzbekistan, Venezuela, Yugoslavia, Zambia, Zimbabwe

OVERVIEW: The purpose of the convention is to protect human health and the environment against adverse effects resulting from modifications of the ozone layer.

DISCUSSION:

The convention calls for all signatories to cooperate in research concerning substances and processes that modify the ozone layer, specifically with regard to the following:

- Effects on human health
- Effects on the environment
- Alternative substances and technologies
- Systematic observation of the state of the ozone layer

The parties to the convention are called on to cooperate in formulation and implementation of measures to control activities that cause adverse effects through modification of the ozone layer, and, particularly, in the development of protocols for such purposes. The signatories agree to exchange relevant scientific, technical, socioeconomic, commercial and legal information relevant, and to cooperate in the development and transfer of technology and knowledge. In two annexes, key issues ozone-layer research and observation are set forth.

The convention remains open to additional signatories.

REFERENCES:

ACCIS Guide to United Nations Information Sources on the Environment. New York: United Nations Publications, 1989.

Firor, John. *The Changing Atmosphere: A Global Challenge.* New Have, Conn.: Yale University Press, 1992.

Makhijani, Arjun. *Mending the Ozone Hole: Science, Technology, and Policy.* Cambridge, Mass.: MIT Press, 1995.

Newton, David E. *The Ozone Dilemma: A Reference Handbook.* Denver: ABC-Clio, 1995.

Convention for the Protection of the Natural Resources and Environment of the South Pacific Region

SIGNED: November 24, 1986, at Noumea, New Caledonia

SIGNATORIES: Australia, Cook Islands, Federated States of Micronesia, Fiji, France, Marshall Islands, New Zealand, Papua New Guinea, Solomon Islands, Western Samoa, Nauru, Palau, Tuvalu, United Kingdom, United States

IN FORCE: August 18, 1990

OVERVIEW: The convention has as its object the protection and management of the natural resources and natural environment of the South Pacific region.

DISCUSSION:

Signatory parties agree to the following major provisions:

- To take measures to prevent, reduce, and control pollution of the convention area, especially pollution from vessels, from land-based sources, from the exploration and exploitation of the sea bed, from airborne pollution, from dumping, and from the testing of nuclear devices

The last-named pollution source is especially important in the South Pacific region because islands in this area were extensively used during the Cold War period for atmospheric and under-water testing of nuclear and thermonuclear weapons.

- To ensure that the implementation of the convention shall not result in an increase in pollution in the marine environment outside of the convention area
- To establish laws and regulations for the execution of the provisions of the convention
- To prohibit the storage of radioactive wastes in the convention area
- To protect and preserve rare ecosystems and endangered flora and fauna, as well as their habitats, in the convention area
- To cooperate in handling pollution emergencies in the convention area

REFERENCE:

ACCIS Guide to United Nations Information Sources on the Environment. New York: United Nations Publications, 1989.

Montreal Protocol on Substances That Deplete the Ozone Layer

SIGNED: September 16. 1987, at Montreal

IN FORCE: From January 1, 1989

SIGNATORIES: Algeria, Antigua and Barbuda, Argentina, Australia, Austria, Bahamas, Bahrain, Bangladesh, Barbados, Belarus, Belgium, Botswana, Brazil, Brunei Darussalam, Bulgaria, Burkina Faso, Cameroon, Canada, Central African Republic, Chile, China, Congo, Costa Rica, Côte d'Ivoire, Croatia, Cuba, Cyprus, Czech Republic, Denmark (except for the Faeroe Islands and Greenland), Dominica, Ecuador, Egypt, El Salvador, European Economic Community, Fiji, Finland, France, Gambia, Germany, Ghana, Greece, Grenada, Guatemala, Guinea, Hungary, Iceland, India, Indonesia, Iran (Islamic Republic of), Ireland, Israel, Italy, Jamaica, Japan, Jordan, Kenya, Kiribati, Korea (Republic of), Kuwait, Lebanon, Libyan Arab Jamahiriya, Liechtenstein, Luxembourg, Malawi, Malaysia, Maldives, Malta, Marshall Islands, Mauritius, Mexico, Monaco, Morocco, Netherlands (for the Kingdom in Europe, the Netherlands Antilles, and Aruba), New Zealand (The Protocol shall not apply to the Cook Islands and Niue.), Nicaragua, Niger, Nigeria, Norway, Pakistan, Panama, Papua New Guinea, Paraguay, Peru, Philippines, Poland, Portugal, Romania, Russian Federation, Saint Kitts and Nevis, Samoa, Saudi Arabia, Senegal, Seychelles, Singapore, Slovakia, Slovenia, Solomon Islands, South Africa, Spain, Sri Lanka, Sudan, Swaziland, Sweden, Switzerland, Syrian Arab Republic, Thailand, Togo, Trinidad and Tobago, Tunisia, Turkey, Uganda, Ukraine, United Arab Emirates, United Kingdom, United Republic of Tanzania, United States, Uruguay, Uzbekistan, Venezuela, Yugoslavia, Zambia, Zimbabwe

OVERVIEW: The protocol establishes precautionary measures to control global emissions of substances that deplete the ozone layer.

DISCUSSION:

Persuaded of the dangers of damaging the ozone layer of the earth's atmosphere, the signatories, by this protocol, agreed to control:

- The annual consumption and production of certain substances named in the protocol's Annex A, maintaining these at the 1986 annual level
- The annual consumption and production of certain substances enumerated in Annex A, reducing these to 50 percent of the 1986 annual level

The protocol makes special provision for developing countries consuming less than 0.3 kg per capita of the controlled substances; on the entry into force of the protocol for them, they may delay compliance by ten years. Another key timetable established by the protocol is a prohibition on importation of enumerated substances from a nonsignatory party. Developing countries are barred from exporting these substances after January 1993.

The protocol, operating within the framework of the **Vienna Convention for the Protection of the Ozone Layer**, provides for measures of exchange of technology and information, calculation of control levels and assessment and review of the progress achieved. The protocol, which remains open to any state or regional economic integration organization that is signatory to the Vienna Convention for the Protection of the Ozone Layer, has been strengthened and extended by the **London Amendment to the Montreal Protocol on Substances That Deplete the Ozone Layer.**

REFERENCES:

ACCIS Guide to United Nations Information Sources on the Environment. New York: United Nations Publications, 1989.

Firor, John. *The Changing Atmosphere: A Global Challenge.* New Have, Conn.: Yale University Press, 1992.

Makhijani, Arjun. *Mending the Ozone Hole: Science, Technology, and Policy.* Cambridge, Mass.: MIT Press, 1995.

Newton, David E. *The Ozone Dilemma: A Reference Handbook.* Denver: ABC-Clio, 1995.

Protocol to the 1979 Convention on Long-Range Transboundary Air Pollution Concerning the Control of Emissions of Nitrogen Oxides or Their Transboundary Fluxes

SIGNED: November 1, 1988, at Sofia, Bulgaria

SIGNATORIES: Austria, Belarus, Belgium, Bulgaria, Canada,

Czechoslovakia, Denmark, Finland, France, Germany, Hungary, Ireland, Italy, Liechtenstein, Luxembourg, Netherlands, Norway, Poland, Russian Federation, Spain, Sweden, Switzerland, Ukraine, United Kingdom, United States

IN FORCE: Not yet in force

OVERVIEW: The protocol enhances and amplifies the **Convention on Long-Range Transboundary Air Pollution** of 1979 by providing specifically for the control or reduction of nitrogen oxides and their transboundary fluxes.

DISCUSSION:

The protocol embodies measures to control or reduce emissions of nitrogen oxides and their transboundary fluxes at or to the level of the national annual emissions of the calendar year 1987 by December 14, 1994. The protocol also lays down the following:

- Applying national emission standards to new stationary and mobile sources and introduces pollution control measures for existing major stationary sources
- Making unleaded fuel sufficiently available two years after the protocol enters into force
- Assigning high priority to research and monitoring techniques in determining necessary reduction of emissions
- Cooperating to determine critical loads, the reductions required, and measures to achieve those reductions
- Exchanging information and (consistent with national laws) facilitating exchange of technology to reduce nitrogen emission and their transboundary fluxes

The protocol includes a detailed technical annex.

REFERENCES:

Underdal, Arild, and Kenneth Hanf. *International Environmental Agreements and Domestic Policies: The Case of Acid Rain.* Brookfield, VT: Ashgate Publishing Limited, 2000.

Basel Convention on the Control of Transboundary Movements of Hazardous Wastes and Their Disposal

SIGNED: March 22, 1989, at Basel

IN FORCE: May 5, 1992

SIGNATORIES: Afghanistan, Antigua and Barbuda, Argentina, Australia, Austria, Bahamas, Bahrain, Bangladesh, Belgium, Bolivia, Brazil, Canada, Chile, China, Colombia, Cyprus, Czech Republic, Denmark, Ecuador, Egypt, El Salvador, Estonia, European Economic Community, Finland, France, Germany, Greece, Guatemala, Haiti, Hungary, India, Iran (Islamic Republic of), Ireland, Israel, Italy, Jordan, Kuwait, Latvia, Lebanon, Liechtenstein, Luxembourg, Maldives, Mauritius, Mexico, Monaco, Netherlands, New Zealand, Nigeria, Norway, Panama, Philippines, Poland, Portugal, Romania, Russian

Federation, Saudi Arabia, Senegal, Seychelles, Slovakia, Spain, Sri Lanka, Sweden, Switzerland, Syrian Arab Republic, Thailand, Turkey, United Arab Emirates, United Kingdom, United Republic of Tanzania, United States, Uruguay, Venezuela

OVERVIEW: The convention regulates the transboundary shipment and disposal of hazardous wastes.

DISCUSSION:

The convention set up obligations for the signatories as follows:

- To reduce transboundary movements of wastes to a minimum consistent with the environmentally sound and efficient management of such wastes
- To minimize the amount and toxicity of hazardous wastes generated and to ensure their environmentally sound management (including disposal and recovery operations) as close as possible to the source of generation
- To assist developing countries in environmentally sound management of the hazardous and other wastes they generate

The convention established protocols enabling states to prohibit the import of hazardous wastes or other wastes. The non-importation regulation of any signatory is binding on all others.

- Signatories are to prohibit the export of hazardous wastes and other wastes if the state of import does not consent in writing to the specific import, in the case where the State of import has not prohibited the import of such wastes.
- Signatories are to prohibit all persons under their national jurisdiction from transporting or disposing of hazardous wastes or other type of wastes unless such persons are authorized or allowed to perform such types of operations.
- Parties are to designate or establish one or more competent authorities as focal points to receive notifications.
- States of export shall not allow the generator of hazardous wastes or other wastes to commence the transboundary movement until they have received written confirmation that the notifier has received the written consent of the state of import.
- Signatories are to cooperate with each other in order to improve and achieve environmentally sound management of hazardous wastes and other wastes.
- In case of an accident occurring during the transboundary movement of hazardous or other wastes or their disposal that is likely to present risks to human health and the environment in other states, those states must be immediately informed.

The convention includes an annex establishing arbitration procedures for settling disputes between signatories. The convention remains open to all states for signature.

REFERENCE:

ACCIS Guide to United Nations Information Sources on the Environment. New York: United Nations Publications, 1989.

Protocol Concerning Specially Protected Areas and Wildlife to the Convention for the Protection and Development of the Marine Environment of the Wider Caribbean Region

SIGNED: January 1, 1990, at Kingston, Jamaica

SIGNATORIES: Antigua and Barbuda, Bahamas, Colombia, Cuba, France, Guatemala, Jamaica, Mexico, Netherlands, St. Lucia, Trinidad and Tobago, United Kingdom, United States, Venezuela

IN FORCE: Not yet in force

OVERVIEW: The protocol established protected coastal and marine areas of the Wider Caribbean region and protects endangered species of wild fauna and flora in the region.

DISCUSSION:

Each party to this comprehensive environmental protocol undertakes to enact and enforce laws and regulations to protect, preserve and manage in a sustainable way areas, within its jurisdiction, of special value and threatened species of fauna and flora. Furthermore, each signatory undertakes the following:

- To establish protected areas within its jurisdiction to conserve representative coastal and marine ecosystems and habitats critical to the survival of endangered species of flora and fauna
- To take appropriate protection measures in conformity with national laws and international law to ensure the sustainable management of the protected areas
- To cooperate in establishing protected areas, establishing of a list of protected areas, and establishing buffer zones in areas contiguous to international boundaries
- To protect wild flora and fauna by identifying threatened or endangered species and taking appropriate measures to prohibit the taking, killing, possession, or disturbance of such species and to promote captive breeding of such species, where necessary
- To cooperate in protecting wild fauna and flora by taking regulatory action with respect to species enumerated in Annexes I, II and III of the protocol
- To take general measures of international cooperation, including environmental impact assessment, promotion of public awareness, and mutual assistance to achieve the objectives of the protocol

In addition, the signatories established a reporting system and a Scientific and Technical Advisory Committee, both of which with the purpose of carrying out the provisions of the protocol.

REFERENCES:
None

London Amendment to the Montreal Protocol on Substances That Deplete the Ozone Layer

SIGNED: June 29, 1990, at London

IN FORCE: From August 10, 1992

SIGNATORIES: Algeria, Antigua and Barbuda, Argentina, Australia, Austria, Bahamas, Bahrain, Brazil, Cameroon, Canada, Chile, China, Denmark, Dominica, Ecuador, Egypt, European Economic Community, Finland, France, Germany, Ghana, Greece, Guinea, Iceland, India, Indonesia, Ireland, Israel, Italy, Jamaica, Japan, Korea (Republic of), Lebanon, Luxembourg, Malaysia, Maldives, Marshall Islands, Mauritius, Mexico, Monaco, Netherlands*, New Zealand, Norway, Pakistan, Papua New Guinea, Paraguay, Peru, Portugal, Romania, Russian Federation, Saudi Arabia, Senegal, Seychelles, Singapore, Slovenia, South Africa, Spain, Sri Lanka, Sweden, Switzerland, Thailand, United Kingdom, United Republic of Tanzania, United States

OVERVIEW: The amendment strengthens the control procedures under the **Montreal Protocol on Substances that Deplete the Ozone Layer** (1987), establishes financial mechanisms for it, and extends its coverage to new substances.

DISCUSSION:

Signatories to the amendment agree to the following:

- To amend the protocol to phase out the production of fully halogenated chlorofluorocarbons (CFCs) and carbon tetrachloride by the year 2000 and methyl chloroform by the year 2005; these substances are most immediately harmful to the ozone layer.
- To phase out all protocol-controlled substances between 1990 and 2005
- To establish a financial mechanism, including a multilateral fund and a clearing-house function, for the implementation of the protocol, financed by the contributions of the signatories assessed on the basis of the United Nations scale of assessment.
- To provide for tighter provisions on reporting of data, trade with non-parties to the protocol, and the special position of developing countries and transfer of technology
- To adopt a new Annex B to the Protocol, which extends control to 10 chlorofluorocarbons (CFCs), carbon tetrachloride, and methyl chloroform, substances not previously covered by the protocol
- The amendment includes a new annex covering transitional substances.

Signature remains open to the parties to the Montreal Protocol.

REFERENCES:
ACCIS Guide to United Nations Information Sources on the Environment. New York: United Nations Publications, 1989.

Firor, John. *The Changing Atmosphere: A Global Challenge.* New Have, CT: Yale University Press, 1992.

Makhijani, Arjun. *Mending the Ozone Hole: Science, Technology, and Policy.* Cambridge, MA: MIT Press, 1995.

Newton, David E. *The Ozone Dilemma: A Reference Handbook.* Denver: ABC-Clio, 1995.

International Convention on Oil Pollution Preparedness, Response and Cooperation

SIGNED: November 30, 1990, London

IN FORCE: Not yet in force

SIGNATORIES: Australia, Egypt, Seychelles, Sweden, United States

OVERVIEW: The convention strengthens the legal framework for the control of environmental pollution by oil, in general, and marine pollution by oil in particular, by providing a basis for preparedness, and for a response capability, to deal with incidents of oil pollution in the marine environment.

DISCUSSION:

In an era of high-capacity supertankers, oil pollution accidents present the potential for massive environmental catastrophe. The convention provides for the following:

- Prescription for a general duty of the signatory parties to take appropriate measures to prepare for and respond to any oil pollution incident
- Definition of terms used in the convention
- Imposition on the signatories of a duty to ensure that all ships flying their flags have made oil pollution emergency plans as prescribed by the convention
- Requirement that ships flying flags of the signatories report all incidents of oil discharge and that the party receiving the report take appropriate control action and transmit the information to all states whose interests are likely to be affected
- Provisions for collaborative initiatives, in research and development, and in technical operations, in the search for appropriate controls to oil pollution incidents

An annex to the Convention details reimbursement of costs of assistance. The convention remains open to for signature.

REFERENCES:

ACCIS Guide to United Nations Information Sources on the Environment. New York: United Nations Publications, 1989.

Bockholts, P., and I. Heidebrink, eds. *Chemical Spills and Emergency Management at Sea: Proceedings of the First International Conference.* Amsterdam: Kluwer Academic Publishers, 1989.

Convention on Environmental Impact Assessment in a Transboundary Context

SIGNED: February 25, 1991, Espoo, Finland

SIGNATORIES: Albania, Austria, Belarus, Belgium, Bulgaria, Canada, Czechoslovakia, Denmark, European Economic Community, Finland, France, Germany, Greece, Hungary, Iceland, Ireland, Italy, Luxembourg, Netherlands, Norway, Poland, Portugal, Romania, Russian Federation, Spain, Sweden, Ukraine, United Kingdom, United States

IN FORCE: Not yet in force

OVERVIEW: An international convention to promote environmentally sound and sustainable economic development by applying environmental impact assessment with the object of preventing environmental degradation across national boundaries.

DISCUSSION:

After defining key terms, the convention lays down the responsibilities of signatory parties, which include the following:

- To take policy, legal, and administrative measures to control adverse transboundary impact arising from proposed activities
- To notify affected parties, and to confer and negotiate with them, in cases where a proposed activity may create a significant adverse transboundary impact
- To create truly comprehensive environmental impact assessments based on guidelines incorporated in the convention
- To provide for and cooperate in research to improve methods of environmental impact assessment while promoting sustainable economic activity
- To meet regularly with other signatories in order to keep under review the working of the convention

The convention provides guidelines and apparatus for the settlement of disputes and includes the following appendixes, which address specific issues:

I. List of activities likely to create adverse environmental impacts

II. Content of the environmental impact assessment documentation

III. General criteria to assist in the determination of the environmental significance of activities not listed in Appendix I

IV. Inquiry procedure

V. Post-project analysis guidelines

VI. Elements for bilateral and multilateral cooperation

VII. Arbitration rules

REFERENCE:

Modak, Rasad, and Asit K. Biwas, eds. *Conducting Environmental Impact Assessment in Developing Countries.* New York: United Nations Publications, 1999.

Protocol to the Antarctic Treaty on Environmental Protection

SIGNED: October 3, 1991, at Madrid

SIGNATORIES: Australia, Austria, Belgium, Brazil, Canada, Chile, China, Colombia, Denmark, Ecuador, Finland, France, Germany, Greece, Hungary, India, Italy, Korea (Democratic People's Republic), Korea (Republic), Netherlands, New Zealand, Norway, Peru, Poland, Romania, Russian Federation, South Africa, Spain, Sweden, Switzerland, United Kingdom, United States, Uruguay

IN FORCE: Not yet in force

OVERVIEW: A protocol to the **Antarctic Treaty**, reaffirming the status of the Antarctica as a special conservation area and enhancing the framework for the protection of the Antarctic environment.

DISCUSSION:

The protocol focuses on the environmental principles governing the conduct of signatory parties in relation to Antarctica. The principal provision is that of protecting the Antarctic environment and its dependent and associated ecosystems and its status as a place for research. The signatories agree to cooperate in the planning and conduct of activities in the Antarctic Treaty area. Furthermore, the signatories agree to the following:

- A prohibition of mineral resource enterprises in the Antarctic Treaty area, save for purposes of scientific research
- A requirement of environmental impact assessment in the Antarctic Treaty area in respect of activities that are likely to entail significant adverse environmental consequences
- A requirement to consult on and monitor activities undertaken by signatories in Antarctica
- A responsibility to take appropriate action to deal with any emergency that may ensue from activities in Antarctica
- An obligation on signatories to report annually on actions taken by them to implement the protocol

In addition, the protocol lays down dispute settlement procedures and includes a schedule on arbitration. Technical annexes address the following topic areas:

- Environment impact assessment
- Conservation of Antarctic fauna and flora
- Waste disposal and waste management
- Prevention of marine pollution

REFERENCES:

Jorgensen-Dahl, Arnfinn, and Willy Ostreng, eds. *The Antarctic Treaty System in World Politics.* New York: St. Martin's Press, 1991.

National Academy. *Antarctic Treaty System: An Assessment.* Washington, D.C.: National Academy Press, 1986.

Rengger, N. J. Treaties and Alliances of the World, 5th ed. Essex, UK: Longman Group, 1990.

Stokke, Olva Schram, and Davor Vidas, eds. *Governing the Antarctic: The Effectiveness and Legitimacy of the Antarctic Treaty System.* New York: Cambridge University Press, 1997.

Protocol to the 1979 Convention on Long-Range Transboundary Air Pollution Concerning the Control of Emissions of Volatile Organic Compounds or Their Transboundary Fluxes

SIGNED: November 18, 1991, at Geneva

SIGNATORIES: Austria, Belgium, Bulgaria, Canada, Denmark, European Economic Community, Finland, France, Germany, Greece, Hungary, Italy, Liechtenstein, Luxembourg, Netherlands, Norway, Portugal, Spain, Sweden, Switzerland, Ukraine, United Kingdom, United States

IN FORCE: Not yet in force

OVERVIEW: The protocol enhances the **Convention on Long-Range Transboundary Air Pollution** of 1979 by focusing on volatile organic compounds.

DISCUSSION:

After defining key terms, the protocol lays down the basic obligations of signatories, which include the following:

- Taking measures to control and reduce national emissions of volatile organic compounds
- Making cooperative arrangements to control transboundary fluxes of such emissions
- Cooperating to acquire useful information to facilitate the control of such emissions

The signatories undertake to exchange technology as a way of controlling the emission of volatile organic compounds and to monitor and review emission-control arrangements. The protocol provides a mechanism for settling disputes and includes detailed annexes:

- To designate tropospheric ozone management areas (TOMAS)
- To enumerate control measures for emission of volatile organic compounds (VOCs) from stationary sources
- To control measures for emissions of volatile organic compounds (VOCs) from on-road motor vehicles
- To classify volatile organic compounds (VOCs) based on their photochemical ozone creation potential (POCP)

REFERENCES:

ACCIS Guide to United Nations Information Sources on the Environment. New York: United Nations Publications, 1989.

Firor, John. *The Changing Atmosphere: A Global Challenge.* New Haven, Conn.: Yale University Press, 1992.

Makhijani, Arjun. *Mending the Ozone Hole: Science, Technology, and Policy.* Cambridge, Mass.: MIT Press, 1995.

Newton, David E. *The Ozone Dilemma: A Reference Handbook.* Denver: ABC-Clio, 1995.

Convention on the Protection and Use of Transboundary Watercourses and International Lakes

SIGNED: March 17, 1992, at Helsinki

SIGNATORIES: Albania, Austria, Belgium, Bulgaria, Croatia, Denmark, Estonia, European Community, Finland, France, Germany, Greece, Hungary, Italy, Latvia, Lithuania, Luxembourg, Netherlands, Norway, Poland, Portugal, Romania, Russian Federation, Spain, Sweden, Switzerland, United Kingdom

IN FORCE: From October 6, 1996; United States has not yet signed

OVERVIEW: An important international environmental convention addressing inland, non-oceanic bodies of water.

DISCUSSION:

Intended to strengthen national measures for the protection and ecologically sound management of transboundary surface waters and groundwaters, the convention obliges signatories to prevent, control, and reduce water pollution from point as well as non-point sources. The convention includes provisions for monitoring, research and development, consultation and cooperation, warning and alarm systems, mutual assistance, institutional arrangements, and the exchange and protection of information, as well as ensuring public access to information.

As of September 1999, the United States, although a participant in the Helsinki conference that produced the convention, has not signed the agreement.

REFERENCES:
None

United Nations Framework Convention on Climate Change

SIGNED: May 9, 1992, at New York

SIGNATORIES: Algeria, Angola, Antigua and Barbuda, Argentina, Armenia, Australia, Austria, Azerbaijan, Bahamas, Bahrain, Bangladesh, Barbados, Belarus, Belgium, Belize, Benin, Bhutan, Bolivia, Botswana, Brazil, Bulgaria, Burkina Faso, Burundi, Cameroon, Canada, Cape Verde, Central African Republic, Chad, Chile, China, Colombia, Comoros, Congo, Cook Islands, Costa Rica, Côte d'Ivoire, Croatia, Cuba, Cyprus, Czech Republic, Denmark, Djibouti, Dominica, Dominican Republic, Ecuador, Egypt, El Salvador, Estonia, Ethiopia, European Economic Community, Fiji, Finland, France, Gabon, Gambia, Germany, Ghana, Greece, Grenada, Guatemala, Guinea, Guinea-Bissau, Guyana, Haiti, Honduras, Hungary, Iceland, India, Indonesia, Iran, Ireland, Israel, Italy, Jamaica, Japan, Jordan, Kazakhstan, Kenya, Kiribati, Korea (Democratic People's Republic), Korea (Republic), Latvia, Lebanon, Lesotho, Liberia, Libyan Arab Jamahiriya, Liechtenstein, Lithuania, Luxembourg, Madagascar, Malawi, Malaysia, Maldives, Mali, Malta, Marshall Islands, Mauritania, Mauritius, Mexico, Micronesia, Moldova, Monaco, Mongolia, Morocco, Mozambique, Myanmar, Namibia, Nauru, Nepal, Netherlands, New Zealand, Nicaragua, Niger, Nigeria, Norway, Oman, Pakistan, Panama, Papua New Guinea, Paraguay, Peru, Philippines, Poland, Portugal, Romania, Russian Federation, Rwanda, Saint Kitts and Nevis, Samoa, San Marino, Sao Tome and Principe, Senegal, Seychelles, Sierra Leone, Singapore, Slovakia, Slovenia, Solomon Islands, Spain, Sri Lanka, Sudan, Suriname, Swaziland, Sweden, Switzerland, Thailand, Togo, Trinidad and Tobago, Tunisia, Tuvalu, Uganda, Ukraine, United Kingdom, United Republic, United States, Uruguay, Uzbekistan, Vanuatu, Venezuela, Vietnam, Yemen, Yugoslavia, Zaire, Zambia, Zimbabwe

IN FORCE: Not yet in force

OVERVIEW: A convention intended to regulate levels of greenhouse gas concentration in the atmosphere to avoid the occurrence of climate change on a level that would impede sustainable economic development, or compromise initiatives in food production.

DISCUSSION:

As with many ecological conventions, this one begins by defining key terms, then goes on to lay down the principal objective of the convention: Signatories undertake to protect the climate system for present and future generations. The major provisions are as follows:

- Developing countries should be given assistance to enable them to fulfil the terms of the convention.
- Signatories should work in cooperation in order to obtain maximum benefit from initiatives in the control of the climate system.
- Signatories undertake to prepare national inventories on greenhouse gas emissions, and on actions taken to remove them.
- Signatories agree to formulate and implement programs for the control of climate change.
- Signatories will undertake cooperation in technology for the control of change in the climate system.
- Signatories agree to incorporate suitable policies for the control of climate change in national plans.
- Signatories will undertake education and training policies to enhance public awareness of climate change.

The developed state parties to the convention (in addition to other parties listed in annex I) agree to commit themselves to take special measures to limit their anthropogenic emissions of greenhouse gases, and to enhance the capacity of their sinks and reservoirs for the stabilization of such gases. These state parties (and other parties listed in annex II) further undertake to provide financial support to developing state parties, to enable them to comply with the terms of the Convention.

The convention provides for the establishment and promotion of networks and cooperative program of research into and systematic observation of climate change and the establishment of a Conference of Parties, to function as the supreme body of the convention responsible for overseeing its implementation. The convention also includes provisions for a financial mechanism to provide, as appropriate, resources on a grant or concessional basis, and it includes procedures for the settlement of disputes.

REFERENCES:

Mintzer, Irving M. *Confronting Climate Change: Risks, Implications and Responses.* Cambridge, UK, and New York: Cambridge University Press, 1992.

United States Department of State. *Treaties in Force: A List of Treaties and other International Agreements of the United States in Force on January 1, 1997.* Washington, D.C.: U.S. Government Printing Office, 1997.

Convention on Biological Diversity

SIGNED: June 5, 1992, Rio de Janeiro

IN FORCE: Not yet in force

SIGNATORIES: Afghanistan, Algeria, Angola, Antigua and Barbuda, Argentina, Armenia, Australia, Austria, Azerbaijan, Bahamas, Bahrain, Bangladesh, Barbados, Belarus, Belgium, Belize, Benin, Bhutan, Bolivia, Botswana, Brazil, Bulgaria, Burkina Faso, Burundi, Cameroon, Canada, Cape Verde, Central African Republic, Chad, Chile, China, Colombia, Comoros, Congo, Cook Islands, Costa Rica. Côte d'Ivoire, Croatia, Cuba, Cyprus, Czech Republic, Democratic People's Republic of Korea, Denmark, Djibouti, Dominican Republic, Ecuador, Egypt, El Salvador, Estonia, Ethiopia, European Economic Community, Fiji, Finland, France, Gabon, Gambia, Germany, Ghana, Greece, Grenada, Guatemala, Guinea, Guinea-Bissau, Guyana, Haiti, Honduras, Hungary, Iceland, India, Indonesia, Iran, Ireland, Israel, Italy, Jamaica, Japan, Jordan, Kazakhstan, Kenya, Kuwait, Latvia, Lebanon, Lesotho, Liberia, Libyan Arab Jamahirya, Liechtenstein, Lithuania, Luxembourg, Madagascar, Malawi, Malaysia, Maldives, Mali, Malta, Marshall Islands, Mauritania, Mauritius, Mexico, Micronesia, Moldova, Monaco, Mongolia, Morocco, Mozambique, Myanmar, Namibia, Nauru, Nepal, Netherlands, New Zealand, Nicaragua, Niger, Nigeria, Norway, Oman, Pakistan, Panama, Papua New Guinea, Paraguay, Peru, Philippines, Poland, Portugal, Qatar, Republic of Korea, Romania, Russian Federation, Rwanda, Saint Kitts and Nevis, Samoa, San Marino, Sao Tome and Principe, Senegal, Seychelles, Singapore, Slovakia, Slovenia, Solomon Islands, South Africa, Spain, Sri Lanka, Sudan, Suriname, Swaziland, Sweden, Switzerland, Syrian Arab Republic, Thailand, Togo, Trinidad and Tobago, Tunisia, Turkey, Tuvalu, Uganda, Ukraine, United Arab Emirates, United Kingdom, United Republic of Tanzania, United States, Uruguay, Vanuatu, Venezuela, Vietnam, Yemen, Yugoslavia, Zaire, Zambia, Zimbabwe

OVERVIEW: The purpose of the convention is to promote the conservation of biological diversity, to promote the sustainable use of its components, and to encourage equitable sharing of the benefits arising out of the use of genetic resources; such equitable sharing includes appropriate access to genetic resources, as well as appropriate transfer of technology, taking into account existing rights over such resources and such technology.

DISCUSSION:

The conservation of biological diversity is critical to the well-being of the world biome—essentially, the ecology of the planet. Such conservation requires international cooperation and coordination, which this convention seeks to promote. The convention accordingly provides for the following:

- Restatement of the principle of national sovereignty over domestic natural resources, subject to respect for the rights of other States
- Statement of the signatories' duty to conserve biological diversity within their jurisdiction
- Requirement of cooperation between signatories in preserving biological diversity in areas out of national jurisdiction
- Conferment of responsibility on signatories for the formulation and implementation of strategies, plans, or programs for the conservation and sustainable use of biological diversity
- Requirement to monitor the elements of biological diversity, determining the nature of the urgency required in the protection of each category of organism
- The signatories' obligations for research, training, general education, and the fostering of awareness relevant to the identification, conservation, and sustainable use of biological diversity
- The signatories' obligation to provide for environmental impact assessment of projects that are likely to have significant adverse effects on biological diversity
- The signatories' obligation to exchange information and undertake consultation with other states in all cases where proposed national projects are likely to have adverse effects on biological diversity in other states;
- Provisions on financial resources and technological exchange; the convention places a duty on signatories to provide, in accordance with their individual capabilities, financial support for the fulfillment of the objectives of conservation and sustainable use of biological diversity

The convention establishes a conference of signatory parties to keep under review the implementation of the convention. It also provides means and procedures for the settlement of disputes. Two annexes are devoted to details of identification and monitoring, and arbitration and conciliation. The convention remains open to all states and regional economic integration organizations.

REFERENCES:

ACCIS Guide to United Nations Information Sources on the Environment. New York: United Nations Publications, 1989.

Becher, Anne. *Biodiversity: A Reference Handbook.* Denver, CO: ABC-Clio, 1998.

Laurence, William F., and Richard O. Bierregaard, eds. *Tropical Forest Remnants: Ecology, Management, and Conservation of Fragmented Communities.* Chicago: University of Chicago Press, 1997.

Pimm, Stuart L. *The Balance of Nature? Ecological Issues in the Conservation of Species and Communities.* Chicago: University of Chicago Press, 1991.

Sutherland, William J., ed. *Ecological Census Techniques: A Handbook.* New York: Cambridge University Press, 1996.

Wilson, Don E., et al, eds. *Measuring and Monitoring Biological Diversity: Standard Methods for Mammals.* Washington. D.C.: Smithsonian Institution Press, 1996.

Agenda 21

SIGNED: June 14, 1992, at Rio de Janeiro, Brazil

SIGNATORIES: Afghanistan, Algeria, Angola, Antigua and Barbuda, Argentina, Armenia, Australia, Austria, Azerbaijan, Bahamas, Bahrain, Bangladesh, Barbados, Belarus, Belgium, Belize, Benin, Bhutan, Bolivia, Botswana, Brazil, Bulgaria, Burkina Faso, Burundi, Cameroon, Canada, Cape Verde, Central African Republic, Chad, Chile, China, Colombia, Comoros, Congo, Cook Islands, Costa Rica. Côte d'Ivoire, Croatia, Cuba, Cyprus, Czech Republic, Democratic People's Republic of Korea, Denmark, Djibouti, Dominican Republic, Ecuador, Egypt, El Salvador, Estonia, Ethiopia, European Economic Community, Fiji, Finland, France, Gabon, Gambia, Germany, Ghana, Greece, Grenada, Guatemala, Guinea, Guinea-Bissau, Guyana, Haiti, Honduras, Hungary, Iceland, India, Indonesia, Iran, Ireland, Israel, Italy, Jamaica, Japan, Jordan, Kazakhstan, Kenya, Kuwait, Latvia, Lebanon, Lesotho, Liberia, Libyan Arab Jamahirya, Liechtenstein, Lithuania, Luxembourg, Madagascar, Malawi, Malaysia, Maldives, Mali, Malta, Marshall Islands, Mauritania, Mauritius, Mexico, Micronesia, Moldova, Monaco, Mongolia, Morocco, Mozambique, Myanmar, Namibia, Nauru, Nepal, Netherlands, New Zealand, Nicaragua, Niger, Nigeria, Norway, Oman, Pakistan, Panama, Papua New Guinea, Paraguay, Peru, Philippines, Poland, Portugal, Qatar, Republic of Korea, Romania, Russian Federation, Rwanda, Saint Kitts and Nevis, Samoa, San Marino, Sao Tome and Principe, Senegal, Seychelles, Singapore, Slovakia, Slovenia, Solomon Islands, South Africa, Spain, Sri Lanka, Sudan, Suriname, Swaziland, Sweden, Switzerland, Syrian Arab Republic, Thailand, Togo, Trinidad and Tobago, Tunisia, Turkey, Tuvalu, Uganda, Ukraine, United Arab Emirates, United Kingdom, United Republic of Tanzania, United States, Uruguay, Vanuatu, Venezuela, Vietnam, Yemen, Yugoslavia, Zaire, Zambia, Zimbabwe

IN FORCE: From signing

OVERVIEW: One of main documents of the Rio "Earth Summit"; outlines global strategies for environmental clean-up and environmentally sound development.

DISCUSSION:

For background information on this document, see **Rio Declaration on Environment and Development.**

With the **Rio Declaration on Environment and Development**, the **Convention on Biological Diversity**, the **Framework Convention on Climate Change,** and the **Statement of Principles on Forests,** Agenda 21 is one of the five principal documents to emerge from the United Nations Conference on Environment and Development, popularly called the Earth Summit, held at Rio de Janeiro, Brazil, from June 3 to June 14, 1992. The long, detailed, and complex document is an entirely non-binding set of objectives and guidelines for stewardship of the environment in the twenty-first century, especially with regard to development. Paragraph 1.3 of the Preamble to the document sets out the ambitious scope of Agenda 21:

> Agenda 21 addresses the pressing problems of today and also aims at preparing the world for the challenges of the next century. It reflects a global consensus and political commitment at the highest level on development and environment cooperation. Its successful implementation is first and foremost the responsibility of Governments. National strategies, plans, policies and processes are crucial in achieving this. International cooperation should support and supplement such national efforts. In this context, the United Nations system has a key role to play. Other international, regional and subregional organizations are also called upon to contribute to this effort. The broadest public participation and the active involvement of the non-governmental organizations and other groups should also be encouraged.

Underlying Agenda 21 is the notion that humanity has reached a "defining moment in its history." It can continue present policies, which serve to deepen the economic divisions within and between countries—increasing poverty, hunger, sickness, and illiteracy worldwide, while causing the deterioration of the ecosystem. Or it can form a "global partnership" to bring development to the nations that badly need it, but to harmonize that development with protection of the environment. This was a leading theme of the Rio Summit, which recognized that development in the so-called Third World typically proceeds without regard to the needs of environmental protection.

The main principles of Agenda 21 follow:

- A resolve to establish international cooperation to accelerate sustainable development in developing countries
- A commitment to combat poverty worldwide, which causes suffering on every level, even as it damages the ecosystem
- A commitment to changing unsustainable patterns of consumption and production, particularly in the industrialized countries, which aggravate poverty and imbalances

- A commitment to develop strategies to mitigate both the adverse impact on the environment of human activities as well as the adverse impact of environmental change on human populations
- A commitment to promote and protect human health worldwide
- A commitment to improve the social, economic and environmental quality of human settlements and the living and working environments of all people, in particular the urban and rural poor
- The full integration of environmental and developmental issues for government decision-making on economic, social, fiscal, energy, agricultural, transportation, trade and other policies.
- A commitment on the part of governments to seek a broader range of public participation in environmental matters
- A commitment to protect the atmosphere, especially the ozone layer, in part through finding new sources of energy, which do not threaten the ozone layer
- Adoption of an integrated approach to land use that examines all needs so that the most efficient trade-offs can be made
- A resolve to combat deforestation, including that of the rainforests
- A commitment to combat desertification
- A commitment to preserve mountain ecosystems and to protect them from soil erosion, landslides and rapid loss of habitat and genetic diversity
- A resolve to develop agricultural practices that do not destroy the land
- A commitment to strategies for sustaining biological diversity
- Adoption of environmentally sound management of biotechnology
- Commitment to safeguarding the oceans
- Adoption of sound management of freshwater resources
- Commitment to the safe use of toxic chemicals
- Adoption of sound methods of hazardous waste management
- Development of sound methods of solid waste disposal
- Adoption of sound management of radioactive wastes
- A guarantee the full and equal participation of women in all development activities and particularly environmental management
- A commitment to broad public participation in environmental matters
- A commitment to policies of free trade and access to markets, which will help make economic growth and environmental protection mutually supportive for all countries
- A resolve to make environmental technology universally available
- A commitment to science in the service of the environment
- The adoption of programs to promote environmental awareness generally

- A general commitment to "capacity-building": the development of each country's human, scientific, technological, organizational, institutional and resource capabilities
- The strengthening of the ability of present institutions to care for the environment
- The institution of standard legal measures to promote environmentally sound policies
- A commitment to collect and analyze increased amounts of environmental data

The most comprehensive and inclusive international statement of issues of the environment and development, Agenda 21 has been praised as well as criticized for its scope. Many see its holistic, comprehensive view as the only viable approach to environmental problems, while others see it as too broad to produce practical solutions.

REFERENCE:
Robinson, Nicholas A., ed. *Agenda 21: Earth's Action Plan Annotated.* New York: Oceana Publications, 1993.

Rio Declaration on Environment and Development

SIGNED: June 16, 1992, at Stockholm

SIGNATORIES: Afghanistan, Algeria, Angola, Antigua and Barbuda, Argentina, Armenia, Australia, Austria, Azerbaijan, Bahamas, Bahrain, Bangladesh, Barbados, Belarus, Belgium, Belize, Benin, Bhutan, Bolivia, Botswana, Brazil, Bulgaria, Burkina Faso, Burundi, Cameroon, Canada, Cape Verde, Central African Republic, Chad, Chile, China, Colombia, Comoros, Congo, Cook Islands, Costa Rica. Côte d'Ivoire, Croatia, Cuba, Cyprus, Czech Republic, Democratic People's Republic of Korea, Denmark, Djibouti, Dominican Republic, Ecuador, Egypt, El Salvador, Estonia, Ethiopia, European Economic Community, Fiji, Finland, France, Gabon, Gambia, Germany, Ghana, Greece, Grenada, Guatemala, Guinea, Guinea-Bissau, Guyana, Haiti, Honduras, Hungary, Iceland, India, Indonesia, Iran, Ireland, Israel, Italy, Jamaica, Japan, Jordan, Kazakhstan, Kenya, Kuwait, Latvia, Lebanon, Lesotho, Liberia, Libyan Arab Jamahirya, Liechtenstein, Lithuania, Luxembourg, Madagascar, Malawi, Malaysia, Maldives, Mali, Malta, Marshall Islands, Mauritania, Mauritius, Mexico, Micronesia, Moldova, Monaco, Mongolia, Morocco, Mozambique, Myanmar, Namibia, Nauru, Nepal, Netherlands, New Zealand, Nicaragua, Niger, Nigeria, Norway, Oman, Pakistan, Panama, Papua New Guinea, Paraguay, Peru, Philippines, Poland, Portugal, Qatar, Republic of Korea, Romania, Russian Federation, Rwanda, Saint Kitts and Nevis, Samoa, San Marino, Sao Tome and Principe, Senegal, Seychelles, Singapore, Slovakia, Slovenia, Solomon Islands, South Africa, Spain, Sri Lanka, Sudan, Suriname, Swaziland, Sweden, Switzerland, Syrian Arab Republic, Thailand, Togo, Trinidad and

Tobago, Tunisia, Turkey, Tuvalu, Uganda, Ukraine, United Arab Emirates, United Kingdom, United Republic of Tanzania, United States, Uruguay, Vanuatu, Venezuela, Vietnam, Yemen, Yugoslavia, Zaire, Zambia, Zimbabwe

IN FORCE: From signing

OVERVIEW: A statement of 27 non-binding principles intended to guide world environmental policy, based on a major international conference, the Earth Summit, held at Rio de Janeiro from June 3 to June 14, 1992.

DISCUSSION:

The United Nations Conference on Environment and Development, popularly called the Earth Summit, was held at Rio de Janeiro, Brazil, from June 3 to June 14, 1992. It was the largest gathering of world leaders in history, with 117 heads of state and representatives of 178 nations in attendance. The object of the summit was to produce documents to promote the pursuit of economic development in ways that would protect and preserve the environment and nonrenewable resources. The agreements produced include the following:

- **Rio Declaration on Environment and Development**
- **Convention on Biological Diversity**
- **Framework Convention on Climate Change**
- **Agenda 21**
- **Statement of Principles on Forests**

The controlling principle of the Rio Declaration holds that the only way to achieve long-term economic progress is in conjunction with environmental protection. This linkage is possible only through a global partnership involving governments, their people, and key sectors of societies. Beyond this, the Rio Declaration laid down the following:

- All people have the right to a healthy and productive life in harmony with nature.
- Present development must not imperil the developmental and environmental needs of the present or the future.
- While nations have the right to exploit their own resources, doing so must not create environmental damage beyond their borders.
- Nations must agree on international laws to provide compensation for damage that activities under their control cause to areas beyond their borders.
- Nations must take a precautionary approach to protect the environment. Facing threat of environmental damage, cost-effective measures must be taken to prevent environmental degradation, even if a degree of scientific uncertainty concerning the situation exists.
- Sustainable development is inseparable from environmental protection.
- Eradication of poverty and the reduction of disparities in living standards in different parts of the world are essential to achieving sustainable development.

- Nations must cooperate to conserve, protect, and restore the earth's ecosystem. In particular, developed countries acknowledge the responsibility they bear in the international pursuit of sustainable development in view of the disproportionate pressures their societies place on the global environment and of the technologies and financial resources they command.
- Nations must reduce and eliminate unsustainable patterns of production and consumption and instead promote appropriate demographic policies.
- Environmental issues are most successfully addressed with public participation; therefore, states should facilitate public awareness and participation in environmental matters.
- Nations must enact effective environmental laws, including laws regarding liability for the victims of pollution and other environmental damage.
- Nations should cooperate to promote an open international economic system leading to economic growth and sustainable development in all countries.
- As a general principle, the polluter should bear the cost of pollution.
- Nations must warn one another of natural disasters or activities that may have harmful transboundary environmental impacts.
- Sustainable development requires scientific understanding of the problems involved; nations should cooperate to share appropriate knowledge and technologies.
- The full participation of women is essential to achieve sustainable development. The creativity, ideals, and courage of youth, and the knowledge of indigenous people are also needed. Nations should recognize and support the identity, culture, and interests of indigenous people.
- Warfare is inherently destructive of sustainable development, and nations must respect international laws protecting environment in times of armed conflict.
- Peace, development, and environmental protection are interdependent and indivisible.

The declaration is general in nature, and its 27 broad principles are non-binding.

REFERENCE:

Robinson, Nicholas A., ed. *Agenda 21: Earth's Action Plan Annotated.* New York: Oceana Publications, 1993.

Convention on the Transboundary Effects of Industrial Accidents

SIGNED: March 17, 1992, at Helsinki, Finland

SIGNATORIES: Albania, Austria, Belgium, Bulgaria, Canada, Denmark, Estonia, European Economic Community, Finland, France, Germany, Greece, Hungary, Italy, Latvia, Lithuania,

Luxembourg, Netherlands, Poland, Portugal, Russian Federation, Spain, Sweden, Switzerland, United Kingdom, United States

IN FORCE: Not yet in force

OVERVIEW: A convention addressing issues of individual and collective national responsibility and capacity in the prevention and control of industrial accidents, as well as the transboundary effects of such accidents.

DISCUSSION:

This comprehensive international convention begins by defining the term *industrial accident*, as well as such ancillary key terms as *hazardous activity* and *transboundary effects*, then goes on to a statement of matters excluded from coverage by the convention, including nuclear accidents, radiological emergencies, accidents at military installations, dam failures, accidental release of genetically modified organisms, and spills of oil and other harmful substances at sea.

Signatories agree to the following:

- To take measures to protect human beings and the environment from the effects of industrial accidents
- To take appropriate legal and policy measures to prevent industrial accidents
- To consult with, inform, cooperate with, and share in assistance for the purpose of enhancing preparedness for coping with industrial accidents that have transboundary effects
- To cooperate in managing the tasks set out in the convention
- To cooperate in the settlement of disputes

An important part of the convention is its set of annexes:

- Annex I lists hazardous substances for the purposes of defining hazardous activities.
- Annex II lays down the procedures for inquiry commissions.
- Annex III lays down consultation procedures.
- Annex IV lays down preventive measures for purposes of enhancing preparedness to cope with accidents that have transboundary effects.
- Annex V provides guidelines and procedures for analysis and evaluation.
- Annex VI relates to decision making on citing violations of convention regulations.
- Annex VII lays down emergency preparedness measures pursuant.
- Annex VIII provides procedures for disseminating Information to the public.
- Annex IX lays down guidelines for industrial accident notification systems
- Annex X provides guidance on mutual assistance.
- Annex XI lays down procedures for the exchange of information among signatories
- Annex XII enumerates tasks for mutual assistance.
- Annex XIII is devoted to the rules of arbitration.

REFERENCES:
None

North American Agreement on Environmental Cooperation

SIGNED: September 8, 9, 12, 14, 1993, at Mexico City, Washington, and Ottawa

SIGNATORIES: Canada, Mexico, United States

IN FORCE: January 1, 1994

OVERVIEW: An agreement "to facilitate effective cooperation on the conservation, protection and enhancement of the environment."

DISCUSSION:

Article 1 lays down the objectives of this agreement among the three nations of the North American continent:

(a) foster the protection and improvement of the environment in the territories of the Parties for the well-being of present and future generations;

(b) promote sustainable development based on cooperation and mutually supportive environmental and economic policies;

(c) increase cooperation between the Parties to better conserve, protect, and enhance the environment, including wild flora and fauna;

(d) support the environmental goals and objectives of the NAFTA;

(e) avoid creating trade distortions or new trade barriers;

(f) strengthen cooperation on the development and improvement of environmental laws, regulations, procedures, policies and practices;

(g) enhance compliance with, and enforcement of, environmental laws and regulations;

(h) promote transparency and public participation in the development of environmental laws, regulations and policies;

(i) promote economically efficient and effective environmental measures; and

(j) promote pollution prevention policies and practices.

To the end of achieving these objectives, the three nations agreed, in Article 2, as follows:

1. Each Party shall, with respect to its territory:

(a) periodically prepare and make publicly available reports on the state of the environment;

(b) develop and review environmental emergency preparedness measures;

(c) promote education in environmental matters, including environmental law;

(d) further scientific research and technology development in respect of environmental matters;

(e) assess, as appropriate, environmental impacts; and

(f) promote the use of economic instruments for the efficient achievement of environmental goals.

2. Each Party shall consider implementing in its law any recommendation developed by the Council [created by the agreement].

3. Each Party shall consider prohibiting the export to the territories of the other Parties of a pesticide or toxic substance whose use is prohibited within the Party's territory....

A large portion of the agreement is devoted to the creation of a Commission for Environmental Cooperation, charged with the following general functions:

- Serving as a forum for the discussion of environmental matters within the scope of the agreement
- Overseeing the implementation and develop recommendations on the further elaboration of the agreement
- Addressing questions and differences that may arise between the parties regarding the interpretation or application of the agreement
- Promoting and facilitating cooperation between the parties with respect to environmental matters

The agreement specifically charges the commission with "establishing a process for developing recommendations on greater compatibility of environmental technical regulations, standards and conformity assessment procedures in a manner consistent with the NAFTA." *See* **North American Free Trade Agreement (NAFTA).**

REFERENCES:
None

United Nations Convention to Combat Desertification

OFFICIAL TITLE: United Nations Convention to Combat Desertification in those Countries Experiencing Serious Drought and/or Desertification, Particularly in Africa
SIGNED: October 12, 1994, at Paris
SIGNATORIES: Afghanistan, Algeria, Angola, Antigua and Barbuda, Argentina, Armenia, Australia, Austria, Azerbaijan, Bahrain, Bangladesh, Barbados, Belgium, Belize, Benin, Bolivia, Botswana, Brazil, Burkina Faso, Burundi, Cambodia, Cameroon, Canada, Cape Verde, Central African Republic, Chad, Chile, China, Colombia, Comoros, Congo, Cook Islands, Costa Rica, Côte d'Ivoire, Croatia, Cuba, Democratic Republic of the Congo, Denmark, Djibouti, Dominica, Dominican Republic, Ecuador, Egypt, El Salvador, Equatorial Guinea, Eritrea, Ethiopia, European Community, Fiji, Finland, France, Gabon, Gambia, Georgia, Germany, Ghana, Greece, Grenada, Guatemala, Guinea, Guinea-Bissau, Guyana, Haiti, Honduras, Iceland, India, Indonesia, Iran (Islamic Republic of), Ireland,

Israel, Italy, Jamaica, Japan, Jordan, Kazakhstan, Kenya, Kiribati, Korea (Republic), Kuwait, Kyrgyzstan, Lao (PDR), Lebanon, Lesotho, Liberia, Libyan Arab Jamahirya, Luxembourg, Madagascar, Malawi, Malaysia, Mali, Malta, Marshall Islands, Mauritania, Mauritius, Mexico, Micronesia (Federated States of), Mongolia, Morocco, Mozambique, Myanmar, Namibia, Nauru, Nepal, Netherlands, Nicaragua, Niue, Niger, Nigeria, Norway, Oman, Pakistan, Panama, Paraguay, Peru, Philippines, Portugal, Romania, Rwanda, Saint Lucia, Saint Vincent and Grenadines, Samoa, Sao Tome and Principe, Saudi Arabia, Senegal, Seychelles, Sierra Leone, South Africa, Spain, Sri Lanka, St. Kitts and Nevis, Sudan, Swaziland, Sweden, Switzerland, Syrian Arab Republic, Tadjikistan, Togo, Tonga, Tunisia, Turkey, Turkmenistan, Tuvalu, Uganda, United Arab Emirates, United Kingdom, United Republic of Tanzania, United States, Uzbekistan, Vanuatu, Venezuela, Vietnam, Yemen, Zaire, Zambia, Zimbabwe
IN FORCE: From December 26, 1996
OVERVIEW: A convention to promote effective action against desertification, especially in Africa, through local programs and supportive international partnerships.

DISCUSSION:
Desertification is the degradation of land in arid, semi-arid, and dry sub-humid areas. It is caused chiefly by human activities, as well as climatic variations. The term *desertification* is rather misleading in that it does not refer to the expansion of existing deserts, but to the degradation of dryland ecosystems, which are especially vulnerable to over-exploitation and inappropriate land use. These, in turn, are often the result of poverty, political instability, deforestation, overgrazing, and bad irrigation practices.

More than 250 million people are directly affected by desertification, but an additional billion in more than a hundred countries are at risk.

The convention recognizes that past effort to combat desertification have often failed, and that success depends on combining and coordinating innovative local programs with supportive international partnerships.

The signatory nations directly affected by desertification undertake to develop national, sub-regional, and regional action programs, which are detailed in the convention's four "Regional Implementation Annexes" for Africa (where desertification is most severe), Asia, Latin America and the Caribbean, and the Northern Mediterranean.

While the convention provides outline guidance for local programs, it specifies that these must be fully integrated with other national policies for sustainable development as well as consultations among affected countries, donors, and intergovernmental and non-governmental organizations.

The role of developed countries, such as the United States, which, for the most part, are not directly impacted by desertification, is defined as providing encouragement for the mobilization of substantial funding and promoting access to appropriate technologies and expertise.

Ultimately, the aim of the convention is to reverse the progress of desertification through programs of sustainable development, which will be subject to regular review and adjustment.

REFERENCES:

Stiles, Daniel, ed. *Social Aspects of Sustainable Dryland Management.* New York: Wiley, 1995.

Thomas, David S. G. *Desertification: Exploding the Myth.* New York: Wiley, 1994.

Draft Declaration of Principles on Human Rights and the Environment

SIGNED: Draft completed May 16, 1994, at Geneva

SIGNATORIES: Not yet open for signature

IN FORCE: Not yet in force

OVERVIEW: The first-ever declaration of principles on human rights and the environment.

DISCUSSION:

The Draft Declaration was drawn up by an international group of experts on human rights and environmental protection in a conference at the United Nations in Geneva convened by the Sierra Club and with the cooperation of other international organizations concerned with the environment and with human rights. The thesis of the declaration is that accepted environmental and human rights principles embody the right of everyone to a secure, healthy, and ecologically sound environment. "Human rights," the declaration holds, "an ecologically sound environment, sustainable development and peace are interdependent and indivisible." The environmental dimension of established human rights include such basics the rights to life, health, and culture, as well as such procedural rights as the right to participation, which is necessary for realization of the substantive rights. The Draft Declaration holds that certain duties that correspond to the rights enumerated, duties that apply not only to individuals, but to governments, international organizations, and transnational corporations.

The intersection of human and environmental rights is most fully set down in Part II of the Declaration, as follows:

5. All persons have the right to freedom from pollution, environmental degradation and activities that adversely affect the environment, threaten life, health, livelihood, well-being or sustainable development within, across or outside national boundaries.

6. All persons have the right to protection and preservation of the air, soil, water, sea-ice, flora and fauna, and the essential processes and areas necessary to maintain biological diversity and ecosystems.

7. All persons have the right to the highest attainable standard of health free from environmental hazards.

8. All persons have the right to safe and healthy food and water adequate to their well-being.

9. All persons have the right to a safe and healthy working environment.

10. All persons have the right to adequate housing, land tenure and living conditions in a secure, healthy and ecologically sound environment.

11. All persons have the right not to be evicted from their homes or land for the purpose of, or as a consequence of, decisions or actions affecting the environment, except in emergencies or due to a compelling purpose benefitting society as a whole and not attainable by other means. All persons have the right to participate effectively in decisions and to negotiate concerning their eviction and the right, if evicted, to timely and adequate restitution, compensation and/or appropriate and sufficient accommodation or land.

12. All persons have the right to timely assistance in the event of natural or technological or other human-caused catastrophes.

13. Everyone has the right to benefit equitably from the conservation and sustainable use of nature and natural resources for cultural, ecological, educational, health, livelihood, recreational, spiritual or other purposes. This Includes ecologically sound access to nature. Everyone has the right to preservation of unique sites, consistent with the fundamental rights of persons or groups living in the area.

14. Indigenous peoples have the right to control their lands, territories and natural resources and to maintain their traditional way of life. This includes the right to security in the enjoyment of their means of subsistence.

Indigenous peoples have the right to protection against any action or course of conduct that may result in the destruction or degradation of their territories, including land, air, water, sea-ice, wildlife or other resources.

Part III addresses procedural rights, including, chiefly, the right to obtain information relating to environmental impacts and the right to participate in decisions that impact the environment. Part III of the Draft Declaration is closely echoed by **Convention on Access to Information and Justice in Environmental Matters.**

The Draft Declaration has yet to be opened for signature.

REFERENCE:

Sachs, Aaron. *Eco-Justice: Linking Human Rights and the Environment.* Washington, D.C.: Worldwatch Institute, 1995.

International Tropical Timber Agreement

SIGNED: January 26, 1994, at Geneva

SIGNATORIES: Australia, Belgium, Bolivia, Burma, Cambodia, Cameroon, Canada, Central African Republic, China, Colombia, Congo, Côte d'Ivoire, Denmark, Ecuador, Egypt, European Community, Fiji, Finland, France, Gabon, Germany, Ghana, Honduras, India, Indonesia, Japan, Korea, Liberia, Luxembourg,

Malaysia, Netherlands, New Zealand, Norway, Panama, Papua New Guinea, Peru, Philippines, Spain, Sweden, Switzerland, Thailand, Togo, United Kingdom, United States, Zaire

IN FORCE: Provisionally, from January 1, 1997

OVERVIEW: Successor agreement to the **International Tropical Timber Agreement** of 1983.

DISCUSSION:

This successor to the 1983 International Tropical Timber Agreement has as its principal objective that all timber-producing countries meet high standards of sustainable forest management, especially in the tropical regions, where rainforests are particularly threatened. Accordingly, the agreement perpetuates the Tropical Timber Organization and Tropical Timber Council, both created by the 1983 agreement, and expands and defines the scope and function of these bodies to help achieve the following objectives:

(a) To provide an effective framework for consultation, international cooperation and policy development among all members with regard to all relevant aspects of the world timber practices; (b) To provide a forum for consultation to promote non-discriminatory timber trade practices; (c) To contribute to the process of sustainable development; (d) To enhance the capacity of members to implement a strategy for achieving exports of tropical timber and timber products from sustainably managed sources by the year 2000; (e) To promote the expansion and diversification of international trade in tropical timber from sustainable sources by improving the structural conditions in international markets, by taking into account, on the one hand, a long-term increase in consumption and continuity of supplies, an, on the other, prices which reflect the costs of sustainable forest management and which are remunerative and equitable for members, and the improvement of market access; (f) To promote and support research and development with a view to improving forest management and efficiency of wood utilization as well as increasing the capacity to conserve and enhance other forest values in timber producing tropical forests; (g) To develop and contribute towards mechanisms for the provision of new and additional financial resources and expertise needed to enhance the capacity of producing members to attain the objectives of this Agreement; (h) To improve market intelligence with a view to ensuring greater transparency in the international timber market, including the gathering, compilation, and dissemination of trade related data, including data related to species being traded; (i) To promote increased and further processing of tropical timber from sustainable sources in producing member countries with a view to promoting their industrialization and thereby increasing their employment opportunities and export earnings; (j) To encourage members to support and develop industrial tropical timber reforestation and forest management activities as well as rehabilitation of degraded forest land, with due regard for the interests of local communities dependent on forest resources; (k) To improve marketing and distribution of tropical timber exports from sustainably managed sources; (l) To encourage members to develop national policies aimed at sustainable utilization and conservation of timber producing forests and their genetic resources and at maintaining the ecological balance in the regions concerned, in the context of tropical timber trade; (m) To promote the access to, and transfer of, tech-

nologies and technical cooperation to implement the objectives of this Agreement, including technical cooperation to implement the objectives of this Agreement, including on confessional and preferential terms and conditions, as mutually agree; and (n) To encourage information-sharing on the international timber market.

REFERENCES:

Gale, Fred P. *The Tropical Timber Regime.* New York: St. Martin's Press, 1998.

Panayotou, Theodore. *Not by Timber Alone: Economics and Ecology for Sustaining Tropical Forests.* Washington, D.C.: Island Press, 1992.

Kyoto Protocol to the United Nations Framework Convention on Climate Change

SIGNED: December 10, 1997, at Kyoto, Japan

SIGNATORIES: Antigua and Barbuda, Argentina, Australia, Austria, Bahamas, Belgium, Bolivia, Brazil, Bulgaria, Canada, Chile, China, Cook Islands, Costa Rica, Croatia, Cuba, Czech Republic, Cyprus, Denmark, Ecuador, Egypt, El Salvador, Estonia, European Community, Fiji, Finland, France, Georgia, Germany, Greece, Guatemala, Honduras, Indonesia, Ireland, Israel, Italy, Jamaica, Japan, Kazakhstan, Korea (Republic), Latvia, Liechtenstein, Lithusania, Luxembourg, Malaysia, Maldives, Mali, Malta, Marshall Islands, Mexico, Micronesia (Federal States), Monaco, Netherlands, New Zealand, Nicaragua, Niger, Niue, Norway, Panama, Papua New Guinea, Paraguay, Peru, Philippines, Poland, Portugal, Romania, Russian Federation, Saint Lucia, Saint Vincent and the Grenadines, Samoa, Seychelles, Slovakia, Slovenia, Solomon Islands, Spain, Sweden, Switzerland, Thailand, Trinidad and Tobago, Turkmenistan, Tuvalu, Ukraine, United Kingdom, United States, Uruguay, Vietnam, Uzbekistan, Zambia

IN FORCE: Not yet in force

OVERVIEW: A protocol to **United Nations Framework Convention on Climate Change** of 1993 in which certain signatory parties agree to quantified greenhouse-gas emission limitation and reduction commitments to combat global warming.

DISCUSSION:

The signatories to the protocol, all signatories of the **United Nations Framework Convention on Climate Change** of 1993, agree to "implement and/or further elaborate policies and measures in accordance with its national circumstances." Such policies are to include:

(i) Enhancement of energy efficiency in relevant sectors of the national economy;

(ii) Protection and enhancement of sinks and reservoirs of greenhouse gases not controlled by the **Montreal Protocol**, taking into account its commitments under relevant international environmental agreements; promotion of sustainable forest management practices, afforestation and reforestation;

(iii) Promotion of sustainable forms of agriculture in light of climate change considerations;

(iv) Research on, and promotion, development and increased use of, new and renewable forms of energy, of carbon dioxide sequestration technologies and of advanced and innovative environmentally sound technologies;

(v) Progressive reduction or phasing out of market imperfections, fiscal incentives, tax and duty exemptions and subsidies in all greenhouse gas emitting sectors that run counter to the objective of the Convention and application of market instruments;

(vi) Encouragement of appropriate reforms in relevant sectors aimed at promoting policies and measures which limit or reduce emissions of greenhouse gases not controlled by the Montreal Protocol;

(vii) Measures to limit and/or reduce emissions of greenhouse gases not controlled by the Montreal Protocol in the transport sector;

(viii) Limitation and/or reduction of methane emissions through recovery and use in waste management, as well as in the production, transport and distribution of energy;

The signatories to the protocol also agree to "cooperate with other such Parties to enhance the individual and combined effectiveness of their policies and measures."

A key feature of the protocol are its two annexes:
• Annex A lists the greenhouse gases and their chief sources.
• Annex B lists the greenhouse-gas reduction commitment for each signatory; the United States (for example) committed to reducing its greenhouse gas emissions during "the commitment period 2008 to 2012" to 93 percent of its 1990 level.

Implementing the reduction commitments is a complex process, which, perhaps, accounts for the delay in ratifying the protocol so that it may come into force.

REFERENCES:
Brown, Paige. *Climate, Biodiversity and Forests: Issues and Opportunities Emerging from the Kyoto Protocol.* Washington, D.C.: World Resources Institute, 1998.
Grubb, Michael, and Duncan Brack, eds. *Kyoto Protocol: A Guide and Assessment.* London: Earthscan Publications, 1998.

Agreed Minute (with the EU) on Humane Trapping of Animals

SIGNED: December 18, 1997, at Brussels
SIGNATORIES: European Union vs. United States
IN FORCE: From signing
OVERVIEW: An agreement on humane standards for trapping fur-bearing animals.

DISCUSSION:
The Agreed Minute includes technical specifications for trap performance, suggests guidelines for further research into trap design, and envisions phasing out certain trapping devices currently in use. An annex subjoined to the document lays down detailed "standards for the humane trapping of specified terrestrial and semi-aquatic mammals."

REFERENCES:
None

Convention on Access to Information and Justice in Environmental Matters

OFFICIAL TITLE: Convention on Access to Information, Public Participation in Decision-Making and Access to Justice in Environmental Matters
SIGNED: June 23-25, 1998, at Århus, Denmark
SIGNATORIES: Albania, Armenia, Austria, Belarus, Belgium, Bulgaria, Croatia, Cyprus, Czech Republic, Denmark, Estonia, European Community, Finland, Former Yugoslav Republic of Macedonia France, Georgia, Germany, Hungary, Greece, Iceland, Ireland, Italy, Kazakhstan, Latvia, Liechtenstein, Lithuania, Luxembourg, Malta, Monaco, Netherlands, Norway, Poland, Portugal, Republic of Moldova, Romania, Slovenia, Spain, Sweden, Switzerland, Turkmenistan, Ukraine, United Kingdom
IN FORCE: Not yet in force
OVERVIEW: A multilateral convention in which the signatories undertake to "guarantee the rights of access to information, public participation in decision-making, and access to justice in environmental matters."

DISCUSSION:
This proposed convention would ensure public access, on an individual basis, to environmental information and would further guarantee public participation in decision-making related to environmental matters. Finally, signatories would undertake to ensure the provision of "justice in environmental matters." Like a number of recent conventions created under the aegis of the United Nations, this draft convention addresses rights of individuals rather than of states in relation to other states. Such conventions are inherently complex and problematic, since they bypass or override possible issues of state sovereignty. In the case of such a convention relating to environmental matters, problems of sovereignty as well as jurisdiction, even within nations, become particularly complicated.

The first general principal provision is the undertaking by each signatory party to respond to requests for environmental information by making the information fully available. Much of the lengthy convention is devoted to provisions aimed at harmonizing this principal undertaking with national law and with the obligation to protect intellectual property rights as well as the confidentiality of commercial and industrial information.

A second general principal provision is the undertaking by signatories actively to promote, encourage, and enable public participation "concerning plans, programs, and policies relating to the environment," including participation "during the preparation of executive regulations and/or generally applicable legally binding normative instruments."

Finally, signatories agree to provide "any person who considers that his or her request for information . . . has been ignored, wrongfully refused . . . inadequately answered, or otherwise not dealt with . . . access to a review procedure before a court of law or another independent and impartial body established by law."

The United States is among the many nations that have yet to sign the convention.

REFERENCES:
Bryant, Bunyan, ed. *Environmental Justice: Issues, Politics, and Solutions.* Washington, D.C.: Island Press, 1995.
Foreman, Christopher H., Jr. *The Promise and Peril of Environmental Justice.* Washington, D.C.: Brookings Institution, 1998.

Agreement on the International Dolphin Conservation Program

SIGNED: May 15 and 21, 1998, at Washington, D.C.
SIGNATORIES: Costa Rica, Ecuador, Mexico, Nicaraguan, Panama, United States, Venezuela
IN FORCE: Not yet in force
OVERVIEW: An agreement to protect dolphins and other marine species in the eastern Pacific Ocean, which may be killed in the process of commercial fishing for other species.

DISCUSSION:
Large-scale commercial fishing methods, especially in the tuna fisheries, frequently result in incidental mortality among dolphins and some other species. United States law places trade restrictions and even embargoes on the tuna of nations that do not regulate fishing methods harmful to dolphins. The 1998 agreement is intended not only to protect the dolphins, but to enable the lifting of United States trade sanctions against the signatory nations.

The principal objectives of the agreement are as follows:
- "To progressively reduce incidental dolphin mortalities in the tuna purse-seine fishery in the Agreement Area to levels approaching zero through the setting of annual limits"
- "With the goal of eliminating dolphin mortality in this fishery, to seek ecologically sound means of capturing large yellowfin tunas not in association with dolphins"
- "To ensure the long-term sustainability of the tuna stocks in the Agreement Area, as well as that of the living marine resources related to this fishery, taking into consideration the interrelationship among species in the ecosystem with special emphasis on . . . avoiding, reducing and minimizing bycatch and discards of juvenile tunas and non-target species"

REFERENCE:
Grose, K. *Dolphins, Porpoises and Whales: 1994-1998.* Washington, D.C.: World Conservation Union, 1993.

Protocol to the 1979 Convention on Long-Range Transboundary Air Pollution by Heavy Metals

SIGNED: June 24, 1998, at Aarhus, Denmark
SIGNATORIES: Armenia, Austria, Belgium, Bulgaria, Canada, Croatia, Cyprus, Czech Republic, Denmark, European Community, Finland, France, Germany, Greece, Hungary, Iceland, Ireland, Italy, Latvia, Liechtenstein, Lithuania, Luxembourg, Netherlands, Norway, Poland, Portugal, Republic of Moldova, Romania, Slovakia, Slovenia, Spain, Sweden, Switzerland, Ukraine, United Kingdom, United States
In force: Not yet in force
Overview: "The objective of the present Protocol is to control emissions of heavy metals caused by anthropogenic activities that are subject to long-range transboundary atmospheric transport and are likely to have significant adverse effects on human health or the environment . . ."

DISCUSSION:
Under the aegis of the 1979 **Convention on Long-Range Transboundary Air Pollution**, this protocol addresses specifically the problem of transboundary pollution by heavy metals, chiefly cadmium, lead, and mercury. The basic provision of the protocol is an undertaking by each signatory to "reduce its total annual emissions into the atmosphere of . . . heavy metals from the level of the emission in the reference year set in accordance with [an] annex by taking effective measures, appropriate to its particular circumstances." The reference year specified is "1990 or an alternative year from 1985 to 1995 inclusive, specified by a Party upon ratification, acceptance, approval or accession." A set of annexes to the protocol lays down the following:
- The substances covered
- Sources of pollutants
- Best techniques for controlling emissions of heavy metals
- Timescales for achieving reductions
- Limit values for controlling emissions from major stationary sources
- Product control and management measures (such as mandating the use of unleaded gasoline)

In addition to reducing emissions within its borders, each signatory agrees to exchange information and cooperate with other signatories, and to engage in programs of research, both national and international. The convention sets up an authority under the United Nations to accept and evaluate reports of compliance from each signatory, but no international enforcement or disciplinary actions are specified.

REFERENCE:

Jarvis, P. J. Heavy Metal *Pollution: an Annotated Bibliography, 1976-1980*. Norwich, UK: Geo-Books, 1983.

Rotterdam Convention on Prior Informed Consent

OFFICIAL TITLE: Rotterdam Convention on the Prior Informed Consent Procedure for Certain Hazardous Chemicals and Pesticides in International Trade

SIGNED: September 10, 1998, at Rotterdam, Netherlands

SIGNATORIES: Angola, Argentina, Armenia, Australia, Austria, Barbados, Belgium, Benin, Brazil, Burkina Faso, Cameroon, Chad, Chile, Colombia, Congo, Congo (Democratic Republic of the), Côte d'Ivoire, Cuba, Cyprus, Czech Republic, Denmark, Ecuador, El Salvador, European Community, Finland, France, Gambia, Germany, Ghana, Greece, Indonesia, Iran (Islamic Republic), Israel, Italy, Jamaica, Kenya, Kuwait, Kyrgyzstan, Luxembourg, Madagascar, Mali, Mongolia, Namibia, Netherlands, New Zealand, Norway, Panama, Paraguay, Peru, Philippines, Portugal, Senegal, Seychelles, Slovenia, Spain, Sudan, Sweden, Switzerland, Syrian Arab Republic, Tajikistan, Tunisia, Turkey, United Kingdom, United Republic of Tanzania, United States, Uruguay, Yemen

IN FORCE: Not yet in force

OVERVIEW: "The objective of this Convention is to promote shared responsibility and cooperative efforts among Parties in the international trade of certain hazardous chemicals in order to protect human health and the environment from potential harm and to contribute to their environmentally sound use, by facilitating information exchange about their characteristics, by providing for a national decision-making process on their import and export and by disseminating these decisions to Parties."

DISCUSSION:

The convention was an outgrowth of an international commitment made at the 1992 Rio Earth Summit to negotiate a convention to curb the trade in certain hazardous chemicals and pesticides. It specifically addresses the problem that chemicals and pesticides banned or severely restricted in industrialized nations are still exported to other countries, typically in the developing world. The convention requires that pesticides and chemicals that have been banned or severely restricted in at least two countries shall not be exported unless explicitly agreed by the importing country through a prescribed Prior Informed Consent Procedure (PIC). As the convention currently stands, 22 pesticides and five industrial chemicals are subject to PIC. These include the pesticides 2,4,5-T, Aldrin, Captafol, Chlordane, Chlordimeform, Chlorbenzilate, DDT, Dieldrin, Dinoseb, 1,2-dibromoethane (EDB), Fluoroacetamide, HCH, Heptachlor, Hexachlorobenzene, Lindane, Mercury compounds, certain formulations of Monocrotophos, Methamidophos, Phosphamidon, Methyl-parathion, Parathion, and the industrial chemicals Crocidolite, Polybrominated Biphenyls (PBB), Polychlorinated Biphenyls (PCB), Polychlorinated Terphenyls (PCT), Tris (2,3 dibromopropyl) phosphate. The convention includes procedures for adding more hazardous chemicals to the PIC list. Signatories undertake to ensure that exporters transmit to importers appropriate safety data sheets, following an internationally recognized format, setting out the most up-to-date information available on exported PIC substances.

The convention also binds exporting countries to inform importing countries about exports of chemicals banned or severely restricted in the exporting country only. Signatories undertake to enforce the agreement at the national level and to create enforcement mechanisms to control commercial exports and exporters. Disputes between states arising from the implementation of the convention may be settled by arbitration or by the International Court of Justice. Finally, the convention also provides for technical assistance to developing countries to aid in the creation of the infrastructure and capacity necessary to manage chemicals.

REFERENCES:

Bryant, Bunyan, ed. *Environmental Justice: Issues, Politics, and Solutions*. Washington, D.C.: Island Press, 1995.

Foreman, Christopher H., Jr. *The Promise and Peril of Environmental Justice*. Washington, D.C.: Brookings Institution, 1998.

Meteorological, Scientific, and Technological Cooperation

Overview of Treaties in This Category

During the twentieth century, the United States concluded a significant number of bilateral treaties of scientific and technological cooperation and participated in a number of multilateral cooperative agreements. Many of the bilateral agreements were concluded for political as much as scientific or technological reasons. For example, the series of agreements with the Soviet Union (beginning in 1958 with **Agreement [with U.S.S.R.] on Exchanges in the Cultural, Technical, and Educational Fields** and continuing throughout the Cold War period) was aimed at maintaining an ongoing dialogue with the Soviet Union and generally improving relations. Another important category of cooperative agreements relates to the peaceful exploitation of atomic energy. Beginning during the Truman administration, when the Atomic Energy Commission was created to assume civilian control of nuclear-energy matters, United States policy emphasized the development of peaceful uses of atomic energy, especially for the generation of electric power. Beginning in the 1960s, the United States concluded cooperative agreements on nuclear energy with a host of nations, including, for example, the Soviet Union (**Agreement [with the U.S.S.R.] on Cooperation in Desalination, Including the Use of Atomic Energy**, 1964) and Mexico (**Agreement [with IAEA and Mexico] for a Preliminary Study of a Nuclear Electric Power and Desalting Plant**, 1965).

Multilateral agreements to which the United States is signatory include **Convention of the World Meteorological Organization** (1947), which seeks to establish cooperation in global meteorology, and two agreements to foster and facilitate the international circulation and sharing of scientific information, **Agreement for Facilitating the International Circulation of Educational, Scientific, and Cultural Materials** (1949) and **Agreement on the Importation of Educational, Scientific, and Cultural Materials** (1950), by which signatories undertake to exempt various materials from import duties and other barriers.

Agreement (with United Kingdom) on the Exchange of Information on Penicillin

OFFICIAL TITLE: Exchange of Notes Constituting an Agreement on the Exchange of Information on Penicillin

SIGNED: January 25, 1946, at Washington, D.C.
SIGNATORIES: United Kingdom vs. United States
IN FORCE: Retroactively from December 1, 1943
OVERVIEW: An agreement relating to wartime cooperation in the production of penicillin.

DISCUSSION:
This agreement was concluded immediately following World War II, but was made retroactive to December 1, 1943 in order to cover the exchange of information relating to the purification, structure, and synthesis of penicillin that took place between these allies beginning at this time. Since the collaborative work on producing "an adequate supply of high quality synthetic penicillin, or therapeutic equivalent, at reasonable prices" produced results of scientific and commercial value, the retroactive agreement was deemed necessary to address questions of intellectual property and patent rights. The main part of the agreement provides guidelines for the determination of patent awards, based primarily on the nationality of the participants in the program:

(a) The Government of the United States will decide whether or not discoveries and inventions made by the American Participants shall be the subject of patent applications anywhere in the world.

(b) The Government of the United Kingdom will decide whether or not discoveries and inventions made by the British Participants shall be the subject of completed patent applications in Great Britain or of patent applications in any other country.

Beyond this, each government will "appraise and determine the value of the contributions" made by participants of both nations to determine whether those may be covered by patents in ether nation. Following the determination of patent rights, the two governments agree to grant licenses on reasonable terms.

REFERENCES:
None

Convention of the World Meteorological Organization

SIGNED: October 11, 1947, at Washington, D.C.
SIGNATORIES: Algeria, Andorra, Argentina, Ashanti, Australia, Australian Territories, Basutoland, Bechuanaland, Belgian Congo, Belgium, Bermuda, Brazil, British Solomon Islands,

Brunei, Burma, Byelorussian Soviet Socialist Republic, Canada, Chile, China, Colombia, Colony of Aden, Cuba, Czechoslovakia, Denmark, Dominican Republic, Ecuador, Egypt, Falkland Islands and Dependencies, Federation of Malaya, Fiji, Finland, France, Fench Equatorial Africa, French Guiana, French Somaliland, French West Africa, Gibraltar, Gilbert and Ellice Islands, Gold Coast Colony, Gold Coast Northern Territory, Greece. Guatemala, Hong Kong, Hungary, Iceland, India, Indonesia, Iraq, Ireland, Israel, Italy, Kenya Colony, Kenya Protectorate, Lebanon, Madagascar, Malta, Mauritius, Mexico, Morocco, Nauru, Netherlands, New Caledonia, New Zealand, Nigeria Colony, Nigeria Protectorate, Norfolk Island, North Borneo, Northern Rhodesia, Norway, Nyasaland, Pakistan, Papua New Guinea, Paraguay, Peru, Philippines, Poland, Portugal, Protectorate of Aden, Reunion, Romania, Saint Pierre and Miquelon, Seychelles, Siam, Singapore, Southern Rhodesia, Swaziland, Sweden, Switzerland, Syrian Arab Republic, Tanganyika, Territory of New Guinea, Territory of the Cameroons under British Administration, Territory of Togoland under French Administration, Thailand, Togo, Tunisia, Turkey, Uganda Protectorate, Ukrainian Soviet Socialist Republic, Union of South Africa, Union of Soviet Socialist Republics, United Kingdom, United States, Venezuela, Yugoslavia, Zanzibar Protectorate

In force: From March 23, 1950

Overview: An international agreement establishing the World Meteorological Organization, "with a view to coordinating, standardizing, and improving world meteorological activities."

DISCUSSION:

The agreement details the requirements for membership in the WMO and lays down its organization. The purposes of the World Meteorological Organization created by this convention include the following:

- To facilitate worldwide cooperation in the establishment of networks of stations for the making of meteorological and other geophysical observations
- To promote systems for the rapid international exchange of weather information
- To promote standardization of observations and statistics
- To further the application of meteorology to aviation, shipping, agriculture, and other human activities
- To encourage and coordinate international research and training

REFERENCE:

The WMO Achievement: Forty Years in the Service of International Meteorology and Hydrology. Geneva, Switzerland: WMO, 1990.

Agreement for Facilitating the International Circulation of Educational, Scientific, and Cultural Materials

OFFICIAL TITLE: Agreement for Facilitating the International Circulation of Visual and Auditory Materials of an Education, Scientific, and Cultural Character

SIGNED: July 15, 1949, at Lake Success, New York

SIGNATORIES: Afghanistan, Cambodia, Canada, Denmark, Domincan Republic, Ecuador, El Salvador, Greece, Haiti, Iran, Iraq, Lebanon, Netherlands, Norway, Pakistan, Philippines, Syria, United States, Uruguay, Yugoslavia

IN FORCE: From August 12, 1954

OVERVIEW: An agreement to promote educational, scientific, and cultural exchange by facilitating the circulation of educational, scientific, and cultural materials.

DISCUSSION:

The signatory nations agree that the importation of such materials as films, filmstrips, microfilms, audio recordings, glass slides, models, wall charts, maps, and posters of an educational, scientific, or cultural nature shall be duty free. The agreement defines the materials that may enjoy such exemptions and provides a procedure for securing the exemptions.

REFERENCES:
None

Agreement on the Importation of Educational, Scientific and Cultural Materials

SIGNED: November 22, 1950, at Lake Success, New York

SIGNATORIES: Afghanistan, Belgium, Bolivia, Cambodia, Ceylon, Colombia, Cuba, Domincan Republic, Ecuador, Egypt, El Salvador, France, Greece, Guatemala, Haiti, Honduras, Iran, Israel, Laos, Luxembourg, Monaco, Netherlands, New Zealand, Pakistan, Peru, Philippines, Sweden, Switzerland, Syrian Arab Republic, Thailand, United Kingdom, United States, Uruguay, Vietnam, Yugoslavia

IN FORCE: From May 21, 1952

OVERVIEW: An agreement perpetuating and expanding **Agreement for Facilitating the International Circulation of Educational, Scientific, and Cultural Materials** of 1949.

DISCUSSION:

This agreement perpetuates and expands the 1949 agreement whereby materials of an educational, scientific, or cultural could be imported on a duty-free basis.

REFERENCES:
None

Agreement (with U.S.S.R.) on Exchanges in the Cultural, Technical, and Educational Fields

OFFICIAL TITLE: Exchange of Letters Constituting an Agreement on Exchanges in the Cultural, Technical, and Educational Fields
SIGNED: January 27, 1958, at Washington, D.C.
SIGNATORIES: Union of Soviet Socialist Republics vs. United States
IN FORCE: From signing
OVERVIEW: First of several cultural, technical, and educational cooperative agreements between the United States and the Soviet Union.

DISCUSSION:

Both the Soviet Union and the United States recognized that the Cold War between them and the ideologies they represented was highly dangerous, always threatening to trigger an apocalyptic thermonuclear exchange. Early in the Cold War, both nations recognized that establishing programs of cultural, technical, and educational exchange might help to improve relations between them or, at least, lessen tensions.

The 1958 agreement proposed the following kinds of exchanges between the nations:

- Exchanges of radio and television broadcasts
- Exchanges of specialists in industry, agriculture, and medicine
- Cultural exchanges in the form of visits by cultural, civic, youth, and student groups
- Visits of delegations of Deputies of the Supreme Soviet and the U.S. Congress
- Joint conferences of U.S.S.R. and U.S. organizations
- Cooperation in the field of cinematography: an exchange of twelve to fifteen documentary films and other programs

The program of exchange between the two countries was continued in the following agreements: **Agreement (with U.S.S.R.) on Exchange in the Scientific, Technical, Educational, Cultural and Other Fields** (1962); **Agreement (with U.S.S.R.) on Exchange in the Scientific, Technical, Educational, Cultural and Other Fields** (1964); **Agreement (with U.S.S.R.) on Exchange in the Scientific, Technical, Educational, Cultural and Other Fields** (1966); **Agreement (with U.S.S.R.) on Exchange in the Scientific, Technical, Educational, Cultural and Other Fields** (1968); **Agreement (with U.S.S.R.) on Exchange in the Scientific, Technical, Educational, Cultural and Other Fields** (1970); **Agreement (with U.S.S.R.) on Exchange in the Scientific, Technical, Educational, Cultural and Other Fields** (1973); **Agreement (with U.S.S.R.) on Exchange in the Scientific, Technical, Educational, Cultural and Other Fields** (1977).

REFERENCE:
Schweitzer, Glenn E. *Experiments in Cooperation: Assessing U.S.-Russian Programs in Science and Technology.* Washington, D.C.: Brookings Institution, 1997.

Agreement (with Argentina) Relating to a Grant for Procurement of Nuclear Research and Training Equipment and Materials

OFFICIAL TITLE: Exchange of Notes Constituting an Agreement Relating to a Grant for Procurement of Nuclear Research and Training Equipment and Materials
SIGNED: September 9, 1959, and May 23, 1960, at Buenos Aires
SIGNATORIES: Argentina vs. United States
IN FORCE: From May 23, 1960
OVERVIEW: An agreement granting Argentina certain funds for nuclear procurement and research for peaceful purposes.

DISCUSSION:

The late 1950s and the decade of the 1906s saw the Untied States making major worldwide efforts to promote the peaceful use of nuclear energy. Efforts frequently included foreign aid in the form of grants and low-interest loans for the procurement of enriched uranium and for other materials necessary for research into nuclear energy.

REFERENCES:
Cantelon, Philip L., et al, eds. *The American Atom: A Documentary History of Nuclear Policies from the Dicovery of Fission to the Present.* Philadelphia: University of Pennsylvania Press, 1992.
Morone, Joseph G. *The Demise of Nuclear Energy? Lessons for Democratic Control of Technology.* New Haven, CT: Yale University Press, 1989.

General Agreement (with Ghana) for Cooperation in Bio-Medicine

OFFICIAL TITLE: General Agreement for a Program of Scientific Cooperation in the Field of Bio-medicine.
SIGNED: January 3, 1962, at Accra, Ghana
SIGNATORIES: Ghana vs. United States
IN FORCE: From signing
OVERVIEW: An agreement to establish "scientific field units" in Ghana under the collaborative auspices of the U.S. National Institutes of Health, Public Health Service, on the one hand, and the National Institute of Health and Medical Research of the National Research Council of Ghana, on the other.

DISCUSSION:

This agreement is typical of many relating to medical and technical "cooperation" between the United States and developing countries during the height of the Cold War. Although framed as collaborative agreements, they were, for the most parts, de facto aid agreements motivated not only by humanitarian objectives, but for the purpose of developing friendly relations with Third World governments in an effort to block the spread of communist influence and control in these regions.

By this agreement, the United States undertakes to send Institutes of Health personnel to Ghana "to study bio-medical problems in Ghana which are immediately necessary for alleviating the burden of ill-health of the people of Ghana and other parts of Africa and which are of mutual interest to the Government of Ghana and the Government of the United States of America." Provision for supplying equipment and transportation is also made by this agreement. In turn, the National Research Council of Ghana agrees to cooperate in providing "research space and facilities, utilities, access to local clinical and other research resources and housing at reasonable rentals for scientific and technical personnel."

REFERENCES:
None

Agreement (with U.S.S.R.) on Exchange in the Scientific, Technical, Educational, Cultural and Other Fields

SIGNED: March 8, 1962, at Washington, D.C.
SIGNATORIES: Union of Soviet Socialist Republics vs. United States
IN FORCE: Retroactively from January 1, 1962
OVERVIEW: One in a series of exchange agreements with the Soviet Union.

DISCUSSION:

This agreement extends and amplifies the 1958 **Agreement (with U.S.S.R.) on Exchanges in the Cultural, Technical, and Educational Fields.**

REFERENCE:
Schweitzer, Glenn E. *Experiments in Cooperation: Assessing U.S.-Russian Programs in Science and Technology.* Washington, D.C.: Brookings Institution, 1997.

Agreement (with U.S.S.R.) on Exchange in the Scientific, Technical, Educational, Cultural and Other Fields

SIGNED: February 22, 1964, at Moscow
SIGNATORIES: Union of Soviet Socialist Republics vs. United States
IN FORCE: Retroactively from January 1, 1964
OVERVIEW: One in a series of exchange agreements with the Soviet Union.

DISCUSSION:

This agreement extends and amplifies the 1962 **Agreement (with U.S.S.R.) on Exchange in the Scientific, Technical, Educational, Cultural and Other Fields**

REFERENCE:
Schweitzer, Glenn E. *Experiments in Cooperation: Assessing U.S.-Russian Programs in Science and Technology.* Washington, D.C.: Brookings Institution, 1997.

Agreement (with the U.S.S.R.) on Cooperation in Desalination, Including the Use of Atomic Energy

OFFICIAL TITLE: Agreement on Cooperation in the Field of Desalination, Including the Use of Atomic Energy
SIGNED: November 18, 1964, at Moscow
SIGNATORIES: Union of Soviet Socialist Republics vs. United States
IN FORCE: From signing
OVERVIEW: A brief agreement to "engage in wide scientific and technical cooperation in the field of desalination, including the use of atomic energy."

DISCUSSION:

Engaged in a tense, dangerous Cold War, the world's two great superpowers also looked for ways to decrease the tensions between them through programs of cultural and technological cooperation. This brief agreement, an agreement in broad principle rather than in detail, is especially significant in that it proposes cooperation in the peaceful use of atomic energy by two nations that were often pictured as poised on the bring of thermonuclear armageddon.

The text of the major part of the agreement follows:

II. The Parties will conduct scientific research and development work in the field of desalination, including the use of atomic energy, in accordance with their own programs and at their own expense.

III. The Parties will exchange, on a reciprocal basis, scientific accounts, reports, and other documents, including results obtained from work at pilot and demonstration plants of the Parties.

IV. The Parties will periodically organize, on a reciprocal basis, symposia and scientific meetings for discussion of scientific and technical problems and projects in accordance with previously agreed programs.

V. The parties will periodically organize visits, on a reciprocal basis, by technical experts to appropriate installations and laboratories.

VI. In order that the International Atomic Energy Agency (IAEA) and its members receive benefits in full measure from this cooperation, the Parties will give the IAEA copies of accounts, reports, and other documents which they exchange ...

REFERENCES:
Cantelon, Philip L., et al, eds. *The American Atom: A Documentary History of Nuclear Policies from the Dicovery of Fission to the Present.* Philadelphia: University of Pennsylvania Press, 1992.
Morone, Joseph G. *The Demise of Nuclear Energy? Lessons for Democratic Control of Technology.* New Haven, CT: Yale University Press, 1989.

Schweitzer, Glenn E. *Experiments in Cooperation: Assessing U.S.-Russian Programs in Science and Technology.* Washington, D.C.: Brookings Institution, 1997.

Agreement (with IAEA and Mexico) for a Preliminary Study of a Nuclear Electric Power and Desalting Plant

SIGNED: October 7, 1965, at Washington, D.C.

SIGNATORIES: International Atomic Energy Commission (IAEA), Mexico, United States

IN FORCE: From signing

OVERVIEW: An agreement concluded under the aegis of the IAEA to establish a study group "to make a preliminary assessment of the technical and economic practicability of a dual-purpose nuclear power plant designed to produce fresh water and electricity."

DISCUSSION:

The 1960s saw a stream of proposals for finding peaceful, international uses of atomic energy. Of particular interest was the idea of using the atom to generate electricity (see also **Agreement (with the Soviet Union) on Cooperation in Desalination, Including the Use of Atomic Energy**). Since the energy of the reactor-controlled nuclear chain reaction produces heat, which boils water to create steam to drive generator turbines, it was a natural leap to speculate that some portion of the vapor produced could be distilled and recovered in a desalination process.

The 1965 agreement specified that the area to be studied would encompass the arid regions of California and Arizona in the United States and Baja California and Sonora in Mexico. The body of the brief agreement lays down the composition of the study group and its tasks:

- Compiling data in Mexico and the United States on electricity and fresh water requirements
- Determining the "best alternatives for a plant capable of meeting the electricity and fresh water requirements"
- Drawing up a report on present and future electricity and fresh water requirements in the area
- Presenting conclusions and recommendations

REFERENCES:

Cantelon, Philip L., et al, eds. *The American Atom: A Documentary History of Nuclear Policies from the Dicovery of Fission to the Present.* Philadelphia: University of Pennsylvania Press, 1992.

Morone, Joseph G. *The Demise of Nuclear Energy? Lessons for Democratic Control of Technology.* New Haven, CT: Yale University Press, 1989.

Contract with Uruguay for the Lease of Enriched Uranium

OFFICIAL TITLE: Contract for the Lease of Enriched Uranium and for the Transfer of Special Fissionable Material and Certain Equipment for a Research Reactor in Uruguay

SIGNED: September 24, 1965, at Tokyo

SIGNATORIES: International Atomic Energy Agency, United States, Uruguay

IN FORCE: From signing

OVERVIEW: An agreement, under the aegis of the International Atomic Energy Agency, to make fissionable material available to Uruguay for a research reactor.

DISCUSSION:

Uruguay, "desiring to set up a project of a training and research reactor for peaceful purposes," requested assistance from the International Atomic Energy Agency, an agency of the United Nations, in "securing certain equipment and the special fissionable material necessary." Through a 1959 agreement, the United States "undertook to make available to the Agency . . . certain quantities of special fissionable material. Having made arrangements with a United States manufacturer to acquire the reactor, fuel elements, and other equipment, Uruguay concluded the present agreement to obtain fuel material for the reactor.

The agreement specifies the nature and amount of fissionable material to be leased to Uruguay; actual title to the material remains vested in the United States. After a specified period, the leased material is to be returned to the Agency.

In addition to stipulating various safeguards for the fissionable material, the agreement specifies charges due, accounting and auditing procedures, and provisions for the safe return of the material at the end of the lease period.

The agreement is an example of a bilateral treaty effectively moderated by a third-party international agency.

REFERENCES:

Cantelon, Philip L., et al, eds. *The American Atom: A Documentary History of Nuclear Policies from the Dicovery of Fission to the Present.* Philadelphia: University of Pennsylvania Press, 1992.

Morone, Joseph G. *The Demise of Nuclear Energy? Lessons for Democratic Control of Technology.* New Haven, CT: Yale University Press, 1989.

Agreement (with U.S.S.R.) on Exchange in the Scientific, Technical, Educational, Cultural and Other Fields

SIGNED: March 19, 1966, at Washington, D.C.

SIGNATORIES: Union of Soviet Socialist Republics vs. United States

IN FORCE: Retroactively from January 1, 1966

OVERVIEW: One in a series of exchange agreements with the Soviet Union.

DISCUSSION:

This agreement extends and amplifies the 1964 **Agreement (with U.S.S.R.) on Exchange in the Scientific, Technical, Educational, Cultural and Other Fields**.

REFERENCES:
Schweitzer, Glenn E. *Experiments in Cooperation: Assessing U.S.-Russian Programs in Science and Technology.* Washington, D.C.: Brookings Institution, 1997.

Agreement (with France) Concerning Cooperation for the Development of Satellite and Balloon Techniques

OFFICIAL TITLE: Exchange of Notes (with Memorandum of Understanding dated 27 May 1966 and Exchange of Letters Dated 11 and 27 May 1966) Constituting an Agreement Concerning Cooperation on Space Matters for the Development of Satellite and Balloon Techniques for the Study of Meteorological Phenomena
SIGNED: June 16 and 17, 1966, at Washington, D.C.
SIGNATORIES: France vs. United States
IN FORCE: From June 17, 1966
OVERVIEW: An agreement to collaborate on a satellite and balloon project to "study meteorological phenomena on a global scale, particularly the characteristics and movements of air masses."

DISCUSSION:

The agreement gives full national support to a "Memorandum of Understanding" between the space agencies of the two nations, Centre National D'Etudes Spatiales (CNES) and the National Aeronautics and Space Administration (NASA), to launch into earth orbit the EOLE satellite, designed to "gather meteorological data acquired by constant level balloons." The agreement includes provisions for collaboration on the design, fabrication, launch, and operation of the EOLE satellite and of the balloons.

REFERENCES:
None

Agreement (with Italy) for a Cooperative Program in Science

SIGNED: June 19, 1967, at Washington, D.C.
SIGNATORIES: Italy vs. United States
IN FORCE: From signing

OVERVIEW: An agreement to "undertake a broad program of scientific cooperation for peaceful purposes."

DISCUSSION:

No specific areas for cooperation are defined in the agreement, and the nature of the cooperative programs envisioned is only broadly delineated as "exchange of scientists, pursuit of joint research projects and consultation or convening of joint seminars." It is also laid down that "scientific information derived from the cooperative activities . . . shall be made available to the world scientific community."

REFERENCES:
None

Agreement (with Japan) for Cooperation Concerning Civil Uses of Atomic Energy

SIGNED: February 26, 1968, at Washington, D.C.
SIGNATORIES: Japan vs. United States
IN FORCE: From July 10, 1968
OVERVIEW: An agreement to cooperate in a "research and development program looking toward the realization of peaceful and humanitarian uses of atomic energy."

DISCUSSION:

Like the **Agreement (with the Philippines) for Cooperation Concerning Civil Uses of Atomic Energy** concluded later in the year, and like several other similar agreements with other nations, the agreement with Japan is first and foremost an agreement to export enriched uranium isotope material (U-235) for the purpose of fueling nuclear reactors. The principal content of the agreement specifies quantities and prices of U-235 to be exported, with detailed provisions for controlling shipments to ensure that the material is not used in the creation of weapons either by Japan or by third parties. Both governments (Article X) guarantee that no nuclear material, equipment, or devices "will be used for atomic weapons, or for research on or development of atomic weapons, or for any other military purpose."

REFERENCES:
Cantelon, Philip L., et al, eds. *The American Atom: A Documentary History of Nuclear Policies from the Dicovery of Fission to the Present.* Philadelphia: University of Pennsylvania Press, 1992.
Morone, Joseph G. *The Demise of Nuclear Energy? Lessons for Democratic Control of Technology.* New Haven, CT: Yale University Press, 1989.

Agreement (with U.S.S.R.) on Exchange in the Scientific, Technical, Educational, Cultural and Other Fields

SIGNED: July 15, 1968, at Moscow

SIGNATORIES: Union of Soviet Socialist Republics vs. United States

IN FORCE: Retroactively from January 1, 1968

OVERVIEW: One in a series of exchange agreements with the Soviet Union.

DISCUSSION:

This agreement extends and amplifies the 1966 **Agreement (with U.S.S.R.) on Exchange in the Scientific, Technical, Educational, Cultural and Other Fields**

REFERENCE:

Schweitzer, Glenn E. *Experiments in Cooperation: Assessing U.S.-Russian Programs in Science and Technology.* Washington, D.C.: Brookings Institution, 1997.

Agreement (with the Philippines) for Cooperation Concerning Civil Uses of Atomic Energy

SIGNED: June 13, 1968, at Washington, D.C.

SIGNATORIES: Philippines vs. United States

IN FORCE: From July 19, 1968

OVERVIEW: An agreement to cooperate in a "research and development program looking toward the realization of peaceful and humanitarian uses of atomic energy."

DISCUSSION:

The agreement supercedes a 1955 agreement with the Philippines and covers cooperation in developing research programs as well as the "design, construction, and operation of power-producing reactors and research reactors, [and] the exchange of information relating to the development of other peaceful uses of atomic energy."

While prohibiting the exchange of classified information, the agreement provides for the following:

- Provision of the services of experts in the field
- Provision of nuclear reactor fuel (U-235); much of the agreement is devoted to specifying delivery controls, safeguards, schedules, and other regulations
- Provisions for United States review of reactor design and construction and the design and construction of other equipment
- Oversight of facilities for storage of the "special nuclear material"

The agreement is typical of numerous agreements the United States has made with other states to promote the peaceful development of atomic energy. Such cooperation not only effectively blocked a Soviet or Chinese nuclear presence in nations developing nuclear industries, but provided lucrative export markets for the United States' cost-intensive nuclear industry. Most important, the agreements provided safeguards to ensure that nuclear material exported from the United States was not appropriated for the creation of weapons, either by the importing nation or by third parties.

REFERENCES:

Cantelon, Philip L., et al, eds. *The American Atom: A Documentary History of Nuclear Policies from the Dicovery of Fission to the Present.* Philadelphia: University of Pennsylvania Press, 1992.

Morone, Joseph G. *The Demise of Nuclear Energy? Lessons for Democratic Control of Technology.* New Haven, CT: Yale University Press, 1989.

Agreement (with U.S.S.R.) on Exchange in the Scientific, Technical, Educational, Cultural and Other Fields

SIGNED: February 10, 1970, at Washington, D.C.

SIGNATORIES: Union of Soviet Socialist Republics vs. United States

IN FORCE: Retroactively from January 1, 1970

OVERVIEW: One in a series of exchange agreements with the Soviet Union.

DISCUSSION:

This agreement significantly extends and amplifies the 1968 **Agreement (with U.S.S.R.) on Exchange in the Scientific, Technical, Educational, Cultural and Other Fields**. Exchange programs are proposed in the following fields:

- Science
- Scientific and technical problems, including man and his environment; air pollution; management systems; social security; agricultural economics; treatment of water in industry
- Technology, industry, transport, and construction, including high voltage power transmission; bridge and tunnel; construction; transport; production of earth-moving equipment; patent management and licensing; aeronautical engineering; geology; atmospheric modeling; Antarctic research; metrology; fisheries management; building construction
- Agriculture
- Medicine
- Performing arts
- Cinematography
- Publications, exhibits, radio and television
- Government, social, civic, cultural, and professional exchange programs
- Sports
- Tourism

REFERENCE:
Schweitzer, Glenn E. *Experiments in Cooperation: Assessing U.S.-Russian Programs in Science and Technology.* Washington, D.C.: Brookings Institution, 1997.

Agreement for the Operation of a Cooperative Meteorological Observation Program in the Netherlands Antilles

SIGNED: June 15, 1970, at the Hague
SIGNATORIES: Netherlands vs. United States
IN FORCE: Provisionally from signing; definitively, December 11, 1970
OVERVIEW: An agreement to continue and enhance a cooperative program of meteorological observation begun in 1956.

DISCUSSION:

The agreement is intended to facilitate "operation and maintenance of a rawinsonde and pilot balloon observation station in Curaçao and of a rawinsonde station in Saint Maarten, and the international dissemination of reports of the observations from these stations."

REFERENCE:
The WMO Achievement: Forty Years in the Service of International Meteorology and Hydrology. Geneva, Switzerland: WMO, 1990.

Agreement (with U.S.S.R.) on Exchange in the Scientific, Technical, Educational, Cultural and Other Fields

SIGNED: June 21, 1973, at Washington, D.C.
SIGNATORIES: Union of Soviet Socialist Republics vs. United States
IN FORCE: From June 21, 1973
OVERVIEW: One in a series of exchange agreements with the Soviet Union.

DISCUSSION:

This agreement extends and renews the 1970 **Agreement (with U.S.S.R.) on Exchange in the Scientific, Technical, Educational, Cultural and Other Fields.**

REFERENCE:
Schweitzer, Glenn E. *Experiments in Cooperation: Assessing U.S.-Russian Programs in Science and Technology.* Washington, D.C.: Brookings Institution, 1997.

Agreement (with U.S.S.R.) on Scientific and Technical Cooperation in the Field of Peaceful Uses of Atomic Energy

SIGNED: June 21, 1973, at Washington, D.C.
SIGNATORIES: Union of Soviet Socialist Republics vs. United States
IN FORCE: From signing
OVERVIEW: An agreement between the parties to "expand and strengthen their cooperation in research, development and utilization of nuclear energy, having as a primary objective the development of new energy sources."

DISCUSSION:

In the long Cold War following the end of World War II, with the threat of thermonuclear annihilation always looming in the background, many United States and Soviet policy makers were eager to conclude agreements of cultural and scientific cooperation and were especially anxious to show a desire to cooperate on solving major common problems, such as the "energy crisis." The impetus behind this agreement was all the more compelling in that solving the energy crisis allowed the two superpowers to use their expertise concerning atomic energy for peaceful and constructive ends.

Cooperation is to be concentrated in three areas:

• Controlled thermonuclear fusion
• Development of fast breeder reactors
• Research into the fundamental properties of matter

Cooperation is to take the form of the establishment of working groups of scientists, joint experimentation and pilot installations, joint work by theoreticians, organization of international panels and seminars, exchanges of instrumentation and equipment, exchanges of scientists, exchanges of information.

REFERENCE:
Schweitzer, Glenn E. *Experiments in Cooperation: Assessing U.S.-Russian Programs in Science and Technology.* Washington, D.C.: Brookings Institution, 1997.

Joint Statement (with Saudi Arabia) on Cooperation in the Fields of Economics, Technology, Industry, and Defense

SIGNED: June 8, 1974, at Washington, D.C.
SIGNATORIES: Saudi Arabia vs. United States
IN FORCE: From signing
OVERVIEW: A joint statement, constituting an agreement, on

broad United States-Saudi cooperation, with an eye toward stabilizing the situation in the Middle East.

DISCUSSION:
The United States had long been identified as Israel's close ally. By announcing a willingness to cooperate with Saudi Arabia across a broad spectrum of issues, the United States sought to broaden its influence in the Middle East and introduce an element of goodwill and stability there.

Cooperation was to extend to the following:
• Creation of a Joint Commission on Economic Cooperation
• Creation of a Joint Working Group on Industrialization
• Creation of a Joint Working Group on Manpower and Education
• Creation of a Joint Working Group on Technology, Research and Development
• Creation of a Joint Working Group on Agriculture

The statement closes with affirmation of "friendship and understanding" between Saudi Arabia and the United States.

REFERENCE:
Holland, Matthew F., *America and Egypt*. New York: Praeger, 1996.

Agreement (with the U.S.S.R.) on Cooperation in the Field of Energy

SIGNED: June 28, 1974, at Moscow
SIGNATORIES: Union of Soviet Socialist Republic vs. United States
IN FORCE: From signing
OVERVIEW: An agreement to collaborate on innovations to meet the energy needs of the United States and U.S.S.R.

DISCUSSION:
This agreement was concluded during the decade in which the worldwide "energy crisis" reached an especially acute point. The principal provisions include:
• A mutual undertaking to strengthen cooperation in the field of energy
• A mutual undertaking to accelerate efforts to develop existing and alternative energy sources
• A mutual undertaking to understand each other's national programs and outlook

REFERENCE:
Schweitzer, Glenn E. *Experiments in Cooperation: Assessing U.S.-Russian Programs in Science and Technology*. Washington, D.C.: Brookings Institution, 1997.

Memorandum of Understanding (with Brazil) Relating to Scientific and Technical Assistance

SIGNED: September 6, 1974, at Gaithersburg, Maryland, and Sao Paulo, Brazil
SIGNATORIES: Brazil vs. United States
IN FORCE: From signing
OVERVIEW: An agreement whereby the United States undertakes to provide assistance to the "Sao Paulo Project in Science and Technology."

DISCUSSION:
The purposes of the Sao Paulo Project in Science and Technology are as follows:
• To promote the application of basic and applied scientific research and technology to the problems of Brazilian industry and agriculture
• To develop capabilities in industry, government, universities and research institutes providing an increased proportion of this research from Brazilian sources
• To focus effort for increasing capabilities in science and technology most closely on those industrial and agricultural sectors that hold promise for rapidly improving Brazil's economic growth

REFERENCES:
None

Agreement (with Egypt) Relating to Cooperation in the Areas of Technology, Research, and Development

SIGNED: June 6, 1975, at Washington, D.C.
SIGNATORIES: Egypt vs. United States
IN FORCE: From signing
OVERVIEW: A formal agreement, following up on **Joint Statement (with Saudi Arabia) on Cooperation in the Fields of Economics, Technology, Industry, and Defense**, to cooperate in a broad spectrum of projects.

DISCUSSION:
This document puts into the form of a an agreement the substance of the 1974 Joint Statement. Like that statement, however, the agreement deals in the general principle of cooperation rather than in detailed projects.

REFERENCE:
Holland, Matthew F., *America and Egypt*. New York: Praeger, 1996.

Agreement (with Norway) Relating to the Peaceful Applications of Atomic Energy in the Field of Water Reactor Technology

SIGNED: November 3, 1975, at Bethesda, Maryland, and November 28, 1975, at Kjeller, Norway

SIGNATORIES: Norway vs. United States

IN FORCE: From January 1, 1976

OVERVIEW: An agreement to collaborate on the "Halden Project," a boiling water reactor designed to increase knowledge in the field of water reactor technology.

DISCUSSION:

The cooperative agreement is intended mainly to study nuclear fuel performance and reliability and to devise technologies for improving these. The agreement contains an article (Article IV) devoted to the disposition of patent rights in any invention that may result from the collaboration. The Norwegian Institutt for Atomenergi (IFA) is to hold title to patents outside of the United States, while the United States Atomic Energy Commission is to hold rights within the United States.

REFERENCES:

Cantelon, Philip L., et al, eds. *The American Atom: A Documentary History of Nuclear Policies from the Dicovery of Fission to the Present.* Philadelphia: University of Pennsylvania Press, 1992.

Morone, Joseph G. *The Demise of Nuclear Energy? Lessons for Democratic Control of Technology.* New Haven, CT: Yale University Press, 1989.

Joint Agreement (with Israel) for a Prototype Desalting Plant

OFFICIAL TITLE: Joint Agreement for the Design, Construction, Testing and Operation of a Large-Scale Prototype Desalting Plant in Israel

SIGNED: June 27, 1975, at Washington, D.C.

SIGNATORIES: Israel vs. United States

IN FORCE: From signing

OVERVIEW: A cooperative agreement to construct a desalination plant in Israel.

DISCUSSION:

The purposes of the agreement include the following:

(a) To improve existing technology, to develop and advance new technology, and to gain experience in the design and construction of large-scale desalting plants of advanced concept, so as to contribute materially to low-cost desalination in all countries;

(b) To deepen and extend cooperative working relations and to facilitate the exchange of desalting and related technology between the technical and scientific communities of the two countries; and

(c) To make feasible through improvement in technology the large-scale production of desalted water for use in arid and semi-arid areas of the two countries.

The scope of the project includes the following:
- Development of designs for a plant capable of desalting 10,000,000 gallons of seawater daily
- Design, construction, and operation at Ashdod, Israel, of an "intermediate test module"
- Construction of the prototype plant at Ashdod
- Operation and maintenance of the plant for a period not to exceed five years
- Evaluation and reporting of results

The plant is to employ an advanced, experimental desalination process known as the IDE Process. Israel is to own and operate the plant. The United States is to contribute funding up to 50 percent of all costs (but not to exceed $20,000,000 for operation and maintenance) and to supply "technical and administrative expertise." Israel contributes land, the IDE Process, and a financial contribution of approximately $35,000,000. The data resulting from the operation of the plant is to be shared freely by and between the two nations.

REFERENCES:

Mansour, Camille. *Beyond Alliance: Israel in U.S. Foreign Policy.* New York: Columbia University Press, 1994.

Organski, A. F. K. *The $36 Billion Bargain: Strategy and Politics in U.S. Assistance to Israel.* New York: Columbia University Press, 1991.

Memorandum of Arrangement (with Costa Rica) for the Operation of Weather Stations

SIGNED: June 28, 1976, at San Jose, Costa Rica

SIGNATORIES: Costa Rica vs. Untied States

IN FORCE: Retroactively from January 1, 1976

OVERVIEW: An agreement between the National Oceanic and Atmospheric Administration (U.S.) And the Servicio Meterológico de Costa Rica for the "United States-Costa Rica Cooperative Meteorological Program."

DISCUSSION:

By this cooperative agreement, the United States will supply radiosonde (weather balloon) equipment to Costa Rica, which, in turn, shall establish and maintain an observation station for use with the balloons.

REFERENCES:
None

Memorandum of Understanding (with Italy and the United Kingdom) for a Transatlantic Balloon Program

SIGNED: July 21 and 22, 1976, at Washington, D.C.
SIGNATORIES: Italy, United Kingdom, United States
IN FORCE: From July 22, 1976
OVERVIEW: An agreement governing the conduct of cooperative balloon experiments among Italy, the United Kingdom, and the United States.

DISCUSSION:

This agreement initiates and governs a cooperative program of long-duration Transatlantic unmanned balloon flights, primarily to study the atmosphere.

REFERENCES:
None

Agreement (with West Germany) on Cooperation in the Field of Biomedical Research and Technology

OFFICIAL TITLE: Agreement between the Department of Health, Education, and Welfare of the United States of America and the Federal Minister for Research and Technology of the Federal Republic of Germany on Cooperation in the Field of Biomedical Research and Technology
SIGNED: September 22, 1976, at Bonn, West Germany
SIGNATORIES: Federal Republic of Germany (West Germany) vs. United States
IN FORCE: from signing
OVERVIEW: A convention to work "together to resolve common health problems through joint research," with emphasis on cancer and heart disease.

DISCUSSION:

This document is unusual, though not unique, in that it is framed as an agreement between government agencies of the two signatory nations rather than between the governments themselves. The authorizing signatures are those of secretary of the Department of Health, Education, and Welfare and that of the Federal Minister for Research and Technology.

The cooperation agreed to includes the following:
• Research programs
• Exchange of specialists
• Organizations of conferences and lectures
• Exchange of information

Although a free exchange of information is encouraged, the agreement is silent on the subject of patent rights.

REFERENCES:
None

Agreement (with Republic of Korea) Relating to Scientific and Technical Cooperation

SIGNED: November 22, 1976, at Seoul
SIGNATORIES: Republic of Korea vs. United States
IN FORCE: From signing
OVERVIEW: An agreement in principle to create programs of scientific and technical cooperation between the two nations.

DISCUSSION:

As with similar agreements concluded during this period with numerous other nations, the document is a broad statement of principle rather than an agreement on specific collaborative projects.

REFERENCE:
Lee, Manwoo, et al. *Alliance Under Tension: The Evolution of South Korean-U.S. Relations.* Denver: Westview Press, 1988.

Arrangement (with Iran) for Cooperation in Nuclear Safety

OFFICIAL TITLE: Arrangement for the Exchange of Technical Information and Cooperation in Nuclear Safety Matters (with Addenda and Letter of Understanding)
SIGNED: April 11, 1977, at Shiraz, Iran
SIGNATORIES: Iran vs. United States
IN FORCE: From signing
OVERVIEW: An agreement between the United States Nuclear Regulatory Commission and the Atomic Energy Organization of Iran to exchange information and to collaborate on nuclear safety matters.

DISCUSSION:

The principal objective of the arrangement is to establish common standards of nuclear safety in a civil context. Toward this end, the signatories agree to exchange technical information on an ongoing basis, to collaborate in the development of regulatory standards, to cooperate in safety research and development, and to engage in a cooperative training program for Iranian personnel.

Since the Iranian revolution of 1979, the provisions of the arrangement have been unofficially suspended; however, the arrangement has not been denounced by either signatory.

REFERENCES:
Cantelon, Philip L., et al, eds. *The American Atom: A Documentary History of Nuclear Policies from the Dicovery of Fission to the Present.* Philadelphia: University of Pennsylvania Press, 1992.

Morone, Joseph G. *The Demise of Nuclear Energy? Lessons for Democratic Control of Technology.* New Haven, CT: Yale University Press, 1989.

Agreement (with Saudi Arabia) for Technical Cooperation in Desalination

OFFICIAL TITLE: Agreement Among the Saline Water Conversion Corporation and the Ministry of Finance and National Economy, Government of Saudi Arabia, and the Department of the Interior and the Department of the Treasury, United States of America, for Technical Cooperation in Desalination
SIGNED: May 3, 1977, at Washington, D.C.
SIGNATORIES: Saudi Arabia vs. United States
IN FORCE: From August 30, 1977
OVERVIEW: An agreement to cooperate in the research and development of desalination plants in Saudi Arabia.

DISCUSSION:

Desalination has long been an issue of great importance in such desert nations as Israel and Saudi Arabia. This agreement defines two technical cooperation projects between Saudi Arabia and the United States: the establishment of a desalination research, development, and training center in Saudi Arabia and a technology development program for multistage flash distillation single-unit desalination plants with capacities of up to 66 million gallons of fresh water daily. By this agreement, U.S. firms would provide technical, research, engineering, and consulting services. Although any inventions resulting from this work would become the property of the Saline Water Conversion Corporation, a Saudi entity, the United States would be granted a royalty-free, non-exclusive, irrevocable license to such inventions. The total estimated cost of the two projects contemplated in the agreement is stated as $79,000,000.

REFERENCES:
None

Memorandum of Understanding (with Republic of Korea) Relating to Scientific and Technical Cooperation

SIGNED: May 24, 1977, at Seoul
SIGNATORIES: Republic of Korea vs. United States
IN FORCE: From signing
OVERVIEW: An interagency agreement between the National Science Foundation (U.S.) And the Korea Science and Engineering Foundation for a program in science and technology under the broad terms of **Agreement (with the Republic of Korea) Relating to Scientific and Technical Cooperation**.

DISCUSSION:
This interagency agreement, sanctioned by the two governments, provides for programs in the following areas:
• Cooperative research
• Individual exchanges
• Joint seminars and workshops

The agreement further stipulates that "Scientific and technical information derived from cooperative activity . . . shall be made available to the world's scientific community."

REFERENCE:
Lee, Manwoo, et al. *Alliance Under Tension: The Evolution of South Korean-U.S. Relations.* Denver: Westview Press, 1988.

Agreement (with U.S.S.R.) on Exchange in the Scientific, Technical, Educational, Cultural and Other Fields

SIGNED: July 8, 1977, at Washington, D.C.
SIGNATORIES: Union of Soviet Socialist Republics vs. United States
IN FORCE: From signing
OVERVIEW: One in a series of exchange agreements with the Soviet Union.

DISCUSSION:
This agreement extends and renews the 1974 **Agreement (with U.S.S.R.) on Exchange in the Scientific, Technical, Educational, Cultural and Other Fields**.

REFERENCE:
Schweitzer, Glenn E. *Experiments in Cooperation: Assessing U.S.-Russian Programs in Science and Technology.* Washington, D.C.: Brookings Institution, 1997.

Agreement (with Israel) Concerning Cooperation in Defense-Related Research

OFFICIAL TITLE: Memorandum of Agreement Concerning the Principles Governing Mutual Cooperation in Research and Development, Scientist and Engineer Exchange, and Procurement and Logistic Support of Selected Defense Equipment
SIGNED: March 19, 1979, at Washington, D.C.
SIGNATORIES: Israel vs. United States
IN FORCE: From signing
OVERVIEW: An agreement to "increase . . . defense capabilities through more efficient cooperation in the field of research and development."

DISCUSSION:
The agreement has as its principal objective the increase of cooperation between the Untied States and Israel in the area of

defense research and development in order to achieve the following:

- Promote the cost-effective and rational use of funds allocated to defense
- Derive mutual benefits from selected research and development programs that satisfy each nation's defense needs in a cost-effective manner

Beyond providing for technical and scientific cooperation, the agreement includes provisions to allow Israel to continue to purchase from the United States large quantities of defense equipment while ameliorating "the ensuing imbalance in defense trade between the two countries. This amelioration is to take the form of the United States' providing Israel "improved opportunities to compete for agreed upon procurements of the U.S. Department Defense." In effect, the agreement represents a U.S. pledge of its intention to purchase more of its defense equipment from Israeli suppliers.

REFERENCES:
Mansour, Camille. *Beyond Alliance: Israel in U.S. Foreign Policy.* New York: Columbia University Press, 1994.
Organski, A. F. K. *The $36 Billion Bargain: Strategy and Politics in U.S. Assistance to Israel.* New York: Columbia University Press, 1991.

Agreement (with India) on Cooperation in the Conduct of the Monsoon Experiment (MONEX-79)

SIGNED: May 24, 1979, at New Delhi
SIGNATORIES: India vs. United States
IN FORCE: From signing
OVERVIEW: An agreement on a program of cooperation between the Untied States and India on a regional research project conducted under the aegis of the United Nations' World Meteorological Organization.

DISCUSSION:
This agreement specifies certain areas of bilateral cooperation between the signatories in their participation in the Monsoon Experiment (called MONEX-79) to be conducted by WMO. Areas of cooperation include the following:

- Airborne instrumentation
- Study of the boundary layer
- Satellite studies
- Aersol monitoring program

The agreement addresses procedures for facilitating cooperation, including expedited entry and reentry of personnel, tax and other fiscal exemptions, and general financial matters. Also addressed are security and safety issues, especially relating to the operation of United States research aircraft in Indian air space.

REFERENCE:
The WMO Achievement: Forty Years in the Service of International Meteorology and Hydrology. Geneva, Switzerland: WMO, 1990.

Memorandum of Understanding on Cooperation in a 1979 High Plains Cooperative Experiment in Weather Modification

SIGNED: June 11, 1979, at Ottawa, and June 20, 1979, at Washington, D.C.
SIGNATORIES: Canada vs. United States
IN FORCE: From June 20, 1979
OVERVIEW: An agreement "to study methods of increasing rainfall on the High Plains."

DISCUSSION:
The agreement calls for the cooperation of the Bureau of Reclamation of the United States Department of the Interior and Canada's Atmospheric Environment Service and National Research Council in an experiment in weather modification known as the 1979 High Plains Cooperative Experiment, or HIPLEX. The primary responsibility for conducting the experiment is to be borne by the Bureau of Reclamation in and around Miles City, Montana. The Canadian agencies are to cooperate in research planning and data analysis and to provide certain pieces of equipment, as well as technical personnel. Results of the experiment are to be made public.

REFERENCE:
The WMO Achievement: Forty Years in the Service of International Meteorology and Hydrology. Geneva, Switzerland: WMO, 1990.

Memorandum of Understanding (with Israel) for Technical Cooperation in Mineral Technology

SIGNED: August 14, 1979, at Washington, D.C., and September 19, 1979, at Jerusalem
SIGNATORIES: Israel vs. United States
IN FORCE: From September 19, 1979
OVERVIEW: An agreement, between the Bureau of Mines of the United States Department of the Interior and the Ministry of Energy and Infrastructure of Israel , on cooperation in matters relating to mineral technology.

DISCUSSION:
The agreement creates the framework for cooperation in such areas as the following:

- Metal and nonmetal mining research
- Health and safety research in mining

- Metallurgy research
- Ceramics research
- Mineral beneficiation research

REFERENCES:

Mansour, Camille. *Beyond Alliance: Israel in U.S. Foreign Policy.* New York: Columbia University Press, 1994.

Organski, A. F. K. *The $36 Billion Bargain: Strategy and Politics in U.S. Assistance to Israel.* New York: Columbia University Press, 1991.

Memorandum of Understanding (with the United Kingdom) on Cooperation in Earth Science and Environmental Studies

SIGNED: September 21, 1979, at Reston, Virginia, and September 26, 1979, at London

SIGNATORIES: United Kingdom vs. United States

IN FORCE: From September 26, 1979

OVERVIEW: A cooperative agreement between the Geological Survey of the United States Department of the Interior and the Natural Environment Research Council of the United Kingdom.

DISCUSSION:

The agreement calls for cooperation in the following areas of the earth sciences and environmental studies:

- Exchange of technical information
- Joint studies of mutual interest
- Exchange of visits of personnel

REFERENCES:

Cantelon, Philip L., et al, eds. *The American Atom: A Documentary History of Nuclear Policies from the Dicovery of Fission to the Present.* Philadelphia: University of Pennsylvania Press, 1992.

Morone, Joseph G. *The Demise of Nuclear Energy? Lessons for Democratic Control of Technology.* New Haven, CT: Yale University Press, 1989.

Technical and Cooperative Arrangement (with Sweden) in the Field of Nuclear Safety Research and Development

SIGNED: January 27, 1981, at Bethesda, Maryland, and February 23, 1981, at Studsvik, Sweden

SIGNATORIES: Sweden vs. Untied States

IN FORCE: From February 23, 1981

OVERVIEW: An agreement between the United States Nuclear Regulatory Commission and Studsvik Energiteknik AB of Sweden to cooperate in matters relating to nuclear safety in a civil context.

DISCUSSION:

The agreement defines the scope of cooperation in nuclear safety research, to encompass such activities as exchange of information, visits by technical personnel, and meetings. The agreement provides for the security of "nuclear information related to proliferation-sensitive technologies" (that is, weapons), as well as the security of proprietary information; however, in general, the results of any cooperative work are to be made generally available. An appendix subjoined to the agreement enumerates certain specific cooperative projects.

REFERENCES:

Cantelon, Philip L., et al, eds. *The American Atom: A Documentary History of Nuclear Policies from the Dicovery of Fission to the Present.* Philadelphia: University of Pennsylvania Press, 1992.

Morone, Joseph G. *The Demise of Nuclear Energy? Lessons for Democratic Control of Technology.* New Haven, CT: Yale University Press, 1989.

Accord (with China) on Industrial and Technical Cooperation

SIGNED: January 12, 1984, at Washington, D.C.

SIGNATORIES: People's Republic of China vs. United States

IN FORCE: From signing

OVERVIEW: An agreement to "take all appropriate steps to create favorable conditions for strengthening industrial and technological cooperation" between China and the United States.

DISCUSSION:

During 1969-1972, President Richard Nixon stepped back from the longtime hard-line United States Cold War policy of isolation and hostility toward Communist China and embraced a new posture of detente, seeking to improve relations with the People's Republic. In February 1972, President Nixon made a historic visit to China for talks with Mao Tse-tung, and, from this point forward, relations between the two countries not only improved, but China emerged as a major trading partner with the United States. The 1984 Accord recognizes "the development of economic and trade relations between the two countries" and asserts the "desirability of promoting industrial and technological cooperation." Accordingly, the document lays down the following major points:

- Both parties undertake to to strengthen industrial and technological cooperation and "to strive for a balance in their economic interests and attainment of the harmonious development of such cooperation."
- Cooperation may include such projects as construction of new industrial facilities in both countries; production, sale, and leasing of high-tech products; purchase and sale of industrial and consumer goods; license of intellectual property rights; coproduction of high-tech products; joint ventures of various types.

- The agreement nominates agencies of the respective nations to coordinate and implement cooperative projects.

REFERENCE:
Mann, James H. *About Face: A History of America's Curious Relationship with China from Nixon to Clinton.* New York: Knopf, 1999.

APPENDIXES:
Depositories, Web Sources, and Bibliography

Appendix A: Depositories

Two types of depository libraries have substantial treaty holdings, Federal Depository Libraries and United Nations Depository Libraries.

The United States Government Printing Office publishes virtually all treaties to which the United States is signatory, and the GPO distributes these to Federal Depository Libraries. Some 1,350 libraries are designated as depositories; however, you are most likely to find the documents you need at one of the fifty-three Regional Libraries. To find the Federal Depository Library or Regional Library nearest you, log on to Federal Depository Library Program's World Wide Web site at www.access.gpo.gov/su_docs/dpos/adpos003.html and fill out the online request form, which will return a list of nearby libraries.

The United Nations has designated more than 359 depository libraries in 141 countries worldwide. These libraries receive, among many other documents, copies of the 30,000+ treaties currently registered with the United Nations. To find the UN Depository Library nearest you, log on to the United Nations Information Web site at http://cn.net.au/un.htm to locate the depository library nearest you.

Native American treaties and related documents may be found in the collection of the National Indian Law Library, 1522 Broadway, Boulder, CO 80302 (303-447-8790).

Before embarking on a journey to a depository library, the researcher is advised to search for documents on the Internet. See **Appendix B: Web Sources**.

Appendix B: Web Sources

The following Web sites offer collections of treaties, often including full texts. In addition to searching these sites, it may be productive to run keyword searches using any of the available Web search engines. Two of the most useful are Yahoo and Google.

ACDA (U.S. Arms Control and Disarmament Agency): www.acda.gov/initial.html. The texts of many treaties (and other documents) relating to arms control.

Alllaw.net: www.alllaw.net/specialty/aviation.html, a full-text collection of treaties relating to aviation and outer space.

Archimedes Institute Library for Space Law and Policy Research: www.permanent.com/archimedes/LawLibrary.html. An extensive collection of outer-space treaties and legislation relating to space exploration, satellite communication, and so on. Includes many official and analytical documents.

Avalon Project at the Yale Law School: www.yale.edu/lawweb/avalon/avalon.htm. A spectacular Web site offering a very rich collection of historical (and some contemporary) United States treaties, including many Native American treaties. Texts of other historical U.S. documents are also presented. Covers the seventeenth through twentieth centuries.

Berkeley Treaty Guide: www.lib.berkeley.edu/GSSI/trtygde.html. A well-annotated guide to print resources on treaties.

Brandeis Libraries Guide—Treaties: www.library.brandeis.edu/resguides/special/treaties.html. No digital treaty texts, but an excellent guide to print treaty collections, broken down by subject area.

Carrow's International Law Links: www.carrow.com/linkINT.html. A handy group of links to international law sites, including many that offer full-text treaty collections. Annotated.

Clamen's Political Archives: www.cs.cmu.edu/afs/cs.cmu.edu/user/clamen/misc/politics/. A miscellaneous but very useful collection of treaties, including many full text versions.

Creek Treaties Related to Georgia: www.cviog.uga.edu/Projects.gainfo/crtreaty.htm. A very extensive collection of Creek Indian treaties, from 1733 to 1832.

Dispatch (United States Department of State): www.state.gov/www/publications/dispatch/index.html. *Dispatch* is an official State Department publication that contains recent treaty and foreign relations information. This site also contains links to the archive of older *Dispatch* issues.

Electronic Research Collection (ERC): http://dosfan.lib.uic.edu/ERC/index.html. A collaborative endeavor of the United States Department of State, University of Illinois at Chicago Library, and the Federal Depository Library Program, the site includes treaty texts and many other documents related to foreign policy.

ENTRI Treaty Texts: http://sedac.ciesin.org/pidb/texts-home.html. Texts of more than 169 environmental agreements.

FedLaw: www.legal.gsa.gov/. Provides access to many law-related documents, including some treaties and treaty-related legislation.

GPO Access: Library Services: www.access.gpo.gov/su_docs/libpro.html. A U.S. Government Printing Office site that allows users to identify and locate Federal Depository libraries, which include print collections of U.S. treaties.

Institute of American Indian Studies: http://usd.edu/iais/siouxnation/treatiesindex.html. Access to the full text of a few important American Indian treaties.

International Humanitarian Law (International Committee of the Red Cross): www.icrc.org/eng/ihl. Includes many human rights treaty texts and the texts of the Geneva and Hague conventions, as well as other rules-of-war documents.

International Treaties and Charters on Narcotics and Human Rights: www.drugtext.org/legal/treat.html. Offers full-text versions of various international conventions relating to narcotics and psychotropic substances; also includes a small selection of human rights treaties.

Israel Jewish Community Relations Council: www.jcrc.org/main/peacedox.htm. Offers full texts of Middle East peace documents and treaties, including those brokered by the United States.

Legal Information Institute of Cornell Law School: www.law.cornell.edu/. Full text versions of *many* key treaties, with an emphasis on twentieth-century multilateral conventions. A valuable site.

Lex Mercatoria: www.jus.uio.no/lm/toc/x.00-free.trade.html. A collection of treaties related to free trade and/or economic union.

Multilaterals Project: www.tufts.edu/fletcher/multilaterals.html. An extremely rich collection of full treaty texts, concentrating on human rights, commerce and trade, laws of war, arms control, and other areas. There is also an interesting collection of early European treaties, dating to the seventeenth century.

Native American Rights Fund: www.narf.org/main_top.html. Includes links to collections of Native American treaties and documents.

Native American Constitution and Law Digitization Project: http://thorpe.ou.edu/. Provides Internet access to the Constitutions, Tribal Codes, and some treaties of Native American tribes.

North American Free Trade Agreement: www.sice.oas.org/trade/nafta/naftatce.stm. This site, sponsored by the OAS, contains the full and fully annotated text of NAFTA and associated documents.

Oceana Publications, Inc.: www.oceanalaw.com/home.htm. A for-fee service that contains a searchable database of treaties to which the United States is signatory from 1989 to the present. Full text copies may be ordered for delivery via e-mail or fax.

Oceans and Marine Conservation: www.state.gov/www/global/oes/oceans/index.html. From the Bureau of Oceans and International Environmental and Scientific Affairs, a full-text collection of treaties relating to the law of the sea, fisheries, and marine conservation.

Oneida Indian Nation—Treaties: www.oneida-nation.net/treat-1777.html. Full-text versions of important early Indian treaties.

Organization of American States: www.oas.org/. This, the homepage of the OAS, includes a text archive of OAS treaties as well as other treaties relating to OAS member states. A valuable resource.

Pace University School of Law Database on the CISG and International Commercial Law: http://cisgw3.law.pace.edu/. The CISG is the United Nations Convention on Contracts for the International Sale of Goods. This site deals with that document, as well as other treaties relating to international commercial law.

SICE—Foreign Trade Information System: www.sice.oas.org/. Full text of trade agreements among countries of the Western Hemisphere.

Treaties and International Law: http://law.house.gov/89.htm. A modest collection of treaties from the Villanova Center for Information Law and Policy.

Treaties with Minnesota Indians: http://indy4.fdl.cc.mn.us/~isk/maps/mn/treaties.html. An extensive collection of treaties with Minnesota tribes.

Treaties in Force: www.acda.gov/state. A Web-based version of the print annual, *Treaties in Force*, published by the U.S. Department of State. An essential site for checking the status of United States treaties.

U.S. Historical Documents Archive: http://w3.one.net/~mweiler/ushda/ushda.htm. Many significant historical documents, including a few treaties.

U.S. House of Representatives Internet Law Library: http://law.house.gov/89.htm. Contains numerous treaties, as well as legislation relating to certain international agreements.

U.S. Department of State Web Site Index: www.state.gov/www/ind.html. A list of links to many documents and treaties on a wide variety of subjects, conveniently broken down and alphabetized.

Unidroit Home Page: www.unidroit.org/english/conventions/c-main.htm. Full-text collection of conventions drawn up by Unidroit, the International Institute for the Unification of Private Law.

United Nations Demining Database: www.un.org/Depts/Landmine/open.htm. A UN site devoted to documents on land mines, including relevant treaties.

United Nations Treaty Data Base: http://untreaty.org. Certainly the single most important Web-based source of treaty status information and full texts, this site offers graphics-based images of some 30,000 treaties registered with the United Nations. Also available: information of the current status of treaties. A fee-based subscription is required.

University of Michigan Documents Center/International Agencies and Information on the Web: www.lib.umich.edu /libhome/Documents.center/intl.html. This is an extensive, well-analyzed collection of links to Web sites relating to international politics. An excellent gateway to specialized sites containing treaty texts and information.

University of Minnesota Human Rights Library: http://www1.umn.edu/humanrts/. An extensive collection of human rights treaties and other documents.

Washburn University School of Law Library: www.washlaw.edu/forint/. Links to various treaty sites.

Welcome to NATO: www.nato.int/. The official NATO Web site, includes many documents, including NATO-related treaties.

WIPO Administered Treaties: Index: www.wipo.org/eng/iplex/index.htm. Links to full-text versions of all intellectual property treaties administered by the World Intellectual Property Organization.

Appendix C: Bibliography

The following are general guides to treaty research, indexes of treaties, and collections of United States treaty texts. For works relating to specific treaties, please consult the listings that follow the **References** subhead of the relevant treaty entry in the main text of this book.

Bevans, Charles I., comp. *Treaties and other International Agreements of the United States of America, 1776-1949.* Washington, D.C.: U.S. Government Printing Office, 1968-76.

Bowman, M.J. and D.J. Harris. *Multilateral Treaties: Index and Current Status.* London: Butterworths, 1984-.

Burns, Richard Dean, ed. *Encyclopedia of Arms Control and Disarmament.* New York: Scribners, 1993.

Copyright Laws and Treaties of the World. Paris: UNESCO and BNA, 1956-.

European Conventions and Agreements. Strasbourg: Council of Europe, 1971-.

Federal Register. Washington, D.C.: Office of the Federal Register, 1936-.

Hein's U.S. Treaty Index on CD-ROM. Buffalo, NY: William S. Hein, 1993-.

Industrial Property Law and Treaties. Geneva: World Intellectual Property Organization, 1978-.

Inter-American Treaties and Conventions. Washington, D.C.: Organization of American States, 1989.

International Legal Materials. Washington, D.C.: American Society of International Law, 1962-.

Kavass, Igor. *Current Treaty Index.* Buffalo, NY: William S. Hein, 1982-.

_____. *United States Treaty Index: 1776–1990 Consolidation (with Supplements).* Buffalo, NY: William S. Hein, 1991-

League of Nations Treaty Series-General Index. Geneva: League of Nations, 1920-1946.

Malloy, William M., comp. *Treaties, Conventions, International Acts, Protocols, and Agreements Between the United States of America and Other Powers.* Washington, D.C.: U.S. Government Printing Office, 1910-_.

Miller, Hunter, ed. *Treaties and Other International Acts of the United States of America.* Washington, D.C.: U.S. Government Printing Office, 1931-1948.

Multilateral Treaties Deposited with the Secretary General: Status as at 31 December.... New York: United Nations, 1968.

Nash, Marian L. "Treaty Research Guide," in *Basic Documents of International Economic Law.* Chicago: CCH. 1990.

Parry, Clive. *Consolidated Treaty Series.* Dobbs Ferry, NY: Oceana, 1969-1981.

Prucha, Francis Paul, ed. *Documents of United States Indian Policy.* 2d ed, expanded. Lincoln: University of Nebraska Press, 1990.

Rengger, N. J. *Treaties and Alliances of the World.* Harlow, U.K.: Longman Group, 1990.

Rohn, Peter. *World Treaty Index.* 2d ed. Santa Barbara, CA: ABC-CLIO, 1983-1984.

Scott, James Brown. *The Hague Peace Conferences of 1899 and 1907.* Baltimore: Johns Hopkins University Press, 1909.

Sklar, Barry, and Virginia Hagen, comps. *Collection of Documents, Legislation, Descriptions of Inter-American Organizations, and Other Material Pertaining to Inter-American Affairs.* Washington, D.C.: U.S. Government Printing Office, 1972.

Sohn, Louis, and Manley O. Hudson. *International Legislation.* New York: Carnegie, 1931-1950.

Tansill, Charles C., comp. *Documents Illustrative of the Formation of the Union of the American States.* Washington, D.C.: U.S. Government Printing Office, 1927.

Tax Notes International. Arlington, VA: Tax Analysts, 1989.

Thorpe, Francis Newton. *The Federal and State Constitutions, Colonial Charters, and Other Organic Laws of the State[s], Territories, and Colonies Now or Heretofore Forming the United States of America.* Washington, D.C.: U.S. Government Printing Office, 1909.

Treaties and Other International Acts Series. Washington, D.C.: U.S. Government Printing Office, 1946-.

United Nations Treaty Series-Cumulative Indexes. New York: United Nations, 1946-.

U.S. Department of State Dispatch. Washington, D.C.: U.S. Department of State, 1990-.

United States Department of State. *Foreign Relations of the United States,* 300 volumes. Washington, D.C.: U.S. Government Printing Office, 1948-.

United States Department of State. *Treaties in Force: A List of Treaties and other International Agreements of the United States in Force on January 1, 1997.* Washington, D.C.: U.S. Government Printing Office, annual.

United States Statutes at Large. Washington, D.C.: U.S. Government Printing Office, 1846-.

United States Treaties and Other International Agreements. Washington, D.C.: U.S. Department of State, 1952-.

United States Senate, Committee on Foreign Relations. *Treaties and Other International Agreements: the Role of the United States Senate.* Washington, D.C.: Government Printing Office, 1993.

Wiktor, Christian L. *Unperfected Treaties of the United States of America. 1776–1976.* Dobbs Ferre NY: Oceana 1976-1981. Includes the texts of almost four hundred treaties "which have been signed on the part of the United States, or have been submitted to the Senate, but which have, for one reason or another, definitely failed to go into force."

Worldwide Tax Treaty Index. Arlington, VA: Tax Analysts, 1993.

Zamora, Stephen and Ronald Brand. *Basic Documents on International Economic Law.* Chicago: CCH, 1990.

INDEX